W9-ASU-103

PAGE 50 — ON THE ROAD

YOUR COMPLETE DESTINATION GUIDE
In-depth reviews, detailed listings
and insider tips

Cantabria & Asturias p455

Galicia p500

Basque Country, Navarra & La Rioja p398

Castilla y León p123

Catalonia p302

Aragón p360

⊙ Barcelona p227

★ Madrid p52

Castilla-La Mancha p194

Valencia p544

Mallorca, Menorca & Ibiza p594

Extremadura p784

Murcia p644

Andalucía p657

TOP EXPERIENCES MAP — NEXT PAGE

PAGE 875 — SURVIVAL GUIDE

YOUR AT-A-GLANCE REFERENCE
How to get around, get a room,
stay safe, say hello

KEY PATTERN

To get by in Spanish,
these simple patterns
your choice:

When's (the next flight)?
¿Cuándo sale   kwa
(el próximo vuelo)?   (el

Where's (the station
…nde está

THIS EDITION WRITTEN AND RESEARCHED BY

Anthony Ham

Stuart Butler, John Noble, Zora O'Neill, Josephine Quintero,

Miles Roddis, Brendan Sainsbury, Damien Simonis

›Spain

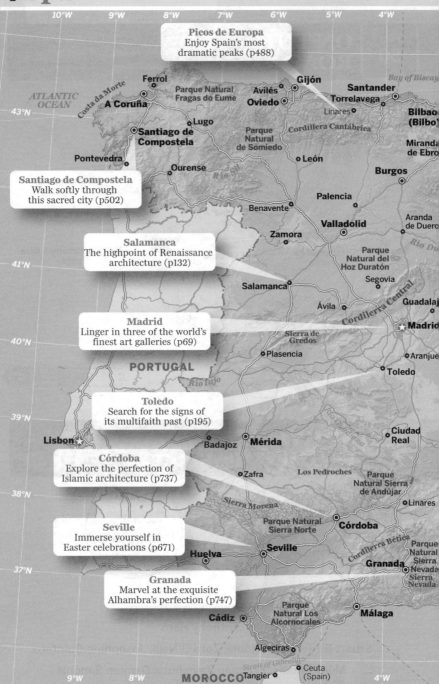

Picos de Europa
Enjoy Spain's most dramatic peaks (p488)

Santiago de Compostela
Walk softly through this sacred city (p502)

Salamanca
The highpoint of Renaissance architecture (p132)

Madrid
Linger in three of the world's finest art galleries (p69)

Toledo
Search for the signs of its multifaith past (p195)

Córdoba
Explore the perfection of Islamic architecture (p737)

Seville
Immerse yourself in Easter celebrations (p671)

Granada
Marvel at the exquisite Alhambra's perfection (p747)

Top Experiences ›

2°W

San Sebastián
Eat in Spain's culinary
capital (p422)

FRANCE

Nîmes

Aragonese Pyrenees
Hike the Pyrenean
high country (p377)

Montpellier

Biarritz

San
Sebastián

Perpignan

Pamplona
(Iruña)

Pyrenees

ANDORRA

Golfe du Lion

Logroño

Andorra
la Vella

Figueras

Río Segre

Girona

Costa Brava

Río Ter

Zaragoza

Lleida

Parc Natural
del Montseny

La Rioja
Meander through Spain's
premier wine region (p451)

Río Ebro

Barcelona

Costa Daurada

Golfo de Valencia

Teruel

Costa del Azahar

Barcelona
Admire the extraordinary
Sagrada Família (p247)

Menorca

Cuenca

Río Turia

Valencia
Experience the finest
modern architecture (p546)

Palma de
Mallorca

Valencia

Mallorca

Balearic Islands (Islas Baleares)

Río Júcar

Ibiza

Río Chorel

Albacete

Menorca
Laze on the Mediterranean's
best beaches (p642)

Parque Natural
Sierras de Cazorla,
Segura y las Villas

Alicante
(Alacant)

Formentera

Elche
(Elx)

Costa Blanca

MEDITERRANEAN
SEA

Río Segura

Murcia

Cartagena

Costa Cálida

ELEVATION

2700m
2400m
2100m
1500m
1200m
900m
600m
300m
0

Almería

Parque Natural
de Cabo de
Gata-Níjar

ALGERIA

N

0   100 km
0   80 miles

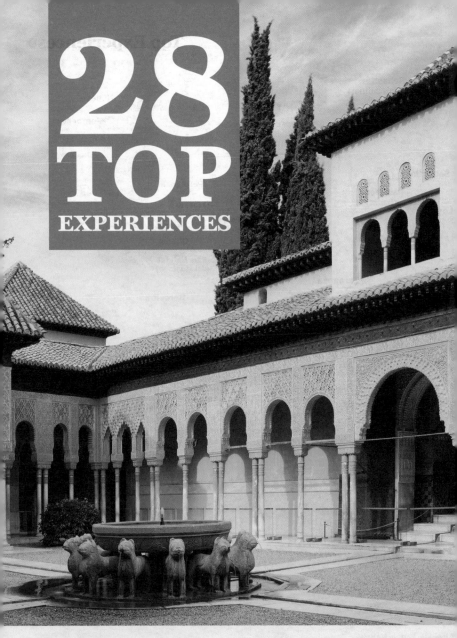

28 TOP EXPERIENCES

Alhambra

1 The palace complex of Granada's Alhambra (p747) is close to architectural perfection. It is perhaps the most refined example of Islamic art anywhere in the world, not to mention the most enduring symbol of 800 years of Moorish rule in what was known as Al-Andalus. From afar, the Alhambra's red fortress towers dominate the Granada skyline, set against a backdrop of the Sierra Nevada's snow-capped peaks. Up close, the Alhambra's perfectly proportioned Generalife gardens complement the exquisite detail of the Palacio Nazaríes. Put simply, this is Spain's most beautiful monument.

La Sagrada Família

2 One of Spain's top sights, the Modernista brainchild of Antoni Gaudí remains a work in progress more than 80 years after its creator's death. Fanciful and profound, inspired by nature and barely restrained by a Gothic style, Barcelona's quirky temple (p247) soars skyward with an almost playful majesty. The improbable angles and departures from architectural convention will have you shaking your head in disbelief, but the detail of the decorative flourishes on the Passion Facade, Nativity Facade and elsewhere are worth studying for hours.

Mezquita

3 Córdoba's astonishing Mezquita (Mosque; p737), founded in 785, is easily the most beautiful mosque on European soil and rivals anything elsewhere in the Islamic World. So important was this mosque to the premier city of Islamic Al-Andalus that caliph after caliph left their mark – the most striking additions are the arches and domes of the 10th-century royal prayer enclosure. The 16th-century intrusion of the Christian cathedral in the heart of the Mezquita aside, this is Moorish architecture at its most graceful.

JEAN-PIERRE LESCOURRET

Easter in Seville

4 Return to Spain's medieval Christian roots and join Seville's masses for the dramatic Easter celebration of Semana Santa (p671). Religious fraternities parade elaborate *pasos* (figures) of Christ and the Virgin Mary around the city to the emotive acclaim of the populace; the most prestigious procession is the *madrugada* (early hours) of Good Friday. Seen for the first time, it's an unforgettable experience, an exotic and utterly compelling fusing of pageantry, solemnity and deep religious faith. There are processions in towns across Spain, but none on the scale of Seville.

RICHARD ROSS

Madrid Nightlife

5 Madrid's not the only European city with nightlife (p99 and p105) but few can match its intensity and street clamour. As Ernest Hemingway said, 'Nobody goes to bed in Madrid until they have killed the night'. There are wall-to-wall bars, small clubs, live venues, cocktail bars and mega-clubs beloved by A-list celebrities all across the city, with unimaginable variety to suit all tastes. But it's in Huertas, Malasaña, Chueca and La Latina that you'll really understand what we're talking about. Why Not? bar (see the boxed text, p89)

KRZYSZTOF DYDYNSKI

DALLAS STRIBLEY

Pintxos in San Sebastián

6 Chefs here have turned bar snacks into an art form. Often called 'high cuisine in miniature', *pintxos* (Basque tapas) are piles of flavour often mounted on a slice of baguette. As you step into any bar in central San Sebastián (p422), the choice lined up along the counter will leave first-time visitors gasping. In short, this is Spain's most memorable eating experience. Although the atmosphere is always casual, the serious business of experimenting with taste combinations (a Basque trademark) ensures that it just keeps getting better.

Ciudad de las Artes y las Ciencias

7 Created by Santiago Calatrava, one of the nation's star architects, the City of Arts and Sciences in Valencia (p546) has helped transform Spain's third-largest city into one of the country's most vibrant. A daring and visually stunning piece of contemporary architecture, the complex includes a state-of-the-art theatre (Palau de les Arts Reina Sofía), grand aquarium (Oceanogràfic), planetarium (Hemisfèric) and science museum (Museo de las Ciencias Príncipe Felipe).

La Rioja Wine Country

8 La Rioja (p451) is the sort of place where you could spend weeks meandering along quiet roads in search of the finest drop. Bodegas offering wine-tastings and picturesque villages that shelter excellent wine museums are the mainstay in this region. The Frank Gehry–designed Hotel Marqués de Riscal (p453), close to Elciego, has been likened to Bilbao's Guggenheim in architectural scale and ambition, and has become the elite centre for wine tourism in the region.

OLIVER CIRENDINI

Renaissance Salamanca

9 Luminous when floodlit, the elegant central square of Salamanca, the Plaza Mayor (p132), is possibly the most attractive in all of Spain. It is just one of many highlights in a city whose architectural splendour has few peers in the country. The city is home to one of Europe's oldest and most prestigious universities so student revelry also lights up the nights. It's this combination of grandeur and energy that makes so many people call Salamanca their favourite city in Spain.

Sierra Nevada & Las Alpujarras

10 Dominated by the Mulhacén (3479m), mainland Spain's highest peak, the Sierra Nevada (p764) makes a stunning backdrop to the warm city of Granada. Skiing in winter and hiking in summer can be mixed with exploration of the fascinating villages of Las Alpujarras (p766), arguably Andalucía's most engaging collection of *pueblos blancos* (white villages). Suitably for one of the last outposts of Moorish settlement on Spanish soil, the hamlets of Las Alpujarras resemble North Africa, oasis-like and set amid woodlands and the deep ravines for which the region is renowned.

Madrid's Golden Art Triangle

11 Madrid may lack architectural landmarks, but it more than compensates with an extraordinary collection of art galleries. Housing works by Goya, Velázquez, El Greco and masters from across Europe, the showpiece is the Museo del Prado (p69), but also within a short stroll are the Centro de Arte Reina Sofía (p68), showcasing Picasso's Guernica, plus works by Dalí and Miró, and the Museo Thyssen-Bornemisza (p73), which carries all the big names spanning centuries. Museo del Prado (p69)

Asturian Coast

12 According to one count, the emerald-green northern Spanish region of Asturias (p470) boasts 211 beaches. While the coolness of the Atlantic may be a drawback for those planning on catching some sun, the beauty of many of these frequently wild and unspoiled stretches is utterly breathtaking. Even better, the villages of the coast and hinterland are among the prettiest anywhere along the Spanish shoreline, and the food served in this part of the country is famous throughout Spain. Coastline near Llanes (p483)

Flamenco in Andalucía

13 Uplifting and melancholic, the soul-stirring strains of flamenco (p870) originated in Andalucía and it's still here in southern Spain that you're most likely to hear the genre at its best. Flamenco's heartland lies along the Seville, Cádiz and Jerez de la Frontera axis and live flamenco lights up the nights in all three cities, with Seville hosting a particularly wide selection of accessible flamenco venues. Performances are electrifying and will live long in your memory.

PAUL BERNHARDT

ALEX SCHLEIF/ALAMY

Hiking the Aragonese Pyrenees

14 Spain is a walker's destination of exceptional variety, but we reckon Aragón's Pyrenees offer the most special hiking country. The Parque Nacional de Ordesa y Monte Perdido (p377) is one of the high points (pun intended) of the Pyrenees. Centred on Monte Perdido (3348m), it offers plenty of opportunities for tough excursions along great rock walls and glacial cirques, accompanied by the occasional chamois. Even better, there are limits on the number of people in the park at any one time.

Staying in a Beautiful Parador

15 Sleeping like a king has never been easier than in Spain's state-run chain of *paradores* (p878) – often palatial, always supremely comfortable former castles, palaces, monasteries and convents. There are 86 of them scattered across the country. Ranking among Europe's most atmospheric sleeping experiences, many are sited on prime real estate (eg inside the grounds of Granada's Alhambra) and prices are more reasonable than you might imagine, especially if you book online and far in advance. Parador de Ronda (p732)

DAVID TOMLINSON

MATTHEW SCHOENFELDER

Picos de Europa

16 Jutting out in compact form just back from the rugged and ever-changing coastline of Cantabria and Asturias, the Picos (p488) comprise three dramatic limestone massifs, unique in Spain but geologically similar to the Alps and jammed with inspiring trails. These ridgelines, an integral part of Spain's second-largest national park, boast some of the most spectacular mountain scenery in the country – no small claim considering the presence of the Pyrenees and Sierra Nevada. The Picos de Europa deservedly belong in such elite company.

Beaches of Menorca

17 At a time when the Spanish Mediterranean has become a byword for mass tourism, Menorca is just a little bit different. Saved from the worst effects of overdevelopment, most of the island is a Unesco Biosphere Reserve with 216km of coastline and beaches that defy description. Some assert that reaching them by sea is the height of pleasure, but happening upon them from the interior brings equal joy. Among the best are Cala Macarelleta (p643) and Cala en Turqueta (p643).

Santiago de Compostela

18 As the reputed final resting place of St James, one of the 12 Apostles, Santiago de Compos(p502) in the far northwest of Galicia resonates with the sacred like nowhere else in the country. Its splendid cathedral bears an unusually rich Romanesque facade and a distinguished gathering of spires; the cathedral is the suitably extravagant objective of pilgrims traversing the Camino de Santiago across northern Spain. But look beyond the cathedral and you'll find a smattering of other gilt-edged monuments and an eating culture that is Galicia in a nutshell.

HANNAH LEVY

Las Fallas

19 Spain's noisiest festival is also one of its most spectacular. Taking place every March in Valencia, Las Fallas (see the boxed text, p556) is an explosive fiesta of fireworks, music and bonfires that light up the sky for almost a week. But this is more than just noise. A festival with deep cultural roots and great inventiveness, Las Fallas sees each Valencia neighbourhood try to outdo each other in elaborate wood-and-papier-mâché sculptures that go up in flames in an extraordinary climax.

Sample the Best Jamón

20 *Jamón* (p853; cured ham) is Spain's culinary constant and one of the few things that unite the country. If there is a national dish, this is it, more so even than paella. Nearly every bar and restaurant in Spain has at least one *jamón* on the go at any one time, strapped into a cradlelike frame called a *jamónera*. Wafer-thin slices of the best *jamón* (known as *jamón ibérico de bellota*, although there are many different kinds) is simplicity itself and our idea of Spanish culinary heaven.

KRZYSZTOF DYDYNSKI

Cabo de Gata

21 Cabo de Gata (p780), a wild stretch of protected coastline east of Almería, is legendary among Spaniards. For most of the year the beaches, strung between imposing cliffs, are nearly deserted and they offer some decent diving and fine hiking as well. Indeed, Cabo de Gata is something of an oasis, a reassuring retreat to a time along the Andalucian coast when no one from beyond Spanish shores had ever heard of the Costa del Sol. Best of all, there's not a tourist resort in sight. Playa de Mónsul (p781)

MAN/IMAGEBROKER

ROBERTO SONCIN GEROMETTA

Segovia

23 One of the most beautiful medium-sized towns in Spain, Segovia (p144) has the usual glittering array of Castilian churches and a fine location, strung out along a ridge against a backdrop of often snow-capped mountains. But two buildings of legend set Segovia apart. Its multi-turreted Alcázar provided the inspiration for Walt Disney's castle confection, while a gigantic but elegant Roman aqueduct of granite blocks (held together by not a drop of mortar) has stood the test of time in the heart of town for almost 2000 years. Segovia's cathedral (p148)

STEPHEN SAKS

Camino de Santiago

22 Every year, tens of thousands of pilgrims and walkers with all manner of motivations set out to walk across northern Spain. Their destination, Santiago de Compostela, is a place of untold significance for Christians, but the appeal of this epic walk (p37) goes far beyond the religious. With numerous routes across the north, there is no finer way to get under Spain's skin and experience the pleasures and caprices of its natural world. And even completing one small stage will leave you with a lifetime of impressions. Approaching Espinal (see the boxed text, p432)

Hanging out in Cádiz

24 Cádiz (p688) has a laid-back, almost rakish live-for-the-present feel that makes its somewhat decayed 18th-century centre instantly likeable. Locals party the sweltering summer nights away in the old town squares and waterfront bars, while Cádiz' celebrations of Carnaval are renowned throughout the country for their fun and fervour. And the city itself has charm as well – fascinating historical monuments, snaking white-washed lanes, panoramic viewpoints and a cathedral square as beautiful as any in Spain are even better when cooled by Cádiz' salty sea breeze.

Galicia's Costa da Morte & Cabo Ortegal

25 The wild Atlantic bluffs of the Galician coast remind us of how small we are. Close to Cabo Ortegal (p520), powerful winds whip around you and great Atlantic rollers seem little more than sea spray as they crash against the walls of the cape far below. And along the Costa da Morte (p522; Coast of Death) where the stories of shipwrecks are legion, long and empty sweeps of sand are separated by dramatic rocky headlands. If only all stretches of Spain's coastline were this unspoiled.

Shopping in Barcelona

26 Barcelona has spent decades as a leading European icon of cool, and its fashion designers have played a leading role in ensuring that reputation never goes stale. As a result, Barcelona is one of the great shopping cities of the world, a place where originality is the watchword. Shop till you drop along Barcelona's boulevards (Passeig de Gràcia, Rambla de Catalunya and Avinguda Diagonal) as well as in countless independent stores and bijou boutiques in the Barri Gòtic, around Passeig del Born and Gràcia (p289). Custo Barcelona (p290)

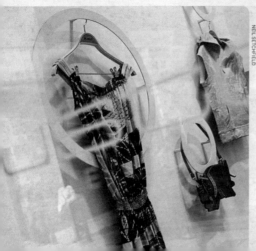

Three Cultures in Toledo

27 Symbolic home to Spain's Catholic Church and the army, the medieval core of Toledo (p195) is an extraordinary piece of world heritage. Known as the city of the three cultures (where Muslims, Jews and Christians once rubbed shoulders), it remains a fascinating labyrinth today with former mosques, synagogues and churches; the latter are still very much in use and the cathedral is one of Spain's most imposing. Given Toledo's proximity to Madrid, the city can get overrun with day-trippers. Stay overnight and that's when Toledo really comes into its own.

CHRISTOPHER GROENHOUT

Costa Brava

28 Easily accessible by air and by land from the rest of Europe and filled with villages and beaches of the kind that spawned Northern Europe's summer obsession with the Spanish coast, the Costa Brava (p303) in Catalonia is one of our favourite corners of the Mediterranean. Beyond this, however, the spirit of Salvador Dalí lends so much personality and studied eccentricity to the Costa Brava experience, from his one-time home in Cadaqués (p321) to Dalí-centric sites in Figueres (p324) and Castell De Púbol (p312). Sa Tuna (p311)

welcome to Spain

Passionate, sophisticated and devoted to living the good life, Spain is at once a stereotype come to life and a country more diverse than you ever imagined.

An Epic Land

Spain's diverse landscapes stir the soul. The Pyrenees and the Picos de Europa are as beautiful as any mountain range on the continent, while the snow-capped Sierra Nevada rises up improbably from the sun-baked plains of Andalucía; these are hiking destinations of the highest order. The wildly beautiful cliffs of Spain's Atlantic northwest are the scene for some of Europe's most spectacular drives, even as the charming coves of the Mediterranean are still the continent's summer destination of choice; despite decades of overdevelopment, numerous unspoiled corners remain. And everywhere you go, villages of timeless beauty perch on hilltops, huddle in valleys and cling to coastal outcrops as tiny but resilient outposts of Old Spain. Spend as long as you can in places like these.

A Culinary Feast

Food and wine are national obsessions in Spain and with good reason. Yes, there's paella, tapas, *jamón* and olive oil in abundance, but these are merely the best-known ingredients of a national cuisine that continues to take the world by storm. The touchstones of Spanish cooking are deceptively simple: incalculable variety, strong traditions of recipes handed down through the generations, and an innate willingness to experiment and see what comes out of the kitchen-laboratory. You may experience the best meal ever over tapas in an earthy bar where everyone's shouting, or over a meal prepared by a celebrity chef in the refined surrounds of a Michelin-starred restaurant. Either way, the breadth of gastronomic experience that awaits you is breathtaking.

Art Imitates Life

Spain's story is told with endless creativity through its arts and architecture. Poignantly windswept Roman ruins, cathedrals of rare power and incomparable jewels of Islamic architecture speak of a country where the great civilisations of history have always risen, fallen and left behind their indelible mark. More recently, what other country could produce such rebellious and relentlessly creative spirits as Salvador Dalí, Pablo Picasso and Antoni Gaudí and place them front and centre in public life? Here, grand monuments to the past coexist alongside architectural creations of such daring that it becomes clear that Spain's future will be every bit as original as its past. For all such talk, this is a country that lives very much in the present. Perhaps you'll sense it along a crowded postmidnight street when all the world has come out to play. Or maybe that moment will come when a flamenco performer touches something deep in your soul. Whenever it happens, you'll find yourself nodding in recognition: *this* is Spain.

need to know

Currency
» The euro (€)

Language
» Spanish (Castellano). Also Catalan, Basque and Gallego (Galician).

When to Go

Santiago de Compostela
GO May-Sep

Barcelona
GO year-round

Madrid
GO Mar-May, Sep & Oct

Valencia
GO year-round

Seville
GO Oct-Apr

Dry climate
Warm to hot summers, cold winters
Mild to hot summers, cold winters
Cold climate

High Season
(Jun–Aug, public holidays)

» Accommodation books out and prices increase by up to 50%.

» Low season in parts of inland Spain.

» Expect warm, dry and sunny weather; more humid in coastal areas.

Shoulder
(Mar–May, Sep & Oct)

» A good time to travel with mild, clear weather and fewer crowds.

» Local festivals can send prices soaring.

Low Season
(Nov–Feb)

» Cold in central Spain; rain in the north and northwest.

» Mild temperatures in Andalucía and the Mediterranean Coast.

» This is high season in ski resorts.

Your Daily Budget

Budget less than

€70

» Dorm beds: €15–20

» Doubles in *hostales*: €45–60

» Supermarkets and lunch *menú del día*

» Use museum and gallery 'free admission' afternoons

Midrange

€70–150

» Room in midrange hotel: €60–120

» Lunch and/or dinner in local restaurant

» Car rental: from €25 per day

Top end over

€150

» Room in top-end hotel: €120 and up (€200 in Madrid and Barcelona)

» Fine dining for lunch and dinner

» Regularly stay in *paradores*

Money

» ATMs widely available. Credit cards accepted in most hotels, restaurants and shops.

Visas

» Generally not required for stays up to 90 days (not at all for members of EU or Schengen countries). Some nationalities need a Schengen visa.

Mobile Phones

» Local SIM cards widely available and can be used in European and Australian mobile phones.

Driving

» Drive on the right; steering wheel is on the left side of the car.

Websites

» **Fiestas.net** (www. fiestas.net) Festivals around the country.

» **LonelyPlanet. com** (www. lonelyplanet.com/ spain) Destination information, hotel bookings, traveller forums and more.

» **Renfe** (Red Nacional de los Ferrocarriles Españoles; www. renfe.es) Spain's rail network.

» **Tour Spain** (www. tourspain.org) Culture, food and links to hotels and transport.

» **Turespaña** (www. spain.info) Spanish tourist office's site.

Exchange Rates

Australia	A$1	€0.69
Canada	C$1	€0.76
Japan	¥100	€0.89
New Zealand	NZ$1	€0.57
UK	UK£1	€1.19
US	US$1	€0.79

For current exchange rates see www.xe.com.

Important Numbers

There are no area codes in Spain.

International access code	+00
Country code	+34
International directory inquiries	+11825
Domestic operator	+1009
National directory inquiries	+11818
Emergencies	+112

Arriving in Spain

» **Barajas airport, Madrid (p114)**
Metro & Buses – €2; every five to 10 minutes from 6.05am to 2am; 30 to 40 minutes to the centre
Taxis – €25 to €35; 20 minutes to the centre

» **Aeroport del Prat, Barcelona (p294)**
Buses – €5; every six to 15 minutes from 6.05am to 1.05am; 30 to 40 minutes to the centre
Trains – €3; from 6.08am to 11.38pm; 35 minutes to the centre
Taxis – €20 to €25; 30 minutes to the centre

Staying in Touch

Internet access in Spain is reasonably easy with some cafes, most hotels and even some budget accommodation having (usually) free wireless internet access for guests. Be wary, however, of hotels promising in-room wi-fi as connection speeds can vary considerably from room to room; always make clear that you require a room with a fast connection when making a reservation. Good internet cafes are increasingly difficult to find; most corner *locutorios* (private call centres) have a few computer terminals out the back. Internet-connected telephone calls (eg Skype) are easily the cheapest way to call home. Otherwise, phone cards are your next best bet (*locutorios* have the widest selection). Buying a local prepaid SIM card for your mobile phone will work out much cheaper than racking up (often exorbitant) roaming charges.

what's new

For this new edition of Spain, our authors have hunted down the fresh, the transformed, the hot and the happening. These are some of our favourites. For up-to-the-minute recommendations, see lonelyplanet.com/spain.

The Greening of Seville

1 With the opening of a new metro system and the pedestrianisation of many streets, Seville is now easier to negotiate and its monuments are free of grime (see the boxed text, p679).

New Flamenco Museum, Seville

2 Seville's Museo del Baile Flamenco fills an 18th-century palace with memorabilia and true flamenco spirit. It's the work of renowned Seville flamenco dancer Cristina Hoyos. It also runs classes (p669).

Learn to Cook Like a Basque

3 Time spent in San Sebastián is never enough, but at least you can take home the secret of its legendary *pintxos:* the tourist office now runs tapas cookery classes (p419).

Museu del Modernisme Català, Barcelona

4 Suitably housed in a fine Modernista building, this new museum displays artworks and furnishings by a catalogue of Modernista luminaries. It's the perfect complement to Barcelona's showpiece architecture (p255).

Museo Teatro Romano, Cartagena

5 Designed by Pritzker Prize–winning architect Rafael Moneo, this new museum ingeniously incorporates numerous archaeological remains, including several galleries of Roman sculpture and artefacts, and the recently restored Roman Theatre (p650).

La Conservera Centro de Arte Contemporáneo, Ceutá

6 A major new art centre housed in a former cannery, this exciting new museum serves as a showcase for Spanish and international contemporary artists and sculptors (see the boxed text, p655).

Boutique Benidorm

7 Benidorm has acquired a touch of class. The five-star Villa Venecia is about luxury and views that reminds you why people started coming to Benidorm in the first place (p580).

Fast Train to Valencia

8 Spain just keeps getting smaller. The December 2010 inauguration of the AVE service between Madrid and Valencia cuts travel time from the capital to the Mediterranean to just 95 minutes (p901).

Real Casino de Murcia, Murcia

9 Reopened by King Juan Carlos in November 2009, Murcia's resplendent 19th-century casino is an ornate architectural combination of cultures and countries, including a Moorish-style patio and splendid ballroom (p646).

Mérida Hotels

10 Mérida finally has two hotels whose standards of excellence provide a suitable companion to the city's ancient Roman sites – budget La Flor de al-Andalus and boutique Hotel Adealba (p806).

if you like...

Art Galleries

Spain's artistic tradition is one of Europe's richest and most original, with Goya, Velázquez, Picasso and Dalí among the better-known Spanish masters. Royal patronage of the arts ensured that works by the great painters from all over Europe also found a home in Spain. The result? Art galleries of astonishing depth.

Museo del Prado, Madrid Quite simply one of the world's best galleries (p69)

Centro de Arte Reina Sofía, Madrid Picasso's *Guernica,* Dalí and Miró (p68)

Museo-Thyssen-Bornemisza, Madrid Works by seemingly every European master (p73)

Museo Picasso Málaga Over 200 works by Picasso, Málaga's favourite son (p720)

Museu Picasso, Barcelona Unrivalled collection from Picasso's early years (p241)

Teatre-Museu Dalí, Figueres As weird-and-wonderful as Salvador Dalí himself (p324)

Museo Guggenheim, Bilbao Showpiece architecture and world-class contemporary art (p401)

Museo de Bellas Artes, Valencia Another stunning gallery with many big names (p552)

Islamic Architecture

For almost seven centuries much of Spain was ruled by a succession of Muslim caliphs and empires and they left behind the finest accumulation of Islamic architecture on European soil. Outstanding extant remains are found in the former Moorish heartland of al-Andalus (Andalucía), especially in Unesco World Heritage–listed Granada, Córdoba and Seville.

Alhambra, Granada An extraordinary monument to the extravagance of al-Andalus (p747)

Mezquita, Córdoba Perfection wrought in stone in Córdoba's one-time Great Mosque (p737)

Albayzín, Granada Like a white-washed North African medina climbing up the hillside (p757)

Alcázar, Seville Exquisite detail amid a perfectly proportioned whole (p668)

Giralda, Seville The former minaret represents a high point in Seville's Islamic skyline (p663)

Aljafería, Zaragoza A rare Moorish jewel in the north (p365)

Alcazaba, Málaga An 11th-century palace-fortress (p721)

Roman Ruins

Spain, or Hispania as it was then called, was an important part of the Ancient Roman Empire for almost five centuries and it left behind a legacy of extraordinary sites scattered around the country. Where modern cities have been built upon the ancient sites, there is a curious juxtaposition between ancient ruins and the clamour of modern Spain, while those ruins abandoned to their fate in the countryside speak eloquently of the long-distant past.

Mérida The most extensive Roman remains in the country (p804)

Tarragona Major public buildings peek out from beneath the new (p352)

Segovia Astonishing Roman aqueduct bisects the city (p144)

Lugo Spain's finest preserved Roman walls (p541)

Itálica Iberia's oldest Roman town with a fine amphitheatre (see the boxed text, p681)

Baelo Claudia, Bolonia Intact Roman town with views of Africa (p711)

» Museo Guggenheim (p401), Bilbao

OLIVER STREWE

Cathedrals

It is difficult to overestimate the significance of Catholicism in forging the Spanish identity and cathedrals have for centuries stood as the monumental and spiritual centrepiece of so many Spanish towns. This legacy of profound faith has been wedded to a rich accumulation of architectural styles. As such, Spain's soaring cathedrals are the story of the country's past writ large.

La Sagrada Família, Barcelona Gaudí's unfinished masterpiece rises above Barcelona like an apparition (p247)

Catedral de Santiago de Compostela One of Spain's most sacred (and beautiful) sites (p503)

León Cathedral Perfectly proportioned and truly astonishing stained-glass windows (p169)

Catedral, Burgos A Gothic highpoint with legends of El Cid (p178)

Catedral Nueva & Catedral Vieja, Salamanca Sandstone Gothic and Romanesque splendour side by side (p133)

Catedral de Toledo Extravagant monument to the power of Catholic Spain (p197)

Capilla Real, Granada An Isabelline-Gothic fantasy adjoining the main cathedral (p751)

Beaches

Nearly 50 million foreign tourists come to Spain every year, and an overwhelming proportion of these (and a large percentage of Spain's own population) come in summer to lie on a near-perfect stretch of Mediterranean sand. Most of Spain's beaches are, as a consequence, dreadfully overcrowded. But if you know where to look, the beach experience that made the Spanish coastline world famous is still a possibility.

Cabo de Gata, Almería A wildly beautiful reminder of the Andalucian coast as it once was (p780)

Costa de la Luz, Andalucía Unbroken stretches of sand along a beautiful coast (p708)

Playa de la Concha, San Sebastián One of the most beautiful city beaches anywhere in the world (p415)

Menorca The Balearics before mass tourism arrived and an insight into why it did (see the boxed text, p612)

Rías Altas, Galicia Spain's most breathtaking coast with cliffs and isolated, sweeping beaches (p513)

Nightlife

Among the most enduring and most easily accessible symbols of the Spanish good life are nights that never seem to end. From sophisticated cocktail bars to beachside *chiringuitos* (bars), from dance-until-dawn nightclubs to outdoor *terrazas* (pavement cafes) on a summer's evening when the night belongs not just to the young, the Spanish night is a diverse, relentless and utterly intoxicating phenomenon. Even the smallest villages seem to have their focal points of night-time *marcha* (action), but the following places are where Spanish nightlife takes on the quality of a legend.

Ibiza Europe's after-dark club and chill-out capital (p618)

Madrid Bars, nightclubs, live music venues and nights that never end (p99 & p105)

Valencia Barrio del Carmen nights are famous throughout Spain (p561)

Barcelona Glamorous and gritty nightspots for an international crowd (p285)

Salamanca Feel-good nights with the university crowd beneath floodlit Renaissance buildings (p140)

If you like... unspoiled coastlines
Galicia's Atlantic shoreline is wildly beautiful, especially the Costa da Morte (p522)

If you like... flamenco
Seville in Andalucía is the best place to catch flamenco live (p677)

Spanish Food

Spanish cuisine may have taken the world by storm, from its celebrity chefs to that winning combination of paella, tapas and *jamón* (cured ham). But eating Spanish food in the country of its birth is another story altogether. This is a country that obsesses about food and one that keeps a watchful eye over its chefs, with an eating public always eager to try something new but wary lest they stray too far from one of Europe's richest culinary traditions. For more information, turn to p850.

Pintxos in San Sebastián Spain's culinary capital with more Michelin stars than Paris and the country's best *pintxos* (tapas; p422)

Paella in Valencia The birthplace of paella and still the place for the most authentic version (p559)

Catalonian cooking in Barcelona Home city for Catalonia's legendary cooking (p277)

Tapas in La Latina, Madrid The best tapas from around Spain (p93)

Spanish Wine

Spanish wines have a devoted international following and in many parts of the country you won't find anything *but* wines from Spain – many Spaniards simply don't see the need for anything else. La Rioja is the king of Spanish wine regions, but the Ribera del Duero (Castilla y León), Somontano (Aragón) and Penedès (near Barcelona) wine-producing regions are also world-class. For more on Spanish wines, see p863.

La Rioja wine region Bodegas, wine museums and vineyards to the horizon (p451)

Cava bodegas, Penedès Wine Country The sparkling wines that are Spain's favourite Christmas drink (p300)

Sherry bodegas, El Puerto de Santa María One of the sherry capitals of the world (p694)

Cider-drinking, Asturias A local passion poured straight from the barrel (see the boxed text, p476)

Zalacaín, Madrid Three Michelin stars, 35,000 bottles and 800 different wine varieties (p99)

Hiking

The clamour of modern Spain can seem all-consuming, but near-pristine wilderness is often just a short bus- or train-ride away. Landscapes almost continental in their variety make Spain one of Europe's premier hiking destinations, from the Pyrenees in the north to the quiet hills and valleys of Andalucía in the south. A superb network of national parks and other protected areas also shelter a surprising range of wildlife.

Parque Nacional de Ordesa y Monte Perdido Pyrenean high country at its most spectacular (p377)

Camino de Santiago Arguably the world's most famous walk, which can last a day or weeks (p37)

Picos de Europa Jagged peaks and steep trails inland from the Bay of Biscay (p488)

Serra de Tramuntana The finest hiking in the Balearics (p604)

Sierra Nevada Wildlife and stunning views in the shadow of Spain's highest mountain (p764)

Sierra de Grazalema White villages and precipitous mountains in Andalucía (p703)

month by month

January

In January, the ski resorts in the Pyrenees in the northeast and the Sierra Nevada, close to Granada in the south, are in full swing. School holidays run until around 8 January so book ahead.

Three Kings

The Día de los Reyes Magos (Three Kings' Day), or simply Reyes, on 6 January, is the most important day on a Spanish kid's calendar. The evening before, three local politicians dress up as the three wise men and lead a sweet-distributing frenzy of Cabalgata de Reyes through the centre of most towns.

February

This is often the coldest month in Spain, with temperatures close to freezing, especially in the north and inland regions such as Madrid. If you're heading to Carnaval, you'll find accommodation at a premium in Cádiz, Sitges and Ciudad Rodrigo in particular.

Life's a Carnaval

Riotously fun Carnaval, ending on the Tuesday 47 days before Easter Sunday, involves fancy-dress parades and festivities. It's wildest in Cádiz (p691), Sitges (p296) and Ciudad Rodrigo (p141). Other curious celebrations are held at Vilanova i La Geltrú (p351) and Solsona (p347).

Return to the Middle Ages

In one of Spain's coldest corners, Teruel's inhabitants don their medieval finery and step back to the Middle Ages with markets, food stalls and a re-enactment of a local lovers' legend during the Fiesta Medieval (p392).

Contemporary Art Fair

One of Europe's biggest celebrations of contemporary art, Madrid's Feria Internacional de Arte Contemporánea (Arco; p85) draws gallery reps and exhibitors from all over the world. It's a thrilling counterpoint to the old masters on display year-round in galleries across the capital.

March

With the arrival of spring, Spain begins to shake off its winter blues (such as they are), the weather starts to warm up ever so slightly and Spaniards start dreaming of a summer by the beach.

Las Fallas

The extraordinary festival of Las Fallas consists of several days of all-night dancing and drinking, first-class fireworks and processions from 15 to 19 March. Its principal stage is Valencia city (see the boxed text, p556) and the festivities culminate in the ritual burning of effigies in the streets.

April

Spain has a real spring in its step with wildflowers in full bloom, Easter celebrations and school holidays. It requires some advance planning (ie book ahead), but it's a great time to be here.

Semana Santa (Holy Week)

Easter (the dates change each year) entails parades of *pasos* (holy figures), hooded penitents and huge crowds. It's extravagantly celebrated in Seville (p671), as well as Málaga (p724), Córdoba (p742), Toledo (p200), Ávila (p128), Cuenca (p217), Lorca (p654) and Zamora (p163).

Dance of Death

The Dansa de la Mort (Dance of Death) on Holy Thursday in the Catalan village of Verges (p317) is a chilling experience. This nocturnal dance of skeleton figures is the centrepiece of Holy Week celebrations.

Los Empalaos

On Holy Thursday, Villanueva de la Vera, in northeast Extremadura, plays out an extraordinary act of Easter abnegation; the devotion and self-inflicted suffering of the barefoot penitents leaves most onlookers breathless. See the boxed text, p787, for details.

Moros y Cristianos (Moors & Christians)

Late-April colourful parades and mock battles between Christian and Muslim 'armies' in Alcoy (see the boxed text, p590), near Alicante, make this one of the most spectacular of many such festivities staged in Valencia and Alicante provinces.

Feria de Abril (April Fair)

This week-long party (p671), held in Seville in the second half of April, is the biggest of Andalucía's fairs. *Sevillanos* ride around on horseback and in elaborate horse-drawn carriages by day and, dressed up in their best traditional finery, dance late into the night.

Feria del Queso (Cheese Fair)

On the last weekend in April, medieval Trujillo, in Extremadura, hosts this pungent cheese fair (p800) with the overwhelming aroma of cheeses from all over Spain. It's sometimes held at the beginning of May.

Romería de la Virgen

On the last Sunday in April, hundreds of thousands of people make a mass pilgrimage to the Santuario de la Virgen de la Cabeza near Andújar, in Jaén province. A small statue of the Virgin is paraded about, exciting great passions.

May

A glorious time to be in Spain, May sees the countryside carpeted with spring wildflowers and the weather can feel like summer's just around the corner. In Jerez de la Frontera, the Feria de Caballo is one of Spain's most iconic festivals and you'll need to book accommodation weeks, if not months in advance.

Feria del Caballo (Horse Fair)

A colourful equestrian fair in Andalucía's horse capital, Jerez de la Frontera (p699), the Feria del Caballo is one of Andalucía's most festive and extravagant fiestas. It features parades, horse-shows, bullfights and plenty of music and dance.

World Music in Cáceres

For three days Cáceres is taken by musical storm for the World of Music, Arts and Dance festival (Womad; p796). Performers from all over the planet take to stages in the medieval squares of the city.

Córdoba's Courtyards Open Up

Scores of beautiful private courtyards are opened to the public for two weeks in Córdoba for the Concurso de Patios Cordobeses (p742). It's a rare chance to see an otherwise-hidden side of Córdoba strewn with flowers and freshly painted.

Muslim Pirates

Sóller, in northern Mallorca, is invaded by Muslim pirates in early May. The resulting 'battle' between townsfolk and invaders (see boxed text, p607), known as Es Firó, recreates an infamous (and unsuccessful) 16th-century assault on the town.

Fiesta de San Isidro

Madrid's major fiesta (p86) celebrates the city's patron saint with bullfights, parades, concerts and more. Locals dress up in traditional costumes and some of the events, such as the bullfighting season, last for a month.

June

By June, the north is shaking off its winter chill and the Camino de Santiago's trails are becoming crowded. In the south, it's warming up as the coastal resorts ready themselves for the summer onslaught.

Romería del Rocío

Focused on Pentecost weekend, the seventh after Easter, this festive pilgrimage is made by up to one million people to the shrine of the Virgin in El Rocío (p685). This is Andalucía's Catholic tradition at its most curious and compelling.

Feast of Corpus Cristi

On the Thursday in the ninth week after Easter, religious processions and celebrations take place in Toledo (p200) and other cities. The strangest celebrations are the baby-jumping tradition of Castrillo de Murcia (see the boxed text, p177).

Bonfires & Fireworks

Midsummer bonfires and fireworks feature on the eve of the Fiesta de San Juan (24 June; Dia de Sant Joan), notably along the Mediterranean coast, including in Barcelona (p272) and in Ciutadella, Menorca (p639), where you can see splendid horsemanship in multitudinous parades.

Electronica Festival

Performers and spectators come from all over the world for Sónar (p272), Bar-celona's two-day celebration of electronic music and said to be Europe's biggest festival of its kind. Dates vary each year.

Wine Battle

On 29 June Haro, one of the premier wine towns of La Rioja, enjoys the Batalla del Vino (p451), squirting wine all over the place in one of Spain's messiest playfights, pausing only to drink the good stuff.

July

Temperatures in Andalucía and much of the interior can be fiercely hot, but it's a great time to be at the beach and is one of the best months for hiking in the Pyrenees.

Festival Internacional de Guitarra

Córdoba's contribution to Spain's impressive calendar of musical events, this fine international guitar festival (p742) ranges from flamenco and classical to rock, blues and beyond. Headline performances take place in the Alcázar gardens at night.

Running of the Bulls

The Fiesta de San Fermín (Sanfermines) is the week-long nonstop festival and party in Pamplona (see the boxed text, p436) with the daily *encierro* (running of the bulls) as its centrepiece. Similar, smaller-scale events occur elsewhere through the summer.

Celtic Pride

Groups from as far off as Nova Scotia come to celebrate their Celtic roots with the *gallegos* in this bagpipe- and fiddler-filled music fest in the Festival de Ortigueira (see the boxed text, p521) in Galicia.

Día de la Virgen del Carmen

Around 16 July in most coastal towns, particularly in some parts of Andalucía, the image of the patron of fisherfolk is carried into the sea or paraded on a flotilla of small boats.

Feast of St James

The Día de Santiago marks the day of Spain's national saint and is spectacularly celebrated in Galicia at Santiago de Compostela (p507). With so many pilgrims in town, it's the city's most festive two weeks of the year.

Festival Internacional de Jazz e Blues de Pontevedra

Top jazz and blues musicians converge on the pretty Galician town of Pontevedra for four days of good listening (p529) near the end of July. The international get-together is preceded by several days of local acts.

Festival Internacional de Benicàssim

Spain is awash with outdoor concert festivals attracting big-name acts from around the country and abroad, especially in summer. This one, in the Valencian town of Benicàssim (p570), remains one of the original and best.

August

Spaniards from all over the country join Europeans in converging on the coastal resorts of the Mediterranean. Although the weather can be unpredictable, Spain's northeastern Atlantic coast offers a more nuanced summer experience.

 Festival de Teatro Clásico

The peerless Roman theatre and amphitheatre in Mérida, Extremadura (p805), become the stage for the classics of ancient Greece and Rome, and the occasional newbie such as Will Shakespeare. Performances are held most nights during July and August.

 More Muslim Pirates

In northwest Mallorca, Pollença (p608) is the scene of fierce mock combat between invading Muslim pirates and townsfolk during the Festes de la Patrona. The afternoon of processions and combat in the streets of the town is preceded by much all-night merriment.

 La Tomatina

Buñol's massive tomato-throwing festival (see the boxed text, p566), held in late August, must be one of the messiest get-togethers in the country. Thousands of people launch about 100 tonnes of tomatoes at one another in just an hour or so!

 All About Cheese

In Arenas de Cabrales (p495) at the foot of the Picos de Europa, cheese-lovers are treated to cheese tasting, making, judging and more. They live for their cheese and cider in this part of the world and there are both in abundance.

 Give Thanks to the Virgin

In Morella the good folk come together every six years (next in 2012) for Sexenni, nine days of exuberant baroque festivities (p574) to give thanks to the Virgin Mary for saving Morella from the plague in 1672.

 Natural Cider Festival

Gijón's Fiesta de la Sidra Natural (p479) gives expression to the Asturian obsession with cider and even includes an annual world-record attempt for the number of people simultaneously pouring cider in one place. It also involves musical concerts.

September

This is the month when Spain returns to work after a seemingly endless summer. Numerous festivals take advantage of the fact that weather generally remains warm until late September at least.

 Bienal de Flamenco

There are flamenco festivals all over Spain throughout the year, but this is the most prestigious of them all. Held in Seville (p672) in even-numbered years (and Málaga every other year) it draws the biggest names in the genre.

 Fiesta de la Virgen de Guadalupe

The pretty town of Guadalupe in Extremadura celebrates its very own Virgin Mary (p803). A statue is paraded about on the evening of the 6th and again on the 8th, which also happens to be Extremadura's regional feast day.

 Feria de Pedro Romero

The honouring of Pedro Romero, one of the legends of bullfighting, is a good excuse for the people of Ronda to host weeks of partying (p731). Highlights include a flamenco festival, an unusual program of bullfighting and much all-night partying.

 La Rioja's Grape Harvest

Logroño celebrates the feast day of St Matthew (Fiesta de San Mateo) and the year's grape harvest (p447). There are grape-crushing ceremonies and endless opportunities to sample the fruit of the vine in liquid form.

 Barcelona's Big Party

Barcelona's Festes de la Mercè (p272) marks the end of summer with four days of parades, concerts, theatre, fire running and more. Barcelona's always fun, but this is a whole new level.

☆ **San Sebastián Film Festival**

It may not be Cannes, but San Sebastián's annual, two-week celebration of film (p420) is one of the most prestigious dates on Europe's film-festival circuit. It's held in the second half of the month and has been gathering plaudits since 1957.

★★ Romans & Carthaginians

In the second half of the month, locals dress up to re-enact ancient battles during the festival of Carthagineses y Romanos in Cartagena (p651). It's among the more original mock battles staged around Spain to honour the distant past.

October

Autumn can be a lovely time to be in Spain, with generally mild temperatures throughout the country, although the winter chill can start to bite in central and northern parts of the country.

★★ Día de Nuestra Señora del Pilar

In Zaragoza on 12 October, the faithful mix with hedonists to celebrate this festival dedicated to Our Lady of the Pillar (p365); the pillar in question is in the cathedral, but much of the fun happens in the bars nearby.

★★ Fiesta de Santa Teresa

The patron saint of Ávila is honoured with 10 days of processions, concerts and fireworks around her feast day (p128). Huddled behind medieval walls, the festival brings to life the powerful cult of personality surrounding Ávila's most famous daughter.

November

A quiet time on the festival calendar, November is cool throughout the country. Depending on the year, the ski season usually begins in this month in the Pyrenees and Sierra Nevada.

☆ Festival Jazz Madrid

One of two annual jazz festivals in the capital (the other is in the spring), this increasingly prestigious jazz festival (p87) plays out in the famous jazz clubs and larger theatres across the city.

itineraries

Whether you've got six days or 60, these itineraries provide a starting point for the trip of a lifetime. Want more inspiration? Head online to lonelyplanet.com/thorntree to chat with other travellers.

One Month
The Grand Tour

❯ So many Spanish trails begin in **Barcelona**, Spain's second-biggest city. Explore the architecture and sample the food, then embark on a coast crawl with stops in **Tarragona** for the Roman ruins, **Peñíscola** for the beach, and **Valencia** for another dose of nightlife and the 21st-century wonders of the Ciudad de las Artes y las Ciencias. From here, flee deep into Castilla-La Mancha, halting en route at craggy **Cuenca**. Push on to the capital, mighty **Madrid**, for the hedonism and museums before continuing to **Toledo**, a medieval jewel. The road sweeps through La Mancha's plains and olive groves, before tilting at windmills like Don Quijote in **Consuegra**. Striking **Almagro**, deep in Almodóvar territory, has a beguiling charm, before you take the A4 to **Jaén** and its gorgeous cathedral. Nearby, **Baeza** and **Úbeda** are enticing Renaissance gems, while the Islamic glories of **Granada** and **Córdoba** are not far away to the south and west, respectively. The colourful capital of the south, **Seville**, also beckons. Hear the call of Africa? Drop down to **Cádiz** and proceed east to lovely **Tarifa** for the boat to Morocco and a whole new adventure.

One Month
Andalucian Adventure

❭ If you're arriving by air, the natural starting point for any Andalucía trip is **Málaga**, whose airport receives flights from almost every conceivable corner of Europe. While in town, don't miss the exceptional Museo Picasso. Head north to the stunning Mudéjar architecture of **Antequera**, then east to **Granada**, the first in Andalucía's triumvirate of Unesco World Heritage–listed cities (the other two are Seville and Córdoba). In Granada, marvel at the peerless Alhambra, be overwhelmed by the gilded Capilla Real and linger in the medieval Muslim quarter of Albayzín. A detour south and then east takes you to the otherworldly valleys of **Las Alpujarras** with their fine mountain scenery and North African–style villages; explore these on foot if you've got the time and the energy. Away to the southeast, **Almería** is one of Spain's most agreeable provincial towns, while **Cabo de Gata** is one of the most dramatic sections of the country's Mediterranean coast and an antidote to its otherwise overdeveloped shoreline.

Returning into the Andalucian heartland, via Granada, make for **Córdoba**, home to the magnificent Mezquita and an enchanted *judería* (Jewish Quarter). Next stop, **Seville**, the heartbeat of Andalucía with its glorious architecture (especially the Alcázar and cathedral), fine tapas and soul-stirring live flamenco. There's more flamenco, as well as fine Andalucía horsemanship, at **Jerez de la Frontera**, while **Cádiz** is at once fun-loving and Europe's oldest settlement; if you're in Cádiz during Carnaval in particular you'll understand what we mean. The region's hill villages don't come any more beautiful than cliff-top **Arcos de la Frontera** that conforms wonderfully to the stereotype of Andalucía's *pueblos blancos* (white villages). After breaking up your journey here, meander along quiet country roads east through the pretty whitewashed villages and mountain trails of the **Parque Natural Sierra de Grazalema** and on to spectacularly sited **Ronda**, where a night in its palatial and precipitous parador is one of Spain's great sleeping experiences. **Vejer de la Frontera** is another hill town par excellence, while the sandy Atlantic beaches of the **Costa de la Luz** are some of Spain's best. End your journey in hip **Tarifa**, the southernmost tip of mainland Spain, and a centre for summer whale-watching, windsurfing and, of course, much lazing on the fine beach.

One Month
Spain's Northeast

❭ Spain's well-drenched northern coast, at times rugged and wildly beautiful, forms a green band from the Basque Country to Galicia, backed by the Cordillera Cantábrica. This route takes you through what is arguably Spain's most spectacular (and certainly least developed) stretch of coastline, with gorgeous villages and fine food thrown in for good measure.

There is no finer introduction to the country than **San Sebastián**, its two dramatic headlands giving way to a perfect crescent bay. Its old town is arguably Spain's spiritual home of tapas (or *pintxos* as they call them here) and spending an evening wandering from bar to bar with their counters groaning under the weight of bit-sized morsels is close to gastronomic paradise. West of San Sebastián, **Bilbao** is best known as the home of the showpiece Guggenheim Museum. Heading west, hug the coast of Cantabria and Asturias and drop by the old centre of **Castro Urdiales**, to surf at **Oriñón** and to promenade along the waterfront at **Santander**. Following Cantabria's eastern coast, explore the cobblestone medieval marvel that is **Santillana del Mar** and admire the Modernista architecture in **Comillas**. The eastern Asturias coast is best travelled by train, stopping off at **Llanes** and **Ribadesella**. **Arriondas**, the next stop, is one gateway to the majestic **Picos de Europa** with their vertiginous rock walls, outstanding scenery and fine hiking opportunities. Next make your way to **Oviedo**, Asturias' capital, for its pre-Romanesque architecture and **Gijón**, a substantial port where cider, one of the great Asturian passions, flows freely. West of Gijón, secluded beaches await between the picturesque fishing harbours of **Cudillero** and **Luarca**. Galicia's coastline is one of Spain's great natural wonders, punctuated with secluded fishing villages and stunning cliffs. As you make your way around the coast, don't miss **Cabo Ortegal**, dynamic **A Coruña** and the **Costa da Morte**. **Pontevedra** and **Vigo**, on the cusp of Portugal, are worth continuing down the coastline for, before doubling back to **Santiago de Compostela**, a thoroughly Galician city, a place of pilgrim footfalls, fine regional cuisine and a cathedral of rare power.

Those with more time could make the final approach on foot along the Camino Portugues route of the **Camino de Santiago** pilgrim route. Alternatively, discover the area with the Transcantábrico scenic train.

Three Weeks
Extreme West

❯ From **Madrid**, travel north through the cathedral towns of **Burgos** and **León** before sweeping through the heart of Castilla y León to the enchanted medieval village of **Puebla de Sanabria**, one of Spain's best-kept secrets. Provincial **Zamora** is a little-visited Romanesque gem, but it's a mere entrée to the main event in southwestern Castilla y León: **Salamanca**. Wander with wonder at night through the pulsating streets of this vibrant university town, amid its splendid plateresque public buildings, luminous and floodlit. If you can tear yourself away, Salamanca is also a gateway to some of Spain's least-visited back-country villages, especially in the timeworn Sierra de Francia. **La Alberca** is probably the pick of a very fine bunch. You would never guess that until recent decades misery ruled in this quiet rural retreat that was one of the poorest regions of Spain.

The road continues to climb and then suddenly drops through woods into Extremadura, passing into the once equally poor Las Hurdes region to reach **Plasencia** to the southeast. Jammed with noble buildings, churches and convents, it was for centuries the region's principal city, and makes a good base for excursions up the northeast valleys. From Plasencia, a circuit takes you first to the birders' paradise that is the **Parque Nacional de Monfragüe** and then on to the charming hill town and pilgrims' destination of **Guadalupe**, lorded over by the monastery complex dedicated to Our Lady of Guadalupe. Country roads then lead westwards to the medieval town of **Trujillo**, a warren of cobbled lanes, churches and the newer Renaissance-era additions that were the fruit of conquistador gold. A short drive further west lies the ochre-coloured medieval jewel of **Cáceres**, a town with a lively student nightlife scene, too. To the south stand some of Spain's most impressive Roman ruins in **Mérida**. Further south again across the dry plains lies the white town of **Zafra**, a precursor to Andalucía in both spirit and geography. Rather than continue straight into Andalucía, make a westwards detour to the hilly town of **Jerez de los Caballeros** before finally heading south for magical **Seville**.

Two to Three Weeks
Madrid to El Maestrazgo

❯ Escape **Madrid** and start this adventure in nonconformist fashion with a night or two in **Segovia** (rather than as the usual day trip from Madrid), with its Disney-esque Alcázar and Roman aqueduct, then repeat the dose huddled behind the perfect medieval walls of **Ávila**. Brooding and monumental **Toledo**, too, is at its best when the day-trippers head home, enabling you to catch the whispering legends of its multifaith past. Wander further from convention by taking the road south to **Orgaz** and then a detour southeast to **Consuegra** and **Almagro**, an enchanting stop for a night or two. From Almagro, the trail takes you east towards the **Parque Natural de las Lagunas de Ruidera** with its lagoons, and then swing back northwest to Quijote territory, checking out **Campo de Criptana**, **El Toboso** and **Mota del Cuervo**. The road continues east to **Belmonte** and its castle. For a castle you can sleep in, press on to **Alarcón**.

Make the loop southeast to reach **Alcalá del Júcar**, on the stunning Río Júcar, which you can then follow west before heading back north for **Cuenca** and its hanging houses. A pretty riverside route takes you north along the CM2105 road into the hilly territory of the Serranía de Cuenca and then east to the ochre town of Muslim origin, **Albarracín** – there are few more beautiful villages in Spain than Albarracín, with its walls strung out along the high ridges that encircle this wonderful place. Next stop is **Teruel**, remarkable for its old town's Mudéjar architecture and far from well-worn travel routes; if you can be here for its February Fiesta Medieval you will, apart from being very cold, catch the essence of its appeal. The theme of leaving behind roads well travelled continues as you head east past hamlets of the high country of El Maestrazgo, including spectacularly sited **Cantavieja** and quieter-than-quiet **Mirambel**, where you'll feel as if you've arrived in one of the most secluded corners of the Spanish interior. Crossing into Valencia (but still in El Maestrazgo), our route takes you on to the pretty, castle-dominated town of **Morella** and finally to the coast at **Peñíscola**.

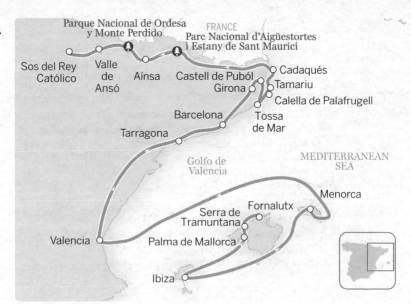

One Month
Balearics to the Pyrenees

❭ You could spend weeks exploring the Balearic Islands depending, of course, on how long you need passing long, lazy days on its wonderful beaches. Begin, like so many holidaymakers, in pretty **Palma de Mallorca**, lingering in particular over its astonishing cathedral. Before leaving the island, set aside time to leave the crowds behind by trekking into the **Serra de Tramuntana** and exploring the villages of Mallorca's northwestern coast, such as **Fornalutx**, and the fine coastal scenery at Cap de Formentor. Take a ferry to **Ibiza** and dive into its world-famous nightlife, before island-hopping again, this time to **Menorca** and its wonderful south coast beaches.

Catch one last ferry from Menorca to **Valencia** and dine on paella by the sea, admire the breathtaking Ciudad de las Artes y las Ciencias and stay out late in the Barrio del Carmen. Follow the Mediterranean northeast to **Tarragona**, one of the most significant Roman sites in the country. Follow the Costa Brava, acquaint yourself with **Barcelona**, then head inland to **Girona** and Salvador Dalí's fantasy castle **Castell de Puból**. Returning to the coast, dip into pretty villages such as **Tossa de Mar**, **Calella de Palafrugell** and **Tamariu** en route to **Cadaqués**, Dalí's beautiful one-time home.

Leave the Mediterranean behind and climb up into the Pyrenees, passing through the increasingly spectacular northwestern valleys to the **Parc Nacional d'Aigüestortes i Estany de Sant Maurici**, before crossing the provincial frontier into Aragón. Medieval, stone-built **Aínsa** is the prettiest among many Aragonese villages in the Pyrenean foothills; linger here for a couple of days before drawing near to the **Parque Nacional de Ordesa y Monte Perdido**, perhaps the most shapely mountains of all on the Spanish side of the frontier. Apart from being staggeringly beautiful, this is one of Europe's premier hiking destinations and its restrictions on the number of visitors make this a premier wilderness destination. As you head west in the shadow of the snow-capped peaks, detour up the **Valle de Ansó** and then end your journey in the idyllic hill village of **Sos del Rey Católico**.

Spain Outdoors

Best Bases for Thrill Seekers

Tarifa (p710), a wind- and kitesurfing centre par excellence

Espot (p340), a gateway to some superb Pyrenean trekking

Las Alpujarras (p766), for snow-white villages surrounded by ski slopes and trekking routes

L'Estartit (p317), for some of the most colourful diving in the Mediterranean

Torla (p380), a launch pad for some outstanding Pyrenean trekking

Mundaka (p411), the finest surf spot in Europe

Vall de la Noguera Pallaresa (p339), for raging white waters perfect for rafting

Cangas de Onís (p493), for canoeing, canyoning, horse riding and caving in the heart of the Picos

El Rocío (p684), for wildlife safaris, horse riding and birdwatching in Spain's flagship national park

Few countries in Europe can match Spain's diversity of landscapes. Its never-ending coastline takes in everything from the snakelike *rías* (inlets or estuaries) of rugged Galicia to the olive-backed shores of the Mediterranean, while jagged mountain ranges, such as Andalucía's mighty Sierra Nevada and the Pyrenean peaks in the north, reach for the skies. This landscape makes for a wonderful adventure playground; there's something for everyone no matter what age or fitness level.

Spain is famous for superb walking trails that criss-cross mountains and hills from the snowy Pyrenees and Picos to the sultry Cabo de Gata coastal trail in Andalucía, but none come more famous than the Camino de Santiago – the pilgrimage route to the cathedral in Galicia's Santiago de Compostela.

Away from hiking boots, Spain's beaches offer fantastic opportunities for watersports, whether hanging in the tube at Mundaka or reef diving in Catalonia.

Other heart-pumping activities include superb skiing, cycling and river rafting, as well as a string of national parks offering the best wildlife viewing in Western Europe.

Walking

Spain is one of the premier walking destinations in Europe and a snapshot of the possibilities shows why: conquering Spain's highest mainland peak, Mulhacén

CAMINO BOOKS

Camino books abound. The best of each category is suggested below.

» Background history: William Melczer's essential history and translation of the 12th-century *Pilgrim's Guide to Santiago de Compostela*.

» Culture: David Gitlitz and Linda Davidson's *The Pilgrimage Road to Santiago: The Complete Cultural Handbook* is well worth its weight.

» Analysis: anthropologist Nancy Frey explores the pilgrimage's modern resurgence in *Pilgrim Stories: On and Off the Road to Santiago*.

» Guidebook: Millán Bravo Lozano's *A Practical Guide for Pilgrims* provides great maps and route descriptions.

» Religious/spiritual account: Joyce Rupp gives a compelling account of the inner journey in *Walk in a Relaxed Manner*.

» Esoteric: Paulo Coelho's mystical journey described in *The Pilgrimage* is an international best seller.

(3479m; p764) above Granada; following in the footsteps of Carlos V in Extremadura (p788); walking along Galicia's Costa da Morte (Death Coast; p522); or sauntering through alpine meadows anywhere in the Pyrenees.

When to Go

Spain encompasses a number of different climate zones, ensuring that it's possible to hike year-round. In Andalucía conditions are at their best from March to June and in September and October; they're unbearable in midsummer, but in winter most trails remain open, except in the high mountains. If you prefer to walk in summer, do what Spaniards have traditionally done and escape to the north. The Basque Country, Asturias, Cantabria and Galicia are best from June to September. The Pyrenees are accessible from mid-June, while July and August are the ideal months for the high Sierra Nevada. August is the busiest month on the trails, so if you plan to head to popular national parks and stay in *refugios* (mountain refuges), book ahead.

Prime Spots

For good reason, the Pyrenees, separating Spain from France, are most famous for walking. The range is utterly beautiful: prim and chocolate-box pretty on the lower slopes, wild and bleak at higher elevations, and relatively unspoilt in comparison with some European mountain ranges. The Pyrenees contain two outstanding national parks, Aigüestortes i Estany de Sant Maurici (p340) and Ordesa y Monte Perdido (p377). The spectacular GR11 (Senda Pirenáica) traverses the range, connecting the Atlantic (at Hondarribia in the Basque Country) with the Mediterranean (at Cap de Creus in Catalonia). Walking the whole 45-day route is an unforgettable challenge, but there are some magnificent day hikes in the national parks and elsewhere.

Breathtaking and accessible limestone ranges with distinctive craggy peaks (usually hot climbing destinations, too) are the hallmark of Spain's first national park, the Picos de Europa (p488), which straddles the Cantabria, Asturias and León provinces and is fast gaining a reputation as *the* place to walk in Spain. Less well known, but just as rewarding, are Valencia's Els Ports area (p572), and the Sierra de Cazorla (p776) and Sierra de Grazalema (p703) in Andalucía.

To walk in mountain villages, the classic spot is Las Alpujarras (p766), near the Parque Nacional Sierra Nevada in Andalucía.

Great coastal walking abounds, even in heavily visited areas such as the south coast (try Cabo de Gata, p780) and Mallorca (p604).

Information

For the full low-down on all of the walks in this chapter plus many others, including the Camino de Santiago, check out Lonely Planet's recently updated *Hiking in Spain*. Region-specific walking (and climbing) guides are published by **Cicerone Press** (www.cicerone.co.uk). Madrid's **La Tienda Verde** (www.tiendaverde.es; Calle de Maudes 23 & 38, Madrid) and **Librería Desnivel** (www.libreriadesnivel.com, in Spanish; Plaza de Matute 6, Madrid) both sell maps (the best Spanish ones are Prames and Adrados) and guides. In Spanish, the website www.andarines.com gives route descriptions and useful links for books, sports shops and Spanish mountaineering associations.

Camino de Santiago

The door is open to all, to sick and healthy, not only to Catholics but also to pagans, Jews, heretics and vagabonds.

So go the words of a 13th century poem describing the Camino. Eight hundred years later these words still ring true. The Camino de Santiago (Way of St James) originated as a medieval pilgrimage and, for more than 1000 years, people have taken up the Camino's age-old symbols – the scallop shell and staff – and set off on the adventure of a lifetime to the tomb of St James the apostle, in Santiago de Compostela, in the Iberian Peninsula's far northwest.

Today this magnificent long-distance walk, spanning 783km of Spain's north from Roncesvalles, on the border with France, to Santiago de Compostela in Galicia, attracts walkers of all backgrounds and ages, from countries across the world. And no wonder. Its laundry list of assets (culture, history, nature) is impressive, as are its accolades. Not only is it Europe's first Cultural Itinerary and a Unesco World Heritage Site but, for pilgrims, it's a pilgrimage equal to one to Jerusalem and by finishing it you're guaranteed a healthy chunk of time off purgatory.

To feel, absorb, smell and taste northern Spain's diversity, for a great physical challenge, for a unique perspective on rural and urban communities, and to meet intriguing travel companions, this is an incomparable walk. *The door is open to all,* so step on in.

PILGRIM HOSTELS

There are around 300 *refugios* along the Camino, owned by parishes, 'friends of the Camino' associations, private individuals, town halls and regional governments. While in the early days these places were run on donations and provided little more than hot water and a bed, today's pilgrims are charged €5 to €10 and expect showers, kitchens and washing machines. Some things haven't changed though – the *refugios* still operate on a first come, first served basis and are intended for those doing the Camino solely on their own steam.

History

In the 9th century a remarkable event occurred in the poor Iberian hinterlands: following a shining star, Pelayo, a religious hermit, unearthed the tomb of the apostle James the Greater (or, in Spanish, Santiago). The news was confirmed by the local bishop, the Asturian king and later the Pope. Its impact is hard to truly imagine today, but it was instant and indelible: first a trickle, then a flood of Christian Europeans began to journey towards the setting sun in search of salvation.

Compostela became the most important destination for Christians after Rome and Jerusalem. Its popularity increased with an 11th-century papal decree granting it Holy Year status: pilgrims could receive a plenary

Camino de Santiago

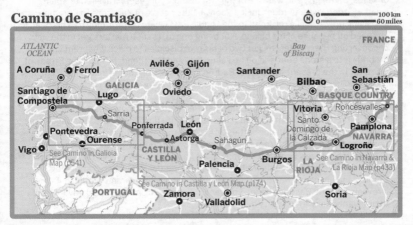

indulgence – a full remission of one's life-time's sins – during a Holy Year. These occur when Santiago's feast day (25 July) falls on a Sunday: the next one isn't until 2021.

The 11th and 12th centuries marked the pilgrimage's heyday. The Reformation was devastating for Catholic pilgrimages and, by the 19th century, the Camino nearly died out. In its startling late-20th-century re-animation, which continues today, it's most popular as a personal-cum-spiritual journey of discovery rather than one primarily motivated by religion.

Routes

Although in Spain there are many *caminos* (paths) to Santiago, by far the most popular is, and was, the Camino Francés, which originated in France, crossed the Pyrenees at Roncesvalles and then headed west for 783km across the regions of Navarra, La Rioja, Castilla y León and Galicia.

Waymarked with cheerful yellow arrows and scallop shells, the 'trail' is a mishmash of rural lanes, paved secondary roads and footpaths all strung together.

Starting at Roncesvalles, the Camino takes roughly two weeks cycling or five weeks walking.

A very popular alternative is to walk only the last 100km (the minimum distance al-lowed) from Sarria in Galicia in order to earn a Compostela certificate of completion given out by the Catedral de Santiago de Compostela.

Information

For information on the various stages of the walk, see the boxed texts on p432, p174 and p540.

For more information about the Creden-cial and the Compostela certificate, visit the cathedral's **Oficina de Acogida de Peregri-nos** (Pilgrim's Office; www.peregrinossantiago.es; Rúa do Vilar 1, Santiago de Compostela).

There are a number of excellent Camino websites packed with useful practical in-formation for the would-be pilgrim. Try www.caminolinks.co.uk for a complete, an-notated guide to many Camino websites; www.mundicamino.com has excellent, thorough descriptions and maps of all of the Caminos; and www.caminodesanti-ago.me contains a huge selection of news groups, where you can get all of your ques-tions answered.

When to Walk

People walk and cycle the Camino year-round. In May and June the wildflowers are glorious and the endless fields of cereals turn from green to toasty gold, making the

---

THE STONE BOAT OF THE MOOR SLAYER

That the Camino de Santiago has had a huge impact on northern Spain is without doubt, but one obvious question persists: what were the remains of Santiago, mar-tyred in Jerusalem in AD 44, doing in northwest Iberia? Here, medieval imagination and masterminding take over. The accepted story suggests that after the crucifixion of Jesus, Santiago (who was one of the first disciples of Jesus) travelled to Spain, where he tried, without much luck, to convert the people of Zaragoza to Christian-ity. Giving up, he finally returned to the Middle East where he promptly had his head chopped off because of his beliefs. Not being one to let such matters get in the way of converting the masses, he got two of his own disciples to place what remained of his body into a stone boat and off he set up the Mediterranean, through the Straits of Gibraltar to the present-day port of Padrón in Galicia. Continuing inland for 17km, he finally had his body buried in a forest named Libredon (present-day Compostela). All was forgotten until Pelayo saw the star.

The Camino even helped in the Christian Reconquista (reconquest) of Muslim Spain. Directly linked to the Reconquista as the Christians' holy hero, Santiago made several appearances at major battles as Matamoros (Moor Slayer). With sword raised, he would descend from the clouds on a white charger to save the day.

As if all this weren't enough, Santiago also gave birth to the very first guidebook to Spain. This medieval guidebook offered both practical advice on completing the Camino and an insight into local cultures and peoples. In one memorable instance it reveals how the Basques have to protect their mules from the sexual advances of their neighbours with chastity belts!

landscapes a huge draw. July and August bring crowds of summer holidaymakers and scorching heat, especially through Castilla y León. September is less crowded and the weather is generally pleasant. From November to May there are fewer people on the road as the season can bring snow, rain and bitter winds. Santiago's feast day, 25 July, is a popular time to converge on the city.

National & Natural Parks

Much of Spain's most spectacular and ecologically important terrain – about 40,000 sq km or 8% of the entire country, if you include national hunting reserves – is under some kind of official protection. Nearly all of these areas are at least partly open to walkers, naturalists and other outdoor enthusiasts, but degrees of conservation and access vary.

The *parques nacionales* (national parks) are areas of exceptional importance and are the country's most strictly controlled protected areas. Spain has 14 national parks – nine on the mainland, four on the Canary Islands and one in the Balearic Islands. The hundreds of other protected areas fall into at least 16 classifications and range in size from 100-sq-metre rocks off the Balearics to Andalucía's 2140-sq-km Parque Natural de Cazorla.

Other Activities

Peddle up a mountain and then blast back down on a pair of skis, clamber up a chasm and then sail above it on a hang-glider, go below the waves on a scuba-diving course or get above them on a surfboard or kayak. If walking isn't your thing, then Spain has plenty of other opportunities to work off that lunch.

Cycling

Spain has a rich variety of cycling possibilities, from gentle family rides to challenging two-week expeditions. If you avoid the cities (where cycling can be somewhat nerve-racking), Spain is also a cycle-friendly country, with drivers accustomed to sharing the roads with platoons of Lycra-clad cyclists. The excellent network of secondary roads, usually with a comfortable shoulder, is ideal for road touring.

CLASSIC CYCLING SPOTS

Every Spanish region has both off-road (called BTT in Spanish, from *bici todo terreno*, meaning 'mountain bike') and touring trails and routes. Mountain bikers can head to just about any sierra (mountain range) and use the extensive *pistas forestales* (forestry tracks). One highly recommended and challenging off-road excursion takes you across the snowy Sierra Nevada (p764). Classic long-haul touring routes include the Camino de Santiago (p37), the Ruta de la Plata (see the boxed text, p797) and the 600km Camino del Cid, which follows in the footsteps of Spain's epic hero from Burgos to Valencia. Guides in Spanish exist for all of these, available at bookshops and online.

Information

An indispensable website for readers of Spanish is www.amigosdelciclismo.com, which gives useful information on restrictions, updates on laws, circulation norms, contact information for cycling clubs and lists of guidebooks, as well as a lifetime's worth of route descriptions organised region by region. There are many cycling guidebooks in publication (the vast majority in Spanish): *España en Bici,* by Paco Tortosa and María del Mar Fornés, is a good overview guide, but it's quite hard to find; *Cycle Touring in Spain: Eight Detailed Routes,* by Harry Dowdell, is a helpful planning tool, as well as being practical once you're in Spain; and another good resource is *The Trailrider Guide – Spain: Single Track Mountain Biking in Spain,* by Nathan James and Linsey Stroud.

For information on bicycle purchase and transport in Spain, see p894. Bike Spain (p83) in Madrid is one of the better cycling tour operators.

Skiing & Snowboarding

For winter powder, Spain's skiers (including the royal family) head to the Pyrenees of Aragón and Catalonia. Outside of the peak periods (the beginning of December, 20 December to 6 January, Carnaval and Semana

PARK	FEATURES	ACTIVITIES	BEST TIME TO VISIT	PAGE
Parc Nacional d'Aigüestortes i Estany de Sant Maurici	beautiful Pyrenees lake region	walking, wildlife spotting	Jun-Sep	p340
Parque Nacional de Doñana	bird and mammal haven in Guadalquivir delta	4WD tours, walking, wildlife watching, horse riding	year-round	p684
Parque Nacional de Ordesa y Monte Perdido	spectacular section of the Pyrenees, with chamois, raptors and varied vegetation	walking, rock climbing	mid-Jun–Jul & mid-Aug–Sep	p377
Parque Nacional de los Picos de Europa	beautiful mountain refuge for chamois, and a few wolves and bears	walking, rock climbing, caving	May-Jul & Sep	p488
Parques Nacional and Natural Sierra Nevada	mainland Spain's highest mountain range, with ibexes, 60 endemic plants and the beautiful Alpujarras valleys on its southern slopes	walking, rock climbing, mountain biking, skiing, horse riding	year-round, depending on activity	p764
Parque Natural de Cazorla	abundant wildlife, 2300 plant species and beautiful mountain scenery	walking, driving, mountain biking, wildlife watching, 4WD tours	Apr-Oct	p776
Áreas Naturales Serra de Tramuntana	spectacular mountain range on Mallorca	walks, birdwatching	late Feb- early Oct	p604
Parque Nacional de Monfragüe	spectacular birds of prey	birdwatching	Mar-Oct	p792
Parque Natural Sierra de Grazalema	lovely, green, mountainous area with rich bird life	walking, caving, canyoning, birdwatching, paragliding, rock climbing	Sep-Jun	p703
Parc Natural del Cadí-Moixeró	steep pre-Pyrenees range	rock climbing, walking	Jun-Sep	p336
Parc Natural de la Zona Volcànica de la Garrotxa	beautiful wooded region with 30 volcanic cones	walking	Apr-Oct	p330
Parque Natural Sierra de Gredos	beautiful mountain region, home to Spain's biggest ibex population	walking, rock climbing, mountain biking	Mar-May & Sep-Nov	p130
Parque Natural de Somiedo	dramatic section of Cordillera Cantábrica	walking	Jul-Sep	p487
Parque Natural de Cabo de Gata-Níjar	sandy beaches, volcanic cliffs, flamingo colony and semidesert vegetation	swimming, birdwatching, walking, horse riding, diving, snorkelling	year-round	p780

Santa), Spain's top resorts are relatively quiet, cheap and warm in comparison with their counterparts in the Alps. The season runs from December to April, though January and February are generally the best, most reliable times for snow. However, in recent years snow fall has been a bit unpredictable.

Prime Spots

In Aragón, two popular resorts are Formigal (p371) and Candanchú (p371); just above the town of Jaca, Candanchú has some 42km of runs with 51 pistes (as well as 35km of cross-country track). In Catalonia, Spain's first resort, La Molina (p335), is still going strong and is ideal for families and beginners. Considered by many to have the Pyrenees' best snow, the 72-piste resort of Baqueira-Beret (p345) boasts 30 modern lifts and 104km of downhill runs for all levels.

Spain's other major resort is Europe's southernmost: the Sierra Nevada (p764), outside Granada. The 80km of runs are at their prime in March and the slopes are particularly suited for families and novice-to-intermediate skiers.

Information

If you don't want to bring your own gear, Spanish resorts have equipment hire, as well as ski schools. Lift tickets cost between €35 and €40 per day for adults, and €25 and €30 for children; equipment hire costs from around €20 per day. If you're planning ahead, Spanish travel agencies frequently advertise affordable single- or multi-day packages with lodging included. An excellent source of information on snowboarding and skiing in Spain (and the rest of Europe) is www.skisnowboardeurope.com.

Water Sports
Scuba-Diving & Snorkelling

There's more to Spain than what you see on the surface – literally! Delve under the ocean waves anywhere along the country's almost 5000km of shoreline and a whole new Spain opens up, crowded with marine life and including features such as wrecks, sheer walls and long cavern swim-throughs. The numerous Mediterranean dive centres cater to an English-speaking market and offer single- and multi-day trips, equipment rental and certification courses. Their Atlantic counterparts (in San Sebastián, Santander and A Coruña) deal mostly in Spanish but, if that's not an obstacle for you, the colder waters of the Atlantic will offer a completely different, and very rewarding, underwater experience.

A good starting point is the reefs along the Costa Brava, especially around the Illes Medes marine reserve (p317), off L'Estartit (near Girona). On the Costa del Sol (p727), operators launch to such places as La Herradura Wall, the *Motril* wreck and the Cavern of Cerro Gordo. Spain's Balearic Islands are also popular dive destinations with excellent services.

HANG-GLIDING & PARAGLIDING

It's not what most people do on their summer holidays but, if you want to take to the skies either *ala delta* (hang-gliding) or *parapente* (paragliding), there are a number of specialised clubs and adventure-tour companies. The **Real Federación Aeronáutica España** (www.rfae.org, in Spanish) gives information on recognised schools and lists clubs and events.

Paco Nadal's *Buceo en España* provides information province by province, with descriptions of ocean floors, dive centres and equipment rental.

Surfing

The opportunity to get into the waves is a major attraction for beginners and experts alike along many of Spain's coastal regions. The north coast of Spain has, debatably, the best surf in mainland Europe.

The main surfing region is the north coast, where numerous high-class spots can be found, but Atlantic Andalucía gets decent winter swells. Despite the flow of vans loaded down with surfboards along the north coast in the summer, it's actually autumn through to spring that's the prime time for decent swell, with October probably the best month overall. The variety of waves along the north coast is impressive: there are numerous open, swell-exposed beach breaks for the summer months, and some seriously heavy reefs and points that only really come to life during the colder, stormier months.

Prime Spots

The most famous wave in Spain is the legendary river-mouth left at Mundaka (p411). On a good day, there's no doubt that it's one of the best waves in the world. However, it's not very consistent and, when it's on, it's always very busy and ugly.

Heading east, good waves can be found throughout the Basque Country. Going west, into neighbouring regions of Cantabria and Asturias, you'll also find a superb range of well-charted surf beaches, such as Rodiles in Asturias (p481) and Liencres in Cantabria. If you're looking for solitude, some isolated beaches along Galicia's beautiful Costa da Morte (p522) remain empty even in summer. In southwest Andalucía there are a number of powerful, winter beach breaks, and weekdays off Conil de la Frontera (located just northwest of Cabo de Trafalgar, p708) can be sublimely lonely.

Information

In summer a shortie wetsuit (or, in the Basque Country, just board shorts) is sufficient along all coasts except Galicia (which picks up the icy Canaries current – you will need a light full suit).

Surf shops abound in the popular surfing areas and usually offer board and wetsuit hire. If you're a beginner joining a surf school, ask the instructor to explain the rules and to keep you away from the more experienced surfers.

There are a number of excellent surf guidebooks to Spain. Check out Stuart Butler's English-language *Big Blue Surf Guide: Spain,* José Pellón's Spanish-language *Guía del Surf en España* and Low Pressure's superb *Stormrider Guide: Europe – the Continent.*

Windsurfing & Kitesurfing

Spain is blessed with excellent windsurfing and kitesurfing (kiteboarding) conditions along much of its Mediterranean coast.

Prime Spots

The best sailing conditions are to be found around Tarifa (p710), which has such strong and consistent winds that it's said that the town's formerly very high suicide rate was due to the wind turning people mad. Whether or not this is true, one thing is without doubt: Tarifa's 10km of white, sandy beaches and perfect year-round conditions have made this small town the windsurfing capital of Europe. The town is crammed with windsurf and kite shops, windsurfing schools and a huge contingent of passing surfers. However, the same wind that attracts so many devotees also makes it a less than ideal place to learn the art.

If you can't make it as far south as Tarifa, then the less-well-known Empuriabrava in Catalonia also has great conditions, especially from March to July, while the family resort of Oliva near Valencia is also worth considering. If you're looking for waves, try

---

SPAIN'S TOP BEACHES

With 4964km of coastline (including offshore islands) and a never-ending variety of pebbly coves, sandy strips and hidden bays, any discussion about the best beaches in Spain is sure to lead to arguments.

» **Playa de la Concha** (p419), a scallop-shaped stretch of sand in the heart of San Sebastián, might well be the finest city beach in Europe.

» **Playa del Silencio** (p484) has a long sandy cove backed by a natural rock amphitheatre, making this Asturian jewel hard to beat.

» **Praia de Lourido** (p523) won't be beaten for lonely walks along a mist-shrouded beach, although Galicia's bleak Costa da Morte is no place for a swim.

» **Illas Cíes** (p534), a pocket-sized, highly protected archipelago off the end of Spain, has beaches so stunning they'll have you rubbing your eyes in disbelief.

» **Aiguablava** (p311) and **Fornells** (p311), two neighbouring Costa Brava beaches, are so divine we couldn't choose between them. Can you?

» **Benidorm** (p580), the king of package-holiday beach resorts, might not be to everyone's taste, but with over two million visitors a year it must be doing something right.

» **Menorca's north coast** (p641), rugged, rocky and dotted with scenic coves, is the Balearic Islands before the tourists arrived.

» **Cabo de Gata** (p780) is Andalucía's most dramatic and remote Mediterranean corner.

» **Zahara de los Atunes** (p709) has a crumbling old castle and a 12km stretch of quiet beach, making it the best of Atlantic Andalucía's enviable bunch.

Spain's northwest coast, where Galicia can have fantastic conditions.

Information

An excellent guidebook to windsurfing and kitesurfing spots across Spain and the rest of Europe is Stoked Publications' *The Kite and Windsurfing Guide: Europe*. The Spanish-language website www.windsurfesp.com gives very thorough descriptions of spots, conditions and schools all over Spain.

Kayaking, Canoeing & Rafting

With 1800 rivers and streams, opportunities abound in Spain to take off downstream in search of white-water fun. As most rivers are dammed for electric power at some point along their flow, there are many reservoirs with excellent low-level kayaking and canoeing, where you can also hire equipment.

In general, May and June are best for kayaking, rafting, canoeing and hydrospeeding (water tobogganing). Top white-water rivers include Catalonia's turbulent Noguera Pallaresa (p339), Aragón's Gállego, Cantabria's Carasa and Galicia's Miño. For fun and competition, the crazy 22km, en-masse Descenso Internacional del Sella

If merely hiking up and down mountains sounds no more exciting than a stroll in the park, then Spain offers plenty of opportunities to see the mountains and gorges from a more vertical perspective.

For a general overview of Spanish rock climbing, check out the Spain information on the websites of **Rockfax** (www.rockfax.com) and **Climb Europe** (www.climb-europe.com). Both include details on the best climbs in the country. Rockfax also publishes various climbing guidebooks covering Spain.

canoe race (p492) is a blast, running from Arriondas in Asturias to coastal Ribadesella. It's held on the first weekend in August. Kayaking in the Parque Natural Fragas do Eume (p519) is a great opportunity for families to get paddling together on a beautiful reservoir in the middle of a dense Atlantic forest.

Patrick Santal's *White Water Pyrenees* thoroughly covers 85 rivers in France and Spain for kayakers, canoeists and rafters.

regions at a glance

Madrid

Galleries ✓✓✓
Nightlife ✓✓✓
Food ✓✓

Art's Golden Mile
Madrid is one of the world's premier cities for public art. World-class galleries scattered across the city exist in the long shadow cast by the Museo del Prado, the Centro de Arte Reina Sofía and the Museo Thyssen-Bornemisza. Together these three museums, all within easy walking distance of each other, are like a roll-call of fine art's grand elite and a fascinating journey through the Spanish soul.

p52

Killing the Night
Nightclubs that don't really get busy until 3am. Sophisticated cocktail bars where you mingle with A-list celebrities while sipping your mojito. A live-music scene that begins with flamenco before moving on to jazz and every other genre imaginable. In this city with more bars than any other city in the world, nights are the stuff of legend, reflecting as they do the *madrileño* passion for having a good time.

Spain's Table
You could travel all around Spain to try the best in regional cuisine, or you could simply come to Madrid. Traditional Madrid food is nothing to get excited about, but the best cooking from every corner of Spain and further afield finds a home here. And the neighbourhood of La Latina is one of the country's finest concentrations of tapas bars.

Castilla y León

Medieval Towns ✓✓
Villages ✓✓✓
Food ✓✓

City as Art
Rich in history, cathedrals and other grand public monuments, the heart of old Castile is home to some of Spain's prettiest medium-sized towns. Salamanca, Ávila, Segovia, León and Burgos are only the start.

Quiet Pueblos
The villages of Castilla y León feel like Spain before mass tourism and the modern world arrived on Iberian shores, from the Sierra de Francia in the far southwest to quiet, medieval hamlets like Covarrubias, Puebla de Sanabria and Calatañazor.

Hearty Inland Fare
Roasted and grilled meats are a specialty in the Spanish interior, so much so that Spaniards travel here from all over the country for a special meal. *Jamón* and other cured meats are also a regional passion and some of the best of their kind come from here.

p123

Castilla-La Mancha

History ✓✓
Literature ✓✓✓
Villages & Castles ✓

Three Faiths City
In the Middle Ages, Toledo was one of the most cosmopolitan cities in Spain, as shown by some fine landmarks to the era – a poignant mosque, fine Jewish sites and a cathedral of real power adorned with works by El Greco and Velázquez.

Tilting at Windmills
The Don Quijote trail through Castilla-La Mancha offers the rare opportunity to follow the terrain trod by one of literature's most eccentric figures. Windmills and sweeping plains evoke Cervantes' novel to such an extent that you can almost hear Sancho Panza's patter.

Beautiful Villages
Amid the often-empty horizons of La Mancha, pretty villages and smaller towns can seem like oases. Cuenca, Almagro, Sigüenza and Alcalá del Júcar are our favourites, while the region's castles are simply magnificent.

p194

Barcelona

Architecture ✓✓✓
Food ✓✓✓
Art ✓✓

Gaudí's Masterclass
Architecture defines Barcelona as it does few other cities on earth. Antoni Gaudí's wonderfully zany creations are the highpoints of the Modernista architectural style – especially La Sagrada Família, Casa Batlló and Park Güell – but there are masterpieces rendered in stone at seemingly every turn.

Food as Art
So much of Catalonia's celebrated cuisine springs from Barcelona kitchens. Food markets offer up an astonishing variety of tastes, as do the restaurants where chefs play on traditional themes with great originality. The seaside district of La Barceloneta is where much of it happens.

Great Galleries
With a museum devoted solely to Pablo Picasso and art galleries that span centuries of Catalan and wider European masters, Barcelona is an art-lover's destination par excellence.

p227

Catalonia

Food ✓✓✓
Beaches ✓✓
Hiking ✓✓

The Catalan Kitchen
Vying with the Basque Country for Spain's highest per-capita ratio of celebrity chefs, Catalonia is something of a pilgrimage for gastronomes. Here, even in the smallest family establishments, they fuse ingredients from land and sea, always keeping faith with rich culinary traditions even as they head off in innovative new directions.

The Catalan Coast
The fine coastlines known as the Costa Brava and Costa Daurada are studded with pretty-as-a-postcard villages and beaches that are generally less crowded than those further south. And not far away, signposts to Salvador Dalí and the Romans make for fine day trips.

Spain's Table
Northern Catalonia means the Pyrenees, where shapely peaks and quiet valleys offer some of the best hiking anywhere in the country.

p302

Aragón

Mountains ✓✓✓
Villages ✓✓
History ✓

Head for the Hills
The prettiest corner of the Pyrenees, northern Aragón combines the drama of impossibly high summits with the quiet pleasures of deep valleys and endless hiking trails. The Parque Nacional de Ordesa y Monte Perdido is perhaps Spain's most picturesque national park.

Stone Villages
Aragón has numerous finalists in the competition for Spain's most beautiful village, among them Aínsa, Sos del Rey Católico and Albarracín. Many sit in the Pyrenean foothills against a backdrop of snow-capped mountains.

Romans, Moors & Christians
Centred on one of Spain's most important historical kingdoms, Aragón is strewn with landmarks from the great civilisations of ancient and medieval times. Zaragoza in particular spans the millennia with grace and fervour, but Mudéjar Teruel is an often-missed jewel.

p360

Basque Country, Navarra & La Rioja

Food ✓✓✓
Wine ✓✓✓
Villages ✓✓

Spain's Culinary Capital
To understand the buzz surrounding Spanish food, head for San Sebastián, at once *pintxo* (Basque tapas) heaven and home to outrageously talented chefs. You eat well everywhere in the Basque Country, with seafood and perfectly prepared meats the mainstay.

The Finest Drop
La Rioja is to wine what the Basque Country is to food. Wine museums, wine tastings and vineyards stretching to the horizon make this Spain's most accessible wine region. And, of course, it accompanies every meal here, from picnics to bars and restaurants.

Villages
There are stunning villages to be found throughout the Basque Country and La Rioja, but those in the Pyrenean foothills and high valleys of Navarra are a match for anything France or the rest of Spain have to offer.

p398

Cantabria & Asturias

Coastal Scenery ✓✓✓
Mountains ✓✓✓
Food ✓✓

The Scenic Coast
While beach-lovers head for the Mediterranean, those looking for something more head to Cantabria and Asturias. It's all about dramatic landforms, gorgeous villages and marvellous sights in the hinterland (including the astonishing Cueva de Altamira).

Picos de Europa
The vertiginous Picos de Europa may not be Spain's most extensive mountain range, but they're easily one of the most beautiful. Jagged summits and ridgelines are the perfect drawcard for hikers and day-trippers alike.

Cheese & Cider
Mention to any Spaniard that you're on your way to Asturias and chances are they'll start waxing lyrical about the pleasures of Asturian food. The tangy Cabrales cheese is one of Spain's best, while cider poured straight from the barrel is a much-lauded Asturian institution.

p455

Santiago de Compostela & Galicia

Coastal Scenery ✓✓✓
Food ✓✓✓
History ✓✓

The Wildest Coast
Galicia's wild and windswept coast is one of Europe's most dramatic. Cliffs plunge from a great height into the roiling waters of the Atlantic, and elsewhere shelter isolated fishing villages and deserted beaches of rare beauty.

Fruits of the Sea
Food dominates life in Galicia, even more than elsewhere in Spain. The culture here owes much to the fishing fleets that have sustained the region through the centuries, while most of the region's festivals have food as their centrepiece.

A Sacred Past
There's no more sacred site in Spain than Santiago de Compostela, the reputed birthplace of St James and endpoint of that great pilgrimage, the Camino de Santiago. And don't forget Lugo, encircled as it is by fine Roman-era walls.

p500

Valencia

Fiestas ✓✓✓
Cuisine ✓
Beaches ✓✓

Bulls, Fire & Knights in Armour
The biggest and noisiest party is Valencia city's Las Fallas in March. But almost every *pueblo* has its fiesta, usually with fireworks, often with bulls and, in the south, with the pomp and elaborate costumes of Moros y Cristianos (Moors and Christians) parades.

Simmering Rice & Bounty from the Sea
Paella first simmered over an open fire in Valencia. Rice dishes (or *fideuá,* a short noodle alternative) are everywhere, supplemented by fish and seafood from the Mediterranean and the freshest of vegetables grown in fertile coastal strip.

Strands & Rocky Coves
From small bays to vast beaches stretching over kilometres, from tiny rocky coves to the sandy sweeps of Denia or Benidorm, there's always room to stretch out your towel.

p544

Mallorca, Menorca & Ibiza

Beaches ✓✓
Walking & Cycling ✓✓
Nightlife ✓✓

Beaches
White sand, black sand, pebbles or rocky inlets, each of the islands offers variety with, in general, fine sand on their southern shores, rougher stuff to the north.

Outdoor Adventure
Watery fun, sailing, windsurfing, diving or simply splashing about in all the major coastal resorts. Magnificent trekking in the Tramontana, Mallorca's wild, craggy north, and more gentle striding in the hills of Menorca. Cycling too along the well-signed routes of all four islands.

Through the Night
It's not only the mega-venues of Ibiza that pound until dawn. In season, Ciutadella, on Menorca, draws in clubbers from all over the island, Palma de Mallorca is the big draw for locals there, while the smaller music bars of diminutive Formentera hold their own.

p594

Murcia

History ✓✓
Festivals ✓✓
Food ✓

Romans & Carthaginians

The area around Cartagena is one of the longest-inhabited corners of the Iberian Peninsula, and Cartagena itself is replete with ruins and a fine new museum to help make sense of it all.

Holy Week & Ancient Battles

Lorca makes for a fine and often less-crowded alternative to Andalucía for utterly compelling Semana Santa (Holy Week) festivities. And of Cartagena's numerous festivals, the September fight between Romans and Carthaginians has the quality of an epic.

Spain's Breadbasket

Murcia is often referred to as Spain's *huerta* (garden) and the produce from the region's vast agricultural fields invariably find their way first and freshest onto the tables of Murcia's restaurants. In Murcia City, the tapas experience is one of Spain's most underrated.

p644

Andalucía

Architecture ✓✓✓
Festivals ✓✓✓
National Parks ✓✓

The Glories of Al-Andalus

Unesco World Heritage–listed sites don't come any more beautiful than Granada's Alhambra and Córdoba's Mezquita. But these are merely the most exquisite showpieces among many that stand as testament to the enlightenment of seven centuries of Moorish rule on Spanish soil.

Fiestas & Festivals

Andalucía is home to many of the irresistible passions of Spanish life and they find expression in a full calendar of festivals, fiestas and ferias. They range from world-famous Semana Santa processions to flamenco festivals.

Wilderness Areas

Hiking trails fan out across Andalucía, leaving behind the clamour of the cities. En route, you pass through the countless *pueblos blancos* (white villages) for which the region is famous, and enter the realm of some of Spain's signature wildlife species.

p657

Extremadura

Medieval Towns ✓✓
Roman Ruins ✓✓
Forgotten Corners ✓

Medieval Film Sets

Spain may be replete with wonderfully preserved old towns that date back to the Middle Ages, but Cáceres and Trujillo are up there with the best. Meandering along their cobblestone lanes is a journey back into an epic past.

Roman Mérida

Spain's most beautiful Roman theatre, its longest Roman-era bridge, a breathtaking museum and a slew of other ruined glories – welcome to Emerita Augusta, now known as Mérida and Spain's finest Roman site.

Leave the Beaten Track

Extremadura gets far fewer tourists than most other Spanish regions, and that means you'll find some of Spain's least frequented and least-spoiled corners here. From Zafra in the south to La Vera, Las Hurdes and the Sierra de Gata in the north, this is Spain as it used to be.

p784

Look out for these icons:

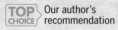 Our author's recommendation

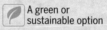 A green or sustainable option

 No payment required

See the Index for a full list of destinations covered in this book.

On the Road

Madrid

Best Places to Eat

» Restaurante Sobrino de Botín (p92)

» Estado Puro (p96)

» Sula Madrid (p96)

» La Musa (p97)

» Mercado de San Miguel (p92)

Best Places to Stay

» Hotel Meninas (p87)

» Hotel Óscar (p91)

» Hotel Urban (p88)

» Cat's Hostel (p89)

» Hotel Abalú (p91)

Why Go?

No city on earth is more alive than Madrid, a beguiling place whose sheer energy carries a simple message: this city knows how to live.

It's true Madrid doesn't have the immediate cachet of Paris, the monumental history of Rome or the reputation for cool of that other city up the road. But it's a city whose contradictory impulses are legion, the perfect expression of Europe's most passionate country writ large.

This city has transformed itself into Spain's premier style centre and its calling cards are many: astonishing art galleries; relentless nightlife; an exceptional live-music scene; a feast of fine restaurants and tapas bars; and a population that's mastered the art of the good life. It's not that other cities don't have these things. It's just that Madrid has all of them in bucket-loads.

When to Go
Madrid

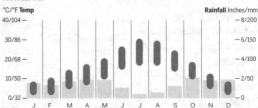

°C/°F **Temp** — 40/104, 30/86, 20/68, 10/50, 0/32 — J F M A M J J A S O N D — **Rainfall** Inches/mm — 8/200, 6/150, 4/100, 2/50, 0

February Five days of Spain's best flamenco during the Festival Flamenco Caja Madrid

May Two of Madrid's biggest fiestas: Fiesta de la Comunidad de Madrid and Fiesta de San Isidro

September Madrid shakes off its summer torpor with (usually) lovely autumn weather

Madrid Baroque

The Spanish capital's contribution to world architectural textbooks is known as *barroco madrileño* (Madrid baroque). Its creation is largely attributed to Juan de Herrera (1530–97), perhaps the greatest figure of the Spanish Renaissance, who fused the sternness of the Renaissance style with a muted approach to its successor, the more voluptuous, ornamental baroque. Prime examples in Madrid include the Plaza Mayor, the former *ayuntamiento* (town hall) on Plaza de la Villa and the Convento de la Encarnación.

MADRID'S BARRIOS IN A NUTSHELL

Los Austrias, Sol and Centro form Madrid's oldest quarter, home to some of Madrid's grandest monuments, as well as bars, restaurants and hotels. Next door, the **La Latina and Lavapiés** neighbourhood is the preserve of narrow medieval streets, great bars for tapas, drinking and restaurants. Away to the east, the **Huertas and Atocha** area is one of Madrid's nightlife capitals and home to the Centro de Arte Reina Sofía.

Down the hill and a world away, **Paseo del Prado and El Retiro** is downtown Madrid's greenest corner, with world-class art galleries along the Paseo's shores and the Parque del Buen Retiro up the hill to the east. **Salamanca** is upmarket and Madrid's home of old money, not to mention Madrid's home of designer shopping, while **Malasaña and Chueca** are two inner-city *barrios* with eclectic nightlife, shopping and outstanding eating options; the latter is the heartbeat of Madrid's gay community.

To the north, **Chamberí and Argüelles** are residential *barrios* with a glimpse of Madrid away from the tourist crowds, while **Northern Madrid** has high-class restaurants and is the home of Real Madrid football club.

Madrid's Best Art Galleries

» **Museo del Prado** (p69) One of the great art galleries of the world, with Goya and Velázquez the highlights.

» **Centro de Arte Reina Sofía** (p68) Stunning art gallery that's home to Picasso's *Guernica*.

» **Museo Thyssen-Bornemisza** (p73) Private art gallery with masters from every era.

» **Real Academia de Bellas Artes de San Fernando** (p63) Goya, Picasso, Velázquez, Rubens...

» **Ermita de San Antonio de la Florida** (p77) Exquisite Goya frescoes in their original setting.

DON'T MISS

La Latina, the tangle of medieval streets southwest of Plaza Mayor, ranks among Spain's finest hunting grounds for tapas. Start along Calle de la Cava Baja, and finish with a mojito on Plaza de la Paja.

Fast Facts

» Population: 3.6 million (city), 6.2 million (Comunidad)

» Area: 505 sq km (city), 7995 sq km (Comunidad)

» Number of visitors (2009): 7.2 million

» Annual income: €22,870

Planning Your Trip

» Book your accommodation at hotels.lonelyplanet.com.

» Avoid the queues and book your tickets online to the Museo del Prado (www.museodelprado.es).

» Beat the rush and book your tickets in advance to see Real Madrid play (p110).

Resources

» Tourism in Madrid city (www.esmadrid.com)

» Tourism in Madrid region (www.turismomadrid.es)

» English-language guide to what's happening (www.in-madrid.com)

Madrid Highlights

1 Watch the masterpieces of Velázquez and Goya leap off the canvas at the world-famous **Museo del Prado** (p69)

2 Search for treasure in the Sunday **El Rastro flea market** (p64), then join the crowds in the **Parque del Buen Retiro** (p74)

3 Soak up the buzz with a *caña* (small beer) or glass of Spanish wine on **Plaza de Santa Ana** (p67)

4 Go on a **tapas crawl** (p95) in the medieval *barrio* (district) of La Latina

5 Order *chocolate con churros* (deep-fried doughnut strips dipped in hot chocolate) close to dawn at the **Chocolatería de San Ginés** (p99)

6 Make a sporting pilgrimage to see the stars of Real Madrid play at **Estadio Santiago Bernabéu** (p110)

7 Dance the night away in one of the city's world-famous **nightclubs** (p105)

8 Feast on roast suckling pig at **Café de la Iberia** (p120) in Chinchón

LA MOVIDA MADRILEÑA

Anyone who went wild when they first moved out of their parents' house can identify with *la movida madrileña* (literally, 'the Madrid scene'). After the long, dark years of dictatorship and conservative Catholicism, Spaniards, especially *madrileños*, emerged onto the streets in the late 1970s with all the zeal of ex-convent schoolgirls. Nothing was taboo as *madrileños* discovered the '60s, '70s and early '80s all at once. Drinking, drugs and sex suddenly were OK. All-night partying was the norm, cannabis was virtually legalised and the city howled.

La movida was presided over by Enrique Tierno Galván, an ageing former university professor who had been a leading opposition figure under Franco and was affection-ately known throughout Spain as 'the old teacher'. A socialist, he became mayor of Madrid in 1979 and, for many, launched *la movida* by telling a public gathering '*a colo-carse y ponerse al loro*', which loosely translates as 'get stoned and do what's cool'. Not surprisingly, he was Madrid's most popular mayor ever. When he died in 1986, a million *madrileños* turned out for his funeral.

But *la movida* was not just about rediscovering the Spanish art of *salir de copas* (going out to drink). It was also accompanied by an explosion of creativity among the country's musicians, designers and film-makers.

The most famous of these was film director Pedro Almodóvar. Still one of Europe's most creative directors, his riotously colourful films captured the spirit of *la movida*, featuring larger-than-life characters who pushed the limits of sex and drugs. When he wasn't making films, Almodóvar immersed himself in the spirit of *la movida*, doing drag acts in smoky bars. Among the other names from *la movida* that still resonate, the designer Agatha Ruiz de la Prada stands out. And start playing anything by Alas-ka, Los Rebeldes, Radio Futura or Nacha Pop and watch *madrileños'* eyes glaze over with nostalgia.

History

When Iberia's Christians began the Recon-quista (c 722) – the centuries-long campaign by Christian forces to reclaim the peninsula – the Muslims of Al-Andalus constructed a chain of fortified positions through the heart of Iberia. One of these was built by Muham-mad I, emir of Córdoba, in 854, on the site of what would become Madrid. The name they gave to the new settlement was Mayrit (or Magerit), which comes from the Arabic word *majira,* meaning water channel.

A WORTHY CAPITAL?

Madrid's strategic location in the centre of the peninsula saw the city change hands repeatedly, but it was not until 1309 that the travelling Cortes (royal court and par-liament) sat in Madrid for the first time. Despite the growing royal attention, medi-eval Madrid remained dirt poor and small-scale: 'in Madrid there is nothing except what you bring with you', observed one 15th-century writer. It simply bore no com-parison with other major Spanish, let alone European, cities.

By the time Felipe II ascended the Span-ish throne in 1556, Madrid was surrounded by walls that boasted 130 towers and six stone gates, but these fortifications were largely built of mud and designed more to impress than provide any meaningful de-fence of the city. Madrid was nonetheless chosen by Felipe II as the capital of Spain in 1561.

Madrid took centuries to grow into its new role and despite a handful of elegant churches, the imposing Alcázar and a smat-tering of noble residences, the city consist-ed of, for the most part, precarious white-washed houses. The monumental Paseo del Prado, which now provides Madrid with so much of its grandeur, was a small creek.

During the 17th century, Spain's golden age, Madrid began to take on the aspect of a capital and was home to 175,000 people, making it the fifth-largest city in Europe (after London, Paris, Constantinople and Naples).

Carlos III (r 1759–88) gave Madrid and Spain a period of comparatively common-sense government. After he cleaned up the city, completed the Palacio Real, inaugu-rated the Real Jardín Botánico and car-ried out numerous other public works, he became known as the best 'mayor' Madrid had ever had.

Madrileños (residents of Madrid) didn't take kindly to Napoleon's invasion and subsequent occupation of Spain in 1805 and, on 2 May 1808, they attacked French troops around the Palacio Real and what is now Plaza del Dos de Mayo. The ill-fated rebellion was quickly put down by Murat, Napoleon's brother-in-law and the most powerful of his military leaders.

WARS, FRANCO & TERRORISM

Turmoil continued to stalk the Spanish capital. The upheaval of the 19th-century Carlist Wars was followed by a two-and-a-half-year siege of Madrid by Franco's Nationalist forces from 1936 to 1939, during which the city was shelled regularly from Casa de Campo and Gran Vía became known as 'Howitzer Alley'.

After Franco's death in 1975 and the country's subsequent transition to democracy, Madrid became an icon for the new Spain as the city's young people unleashed a flood of pent-up energy. This took its most colourful form in the years of *la movida* (see the boxed text, p56), the endless party that swept up the city in a frenzy of creativity and open-minded freedom that has in some ways yet to abate.

On 11 March 2004, just three days before the country was due to vote in national elections, Madrid was rocked by 10 bombs on four rush-hour commuter trains heading into the capital's Atocha station. When the dust cleared, 191 people had died and 1755 were wounded, many seriously. Madrid was in shock and, for 24 hours at least, this most clamorous of cities fell silent. Then, 36 hours after the attacks, more than three million *madrileños* streamed onto the streets to protest against the bombings, making it the largest demonstration in the city's history. Although deeply traumatised, Madrid's mass act of defiance and pride began the process of healing. Visit Madrid today and you'll find a city that has resolutely returned to normal.

In the years since, Madrid has come agonisingly close in the race to host the Summer Olympics, coming third behind London and Paris in the race for 2012 and second behind Rio for 2016. The town hall has yet to decide whether to mount another bid, but many *madrileños* are hoping it will be third time lucky. And, of course, Madrid was the scene of one of the biggest celebrations in modern Spanish history when the Spanish World Cup–winning football team returned home in July 2010.

⊙ Sights

Madrid has three of the finest art galleries in the world – if ever there existed a golden mile of fine art, it would have to be the combined charms of the Museo del Prado, the Centro de Arte Reina Sofía and the Museo Thyssen-Bornemisza. Beyond the museums' walls, the combination of stunning architecture and feel-good living has never been easier to access than in the beautiful plazas, where *terrazas* (cafes with outdoor tables) provide a front-row seat for Madrid's fine cityscape and endlessly energetic streetlife. Throw in some outstanding city parks (the Parque del Buen Retiro, in particular) and areas like Chueca, Malasaña and Salamanca, which each have their own identity, and you'll quickly end up wondering why you decided to spend so little time here.

MADRID IN TWO DAYS

Begin in **Plaza Mayor**, with its architectural beauty, fine *terrazas* (cafes or bars with outdoor tables) and endlessly fascinating passing parade. Wander down Calle Mayor, passing the delightful **Plaza de la Villa**, and head for the **Palacio Real**. There's no finer place to rest than in **Plaza de Oriente**. Double back up towards the **Puerta del Sol**, and then on to **Plaza de Santa Ana**, the ideal place for a long, liquid lunch. Time for some high culture, so stroll down the hill to the incomparable **Museo del Prado**, one of the best art galleries in the world. In anticipation of a long night ahead, catch your breath in the **Parque del Buen Retiro** before heading into **Chueca** or **Malasaña** for great restaurants, followed by some terrific live jazz.

On day two, cram in everything you didn't have time for on day one. Choose between the **Centro de Arte Reina Sofía** and the **Museo Thyssen-Bornemisza**, then jump on the metro for a quick ride across town to the astonishing Goya frescoes in the **Ermita de San Antonio de la Florida**. Finish off with tapas in **La Latina** and drinks at **Museo Chicote**.

MADRID CARD

If you intend to do some intensive sightseeing and travelling on public transport, it might be worth looking at the Madrid Card (☎91 588 29 00, 91 360 47 72; www.madridcard.com). It includes free entry to more than 40 museums in and around Madrid (including the Museo del Prado, Museo Thyssen-Bornemisza, Centro de Arte Reina Sofía, Estadio Santiago Bernabéu and Palacio Real) and free Descubre Madrid walking tours, as well as discounts on public transport, on the Madrid Visión tourist bus and in certain shops and restaurants. The ticket is available for one/two/three days (€47/60/74). There's also a cheaper version (€31/35/39), which just covers cultural sights. The Madrid Card can be bought online, over the phone, or in person at the tourist offices on Plaza Mayor and Terminal 4 in Barajas airport, and in some tobacconists and hotels – a list of major sales outlets appears on the website.

LOS AUSTRIAS, SOL & CENTRO

These *barrios* are where the story of Madrid began. As the seat of royal power, this is where the splendour of Imperial Spain was at its most ostentatious and where Spain's overarching Catholicism was at its most devout – think expansive palaces, elaborate private mansions, ancient churches and imposing convents amid the raucous clamour of modern Madrid.

This is Madrid at its most riotous and diverse: the tangle of streets tumbling down the hillside of Madrid de Los Austrias (named for the Habsburg dynasty, which ruled Spain from 1517 to 1700); the busy shopping streets around Plaza de la Puerta del Sol (more commonly known as Puerta del Sol, the Gate of the Sun); the monumental Gran Vía, marking the northern border of central Madrid. If other *barrios* have their own distinctive character traits, then Los Austrias, Sol and Centro are the sum total of all Madrid's personalities. It's also where the *madrileño* world most often intersects with that of tourists and expats drawn to that feel-good Madrid vibe.

Plaza Mayor   SQUARE
(Map p60; ⓂSol) Designed in 1619 by Juan Gómez de Mora, the stunningly beautiful Plaza Mayor is a highlight of any visit to Madrid. The grandeur of its buildings is one thing, but this is a living, breathing entity, from the outdoor tables of the *terrazas* to the students strewn across the cobblestones on a sunny day.

The plaza's first public ceremony was the beatification of San Isidro Labrador, Madrid's patron saint. Thereafter, bullfights watched by 50,000 spectators were a recurring spectacle until 1878, while the autos-da-fé (the ritual condemnation of heretics) of the Spanish Inquisition also took place here. Fire largely destroyed the square in 1790, but it was rebuilt and became an important market and hub of city life. Today, the uniformly ochre-tinted apartments with wrought-iron balconies are offset by the exquisite frescoes of the 17th-century Real Casa de la Panadería (Royal Bakery); the present frescoes were added in 1992.

Palacio Real   ROYAL PALACE
(Royal Palace; www.patrimonionacional.es; Calle de Bailén; adult/child, student & EU senior €10/3.50, adult without guided tour €8, EU citizen free Wed; ⊙9am-6pm Mon-Sat, 9am-3pm Sun & holidays Apr-Sep; ⓂÓpera) Spain's lavish Palacio Real is a jewel box of a palace, although it's used only occasionally for royal ceremonies; the royal family moved to the modest Palacio de la Zarzuela years ago.

When the Alcázar burned down on Christmas Day 1734, Felipe V, the first of the Bourbon kings, decided to build a palace that would dwarf all its European counterparts. Felipe died before the palace was finished, which is perhaps why the Italianate baroque colossus has a mere 2800 rooms, just one-quarter of the original plan.

The official tour leads through 50 of the palace rooms, which hold a good selection of Goyas, 215 absurdly ornate clocks and five Stradivarius violins still used for concerts and balls. The **main stairway** is a grand statement of imperial power, leading first to the Halberdiers' rooms and eventually to the sumptuous **Salón del Trono** (Throne Room), with its crimson-velvet wall coverings and Tiepolo ceiling. Shortly after, you reach the **Salón de Gasparini**, with its exquisite stucco ceiling and walls resplendent with embroidered silks.

Outside the main palace, visit the **Farmacia Real** (Royal Pharmacy) at the southern end of the patio known as the **Plaza de la Armería** (or Plaza de Armas). Westward across the plaza is the **Armería Real** (Royal Armoury), a shiny collection of weapons and armour, mostly dating from the 16th and 17th centuries.

Plaza de Oriente   PUBLIC SQUARE

(Map p60; MÓpera) A royal palace that once had aspirations to be the Spanish Versailles. Sophisticated cafes watched over by apartments that cost the equivalent of a royal salary. The Teatro Real, Madrid's opera house and one of Spain's temples to high culture. Some of the finest sunset views in Madrid. Welcome to Plaza de Oriente, a gloriously alive monument to imperial Madrid.

At the centre of the plaza, which the palace overlooks, is an equestrian statue of Felipe IV, designed by Velázquez. If you're wondering how a heavy bronze statue of a rider and his horse rearing up can actually maintain that stance, the answer is simple: the hind legs are solid while the front ones are hollow. That idea was Galileo Galilei's.

Nearby are some 20 marble statues of mostly ancient monarchs. Local legend has it that these ageing royals get down off their pedestals at night to stretch their legs.

The adjacent **Jardines Cabo Naval** is a great place to watch the sun set.

Campo del Moro & Jardines de Sabatini
PUBLIC GARDENS

In proper palace style, lush gardens surround the Palacio Real. To the north are the formal French-style Jardines de Sabatini (⊙9am-9pm May-Sep; MÓpera). Directly behind the palace are the fountains of the Campo del Moro (Paseo de la Virgen del Puerto; ⊙10am-8pm Mon-Sat, 9am-8pm Sun & holidays Apr-Sep; MPríncipe Pío), so named because this is where the Muslim army camped before a 12th-century attack on the Alcázar. Now, shady paths, a thatch-roofed pagoda and palace views are the main attractions.

Catedral de Nuestra Señora de la Almudena   CATHEDRAL, VIEWS

(Calle de Bailén; ⊙9am-8.30pm; MÓpera) Paris has Notre Dame and Rome has St Peter's Basilica. In fact, almost every European city of stature has its signature cathedral, one that is a standout monument to the city's glorious Christian past. Not Madrid. Its Catedral de Nuestra Señora de la Almudena, south of the Palacio Real, is cav-

ernous and laden with more adornment than charm, its colourful, modern ceilings doing little to make up for the lack of old-world gravitas that so distinguishes the world's great cathedrals.

Carlos I first proposed building a cathedral here back in 1518, but construction didn't get under way until the 1880s. Other priorities got in the way and it wasn't finished until 1992. Not surprisingly, the pristine, bright-white neo-Gothic interior holds no pride of place in the affections of *madrileños*.

It's possible to climb to the cathedral's summit with fine views. En route you climb up through the cathedral's museum; follow the signs to the Museo de la Catedral y Cúpola (adult/child €6/4; ⊙10am-2.30pm Mon-Sat) on the northern facade that faces the Palacio Real.

Muralla Árabe   CITY WALLS

(Arab Wall; MÓpera) Behind the cathedral apse, down Cuesta de la Vega, is a short stretch of the so-called Muralla Árabe, the fortifications built by Madrid's early medieval Islamic rulers. Some of it dates as far back as the 9th century, when the initial Islamic fort was raised. Other sections date from the 12th and 13th centuries, by which time the city was in Christian hands.

Plaza de la Villa   PUBLIC SQUARE

(Map p60; MÓpera) There are grander squares elsewhere, but the intimate Plaza de la Villa is one of Madrid's prettiest. Enclosed on three sides by wonderfully preserved examples of 17th-century *barroco madrileño* (Madrid-style baroque architecture: a pleasing amalgam of brick, exposed stone and wrought iron), it was the permanent seat of Madrid's city government from the Middle Ages until recent years when Madrid's city council relocated to the grand Palacio de Comunicaciones on Plaza de la Cibeles.

On the western side of the square is the 17th-century former ayuntamiento (town hall), in Habsburg-style baroque with Herrerian slate-tile spires. On the opposite side of the square is the Gothic Casa de los Lujanes, whose brickwork tower is said to have been 'home' to the imprisoned French monarch François I after his capture in the Battle of Pavia (1525). The plateresque (15th- and 16th-century Spanish baroque) Casa de Cisneros, built in 1537 with later Renaissance alterations, also catches the eye.

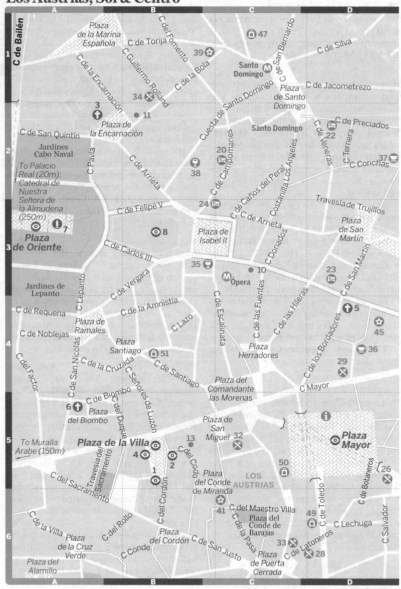

Convento de las Descalzas Reales

CONVENT

(Convent of the Barefoot Royals; Map p60; www.
patrimonionacional.es; Plaza de las Descalzas 3;
adult/child €5/2.50, incl Convento de la Encarnación €6/3.40, EU citizen free Wed; ☺10.30am-

12.45pm & 4-5.45pm Tue-Thu & Sat, 10.30am-
12.45pm Fri, 11am-1.45pm Sun; Ⓜ Ópera or Sol)
The grim plateresque walls of the Convento
de las Descalzas Reales offer no hint that
behind the facade lies a sumptuous stronghold of the faith. Founded in 1559 by Juana

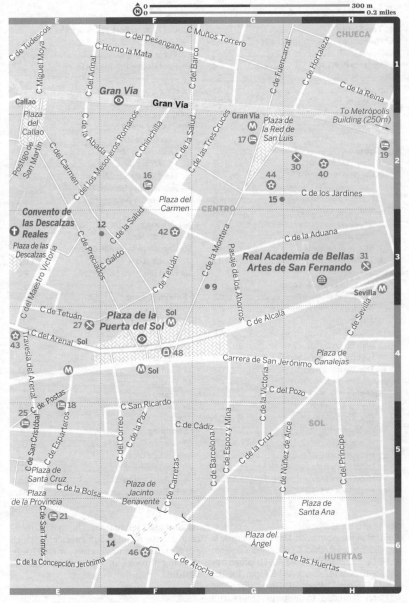

of Austria, the widowed daughter of the Spanish king Carlos I, the convent quickly became one of Spain's richest religious houses thanks to gifts from Juana's noble friends. On the obligatory guided tour you'll see a gaudily frescoed Renaissance stairway, a number of extraordinary tapestries based on works by Rubens, and a wonderful painting entitled *The Voyage of the 11,000 Virgins*. Some 33 nuns still live here and there are 33 chapels dotted around the convent.

Convento de la Encarnación CONVENT
(Convent of the Incarnation; Map p60; Plaza de la
Encarnación; adult/child €3.60/2, incl Convento
de las Descalzas Reales €6/3.40, EU citizen free
Wed; ⊘10.30am-12.45pm & 4-5.45pm Tue-Thu
& Sat, 10.30am-12.45pm Fri, 11am-1.45pm Sun;
ⓂÓpera) Founded by Empress Margarita
of Austria, the Convento de la Encarnación
occupies a 17th-century mansion built in
barroco madrileño style. It's still inhabited
by nuns of the Augustine order (Agustinas
Recoletas). Inside there's a unique collection of 17th- and 18th-century sculptures
and paintings, as well as a handful of sil-

ver and gold reliquaries. The most famous
contains the blood of San Pantaleón, which
purportedly liquefies every year on 27 July,
drawing throngs of the curious and the
faithful.

Iglesia de San Nicolás de los Servitas
CHURCH
(Map p60; Plaza de San Nicolás 6; ⊘8am-1.30pm
& 5.30-8.30pm Mon, 8-9.30am & 6.30-8.30pm
Tue-Sat, 9.30am-2pm & 6.30-9pm Sun & holidays; ⓂÓpera) Considered Madrid's oldest
surviving church, Iglesia de San Nicolás
de los Servitas may have been built on the

site of Muslim Magerit's second mosque. It offers a rare glimpse of medieval Madrid, although apart from the restored 12th-century Mudéjar bell tower, most of the present church dates back to the 15th century.

Iglesia de San Ginés
CHURCH

(Map p60; Calle del Arenal 13; M Sol or Ópera) Due north of Plaza Mayor, Iglesia de San Ginés is one of Madrid's oldest churches: it has been here in one form or another since at least the 14th century. What you see today was built in 1645 but largely reconstructed after a fire in 1824. The church houses some fine paintings, including El Greco's *Expulsion of the Moneychangers from the Temple* (1614), which is beautifully displayed: the glass is just 6mm from the canvas to avoid reflections. Sadly, the church opens to the public only during Mass; times are posted outside the door.

Plaza de la Puerta del Sol
PUBLIC SQUARE

(Map p60; M Sol) The official centre point of Spain is a gracious hemisphere of elegant facades that's often very crowded. It is, above all, a crossroads. People here are forever heading somewhere else, on foot, by metro (three lines cross here) or by bus (many lines terminate and start close to here). In Madrid's earliest days, the Puerta del Sol (Gate of the Sun) was the eastern gate of the city. Plaza de la Puerta del Sol comes into its own on New Year's Eve, when *madrileños* pack into the square in their tens of thousands, waiting for the clock that gives Spain its official time to strike midnight, as the rest of the country watches on TV. Look out for the statue of a bear nuzzling a *madroño* (strawberry tree); this is the official symbol of the city.

Real Academia de Bellas Artes de San Fernando
ART GALLERY

(Map p60; http://rabasf.insde.es, in Spanish; Calle de Alcalá 13; adult/senior & under 18yr €3/ free; ⊘9am-5pm Tue-Sat, 9am-2.30pm Sun & Mon Sep-Jun, hr vary Jul & Aug; M Sevilla) In any other city, the Real Academia de Bellas Artes de San Fernando would be a standout attraction, but in Madrid it too often gets forgotten in the rush to the Prado, Thyssen or Reina Sofía. An academic centre for up-and-coming artists since Fernando VI founded it in the 18th century (both Picasso and Dalí studied here), it houses works by some of the best-loved old masters. Highlights include works by Zurbarán, El Greco,

Rubens, Tintoretto, Goya, Sorolla and Juan Gris, not to mention a couple of minor portraits by Velázquez and a few drawings by Picasso.

Gran Vía
BOULEVARD

It's difficult to imagine Madrid without Gran Vía, the grand boulevard that climbs through the city centre from Plaza de España down to Calle de Alcalá, but it has only existed since 1910, when it was bulldozed through what was then a lively labyrinth of old streets. On a rise about one-third of the way along stands the 1920s-era Telefónica building (Edificio Telefónica; Map p80), which was for years the tallest building in the city. During the civil war, the boulevard became known as 'Howitzer Alley' as shells rained down from Franco's forces in the Casa de Campo. At the southern end of Gran Vía, the stunning French-designed 1905 Metrópolis building (Edificio Metrópolis) has a winged statue of victory sitting atop its dome.

LA LATINA & LAVAPIÉS

La Latina combines some of the best things about Madrid: the Spanish capital's best selection of tapas bars and a medieval streetscape studded with elegant churches. The *barrio*'s heartland is centred on the area between (and very much including) Calle de la Cava Baja and the beautiful Plaza de la Paja.

MOST BEAUTIFUL PLAZAS

» **Plaza Mayor** (p58) – the elegant focal point of central Madrid.

» **Plaza de Oriente** (p59) – the glorious centrepiece of imperial Madrid.

» **Plaza de Santa Ana** (p67) – the heartbeat and cultural hub of Huertas.

» **Plaza de la Villa** (p59) – a small square surrounded by stunning local architecture.

» **Plaza de la Paja** (p65) – the villagelike intimacy of old Madrid.

» **Plaza de la Puerta del Sol** (p63) – the clamorous crossroads of the city centre.

» **Plaza de la Cibeles** (p75) – a monument to Madrid's cults of excess and extravagance.

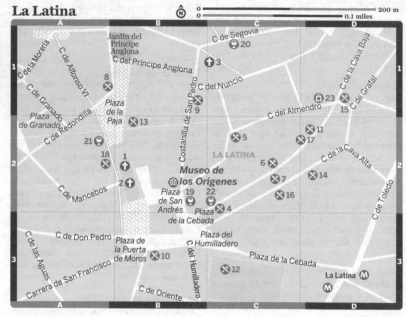

Lavapiés, on the other hand, is a world away from the sophistication of modern Madrid. This is at once one of the city's oldest and most traditional *barrios* and home to more immigrants than any other central-Madrid *barrio*. It's quirky, alternative and a melting pot all in one. It's not without its problems and the *barrio* has a reputation both for antiglamour cool and as a no-go zone, depending on your perspective.

El Rastro
FLEA MARKET

(☺8am-3pm Sun; MLa Latina) A Sunday morning at El Rastro, Europe's largest flea market, is a Madrid institution. El Rastro (the Stain) owes its name to the blood that once trickled down these streets from the slaughterhouses, which sat up the hill. It's been an open-air market for half a millennium.

The madness begins at Plaza de Cascorro, near La Latina metro stop, and you could easily spend an entire morning inching your way down Calle de la Ribera de Curtidores and the maze of streets branching off it. Cheap clothes, luggage, antiques, old photos of Madrid, old flamenco records, faux designer purses, grungy T-shirts, household goods and electronics are the main fare, but for every 10 pieces of junk, there's a real gem waiting to be found. For many *madrileños,* the best of El Rastro

comes after the stalls have shut down and everyone crowds into nearby bars for an *aperitivo* (aperitif) of vermouth and tapas, turning the *barrio* into the site of a spontaneous Sunday fiesta.

A word of warning: pickpockets love El Rastro as much as everyone else.

Viaducto & Jardines de las Vistillas
VIADUCT, GARDENS

For a great view out to the west, take a stroll down Calle de Segovia, where a *viaducto* (viaduct) provides a good vantage point. The outdoor tables in the adjacent Jardines de las Vistillas are another good spot, with views out towards Sierra de Guadarrama. During the civil war, Las Vistillas was heavily bombarded by Nationalist troops from the Casa de Campo, and they in turn were shelled from a Republican bunker here.

La Morería
MOORISH QUARTER

The area stretching southeast from the *viaducto* to the Iglesia de San Andrés was the heart of the *morería* (Moorish quarter). Strain the imagination a little and the maze of winding and hilly lanes even now retains a whiff of the North African medina. This is where the Muslim population of Magerit was concentrated in the wake of the 11th-century Christian takeover of the town.

La Latina

Basílica de San Francisco El Grande
CHURCH

(Plaza de San Francisco 1; adult/senior & child €3/2; ⊙Mass 8am-10.30am Mon-Sat, museum 10.30am-12.30pm & 4-6pm Mon-Sat; Ⓜ La Latina or Puerta de Toledo) One of the largest churches in the city, the Basílica de San Francisco El Grande dominates the skyline at the southern reaches of La Latina. Its extravagantly frescoed dome is, by some estimates, the largest in Spain and the fourth-largest in the world, with a height of 56m and diameter of 33m. The baroque basilica has some outstanding features, including frescoed cupolas and chapel ceilings by Francisco Bayeu. Goya's *The Prediction of San Bernardino of Siena for the King of Aragón* is here, too, in the Capilla de San Bernardino. According to legend, the basilica sits atop the site where St Francis of Assisi built a chapel in 1217.

Although entry is free during morning Mass times, there is no access to the museum then, and the lights in the Capilla de San Bernardino won't be on to illuminate the Goya.

Iglesia de San Andrés & Around
CHURCH, MUSEUM

(Map p64; Plaza de San Andrés 1; ⊙8am-1pm & 6-8pm Mon-Sat, 8am-1pm Sun; Ⓜ La Latina) The stately Iglesia de San Andrés crowns the plaza of the same name, providing a lovely backdrop for the impromptu parties that fill this square on Sunday afternoons as the El Rastro crowd drifts in. Gutted during Spain's civil war, it was restored to its former glory and is at its best when illuminated at night. Around the back, overlook-ing the delightful Plaza de la Paja, is the Capilla del Obispo, considered the best Renaissance church in Madrid, though it's not strictly of the period. Look out for the mostly Gothic vaulting in the ceilings, the plateresque tombs and the fine Renaissance *reredos* (screen behind the altar). Restoration of the chapel was nearing completion at the time of writing.

The nearby Museo de los Orígenes (Map p64; ☑91 366 74 15; www.munimadrid.es/museo sanisidro, in Spanish; Plaza de San Andrés 2; admission free; ⊙10am-8pm Tue-Fri, 10am-2pm Sat & Sun; Ⓜ La Latina) occupies the spot where San Isidro Labrador (the patron saint of Madrid) is said to have ended his days in 1172. Displays range from archaeological finds from the Roman period to maps, scale models, paintings and photos of Madrid down through the ages. A particular highlight is the large model based on Pedro Teixeira's famous 1656 map of Madrid. Major renovations are planned, so expect some disruptions.

Iglesia de San Pedro El Viejo
CHURCH

(Map p64; Costanilla de San Pedro; Ⓜ La Latina) With its clearly Mudéjar bell tower, Iglesia de San Pedro El Viejo is one of the few remaining windows onto the world of medieval Madrid. The church was built atop the site of the old Mezquita de la Morería (Mosque of the Muslim Quarter).

HUERTAS & ATOCHA

If Huertas is known for anything, it's for nightlife that never seems to abate once

MADRID

Huertas

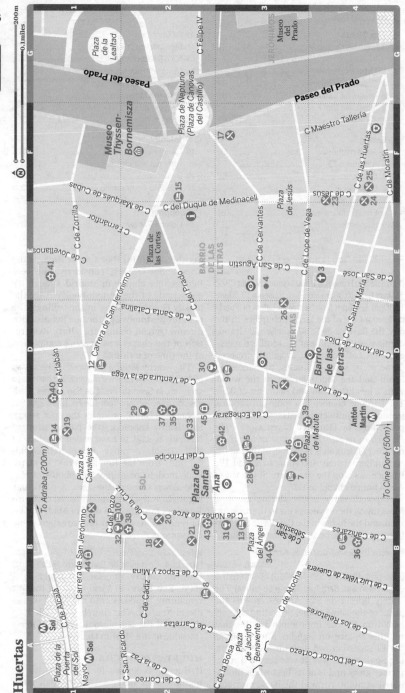

the sun goes down. Such fame is well deserved, but there's so much more to Huertas than immediately meets the eye. Enjoy the height of sophisticated European cafe culture in the superb Plaza de Santa Ana, then go down the hill through Barrio de las Letras to the Centro de Arte Reina Sofía, one of the finest contemporary art galleries in Europe. Across the Plaza del Emperador Carlos V from the gallery, the Antigua Estación de Atocha marks the beginning of the Atocha district.

Plaza de Santa Ana PUBLIC SQUARE
(Map p66; MSol, Sevilla or Antón Martín) A delightful confluence of elegant architecture and irresistible energy, Plaza de Santa Ana is a gem. What it lacks in a distinguished history (it was laid out in 1810 during the reign of Joseph Bonaparte, giving breath-

ing space to what had hitherto been one of Madrid's most claustrophobic *barrios*), it more than compensates for as a focal point of the *barrio*'s intellectual life, overlooked by the Teatro Español and surrounded by a host of live-music venues.

Barrio de las Letras LITERARY NEIGHBOURHOOD
The area that unfurls down the hill east of Plaza de Santa Ana is referred to as the Barrio de las Letras (District of Letters), because of the writers who lived here during Spain's golden age of the 16th and 17th centuries. Miguel de Cervantes Saavedra (1547–1616), the author of *Don Quijote,* spent much of his adult life in Madrid and lived and died at Calle de Cervantes 2 (Map p66; MAntón Martín); a plaque (dating from 1834) sits above the door. Sadly, the original building was torn down in the

early 19th century. When Cervantes died his body was interred around the corner at the Convento de las Trinitarias (Map p66; Calle de Lope de Vega 16; MAntón Martín), which is marked by another plaque. Still home to cloistered nuns, the convent is closed to the public, which saves the authorities' embarrassment: no one really knows where in the convent the bones of Cervantes lie. A commemorative Mass is held for him here every year on the anniversary of his death, 23 April. Another literary landmark is the Casa de Lope de Vega (Map p66; Calle de Cervantes 11; admission free; ☺guided visits every 30min 10am-2pm Tue-Sat; MAntón Martín), the former home of Lope de Vega (1562–1635), Spain's premier playwright. It's now a museum containing memorabilia from Lope de Vega's life and work.

Antigua Estación de Atocha   GARDEN
(Old Atocha Train Station; Map p68; Plaza del Emperador Carlos V; MAtocha Renfe) The Antigua Estación de Atocha is a towering iron-and-glass relic from the 19th century. Lovingly preserved and artfully converted in 1992 into a surprising tropical garden with more than 500 plant species, it now feels more like a lush greenhouse than a transport hub, although the cavernous ceiling resonates with the grand old European train stations of another age.

Centro de Arte Reina Sofía   ART GALLERY
(Map p68; www.museoreinasofia.es; Calle de Santa Isabel 52; adult/student, under 18yr & over 65yr €6/free, free to all Sun, 7-9pm Mon & Wed-Fri, 2.30-9pm Sat, audioguide adult/student €4/3; ☺10am-9pm Mon & Wed-Sat, 10am-2.30pm Sun; MAtocha)Home to Picasso's *Guernica,* arguably Spain's single-most famous artwork, and a host of other important Spanish artists, the Centro de Arte Reina Sofía is Madrid's premier collection of contemporary art. The collection principally spans the 20th century up to the 1980s (for more recent works, visit the Museo Municipal de Arte Contemporáneo).

In addition to Picasso's *Guernica,* which is worth the admission fee on its own, don't neglect the artist's preparatory sketches in the rooms surrounding Room 206. If Picasso's cubist style has captured your imagination, the work of the Madrid-born Juan Gris (1887–1927) or Georges Braque (1882–1963) may appeal.

The work of Joan Miró (1893–1983) is defined by often delightfully bright primary colours, but watch out also for a handful of his equally odd sculptures; his paintings became a symbol of the Barcelona Olympics in 1992.

The Reina Sofía is also home to 20 or so canvases by Salvador Dalí, of which the most famous is perhaps the surrealist extravaganza that is *El Gran Masturbador* (1929).

If you can tear yourself away from the big names, the Reina Sofía offers a terrific opportunity to learn more about sometimes lesser-known 20th-century Spanish artists. Among these are: Miquel Barceló (b 1957); *madrileño* artist José Gutiérrez Solana (1886–1945); the renowned Basque painter Ignazio Zuloaga (1870–1945); Benjamin Palencia (1894–1980), whose paintings capture the turbulence of Spain in the 1930s; Barcelona painter Antoni Tàpies (b 1923); the pop art of Eduardo Arroyo (b 1937); and abstract painters such as Eusebio Sempere (1923–85) and members of the Equipo 57 group (founded in 1957 by a group of Spanish artists in exile in Paris), such as Pablo Palazuelo (1916–2007). Although better known as a poet and playwright, Federico

Atocha

N 0 —— 100 m
0 —— 0.05 miles

Atocha

◉ **Top Sights**

✪ **Eating**

◉ **Entertainment**

» **Guernica** (Pablo Picasso; Room 206)

» **Naturaleza Muerta** (Pablo Picasso; 1912)

» **El Gran Masturbador** (Salvador Dalí; 1929)

» **Muchacha en la Ventana** (Salvador Dalí; 1925)

» **Monumento Imperial a la Mujer Niña** (Salvador Dalí; 1929)

» **Pastorale** (Joan Miró; 1923–24)

» **Danseuse Espagnole** (Joan Miró; 1928)

» **L'atelier aux Sculptures** (Miquel Barceló; 1993)

» **Los Cuatro Dictadores** (Eduardo Arroyo; 1963)

» **Retrato de Josette** (Juan Gris; 1916)

» **Cartes et Dés** (Georges Braque; 1914)

» **El Peine del Viento I** (Eduardo Chillida; 1962)

» **Homenaje a Mallarmé** (Jorge Oteiza; 1958)

» **Pintura** (Antoni Tàpies; 1955)

» **Otoños** (Pablo Palazuelo; 1952)

García Lorca (1898–1936) is represented by a number of his sketches.

Of the sculptors, watch in particular for Pablo Gargallo (1881–1934), whose work in bronze includes a bust of Picasso, and the renowned Basque sculptors Jorge Oteiza (1908–2003) and Eduardo Chillida (1924–2002).

PASEO DEL PRADO & EL RETIRO
If you've just come down the hill from Huertas, you'll feel like you've left behind a madhouse for an oasis of greenery, fresh air and high culture. The Museo del Prado and the Museo Thyssen-Bornemisza are among the richest galleries of fine art in the world, and other museums lurk in the quietly elegant streets just behind the Prado. Rising up the hill to the east are the stately gardens of the glorious Parque del Buen Retiro.

Museo del Prado   ART GALLERY
(Map p73; www.museodelprado.es; Paseo del Prado; adult/under 18yr & EU senior over 65yr €8/free, free to all 6-8pm Tue-Sat & 5-8pm Sun, audioguide €3.50; ⊗9am-8pm Tue-Sun; Ⓜ Banco de España) Welcome to one of the premier art galleries anywhere in the world. The more than 7000 paintings held in the Museo del Prado's collection (although only around 1500 are currently on display) are like a window on the historical vagaries of the Spanish soul, at once grand and imperious in the royal paintings of Velázquez, darkly tumultuous in Las Pinturas Negras (the Black Paintings) of Goya and outward-looking with sophisticated works of art from all across Europe. Spend as long as you can at the Prado or, better still, plan to make a couple of visits – it can be a little overwhelming if you try to absorb it all at once.

Entrance to the Prado is via the eastern Puerta de los Jerónimos or northern Puerta de Goya. Either way tickets must first be purchased from the ticket office at the northern end of the building. The Prado's curators are, until 2012, in the process of reorganising the collection and some room numbers are subject to change. The only sure way to find what you're looking for is to pick up the free 'Plan' from the ticket office or information desk just inside the entrance – it lists the location of 50 of the Prado's most famous works and gives current room numbers for all major artists.

The western wing of the Prado (Edificio Villanueva) was completed in 1785, as the neoclassical Palacio de Villanueva. Originally conceived as a house of science, it later served, somewhat ignominiously, as a cavalry barracks for Napoleon's troops during their occupation of Madrid between 1808 and 1813. In 1814 King Fernando VII decided to use the palace as a museum and five years later the Museo del Prado opened with 311 Spanish paintings on display.

Museo del Prado

PLAN OF ATTACK

Begin on the 1st floor with *Las Meninas* **1** by Velázquez. Although alone worth the entry price, it's a fine introduction to the 17th-century golden age of Spanish art; nearby are more of Velázquez' royal paintings and works by Zurbarán and Murillo. While on the 1st floor, seek out Goya's *La Maja Vestida* and *La Maja Desnuda* **2** with more of Goya's early works in neighbouring rooms. Downstairs at the southern end of the Prado, Goya's anger is evident in the searing *El Dos de Mayo* and *El Tres de Mayo* **3**, and the torment of Goya's later years find expression in the adjacent rooms with his *Pinturas Negras* **4**, or Black Paintings. Also on the lower floor, Hieronymus Bosch's weird-and-wonderful *Garden of Earthly Delights* **5** is one of the Prado's signature masterpieces. Returning to the 1st floor, El Greco's *Adoration of the Shepherds* **6** is an extraordinary work, as is Peter Paul Rubens' *Las Tres Gracias* **7** which forms the centrepiece of the Prado's gathering of Flemish masters (This painting may have been moved to the 2nd floor.) A detour to the 2nd floor takes in some lesser-known Goyas, but finish in the Edificio Jerónimos **8** with a visit to the cloisters and the outstanding bookshop.

ALSO VISIT:

Nearby are Museo Thyssen-Bornemisza and Centro de Arte Reina Sofía. They form an extraordinary trio of galleries.

TOP TIPS

» **Book online** Purchase your ticket online (www.museodelprado.es), save €1 and avoid the queues.

» **Best time to visit** As soon after opening time as possible.

» **Free tours** The website (www.museo delprado.es/coleccion/que-ver/) has self-guided tours for one- to three-hour visits.

Las Tres Gracias (Rubens)
A late Rubens masterpiece, *The Three Graces* is a classical and masterly expression of Rubens' preoccupation with sensuality, here portraying Aglaia, Euphrosyne and Thalia, the daughters of Zeus.

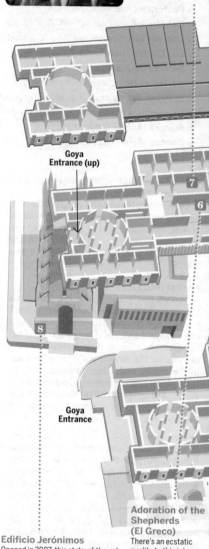

Goya Entrance (up)

Goya Entrance

Edificio Jerónimos
Opened in 2007, this state-of-the-art extension has rotating exhibitions of Prado masterpieces held in storage for decades for lack of wall space, and stunning 2nd-floor granite cloisters that date back to 1672.

Adoration of the Shepherds (El Greco)
There's an ecstatic quality to this intense painting. El Greco's distorted rendering of bodily forms came to characterise much of his later works.

Las Meninas (Velázquez)

This masterpiece depicts Velázquez and the infant Margarita, with the king and queen whose images appear, according to some experts, in mirrors behind Velázquez.

GIANNI DAGLI ORTI/ALAMY

La Maja Vestida & La Maja Desnuda (Goya)

These enigmatic works scandalised early-19th-century Madrid society, fuelling the rumour mill as to the woman's identity and drawing the ire of the Spanish Inquisition. (La Maja Vestida pictured above.)

Edificio Villanueva

Jeronimos Entrance

El Dos de Mayo & El Tres de Mayo (Goya)

Few paintings evoke a city's sense of self quite like Goya's portrayal of Madrid's valiant but ultimately unsuccessful uprising against French rule in 1808. (El Dos de Mayo pictured above.)

RICHARD NEBESKY

Murillo Entrance

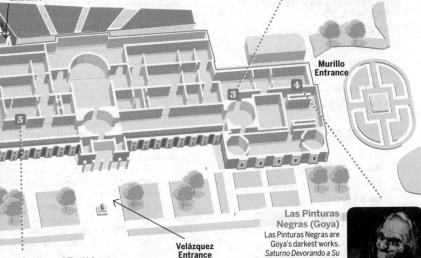

Velázquez Entrance

The Garden of Earthly Delights (Bosch)

A fantastical painting in triptych form, this overwhelming work depicts the Garden of Eden and what the Prado describes as 'the lugubrious precincts of Hell' in exquisitely bizarre detail.

Las Pinturas Negras (Goya)

Las Pinturas Negras are Goya's darkest works. *Saturno Devorando a Su Hijo* evokes a writhing mass of tortured humanity, while *La Romería de San Isidro* and *El Akelarre* are profoundly unsettling.

PETER BARRITT/ALAMY

In contrast, the eastern wing (Edificio Jerónimos) is part of the Prado's stunning modern extension, which opened in 2007. Dedicated to temporary exhibitions, and home to the excellent bookshop and cafe, its main attraction is the 2nd-floor cloisters. Built in 1672 of local granite, the cloisters were until recently attached to the adjacent Iglesia de San Jerónimo El Real.

Goya

Francisco José de Goya y Lucientes is found on all three floors of the Prado. In Rooms 64 and 65, Goya's *El Dos de Mayo* and *El Tres de Mayo* rank among Madrid's most emblematic paintings; they bring to life the 1808 anti-French revolt and subsequent execution of insurgents in Madrid. Alongside, in Rooms 66 and 67, are some of his darkest and most disturbing works, Las Pinturas Negras; they are so-called in part because of the dark browns and black that dominate, but more for the distorted animalesque appearance of their characters.

On the 1st floor, there are more Goyas in Rooms 32 and 34 to 38, among them, in Room 36, two more of Goya's best-known and most intriguing oils: *La Maja Vestida* and *La Maja Desnuda*. These portraits of an unknown woman commonly believed to be the Duquesa de Alba (who may have been Goya's lover) are identical save for the lack of clothing in the latter. There are further Goyas, including *The Parasol* in Room 85, on the top floor.

Velázquez

Diego Rodriguez de Silva y Velázquez is another of the grand masters of Spanish art who brings so much distinction to the Prado. Of all his works, *Las Meninas* is what most people come to see. Completed in 1656, it is more properly known as *La Família de Felipe IV* (The Family of Felipe IV). His mastery of light and colour is never more apparent than here.

The rooms surrounding *Las Meninas* (most likely Rooms 14, 15, 16 and 18) contain more fine works by Velázquez. Watch in particular for his paintings of various members of royalty – Felipe II, Felipe IV, Margarita de Austria (a younger version of whom appears in *Las Meninas*), El Príncipe Baltasar Carlos and Isabel de Francia – who seem to spring off the canvas.

Other Artists

Having captured the essence of the Prado, you're now free to select from the astonishingly diverse works that remain. If Spanish painters have piqued your curiosity, Bartolomé Esteban Murillo, José de Ribera and the stark figures of Francisco de Zurbarán should be on your itinerary. The vivid, almost surreal works by the 16th-century master and adopted Spaniard El Greco, whose figures are characteristically slender and tortured, are also perfectly executed.

Another alternative is the Prado's outstanding collection of Flemish art. The fulsome figures and bulbous cherubs of Peter Paul Rubens (1577–1640) provide a playful antidote to the darkness of many of the other Flemish artists. His signature works are *Las Tres Gracias* (The Three Graces) and *Adoración de los Reyes Magos*. Other fine works in the vicinity include *The Triumph of Death* by Pieter Bruegel, Rembrandt's *Artemisa,* and those by Anton Van Dyck.

And on no account miss the weird-and-wonderful *The Garden of Earthly Delights* by Hieronymus Bosch (c1450–1516). No one has yet been able to provide a definitive explanation for this hallucinatory work, although many have tried. While it is, without doubt, the star attraction of this fantastical painter's collection, all his work rewards inspection, especially the *Table of the Seven*

DON'T MISS

PAINTINGS IN THE MUSEO DEL PRADO

» **Las Meninas** (Velázquez)

» **La Rendición de Breda** (Velázquez)

» **La Maja Desnuda & La Maja Vestida** (Goya)

» **El Tres de Mayo** (Goya)

» **Las Pinturas Negras** (the Black Paintings, Goya)

» **The Garden of Earthly Delights** (*El Jardín de las Delicias*, Hieronymus Bosch)

» **Adam & Eve** (Adán y Eva, Dürer)

» **El Lavatorio** (Tintoretto)

» **La Trinidad** (El Greco)

» **David Vencedor de Goliath** (Caravaggio)

» **El Sueño de Jacob** (Ribera)

» **Las Tres Gracias** (*The Three Graces*, Rubens)

» **Artemisa** (Rembrandt)

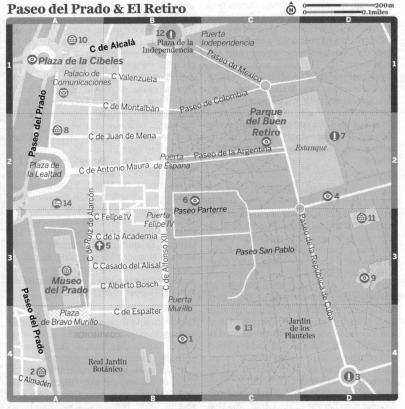

Deadly Sins. The closer you look, the harder it is to escape the feeling that he must have been doing some extraordinary drugs.

And then there are the paintings by Dürer, Rafael, Tiziano (Titian), Tintoretto, Sorolla, Gainsborough, Fra Angelico, Tiepolo...

Museo Thyssen-Bornemisza ART GALLERY
(Map p66; www.museothyssen.org; Paseo del Prado 8; adult/under 12yr €8/free, audioguide €5; ⊙10am-7pm Tue-Sun; ⓂBanco de España) One of the most extraordinary private collections of predominantly European art in

the world, the Museo Thyssen-Bornemisza is a worthy member of Madrid's 'Golden Triangle' of art. Where the Museo del Prado or Centro de Arte Reina Sofía enable you to study the body of work of a particular artist in depth, the Thyssen is a place to immerse yourself in a breathtaking breadth of artistic styles. Most of the big names are here, sometimes with just a single painting, but the Thyssens' gift to Madrid and the art-loving public is to have them all under one roof. Not surprisingly, it often ends up being many visitors' favourite Madrid art gallery.

2nd Floor

The 2nd floor, which is home to medieval art, includes some real gems hidden among the mostly 13th- and 14th-century and predominantly Italian, German and Flemish religious paintings and triptychs. Unless you have a specialist's eye, pause in Room 5 where you'll find one work by Italy's Piero della Francesca (1410–92) and the instantly recognisable *Portrait of King Henry VIII* by Holbein the Younger (1497–1543), before continuing on to Room 10 for the evocative 1586 *Massacre of the Innocents* by Lucas Van Valckenberch. Room 11 is dedicated to El Greco (with three pieces) and his Venetian contemporaries Tintoretto and Titian, while Caravaggio and the Spaniard José de Ribera dominate Room 12. A single painting each by Murillo and Zurbarán add further Spanish flavour in the two rooms that follow, while the exceptionally rendered views of Venice by Canaletto (1697–1768) should on no account be missed.

Best of all on this floor is the extension (Rooms A to H) built to house the collection of Carmen Thyssen-Bornemisza. Room C houses paintings by Canaletto, Constable and Van Gogh, while the stunning Room H includes works by Monet, Sisley, Renoir, Pissarro and Degas.

Before heading downstairs, a detour to Rooms 19 through to 21 will satisfy those devoted to 17th-century Dutch and Flemish masters, Anton van Dyck, Jan Brueghel the Elder, Rubens and Rembrandt (one painting).

1st Floor

If all that sounds impressive, the 1st floor is where the Thyssen really shines. There's a Gainsborough in Room 28 and a Goya in Room 31, but if you've been skimming the surface of this at times overwhelming collection, Room 32 is the place to linger over each and every painting. The astonishing texture of Van Gogh's *Les Vessenots* is a masterpiece, but the same could be said for *Woman in Riding Habit* by Manet, *The Thaw at Vétheuil* by Monet, Renoir's *Woman with a Parasol in a Garden,* and Pissarro's quintessentially Parisian *Rue Saint-Honoré in the Afternoon*. Room 33 is also something special with Cezanne, Gauguin, Toulouse-Lautrec and Degas, while the big names continue in Rooms 34 (Picasso, Matisse and Modigliani) and 35 (Edvard Munch and Egon Schiele).

In the 1st floor's extension (Rooms I to P), the names speak for themselves. Room K has works by Monet, Pissaro, Sorolla, and Sisley, while Room L is the domain of Gauguin (including his iconic *Mata Mua*), Degas and Toulouse-Lautrec. Rooms M (Munch), N (Kandinsky), O (Matisse and Georges Braque) and P (Picasso, Matisse, Edward Hopper and Juan Gris) round out an outrageously rich journey through the masters. On your way to the stairs there's Edward Hopper's *Hotel Room*.

Ground Floor

On the ground floor, the foray into the 20th century that you began in the 1st-floor extension takes over with a fine spread of paintings from cubism through to pop art.

In Room 41 you'll see a nice mix of the big three of cubism, Picasso, Georges Braque and Madrid's own Juan Gris, along with several other contemporaries. Kandinsky is the main drawcard in Room 43, while there's an early Salvador Dalí alongside Max Ernst and Paul Klee in Room 44. Picasso appears again in Room 45, another one of the gallery's standout rooms; its treasures include works by Marc Chagall and Dalí's hallucinatory *Dream caused by the Flight of a Bee around a Pomegranate, one Second before Waking up*.

Room 46 is similarly rich, with Joan Miró's *Catalan Peasant with a Guitar,* the splattered craziness of Jackson Pollock's *Brown and Silver I* and the deceptively simple but strangely pleasing *Green on Maroon* by Mark Rothko taking centre stage. In Rooms 47 and 48 the Thyssen builds to a stirring climax, with Francis Bacon, Roy Lichtenstein, Henry Moore and Lucian Freud, Sigmund's Berlin-born grandson, all represented.

Parque del Buen Retiro   PUBLIC GARDENS
(Map p73; ☉6am-midnight May-Sep, 6am-11pm Oct-Apr; MRetiro, Príncipe de Vergara, Ibiza or

Atocha) The splendid gardens of El Retiro are littered with marble monuments, landscaped lawns, the occasional elegant building and abundant greenery. It's quiet and contemplative during the week, but comes to life on weekends. Put simply, this is one of our favourite places in Madrid.

Laid out in the 17th century by Felipe IV as the preserve of kings, queens and their intimates, the park was opened to the public in 1868 and ever since, whenever the weather's fine and on weekends in particular, *madrileños* from all across the city gather here to stroll, read the Sunday papers in the shade, take a boat ride or nurse a cool drink at the numerous outdoor *terrazas*.

The focal point for so much of El Retiro's life is the artificial lake *(estanque)*, which is watched over by the massive ornamental structure of the Monument to Alfonso XII on the east side of the lake, complete with marble lions.

On the southern end of the lake, the odd structure decorated with sphinxes is the Fuente Egipcia (Egyptian Fountain); legend has it that an enormous fortune buried in the park by Felipe IV in the mid-18th century rests here. Hidden among the trees south of the lake, the Palacio de Cristal, a magnificent metal and glass structure, is arguably one of El Retiro's most beautiful architectural monuments. It was built in 1887 as a winter garden for exotic flowers and is now used for temporary exhibitions organised by the Centro de Arte Reina Sofía. Just north of here, the 1883 Palacio de Velázquez is also used for temporary exhibitions.

At the southern end of the park, near **La Rosaleda** (Rose Garden) with its more than 4000 roses, is a statue of El Ángel Caído (the Fallen Angel, aka Lucifer), one of the few statues to the devil anywhere in the world. Strangely, it sits 666m above sea level...

West of here is moving Bosque del Recuerdo (Memorial Forest), an understated memorial to the 191 victims of the 11 March 2004 train bombings. For each victim stands an olive or cypress tree. To the north, just inside the Puerta de Felipe IV, stands what is thought to be Madrid's oldest tree, a Mexican conifer *(ahuehuete)* planted in 1633.

In the northeastern corner of the park is the Ermita de San Isidro, a small country chapel noteworthy as one of the few, albeit modest, examples of Romanesque architecture in Madrid. When it was built Madrid was a small village more than 2km away.

Real Jardín Botánico   BOTANICAL GARDENS
(Royal Botanical Garden; Map p73; ☎91 420 30 17; Plaza de Bravo Murillo 2; adult/child/concession €2.50/free/1.25; ☺10am-9pm May-Aug; ⓂAtocha) With its manicured flower beds and neat paths, the Real Jardín Botánico is more intimate than El Retiro. First created in 1755 on the banks of Río Manzanares, the garden was moved here in 1781 by Carlos III. These days you can see thousands of plant species.

FREE Caixa Forum   MULTIMEDIA CENTRE
(Map p73; www.fundacio.lacaixa.es, in Spanish; Paseo del Prado 36; ☺10am-8pm; ⓂAtocha) The extraordinary Caixa Forum, which opened in early 2008, is one of the most exciting architectural innovations to emerge in Madrid in recent years. Seeming to hover above the ground, this brick edifice is topped by an intriguing summit of rusted iron. On an adjacent wall is the *jardín colgante* (hanging garden), a lush vertical wall of greenery almost four storeys high. Inside are four floors of exhibition and performance space awash in stainless steel and with soaring ceilings. Exhibitions range from photography and multimedia to retrospectives of major contemporary painters.

Plaza de la Cibeles   ROUNDABOUT
(Map p73; ⓂBanco de España) Of all the grand roundabouts that punctuate the elegant boulevard of Paseo del Prado, Plaza de la

---

BEST MUSEUMS FOR SPANISH ARTISTS

» **Museo del Prado** (p69) – Goya, Velázquez, Zurbarán...

» **Centro de Arte Reina Sofía** (p68) – Picasso, Dalí, Miró...

» **Real Academia de Bellas Artes de San Fernando** (p63) – Goya, Velázquez, Picasso, Juan Gris

» **Ermita de San Antonio de la Florida** (p77) – Goya

» **Museo Sorolla** (p79) – Joaquín Sorolla

» **Museo Municipal de Arte Contemporáneo de Madrid** (p77) – contemporary artists

Cibeles most evokes the splendour of imperial Madrid.

The jewel in the crown is the astonishing Palacio de Comunicaciones. Completed in 1917 by Antonio Palacios, Madrid's most prolific architect of the belle époque, it combines elements of the North American monumental style of the period with Gothic and Renaissance touches. It serves as Madrid's town hall *(ayuntamiento)*, with the central post office occupying the southwestern corner. Other landmark buildings around the plaza's perimeter include the Palacio de Linares, Casa de América, Palacio de Buenavista, Casa de las Siete Chimeneas and the national Banco de España. The views east towards the Puerta de Alcalá or west towards the Metrópolis building are some of Madrid's finest.

The spectacular fountain of the goddess Cybele at the centre of the plaza is also one of Madrid's most beautiful. Ever since it was erected in 1780 by Ventura Rodríguez, it has been a Madrid favourite. Carlos III tried to move it to the gardens of the Granja de San Ildefonso, near Segovia, but the *madrileños* kicked up such a fuss that he abandoned the idea. The Cibeles fountain has also long been the venue for joyous and often destructive celebrations by players and supporters of Real Madrid whenever the side wins anything of note.

FREE **Museo Naval**   NAVAL MUSEUM
(Map p73; www.museonavalmadrid.com, in Spanish; Paseo del Prado 5; ⊙10am-2pm Tue-Sun; MBanco de España) A block south of Plaza de la Cibeles, this museum will appeal to those who love their ships or who have always wondered what the Spanish armada really looked like. On display are quite extraordinary models of ships from the earliest days of Spain's maritime history to the 20th century. Lovers of antique maps will also find plenty of interest, especially Juan de la Cosa's parchment map of the known world, put together in 1500. The accuracy of Europe and Africa is astounding, and it's supposedly the first map to show the Americas (albeit with considerably greater fantasy than fact).

Iglesia de San Jerónimo el Real   CHURCH
(Map p73; Calle de Ruiz de Alarcón 19; ⊙10am-1pm & 5-8.30pm Mon-Sat Oct-Jun, hr vary Jul-Sep; MAtocha or Banco de España) Tucked away behind the Museo del Prado, this chapel was traditionally favoured by the Spanish royal family, and King Juan Carlos I was crowned here in 1975 upon the death of Franco. The sometimes-sober, sometimes-splendid mock-Isabelline interior is actually a 19th-century reconstruction that took its cues from the Iglesia de San Juan de los Reyes in Toledo; the original was largely destroyed during the Peninsular War.

Puerta de Alcalá   MONUMENTAL GATE
(Map p73; Plaza de la Independencia; MRetiro) The first triumphal gate to bear this name was built in 1599, but Carlos III was singularly unimpressed and had it demolished in 1764 and replaced by another, the one you see today. Twice a year, in autumn and spring, cars abandon the roundabout and are replaced by flocks of sheep being transferred in an age-old ritual from their summer to winter pastures (and vice versa).

SALAMANCA

The *barrio* of Salamanca is Madrid's most exclusive quarter, defined by grand and restrained elegance. This is a place to put on your finest clothes and be seen (especially along Calle de Serrano or Calle de José Ortega y Gasset), to stroll into shops with an affected air and resist asking the prices, or to promenade between the fine museums and parks that make you wonder whether you've arrived at the height of civilisation.

Museo Arqueológico Nacional

ARCHAEOLOGICAL MUSEUM
(Map p78; http://man.mcu.es, in Spanish; Calle de Serrano 13; admission free until renovations complete; ⊙9.30am-8pm Tue-Sat, 9.30am-3pm Sun & holidays; MSerrano) The showpiece National Archaeology Museum contains a sweeping accumulation of artefacts behind its towering facade. The large collection includes stunning mosaics taken from Roman villas across Spain, intricate Muslim-era and Mudéjar handiwork, sculpted figures such as the Dama de Ibiza and Dama de Elche, examples of Romanesque and Gothic architectural styles and a partial copy of the prehistoric cave paintings of Altamira (Cantabria).

Sadly, until 2012 (and more likely 2013), only a small sample of the museum's riches will be on display as the building undergoes major (and long-overdue) renovations.

Museo Lázaro Galdiano   PRIVATE MUSEUM
(www.flg.es, in Spanish; Calle de Serrano 122; adult/student €4/3, Sun free; ⊙10am-4.30pm Wed-Mon; MGregorio Marañón) In an imposing

early-20th-century Italianate stone mansion, the Museo Lázaro Galdiano has some 13,000 works of art and objets d'art. Apart from works by Bosch, Zurbarán, Goya, Claudio Coello, El Greco and Constable, this is a rather oddball assembly of all sorts of collectables. In Room 14 some of Goya's more famous works are hung together to make a collage, including *La Maja* and the frescoes of the Ermita de San Antonio de la Florida.

Museo de la Escultura Abstracta
OPEN-AIR GALLERY
(Map p78; www.munimadrid.es/museoairelibre/; Ⓜ Rubén Darío) This fascinating open-air collection of 17 abstracts includes works by the renowned Basque artist Eduardo Chillida, the Catalan master Joan Miró as well as Eusebio Sempere and Alberto Sánchez, one of Spain's foremost sculptors of the 20th century. The sculptures are beneath the overpass where Paseo de Eduardo Dato crosses Paseo de la Castellana, but somehow the hint of traffic grime and pigeon shit only adds to the appeal. All but one of the sculptures are on the eastern side of Paseo de la Castellana.

MALASAÑA & CHUECA
The inner-city *barrios* of Malasaña and Chueca are where Madrid gets up close and personal. Yes, there are rewarding museums and examples of landmark architecture sprinkled throughout. But these *barrios* are more about doing than seeing, more about experiencing life as it's lived by *madrileños* than ticking off a list of wonderful, if more static, attractions. These attractions may have made the city famous, but they only tell half the story. These are neighbourhoods with attitude and personality, where Madrid's famed nightlife, shopping and eating thrive. Malasaña is streetwise and down to earth, while Chueca, as Madrid's centre of gay culture, is more stylish and flamboyant.

Museo de Historia
MUSEUM
(Map p80; www.munimadrid.es/museomunicipal, in Spanish; Calle de Fuencarral 78; Ⓜ Tribunal) The fine Museo de Historia (formerly the Museo Municipal) has an elaborate and restored baroque entrance, raised in 1721 by Pedro de Ribera. The interior is dominated by paintings and other memorabilia charting the historical evolution of Madrid, of which the highlight is Goya's *Allegory of the City of Madrid*. Also worth lingering over

is the expansive model of 1830s Madrid on the ground floor. Sadly, the museum was closed for extensive renovations and may not reopen until at least 2011, but possibly not until 2012.

Sociedad General de Autores y Editores
MODERNIST ARCHITECTURE
(General Society of Authors & Editors; Map p80; Calle de Fernando VI 4; Ⓜ Alonso Martínez) The swirling, melting wedding cake of a building that is the Sociedad General de Autores y Editores is as close as Madrid comes to the work of Antoni Gaudí. It's a joyously self-indulgent ode to Modernisme and one of a kind in Madrid. It's far more impressive from the street, which is just as well because it's only open on the first Monday of October (International Architecture Day) and during the Noche en Blanco festivities.

Antiguo Cuartel del Conde Duque
FORMER BARRACKS
(Map p80; Calle del Conde Duque 9; Ⓜ Plaza de España, Ventura Rodríguez or San Bernardo) Dominating the western edge of the Malasaña district, this formidable former barracks houses government archives, libraries and the Hemeroteca Municipal (the biggest collection of newspapers and magazines in Spain) behind its 228m facade. Also contained within its walls is the Museo Municipal de Arte Contemporáneo de Madrid (Map p80; www.munimadrid.es/museoartecontemporaneo, in Spanish; admission free; ⊙10am-2pm & 5.30-9pm Tue-Sat, 10.30am-2.30pm Sun), with contemporary Spanish and international paintings, sculpture, photography and graphic art.

CHAMBERÍ & ARGÜELLES
You don't come to Chamberí or Argüelles for the sights, although there are some fine museums, as well as outstanding places to eat, drink and watch live music. Chamberí and, to a lesser extent, Argüelles may be fairly well off today, but they lack the snootiness of Salamanca. As such, it's here perhaps more than anywhere else in Madrid that you get a sense of the city as the *madrileños* experience it, away from the tourist crowds.

Ermita de San Antonio de la Florida
CHURCH, GALLERY
(Glorieta de San Antonio de la Florida 5; ⊙9.30am-8pm Tue-Fri, 10am-2pm Sat & Sun Sep-Jun, hr vary Jul & Aug; Ⓜ Príncipe Pío) The frescoed ceilings of the Ermita de San Antonio de la Florida

0   200 m
0   0.1 miles

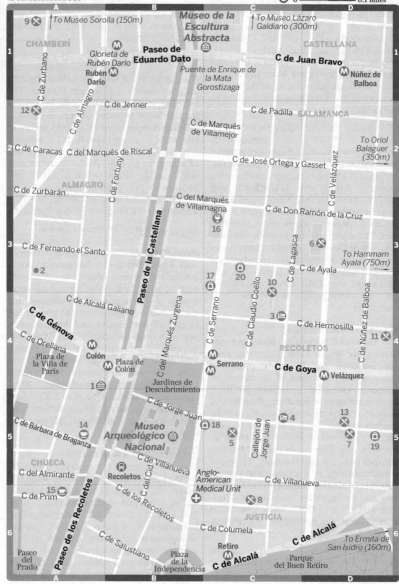

To Museo Sorolla (150m)

Museo de la Escultura Abstracta

To Museo Lázaro Galdiano (300m)

CHAMBERÍ

Glorieta de Rubén Darío

Paseo de Eduardo Dato

CASTELLANA

C de Juan Bravo

9

Rubén Darío

Puente de Enrique de la Mata Gorostizaga

Núñez de Balboa

C de Zurbano

C de Almagro

C de Jenner

C de Padilla   SALAMANCA

12

C de Marqués de Villamejor

To Oriol Balaguer (350m)

C de Caracas   C del Marqués de Riscal

C de José Ortega y Gasset

C de Velázquez

C de Zurbarán

ALMAGRO

C de Fortuny

C del Marqués de Villamagna

C de Don Ramón de la Cruz

16

C de Fernando el Santo

C de Lagasca

6

To Hammam Ayala (750m)

●2

17

20

10

C de Ayala

C de Claudio Coello

C de Serrano

Paseo de la Castellana

C de Alcalá Galiano

3

C de Hermosilla

11

C de Génova

C del Marqués Zurgena

RECOLETOS

C de Núñez de Balboa

C de Orellana

Colón

Plaza de la Villa de París

Plaza de Colón

Serrano

C de Goya

Velázquez

1

Jardines de Descubrimiento

C de Jorge Juan

13

C de Bárbara de Braganza

14

18

Callejón de Jorge Juan

4

Museo Arqueológico Nacional

5

7

19

CHUECA

C de Villanueva

C del Almirante

Recoletos

Anglo-American Medical Unit

C de Villanueva

15

C de Prim

C del Cid

C de los Recoletos

8

JUSTICIA

Paseo de los Recoletos

C de Columela

Paseo del Prado

C de Salustiano

Plaza de la Independencia

Retiro

C de Alcalá

Parque del Buen Retiro

C de Alcalá

To Ermita de San Isidro (160m)

---

are one of Madrid's most surprising secrets. Also known as the Panteón de Goya, the southern of the two small chapels is one of the few places to see Goya's work in its original setting, as painted by the master in 1798 on the request of Carlos IV.

The frescoes on the dome depict the miracle of St Anthony, who is calling on a young man to rise from the grave and absolve his father, unjustly accused of his murder. Around them swarms a typical Madrid crowd.

The painter is buried in front of the altar. His remains (minus the mysteriously missing head) were transferred in 1919 from Bordeaux (France), where he died in self-imposed exile in 1828.

FREE **Templo de Debod** EGYPTIAN TEMPLE
(www.munimadrid.es/templodebod, in Spanish; Paseo del Pintor Rosales; ⊘10am-2pm & 6-8pm Tue-Fri, 10am-2pm Sat & Sun Apr-Sep; ⓂVentura Rodríguez) Remarkably, this authentic 4th-century-BC Egyptian temple sits in the heart of Madrid, in the Parque de la Montaña. The Templo de Debod was saved from the rising waters of Lake Nasser, after the Aswan High Dam was built, and was sent block by block to Spain in 1968. The views from the surrounding gardens towards the Palacio Real are quite special.

Museo de América COLONIAL MUSEUM
(http://museodeamerica.mcu.es, in Spanish; Avenida de los Reyes Católicos 6; adult/child €3/free, Sun free; ⊘9.30am-3pm Tue, Wed, Fri & Sat, 9.30am-3pm & 4-7pm Thu, 10am-3pm Sun & holidays; ⓂMoncloa) Travel to and trade with the newly discovered Americas was a central part of Spain's culture and economy from 1492 until the early 20th century. The Museo de América has a representative display of ceramics, statuary, jewellery and instruments of hunting, fishing and war, along with some of the paraphernalia brought back by the colonisers. The Colombian gold collection,

dating back to the 2nd century AD, and a couple of shrunken heads are particularly eye-catching.

Museo Sorolla ART GALLERY
(http://museosorolla.mcu.es, in Spanish; Paseo del General Martínez Campos 37; adult/under 18yr & senior €3/free, Sun free; ⊘9.30am-8pm Tue-Sat, 9.30am-6pm Wed, 10am-3pm Sun & holidays; ⓂIglesia or Gregorio Marañón) The Valencian artist Joaquín Sorolla immortalised the clear Mediterranean light of the Valencian coast. His Madrid mansion, now a museum, is home to the largest collection of his works. On the ground floor you enter a cool *patio cordobés,* an Andalucian courtyard off which is a room containing collections of Sorolla's drawings. The 1st floor was mostly decorated by the artist himself and Sorolla used the three separate rooms as studios. In the second one is a collection of his Valencian beach scenes. Upstairs, works spanning Sorolla's career are organised across four adjoining rooms.

BEYOND THE CENTRE
Casa de Campo PARK
(ⓂBatán) This 1700-hectare, somewhat unkempt semi-wilderness stretches west of Río Manzanares. There are prettier and more central parks in Madrid, but such is its scope that nearly half a million *madrileños* visit every weekend, when cyclists, walkers and picnickers overwhelm the byways and trails that criss-cross the park.

MADRID

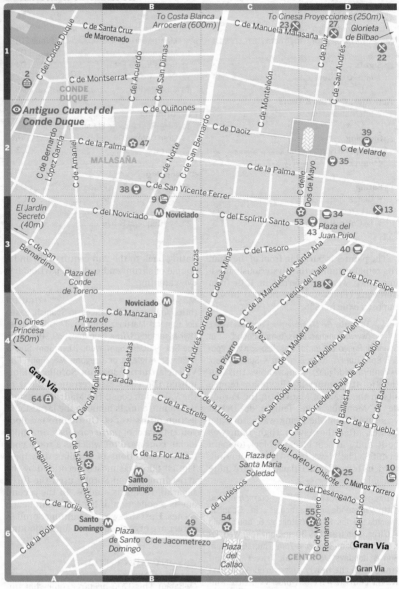

Inside the Casa de Campo is the **Zoo Aquarium de Madrid** (www.zoomadrid.com; adult/3-7yr & senior €18.65/15.10; ⊙hr vary; MCasa de Campo), home to around 3000 animals, and the **Parque de Atracciones** (www.parquedeatracciones.es, in Spanish; admis-

sion €10.60, incl unlimited rides adult/under 7yr €29/22; ⊙hr vary; MBatan), a decent amusement park sure to keep the kids entertained. Opening hours vary at both places.

A fun way to get to the Casa de Campo is the **teleférico** (cable car; www.teleferico.com, in

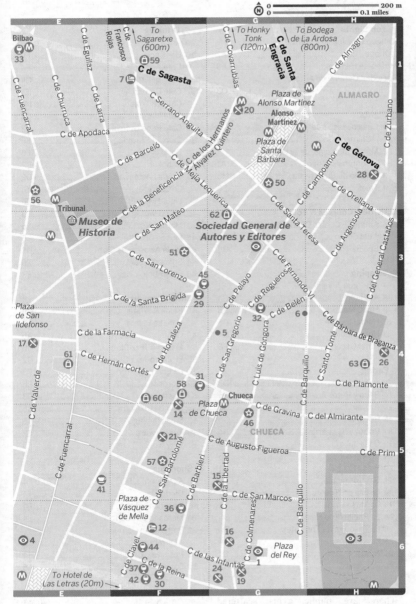

🏃 Activities

Madrid is not Europe's most bicycle-friendly city, but a ride in the Casa de Campo or El Retiro is a fantastic way to spend an afternoon.

MADRID

There are public gyms scattered throughout Madrid. They generally charge a modest €3.50 to €7 for one-day admission. Privately owned health centres are more expensive (€10 to €15), but usually have less-crowded workout rooms.

Madrid Xanadú SKI CENTRE
(www.madridsnowzone.com, in Spanish; Calle Puerto de Navacerrada, Arroyomolinos; adult/child 1hr €19/16, day pass €33/30, equipment rental per hr/day €36/50; ⊙10am-midnight Fri & Sat) The largest covered ski centre in Europe. Open year-round, it's kept at a decid-

edly cool -2°C. Within the same complex is a mammoth mall, cinemas, a kart track and an amusement park. Madrid Xanadú is approximately 23km west of Madrid, just off the A5. To get here, take bus 528 or 534 from the Intercambiador de Príncipe Pío.

Hammam Medina Mayrit
HAMMAM

(Map p60; www.medinamayrit.com; Calle de Atocha 14; ⊙10am-midnight; Ⓜ Sol) A traditional Arab bathhouse; bookings required.

Hammam Ayala
HAMMAM

(www.hammamayala.com, in Spanish; Calle de Ayala 126; ⊙10am-8pm Tue & Thu, 1-10pm Wed, Fri & Sat, 1-8pm Sun; Ⓜ Manuel Becerra) Another Arab-style bathhouse.

Spa Relajarse
DAY SPA

(Map p80; www.sparelajarse.es, in Spanish; Calle de Barquillo 43; ⊙11am-11pm Mon-Sat, 1-9pm Sun; Ⓜ Chueca)

By Bike
BICYCLE RENTAL

(www.bybike.info; Avenida de Menéndez Pelayo 35; per hr/day €4/20; ⊙10am-9pm Mon-Fri & 9.30am-9.30pm Sat & Sun Jun-Sep; Ⓜ Ibiza) Ideally placed for the Parque del Buen Retiro.

Bike Spain
BICYCLE RENTAL

(Map p60; www.bikespain.info; Plaza de la Villa 1 (Calle del Codo); half-/full day/weekend €10/15/30; ⊙10am-2pm & 4-7pm Mon-Fri; Ⓜ Ópera) Also organises cycling tours.

Trixi.com
BICYCLE RENTAL

(Map p60; www.trixi.com; Calle de los Jardines 12; 4/8/24hr €8/12/15, helmet €2.50; ⊙10am-2pm & 4-8pm Mon-Fri, 10am-8pm Sat & Sun Mar-Oct; Ⓜ Gran Vía)

Polideportivo La Chopera
SPORTS CENTRE

(Map p73; Parque del Buen Retiro; 1/10 sessions €4.35/37; ⊙9am-9pm Mon-Sat, 9am-3pm Sun, closed Aug; Ⓜ Atocha) One of Madrid's best sports centres, boasting a fine new workout centre, in the southwestern corner of El Retiro.

Casa de Campo
SWIMMING POOL

(Avenida Ángel; admission €4. 50; ⊙11.30am-9pm May-Sep; Ⓜ Batán) There are indoor and outdoor pools.

Canal de Isabel II
SWIMMING POOL

(Avenida de Filipinas 54; admission €4; ⊙11am-8pm Jun-early Sep; Ⓜ Ríos Rosas or Canal) If you're clamouring for respite during the dry heat of Madrid's endless summer, head to the huge outdoor pool in northern Madrid.

 Courses

Spanish-language schools of all possible categories abound in Madrid. Non-EU citizens who are wanting to study at a university or language school in Spain should, in theory, have a study visa. Language schools include the following:

Academia Inhispania
LANGUAGE

(Map p60; www.inhispania.com; Calle de la Montera 10-12; Ⓜ Sol)

Academia Madrid Plus
LANGUAGE

(Map p60; www.madridplus.es; 6th fl, Calle del Arenal 21; Ⓜ Ópera)

International House
LANGUAGE

(Map p78; www.ihmadrid.es; Calle de Zurbano 8; Ⓜ Alonso Martínez)

Universidad Complutense
LANGUAGE

(www.ucm.es/info/cextran/Index.htm; Secretaria de los Cursos para Extranjeros, Facultadole Filologia [Edificio A] Universidad Complutense, Cuidad Universitaria; Ⓜ Cuidad Universitaria)

Other courses:

Fundación Conservatorio Casa Patas
FLAMENCO

(Map p66; www.conservatorioflamenco.org, in Spanish; Calle de Cañizares 10; Ⓜ Antón Martín or Tirso de Molina) The best place to learn to dance *sevillanas* (a popular dance with high, twirling arm movements) or strum the guitar like the greats.

Alambique
COOKING

(Map p60; www.alambique.com; Plaza de la Encarnación 2; Ⓜ Ópera or Santo Domingo) Cooking classes start at around €50, with a handful of English-language courses.

HAVE YOUR SAY

Found a fantastic restaurant that you're longing to share with the world? Disagree with our recommendations? Or just want to talk about your most recent trip?

Whatever your reason, head to lonelyplanet.com, where you can post a review, ask or answer a question on the Thorntree forum, comment on a blog, or share your photos and tips on Groups. Or you can simply spend time chatting with like-minded travellers. So go on, have your say.

Walking Tour
Historic Madrid

❯ Start in the pulsating, geographic centre of Spain, ① **Plaza de la Puerta del Sol**, then head northwest along Calle del Arenal to the ② **Iglesia de San Ginés**, the site of one of Madrid's oldest places of Christian worship. Behind it is the wonderful ③ **Chocolatería de San Ginés**, a place of worship for lovers of *chocolate con churros* (deep-fried doughnut strips dipped in hot chocolate).

Continue up to and across Calle Mayor until you reach ④ **Plaza Mayor**, then turn west and head down the hill to the historic ⑤ **Plaza de la Villa**, home to some of the city's oldest surviving buildings.

Take the street down the left side of the Casa de Cisneros, cross Calle del Sacramento at the end, go down the stairs and follow the cobbled Calle del Cordón out onto Calle de Segovia. Almost directly in front of you is the Mudéjar tower of the 15th-century ⑥ **Iglesia de San Pedro El Viejo**; proceed up Costanilla de San Pedro, lingering en route in the charming ⑦ **Plaza de la Paja**.

From here, twist down through lanes of La Morería to Calle de Bailén and the wonderful, if expensive, *terrazas* (cafes with outdoor tables) on the edge of the ⑧ **Jardines de las Vistillas**. After a soothing *cerveza* (beer), follow Calle de Bailén past the cathedral and royal palace to the supremely elegant ⑨ **Plaza de Oriente**.

Head to the western side of the square and follow the walkway extension of Calle de Bailén, which leads into ⑩ **Plaza de España**, surrounded by monumental towers. The eastern flank of Plaza de España marks the start of ⑪ **Gran Vía**, a Haussmann-esque boulevard that was slammed through tumbledown slums in the 1910s and 1920s. Head up and then down the hill past the elegant facades to the superb dome of the ⑫ **Metrópolis building**, where Gran Vía meets Calle de Alcalá. Down the hill you go to ⑬ **Plaza de la Cibeles**, Madrid's favourite roundabout.

Apunto – Centro Cultural del Gusto
COOKING

(Map p80; www.apuntolibreria.com, in Spanish; Calle de Pelayo 60; MChueca) Classes across a range of cuisines start at €25.

☞ Tours

If you're pushed for time and want to fit a lot of sightseeing into a short visit, guided tours may be the ideal way to see the city.

Descubre Madrid
WALKING TOUR

(Discover Madrid; ☑91 588 29 06; www.esmadrid.com/descubremadrid; walking tours adult/concession €3.90/3.12, bus tours €6.45/5.05, bicycle tours €3.90/3.12 plus bike rental €6) The city tourist office offers 20 guided walking, cycling and bus itineraries.

Wellington Society
WALKING TOUR

(☑609 143 203; www.wellsoc.org; tours from €60) A handful of quirky historical tours laced with anecdotes and led by the inimitable Stephen Drake-Jones. Possibilities include 'Bullfights', 'Hemingway's Madrid', and 'Curiosities & Anecdotes of Old Madrid'.

Letango Tours
WALKING TOUR

(☑91 369 47 52; www.letango.com; weekdays/weekends €95/135) Walking tours through Madrid, including tapas tours, with additional excursions to San Lorenzo El Escorial, Segovia and Toledo.

Insider's Madrid
WALKING TOUR

(☑91 447 38 66; www.insidersmadrid.com; tours from €55) Tailor-made tours that include walking, tapas, flamenco and bullfighting.

Madrid Bike Tours
CYCLING TOUR

(☑680 581 782; www.madridbiketours.com; 4hr tours €55) Londoner Mike Chandler organises guided two-hour tours of Madrid.

Bike Spain
CYCLING TOUR

(Map p60; ☑91 559 06 53; www.bikespain.info; Plaza de la Villa 1 (Calle del Codo); tours €35; ☺10am-2pm & 4-7pm Mon-Fri, 10am-2pm Sat & Sun; MÓpera) English-language guided city tours by bike.

Seg City Tours
SEGWAY TOUR

(Map p66; ☑91 127 43 93; www.segcity.es; Calle de Cervantes 22; 2-/4hr tours from €36/60; MAntón Martín) Authorised Segway operator using the latest Segway i2 PT.

Madrid Vision
BUS TOUR

(www.madridvision.es; 1-/2-day ticket adult €16/19, 7-16yr & over 65yr €7.50/10, under 7yr free; ☺9.30am-midnight 21 Jun-20 Sep, 10am-5pm 21 Dec-20 Mar, 10am-6.30pm rest of year)

Hop-on, hop-off open-topped bus tours. Information is available at tourist offices and some hotels, and you can get tickets on the bus.

Adventurous Appetites
CULINARY TOUR

(☑639 331 073; www.adventurousappetites.com; 4hr tours €50; ☺8pm-midnight Mon-Sat) English-language tapas tours through central Madrid. Prices include the first drink but exclude food.

Alambique
CULINARY TOUR

(Map p60; ☑91 547 42 20; www.alambique.com; 3½hr tours from €50; Plaza de la Encarnación 2; MÓpera or Santo Domingo) The 'Foodies Walking Tour' visits traditional bakeries and the Mercado de San Miguel; these can be extended to include lunch and a cooking class.

🎊 Festivals & Events

Madrid loves to party, and seemingly any excuse is good for a fiesta. For details about national festivals see p24, but here in the city be sure to look out for the following events. There's more information online at www.esmadrid.com.

February

Festival Flamenco Caja Madrid
FLAMENCO

Five days of fine flamenco music in one of the city's theatres. The dates are movable and big names in recent years have included Enrique Morente, Carmen Linares and Diego El Cigala.

Arco
CONTEMPORARY ART

(Feria Internacional de Arte Contemporánea; www.arco.ifema.es, in Spanish) One of Europe's biggest celebrations of contemporary art, Arco draws galleries and exhibitors from all over the world to the Parque Ferial Juan Carlos I exhibition centre near Barajas airport. It's held mid-February.

March

Jazz es Primavera
JAZZ

(www.sanjuanevangelista.org) Three weeks of jazz in leading jazz venues across the city. It sometimes spills over into April.

La Noche de los Teatros
STREET THEATRE

On 'The Night of the Theatres', Madrid's streets become the stage for all manner of performances, with a focus on comedy and children's plays. It usually takes place on the last Saturday of March.

MADRID FOR CHILDREN

Madrid has plenty to keep the little ones entertained. A good place to start is Casa de Campo (p79), where there are swimming pools, the Zoo Aquarium de Madrid and the Parque de Atracciones, which has a 'Zona Infantil' with sedate rides for the really young. To get to Casa de Campo, take the *teleférico*, one of the world's most horizontal cable cars, which putters for 2.5km out from the slopes of La Rosaleda.

Another possibility is Faunia (www.faunia.es, in Spanish; Avenida de las Comunidades 28; adult/under 12yr €24.90/19.10; ⊙hr vary; ⓂValdebernardo), a modern animal theme park with an 'Amazon jungle' and 'Polar Ecosystem'. Faunia is located east of the M-40, about 7km from the city centre.

The Museo del Ferrocarril (Railway Museum; www.museodelferrocarril.org; Paseo de las Delicias 61; adult/child €4.50/3; ⊙10am-3pm Tue-Sun Sep-Jul; ⓂDelicias) is home to old railway cars, train engines and more. The free Museo Naval (p76) will appeal to those fascinated by ships.

The Museo de Cera (Wax Museum; Map p78; www.museoceramadrid.com; Paseo de los Recoletos 41; adult/under 10yr €16/12; ⊙10am-2.30pm & 4.30-8.30pm Mon-Fri, 10am-8.30pm Sat & Sun; ⓂColón) is Madrid's modest answer to Madame Tussaud's, with more than 450 wax characters.

Other possibilities include seeing Real Madrid play at the Estadio Santiago Bernabéu (p110), wandering through the soothing greenery of the Parque del Buen Retiro (p74), where in summer there are puppet shows and boat rides, or skiing at Madrid Xanadú (p82).

May & June

Fiesta de la Comunidad de Madrid

CITY FESTIVAL

On 2 May 1808 Napoleon's troops put down an uprising in Madrid, and commemoration of the day has become an opportunity for much festivity. The day is celebrated with particular energy in the bars of Malasaña.

Fiesta de San Isidro

PATRON SAINT

Around 15 May Madrid's patron saint is honoured with a week of nonstop processions, parties and bullfights. Free concerts are held throughout the city, and this week marks the start of the city's bullfighting season.

Festimad

INDIE MUSIC

(www.festimad.es, in Spanish) Bands from all over the country and beyond converge on Móstoles or Leganés (on the MetroSur train network) for two days of indie music indulgence. Although usually held in May, Festimad sometimes spills over into April or June.

Fiesta de Otoño en Primavera

MUSIC, THEATRE

(www.esmadrid.com) The 'Autumn Festival in Spring' involves a busy calendar of musical and theatrical activity.

Suma Flamenca

FLAMENCO

(www.madrid.org/sumaflamenca, www.teatros delcanal.org) Another soul-filled flamenco festival that draws some of the biggest names in the genre to the Teatros del Canal in June.

Día del Orgullo de Gays, Lesbianas y Transexuales

GAY PRIDE

(www.orgullogay.org, in Spanish, www.gaypride madrid.com) The colourful Gay Pride Parade, on the last Saturday in June, sets out from the Puerta de Alcalá in the early evening, and winds its way around the city in an explosion of music and energy, ending up at the Puerta del Sol.

July & August

Veranos de la Villa

CULTURE

(www.esmadrid.com/veranosdelavilla/) Madrid's town hall stages a series of cultural events, shows and exhibitions throughout July and August, known as Summers in the City.

Summer Festivals

NEIGHBOURHOOD FESTIVALS

Small-time but fun, the neighbourhood summer festivals (held during the period from mid-August to September), such as San Cayetano in Lavapiés, and San Lorenzo and La Paloma in La Latina, are great for cheap entertainment.

September–November

La Noche en Blanco ALL-NIGHT FESTIVAL

On September's White Night, Madrid stays open all night with a citywide extravaganza of concerts and general revelry in 120 venues.

Festival Jazz Madrid JAZZ

(www.esmadrid.com/festivaljazzmadrid/) Madrid loves its jazz too much to be confined to just one festival (Jazz es Primavera in spring is the other one). This one in November is arguably the more prestigious and groups from far and wide converge on the capital for a series of concerts in venues across town.

🛏 Sleeping

Madrid has high-quality accommodation across all price ranges and caters to every taste. Where you decide to stay will play an important role in your experience of Madrid. Los Austrias, Sol and Centro put you in the heart of the busy downtown area, while La Latina (the best *barrio* for tapas), Lavapiés and Huertas (good for nightlife) are ideal for those who love Madrid nights and don't want to stagger too far to get back to their hotel in the wee small hours. Staying along the Paseo del Prado is ideal for those here to spend most of their time in galleries, while Salamanca is quiet, upmarket and perfect for serial shoppers. You don't have to be gay to stay in Chueca, but you'll love it if you are, while Malasaña is another inner-city *barrio* with great restaurants and bars.

LOS AUSTRIAS, SOL & CENTRO

TOP CHOICE **Hotel Meninas** BOUTIQUE HOTEL €€

(Map p60; ☎91 541 28 05; www.hotel meninas.com; Calle de Campomanes 7; s/d from €109/129; ✳🖥; MÓpera) This is the sort of place where an interior designer licked his or her lips and created a masterwork of understated minimalist luxury. The colour scheme is blacks, whites and greys, with dark-wood floors and splashes of fuchsia and lime-green. Flat-screen TVs are in every room, along with the latest bathroom fittings and internet access points (there's even a laptop in some rooms), all rounding out the effect of clean lines and the latest innovations.

Hostal Madrid HOSTAL, APARTMENTS €

(Map p60; ☎91 522 00 60; www.hostal-madrid. info; 2nd fl, Calle de Esparteros 6; s €40-60, d €50-78, apt per night €60-150, per month €1200-2100; MSol) The 19 excellent apartments here range in size from 33 sq metres to 200 sq metres and each has a fully equipped kitchen, its own sitting area, bathroom and, in some, an expansive terrace with good rooftop views. The double *hostal* (budget hotel) rooms are comfortable and well sized and the service is extremely friendly.

Hotel Plaza Mayor HOTEL €€

(Map p60; ☎91 360 06 06; www.h-plazamayor. com; Calle de Atocha 2; s €50-70, d €60-130; ✳; MSol or Tirso de Molina) Sitting just across from Plaza Mayor, here you'll find stylish decor, charming original elements from the 150-year-old building, and extremely helpful staff. The rooms are attractive, some with a light colour scheme and wrought-iron furniture. The designer attic rooms have lovely little terraces with wonderful rooftop views of central Madrid.

Los Amigos Sol Backpackers' Hostel HOSTAL €

(Map p60; ☎91 559 24 72; www.losamigoshostel. com; Calle de Arenal 26, 4th fl; dm incl breakfast €17-20; ▣; MÓpera or Sol) If you arrive in Madrid keen for company, this could be the place for you – lots of students stay here, the staff are savvy (and speak English) and there are bright dorm-style rooms (with free lockers). Prices include breakfast and there's a kitchen for use by guests. A steady stream of repeat visitors is the best recommendation we can give.

Hotel de Las Letras HOTEL €€

(Map p60; ☎91 523 79 80; www.hoteldelasletras. com; Gran Vía 11; d from €100; MGran Vía) If you want to cause a stir with a new hotel in Madrid at the moment, make sure it has a rooftop bar overlooking the city. They're all the rage, but Hotel de las Letras started the craze. The bar's wonderful, but the whole hotel is excellent, with individually styled rooms, each with literary quotes from famous writers on the walls.

Mario Room Mate BOUTIQUE HOTEL €€

(Map p60; ☎91 548 85 48; www.room-mate hoteles.com; Calle de Campomanes 4; s €90-120, d €100-140; ✳🖥; MÓpera) Entering this swanky boutique hotel is like crossing the threshold of Madrid's latest nightclub – staff dressed all in black, black walls and swirls of red lighting in the lobby. Rooms can be small but with high ceilings and simple furniture, light tones contrasting smoothly with muted colours and dark surfaces; some rooms are pristine white, others have splashes of colour with zany murals. The first of the Room Mate chain of hotels to open, Mario prides itself on being 'intimate, elegant and serene', and we have to agree with it.

Hostal Luis XV HOSTAL €
(Map p60; ☎91 522 10 21; www.hrluisxv.net, in Spanish; 8th fl, Calle de la Montera 47; s/d from €45/59; MGran Vía) Everything here – the views, the spacious rooms and the attention to detail – makes this family-run place feel pricier than it is. Exterior rooms have balconies from where the views are superb (especially from the triple room 820); you'll find it hard to tear yourself away.

Hostal Acapulco HOSTAL €
(Map p60; ☎91 531 19 45; www.hostalacapulco.com; Calle de la Salud 13, 4th fl; s/d €52/62; ❄📶; MGran Vía) This immaculate little *hostal* is a cut above many in town, with marble floors, recently renovated bathrooms, double-glazed windows and comfortable beds. Street-facing rooms have balconies overlooking sunny Plaza del Carmen and are flooded with natural light.

Petit Palace Posada del Peine BOUTIQUE HOTEL €€
(Map p60; ☎91 523 81 51; www.hthoteles.com; Calle de Postas 17; d from €130; ❄📶; MSol) This outstanding hotel combines a splendid historic building (dating to 1610), a brilliant location (just 50m from the Plaza Mayor) and modern hi-tech rooms. The bathrooms sparkle with stunning fittings and many historical architectural features remain in situ in the public areas. It's just a pity some of the rooms aren't larger.

Hotel Preciados BUSINESS HOTEL €€
(Map p60; ☎91 454 44 00; www.preciadoshotel.com; Calle de Preciados 37; d from €125; ❄📶; MSanto Domingo or Callao) This hotel has a classier feel than many of the other business options around town and it gets rave reviews for its service. Soft lighting, light shades and plentiful glass personalise the rooms and provide an intimate feel.

Hostel Metropol HOSTEL €
(Map p60; ☎91 521 29 35; www.metropolhostel.com; Calle de la Montera 47, 1st fl; dm €16-21, s/d €45/60; @; MGran Vía) This easygoing place attracts a host of young travellers, not because of its rooms (which are simple and don't have a whole lot of character), but because it offers a special something that few hostels have: attitude and a real sense of fun.

LA LATINA & LAVAPIÉS

Mad Hostel HOSTEL €
(☎91 506 48 40; www.madhostel.com; Calle de Cabeza 24; dm from €15; ❄@; MAntón Martín) From the same people who brought you Cat's Hostel, Mad Hostel is similarly filled with a buzzing vibe. The 1st-floor courtyard – with retractable roof – is a wonderful place to chill, while the four- to eight-bed rooms are smallish but new and clean. There's a small rooftop gym complete with state-of-the-art equipment.

HUERTAS & ATOCHA

TOP CHOICE **Alicia Room Mate** BOUTIQUE HOTEL €€
(Map p66; ☎91 389 60 95; www.room-matehoteles.com; Calle del Prado 2; d €105-165, ste from €200; ❄📶; MSol or Antón Martín) One of the landmark properties of the designer Room Mate chain of hotels, Hotel Alicia overlooks Plaza de Santa Ana with beautiful, spacious rooms. The style (the work of Pascua Ortega) is a touch more muted than in other Room Mate hotels, but the super-modern look remains intact, the downstairs bar is oh-so-cool, and the service young and switched on.

TOP CHOICE **Quo** BOUTIQUE HOTEL €€
(Map p66; ☎91 532 90 49; www.hotelesquo.com; Calle de Sevilla 4; d €90-217; ❄📶; MSevilla) Quo is one of Madrid's boutique hotels of longer standing and it's still deservedly popular. The rooms have minimalist designer furniture, tall ceilings and huge windows that let light flood in. The colour scheme is black and red, with light surfaces providing perfect contrast and a resolutely contemporary look. We're also big fans of the bathrooms, with glass doors, glass benches and stainless-steel basins. All rooms have flat-screen TVs, black-and-white photos of Madrid, dark-wood floors and comfy armchairs; rooms on the 7th floor have Jacuzzis and private terraces with terrific views over the rooftops.

Hotel Urban LUXURY HOTEL €€€
(Map p66; ☎91 787 77 70; www.derbyhotels.com; Carrera de San Jerónimo 34; d/ste from €190/250; ❄📶🏊; MSevilla) The towering glass edifice of Hotel Urban is the epitome of art-inspired, superstylish designer cool. With its clean lines, modern art and antiques from around the world, it's a wonderful antidote to the more classic charm of Madrid's five-star hotels of longer standing. Dark-wood floors and dark walls are offset by plenty of light, while the bathrooms have

Madrid is one of Europe's most gay-friendly cities. The heartbeat of gay Madrid is the inner-city *barrio* (district) of Chueca, where Madrid didn't just come out of the closet, but ripped the doors off in the process. But even here the crowd is almost always mixed gay/straight. The best time of all to be in town if you're gay or lesbian is around the last Saturday in June, for Madrid's gay and lesbian pride march (p86).

Chueca has an abundance of gay-friendly bars, restaurants and shops. Librería Berkana (Map p80; ☎ 91 522 55 99; www.libreriaberkana.com, in Spanish; Calle de Hortaleza 64; ☺ 10.30am-9pm Mon-Fri, 11.30am-9pm Sat, noon-2pm & 5-9pm Sun; Ⓜ Chueca) operates like an unofficial information centre for gay Madrid; here you'll find the biweekly *Shanguide*, jammed with listings and contact ads, as well as books, magazines and videos. A Different Life (Map p80; www.adifferentlife.es, in Spanish; Calle de Pelayo 30; ☺ 11am-10pm Mon-Fri, 11am-midnight Sat, 11am-3pm & 5-10pm Sun; Ⓜ Chueca) is another bookshop geared towards gays and lesbians.

Another good place to get the low-down on gay Madrid is the laid-back Mamá Inés (Map p80; www.mamaines.com, in Spanish; Calle de Hortaleza 22; ☺ 10am-2pm Sun-Thu, 10am-3am Fri & Sat; Ⓜ Gran Vía or Chueca), a cafe where you'll hear the gossip on where that night's hot spot will be. Café Acuarela (Map p80; Calle de Gravina 10; ☺ 11am-2am Sun-Thu, 11am-3am Fri & Sat; Ⓜ Chueca) is a dimly lit centrepiece of gay Madrid – a huge statue of a nude male angel guards the doorway. Also good for a low-key night out is the sophisticated Café La Troje (Map p80; Calle de Pelayo 26; ☺ 2pm-2am; Ⓜ Chueca).

Two of the most popular Chueca nightspots are Club 54 Studio (Map p80; www.studio54madrid.com, in Spanish; Calle de Barbieri 7; ☺ 11.30pm-3.30am Thu-Sat; Ⓜ Chueca), which is modelled on the famous New York club Studio 54, and Liquid Madrid (Map p80; www.liquid.es; Calle de Barbieri 7; ☺ 9am-3am Mon-Thu, 9am-3.30am Fri & Sat; Ⓜ Chueca). For something that stays open later, Why Not? (Map p80; Calle de San Bartolomé 7; ☺ 10.30pm-6am; admission €10; Ⓜ Chueca) is the sort of place where nothing's left to the imagination (the gay and straight crowd who come here are pretty amorous) and it's full nearly every night of the week. Pop and top-40s music are the standards here.

Other clubs popular with a predominantly gay crowd include Sala Bash/Ohm (Map p80; Plaza del Callao 4; ☺ midnight-6am Fri & Sat; Ⓜ Callao), Black & White (Map p80; www.discoblack-white.net; Calle de la Libertad 34; ☺ 10pm-5.30am Sun-Thu, 10pm-6am Fri & Sat; Ⓜ Chueca) and Saturday nights at Cool (p105).

For a place to rest your head, look no further than the excellent Hostal La Zona (p91), which has a mainly gay clientele.

---

wonderful designer fittings – the wash basins are sublime. The rooftop swimming pool is Madrid's best and the gorgeous terrace is heaven on a candlelit summer's evening.

Chic & Basic Colors HOSTEL €€
(Map p66; ☎ 91 429 69 35; www.chicandbasic.com; Calle de las Huertas 14, 2nd fl; s/d/apt from €62/78/96; ❄ 🛜 ✉; Ⓜ Antón Martín) It's all about colours here at this fine little hostel. The rooms are white in a minimalist style, with free internet, flat-screen TVs, dark hardwood floors with a bright colour scheme superimposed on top with every room a different shade. It's all very comfortable, contemporary and casual. Prices increase by €10 per room on Friday and Saturday. It also has apartments in the same building.

Cat's Hostel HOSTEL €
(Map p66; ☎ 91 369 28 07; www.catshostel.com; Calle de Cañizares 6; dm/d from €15/42; ❄ @; Ⓜ Antón Martín) Forming part of a 17th-century palace, the internal courtyard here is Madrid's finest – lavish Andalucian tilework, a fountain, a spectacular glass ceiling and stunning Islamic decoration, surrounded on four sides by an open balcony. There's a super-cool basement bar with free internet connections and fiestas, often with live music.

Hostal Adriano HOSTEL €
(Map p66; ☎ 91 521 13 39; www.hostaladriano.com; Calle de la Cruz 26, 4th fl; s/d €53/65; Ⓜ Sol) They don't come any better than this bright and cheerful *hostal* wedged in the streets that mark the boundary between Sol and

Huertas. Most rooms are well sized and each has its own colour scheme.

Hostal Sardinero
HOSTAL €

(Map p66; ☑91 429 57 56; www.hostalsardinero. com; Calle del Prado 16; s/d from €42/50; ☒; ⓂSol or Antón Martín) A change of owners here has brought more than just a fresh lick of paint, new mattresses and new TVs. The cheerful rooms, which have high ceilings, air-conditioning, a safe, hairdryers and renovated bathrooms, are complemented nicely by the equally cheerful Nieves and Jimmy, who are attentive without being in your face.

Hostal Adria Santa Ana
HOSTAL €€

(Map p66; ☑91 521 13 39; www.hostaladriasanta ana.com; Calle de la Cruz 26, 4th fl; s/d €60/70; ⓂSol) The owners of Hostal Adriano also run this place. It's on the same floor, but a step up in price, style and luxury. Put the two *hostales* together and they're a great combination.

Me by Meliá
HOTEL €€€

(Map p66; ☑91 701 60 00; www.me-by-melia. com; Plaza de Santa Ana 14; d without/with plaza view from €182/230; ⓂSol or Antón Martín) Until recently the landmark Gran Victoria Hotel, the Madrid home of many a famous bullfighter, this audacious hotel is fast becoming a landmark of a different kind. Overlooking the western end of Plaza de Santa Ana, this luxury hotel is decked out in minimalist white with curves and comfort in all the right places. This is one place where it's definitely worth paying extra for a room with a view.

Hotel Miau
BOUTIQUE HOTEL €€

(Map p66; ☑91 369 71 20; www.hotelmiau.com; Calle del Príncipe 26; s/d incl breakfast €85/95; ☒@; ⓂSol or Antón Martín) If you want to be close to the nightlife of Huertas or you can't tear yourself away from the beautiful Plaza de Santa Ana, then this is your place. Light tones, splashes of colour and elegant modern art adorn the rooms, which are large and well equipped. It can be noisy, but you chose Huertas...

Hotel El Pasaje
HOTEL €€

(Map p66; ☑91 521 29 95; www.elpasajehs.com; Calle del Pozo 4; d incl breakfast €91-113; ⓂSol) If you were to choose your ideal location in Huertas, Hotel El Pasaje would be hard to beat. Set on a quiet lane largely devoid of bars, yet just around the corner from the Plaza de la Puerta del Sol, it combines a

central location with a quiet night's sleep, at least by the standards of Huertas. The feel is intimate and modern (except for the tired-looking bedspreads – what were they thinking?), with good bathrooms, minibars and enough space to leave your suitcase without tripping over it.

PASEO DEL PRADO & EL RETIRO

Hotel Ritz
LUXURY HOTEL €€€

(Map p73; ☑91 701 67 67; www.ritzmadrid.com; Plaza de la Lealtad 5; d from €280, ste €1100-5000; ☒☎; ⓂBanco de España) The grand old lady of Madrid, the Hotel Ritz is the height of exclusivity. One of the most lavish buildings in Madrid, its classic style and impeccable service are second to none. Not surprisingly, it's the hotel of choice for presidents, kings and celebrities. The public areas are palatial and awash with antiques, while the rooms are extravagantly large, opulent and supremely comfortable.

Westin Palace
LUXURY HOTEL €€€

(Map p66; ☑91 360 80 00; www.westinpalace madrid.com; Plaza de las Cortes 7; d from €215, ste from €650; ☒☎; ⓂBanco de España or Antón Martín) An old Madrid classic, this former palace of the Duque de Lerma opened as a hotel in 1911 and was Spain's second luxury hotel. Ever since it has looked out across Plaza de Neptuno at its rival, the Ritz, like a lover unjustly scorned. Its name may not have the world-famous cachet of the Ritz, but it's not called the Palace for nothing and is extravagant in all the right places.

SALAMANCA

Petit Palace Art Gallery
TOP CHOICE
ART HOTEL €€

(Map p78; ☑91 435 54 11; www.hthoteles.com; Calle de Jorge Juan 17; d €120-220; ☒☎; ⓂSerrano) Occupying a stately 19th-century Salamanca building, this lovely designer hotel combines hi-tech facilities with an artistic look, with loads of original works dotted around the public spaces and even in some of the rooms. Hydro-massage showers, laptop computers and exercise bikes in many rooms are just some of the extras, and the address is ideal for getting out among the best of Salamanca.

Hesperia Hermosilla
HOTEL €€

(Map p78; ☑91 246 88 00; www.hesperia.com; Calle de Hermosilla 23; d from €84; ☒☎; ⓂSerrano) If you're here on a mission to shop in Salamanca, or you value quiet, exclusive streets away from the noise of central Madrid, this modern and subtly stylish hotel is a terrific choice. The furnishings are vaguely minimalist, especially in the public areas, and LCD flat-screen TVs and other creature comforts are rare luxuries in this price range.

MALASAÑA & CHUECA

TOP CHOICE **Hotel Óscar** BOUTIQUE HOTEL **€€**
(Map p80; ☑91 701 11 73; www.room -matehoteles.com; Plaza de Vázquez de Mella 12; d €90-200, ste €150-280; ※☎; MGran Vía) Simply outstanding. Hotel Óscar's designer rooms ooze style and sophistication. Some have floor-to-ceiling murals, the lighting is always funky and the colour scheme is awash with pinks, lime-greens, oranges or a more minimalist black-and-white. The facade – with thousands of hanging Coca-Cola bottles – is a striking local landmark, there's a fine street-level tapas bar and a rooftop terrace.

TOP CHOICE **Antigua Posada del Pez** HOTEL **€€**
(Map p80; ☑91 531 42 96; www.antigua posadadelpez.com; Calle de Pizarro 16; s €40-120, d €50-150; MNoviciado) If only all places to stay were this good. This place inhabits the shell of a historic Malasaña building, but the rooms are slick and contemporary with designer bathrooms. You're also just a few steps up the hill from Calle del Pez, one of Malasaña's most happening streets. It's an exceptionally good deal, even when prices head upwards.

Hotel Abalú BOUTIQUE HOTEL **€€**
(Map p80; ☑91 531 47 44; www.hotelabalu.com; Calle del Pez 19; s/d/ste from €74/90/140; ※☎; MNoviciado) Malasaña's stand-out boutique hotel is an oasis of style amid the *barrio*'s time-worn feel. Each room has its own design drawn from the imagination of Luis Delgado, from retro chintz to Zen, baroque to pure white, and most aesthetics in between. Some of the suites have Jacuzzis and large-screen home cinemas. You're close to Gran Vía, but away from the tourist scrum.

Hostal La Zona HOSTAL **€**
(Map p80; ☑91 521 99 04; www.hostallazona. com; Calle de Valverde 7, 1st fl; s/d €50/60; ※☎; MGran Vía) Catering primarily to a gay clientele, the stylish Hostal La Zona has exposed brickwork, wooden pillars and a subtle colour scheme. We like a place where a sleep-in is encouraged – breakfast (included in

room price) is from 9am to noon, which is exactly the understanding Madrid's nightlife merits. Other highlights include free internet, helpful staff and air-conditioning/heating in every room.

Albergue Juvenil HOSTEL **€**
(Map p80; ☑91 593 96 88; www.ajmadrid.es; Calle de Mejía Lequerica 21; dm incl breakfast €19-25; ※@☎; MBilbao or Alonso Martínez) If you're looking for dormitory-style accommodation, you'd need a good reason to stay anywhere other than here while you're in Madrid. Opened in 2007, the slick Albergue's rooms are spotless, no dorm houses more than six beds (and each dorm has its own bathroom), and the supermodern facilities include a pool table, a gymnasium, wheelchair access, free internet, laundry and a TV/DVD room with a choice of movies.

Flat 5 Madrid HOSTAL **€**
(Map p80; ☑91 127 24 00; www.flat5madrid. com; Calle de San Bernardo 55, 5th fl; d without bathroom €40-60, with bathroom €60-100; ※☎; MNoviciado) Unlike so many other *hostales* in Madrid where the charm depends on a timeworn air, Flat 5 Madrid has a fresh, clean-lined look with bright colours, flatscreen TVs, free wi-fi, air-con and heating and flower boxes on the window sills. Even the rooms that face onto a patio have partial views over the rooftops. If the rooms and bathrooms were a little bigger, we'd consider moving in.

BEYOND THE CENTRE

Hotel Puerta América DESIGNER HOTEL **€€**
(☑91 744 54 00; www.hotelpuertamerica.com; Avenida de América 41; d/ste from €117/235; P※☎; MCartagena) When the owners of this hotel looked at its location halfway between the city and the airport, they knew they had to do something special. Their idea? Take some of world architecture's most innovative names and give them a floor each to design. The result? An extravagant pastiche of styles, from curvy minimalism and zany montages of 1980s chic to bright-red bathrooms that feel like a movie star's dressing room. Even the bar ('a temple to the liturgy of pleasure'), restaurant, facade, gardens, public lighting and parking garage each had their own architect (including Jean Nouvel, Ron Arad, David Chipperfield, Sir Norman Foster and Zaha Hadid).

✕ Eating

After holding fast to its rather unexciting local cuisine for centuries (aided, it must be said, by loyal locals who never saw the need for anything else), Madrid has finally become a worthy culinary capital.

BEST FOR...

Cocido a la Madrileña (meat & chickpea stew)

Taberna La Bola

Lhardy (p96)

Roast lamb or suckling pig

Restaurante Sobrino de Botín

Posada de la Villa

Tortilla de patatas (potato & onion omelette)

Juanalaloca (boxed text, p95)

Bodega de La Ardosa (boxed text, p95)

Estado Puro (p96)

Las Tortillas de Gabino (p98)

Croquetas

Casa Julio (p95)

Casa Labra (boxed text, p95)

Casa Alberto (p95)

Baco y Beto (boxed text, p95)

Las Tortillas de Gabino (p98)

Patatas bravas (roast potatoes in a spicy tomato sauce)

Las Bravas (boxed text, p95)

Le Cabrera (boxed text, p95)

Bodega de la Ardosa (boxed text, p95)

Huevos rotos (fried eggs with potato & jamón)

Almendro 13 (boxed text, p95)

Casa Lucio

Rice & Paella

Costa Blanca Arrocería (p98)

La Paella de la Reina (p97)

Chocolate con churros

Chocolatería de San Ginés (p99)

Chocolatería Valor (p99)

El Brillante (p96)

There's everything to be found here, not least the rich variety of regional Spanish specialities from across the country. And there's not a *barrio* where you can't find a great meal. Restaurants in Malasaña, Chueca and Huertas range from glorious old *tabernas* (taverns) to boutique eateries across all price ranges. For more classically classy surrounds, Salamanca and Northern Madrid are generally pricey but of the highest standard, and ideal for a special occasion or for spotting royalty and celebrities. In the central *barrios* of Los Austrias, Sol and Centro there's a little bit of everything. Splendid tapas bars abound everywhere, but La Latina is the undoubted queen.

LOS AUSTRIAS, SOL & CENTRO

TOP CHOICE Mercado de San Miguel

TAPAS, DELICATESSEN €€

(Map p60; www.mercadodesanmiguel.es; Plaza de San Miguel; meals €15-35; ☺10am-midnight Sun-Wed, 10am-2am Thu-Sat; Ⓜ Sol) One of Madrid's oldest and most beautiful markets, the Mercado de San Miguel has undergone a stunning major renovation and bills itself as a 'culinary cultural centre'. Within the early-20th-century glass walls, the market has become an inviting space strewn with tables (difficult to nab) where you can enjoy the freshest food or a drink. Apart from the fresh fish corner, you can order tapas at most of the counter-bars.

TOP CHOICE Restaurante Sobrino de Botín

ROAST MEATS €€

(Map p60; ☎91 366 42 17; www.botin.es; Calle de los Cuchilleros 17; meals €40-45; Ⓜ La Latina or Sol) It's not every day that you can eat in the oldest restaurant in the world (1725), which also appears in many novels about Madrid, most notably Hemingway's *The Sun Also Rises*. The secret of its staying power is fine *cochinillo* (suckling pig; €22.90) and *cordero asado* (roast lamb; €22.90) cooked in wood-fired ovens. Eating in the vaulted cellar is a treat.

La Terraza del Casino

NOUVELLE SPANISH €€€

(Map p60; ☎91 521 87 00; www.casinodemadrid. es; Calle de Alcalá 15; meals €100-140; ☺lunch & dinner Mon-Fri, dinner Sat; Ⓜ Sevilla) Perched atop the landmark Casino de Madrid building, this temple of haute cuisine is overseen, albeit from afar, by Fernan Adrìa (Spain's premier celebrity chef) and mostly in the hands of his acolyte Paco Roncero.

It's all about culinary experimentation and a menu that changes with each new idea that emerges from the laboratory and into the kitchen. You may not eat here often, but doing so just once will leave you in raptures.

Cervecería 100 Montaditos
BOCADILLOS €

(Map p60; www.cerveceria100montaditos.com; Calle Mayor 22; meals €5-10; MSol) This bar with outlets all across the city serves up no fewer than 100 different varieties of mini-*bocadillos* (filled rolls, without butter) that span the full range of Spanish staples, such as chorizo, *jamón*, tortilla, a variety of cheeses and seafood. Each one costs a princely €1 to €2 and four will satisfy most stomachs. You fill out your order, take it up to the counter and your name is called in no time.

La Gloria de Montera
TRADITIONAL, FUSION €€

(Map p60; Calle del Caballero de Gracia 10; meals €25-30; MGran Vía) La Gloria de Montera combines classy decor with eminently reasonable prices. The food's not especially creative, but the tastes are fresh, the surroundings are sophisticated and you'll get a good initiation into Spanish cooking without paying over the odds. It doesn't take reservations, so turn up early or be prepared to wait.

Taberna La Bola
TRADITIONAL SPANISH €€

(Map p60; 91 547 69 30; www.labola.es; Calle de la Bola 5; meals €30-35; lunch & dinner Mon-Sat, lunch Sun, closed Aug; MSanto Domingo) In any poll of food-loving locals seeking the best and most traditional Madrid cuisine, Taberna La Bola (going strong since 1870 and run by the sixth generation of the Verdasco family) always features near the top. We're inclined to agree and if you're going to try *cocido a la madrileña* (€19) while in Madrid, this is a good place to do so. It's busy and noisy and very Madrid. It serves other Madrid specialities, such as *callos* (tripe) and *sopa castellana* (garlic soup).

LA LATINA & LAVAPIÉS

TOP CHOICE   Naïa Restaurante
FUSION €€

(Map p64; 91 366 27 83; www.naiarestaurante.com, in Spanish; Plaza de la Paja 3; meals €30-35; lunch & dinner Tue-Sun; MLa Latina) On the lovely Plaza de la Paja, Naïa has real buzz about it, with a cooking laboratory overseen by Carlos López Reyes, delightful modern Spanish food and a chill-out lounge downstairs. The emphasis throughout is on natural ingredients, healthy cooking and exciting tastes.

Viva La Vida
VEGETARIAN €

(Map p64; www.vivalavida.vg; Costanilla de San Andrés 16; buffet per 100g €2.10; noon-midnight; ; MLa Latina) This organic food shop has as its centrepiece an enticing vegetarian buffet with hot and cold food that's always filled with flavour. On the cusp of Plaza de la Paja, and with a laid-back vibe, it's a great place at any time of the day, especially outside normal Spanish eating hours when your stomach's rumbling.

El Estragón
VEGETARIAN €€

(Map p64; 91 365 89 82; Plaza de la Paja 10; meals €20-25; ; MLa Latina) A delightful spot for crêpes and other vegetarian specialities, El Estragón is undoubtedly one of Madrid's best vegetarian restaurants, although attentive vegans won't appreciate the use of butter. Apart from that, we're yet to hear a bad word about it, and the *menu del día* (daily set menu; from €8) is one of Madrid's best bargains.

Casa Lucio
TRADITIONAL SPANISH €€

(Map p64; 91 365 32 52; www.casalucio.es, in Spanish; Calle de la Cava Baja 35; meals €45-50; lunch & dinner Sun-Fri, dinner Sat, closed Aug; MLa Latina) Lucio has been wowing *madrileños* with his light touch, quality ingredients and home-style local cooking for ages – think seafood, roasted meats and eggs (a Lucio speciality) in abundance. Casa Lucio draws an august, always well-dressed crowd that has included the king of Spain, former US president Bill Clinton and Penélope Cruz.

Posada de la Villa
TRADITIONAL SPANISH €€€

(Map p64; 91 366 18 60; Calle de la Cava Baja 9; meals €50-55; lunch & dinner Mon-Sat, lunch Sun, closed Aug; MLa Latina) This wonderfully restored 17th-century *posada* (inn) is something of a local landmark. The atmosphere is formal, the decoration sombre and traditional (heavy timber and brickwork), and the cuisine decidedly local – roast meats, *cocido* (meat and chickpea stew), *callos* and *sopa de ajo*.

Nunc est Bibendum
SPANISH, INTERNATIONAL €€

(Map p64; 91 366 52 10; Calle de la Cava Alta 13; meals €30-35; lunch & dinner Mon-Sat, lunch Sun; MLa Latina) Nunc est Bibendum combines a classy, clean-lined look with a varied menu that defies categorisation –

A TAPAS TOUR OF MADRID

La Latina

Madrid's home of tapas is La Latina, especially along Calle de la Cava Baja and the surrounding streets. Almendro 13 (Map p64; Calle del Almendro 13; meals €15-20; MLa Latina) is famous for quality rather than frilly elaborations, with cured meats, cheeses, tortillas and *huevos rotos* (literally, 'broken eggs') the house specialties. Down on Calle de la Cava Baja, Txacolina (Map p64; Calle de la Cava Baja 26; meals €15-20; ⊙lunch & dinner Sat, dinner Mon & Wed-Fri; MLa Latina) does Basque 'high cuisine in miniature', although these are some of the biggest *pintxos* (Basque tapas) you'll find; wash it all down with a *txacoli,* a sharp Basque white. On the same street, Casa Lucas (Map p64; Calle de la Cava Baja 30; meals €20-30; ⊙lunch & dinner Thu-Tue, dinner Wed; MLa Latina) and La Chata (Map p64; Calle de la Cava Baja 24; meals €25-30; ⊙lunch & dinner Thu-Mon, dinner Wed; MLa Latina) are also hugely popular. Not far away, Juanalaloca (Map p64; Plaza de la Puerta de Moros 4; meals €25-35; ⊙lunch & dinner Tue-Sun, dinner Mon; MLa Latina) does a magnificent *tortilla de patatas* (potato and onion omelette), and Taberna Matritum (Map p64; Calle de la Cava Alta 17; meals €25-30; ⊙lunch & dinner Thu-Sun, dinner Mon-Wed; MLa Latina) serves great tapas and desserts by the master chocolatier Oriol Balaguer.

Los Austrias, Sol & Centro

La Latina's tapas experience spills over into neighbouring Los Austrias, Sol and Centro, with Amaya (Map p60; Plaza de la Provincia 3; meals €25-30; ⊙noon-5pm & 8pm-late Tue-Sat, noon-5pm Sun; MSol) combining traditional Spanish flavours with some surprising twists. For *bacalao* (cod), Casa Labra (Map p60; Calle de Tetuán 11; meals €15-20; ⊙11am-3.30pm & 6-11pm; MSol) has been around since 1860 and was a favourite of the poet Federico García Lorca. However, many *madrileños* (residents of Madrid) wouldn't eat *bacalao* anywhere except Casa Revuelta (Map p60; Calle de Latoneros 3; meals €15-20; ⊙10.30am-4pm & 7-11pm Mon & Wed-Sat, 10.30am-4pm Sun, closed Aug; MLa Latina or Sol), clinched by the fact that the owner painstakingly extracts every fish bone in the morning.

Huertas

In Huertas, La Casa del Abuelo (Map p66; Calle de la Victoria 12; meals €15-25; ⊙8.30am-midnight; MSol) is famous for *gambas a la plancha* (grilled prawns) or *gambas al ajillo* (prawns sizzling in garlic on little ceramic plates) and a *chato* (small glass) of the heavy, sweet El Abuelo red wine; they cook over 200kg of prawns here on a good day. For *patatas bravas* (fried potatoes lathered in a spicy tomato sauce), Las Bravas (Map p66; Callejón de Álvarez Gato 3; meals €15; MSol) is the place, while La Trucha (Map p66; Calle de Núñez de Arce 6; meals €20-25; ⊙lunch & dinner Tue-Sat; MSol) has a counter overloaded

sometimes it's a Basque base, other flavours come from the south or from France – but is always good. The wine list is thoughtfully chosen, with some lesser-known Spanish wines.

Ene Restaurante TAPAS, FUSION €€
(Map p64; ☑91 366 25 91; www.enerestaurante.com; Calle del Nuncio 19; meals €35-40; MLa Latina) Just across from Iglesia de San Pedro El Viejo, one of Madrid's oldest churches, Ene is anything but old-world. The design is cutting-edge and awash with reds and purples, while the young waiters circulate to the tune of lounge music. The food is Spanish-Asian

fusion and there are also plenty of *pintxos* (Basque tapas) to choose from. The chill-out beds downstairs are great for an after-dinner cocktail or even a meal, although they're always reserved well in advance.

HUERTAS & ATOCHA

TOP CHOICE Vinos Gonzalez

TAPAS, DELICATESSEN €€
(Map p66; Calle de León 12; meals €20-25; ⊙9am-midnight Tue-Thu, 9am-1am Fri & Sat; MAntón Martín) Ever dreamed of a deli where you could choose a tasty morsel and sit down and eat it right there? Well, here you can.

with enticing Andalucian tapas and 95 items on the menu. Another good choice down the bottom of the Huertas hill is Los Gatos (Map p66; Calle de Jesús 2; meals €25-30; ⊘noon-1am; MAntón Martín) with eclectic decor and terrific canapés.

Paseo del Prado & Salamanca

Along the Paseo del Prado, there's only one choice for tapas and it's one of Madrid's best: Estado Puro (p96). In Salamanca, Biotza (Map p78; Calle de Claudio Coello 27; ⊘9am-midnight Mon-Sat; MSerrano) offers creative Basque *pintxos* in stylish surrounds, while La Colonial de Goya (Map p78; Calle de Jorge Juan 34; meals €30-35; ⊘1pm-midnight Mon-Sat; MVelázquez) serves up a staggering choice of *pintxos*, including 63 varieties of canapés. Also excellent are Restaurante Estay (Map p78; Calle de Hermosilla 46; meals €20-30; ⊘8am-12.30am Mon-Sat; MVelázquez) and El Lateral (Map p78; www.cadenalateral.es; Calle de Velázquez 57; meals €20-30; ⊘1pm-midnight; MVelázquez or Nuñez de Balboa).

Chueca

Chueca is another stellar tapas *barrio* (district). Don't miss Bocaito (Map p80; Calle de la Libertad 4-6; meals €20-25; ⊘lunch & dinner Mon-Fri, dinner Sat; MChueca), another purveyor of Andalucian *jamón* (ham) and seafood and a favourite haunt of film-maker Pedro Almodóvar. Bodega de La Ardosa (Map p80; Calle de Colón 13; meals €15-25; ⊘8.30am-1am; MTribunal) is extremely popular for its *salmorejo, croquetas, patatas bravas* and *tortilla de patatas*, while Casa Julio (Map p80; Calle de la Madera 37; meals €10-15; ⊘lunch & dinner Mon-Sat; MTribunal) is widely touted as the home of Madrid's best *croquetas*. Other brilliant choices include Le Cabrera (Map p80; www.lecabrera.com, in Spanish; Calle de Bárbara de Braganza; meals €25-35; ⊘lunch & dinner Tue-Sat; MColón or Alonso Martínez), Baco y Beto (Map p80; www.bacoybeto.com, in Spanish; Calle de Pelayo 24; meals €20-25; ⊘lunch & dinner Fri & Sat, dinner Mon-Thu; MChueca) and Gastromaquia (Map p80; Calle de Pelayo 8; meals €15-20; ⊘lunch & dinner Tue-Thu & Sat, lunch Mon, dinner Fri; MChueca).

Chamberí

Sagaretxe (Calle de Eloy Gonzalo 26; meals €15-25; ⊘noon-5pm & 7pm-1am; MIglesia) is one of Madrid's better Basque *pintxo* bars of long standing, with tempting choices lined up along the bar; the *surtido de pintxos* (your own selection of 8/12 tapas) costs €14/20. Bodega de La Ardosa (Calle de Santa Engracia 70; meals €10-15; ⊘9am-3pm & 6-11.30pm Thu-Tue; MIglesia) is another *barrio* classic with an extravagantly tiled facade (the shrapnel pockmarks date back to the Spanish Civil War), vermouth on tap and some of the best traditional Spanish *patatas bravas* in town.

On offer are a tempting array of cheeses, cured meats and other typically Spanish delicacies, and there's an all-you-can-eat buffet (€10) from 1pm to 4pm Tuesday to Friday.

TOP CHOICE Casa Alberto

TRADITIONAL SPANISH €€

(Map p66; ☎91 429 93 56; www.casaalberto.es, in Spanish; Calle de las Huertas 18; meals €25-30; ⊘noon-1.30am Tue-Sat, noon-4pm Sun; MAntón Martín) One of the most atmospheric old *tabernas* of Madrid, Casa Alberto has been around since 1827 and occupies a building where Cervantes is said to have written one of his books. The secret to its staying power is vermouth on tap, excellent tapas and fine sit-down meals; *rabo de toro* (bull's tail) is a good order. As the antique wood-pannelled decoration will suggest straight away, the *raciones* (large tapas servings) have none of the frilly innovations that have come to characterise Spanish tapas, and *jamón*, Manchego cheese and *croquetas* are recurring themes.

Maceiras

GALICIAN €€

(Map p66; ☎91 429 15 84; Calle de las Huertas 66; meals €20-30; MAntón Martín) Galician tapas (think octopus, green peppers etc) never tasted so good as in this agreeably rustic bar down the bottom of the Huertas hill, especially when washed down with a crisp white Ribeiro. The simple wooden tables, loyal customers and handy location make for a fine atmosphere. There's another branch around the corner at Calle de Jesús 7, which keeps the same hours.

Sidrería Vasca Zeraín
BASQUE €€

(Map p66; ☎91 429 79 09; Calle Quevedo 3; meals €35-40; ☺lunch & dinner Mon-Sat, closed Aug; ⓜAntón Martín) Right in the heart of the Barrio de las Letras, this sophisticated Basque restaurant is one of the best places in the area to sample the region's cuisine. The staples include cider, *bacalao* (cod) and wonderful steaks, while there are also a few splashes of creativity thrown in (the secret is in the sauce). We highly recommend the Menú Sidrería (cider-house menu; €36.50).

Lhardy
TRADITIONAL MADRILEÑO €€€

(Map p66; ☎91 521 33 85; www.lhardy.com; Carrera de San Jerónimo 8; meals €60-70; ☺lunch & dinner Mon-Sat, lunch Sun, closed Aug; ⓜSol or Sevilla) This Madrid landmark (since 1839) is an elegant treasure-trove of takeaway gourmet tapas. Upstairs is the upscale preserve of house specialities such as *callos*, *cocido*, pheasant in grape juice and lemon soufflé. It's expensive, but the quality and service are unimpeachable and the great-and-good of Madrid have all eaten here at some stage.

El Brillante
BOCADILLOS, CHURROS €

(Map p68; Calle del Doctor Drumén 7; bocadillos €4.50-6.50, raciones €6-10; ☺6.30am-12.30am; ⓜAtocha) Just by the Centro de Arte Reina Sofía, this breezy and no-frills bar-eatery is a Madrid institution for *bocadillos* (the *bocadillo de calamares* is an old favourite) and other snacks. It's also famous for *chocolate con churros* or *porras* (deep-fried doughnut strips).

La Finca de Susana
SPANISH, MEDITERRANEAN €€

(Map p66; www.lafinca-restaurant.com; Calle de Arlabán 4; meals €20-25; ⓜSevilla) It's difficult to find a better combination of price, quality cooking and classy atmosphere anywhere in Huertas. The softly lit dining area is bathed in greenery and the sometimes innovative, sometimes traditional food draws a hip young crowd. It doesn't take reservations.

PASEO DEL PRADO & EL RETIRO

Estado Puro
TAPAS €€

(Map p66; ☎91 330 24 00; www.tapasenestadopuro.com, in Spanish; Plaza de Cánovas del Castillo 4; tapas €1.95-9.50; ☺11am-1am Tue-Sat, 11am-4pm Sun; ⓜBanco de España or Atocha) Most places to eat along or around the Paseo del Prado are either tourist traps or upmarket temples to fine dining, but this place bucks the trend. A slick but casual tapas bar, Estado Puro serves up fantastic tapas, many of which have their origins in Catalonia's world-famous El Bulli restaurant, such as the *tortilla española siglo XXI* (21st-century Spanish omelette, served in a glass). The kitchen here is overseen by Paco Roncero, the head chef at La Terraza del Casino and who learned his trade with master-chef Ferran Adrìa. Most of the tapas involve spectacular variations on traditional Spanish themes. There's a funky indoor area and outdoor tables (often reserved and with higher prices).

SALAMANCA

TOP CHOICE Sula Madrid
SPANISH FUSION €€€

(Map p78; ☎91 781 61 97; www.sula.es; Calle de Jorge Juan 33; meals €60-70; ☺lunch & dinner Mon-Sat; ⓜVelázquez) A gastronomic temple that combines stellar cooking with clean-lined sophistication, Sula Madrid – a gourmet food store, super-stylish tapas bar and top-notch restaurant all rolled into one – is one of our favourite top-end restaurants in Madrid. It's the sort of place where Madrid celebrities are on first-name terms with the waiters, and the name-dropping continues in the kitchen where wunderkind Quique Dacosta (voted Spain's best chef in 2005) prepares a range of Mediterranean dishes – some traditional, some with the most creative of twists – that you won't find anywhere else. Design touches added by Amaya Arzuaga help to make this one of Madrid's coolest, black-clad spaces.

La Galette
VEGETARIAN, EUROPEAN €€

(Map p78; ☎91 576 06 41; Calle del Conde de Aranda 11; meals €30-35; ☺lunch & dinner Mon-Sat, lunch Sun; ☑; ⓜRetiro) This lovely little restaurant combines an intimate dining area with checked tablecloths and cooking that the owner describes as 'baroque vegetarian'. The food is a revelation, blending creativity with a strong base of traditional home cooking. The *croquetas de manzana* (apple croquettes) are a house speciality, but everything on the extensive menu is good. The only problem is that the tables are too close together.

MALASAÑA & CHUECA

TOP CHOICE La Musa   SPANISH FUSION €€

(Map p80; ✆91 448 75 58; www.lamusa. com.es; Calle de Manuela Malasaña 18; meals €25-30; ⊙9am-1.30am; Ⓜ San Bernardo) Snug yet loud, a favourite of Madrid's hip young crowd yet utterly unpretentious, La Musa is all about designer decor, lounge music on the sound system and food (breakfast, lunch or dinner) that is always fun and filled with flavour. The menu is divided into three types of tapas – hot, cold and BBQ; among the hot varieties is the fantastic *jabalí con ali-oli de miel y sobrasada* (wild boar with mayonnaise of honey and sobrasada). It doesn't take reservations, so sidle up to the bar, add your name to the waiting list and soak up the ambient buzz of Malasaña at its best.

Bazaar   NOUVELLE SPANISH €€

(Map p80; www.restaurantbazaar.com; Calle de la Libertad 21; meals €20-25; Ⓜ Chueca) Bazaar's popularity among the well-heeled and often-famous shows no sign of abating. Its pristine white interior design with theatre lighting may draw a crowd that looks like it stepped out of the pages of *¡Hola!* magazine, but the food is extremely well priced and innovative. It doesn't take reservations, so get here early or be prepared to wait, regardless of whether you're famous or not.

Nina   MEDITERRANEAN FUSION €€

(Map p80; ✆91 591 00 46; Calle de Manuela Malasaña 10; meals €30-40; Ⓜ Bilbao) Sophisticated, intimate and wildly popular, Nina has an extensive menu (available in English) of nouvelle Mediterranean cuisine that doesn't miss a trick. We like the decor, all exposed brick and subtle lighting, we love just about everything on the menu, but we adore the honey-and-sobrasada-glazed grilled ostrich steak with a salmon and raspberry crust. What we're not so keen on is the policy of two sittings (at 9.15pm and 11.30pm), which inevitably means that staff can start to hover when your time's nearly up. The weekend brunch (€21.90, noon to 5.30pm Saturday and Sunday) is excellent.

La Tasquita de Enfrente

TRADITIONAL, FUSION €€€

(Map p80; ✆91 532 54 49; www.latasquitade enfrente.com, in Spanish; Calle de la Ballesta 6; meals €70; Ⓜ Gran Vía) To succeed on the international stage, Spain's celebrity chefs have to take experimentation to new levels, but to succeed at home they usually have

to maintain a greater fidelity to traditional bases before heading off in new directions. And therein lies the success – it's difficult to overstate how popular this place is among people-in-the-know in Madrid's food scene – of chef Juanjo López. His seasonal menu never ceases to surprise (he was preparing cream of pea soup with caviar and hamburgers with foie gras and truffles when we were there) but also combines simple Spanish staples such as squid with broad beans to stunning effect. His *menu degustación* (€48) and *menú de Juanjo* (€65) would be our choice if this is your first time. Reservations are essential.

A Dos Velas   SPANISH, INTERNATIONAL €€

(Map p80; ✆91 446 18 63; www.adosvelas.net, in Spanish; Calle de San Vicente Ferrer 16; meals €20-30; ⊙lunch & dinner Mon-Sat; Ⓜ Tribunal) The food here is always creative, with Mediterranean cooking fused with occasional Indian or even Argentinian flavours. There's a lovely dining area with soft lighting and exposed brick, and service is attentive without being intrusive.

La Isla del Tesoro   VEGETARIAN €€

(Map p80; ✆91 593 14 40; www.isladeltesoro.net; Calle de Manuela Malasaña 3; meals €30-40; ✐; Ⓜ Bilbao) La Isla del Tesoro is loaded with quirky charm – the dining area is like someone's fantasy of a secret garden come to life. The cooking here is assured and wide-ranging in its influences; the jungle burger is typical in a menu that's full of surprises. The weekday, lunchtime *menú del día* (€10) is more varied than most in Madrid. Our only complaint? The otherwise friendly waiters are often too keen to free up your table for the next punters on weekends.

El Original   TRADITIONAL SPANISH €€

(Map p80; ✆91 522 90 69; www.eloriginal.es, in Spanish; Calle de las Infantas 44; meals €25-30; ⊙lunch & dinner Mon-Sat; Ⓜ Chueca or Banco de España) With the best products and signature dishes from each of the regions of Spain, you might expect El Original to be a bastion of traditionalism. Indeed, it describes its food as classic Spanish cooking. But the classic theme ends when you step into the restaurant and find trees growing in the sleek dining room.

La Paella de la Reina   RICE DISHES €€

(Map p80; ✆91 531 18 85; www.lapaelladela reina.com, in Spanish; Calle de la Reina 39; meals €25-30; Ⓜ Banco de España) Madrid is not renowned for its paella (Valencia is king in that regard), but *valencianos* who can't make it home are known to frequent La Paella de la Reina. Like any decent paella restaurant, you need two people to make an order but, that requirement satisfied, you've plenty of choice. The typical Valencia paella is cooked with beans, chicken and rabbit, but there are also plenty of seafood varieties on offer, including *arroz negro* (black rice whose colour derives from squid ink).

Fresc Co   BUFFET €
(Map p80; www.frescco.com; Calle de Sagasta 30; meals from €8.95; ⊙noon-5pm & 8-11.30pm; ⓂAlonso Martínez) If you just can't face deciphering another Spanish menu or are in dire need of a do-it-yourself salad, Fresc Co is a fresh, well-priced, all-you-can eat antidote. An extensive buffet of salads, soups, pasta and pizza is on offer, and the price includes a drink. Queues often form out the door at lunchtime.

CHAMBERÍ & ARGÜELLES

TOP CHOICE **Sergi Arola Gastro**
NOUVELLE SPANISH €€€
(Map p78; ☑91 310 21 69; www.sergiarola.es; Calle de Zurbano 31; meals €95-235; ⊙lunch & dinner Mon-Fri, dinner Sat; ⓂAlonso Martínez) Sergi Arola, a young Catalan acolyte of the world-renowned chef Ferran Adrià, has opened his very own personalised temple to all that's

---

SELF-CATERING

Some of the better food markets in town:

Mercado de la Cebada (Map p64; Plaza de la Cebada; ⊙9am-2pm & 5.30-8.30pm Mon-Fri, 9am-2.30pm Sat; ⓂLa Latina) Slated for long-overdue major renovations.

Mercado de la Paz (Map p78; off Calle de Ayala; ⊙9am-8pm Mon-Sat; ⓂSerrano)

Other specialist food stores include **Mantequería Bravo** (p113) and **Alma de Ibérico** (Map p64; www.julian-becerro.com, in Spanish; Calle de la Cava Baja 41; ⊙10am-10pm; ⓂLa Latina). For Spanish and other European cheeses, **Poncelet** (Map p80; ☑91 308 02 21; www.poncelet.es; Calle de Argensola 27; ⊙10.30am-8.30pm Mon-Sat; ⓂAlonso Martínez) should be your first stop.

---

innovative in Spanish gastronomy. You pay for the privilege of eating here – the showpiece Menú Gastro costs €160 without wine and taxes, although the 'Basico' menu covers seven signature dishes for €105. But this is culinary indulgence at its finest, the sort of place where creativity, presentation and taste are everything. And oh, what tastes...

Las Tortillas de Gabino
TRADITIONAL SPANISH €€
(Map p78; ☑91 319 75 05; www.lastortillasde gabino.com, in Spanish; Calle de Rafael Calvo 20; meals €35-40; ⊙lunch & dinner Mon-Fri, dinner Sat; ⓂIglesia) It's a brave Spanish chef who fiddles with the iconic *tortilla de patatas,* but the results here are delicious – tortilla with cockles, with octopus, with all manner of surprising combinations. This place also gets rave reviews for its *croquetas*. The service is excellent and the bright yet classy dining area adds to the sense of a most agreeable eating experience. Reservations are highly recommended.

Costa Blanca Arrocería   RICE DISHES €€
(☑91 448 58 32; Calle de Bravo Murillo 3; meals €20-30; ⓂQuevedo) Even if you've no plans to be in Chamberí, it's worth a trip across town to this casual bar-restaurant, which serves outstanding rice dishes, including paella. The quality is high and prices (around €11 per person) are among the cheapest in town. Start with *almejas a la marinera* (baby clams) and follow it up with a *paella de marisco* (seafood paella) for the full experience. As always in such places, you'll need two to make up an order.

NORTHERN MADRID

TOP CHOICE **Santceloni**   CATALAN €€€
(☑91 210 88 40; www.restaurantesant celoni.com; Paseo de la Castellana 57; meals from €125, set menús €132-165; ⊙lunch & dinner Mon-Fri, dinner Sat; ⓂGregorio Marañón) The Michelin-starred Santceloni is one of Madrid's best restaurants, with luxury decor that's the work of star interior designer Pascual Ortega, and nouvelle cuisine from the kitchen of master Catalan chef Santi Santamaría. Primary responsibility for the kitchen has passed to one of his acolytes, Óscar Velasco, but the quality hasn't dipped at all and Santamaría flourishes still make regular appearances. Each dish is an exquisite work of art and the menu changes with the seasons, but we'd recommend one of the set *menús gastronómicos* to really sample the breadth of surprising tastes on offer.

Zalacaín
BASQUE, NAVARRAN €€€

(☑91 561 48 40; www.restaurantezalacain.com; Calle de Álvarez de Baena 4; meals €90-100; ⏰lunch & dinner Mon-Fri, dinner Sat, closed Aug; MGregorio Marañón) Where most other fine-dining experiences centre on innovation, Zalacaín is a bastion of tradition with a refined air and a loyal following among Spain's great and good. Everyone who's anyone in Madrid, from the king down, has eaten here since the doors opened in 1973; it was the first restaurant in Spain to receive three Michelin stars. The pig's trotters filled with mushrooms and lamb is a house speciality, as is the lobster salad. The wine list is purported to be one of the best in the city (it stocks an estimated 35,000 bottles with 800 different varieties). You should certainly dress to impress (men will need a tie and a jacket).

🍷 Drinking

To get an idea of how much *madrileños* like to go out and have a good time, consider one simple statistic: Madrid has more bars than any city in the world – six, in fact, for every 100 inhabitants.

LOS AUSTRIAS, SOL & CENTRO

Old taverns and the odd hidden gem rub shoulders in Madrid's centre. As a general rule, the further you stray from Plaza Mayor, the more prices drop and the fewer tourists you'll see.

☐TOP CHOICE Chocolatería de San Ginés
CHURROS CAFE

(Map p60; Pasadizo de San Ginés 5; ⏰9.30am-7am; MSol) Perhaps the best known of Madrid's *chocolate con churros* vendors, this Madrid institution is at its most popular from 3am to 6am as clubbers make a last stop for sustenance on their way home. Only in Madrid.

Café del Real
BAR-CAFE

(Map p60; Plaza de Isabel II 2; ⏰9am-1am Mon-Thu, 9am-3am Fri & Sat; MÓpera) One of the nicest bar-cafes in central Madrid, this place serves a rich variety of creative coffees and a few cocktails to a soundtrack of chill-out music. The best seats are upstairs, where the low ceilings, wooden beams and leather chairs make a great place to pass an afternoon.

Chocolatería Valor
CHURROS CAFE

(Map p60; Postigo de San Martín; ⏰9am-10.30pm Sun, 8am-10.30pm Mon-Thu, 8am-1am Fri, 9am-1am Sat; MCallao) It may be Madrid tradition to indulge in *chocolate con churros* around sunrise on your way home from a nightclub, but for everyone else who prefers a more reasonable hour, this is possibly the best *chocolatería* in town. That's because it serves traditional *churros* but they're only the side event to the astonishing array of chocolates in which to dip them.

El 44 Bar
BAR

(Map p60; Cuesta de Santo Domingo 8; ⏰8pm-2.30am Tue-Sat; MÓpera or Santo Domingo) An intimate bar experience tucked away on a quiet street that leads down towards the opera house, El 44 Bar ranks among our favourite little bars in the centre. The cocktails are well priced (€5 to €7) and original (including *caipipretas,* a Lisbon staple that riffs on the caipirinha with black rum). The music includes '70s and '80s and detours into lounge (Gotan Project seems a particular favourite), Brazilian jazz and deep house, picking up speed as the night wears on.

LA LATINA & LAVAPIÉS

Most nights (and Sunday afternoons), crowds of happy *madrileños* hop from bar to bar across La Latina. This is a *barrio* beloved by discerning 20- and 30-something urban sophisticates who ensure there's little room to move in the good places and the bad ones don't survive long. The crowd is a little more diverse on Sundays as hordes fan out from El Rastro. Most of the action takes place along Calle de la Cava Baja (where the dividing line between drinking and tapas bars is decidedly blurred), the western end of Calle del Almendro and Plaza de la Paja. Working-class, multicultural Lavapiés is a completely different kettle of fish – quirky bars brimful of personality that draw an alternative, often bohemian crowd. Not everyone loves Lavapiés, but we do.

☐TOP CHOICE Delic
BAR-CAFE

(Map p64; Costanilla de San Andrés 14; ⏰11am-2am Fri-Sun & Tue-Thu, 7pm-2am Mon; MLa Latina) We could go on for hours about this long-standing cafe-bar, but we'll reduce it to its most basic elements: nursing an exceptionally good mojito (€8) or three on a warm summer's evening at Delic's outdoor tables on one of Madrid's prettiest plazas is one of life's great pleasures. Bliss. Due to local licensing restrictions, the outdoor tables close two hours before closing time, whereafter the intimate interior is almost as good.

TOP CHOICE Gaudeamus Café CAFE
(www.gaudeamuscafe.com, in Spanish; Calle de Tribulete 14, 4th fl; ⊙3pm-midnight Mon-Fri, 6pm-midnight Sat; ⓜLavapiés) Decoration that's light and airy, with pop-art posters of Audrey Hepburn and James Bond. A large terrace with views over the Lavapiés rooftops. A stunning backdrop of a ruined church atop which the cafe sits. With so much else going for it, it almost seems incidental that this cafe serves great teas, coffees and snacks.

La Escalera de Jacob COCKTAIL BAR
(Calle de Lavapiés 11; ⊙6pm-2am; ⓜAntón Martín or Tirso de Molina) With magicians, storytellers, children's theatre (on Saturdays and Sundays at noon) and live jazz and other musical genres, 'Jacob's Ladder' is one of Madrid's most original bars. And regardless of what's on, it's worth stopping by here for creative cocktails that you won't find anywhere else – the *fray aguacate* (Frangelico, vodka, honey, avocado and vanilla) should give you an idea of how far they go.

Bonanno WINE BAR
(Map p64; Plaza del Humilladero 4; ⊙noon-2am; ⓜLa Latina) If much of Madrid's nightlife starts too late for your liking, Bonanno could be for you. It made its name as a cocktail bar, but many people come here for the great wines and it's usually full with young professional *madrileños* from early evening onwards. Be prepared to snuggle up close to those around you if you want a spot at the bar.

Café del Nuncio BAR-CAFE
(Map p64; Calle de Segovia 9; ⊙noon-2am Sun-Thu, noon-3am Fri & Sat; ⓜLa Latina) Café del Nuncio straggles down a stairway passage to Calle de Segovia. You can drink on one of several cosy levels inside or, better still in summer, enjoy the outdoor seating that one local reviewer likened to a slice of Rome. By day it's an old-world cafe, but by night it's one of the best bars in the *barrio*.

La Inquilina BAR
(Calle del Ave María 39; ⊙7pm-1.30am Tue-Thu, 7pm-2.30am Fri & Sat, 1pm-1am Sun; ⓜLavapiés) This could just be our favourite bar in Lavapiés. It's partly about the cool-and-casual vibe and partly its community spirit with deep roots in the Lavapiés soil. Contemporary artworks by budding local artists adorn the walls and you can either gather around the bar or take a table out the back.

It's a small slice of sophistication in a *barrio* not known for such characteristics.

Taberna Tempranillo WINE BAR
(Map p64; Calle de la Cava Baja 38; ⊙1-3.30pm & 8pm-midnight Tue-Sun, 8pm-midnight Mon; ⓜLa Latina) You could come here for the tapas, but we are recommending Taberna Tempranillo primarily for its wines, of which there is a selection that puts most other Spanish bars to shame. It's not a late-night place, but it's always packed with an early-evening crowd and on Sundays after El Rastro.

HUERTAS & ATOCHA

Huertas comes into its own after dark and stays that way until close to sunrise. Bars are everywhere, from Sol down to the Paseo del Prado hinterland, but it's in Plaza de Santa Ana and along Calle de las Huertas that most of the action is concentrated.

TOP CHOICE Penthouse ROOFTOP BAR
(Map p66; Plaza de Santa Ana 14, 7th fl; ⊙9pm-1.30am Mon-Thu, 9pm-2.30am Fri & Sat, 5pm-1.30am Sun; ⓜAntón Martín or Sol) High above the Plaza de Santa Ana, this sybaritic rooftop (7th floor) cocktail bar has terrific views over Madrid's rooftops. It's a place for sophisticates with chill-out areas strewn with cushions, funky DJs and a dress policy designed to sort out the classy from the wannabes, although they're less strict when things are quiet. If you suffer from vertigo, consider the equally classy Midnight Rose on the ground floor.

TOP CHOICE La Venencia SHERRY BAR
(Map p66; Calle de Echegaray 7; ⊙1-3.30pm & 7.30pm-1.30am; ⓜSol) This is how sherry bars should be – old-world, drinks poured straight from the dusty wooden barrels and none of the frenetic activity for which Huertas is famous. La Venencia is a *barrio* classic, with fine sherry from Sanlúcar and *manzanilla* from Jeréz. There's no music, no flashy decorations; it's all about you, your *fino* (sherry) and your friends.

El Imperfecto BAR
(Map p66; Plaza de Matute 2; ⊙3pm-2am Sun-Thu, 3pm-3am Fri & Sat; ⓜAntón Martín) Its name notwithstanding, the 'Imperfect One' is our ideal Huertas bar, with live jazz most Tuesdays at 9pm and a drinks menu as long as a saxophone, ranging from cocktails (€6.50) and spirits to milkshakes, teas and creative coffees.

Taberna Alhambra
FLAMENCO BAR

(Map p66; www.tabernaalhambra.es, in Spanish; Calle de la Victoria 9; ☺11am-1.30am Sun-Thu, 11am-2.30am Fri & Sat; Ⓜ Sol) There can be a certain sameness about the bars between Sol and Huertas, which is why this fine old *taberna* stands out. The striking facade and exquisite tilework of the interior are quite beautiful; however, this place is anything but stuffy and the vibe is cool, casual and busy. It serves tapas and late at night there are some fine flamenco tunes.

Cervecería Alemana
BEER BAR

(Map p66; Plaza de Santa Ana 6; ☺11am-12.30am Sun-Thu, 11am-2am Fri & Sat, closed Aug; Ⓜ Antón Martín or Sol) If you've only got time to stop at one bar on Plaza de Santa Ana, let it be this classic *cervecería* (beer bar) renowned for its cold, frothy beers. It's fine inside, but snaffle a table outside in the square on a summer's evening and you won't be giving it up without a fight. This was one of Hemingway's haunts, and neither the wood-lined bar nor the bow-tied waiters have changed since his day.

Viva Madrid
BAR

(Map p66; www.barvivamadrid.com; Calle de Manuel Fernández y González 7; ☺1pm-2am; Ⓜ Antón Martín or Sol) The tiled facade of Viva Madrid is one of Madrid's most recognisable and it's an essential landmark on the Huertas nightlife scene. It's packed to the rafters on weekends and you come here in part for fine mojitos and also for the casual, friendly atmosphere.

Ølsen
VODKA BAR

(Map p66; www.olsenmadrid.com; Calle del Prado 15; ☺1-4pm & 8pm-2am Tue-Sun; Ⓜ Antón Martín) This classy and clean-lined bar is a temple to Nordic minimalism and comes into its own after the Scandinavian restaurant out the back closes. We think the more than 80 varieties of vodka are enough to satisfy most tastes. You'll hate vodka the next day, but Madrid is all about living for the night.

MALASAÑA & CHUECA

Drinking in Malasaña and Chueca is like a journey through Madrid's multifaceted past. Around the Glorieta de Bilbao and along the Paseo de los Recoletos you encounter stately old literary cafes that revel in their grandeur and late-19th-century ambience. Throughout Malasaña, *rockers* (rockers) nostalgic for the hedonistic Madrid of the 1970s and 1980s will find ample

---

> ## CHUECA COCKTAIL BARS
>
> Chueca has Madrid's richest concentration of sophisticated cocktail bars beloved by the city's A-list celebrities. In addition to **Museo Chicote** there's **Del Diego** (Map p80; Calle de la Reina 16; ☺8pm-3am; Ⓜ Gran Vía), where the decor blends old-world-cafe with New York style and there are 75 cocktails to choose from. Other places we highly recommend include old-world **Bar Cock** (Map p80; Calle de la Reina 16; ☺8pm-3am; Ⓜ Gran Vía), achingly chic **Le Cabrera** (Map p80; www.lecabrera.com, in Spanish; Calle de Bárbara de Braganza 2; ☺4pm-2.30am Mon-Sat; Ⓜ Colón or Alonso Martínez) and **Stromboli** (Map p80; Calle de Hortaleza 96; ☺6pm-3am Mon-Sat; Ⓜ Chueca or Tribunal).

bars to indulge their memories. At the same time, across both *barrios* but especially in gay Chueca and away to the west in Conde Duque, modern Madrid is very much on show, with chill-out spaces and swanky, sophisticated cocktail bars.

TOP CHOICE Museo Chicote
COCKTAIL BAR

(Map p80; www.museo-chicote.com; Gran Vía 12; ☺6pm-3am Mon-Thu, 6pm-3.30am Fri & Sat; Ⓜ Gran Vía) The founder of this Madrid landmark is said to have invented more than a hundred cocktails, which the likes of Hemingway, Ava Gardner, Grace Kelly, Sophia Loren and Frank Sinatra all enjoyed at one time or another. It's still frequented by film stars and top socialites, and it's at its best after midnight when a lounge atmosphere takes over, couples cuddle on the curved benches and some of the city's best DJs do their stuff. The 1930s-era interior only adds to the cachet of this place.

TOP CHOICE Café Comercial
LITERARY CAFE

(Map p80; Glorieta de Bilbao 7; ☺7.30am-midnight Mon-Thu, 7.30am-2am Fri, 8.30am-2am Sat, 9am-midnight Sun; Ⓜ Bilbao) This glorious old Madrid cafe proudly fights a rearguard action against progress with heavy leather seats, abundant marble and old-style waiters. As close as Madrid came to the intellectual cafes of Paris' Left Bank, Café Comercial now has a clientele that has broadened to include just about anyone.

Madrid – Killing the Night

An All-Night Itinerary

Nights in the capital are long and loud and what Hemingway wrote in the '30s remains true to this day: 'Nobody goes to bed in Madrid until they have killed the night.'

» Start late afternoon with a quiet drink at **Café Comercial** (p101), one of Madrid's grandest old cafes.

» Move on to something a little stronger, namely a mojito at **Café Belén** (p104), the epitome of Chueca cool.

» Head next for one of Europe's most famous bars, **Museo Chicote** (p101), with its creative cocktails, fine lounge music and celebrity crowd.

» Not far away, **Costello Café & Niteclub** (p109) is New York style wedded to an irresistible Madrid buzz.

» It's time for some live jazz at the art-deco **Café Central** (p109), one of Europe's most prestigious live-music venues.

» You've just enough time for an atmospheric tipple at the timeless **La Venencia** (p100) before it closes.

» Resist the urge to linger in the nearby Plaza de Santa Ana and climb up to look down upon it all from on high at the sophisticated **Penthouse** (p100).

» It's time for a dance and **Kapital** (p106) is one of the biggest and the best of Madrid's mega nightclubs.

» New on the scene but already a place of legend, **Adraba** (p106) will keep you going until dawn.

» And no Madrid night is complete without a *chocolate con churros* (deep-fried doughnut strips dipped in hot chocolate) close to sunrise at **Chocolatería de San Ginés** (p99).

Clockwise from top left
1. Mercado de San Miguel (p92) 2. Teatro Joy Esleva (p105) 3. Café Central (p109) 4. Malasaña street (p101)

Splash Óscar
ROOFTOP BAR

(Map p80; Plaza de Vázquez de Mella 12; ⏰4.30pm-12.30am; ⓜGran Vía) Another of the stunning rooftop terraces (although this one with a small swimming pool), atop Hotel Óscar, this chilled space with gorgeous skyline views has become the bar of choice among A-list celebrities.

Kabokla
BRAZILIAN BAR

(Map p80; www.kabokla.es, in Spanish; Calle de San Vicente Ferrer 55; ⏰10pm-1am Tue-Thu, 6pm-3am Fri, 2.30-6.30pm & 10.30pm-3.30am Sat, 2.30pm-10pm Sun; ⓜNoviciado) Run by Brazilians and dedicated to all things Brazilian, Kabokla is terrific. Live Brazilian groups play some nights from around 10pm (from percussion to samba and cover bands playing Chico Buarque). When there's no live music, the DJ gets the crowd dancing. It also serves Madrid's smoothest caipirinhas and runs samba and capoeira classes outside opening hours.

El Jardín Secreto
BAR-CAFE

(Calle de Conde Duque 2; ⏰5.30pm-12.30am Sun-Thu & Sun, 6.30pm-2.30am Fri & Sat; ⓜPlaza de España) 'The Secret Garden' is all about intimacy and romance in a *barrio* that's one of Madrid's best-kept secrets. Lit by Spanish designer candles, draped in organza from India and serving up chocolates from the Caribbean, it's at its best on a summer's evening, but the atmosphere never misses a beat. It attracts a loyal and young professional crowd.

Café Belén
CHILL-OUT BAR

(Map p80; Calle de Belén 5; ⏰3.30pm-3am; ⓜChueca) Café Belén is cool in all the right places – lounge and chill-out music, dim lighting, a great range of drinks (the mojitos are especially good) and a low-key crowd that's the height of casual sophistication. In short, it's one of our favourite Chueca watering holes.

La Vía Láctea
BAR-NIGHTCLUB

(Map p80; Calle de Velarde 18; ⏰9pm-3am; ⓜTribunal) Another living, breathing and somewhat grungy relic of *la movida,* La Vía Láctea remains a Malasaña favourite for a mixed, informal crowd who seems to live for the 1980s, and the music here ranges across rock, pop, garage, rockabilly and indie. There are plenty of drinks to choose from and by late Saturday night anything goes. Expect long queues to get in on weekends.

Café-Restaurante El Espejo
LITERARY CAFE

(Map p78; Paseo de los Recoletos 31; ⏰11am-2am Sun-Thu, 11am-3am Fri & Sat; ⓜColón) Once a haunt of writers and intellectuals, this architectural gem blends Modernista and art deco styles and its interior could well overwhelm you with all the mirrors, chandeliers and bow-tied service of another era. The atmosphere is suitably quiet and refined, although our favourite corner is next to the elegant glass pavilion out on Paseo de los Recoletos.

Café Pepe Botella
CAFE-BAR

(Map p80; Calle de San Andrés 12; ⏰noon-2am; ⓜBilbao or Tribunal) Pepe Botella has hit on a fine formula for success. As good in the hours around midnight as it is in the afternoon when its wi-fi access draws the laptop-toting crowd, it's a classy bar with green-velvet benches, marble-topped tables, and old photos and mirrors covering the walls. The faded elegance gives the place the charm that's made it one of the most enduringly popular drinking holes in the *barrio.*

Areia
BAR, NIGHTCLUB

(Map p80; www.areiachillout.com, in Spanish; Calle de Hortaleza 92; ⏰1pm-3am; ⓜChueca or Alonso Martínez) The ultimate lounge bar by day (cushions, chill-out music and dark, secluded corners where you can hear yourself talk, or even snog quietly), this place is equally enjoyable by night. That's when groovy DJs take over (from 11pm Sunday to Wednesday, and from 9pm the rest of the week) with deep and chill house, nu jazz, bossa and electronica. It's cool, funky and low-key all at once.

Gran Café de Gijón
LITERARY CAFE

(Map p78; Paseo de los Recoletos 21; ⏰7am-1.30am; ⓜChueca or Banco de España) This graceful old cafe has been serving coffee and meals since 1888 and has long been a favourite with Madrid's literati for a drink or a meal – all of Spain's great literary figures of the 20th century came here for coffee and *tertulias* (literary discussions). You'll find yourself among intellectuals, conservative Franco diehards and young *madrileños* looking for a quiet drink.

Ojalá Awareness Club
CHILL-OUT BAR

(Map p80; Calle de San Andrés 1; ⏰8.30am-1am Sun-Wed, 8.30am-2am Thu-Sat; ⓜTribunal) Ojalá is funky. We love it first and foremost for a drink (especially a daiquiri) at any time of the day. Its lime-green colour scheme, zany lighting and hip, cafe-style ambience all make it an extremely cool place to hang out, but the sandy floor and cushions downstairs take chilled to a whole new level.

Café Manuela
CAFE

(Map p80; Calle de San Vicente Ferrer 29; ⊗4pm-2am Mon-Fri, noon-3am Sat, noon-2am Sun; MTribunal) Stumbling into this graciously restored throwback to the 1950s along one of Malasaña's grittier streets is akin to discovering hidden treasure. There's a luminous quality to it when you come in out of the night and, like so many Madrid cafes, it's a surprisingly multifaceted space, serving cocktails, delicious milkshakes and offering board games atop the marble tables in the unlikely event that you get bored.

Lolina Vintage Café
CAFE

(Map p80; Calle del Espíritu Santo 9; ⊗10am-1am Sun-Tue, 10am-2am Wed-Sat; MTribunal) Close to being our favourite recent discovery in Malasaña, Lolina Vintage Café seems to have captured the essence of the *barrio* in one small space. With a studied retro look (comfy old-style chairs and sofas, gilded mirrors and 1970s-era wallpaper), it confirms that the new Malasaña is not unlike the old but a whole lot more sophisticated.

☆ Entertainment

All of the following publications and websites provide comprehensive, updated listings of showings at Madrid's theatres, cinemas and concert halls:

EsMadrid Magazine (www.esmadrid.com) Monthly tourist office listings for concerts and other performances; available at tourist offices, some hotels and online.

Guía del Ocio (www.guiadelocio.com, in Spanish) A Spanish-only weekly magazine available for €1 at news kiosks.

In Madrid (www.in-madrid.com) This monthly English-language expat publication is given out free (check the website for locations) and has lots of information about what to see and do in town.

La Netro (http://madrid.lanetro.com, in Spanish) Comprehensive online guide to what's happening in Madrid.

Metropoli (www.elmundo.es/metropolis, in Spanish) *El Mundo*'s Friday supplement magazine has information on the week's offerings.

On Madrid (www.elpais.com, in Spanish) *El País* also has a Friday supplement with weekly listings.

What's on When (www.whatsonwhen.com) The Madrid page covers the highlights of sport and cultural activities, with some information on getting tickets.

Nightclubs

No *barrio* in Madrid is without a decent club or disco, but the most popular dance spots are in the centre. Don't expect the dance clubs or *discotecas* to really get going until after 1am, and some won't even bat an eyelid until 3am, when the bars elsewhere have closed.

Club prices vary widely, depending on the time of night you enter, the way you're dressed and the number of people inside. The standard admission fee is €10, which usually includes the first drink, although megaclubs and swankier places charge a few euros more. Even those that let you in free will play catch-up with hefty prices for drinks, so don't plan your night around looking for the cheapest ticket.

LOS AUSTRIAS, SOL & CENTRO

TOP CHOICE **Teatro Joy Eslava**
NIGHTCLUB

(Map p60; www.joy-eslava.com; Calle del Arenal 11; admission €12-15; ⊗11.30pm-6am; MSol) The only things guaranteed at this grand old Madrid dance club (housed in a 19th-century theatre) are a crowd and the fact that it will be open. (The club claims to have opened every single day for the past 29 years.) The music and the crowd are a mixed bag, but queues are long and invariably include locals and tourists, and even the occasional *famoso*.

Cool
NIGHTCLUB

(Map p80; www.fsmgroup.es; Calle de Isabel la Católica 6; admission from €10; ⊗11pm-6am Thu-Sat; MSanto Domingo) Cool by name, cool by nature. One of the hottest clubs in the city, the Phillipe Starck–designed curvy white lines, discreet lounge chairs in dark corners and pulsating dance floor are decked by gorgeous people, gorgeous clothes and a strict entry policy. Thursday is given over to 'Sunflower Dance Sessions' (house music and a fashionista crowd), Friday is 'Stardust' (electronica and techno), while Saturdays are called 'Royal' with new house music and a predominantly gay clientele. Things don't really get going until 3am.

Charada NIGHTCLUB

(Map p60; www.charadaclubdebaile.com, in Spanish; Calle de la Bola 13; admission €10-15; ☺midnight-6am Thu-Sat; MSanto Domingo) Charada took the Madrid nightlife scene by storm in 2009 and has never looked back. Its decor is New York chic (with no hint of its former existence as a brothel), the cocktails are highly original, the clientele is well heeled and often famous, it's the home turntable for some of the best house DJs in town. Thursday's 'Future Disco Jams' (discofunk) is our pick of the nights.

Palacio Gaviria NIGHTCLUB

(Map p60; www.palaciogaviria.com; Calle del Arenal 9; admission €10-15; ☺midnight-6am; MSol) A recently renovated palace converted into one of the most popular dance clubs in Madrid, this is the kind of place where the crowd can be pretty young and boisterous and the queues long. Thursday is international student and house music night – international relations have never been so much fun.

HUERTAS & ATOCHA

TOP CHOICE Adraba NIGHTCLUB

(www.fsmgroup.es, in Spanish; Calle de Alcalá 20; admission €15-18; ☺midnight-6am Wed-Sun; MSevilla) This nightclub has history. It was one of the most famous nightclubs of *la movida madrileña* until it burned down (killing 81 revellers in the process) in 1983. It finally reopened to much fanfare in 2010 and has rapidly re-established itself as one of the city's best. The designer decor is stunning, the safety provisions second to none and there's five nights of dancing with a sophisticated crowd. Thursday night is 'Vanité' (which comes with the attached subtitle of 'The Most Fashion Night' and is devoted to glamour and lounge-bar sounds), while Friday and Saturday take you through the last three decades of dance tunes. Bookends to the rather long Adraba weekend are provided by Wednesday ('Fever', with music from the 1970s through to the 1990s) and Sunday ('Queen's Club', an elitist party with a door policy to match). Whatever the night, the resident DJs are among the best in Madrid.

Kapital NIGHTCLUB

(Map p68; www.grupo-kapital.com, in Spanish; Calle de Atocha 125; admission €20; ☺6-10pm & midnight-6am Thu-Sun; MAtocha) One of the most famous megaclubs in Madrid, this massive seven-storey nightclub has something for everyone: from cocktail bars and dance music to karaoke, salsa, hip hop and more chilled spaces for R&B and soul, as well as a section devoted to 'Made in Spain' music. It's such a big place that a cross-section of Madrid society (VIPs and the Real Madrid set love this place) hangs out here without ever getting in each other's way.

Stella NIGHTCLUB

(Map p66; www.theroomclub.com; Calle de Arlabán 7; admission €13-15; ☺12.30-6am Thu-Sat; MSevilla) If you arrive here after 3am, there simply won't be room and those inside have no intention of leaving until dawn. The DJs here are some of Madrid's best, and the great visuals will leave you cross-eyed if you weren't already from the music in this heady place. Thursday and Saturday nights ('Mondo', for electronica) rely on resident and invited DJs, while Friday nights ('The Room') is usually the preserve of Ángel García, one of the celebrated stalwart DJs of the Madrid night.

SALAMANCA

Serrano 41 NIGHTCLUB

(Map p78; ☎91 578 18 65; www.serrano41.com, in Spanish; Calle de Serrano 41; admission €10; ☺11pm-5.30am Wed-Sun; MSerrano) If bullfighters, Real Madrid stars and other A-listers can't drag themselves away from Salamanca, chances are that you'll find them here. Danceable pop and house dominate the most popular Friday and Saturday nights, funk gets a turn on Sunday and it's indie night on Thursday. As you'd imagine, the door policy is stricter than most.

MALASAÑA & CHUECA

There's more information about Chueca's nightclubs in the boxed text, p89.

Morocco NIGHTCLUB

(Map p80; www.morocco-madrid.com, in Spanish; Calle del Marqués de Leganés 7; admission €10; ☺midnight-6am Fri & Sat; MSanto Domingo or Noviciado) Owned by the zany Alaska, the standout musical personality of *la movida*, Morocco has decor that's so kitsch it's cool, and a mix of musical styles that never strays too far from 1980s Spanish and international tunes with electronica another recurring theme. The bouncers have been known to show a bit of attitude, but then that kind of comes with the profession.

Nasti Club NIGHTCLUB

(Map p80; www.nasti.es, in Spanish; Calle de San Vicente Ferrer 33; admission free-€10; ☺11pm-5.30am Thu-Sat; MTribunal) It's hard to think of a more off-putting entrance with Nasti Club's graffiti and abandoned-building look. Its staple, appropriately, is a faithfully grungy approach to the 1970s (pop, rock and punk), both in terms of music and decor. But it's not as nasty as it sounds and the crowd can span the full range of 1970s throwbacks from a Who's Who of Madrid's underground to some surprisingly respectable types. Above all it's a place with attitude, and as its own publicity says, it's *not* from Barcelona, it *doesn't* play electronica, people who come here *are* cool and no one's ever heard of the live acts who appear here until they become famous two years later. Says it all really. Very Malasaña.

Sala Flamingo
NIGHTCLUB

(Map p80; Calle de Mesonero Romanos 13; admission €10; ⊙midnight-5.30am Thu, Fri & Sat; ⓂCallao or Gran Vía) One of the most 'in' places in Madrid for many years, Sala Flamingo is famous above all for its Friday night 'Ochoy-Media' session, which seamlessly blends indie rock with electronica to create its own genre, *rockotrónica* – this is the night when local celebrities flood through the doors. For a complete change of pace and clientele, 'Darkhole' on Saturday is all black and Gothic, while Thursday kicks it all off with 'Playback', where dressing down seems to be the only requirement.

Tupperware
BAR-NIGHTCLUB

(Map p80; Corredera Alta de San Pablo 26; ⊙9pm-3am; ⓂTribunal) A Malasaña stalwart and prime candidate for the bar that best catches the enduring *rockero* spirit of Malasaña, Tupperware draws a 30-something crowd, spins indie rock with a bit of soul and classics from the '60s and '70s, and generally revels in its kitsch (eyeballs stuck to the ceiling, and plastic TVs with action-figure dioramas lined up behind the bar). By the way, locals pronounce it 'Tupper-warry'.

Cinemas

Cine Doré
CINEMA

(Calle de Santa Isabel 3; ⊙Tue-Sun; ⓂAntón Martín) The National Film Library offers fantastic classic and vanguard films for just €2.50.

Cinesa Proyecciones
CINEMA

(☎902 33 32 31; www.cinesa.es, in Spanish; Calle de Fuencarral 136; ⓂBilbao or Quevedo) Wonderful art-deco exterior; modern cinema within.

La Enana Marrón
CINEMA

(Map p80; www.laenanamarron.org; Travesía de San Mateo 8; ⓂAlonso Martínez) There's no beating this great arty, alternative theatre, showing documentaries, animated films, international flicks and oldies.

Cines Princesa
CINEMA

(www.cinesrenoir.com, in Spanish; Calle de la Princesa 3; ⓂPlaza de España) Screens all kinds of original-version films, from Hollywood blockbusters to arty flicks.

Yelmo Cineplex Ideal
CINEMA

(Map p60; www.yelmocines.es, in Spanish; Calle del Doctor Cortezo 6; ⓂSol or Tirso de Molina) Close to Plaza Mayor; offers a wide selection of films.

Theatre & Dance

Madrid's theatre scene is a year-round affair. Most shows are in Spanish, but those who don't speak the language may still enjoy musicals or *zarzuela,* Spain's own singing and dancing version of musical theatre. Tickets for all shows start at around €10 and run up to around €50.

Compañía Nacional de Danza
DANCE COMPANY

(☎91 354 50 53; http://cndanza.mcu.es) Under director Nacho Duato, this dynamic company performs worldwide and has won accolades for its innovation and marvellous technicality and style. The company, made up mostly of international dancers, performs original, contemporary pieces and is considered a leading player on the international dance scene. When it is in town, which is unfortunately not often, it performs at various venues, including the Teatro de la Zarzuela.

Ballet Nacional de España
BALLET COMPANY

(☎91 517 99 99; balletnacional.mcu.es) A classical company that's known for its unique mix of ballet and traditional Spanish styles, such as flamenco and *zarzuela*. When in Madrid, it's usually on stage at the Teatro Real or the Teatro de la Zarzuela.

Teatro de la Zarzuela
THEATRE

(Map p66; ☎91 524 54 00; teatrodelazarzuela. mcu.es; Calle de Jovellanos 4; ⓂBanco de España) This theatre, built in 1856, is the premier place to see *zarzuela*. It also hosts a smattering of classical music and opera, as well as the cutting-edge Compañía Nacional de Danza.

Teatro Español THEATRE
(Map p66; ☎91 360 14 84; www.esmadrid.com/
teatroespanol; Calle del Príncipe 25; Ⓜ Sevilla, Sol
or Antón Martín) This theatre has been here
since the 16th century and is still one of the
best places to catch mainstream Spanish
drama, from the works of Lope de Vega to
more-recent playwrights.

Teatros del Canal THEATRE
(☎91 308 99 99; www.teatrosdelcanal.org, in
Spanish; Calle de Cea Bermúdez 1; Ⓜ Canal) A
state-of-the-art theatre complex opened in
2009, Teatros del Canal does major theatre
performances, as well as musical and dance
concerts. It's also the main venue for the
Suma Flamenca festival (p86) in June.

Live Music
FLAMENCO

Madrid may not be the spiritual home of
flamenco, and its big names may feel more
at home in the atmospheric flamenco taverns of Andalucía, but Madrid remains one
of Spain's premier flamenco stage.

Seeing flamenco in Madrid is, with some
worthy exceptions, expensive – at the *tablaos* (restaurants where flamenco is performed) expect to pay €25 to €35 just to
see the show. The admission price usually
includes your first drink, but you pay extra
for meals (up to €50 per person) that, put
simply, are rarely worth the money. For
that reason, we suggest you eat elsewhere
and simply pay for the show (after having
bought tickets in advance), albeit on the understanding that you won't have a front-row
seat. The other important thing to remember is that most of these shows are geared
towards tourists. That's not to say that the
quality isn't often top-notch. On the contrary, often it's magnificent, spine-tingling
stuff. It's just that they sometimes lack the
genuine, raw emotion of real flamenco.

TOP CHOICE Corral de la Morería FLAMENCO
(☎91 365 84 46; www.corraldelamor
eria.com; Calle de la Morería 17; admission €27-37;
☺8.30pm-2.30am, shows 10pm & midnight Sun-
Fri, 7pm, 10pm & midnight Sat; Ⓜ Ópera) This
is one of the most prestigious flamenco
stages in Madrid, with 50 years as a leading flamenco venue and top performers
most nights. The stage area has a rustic
feel, and tables are pushed up close. We'd
steer clear of the restaurant, which is overpriced (€43), but the performances have a
far higher price-quality ratio. This is where
international celebrities (eg Marlene Dietri-

ch, Marlon Brando, Muhammad Ali, Omar
Sharif) have always gone for their flamenco
fix when in town.

Las Carboneras FLAMENCO
(Map p60; ☎91 542 86 77; www.tablaolascar
boneras.com, in Spanish; Plaza del Conde de Miranda 1; admission €30-35; ☺shows 10.30pm
Mon-Thu, 8.30pm & 11pm Fri & Sat; Ⓜ Sol or La Latina) Like most of the *tablaos* around town,
this place sees far more tourists than locals,
but the quality is top-notch. It's not the
place for gritty, soul-moving spontaneity,
but it's still an excellent introduction and
one of the few places that flamenco aficionados seem to have no complaints about.

Las Tablas FLAMENCO
(☎91 542 05 20; www.lastablasmadrid.com; Plaza
de España 9; admission €24; ☺shows 10.30pm
Sun-Thu, 8pm & 10pm Fri & Sat; Ⓜ Plaza de España) Las Tablas has quickly earned a reputation for quality flamenco. Most nights you'll
see a classic flamenco show, with plenty of
throaty singing and soul-baring dancing.
Antonia Moya and Marisol Navarro, leading lights in the flamenco world, are regular
performers here.

Casa Patas FLAMENCO
(Map p66; ☎91 369 04 96; www.casapatas.com,
in Spanish; Calle de Cañizares 10; admission €30-
35; ☺shows 10.30pm Mon-Thu, 9pm & midnight
Fri & Sat; Ⓜ Antón Martín or Tirso de Molina) One
of the top flamenco stages in Madrid, this
tablao always offers unimpeachable quality that serves as a good introduction to the
art. It's not the friendliest place in town,
especially if you're only here for the show,
and you're likely to be crammed in a little,
but no one complains about the standard of
the performances.

CLASSICAL MUSIC & OPERA
Auditorio Nacional de Música
MUSIC AUDITORIUM
(☎91 337 01 40; www.auditorionacional.mcu.es;
Calle del Príncipe de Vergara 146; Ⓜ Cruz del Rayo)
Resounding to the sounds of classical mu-
sic, this modern venue offers a varied cal-
endar of performances, often by Madrid's
Orquesta Sinfonía (www.osm.es) and led by
conductors from all over the world.

Teatro Real OPERA HOUSE
(Map p60; ☎902 24 48 48; www.teatro-real.com;
Plaza de Oriente; Ⓜ Ópera) The Teatro Real is
as technologically advanced as any venue
in Europe, and is the city's grandest stage
for elaborate operas and ballets. You'll pay

as little as €15 for a spot so far away you'll need a telescope, although the sound quality is consistent throughout. For the best seats, don't expect change from €127.

JAZZ

Madrid was one of Europe's jazz capitals in the 1920s. It's taken a while, but it once again ranks among Europe's elite for live jazz. You'll pay about €10 to get into most places, but special concerts can run up to €20 or more.

TOP CHOICE Café Central
JAZZ CLUB

(Map p66; ☎91 369 41 43; www.cafe centralmadrid.com, in Spanish; Plaza del Ángel 10; admission €10-15; ⏰1pm-2.30am Sun-Thu, 1.30pm-3.30am Fri & Sat; ⓜAntón Martín or Sol) This art-deco bar has consistently been voted one of the best jazz venues in the world by leading jazz magazines, and with almost 9000 gigs under its belt, it rarely misses a beat. Big international names like Chano Domínguez, Tal Farlow and Wynton Marsalis have all played here, and there's everything from Latin jazz and fusion to tango and classic jazz. Performers usually play here for a week and then move on, so getting tickets shouldn't be a problem, except on weekends; shows start at 10pm and tickets go on sale an hour before the set starts.

FREE Populart
JAZZ CLUB

(Map p66; ☎91 429 84 07; www.populart. es, in Spanish; Calle de las Huertas 22; ⏰6pm-2.30am Sun-Fri, 6pm-3.30am Fri & Sat; ⓜAntón Martín or Sol) One of Madrid's classic jazz clubs, this place offers a low-key atmosphere and top-quality music – mostly jazz, but with occasional blues, swing and even flamenco thrown into the mix. Think Compay Segundo, Sonny Fortune and the Canal Street Jazz Band and you'll get an idea of the quality on offer here. Shows start at 10.15pm, but if you want a seat get here early.

El Berlín Jazz Club
JAZZ CLUB

(Map p80; ☎91 521 57 52; www.cafeberlin.es, in Spanish; Calle de Jacometrezo 4; admission €6-10; ⏰7pm-2.30am Tue-Sun; ⓜCallao or Santo Domingo) El Berlín has been something of a Madrid jazz stalwart since the 1950s and it's the kind of place that serious jazz fans rave about as the most authentic in town – it's all about classic jazz here, with none of the fusion performances you find elsewhere. The art-deco interior ads to the charm and the headline acts are a Who's Who of world jazz. The headline acts take to the stage at

11.30pm on Fridays and Saturdays, with other performances sprinkled throughout the week.

FREE El Junco Jazz Club
JAZZ CLUB

(Map p80; ☎91 319 20 81; Plaza de Santa Bárbara 10; ⏰11pm-6am; ⓜAlonso Martínez) El Junco has established itself on the Madrid nightlife scene by appealing as much to jazz aficionados as to clubbers. Its secret is high-quality live jazz gigs from Spain and around the world at 11.30pm every night, followed by DJs spinning funk, soul, nu jazz, blues and innovative groove beats. There are also jam sessions at 11.30pm in jazz (Tuesday) and blues (Sunday).

OTHER LIVE MUSIC

TOP CHOICE Costello Café & Niteclub
LIVE MUSIC

(Map p60; www.costelloclub.com; Calle del Caballero de Gracia 10; admission €5-10; ⏰6pm-1am Sun-Wed, 6pm-2.30am Thu-Sat; ⓜGran Vía) Very cool. Costello Café & Niteclub is smooth-as-silk ambience wedded with an innovative mix of pop, rock and fusion in Warholesque surrounds. There's live music every night of the week (except Sundays) at 9.30pm, with resident and visiting DJs keeping you on your feet until closing time from Thursday to Saturday. Even when there's nothing happening, it's a funky place that draws a sophisticated crowd which usually includes the odd local celebrity.

TOP CHOICE Sala El Sol
LIVE MUSIC

(Map p60; ☎91 532 64 90; www.elsolmad. com, in Spanish; Calle de los Jardines 3; admission €8-25; ⏰11pm-5.30am Tue-Sat Jul-Sep; ⓜGran Vía) Madrid institutions don't come any more beloved than Sala El Sol. It opened in 1979, just in time for *la movida*, and quickly established itself as a leading stage for all the icons of the era, such as Nacha Pop and Alaska y los Pegamoides. *La movida* may have faded into history, but it lives on at El Sol, where the music rocks and rolls and usually resurrects the '70s and '80s while soul and funk also get a run. It's a terrific venue and opening times vary – most concerts start around 11pm but can be as 'early' as 10pm. Check the website (which also allows you to book online) for upcoming acts.

ContraClub
LIVE MUSIC

(☎91 365 55 45; www.contraclub.es, in Spanish; Calle de Bailén 16; admission €6-12; ⏰10pm-6am Wed-Sat; ⓜLa Latina) ContraClub is a crossover live music venue and nightclub, with live flamenco on Wednesday and an eclectic mix of other live music (jazz, blues, world music and rock) from Thursday to Sunday; after the live acts (which start at 10.30pm), the resident DJs serve up equally eclectic beats (indie, pop, funk and soul) to make sure you don't move elsewhere.

Café La Palma
LIVE MUSIC

(Map p80; ☑91 522 50 31; www.cafelapalma.com, in Spanish; Calle de la Palma 62; admission free-€12; ☺4.30pm-3am; Ⓜ Noviciado) It's amazing how much variety Café La Palma has packed into its labyrinth of rooms. Live shows featuring hot local bands are held at the back, while DJs mix up the front. You might find live music other nights, but there are always two shows at 10pm and midnight from Thursday to Saturday. Every night is a little different.

Clamores
LIVE MUSIC

(☑91 445 79 38; www.clamores.es, in Spanish; Calle de Alburquerque 14; admission €5-15; ☺6pm-3am; Ⓜ Bilbao) This one-time classic jazz cafe has morphed into one of the most diverse live-music stages in Madrid. Jazz is still a staple, but world music, flamenco, soul fusion, singer-songwriter, pop and rock all make regular appearances. Live shows can begin as early as 9pm.

FREE Honky Tonk
LIVE ROCK

(☑91 445 61 91; www.clubhonky.com, in Spanish; Calle de Covarrubias 24; ☺9pm-5am; Ⓜ Alonso Martínez) Despite the name, this is a great place to see local rock and roll, though many acts have a little country or blues thrown into the mix too. It's a fun vibe in a smallish club that's been around since the heady 1980s. Arrive early, as it fills up fast.

La Boca del Lobo
LIVE MUSIC

(Map p66; ☑91 429 70 13; www.labocadellobo. com, in Spanish; Calle de Echegaray 11; admission free-€10; ☺9pm-3am; Ⓜ Sevilla) Known for offering mostly rock and alternative concerts, La Boca del Lobo (The Wolf's Mouth) is as dark as its name suggests and has broadened its horizons to include just about anything – roots, reggae, jazz, soul, ska, flamenco, funk and fusion. Amid all the variety are some mainstays – Wednesdays at 11pm is set aside for a roots and groove jam session, while Sunday nights are dedicated to soul music. Concerts start between 9.30pm and 11pm (check the website) most nights, and DJs take over until closing time.

Sport
BULLFIGHTING

From the Fiesta de San Isidro in mid-May until the end of October, Spain's top bullfighters come to swing their capes at Plaza de Toros Monumental de Las Ventas (☑91 356 22 00; www.las-ventas.com, in Spanish; Calle de Alcalá 237; Ⓜ Ventas), one of the largest rings in the bullfighting world. Las Ventas has a grand Mudéjar exterior and a suitably Colosseum-like arena surrounding the broad, sandy ring. During the six weeks of the fiesta's main bullfighting season that begins with the Fiestas de San Isidro, there are *corridas* (bullfights) almost every day.

Tickets for *corridas* are divided into *sol* (sun) and *sombra* (shade) seating. The cheapest tickets (around €5) are for standing-room *sol,* though on a broiling-hot summer day it's infinitely more enjoyable to pay the extra €4 for *sombra* tickets. The very best seats – in the front row in the shade – are the preserve of celebrities and cost more than €100.

Ticket sales begin a few days before the fight, at Plaza de Toros Monumental de Las Ventas ticket office (☺10am-2pm & 5-8pm). A few agencies sell before then, adding an extra 20% for their trouble; one of the best is Localidades Galicia (Map p60; ☑91 531 91 31; www.bullfightticketsmadrid.com; Plaza del Carmen 1; ☺9.30am-1pm & 4.30-7pm Mon-Sat, 9.30am-1pm Sun; Ⓜ Sol). You can also get tickets at La Central Bullfight Ticket Office (Map p66; ☑91 531 33 66; Calle de la Victoria).

For further discussion of Spain's most controversial pastime, see p865.

FOOTBALL

The home of **Real Madrid**, Estadio Santiago Bernabéu is a temple to football and is one of the world's great sporting arenas; watching a game here is akin to a pilgrimage for sports fans. When the players strut their stuff with 80,000 passionate *madrileños* in attendance, you'll get chills down your spine. If you're fortunate enough to be in town when Real Madrid wins a major trophy, head to Plaza de la Cibeles and wait for the all-night party to begin.

Named after the club's long-time president, the Estadio Santiago Bernabéu (☑91 398 43 00; www.realmadrid.com; Avenida de Concha Espina 1; tour adult/under 14yr €15/10; ☺10am-7pm Mon-Sun; Ⓜ Santiago Bernabéu) is a mecca for *madridistas* (Real

Madrid football fans) worldwide. For a self-guided tour of the stadium, buy your ticket at ticket window 10 (next to Gate 7). The tour takes you through the extraordinary **Exposición de Trofeos** (Trophy Exhibit), the presidential box, the press room, dressing rooms and the players' tunnel, and even onto the pitch itself. On match days, tours cease five hours before the game is scheduled to start, although the Exposición de Trofeos is open until two hours before game time.

Tickets for matches start at around €40 and run up to the rafters for major matches. Unless you book through a ticket agency, turn up at the ticket office at Gate 42 on Avenida de Concha Espina early in the week before a scheduled game. The all-important telephone number for booking tickets (which you later pick up at Gate 42) is ☎902 32 43 24, which only works if you're calling from within Spain. If you're booking from abroad and don't have any luck online, try Localidades Galicia (Map p60; ☎91 531 91 31; www.bullfightticketsmadrid. com; Plaza del Carmen 1; ☺9.30am-1pm & 4.30-7pm Mon-Sat, 9.30am-1pm Sun; MSol). Numerous websites also sell tickets to Real Madrid games, including www.madrid-tickets.net, www.madrid-tickets.com and www.ticket-finders.com.

The city's other big club, **Atlético de Madrid**, may have long existed in the shadow of its more illustrious city rival, but it has been one of the most successful teams in Spanish football history in its own right; it won the Europa League in 2010. The first-division team's home, Estadio Vicente Calderón (☎91 366 47 07; www.clubatleticodemadrid.com; Paseo de la Virgin del Puerto; MPirámides), isn't as large as Real Madrid's (Vicente Calderón seats a mere 60,000), but what it lacks in size it makes up for in raw energy. To see an Atlético de Madrid game, try calling ☎91 366 47 07 or ☎902 530 500, but you're most likely to manage a ticket if you turn up at the ground a few days before the match.

🔒 Shopping

Eager to change your look to blend in with the casual-but-sophisticated Spanish crowd? Tired of bull postcards and tacky flamenco posters? Convinced that your discerning friends back home have taste that extends beyond a polka-dot flamenco dress? In Madrid, you'll find it all.

This is a fantastic city in which to shop and *madrileños* are some of the finest exponents of the art.

The peak shopping season is during *las rebajas,* the annual winter and summer sales when prices are slashed on just about everything. The winter sales begin around 7 January, just after Three Kings' Day, and last well into February. Summer sales begin in early July and last into August.

All shops may (and most usually do) open on the first Sunday of every month and throughout December.

LOS AUSTRIAS, SOL & CENTRO

TOP CHOICE Antigua Casa Talavera
TRADITIONAL CERAMICS
(Map p60; Calle de Isabel la Católica 2; ☺10am-1.30pm & 5-8pm Mon-Fri, 10am-1.30pm Sat; MSanto Domingo) The extraordinary tiled facade of this wonderful old shop conceals an Aladdin's cave of ceramics from all over Spain. This is not the mass-produced stuff aimed at the tourist market, but comes from the small family potters of Andalucía and Toledo, and ranges from the decorative (tiles) to the useful (plates, jugs and other kitchen items).

TOP CHOICE El Arco Artesanía
CONTEMPORARY SOUVENIRS
(Map p60; www.elarcoartesania.com; Plaza Mayor 9; ☺11am-9pm; MSol or La Latina) This original shop in the southwestern corner of Plaza Mayor sells an outstanding array of homemade designer souvenirs, from stone and glasswork to jewellery and home fittings. The papier-mâché figures are gorgeous, but there's so much here to turn your head.

El Flamenco Vive
FLAMENCO
(Map p60; www.elflamencovive.es; Calle Conde de Lemos 7; ☺10am-2pm & 5-9pm Mon-Sat; MÓpera) This temple to flamenco has it all, from guitars, songbooks and well-priced CDs to polka-dotted dancing costumes, shoes, colourful plastic jewellery and literature about flamenco. It's the sort of place that will appeal as much to curious first-timers as to serious students of the art.

Casa de Diego
SPANISH FANS
(Map p60; www.casadediego.com; Plaza de la Puerta del Sol 12; ☺9.30am-8pm Mon-Sat; MSol) This classic shop has been around since 1858, selling and repairing Spanish fans, shawls, umbrellas and canes. Service is old-style and the staff occasionally grumpy, but the fans are works of antique art.

Salvador Bachiller LEATHER GOODS
(Map p80; www.salvadorbachiller.com; Gran Vía 65; ⊙10am-9.30pm Mon-Sat; MPlaza de España or Santo Domingo) The stylish and high-quality leather bags, wallets, suitcases and other accessories of Salvador Bachiller are a staple of Spanish shopping aficionados. This is leather with a typically Spanish twist – the colours are dazzling in bright pinks, yellows and greens. Sound garish? You'll change your mind once you step inside.

Casa Hernanz ESPADRILLES
(Map p60; Calle de Toledo 18; ⊙9am-1.30pm & 4.30-8pm Mon-Fri, 10am-2pm Sat; MLa Latina or Sol) Comfy, rope-soled *alpargatas* (espadrilles), Spain's traditional summer footwear, are worn by everyone from the King of Spain down, and you can buy your own pair at this humble workshop, which has been handmaking the shoes for five generations; you can even get them made to order. Prices range from €5 to €40 and queues form whenever the weather starts to warm up.

LA LATINA & LAVAPIÉS

TOP CHOICE El Rastro FLEA MARKET
(Calle de la Ribera de Curtidores; ⊙8am-3pm Sun; MLa Latina, Puerta de Toledo or Tirso de Molina) A Sunday morning at El Rastro is a Madrid institution. You could easily spend an entire morning inching your way down the Calle de la Ribera de Curtidores and through the maze of streets that hosts El Rastro flea market every Sunday morning. Cheap clothes, luggage, old flamenco records, even older photos of Madrid, faux designer purses, grungy T-shirts, household goods and electronics are the main fare, but for every 10 pieces of junk, there's a real gem (a lost masterpiece, an Underwood typewriter) waiting to be found.

A word of warning: pickpockets love El Rastro as much as everyone else, so keep a tight hold on your belongings and don't keep valuables in easy-to-reach pockets.

Helena Rohner JEWELLERY
(Map p64; www.helenarohner.com; Calle del Almendro 4; ⊙9am-8.30pm Mon-Fri, noon-2.30pm & 3.30-8pm Sat, noon-3pm Sun; MLa Latina or Tirso de Molina) One of Europe's most creative jewellery designers, Helena Rohner has a spacious boutique in La Latina. Working with silver, stone, porcelain, wood and Murano glass, she makes inventive pieces and her work is a regular feature of Paris fashion shows. In her own words, she seeks to re-create 'the magic of Florence, the vitality of London and the luminosity of Madrid'. She has also recently branched out into homewares.

HUERTAS & ATOCHA

TOP CHOICE Gil SPANISH SHAWLS
(Map p66; Carrera de San Jerónimo 2; ⊙9.30am-1.30pm & 4.30-8pm Mon- Sat; MSol) You don't see them much these days, but the exquisite fringed and embroidered *mantones* and *mantoncillos* (traditional Spanish shawls worn by women on grand occasions) and delicate *mantillas* (Spanish veils) are stunning and uniquely Spanish gifts. Gil also sells *abanicos* (Spanish fans). Inside this dark shop, dating back to 1880, the sales clerks still wait behind a long counter to attend to you; the service hasn't changed in years and that's no bad thing.

María Cabello WINE
(Map p66; Calle de Echegaray 19; ⊙9.30am-2.30pm & 5.30-9pm Mon-Fri, 10am-2.30pm & 6.30-9.30pm Sat; MSevilla or Antón Martín) All wine shops should be like this. This family-run corner shop really knows its wines and the decoration has scarcely changed since 1913, with wooden shelves and even a faded ceiling fresco. There are fine wines in abundance (mostly Spanish, and a few foreign bottles) with some 500 labels on show or tucked away out the back.

SALAMANCA

TOP CHOICE Agatha Ruiz de la Prada
  CLOTHING
(Map p78; www.agatharuizdelaprada.com; Calle de Serrano 27; ⊙10am-8.30pm Mon-Sat; MSerrano) This boutique has to be seen to be believed, with pinks, yellows and oranges everywhere you turn. It's fun and exuberant, but it's not just for kids: it's also serious and highly original fashion. Agatha Ruiz de la Prada is one of the enduring icons of Madrid's 1980s outpouring of creativity known as *la movida madrileña*.

Gallery MEN'S FASHION
(Map p78; www.gallerymadrid.com; Calle de Jorge Juan 38; ⊙10.30am-8.30pm Mon-Sat; MPríncipe de Vergara or Velázquez) This stunning showpiece of men's fashions and accessories (shoes, bags, belts and the like) is the new Madrid in a nutshell – stylish, brand-conscious and all about having the right look. With an interior designed by Tomas Alia, it's one of the city's coolest shops for men.

Oriol Balaguer
CHOCOLATE

(www.oriolbalaguer.com; Calle de José Ortega y Gasset 44; ⊙9am-9pm Mon-Sat, 9am-2.30pm Sun; MNuñez de Balboa) Catalan pastry chef Oriol Balaguer has a formidable CV – he worked with Ferran Adrià and won the prize for the World's Best Dessert in 2001. His much-awaited chocolate boutique opened in Madrid in March 2008 and is a combination of small art gallery and fashion boutique, except that it's dedicated to exquisite chocolate collections and cakes. You'll never be able to buy ordinary chocolate again after a visit here.

Camper
SHOES

(Map p78; www.camper.es; Calle de Serrano 24; ⊙10am-8.30pm Mon-Sat; MSerrano) Spanish fashion is not all haute couture, and this world-famous cool and quirky shoe brand from Mallorca has shops all over Madrid. The designs are bowling-shoe chic, with colourful, fun styles that are all about comfort. There are other outlets throughout the city – check out the website for locations.

Mantequería Bravo
FOOD, WINE

(Map p78; Calle de Ayala 24; ⊙9.30am-2.30pm & 5.30-8.30pm Mon-Fri, 9.30am-2.30pm Sat; MSerrano) Behind the attractive old facade lies a connoisseur's paradise, filled with local cheeses, sausages, wines and coffees. The products here are great for a gift, but everything's so good that you won't want to share. Mantequería Bravo won the 2007 prize for Madrid's best gourmet food shop or delicatessen – it's as simple as that.

MALASAÑA & CHUECA

TOP CHOICE Mercado de Fuencarral
CLOTHING

(Map p80; www.mdf.es, in Spanish; Calle de Fuencarral 45; ⊙11am-9pm Mon-Sat; MTribunal) Madrid's home of alternative club-cool is still going strong, revelling in its reverse snobbery. With shops like Fuck, Ugly Shop and Black Kiss, it's funky, grungy and filled to the rafters with torn T-shirts and more black leather and silver studs than you'll ever need. This is a Madrid icon and when it was threatened with closure in 2008, there was nearly an uprising.

Patrimonio Comunal Olivarero
OLIVE OILS

(Map p80; Calle de Mejía Lequerica 1; ⊙10am-2pm & 5-8pm Mon-Fri, 10am-2pm Sat; MAlonso Martínez) To catch the real essence of Spain's olive oil varieties, Patrimonio Comunal

Olivarero is perfect. With examples of the extra-virgin variety (and nothing else) from all over Spain, you could spend ages agonising over the choices. The staff know their oil and are happy to help out if you speak a little Spanish.

CHAMBERÍ & ARGÜELLES

Diedro
CLOTHING, ACCESSORIES

(Map p80; www.diedro.com; Calle de Sagasta 17; ⊙10am-10pm Mon-Sat, noon-10pm Sun; MBilbao or Alonso Martínez) One of the most innovative gift shops in Madrid, Diedro has designer jewellery, clothes, stationery and homewares. It's a wonderful space spread over three floors that span just about every taste, as long as it's design-conscious. Leading brand names include Calvin Klein, Pandora, Guess, Bodum and Alessi.

NORTHERN MADRID

Tienda Real Madrid
FOOTBALL MEMORABILIA

(Gate 57, Estadio Santiago Bernabéu, Avenida de Concha Espina 1; ⊙10am-8.30pm; MSantiago Bernabéu) The club shop of Real Madrid sells replica shirts, posters, caps and just about everything under the sun to which they could attach a club logo. From the shop window, you can see down onto the stadium itself.

① Information

Dangers & Annoyances

Madrid is a generally safe city although you should, as in most European cities, be wary of pickpockets in the city centre, on the metro and around major tourist sights. You need to be especially careful in the most heavily touristed parts of town, notably the Plaza Mayor and surrounding streets, the Puerta del Sol, El Rastro and the Museo del Prado. Tricks abound and they usually involve a team of two or more (sometimes one of them is an attractive woman to distract male victims). While one diverts your attention, the other empties your pockets. But don't be paranoid: remember that the overwhelming majority of travellers to Madrid rarely encounter any problems.

More unsettling than dangerous, the central Calle de la Montera has long been the haunt of prostitutes, pimps and a fair share of shady characters, although the street has recently been pedestrianised, and furnished with CCTV cameras and a police station.

The *barrio* of Lavapiés is a gritty, multicultural melting pot. We love it, but it's not without its problems, with drug-related crime an occasional but persistent problem. It's probably best avoided if you're on your own at night.

Emergency

Emergency (☏112)

Policía Nacional (☏091)

Servicio de Atención al Turista Extranjero (Foreign Tourist Assistance Service; ☏91 548 85 37/80 08; www.esmadrid.com/satemadrid; Calle de Leganitos 19; ⊗9am-10pm; MPlaza de España or Santo Domingo) To report thefts or other crime-related matters, cancel your credit cards, contact your embassy and other related matters, this is your best bet.

Teléfono de la Víctima (☏902 180 995) Hot-line for victims of racial or sexual violence.

Internet Access

In this era of wi-fi and laptop-bearing travellers, most of Madrid's better internet cafes have fallen by the wayside. You'll find plenty of small *locutorios* (small shops selling phonecards and cheap phone calls) all over the city and many have a few computers out the back, but we haven't listed these as they come and go with monotonous regularity. In the downtown area, your best options:

Centro de Turismo de Madrid (p114) Free internet for up to 15 minutes at the branch on Plaza Mayor, or free and unlimited access at the Plaza de Colón branch.

Café Comercial (Glorieta de Bilbao 7; per 50min €1; ⊗7.30am-midnight Mon, 7.30am-1am Tue-Thu, 7.30am-2am Fri, 8.30am-2am Sat, 9am-midnight Sun; MBilbao) One of Madrid's grandest old cafes, with internet upstairs.

Media

European newspapers are available at news-stands all over central Madrid.

ABC (www.abc.es, in Spanish) Right-leaning Spanish-language daily.

El Mundo (www.elmundo.es, in Spanish) Centre-right Spanish-language daily.

El País (www.elpais.com, in Spanish) Centre-left Spanish-language daily; Spain's largest-circulation newspaper.

InMadrid (www.in-madrid.com) Free English-language monthly newspaper available from some hotels, bars and tourist offices; has articles on and listings for Madrid.

International Herald Tribune (www.iht.com) Includes a daily eight-page supplement of articles from *El País* translated into English (www.elpais.com/misc/herald/herald.pdf).

Madriz (www.madriz.com) Bilingual, biannual magazine about Madrid.

Marca (www.marca.com, in Spanish) Daily Spanish-language sports newspaper.

Medical Services

Anglo-American Medical Unit (Unidad Medica; ☏91 435 18 23; www.unidadmedica.com; Calle del Conde de Aranda 1; ⊗9am-8pm Mon-Fri, 10am-1pm Sat for emergencies; MRetiro) Private clinic with Spanish- and English-speaking staff. Consultations cost around €125.

Farmacia Mayor (☏91 366; Calle Mayor 13; ⊗24hr; MSol)

Farmacia Velázquez 70 (☏91 575 60 28; Calle de Velázquez 70; ⊗24hr; MVelázquez)

Hospital General Gregorio Marañón (☏91 586 80 00; www.hggm.es, in Spanish; Calle del Doctor Esquerdo 46; MSáinz de Baranda or O'Donnell) One of the city's main public hospitals.

Post

Main post office (www.correos.es; Paseo del Prado 1; MBanco de España)

Tourist Information

Centro de Turismo de Madrid (Map p60; ☏91 588 16 36 51; www.esmadrid.com; Plaza Mayor 27; ⊗9.30am-8.30pm; MSol) Excellent city tourist office with a smaller office underneath Plaza de Colón and information points at Plaza de la Cibeles, Plaza de Callao, outside the Centro de Arte Reina Sofía and at the T4 terminal at Barajas airport.

Comunidad de Madrid Regional Information Line (☏012, Spanish only)

Regional Tourist Office (Map p66; ☏91 429 49 51, 902 10 00 07; www.turismomadrid.es; Calle del Duque de Medinaceli 2; ⊗8am-8pm Mon-Sat, 9am-2pm Sun; MBanco de España) Further offices at Barajas airport (T1 and T4), and Chamartín and Atocha train stations.

Town Hall City Information Line (☏010 or 91 540 40 10, Spanish only) Deals with everything from public transport to shows

Websites

EsMadrid.com (www.esmadrid.com) The *ayuntamiento*'s supersexy website with info on upcoming events.

In Madrid (www.in-madrid.com) A direct line to Madrid's expat community with upcoming events, nightlife reviews, articles, a forum, classifieds and some useful practical information.

Le Cool (www.lecool.com) Weekly updates on upcoming events in Madrid with an emphasis on the alternative, offbeat and avant-garde.

Lonely Planet (www.lonelyplanet.com) An overview of Madrid with hundreds of useful links, including to the Thorn Tree, Lonely Planet's online bulletin board.

WANT MORE?

For in-depth information, reviews and recommendations at your fingertips, head to the Apple App Store to purchase Lonely Planet's Madrid City Guide iPhone app.

Alternatively, head to Lonely Planet (www.lonelyplanet.com/spain/madrid) for planning advice, author recommendations, traveller reviews and insider tips.

Turismo Madrid (www.turismomadrid.es) Portal of the regional Comunidad de Madrid tourist office that's especially good for areas outside the city but still within the Comunidad de Madrid.

Vive Madrid (www.guiavivemadrid.com) A privately run site that has some moderately useful info on bars, restaurants, hotels and transport, as well as a booking service.

🛈 Getting There & Away

Air

Madrid's **Barajas airport** (Aeropuerto de Barajas; ☑902 40 47 04; www.aena.es) lies 15km northeast of the city. It's Europe's fourth-busiest hub (more than 52 million passengers pass through here annually), trailing only London Heathrow, Paris Charles de Gaulle and Frankfurt.

Although all airlines conduct check-in *(facturación)* in the airport's departure areas, some also allow check-in at the Nuevos Ministerios metro stop and transport interchange in Madrid itself – ask your airline.

A full list of airlines flying to Madrid (and which of Madrid's four terminals they use) is available on the Madrid-Barajas section of www.aena.es; click on 'Airlines'. Major airlines:

Aer Lingus (☑902 502 737; www.aerlingus.com)

Air Berlin (☑902 320 737; www.airberlin.com)

Air Europa (☑902 401 501; www.aireuropa.com)

Air France (☑902 207 090; www.airfrance.com)

Alitalia (☑902 100 323; www.alitalia.it)

American Airlines (☑902 887 300; www.aa.com)

Andalus (☑902 887 300; www.andalus.es)

Austrian Airlines ☑902 551 257; www.aua.com)

British Airways (☑902 111 333; www.britishairways.com)

Continental Airlines (☑900 961 266; www.continental.com)

EasyJet (☑807 260 026; www.easyjet.com)

Emirates (www.emirates.com)

German Wings (☑807 070 025; www.germanwings.com)

Iberia (☑902 400 500; www.iberia.es)

KLM (☑902 222 747; www.klm.com)

Lufthansa (☑902 883 882; www.lufthansa.com)

Qatar Airways (☑902 627 070; www.qatarairways.com)

Royal Air Maroc (☑902 210 010; www.royalairmaroc.com)

Ryanair (☑807 220 032; www.ryanair.com)

Spanair (☑902 131 415; www.spanair.com)

Swiss International Airlines (☑901 116 712; www.swiss.com)

TAP Air Portugal (☑901 116 718; www.flytap.com)

Thai Airways (☑91 782 05 21; www.thaiairways.com)

Turkish Airlines (☑902 124 440; www.turkishairlines.com)

Vueling (☑807 200 200; www.vueling.com)

Bus

Estación Sur de Autobuses (☑91 468 42 00; www.estaciondeautobuses.com, in Spanish; Calle de Méndez Álvaro 83; Ⓜ Méndez Álvaro), just south of the M30 ring road, is the city's principal bus station. It serves most destinations to the south and many in other parts of the country. Most bus companies have a ticket office here, even if their buses depart from elsewhere.

Major bus companies:

ALSA (☑902 422 242; www.alsa.es)

Avanzabus (☑902 020 052; www.avanzabus.com)

Car & Motorcycle

The city is surrounded by two main ring roads, the outermost M-40 and the inner M-30; there are also two additional partial ring roads, the M-45 and the more-distant M-50. The R-5 and R-3 are part of a series of toll roads built to ease traffic jams.

The big-name car-rental agencies have offices all over Madrid. Avis, Budget, Hertz and Europcar have booths at the airport and some have branches at Atocha and Chamartín train stations. Car-hire companies:

Avis (☑902 180 854; www.avis.es; Gran Vía 60; Ⓜ Santo Domingo or Plaza de España)

Europcar ([📞]902 105 055; www.europcar.es; Calle de San Leonardo de Dios 8; [M]Plaza de España)

Hertz ([📞]902 402 405; www.hertz.es; Edificio de España, Plaza de España 18; [M]Plaza de España)

National/Atesa ([📞]902 100 101; www.atesa. es; underground parking area, Plaza de España; [M]Plaza de España)

Pepecar ([📞]807 414 243; www.pepecar.com; underground parking area, Plaza de España; [M]Plaza de España)

Train

Madrid is served by two main train stations. The bigger of the two is **Puerta de Atocha** (Map p68; [M]Atocha Renfe), at the southern end of the city centre. **Chamartín train station** ([M]Chamartín) lies in the north of the city. The bulk of trains for Spanish destinations depart from Atocha, especially those going south. International services arrive at and leave from Chamartín. For bookings, contact **Renfe** ([📞]902 24 02 02; www. renfe.es) at either train station.

High-speed Tren de Alta Velocidad Española (AVE) services connect Madrid with Seville (via Córdoba), Valladolid (via Segovia), Toledo, Valencia, Málaga and Barcelona (via Zaragoza and Tarragona). Most high-speed services operate from Madrid's Puerta de Atocha station. The Madrid–Segovia/Valladolid service leaves from the Chamartín station.

ℹ Getting Around

Madrid is well served by an excellent and ever-expanding underground rail system (metro) and an extensive bus service. In addition, you can get from the north to the south of the city quickly by using *cercanías* (local trains) between Chamartín and Atocha train stations. Taxis are also a reasonably priced option.

To/From the Airport

Metro (www.metromadrid.es, in Spanish; entrances in T2 & T4) Line 8 of the metro to the Nuevos Ministerios transport interchange, which connects with lines 10 and 6. It operates from 6.05am to 2am. A single ticket costs €1 (10-ride Metrobús ticket €9); there's a €1 supplement if you're travelling to/from the airport in addition to the prices listed above. The journey to Nuevos Ministerios takes around 15 minutes, around 25 minutes from T4.

Bus From T1, T2 and T3 take bus 200 to/from the Intercambiador de Avenida de América (transport interchange on Avenida de América). From T4 take bus 204. The same ticket prices apply as for the metro. There's also a free bus service connecting all four terminals.

AeroCITY ([📞]91 747 75 70; www.aerocity.com; €5-19 per person) A private minibus service that takes you door-to-door between central Madrid and the airport.

Taxi A taxi to the city centre will cost you around €25 in total (up to €35 from T4), depending on traffic and where you're going; in addition to what the meter says, you pay a €5.50 airport supplement.

Bus

Buses operated by **Empresa Municipal de Transportes de Madrid** (EMT; [📞]902 50 78 50; www.emtmadrid.es, in Spanish) travel along most city routes regularly between about 6.30am and 11.30pm. Twenty-six night-bus *búhos* (owls) routes operate from midnight to 6am, with all routes originating in Plaza de la Cibeles.

Cercanías

The short-range *cercanías* regional trains operated by **Renfe** (www.renfe.es/cercanias, in Spanish) go as far afield as El Escorial, Alcalá de Henares, Aranjuez and other points in the Comunidad de Madrid. Tickets range between €1.25 and €4.25 depending on how far you're travelling. In Madrid itself they're handy for making a quick, north–south hop between Chamartín and Atocha train stations (with stops at Nuevos Ministerios and Sol).

Metro

Madrid's modern **metro** ([📞]902 444 403; www. metromadrid.es), Europe's second-largest, is a fast, efficient and safe way to navigate Madrid, and generally easier than getting to grips with bus routes. There are 11 colour-coded lines in central Madrid, in addition to the modern southern suburban MetroSur system, as well as lines heading east to the major population centres of Pozuelo and Boadilla del Monte. Colour maps showing the metro system are available from any metro station. The metro operates from 6.05am to 2am. A single ticket costs €1; a 10-ride Metrobús ticket is €9.

Taxi

You can pick up a taxi at ranks throughout town or simply flag one down. Flag fall is €2.05 from 6am to 10pm daily, €2.20 from 10pm to 6am Sunday to Friday and €3.10 from 10pm Saturday to 6am Sunday. You pay between €0.98 and €1.18 per kilometre depending on the hour. Several supplementary charges, usually posted inside the taxi, apply; these include €5.50 to/from the airport; €2.95 from taxi ranks at train and bus stations, and €2.95 to/from the Parque Ferial Juan Carlos I. There's no charge for luggage.

Taxi services:

Radio-Teléfono Taxi ([📞]91 547 82 00, 91 547 82 00; www.radiotelefono-taxi.com)

Tele-Taxi ([📞]91 371 21 31, 902 501 130)

AROUND MADRID

The Comunidad de Madrid may be small but there are plenty of rewarding excursions that allow you to escape the clamour of city life without straying too far. Imposing San Lorenzo de El Escorial and graceful Aranjuez guard the western and southern gateways to Madrid. Also to the south, the beguiling village of Chinchón is a must-see, while Alcalá de Henares is a stunning university town east of the capital. To the north, picturesque villages (and skiing opportunities) abound in Sierra de Guadarrama and Sierra del Pobre.

San Lorenzo de El Escorial

POP 17,100 / ELEV 1032M

The imposing palace and monastery complex of San Lorenzo de El Escorial is an impressive place, rising up from the foothills of the mountains that shelter Madrid from

the north and west. The one-time royal getaway is now a prim little town overflowing with quaint shops, restaurants and hotels catering primarily to throngs of weekending *madrileños*. The fresh, cool air here has been drawing city dwellers since the complex was first ordered to be built by Felipe II in the 16th century. Most visitors come on a day trip from Madrid.

History

After Felipe II's decisive victory in the Battle of St Quentin against the French on St Lawrence's Day, 10 August 1557, he ordered the construction of the complex in the saint's name above the hamlet of El Escorial. Several villages were razed to make way for the huge monastery, royal palace and mausoleum for Felipe's parents, Carlos I and Isabel. It all flourished under the watchful eye of the architect Juan de Herrera, a towering figure of the Spanish Renaissance.

Comunidad de Madrid

The palace-monastery became an important intellectual centre, with a burgeoning library and art collection, and even a laboratory where scientists could dabble in alchemy. Felipe II died here on 13 September 1598.

In 1854 the monks belonging to the Hieronymite order, who had occupied the monastery from the beginning, were obliged to leave during one of the 19th-century waves of confiscation of religious property by the Spanish state, only to be replaced 30 years later by Augustinians.

◉ Sights

The main entrance to the Real Monasterio de San Lorenzo (www.patrimonionacional.es; admission €8, EU citizen free Wed; ⊙10am-6pm Apr-Sep, 10am-5pm Oct-Mar, closed Mon) is on its western facade. Above the gateway a statue of St Lawrence stands guard, holding a symbolic gridiron, the instrument of his martyrdom (he was roasted alive on one). From here you'll first enter the **Patio de los Reyes**, which houses the statues of the six kings of Judah.

Directly ahead lies the sombre **basilica**. As you enter, look up at the unusual flat vaulting by the choir stalls. Once inside the church proper, turn left to view Benvenuto Cellini's white Carrara marble statue of Christ crucified (1576).

The remainder of the ground floor contains various treasures, including some tapestries and an El Greco painting – impressive as it is, it's a far cry from El Greco's dream of decorating the whole complex – and then downstairs to the northeastern corner of the complex. You pass through the **Museo de Arquitectura** and the **Museo de Pintura**. The former tells (in Spanish) the story of how the complex was built, the latter contains a range of 16th- and 17th-century Italian, Spanish and Flemish art.

Head upstairs into a gallery around the eastern part of the complex known as the **Palacio de Felipe II** or **Palacio de los Austrias**. You'll then descend to the 17th-century **Panteón de los Reyes** (Crypt of the Kings), where almost all Spain's monarchs since Carlos I are interred. Backtracking a little, you'll find yourself in the **Panteón de los Infantes** (Crypt of the Princesses).

Stairs lead up from the **Patio de los Evangelistas** (Patio of the Gospels) to the **Salas Capitulares** (chapterhouses) in the southeastern corner of the monastery. These bright, airy rooms, whose ceilings are richly frescoed, contain works by El Greco, Titian, Tintoretto, José de Ribera and Hieronymus Bosch (known as El Bosco to Spaniards).

Just south of the monastery is the Huerta de los Frailes (Friars Garden; ⊙10am-7pm Apr-Sep), which merits a stroll, while the Jardín del Príncipe (⊙10am-7pm Apr-Sep), which leads down to the town of El Escorial (and the train station), contains the Casita del Príncipe (guided visits adult/student €3.60/2; ⊙10am-1pm & 4-6.30pm Tue-Sun), a little neoclassical gem built in 1772 by Juan de Villanueva under Carlos III for his heir, Carlos IV.

❶ Information

Tourist office (☑91 890 53 13; www.sanlorenzoturismo.org; Calle de Grimaldi 2; ⊙10am-2pm & 3-6pm Tue-Sat, 10am-2pm Sun)

❶ Getting There & Away

Every 15 minutes (every 30 minutes on weekends) **Herranz** (☑91 890 41 00) sends buses 661 and 664 to El Escorial (€3.35, one hour) from platform 30 at the Intercambiador de Autobuses de Moncloa.

San Lorenzo de El Escorial is 59km northwest of Madrid and it takes 40 minutes to drive there. Take the A6 highway to the M600, then follow the signs to El Escorial.

A few dozen **Renfe** (☑902 24 02 02; www.renfe.es) C8 *cercanías* make the trip daily from Madrid's Atocha or Chamartín train station to El Escorial (€1.25, one hour).

South of Madrid

Warner Brothers Movie World   THEME PARK
(☑902 024 100; www.parquewarner.com; San Martín de la Vega; adult/child €38/29; ⊙hr vary) Disney World it ain't but this movie theme-park, 25km south of central Madrid, has much to catch the attention. Kids will love the chance to hang out with Tom and Jerry, while the young-at-heart film buffs among you will be similarly taken with the Wild West or remakes of the studio sets for such Hollywood 'greats' as *Police Academy*. Entrance to the park is via Hollywood Boulevard, not unlike LA's Sunset Boulevard, whereafter you can choose between Cartoon World, the Old West, Hollywood Boulevard, Super Heroes (featuring Superman, Batman and the finks of Gotham City) and finally Warner Brothers Movie World Studios. It's all about the stars of the silver screen coming to life as life-sized cartoon

characters roam the grounds, and rides and high-speed roller coasters distract you if attention starts to wane. There are also restaurants and shops. Opening times are complex and do change – check before heading out.

To get here by public transport, take the *cercanías* train C3 for Aranjuez from Atocha station, then change at Pinto for the 3a line to Parque de Ocio station.

ARANJUEZ
POP 49,100

Aranjuez was founded as a royal pleasure retreat, away from the riff-raff of Madrid, and it remains an easy day trip to escape the rigours of city life. The palace is opulent, but the fresh air and ample gardens are what really stand out.

◉ Sights

Palacio Real PALACE
(www.patrimonionacional.es; adult/child, EU senior & student €5/2.55, EU citizen free Wed, gardens free; ☺palace 10am-6.15pm Tue-Sun Apr-Sep, gardens 8am-8.30pm mid-Jun–mid-Aug) The Royal Palace started as one of Felipe II's modest summer palaces but took on a life of its own as a succession of royals, inspired by the palace at Versailles in France, lavished money upon it. By the 18th century its 300-plus rooms had turned the palace into a sprawling, gracefully symmetrical complex filled with a cornucopia of ornamentation. Of all the rulers who spent time here, Carlos III and Isabel II left the greatest mark.

The obligatory guided tour (in Spanish) provides insight into the palace's art and history. And a stroll in the lush **gardens** takes you through a mix of local and exotic species, the product of seeds brought back by Spanish botanists and explorers from Spanish colonies all over the world. Within their shady perimeter, which stretches a few kilometres from the palace, you'll find the **Casa de Marinos**, which contains the Museo de Falúas (admission €3; ☺10am-4pm Oct-Mar, 10am-6.15pm Apr-Sep), a museum of royal pleasure boats from days gone by. The 18th-century neoclassical Casa del Labrador (adult/child, senior or student €5/2.50; ☺10am-6pm Tue-Sun Apr-Sep) is also worth a visit. Further away, towards Chinchón, is the Jardín del Príncipe, an extension of the massive gardens. The Chiquitren (www.arantour.com; adult/child €5/3; ☺10am-8pm Tue-Sun Mar-Sep), a small tourist train, loops through town and stops at all the major sites.

✕ Eating

Casa José LOCAL CUISINE €€€
(☏91 891 14 88; www.casajose.es; Calle de Abastos 32; meals €50-60; ☺lunch & dinner Tue-Sat, lunch Sun) The quietly elegant Casa José is the proud owner of a Michelin star and is packed on weekends with *madrileños* drawn here by the beautifully prepared meats and local dishes.

Pabelete TAPAS €€
(Calle de Stuart 108; meals €25-30; ☺lunch & dinner Wed-Mon) Going strong since 1946, this casual tapas bar has a loyal following far beyond Aranjuez. Its *croquetas* are a major drawcard, as is the stuffed squid. It's all about traditional cooking at its best without too many elaborations.

❶ Information

Tourist office (☏91 891 04 27; www.aranjuez. es, in Spanish; Antigua Carretera de Andalucía; ☺10am-8.30pm May-Oct)

❶ Getting There & Away

Coming by car from Madrid, take the N-IV south to the M-305, which leads to the city centre.

The **AISA bus company** (☏902 198 788; www.aisa-grupo.com, in Spanish) sends buses (route number 423) to Aranjuez from Madrid's Estación Sur every 15 minutes or so. The 45-minute trip costs €3.35.

From Madrid's Atocha station, C3 *cercanías* trains leave every 15 or 20 minutes for Aranjuez. The 45-minute trip costs €3.20.

CHINCHÓN
POP 5100

Chinchón is just 45km from Madrid but worlds apart. Although it has grown beyond its village confines, visiting its antique heart is like stepping back into a charming, ramshackle past. It's worth an overnight stay to really soak it up, and lunch in one of the *méson* (tavern)-style restaurants around the plaza is another must.

◉ Sights

The heart of town is its unique, almost circular Plaza Mayor, which is lined with sagging, tiered balconies – it wins our vote as one of the most evocative *plazas mayores* in Spain. In summer the plaza is converted into a bullring, and it's also the stage for a popular Passion play shown at Easter.

Chinchón's historical monuments won't detain you long, but you should take a quick look at the 16th-century Iglesia de la Asunción, which rises above Plaza Mayor, and

THE STRAWBERRY TRAIN

You could take a normal train from Madrid to Aranjuez, but for romance it's hard to beat the **Tren de la Fresa** (Strawberry Train; ☎902 240 202, 902 228 822; www.museo delferrocarril.org, in Spanish; adult/child return €26/18; ☉May-Oct). Begun in 1985 to commemorate the Madrid–Aranjuez route – Madrid's first and Spain's third rail line, which was inaugurated in the 1850s – the Strawberry Train is a throwback to the time when Spanish royalty would escape the summer heat and head for the royal palace at Aranjuez.

The journey begins at 10am on Saturday and Sunday between early May and late October when an antique Mikado 141F-2413 steam engine pulls out from Madrid's Museo del Ferrocarril (see the boxed text, p86), pulling behind it four passenger carriages that date from the early 20th century and have old-style front and back balconies. During the 50-minute journey, rail staff in period dress provide samples of local strawberries – one of the original train's purposes was to allow royalty to sample the summer strawberry crop from the Aranjuez orchards. Upon arrival in Aranjuez, your ticket fare includes a guided tour of the Palacio Real, Museo de Falúas and other Aranjuez sights, not to mention more strawberry samplings. The train leaves Aranjuez for Madrid at 6.25pm for the return journey.

the late-16th-century Renaissance **Castillo de los Condes**, out of town to the south. The castle was abandoned in the 1700s and was last used as a liquor factory. Ask at the tourist office to see if they're open.

✦ Festivals & Events

Fiesta Mayor   VILLAGE FESTIVAL

The town's main plaza is turned into a bullring during the annual fiesta, held from the 12th to the 18th of August.

🛏 Sleeping

Hostal Chinchón   HOSTAL €

(☎91 893 53 98; www.hostalchinchon.com, in Spanish; Calle Grande 16; s/d €40/48; ⊠) The public areas here are nicer than the smallish rooms, which are clean but worn around the edges. The highlight is the surprise rooftop pool overlooking Plaza Mayor.

Parador Nacional   PARADOR €€

(☎91 894 08 36; www.parador.es; Avenida Generalísimo 1; d from €137) The former Convento de Agustinos (Augustine Convent), Parador Nacional is one of the town's most important historical buildings and can't be beaten for luxury. It's worth stopping by for a meal or coffee (and a peek around) even if you don't stay here.

🍴 Eating

Chinchón is loaded with traditional-style restaurants dishing up *cordero asado* (roast lamb). But if you're after something a little lighter, there is nothing better than

savouring a few tapas and drinks on sunny Plaza Mayor.

Mesón Cuevas del Vino   LOCAL FOOD €€

(☎91 894 02 06; www.cuevasdelvino.com; Calle Benito Hortelano 13; meals €35-40; ☉lunch & dinner Wed-Sat & Mon, lunch Sun) From the huge goatskins filled with wine and the barrels covered in famous signatures to the atmospheric caves underground, this is sure to be a memorable eating experience with delicious home-style cooking.

Café de la Iberia   ROAST MEAT €€

(☎91 894 08 47; www.cafedelaiberia.com; Plaza Mayor 17; meals €35-40) This is definitely our favourite of the *mesones* on the Plaza Mayor perimeter. It offers wonderful food, attentive staff and an atmospheric dining area – eat in the light-filled internal courtyard (where Goya is said to have visited) or on the balcony. The speciality is succulent *cochinillo asado* (roast suckling pig).

ℹ Information

Tourist office (☎91 893 53 23; www.ciudad -chinchon.com; Plaza Mayor 6; ☉10am-7pm)

ℹ Getting There & Away

La Veloz (☎91 409 76 02) has half-hourly services (bus 337) to Chinchón (€3.35, 50 minutes). The buses leave from Avenida del Mediterráneo, 100m east of Plaza del Conde de Casal.

Sitting 45km southeast of Madrid, Chinchón is easy to reach by car. Take the N-IV motorway and exit onto the M404, which makes its way to Chinchón.

Alcalá de Henares

POP 199.500

East of Madrid, Alcalá de Henares is full of surprises with historical sandstone buildings seemingly at every turn. Throw in some sunny squares and a legendary university, and it's a terrific place to escape the capital for a few hours.

◉ Sights

FREE **University** UNIVERSITY
(☏91 883 43 84; 6 free guided tours per day Mon-Fri, 11 per day Sat & Sun; ⊙9am-9pm) Founded in 1486 by Cardinal Cisneros, this is one of the country's principal seats of learning. A guided tour gives a peek into the *mudéjar* **chapel** and the magnificent **Paraninfo** auditorium, where the King and Queen of Spain give out the prestigious Premio Cervantes literary award every year.

FREE **Museo Casa Natal de Miguel de Cervantes** MUSEUM
(www.museo-casa-natal-cervantes.org; Calle Mayor 48; ⊙10am-6pm Tue-Sun) The town is dear to Spaniards because it is the birthplace of literary figurehead Miguel de Cervantes Saavedra. The site believed by many to be Cervantes' birthplace is re-created in this illuminating museum, which lies along the beautiful, colonnaded Calle Mayor.

✗ Eating

Baratería TAPAS €€
(☏91 888 59 25; Calle de los Cerrajeros 18; meals €25-35; ⊙lunch & dinner Mon-Sat, lunch Sun) A wine bar, tapas bar and restaurant all rolled into one, Baratería is a fine place to eat whatever your mood. Grilled meats are the star of the show, with the ribs with honey in particular a local favourite.

Hostería del Estudiante CASTILIAN €€
(☏91 888 03 30; Calle de los Colegios 3; menús €40-50) Based in the *parador*, this charming restaurant has wonderful Castilian cooking and a classy ambience in a dining room decorated with artefacts from the city's illustrious history.

ℹ Information

Tourist office (☏91 881 06 34; www.turismo alcala.com, in Spanish; Plaza de los Santos Niños; ⊙10am-2pm & 5-7.30pm Jun-Sep)

ℹ Getting There & Away

Alcalá de Henares is just 35km east of Madrid, heading towards Zaragoza along the A2.

There are regular bus departures (every five to 15 minutes) from Madrid's Intercambiador de Avenida de América. The trip takes about one hour (€2.99).

Train C2 and C7 *cercanías* trains (€1.25) make the 50-minute trip to Alcalá de Henares daily.

Sierra de Guadarrama

North of Madrid lies the Sierra de Guadarrama, a popular skiing destination and home of several charming towns. In Manzanares El Real you can explore the small 15th-century Castillo de los Mendoza (Manzanares El Real; admission incl guided tour €2.50; ⊙10am-2pm & 3-6pm Tue-Sun Apr-Sep, 10am-5pm Tue-Sun Oct-Mar), a storybook castle with round towers at its corners and a Gothic interior patio.

Cercedilla is a popular base for hikers and mountain bikers. There are several marked trails, the main one known as the **Cuerda Larga** or **Cuerda Castellana**. This is a forest track that takes in 55 peaks between the Puerto de Somosierra in the north and Puerto de la Cruz Verde in the southwest. Small ski resorts, such as Valdesqui (www. valdesqui.es, in Spanish; Puerto de Cotos; day/afternoon lift tickets €36/21; ⊙9am-4pm) and Navacerrada (www.puertonavacerrada.com, in Spanish; lift tickets €25-30; ⊙9.30am-5pm) welcome weekend skiers from the city.

From Madrid's Chamartín train station, you can get to Puerto de Navacerrada on the C8B *cercanías* line (€1.85, two hours with train change in Cercedilla, four daily). Bus 691 from platform 14 of Madrid's Intercambiador de Autobuses de Moncloa also runs here regularly (€2.75, one hour).

ℹ Information

Centro de Información Valle de la Fuenfría (☏91 852 22 13; Carretera de las Dehesas; ⊙10am-6pm) Located 2km outside Cercedilla on the M-614.

Navacerrada Tourist Office (☏91 856 03 08; www.navacerrada.es, in Spanish)

ℹ Getting There & Away

By car from Madrid, take the A-6 motorway to Cercedilla.

Bus 724 runs to Manzanares El Real from Plaza de Castilla in Madrid (€2.90, 45 minutes). From Madrid's Intercambiador de Autobuses de Moncloa, bus 691 heads to Navacerrada (€3.70, one hour) and bus 684 runs to Cercedilla (€3.70, one hour).

From Chamartín station you can get to Puerto de Navacerrada (C8B *cercanías* line; €6, two hours with train change in Cercedilla, four daily) and Cercedilla (C2 *cercanías* line; €3.20, one hour 20 minutes, 15 daily).

Palacio Real de El Pardo

Built in the 15th century and remodelled in the 17th, this opulent palace (www.patrimonionacional.es; Calle de Manuel Alonso; admission incl guided tour €4; ☉10.30am-5.45pm Mon-Sat, 9.30am-1.30pm Sun Apr-Sep) was Franco's favourite residence. It's surrounded by lush gardens (which close one hour later than the palace) and on Sunday fills with *madrileño* families looking for a bit of fresh air and a hearty lunch. Of the art on display inside, the tapestries stand out, particularly those based on cartoons by Goya.

If you're driving from Madrid take the M40 to the C601, which leads to El Pardo. The 13km trip takes just 15 minutes. You can also take bus 601 (€1.40, 25 minutes), which leaves every five to 10 minutes from Madrid's Intercambiador de Autobuses de Moncloa.

Buitrago & Sierra Pobre

The 'Poor Sierra' is a toned-down version of its more refined western neighbour, the Sierra de Guadarrama. Popular with hikers and others looking for nature without quite so many creature comforts or crowds, the sleepy Sierra Pobre has yet to develop the tourism industry of its neighbours. And that's just why we like it.

Head first to Buitrago, the largest town in the area, where you can stroll along part of the old city walls. You can also take a peek into the 15th-century *mudéjar* and Romanesque Iglesia de Santa María del Castillo and into the small and unlikely Picasso Museum (Plaza Picasso 1; admission free; ☉11am-1.45pm & 4-6pm Tue, Thu & Fri, 11am-1.45 Wed, 10am-2pm & 4-7pm Sat, 10am-2pm Sun), which contains a few works that the artist gave to his barber, Eugenio Arias.

Hamlets are scattered throughout the rest of the sierra; some, like Puebla de la Sierra and El Atazar, are pretty walks and are the starting point for winding hill trails.

✕ Eating

El Arco   LOCAL FOOD **€€**
(☑91 868 09 11; Calle Arco 6; meals €35-45; ☉lunch Fri-Sun mid-Sep–mid-Jun, lunch & dinner Tue-Sat & lunch Sun mid-Jun–mid-Sep) The best restaurant in the region, El Arco is located in Villavieja del Lozoya, close to Buitrago, and is known for its fresh, creative cuisine based on local ingredients and traditional northern Spanish dishes. The desserts and wine list also stand out.

❶ Information

Buitrago Tourist Office (☑91 868 16 15; ☉9am-3pm Jul-Sep)

❶ Getting There & Away

By car from Madrid, take the N-I highway to Buitrago.

Buses (line 191) leave hourly from Madrid's Plaza de la Castilla to Buitrago (€4.90, 1½ hours).

Castilla y León

Best Places to Eat

» Restaurante El Fogón Sefardí (p152)
» El Caballo de Troya (p157)
» El Llar (p172)

Best Places to Stay

» El Milano Real (p131)
» Hotel El Rastro (p128)
» Hospedería La Gran Casa Mudéjar (p149)

Why Go?

If you're looking for a window on the Spanish soul, head to Castilla y León. This is red-blooded Spain without the stereotypes, with vast plains, spectacular mountain peaks and evocative medieval towns. Experience fabled cities like Salamanca, with its lively student population, and Segovia, famed for a fairy-tale fortress that inspired Disneyland's Sleeping Beauty castle. The multiturreted walls of Avila have similar magical appeal, while the lofty cathedrals of León and Burgos are among Europe's most impressive.

But the region's story is also told through quiet back roads, half-timbered hamlets and imposing isolated castles. From the scenic Sierra de Francia in the southwest to Covarrubias, Calatañazor and Medinaceli in the east, this is the hidden Spain most travellers never imagined still existed.

This is also serious meat-and-no-veg country, with Spaniards travelling from afar to sample the region's famed roast lamb and suckling pig, served in traditional wood-panelled *asadores*.

When to Go

Leon

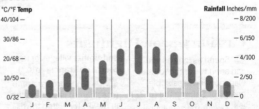

March-April
Enjoy wild flowers in the countryside and soul-stirring Semana Santa processions.

June Get into holiday mode during annual fiesta time in Burgos, Soria and Segovia.

September Capture the youthful buzz of Salamanca and the university cities.

THE SOUTHWEST

You could easily spend a week or more in southwestern Castilla y León, one of the region's most engaging corners. Salamanca and Ávila are two of the most appealing towns in central Spain, but the beautiful Sierra de Gredos and the time-worn villages of the Sierra de Francia and Sierra de Béjar promise fascinating breaks from city life.

Ávila

POP 56,900 / ELEV 1130M

Ávila's old city, surrounded by imposing city walls comprising eight monumental

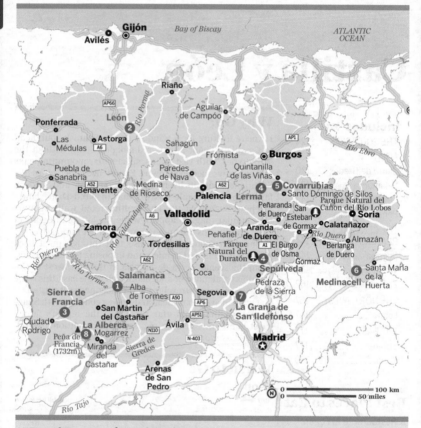

Castilla y León Highlights

1 Spend as long as you can amid the architectural elegance and irresistible energy of **Salamanca** (p132)

2 Savour the sepulchral light in León's **cathedral** (p166), a kaleidoscopic vision of glass and stone

3 Lose yourself in the land time forgot amid the stone-and-timber villages of the **Sierra de Francia** (p142)

4 Dine on *cordero asado* (roast lamb) like a Castilian in the pretty hilltop towns of **Lerma** (p184) or **Sepúlveda** (p186)

5 Escape city life in the exquisite historic village of **Covarrubias** (p182)

6 Stroll along the tranquil cobbled streets at **Medinaceli** (p192)

7 Play hide and seek at **La Granja de San Ildefonso's** classic maze (p154)

8 Shop for honey and other local gourmet goodies at the Saturday morning market in picturesque **La Alberca** (p142)

gates, 88 watchtowers and more than 2500 turrets, is one of the best-preserved medieval bastions in all Spain. In winter, when an icy wind whistles in off the plains, the old city huddles behind the high stone walls as if seeking protection from the harsh Castilian climate. At night, when the walls are illuminated to magical effect, you will wonder if you've stumbled into a fairy tale.

Within the walls, Ávila can appear caught in a time warp. It's a deeply religious city that, for centuries, has drawn pilgrims to the cult of Santa Teresa de Ávila, with many churches, convents and high-walled palaces. As such, Ávila is the essence of Castilla, the epitome of old Spain.

History

According to myth, one of Hercules' sons founded Ávila. The more prosaic truth credits obscure Iberian tribes, who were later Romanised, then Christianised. For almost 300 years Ávila changed hands between Muslims and Christians, until the fall of Toledo to Alfonso VI in 1085. 'Ávila of the Knights' became an important commercial centre with a well-established noble class, although the 1492 edict expelling all Jews from Spain robbed the city of much of its lifeblood.

⊙ Sights

Just about all the main sights are located in the old centre which fans out west of the *catedral* (cathedral).

Murallas   DEFENSIVE WALLS

(adult/child €4/2.50) Ávila's splendid 12th-century walls rank among the world's best-preserved medieval defensive perimeters. Raised to a height of 12m between the 11th and 12th centuries, the walls stretch for 2.5km atop the remains of earlier Roman and Muslim battlements. They have been much restored and modified, with various Gothic and Renaissance touches, and even some Roman stones re-used in the construction. At dusk the walls attract swirls of swooping and diving swallows.

The two access points are at the Puerta del Alcázar and the Puerta de los Leales (⊘10am-8pm Tue-Sun for both), with walks of 300m and 1200m, respectively. The same ticket allows you to climb both sections; the last ones are sold at 7.30pm.

FREE Convento de Santa Teresa
                                              CONVENT
(Plaza de la Santa; ⊘8.45am-1.30pm & 3.30-9pm Tue-Sun) Built in 1636 over the saint's birth-

place, this is the epicentre of the cult surrounding Teresa. The room where she was born in 1515 is now a chapel smothered in gold; it is lorded over by a baroque altar by Gregorio Fernández and features a statue of the saint. An adjoining relics room (⊘10am-2pm & 4-7pm) is crammed with Teresa relics, some of which, such as her ring finger (complete with ring), border on the macabre (but that didn't stop Franco from keeping it by his bedside throughout his rule). There's also a small museum (admission €2; ⊘10am-2pm & 4-7pm) dedicated to the saint and accessible from Calle Aizpuru.

Monasterio de la Encarnación   MONASTERY

(Calle de la Encarnación; admission €1.70; ⊘9.30am-1.30pm & 3.30-6pm) North of the city walls, this unadorned monastery is where Santa Teresa fully took on the monastic life and lived for 27 years. A Renaissance complex modified in the 18th century, it contains further mementoes of her life, as well as a replica of her suitably spartan cell. To reach here, head north from Plaza de Fuente el Sol, via Calle de la Encarnación, for approximately half a kilometre.

Iglesia de Santo Tomé El Viejo   CHURCH

(Plaza de Italia; admission €1.20; ⊘10am-2pm & 4-7pm Tue-Sat, 10am-2pm Sun) This church dates from the 13th century, and it was from this pulpit that Santa Teresa was castigated most vehemently for her reforms. It has been impressively restored to house mostly Roman foundation stones and a splendid floor mosaic.

Los Cuatro Postes   BEST VIEWS

Northwest of the city, on the road to Salamanca, this camera-clicking spot provides fine views of Ávila's walls. It also marks the place where Santa Teresa and her brother were caught by their uncle as they tried to run away from home (they were hoping to achieve martyrdom at the hands of the Muslims). The best views are at night.

Real Monasterio de Santo Tomás
                                              MONASTERY
(www.monasteriosantotomas.com; Plaza de Granada 1; admission €3; ⊘10am-1pm & 4-8pm) Although it is a good 10 minutes' walk southeast from the city walls, this monastery is well worth the side step. Commissioned by the Reyes Católicos (Catholic Monarchs), Fernando and Isabel, and completed in 1492, it is an exquisite example of Isabelline architecture, rich in historical resonance. Three interconnected cloisters

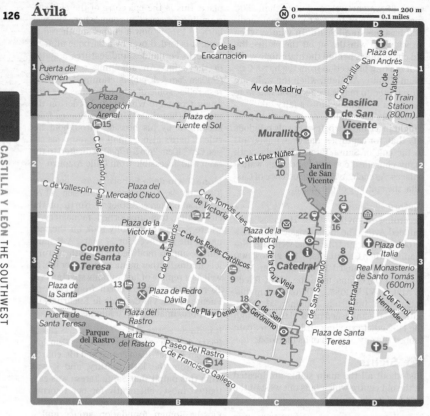

Ávila

Teresa de Cepeda y Ahumada, probably the most important woman in the history of the Spanish Catholic Church, was born in Ávila on 28 March 1515, one of 10 children of a merchant family. Raised by Augustinian nuns after her mother's death, she joined the Carmelite order at age 20. After her early, undistinguished years as a nun, she was shaken by a vision of hell in 1560, which crystallised her true vocation: she would reform the Carmelites.

In stark contrast to the opulence of the church in 16th-century Spain, her reforms called for the church to return to its roots, taking on the suffering and simple lifestyle of Jesus Christ. The Carmelites demanded the strictest of piety, went *descalzadas* (barefoot), lived in extremely basic conditions and even employed flagellation to atone for their sins. Not surprisingly, all this proved extremely unpopular with the mainstream Catholic Church.

With the help of many supporters, Teresa founded convents of the Carmelitas Descalzas (Shoeless Carmelites) all over Spain. She also co-opted San Juan de la Cruz (St John of the Cross) to undertake a similar reform in the masculine order, a task that earned him several stints of incarceration. Santa Teresa's writings were first published in 1588 and proved enormously popular, perhaps partly for their earthy style. She died in 1582 in Alba de Tormes, where she is buried and was canonised by Pope Gregory XV in 1622.

Unsurprisingly, Santa Teresa casts a long shadow over Ávila. From the convent, plaza and gate that bear her name, to the sweet *yemas de Santa Teresa* (yummy cookies made with egg yolk and supposedly invented by the saint), her trail covers every inch of the city.

lead up to the church that contains the alabaster tomb of Don Juan, the monarchs' only son. It is backed by an altarpiece by Pedro de Berruguete depicting scenes from the life of St Thomas Aquinas. The magnificent choir stalls, in Flemish Gothic style, are accessible from the upper level of the third cloister, the Claustro de los Reyes, so called because Fernando and Isabel often attended Mass here. It's thought that the Grand Inquisitor Torquemada is buried in the sacristy. The admission price also covers the entrance to the impressive Museo Oriental (Oriental Museum) with 11 galleries of art from the Far East, as well as a more modest Museo de Historia Natural (Natural History Museum); both are located within the monastery complex. To get here, head southeast from Jardín de San Vicente along Calle de Ferrol Hernandez and Avenida del Alférez Provisional.

Ávila Catedral
CATHEDRAL

(Plaza de la Catedral; admission €4; ☺10am-7pm Mon-Sat, noon-6pm Sun) Ávila's 12th-century cathedral is not just a house of worship, but also an ingenious fortress: its stout granite apse forms the central bulwark in the heavily fortified eastern wall of the town. Although the main facade hints at the cathedral's 12th-century, Romanesque origins, the church was finished 400 years later in a predominantly Gothic style, making it the first Gothic church in Spain. The sombre grey facade betrays some unhappy 18th-century meddling in the main portal.

The interior is a different story, with playful red-and-white limestone columns along the long, narrow central nave that makes the soaring ceilings seem all the more majestic. Renaissance-era carved walnut choir stalls and a dazzling altar painting begun by Pedro de Berruguete, showing the life of Jesus in 24 scenes, are other highlights of the inner sanctum. Off the fine cloisters, a small museum contains a painting by El Greco and a splendid silver monstrance by Juan de Arfe.

Basílica de San Vicente
ROMANESQUE CHURCH

(www.basilicasanvicente.com; Plaza de San Vicente; admission €2; ☺10am-1.30pm & 4-6pm) Much of Ávila's religious architecture is sombre and brooding, but this graceful Romanesque church is a masterpiece of the subdued elegance of Romanesque style: a series of largely Gothic modifications in sober granite contrast with the warm sandstone of the Romanesque original. Work started in the 11th century, supposedly on the site where three martyrs – San Vicente and his sisters – were slaughtered by the Romans in the early 4th century. Their canopied cenotaph is an outstanding piece of Romanesque with nods to the Gothic; don't forget to take a peek at the crypt. The Jardín de San Vicente across the road was once a Roman cemetery.

FIglesia de San Juan Bautista   CHURCH
(Plaza de la Victoria; ⊙before & after Mass) Dates from the 16th century and contains the font in which Santa Teresa was baptised.

Iglesia de San Pedro   CHURCH
(Plaza de Santa Teresa; ⊙10.30am-noon & 7-8pm) One of the city's later churches, its light, sandstone exterior is a pleasant complement to the granite austerity that reigns inside the city walls. An ugly block of modern offices on an adjacent side of the plaza has caused local outrage because of its inappropriateness.

Iglesia de San Andrés   OLDEST CHURCH
(Plaza de San Andrés; ⊙10am-2pm & 4-6pm Mon-Sat) Located north of the old city and dating from the 12th century, this is Ávila's oldest church and a pure example of Romanesque architecture.

FREE Palacio Los Serrano   CULTURAL CENTRE
(Plaza de Italia; ⊙7.30-9.30pm Mon-Fri, noon-2pm & 7.30-9.30pm Sat & Sun) A cultural centre, also used for contemporary art exhibitions.

Museo Provincial   PROVINCIAL MUSEUM
(admission €1.20, Sat & Sun free; ⊙10am-2pm & 4-7pm Tue-Sat, 10am-2pm Sun) Includes Roman artefacts and some fine medieval paintings.

Murallito   TOURIST TRAIN
(www.murallitoavila.com, in Spanish; adult/child €4/3; ⛟) This nifty tourist train makes a complete circuit of the city walls with a few other sights thrown in.

Festivals & Events
Ávila has two principal festivals:

Semana Santa   EASTER WEEK
Ávila is one of the best places in Castilla y León to watch the solemn processions of Easter. It all begins on Holy Thursday and the most evocative event is the early morning (around 5am) Good Friday procession which circles the city wall.

Fiesta de Santa Teresa   PATRON SAINT
Annual festival during the second week of October honouring the city's patron saint with processions, concerts and fireworks.

Sleeping
Staying overnight at a hotel within Ávila's historic walls immerses you in the medieval tranquillity that is the city's hallmark.

TOP CHOICE Hotel Las Leyendas   HISTORIC HOTEL €€
(☎920 35 20 42; www.lasleyendas.es; Calle de Francisco Gallego 3; s/d €69/89; ❋☎) Occupying the house of 16th-century Ávila nobility, this intimate hotel overflows with period touches (original wooden beams, exposed brick and stonework) wedded to modern amenities. Some rooms have marvellous views out across the plains, while others look onto an internal garden. The hotel's restaurant, La Bruja (www.la-bruja.es), has some tempting appetisers, including a *selección de quesos artesanos* (selection of local cheeses; €14).

Hotel El Rastro   HISTORIC HOTEL €€
(☎920 35 22 25; www.elrastroavila.com; Calle Cepedas; s/d from €55/65; ❋☎) Not to be confused with the *hostal* (budget hotel) of the same name (run by the same owners), this superb choice is located in a former 16th-century palace. Natural stone, exposed brickwork and a warm colour scheme of earth tones exude a calming understated elegance. The rooms are spacious and stylish.

Hostal Arco San Vicente   BUDGET HOTEL €€
(☎920 22 24 98; www.arcosanvicente.com; Calle de López Núñez 6; s/d €55/65; P☎) This gleaming *hostal* has small, blue-carpeted rooms with pale paintwork and wrought-iron bed heads. The location, just inside Puerta de San Vicente, and the parking (€10), are additional perks.

Parador Raimundo de Borgoña   HISTORIC PARADOR €€€
(☎920 21 13 40; www.parador.es; Marques de Canales y Chozas 2; d/ste €150/285; ❋☎) Occupying a 16th-century palace hard up against the wall in the north of the old town, Parador Raimundo de Borgoña has all the essential elements of the *parador* chain: elegant public areas, helpful staff and stylish bedrooms.

Hostal San Juan   BUDGET HOTEL €
(☎920 25 14 75; www.hostalsanjuan.es; Calle de los Comuneros de Castilla 3; s/d €30/48; ☎)

With warm tones throughout, Hostal San Juan is pleasant, friendly and close to everything in Ávila. The recent addition of a small fitness room, complete with exercise machines, is a real one-off in this budget category.

Hospedería La Sinagoga
BOUTIQUE HOTEL €€

(☎920 35 23 21; Calle de los Reyes Católicos 22; s/d/tr €53/74/106; ❄) Delightful small hotel incorporates details from Ávila's main 15th-century synagogue. Choose carefully as some rooms can be a little dark.

Hostería Las Cancelas
CLASSIC HOTEL €€

(☎920 21 22 49; www.lascancelas.com; Calle de la Cruz Vieja 6; s/d/tr €53/76/107; ☺Feb-Dec) Tucked away behind the cathedral, this place has large rooms with traditional furniture and a superb restaurant.

Hostal El Rastro
BUDGET HOTEL €

(☎920 21 12 18; www.elrastroavila.com; Plaza del Rastro 4; s/d €33/50; ❄) The whole place oozes old-world charm with seven quaint rooms overlooking a quiet central square.

✗ Eating

Ávila is famous for its *chuleton de Ávila* (T-bone steak) and *judías del barco de Ávila* (white beans, often with chorizo, in a thick sauce). There is a wide selection of restaurants within Ávila's historic walls, while the perimeter road – Calle de San Segundo – also has a reliable choice of eateries, especially around Puerta de los Leales.

Hostería Las Cancelas
SOPHISTICATED REGIONAL €€

(☎920 21 22 49; www.lascancelas.com; Calle de la Cruz Vieja 6; meals €30-40; ☺Feb-Dec) Part of the hotel of the same name, this courtyard restaurant occupies a delightful interior patio dating back to the 15th century. Renowned for being a mainstay of Ávila cuisine, traditional meals are prepared with a salutary attention to detail. Reservations recommended.

La Flor de Castilla
LIGHT MEALS €

(Calle de San Gerónimo; ☺9am-10pm; meals €15-20; ☎) This patisserie-cum-restaurant is not only a fine place to buy a *yema de Santa Teresa,* (a sticky, ultra sweet cookie made of egg yolk and sugar), but also a rare place that serves red-meat alternatives like quiches and fettuccini with a choice of sauces.

Mesón del Rastro
TRADITIONAL CASTILIAN €€

(Plaza del Rastro 1; menú del día €12; ☺Thu-Sat, lunch only Sun-Wed) The dark-wood beamed interior announces immediately that this is a bastion of robust Castilian cooking. Expect delicious mainstays such as *judías del barco de Ávila* and *cordero asado* (roast lamb) and, regrettably, the occasional coach tour.

Restaurante Reyes Católicos
CREATIVE REGIONAL €€

(www.restaurante-reyescatolicos.com, in Spanish; Calle de los Reyes Católicos 6; menú del día €15, meals €25-35) Fronted by a popular tapas bar, this place has bright decor and an accomplished kitchen that churns out traditional dishes that benefit from a creative tweak.

Posada de la Fruta
TRADITIONAL CASTILIAN €

(www.posadadelafruta.com, in Spanish; Plaza de Pedro Dávila 8; meals €10-15) Simple tasty meals can be had in a light-filled, covered courtyard, while the traditional *comedor* (dining room) caters to a conservative palate.

Casa de Postas
TRADITIONAL CASTILIAN €€

(www.casadepostas.com, in Spanish; Calle de San Segundo 40; menú del día €12, meals €30-35; ☺Wed-Mon) A busy tavern for tapas with an elegant restaurant upstairs for deftly executed traditional dishes.

☕ Drinking

Ávila is long on saints but short on discos, so nights aren't particularly lively. There are a few spots worth seeking out.

TOP CHOICE La Bodeguita de San Segundo
WINE BAR

(www.vinoavila.com, in Spanish; Calle de San Segundo 19; ☺11am-midnight Thu-Tue) Situated in the 16th-century Casa de la Misericordia, this superb wine bar is standing-room only most nights and more tranquil in the quieter afternoon hours when you can head for the clutch of chairs near the kitchen and enjoy unusual *raciones* (large tapas) like four cheese fondue.

Café del Adarve
MUSIC BAR

(Calle de San Segundo 40; ☺5pm-3am) About as lively as Ávila gets, Café del Adarve has quirky decor, edgy art exhibitions, weekend DJs and regular live jazz on Thursdays. There's a terrace for al fresco quaffing in summer.

WHAT'S COOKING IN CASTILLA Y LEÓN?

Castilla y León's cuisine owes everything to climate. There's no better way to fortify yourself against the bitterly cold winters of the high plateau than with *cordero asado* (roast lamb), a signature dish from Sepúlveda to Burgos and every town in between. *Cochinillo asado* (roast suckling pig) is a speciality of Segovia. Other regional specialities include *morcilla de Burgos* (blood sausage mixed with rice, from Burgos), *chuleton de Ávila* (T-bone steak, from Ávila) and *embutidos* (cured meats such as *jamón* and chorizo). The *jamón* (cured ham) from Guijelo, south of Salamanca, is recognised throughout Spain as belonging to the elite. Vegetarians have a tough time, although most restaurant menus include salads, cheese, omelettes and *menestra de verduras* (vegetable stew), although the latter can include ham. Vegans may get very hungry indeed...

❶ Information

The official site of the city of Ávila is www.avila.es.

Centro de Recepción de Visitantes (tourist office; ☎902 10 21 21; www.avilaturismo.com; Avenida de Madrid 39; ☉8am-8pm) Covers all aspects of information on the town with maps and brochures.

Regional tourist office (☎920 21 13 87; www.turismocastillayleon.com; Calle San Segundo 17; ☉9am-8pm Sun-Thu, 9am-9pm Fri & Sat).

❶ Getting There & Away

BUS From Ávila's bus station, there are frequent services to Segovia (€5.45, 55 minutes) and Salamanca (€6.76, 1½ hours). A couple of daily buses also head for the main towns in the Sierra de Gredos.

CAR & MOTORCYCLE From Madrid the driving time is around one hour; the toll costs €7.45.

TRAIN More than 30 trains run daily to Madrid (from €8.25, 1¼ to two hours) and to Salamanca (€9.65, one to 1½ hours, nine daily).

❶ Getting Around

Local bus 1 runs past the train station to Plaza de la Catedral. There are several well-signposted car parks outside the city walls. There's also the Murallito.

Sierra de Gredos

West of Madrid and south of Ávila, the plains of Castilla yield to the precipitous Sierra de Gredos, a secret world of lakes and granite mountains rising up to the Pico de Almanzor (2592m). While the occasional castle or sanctuary may catch the eye, the overriding appeal is the scenery. The sierra is also popular with walkers, mountain bikers and rock climbers; the best seasons being spring (March to May) and autumn (September to November). Summer (June to August) can be stifling, while in winter (December to February) the trails are covered in snow. The region overflows with Spanish tourists on weekends but sees very few foreign tourists.

Public transport to and throughout the sierra is intermittent at best (and almost nonexistent on weekends), so renting a car is essential to getting the best from the region. Of the three main routes through the sierra, the N502 travels north–south, paralleling an old Roman road (still visible in parts) through a steep valley. Cutting across the northern foothills, the C500 affords scenic views of the mountains, while the C501 follows the southern flank and passes through some outstanding scenery en route to Extremadura's La Vera.

ARENAS DE SAN PEDRO & AROUND

A convenient gateway to the southern Sierra de Gredos, Arenas de San Pedro (population 6778, elevation 620m) does have its pretty corners, but it's more the sort of place you would use as a base than visit for its own sake.

In the town centre, sights worth a quick look include the stout 15th-century Castillo de la Triste Condesa, the sober 14th-century Gothic parish church and the Roman bridge. A 10-minute walk north of here is the neoclassical Palacio del Infante Don Luis de Borbón, a gilded cage for Carlos III's imprisoned brother.

Not far from Arenas de San Pedro, Guisando, El Hornillo and El Arenal, a trio of villages at a distance of 5km, 6km and 9km from Arenas, respectively, have access to walking trails. All three are served by a bus (weekdays only).

One popular **walking trail** leads from El Arenal to Puerto de la Cabrilla. Gaining some 1000m over a distance of 4.5km, it's a strenuous five- to seven-hour workout.

🛏 Sleeping & Eating

El Fogon de Gredos   RURAL HOTEL €
(☎920 37 40 18; Carretera Linarejos, Guisando; s/d/ste €28/52/100) This is the most attractive option in Guisando, offering attractive, spacious rooms with sweeping pine-clad mountain views. The suite is overpriced, however. The hostal is even better known as a restaurant (meals €20) for satisfying, meat-dominated local cuisine. It is located around 1.5km beyond the town centre, by the Rio Pelayo. Follow the signs.

Camping Los Galayos   CAMPSITE €
(☎920 37 40 21; www.campinglosgalayos.com; Carretera Linarejos, Guisando; adult/sites/car €3.90/3.80/3.60, 4-person bungalow €93; 🐾) One of the best campsites in the region, Los Galayos has a stunning position on the Rio Pelayo with mountain views. Ideal for families, there is easy access to a small waterfall and pools of shallow turquoise water for paddling tots. The restaurant offers a reduced-price menu for campers (€9.90).

Hostal El Castillo   BUDGET HOTEL €
(☎920 37 00 91; Carretera de Candeleda 2, Arenas de San Pedro; s/d €28/38) On the main road through Arenas, El Castillo has simple, clean rooms with castle views fit for a king.

ℹ Information
Tourist office (☎920 37 23 68; www.turismo castillayleon.com; Plaza de San Pedro, Arenas; ⊙10am-1pm & 4-8pm) Has walking suggestions, as does Ávila's regional tourist office.

ℹ Getting There & Away
BUSES Daily from Arenas de San Pedro to Madrid (€11.10, 2½ hours, two daily) and Ávila (€5.90, 1¼ hours), except on Sunday.

NORTHERN FLANK OF THE SIERRA DE GREDOS
To escape the weekend and summer crowds, head for the Sierra de Gredos' less-frequented northern flank of mountains, normally snow-capped until Easter. The sierra is famed for its spectacular views, fine walks and excellent hotels. You will need your own wheels; public transport is even less frequent here than further south.

Running west off the N502, near Puerta de Pico, the scenic C500 leads past Navarredonda de Gredos and on to Hoyos del Espino, from where the small AV931 leads into the sierra, ending after 12km at La Platafor-

ma. This is the jumping-off point for one of the most picturesque walks, leading to the **Laguna Grande**, a glassy mountain lake in the shadow of the Pico de Almanzor. The easy-to-moderate walk along a well-marked 8km trail takes about 2½ hours each way. Next to the lake is a *refugio* (mountain shelter), which is often full, and good camping. From here it's possible to climb to the top of the **Pico de Almanzor** (2592m; difficult) in about two hours or continue for two hours west to the **Circo de Cinco Lagunas** (easy to moderate). From there you could either backtrack or descend via the Garganta del Pinar towards the town of Navalperral de Tormes, a rigorous undertaking that can take five hours.

For organised activities, including **horse riding**, **trekking** and **abseiling**, check out Alternativas en el Medio Natural (☎920 34 83 85; www.amngredos.com; Km 0.2, Hoyos del Espino).

🛏 Sleeping & Eating
Navarredonda de Gredos is an unexceptional town but has the best choice of accommodation; smarter Hoyos del Espino makes another good base.

📋TOP CHOICE El Milano Real   SPA HOTEL €€
(☎920 34 91 08; www.elmilanoreal. com; Calle de Toledo, Hoyos del Espino; ste €110; P🐾❋🐾🐾) This is a gorgeous place to stay, with wonderful views, a peaceful setting and a fine restaurant (meals around €35). The accommodation is super stylish hiding behind the old-world facade. Each room's decor reflects the name it has been given; there is a Zen-feel Japanese room, the minimalist-look Manhattan suite and an English suite decorated in country garden-style floral fabrics. All have luxuries like hydro-massage baths and DVD players, and breakfast is a gourmet affair. There is also a spa. Prices drop mid-week.

La Casa de Arriba   RUSTIC HOTEL €€
(☎920 34 80 24; www.casadearriba.com; Calle de la Cruz 19, Navarredonda de Gredos; s/d €67/79; 🐾) Located at the top of the village and well signposted, this lovely hotel brims with rustic charm: wooden beams, wood floors, antique furnishings and thick stone walls. The restaurant is highly regarded.

Albergue Juvenil   YOUTH HOSTEL €
(☎920 34 80 05; www.juventud.jcyl.es; Km10.5, Navarredonda de Gredos; dm under/over 30yr €8.50/11.60, full board €15.70/21.10; ⊙15 Mar-15

Dec; 🏊) Situated just past the *parador*, this place has spotless rooms, its own Olympic-sized swimming pool, a tennis court and breathtaking mountain views.

ℹ️ Information

For maps and further information on walks in the area, visit the tourist offices in Arenas de San Pedro or Ávila or check the website (www.naver redondadegredos.net).

Salamanca

POP 156,000

Whether floodlit by night or bathed in mid-day sun, Salamanca is a dream destination. This is a city of rare architectural splen-dour, awash with golden sandstone overlaid with Latin inscriptions in ochre, and with an extraordinary virtuosity of plateresque and Renaissance styles. The monumental highlights are many, with the exceptional Plaza Mayor (illuminated to stunning ef-fect at night) an unforgettable highlight. But this is also Castilla's liveliest city; home to a massive Spanish and international stu-dent population which throng the streets at night and provide the city with so much youth and vitality.

History

In 220 BC Celtiberian Salamanca was be-sieged by Hannibal. Later, under Roman rule, it was an important staging post on the Via Lata (Ruta de la Plata, or Silver Route) from the mines in Asturias to Anda-lucía. After the Muslim invasion of Spain, it changed hands repeatedly. The greatest turning point in the city's history was the founding of the university in 1218. It became the equal of Oxford and Bologna and, by the end of the 15th century, was the focal point of some of the richest artistic activity in the country. The city followed the rest of Castil-la into decline in the 17th century although, by the time Spanish literary hero Miguel de Unamuno became rector at the university in 1900, Salamanca had essentially recovered. Throughout the 20th century, especially during the Civil War and the almost four decades of Franco's rule that followed, Sala-manca's university became both the centre for liberal resistance to fascism and the object of Franco's efforts to impose a com-pliant academic philosophy in Spain's most prestigious university. To a small degree, that liberal–conservative tension still sur-vives and defines the character of the town.

⊙ Sights & Activities

Salamanca is an easy city to explore on foot, but a good way to get an overview is to don the blinkers (in case you are recog-nised) and climb aboard the **Tren Turístico** (tourist train; Plaza Anaya; adult/child €3.75/1.75; ⊙10am-2pm & 4-8pm; ♿). Trips last for 20 minutes, and the service runs for longer hours in summer. Most major monuments are close to Plaza Mayor.

Plaza Mayor   MAIN SQUARE
Built between 1729 and 1755, Salamanca's ex-ceptional grand square is widely considered Spain's most beautiful central plaza, even more stunning than Madrid's. The square is particularly memorable at night when it's illuminated (until midnight) to magical ef-fect. Designed by Alberto Churriguera, it's a remarkably harmonious and controlled baroque display. The medallions placed around the plaza bear the busts of famous figures. Look for the controversial inclusion of Franco in the northeast corner. It looks different from the others, being moulded in a special easy-to-clean plastic to counter its regular subjection to vandalism. Bullfights were held here well into the 19th century; the last ceremonial *corrida* (bullfight) took place here in 1992. The plaza's outdoor ta-bles are a place to linger, watch the passing parade and marvel at the beguiling beauty of the architecture. Poor local students can't afford to drink here, so sit in jovial huddles on the ground. If you're lucky, you may be entertained by the *Tunas* (student musi-cians dressed in Renaissance costume).

Just off the square, the pretty 12th-cen-tury Romanesque **Iglesia de San Martín** (Plaza del Corrillo; ⊙11am-2pm & 4-7pm Tue-Sun) is wedged among houses.

Universidad Civil   UNIVERSITY
(Calle de los Libreros; adult/child €4/2, Mon morn-ing free; ⊙9.30am-1pm & 4-6.30pm Mon-Sat, 10am-1pm Sun; ♿) The visual feast of the en-trance facade to Salamanca's university is a tapestry in sandstone, bursting with imag-es of mythical heroes, religious scenes and coats of arms. It's dominated in the centre by busts of Fernando and Isabel. It's the elusive frog that draws the crowds (see the boxed text, p138), but don't let that distract you from the overall magnificence.

Founded initially as the Estudio Generál in 1218, the university came into being in 1254 and reached the peak of its renown in the 15th and 16th centuries. Behind the facade, the highlight of an otherwise modest collection of rooms lies upstairs: the extraordinary **university library**, one of the oldest university libraries in Europe. With some 2800 manuscripts gathering dust, it's a real cemetery of forgotten books. Note the fine late-Gothic features and beautiful *techumbre* (carved wooden ceiling).

Among the small lecture rooms arranged around the courtyard downstairs, the **Aula de Fray Luis de León** was named after the celebrated 16th-century theologian and writer whose statue adorns the Patio de las Escuelas Menores outside. It conserves the original benches and lectern from Fray Luis' day. Arrested by the Inquisition for having translated the *Song of Solomon* into Spanish, the sardonic theologian returned to his class after five years in jail and resumed lecturing with the words, 'As I was saying yesterday...'. It was here, too, that the famous Spanish philosopher and essayist, Miguel de Unamuno, claimed the Nationalist rising was 'necessary to save Western Civilization', and was saved from the fury of the crowd by Franco's wife.

The **Escalera de la Universidad** (University Staircase) that connects the two floors has symbols carved into the balustrade, seemingly of giant insects having a frolic with several bishops – to decode them was seen as symbolic of the quest for knowledge.

Catedral Nueva
NEW CATHEDRAL

(Plaza de Anaya; ☺9am-8pm) The tower of the late Gothic Catedral Nueva lords over the centre of Salamanca, its compelling *churrigueresco* (ornate style of baroque) dome visible from almost every angle. It is, however, the magnificent Renaissance doorways, particularly the **Puerta del Nacimiento** on the western face, that stand out as one of several miracles worked in the city's native sandstone. The **Puerta de Ramos**, facing Plaza Anaya, contains an encore to the 'frog spotting' challenge on the university facade (see the boxed text, p138). Look for the little astronaut and ice-cream cone chiselled into the portal by stonemasons during recent restorations.

Inside, the most notable features include the elaborate choir stalls, main chapel and retrochoir, all courtesy of the prolific José Churriguera. The ceilings are also exceptional.

Catedral Vieja
OLD CATHEDRAL

(admission €4.75; ☺10am-7.30pm) The Catedral Nueva's largely Romanesque prede-cessor, the Catedral Vieja is adorned with an exquisite 15th-century altarpiece, with 53 panels depicting scenes from the lives of Christ and Mary, topped by a representation of the Final Judgment – it's one of the most beautiful Renaissance altarpieces outside Italy. The cathedral was begun in 1120 and remains something of a hybrid: there are Gothic elements, while the unusual ribbed cupola, the Torre del Gallo, reflects a Byzantine influence. The cloister was largely ruined in the 1755 earthquake, but the Capilla de Anaya houses an extravagant alabaster sepulchre and one of Europe's oldest organs, a Mudéjar work of art dating from the 16th century. The entrance is inside the Catedral Nueva.

Puerta de la Torre
VIEWS

(Jeronimus; Plaza de Juan XXIII; admission €3.25; ☺10am-7.15pm; ⓘ) For fine views over Salamanca, head to the tower at the southwestern corner of the Catedral Nueva's facade. From here, stairs lead up through the tower, past labyrinthine but well-presented exhibitions of cathedral memorabilia, then along the interior balconies of the sanctuaries of the Catedral Nueva and Catedral Vieja and out onto the exterior balconies. There's another entrance inside the Catedral Vieja.

Convento de San Esteban
CONVENT

(Plaza de los Basilios; adult/concession €3/2; ☺10am-1.15pm & 4-7.15pm) Rising above the southeastern corner of the old city, the Convento de San Esteban's church has an extraordinary altarlike facade with the stoning of San Esteban (St Stephen) as its central motif. Inside is a well-presented museum dedicated to the Dominicans and their missionary work in the Americas. The splendid Gothic-Renaissance cloister has strategically placed mirrors that enable you to appreciate fully the fine ceiling.

Convento y Museo de las Úrsulas
CONVENT

(Calle de las Úrsulas 2; museum admission €2; ☺11am-1pm & 4.30-6pm Tue-Sun) A late-Gothic nunnery founded by Archbishop Alonso de Fonseca in 1512. The religious museum is fairly modest, but do take a look at the magnificent marble tomb within the church, sculpted by Diego de Siloé.

FREE Casa de las Conchas
HISTORICAL BUILDING

(Calle de la Compañia 2; ☺9am-9pm Mon-Fri, 9am-2pm & 4-7pm Sat, 10am-2pm & 4-7pm Sun) One of the city's most endearing buildings, named after the scallop shells clinging to

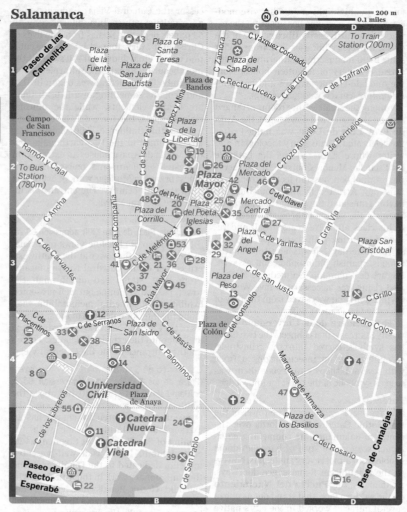

its facade. Its original owner, Dr Rodrigo Maldonado de Talavera, was a doctor at the court of Isabel and a member of the Order of Santiago, whose symbol is the shell. It now houses the public library, entered via a charming bi-level courtyard.

Museo de Salamanca CITY MUSEUM
(Patio de las Escuelas Menores 2; admission €1.20, Sat & Sun free; ☺10am-2pm & 4-7pm Tue-Sat, 10am-2pm Sun). Housed in the former residence of Queen Isabel's doctor, this museum is more interesting for the picture of tranquil Salamanca residential life in its attractive patios than for the paintings and sculptures within.

Museo de la Universidad
UNIVERSITY MUSEUM
(Patio de las Escuelas Menores; incl Universidad Civil €3; ☺9.30am-1pm & 4-6.30pm Mon-Sat, 10am-1pm Sun) The main attraction here is the beautiful pale-blue ceiling fresco of the zodiac; give yourself a few minutes to adjust to the light before gazing aloft.

Convento de Santa Clara CONVENT MUSEUM
(admission €3; ☺9.30am-2pm & 4.15-7pm Mon-Fri, 9.30am-3pm Sat & Sun). This much-modified convent started life as a Romanesque structure and now houses a small museum. You can admire the beautiful frescoes and climb

Salamanca

Top Sights
- Catedral Nueva ... B5
- Catedral Vieja ... A5
- Plaza Mayor ... C2
- Universidad Civil ... A4

Sights
1. Casa de las Conchas ... B3
2. Convento de las Dueñas ... C4
3. Convento de San Esteban ... C5
4. Convento de Santa Clara ... D4
5. Convento y Museo de las Úrsulas ... A2
6. Iglesia de San Martín ... B3
7. Museo de Art Nouveau y Art Decó ... A5
8. Museo de la Universidad ... A4
9. Museo de Salamanca ... A4
10. Museo Taurino ... C2
11. Puerta de la Torre ... A5
12. Real Clericía de San Marcos ... A4
13. Torre del Clavero ... C3
14. Tren Turístico ... B4

Activities

15. University of Salamanca (Cursos Internacionales) ... A4

Sleeping

16. Albergue Juvenil ... D5
17. Aparthotel El Toboso ... C2
18. Hostal Catedral ... B4
19. Hostal Concejo ... B2
20. Hostal Plaza Mayor ... B2
21. Hostal Sara ... B3
22. Hotel Rector ... A5
23. Microtel Placentinos ... A4
24. NH Palacio de Castellanos ... B5
25. Pensión Los Ángeles ... C2
26. Petit Palace Las Torres ... C2
27. RoomMate Vega Hotel ... C3
28. Rúa Hotel ... B3

Eating

29. Casa Paca ... C3
30. El Bardo ... B3
31. El Grillo Azul ... D3
32. El Pecado ... C3
33. Mandala Café ... A4
34. Mater Asturias ... B2
35. Mesón Cervantes ... C2
36. Mesón Las Conchas ... B3
37. Patio Chico ... B3
38. Restaurante La Luna ... A4
39. Victor Gutierrez ... B5
40. Zazu Bistro ... B2

Drinking

41. Café El Corrillo ... B3
42. Chido's Bar ... C2
43. Litre Bars ... B1
44. O'Hara's ... C2
45. Taberna La Rayuela ... B3
46. Tío Vivo ... C2
47. Vinodiario ... C4

Entertainment

48. Cum Laude ... B2
49. Garamond ... B2
50. Posada de las Almas ... C1
51. Potemkin ... C3
52. Sala Klimt Gallery ... B1

Shopping

53. El Fotografo ... B3
54. La Despensa ... B3
55. Universitatis Salamantinae Mercatus ... A5

up some stairs to inspect at close quarters the 14th- and 15th-century *artesonado* (wooden Mudéjar ceiling).

Colegio del Arzobispo Fonseca HISTORICAL BUILDING
(Plaza de Fonseca 4; admission €2; 10am-2pm & 4-7pm) The 16th-century Colegio has a plateresque facade, a lovely courtyard and a sophisticated restaurant (meals €40).

Convento de las Dueñas CONVENT
(Calle Gran Vía; admission €2; 11am-12.45pm & 4.30-6.45pm Mon-Sat) This Dominican convent is home to the city's most beautiful cloister, with some decidedly ghoulish carvings on the capitals.

Museo de Art Nouveau y Art Decó MUSEUM
(Casa Lis; Calle de El Expolio 14; adult/concession €3/2, Thu morning free; 11am-2pm & 5-9pm Tue-Fri, 11am-9pm Sat & Sun) Gallery devoted to both styles in a Modernista (Catalan art nouveau) house.

Real Clericía de San Marcos BAROQUE CHURCH
(Universidad Pontificia; Calle de la Compañía; admission €3; 10.30am-12.45pm & 5-6.30pm Tue-Fri, 10am-1pm & 5-7.15pm Sat, 10am-1pm Sun) A colossal baroque church where obligatory guided tours run every 45 minutes.

CASTILLA Y LEÓN THE SOUTHWEST

Torre del Clavero
HISTORIC TOWER

(Calle del Consuelo) A 15th-century octagonal fortress with an unusual square base and smaller cylindrical towers.

Museo Taurino
BULLFIGHTING MUSEUM

(Calle de Doctor Piñuela 5-7; adult/child €3/free; ⊙11.30am-1.30pm & 6-8pm Tue-Sat, 11.30am-1.30pm Sun; ▣) Packed with bullfighting memorabilia.

Courses

Salamanca is one of the most popular places in Spain to study Spanish and the University of Salamanca (Cursos Internacionales, Universidad Civil; ☑923 29 44 18; www.usal.es; Patio de las Escuelas Menores) is the most respected language school. Courses range from a three-hour daily course spread over two weeks (€365) to a 10-week course of five hours daily (€1650). Accommodation can also be arranged.

The municipal tourist office has a list of accredited private colleges.

🛏 Sleeping

Salamanca has outstanding accommodation, especially in the midrange category. Overall, prices increase on weekends.

TOP CHOICE Microtel Placentinos
BOUTIQUE HOTEL €€

(☑923 28 15 31; www.microtelplacentinos.com; Calle de Placentinos 9; s/d incl breakfast €80/95; ❄🖥) One of Salamanca's most charming boutique hotels, Microtel Placentinos is tucked away on a quiet street and has rooms with exposed stone walls and wooden beams. The service is faultless, and the overall atmosphere one of intimacy and discretion. All rooms have a hydromassage shower or tub and there is a summer-only outside whirpool spa.

Aparthotel El Toboso
APARTMENT HOTEL €

(☑923 27 14 62; www.hoteltoboso.com; Calle del Clavel 7; s/d from €30/52, 3-/5-person self-contained apt €76/93; ❄🖥) These rooms have a homey spare-room feel and are super value, especially the enormous apartments, which come with kitchens (including washing machines) and renovated bathrooms. It's ideal for families or if you're planning to stay in Salamanca for more than a night. Don't miss the fabulous 100-year-old tiled mural of Don Quijote in the bar.

Hostal Concejo
SMALL HOTEL €€

(☑923 21 47 37; www.hconcejo.com, in Spanish; Plaza de la Libertad 1; s/d/tr €45/62/80; P❄@🖥) A cut above the average *hostal*, the stylish Concejo has polished-wood floors, tasteful furnishings and a superb central location. Try and snag one of the corner rooms (like number 104) with its traditional glassed-in balcony, complete with a table, chairs and people-watching views. Parking costs €8.

Pensión Los Ángeles
BUDGET HOTEL €

(☑923 21 81 66; Plaza Mayor 10; s/d without bathroom €18/30, with bathroom €28/35) In a prime location on Plaza Mayor and with cheap prices to boot, this place is a winner. The rooms have original colourful floor tiles and the larger rooms sleep from three to five people (up to €95) with balconies overlooking the plaza. On the downside, it's a steep climb if you're lugging heavy luggage.

Hostal Catedral
BUDGET HOTEL €

(☑923 27 06 14; Rúa Mayor 46; s/d €30/48; ❄) Just across from the cathedrals, this pleasing *hostal* has just six extremely pretty, clean-as-a-whistle, bright bedrooms with showers. All look out onto the street or cathedral, which is a real bonus, as is the motherly owner, who treats her visitors as honoured guests.

Hotel Rector
CLASSIC HOTEL €€€

(☑923 21 84 82; www.hotelrector.com; Paseo del Rector Esperabé 10; r incl breakfast €152; P❄@🖥) This luxurious hotel is an oasis of calm and luxury, and the antithesis of the cookie-cut homogeneity of the five-star chains. Expect vases of orchids, stained-glass windows, intricately carved antiques and excellent service, as well as sumptuous, carpeted rooms.

Albergue Juvenil
YOUTH HOSTEL €

(☑923 26 91 41; www.alberguesalamanca.com; Calle de Escoto 13-15; dm/s/d €14/28/38) Salamanca's youth hostel is a popular, well-run place with large, clean dorms. It's a 10-minute walk down the hill from the old town.

Petit Palace Las Torres
MODERN HOTEL €€

(☑923 21 21 00; www.hthotels.com; Calle de Concejo 4-6; d from €85; ❄@🖥) Part of the quality High-Tech chain, this slick hotel has designer lamps, computers and a sophisticated feel. On the downside, the rooms overlooking Plaza Mayor equal a considerable hike in price and some interior rooms are a little small. Guests have the free use of bikes.

Hostal Sara
SMALL HOTEL €€

(☑923 28 11 40; www.hostalsara.org; Calle de Meléndez 11; s/d €53/60, d with kitchen from €65;

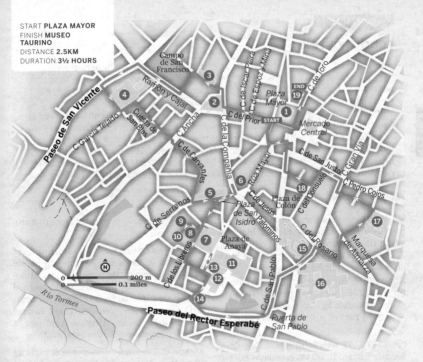

Walking Tour
Salamanca's Historical Highlights

❯ Start your exploration of Salamanca in the incomparable **①** **Plaza Mayor**. Heading west off the southwestern corner of the plaza, take Calle del Prior, which leads to the **②** **Palacio de Monterrey**, a 16th-century holiday home of the Dukes de Alba and a seminal piece of Spanish Renaissance architecture. It's not open to the public but the facade is superb. A short detour north yields the **③** **Convento y Museo de las Úrsulas**. Across the Campo de San Francisco is the **④** **Colegio del Arzobispo Fonseca**.

Descend Cuesta de San Blas and then wind your way southeast to the **⑤** **Real Clerícia de San Marcos**. Directly opposite is the **⑥** **Casa de las Conchas**.

From Plaza de San Isidro, head southwest along Calle de los Libreros to the **⑦** **Universidad Civil**, which faces onto the **⑧** **Patio de las Escuelas Menores**, a small square where you'll find the **⑨** **Museo de Salamanca**. Almost next

door, off a small cloister, check out the fresco at the **⑩** **Museo de la Universidad**.

After visiting the **⑪** **Catedral Nueva** and the **⑫** **Catedral Vieja**, and climbing up through the **⑬** **Puerta de la Torre**, head southwest down the hill to the **⑭** **Museo de Art Nouveau y Art Decó**.

Walking east along Paseo del Rector Esperabé, then north along Calle de San Pablo, brings you to the **⑮** **Convento de las Dueñas**. Directly opposite is the sublime **⑯** **Convento de San Esteban**; from here, quiet streets lead away to the northeast, a shabbier part of town, popular with amateur graffitists. It is also home to the **⑰** **Convento de Santa Clara**.

As you make your way northwest to the old town, pause at the **⑱** **Torre del Clavero** then continue up Calle de San Pablo, skirt Plaza Mayor and seek out the **⑲** **Museo Taurino**.

FROG SPOTTING

Arguably a lot more interesting than trainspotting (and you don't have to drink tea from a thermos flask), a compulsory task facing all visitors to Salamanca is to search out the frog sculpted into the facade of the Universidad Civil. Once pointed out, it's easily enough seen, but the uninitiated can spend considerable time searching.

Why bother? Well, they say that those who detect it without help can be assured of good luck and even marriage within a year. Some hopeful students see a guaranteed examination's victory in it. If you believe all this, stop reading now: if you need help, look at the busts of Fernando and Isabel. From there, turn your gaze to the largest column on the extreme right of the front. Slightly above the level of the busts is a series of skulls, atop the leftmost of which sits our little amphibious friend (or what's left of his eroded self).

❋) This place has friendly staff, large and prettily decorated rooms, tasteful blue-and-white tiled bathrooms and a fine location. The minimal extra cost for a modest kitchen is well worth it for longer stays.

RoomMate Vega Hotel   MODERN HOTEL **€€**
(☎923 27 22 50; www.room-matehotels.com; Plaza del Mercado 16; r incl breakfast €80; ➲❋@🖙) Part of a stylish hotel chain.

Rúa Hotel   SMALL HOTEL **€€**
(☎923 27 22 72; www.hotelrua.com; Calle de Sánchez Barbero 11; s/d incl breakfast €80/100; ❋@🖙) The former apartments here have been converted to seriously spacious rooms. Light wood floors, pastel painted walls and arty prints set the tone.

NH Palacio de Castellanos
   CLASSIC HOTEL **€€€**
(☎923 26 18 18; www.nh-hotels.com; Calle de San Pablo 58-64; s from €99, d €130; ❋@🖙) All lofty patios and antique staircases.

Hostal Plaza Mayor   BUDGET HOTEL **€**
(☎923 26 20 20; www.hostalplazamayor.es, in Spanish; Plaza del Corrillo 20; s/d €36/60; P❋@🖙) Near Plaza Mayor, this *hostal* has stylish rooms washed in pale peach with dark wood furniture and beams.

✕ Eating

Salamanca has an excellent range of restaurants to suit all budgets. Restaurants in and around Plaza Mayor concentrate on traditional grilled meats and tend to be more expensive, although the quality is generally high. Prices drop the further away you are from the square. Pedestrian Calle Meléndez and Rúa Mayor are home to more economical restaurants with outside seating while the streets around the university, including Calle de Serranos, are a good, inexpensive bet as restaurants here cater more to a student crowd.

Mesón Las Conchas   GRILLED MEATS **€€**
(Rúa Mayor 16; meals €25-30) Enjoy a choice of outdoor tables (in summer), an atmospheric bar or the upstairs, wood-beamed dining area. The bar caters mainly to locals who know their *embutidos* (cured meats). For sit-down meals, there's a good mix of roasts, *platos combinados* and *raciones*.

Mesón Cervantes   TRADITIONAL CASTILIAN **€€**
(Plaza Mayor 15; meals €15-20; ⊙10am-midnight) This is another great place where you can eat at the outdoor tables on the plaza, but the dark wooden beams and atmospheric buzz of the Spanish crowd on the 1st floor should be experienced at least once. The food's a mix of *platos combinados,* salads and *raciones*.

El Pecado   MODERN CREATIVE **€€**
(☎923 26 65 58; Plaza de Poeta Iglesias 12; meals €40, menú de degustación €45; ➲) A trendy place that regularly attracts Spanish celebrities (eg Pedro Almodóvar and Ferran Adrià). El Pecado ('The Sin') has an intimate dining room and a quirky, creative menu. The hallmarks are fresh tastes, intriguing combinations and dishes that regularly change according to what is fresh in the market that day. Reservations recommended.

El Grillo Azul   VEGETARIAN **€**
(Calle Grillo 1; menú de día €9, meals €15-20; ⊙Tue-Sat, lunch only Sun; ➲🖉) Vegetarian visitors to Salamanca have a treat that's rare in Castilian towns – a real-life vegetarian restaurant. It's a buzzy place with attractive blue-and-white decor and a creative menu that includes a *plato degustación* (€11.50):

a veritable veggie feast for two with taster portions of dishes like grilled seitan or tofu, vegetable soufflé, wild mushrooms and inventive salads.

Restaurante La Luna
MODERN SOPHISTICATED €

(Calle de los Libreros 4; meals €15; ⊙Tue-Sun, lunch only Mon; ☑) This place has an upbeat young vibe with a background of cool jazz and interesting dishes that deviate from the grilled meats' norm, like salmon prepared a variety of ways and stuffed vegetables, including aubergines, topped with cheese. The downstairs is crowded and intimate; the upstairs bright and modern.

Zazu Bistro
MODERN EUROPEAN €€

(www.restaurantezazu.com, in Spanish; Plaza de la Libertad 8; meals €25-30) Expect smooth sounds on the stereo, and Italian-inspired dishes including exceedingly moreish risottos (with wild mushrooms and similar). There are some culinary surprises as well, like that delectable British standard, sticky toffee pudding, for dessert.

Mandala Café
MODERN MEDITERRANEAN €

(Calle de Serranos 9-11; menú €10; ☑ ⊞) Cool and casual Mandala specialises in a superb daily menu with choices like black rice with prawns and *calamares* (squid), and vegetarian moussaka. There are also more salads than you can shake a carrot-stick at, as well as cakes and fancy ice creams.

Mater Asturias
ASTURIAN €€

(Calle de Concejo 3; menú asturiano €22, meals €20-25) The tastes here are fresh and straight from Spain's northern coast, with a few staples from Asturias. The selection of brochettes, pâtés and toasts come warmly recommended.

Casa Paca
GRILLED MEATS €€

(☑923 21 89 93; Plaza del Peso 10; meals €40-50) Established in 1928 and still going strong, Casa Paca is rumoured to be where the king dines when in town. Both the restaurant and its most famous patron are known for their love of hearty dishes like *cochinillo asado* (roast suckling pig). Reservations essential.

Victor Gutierrez
MODERN €€€

(☑923 26 29 73; Calle de San Pablo 66-80; meals €50) Justifiably exclusive vibe with emphasis on innovative dishes with plenty of colourful drizzle. Reservations essential.

El Bardo
TAPAS €€

(Calle de la Compañía 8; tapas €2.50, menú del día €15) High-calibre tapas and a reliable daily menu aimed at the locals.

Patio Chico
REGIONAL CUISINE €€

(Calle de Meléndez 13; menú del día €12, meals €20-25) Prompt service and excellent value accompany a range of well-prepared local dishes.

Drinking

Salamanca, with its myriad bars and large student population, is the perfect after-dark playground. Nightlife here starts very late, with many bars not filling until after midnight. The so-called 'litre bars' on Plaza de San Juan Bautista are fun night-time hang-outs mainly for students (who clearly have better things to do than hit the books).

Tío Vivo
TOP CHOICE

MUSIC BAR

(Calle del Clavel 3; ⊙4pm-late) Sip drinks by flickering candlelight to a background of '80s music, enjoying the whimsical decor of carousel horses and oddball antiquities. There is live music Tuesdays to Thursdays from midnight.

Chido's Bar
COCKTAIL BAR

(Plaza del Mercado 26; ⊙11am-late) A popular place for American students seeking their Tex Mex fix with tacos, nachos and guacamole, accompanied by cocktails or Corona beer. Head downstairs to the great barrel-vault space with its intriguing ancient tunnel entrance that leads to Plaza Mayor.

Vinodiario
WINE BAR

(Plaza de los Basilios 1; ⊙10am-1am) Away from the crowds of the old-city centre, this delightfully chilled wine bar is staffed by knowledgeable bar staff and loved by locals who, in summer, fill the outdoor tables for early evening drinks. The tapas are innovative and delicious.

Café El Corrillo
LIVE MUSIC

(www.cafecorrillo.com, in Spanish; Calle de Meléndez 18; ⊙8.30am-late) Great for a beer and tapas at any time, with live music on Friday nights from 11.30pm. The *terraza* (terrace) out back is perfect on a warm summer's evening.

O'Hara's
IRISH PUB

(Calle Zamora 14; ⊙11am-late) On Thursdays and Sundays there is live music from 11pm.

Taberna La Ruyuela
BAR

(Rúa Mayor 19; ⊙6pm-1am Sun-Thu, 6pm-2am Fri & Sat) Buzzes with a 20-something crowd.

☆ Entertainment

Many of Salamanca's cafe-bars morph into dance clubs after midnight; there's usually no cover charge.

Posada de las Almas CLUB
(Plaza de San Boal; ⊙6pm-late) Decked out in a curious design mix of looming papier-mâché figures, dollhouses and velvet curtains, this place attracts a mixed crowd – gay and straight, Spanish and foreign.

Potemkin LIVE MUSIC
(Calle del Consuelo; ⊙11pm-late) Salamanca's grungy alternative to the sophisticates elsewhere can be found at Potemkin, where you'll catch live rock music most nights. The neighbouring bars are similar, so dress down.

Cum Laude CLUB
(Calle del Prior 7; ⊙10pm-late Tue-Sun) Sprawling mock-palace interior.

Garamond CLUB
(Calle del Prior 24; ⊙9pm-late) Medieval-style decor.

Sala Klimt Gallery CLUB
(Calle de Iscar Peira 30; ⊙midnight-6am Fri & Sat) House, electro, techno and two dance floors.

🛍 Shopping

Salamanca overflows with souvenir shops, running the whole gamut from the tasteful to the tacky.

Universitatis Salamantinae Mercatus
SOUVENIRS
(Calle de Cardenal Pla y Deniel) The official shop of the University of Salamanca has a stunning range of stationery items, leather-bound books and other carefully selected reminders of your Salamanca visit.

La Despensa DELICATESSEN
(Rua Mayor 23) This small delicatessen has top-quality hams, chorizo and cheeses, as well as boxes of *yemas,* the traditional sweets made by the local nuns. They will ship.

El Fotografo PHOTOGRAPHY
(Calle de Meléndez 5) This small photography shop sells beautiful B&W photos of Salamanca, coffee-table books and photographic equipment.

ℹ Information

An informative website that includes 'what's on'-style information is www.aboutsalamanca.com.

Ciberplace (Plaza Mayor 10; per hr €1.50; ⊙11am-midnight Mon-Fri, noon-midnight Sat & Sun) Internet access.

Municipal tourist office (☎923 21 83 42; www.salamanca.es; Plaza Mayor 14; ⊙9am-2pm & 4.30-8pm Mon-Fri, 10am-8pm Sat, 10am-2pm Sun)

Regional tourist office (☎923 26 85 71; www.turismocastillayleon.com; Casa de las Conchas, Rúa Mayor; ⊙9am-8pm Sun-Thu, 9am-9pm Fri & Sat)

Both tourist offices organise multilingual guided tours of the city. These depart at noon daily and cost €8. The duration is roughly 1½ hours but you must reserve in advance.

ℹ Getting There & Away

The bus and train stations are a five- and 10-minute walk northwest and northeast, respectively, of the cathedral in the new town.

BUS The **bus station** (Avenida de Filiberto Villalobos 71-85) is approached via Calle Ramón y Cajal. Buses run hourly to Madrid (regular/express €14.80/21.90, 3/2½ hours) and there are regular services to other cities, including Ávila (€6.76, 1½ hours, four daily Monday to Friday, one or two on weekends) and Segovia (€10.96, 2¾ hours, two daily). There is a limited service to smaller towns with just one daily bus, except on Sunday, to La Alberca (€5.10, around 1½ hours), with stops in the villages of the Sierra de Francia such as Mogarraz and San Martín del Castañar.

TRAIN Up to eight trains depart daily for Madrid's Chamartín station (€19.10, 2½ hours) via Ávila (€9.65, one hour). There are also frequent services to Valladolid (from €8.25, 1½ hours). The train station is 600m beyond Plaza de España.

ℹ Getting Around

BUS Bus 4 runs past the bus station and around the old-town perimeter to Calle Gran Vía. From the train station, the best bet is bus 1, which heads into the centre along Calle de Azafranal. Going the other way, it can be picked up at the Mercado Central.

CAR & MOTORCYCLE There are few underground parking stations (€9 to €13 for 12 hours) in the old part of town – your best bet is along or just off Paseo del Rector Esperabé.

Around Salamanca

The town of Alba de Tormes makes for an interesting and easily accomplished half-day excursion from Salamanca. People come here from far and wide to pay homage to Santa Teresa, who is buried in the Convento de las Carmelitas she founded in 1570. There's also the stout and highly visible Torreón, the only surviving section of the former castle of the Dukes of Alba. There are regular buses (every two hours on weekends) from Salamanca's bus station to Alba de Tormes.

Ciudad Rodrigo

POP 14,100

Close to the Portuguese border and away from well-travelled tourist routes, somnambulant Ciudad Rodrigo is one of the prettier towns in western Castilla y León. It's an easy day trip from Salamanca, 80km away, but sleeping within the sanctuary of its walls enables you to better appreciate its medieval charm – and you'll have the sloping Plaza Mayor all to yourself after the tourist crowds return home.

The elegant cathedral (Plaza de San Salvador; admission €3, Sun afternoon free; ⊙11.45am-2pm & 4-7pm Tue-Sat, 12.45am-2pm & 4-6pm Sun), begun in 1165, towers over the old walled town. Of particular interest are the Puerta de las Cadenas, with Gothic reliefs of Old Testament figures; the elegant Pórtico del Perdón; and, inside, the exquisite carved-oak choir stalls.

Even if you've nothing to post, the correos (post office; Calle de Dámaso Ledesma 12) is worth passing by to admire the artesonado (wooden Mudéjar ceiling), while the 1st-floor gallery of the ayuntamiento (town hall) is a prime vantage point overlooking Plaza Mayor. The fusion of 12th-century Romanesque-Mudéjar elements with later Gothic modifications makes the Iglesia de San Isidoro worth seeking out. Don't miss the porticoes in the cloister. Discovered in 1994, the 12th-century reliefs of a Roman queen, Arab king and Catholic bishop reflect the various cultures of the region over the years. The 16th-century Palacio de los Castro (Plaza del Conde 3; ⊙9am-7pm Mon-Sat) boasts one of the town's most engaging plateresque facades; only the patio is open to visitors.

You can also climb the city walls and follow their length of about 2.2km around the town for good views over the surrounding plains.

🎊 Festivals & Events

Carnaval   FESTIVAL
Celebrated with great enthusiasm in Ciudad Rodrigo in February. In addition to the outlandish fancy dress, you can witness (or join in) a colourful encierro (running of the bulls) and capeas (amateur bullfights).

🛏 Sleeping

TOP CHOICE **Hotel Conde Rodrigo 1**
                            HISTORIC HOTEL €€
(☎923 46 14 08; www.hotelesciudadrodrigo.com; Plaza de San Salvador 9; r €70; P🅿❄🛜) Housed in a magnificent 16th-century former palace, the refurbished rooms are washed in pale yellow with dark wood furnishings, shiny parquet floors and burgundy-and-white fabrics. The large flat-screen TV, minibar and well-equipped bathroom are similarly agreeable, given the price.

Parador Enrique II   PARADOR €€
(☎923 46 01 50; www.parador.es; Plaza del Castillo 1; r €100; P❄@🛜) Ciudad Rodrigo's premier address is a plushly renovated castle built into the town's western wall. Converted in 1931, it's the third-oldest parador in Spain. The views are good, the rooms brimful of character and the restaurant easily the best in town. The delightful terraced gardens out back overlook the Rio Agueda.

Hospedería Audiencia Real
                            HISTORIC HOTEL €€
(☎923 49 84 98; www.audienciareal.com, in Spanish; Plaza Mayor 17; d €80; ❄) Right on Plaza Mayor, this fine 16th-century hospedería (inn) has been aesthetically reformed and retains a tangible historic feel. Rooms have wrought-iron furniture and exposed brickwork. Several have balconies overlooking the plaza.

Hostal Puerta del Sol   SMALL HOTEL €€
(☎923 46 06 71; www.puertadelsolhostal.com; Rúa del Sol 33; s/d €50/60) Attractive hostal with comfortable bright rooms featuring modern pine furniture, sunny yellow paintwork, and elegant cream fabrics. The bathrooms are expensively marbled in natural colours.

🍴 Eating & Drinking

Head for Plaza Mayor, Rúa del Sol and the surrounding pedestrian streets for the best choice of restaurants.

Mayton   TRADITIONAL CASTILIAN €€
(Calle Colada 9; menú del día €12, meals €25) Set in an old stone mansion – but without the prohibitive price tag you would expect to find – Mayton promises quality traditional cooking. The region's outstanding embutidos

DON'T MISS

GOING POTTY

Chamber pots, commodes, bed pans... Ciudad Rodrigo's Museo del Orinal (Chamber Pot Museum; Plaza de Herrasti: ☉11am-2pm Mon-Wed & Fri, 11am-2pm & 4-7pm Sat & Sun; admission €2; ⓘ) may be located opposite the cathedral, but its theme is definitely more down-to-earth than otherworldly. This city is home to Spain's (possibly the world's) only museum dedicated to the not-so-humble chamber pot (or potty, as it is known in the UK). The private collection of former local resident José Maria del Arco, the collection comprises a staggering 1300 exhibits. Originating from 27 countries, there are some truly historic pieces here, including a 12th-century Islamic version from Cordoba and some wonderful one-offs, like a 19th-century French chamber pot shaped like a bra and a Chinese example with a narrow opening, apparently used on rice boats. José Maria's wife is from Wales so, unsurprisingly, there is a considerable number of UK potties here, including beautifully painted Victorian ceramic pieces and the more rustic wooden-seated style. Incidentally, if you need a tinkle yourself, you will have to go elsewhere; there are no public toilets at the Museo del Orinal.

feature alongside *cordero* (lamb) and there is an overflowing, atmospheric wine cellar.

El Sanatorio   TRADITIONAL BAR €
(Plaza Mayor 12; tapas €1.10, raciones €4.50; ☉11am-late) Dating from 1937, the interior here doubles as a fascinating social history of the town. The walls are papered floor-to-ceiling with black-and-white photos (the oldest dated 1928), mainly of the annual Carnaval when the plaza used to be used as a bullring. Order a beer and peruse the pics. The tapas and *raciones* are good, as well.

La Artesa   TAPAS €
(Rúa del Sol 1; pinchos €1; ⓘ) If you are hungry and euro-economising, the €1 pinchos (small slices of bread with varying toppings) here are excellent value. There are 20 to choose from, ranging from *pulpo a la vinagreta* (octupus in vinaigrette) to *patatas al roquefort* (roast potatoes in a roquefort sauce). The portions are generous; the house wine (€1 a glass) surprisingly palatable.

ⓘ Information

Tourist office (☎923 49 84 00; www.aytociud adrodrigo.es; Plaza Mayor 27; ☉10am-1.30pm & 4-7pm Tue-Sun) Good for brochures and very helpful.

ⓘ Getting There & Away

BUS From the **bus station** (Campo de Toledo) there are up to 12 daily services (fewer on weekends) to Salamanca (€6, 1½ hours). For the Sierra de Francia, you'll need to go via Salamanca.

Sierra de Francia

Hidden away in a remote corner of southwestern Castilla y León and, until recently, secluded for centuries, this mountainous region with wooded hillsides and pretty stone and timber villages is among Castilla y León's best-kept secrets. Quiet mountain roads connect villages that you could easily spend days exploring and where the pace of life remains relatively untouched by the modern world. Best of all, its architecture is yet to succumb to the ill-conceived developments that have come to blight other once-idyllic corners of Spain.

This was once one of Spain's most godforsaken regions. Malaria-ridden until the early 20th century, the region hadn't improved much in 1932 when Luís Buñuel came to film *Las Hurdes – Terre Sans Pain* (Land Without Bread). When King Alfonso XIII visited in June 1922, the only milk available for his coffee was human! Touched by this abject misery, or perhaps hoping for something a little more palatable on his next visit, he was supposedly responsible for the introduction of the area's first cows.

La Alberca

POP 1160 / ELEV 1048M

La Alberca is one of the largest and most beautifully preserved of the Sierra de Francia's villages, a historic and harmonious huddle of narrow alleys flanked by gloriously ramshackle houses built of stone, wood beams and plaster. Look for the date they were built (typically around 1794) carved into the door lintels. Numerous stores sell local products such as *jamón* and *turrón* (nougat), as well as baskets and the inevitable tackier souvenirs. The centre is pretty-as-a-postcard Plaza Mayor; there's a market here on Saturday mornings. If you fancy wafting over the village in a hot-air balloon with your beloved, contact Las Batuecas (☑923 42 31 07; Carretera Mogarraz; €312 for two people).

🛏 Sleeping & Eating

Weekends are the busiest time, when Spanish tourists threaten to overwhelm the town. Come during the week and make an overnight stop to see La Alberca at its best. Restaurants and hotels are concentrated in and around Plaza Mayor.

Hotel Doña Teresa   MODERN HOTEL €€
(☑923 41 53 08; www.hoteldeteresa.com, in Spanish; Carretera Mogarraz; s/d €60/90; P❄🛜) A perfect modern fit for the village's old-world charm and just a short stroll from Plaza Mayor. The large rooms combine character (wooden beams and exposed stonework) with all the necessary mod-cons. There's also a small fitness centre with sauna and Turkish bath, and a good restaurant. It is, less happily, popular with Spanish tour groups.

Hostal La Alberca   SMALL HOTEL €
(☑923 41 51 16; www.hostallaalberca.com; Plaza Padre Arsenio; s/d/tr €29/35/49) Housed in one of La Alberca's most evocative half-timbered buildings, this charming place has comfortable, renovated rooms and small

balconies overlooking the plaza. There's a handy restaurant and bar downstairs.

El Sopotal   TRADITIONAL CASTILIAN €
(Plaza Mayor 7; meals €15-20) Rumbling tummies may want to consider the gut-busting *parrillada* (grill) of various meats, plus potatoes and peppers (€24 for two) at this central spot.

Getting Here & Away

Buses travel between La Alberca and Salamanca (€5.10, around 30 minutes) twice daily on weekdays and once a day on weekends.

Valle de las Batuecas

The drive south into Extremadura through this dreamy valley is spectacular. Just beyond La Alberca, a sweeping panorama of cascading lower mountain ranges opens up before you. The road corkscrews down into the valley before passing through beautiful terrain that has been praised by poets and the writer/academic Miguel de Unamuno. Time your visit for spring when purple heather and brilliant yellow rapeseed blanket the hillsides.

Peña de Francia

Head north from La Alberca along the C512 and you'll soon strike the turn-off to the highest peak in the area, Peña de Francia (1732m), topped by a monastery and reached by a road that turns perilous after rain. Views extend east to the Sierra de Gredos, south into Extremadura and west towards Portugal.

IDYLLIC VILLAGES

Having your own car enables you to immerse yourself in quiet villages such as Mogarraz, east of La Alberca, which has some of the most evocative old houses in the region and is famous for its *embutidos* (cured meats). Miranda del Castañar, further east again, is similarly intriguing, strung out along a narrow ridge, but San Martín del Castañar is the most enchanting, with half-timbered stone houses, flowers cascading from balconies, a bubbling stream and a small village bullring at the top of the town, next to the ruined castle (now a cemetery).

Hotels are rare in these parts, but *casas rurales* (village or farmstead accommodation) abound, with a handful in each village. Alternatively, La Posada de San Martín (☑923 43 70 36; laposadadesanmartin@gmail.com; Calle Largo 1; r incl breakfast €50; @) in San Martín del Castañar is a wonderful choice. The building dates from the 14th century and the rooms are all warm wood and rustic tiles.

For further information and maps of this area, visit the tourist offices in Salamanca or Ciudad Rodrigo.

DON'T MISS

PICTURESQUE PERFECT VILLAGES

» **San Martín del Castañar** (boxed text, p143) – Sierra de Francia's prettiest village

» **Candelario** (p144) – stone-and-wood village huddling beneath the Sierra de Béjar

» **Pedraza de la Sierra** (p152) – lovely walled hamlet watched over by a castle

» **Puebla de Sanabria** (p164) – a return to the past with medieval streetscapes

» **Castrillo de los Polvazares** (boxed text, p176) – rustic stone buildings emblematic of northwestern Castilla y León

» **Covarrubias** (p182) – arguably Castilla y León's most postcard-perfect village

» **Santo Domingo de Silos** (p183) – quiet streets, a stunning cloister and Gregorian chants in the Burgos hinterland

» **Peñaranda de Duero** (p185) – a palace, churches and a ruined castle on the banks of the Río Duero

» **Calatañazor** (p191) – movie-set, cobbled charm just off the highway but a world away

» **Medinaceli** (p192) – splendid old-world feel high above eastern Castilla y León

Sierra de Béjar

Between the Sierra de Francia and the Sierra de Gredos, the Sierra de Béjar is home to more delightful villages and rolling mountain scenery, normally snow-capped until well after Easter. It is an excellent region for outdoor activities.

The centre of the region is Béjar, whose partly-walled old quarters straddle the western end of a high ridge. Among the worthwhile sights is the eye-catching 16th-century Palacio Ducal, just west of Plaza Mayor. A charming place to stay in town is the Hospedaría Real de Béjar (⊘923 40 84 94; www.hospederiarealdebejar.com; Plaza de la Piedad 34; s/d €80/100; P❋🛜) with elegant rooms and a good restaurant (lunch menú €10). Parking costs €10.

Just east of the mountains, the C500 leads to El Barco de Ávila, which has an appealing setting on Río Tormes and is lorded over by a proud, if ruined, castle.

The most scenic village in the region is tiny Candelario (population 1020), a 5km detour from Béjar. Nudging against a steep rock face, this charming village is dominated by mountain architecture of stone-and-wood houses clustered closely together to protect against the harsh winter climate. It is a popular summer resort and a great base for hiking. Contact Tormes (⊘923 40 80 89; www.aventur.es; Calle Tormes 7, Béjar) for organised hikes and other activities.

Hotel Cinco Castaños (⊘923 41 32 04; www.candelariohotel.com; Carretera de la Sierra; s/d €54/60, sites per person €19, 4-person bungalows €90; P❋🛜) is a tranquil place set amid the hills but within walking distance of the village. The pine-furnished rooms are pleasant and the views are sublime. There's a fine restaurant (menú del día €15) and a playground for children.

Béjar and Candelario are served by sporadic bus services from Salamanca and various other destinations, including Madrid and Plasencia.

THE CENTRAL PLATEAU

There's something soul-stirring about the high *meseta* (plateau) with its seemingly endless horizon. But from the plains spring the delightful towns of the Castilla y León heartland – magical Segovia, energetic Valladolid, the Romanesque glories of Zamora and the exceptional cathedral of Palencia.

Segovia

POP 56,100 / ELEV 1002M

Unesco World Heritage–listed Segovia has always had a whiff of legend about it, not least in the myths that Segovia was founded by Hercules or by the son of Noah. It may also have something to do with the fact that nowhere else in Spain has such a stunning monument to Roman grandeur (the soaring aqueduct) survived in the heart of a vibrant modern city. Or maybe it's because art really has imitated life Segovia-style – Walt Disney is said to have modelled Sleeping Beauty's castle in California's Disneyland on Segovia's Alcázar. Whatever it is, the effect is stunning: a city of warm terracotta and sandstone hues set amid the rolling hills of Castilla and against the backdrop of the Sierra de Guadarrama.

History

Founded by Celtiberian tribes, Segovia was occupied by the Romans in 80 BC and rose to become an important town of Roman Hispania. As Christian Spain recovered from the initial shock of the Muslim attack, Segovia became something of a frontline city until the invaders were definitively evicted in 1085. Later a favourite residence of Castilla's roaming royalty, the city backed Isabel and saw her proclaimed queen in the Iglesia de San Miguel in 1474. After backing the wrong side in the Guerra de las Comunidades (War of the Communities) in 1520, Segovia slid into obscurity until the 1960s, when tourism helped regenerate the town. This rebirth gained added momentum in 1985 when the old town and aqueduct were added to Unesco's World Heritage list, bringing Segovia to the attention of the world and sparking a tourist boom that has not yet abated.

◎ Sights

The old town of Segovia rises in the east and ends in the fanciful towers of the Alcázar (Islamic-era fortress) to the west. Calle de Juan Bravo, the road connecting Plaza Mayor and the aqueduct, is a pedestrian thoroughfare that locals know simply as Calle Real. The shady Plaza Mayor is the hub of old Segovia, lined by an eclectic assortment of buildings, arcades and cafes with an open pavilion in its centre. Most of the sights are within easy strolling distance of each other in the historic centre.

El Acueducto
AQUEDUCT

Segovia's most recognisable symbol is El Acueducto (Roman aqueduct), an 894m-long engineering wonder that looks like an enormous comb plunged into Segovia. First raised here by the Romans in the 1st century AD, the aqueduct was built with not a drop of mortar to hold the more than 20,000 uneven granite blocks together. It's made up of 163 arches and, at its highest point in Plaza del Azoguejo, rises 28m high. It was most probably built around AD 50 as part of a complex system of aqueducts and underground canals that brought water from the mountains more than 15km away. By some accounts, it once reached as far as the Alcázar. The aqueduct's pristine condition is attributable to a major restoration project in the 1990s. Sadly, the aqueduct and other monuments are only illuminated at night on weekends and during Easter.

Alcázar
CASTLE

(www.alcazardesegovia.com; Plaza de la Reina Victoria Eugenia; adult/concession €4/3, tower €2, EU citizens 3rd Tue of month free; ◷10am-7pm; ♿) Rapunzel towers, turrets topped with slate witches' hats and a *deep* moat at its base make the Alcázar a prototype fairy-tale castle, so much so that its design inspired Walt Disney's vision of Sleeping Beauty's castle. Fortified since Roman days, the site takes its name from the Arabic *al-qasr* (fortress). It was rebuilt and expanded in the 13th and 14th centuries, but the whole lot burned down in 1862. What you see today is an evocative, over-the-top reconstruction of the original.

Highlights include the **Sala de las Piñas**, with its ceiling of 392 pineapple-shaped 'stalactites', and the **Sala de Reyes**, featuring a three-dimensional frieze of 52 sculptures of kings who fought during the Reconquista. The views from the summit of the **Torre de Juan II** are truly exceptional and put the old town's hilltop location into full context.

THE DEVIL'S WORK

Although no one really doubts that the Romans built the aqueduct, a local legend asserts that two millennia ago a young girl, tired of carrying water from the well, voiced a willingness to sell her soul to the devil if an easier solution could be found. No sooner said than done. The devil worked through the night, while the girl recanted and prayed to God for forgiveness. Hearing her prayers, God sent the sun into the sky earlier than usual, catching the devil unawares with only a single stone lacking to complete the structure. The girl's soul was saved, but it seems like she got her wish anyway. Perhaps God didn't have the heart to tear down the aqueduct.

Segovia

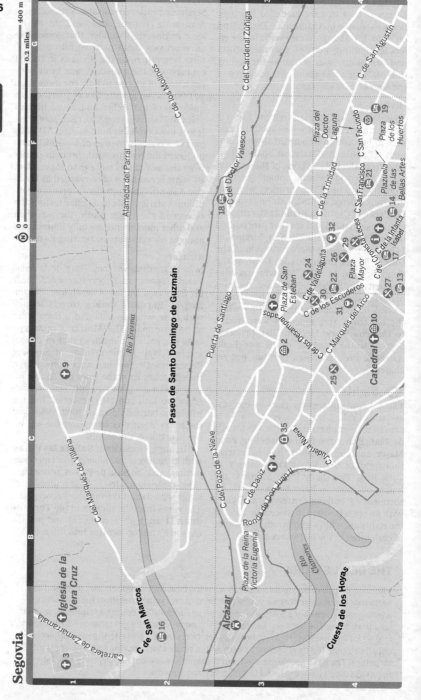

Segovia

CASTILLA Y LEÓN SEGOVIA

BEST VIEW OF TOWN

For *the* shot of Segovia to impress the folks back home, head out of town due north (towards Cuéllar) for around 2km. The view of the city unfolds in all its movie-style magic, with the aqueduct taking a star role – as well it should.

Iglesia de la Vera Cruz
CHURCH

(Carretera de Zamarramala; admission €1.75; ☺10.30am-1.30pm & 4-7pm Tue-Sun, closed Nov). This 12-sided church is the most interesting of Segovia's churches, and one of the best-preserved of its kind in Europe. Built in the early 13th century by the Knights Templar and based on the Church of the Holy Sepulchre in Jerusalem, it long housed what is said to be a piece of the Vera Cruz (True Cross), now in the nearby village church of Zamarramala (on view only at Easter). The curious two-storey chamber in the circular nave (the inner temple) is where the knights' secret rites took place and where they stood vigil over the holy relic. For fantastic views of the town and the Sierra de Guadarrama, walk uphill behind the church for approximately 1km.

Plaza de San Martín
IMPORTANT SQUARE

A little further on from Plaza Mayor is one of the most captivating small plazas in Segovia. The square is presided over by a statue of Juan Bravo and the 14th-century Torreón de Lozoya (admission free; ☺5-9pm Tue-Fri, noon-2pm & 5-9pm Sat & Sun), a tower that was once an armoury and now houses exhibitions.

Museo de Arte Contemporáneo Esteban Vicente
CONTEMPORARY ART MUSEUM

(www.museoestebanvicente.es; Plazuela de las Bellas Artes; adult/concession €3/1.50, Thu free; ☺10am-2pm & 4-7pm Tue & Wed, 11am-2pm & 4-8pm Thu & Fri, 11am-8pm Sat, 11am-3pm Sun) Occupies a 15th-century palace of Enrique IV, complete with Renaissance chapel and Mudéjar ceiling. Some 153 abstract paintings, lithographs and sculptures by Segovia-born artist Esteban Vicente (1903–2000), a fine painter of the abstract expressionist school, form the core of the exhibit. Vicente spent most of his life on Long Island in the USA, but left instructions in his will that his artwork be returned to his native town.

Casa-Museo de Antonio Machado
LITERARY MUSEUM

(Calle de los Desamparados 5; admission €1.50, Wed free; ☺11am-2pm & 4.30-7.30pm Wed-Sun) This is another museum that commemorates a native son: Antonio Machado is one of Spain's pre-eminent 20th-century poets. He lived here from 1919 to 1932 and his former home contains his furnishings and personal effects.

Catedral
CATHEDRAL

(Plaza Mayor; adult/concession €3/2, 9.30am-1.15pm Sun free; ☺9.30am-6.30pm) Started in 1525 after its Romanesque predecessor had burned to the ground in the War of the Communities, Segovia's cathedral is a final, powerful expression of Gothic architecture in Spain that took almost 200 years to complete. The austere three-nave interior is anchored by an imposing choir stall and enlivened by 20-odd chapels. One of these, the **Capilla del Cristo del Consuelo**, houses a magnificent Romanesque doorway preserved from the original church. The **Capilla de la Piedad** contains an important altarpiece by Juan de Juni, while the **Capilla del Cristo Yacente** and **Capilla del Santísimo Sacramento** are also especially beautiful. The Gothic cloister is lovely, while the attached Museo Catedralicio will appeal to devotees of religious art.

Convento de los Carmelitas Descalzos
CONVENT

(Carretera de Zamarramala; admission by donation; ☺10am-1.30pm & 4-7pm Tue-Sun, 4-7pm Mon, closed 1hr earlier in winter) This is where San Juan de la Cruz is buried. The area immediately south of the convent affords fine views up to the Alcázar.

Monasterio del Parral
MONASTERY

(Calle Del Marqués de Villena; admission by donation; ☺10am-12.30pm & 4.15-6.30pm Mon-Sat, 10-11.30am & 4.15-6.30pm Sun). Ring the bell to see part of the cloister and church; the latter is a proud, flamboyant Gothic structure. The monks chant a Gregorian Mass at noon on Sundays, and at 1pm daily in summer.

Convento de San Antonio El Real
CONVENT

(off Avenida de Padre Claret; adult/child €3/free, 9.30am-1.15pm Sun free; ☺10am-2pm & 4-7pm Tue-Sat, 9.30am-2pm Sun) About 1.3km southeast of the aqueduct, this was once the summer residence of Enrique IV. The Gothic-Mudéjar church has a splendid ceiling.

Casa de los Picos
MANSION

(Calle de Juan Bravo; ⊙noon-2pm & 7-9pm Mon-Fri) A grand Renaissance mansion with a diamond-patterned facade that's home to a school of applied arts, and hosts free contemporary art exhibitions.

There are a few Romanesque churches worth checking out:

Iglesia de San Millán
CHURCH

Located off Avenida de Fernández Ladreda, this church is a time-worn example of the Romanesque style typical of Segovia, with porticoes and a Mudéjar bell tower.

Iglesia de San Miguel
CHURCH

(⊙before & after Mass) On Plaza Mayor, this church – where Isabel was proclaimed Queen of Castilla – recedes humbly into the background before the splendour of the cathedral across the square.

Iglesia de San Esteban
CHURCH

(Plaza de San Esteban; ⊙before & after Mass) Has a lovely six-level sandstone tower and baroque interior.

Iglesia de San Martín
CHURCH

(Plaza de San Martín; ⊙before & after Mass) Among the town's churches, this is pièce de Romanesque résistance with its *segoviano* touch of a Mudéjar tower and arched gallery. The interior boasts a Flemish Gothic chapel.

Iglesia de San Justo
CHURCH

(Plaza de San Justo; admission by donation; ⊙11am-2pm & 4-6pm Mon-Sat) The church lies southeast of the centre. From the Plaza del Azoguejo (home of the Centro de Recepción de Visitantes), head south down Calle de Teodosio El Grande and take your first left towards Plaza de San Justo.

Iglesia de San Clemente
CHURCH

(Plaza de San Clemente; ⊙before & after Mass)

☆ Festivals & Events

Segovianos have two major annual festivals.

Fiestas de San Juan y San Pedro
PILGRIMAGE

Celebrated from 24 to 29 June, on San Juan's day, a pilgrimage takes place to a hermitage outside town, where, says a tourist office handout, 'according to tradition and owing to the profound state of merriment caused by the abundant consumption of spirits, the sun is supposed to rise going around in circles'. Throughout the six days of festivities, there are parades, concerts and bullfights.

Fiesta San Frutos
CHORAL SINGING

On 25 October Segovia celebrates the town's patron saint, who is said to be the healer of hernias and bodily fractures. The event is marked in the cathedral with choral singing.

🛏 Sleeping

Segovia's accommodation just gets better all the time, whatever your price range, whatever your taste, but especially in the midrange category. Most hotels are located within the old city.

Hospedería La Gran Casa Mudéjar
HISTORIC HOTEL €€

(☎921 46 62 50; www.lacasamudejar.com; Calle de Isabel La Católica 8; r €90; ❋@🖵) Spread over two buildings, this place has been magnificently renovated, blending genuine, 15th-century Mudéjar carved wooden ceilings in some rooms with modern amenities. In the newer wing, where the building dates from the 19th century, the rooms on the top floors have fine mountain views out over the rooftops of Segovia's old Jewish quarter. A small spa opened here in September 2010 and the hotel's El Fogón Sefardí restaurant comes highly recommended.

Hotel Alcázar
BOUTIQUE HOTEL €€€

(☎921 43 85 68; www.alcazar-hotel.com; Calle de San Marcos 5; s/d incl breakfast €135/163; ❋🖵) Sitting by the riverbank in the valley beneath the Alcázar, this charming, tranquil little hotel have lavish rooms beautifully styled to suit those who love old-world luxury. Breakfast on the back terrace is a lovely way to pass the morning, and there's an intimacy and graciousness about the whole experience.

Las Sirenas
CLASSIC HOTEL €€

(☎921 46 26 63; www.hotelsirenas.com; Calle de Juan Bravo 30; s/d €58/75; P❋🖵) Dating from the 1950s, the public spaces have real old-world elegance with the original floor tiles, chintzy armchairs, chandeliers, and a ponderous grandfather clock. The rooms are more straightforward with a successful marriage of dark-wood furniture and pale paintwork. Parking costs €15.

1. Salamanca (p132)
A city of rare architectural splendour, with a virtuosity of plateresque and Renaissance styles.

2. León Cathedral (p169)
A 13th-century cathedral with soaring towers, flying buttresses and a truly breathtaking interior.

3. Covarrubias (p182)
A picturesque hamlet with distinctive arcaded half-timbered houses and cobblestone squares.

4. Peñaranda de Duero (p185)
Originally a Celtic fortress village, there are superb views from its 15th-century castle ruins.

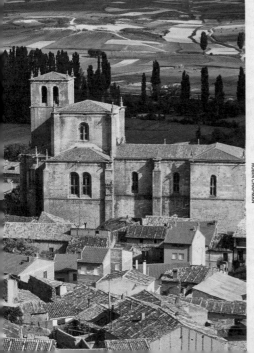

ROBIN CHAPMAN

Hostal Fornos
SMALL HOTEL **€**

(📞921 46 01 98; www.hostalfornos.com, in Spanish; Calle de la Infanta Isabel 13; s/d €41/55; ❄) This tidy little *hostal* is a cut above most other places in this price category. It has a lovely cheerful air and rooms with a fresh white-linen-and-wicker-chair look. Some rooms are larger than others, but the value is unbeatable.

Natura – La Hostería
SMALL HOTEL **€**

(📞921 46 67 10; www.naturadesegovia.com, in Spanish; Calle de Colón 5-7; r €60; ❄🛜) An eclectic choice a few streets back from Plaza Mayor. The owner obviously has a penchant for Dalí prints and the rooms have plenty of character, with chunky wooden furnishings and bright paintwork.

Hotel Palacio San Facundo
HISTORIC HOTEL **€€**

(📞921 46 30 61; www.hotelpalaciosanfacundo.com; Plaza San Facundo 4; s/d €82/102; ❄@🛜) Segovia's hotels are proving adept at fusing stylishly appointed modern rooms onto centuries-old architecture. This place is one of the best, with an attractive columned courtyard, a warm colour scheme, friendly service and a central location.

Hostal Juan Bravo
BUDGET HOTEL **€**

(📞921 46 34 13; Calle de Juan Bravo 12; d with washbasin/bathroom €35/43) This great-value *hostal* has sparkling rooms with plush chenille bedspreads and cheery art prints. Several of the back rooms have stunning views of the Sierra de Guadarrama. The owner is friendly, the location superb.

Hotel Infanta Isabel
HISTORIC HOTEL **€€**

(📞921 46 13 00; www.hotelinfantaisabel.com; Plaza Mayor 12; s/d €85/95; 🅿❄🛜) The colonnaded building fits well with the hotel's interior of period furnishings in most of the spacious rooms. Some overlook Plaza Mayor. Parking costs €13.

Pensión Odeón
BUDGET HOTEL **€**

(📞664 886644; www.pensionodeon.com; Calle de los Escuderos 10; s/d €30/39) Occupying the ground floor of an old house, this simple *hostal* has tasteful furnishings and a dynamic colour scheme.

Hotel Los Linajes
HISTORIC HOTEL **€€**

(📞921 46 04 75; www.hotelloslinajes.com; Calle del Doctor Velasco 9; s/d €86/117; ❄🛜) The rooms here are large and filled with character, and all look out onto the hills; many also have cathedral and/or Alcázar views.

Eating

Segovianos love their pigs to the point of obsession. Just about every restaurant boasts its *horno de asar* (roasts). The main speciality is *cochinillo asado* (roast suckling pig), but *judiones de la granja* (butter beans with pork chunks) also looms large. For a good range of restaurants head for Plaza de San Martín and Plaza Mayor and the web of narrow streets in and around the two squares, including Calle Infanta Isabel, which is home to more economical restaurants.

TOP CHOICE ☆ Restaurante El Fogón Sefardí
SEPHARDIC **€€**

(📞921 46 62 50; www.lacasamudejar.com; Calle de Isabel La Católica 8; meals €30-40; 🍴) Located within the Hospedería La Gran Casa Mudéjar, this is one of the most original places in town. Sephardic cuisine is served in either the intimate patio or splendid dining hall with original, 15th-century Mudéjar flourishes. The theme in the bar is equally diverse with dishes from all the continents, including cous cous from Africa and Argentinean steak from the Americas. Reservations recommended.

Di Vino
MODERN SOPHISTICATED **€€**

(📞921 46 16 50; www.restaurantedivino.com; Calle Valdeláguila 7; meals €25; ⏱lunch & dinner Wed-Mon; 🍴) Dine in snazzy modern surroundings on dishes that combine the traditional, like *pierna de cabrito al horno* (roasted leg of lamb), with the innovative, like the starter of *bacalau bloody mary* (cod-infused bloody mary) or risotto with artichokes and prawns. The restaurant prides itself on its extensive wine list. Reservations recommended.

Casa Duque
GRILLED MEATS **€€**

(📞921 46 24 87; www.restauranteduque.es; Calle de Cervantes 12; menús del día €21-40, meals €25-35) They've been serving *cochinillo asado* here since the 1890s. For the uninitiated, try the *menú segoviano* (€31), which includes *cochinillo*, or the *menú gastronómico* (€40). Downstairs is the informal *cueva* (cave), where you can get tapas and full-bodied *cazuelas* (stews). Reservations recommended.

Mesón de Cándido
GRILLED MEATS **€€**

(📞921 42 81 03; www.mesondecandido.es; Plaza del Azoguejo 5; meals €30-40; 🍴) Set in a delightful 18th-century building in the shadow of the aqueduct, Mesón de Cándido is another place famous throughout Spain for its suckling pig and the more unusual roast boar with apple. Reservations recommended.

DON'T MISS

SWEET TREATS

If you are one of those people who scoffs all the marzipan off the Christmas cake, you will love Segovia's speciality: *ponche segoviano* (literally 'Segovian punch'), but far removed from that insipid low-alcohol drink you used to consume as a spotty teenager. This is a rich lemon-infused sponge cake coated with marzipan and topped in icing sugar with a distinctive criss-cross pattern. A good place to indulge in your *ponche* passion is the patisserie **Limón y Menta** (Calle de Isabel La Católica 2; ⊙8am-11pm), just off Plaza Mayor.

La Almuzara   MODERN LIGHT €
(Calle Marqués del Arco 3; meals €15; ⊙Tue-Sat, dinner only Sun; ⊝🖉) If you're a vegetarian, you don't need to feel like an outcast in this resolutely carnivorous city. La Almuzara features lots of vegetarian dishes, pastas and salads, and the ambience is warm and artsy.

Mesón José María   GRILLED MEATS €€
(www.rtejosemaria.com, in Spanish; Calle del Cronista Lecea 11; meals €30-40) Offers great tapas in the bar and five dining rooms serving exquisite *cochinillo* and other local specialities.

La Taurina   GRILLED MEATS €€
(Plaza Mayor 8; meals €20; 🐟) An unpretentious place that has been churning out hearty traditional food since 1939. The mounted bull's head gives an idea of the carnivorous emphasis.

Zarzamora   HOME STYLE €
(Calle de Valdeláguila; meals €10-15; ⊙6pm-midnight Tue-Sun) Offers healthy pasta and meat dishes, fruit tarts and other home cooking. It's like eating in your own cosy kitchen.

🍷 Drinking & Entertainment

In fine weather Plaza Mayor is the obvious place for hanging out and people-watching. Calle de la Infanta Isabel is one of those Spanish streets that you'll definitely hear before you see it; locals call it 'Calle de los Bares' (Street of the Bars). Another good street for bars and nightclubs is nearby Calle de los Escuderos.

La Tasquina   WINE BAR
(Calle de Valdeláguila 3; ⊙9pm-late) This wine bar draws crowds large enough to spill out onto the pavement nursing their good wines, *cavas* (sparkling wines) and cheeses.

Sala Joplin   LIVE MUSIC
(Calle de Juan Bravo 11; ⊙10.30pm-late Thu-Sat) This is one of the rare venues in town where you can regularly hear live bands.

Buddha Bar   CLUB
(Calle de los Escuderos 3; ⊙9pm-late) This place has lounge music that can turn more towards house as the night wears on.

🔒 Shopping

Artesanía La Gárgola   CRAFTS
(www.gargolart.com, in Spanish; Calle Judería Vieja 4) There are many shops worth browsing in Segovia but make sure you check out these unusual, high-quality handmade crafts and souvenirs in ceramic, wood and textile.

Montón de Trigo Montón de Paja
    SOUVENIRS
(www.montondetrigomontondepaja.com; Plaza de la Merced 1) With handcrafted handbags, block prints of Segovia and a host of other artsy, locally made items, this shop is ideal for creative gifts.

ℹ Information

InternetCaf (Calle de Teodosio El Grande 10; per hr €2; ⊙9am-1.30pm & 3-7pm Mon-Fri, noon-4pm Sat) Internet access.

Centro de Recepción de Visitantes (tourist office; ☎921 46 67 20; www.turismodesego via.com; Plaza del Azoguejo 1; ⊙10am-7pm Sun-Fri, 10am-8pm Sat). Guided city tours are available (€12 per person; 2¼ hours), departing daily at 11.15 for a minimum of four persons.

Regional tourist office (☎921 46 03 34; www. segoviaturismo.es; Plaza Mayor 10; ⊙9am-8pm Sun-Thu, 9am-9pm Fri & Sat)

ℹ Getting There & Away

BUS The bus station is just off Paseo de Ezequiel González, near Avenida de Fernández Ladreda. Buses run half-hourly to Segovia from Madrid's Paseo de la Florida bus stop (€6.70, 1½ hours). Buses depart to Ávila (€5.45, 1¼ hours, five daily), Salamanca (€10.96, 2¾ hours, two daily) and almost hourly to Valladolid (€8.05, 2¾ hours), with just six departures on Sunday.

ℹ️ SEGOVIA BY BIKE

Pedal power is a great way to visit the city. The Segovia de bicio (Segovia by bike; http://segovia.onroll.info/) scheme allows you to borrow (and drop off) a bicycle from eight places throughout the centre of town. And it costs just €3 for a day's rental and €6 for an entire week. All you have to do is register at the tourist office and show ID, and you're ready to explore one of Spain's most bike-friendly cities.

CAR & MOTORCYCLE Of the two main roads down to the AP6, which links Madrid and Galicia, the N603 is the prettier. The alternative N110 cuts southwest across to Ávila and northeast to the main Madrid–Burgos highway.The nearest underground car park to the historic centre is in Plaza de la Artillería near the aqueduct.

TRAIN There are two options by train: up to nine normal trains run daily from Madrid to Segovia (€6.50 one way, two hours), leaving you at the main train station 2.5km from the aqueduct. The faster option is the high-speed AVE (€9.90 one-way, 35 minutes), which deposits you at the newer Segovia-Guiomar station, 5km from the aqueduct.

ℹ️ Getting Around

BUS Bus 9 (€1, half-hourly, 10am to 1pm and 4.30pm to 7pm) does a circuit through the old town from just outside the aqueduct, while bus 8 (€1, every 15 minutes, 6.45am to 9.45pm) connects Segovia-Guiomar station with just outside the aqueduct.

Around Segovia

LA GRANJA DE SAN ILDEFONSO

It's not hard to see why the Bourbon King Felipe V chose this site to re-create in miniature his version of Versailles, the palace of his French grandfather Louis XIV. In 1720 French architects and gardeners, together with some Italian help, began laying out the elaborate and decidedly baroque gardens (admission free; ◷10am-8pm; 🏢) in the western foothills of the Sierra de Guadarrama, 12km southeast of Segovia. La Granja's most famous for its 28 extravagant fountains, situated throughout the gardens, that depict ancient myths, such as those featuring Apollo and Diana. There is also a maze. If you time your visit for Wednesday, Saturday or Sunday at 5.30pm you can see the fountains in action (adult/child €3.40/1.70).

The 300-room Palacio Real (www.patrimonionacional.es; adult/child €5/2.50), once a favoured summer residence for Spanish royalty and restored after a fire in 1918, is impressive but perhaps the lesser of La Granja's jewels. The palace includes the colourful Museo de Tapices (Tapestry Museum).

Up to a dozen daily buses to La Granja depart regularly from Segovia's main bus station (€1.35, 20 minutes).

PEDRAZA DE LA SIERRA
POP 120

The captivating walled village of Pedraza de la Sierra, about 37km northeast of Segovia, is eerily quiet during the week; its considerable number of restaurants, bars and eclectic shops spring to life with the swarms of weekend visitors. At the far end of town stands the lonely Castillo de Pedraza (admission €5; ◷11am-2pm & 5-8pm), unusual for its intact outer wall. The 14th-century Plaza Mayor is similarly evocative with its ancient columned arcades. For a wonderful rural shopping experience, visit De Natura (www.casayjardin.es/denatura.htm, in Spanish; Calle Calzada 8), a three-storey barn-house filled with quality Castilian bric-a-brac, including furnishings, and traditional clay and porcelain crockery.

On the first and second Saturdays of July, Pedraza hosts the atmospheric **Conciertos de las Velas**, when the electricity is shut down and live music is performed in a village lit only by candles.

The excellent Hospedería de Santo Domingo (📞921 50 99 71; www.hospederiadesantodomingo.com; Calle Matadero 3; s/d €95/114; ⊝❄️🛜) has terrific rooms decked out in warm ochre and earth colours. Most have large terraces overlooking the low hills across the way, criss-crossed with dry stone walls. Nearby El Hotel de la Villa (📞921 50 86 53; www.elhoteldelavilla.com; Calle Calzada 5; s/d €90/120; ⊝❄️🛜) is a similarly stylish boutique hotel.

Bus services to Pedraza are sporadic at best.

TURÉGANO
POP 1160

Turégano, about 30km north of Segovia, is dominated by a unique 15th-century castle-church complex built by the then Archbishop of Segovia, Juan Arias Dávila, who decided to make a personal fortress of the town. Conversely, both cutesy and formidable, the castle walls, with their sturdy ramparts and rounded turrets, are built around the facade of the Iglesia de San Miguel; ruined sections of the wall fan out across the surrounding countryside.

COCA
POP 2100

A typically dusty, inward-looking Castilian village, 50km northwest of Segovia, Coca is presided over by a stunning all-brick castle (guided tours €2.70; ⊗tours 10.30am-1pm & 4.30-7pm), a virtuoso piece of Gothic-Mudéjar architecture. Built in 1453 by the powerful Fonseca family, it's surrounded by a deep moat. Although part of the castle is now used as a forestry college, most of the castle may be visited by guided tour – tours start when there are enough people in a group – and it closes one hour earlier in the evening in winter. Up to five buses run daily between Coca and Segovia (€3.45, one hour).

Valladolid
POP 316.600

Connected by air to London, Brussels and Milan, and by fast train to Madrid, Valladolid is a city on the upswing and a convenient gateway to northern Spain. An attractive place with a very Spanish character, the city's appeal is in its sprinkling of monuments, the fine Plaza Mayor and its excellent museums. By night, Valladolid comes alive as its large student population overflows from the city's boisterous bars.

⊙ Sights

Museo Nacional de Escultura
SCULPTURE MUSEUM
(www.mne.es; Calle de San Gregorio 2; adult/concession €3/1.50, Sat afternoon & Sun free; ⊗10am-2pm & 4-9pm Tue-Sat, 10am-2pm Sun) This museum, Spain's premier showcase of polychrome wood sculpture, is housed in the former Colegio de San Gregorio (1496), a flamboyant example of the Isabelline Gothic style where exhibition rooms line a splendid two-storey galleried courtyard.

Works by Alonso de Berruguete, Juan de Juní and Gregorio Fernández are the star attractions, especially some enormously expressive fragments from Berruguete's high altar for Valladolid's Iglesia de San Benito. Downstairs is a small wing dedicated to Fernández, whose melodramatic intensity

is especially well reflected in his painfully lifelike sculpture of a dead Christ.

Plaza de San Pablo
HISTORIC SQUARE
Virtually next to the Museo Nacional de Escultura, this open square is dominated by the exquisite Iglesia de San Pablo. The church's main facade is an extravagant masterpiece of Isabelline Gothic, with every square inch finely worked, carved and twisted to produce a unique fabric in stone. Also fronting the square is the Palacio de Pimentel, where, on 12 July 1527, Felipe II was born. A tiled mural in the palace's entrance hall depicts scenes from the life of the king. The palace hosts occasional exhibitions.

Museo Patio Herreriano
ART MUSEUM
(www.museopatioherreriano.org, in Spanish; Calle de Jorge Guillén 6; adult/concession €3/2, Wed €1; ⊗11am-8pm Tue-Fri, 10am-8pm Sat, 10am-3pm Sun) Dedicated to post-WWI Spanish art, this museum contains works by Salvador Dalí, Joan Miró, Basque sculptor Eduardo Chillida, Jorge Oteiza, Antoni Tápies and Esteban Vicente, arrayed around the cloisters of a former monastery.

Casa-Museo de Colón
HISTORIC MUSEUM
(Calle de Colón; adult/child €2/free, Wed €1; ⊗10am-2pm & 5-8.30pm Tue-Sun; ⚐) The Casa-Museo de Colón is a superb museum spread over four floors. It has interactive exhibits, and wonderful old maps take you on a journey through Christopher Columbus' (Cristóbal Colón in Spanish) journeys to the Americas. The top floor describes Valladolid in the days of the great explorer (who died here in 1506). The explanations are in Spanish only.

Catedral
CATHEDRAL
(Calle de Arribas 1; museum admission €2.50; ⊗10am-1.30pm & 4.30-7pm Tue-Fri, 10am-2pm Sat & Sun). Valladolid's 16th-century cathedral is not Castilla's finest, but it does have a fine altarpiece by Juní and a processional monstrance by Juan de Arfe in the attached Museo Diocesano y Catedralicio. Arguably more interesting are the 13th-century ruins of the old Collegiate Church (atop which the cathedral was built) on the cathedral's northeastern perimeter.

Casa de Cervantes
CERVANTES' HOUSE
(Calle del Rastro; adult/child €3/free, Sun free; ⊗9.30am-3pm Tue-Sat, 10am-3pm Sun) Cervantes was briefly imprisoned in Valladolid; his house is happily preserved behind a quiet little garden.

Valladolid

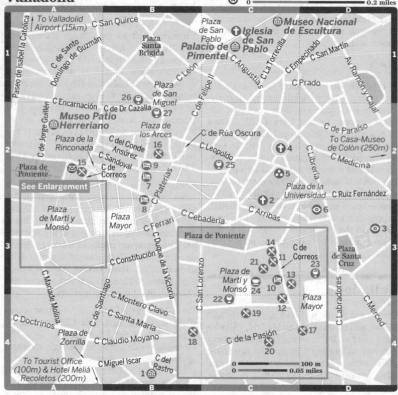

FREE Colegio de Santa Cruz

HISTORIC BUILDING

(Calle Cardenal Mendoza; ⊙sporadic) Check out the colonnaded patio and chapel with super-realistic *Cristo de la Luz* sculpture. The Colegio is located just east of Plaza de Santa Cruz.

Iglesia de Santa María la Antigua

CHURCH

(Calle Antigua 1; ⊙before & after Mass) Stunning 14th-century Gothic church with elegant Romanesque tower.

🛏 Sleeping

Valladolid's hotels see more businesspeople than tourists during the week, so prices at many hotels drop considerably from Friday to Sunday.

Hostal París

BOUTIQUE HOTEL €€

(📞983 37 06 25; www.hostalparis.com, in Spanish; Calle de la Especería 2; s/d €51/69; 🕸🛜)

One of the closest places to Plaza Mayor, Hostal París has had the interior designers in. Washed in pale pastel colours with striking abstract art panels, good-size desks and flat-screen TVs, the rooms successfully combine comfort with a corporate feel. There's nearby parking in Plaza Mayor.

Hotel Meliá Recoletos

CLASSIC HOTEL €€

(📞983 21 62 00; www.solmelia.com; Acera de Recoletos 13; s/d €75/100; 🅿🕸@🛜) This excellent four-star hotel has a touch of class that elevates it above other hotels in this category. Part of a chain but with a boutique-hotel intimacy, it offers large luxurious rooms and impeccable service. With a predominantly business clientele, the hotel lowers its rates considerably from Friday to Sunday. Parking costs €14.

Hostal Del Val

BUDGET HOTEL €

(📞983 37 57 52; Plaza del Val 6; s/d with washbasin €18/33, with bathroom €33/42) Situated in an old building, without a lift, so do specify a lower floor if you have heavy luggage. Rooms are small, pink and comfortable with traditional glassed-in terraces overlooking the quiet square. The same owner runs a similarly-priced *hostal* near by.

Hotel El Nogal   MODERN HOTEL €€
(☏983 34 03 33; www.hotelelnogal.com, in Spanish; Calle del Conde Ansúrez 10-12; s/d €50/72; P❄) Hotel El Nogal has revamped its rooms which now sport polished floorboards, colourful crimson drapes and bedspreads, and modern bathrooms, most with hydro-massage showers. All rooms face out onto either a plaza or a quiet street. Parking costs €11.

Hotel Imperial   CLASSIC HOTEL €€
(☏983 33 03 00; www.himperial.com, in Spanish; Calle Peso 4; s/d €60/70; ❄❄) This solid, comfortable hotel has a warm old-fashioned feel in the public spaces, while the carpeted rooms are more modern, with sunny cream-and-yellow paintwork. The bathrooms are large and glossy.

✗ Eating

Valladolid is a great town to get into the tapas habit and you need look no further than the bars west of Plaza Mayor, especially around Plaza Martí y Monsó. You can easily fill up on a meal's worth of delicious light bites here. Restaurants are also found in this region and many of the tapas bars have more formal *comedores* (dining rooms), as well.

TOP CHOICE **El Caballo de Troya**
                        REGIONAL DISHES €€
(☏983 33 93 55; Calle de Correos 1; meals €30-45; ⊙Mon-Sat) The 'Trojan Horse' is a Valladolid treat, ranged around a stunning Renaissance-style courtyard with a *taberna* downstairs for brilliant *raciones* – choose the *bandeja surtidas* (tasting platters) for a rich and varied combination of tastes. The restaurant is as sophisticated in flavours as the dining room is classy in design. Reservations recommended.

Herbe   REGIONAL DISHES €
(Calle de Correos 6; menu €12, meals €15; ⊙Mon-Sat) A tad more down-to-earth than some of its grander neighbours, Herbe's menu is, unusually, available both lunchtime and evening. The choice will typically include starters like *menestra de verduras* (fresh vegetable stew), followed by meat and fish mains and dessert. The €6 house wine is perfectly drinkable and the friendly service a delight.

Vinotinto   GRILLED MEATS €€
(www.vinotinto.es, in Spanish; Calle de Campanas 4; meals €25-30) This is where wine bar meets steakhouse, sizzling nightly with local gossip, spare ribs and other grilled meats in

THE DARK PRINCE OF THE INQUISITION

There were few more notorious personalities of the Spanish Inquisition than the zealot Fray Tomás de Torquemada (1420–98). Immortalised by Dostoevsky as the articulate Grand Inquisitor who puts Jesus himself on trial in *The Brothers Karamazov*, and satirised by Monty Python in the *Flying Circus*, Torquemada was born in Valladolid to well-placed Jewish *conversos* (converts to Christianity).

A Dominican, Fray Tomás was appointed Queen Isabel's personal confessor in 1479. Four years later, Pope Sixtus IV appointed this rising star to head the Castilian Inquisition.

Deeply affected by the Spanish cult of *sangre limpia* (pure blood), the racist doctrine that drove the 800-year struggle to rid Spain of non-Christian peoples, Torquemada gleefully rooted out *conversos* and other heretics, including his favourite targets, the *marranos* (Jews who pretended to convert but continued to practise Judaism in private).

The 'lucky' sinners had their property confiscated, which served as a convenient fund-raiser for the war of Reconquista against the Muslims. They were paraded through town wearing the *sambenito*, a yellow shirt emblazoned with crosses that was short enough to expose their genitals, then marched to the doors of the local church and flogged.

If you were unlucky, you underwent unimaginable tortures before going through an auto-da-fé, a public burning at the stake. Those who recanted and kissed the cross were garrotted before the fire was set, while those who recanted only were burnt quickly with dry wood. If you stayed firm and didn't recant, the wood used for the fire was green and slow-burning.

In the 15 years Torquemada was Inquisitor General of the Castilian Inquisition, he ran some 100,000 trials and sent about 2000 people to burn at the stake. Many of the trials were conducted in Valladolid's Plaza Mayor; the executions in Plaza de Zorrilla. On 31 March 1492 Fernando and Isabel, on Torquemada's insistence, issued their Edict of Expulsion, forcing all Jews to leave Spain within two months on pain of death.

The following year Torquemada retired to the monastery of Santo Tomás in Ávila, from where he continued to administer the affairs of the Inquisition. In his final years he became obsessed with the fear that he might be poisoned, and refused to eat anything without having (what he believed to be) a unicorn's horn nearby as an antidote. Unlike many of his victims, he died in his sleep in 1498.

a cavernous tavern atmosphere. The local *jamón ibérico,* is particularly good, sliced so finely as to melt in the mouth. The modern Vinotinto Joven, opposite, has a more intimate, younger feel.

La Parrilla de San Lorenzo

SOPHISTICATED CASTILIAN €€

(☎983 33 50 88; Calle de Pedro Niño; meals €25-35; ☉bar 10.30am-late, restaurant Mon-Sat, lunch Sun) Both a rustic stand-up bar and a much-lauded restaurant in the evocative setting of a former monastery, La Parilla de San Lorenzo specialises in upmarket Castilian cuisine (hearty stews, legumes and steaks). Reservations recommended.

Los Zagales de Abadía

SOPHISTICATED CASTILIAN €€

(☎983 38 08 92; www.loszagales.com; Calle de la Pasión 13; meals €25-30; ☉Mon-Sat, lunch

Sun) The bar here is awash with hanging local produce, all represented in the prize-winning tapas displayed along the bar. Notwithstanding, Los Zagales is best known for its restaurant, where the servings are generous and the food excellent. Reservations recommended.

Valladolid is superb for tapas bars; as well as the following listed ones, many of the aforementioned restaurants are also fronted by more informal tapas bars.

Bar Zamora TAPAS €€

(Calle de Correos 5; ☉Thu-Tue) This prize-winning tapas bar courts flavours from western Castilla.

El Corcho TAPAS €

(Calle de Correos 2) A few doors up from Bar Zamora, this spit-and-sawdust place wins the prize of public opinion with its excellent selection of *tostas* (toasts), with tasty toppings, from just €1.40.

La Mejillonera   SEAFOOD TAPAS **€**
(Calle de la Pasión 13) It's said that Spaniards consume 30 million kilograms of mussels every year; at a guess, a fair proportion of these are downed here.

La Tasquita II   TAPAS **€**
(Calle Caridad 2; ⊘Tue-Sun) Another good place to try for its range of *tostas* is this popular place.

Jero   TAPAS **€**
(Calle de Correos 11) For an excellent range of Basque-style *pinchos* check out Jero, with innovative choices like *crema de yogur con gambas y melocotón* (creamy yoghurt with shrimps and peach).

La Jamónería   TAPAS **€**
(Calle del Conde Ansúrez 11) Go back to basics and head for this place, popular for its cured meats.

🍷 Drinking

Central Valladolid brims with welcoming bars and cafes.

El Minuto   CAFE BAR
(Calle de Macias Picavea 15; ⊘9am-late) Near Valladolid's cathedral, this smooth cafe-bar is popular with students and is flanked by several other prospects for late-night drinking. The nearby Calle de Librería is an epicentre of early-evening student drinking.

Café Continental   CLUB
(Plaza Mayor 23; ⊘8am-late) This hip spot on the plaza features live music most nights.

El Soportal   BAR
(Plaza de San Miguel; ⊘4pm-1am Sun-Thu, 4pm-3am Fri & Sat) A large, diverse space that attracts all ages.

Harlem Music Club   CLUB
(Calle de San Antonio de Padua; ⊘4pm-1am Sun-Thu, 4pm-3am Fri & Sat) Has black glossy decor and music from America's Deep South.

Café de la Comedia   CLUB
(Plaza de Martí y Monsó; ⊘10am-1am) Has that winning combo of a convivial atmosphere with killer cocktails.

Be Bop   CLUB
(Plaza de Martí y Monsó; ⊘4pm-late) All pink stilettos and a super-cool crowd.

ℹ Information

The independent tourism site www.vallodolid turismo.com has useful up-to-date information on the city.

Tourist office (☑983 21 93 10; www.asomate avalladolid.org; Acera de Recoletos; ⊘9am-2pm & 5-8pm) Good for sightseeing advice, activities in the city and a map.

ℹ Getting There & Away

AIR Ryanair (www.ryanair.com) has flights to Valladolid from London (Stansted), Brussels (Charleroi) and Milan (Bergamo).

  Iberia (www.iberia.es) operates up to five daily flights to Barcelona, with connections to other cities in Spain.

BUS With such good train connections, it's hard to see why you'd need the bus. For the record, buses travel to Madrid almost hourly between 6.30am and 9.30pm (€12.95, 2¼ hours), while others go hourly to Palencia (€3.80, 45 minutes).

CAR & MOTORCYCLE There's a convenient underground car park in Plaza Mayor.

TRAIN Five daily high-speed AVE train services connect Valladolid with Madrid (€35.10, one hour), but there are slower services (2½ hours) for as little as €16.20. Other regular trains run to León (from €12.15, about two hours), Burgos (from €9, about 1½ hours) and Salamanca (from €8.25, 1½ hours).

ℹ Getting Around

Valladolid's airport is 15km northwest of the city centre. **Linecar** (www.linecar.es) has up to five daily bus services from Valladolid to the airport (€3.80). A taxi between the airport and the city centre costs around €20, a little more on Sunday and holidays.

  Local buses 2 and 10 pass the train and bus stations on their way to Plaza de España.

Around Valladolid

MEDINA DE RIOSECO
POP 5010

Medina de Rioseco, a once-wealthy trading centre, still has a tangible medieval feel, particularly along the narrow pedestrian main street with its colonnaded arcades held up by ancient wooden columns. It is well worth some strolling time; you can pick up a map at the tourist office.

⊙ Sights

Iglesia de Santa María de Mediavilla   CHURCH
(⊘11am-2pm & 5-8pm Tue-Sun) This is a grandiose Isabelline Gothic work with three

IT COULD HAVE BEEN SO DIFFERENT

Wondering why some of the great names of Spanish history – El Cid, Cervantes, Christopher Columbus and the merciless Inquisitor General Fray Tomás de Torquemada – were all connected with Valladolid? It's because the city was considered Spain's capital-in-waiting. In short, Valladolid could have been Madrid.

Fernando of Aragón and Isabel of Castilla (the Reyes Católicos, or Catholic Monarchs) discreetly married here in 1469. As Spain's greatest-ever ruling duo, they carried Valladolid to the height of its splendour. Its university was one of the most dynamic on the peninsula and Carlos I made Valladolid the seat of imperial government. Felipe II was born here in 1527 but, 34 years later, chose to make Madrid the capital, even though Madrid was considerably smaller. Valladolid, which had become too powerful for its own good, was aghast. In 1601 Felipe III moved the royal court back to Valladolid, but the move was so unpopular that the court returned to Madrid, there to remain in perpetuity.

With Spain's return to democracy after 1975, the *vallasoletanos* (people from Valladolid) had to be content with their city becoming the administrative capital of the Autonomía de Castilla y León.

star-vaulted naves and the famous **Capilla de los Benavente** chapel. Anchored by a grandiose altarpiece by Juan de Juní, it's sometimes referred to as 'the Sistine Chapel of Castilla'.

Museo de Semana Santa MUSEUM
(www.museos-medinaderioseco.com; Calle de Lázaro Alonso; admission €3; ⊙11am-2pm & 4-7pm Tue-Sun) Medina de Rioseco is famous for its Easter processions, but if you can't be here during Holy Week, this museum provides an insight into the ceremonial passion of Easter here. Like its sister museum in Zamora, it's dedicated to *pasos* (figures carried in Semana Santa processions) and an extensive range of other Easter artefacts.

Iglesia de Santiago CHURCH
(admission €1.80; ⊙11am-2pm & 4-7pm Tue-Sun Oct-Apr, 11am-2pm & 5-8pm May-Sep) Down the hill from the Iglesia de Santa María, the portals of this light-flooded church blend Gothic, neoclassical and plateresque architectural styles.

🛏 Sleeping & Eating

Vittoria Colonna MODERN HOTEL €€
(☑983 72 50 87; www.hotelvittoriacolonna.es; s/d €55/75; ❋❂) This supremely elegant hotel opened in 2009 and offers luxurious modern rooms with plush furnishings and smart grey-and-white bathrooms.

Hostal Duque de Osuna BUDGET HOTEL €
(☑983 70 01 79; www.hostalduquedeosuna.com; Avenida de Castilviejo 16; s/d €20/35; ❂) Hand-

ily situated for the bus station, with clean, simply decorated rooms.

Restaurante Pasos TRADITIONAL CASTILIAN €€
(☑983 72 00 21; Calle de Lázaro Alonso 44; meals €20) Recognised as the town's top restaurant, where you can expect well-prepared typical Castilian fare that courts various flavours but stays firmly in classical mould. Reservations recommended.

The town is famous for its delicious biscuits and cakes. Try a selection at centrally located La Espiga (Calle Lázaro Alonso 30).

ⓘ Information

Tourist office (☑983 72 03 19; www.medinaderioseco.com, in Spanish; Paseo de San Francisco 1; ⊙10am-2pm & 5-8pm Tue-Sat, 10am-2pm Sun) Located within a monastery, can provide a town map and information on the sights.

ⓘ Getting There & Away

Up to eight buses run to León (€6.40, 1¼ hours, daily) and up to 10 go to Valladolid (€4.10, 30 minutes, daily).

TORDESILLAS
POP 8710

Commanding a rise on the northern flank of Río Duero, this charming little town has a historical significance that belies its size. Originally a Roman town, it later played a major role in world history when, in 1494, Isabel and Fernando, the Catholic Monarchs, sat down with Portugal here to hammer out a treaty determining who got what in Latin America. Portugal got Brazil and much of the rest went to Spain.

Sights

The heart of town is formed by the pretty, porticoed Plaza Mayor, its mustard-yellow paintwork offset by dark-brown woodwork and black grilles.

Real Convento de Santa Clara CONVENT
(adult/concession €3.60/2, EU citizens free Wed; ☺10am-1.15pm & 3.45-5.45pm Tue-Sat, 10.30am-1.15pm Sun) The history of Tordesillas has been dominated by this Mudéjar-style convent, which is still home to a few Franciscan nuns living in near-total isolation from the outside world. First begun in 1340 as a palace for Alfonso XI, it was here, in 1494, that the Treaty of Tordesillas was signed. A guided tour (included in the entry fee) of the convent takes in some remarkable rooms, including a wonderful Mudéjar patio left over from the palace, and the church – the stunning *techumbre* (roof) is a masterpiece. The Mudéjar door, Gothic arches and Arabic inscriptions are superb, as are the Arab baths (☎983 77 00 71; admission €2.25, incl convent €4.60; ☺by appointment).

Museo del Tratado del Tordesillas
MUSEUM
(Calle de Casas del Tratado; admission free; ☺10am-1.30pm & 5-7.30pm Tue-Sat, 10am-2pm Sun) Dedicated to the 1494 Treaty of Tordesillas, the informative displays in this museum look at the world as it was before and after the treaty. There's a reproduction of the treaty itself and a map that suggests Spain did very well out of the negotiations.

FREE Museo de La Radio RADIO MUSEUM
(Calle San Antón 1; ☺5.30-7.30pm Fri, 12.30-2.30pm & 5.30-7.30pm Sat, 12.30-2.30pm Sun) A quirkier style of museum, this is for serious radio heads with more than 450 wirelesses on display, dating from 1916 to 1980.

Sleeping & Eating

Parador de Tordesillas PARADOR €€
(☎983 77 00 51; www.parador.es; Carretera de Salamanca 5; r €135; P ✳ ☜) Tordesillas' most sophisticated hotel is the low-rise ochre-toned *parador*, surrounded by pine trees just outside town. Some rooms have four-poster beds and many look out onto the tranquil gardens. This is one of the flagship *paradores* and is worth every euro. The set menu costs €31.

Hostal San Antolín SMALL HOTEL €
(☎983 79 67 71; www.hostalsanantolin.com; Calle San Antolín 8; s/d €30/45; ✳ ☜) This is the best place to stay in the old town, although the overall aesthetic is modern. The attached restaurant, the Mesón San Antolín, is one of the most popular eateries here, with good *raciones* downstairs, a pretty flower-decked inner patio and a fancy restaurant upstairs. It's just off Plaza Mayor.

A few pleasant cafes and restaurants surround the perimeter of Plaza Mayor, including Don Pancho (Plaza Mayor 9; menú €10, meals €20-25), with its atmospheric tiled bar and home cooking, including meats roasted in a wood-fire oven. For tapas, try Viky (Plaza Mayor 14; raciones €5-7, meals €20; ☺Tue-Sun).

Shopping

Muelas de Tordesillas WINE SHOP
(Calle Santa Maria 3-5) Just off the Plaza Mayor, the main shopping street is home to a bodega selling the excellent wines of this small family-owned label (from €4.50 a bottle). Tasting available.

Information

Tourist office (☎983 77 10 67; www.tordesillas.net; ☺10am-1.30pm & 5-7.30pm Tue-Sat, 10am-2pm Sun May-Sep) In Casas del Tratado, near the Iglesia de San Antolín.

Getting There & Away

The bus station (Avenida de Valladolid) is near Calle de Santa María. Regular buses depart for Madrid (€11.25, 2¼ hours), Salamanca (€6.15, 1¼ hours), Valladolid (€3.35, 30 minutes) and Zamora (€5.75, one hour).

TORO
POP 9740

Toro is your archetypal Castilian town in more than just name. Modern Toro, which lies north of Río Duero, is one of those Castilian towns whose past overshadows its present – it was here that Fernando and Isabel cemented their primacy in Christian Spain at the Battle of Toro in 1476. Since then, the town has settled rather comfortably into provinciality at the heart of a much-loved wine region. It has a charming historic centre with several architectural gems.

Sights

Romanesque churches appear on seemingly every street corner in Toro.

Colegiata Santa María La Mayor CHURCH
(admission €1; ☺10.30am-2pm & 5-7.30pm Tue-Sun) This 12th-century church rises above the town and boasts the magnificent

DON'T MISS

WINE TASTING

The great **Ribero del Duero** vintage wines are possibly the oldest in Spain and their sensuous appeal is well known. This is the largest wine-growing region in Castilla y León, covering some 9229 hectares. Tempranillo, cabernet-sauvignon, malbec and merlot are the most popular grape varieties and Spain's most celebrated (and expensive) wine, Vega Sicilia, comes from here. Not all the 200-plus wineries here are open for tours and tasting (including, unfortunately, Vega Sicilia), but several are. For a comprehensive list, check the www.rutasdevino.com/enoturismo/riberabodegas. htm website. Meanwhile, if you are ordering wine in a restaurant or bar, forget the familiar play-it-safe Rioja option, and go for the Ribero del Duero region instead. In general, the *vino de la casa* (house wine) will be local and a good bet.

Romanesque-Gothic **Pórtico de la Majestad**. Treasures inside include the famous 15th-century painting called *Virgen de la Mosca* (Virgin of the Fly); see if you can spot the fly on the virgin's robe. From behind the church you have a superb view south across the fields to the Romanesque bridge over Río Duero.

Monasterio Sancti Spiritus MONASTERY (admission €4.50; ⏱guided tours 10.30am-12.30pm & 4.30-6.30pm Tue-Sun) Southwest of town, this monastery features a fine Renaissance cloister and the striking alabaster tomb of Beatriz de Portugal, wife of Juan I. Guided tours run regularly during the hours indicated.

Near the Colegiata, the **Alcázar**, dating from the 10th century, retains its original walls and seven towers.

🛏 Sleeping & Eating

Plaza Mayor and nearby streets bustle with plenty of places to eat and sample local wines.

Hotel Juan II CLASSIC HOTEL €€ (☎980 69 03 00; http://hoteljuanii.com; Paseo del Espolón 1; s/d from €51/72; P🅿🐕☎🖥) Request room 201 if you can for its fabulous double-whammy vista of the River Duero to one side and the Colegiata to the other. The rooms have warm terracotta-tiled floors, dark-wood furniture and large terraces. The restaurant is one of Toro's best.

Zaravencia BUDGET HOTEL € (☎980 69 49 98; Plaza Mayor 17; s/d incl breakfast €45/60; ❄) Overlooking the lovely main square, this friendly place has a bar-restaurant downstairs and good size rooms with an, albeit, anaemic decor of light pine furniture and cream walls.

ℹ Information
Tourist office (☎980 69 47 47; www.turismo castillayleon.com; Plaza Mayor 6; ⏱10am-2pm & 4-7pm Tue-Sat, 10am-2pm Sun) Can provide general city information and a map.

ℹ Getting There & Away
Regular buses operate to Valladolid (€4.50, one hour) and Zamora (€2, 30 minutes), and there are two direct services to Salamanca (€5.40, 1½ hours) on weekdays.

Zamora
POP 66,200

As in so many Spanish towns, your first introduction to provincial Zamora is likely to be nondescript apartment blocks, but don't be put off: the *casco historico* (old town) is hauntingly beautiful with sumptuous medieval monuments that have earned Zamora the popular sobriquet 'Romanesque Museum'. It's a subdued encore to the monumental splendour of Salamanca and one of the best places to be during Semana Santa.

👁 Sights

Catedral CATHEDRAL (adult/concession €3/1.50; ⏱10am-2pm & 5-8pm) Crowning medieval Zamora's southwestern extremity, the largely Romanesque cathedral features a square tower, an unusual Byzantine-style dome surrounded by turrets, and the ornate Puerta del Obispo. To enter the cathedral, you pass through the **Museo Catedralicio** (⏱same hr), where the star attraction (on the 2nd floor) is the collection of Flemish tapestries. The oldest tapestry depicts the Trojan War and dates from the 15th century.

Inside the 12th-century cathedral itself, the early-Renaissance choir stalls are a masterpiece: carvings depict clerics, animals and a naughty encounter between a monk and a nun. The other major highlights are the Capilla de San Ildefonso, with its lovely Gothic frescoes, and some fine Flemish tapestries in the adjoining antechamber.

Museo de Semana Santa   EASTER MUSEUM
(Plaza de Santa María La Nueva; adult/concession €3/1.50; ⏱10am-2pm & 5-8pm Tue-Sat, 10am-2pm Sun) This museum will initiate you into the weird-and-wonderful rites of Easter, Spanish-style. It showcases the carved and painted *pasos* that are paraded around town during the colourful processions. The hooded models are eerily lifelike.

Churches   CHURCHES
(⏱10am-1pm & 5-8pm Tue-Sun) Zamora's churches are of Romanesque origin, but all have been subjected to other influences. Their steeples and towers are home to many happy nesting storks. Among those churches retaining some of their Romanesque charm are the Iglesia de San Pedro y San Ildefonso (with Gothic touches), Iglesia de la Magdalena (the southern doorway is considered the city's finest, with its preponderance of floral motifs) and Iglesia de San Juan de Puerta Nueva on Plaza Mayor. Iglesia de Santa María La Nueva (Calle de San Martín Carniceros) is actually a medieval replica of a 7th-century church destroyed by fire in 1158.

If you're here in January or February, apart from being *extremely* cold, you'll find most of Zamora's churches closed while church authorities sort out the year's opening hours. Check with either of the tourist offices.

FREE Castillo   CASTLE
(⏱11am-2pm & 6-10pm Tue-Sun; 🚻) After years of closure, this magnificent 11th-century castle has had the restoration folk in and is open to visitors. An ongoing project, at the time of research there were some local sculptures on display and visitors could climb the tower and walk the ramparts. There are ambitious plans afoot, however, including a museum. Check at the tourist office for an update.

Festivals & Events

Semana Santa   EASTER WEEK
If you're in Spain during Easter Week, make your way to Zamora, a town made famous for its elaborate celebrations; it's one of the most evocative places in the country to view the hooded processions. Watching the penitents weave their way through the historic streets, sometimes in near-total silence, is an experience you'll never forget. During the rest of the year, the Museo de Semana Santa will provide the appropriate initiation.

Sleeping
Zamora has a decent spread of accommodation. Prices can almost double during Semana Santa.

NH Palacio del Duero   MODERN HOTEL €€
(☎980 50 82 62; www.nh-hotels.com; Plaza de la Horta 1; s/d €65/75; P✳@✱) As usual, NH has snagged a superb position for one of its latest hotels. Next to a lovely Romanesque church, the seemingly modern building has cleverly encompassed part of the former convent, as well as (somewhat bizarrely) a 1940s power station; the lofty brick chimney still remains. Rooms are large and plushly furnished.

Parador Condes de Alba y Aliste
HISTORIC PARADOR €€€
(☎980 51 44 97; www.parador.es; Plaza Viriato 5; s/d €125/160; ✳@✱✱) Set in a sumptuous 15th-century palace (previous 'guests' included Isabel and Fernando), this is modern luxury with myriad period touches (mostly in the public areas). There's a swimming pool out the back and, unlike many *paradores*, it's right in the heart of town. On the downside, there is very limited parking available (just eight places).

Hotel Dos Infantas   MODERN HOTEL €€
(☎980 50 98 98; www.hoteldosinfantas.com, in Spanish; Calle Cortinas de San Miguel 3; s/d €60/80; P✳✱) They won't win any style awards here, but the rooms are modern, large and comfortable and you're not too far from the old town. Parking costs €8.

Eating & Drinking
Several cafe-restaurants line Plaza Mayor and can be found in the side streets around Calle Santa Clara. A good area for tapas bars is around Plaza del Maestro.

Restaurante París   GRILLED MEATS €€
(☎980 51 43 25; Avenida de Portugal 14; menú del día €15, menú turístico €24; ⏱Mon-Sat) This is one of Zamora's best restaurants and was once voted one of the best 1000 restaurants in Spain. That may not sound like much, but given the number of restaurants in this food-obsessed country... Castilian specialities (steaks, salads and roasted meats) rule

and *arroz a la zamorana* (a local rice dish with pork and ham) is a popular choice. Reservations recommended.

Restaurante El Rincón de Antonio

SOPHISTICATED CASTILIAN €€

(☑980 53 53 70; www.elrincondeantonio.com, in Spanish; Rúa de los Francos 6; meals €28-50; ⊙Mon-Sat, lunch Sun) Another fine place boasting one Michelin star and offering tapas as well as sit-down meals in a classy, softly lit dining area. À la carte choices can be pricey, more modest choices include a tasty *ración* of local cheese (€15) and the tasting menu of four tapas (€11, including a glass of wine). Reservations recommended.

Plaza Mayor and the streets emanating from it are great places for cafes and bars. One particular street abuzz with evening *marcha* (action) is Calle de los Herreros. Elsewhere, Café Marlene (Calle de la Reina 1; ⊙4pm-1am) is an oasis of sophistication that fronts onto Plaza Mayor.

❶ Information

Municipal tourist office (☑980 54 82 00; www.turismocastillayleon.com; Plaza de Arias Gonzalo; ⊙10am-2pm & 4-7pm Oct-Mar, 10am-2pm & 5-8pm Apr-Sep)

Regional tourist office (☑980 53 18 45; www.zamora.es; Avenida Príncipe de Asturias 1; ⊙9am-8pm Sun-Thu, 9am-9pm Fri & Sat) Organises guided tours (free to €5); check with the office for timings.

❶ Getting There & Away

BUS Almost hourly bus services operate to/from Salamanca (€4.95, one hour), with less-frequent departures on weekends. Other regular services include: to León (€7.75, 1½ hours), Valladolid (€7.20, 1½ hours) and Burgos (€15.10, 4½ hours).

TRAIN Trains head to Valladolid (€9.75, 1½ hours, one daily), Madrid (€29.10, 3¾ hours, three daily) and Ávila (€21.40, two hours, two daily).

Around Zamora

SAN PEDRO DE LA NAVE

This lonely 7th-century church (⊙10am-1pm & 5-8pm Tue-Sun), about 24km northwest of Zamora, is a rare and outstanding example of Visigoth church architecture, with blended Celtic, Germanic and Byzantine elements. Of special note are the intricately sculpted capitals. The church was moved to its present site in Campillo during the con-

struction of the Esla reservoir in 1930. To get there from Zamora, take the N122, then follow the signs to Campillo.

PUEBLA DE SANABRIA

POP 1620

Nestled between the Sierra de la Culebra and Sierra de la Cabrera, and close to the Portuguese border, this captivating little village is a tangle of medieval alleyways that unfold around a 15th-century castle and trickle down the hill. You can enter the castle at will and wander around the walls, while the view up towards town from the bridge is very pretty indeed. Puebla de Sanabria also serves as the gateway to Lago de Sanabria, Spain's largest glacier lake at 368 hectares and an astonishing 55m deep. It's a beautiful spot around 15km north of town that gets overrun on summer weekends.

It's well worth stopping overnight: the quiet cobblestone lanes make it feel like you've stepped back centuries. Posada Real la Cartería (☑980 62 03 12; www.lacarteria.com; Calle de Rúa 16; r €125; ⊙❈🐾) is one of the best hotels in this part of the country. It blends modern comforts with all the old-world atmosphere of the village itself, featuring delightful, large rooms with exposed stone walls and wooden beams, not to mention a gym, a good restaurant and professional service.

The village has a helpful tourist office (☑980 62 07 34; www.pueblasanabria.org, in Spanish; Calle de Rúa 3; ⊙11am-2pm & 5-8pm).

There are sporadic bus services to Puebla de Sanabria from Zamora (from €7, 1¼ hours).

Palencia

POP 82,300

Subdued Palencia boasts an immense Gothic cathedral, the sober exterior of which belies the extraordinary riches that await within; it's widely known as 'La Bella Desconocida' (Unknown Beauty). Otherwise, you'll find some pretty squares, a colonnaded main street (Calle Mayor) and a slew of other churches. King Alfonso VIII founded Spain's first university here in 1208.

◉ Sights

Catedral

CATHEDRAL

(Calle Mayor Antigua 29; admission €2; ⊙10am-1.30pm & 4.30-7.30pm Mon-Fri, 10am-2pm &

4-5.30pm Sat, 4.30-8pm Sun) The **Puerta del Obispo** (Bishop's Door) is the highlight of the facade of the imposing cathedral which, at 130m long, 56m wide and 30m high, is one of the largest of the Castilian cathedrals. The interior contains a treasure trove of art. One of the most stunning chapels is the **Capilla El Sagrario**: its ceiling-high altarpiece tells the story of Christ in dozens of exquisitely carved and painted panels. The stone screen behind the choir stalls (*trascoro*), is a masterpiece of bas-relief attributed to Gil de Siloé and is considered by many to be the most beautiful retrochoir in Spain.

From here, a platesresque stairwell leads down to the **crypt**, a remnant of the original, 7th-century Visigoth church and a later Romanesque replacement. Near the stairwell is the oak pulpit, with delicate carvings of the Evangelists by Juan de Ortiz.

In the attached Museo Catedralicio (guided tours €3; 9am-2pm & 4-8pm) you'll see some fine Flemish tapestries and a painting of San Sebastián by El Greco. A whimsical highlight is a trick painting by 16th-century German artist Lucas Cranach the Elder. Looking straight on, it seems to be a surreal dreamscape that predates Dalí by some 400 years. Only when viewed from the side is the true image revealed – a portrait of Emperor Carlos V. Tours run hourly and last 45 minutes.

Iglesia de San Miguel CHURCH
(Calle de Mayor Antigua; 9.30am-1.30pm & 6-7.30pm) This church stands out for its tall Gothic tower with a castle-like turret. San Miguel's interior is unadorned and austerely beautiful, a welcome antidote to the extravagant interiors of other Castilian churches. According to legend, El Cid was betrothed to his Doña Jimena here.

Museo Diocesano ART MUSEUM
(Calle de Mayor Antigua; guided tours €2; tours 10am-1.30pm & 4.30-7.30) Located within the 18th-century Palacio Episcopal, this museum showcases art from the Middle Ages through to the Renaissance. Pride of place goes to works by Pedro de Berruguete and an altarpiece starring the Virgin (attributed to Diego de Siloé).

Modernista Architecture
ARCHITECTURAL GEMS
Palencia is embellished with some real architectural gems. You can follow a numbered route around the centre; look for the large rectangular signs: **Reencuentra La Belleza** (Rediscover the Beauty). The itinerary includes stops at the 19th-century Modernista Mercado de Abastos (fresh food market) on Calle Colón and the extraordinarily ornate neo-plateresque Palacio Provincial on Calle Burgos. Step into the lobby here to admire the ceiling frieze of the city under attack by the Roman legions dating from 1904 and painted by local artist Eugenio Oliva. The tourist office can provide you with more information and references.

Iglesia de San Pablo CHURCH
(Plaza de San Pablo; 7.30am-12.30pm & 6.30-8.15pm) Has a Renaissance facade and an enormous platesresque altarpiece in the main chapel.

🛏 Sleeping

TOP CHOICE Hotel Colón 27 MODERN HOTEL €
(979 74 07 00; www.hotelcolon27.com; Calle de Colón 27; s/d €33/45; ❊❀) This place is excellent value with comfortable carpeted rooms sporting light pine furniture, good firm mattresses, shiny green-tiled bathrooms and small flat-screened TVs.

Hotel Plaza Jardinillos BUDGET HOTEL €
(979 75 00 22; www.palencia.com/hotelplaza jardinillos.com; Calle de Eduardo Dato 2; s/d €30/36; P❊) The rooms here are large and clean but could do with some loving DIY and a touch of paint. A real bonus is the inexpensive parking (€5) and the location, just off pedestrian Calle Mayor and close to the cathedral.

Diana Palace MODERN HOTEL €€
(979 01 80 50; www.eurostarsdianapalace. com; Avenida Santander 12; s/d incl breakfast €60/80; P❊❀) A comfortable, albeit modern, block of a hotel within walking distance of the centre.

🍴 Eating & Drinking

Head for Plaza Mayor, one of the most agreeable places to eat, drink and people-watch. The surrounding streets are also home to the bulk of the better dining options.

Restaurante Casa Lucio
CASTILIAN SPECIALITIES €€
(979 74 81 90; Calle de Don Sancho 2; meals €30-35; closed Sun) That great Spanish tradition of an overcrowded bar laden with tapas yielding to a quieter, more elegant restaurant is alive and well. Sidle up to the bar for creative tapas or consider the

Castilian speciality of *cordero asado* (€41 for two) at this, Palencia's most famous restaurant. Reservations recommended.

Casa Damian REGIONAL DISHES €€
(Calle de Martínez de Azcoita 9; meals €20-25; ☺lunch Tue, Wed & Sun, lunch & dinner Thu-Sat) This timeless classic of a restaurant has elderly bow-tied waiters, a smart wood-panelled dining room and a menu of classic local dishes. Folk travel from far and wide for the house speciality starter: *menestra Damien* (fresh vegetable stew), generally followed by a grilled meat main.

Ponte Vecchio ITALIAN €€
(Calle de Doctrinus 1; meals €20-25; ☺Tue-Sun) If you're craving upper-crust pizza and well-cooked pasta in classy surrounds, Ponte Vecchio is Palencia's best Italian restaurant. Low ceilings, muted lighting and a warm colour scheme equal a romantic dinner for two. There is live music, ranging from flamenco to jazz, on Thursdays. Note that if you order fish or steak, your bill can double.

El Templo del Café WORLD COFFEES €
(Calle de Martínez de Azcoita 5; ☺Tue-Sun) This is the place to come if you are into exotic coffees and teas, delectable cakes, head-spinning cocktails or the simple pleasure of that irresistible combination of *chocolate con churros* (deep-fried donut strips dipped in hot chocolate; €3). Regular art exhibitions are also held here.

Taberna Plaza Mayor RACIONES €
(Plaza Mayor 8; menú del día €10, meals €20) Grab an outdoor table here and choose from a selection of *raciones*, ranging from sardines stuffed with cured ham to a hearty bowl of lentil stew; the tapas and house wine are also good.

ℹ Information

Locutorio (Calle de Eduardo Dato 1; per hr €1; ☺10am-4pm & 1.30-10.30pm) Internet access and telephone booths.

Municipal tourist office (☎979 74 99 74; www.palencia-turismo.com; Plaza de San Pablo; ☺10.30am-2pm & 5-8.30pm) Covers the city with plenty of information and a map.

Patronato de Turismo (☎979 70 65 23; www.palencia.es; Calle Mayor 31; ☺9am-2pm & 5-8pm Mon-Sat, 9am-2pm Sun) Information about Palencia province.

ℹ Getting There & Away

BUS From the **bus station** (Carerra del Cementerio) there are regular services to Valladolid (€3.80, 45 minutes), Madrid (€15.95, 3¼ hours), Aguilar de Campóo (€5.30, 1½ hours), Frómista (€3.15, 30 minutes) and Paredes de Nava (€1.45, 25 minutes).

TRAIN Regular trains run to Madrid (€20.20, 3¼ hours), Burgos (from €4.85, one hour), León (from €7.85, 1¾ hours) and Valladolid (€4.05, 45 minutes).

Around Palencia

BAÑOS DE CERRATO

Close to the singularly unattractive rail junction of Venta de Baños lies Spain's oldest church, the 7th-century Basílica de San Juan (admission €1, Wed free; ☺10.30am-1.30pm & 4-6pm Tue-Sun) in Baños de Cerrato. Built by the Visigoths in 661 and modified many times since, its stone-and-terracotta facade exudes a pleasing, austere simplicity and features a 14th-century alabaster statue of St John the Baptist. To get there, take a train from Palencia to Venta de Baños, then walk the final 2km.

PAREDES DE NAVA
POP 2150

The eminent 16th-century sculptor Alonso de Berruguete was born in Paredes in 1488. Sadly, most of the town's churches are in great disrepair, save for the eclectic 13th-century Iglesia de Santa Eulalia (Plaza de España; admission €2; ☺10.30am-1.30pm & 4-7pm Mar-Sep, by appointment rest of yr), with its pretty steeple with arched windows. Its museum contains several pieces by Berruguete.

Several trains travel daily to Palencia (€2.55, 15 minutes), and a couple of buses (€1.75) also ply the route.

FRÓMISTA
POP 840

The main (and some would say only) reason for stopping here is the exceptional Romanesque Iglesia de San Martín (admission €1; ☺9am-2pm & 4.30-8pm). Dating from 1066 and restored in the early 20th century, this harmoniously proportioned church is adorned with a veritable menagerie of human and zoomorphic figures just below the eaves. The capitals within are also richly decorated.

If you get stuck here overnight or just meal time, Pensión Marisa (☎979 81 00 23;

Plaza Obispo Almaraz 2; s/d without bathroom €18/30; menú del día €9) has spotless, bright rooms and great home cooking.

There are two buses daily from Palencia (€3.15, 30 minutes).

Montaña Palentina

These hills in the far north of Castilla y León offer a beautiful preview of the Cordillera Cantábrica, which divides Castilla from Spain's northern Atlantic regions.

AGUILAR DE CAMPÓO
POP 7270

Aguilar de Campóo wouldn't win a beauty contest, but it does boast a medieval castle and serves as a good base for exploring the region: there are no fewer than 55 Romanesque churches in the cool, hilly countryside.

The elongated Plaza de España is capped at its eastern end by the Colegiata de San Miguel, a 14th-century Gothic church with a fine Romanesque entrance.

Downhill from the castle is the graceful Romanesque Ermita de Santa Cecilia. Just outside town, on the highway to Cervera de Pisuerga, is the restored Monasterio de Santa María la Real (Carretera de Cervera; admission €5; ⊘10.30am-2pm & 4.30-8pm) of Romanesque origin. Its 13th-century Gothic cloister with delicate capitals is glorious.

There's plenty of accommodation around town and the square is swarming with cafes, bars and a couple of restaurants. The sprawling, central Hotel Restaurante Valentín (⌨979 12 21 25; www.hotelvalentin.com; Avenida Ronda 23; s/d €44/60; P❄☎) is easily the best choice, with large comfortable rooms. Parking costs €6.

There's a tourist office (www.turismo castillayleon.com; Plaza de España 30; ⊘10am-1.45pm & 4-5.45pm Tue-Sat, 10am-1.45pm Sun).

Regular trains link Aguilar de Campóo with Palencia (€5.30, 1¼ hours), but the station is 4km from town. Buses bound for Burgos, Palencia and Santander depart at least once daily.

ROMANESQUE CIRCUIT

The area around Aguilar is studded with little villages and churches. At Olleros de Pisuerga there's a little church carved into rock, while further south, on a quiet back road, the Benedictine Monasterio de Santa María de Mave (admission free; ⊘10am-2pm & 4-7pm Tue-Sun) has an inter-

BEST CITY FOR...

» **Medieval walls** – Ávila (p125)

» **Cathedrals** – León (p166), Burgos (p178), Palencia (p164) and Salamanca (p132)

» **Stunning architecture** – Salamanca (p132), Zamora (p162) and Segovia (p145)

» **Restaurants and nightlife** – Salamanca (p138), León (p171), Segovia (p152) and Valladolid (p157)

» **Pretty plazas** – Salamanca (p132) and Valladolid (p155)

» **Provincial atmosphere** – Soria (p189)

esting 13th-century Romanesque church. The Monasterio de San Andrés de Arroyo (guided tours €2.50; ⊘10am-12.30pm & 3-6pm) is an outstanding Romanesque gem, especially its cloister, which dates from the 13th century. Guided tours run hourly.

The C627 highway heading to Cervera de Pisuerga is lined with still more little churches dating from as far back as the 12th century. Cervera de Pisuerga itself is dominated by an imposing late-Gothic church, the Iglesia de Santa María del Castillo.

The N621 north from Cervera is a lovely road into Cantabria and to the southern face of the Picos de Europa.

THE NORTHWEST

The city of León stands like a sentinel at the rim of the great Castilian heartland and its breathtaking cathedral provides a major focal point for pilgrims along the Camino de Santiago, before the trail climbs west into the sierras that separate Castilla from Galicia. León's hinterland is full of gems such as Astorga and the otherworldly minescapes of Las Médulas.

León

POP 135,000 / ELEV 527M

León is a wonderful city, combining stunning historical architecture with an irresistible energy. Its standout attraction is the cathedral, one of the most beautiful in all of Spain. By day you'll encounter a city with its roots firmly planted in the soil of northern

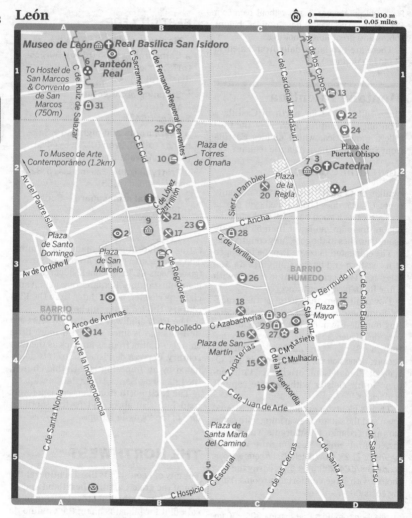

Castilla, with its grand monuments, loyal Catholic heritage and role as an important staging post along the Camino de Santiago. By night León is taken over by its large student population, who provide it with a deep-into-the-night soundtrack of revelry that floods the narrow streets and plazas of the picturesque old quarter, the Barrio Húmedo. It's a wonderful mix.

History

A Roman legion set up camp here in AD 70 as a base for controlling the goldmines of Las Médulas. In the 10th century the Asturian king Ordoño II moved his capital here from Oviedo and, although it was later sacked by the Muslim armies of Al-Mansour, León was maintained by Alfonso V as the capital of his growing kingdom. As the centre of power shifted south, León went into decline. Mining brought the city back to life in the 1800s. Throughout the 20th century, León's fame revolved around its role as a major staging post along the Camino de Santiago. The city came within the newly autonomous region of Castilla y León in 1983, which some locals saw as an indignity after its proudly independent history.

León

Sights

Catedral CATHEDRAL
(www.catedraldeleon.org, in Spanish; ◷8.30am-1.30pm & 4-8pm Mon-Sat, 8.30am-2.30pm & 5-8pm Sun) León's 13th-century cathedral, with its soaring towers, flying buttresses and truly breathtaking interior, is the city's spiritual heart. Whether spotlit by night or bathed in the glorious northern sunshine, the cathedral, arguably Spain's premier Gothic masterpiece, exudes a glorious, almost luminous quality.

The extraordinary facade has a radiant rose window, three richly sculpted doorways and two muscular towers. After going through the main entrance, lorded over by the scene of the Last Supper, an extraordinary gallery of *vidrieras* (stained-glass windows) awaits. French in inspiration and mostly executed from the 13th to the 16th centuries, the windows evoke an atmosphere unlike that of any other cathedral in Spain; the kaleidoscope of coloured light is offset by the otherwise gloomy interior. There seems to be more glass than brick – 128 windows with a surface of 1800 sq metres in all – but mere numbers cannot convey the ethereal quality of light permeating this cathedral.

Other treasures include a silver urn on the altar, by Enrique de Arfe, containing the remains of San Froilán, León's patron saint. Also note the magnificent choir stalls and the rich chapels in the ambulatory behind the altar, especially the one containing the tomb of Ordoño II.

The peaceful, light-filled **claustro** (cloister; admission €1), with its 15th-century frescoes, is a perfect complement to the main sanctuary and an essential part of the cathedral experience. The **Museo Catedralicio-Diocesano** (admission incl claustro €3.50; ◷9.30am-1.30pm & 4-7.30pm Mon-Sat), off the cloisters, has an impressive collection encompassing works by Juní and Gaspar Becerra alongside a precious assemblage of early-Romanesque carved statues of the Virgin Mary.

Real Basílica de San Isidoro
ROMANESQUE CHURCH
Older even than the cathedral, the Real Basílica de San Isidoro provides a stunning Romanesque counterpoint to the former's

Gothic strains. Fernando I and Doña Sancha founded the church in 1063 to house the remains of the saint, as well as the remains of themselves and 21 other early Leónese and Castilian monarchs. Sadly, Napoleon's troops sacked San Isidoro in the early 19th century, leaving behind just a handful of sarcophagi, although there's still plenty to catch the eye.

The main basilica is a hotchpotch of styles, but the two main portals on the southern facade are pure Romanesque. Of particular note is the **Puerta del Perdón** (on the right), which has been attributed to Maestro Mateo, the genius of the cathedral at Santiago de Compostela. The church remains open night and day by historical royal edict.

The attached Panteón Real (admission €4, Thu afternoon free; ☉10am-1.30pm & 4-6.30pm Mon-Sat, 10am-1.30pm Sun) houses the remaining sarcophagi, which rest with quiet dignity beneath a canopy of some of the finest Romanesque frescoes in Spain. Motif after colourful motif drenches the vaults and arches of this extraordinary hall, held aloft by marble columns with intricately carved capitals. Biblical scenes dominate and include the Annunciation, King Herod's slaughter of the innocents, the Last Supper and a striking representation of Christ Pantocrator. The agricultural calendar on one of the arches is equally superb.

The pantheon, which once formed the portico of the original church, also houses a small museum where you can admire the shrine of San Isidoro, a mummified finger of the saint (!) and other treasures. A library houses a priceless collection of manuscripts.

Abutting the southwestern corner of the basilica is a fragment of the former **muralla** (old city wall), a polyglot of Roman origins and medieval adjustments.

Barrio Gótico   HISTORIC QUARTER

On the fringes of León's old town (also known as the Barrio Gótico), Plaza de San Marcelo is home to the ayuntamiento (town hall), which occupies a charmingly compact Renaissance-era palace. The Renaissance theme continues in the form of the splendid Palacio de los Guzmanes (1560), where the facade and patio stand out. Next door is Antoni Gaudí's contribution to León's skyline, the castle-like, neo-Gothic Casa de Botines (1893). The zany

architect of Barcelona fame seems to have been subdued by sober León.

Down the hill, the delightful Plaza de Santa María del Camino (also known as Plaza del Grano) feels like a cobblestone Castilian village square and is overlooked by the Romanesque Iglesia de Santa María del Mercado.

At the northeastern end of the old town is the beautiful and time-worn 17th-century Plaza Mayor. Sealed off on three sides by porticoes, this sleepy plaza is home to a bustling fruit-and-vegetable market on Wednesday and Saturday. On the west side of the square is the superb late-17th-century baroque old town hall.

FREE Museo de Arte Contemporáneo
ART MUSEUM

(Musac; www.musac.org.es; Avenida de los Reyes Leóneses 24; ☉11am-8pm Tue-Thu, 11am-9pm Fri, 10am-9pm Sat & Sun) León's showpiece Museo de Arte Contemporáneo belongs to the new wave of innovative Spanish architecture. A pleasing square-and-rhombus edifice of colourful glass and steel, the museum won the Spanish architecture prize a few years back. It has been acclaimed for the 37 shades of coloured glass that adorn the facade; they were gleaned from the pixelisation of a fragment of one of the stained-glass windows in León's cathedral.

Although the museum has a growing permanent collection, it mostly houses temporary displays of cutting-edge Spanish and international photography, video installations and other similar forms. For many, the building may appeal more than the works it contains. Musac also hosts musical performances and is fast becoming one of northern Spain's most dynamic cultural spaces. Guided tours for groups may be arranged with prior arrangement. To get here, head northwest of the centre along Avenida del Padre Isla and follow the signs.

Museo de León   CITY MUSEUM

(Plaza de Santo Domingo 8; admission €1.20, Sat & Sun free; ☉10am-2pm & 4-7pm Tue-Sat) After years of looking for a suitable home, the Museo de León has found a space worthy of the city's history. Spread over four floors, the exhibits begin with stunning stone artefacts in the basement, and thereafter journey through the Middle Ages up to the 19th century. It's wonderfully presented and the informative descriptions are in Spanish and English.

Convento de San Marcos
CONVENT

More than 100m long and blessed with a glorious facade, the Convento de San Marcos (lying within the Hostal de San Marcos) looks more like a palace than the pilgrim's hospital it was from 1173. The plateresque exterior, sectioned off by slender columns and decorated with delicate medallions and friezes, dates to 1513, by which time the edifice had become a monastery of the Knights of Santiago. Much of the former convent is now a supremely elegant *parador*. Non-guests can visit the former chapter house and the magnificent cloister (adult/concession €0.60/free, Thu free; ⊙10am-2pm & 4-7pm Tue-Sat, 10am-2pm Sun).

FREE Cripta de Puerta Obispo
CRYPT

(Calle Ancha) Beneath the footpath below the southern wall of the cathedral is the Cripta de Puerta Obispo, the foundations from the northern gate of the Roman camp where León was founded. It's an ongoing archeological site, so opening times vary. Immediately east of the crypt are the foundations of the **Puerta Obispo**, one of the main city gates in Roman times.

⚜ Festivals & Events

León is famous for its solemn processions of hooded devotees during **Semana Santa**, while the city really lets its hair down from 21 to 30 June for the **Fiestas de San Juan y San Pedro**.

🛏 Sleeping

León has a solid range of centrally located accommodation. If you would prefer rural accommodation near the city, check out the comprehensive website (www.castillay leonesvida.com).

TOP CHOICE Hostal San Martín
HISTORIC HOTEL €

(🕿987 87 51 87; www.sanmartinhostales. com; 2nd fl, Plaza de Torres de Omaña 1; s without bathroom €20, s/d with bathroom €31/43) In a splendid central position, this recently overhauled 18th-century building has light, airy rooms painted in candy colours with small terraces. The spotless bathrooms have excellent water pressure and tubs, as well as showers. There is a comfortable sitting area and the friendly owner can provide advice and a map.

La Posada Regia
HISTORIC HOTEL €€

(🕿987 21 31 73; www.regialeon.com, in Spanish; Calle de Regidores 9-11; s/d €65/120; ✳🛜) You won't find many places better than this in northern Spain. The secret is a 14th-century building, magnificently restored (wooden beams, exposed brick and understated antique furniture), with individually styled rooms, character that overflows into the public areas and supremely comfortable beds and bathrooms. Even the artwork is well thought out, including abstract and classical styles.

QH
SPA HOTEL €€

(🕿987 87 55 80; www.qhhoteles.com; Avenida de los Cubos 6; s/d €45/60; ✳🛜🛜) Located within confessional distance of the cathedral, this boutique spa hotel opened in March 2010. The historic 19th-century building provided a suitable aesthetic canvas for the sharp modern design of the interior. Rooms have cathedral views, a bold accented colour scheme and steely grey bathrooms. Prices increase with use of the spa and treatments.

Hostal de San Marcos
HISTORIC PARADOR €€€

(🕿987 23 73 00; www.parador.es; Plaza de San Marcos 7; d from €198; ✳@🛜) León's sumptuous *parador* is one of the finest hotels in Spain. With palatial rooms fit for royalty and filled with old-world charm, this is one of the Parador chain's flagship properties. It also houses the Convento de San Marcos.

Hostal Bayón
BUDGET HOTEL €

(🕿987 23 14 46; Calle del Alcázar de Toledo 6; s/d with washbasin €15/30, with shower €25/37) At this long-standing León favourite, the laid-back owner presides over inviting, functional rooms with bright fabrics and pine floors. You're surrounded by modern León, but just a five-minute walk from the old town. To reach the *hostal* head west from Plaza de Santo Domingo along Avenida de Ordoño II and right on Calle del Alcázar de Toledo; the *hostal* is on your right.

NH Plaza Mayor
CLASSIC HOTEL €€

(🕿987 34 43 57; www.nh-hoteles.es; Plaza Mayor 15; s/d €67/87; ✳@🛜) Part of the stylish NH chain, which has a knack for finding a great location, this hotel has the perfect combination of comfort, muted colour schemes, great service and an intimate ambience. The glossy bathrooms have tubs and double sinks, as well as showers. Nineteen rooms overlook the plaza.

🍴 Eating

The most atmospheric part of town for restaurants is the Barrio Húmedo, which lies immediately south of the cathedral. You can easily fill up on tapas here, but if you would like something more substantial, there is a good choice of restaurants as well. A good place to head is Plaza de San Martín.

La Parrilla del Humedo　TRADITIONAL TAPAS €
(Calle Azabacheria 6; raciones €7-13) This place is always packed with euro-economising *leonéses,* here for the remarkably good house wine and accompanying free and good-size tapas; both for the bargain-basement price of €1.50. These tasty bites include fried potatoes with *alioli* (garlic mayonnaise) and sauteed mushrooms. Head for the dining room out back for heartier portions, including the city's fabled *el morcilla de León* (León-style blood sausage) or, for lightweights, a plate of tasty *pimientos de padrón* (small roasted peppers).

TOP CHOICE **El Llar**　TRADITIONAL TAPAS €€
(Plaza de San Martín 9; meals €25-30; 📷) This old León *taberna* is a great place to *tapear* (eat tapas) with its innovative selection of *raciones* that includes baked potatoes filled with wild mushrooms and prawns *au gratin*. The upstairs restaurant has a fine classic look and the menu includes vegetarian options like fresh leeks prepared in puff pastry and a seven salad choice. There is an excellent wine list to complement your meal.

Estrella de Galicia　SPANISH €
(Calle Ancha 20; menú del día €11, meals €15; 🕐Tue-Sun) This sprawling modern restaurant is located in the middle of this popular shopping street and attracts a mix of the lunchbreak business bunch and shoppers. All that's good about northwestern Spanish cuisine can be found here, with Galician seafood, Cantabrian fish and cured meats from the northern interior. The *pulpo* (octopus) is a great order but Estrella also does salads, mini-rolls and a host of *raciones.*

Alfonso Valderas　SEAFOOD €€
(📷987 20 05 05; Calle Arco de Ánimas 1; meals €35-40) The city's most famous restaurant for *bacalao* (salt cod) prepared around 20 different ways, including *al pil-pil* (with a spicy chilli sauce), with the local *queso valdeóon* cheese and with a *salsa de oricios* (sea urchin sauce). There are also meat, fish and rice mains. The dining room is grandly elegant, with a magnificent grandfather clock and a baffling display cabinet of antique shoes. Reservations recommended.

El Tizón　REGIONAL SPECIALITIES €€
(📷987 25 60 49; Plaza de San Martín 1; raciones €10-15, meals €25-30; 🕐Mon-Sat, lunch Sun) The tapas are good here, but the small sit-down restaurant, with its abundant range of *raciones,* is even better. House specialities include the local *embutidos.* More adventurous souls can order *caracoles* (snails) or *ancas de rana* (frog legs). There's an extensive wine list. Reservations recommended.

Restaurante Zuloaga
SOPHISTICATED MODERN €€
(📷987 23 78 14; Sierra Pambley 3; meals €35-40; 🕐Tue-Sat) Located in the vaults of an early-20th-century palace, this sophisticated place has a well-stocked cellar and classy adventurous menu. Starters include Andalusian-style partridge salad followed by mains like duck confit with dried fruits. Reservations recommended.

Susi　CONTEMPORARY CUISINE €€
(📷987 27 39 96; Calle de López Castrillión 1; meals €25-30) Intimate dining and creative cooking. Reservations recommended.

Palacio Jabal Quinto　MODERN €€
(📷987 21 53 22; www.palaciojabalquinto.com, in Spanish; Calle de Juan de Arfe 2; meals €35; 🕐Tue-Sat) One of the classier places to eat, located in a renovated 17th-century palace. Reservations recommended.

🍸 Drinking & Entertainment

The Barrio Húmedo's night-time epicentre is Plaza de San Martín – prise open the door of any bar here or in the surrounding streets (especially Calle de Juan de Arfe and Calle de la Misericordia), inch your way to the bar and you're unlikely to want to leave until closing time. The crowds will tell you where the buzz is, but a good night could begin at **Rebote** (Plaza de San Martín 9; 🕐8pm-1am Mon-Sat), then move on to the nightly live music and Guinness on tap at **Molly Malone's** (Calle Cardiles 2; 🕐11am-late) before ending up at **Club Danzatoria** (Calle de Ramirez III 9; 🕐11pm-3am Wed-Sat).

Tucked away behind the cathedral to the east, **Big John's** (Avenida de los Cubos 4; 🕐7pm-2am) is a jazz hang-out with a vigorous sound mix including bee bop, Latin and Dixieland, while adjacent **Ébanno** (Avenida de los Cubos 2; 🕐4pm-late) is classy and as good for laptop-toting wi-fi hunters as for late-night sophisticates.

CRIPPLING CAR PARK COSTS

Drivers should note that León's central city underground car parks are privately owned and costlier than most (€1.35 an hour) with, unusually, no reduction for overnight stays. You may want to consider a hotel with private parking instead.

Elsewhere, Ékole Café (Plaza de Torres de Omaña; ☺4.30pm-1.30am Sun-Thu, 4.30pm-3.30am Fri & Sat) is another favourite León drinking hole with an old Parisian feel. It serves cocktails (€5), ice creams and hot drinks and has a lovely interior patio.

A great place for a drink, day or night, is Capitán Haddock (Calle Ancha 8; ☺noon-late), with red velvet curtains, candlelight, mirrors, a collection of antiquated wirelesses and an ambience somewhere between boudoir and retro.

Shopping

The main pedestrian shopping street is Calle Ancha. Don't miss the fabulous Farmacia Alonso Nuñez at number 3. It dates from 1827 and, aside from the displays of anti-wrinkle creams and condoms, the sumptuous interior hasn't changed a bit.

La Casa de los Quesos   CHEESE
(Calle Plegarias 14) Cheese-lovers will want to make a stop here; you'll find every imaginable variety, including low-fat for those counting cholesterol numbers.

Tejuelo   FINE STATIONERY
(Calle de Ruiz de Salazar 18) Handmade paper products, fountain pens, leather-bound books and a small but rich range of classically upmarket stationery make this place stand out.

Iguazú   TRAVEL BOOKS
(Calle de Plegarias 7; ☺10am-2pm & 5-8.30pm Mon-Fri, 10.30am-2.30pm Sat) A fine little travel bookshop.

Information

Locutorio La Rua (Calle de Varillas 3; per 1/5hr €2/5; ☺9.30am-9.30pm Mon-Fri, 10.30am-2.30pm & 5.30-9.30pm Sat) Internet access.

Tourist office (☎987 23 70 82; www.turismo castillayleon.com; Calle el Cid 2; ☺9am-8pm) Has contact information for guided tour companies.

Getting There & Away

The train and bus stations lie on the western bank of Río Bernesga.

BUS From the bus station (Paseo del Ingeniero Sáez de Miera) there are numerous daily buses to Madrid (€22, 3½ hours), Burgos (€14.10, 3¾ hours), Ponferrada (€8.15, two hours), and Valladolid (€9.25, two hours).

CAR & MOTORCYCLE Parking bays (€9 to €13 for 12 hours) are found in the streets surrounding Plaza de Santo Domingo.

TRAIN Regular daily trains travel to Valladolid (from €12.15, two hours), Burgos (from €20.10, two hours), Oviedo (from €18.80, two hours), Madrid (from €28.30, 4¼ hours) and Barcelona (from €68.40, nine hours).

East of León

IGLESIA DE SAN MIGUEL DE ESCALADA

Rising from Castilla's northern plains, this beautifully simple church (☺10.15am-2pm & 4.30-8pm Tue-Sun) was built in the 9th century by refugee monks from Córdoba on the remains of a Visigoth church dedicated to the Archangel Michael. Although little trace of the latter remains, the church is notable for its Islamic-inspired horseshoe arches, rarely seen so far north in Spain. The graceful exterior porch with its portico is balanced by the impressive marble columns within. The entrance dates from the 11th century. To get here, take the N601 southeast of León. After about 14km, take the small LE213 to the east; the church is 16km after the turn-off.

SAHAGÚN
POP 2850 / ELEV 807M

An unremarkable place today, Sahagún was once home to one of Spain's more powerful abbeys. Its more important remnants are kept in the small Museo Benedictinas (admission by donation; ☺10am-noon & 4-6pm Tue-Sat, 10am-noon Sun).

Next to the former abbey is the early-12th-century Iglesia de San Tirso (☺10.15am-2pm & 4.30-8pm Wed-Sat, 10.15am-2pm Sun), an important stop on the Camino de Santiago, known for its pure Romanesque design and Mudéjar bell tower laced with rounded arches. The Iglesia San Lorenzo, just north of Plaza Mayor, has a similar bell tower.

Right across the road from the tourist office, comfortable Hostal La Codorniz (☎987 78 02 76; www.hostallacodorniz.com; Avenida de la Constitución 97-99; s/d €40/50; ❄) has a traditional restaurant complete with

CAMINO DE SANTIAGO

Burgos to León

Many pilgrims avoid this stretch of the camino and take the bus, which is a pity as they are missing out on a unique experience of nature with the beauty lying in the subtle and ever-changing play of colours on the *meseta* (the high tableland of central Spain). Contrary to popular opinion, it is not flat. Villages are set low in long valleys, with occasional rivers, which rise up to the high barren plains. There are large limestone rocks everywhere and evocative sights, such as flocks of sheep led by solitary shepherds and isolated adobe villages. The path passes via Castrojeriz, with its castle dominating the town, while, in better-known Fromista, the Iglesia de San Martín is one of the jewels of early Spanish Romanesque architecture with its 315 well-preserved corbels and fine interior capitals. Between Carrión de los Condes and Calzadilla de la Cueza, the Camino coincides with a stretch of Roman road. Further on, despite appearances, Sahagún was an immensely powerful and wealthy Benedictine centre by the 12th century. The Mudéjar-influenced brick Romanesque churches merit a visit (look for the horseshoe arches and the clever way the bricks are placed in geometric patterns). Before reaching León, the Camino becomes monotonous, running through a long series of villages along paved, busy roads.

Day Walk

If you fancy being a pilgrim for a day, you can consider embarking on the comparatively short stretch between Rabé de las Calzadas and Hontanas (18.8km/five hours). Best in spring time, this rolling *meseta* walk brings solitude amid the wheat, allowing you to appreciate the region's uniquely lonely landscapes and villages.

original Mudéjar ceiling and is a haven from dusty Camino trails.

For more information, visit the local **tourist office** (☑987 78 21 17; www.sahagun. org; Calle del Arco 87; ◐10am-2pm & 4.30-7pm) located within the Albergue de Peregrinos (Hostel for Pilgrims).

Trains run regularly throughout the day from León (€4.85, 40 minutes) and Palencia (€4.30, 35 minutes).

West of León

ASTORGA
POP 12,200 / ELEV 870M

Perched on a hilltop on the frontier between the bleak plains of northern Castilla and the mountains that rise up to the west towards Galicia, Astorga is a fascinating little town with a wealth of attractions, out of proportion to its size. In addition to its fine cathedral, the city boasts a Gaudí-designed palace, a smattering of Roman ruins and a personality dominated by the Camino de Santiago.

HISTORY

The Romans built the first settlement, Astúrica Augusta, at the head of the Ruta del Oro. During the Middle Ages Astorga was well established as a waystation along one of Europe's most important pilgrimage routes. By the 15th century its growing significance inspired the construction of the cathedral and the rebuilding of its 3rd-century walls.

◉ Sights

Catedral   CATHEDRAL

(Plaza de la Catedral; ☺9.30am-noon & 5-6.30pm) The cathedral's striking plateresque southern facade is made from caramel-coloured sandstone with elaborate sculptural detail. Work began in 1471 and proceeded in stop-start fashion over three centuries, resulting in a mix of styles. The mainly Gothic interior has soaring ceilings and a superb 16th-century altarpiece by Gaspar Becerra. The attached **Museo Catedralicio** (admission €2.50, incl Museo de los Caminos €4; ☺10am-2pm & 4-8pm) features the usual religious art, documents and artefacts.

Palacio Episcopal   EPISCOPAL PALACE

(Calle de Los Sitios; ☺10am-2pm & 4-8pm Tue-Sat, 10am-2pm Sun) The Catalan architect Antoni Gaudí may have spurned Madrid, but he left his mark on Astorga in the fairy-tale turrets, frilly facade and surprising details of the Palacio Episcopal. Built for the local bishop from the end of the 19th century, it now houses the **Museo de los Caminos** (admission €2.50, incl Museo Catedralicio €4), an eclectic collection with Roman artefacts and coins in the basement; contemporary paintings on the top floor; and medieval sculpture, Gothic tombs and silver crosses dominating the ground and 1st floors. The highlight is the chapel, with its stunning murals, tilework and stained glass.

Museo del Chocolate   CHOCOLATE MUSEUM

(Calle de José María Goy 5; admission €1; ☺10.30am-2pm & 4-6pm Tue-Sat, 11am-2pm Sun; 🚼) Proof that Astorga does not exist solely for the virtuous souls of the Camino comes in the form of this small and quirky private museum. Chocolate ruled Astorga's local economy in the 18th and 19th centuries, as evidenced by this eclectic collection of old machinery, colourful advertising and fascinating lithographs. It offers a refreshing, indulgent (some would say sinful) break from Castilla's religious-art circuit. Best of all, you get a free chocolate sample at the end.

✦ Festivals & Events

Festividad de Santa Marta   PATRON SAINT

During the last week of August, Astorga awakes from its customary slumber to celebrate this saint with fireworks and bullfights.

⨝ Sleeping

Casa de Tepa   HISTORIC HOTEL €€

(☎987 60 32 99; www.casadetepa.com; Calle de Santiago Postas 2; s/d €80/100; ❂❋@☎) This handsome 18th-century building has been reinvented several times. Originally built as the residence of the Earl of Tepas, it subsequently housed a convent and, later, a hospital for pilgrims. Sumptuously restored with antiques, plush fabrics and tasteful art work, the posada offers luxurious large rooms.

Hotel Gaudí   CLASSIC HOTEL €€

(☎987 61 56 54; www.hotelgaudiastorga.com; Calle de Eduardo de Castro 6; s/d from €48/65; ❋☎) There aren't many places in the world where you can see a Gaudí flight of fancy from your bed, so ask for a street-facing room. The large rooms have been given a facelift and sparkle with glossy wooden floors, dazzling white bedspreads and pale pine furnishings. The downstairs bar and cafeteria has a welcoming clubby look with its black leather and dark wood decor.

Hotel Astur Plaza   MODERN HOTEL €€

(☎987 61 89 00; www.asturplaza.com; Plaza de España 2; s/d/ste from €65/90/100; ❋@☎) This modern hotel is supremely comfortable, with some rooms facing pretty Plaza de España. Breakfast is best taken in the Taverna Los Hornas where you can go for a rare egg-and-bacon choice, upon request.

✗ Eating

The local speciality is *cocido maragato,* a stew of chickpeas, various meats, potatoes and cabbage. Portions are huge, so one order usually feeds two. Several pastry shops sell the traditional local *mantecadas,* a cake-like sweet peculiar to Astorga.

Restaurante Serrano

GOURMET MEDITERRANEAN €€

(☎987 61 78 66; www.restauranteserrano.es; Calle de la Portería 2; meals €30; ☺Tue-Sun) The upmarket Restaurante Serrano is a little different from the other more homey restaurants around town. The menu has

WORTH A TRIP

HISTORIC VILLAGES

For a glimpse of unspoiled 17th-century Castilla, head west out of Astorga following the *Camino de Santiago* signs towards Castrillo de los Polvazares. After around 4.5km you arrive at the blink-and-you-miss it hamlet of Murias de Rechivaldo with its hauntingly beautiful church to the right of what must be the most modest Plaza Mayor in Spain. There's a lovely picnic ground by the river just beyond here. Alternatively, Casa Botas (Plaza Mayor 4; meals from €8) has a glorious vine-festooned terrace and serves hearty local food. Continue on to Castrillo de los Polvazares, a larger 17th-century hamlet built from ferrous stone, its soft orange colour made all the more striking by the brilliant green paint job on the doors and window frames. At weekends, this is a popular venue for city folk to come to eat at restaurants like Hostería Cuca La Vaina (☎987 69 10 34; www.cucalavaina.com; Calle de Jardín; meals €25; d €55), which serves up the local speciality *cocido maragato* and also has comfortable rooms. Book ahead for meals. Semi-regular buses (€1.10, 15 minutes) run from Astorga's bus station.

a definite gourmet flourish, with fresh summery starters like *ensalada de mango y centollo con vinagreta de frambuesa* (mango and crab salad with raspberry vinaigrette), innovative meat and fish mains, and plenty of tempting desserts with chocolate. Reservations recommended.

Restaurante Las Termas REGIONAL CUISINE €€ (Calle de Santiago Postas 1; meals from €20; ⊙Tue-Sun; 🖗) This restaurant is housed in a fine 18th-century stone building where owner Santiago (a popular name in these parts) is a charming host. The dining room is similarly inviting with its warm ochre-and-yellow colour scheme. The menu is renowned for the quality of its *cocido* and *ensalada maragata* (salad of chickpeas and cod).

Cervecería La Esquina BEER HOUSE € (Plaza de España 5; meals €10-20) Best for local tapas specialities, including the unsurpassed *patatas esquinadas* (lightly-seasoned potato slices), plus 18 varieties of beer.

La Peseta REGIONAL CUISINE € (www.restaurantelapeseta.com; Plaza de San Bartolomé 3; meals €20) Serves local dishes with cheaper *menús* for pilgrims. Rooms available (doubles from €55).

ⓘ Information
Tourist office (☎987 61 82 22; www.turismo castillayleon.com; ⊙10am-2pm & 4-8pm) In the northwestern corner of the old town.

ⓘ Getting There & Away
Regular bus services connect Astorga with León (€3.50, 45 minutes, up to 16 daily) and Madrid (€21.60, 4½ hours, five daily). The train station is inconveniently a couple of kilometres north of town.

PONFERRADA
POP 66.900 / ELEV 508M

Ponferrada, 60km west of Astorga, is not the region's most enticing town, but its castle and remnants of the old town centre (around the stone clock tower) make it worth a brief stop en route to or from Galicia. Built by the Knights Templar in the 13th century, the walls of the fortress-monastery Castillo Templario (adult/concession €3/1.50; ⊙11am-2pm & 5-9pm Tue-Sat, 11am-2pm Sun) rise high over Río Sil, and the square, crenulated towers ooze romance and history. The castle has a lonely and impregnable air, and is a striking landmark in Ponferrada's otherwise bleak urban landscape.

Among Ponferrada's churches, the Gothic-Renaissance Basílica de Nuestra Señora de la Encina (⊙9am-2pm & 4.30-8.30pm), up the hill past the tourist office, is the most impressive, especially its 17th-century painted wood altarpiece from the school of Gregorio Fernández.

For meals, sophisticated Menta y Canela (☎987 40 32 89; Calle Alonso Cana 10; meals €40) is famed for its unconventional preparations of traditional ingredients. Reservations recommended.

Regular buses connect Ponferrada with León (€8.15, two hours) and Madrid (€25.20, five hours, seven daily)

LAS MÉDULAS
The ancient Roman goldmines at Las Médulas, about 20km southwest of Ponferrada, once served as the main source of gold for the entire Roman Empire – the final tally came to a remarkable 3 million kilograms. An army of slaves honeycombed the area

with canals and tunnels (some over 40km long!) through which they pumped water to break up the rock and free it from the precious metal. The result is a singularly unnatural natural phenomenon and one of the more bizarre landscapes you'll see in Spain. It's breathtaking at sunset.

To get to the heart of the former quarries, drive beyond Las Médulas village (4km south of Carucedo and the N536 highway). Several trails weave among chestnut trees and bizarre formations left behind by the miners.

THE EAST

Eastern Castilla y León is where you can leave behind tourist Spain and immerse yourself in a world of charming villages, isolated monasteries and castles, quiet roads and scenic landscapes. Beautiful Burgos and provincial Soria serve as the urban bookends to the region.

Burgos

POP 174,000 / ELEV 861M

The extraordinary Gothic cathedral of Burgos is one of Spain's glittering jewels of religious architecture. It looms large over the city and skyline. On the surface, conservative Burgos seems to embody all the stereotypes of a north-central Spanish town, with sombre grey-stone architecture, the fortifying cuisine of the high *meseta* (plateau) and a climate of extremes. But this is a city that rewards deeper exploration: below the surface lie vibrant nightlife, good restaurants and, when the sun's shining, pretty streetscapes that extend far beyond the landmark cathedral. There's even a whiff of legend about the place: beneath the majestic spires of the cathedral lies Burgos' favourite and most roguish son, El Cid.

History

Burgos began life in 884 as a strategic fortress on the frontline between the Muslims and the rival kingdom of Navarra. It was surrounded by several *burgos* (villages), which eventually melded together to form the basis of a new city. Centuries later, Burgos thrived as a staging post for pilgrims on the Camino de Santiago and as a trading centre between the interior and the northern ports. During the Spanish Civil War, General Franco used Burgos as the base for his government-in-waiting.

◉ Sights

Old Quarter HISTORIC NEIGHBOURHOOD

Burgos' old quarter, on the north bank of Río Arlanzón, is austerely elegant in the manner of so many cathedral towns of old Castilla. Coming from the south, it can be accessed via two main bridges. One of these is the **Puente de San Pablo**, beyond which looms a romanticised **statue of El Cid** with his swirling cloak and his sword held aloft. About 300m to the west, the **Puente de Santa María** leads to the splendid **Arco de Santa María** (⊙11am-1.50pm & 5-9pm Tue-Sat, 11am-1.50pm Sun), once the main gate to the old city and part of the 14th-century walls. It now hosts temporary exhibitions. Running along the riverbank between the two bridges is the **Paseo del Espolón**, a lovely tree-lined pedestrian area. Just back from the *paseo* (promenade) is the oddly shaped **Plaza Mayor**, with some lovely facades.

ONLY IN SPAIN...

Spain's weird and wonderful fiestas have always left the rest of the world shaking their heads, from the Running of the Bulls in Pamplona (p436) to the tomato-throwing extravaganza of La Tomatina (p566) in Buñol. But surely there's no festival quite as strange as the baby-jumping festival of Castrillo de Murcia, a small village just south of the A231, 25km west of Burgos.

Every year since 1620, this tiny village of around 250 inhabitants has marked the feast of Corpus Cristi by lining up the babies of the village on a mattress, while grown men dressed as 'El Colacho', a figure representing the devil, leap over up to six prostrate and, it must be said, somewhat bewildered babies at a time. Like all Spanish rites, it does have a purpose: the ritual is thought to ward off the devil. But why jumping over babies? We have no idea and the villagers aren't telling. They do, however, assure us that no baby has been injured in the recorded history of the fiesta.

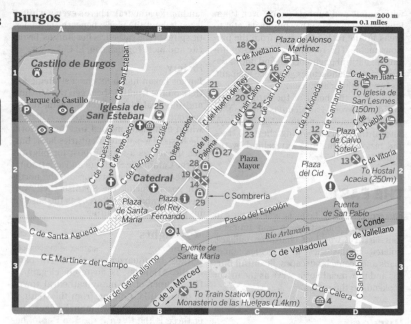

Burgos

◎ Top Sights

Castillo de Burgos	A1
Catedral	B2
Iglesia de San Esteban	B2

◎ Sights

1	Arco de Santa María	B3
2	Iglesia de San Nicolás	B2
3	Mirador	A2
4	Museo de Burgos	D3
5	Museo del Retablo	B2
6	Parque de Castillo	A1
7	Statue of El Cid	D2

🛏 Sleeping

8	Hotel Jacobeo	D1
9	Hotel La Puebla	D1
10	Hotel Meson del Cid	B2
11	Hotel Norte y Londres	C1

🍴 Eating

12	Casa Babylon	D2
13	Casa Ojeda	D2
14	Cervecería Morito	B2
15	El Jardín del Ecocentro	B3
16	La Comidilla de San Lorenzo	C1
17	La Fabula	D2
18	La Favorita	C1
19	La Mejillonera	B2
20	Royal	C1

🍷 Drinking

21	Buddha	C1
22	Café de las Artes	C1
23	Café España	C2
24	Café Latino	C1
	Café Marmedi	(see 9)
25	Chocolatería Candilejas	B1
26	El Bosque Encantado	D1

🛍 Shopping

27	Casa Quintanilla	C2
28	Jorge Revilla	B2
29	Teodoro	B2

Catedral   CATHEDRAL
(Plaza del Rey Fernando; adult/child €5/2.50;
⊙9.30am-6.30pm) The Unesco World Heritage-listed cathedral is a masterpiece
that's probably worth the trip to Burgos on
its own. It had humble origins as a modest
Romanesque church, but work began on a
grander scale in 1221. Remarkably, within
40 years most of the French Gothic structure that you see today had been complet-

ed. The twin towers, which went up later in the 15th century, each represent 84m of richly decorated Gothic fantasy and they're surrounded by a sea of similarly intricate spires. Probably the most impressive of the portals is the **Puerta del Sarmental**, the main entrance for visitors, although the honour could also go to the **Puerta de la Coronería**, on the northwestern side, which shows Christ surrounded by the Evangelists.

It's possible to enter the cathedral from Plaza de Santa María for free, but doing so leaves the most worthwhile sections off-limits. Nonetheless, you'll still have access to the **Capilla del Santísimo Cristo**, which harbours a much-revered 13th-century crucifix (known as the *Cristo de Burgos*) made from buffalo hide, and the **Capilla de Santa Tecla**, with its extraordinary ceiling.

Inside the main sanctuary, a host of other chapels showcase the diversity of the interior, from the light and airy **Capilla de la Presentación** to the **Capilla de la Concepción** with its impossibly gilded, 15th-century altar. The main altar is a typically overwhelming piece of gold-encrusted extravagance, while directly beneath the star-vaulted central dome lies the **tomb of El Cid**. Another highlight is the **Escalera Dorada** (Gilded Stairway; 1520) on the cathedral's northwestern flank, the handiwork of Diego de Siloé.

The **Capilla del Condestable**, on the eastern end of the ambulatory behind the main altar, is a remarkable late-15th-century production. Bridging Gothic and plateresque styles, its highlights include three altars watched over by unusual star-shaped vaulting in the dome. The sculptures facing the entrance to the chapel are astonishing 15th- and 16th-century masterpieces of stone carving, portraying the passion, death, resurrection and ascension of Christ.

Also worth a look is the peaceful **cloister**, with its sculpted medieval tombs. Off the cloister is the **Capilla de Corpus Cristi**, where, high on the northwestern wall, hangs the coffin of El Cid.

The adjoining Museo Catedralicio has a wealth of oil paintings, tapestries and ornate chalices, while the lower cloister, downstairs, covers the history of the cathedral's development, with a **scale model** to help you take it all in.

Monasterio de las Huelgas   MONASTERY

(Calle Compases; guided tours adult/concession €5/2.50, Wed free; ⊙10am-1pm & 3.45-5.30pm Tue-Sat, 10.30am-2pm Sun) A 30-minute walk west of the city centre on the southern bank of Río Arlanzón, this monastery was once among the most prominent monasteries in Spain. Founded in 1187 by Eleanor of Aquitaine, daughter of Henry II of England and wife of Alfonso VIII of Castilla, it's still home to 35 Cistercian nuns.

If you've come this far, join a guided tour (otherwise only a small section of the church is accessible), which takes you through the three main naves of the church. This veritable royal pantheon contains the tombs of numerous kings and queens, as well as a spectacular gilded Renaissance altar topped by a larger-than-life Jesus being taken off the cross. The highlight, though, is the Museo de Ricas Telas, reached via a lovely Romanesque cloister known as Las Claustrillas. It contains bejewelled robes and royal garments.

To get here follow the river via Calle de la Merced and Avenida de Palencia, turning left on Calle Reina Leonor. The Monastery is signposted.

Iglesia de San Esteban   GOTHIC CHURCH

(Calle de Pozo Seco; admission incl museum €2; ⊙10am-2pm & 5-8pm) Located just west of the cathedral, this is a solid 14th-century Gothic structure with an unusual porch and a Museo del Retablo (Altar Museum; ⊙same hr) with a display of some 15 altars dating from the 15th to 18th centuries.

Cartuja de Miraflores   MONASTERY

(⊙10.15am-3pm & 4-6pm) Located in peaceful woodlands 4km east of the city centre, this contains a trio of 15th-century masterworks by Gil de Siloé. The walk to the monastery along Río Arlanzón takes about one hour. To get here, head north along Paseo de la Quinta (flanking the river) from where the monastery is clearly signposted.

Castillo de Burgos   CASTLE

(adult/concession €3.70/2.60; ⊙11am-2pm & 4-7pm Sat & Sun; ⊞) Crowning the leafy hilltop Parque de Castillo are the massive fortifications of the rebuilt Castillo de Burgos. Dating from the 9th century, the castle has witnessed a turbulent history, suffering a fire in 1736 before finally being blown up by Napoleon's retreating troops in 1813. There's a small museum here covering the history of the town and, thanks to recent

EL CID: THE HEROIC MERCENARY

Few names resonate through Spanish history quite like El Cid, the 11th-century soldier of fortune and adventurer whose story tells in microcosm the tumultuous years when Spain was divided into Muslim and Christian zones. That El Cid became a romantic, idealised figure of history, known for his unswerving loyalty and superhuman strength, owes much to the 1961 film starring Charlton Heston and Sophia Loren. Reality, though, presents a different picture.

El Cid (from the Arabic *sidi* for 'chief' or 'lord') was born Rodrígo Diaz in Vivar, a hamlet about 10km north of Burgos, in 1043. After the death of Ferdinand I, he dabbled in the murky world of royal succession, which led to his banishment from Castilla in 1076. With few scruples as to whom he served, El Cid offered his services to a host of rulers, both Christian and Muslim. With each battle, he became ever more powerful and wealthy.

It's not known whether he suddenly developed a loyalty to the Christian kings or smelled the wind and saw that Spain's future would be Christian. Either way, when he heard that the Muslim armies had taken Valencia and expelled all the Christians, El Cid marched on the city, recaptured it and became its ruler in 1094 after a devastating siege. At the height of his powers and reputation, the man also known as El Campeador (Champion) retired to spend the remainder of his days in Valencia, where he died in 1099. His remains were returned to Burgos, where he lies buried along with his wife, Jimena, in the cathedral.

excavations, some of the original foundations of the castle are on view. Just south of the car park is a **mirador** (lookout), which offers fine views over the town.

Museo de Burgos MUSEUM
(Calle de Calera 25; admission €1.20, Sat & Sun free; ⏲10am-2pm & 5-8pm Tue-Sat, 10am-2pm Sun) This museum, housed in the 16th-century Casa de Miranda, contains some fine Gothic tombs and other archeological artefacts covering a wide period.

Iglesia de San Nicolás CHURCH
(Calle de San Nicolás; ⏲12-1.30pm & 5-7pm) Boasts an enormous stone-carved altar by Francisco de Colonia, with scenes from the life of St Nicolas.

Iglesia de San Lesmes CHURCH
(Plaza de San Juan; ⏲before & after Mass) Dates to the 15th century and is notable for its three naves and rustic charm.

Festivals & Events

Burgos' big fiestas occur in late June and early July. The **Festividad de San Pedro y San Pablo** (Feast of Saints Peter and Paul) is celebrated with bullfights, processions and much merry-making, particularly on the first Sunday of July, the **Día de las Peñas**. Slightly more low-key is the **Festividad de San Lesmes** (for the city's patron saint) on 30 January.

Sleeping

TOP CHOICE **Hotel Norte y Londres** HISTORIC HOTEL €€
(☎947 26 41 25; www.hotelnorteylondres.com; Plaza de Alonso Martínez 10; s/d €66/100; P@Wi-Fi) Set in a former 16th-century palace and with understated period charm, this fine hotel promises spacious rooms with antique furnishings, polished wooden floors and pretty balconies; those on the 4th floor are more modern. The bathrooms are exceptionally large, the service exceptionally efficient. Parking costs €11.50.

Hotel Jacobeo SMALL HOTEL €
(☎947 26 01 02; www.hoteljacobeo.com; Calle de San Juan 24; s/d incl breakfast €47/58; ⊖❄Wi-Fi) This stylish small hotel has gleaming rooms of burgundy-and-white-washed walls, terracotta tiles and parquet floors. Bathrooms are well equipped, if on the small side. The public areas are tasteful with gilt mirrors, historic oil paintings and a warm colour scheme of dark purples and pinks.

Hotel Meson del Cid HISTORIC HOTEL €€
(☎947 20 87 15; www.mesondelcid.es; Plaza de Santa María 8; s/d €70/100; P⊖❄Wi-Fi) Housed in the oldest non-municipal building in the city (dating from 1483), the rooms have Regency-style burgundy-and-cream fabrics, aptly combined with dark wood furnishings and terracotta tiles. Most have stunning front row seats of the cathedral. The

dated bathrooms are due for a slick make-over in 2011. Parking costs €12.

Hotel La Puebla
BOUTIQUE HOTEL €€

(☑947 20 00 11; www.hotellapuebla.com; Calle de la Puebla 20; s/d €70/95; P✷@☎) This boutique hotel adds a touch of style to the Burgos hotel scene. The rooms aren't huge and most don't have views, but they're softly lit and supremely comfortable. They come in a range of styles, from colourful to minimalist black-and-white. Parking costs €10.

Hostal Acacia
BUDGET HOTEL €

(☑947 20 51 34; www.hostalacacia.com; Calle de Bernabé Perez Ortiz 1; s/d with bathroom €25/59) This *hostal* is especially popular with pilgrims. The simple rooms have plain bedspreads and renovated bathrooms, and some have attractive ochre-painted walls. Bike rental available.

Eating

Burgos is famous for its *queso, morcilla* and *cordero asado.* The city has an excellent choice of restaurants, particularly around Plaza de Calvo Sotelo, Plaza de Alonso Martínez and Plaza Mayor. For tapas bars head for Calle de San Lorenzo, Calle de Avellanos and Calle de la Paloma, near the cathedral.

Cervecería Morito
TRADITIONAL TAPAS €

(Calle de la Sombrerería 27; tapas €3, raciones €5-7) Cervecería Morito is the undisputed king of Burgos tapas bars and it's always crowded. A typical order is *alpargata* (lashings of cured ham with bread, tomato and olive oil) or *calamares fritos* (fried calamari). The presentation is surprising nouvelle, especially the visual feast of salads.

TOP CHOICE La Fabula
MODERN CASTILLIAN €€

(☑947 26 30 92; Calle de la Puebla 18; menú del día €15, meals €25-30; ☻) With local celebrity chef Isabel Alvarez at the helm, fabulous La Fabula offers innovative slimmed-down dishes in a bright, modern dining room filled with classical music. The menu includes tasty rice dishes and summery light eats, like crispy vegetable spring rolls. Fortunately this should leave plenty of space for one of the delectable desserts. The chocolate soufflé with mango ice cream and yoghurt mousse comes plumply recommended. Reservations essential.

La Comidilla de San Lorenzo
MODERN CASTILIAN €€

(Calle San Lorenzo 29; meals €18-25) Opened in early 2010, this place has a young upbeat

vibe with art exhibitions, cool modern decor and a menu that includes accomplished and innovative dishes like *secreto con salsa de frambuesa* (steak with raspberry sauce) and *tacos de atun con puré de patatas y pimiento* (tuna tacos with mashed potatoes and peppers).

El Jardín del Ecocentro
VEGETARIAN €

(☑947 25 54 81; Calle de la Merced 19; meals €15; ☻Tue-Wed 1.30-3pm, Thu-Sat 9.30am-11pm; ☻) Simple well-executed vegetarian *platos combinados,* fresh vegetable and fruit juices and healthy puds are available at this haven of an eco-centre which also offers yoga, pilates, ayuvedic massages etc.

La Mejillonera
MUSSELS €

(Calle de la Paloma 33; mussels per portion €2.35) Another popular stand-up place, La Mejillonera serves great mussels, while the *patatas bravas* (potatoes with spicy tomato sauce) and *calamares* are other popular orders.

Casa Ojeda
ROAST LAMB €€

(☑947 20 90 52; www.grupojeda.com, in Spanish; Calle de Vitoria 5; meals €30-40; ☻Mon-Sat, lunch Sun) Dating from 1912, this Burgos institution, all sheathed in dark wood with stunning mullioned windows, is one of the best places in town to try *cordero asado.* The upstairs dining room has outstanding food and faultless service. A more limited range of *platos combinados* is available in the downstairs bar. Reservations recommended.

La Favorita
CURED MEATS €€

(www.lafavorita-taberna.com, in Spanish; Calle de Avellanos 8; meals €18-25) Away from the main Burgos tapas hub and close to the cathedral, La Favorita has a barn-like interior of exposed brick and wooden beams, and attracts slicked-back-hair businessmen at midday. The emphasis is on local cured meats and cheeses, and wine by the glass starts at €1.50.

Casa Babylon
FUSION €€

(www.casababylon.es; Plaza de Santo Domingo 3; menús €15-20; ☑☻) Serves well-executed Asian-inspired dishes (including sushi), Tex Mex and Italian, the latter including risottos.

Royal
LIGHT MEALS €

(Calle del Huerto del Rey 23; meals €10-15) If you can withstand the brightly lit retro '70s dining area, Royal has a surprising gourmet flourish among the old culinary classics.

Drinking

With its old-world elegance, Café España (Calle de Lain Calvo 12; ⊙10am-11pm) has been a bastion of the Burgos cafe scene for more than 80 years. A pianist plays jazz here at weekends. Other good options include Café Latino (Calle de Lain Calvo 16; ⊙10am-11pm) and Café de las Artes (Calle de Lain Calvo 31; ⊙10am-midnight); the latter has an artsy vibe and occasional live music. For killer milkshakes, including unusual flavours like raspberry and walnut, check out Chocolatería Candilejas (Calle de Fernán González 36; ⊙6.30-11pm Thu-Mon; 🖳).

There are two main hubs of nightlife. The first is along Calle de San Juan and Calle de la Puebla. Good early evening options include El Bosque Encantado (Calle de San Juan 31; ⊙4.30pm-1am), which revels in its kitsch decor, and Café Marmedi (Calle de le Puebla 20; ⊙4pm-1am), serving heady *mojitos*.

For later nights on weekends, Calle del Huerto del Rey, northeast of the cathedral, has dozens of bars. Buddha (Calle del Huerto del Rey 8; ⊙11pm-4am Thu-Sat) comes particularly recommended.

Pick up a copy of the Burgos edition of *Go!* (www.laguiago.com in Spanish) from the tourist office to find out what's on.

Shopping

Jorge Revilla JEWELLERY
(www.jorgerevilla.com; Calle de la Paloma 29; ⊙10am-2pm & 5-8pm Mon-Fri, 10am-2pm Sat) Local Burgos jewellery designer Jorge Revilla is becoming a global name with his exquisite and sophisticated silver pieces.

Casa Quintanilla DELICATESSEN
(Calle de la Paloma 22; ⊙10am-8.30pm Mon-Sat, 10am-2pm Sun) This is the pick of many stores around the centre offering local produce that's ideal for a picnic or a gift for back home.

Teodoro HATS
(Calle Sombreria 4; ⊙10am-2pm & 5-8pm Mon-Fri, 10am-2pm Sat) Step back in time at this 1860s hat shop with its original interior, including the magnificent American-made (National) cash register. The elderly owner Teodoro is a charmer, the hats a delight.

ℹ Information

Ciber-Café Cabaret (Calle de la Puebla 21; per hr from €2.50; ⊙noon-1am Sun-Thu, 7pm-4am Fri & Sat) Internet access.

Municipal tourist office (947 28 88 74; www.aytoburgos.es, in Spanish; Plaza del Rey Fernando 2; ⊙10am-2pm & 4.30-7.30pm Mon-Fri, 10am-1.30pm & 4-7.30pm Sat & Sun)

Regional tourist office (947 20 31 25; www.turismocastillayleon.com; Plaza de Alonso Martínez 7; ⊙9am-8pm Sun-Thu, 9am-9pm Fri & Sat)

ℹ Getting There & Away

The bus and train stations lie south of the river, in the newer part of town.

BUS From Burgos' **bus station** (Calle de Miranda 4) regular buses run to major Spanish cities including Madrid (€16.25, 2¾ hours), Bilbao (€11.86, two hours) and León (€14.10, 3¾ hours).

CAR & MOTORCYCLE There are several underground car parks, including at Plaza Mayor.

TRAIN Burgos is connected to major cities, including Madrid (from €25.60, four hours, up to seven daily), Bilbao (from €18.70, three hours, five daily), León (from €20.10, two hours, four daily) and Salamanca (from €20.90, 2½ hours, three daily).

Renfe (Red Nacional de los Ferrocarriles Españoles; Calle de la Moneda 21; ⊙9.30am-1.30pm & 4.30-7.30pm Mon-Fri, 9.30am-1.30pm Sat) The national rail network has a convenient sales office in the centre of town.

Around Burgos

ERMITA DE SANTA MARÍA DE LARA

If you take the N234 southeast out of Burgos, a worthwhile stop some 35km out is the 7th-century Ermita de Santa María de Lara close to Quintanilla de las Viñas. This modest Visigothic hermitage has some fine bas-reliefs around its external walls, which are among the best surviving regional examples of religious art from the 7th century.

COVARRUBIAS
POP 640 / ELEV 975M

The picturesque hamlet of Covarrubias is one of Castilla y León's hidden gems. Spread out along the shady banks of Río Arlanza, its distinctive arcaded half-timbered houses overlook intimate cobblestone squares.

A good time to be here is the second weekend of July, when the village hosts its **Medieval Market & Cherry Festival**.

⊙ Sights

Although the main attraction of Covarrubias is simply wandering its charming cobbled streets, there are a few sights to provide focus for your visit.

Torreón de Doña Urraca TOWER

This squat 10th-century tower dominates the remains of the town's medieval walls.

Colegiata de San Cosme y Damián
CHURCH

(admission €2; ☉10.30am-2pm & 4-7pm Wed-Mon) This late-Gothic church hosts Castilla's oldest still-functioning church organ and has attractive cloisters. It also contains the stone tomb of Fernán González, the 10th-century founder of Castilla.

🛏 Sleeping & Eating

Casa Galín SMALL HOTEL €

(☎947 40 65 52; www.casagalin.com, in Spanish; Plaza de Doña Urraca 4; s/d €25/42) A cut above your average provincial Castilian *hostal,* Casa Galín has comfortable, pastel-painted rooms in an old-fashioned timbered building overlooking the main plaza. It's home to a popular restaurant for tapas, fish and roasted meats, with a well-priced *menú* (€10).

Hotel Rey Chindasvinto CLASSIC HOTEL €

(☎947 40 65 60; hotelchindas@wanadoo.es; Plaza del Rey Chindasvinto 5; s/d incl breakfast €35/55; ❄🛜) The classiest hotel in town, the Rey Chindasvinto has lovely spacious rooms with wooden beams, exposed brickwork, friendly owners and a good restaurant.

La Posada del Conde CASA RURAL €

(☎609 406698; www.laposadadelconde.es; Calle Fernán González 8; s/d incl breakfast €50/60; 🛜) Opened in 2010, the large rooms are brightly painted, while the bathrooms have a designer touch. The communal sitting room is large and comfortable although the snarling mounted wolf's head may not appeal to all. Activities, ranging from mountain-climbing to fishing, can be organised.

Restaurante de Galo TRADITIONAL DISHES €€

(Plaza Mayor; menú €10.50, meals €20-25) This fine restaurant in the heart of the village is recommended for its robust traditional dishes cooked in a wood-fired oven. This is a good place to sample the regional speciality of *cordero asado.*

🛍 Shopping

La Alacena DELICATESSEN

(Calle de Monseñor Vargas 8; ☉10am-2pm & 5-7.30pm Tue-Sun) For homemade chocolates, local honey and other gourmet goodies, step inside this friendly shop.

ℹ️ Information

Tourist office (☎947 40 64 61; www.ecov arrubias.com, in Spanish; Calle de Monseñor Vargas; ☉10.30am-2pm & 4-7pm Tue-Sat, 11am-2.30pm Sun) Located under the arches of the village's imposing northern gate, pick up the free *Covarrubias: Castile Birthplace,* a handy pocket-sized guide to the sights around town.

ℹ️ Getting There & Away

Two buses travel between Burgos and Covarrubias on weekdays, and one runs on Saturday (€2.95, one hour).

SANTO DOMINGO DE SILOS
POP 320

Nestled in the rolling hills south of Burgos, this tranquil, pretty village has an unusual claim to fame: monks from its monastery made the British pop charts in the mid-1990s with recordings of Gregorian chants. The monastery is one of the most famous in central Spain, known for its stunning cloister.

👁 Sights

For sweeping views over the town, pass under the Arco de San Juan and climb the grassy hill to the south to the Ermita del Camino y Via Crucis.

Church CHURCH

(☉6am-2pm & 4.30-10pm) Notable for its pleasingly unadorned Romanesque sanctuary dominated by a multidomed ceiling, this is where you can hear the monks chant (admission free; ☉9am Mon-Fri, 1pm Sat, noon Sun).

Cloister CLOISTER

(admission €3; ☉guided tours 10am-1pm & 4.30-6pm Tue-Sat, 4.30-6pm Sun) The jewel in the attached monastery's crown is this two-storey treasure chest of some of the most imaginative Romanesque art anywhere in the country. Although the overall effect is spectacular, the sculpted capitals are especially exquisite, with lions intermingled with floral and geometrical motifs betraying the never-distant influence of Islamic art in Spain. Look for the unusually twisted column on the western side. The pieces executed on the corner pillars represent episodes from the life of Christ, while the galleries are covered by Mudéjar ceilings from the 14th century. In the northeastern corner sits a 13th-century image of the Virgin Mary carved in stone, and nearby is the original burial spot of Santo Domingo.

Although much of the monastery is off-limits to visitors, the compulsory guided tour will show you inside the 17th-century **botica** (pharmacy) and a small **museum** containing religious artworks, Flemish tapestries and the odd medieval sarcophagus. Tours are available within the hours listed and begin when there are enough people.

Sleeping & Eating

Hotel Tres Coronas HISTORIC HOTEL €€
(☎947 39 00 47; www.hoteltrescoronasdesilos.com, in Spanish; Plaza Mayor 6; s/d incl breakfast €57/72; ❄📶) Set in a former 17th-century palace, this hotel is brimming with character (the suit of armour at the top of the grand staircase sets the scene), with rooms of thick stone walls and old-world charm. The rooms at the front have lovely views over the plaza.

Hotel Santo Domingo de Silos HOSTAL, HOTEL €€€
(☎947 39 00 53; www.hotelsantodomingodesilos.com, in Spanish; Calle de Santo Domingo; hostal s/d €36/52, hotel s/d €52/62; P❄📶) This place combines a simple *hostal* with a three-star hotel with large, luxurious rooms, some with whirlpool bathtubs, right opposite the monastery. It's a popular place so book ahead.

Hostal Cruces BUDGET HOTEL €
(☎947 39 00 64; Plaza Mayor 2; s/d €23/42) Decent if simple rooms – the cheapest in town – and friendly owners make this a good choice right in the heart of the village.

Padre Hospedero MONASTERY €
(☎947 39 00 68, r with meals €30) Men can rent a heated room in the monastery, but you'll need to book well ahead. Call between 10am and 1.30pm Monday to Friday. You can stay for a period of three to 10 days.

The village's best, most atmospheric and most expensive restaurant is at the **Hotel Tres Coronas** (meals €20-30), although the cheaper **Hotel Santo Domingo de Silos** (meals €15-20) is not bad.

Information

Tourist office (☎947 39 00 70; www.turismocastillayleon.com; Calle de Cuatro Cantones 10; ⏲10am-1.30pm & 4-6pm Tue-Sun) Centrally located and helpful.

Getting There & Away

There is one daily bus from Burgos to Santo Domingo de Silos (€5.70, 1½ hours) from Monday to Saturday.

DESFILADERO DE YECLA

A mere 1.3km down the back road (BU911) to Caleruega from Santo Domingo, the spectacular Desfiladero de Yecla, a splendid gorge of limestone cliffs, opens up. It's easily visited thanks to a walkway – the stairs lead down from just past the tunnel exit.

South to Río Duero

LERMA

POP 2720 / ELEV 827M

If you're travelling between Burgos and Madrid and finding the passing scenery none too eye-catching, Lerma rises up from the roadside like a welcome apparition.

An ancient settlement, Lerma hit the big time in the early 17th century when Grand Duke Don Francisco de Rojas y Sandoval, a minister under Felipe II, launched an ambitious project to create another El Escorial (see p117). He failed, but the cobbled streets and delightful plazas of the old town are his most enduring legacy.

Sights

Pass through the **Arco de la Cárcel** (Prison Gate), off the main road to Burgos, climbing up the long Calle del General Mola to the massive **Plaza Mayor**, which is fronted by the oversized **Palacio Ducal**, now a *parador* notable for its courtyards and 210 balconies. To the right of the square is the Dominican nuns' **Convento de San Blas**, which can be visited as part of the tourist office tour.

A short distance northwest of Plaza Mayor, a pretty passageway and viewpoint, **Mirador de los Arcos**, opens up over Río Arlanza. Its arches connect with the 17th-century **Convento de Santa Teresa**.

The **Pasadizo de Duque de Lerma** (admission €2) is a restored 17th-century subterranean passage that connects the palace with the **Iglesia Colegial de San Pedro Apóstol** – buy tickets at the tourist office.

Sleeping & Eating

Posada La Hacienda de Mi Señor HISTORIC HOTEL €€
(☎947 17 70 52; www.lahaciendademisenor.com, in Spanish; Calle El Barco 6; s/d with breakfast €50/75; ❄@📶) Apart from a few *casas rurales* dotted around the old town, this is your best midrange bet, with enormous rooms with free wi-fi in a renovated, historic building. The candy-floss colour scheme will start to grate if you stay too long; request room 205 for a more muted paint palette.

HIDDEN VILLAGES

The N623 highway carves a pretty trail from Burgos, particularly between the mountain passes of **Portillo de Fresno** and **Puerto de Carrales**. About 15km north of the former, a side road takes you through a series of intriguing villages in the **Valle de Sedano**. The town of the same name has a fine 17th-century church, but more interesting is the little Romanesque one above **Moradillo de Sedano**: the sculpted main doorway is outstanding.

Villages flank the highway on the way north, but **Orbaneja del Castillo** is the area's best-kept secret. Take the turn-off for Escalada and follow the bumpy road until you reach the waterfall. Park where you can, then climb up beside the waterfall to the village, which is completely hidden from the road. A dramatic backdrop of strange rock walls lends this spot an enchanting air.

Parador de Lerma HISTORIC PARADOR **€€€**
(☑947 17 71 10; www.parador.es; Plaza Mayor 1; s/d €128/160; P✳@⚡) Undoubtedly the most elegant place to stay is this *parador*, which occupies the renovated splendour of the old Palacio Ducal. As in any *parador*, the rooms have luxury and character, and the service is impeccable.

El Zaguan CASA RURAL **€€**
(☑947 17 21 65; www.elzaguanlerma.com; Calle Baquilo 6; d with breakfast €66) A friendly place to stay in the centre.

You're in the heart of Castilian wood-fired-oven territory and Plaza Mayor is encircled by high-quality restaurants with *cordero asado* on the menu (€35 for two is a good price to pay). A favourite is the cosy and friendly **Asador Casa Brigante** (Plaza Mayor 5; meals €25; ☺lunch) – you won't taste better roast lamb anywhere.

ℹ Information
Tourist office (☑947 17 70 02; www.citlerma. com, in Spanish; Convento de Santa Teresa, Plaza de Santa Clara; ☺10am-2pm & 4-7pm Tue-Sun) Offers guided tours (€3) of the town and most of its monuments, departing from here.

ℹ Getting There & Away
There are eight daily buses from Burgos (€3.15, 30 minutes), with only four on Saturday or Sunday. Some buses coming from Aranda de Duero or Madrid also pass through.

ARANDA DE DUERO
POP 32,000 / ELEV 802M

The big attraction in this otherwise unattractive crossroads town is the main portal of the late-Gothic **Iglesia de Santa María** (☺10am-2pm & 5-8pm Tue-Sun). Its remarkably rich sculptural flourish was executed in the 15th and 16th centuries.

Other than that, Aranda de Duero is renowned as a bastion of classic Castilian cooking. Most of the better places serving *cordero* are on and around Plaza del Arco Isilla; look for the 'Asador' signs. Probably Aranda's premier *asador* is **Mesón de la Villa** (☑947 50 10 25; Calle de Rodríguez Valcarcel 3; meals €40; ☺Tue-Sun), which does succulent lamb and complements it with excellent local wines. Reservations are essential on weekends.

For more information on the city, visit the **tourist office** (☑947 51 04 76; Plaza Mayor; ☺9am-2pm & 3.30-7pm).

Numerous buses and trains connect Aranda with Madrid (€11.26, two hours) and most major cities in Castilla y León.

PEÑARANDA DE DUERO
POP 560 / ELEV 877M

About 20km east of Aranda on the C111, the village of Peñaranda de Duero exudes considerable charm. Originally a Celtic fortress village, most of its surviving riches are grouped around the stately Plaza Mayor. The **Palacio Condes de Miranda** (admission free; ☺10am-2pm & 4-7.30pm Tue-Sun) is a grand Renaissance palace with a fine plateresque entrance, double-arched patio and beautiful ceilings in various styles. Obligatory guided tours run on the hour.

The 16th-century **Iglesia de Santa Ana** integrates columns and busts found at the Roman settlement of Clunia into an otherwise baroque design. Enjoy superb views of the village and surrounding country by taking a walk up to the sprawling 15th-century **castle ruins**.

For more information, visit the **tourist office** (☑947 55 20 63; Calle de Trinquete 7; ☺10am-2pm & 4-8pm Tue-Sun).

A SLOW DEATH

Many tranquil villages of Castilla y León have a dark secret: they could soon be extinct. Spain's economic boom in the late 1990s and beyond drove a massive shift from rural villages into urban centres. In the last 50 years, Spain's largest autonomous region has lost a million inhabitants. Its population of just over 2.5 million people is now the same as it was in 1901.

Award-winning documentary film-maker Mercedes Alvarez is one of just 43 inhabitants in the village of Aldealsenor and, in a recent interview with *El País* newspaper, warned of 'the dying without sound of a culture with over a thousand years of history'. At the same time, the renowned Spanish writer Julio Llamazares, a Castilla y León native, blamed 'the uncontrolled development of the 1960s and 1970s, which generated a total disdain for everything rural'.

The regional Castilla y León government has set up a commission to study the problem and attempts are being made to lure more immigrants to smaller communities – just 2.5% of Castilla y Leon's population are immigrants, compared with a national average of around 10%.

There are half a dozen or so *casas rurales* in the area for you to choose from should you wish to stay. Most buses between Valladolid (€6.35, 1½ hours) and Soria (€6.25, 1½ hours) pass through town.

SEPÚLVEDA
POP 1320 / ELEV 1313M

With its houses staggered along a ridge carved out by the gorge of Río Duratón, and famous for its *cordero asado* and *cochinillo,* Sepúlveda is a favourite weekend escape for *madrileños* (Madrid residents). Indeed, the Tuscan-style warm tones of Sepúlveda's buildings, fronting the central Plaza de España, are an enviable setting for a hot Sunday roast. Wednesday is market day.

The *ayuntamiento* backs onto what remains of the old castle, while high above it all rises the 11th-century Iglesia del Salvador. It's considered the prototype of Castilian Romanesque, marked by the single arched portico.

Most visitors don't stay overnight, but if you'd like to enjoy the town's sleepy post-crowd aspect, Mirador del Castilla (☎921 54 03 53; Calle del Conde Sepúlveda 26; s/d €35/45), just off Plaza de España, has comfortable rooms, several with views (number 4 is a good choice).

For the *cordero* feast, take your pick around Plaza de España (places serving mediocre *cordero* don't last long here), but Restaurante Cristóbal (☎921 54 01 00; Calle del Conde de Sepúlveda 9; meals €35) and Restaurante Figón Zute el Mayor (☎921 54 01 65; Calle de Lope Tablada 6; meals €28) under

the arches are both long-standing favourites with good wine lists. Reservations are essential on weekends.

At least two buses link Sepúlveda daily with Madrid.

PARQUE NATURAL DEL HOZ DEL DURATÓN

A sizeable chunk of land northwest of Sepúlveda has been constituted as a natural park, the centrepiece of which is the Hoz del Duratón (Duratón Gorge). A dirt track leads 5km west from the hamlet of Villaseca to the Ermita de San Frutos. In ruins now, the hermitage was founded in the 7th century by San Frutos and his siblings, San Valentín and Santa Engracia. They lie buried in a tiny chapel nearby. This is a magical place, overlooking one of the many serpentine bends in the gorge, with squadrons of buzzards and eagles soaring above. The Parque Natural del Hoz del Duratón is a popular weekend excursion and some people take kayaks up to Burgomillodo to launch themselves down the waters of the canyon.

There is an excellent and informative Centro de Interpretación (☎921 54 05 86; www.miespacionatural.es; Calle del Conde de Sepúlveda 34; ☺10am-7pm; 🖩) in Sepúlveda that also has an informative permanent exhibition about all aspects of the natural park, including the flora and fauna. It is housed in part of the Iglesia de Santiago. Beneath part of the display area, visitors can see the glassed-over **10th-century crypt**.

West along Río Duero

PEÑAFIEL

POP 5520 / ELEV 758M

At the heart of the Ribera del Duero wine region, Peñafiel is home to the state-of-the-art Museo Provincial del Vino (www.museodelvinodevalladolid.es), cleverly ensconced within the walls of the mighty Castillo de Peñafiel (admission castle €3, incl museum €6; ⊙11am-2.30pm & 4.30-8.30pm Tue-Sun). Telling a comprehensive story of the region's wines, this wonderful museum is informative and entertaining with interactive displays, dioramas, backlit panels and computer terminals. The pleasures of the end product are not neglected: wine tasting costs €9.

The castle itself, one of the longest and narrowest in Spain, is also worth exploring. Its crenulated walls and towers stretch over 200m, but are little more than 20m across, and were raised and modified over 400 years from the 11th century onwards. The sight of it in the distance alone is worth the effort of getting here.

Like the wine museum, the cool, classy Hotel Convento Las Claras (☑983 87 81 68, www.hotelconventolasclaras.com; Plaza de los Comuneros 1; r €110) is an unexpected find in little Peñafiel. A former convent, the rooms are luxurious and there is a full spa available with thermal baths and treatments. The restaurant is similarly excellent.

Just north of Peñafiel, in the village of Curiel de Duero, Hotel Castillo de Curiel (☑983 88 04 01; www.castillodecuriel.com; d from €140; ✲⑯✳) should be the hotel of choice for castle romantics. No surprise then that it is a top choice for weddings. Occupying the oldest castle, dating from the 9th century, in the region (albeit extensively reformed), the hotel has lovely antique-filled rooms, all with sweeping views.

Four or five buses a day run to Valladolid (€4.45, 45 minutes), 60km west of here.

East along Río Duero

SAN ESTEBAN DE GORMAZ

POP 3290 / ELEV 911M

The dusty little town of San Esteban de Gormaz contains a couple of Romanesque gems hidden away in its centre: the 11th-century Iglesia de San Miguel and Iglesia de Nuestra Señora del Rivero (⊙11am-2pm & 5-7pm for both churches). The two churches sport the porticoed side galleries that char-

acterise the Romanesque style of the Segovia and Burgos areas.

EL BURGO DE OSMA

POP 5060 / ELEV 943M

Some 12km east of San Esteban de Gormaz, El Burgo de Osma is a real surprise. Once important enough to host its own university, it's now a somewhat rundown little old town, dominated by a quite remarkable cathedral and infused with an air of decaying elegance.

⊙ Sights

Your initiation into the old town is likely to be along the broad Calle Mayor, its portico borne by an uneven phalanx of stone and wooden pillars. Not far along, it leads into Plaza Mayor, fronted by the 18th-century ayuntamiento and the more sumptuous Hospital de San Agustín.

Catedral   CATHEDRAL

(⊙10am-1pm & 4-7pm Tue-Sun) On Plaza de San Pedro de Osma, this cathedral was begun in the 12th century as a Romanesque building, continued in a Gothic vein and finally topped with a weighty baroque tower that rivals many of the great cathedrals of Spain. The sanctuary is filled with art treasures, including the 16th-century main **altarpiece** and the so-called **Beato de Osma**, a precious 11th-century codex (manuscript) that can be seen in the Capilla Mayor. Also of note is the light-flooded, circular **Capilla de Palafox**, a rare example of the neoclassical style in this region. If you continue south, after around 150m you come to the river Ucero flanked by grassy banks and popular for picnicking in summer.

If you exit El Burgo from near Plaza de San Pedro de Osma, take a left for the village of Osma, high above which stand the ruins of the 10th-century Castillo de Osma.

🛏 Sleeping & Eating

Posada del Canónigo   HISTORIC HOTEL €€

(☑975 36 03 62; www.posadadelcanonigo.es; Plaza San Pedro de Osma 19; s/d incl breakfast €70/80; ✲⑯) This is certainly the most imaginative choice, with some rooms overlooking the cathedral from a handsome 16th-century building. There are two comfortable sitting rooms, one with a fireplace and library, and the rooms are overflowing with charm.

Hotel Il Virrey
CLASSIC HOTEL €€

(☑975 34 13 11; www.virreypalafox.com; Calle Mayor 2; s/d/ste €65/95/135; P❋✿) This place has old Spanish charm, verging on kitsch, with its heavily gilded furniture, porcelain cherubs, dripping chandeliers and sweeping staircase. The rooms are more muted with hardwood floors and wrought-iron furnishings. Room rates soar on weekends in February and March, when people flock here for the ritual slaughter (matanza) of pigs, after which diners indulge in all-you-can-eat feasts. At €46 per head it's not bad for one of the more unusual dining experiences. There's even a pig museum.

Casa Engracia
GRILLED MEATS €

(Calle Ruiz Zorrilla 3; meals €20-25; ☺Tue-Sun, lunch Mon) One of a rare breed of restaurants in this town that is open during the week. Expect sound rather than sensational meals, with an emphasis on grilled meats and fish.

Hospederia El Fielato
MODERN HOTEL €

(☑975 36 82 36; www.hospederiaelfielato.es; Avenida Juan Carlos 1; s/d €55/65; ❋✿) Pleasant modern rooms in an aesthetically reformed historic building.

Hostal Mayor 71
BUDGET HOTEL €

(☑975 36 80 24; www.mayor71.es, in Spanish; Calle Mayor 71; s/d €32/38) This is a good central option, although the whole place has a sterile institutional air.

ℹ Information

Tourist office (☑975 36 01 16; www.burgosma. es; Plaza Mayor 9; ☺10am-2pm & 4-8pm Wed-Sun) Should be your first port of call.

ℹ Getting There & Away

Buses link El Burgo with Soria (€3.30, 50 minutes, two daily, one on Sunday) and Valladolid (€9.30, two hours, three daily).

PARQUE NATURAL DEL CAÑÓN DEL RÍO LOBOS

Some 15km north of El Burgo de Osma, this park promises forbidding rockscapes and a magnificent, deep river canyon, not to mention abundant vultures and various other birds of prey. About 4km in from the road stands the Romanesque Ermita de San Bartolomé. You can walk deeper into the park but free camping is forbidden.

Camping Cañón del Río Lobos (☑975 36 35 65; sites per person/tent/car €5/5/6.25; ☺Easter–mid-Sep; ❋) is near Ucero. If you're heading north along the switchback road

that climbs up the canyon, you'll have some fine views back towards Ucero.

GORMAZ
POP 20

Some 14km south of El Burgo, on Río Duero, is the virtual ghost town of Gormaz. The sprawling low-lying castle has 21 towers, and was built by the Muslims in the 10th century and altered in the 13th. Its ruins still convey enormous dignity and the views alone justify the effort of getting here – this must have been a great perch for defending the surrounding country. The castle is reached via a winding road about 2km beyond the modern village.

BERLANGA DE DUERO
POP 1060 / ELEV 978M

About 15km east of Gormaz, Berlanga de Duero is lorded over by an imposing but ruined castle made larger by its continuous ramparts at the base of its hill. Down below, the squat Colegiata de Santa María del Mercado is a fine late-Gothic church, with star-shaped vaulting inside. The area around the pretty Plaza Mayor, with the occasional Renaissance house, has a certain dusty charm. To find out more, visit the tourist office (☑975 34 34 33; ☺10am-2pm & 4-8pm Mon-Sat).

AROUND BERLANGA DE DUERO

About 8km southeast of Berlanga de Duero stands the Ermita de San Baudelio (admission €1; ☺10am-2pm & 4-8pm Wed-Sat, 10am-2pm Sun Apr-Sep), whose simple exterior conceals a remarkable 11th-century Mozarabic interior. A great pillar in the centre of the only nave opens up at the top like a palm tree to create delicate horseshoe arches.

Another 17km south, the hilltop stone village of Rello retains much of its medieval defensive wall and feels like the place time forgot. The views from the village's southern ledge are superb. There's at least one casa rural if you love peace and quiet.

THE ROAD TO MADRID

The N110 winds southwest from San Esteban de Gormaz to join up with the A1 highway between Madrid and Burgos.

The first village of note you'll come to is Ayllón, some 50km southwest of El Burgo de Osma; it bathes in the same orange glow that characterises El Burgo's townscape. You enter by a medieval archway and are immediately confronted on the right by the ornate facade of a late-15th-century

THE OLDEST EUROPEAN

The archeological site of Atapuerca (☎902 02 42 46; www.atapuerca.org; guided tours in Spanish €6; ☺10am-2pm & 4-8pm Mon-Fri, 10am-2pm Sat & Sun; ⓘ), around 15km west of Burgos, has long excited students of early human history. But archeologists made their greatest discovery here in July 2007 when they uncovered a jawbone and teeth of what is believed to be the oldest-known European: 1.2 million years old, some 500,000 years older than any other remains discovered in Western Europe. A Unesco World Heritage–listed site, there are also remains of occupation in the area by homo-sapiens around 40,000 years ago and human settlements from the Neolithic age. Ceramics, cave paintings, carvings and burial sites have been discovered here, as well as evidence of cannibalism. Although Atapuerca is still under excavation, the site is open to visitors. There's a diverse programme of courses and study groups for adults, students and children (in Spanish). Advance reservations are essential for all visitors.

noble family's mansion, built in Isabelline style. The uneven, porticoed Plaza Mayor is capped at one end by the Romanesque Iglesia de San Miguel, and nearby stands the Renaissance-era Iglesia de Santa María la Mayor. Turn right behind this and follow the narrow street for about 500m and you'll come to the extensive remains of another Romanesque church. For tapas or hearty local meals, join the locals at Pemar (Plaza Mayor 1; tapas €0.50, meals €15). Modern Hostal Vellosillo (☎921 55 30 62; Avenida Conde Vallellano; s/d with washbasin €15/25, d with bathroom €35) over the bridge in the new town is a sound place to stay.

About 20km south of Ayllón, Riaza has a pretty circular Plaza Mayor surrounded by restaurants and bars; the sandy arena in the centre is still used for bullfights during the town's annual September fair.

Soria

POP 38,200 / ELEV 1055M

Small-town Soria is one of Spain's smaller and least-visited provincial capitals. Set on Río Duero in the heart of backwoods Castilian countryside, it's a great place to escape tourist Spain, with an appealing and compact old centre, and a sprinkling of stunning monuments. Calm and laid-back by day, Soria has a surprisingly lively nightlife.

◎ Sights

Monasteries & Churches

RELIGIOUS MONUMENTS

The most striking of Soria's sights has to be the 12th-century Monasterio de San Juan de Duero (Camino Monte de las Ánimas; admission €0.60, Sat & Sun free; ☺10am-2pm & 5-8pm Tue-Sat, 10am-2pm Sun). What most catch the eye are the exposed and gracefully interlaced arches of the monastery's partially ruined cloister which artfully blends Mudéjar and Romanesque influences. Inside the church, the capitals are worth a closer look for their intense iconography.

A lovely riverside walk south for 2.3km will take you past the 13th-century church of the former Knights Templar, the Monasterio de San Polo (not open to the public), and on to the fascinating, baroque Ermita de San Saturio (Paseo de San Saturio; admission free; ☺10.30am-2pm & 4.30-7.30pm Tue-Sat, 10.30am-2pm Sun). This octagonal structure perches right over the cave where Soria's patron saint spent much of his life.

Casco Viejo HISTORIC QUARTER

The narrow streets of Soria's casco viejo (old town) centre on Plaza Mayor. The plaza's appeal lies in its lack of uniformity, and in the attractive Renaissance-era ayuntamiento and the Iglesia de Santa María la Mayor, with its unadorned Romanesque facade and gloomy, though gilt-edged, interior. On the downside, it's a shame that there aren't more local bars here with chairs on the square. A block north is the majestic, sandstone, 16th-century Palacio de los Condes Gomara (Calle de Aguirre).

Churches CHURCHES

North of the centre is Soria's most beautiful church, the Romanesque Iglesia de Santo Domingo (Calle de Santo Tomé Hospicio; ☺7am-9pm). Its small but exquisitely sculpted portal is something special, particularly at sunset when its reddish stone seems to be aglow.

At the **Iglesia de San Juan de Rabanera** (Calle de San Juan de Rabanera), which was first built in the 12th century, hints of Gothic and even Byzantine art gleam through the mainly Romanesque hue.

Heading east towards Río Duero you pass the **Concatedral de San Pedro** (Calle de San Agustín), with its plateresque facade. The 12th-century **cloister** (admission €1; ⊙11am-1pm Mon, 10.30am-1.30pm & 4.30-7.30pm Tue-Sun) is the most charming feature here. Its delicate arches are divided by slender double pillars topped with capitals adorned with floral, human and animal motifs.

Museo Numantino ARCHEOLOGICAL MUSEUM
(Paseo del Espolón 8; adult/concession €1.20/free; ⊙10am-2pm & 5-8pm Tue-Sat, 10am-2pm Sun) Archeology buffs with a passable knowledge of Spanish should enjoy this well-organised museum, dedicated to finds from ancient sites across the province of Soria (especially Numancia; see p191). It has everything from mammoth bones to ceramics and jewellery, accompanied by detailed explanations of the historical developments in various major Celtiberian and Roman settlements.

🎊 Festivals & Events

Fiestas de San Juan y de la Madre de Dios TRADITIONAL FESTIVAL
Since the 13th century, the 12 *barrios* of Soria have celebrated this annual festival with considerable fervour. Held during the second half of June, the main festivities take place on *Jueves* (Thursday) *La Saca,* when each of the districts presents a bull to be fought the next day. The day following the bullfight some of the animals' meat is auctioned off, after which general carousing continues until the small hours of Sunday – and beyond.

🛏 Sleeping

Hostería Solar de Tejada
BOUTIQUE HOTEL €€
(☑975 23 00 54; www.hosteriasolardetejada.com; Calle de Claustrilla 1; s/d €52/56; ❄🛜) This handsome boutique hotel right in the middle of the pedestrianised zone is one of the best choices in Soria. Individually designed rooms have whimsical decor, Bohemian touches and beautifully tiled bathrooms.

Hotel Soria Plaza Mayor CLASSIC HOTEL €€
(☑975 24 08 64; www.hotelsoriaplazamayor.com; Plaza Mayor 10; s/d/ste €95/105/115; ❄@)

This hotel has terrific rooms, each with its own style of decor, overlooking either Plaza Mayor or a quiet side street. There are so many balconies that even some bathrooms have them. The suites are *very* comfortable.

Hotel Ruiz SMALL HOTEL €
(☑975 22 67 01; www.hostalruiz.com; Calle Numancia 49; s/d €46/68; ❄@) A good choice a few minutes from the bustle of the centre, rooms here are polished and comfortable with light-wood floors and dazzling white fabrics.

🍴 Eating

Soria's restaurants are mainly centred around the main squares, namely Plaza El Salvador, Plaza Ramón Benito Aceñal and Plaza Mayor.

Fogon del Salvador TRADITIONAL DISHES €€
(Plaza El Salvador 1; meals €25-30; ✍) A Soria culinary stalwart, Fogon del Salvador has a wine list as long as your arm (literally) and a fabulous wood-fired oven churning out succulent meat-based dishes. There is also (surprisingly) a healthy list of vegetarian dishes including *verduras en tempura* (tempura vegetables).

Casa Augusto SOPHISTICATED CASTILLIAN €€
(☑975 21 30 41; www.casaaugusto.com; Plaza Mayor 5; meals €15-25) This is a classy alternative, with an intimate dining area, an extensive wine list and professional service. If you can't decide what to eat, ask the waiter for the list of the year's most popular orders. For some reason, *pie sucio rellenos* (stuffed pigs trotters) is always there. Pasta dishes are also available (phew!). Reservations recommended.

Mesón Castellano TRADITIONAL CASTILLIAN €€
(Plaza Mayor 2; meals €25-35) With beamed ceilings, dangling flanks of ham, and the wall papered with proud photos of the local football team, this local institution serves some of the best tapas in town and delicious full meals in its *comedor.* The *cabrito asado* (roast goat kid) is a good order.

Iruna Plaza TRADITIONAL CASTILLIAN €€
(Plaza Ramón Benito Aceña 2; menú del día €22) One of the most popular spots in town; head for the restaurant out back to enjoy a healthy variety of dishes, ranging from the deeply traditional *cabrito frito* (fried baby goat; €15) to an Italian-inspired creamy *risotto de hongos* (mushroom risotto).

Capote

OPEN SANDWICHES €

(Plaza Ramón Benito Aceñal; montaditos €1;) You will have to fight through the crowd to reach the counter at this popular (cheap) bar where you can fill up happily on the tasty and varied *montaditos* (open sandwiches).

Drinking

Plaza San Clemente is perfect for kicking off the *marcha*. Of the handful of bars around here, Bar Patata (Plaza San Clemente 1) has the best range of tapas to go with your drinks.

Another good spot to start the evening is Plaza Ramon Benito Aceña, where you'll find the hugely popular Apolonia and the very cool Cafe Latino.

A see-and-be-seen alternative is Café-Bar Soho (Calle de Campo 16; ☺8am-late Mon-Sat), which is good at any time of the day.

ℹ Information

Tourist office (☑975 21 20 52; www.turismo castillayleon.com; Calle de Medinaceli 2; ☺9am-2pm & 5-8pm) Can provide a map and plenty of up-to-date information.

ℹ Getting There & Away

From the **bus station** (Avenida de Valladolid), a 15-minute walk west of the centre, there are regular services to Burgos (€11.20, 2¼ hours), Madrid (€14.80, 2½ hours) and Valladolid (€14.90, three hours), as well as main provincial towns.

The **train station** (Carretera de Madrid) is 2.5km southwest of the city centre. Trains connect Soria with Madrid (€13.85, three hours, three daily), but there are few other direct services.

Around Soria

NUMANCIA

The mainly Roman ruins of Numancia (adult/child €0.60/free, free Sat & Sun; ☺10am-2pm & 4-8pm Tue-Sat, 10am-2pm Sun;), 8km north of Soria, have a lonely, windswept aspect with little to suggest the long history of a settlement inhabited as early as the Bronze Age. Numancia proved one of the most resistant cities to Roman rule. Finally Scipio, who had crushed Carthage, starved the city into submission in 134 BC. Under Roman rule, Numancia was an important stop on the road from Caesaraugustus (Zaragoza) to Astúrica Augusta (Astorga). Now the city exists in outline only and will appeal more to budding archeologists than to casual visitors.

To get here, take the N111 for around 5km north of Soria, then follow the signs to Garray.

SIERRA DE URBIÓN & LAGUNA NEGRA

The Sierra de Urbión, northwest of Soria, is home to the beautiful Laguna Negra (Black Lake), a small glacial lake that resembles a black mirror at the base of brooding rock walls amid partially wooded hills. Located 18km north of the village of Vinuesa, the lake is reached by a winding and scenic road (there's no public transport) that's bumpy in patches. The road ends at a car park, where there's a small **information office** (☺June-Oct). It's a further 2km uphill to the lake, either on foot or via the bus (return €1, departing every half-hour from 10am to 2pm and 4pm to 6.30pm June to October), which leaves you 300m short of the lake. From the lake, a steep trail leads up to the Laguna de Urbión in La Rioja or to the summit of the Pico de Urbión, above the village of Duruelo de la Sierra, and on to a series of other tiny glacial lakes.

Vinuesa makes a good base for the area. Hostal Virginia (☑975 37 85 55; www.hotelvir ginia.net; Avenida de la Generalitat 139; s/d €48/65) offers bright and pleasant rooms with wrought-iron beds; the same owners run a popular bar and restaurant opposite. Hostal Visontium (☑975 37 83 54; Ctra de la Laguna Negra; s/d €32/55) has attractive rustic-style rooms and an excellent restaurant.

Camping El Cobijo (☑975 37 83 31; www. campingcobijo.com; sites from €4.60, 4-person bungalows €86; ☺Easter-Oct; ⓢ) is the nearest camping ground to the Laguna Negra (free camping is not permitted). It's a pleasant place set among pine trees, 2km northwest of Vinuesa.

CALATAÑAZOR

POP 60 / ELEV 1071M

One of Castilla y León's most romantic tiny hilltop villages, Calatañazor, about 30km west of Soria, is a charming detour off the main road. It's not visible from the highway, just a kilometre away, and has a crumbling medieval air. Pass through the town gate and climb the crooked, cobbled lanes, wandering through narrow streets lined by ochre stone and adobe houses topped with red-tiled roofs and conical chimneys. Scenes from the movie *Doctor Zhivago* were shot here.

Towering above the village is the one-time Muslim fortress that gave Calatañazor its name (which comes from the Arabic *Qala'at an-Nassur*, literally 'the vulture's citadel'). Now in ruins, it has exceptional views from the walls and watchtowers, both down over the rooftops and north over a vast field called Valle de la Sangre (Valley of Blood). This was the setting of an epic 1002 battle that saw the Muslim ruler Almanzor defeated.

There's also a church and a handful of artisan shops selling local products, including La Casa de Queso selling cheese pronounced the '*mas fuerte de España*' (strongest in Spain) and La Alacena, specialising in local and wild mushrooms. There are three well-signposted *casas rurales* if you fancy staying the night.

There's no regular public transport to Calatañazor. If you're driving, the village lies around 1km north of the N122 – the well-signposted turn-off is about 29km west of Soria and about 27km northeast of El Burgo de Osma.

South of Soria

ALMAZÁN
POP 5830 / ELEV 940M

Three of this small town's massive gates remain to testify to a past more illustrious than the present in this quiet backwater. It frequently changed hands between the Muslims and Christians and, improbably, for three short months was chosen by Fernando and Isabel as their residence.

The Romanesque Iglesia de San Miguel (Plaza Mayor; ☉10.30am-2pm & 5-7pm Tue-Sun) sports an unusual octagonal cupola–bell tower that reveals Mudéjar influences and a lovely circular apse. Inside is a bas-relief depicting the killing of Thomas à Becket at the hands of the British king Henry II. The work was commissioned by Henry's daughter, Eleanor of Aquitaine, the wife of Alfonso VIII, as a gesture of penance on behalf of her father.

The attractive facade of the Gothic-Renaissance Palacio de los Hurtado de Mendoza looks out over Plaza Mayor.

Hotel Villa de Almazán (☑975 30 06 11; www.hotelvilladealmazan.com; Avenida de Soria 29; s/d €58/77; ❋🐾) promises large, well-appointed modern rooms and the best restaurant in town.

There are four daily buses to/from Soria (€2.15, 30 minutes).

MEDINACELI
POP 750 / ELEV 1270M

Modern Medinaceli, along a slip road just north of the A2 motorway, is the contemporary equivalent of a one-horse town, but don't be fooled: old Medinaceli is one of Castilla y León's most rustic and beautiful *pueblos* (villages), draped along a high, windswept ridge 3km to the north. Its most incongruous landmark is a 1st-century-AD Arco Romano (Roman triumphal arch), while there's also the moderately interesting Gothic Colegiata de Santa María, and the evocative remains of a synagogue: San Román. But Medinaceli's charm consists of rambling through tranquil cobblestone lanes and being surrounded by delightful stone houses redolent of the noble families that lived here after the town fell to the Reconquista in 1124. The area between Plaza de Santiueste and the lovely, partly colonnaded Plaza Mayor is Medinaceli at its best. The plaza appears incongruously large compared to its surroundings and is very quiet, aside from when David Beckham filmed his Pepsi ad here a few years back... The oldest remaining building is the 16th-century Alhónidga formerly used for storing and selling grain.

Lovely La Ceramica (☑975 32 63 81; www.laceramicacasarural.es, in Spanish; Calle de Santa Isabel 2; s/d €50/55, d incl breakfast & dinner €91) wins our vote for the friendliest staff, best location in the old town and all-round best deal. The rooms are intimate and comfortable, with a strong dose of rustic charm. There's usually a two-night minimum stay.

The style of the rooms at Hostal Rural Bavieca (☑975 32 61 06; www.hostalrural babieca.com, in Spanish; Calle Campo de San Nicolás 6; s/d incl breakfast €55/75, incl dinner €65/120) may not be to everyone's taste, but this is unmistakably a boutique hotel that offers high-quality rooms and ambience.

Both of the above sleeping options have good restaurants – again, La Ceramica is cosier – but consider also the well signposted Asador de la Villa El Granero (Calle de Yedra 10; meals €25-30; ☉Jul & Aug, lunch Wed-Mon Sep-Jun,), which is thought by many to be Medinaceli's best restaurant. The *setas de campo* (wild mushrooms) are something of a local speciality.

You can't miss the tourist office (☑689 734176; Calle Campo de San Nicolás; ☉10am-2pm & 4-8pm Wed-Sun) at the entrance to town, just around the corner from the arch.

Two daily buses to Soria (€4.95, 45 minutes) leave from outside the *ayuntamiento* in the new town. There's no transport between the old and new towns; it's quite a steep hike.

SANTA MARÍA DE LA HUERTA
POP 390 / ELEV 818M

This largely insignificant village, just short of the Aragonese frontier, contains a wonderful Cistercian monastery (admission €3; ☺10am-1pm & 4-6.30pm Mon-Sat, 10-11.30am & 4-6.30pm Sun), founded in 1162, where monks lived until the monastery was expropriated in 1835. The order was allowed to return in 1930 and 25 Cistercians are now in residence. Before entering the monastery, note the church's impressive 12th-century facade with its magnificent rose window.

Inside the monastery you pass through two cloisters, the second of which is the more beautiful. Known as the **Claustro de los Caballeros**, it's Spanish-Gothic in style, although the medallions on the 2nd floor, bearing coats of arms and assorted illustrious busts, such as that of Christopher Columbus, are a successful plateresque touch. Off this cloister is the *refectorio* (dining hall). Built in the 13th century, it's notable for the absence of columns to support the vault.

A couple of buses per day connect the village with Almazán and Soria.

Castilla-La Mancha

Includes »

Best Places to Eat

» Manolo de la Osa (p219)

» Alfileritos 24 (p202)

» El Corregidor (p210)

Best Places to Stay

» Casa de Cisneros (p200)

» La Casa del Rector (p210)

» Posada de San José (p217)

Why Go?

Castilla-La Mancha's landscape is richly patterned and dramatic: undulating plains of rich henna-coloured earth, neatly striped and spotted with olive groves, and golden wheat fields and grapevines – all stretching to a horizon you never seem to reach. The story-book quality is intensified by the presence of solitary windmills and abundant (mostly ruined) castles. There are quiet mountainous stretches here as well, including the Montes de Toledo and the thickly carpeted valleys around Alcalá del Júcar.

The area's best-known city is glorious Toledo, Spain's spiritual capital and an open-air museum of medieval buildings and cultural sights. Cuenca is another wondrous place, seemingly about to topple off its eagle's-eyrie perch high above a gorge.

On a more sensory level, this is the region where saffron is grown and it's also the capital of Spain's unrivalled Manchego cheese. The latter makes the perfect accompaniment to the local wines – Spain's largest vineyard is located here.

When to Go

Toledo

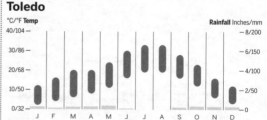

March–April
Enjoy the countryside's colourful dazzle of wild flowers against a lush green landscape.

May Stroll the evocative streets of medieval Toledo and Cuenca before the sizzle of high summer.

September–October Hike across Castilla-La Mancha's natural parks and picturesque villages.

Toledo

POP 82,300 / ELEV 655M

Toledo is Spain's equivalent of a downsized Rome. All you need to cover the city's sights is a pair of sturdy cobble-proof shoes. The city's labyrinth of narrow streets, plazas and inner patios is also reminiscent of the *medinas* (towns) of Damascus, Cairo or Morocco's Fez, although the historic diversity of Christians, Jews and Muslims equals an intriguing combination of churches, synagogues and mosques. Add to this a lofty

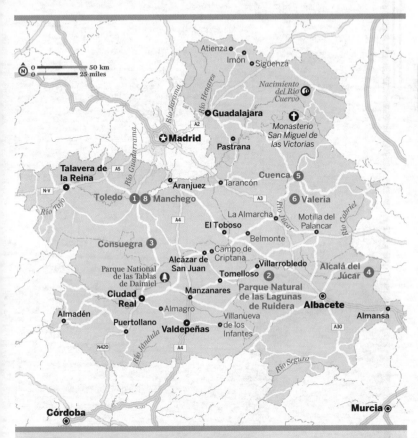

Castilla-La Mancha Highlights

❶ Stroll the tangle of medieval streets and explore the museums and monuments of **Toledo** (p195)

❷ Revel in the unspoilt beauty of the **Parque Natural de las Lagunas de Ruidera** (p210), with its crystal-clear turquoise lakes

❸ Take *the* Don Quijote shot of the windmills overlooking **Consuegra** (p212)

❹ Kick back with a beer at a riverside bar in **Alcalá del Júcar** (p213) beneath the cascade of houses and the castle

❺ Visit the exceptional Museo de Arte Abstracto Español, housed in one of extraordinary hanging houses of **Cuenca** (p215)

❻ Step back in time and explore little-known Roman excavations in **Valeria** (p218)

❼ Be king or queen of the castle, several times over, by visiting the province's fascinating **castillos** (p204)

❽ Enjoy the local wines with the perfect accompaniment: a crumbly wedge of well-aged, locally produced **Manchego** (p205) cheese

CASTILLA-LA MANCHA

Toledo

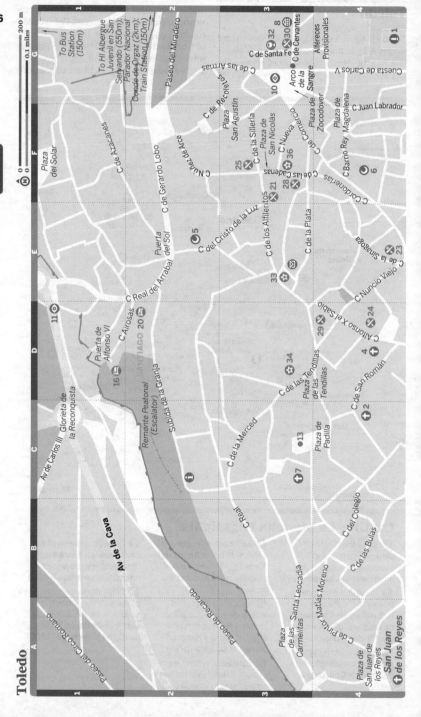

0   200 m
0   0.1 miles

setting, high above Río Tajo, and it's no surprise that Toledo is one of Spain's most-visited cities.

Toledo's charms can be dampened when the streets are choked with tour groups. Try to stay till dusk, when the city returns to the locals and the streets take on a moody, other-worldly air.

History

After the Visigothic nobles sent the kingdom into decline, the Muslims succeeded in conquering Toledo in 711. The city rapidly grew to become the capital of an independent Arab *taifa* (small kingdom) and *the* centre of learning and arts in Spain.

Alfonso VI marched into Toledo in 1085 and, shortly thereafter, the Vatican recognised Toledo as a seat of the Spanish Church. Initially, Toledo's Christians, Jews and Muslims coexisted tolerably well. However, in 1492, Spain's Muslims and Jews were compelled to convert to Christianity or flee – a grievous tragedy in this city of many faiths.

In the 16th century Carlos I considered making Toledo his permanent capital, but his successor, Felipe II, dashed such ideas with his definitive move to Madrid, and Toledo again went into decline.

In the early months of the 1936–39 civil war, Nationalist troops (and some civilians) were kept under siege in the Alcázar.

In 1986 Unesco declared Toledo a monument of world interest.

◉ Sights

Most of Toledo's sights are within easy strolling distance of each other in the old town. Plaza del Ayuntamiento is the convenient home to the tourist office and cathedral, making it an ideal place from which to set out.

Catedral de Toledo CATHEDRAL
(Plaza del Ayuntamiento; adult/child €7/free; ⏱10.30am-6.30pm Mon-Sat, 2-6.30pm Sun) Toledo's cathedral dominates the skyline, reflecting the city's historical significance as the heart of Catholic Spain.

From the earliest days of the Visigothic occupation, the current site of the cathedral has been a centre of worship. During Muslim rule, it contained Toledo's central mosque, destroyed in 1085. Dating from the 13th century and essentially a Gothic structure, the cathedral is nevertheless a melting pot of styles, including Mudéjar and the Spanish Renaissance.

CASTILLA-LA MANCHA TOLEDO

The main nave is dominated by the **coro** (choir stalls), a feast of sculpture and carved wooden stalls. The 15th-century lower tier depicts the conquest of Granada.

Opposite is the **Capilla Mayor**, an extravagant work of art dating back to 1498. The masterpiece is the *retablo* (altarpiece) in Flemish Gothic style, depicting scenes from the lives of Christ and the Virgin Mary. The oldest of the cathedral's magnificent stained-glass pieces is the rose window above the **Puerta del Reloj**. Behind the main altar lies a mesmerising piece of 18th-century *churrigueresco* (lavish Baroque ornamentation), the **Transparente**, which also provides welcome light.

Other highlights include the gilded **Capilla de Reyes Nuevos**, the **Capilla de la Torre** and the **sacristía** (sacristy). The last contains a small gallery with paintings by such masters as El Greco, Zurbarán, Titian, Rubens and Velázquez, while the Capilla de Reyes Nuevos houses the extraordinary **Custodia de Arfe**, by the celebrated goldsmith Enrique de Arfe. With 18kg of pure gold and 183kg of silver, this 16th-century religious jewel bristles with some 260 statuettes. Its big day out is the Feast of Corpus Christi (p200), when it is paraded around Toledo's streets.

The **sala capitular** (chapter house) features a remarkable 500-year-old *artesonado* (wooden Mudéjar ceiling) and Renaissance religious murals.

Sinagoga del Tránsito   SYNAGOGUE
(www.museosefardi.net, in Spanish; Calle Samuel Leví; adult/child €2.40/1.20, audioguide €3; ☉10am-9pm Tue-Sat, 10am-2pm Sun; 🚻) This magnificent synagogue was built in 1355 by special permission of Pedro I (construction of synagogues was prohibited in Christian Spain). Toledo's former *judería* (Jewish quarter) was once home to 11 synagogues. The bulk of Toledo's Jews were tragically expelled in 1492. From 1492 until 1877, it was variously used as a priory, hermitage

and military barracks. The synagogue now houses the Museo Sefardi, open the same hours as the synagogue. The vast main prayer hall has been expertly restored and the Mudéjar decoration and intricately carved wooden ceiling are striking. Exhibits provide an insight into the history of Jewish culture in Spain, and include archaeological finds, a memorial garden, costumes and ceremonial artefacts.

Sinagoga de Santa María La Blanca
SYNAGOGUE

(Calle de los Reyes Católicos 4; admission €2.30; ☉10am-6pm) A more modest synagogue, characterised by the horseshoe arches that delineate the five naves – classic Almohad architecture. Originally the upper arches opened onto rooms where women worshipped; the men worshipped down below.

San Juan de los Reyes
FRANCISCAN MONASTERY

(Plaza de San Juan de los Reyes 2; admission €2.30; ☉10am-6pm) North of the synagogues lies the early-17th-century Franciscan monastery and church of San Juan de los Reyes, notable for its delightful cloisters, which encircle a classic garden with a fountain, orange trees and roses.

Provocatively built in the heart of the Jewish quarter, the monastery was founded by Isabel and Fernando to demonstrate the supposed supremacy of the Catholic faith. The rulers had planned to be buried here but, when they took the greater prize of Granada in 1492, opted for the purpose-built Capilla Real.

Throughout the church and cloister, the coat of arms of Isabel and Fernando dominates. The chains of Christian prisoners liberated in Granada dangle from the outside walls. The prevalent late Flemish Gothic style is enhanced with lavish Isabelline ornament, counterbalanced by Mudéjar decoration, like the magnificent wooden ceiling in the upper cloister.

Alcázar
FORTRESS

At the highest point in the city, looms the foreboding Alcázar. Abd ar-Rahman III raised an *al-qasr* (fortress) here in the 10th century, which was thereafter altered by the Christians. Alonso Covarrubias and Herrera rebuilt it as a royal residence for Carlos I, but the court moved to Madrid and the fortress became a white elephant, eventually becoming the Academia de la Infantería (Military Academy).

TAKE THE ESCALATOR
199

A remonte peatonal (escalator; ☉7am-10pm Mon-Fri, 8am-2am Sat, 8am-10pm Sun), which starts near the Puerta de Alfonso VI and ends near the Monasterio de Santo Domingo El Antiguo, is a good way to avoid the steep uphill climb to reach the historic quarter of town.

The Alcázar was largely destroyed during the siege of Franco's forces in 1936 but Franco had it rebuilt and turned into a military museum. At the time of research the museum was closed for major renovations, with no completion date available.

Mezquita del Cristo de la Luz
MOSQUE

(Cuesta de Carmelitas Descalzos 10; admission €1.90; ☉2-8pm Fri, 10am-2pm & 3-8pm Sat & Sun) On the northern slopes of town you'll find a modest, yet beautiful, mosque, where architectural traces of Toledo's medieval Muslim conquerors are still in evidence. Built in the 10th century, it suffered the usual fate of being converted to a church (hence the religious frescoes), but the original vaulting and arches survived. The narrow, steep Calle del Cristo de la Luz continues via the Islamic-named Bab al-Mardum gate.

Plaza de Zocodover
MAIN SQUARE

This lively square is flanked by cafes that are prime places for people-watching.

From 1465 until the 1960s Zocodover was the scene of the city's Tuesday market and successor to the Arab *souq ad-dawab* (livestock market), hence the name. It was also here that *toledanos* for centuries enjoyed their bullfights or, morbidly, gathered to witness public burnings at the stake carried out by the Inquisition.

The southern flank dates from the 17th century – the McDonald's certainly does not.

FREE Museo de Santa Cruz
CITY MUSEUM

(Calle de Cervantes 3; ☉10am-6.30pm Mon-Sat, 10am-2pm Sun) Just off the Plaza de Zocodover, the 16th-century Museo de Santa Cruz is a beguiling combination of Gothic and Spanish Renaissance styles. The cloisters and carved wooden ceilings are superb, as are the upstairs displays of Spanish ceramics. The ground-level gallery contains a number of El Grecos (look for the *Asunción de la Virgen* and the superbly rendered *La Veronica*), a painting attributed to Goya *(Cristo Crucificado),* and the wonderful 15th-century *Tapestry of the Astrolabes.*

DON'T MISS

TOP VISTAS

For superb city views, head over the Puente de Alcántara to the other side of Río Tajo. Alternatively, hop on the free **cable ferry** (⊙10am-1.30pm & 3-6pm) from near Hotel El Diamantista and walk up the opposite bank. For a pleasant riverside stroll, head west along the banks from the ferry as far as the Puente de San Martín, a pretty grassy stretch popular with joggers and fishermen, with all the drama of the city looming above. You can also climb the tower at the **Iglesia San Ildefonso** (Plaza Juan de Mariana 1; admission €1.90; ⊙10am-6.45pm), for more camera-clicking views.

Courses

University Castilla-La Mancha   SPANISH
(www.uclm.es/fundacion/esto) The University Castilla-La Mancha runs an ESTO (Spanish in Toledo) program with various language courses. Visit its website for more details.

Festivals & Events
Toledo has several annual festivals worthy of your attention.

Feast of Corpus Christi   CORPUS CHRISTI
This is one of the finest Corpus Christi celebrations in Spain, taking place on the Thursday of the ninth week after Easter. Several days of festivities reach a crescendo with a procession featuring the massive *Custodia de Arfe* (see p197).

Semana Santa   HOLY WEEK
Easter week is marked by several days of solemn processions by masked members of *cofradías* (brotherhoods), including several that take place around midnight.

Feast of the Assumption
ASSUMPTION DAY
Taking place on 15 August, this is when you can drink of the cathedral's well water, believed to have miraculous qualities – the queues for a swig from an earthenware *botijo* (jug) can be equally astonishing.

Sleeping
Toledo's plentiful accommodation is offset by the visiting tourists, especially from July to September. Book ahead to avoid endless suitcase-trundling over cobbles.

TOP CHOICE **Casa de Cisneros**   BOUTIQUE HOTEL **€€**
(☏925 22 88 28; www.hostal-casa-de-cisneros.com; Calle del Cardenal Cisneros; s/d €50/80; ❀❄❂) Across from the cathedral, this seductive hotel is built on the site of an 11th-century Islamic palace, parts of which can be spied via a glass porthole in the lobby floor. In comparison, this building is a 16th-century youngster, with pretty stone-and-wood-beamed rooms and exceptionally voguish bathrooms.

Hostal Santo Tomé   BUDGET HOTEL **€**
(☏925 22 17 12; www.hostalsantotome.com; Calle de Santo Tomé 13; s/d €42/55; P❄) This good-value *hostal*, above a souvenir shop, has larger-than-most rooms with light wood floors and furniture, plus bathrooms with five-star attitude, offering extras like shoe polish and hairdryers. Parking costs €10.

Hostal del Cardenal   HISTORIC HOTEL **€€**
(☏925 22 49 00; www.hostaldelcardenal.com; Paseo de Recaredo 24; s/d €77/113; P❄❂) This wonderful 18th-century mansion has soft ochre-coloured walls, arches and columns. The rooms are grand, yet welcoming, with dark furniture, plush fabrics and parquet floors. Several overlook the glorious terraced gardens.

La Posada de Manolo   BOUTIQUE HOTEL **€€**
(☏925 28 22 50; www.laposadademanolo.com; Calle de Sixto Ramón Parro 8; s/d incl breakfast €42/66; ❄❂) This memorable hotel has themed each floor with furnishings and decor reflecting one of the three cultures of Toledo: Christian, Islamic and Jewish. There are stunning views of the old town and cathedral from the terrace.

Parador Nacional Conde de Orgaz
PARADOR **€€€**
(☏925 22 18 50; www.parador.es; Cerro del Emperador; s/d €159/171; P❄❂❀) High above the southern bank of Río Tajo, Toledo's low-rise *parador* (luxurious state-owned hotel) boasts a classy interior and breathtaking city views. To get here, cross the Puente de Alcántara bridge and follow the signs.

Virgen de la Estrella   BUDGET HOTEL **€**
(☏925 25 31 34; www.pensionarrabal.com; Calle Airosas 1; r without bathroom €30) The owner also runs the nearby restaurant of the

Walking Tour
A Stroll through History

❯ Stock up on Band-Aids and explore Toledo on foot in a walk that could be completed in three hours or last all day.

Start off in central ❶ **Plaza de Zocodover**, then pass through the ❷ **Arco de la Sangre** on the eastern side of the square to the rewarding ❸ **Museo de Santa Cruz** on the left. Up the hill to the south is Toledo's signature ❹ **Alcázar**, beyond which there are some fine views over the Río Tajo. Follow the spires down the hill to the west, passing the remnants of a mosque, ❺ **Mezquita de las Tornerías**, before reaching the ❻ **Catedral de Toledo**, the spiritual home of Catholic Spain. Twist your way northwest to the ❼ **Centro Cultural San Marcos**, housed in the 17th-century San Marcos church where the original domed roof, complete with ceiling frescoes, creates an evocative gallery space for temporary art exhibitions. Southwest of here, the 14th-century ❽ **Taller del Moro** is closed for the fore-

seeable future, but the building is still interesting for its classic Mudéjar architecture.

From here, you can detour northeast to the ❾ **Iglesia de San Román**, an impressive hybrid of Mudéjar and Renaissance styles and home to the Museo de los Concilios y Cultura Visigoda, with Visigothic artefacts. Nearby is the ❿ **Monasterio de Santo Domingo El Antiguo**.

Down the hill is a must-see for El Greco enthusiasts: the wonderful ⓫ **Iglesia de Santo Tomé**. From here you enter the heart of Toledo's old Jewish quarter. The ⓬ **Sinagoga del Tránsito** should not be missed, while the ⓭ **Sinagoga de Santa María La Blanca** is also worth a look. These synagogues take on special poignancy if you continue along Calle de los Reyes Católicos to the splendid ⓮ **San Juan de los Reyes**. Spain's Catholic rulers hoped this church would represent the ultimate finale to the city's history, so it seems a fitting spot to end your walk.

ℹ️ RATING HOTELS

Bear in mind that the hotel rates in Toledo, Cuenca and many other tourist-driven towns and villages in the province vary drastically during the week, being popular weekend destinations for city folk from Valencia, Murcia and Madrid. Prices listed here are for the higher weekend rate, but prices can drop by as much as 30 per cent midweek when hotels tend to cater more to travelling salesmen than tourists.

same name (*menú* €12), as well as a second, equally inexpensive, *pensión*. The plus here is the location opposite the Santiago church, which is pretty and quiet – except when the church bells toll.

Hotel Eurico SMALL HOTEL €€
(☑925 28 41 78; www.hoteleurico.com; Calle de Santa Isabel 3; s/d €59/89; ❄️📶) Pleasant rooms are set around a pretty courtyard.

Hostal Alfonso XII SMALL HOTEL €€
(☑925 25 25 09; www.hostal-alfonso12.com; Calle de Alfonso XII; r €65; 😊❄️📶) Gingerbread cottage of a place, dating from the 18th century.

HI Albergue Juvenil en San Servando
YOUTH HOSTEL €
(☑925 22 45 54; ralberguesto@jccm.es; Subida del Hospital; dm under/over 26yr €9.50/12; @) Good youth hostel in a castle setting.

🍴 Eating

The city is heaving with restaurants. For a good range of choices, head for Calle Alfonso X el Sabio and the surrounding pedestrian streets, including Calle de los Alfileritos and Calle de la Sillería. Avoid the overpriced terraced restaurants on Plaza de Zocodover, as well as those that advertise various types of paella with a brightly-coloured placard outside, as they will generally reflect an indifferent kitchen (these paellas are mass produced).

Alfileritos 24 MODERN INTERNATIONAL €€
(www.alfileritos24.com; Calle de los Alfileritos 24; meals €25-35; 😊) The 14th-century surroundings of columns, beams and barrel-vault ceilings are snazzily coupled with modern artwork and bright dining rooms spread over four floors. The menu demonstrates an innovative flourish in the kitchen, with dishes like red-tuna tartare with seaweed and guacamole, and strawberry 'soup' with Szechuan pepper ice cream.

Aurelio TRADITIONAL SOPHISTICATED €€
(☑925 22 13 92; Plaza del Ayuntamiento 4; meals €35-45; ⏱lunch & dinner Tue-Sun, lunch only Mon) The three restaurants under this name are among the best of Toledo's top-end eateries (the other locations are Calle de la Sinagoga 1 and 6). Game, fresh produce and traditional dishes are prepared with panache. Reservations recommended.

Madre Tierra VEGETARIAN €€
(☑925 21 34 24; www.restaurantemadretierra.com; Bajanda de la Tripería 2; meals €25-35; ⏱lunch & dinner Wed-Sun, lunch Mon; 😊📶) A cool cavernous space, with exposed brick arches, a soft ochre colour scheme and muted light, creates a romantic atmosphere for enjoying Indian-, Asian- and Mediterranean-inspired vegetarian meals, including sushi, moussaka, pastas, *pakoras* (vegetables in a spicy batter) and salads. Reservations recommended.

La Abadía LIGHT DISHES €€
(www.abadiatoledo.com; Plaza de San Nicolás 3; meals €25-30; 📶) In a former 16th-century palace, this atmospheric bar and restaurant is ideal for romancing couples. Arches, niches and subtle lighting are spread over a warren of brick-and-stone-clad rooms. The menu includes lightweight dishes like *verduras a la parrilla* (grilled fresh vegetables) – perfect for small (distracted) appetites.

Palacios HOMESTYLE TRADITIONAL €
(Calle Alfonso X el Sabio 3; menú €13.90, meals €14-18) An unpretentious place, where stained glass, beams and efficient old-fashioned service combine with traditional no-nonsense cuisine. Hungry? Try a gut-busting bowl of traditional *judías con perdiz* (white beans with partridge) for starters.

Mille Grazie ITALIAN €
(Calle de las Cadenas 2; pizzas from €7.50, pastas from €8.50; lunch & dinner Mon-Sat, lunch Sun; 📶) Despite the worrying inclusion of a Hawaiian pizza (with pineapple), the chef here *is* Italian and the dishes are tasty and good. Try the *panzotti Mille Grazie* (ravioli-style pasta stuffed with spinach and walnuts).

Santa Fe HOMESTYLE COOKING €
(Calle de Santa Fe 6; menú €10.50) You can eat better here, and for half the price, than in the restaurants on nearby Zocodover. Try the homemade paella.

La Naviera SEAFOOD €€
(Calle de la Campana 8; meals €20-25; ⏱lunch & dinner Tue-Sat) Diners swoop like seagulls ready for the best seafood in Toledo.

Kumera

SOPHISTICATED MODERN €

(Calle Alfonso X el Sabio 2; meals €18-25)
Diverse, innovative menu and streetside
dining space.

Drinking & Entertainment

Toledo has enough bars and discos to ensure you miss bedtime. Aside from the listings below, the outdoor tables of the bars in
the leafy courtyard just off Plaza de Magdalena are a delight in summer. For student-
oriented nightlife, shimmy down to the
streets around Plaza de San Nicolás.

Enebro

BAR

(Plaza San Justo 9; 8am-midnight Mon-Fri,
noon-1am Sat & Sun) Ease into your evening out with a drink under the trees in
this pretty square, enjoying generous free
tapas and Hendrix (or similar) on the
sound system.

Círculo de Arte

CONCERTS

(www.circuloartetoledo.org; Plaza de San Vicente
2) There are several venues for enjoying
foot-tapping live sounds, including this
classy place in a converted chapel, with its
regular concerts and theatre productions.

El Último

LIVE MUSIC

(Plaza del Colegio de Infantes 4; 5.30pm-late)
Situated in a 16th-century building, El
Último is a hotbed for live jazz, blues and
soul.

El Ambigú

LIVE MUSIC

(Calle de las Tendillas 8; 8pm-late) Plays jazz
and blues in an intimate half-tiled interior with artwork and arches.

La Tabernita

BAR

(Calle de Santa Fe 10) A small chilled-out bar.

Pícaro

CAFE-THEATRE

(www.picarocafeteatro.com; Calle de las Cadenas 6) A laid-back venue for theatre and
other acts.

Shopping

For centuries Toledo was renowned for the
excellence of its swords and you'll see them
for sale everywhere (although be wary of
taking them in your hand baggage through
customs!). Another big seller is anything
decorated with *damasquinado* (dama-
scene), a fine inlay of gold or silver in the
Arab artistic tradition. A reliable outlet is
Pedro Maldonado Gonzalez (Calle de San
Juan de Dios 10).

Information

For official guided tours, check out www.alficen.
com.

Centro Locutorio Santo Tomé (Calle de Santo
Tomé 1; per hr €2; 11am-10.30pm) Internet
access.

Main tourist office (925 25 40 30; www.
toledoturismo.com; Plaza del Ayuntamiento;
10.30am-2.30pm Mon, 10.30am-2.30pm &
4.30-7pm Tue-Sun).

Provincial tourist office (925 25 93 00;
www.diputoledo.es; Subida de la Granja;
10am-5pm Mon-Sat, 10am-3pm Sun)

Getting There & Away

For most major destinations, you'll need to backtrack to Madrid.

BUS From Toledo's **bus station** (Avenida de
Castilla La Mancha), buses depart for Madrid
every half-hour from 6am to 10pm daily (less on
Sundays). Direct buses (€5.25, one hour) run
hourly; other services (1½ hours) go via villages
along the way. There are also services on weekdays and Sunday to Albacete (€14.35, 2¾ hours)
and Cuenca (€11.40, 2¼ hours).

TRAIN Built in 1920, the **train station** (Paseo de
la Rosa) is a pretty introduction to the city. The
high-speed AVE service runs every hour or so to
Madrid (€9.90, 30 minutes).

Getting Around

BUS Handy buses run between Plaza de Zocodover and the bus station (bus 5) and train
station (buses 61 and 62; €0.95).

CAR & MOTORCYCLE The closest underground car park to the centre is on Calle de
Santa Ursula.

TAXI There are taxi ranks south of Plaza de
Zocodover and at the bus station. Or you can call
a taxi on 925 25 50 50.

ALMOND NUTS

Not a marzipan fan? Think again. You probably won't have tasted any so good anywhere else. Toledo is famed for this wonderful almond-based confectionery, which
every shop seems to sell. The **Santo Tomé** marzipan brand is highly reputable and
there are several outlets in town, including one on **Plaza de Zocodover**. Even the local
nuns get in on the marzipan act and most of the convents sell the sweets.

EL GRECO IN TOLEDO

Fortunately El Greco chose to change his name from the singularly unpronounceable Domenikos Theotokopoulos. Born in Crete in 1541, he moved to Venice in 1567 to be schooled as a Renaissance artist.

El Greco came to Spain in 1577 and settled in Toledo, where there were several patrons to support him. The painter liked to hang around with the movers and shakers of the time and, apparently, did not suffer from a lack of modesty: 'As surely as the rate of payment is inferior to the value of my sublime work, so will my name go down to posterity as one of the greatest geniuses of Spanish painting,' he pompously pronounced.

Arrogant and extravagant, El Greco liked the high life and took rooms in a mansion on the Paseo del Tránsito. As Toledo's fortunes declined, however, so did the artist's personal finances (that's karma for you). Although his final paintings are among his best, he often found himself unable to pay the rent. He died in 1614, leaving his works scattered about the city, where many have remained to this day.

Iglesia de Santo Tomé (www.santotome.org; Plaza del Conde; admission €2.30; ☺10am-6pm) contains El Greco's masterpiece *El Entierro del Conde de Orgaz* (The Burial of the Count of Orgaz). When the count was buried in 1322, Saints Augustine and Stephen supposedly descended from heaven to attend the funeral. El Greco's work depicts the event, complete with miracle guests including himself, his son and Cervantes.

One of the oldest convents in Toledo, the 11th-century **Monasterio de Santo Domingo El Antiguo** (Plaza de Santo Domingo el Antiguo; admission €2; ☺11am-1.30pm & 4-7pm Mon-Sat, 4-7pm Sun) includes some of El Greco's early commissions (most are copies). Visible through an iron grating is the crypt and wooden coffin of the painter himself.

Other spots in Toledo where you can contemplate El Greco's works include the Museo de Santa Cruz and the cathedral's *sacristía*.

Around Toledo

The region surrounding Toledo is best explored by car. There is plenty to see here, including Roman ruins and some of the country's most evocative castles.

CARRANQUE

Since 1983 archaeologists at **Carranque** (adult/child €4/free; ☺10am-9pm Tue-Sun) have been excavating what they believe to be the foundations of a late-4th-century **Roman basilica**, which would make it the oldest in Spain. The skeletal remains of Roman villas and temple-fountains are among the site's other highlights, while the remains of a 12th-century monastery with some valuable mosaics are also undergoing excavation. The admission fee includes entrance to a small interpretation centre and museum.

CASTLES

The area around Toledo is rich with castles in varying states of upkeep. Most are only accessible by car.

Situated some 20km southeast of Toledo along the CM42 is the dramatic ruined Arab castle of **Almonacid de Toledo**. There are legends that suggest El Cid lived here, but the lonely ruins have long been abandoned. A few kilometres further down the road is a smaller castle in the village of **Mascaraque**. Continue on to Mora, where the 12th-century **Castillo Peñas Negras**, 3km from town, is on the site of a prehistoric necropolis, currently undergoing extensive archaeological exploration; follow the sandy track to reach the castle for stunning big-sky views of the surrounding plains. Next, head for the pretty small town of **Orgaz**, which has a handsome, well-preserved 15th-century **castle** (☺every 2nd Wed Apr-Nov).

Around 30km southwest of Toledo, the hulking ruin of **Castillo de Montalbán**, believed to have been erected by the 12th-century Knights Templars, stands majestically over the Río Torcón valley. It's open only sporadically, but there's little to stop you wandering around at any time.

The town of **Escalona**, 52km northwest of Toledo on the N403, boasts a castle ruin of Arab origin in a pretty location on the banks of Río Alberche.

THE WEST

Heavily wooded in parts and with a compelling combination of sweeping plains and dramatic mountains, the west of this region has plenty of surprises up its sleeve.

Talavera de la Reina

POP 88,900

Talavera de la Reina, with original city walls and Portuguese-style ceramic facades, has a laid-back appeal, once you get beyond the surrounding modern sprawl. It was overrun by the Muslim Almoravid dynasty in the 12th century. In 1809 the town was the scene of a key battle between the Duke of Wellington's forces and the French.

These days, Talavera has settled into comfortable provinciality and has long been famous for its ceramic work, which adorns many buildings. The finest example is the gold-and-blue facade of the Teatro Victoria, just off Plaza del Padre Juan de Mariana.

Within the old city walls is Museo Ruiz de Luna (Calle de San Agustín el Viejo; admission €1; ⊘10am-2pm & 4-6.30pm Tue-Sat, 10am-2pm Sun), housing local ceramics dating from the 16th to 20th centuries. To buy contemporary ceramics, check out the factories

and shops along the road leading west to the A5 motorway.

The tourist office (www.talavera.org/turismo; Ronda del Cañello; ⊘10.30am-1.30pm & 4-6pm Mon-Sat, 10.30am-12.30pm Sun) doubles as a gallery displaying (you guessed it) ceramics.

The bus station is in the town centre. Regular buses between Madrid and Badajoz stop in Talavera de la Reina, and up to nine leave daily for Toledo (€6.30, 1¼ hours).

Around Talavera de la Reina

OROPESA

The delightful village of Oropesa, 34km west of Talavera, makes a more appealing overnight stop. Head first for a *cerveza* (beer) at one of the bars flanking lovely Plaza del Navarro, before tramping up to the hilltop 14th-century castle (www.e-oropesa.com; adult/child €2.50/free; ⊘10am-2pm & 4-7pm Tue-Sun; ▣). It looks north across the plains to the mighty Sierra de Gredos and is a year-round venue for art exhibitions, with concerts in July and August.

Across from here is a 14th-century palace that houses Spain's second-oldest parador (⊘925 43 00 00; www.parador.es; s/d

---

LA MANCHA'S MANCHEGO

To the uninitiated, Spain's most popular dairy product, Manchego cheese, is a bit of an enigma. Peer into any cheese counter here and you find great wheels of this *queso*, in varying sizes and displaying a baffling range of labels and prices. Whatever happened to good old (recognisable) Cheddar? Or all those different varieties that you find in the UK, USA or, still more, in France and Italy? The answer is that, although you *can* find imported cheese in the larger cities and tourist resorts, the subtleties and variants found in Manchego are sufficiently satisfying for most *queso* aficionados.

For many visitors, their Manchego initiation will be the neat little tapas triangles often served free with a drink. These are usually *semi curado* (semi-cured) rather than the crumbly stronger (and more expensive) *curado* (cured); the former is aged for approximately three to four months, the latter six to eight months. To receive the Manchego *denominación* (brand), the milk must also come from a local Manchegan breed of sheep that has evolved over hundreds of years.

According to artisan cheesemaker Alfonso Alvárez Valera, the best *queso* is made from unpasteurised milk, which prevents the cheese becoming rubbery. Producing some 40,000 wheels annually, Artequeso (⊘925 14 51 92; www.artequeso.com; Finca La Prudenciana, Tembleque) is run by the fourth generation of the Valera family, who produce their cheese following strict artisan tradition. They have also recently introduced several additional non-Manchego cheeses to their production line, including goat's cheese with wine or paprika and a blend of sheep, goat and cow's cheese. You can visit Artequeso and taste their cheese (with prior appointment only). The best time is between March and June, which is the peak of the cheesemaking season.

€105/135; [P][※][🛜]), which has managed to retain a heady historical feel without the 'over-heritaging' that typifies many Spanish *paradores*. The rooms are large and luxurious, with heavy brocade curtains and antiques. Read Somerset Maugham's rave review of the place in the lobby and ask to see San Pedro de Alcántara's sleeping quarters, hidden in the bowels of this former palace.

There's also **La Hostería** ([📞]925 43 08 75; www.lahosteriadeoropesa.com; Plaza del Palacio 5; s/d incl breakfast €50/65; [P][※]), just below the castle, which has pretty, individually decorated rooms with beamed ceilings and a popular restaurant (meals €20) with tables spilling out into a flower-festooned courtyard.

From Talavera de la Reina, buses travel here three or four times daily.

EL PUENTE DEL ARZOBISPO

By Río Tajo, just 14km south of Oropesa, sits El Puente del Arzobispo, another well-known centre for ceramics, with showrooms galore. The multi-arched bridge after which the town is named was built in the 14th century.

Montes de Toledo

ELEV 1400M

The dramatic Montes de Toledo begin at the low foothills south of Toledo, rising westward towards Extremadura. Exploring these hills takes you into the heart of some of the most sparsely populated country of Spain's interior. Long stretches of the region's roads are lined with terracotta-coloured earth criss-crossed with neat lines of olive trees or with fields resembling swathes of soft green velvet, ablaze with wildflowers in spring.

Eleven kilometres short of Navahermosa, a trail leads south to **Embalse del Torcón**, a popular lake-shore picnic spot. Beyond Navahermosa, you have several options for branching south. Some of the heavily wooded areas offer gorgeous vistas and, apart from in the odd tiny *pueblo* (village), you'll see more goats than folk. One longish route that gives a taste of the area starts at Los Navalmorales. Take the CM4155 towards Los Navalucillos and keep heading south past seemingly deserted villages until you hit a T-junction after 48km. Turning right (west), you wind 35km to

the northern reaches of the huge **Embalse de Cijara**, part of a chain of reservoirs fed by Río Guadiana and actually part of Extremadura. Swing north towards **Puerto de San Vicente**, branching off west to the EX102 and the last curvy stretch towards Guadalupe.

THE SOUTH

This is the terrain that typifies La Mancha for many people: flat plains stretching to the horizon, punctuated by the occasional farmhouse or emblematic windmill. The southeast, however, is surprisingly verdant and lush with rivers, natural parks and some of the prettiest villages in the province.

Ciudad Real

POP 74,000

Despite being the one-time royal counterpart of Toledo, these days Ciudad Real is an unspectacular Spanish working town. The centre has a certain charm, however, with its pedestrianised shopping streets and distinctive Plaza Mayor, complete with carillon clock (topped by Cupid), flamboyant neo-Gothic town-hall facade and modern tiered fountain.

◉ Sights

Puerta de Toledo　　　　　　　CITY GATE

Coming from the north, you'll enter Ciudad Real by the Puerta de Toledo (1328), the last remaining gate of the original eight, built in Mudéjar style by Alfonso X.

FREE **Museo del Quijote**　　　　　　MUSEUM

(Ronda de Alarcos 1; ⊙10am-2pm & 6-9pm Mon-Sat, 10am-2pm Sun) For Quijote fans, the Museo del Quijote has audiovisual displays, plus a Cervantes library stocked with hundreds of Don Quijote books, including some in Esperanto and Braille, and others dating back to 1724. It helps if you speak Spanish.

Iglesia de San Pedro　　　　　　CHURCH

(Calle Ramón y Cajal General Rey; ⊙11am-noon & 8-8.30pm Mon-Fri, 11am-noon & 7-7.30pm Sat, 9am-1pm Sun) Of the handful of churches, the most striking is the 14th-century Gothic Iglesia de San Pedro, with its three-part facade and three naves within, plus star-shaped vaults and gleaming 15th-century alabaster altarpiece.

📍 Sleeping & Eating

The restaurants on Plaza Mayor are good for a drink but the food here is indifferent overall. Head for the streets on and around Avenida del Torreón del Alcázar and the parallel Calle de los Hidalgos for the best choice of bars and restaurants. Self-caterers should check out the vast covered mercado (market; Calle de las Postas).

Hostal Plaza   SMALL HOTEL €
(☑926 25 43 35; Plaza de Agustín Salido 2; s/d €35/50; ❄🛜) Situated on a pretty quiet square, this comfortable place has smart rooms and a bustling breakfast bar and cafeteria.

Hotel Silken Alfonso X   CLASSIC HOTEL €€
(☑926 22 42 81; www.hotelalfonsox.com; Calle de Carlos Vázquez 8; s/d €60/75; P❄🛜) This is an upmarket place where old facade meets renovated interior with success. The modern carpeted rooms come with all the swish trimmings, plus glossy marble bathrooms. The restaurant has a reasonable €15 midweek menú (set meal). Parking costs €12.85.

La Casuca   HOMESTYLE TRADITIONAL €
(Calle de Palma 10; meals €15) This is where the locals come. Fronted by a boisterous tapas bar, this down-to-earth restaurant serves solidly reliable and well-priced local dishes.

El Ventero   TAPAS BAR €
(Plaza Mayor 8) Time your chair on the square here to enjoy the carillon-clock display (generally noon, 1pm, 2pm, 6pm and 8pm), when Don Quijote, Sancho and Cervantes emerge for a congenial spin around a small stage. Stick to a drink (and complimentary tapas) instead of a meal.

🍸 Drinking

You'll find clubs, discos and welcoming bars like the Australian Pub (Avenida del Torreón del Alcázar 4; ⏱11am-late) and the adjacent Baston Pub (⏱3.30pm-late Fri & Sat) on lively Avenida del Torreón del Alcázar, flanking a park. Calle de los Hidalgos is another energetic street for bar hopping.

ℹ️ Information

Municipal tourist office (☑926 21 64 86; www.ayto-ciudadreal.es; Plaza Mayor 1; ⏱10am-2pm & 5-7pm Tue-Sat, 10am-2pm Sun) Can advise on city sights, hotels and restaurants.

Provincial tourist office (☑926 20 00 37; www.turismocastillalamancha.com; Calle de Alarcos 21; ⏱10am-2pm & 4-7pm Mon-Sat, 10am-2pm Sun) Similarly helpful to the municipal office.

ℹ️ Getting There & Away

BUS The **bus station** (Carretera Calzada) is southwest of the centre. Services include up to three daily buses to Albacete (€13.95, 2¾ hours) and Toledo (€8.35, 1½ hours), and five per day head off to Madrid (€11.45, 2½ hours).

TRAIN The **train station** (Av Europa) lies east of the town centre. Most trains linking Madrid with Andalucía stop at Ciudad Real. There are regular departures to several cities and towns, including Madrid (€21.15, one hour), Valencia (€38.90, five hours, two daily) and southeast to Almagro (€2.20, 15 minutes).

ℹ️ Getting Around

Local bus 5 swings past both the train and bus stations bound for the town centre; catch it from Plaza del Pilar when you're leaving town.

Ciudad Real Province

ALMAGRO
POP 9100

The jewel in Almagro's crown is the extraordinary Plaza Mayor, with its wavy tiled roofs, stumpy columns and faded bottle-green porticoes. Although it looks quasi-Oriental, the 16th-century plaza has Germanic roots, dating back to the reign of Carlos I, when several well-heeled bankers and traders moved here. The town is a delight to wander around: the relatively traffic-free cobbled streets are flanked by Renaissance palaces and churches, with shops selling local cheese, embroidery and basketry.

👁 Sights

Corral de Comedias   THEATRE
(www.corraldecomedias.com; Plaza Mayor 18; adult/child incl audioguide in English €3/free; ⏱10am-12pm & 5-8pm Mon-Fri, 10am-1pm & 5-7pm Sat & Sun; ♿) Opening onto the plaza is the oldest theatre in Spain: the 17th-century Corral de Comedias, an evocative tribute to the golden age of Spanish theatre, with rows of wooden balconies facing the original stage, complete with dressing rooms. It's still used for performances.

Museo Nacional de Teatro   THEATRE MUSEUM
(http://museoteatro.mcu.es; Calle de Gran Maestre 2; admission €2.50; ⏱10am-2pm & 4-7pm Tue-Fri, 11am-2pm & 4-6pm Sat, 11am-2pm Sun) The theatre is appropriately complemented by the Museo Nacional de Teatro, just across the square, with exhibits on Spanish theatre from the 18th century displayed in rooms surrounding a magnificent 13th-century courtyard.

1. Cuenca (p215)

Casas colgadas (hanging houses) cling like swallows' nests above deep gorges.

2. Consuegra (p212)

Molinos de vientos (windmills) flank Consuegra's 12th-century Knights of Malta's castle.

3. Corpus Christi, Toledo (p200)

One of the finest Corpus Christi celebrations in Spain, with several days of festivities.

4. Alcalá del Júcar (p213)

A landmark 12th-century castle towers over houses that spill down the steep bank of Júcar gorge.

BRUCE BI

Museo de Encale EMBROIDERY MUSEUM
(Callejon del Villar; admission €1.50; ⏲10am-2pm & 5-8pm Tue-Fri, 10am-2pm & 5-7pm Sat, 11am-2pm Sun) Almagro is also famed for its embroidery. Check it out at the Museo de Encale, which has some stunning examples of lacework and embroidery exhibited over three floors of well-lit galleries.

Festivals & Events

Festival Internacional de Teatro Clásico THEATRE FESTIVAL
(www.festivaldealmagro.com, in Spanish) In July the Corral de Comedias holds a month-long international theatre festival, attracting world-class theatre companies performing, primarily, classical plays.

Sleeping

Almagro's hotel prices increase by a whopping 50% during the July theatre festival and Semana Santa.

TOP CHOICE **La Casa del Rector** DESIGNER HOTEL €€
(☎926 26 12 58; www.lacasadelrector.com; s/d from €85/100; ❄@📶) This extraordinary hotel has a wide variety of rooms ranging from sumptuous antique-filled classics to those reflecting cutting-edge modern design, complete with vast private hot tubs and dramatic artwork. Facilities include a classy spa.

Retiro del Maestre CLASSIC HOTEL €€
(☎926 26 11 85; www.retirodelmaestre.com, in Spanish; Calle San Bartolomé 5; s/d incl breakfast €70/87; P❄@📶) Enjoy five-star treatment and style without the hurly-burly of a big hotel. The rooms are spacious and washed in warm yellow and blue; go for those on the upper floor with private balconies.

Parador PARADOR €€€
(☎926 86 01 00; www.parador.es; Ronda de San Francisco 31; s/d €125/154; P❄📶) A sumptuous ivy-clad former convent in a quiet corner of Almagro, this *parador* has a luxurious, old-world charm, despite the mildly incongruous, brightly coloured beams in the rooms.

Hostal Rural San Bartolomé SMALL HOTEL €€
(☎926 26 10 73; www.hostalsanbartolome.com; Calle San Bartolomé 12; s/d €53/64; ❄) Atmospheric and comfortable.

Eating

There are several cafes and bars spilling out onto Plaza Mayor, serving traditional Spanish fare, including meat and seafood dishes, at surprisingly reasonable prices.

TOP CHOICE **El Corregidor** SOPHISTICATED MANCHEGAN €€
(☎926 86 06 48; Calle de Jerónimo Ceballos 2; menú €30, meals €35-40; ⏲closed Mon) The town's best restaurant has several lively bars flanking a leafy courtyard and a hotchpotch decor that somehow works. The upstairs restaurant features high-quality Manchegan cooking; check out the wall of culinary awards. Reservations recommended.

Bar Las Nieves TAPAS BAR €
(Plaza Mayor 52; tapas from €2.50, paella €5) One of the better Plaza Mayor bars, featuring chairs on the square and tasty light eats, plus paella on Sundays in the summer.

Meson Cepa Vieja HOMESTYLE TRADITIONAL €
(Ronda de Santo Domingo 77; meals €14-18) Better for a hot dinner than a hot date, this brightly lit place has a no-fuss, inexpensive menu. Try the excellent *pisto con huevo* (fried peppers, tomatoes and garlic topped with a fried egg), but avoid the house wine.

Information

Tourist office (☎926 86 07 17; www.ciudad-almagro.com, in Spanish; Plaza Mayor 1; ⏲10am-2pm & 5-8pm Tue-Fri, 10am-2pm & 5-7pm Sat, 11am-2pm Sun) Can provide a map and information about the town sights, restaurants and hotels.

Getting There & Away

Two trains go daily to Madrid (€13.28, 2¾ hours); for destinations to the south, change in Ciudad Real. Buses run to Ciudad Real (€2.50, 30 minutes, up to five daily Monday to Saturday).

CASTILLO DE CALATRAVA

FREE **Castillo de Calatrava** (Calatrava La Nueva; ⏲10am-2pm & 4-7pm Tue-Sun), a fortresslike castle-monastery complex about 30km south of Almagro, commands magnificent views across the sierra of the same name. The complex was once a base of the medieval order of knights who controlled this frontier area during the Reconquista.

PARQUE NATURAL DE LAS LAGUNAS DE RUIDERA

This ribbon of 14 small lakes is surrounded by lush parkland, camping grounds, picnic areas and discreetly situated restaurants and hotels. Foreign tourists are rare; it's most popular as a chill-out zone for hot-and-bothered *madrileños* (Madrid residents).

THE WINES OF VALDEPEÑAS

Situated midway between Madrid and Córdoba, the large and otherwise uninviting town of Valdepeñas offers weary travellers one (and only one) good reason to break the journey. Surrounding the town is what some experts believe to be the largest expanse of vineyards in the world, although true aficionados of the humble grape argue that quantity does not easily translate into quality. There's an element of truth to this view – Valdepeñas has historically been to the mass market what La Rioja is to the quality end of the wine trade.

That said, things are changing. You're still more likely to come across Valdepeñas wines in the cheap, cask variety than served in Spain's finest restaurants, but some of the Valdepeñas bodegas have begun making inroads into the quality end of the market. Most of the bodegas offer tours and tastings only by appointment and charge to boot. Check the websites for details to avoid going thirsty.

Bodegas Arúspide (☎926 34 70 75; www.aruspide.com; Calle Franci Morales 102; tour €4.50) offers tours and a tasting of two or more wines.

Bodega de las Estrellas (☎650 552976; www.labodegadelasestrellas.com; Calle Unión 82; tour €6, tour with meal from €17) makes organic wine and also has a tour and tasting option that includes a meal in the bodega.

A great place to stay is **Hotel Albamanjon** (☎926 69 90 48; www.albamanjon.net; Laguna de San Pedro 16; d/ste €117/170; ❄). The windmill suite has a view of the turquoise lake that's worth pushing the boat out for. All the rooms have private terraces and there's an excellent restaurant. The hotel also has a bathing area with a jetty, offering pedal-boat and canoe rentals. Landlubbers can opt for the mountain bikes on loan. Similarly situated **La Vega** (www.restaurantelavega.com; Calle San Pedro 7, Lagunas de Ruidera; meals from €15) overlooks one of the larger lakes, with a sprawling terrace and small beach. Expect a good grilling: barbecued meats are the speciality.

Leafy campsite **Camping Los Batanes** (☎926 69 90 76; www.losbatanes.com; sites per person/tent/car €6.60/6/6.60, 4-person bungalow €85; P❄) is on Laguna Redondilla. During the summer months there's an entertainment program for children.

The **tourist office** (☎926 52 81 16; www.lagunasruidera.com; Avenida Castilla la Mancha, Ruidera; ⊙10am-2pm & 4-6pm Wed-Sat, 10am-2pm Sun) has lots of glossy information on accommodation and activities, such as hiring rowing boats, kayaks or mountain bikes.

VILLANUEVA DE LOS INFANTES
POP 6400

Villanueva de los Infantes is an attractive and busy provincial town. A highlight is **Plaza Mayor**, with its ochre-coloured buildings, wood-and-stone balconies, and lively bars and restaurants.

Like Almagro, Villanueva is studded with the houses of old nobles. On the square stands the 15th-century **Iglesia de San Andrés**, where the 16th-century poet Francisco de Quevedo is buried.

Hospedería El Buscón Quevedo (☎926 36 17 88; www.hosteriasreales.com; Calle Frailes 1; s/d €60/75; P❄) is housed in a 16th-century, former Dominican convent. The handsome regency-style rooms have wrought-iron furniture and the public areas are magnificent, with original tapestries and oil paintings. On the downside, it can seem a little austere. Bicycles are available for hire.

The **tourist office** (☎926 36 13 21; www.infantes.org, in Spanish; Plaza Mayor; ⊙10am-2pm & 5-8pm Mon-Sat, 10am-2pm Sun) organises guided walks of the town.

Buses run to Ciudad Real three times daily from Monday to Friday (€6.45, 1½ hours).

Southeast to Albacete

The sweeping, windswept plains of southeastern Castilla-La Mancha have an unfair reputation for being flat and boring. In fact, this landscape can have a very special drama with its rich abstract patterns and vibrant colours. Once you get off the highway, this is a land of historic windmills, quiet villages and our favourite nutty knight, Don Quijote.

CONSUEGRA

This is *the* place for the novice windmill spotter, where you can get that classic shot of nine *molinos de vientos* (windmills) flanking Consuegra's 12th-century **castle** (adult/child €2/free; ☺9am-6pm Mon-Fri, 10.30am-2pm & 3.30-6pm Sat & Sun; ♿). Consuegra once belonged to the Knights of Malta; a few rooms in the castle have been done up to give a good indication of how the knights would have lived.

The **tourist office** (☎925 47 57 31; www.consuegra.es, in Spanish; ☺9am-2pm & 4.30-7pm Mon-Fri, from 10.30am Sat & Sun) is in the Bolero mill (they all have names), which is the first you come to as the road winds up from the town. It can advise on *casas rurales* (village or farmstead accommodation) if you want to stay overnight. You can also climb the steps here and see the original windmill machinery.

There are regular weekday buses (three on weekends) running between Consuegra and Toledo (€4.80, one hour) and up to seven buses daily to Madrid (€7.60, two hours).

CAMPO DE CRIPTANA & AROUND

Ten windmills straddle the town's summit and their proximity to the surrounding houses makes an interesting contrast with Consuegra. The town is pleasant, if unexceptional.

If you want to stay overnight, lovely **Hospedería Casa de la Torrecilla** (☎926 58 91 30; www.casadelatorrecilla.com; Calle Cardenal Monescillo 17; s/d €37/54; ♿) has a vividly patterned and tiled interior patio. Housed in an early-20th-century nobleman's house, the rooms have parquet floors and are spacious and atmospheric. The restaurant has a choice of four *menús* ranging between €28 and €34.

The **tourist office** (☎926 56 22 31; www.campodecriptana.info; ☺10am-2pm & 5-7pm Tue-Sat, 10am-2pm Sun) is located in a low-rise building opposite the Inca Garcilaso windmill.

Campo de Criptana is served by the odd train and regional bus, but options are greater 8km away in Alcázar de San Juan. About four buses run daily between the two towns but there are none on Sunday.

There are seven more pretty windmills gracing the horizon overlooking **Mota del Cuervo**, 29km northeast of Campo de Criptana, at the junction of the N301.

EL TOBOSO

This is a town that has really cashed in on its Don Quijote heritage. Everywhere you look there seems to be a Quijote bar, a Quijote restaurant and several Quijote-themed small museums. Pilgrim or not, you'll find the most entertaining is the 16th-century **Casa-Museo de Dulcinea** (Calle Don Quijote 1; admission €1; ☺10am-2pm & 4.30-7.30pm Tue-Sat, 10am-2pm Sun). This was apparently the home of Doña Ana, the *señorita* who inspired Cervantes' Dulcinea, the platonic love of Quijote.

There's a small **tourist office** (☎925 56 82 26; www.turismocastillalamancha.com; Calle Daoíz y Velarde 3; ☺10am-2pm & 4-7pm Tue-Sat, 10am-2pm Sun). There are three direct buses every day to Madrid (€7.50, two hours).

BELMONTE

About 25km northeast of Mota del Cuervo, Belmonte has one of the better-preserved 15th-century Castilian **castles** (adult/child €2/free; ☺10am-1.30pm & 5-8pm Tue-Sun). This is how castles *should* look, with turrets, largely intact walls and a commanding position over the village. The castle was once home to France's Empress Eugénie after her husband, Napoleon III, lost the French throne in 1871. Also well worth a visit is **Iglesia Colegial de San Bartolomé** (Colegiata; ☺11am-2pm & 4-8pm Tue-Sat, 4-8pm Sun), a magnificent golden-sandstone church with an impressive altarpiece.

Palacio Buenavista Hospedería (☎967 18 75 80; www.palaciobuenavista.es; Calle José Antonio González 2; s/d/ste incl breakfast from €47/75/94; ♿♻) is a classy boutique hotel set in a 17th-century palace next to the Colegiata. Rooms are stylish and set around a sumptuous central patio with skylight; several have views of the castle. There's an excellent restaurant (traditional *menú* €22).

By bus from Belmonte, you can get to Alcázar de San Juan (€2.50, 30 minutes) and Cuenca (€5.15, 1¼ hours).

Albacete

POP 169,700

This mildly down-at-heel provincial city is no star, but is useful as a transport hub and a place to pause between Spain's central plains and the Mediterranean coast.

If you're passing through, the **cathedral**, with its four Ionic columns, is appealing enough. On a hot summer's afternoon, leafy **Parque de Abelardo Sánchez** (Calle

Part of the charm of a visit to Castilla-La Mancha is the chance to track down the real-life locations in which Miguel de Cervantes placed his picaresque hero. These days it requires less puzzling over maps as, to celebrate the fourth centenary of this epic tale in 2007, the 250km Route of Don Quijote was created, with signposts that direct you along paths, cattle ways and historic routes throughout the region.

Of all the places and sights you can ponder along the way, the *molinos de vientos* (windmills) are the most obvious, for it was these 'monstrous giants' that so haunted El Quijote and with which he tried to battle. Although Consuegra's are the most attractive, those that are specifically mentioned in Cervantes' novel are the windmills of **Campo de Criptana** (p212) and **Mota del Cuervo** (p212). Other highlights on the trail include the castle of **Belmonte** (p212) and **El Toboso** (p212), where the knight discovered the lovely Dulcinea.

If you prefer the idea of tweeting, rather than tilting, at windmills, Cervantes' fabled work went online to the micro-blogging website Twitter in early 2010. It will necessitate some 8200 'tweets' (of just 140 characters each) to complete. The non-profit project, known as Twijote, has recruited Quijote fans from all over the world for the painstaking task of uploading the text.

de Tesifonte Gallego) offers some respite. It is one of several green spaces in town, which no doubt contribute to the city ranking amongst the 10 least-polluted cities (of over 100,000 inhabitants) in Europe. The park is home to the Museo Provincial (admission €1.20; ⊙10am-2pm & 4.30-7pm Mon-Sat, 10am-2pm Sun) with well-documented archaeological exhibits, including a famous collection of articulated dolls, made of amber and ivory, discovered in the Roman necropolis of Ontur.

If you want to stay, Hotel Altozano (☑967 21 04 62; www.hotelaltozano.es; Plaza del Altozano 7; s/d €50/85; P❋❂🖳) has an ace location on a pretty main square. Revamped in 2009, the rooms are modern, with satellite TV. Parking costs €15 and children under nine stay free of charge.

The city has plenty of good restaurants: head for the streets located just north of the main parking area (including Calle Nueva and Calle Tejaras) for a good selection and price range. El Callejón (Calle de Guzmán El Bueno 18; meals €20-25) serves typical Manchegan dishes in a *taurino*-inspired interior.

The tourist office (☑967 58 05 22; www.turismocastillalamancha.com; Calle del Tinte 2; ⊙10am-2pm & 4.30-6.30pm Mon-Sat, 10am-3pm Sun) should be able to muster more enthusiasm for the town than we can.

The bus and train stations are next to each other at the northeastern end of town. Both serve most major cities around the country. Trains to Madrid (€33, three hours) leave hourly.

Around Albacete

Just off the N430 motorway to Valencia, a restored fortress overlooks Chinchilla de Monte Aragón, a whitewashed village with a beautiful Plaza Mayor flanked by restaurants and bars. About 60km further on, a square-turreted castle built by the Muslims stands high above the town of Almansa. Both towns are served by bus from Albacete.

ALCALÁ DEL JÚCAR & AROUND

Northeast of Albacete, the deep, tree-filled gorge of Río Júcar makes a stunning detour. About halfway along the CM3201, the breathtaking town of Alcalá del Júcar comes into view as you descend via hairpin turns. Its landmark 12th-century castle (admission €2; ⊙11am-2pm & 4-8pm) towers over the houses that spill down the steep bank of the Júcar gorge. At the foot of the town there's a flowing river, a Roman bridge and a leafy meeting-and-greeting plaza.

There are several well-priced hotels, including Hotel Pelayo (☑967 47 30 99; Avenida Constitución 4; s/d incl breakfast €45/55; ❋), with large modern rooms, and Hostal Rambla (☑967 47 40 64; Paseo Los Robles 2; s/d incl breakfast €40/50; ❋❂). Both have restaurants; the one at Hostal Rambla (meals €15 to €25) is particularly good, especially the chargrilled meats served with green peppers and potatoes.

La Asomada (☑652 182440; Calle de la Asomada 107; ❒), at the top of the village, should be sought out by eco folks.

Located in a cave and former bodega, owner Pilar Escusa uses organic produce and prepares delicious seasonal dishes. Reservations essential.

The small **tourist office** (☑967 47 30 90; www.turismocastillalamancha.com; La Rambla; ◷10.30am-2.30pm & 4-7pm Fri & Sat, 10.30am-2.30pm Sun) has a wealth of information about *casas rurales,* cave accommodation and activities, including maps showing local walking trails.

For an alternative route back to Albacete, a small back road takes you through the gorge, with houses cut into the cliff face. The more picturesque hamlets are at the western end, where the gorge narrows. Tiny **Cubas** has an intriguing ceramic-tiled and domed church hollowed out of the cliff, while **Alcozarejos** is famed for its trout fishing.

SIERRA DE ALCARAZ
Stretching across the southern strip of Albacete province, the cool, green peaks of the Sierra de Alcaraz, laced with small, intensively farmed plots and dotted with villages, offer a great escape from the dusty plains around Albacete. Donkey-mounted shepherds still watch their small flocks of sheep in the more remote corners of the sierra.

The most scenic countryside is to be found along the CM412, particularly between **Puerto de las Crucetas** (1300m) and **Elche de la Sierra**, although a detour to pretty **Vianos** is also worthwhile. The largest choice of accommodation is in leafy **Riópar**, including the excellent **Camping Río Mundo** (www.campingriomundo.com; sites per person/tent/car €5.50/6.85/6.85; ✹), where you can pick up a booklet of routes for walking and cycling in the region. The campsite is located 6km east of town.

The prettiest place to stay in these parts, however, is in sleepy hilltop **Alcaraz**, with its medieval Plaza Mayor and lattice of narrow cobbled streets. At the top of the village, sporting magnificent views, is modern **Los Rosales** (☑967 38 01 28; www.losrosalesalcaraz.com; Calle Granada; r €48; ℗), with spruce and comfortably furnished rooms. Just down the hill, a handsome, mainly 16th-century building houses the **Mirador Sierra de Alcaraz** (☑967 38 00 17; www.alcarazmirador.com; Calle Padre Pareja; d/ste €65/69; ✹), its central Moorish courtyard dating, incredibly, from the 9th century. The rooms have beamed ceilings, carved wooden bedheads and heavy period-style curtains and furnishings. The sumptuous suite is excellent value.

A BATTY CAVE

Forget stalagmites, cave drawings and coach tours – Alcalá's **Cuevas y Mirador del Diablo** (San Lorenzo 7; admission €3; ⎈) is not your conventional cave. The first inkling comes when owner Juan José Martinez Garcia appears to collect your entrance fee sporting a sweeping Dalí-clone moustache. It transpires he grew up in the maestro's home town of Cadaqués. OK, so that makes sense – sort of.

The real adventure starts with a 70m-long tunnel, which apparently dates back to Moorish times, when it was used for stabling animals. Spy through the porthole on your left and you are met with the astonishing sight of strobe lights in a quasi-disco setting, complete with throbbing music. Next you move into a bar (Juan has 10 adolescent children so there's no shortage of staff). After your free drink you can enjoy an extraordinary museum: a collectables heaven with old cameras, lottery tickets, farming implements, a stuffed hare (in hunter's garb), cash registers, radios, sewing machines, news clippings and Juan's poems.

Next, climb several flights of stairs to emerge at a fabulous mirador set into the side of the cave. Then there's another passage (170m) and another bar (different children) with stuffed goats, boars, foxes, badgers and wild cats, among ancient farming implements and walls papered with photos of Juan with family, friends and uncertain-looking tourists. Juan has a stuffed gorilla as well, currently on show (as King Kong) at his second, rapidly-expanding **Museo del Cine** (Museum of Cinema), just across the road.

There's something particularly apt about finding such an eccentric in the depths of La Mancha country – Cervantes would definitely have approved.

WORTH A TRIP

THE BIRTH OF THE WORLD

Take a photo of yourself standing in front of the Nacimiento del Río Mundo (Birth of the River World; ☺10am-dusk; 🚻), send it to the folks back home and they will think that you have sidestepped to Niagara Falls for the day. To get to these amazing waterfalls, follow the signs just before Riópar for around 8km – past the amusing pictorial 'beware of the amfibos (frogs)' signs – until you reach the entrance and car park. It's a short walk through the forest of mainly coniferous trees to the bottom of the falls, where the water splashes and courses via several rock pools. There are two miradors: the first is at the base of the falls with neck-craning views of the dramatic waterfall above; it's a steep climb to the second mirador, but worth the effort. At some 800m above sea level, the water emerges from the rocks just above the platform, almost close enough to touch, in a dramatic drop of some 24m (spraying you liberally en route). The falls are surrounded by dense forest stretching to a rocky horizon – all those sceptics who say La Mancha is flat and boring should definitely pay a visit here.

THE NORTHEAST

This region has a rich hinterland of craggy mountains and lush green valleys studded by unspoiled, pretty villages. It is also home to some of the country's most enchanting towns and *pueblos*.

Cuenca

POP 53,000

A World Heritage Site, Cuenca is one of Spain's most memorable cities, its old centre a stage set of evocative medieval buildings. Most emblematic are the *casas colgadas,* the hanging houses, which cling like swallows' nests above the deep gorges that surround the town. As in so many Spanish cities, the surrounding new town is modern and forgettable, so keep the blinkers on during the approach – up the hill lies another world.

⊙ Sights & Activities

Cuenca is compact and easily negotiable. The old town is home to all the sights and occupies the narrow hill at the northeastern end of town, between the gorges of Ríos Júcar and Huécar. At the foot of the hill down which the old town tumbles, the new town spreads out to the south.

TOP CHOICE Museo de Arte Abstracto Español ABSTRACT-ART MUSEUM
(www.march.es; adult/child €3/free; ☺11am-2pm & 4-6pm Tue-Fri, 11am-2pm & 4-8pm Sat, 11am-2.30pm Sun) Although strolling around old Cuenca can feel like you've been dropped in the middle of a medieval museum, this is not just a place of ancient history. This impressive contemporary art museum is one of several spaces lauding modern art and sculpture. This is the best known, however, with its galleries occupying one of the *casas colgadas*. Begun as an attempt by Fernando Zóbel to unite the works of his fellow artists from the so-called Abstract Generation of the 1950s and '60s, the museum's constantly evolving displays include works by Chillida, Tápies and Millares. Don't miss the extraordinary landscapes by Eusebio Sempere (1924–85), which really capture the colourful patterned plains of La Mancha.

Casas Colgadas HANGING HOUSES
The most striking element of medieval Cuenca, the *casas colgadas* jut out precariously over the steep defile of Río Huécar. Dating from the 16th century, the houses, with their layers of wooden balconies, seem to emerge from the rock as if an extension of the cliffs. The finest restored examples now house an upmarket restaurant and the abstract-art museum, both of which make excellent use of the former limited living space. For the best views of the *casas colgadas*, cross the Puente de San Pablo footbridge or walk to the mirador at the northernmost tip of the old town.

FREE Fundación Antonio Pérez CONTEMPORARY-ART MUSEUM
(www.dipucuenca.es; Ronda de Julián Romero 20; ☺11am-9pm Mon-Sun) Galleries are spread over four floors within the former San Clemente convent. Spanish and international artists are represented in a mixed bag of mainly abstract paintings and sculptures.

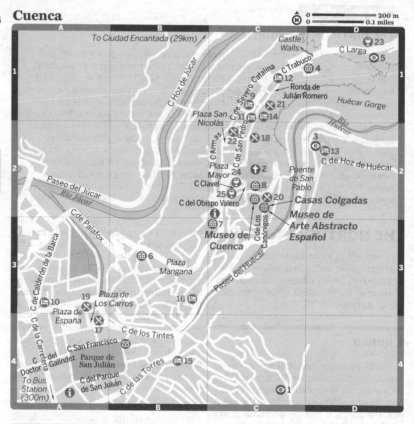

Cuenca

Museo de Cuenca
MUSEUM

(Calle del Obispo Valero 6; adult/child €1.20/free; ⊙10am-2pm & 4-7pm Tue-Sat, 11am-2pm Sun; 👶) Exceptionally well-laid-out and well-documented (in Spanish) exhibits range from the Bronze Age to the 18th century. Sala 7 is particularly awe inspiring, with its original Roman statues, including Emperor Augustus, plus columns and pediments discovered at nearby Segóbriga (p221).

FREE Espacio Torner
ART GALLERY

(Iglesia San Pablo, Calle de Hoz de Huécar; ⊙11am-2pm & 4-6pm Tue-Sat, 11am-2.30pm Sun) Yet another space where the inside feels about five centuries younger than the outside. Located adjacent to the *parador,* it displays abstract paintings and sculptures by Gustavo Torner, one of several abstract artists who made Cuenca their home in the 1960s. The soaring vaulted ceilings and combination of space and height are exceptionally powerful.

Ars Natura
ECOLOGICAL EDUCATION

(www.centroarsnatura.es; Calle Río Gritos 5, Cerro Molina; adult/child €3/free; ⊙10am-2pm & 4-7pm Tue-Sun; 👶) Opened in May 2010, this impressive interpretation centre has several vast galleries with interactive exhibits ranging from local flora and fauna to basket-weaving video demonstrations. Climate change, local geology, environmental impact studies and overall sustainability are given the hands-on approach, which makes this an ideal outing for children and students. Currently all the information is in Spanish, but there are plans to provide English translations.

Museo de la Semana Santa
EASTER MUSEUM

(Calle Andrés de Cabrera; adult/child €3/free; ⊙11am-2pm & 4.30-7.30pm Wed-Sat; 👶) This museum is the next best thing to experiencing Semana Santa firsthand. Spread over two floors are audiovisual displays showing the processions by local brotherhoods, against a background of sombre music. Displays include costumes and a 20-minute film (in Spanish), in which the locals explain their passion for this annual religious ritual.

Museo de Las Ciencias
SCIENCE MUSEUM

(Plaza de la Merced; adult/child €1.20/free; ⊙10am-2pm & 4-7pm Tue-Sat, 10am-2pm Sun; 👶) Another family-friendly museum, there are displays that range from a time-machine to plenty of interactive gadgets to keep the kiddies happy. There is also a planetarium (adult/child €1.20/free).

Museo Diocesano
RELIGIOUS MUSEUM

(Calle del Obispo Valero 3; admission €1.80; ⊙11am-2pm & 4-6pm Tue-Sat, 11am-2pm Sun) Appropriately close to the cathedral, this museum has exhibits of richly embroidered tapestries, plus sculptures, rugs and paintings, including two canvases by El Greco. A 14th-century Byzantine diptych is the jewel in the crown. How such a piece ended up in Cuenca is a mystery.

Catedral
CATHEDRAL

(adult/child €2.50/free, audioguide €0.50; ⊙9am-2pm & 4-7pm) The main facade of Cuenca's cathedral is hardly Spain's finest – a pastiche of unfortunate 16th-century Gothic experimentation and 20th-century restoration. Built on the site of a mosque, highlights within include several stunning stained-glass windows, the result of a competition among local artists in 1990. The abstract designs fuse well with the Gothic architecture and lofty fan vaulting.

✯✯ Festivals & Events

Semana Santa
EASTER WEEK

Cuenca's Easter celebrations are renowned throughout Spain for the eerie, silent processions through the streets of the old town.

Semana de Música Religiosa de Cuenca
SACRED MUSIC

Also gaining international acclaim is this religious music festival, generally held in March or April, that attracts international performers and spectators.

🛏 Sleeping

Aside from the possible disadvantage of lugging bags up the hill, the atmospheric old town is *the* place to stay. Many of the hotel rooms in the old town have stunning views, so always ask for a room with *una vista*. That said, there are some reasonable options down the hill, too.

TOP CHOICE Posada de San José
HISTORIC HOTEL €€

(☎969 21 13 00; www.posadasanjose.com; Ronda de Julián Romero 4; s/d without bathroom €30/43, d with/without views €94/82) Owned by Antonio and his Canadian wife, Jennifer, this 17th-century former choir school retains an extraordinary monastic charm with its labyrinth of rooms, crumbling portal, uneven

VALERIA'S ROMAN RUINS

The fascinating archaeological site **Ruinas Romanas de Valeria** (www.granvaleria. com; admission free; ⏰8am-3pm Mon-Sat; 🅿) is located just outside the village of Valeria, 34km south of Cuenca. It is hardly known to tourists, which equals that rare evocative pleasure of wandering around the site of a former sizeable Roman town without the distraction of coach tours and school groups. The location is fittingly sublime, set amid wild meadows and flanked by dramatic gorges. There are also remains of a medieval castle crowning the hillside. Stretching below this, dating from 82 BC, are remains of a forum (the best preserved in Spain), as well as a basilica, four reservoirs (used for water supply), urban streets and the well-preserved remains of a vast extravagant fountain stretching over 80m in length with 12 spouts. There is also the original *casa colgada* here, its upper floor still clearly constructed to cling to the rock side, with the lower floors visible below. The views of the surrounding ravines are magnificent and probably little changed in 2000 years.

floors and original tiles. The cheaper rooms are in the former priests' cells, while the more costly doubles combine homey comfort with sumptuous old-world charm. Several have balconies with dramatic views of the gorge. The restaurant is recommended and the owners also rent out several tastefully furnished and fully equipped self-contained **apartments** (apt €160-180).

Hostal San Pedro   BUDGET HOTEL €
(☎969 23 45 43, 628 407601; www.hostalsanpedro.es; Calle de San Pedro 34; s/d €35/60) In this excellently priced and positioned *hostal,* rooms have butter-coloured paintwork, wrought-iron bedheads and rustic wood furniture, and the bathrooms are shiny and modern. The owners live elsewhere, so be sure to call first.

Hotel Cueva del Fraile   BOUTIQUE HOTEL €€
(☎969 21 15 71; www.hotelcuevadelfraile.com; Hoz del Huécar; s/d €88/118; 🅿🕸🛜📶) This 16th-century former convent is 5km from Cuenca. It's been resurrected as a chic, welcoming hotel with rooms washed in earthy colours and excellent facilities, including tennis courts, minigolf and mountain bikes.

Posada Huécar   SMALL HOTEL €
(☎969 21 42 01; www.posadahuecar.com; Paseo del Huécar 3; s/d €35/48; 🅿🕸@📶) Feel luxurious on a tight budget. Located squarely between the old and new towns, this upbeat place has large rooms with terracotta tiles, rustic furnishings and river views. There are bicycles for rent (€4 for two hours). The young owners also run a successful Spanish language school, so there are often foreign student groups staying. Parking costs €9.

Hospedería de Cuenca   BOUTIQUE HOTEL €€
(☎969 23 91 17; Calle de San Pedro 27; d/ste incl breakfast €95/125; 🕸📶) This former aristocratic historic home has been aesthetically reformed with a sumptuous colour scheme, with dark burgundies and peacock blues, that creates the ideal backdrop for the traditional furnishings, including four-poster beds, original etchings and beamed ceilings. Fresh flowers in every room are a nice touch.

Parador   PARADOR €€€
(☎969 23 23 20; www.parador.es; Calle de Hoz de Huécar; d €143; 🅿🕸) This majestic former convent commands stunning views of the *casas colgadas.* The aesthetically revamped rooms have a luxury corporate feel, while the public areas are headily historic with giant tapestries and antiques.

Posada de San Julián   BUDGET HOTEL €
(☎969 21 17 04; Calle de las Torres 1; s/d €20/36) Just down the hill from the historic centre, revel in 16th-century surroundings, with lofty ceilings, original columns, creaking staircases and atmospheric heavy-beamed rooms, some with balconies. It's family run and grandpa peels potatoes all day for the bustling restaurant downstairs (*menú* €10).

Leonor de Aquitania Hotel
   HISTORIC HOTEL €€
(☎969 23 10 00; www.hotelleonordeaquitania. com; Calle de San Pedro 60; s/d incl breakfast €85/108; 🕸) In an 18th-century house, this is a well-aged classic in the old town with an excellent restaurant.

Hostal Cánovas   BUDGET HOTEL €
(☎969 21 39 73; www.hostalcanovas.net; Calle Fray Luis de León 38; s/d €45/60; 🕸) This upbeat and welcoming *hostal* in the new

town has spacious rooms and a warm colour scheme.

Eating

Head for a chair in the square at Plaza Mayor (in the old town) or in Plaza de España (in Cuenca's modern quarter) for a drink and tapas before moving on to a restaurant. There is a good choice in and surrounding both squares, although meals in the historic quarter cost more.

TOP CHOICE La Bodeguilla de Basilio

TAPAS BAR €

(Calle Fray Luis de León 3; raciones €10-13; ☺lunch & dinner Mon-Sat, lunch Sun) Arrive here with an appetite, as you're presented with a complimentary plate of tapas when you order a drink, and not just a slice of dried-up cheese – typical freebies are a combo of quail eggs, ham, fried potatoes, lettuce hearts and courgettes. Understandably, it gets packed out, so head to the restaurant out back for more of the same (except you have to pay). If you are bored with conversation, the walls are covered with fascinating clutter, ranging from old pics of Cuenca to farming tools.

TOP CHOICE Manolo de la Osa

SOPHISTICATED TRADITIONAL €€

(☎969 21 95 12; Calle Río Gritos 5, Cerro Molina; meals €40-50) Following the success of his flagship Las Rejas restaurant in nearby Las Pedroñeras, celebrated chef Manuel de la Osa has opened up this superb restaurant at Ars Natura. Osa creates unique dishes using traditional local ingredients, like red partridge salad with butter beans and oyster mushrooms. The decor is suitably elegant. Reservations are essential.

Comedor Posada de San José

INTERNATIONAL SPANISH €

(Ronda de Julián Romero 4; meals €12; ☺7-10pm Tue-Sun) The Canadian owner has sensibly ensured that tourists can eat here according to their timetable back home. The food is uncomplicated and good, ranging from the reliable classic of fried eggs and (homemade) chips to *solomillo de cerdo a la sidra* (pork loin in cider). Desserts include strawberries and cream.

Mesón Casas Colgadas

SOPHISTICATED TRADITIONAL €€

(☎969 22 35 52; Calle de Los Canónigos 3; meals €25-35, menú €27) Housed in one of the *casas colgadas,* Cuenca's gourmet pride and joy fuses an amazing location with delicious traditional food on the menu, such as venison stew and the quaintly translated *boned little pork hands stew* (pig-trotter stew). Reservations are recommended.

American Piccolo

INTERNATIONAL €

(Plaza de Los Carros 4; meals €15; ☺Thu-Tue; ☻) Weary of the ubiquitous meaty fare? This independent restaurant packs in young couples on an affordable date, with its welcoming, diverse menu of Tex-Mex, Italian and Argentinean cuisine. Expect reliably acceptable rather than exceptional cuisine, with more than 125 dishes plus an adventurous wine list with plenty of imports.

Restaurante Figón del Huécar

SOPHISTICATED TRADITIONAL €€

(☎969 24 00 62; Ronda de Julián Romero 6; meals €30-35) This dress-for-dinner place specialises in Castilian specialities, as well as more-unusual plates, like codfish and potatoes with a mango sauce. Reservations are recommended.

El Ajibe

SOPHISTICATED TRADITIONAL €€

(☎969 24 00 62; Calle de San Pedro 12; meals €25-30) Elegant restaurant serving classy traditional cooking, including roast leg of lamb with a creamy mustard sauce. Reserve ahead.

Restaurante San Nicolás

CASTILIAN-MANCHEGAN €€

(☎969 24 05 19; Calle de San Pedro 15; menú €16, meals €25-35) Another fine establishment for solid Castilian-Manchegan food with an emphasis on *bacalao* (cod) and game. Reservations recommended.

Drinking

You can join the under 25s who gather together along Calle de Severo Catalina (old town) or Plaza de España (new town) for loads of noisy evening *copas*. There are several more-sophisticated venues around Plaza Mayor.

Lolita Lounge Bar

FASHIONABLE BAR

(Calle Clavel 7; ☺6pm-4am Thu & Fri, midday-4am Sat & Sun) A slick new bar with lots of steely metal, grey slate and sculpted black (ceiling). Cocktails, imported beers and a good mix of music attract the high-heeled and slicked-back-hair set.

Bar La Tinaja

TAPAS BAR

(Calle del Obispo Valero 4) Enjoying an ace position beside the cathedral, this place is typically crowded with crusty locals here

GOLD ON A PLATE

Saffron is one of the most sensuous spices in the world: its intense colour, aroma and delicacy are accentuated by a wealth of nuances. It's also among the most expensive spices – hardly surprising when you consider that it takes some 160,000 flowers to produce just 1kg of commercial saffron.

Spain leads the European saffron market, while La Mancha is the region where the flowers have been grown and cultivated since Moorish times, primarily around Cuenca and Albacete. Visit here in October and the surrounding fields are a sumptuous blanket of purple blooms.

Saffron is used as a culinary spice around the world. Some typical dishes are, in Italy, *risotto alla milanese;* in France, bouillabaisse; in England, saffron cake; in Sweden, *lusserkatter* cake; and, in Spain, numerous dishes, although the most famous just has to be the all-time traditional paella.

for the delicious (and free) tapas provided with every drink. The pasta dishes (€5.50) are good, too.

Bar Café del Castillo   CAFE-BAR
(Calle Larga 13; ☺closed Sun) Well sited for views from the large terrace, this spirited place is perfect for that late-night coffee, with a dozen of the spiked variety on offer.

☆ Entertainment
If you're looking to improve your dance moves, head for the disco-pubs on **Calle del Doctor Galíndez**, near Plaza de España. There is little to choose between them, but don't even consider shimmying down here until midnight. Early birds can head for nearby **Calle San Francisco**, where an energetic row of terrace bars has a pre-clubbing party feel from around 9pm at weekends.

ℹ Information
La Repro 11 (Calle Fray Luis de León 16; internet access per hr €1.20; ☺10am-2pm & 5-8pm Mon-Sat)

Main tourist office (www.aytocuenca.org, in Spanish; Plaza Mayor; ☺9am-9pm Mon-Sat, 9am-2.30pm Sun) Has a handy free booklet: *7 Paseos por Cuenca* (seven walking itineraries covering the city sights).

Tourist office (Plaza Hispanidad; ☺10am-2pm & 5-8pm Mon-Thu, 10am-8pm Fri-Sun) There's a second slightly smaller office in the new town.

ℹ Getting There & Away
The train and bus stations are located almost across from each other, southwest of Calle de Fermin Caballero.

BUS Services include up to seven buses daily to Madrid (€13.48, two hours) and regular services to Cuenca (€11.40, 2¼ hours).

TRAIN Trains to Madrid's Atocha station (€11.75, 2½ hours) depart six times a day on weekdays and four times a day on weekends. Trains to Valencia leave four times daily (€12.95, 3¼ hours).

ℹ Getting Around
Local buses 1 and 2 do the circuit from the new town to Plaza Mayor (€0.70, every 30 minutes) with numerous stops, including outside the train station. The closest underground car park to both the new and old towns is on Paseo del Huécar.

Around Cuenca
SERRANÍA DE CUENCA
Spreading north and east of Cuenca, the Serranía de Cuenca is a heavily wooded and fertile zone of craggy mountains and green fields. Ríos Júcar and Huécar flow through Cuenca from the high hinterland, through landscapes that are well worth exploring if you have your own transport.

If you are heading to Guadalajara, a pretty route is the minor CM210, which takes you via Priego, a lovely valley town that dates from Roman times and has sights including medieval churches, Roman arches and Moorish towers. Follow the signs from here to the Monasterio San Miguel de las Victorias, built to commemorate the naval battle of Lepanto in 1571 and currently being extensively restored. You can visit the pretty chapel with its original frescoes. If this doesn't stir the soul, the dramatic canyon views sure will.

Another trip from Cuenca is taking the CM2105 about 30km to the extraordinary Ciudad Encantada (Enchanted City; adult/child €3/free; ☺10am-sunset;). Surrounded by pine woods, limestone rocks have been eroded into fantastical shapes by nature. The shaded 40-minute circuit around the open-air rock museum is great for breaking up a car journey. It's crowded with *madrileños* at weekends and there are several (albeit pricey) places to eat and drink.

The CM2105 continues north via the picturesque village of Uña, the crystal-clear waters of Embalse de el Tobar and past the Reserva Natural de El Hosquillo, a protected natural park where brown bears have been roaming wild since being reintroduced in the early 1970s. Continue to the Nacimiento del Río Cuervo (17km), a couple of small waterfalls from which Río Cuervo rises. From here you could loop around towards Beteta (29km) and Hoz de Beteta, the gorge of the same name, encircled by lofty limestone crags and ridges. Around 8km before you reach Beteta, look for the Fuente de los Tilos turn-off to the right. There is a pretty circular 2km *paseo botánico* (botanical trail; two hours and 40 minutes) here, above the Río Guadiela.

Beteta has a charming porticoed Plaza Mayor with half-timbered buildings. There are a couple of *casas rurales* in town or you can opt for the comfortable Hotel Caserío de Vadillos (☎969 31 32 39; www.caseriovadillos.com; Puente de Vadillos; s/d €45/55) in nearby Puente de Vadillos, surrounded by lush gardens. Three kilometres beyond Beteta is Laguna de El Tobar, a pretty small lake surrounded by a trail just beyond the eponymous hamlet. You can return to Cuenca via the CM210, a quiet rural route that passes several traditional villages.

ALARCÓN

One hundred kilometres or so south of Cuenca is the seductive medieval village of Alarcón. The approach is via a narrow road winding through three medieval defensive arches.

The most famous sight here is the triangle-based Islamic castle, which has been converted into a sumptuous parador (☎969 33 03 15; www.parador.es; d €222; P ✱ ☎), offering old-world charm and supremely comfortable rooms with exposed brick-and-stone walls, and plush fabrics and furnishings. Alternatively, Meson Don Julián (☎969 33 03 00; Plaza Autonomo 1, s/d €40/50) across the way has pretty, rustic rooms with balconies and fridges, and sophisticated jet showers in the swing-a-cat-size bathrooms. The best restaurant in town is La Cabaña de Alarcón (Álvaro de

Lara 21; meals €20; lunch & dinner Mon-Sat, lunch Sun; ☻), with its picture windows, dark-pink paintwork, contemporary artwork and well-executed local dishes.

Stop at the tourist office (☎969 33 03 01; Calle Posadas 6; ☉10am-2pm & 5-7pm Wed-Sat, 10am-2pm Sun) for a map of walks around the village and beyond. If the tourist office is closed, there are detailed plaques with maps 150m south of the tourist office.

SEGÓBRIGA

These ruins (www.segobrigaconsocio.ua.es; adult/child €4/free; ☉9am-9pm Tue-Sun) may date as far back as the 5th century BC. The best-preserved structures are a **Roman theatre** and **amphitheatre** on the fringes of the ancient city, looking out over a valley. Other remains include the outlines of a Visigothic basilica and a section of the aqueduct, which helped keep the city green in what was otherwise a desert. There is also a small museum included in the price with some striking exhibits, including, among others, a tiny, exquisitely carved Venus made from bone and life-size sculptures dating from the 1st to 3rd centuries AD.

The site is near Saelices, 2km south of the A3 motorway between Madrid and Albacete. From Cuenca, drive west 55km on the N400, then turn south on the CM202.

Guadalajara

POP 69,600

Despite its romantic name, Guadalajara is, disappointingly, a modern, somewhat scruffy city, of more historical than aesthetic interest.

Guadalajara (from the Arabic *wad al-hijaara,* meaning 'stony river') was, in its

CASTILLA-LA MANCHA GUADALAJARA

WHAT'S WITH THE WICKER?

If you are driving around the Serranía de Cuenca, look in the fields for clusters of approximately 3m-high pyramid-shaped stacks of russet-red-and-brown reeds. Eight Serranía towns, including Priego and Beteta, form part of the Ruta del Mimbre (Wicker Route), so named as this is the country's most important region for the production of willow cane, used for wickerwork and basket weaving throughout Spain.

medieval Muslim heyday, the principal city of a large swath of northern Spain under the green banner of Islam at a time when Madrid was no more than a military observation point. In 1085 Alfonso VI finally took Guadalajara as the Reconquista moved ponderously south. The city was repeatedly sacked during the War of the Spanish Succession (1702–13), the Napoleonic occupation and the Spanish Civil War.

While little remains of Guadalajara's glory days, the much-restored Palacio de los Duques del Infantado (adult/child €2/free; ☉10am-2pm & 4-7pm Tue-Sat, 10am-2pm Sun), where the Mendoza family held court, is worth a visit if you're passing by. Its striking facade is a fine example of Gothic Mudéjar work and the heavily ornamental patio is equally entrancing.

Guadalajara is a simple day trip from Madrid, but, if you're stuck, check into Hotel Pax (☎949 24 80 60; www.hotusa.com; Avenida de Venezuela 15; s/d €55/60; P❄🅟), with its air of all-round poshness and genteel pastel-coloured rooms.

The town's tourist office (☎949 21 16 26; Plaza de los Caídos 6; ☉10am-2pm & 4-7.30pm Mon-Sat, 10am-2pm Sun) is opposite the *palacio*.

The bus station (Calle del Dos de Mayo) is a short walk from the *palacio*. Regular buses depart for Madrid (€4.75, 50 minutes). There are also buses to Sigüenza (€6.30, 1½ hours).

From the train station, 2km north of town, there are regular AVE fast trains to Madrid (€18.40, 30 minutes) from about 5am to 11.30pm and far fewer slower trains (€15, 50 minutes).

Pastrana

POP 1080

Pastrana should not be missed. It's an unspoilt place that has a Tuscan feel, with twisting cobbled streets flanked by honey-coloured stone buildings. Forty-two kilometres south of Guadalajara along the CM200, the heart and soul of the place is the Plaza de la Hora, a large square dotted with acacias and fronted by the sturdy Palacio Ducal; Wednesday morning it is the site of a lively market. It is in Pastrana that the one-eyed princess of Éboli, Ana Mendoza de la Cerda, was confined in 1581 for a love affair with the Spanish king Felipe II's secretary. You can see the caged window of her 'cell', where she died 10 years later, and arrange

a tour (Spanish only; €2) via the tourist office (☎949 37 06 72; www.pastrana.org, in Spanish; Plaza de la Hora 5; ☉10am-2pm & 4-7pm Tue-Fri, 10am-2pm & 4-8pm Sat, 10am-2pm Sun).

Walk from the square along Calle Mayor and you'll soon reach the massive Iglesia de Nuestra Señora de la Asunción (Colegiata). Inside, the interesting little museum (adult/child €2.50/free; ☉10am-2pm & 4-7pm Tue-Fri, 10am-2pm & 4-8pm Sat, 10am-2pm Sun) contains the jewels of the princess, some exquisite 15th-century tapestries and even an El Greco.

Hotel Palaterna (☎949 37 01 27; www.hotelpalaterna.com; Plaza de los Cuatro Caños; s/d €55/70; ❄) is a pleasant modern hotel overlooking a small square complete with bubbling fountain. Rooms are painted in cool colours, contrasting with dark wood furniture. There is wheelchair access

Hostelería Real de Pastrana (☎949 37 10 60; www.hosteriasreales.com; Carretera C200 Pastrana-Zorita, s/d from €53/106; P❄@) should be a *parador*: it's gorgeous, with original oil paintings and antiques throughout, and classic rooms with period touches and plush furnishings. The restaurant concentrates on local dishes like the starter *gachas manchegas* (a kind of porridge with fried pork – and better than it sounds!). There is an adjacent museum of religious artefacts. If this fails to excite, you'll need wheels – Pastrana is 2km away.

Pastrana has plenty of restaurants and bars. Don't miss the locals' local, Casa Seco (Calle Mayor 36; tapas from €2), with all four walls, plus ceiling, papered with faded bullfighting posters. It's run by a wonderfully matriarchal lady who keeps the flat-cap clientele under control. Just down the street, Café de Ruy (Calle Mayor 1; meals from €15) is the pick of the restaurant bunch, run by a dynamic young *madrileño* couple. Dishes feature locally grown and produced ingredients. Fancy teas, coffees and cocktails add to the appeal, together with the chill-out music.

Two buses travel to Madrid (€5.20, 1½ hours) via Guadalajara every weekday morning.

Around Pastrana

Some 20km northeast of Pastrana is the area's main reservoir, the white-rimmed Embalse de Entrepeñas, where swimming is more an attraction than the views. From here you can push north on the CM204 to Cifuentes, with its 14th-century castle.

An alternative, albeit longer, route to the lake goes via Guadalajara, from where you could follow the A2 northeast and turn off at Torija, which has an impressive castle situated on a classic Castilian main square, Plaza de la Villa. From here, take the CM2011 for Brihuega, a leafy village with stretches of its medieval walls intact. The drive east along Río Tajuña is one of the more pleasant in this part of Castilla-La Mancha.

Sigüenza

POP 5020

Sleepy, historic and filled with the ghosts of a turbulent past, Sigüenza is well worth a detour. The town is built on a low hill cradled by Río Henares and boasts a castle, a cathedral and several excellent restaurants set among twisting lanes of honey-coloured medieval buildings. Start your ambling at the beautiful 16th-century Plaza Mayor.

History

Originally a Celtiberian settlement, Segontia (as the town was previously named) became an important Roman and, later, Visigothic military outpost and was in Muslim hands from the 8th century until the 1120s. The town was eventually ceded to the Castilians, who turned Sigüenza and its hinterland into a vast Church property. Sigüenza's decline was long and painful as the town found itself repeatedly in the way of advancing armies: it was a front line during both the War of the Spanish Succession and the Spanish Civil War.

◎ Sights

Catedral   CATHEDRAL
(◎9.30am-2pm & 4-8pm Tue-Sat, noon-5.30pm Sun) Rising up from the heart of the old town is the city's centrepiece, the *catedral*. Begun as a Romanesque structure in 1130, work continued for four centuries as the church was expanded and adorned. The largely Gothic result is laced with elements of other styles, from plateresque through Renaissance to Mudéjar. The church was heavily damaged during the civil war, but was subsequently rebuilt. Take a look at the tall tower opposite the Plaza Mayor where the top slit window is pock-marked by bullets (doubtless trying to hit a sniper).

The dark (and very cold) **nave** has some fine stained-glass windows, including a magnificent rose window, plus an impressive 15th-century altarpiece along the south wall. To enter the chapels, sacristy and Gothic cloister, you'll need to join a Spanish-language-only guided tour (per person €4; ◎11am, noon, 4.30pm & 5.30pm Tue-Sat). The highlights of the tour include the **Capilla Mayor**, home of the reclining marble statue of Don Martín Vázquez de Arce (the statue is named *El Doncel*), who died fighting the Muslims in the final stages of the Reconquista. Particularly beautiful is the **Sacristía de las Cabezas**, with a ceiling adorned with hundreds of heads sculpted by Covarrubias. The **Capilla del Espíritu Santo** boasts a doorway combining plateresque, Mudéjar and Gothic styles; inside is a remarkable dome and an *Anunciación* by El Greco.

Museo Diocesano de Arte   RELIGIOUS ART
(admission €3; ◎11am-2pm & 4-7pm Tue-Sun) Across the square from the cathedral, this museum has an impressive selection of religious art from Sigüenza and the surrounding area, including a series of mainly 15th-century altarpieces.

Castillo   CASTLE
Calle Mayor heads south up the hill from the cathedral to a magnificent-looking castle, which was originally built by the Romans and was, in turn, a Moorish *alcázar* (fortress), royal palace, asylum and army barracks. Virtually destroyed during the Spanish Civil War, it was subsequently rebuilt under Franco as a *parador* (see p224).

🛏 Sleeping

As Sigüenza is a popular weekend jaunt for *madrileños*, accommodation in the handful of hotels here gets quickly booked up.

Hotel El Doncel   MODERN HOTEL €€
(☏949 39 00 01; www.eldoncel.com, in Spanish; Paseo de la Alameda 3; s/d €62/78; ❄☏) With earthy colours, spot lighting, minibar, and marshmallow-soft duvets and pillows, this place has benefited from a sophisticated update. Located opposite the tourist office; note that prices drop substantially midweek.

Hospedería Porta Coeli   HISTORIC HOTEL €€
(☏949 39 18 75; Calle Mayor 50; s/d €57/74; ❄) Housed in a sumptuous historic building, the Hospedería Porta Coeli has light tiles and pale paintwork that provide a bright,

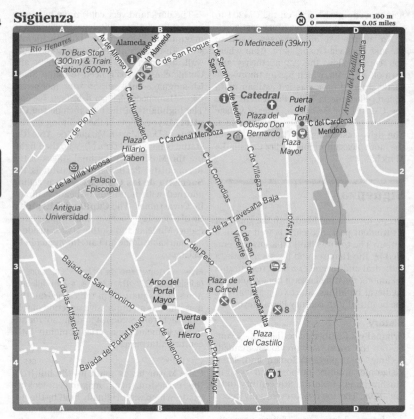

fresh look to the good-sized bedrooms. The restaurant (meals cost €20; open weekends only) serves tasty light dishes, such as mushrooms crêpes with a creamy cheese sauce.

Parador PARADOR €€€

(☎949 39 01 00; www.parador.es; Plaza del Castillo; s/d from €114/124; [P][❄][☎]) Sigüenza's *parador* ably provides its guests with the usual combination of luxury, attentive service and period furnishings. It is set in the castle, which dates back to the 12th century, and overlooks the town. It was in virtual ruins before being extensively rebuilt in the 1970s. Its courtyard is a wonderful place to pass the time. The restaurant *menú* costs a reasonable €31.

🍴 Eating & Drinking

Finding somewhere to eat to fit your timetable can be problematic here. Several restaurants don't open until 10pm (locals eat dinner late), while those in the historic centre are geared more towards the weekend influx from Madrid and close several days during the week. Paseo de la Alameda (flanking the park) has a limited choice of restaurants open daily serving hearty honest grub.

Gurugú de la Plazuela MUSHROOMS €€

(Plaza de la Cárcel; mushroom dishes €12-18, meals €20-25; ⊙lunch & dinner Thu-Sat, lunch Sun; [✍]) Overlooking this atmospheric small square, the speciality here is mushrooms, lots of them, with some 16 varieties on the menu, prepared all sorts of ways. Other choices include *rabo de toro al vino* (oxtail in a wine sauce). There are regular art and photography exhibitions.

Cafe-Bar Alameda TAPAS BAR €

(Paseo de la Alameda 2; snacks €5-10; ⊙10am-midnight) Join the local card players at this down-home bar. Its counter groans with tempting tapas and *pintxos* (Basque tapas),

Sigüenza

including *caracoles* (snails) and *orejas* (pig's ears) for the intrepid, as well as more-digestible, albeit still unusual, choices like tortilla stuffed with bacon and cheese.

Taberna Seguntina
TRADITIONAL MANCHEGAN €€
(www.latabernaseguntina.es; Calle Mayor 43; meals €20-25; ⊙8-11pm Wed-Fri, 1.30-8.30pm Sat & Sun) A swallow's swoop from the castle, this restaurant has a traditional menu that includes local classics like suckling pig, roasted lamb and pheasant.

Los Soportales
TAPAS BAR €
(Plaza Mayor 3; tapas €2-4) Great location under the arches, with tables on the square and free tapas with every drink.

La Flor de Brijhuega
CHEESE SHOP €
(Calle del Cardenal Mendoza 2) Fabulous cheese shop specialising in locally produced *quesos artesanos* (boutique cheese).

ⓘ Information

Locotorio Sigüenza (Calle del Humilladero 21; internet access per hr €1.80; ⊙10am-10pm Mon-Sat, 10am-8pm Sun)

Main tourist office (www.siguenza.es, in Spanish; Paseo de la Alameda; ⊙10am-2pm & 5-7pm Mon-Thu, 10am-2pm & 5-8pm Fri & Sat, 10am-2pm Sun) In the delightful Ermita del Humilladero.

Tourist office (Calle de Medina 9; ⊙10am-2pm & 5-7pm Mon-Thu & Sat, 10am-2pm & 5-8pm Fri, 10am-2pm Sun) This smaller branch is just down the hill from the cathedral.

ⓘ Getting There & Away

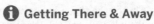

Buses are infrequent and mainly serve towns around Sigüenza, including Guadalajara. They stop on Avenida de Alfonso VI. Up to 10 regional **trains** go to Madrid's Chamartín station (€10.80, 1½ hours); some go on to Soria.

Around Sigüenza

IMÓN
POP 40

This tiny gem of a hamlet, located 7km northwest of Sigüenza, has a surprising amount on offer, including several sophisticated restaurants (for weekending *madrileños*), a superb hotel and spa, and excellent walking and birdwatching potential.

TOP CHOICE **Salinas de Imón** (☑949 39 73 11; www.salinasdeimon.com; Real 49; r from €85; ❀❁❂) is housed in a mid-17th-century stone building. It has 13 rooms, restored with sensitive integrity, that retain a sense of history. There is nothing historic about the luxurious bathrooms or spa, however. A wide range of treatments is available, including massages (ayurvedic, sports, psycho-sensitive and aromatherapy) and reflexology. The garden is secluded and lovely, with lawns, a bower and a pool. A comment in the guest book says it all: 'Because I liked it so much, I will tell my friend Dorothy,' writes Vicente, charmingly. Dinner is available.

For an easy walk, follow Don Quijote's path at the end of the main street (Calle Cervantes), heading north. The 4.5km pleasant stroll through fields leads to a 15th-century castle, **La Riba de Santiuste**, perched high on a rock above the partly abandoned village of the same name. The castle is partly in ruins and is fascinating to explore.

ATIENZA
POP 420

Some 10km northwest of Imón lies Atienza, a charming walled medieval village crowned by yet another castle ruin. The main half-timbered square and former 16th-century market place, Plaza D Bruno Pascual Ruilopez, is overlooked by the Romanesque **Iglesia San Juan Bautista**, which has an impressive organ and lavish gilt *retablo*. For local bars and a couple of cavernous antique and gift shops, head to the adjacent Plaza de España. There are several more mostly Romanesque churches, plus three small **museums** (admission per museum €1.50; ☻10.30am-1.30pm & 4.30-6.30pm) in the Iglesia de San Gil, Iglesia de San Bartolomé and Santísima Trinidad.

The best place to stay is the **Antiguo Palacio de Atienza** (☎949 39 91 80; www.palaciodeatienza.com; Callejuelas de San Gil 47; r €80-120; ✳🌐📶🐾), a former palace with handsome rooms featuring grey stone walls and beams. The variation in price relates to the size of the room and option of a hot tub. Balconies overlook the lawns and pool.

El Mirador (☎949 39 90 38; Calle Barruelo; d with/without bathroom €48/35; 🅿), with small simple rooms, is the cheaper option in a modern whitewashed building on the edge of town. The excellent restaurant (meals €25) has creative dishes, as well as the standard *cordero* (lamb) and *cabrito* (kid), accompanied by panoramic views.

A couple of buses leave early in the morning, bound for Guadalajara, Madrid and Sigüenza.

Barcelona

Best Places to Eat

» Cerveseria Brasseria
Gallega (p280)

» Ipar-Txoko (p281)

» Tapaç 24 (p280)

» Xiringuito d'Escribà
(p279)

» Vaso de Oro (p279)

Best Places to Stay

» Alberg Mare de Déu de
Montserrat (p277)

» Hostal Goya (p275)

» Hotel Banys Orientals
(p274)

» Hotel Constanza (p276)

» Hotel Axel (p275)

Why Go?

Barcelona is a mix of sunny Mediterranean charm and European urban style, where dedicated hedonists and culture vultures feel equally at home. From Gothic to Gaudí, the city bursts with art and architecture; Catalan cooking is among the country's best; summer sun seekers fill the beaches in and beyond the city; and the bars and clubs heave year-round.

From its origins as a middle-ranking Roman town, of which vestiges can be seen today, Barcelona became a medieval trade juggernaut. Its old centre holds one of the greatest concentrations of Gothic architecture in Europe. Beyond this are some of the world's more bizarre buildings: surreal spectacles capped by Antoni Gaudí's La Sagrada Família.

Barcelona has been breaking ground in art, architecture and style since the late 19th century. From Picasso and Miró to the modern wonders of today, the racing heart of Barcelona has barely skipped a beat. Equally busy are the city's avant-garde chefs, who compete with old-time classics for the gourmet's attention.

When to Go

Barcelona

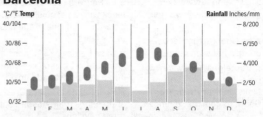

| °C/°F Temp | Rainfall Inches/mm |

May Plaça del Fòrum rocks during Primavera Sound, a long weekend of outdoor concerts.

June Sónar, Europe's biggest celebration of electronic music, is held across the city.

September Festes de la Mercè is Barcelona's end-of-summer finale and biggest party.

DON'T MISS

Head up to the **Eclipse bar** (p274) in the waterfront W Barcelona tower hotel for some of the best views over Barcelona. Enjoy with a watermelon martini.

Fast Facts

» Population: 1.62 million

» Greater metropolitan area: 636 sq km

» Average annual income: €22,000

» Number of visitors (2009): 6.5 million

Best of What's Free

» Park Güell (p257)

» CaixaForum (p267)

» Església de Santa Maria del Mar (p243)

» Estadi Olímpic (p267)

» Castell de Montjuïc (p263)

Resources

» Barcelona Turisme (www.barcelonaturisme. com) Official tourism website.

» Barcelona (www.bcn. cat) Barcelona Town Hall, with links.

» Le Cool (http://lecool. com) What's-on guide.

» Barcelona Yellow (www. barcelonayellow.com) Links on everything from Gaudí to gourmet dining.

A Hidden Portrait at La Sagrada Família

Careful observation of the Passion Facade of Antoni Gaudí's masterpiece, La Sagrada Família (p247), will reveal a special tribute to the genius architect from sculptor Josep Subirachs. In a building dripping with symbology, some of it less than obvious to the uninitiated, this search is not too difficult a task. The central sculptural group (below Christ crucified) shows, from right to left, Christ bearing his cross, Veronica displaying the cloth with Christ's bloody image, a pair of soldiers and, watching it all, a man called the Evangelist. Subirachs used a rare photo of Gaudí, taken a couple of years before his death, as the model for the Evangelist's face.

MANIC MONDAYS

Many attractions shut their doors on Monday, but there are plenty of exceptions. Among the more enticing open attractions are Casa-Museu Gaudí (Park Güell), Gran Teatre del Liceu, Jardí Botànic, Catedral, La Pedrera, La Sagrada Família, Mirador a Colom, Museu d'Art Contemporani de Barcelona, Museu de l'Eròtica, Museu de la Xocolata, Museu del Futbol Club Barcelona, Museu del Modernisme Català, Museu Marítim, Palau de la Música Catalana and the Pavelló Mies van der Rohe.

Top Modernista Gems

» La Sagrada Família (p247), Antoni Gaudí's unfinished symphony, is a soaring cathedral that people love or loathe. Work continues apace on this controversial project.

» Palau de la Música Catalana (p239), a gaudily sumptuous home for music to suit the most eclectic of tastes, is a giddy example of Modernista fantasy.

» La Pedrera (p255), Gaudí's wavy corner apartment block with an exquisite period apartment and crowned by a sci-fi roof, is one of the best examples of the star architect's work.

» Casa Batlló (p254), possibly kookier than La Pedrera, looks at first glance like some strange sea creature frozen into a building facade. Inside, it's all curls and swirls.

» Hospital de la Santa Creu i de Sant Pau (p291), long one of the city's main hospitals, features 16 uniquely decorated pavilions.

History

It is thought that Barcelona may have been founded by the Carthaginians in about 230 BC, taking the surname of Hamilcar Barca, Hannibal's father. Roman Barcelona (known as Barcino) covered an area within today's Barri Gòtic and was overshadowed by Tarraco (Tarragona), 90km to the southwest.

In the wake of Muslim occupation and then Frankish domination, Guifré el Pilós (Wilfrid the Hairy) founded the house of the Comtes de Barcelona (Counts of Barcelona) in AD 878. In 1137 Count Ramon Berenguer IV married Petronilla, heiress of Aragón, creating a joint state and setting the scene for Catalonia's golden age. Jaume I (1213–76) wrenched the Balearic Islands and Valencia from the Muslims in the 1230s to '40s. Jaume I's son Pere II followed with Sicily in 1282.

The accession of the Aragonese noble Fernando to the throne in 1479 augured ill for Barcelona, and his marriage to Queen Isabel of Castilla more still. Catalonia effectively became a subordinate part of the Castilian state. After the War of the Spanish Succession (1702–13), Barcelona fell to the Bourbon king, Felipe V, in September 1714.

MODERNISME, ANARCHY & CIVIL WAR

The 19th century brought economic resurgence. Wine, cotton, cork and iron industries developed, as did urban working-class poverty and unrest. To ease the crush, Barcelona's medieval walls were demolished in 1854, and in 1869 work began on L'Eixample, an extension of the city beyond Plaça de Catalunya. The flourishing bourgeoisie paid for lavish buildings, many of them in the eclectic Modernisme style, whose leading exponent was Antoni Gaudí.

In 1937, a year into the Spanish Civil War, the Catalan communist party (PSUC; Partit Socialista Unificat de Catalunya) took control of the city after fratricidal street battles against anarchists and Trotskyists. George Orwell recorded the events in his classic *Homage to Catalonia*. Barcelona fell to Franco in 1939 and there followed a long period of repression.

FROM FRANCO TO THE PRESENT

Under Franco Barcelona received a flood of immigrants, chiefly from Andalucía. Some 750,000 people came to Barcelona in the '50s and '60s, and almost as many to the rest of Catalonia. Many lived in appalling conditions.

Three years after Franco's death in 1975, a new Spanish constitution created the autonomous community of Catalonia (Catalunya in Catalan; Cataluña in Castilian), with Barcelona as its capital. The 1992 Olympic Games put Barcelona on the map. Under the visionary leadership of popular Catalan Socialist mayor Pasqual Maragall, a burst of public works brought new life to Montjuïc and the once shabby waterfront.

Maragall's successors have maintained the Socialists' hold on the city administration, but only just. The present mayor, Jordi Hereu, governs with a minority government and is tipped to lose the next city polls in 2011, in spite of an ambitious decision to bid for the 2022 Winter Olympic Games.

In 2006, the Catalan regional government negotiated a new autonomy statute with the central government in Madrid. Designed to devolve more powers to Barcelona, it was challenged in the constitutional court by the right-wing Partido Popular. The court took fours years to make a decision, in which it rolled back some of the advances under the new statute, thus aggravating tensions between Barcelona and Madrid.

In July 2010, the regional parliament took a major symbolic step when it outlawed bullfights in Catalonia from 2012.

⊙ Sights

Barcelona could be divided up into thematic chunks. In Ciutat Vella (especially the Barri Gòtic and La Ribera) are clustered the bulk of the city's ancient and medieval splendours. Along with El Raval, on the other side of La Rambla, and Port Vell, where old Barcelona meets the sea, this is the core of the city's life, both by day and by night.

L'Eixample is where the Modernistas went to town. Here the attractions are more spread out. Passeig de Gràcia is a concentrated showcase for some of their most outlandish work, but La Sagrada Família, Gaudí's masterpiece, and other outstanding buildings are scattered about.

The beaches and working-class district of La Barceloneta (which is riddled with seafood restaurants) form a separate summery side of the city, just as Montjuïc, with its gardens, museums, art galleries and Olympic Games sites, forms a microcosm on its own.

Gaudí's Park Güell is just beyond the area of Gràcia, whose narrow lanes and interlocking squares set the scene for much lively nightlife.

Barcelona Highlights

1 Marvel at **La Sagrada Família** (p247), Antoni Gaudí's still-unfolding Modernista masterpiece

2 Drink in the views from Gaudí's **Park Güell** (p257)

3 Head out with the locals for a night of tippling and snacking in **L'Eixample** (p280)

4 Study the earliest of Pablo's portraits in the **Museu Picasso** (p241)

5 Grab your towel and taste buds and head for **La Barceloneta** (p246)

6 Get a spiritual lift in the strange soaring mountains of **Montserrat** (p298)

7 Swan around inside the curvy **Casa Batlló** (p254), Gaudí's kookiest building

8 Explore **Montjuïc** (p261), home to Romanesque art, a brooding fort, Miró and beautiful gardens

9 Head down the coast for **Sitges** (p295), an outrageous beachside party resort

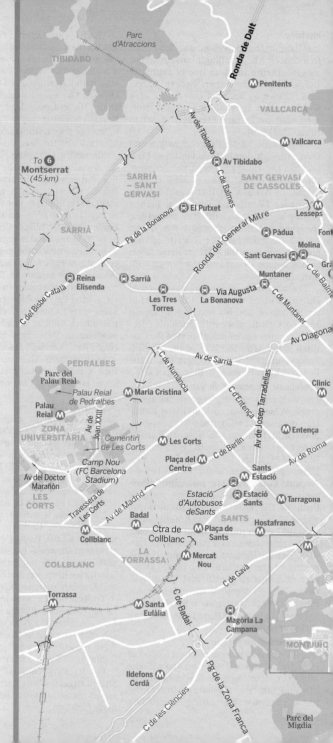

Two Days

Start with the **Barri Gòtic**. After a stroll along **La Rambla**, wade into the labyrinth to admire the **Catedral** and the **Museu d'Història de Barcelona** on historic Plaça del Rei. Cross Via Laietana into **La Ribera** for the city's most beautiful church, the **Església de Santa Maria del Mar**, and the nearby **Museu Picasso**. Round off with a meal and cocktails in the funky **El Born** area.

The following day, start with a walk through Gaudí's unique **Park Güell**, then head for his work in progress, **La Sagrada Família**. Such grandeur may have you reaching for a drink in nearby **Michael Collins Pub**, before heading off for dinner in L'Eixample, say at **Cerveseria Brasseria Gallega**.

Four Days

Start the third day with another round of Gaudí, visiting **Casa Batlló** and **La Pedrera**, followed by beachside relaxation and seafood in **La Barceloneta**. Day four should be dedicated to **Montjuïc**, with its museums, galleries, fortress, gardens and Olympic stadium.

One Week

With three extra days, you can explore further, taking in **El Raval**, **Tibidabo** amusement park and walking in the **Collserola** parklands. A tempting one-day excursion is **Montserrat**, Catalonia's 'sacred mountain'. Another option is to spend a day at the beach at **Sitges**.

Two good landmarks are the hills of Montjuïc and Tibidabo. Montjuïc, the lower of the two, begins about 700m southwest of the bottom (southeast end) of La Rambla. Tibidabo, with its TV tower and church topped by a giant statue of Christ, is 6km northwest of Plaça de Catalunya. It's the high point of the Collserola range of wooded hills that forms the backdrop to the city.

Further sights, ranging from FC Barcelona's Camp Nou football stadium to the peaceful haven of the Museu-Monestir de Pedralbes, glitter like distant stars away from the centre.

LA RAMBLA

Head to Spain's most famous street for that first taste of Barcelona's vibrant atmosphere. Flanked by narrow traffic lanes, La Rambla is a broad pedestrian boulevard, lined with cafes and restaurants, and crowded deep into the night with a cross-section of Barcelona's permanent and transient populace. It has to be said that the average *barcelonin* tends to stay away from La Rambla – under assault by tourists and the late-night party crowd, it has long ceased to be the locals' favourite boulevard for a Sunday stroll. That doesn't detract from its liveliness, however.

La Rambla gets its name from a seasonal stream (*raml* in Arabic) that once ran here. It was outside the city walls until the 14th century and was built up with monastic buildings and palaces in the 16th to 18th centuries. Unofficially La Rambla is divided into five sections with their own names.

La Rambla de Canaletes   STREET

To the north, from Plaça de Catalunya, La Rambla de Canaletes is named after an inconspicuous fount, whose drinking water (despite claims that anyone who drinks it will return to Barcelona) nowadays leaves much to be desired. Delirious football fans gather here to celebrate whenever the main home side, FC Barcelona, wins a cup or the league premiership. A block east along Carrer de la Canuda is Plaça de la Vila de Madrid, with a sunken garden where Roman tombs lie exposed in the Via Sepulcral Romana (Map p240; www.museuhistoria.bcn.cat; Plaça de la Vila de Madrid; admission €2; ☺10am-8pm Tue-Sun, 10am-3pm holidays; Ⓜ Catalunya).

La Rambla dels Estudis   STREET

La Rambla dels Estudis, from Carrer de la Canuda running south to Carrer de la Portaferrissa, is popularly known as La Rambla dels Ocells (Birds) because of its twittering bird market (which was being dismantled in the course of 2010 to be replaced by ice-cream and pastry stands).

La Rambla de Sant Josep   STREET
From Carrer de la Portaferrissa to Plaça de la Boqueria, what is officially called La Rambla de Sant Josep (named after a now nonexistent monastery) is lined with flower stalls, which give it the alternative name La Rambla de les Flors.

The Palau de la Virreina (p285) is a grand 18th-century rococo mansion housing a municipal arts-and-entertainment information and ticket office, and an exhibition space. Next is the Mercat de la Boqueria, one of the best-stocked and most colourful produce markets in Europe. Plaça de la Boqueria, where four side streets meet just north of Liceu metro station, is your chance to walk all over a Miró – the colourful Mosaïc de Miró in the pavement, with one tile signed by the artist.

Barcelona takes pride in being a pleasure centre and in the Museu de l'Eròtica (Map p234; www.erotica-museum.com; La Rambla de Sant Josep 96; adult/senior & student €9/8; ☺10am-9pm; ⓜLiceu) you can observe just how people have been enjoying themselves since ancient times – lots of Kama Sutra and 1920s porn flicks.

La Rambla dels Caputxins   STREET
La Rambla dels Caputxins (named after yet another defunct monastery and also known as La Rambla del Centre) runs from Plaça de la Boqueria to Carrer dels Escudellers. The west side is flanked by the Gran Teatre del Liceu.

Further south, on the east side of La Rambla dels Caputxins, is the entrance to the palm-shaded Plaça Reial. South of this point La Rambla gets seedier.

Gran Teatre del Liceu
(Map p234; www.liceubarcelona.com; La Rambla dels Caputxins 51-59; admission with/without guide €8.70/4; ☺guided tour 10am, unguided visits 11.30am, noon, 12.30pm & 1pm; ⓜLiceu) Barcelona's grand opera house was built in 1847, largely destroyed by fire in 1994 and reopened better than ever in 1999.

The Liceu launched such Catalan stars as Josep (aka José) Carreras and Montserrat Caballé, and can seat up to 2300. On the guided visit you are taken to the grand foyer, and then up the marble staircase to the glittering, neobaroque Saló dels Miralls (Hall of Mirrors). You are then led up to the 4th floor to admire the theatre in all its splendour from the high stalls. You finish off with a modest collection of Modernista art, El Cercle del Liceu.

La Rambla de Santa Mònica   STREET
The southernmost stretch of La Rambla, La Rambla de Santa Mònica, widens out to approach the Mirador a Colom overlooking Port Vell. La Rambla here is named after the Convent de Santa Mònica, a monastery converted into an art gallery and cultural centre, the Centre d'Art Santa Mònica (Map p234; www.artssantamonica.cat; La Rambla de Santa Mònica 7; admission free; ☺11am-9pm Tue-Sun & holidays; ⓜDrassanes).

Museu de Cera
(Map p234; www.museocerabcn.com; Passatge de la Banca 7; adult/senior, student & child €12/7; ☺10am-10pm; ⓜDrassanes) On the east side of La Rambla de Santa Mònica lurks this wax museum, with a hall of horror and everyone from Lady Di to General Franco.

Mirador a Colom
(Plaça del Portal de la Pau; lift adult/senior & child €2.50/1.50; ☺9am-8.30pm; ⓜDrassanes) The bottom end of La Rambla, and the harbour beyond, lie under the supervision of this late-19th-century monument to the glory of Christopher Columbus (who some Catalan historians insist came from Barcelona rather than Genoa in Italy). Take the lift to the top for spectacular views over the city.

BARRI GÒTIC
Barcelona's 'Gothic Quarter', east of La Rambla, is a medieval warren of narrow, winding streets, quaint *plaças* (plazas), and grand mansions and monuments from the city's golden age. Many of its buildings date from the 15th century or earlier. The district is liberally seasoned with restaurants, cafes and bars, so relief from sightseeing is always close to hand.

The Barri Gòtic stretches from La Rambla in the southwest to Via Laietana in the northeast; and from Plaça de Catalunya in the northwest to Passeig de Colom in the southeast. Carrer de Ferran and Carrer de Jaume I, cutting across the middle, form a halfway line: these streets and those to their northwest are peppered with chic little shops, while those to their southeast become marginally seedier (but no less lively).

Plaça de Sant Jaume   SQUARE
It's hard to imagine that on this very spot a couple of thousand years ago folk in togas

BARCELONA

would discuss the day's events and Roman politics. For hereabouts lay the Roman-era forum and the square as you see it today has again been Barcelona's political hub since at least the 15th century. Facing each other across it are the Palau de la Generali-tat (the seat of Catalonia's government) on the north side, and the *ajuntament* (town hall) on the south side.

Palau de la Generalitat
(Map p234; www.gencat.cat; MLiceu or Jaume I)
Founded in the early 15th century, the Pa-

lau de la Generalitat is open on limited occasions only (the second and fourth weekends of the month, plus open-door days). The most impressive of the ceremonial halls is the **Saló de Sant Jordi**, named after St George, the region's patron saint. At any time, however, you can admire the original Gothic main entrance on Carrer del Bisbe. To join weekend visits, book on the website.

Ajuntament
(Map p234; ⊘10am-1pm Sun; ⓂLiceu or Jaume I) Outside, the only feature of the *ajuntament* that's now worthy of note is the disused Gothic entrance on Carrer de la Ciutat. Inside, you can visit the **Saló de Cent**, a fine arched hall created in the 14th century (but since remodelled) for the medieval city council, the Consell de Cent. Guided visits start every 30 minutes; English and French speakers are catered for.

Catedral & Around   CATHEDRAL
(Map p234; Plaça de la Seu; ⊘8am-8pm; ⓂJaume I) You can reach Barcelona's Catedral, one of its most magnificent Gothic structures, by following Carrer del Bisbe northwest from Plaça de Sant Jaume. The narrow old streets around the cathedral are traffic-free and dotted with occasionally very talented buskers.

The best view of the cathedral is from Plaça de la Seu beneath its main **northwest facade**. Unlike most of the building, which dates from between 1298 and 1460, this facade was not created until the 1870s. They say it is based on a 1408 design and it is odd in that it reflects northern-European Gothic styles rather than the sparer, Catalan version.

The interior of the cathedral is a broad, soaring space. It is divided into a central nave and two aisles by lines of elegant, thin pillars.

MUSEUMS WITHIN A MUSEUM

One combined ticket, which has no expiry date, can be used to visit all the components of the Museu d'Història de Barcelona. The main centre is the Plaça del Rei complex, where you can discover parts of Roman and medieval Barcelona. It also includes the Museu-Monestir de Pedralbes (p260), the Centre d'Interpretació in Park Güell (p257), the civil war air raid shelter, Refugi 307 (p261) and the Via Sepulcral Romana (p232).

In the first chapel, on the right from the northwest entrance, the main crucifixion figure above the altar is **Sant Crist de Lepant**, which was carried on the prow of the Spanish flagship at the Battle of Lepanto against the Turks in 1571. It is said the figure acquired its odd stance by dodging an incoming cannonball. Further down along this same wall, past the southwest transept, are the wooden **coffins** of Count Ramon Berenguer I and his wife Almodis, cofounders of the 11th-century Romanesque predecessor to the present cathedral.

Smack in the middle of the central nave is the exquisitely sculpted, late-14th-century timber coro (choir stall; admission €2.20). The coats of arms belong to members of the Barcelona chapter of the Order of the Golden Fleece.

The **crypt** beneath the main altar contains the remarkable alabaster tomb of Santa Eulàlia, one of Barcelona's patron saints and a good Christian lass of the 4th century, who suffered terrible tortures and death at the hands of the pagan Romans (or so the story goes). Some of those gruesome tortures are depicted on the tomb.

For a bird's-eye (mind the poop) view of medieval Barcelona, visit the cathedral's roof and tower (admission €2.20) by a lift from the Capella de les Animes del Purgatori, near the northeast transept.

From the southwest transept, exit to the lovely **claustre** (cloister), with its trees, fountains and geese (there have been geese here for centuries). One of the cloister chapels commemorates 930 priests, monks and nuns martyred in the civil war.

Along the northern flank of the cloister is the Sala Capitular (chapter house; admission €2; ☉10am-12.15pm & 5.15-7pm). Bathed in the rich reds of the carpet and cosseted by fine wooden seating, its rooms contain some artworks of minor interest. Among them is a *Pietat* by Bartolomeo Bermejo.

You can visit the cathedral in one of two ways. In the morning or the late afternoon, entrance is free and you can pay to visit any combination you choose of the choir stalls, chapter house and roof. If you want to visit all three, it costs less (€5) and is less crowded to enter for the so-called 'special visit' between 1pm and 5pm.

Casa de l'Ardiaca, Palau del Bispat & Roman Walls

At the northern end of Carrer del Bisbe, poke your head into the courtyards of the 16th-century Casa de l'Ardiaca (Archdeacon's House) and the 13th-century Palau del Bispat (Bishop's Palace). On the outside of both buildings, at the end of Carrer del Bisbe, the foundations of the rounded towers that flanked a Roman gate are visible. The lower part of the Casa de l'Ardiaca's northwest wall was part of the Roman walls (☉9am-9pm Mon-Fri, 9am-2pm Sat), which ran along present-day Plaça de la Seu. Inside the building itself you can see parts of the wall.

Museu Diocesà

(Diocesan Museum; www.arqbcn.org, in Catalan; Avinguda de la Catedral 4; adult/senior & student €6/3; ☉10am-2pm & 5-8pm Tue-Sat, 11am-2pm Sun; M Jaume I) Housed in the Casa de la Pia Almoina, a medieval almshouse, Museu Diocesà contains a sparse collection of medieval religious art, usually supplemented by a temporary exposition or two.

Temple Romà d'August

(Roman Temple of Augustus; Carrer del Paradis; ☉10am-8pm Tue-Sun, 10am-3pm holidays; M Jaume I) Just beyond the southeast end of the cathedral stand this temple's four mighty columns, built in the first century AD.

TOP CHOICE **Plaça del Rei**   MUSEUM SQUARE
A stone's throw east of the cathedral, Plaça del Rei is the courtyard of the former Palau Reial Major, the palace of the counts of Barcelona and monarchs of Aragón.

Museu d'Història de Barcelona

(Barcelona History Museum; Map p234; www.
museuhistoria.bcn.cat; Carrer del Veguer; adult/
senior & student €7/5; ◎10am-8pm Tue-Sun,
10am-3pm holidays; MJaume I) Most of the tall,
centuries-old buildings surrounding Plaça
del Rei are now open to visitors as the Museu d'Història de Barcelona. This is one of
Barcelona's most fascinating sights, combining large sections of the former palace
with a subterranean walk through Roman
and Visigothic Barcelona. Set aside at least
an hour for the visit. Entry is free from 3pm
Sundays and from 4pm on the first Saturday of the month.

The entrance to the museum is through
16th-century Casa Padellàs, just south of
Plaça del Rei. With its courtyard typical of
Barcelona's late-Gothic and baroque mansions, the house was moved here in the
1930s because of roadworks. The external
courtyard staircase now leads to a restored
Roman tower. Below ground awaits a remarkable walk through excavated Roman
and Visigothic **ruins**, complete with sections of a Roman street, baths and shops,
and remains of a Visigothic basilica. You
emerge, after passing two vaulted halls
containing displays on medieval Barcelona,
inside the former palace on the north side
of Plaça del Rei. To your right is the Saló
del Tinell and to the left ahead of you is the
Capella Reial de Santa Àgata.

The Saló del Tinell was the royal palace's throne hall, a masterpiece of strong,
unfussy Catalan Gothic, built in the mid-
14th century with wide, rounded arches
holding up a wooden roof. The Capella
Reial de Santa Àgata, whose spindly bell
tower rises from the northeast side of Plaça
del Rei, was the palace chapel and dates
from the same period. Rising above the
Saló del Tinell is the multi-tiered Mirador
del Rei Martí (Lookout Tower of King Martin), built in 1555 and closed to the public.

Palau del Lloctinent

(Viceroy's Palace; Map p234; Carrer dels Comtes;
◎10am-7pm; MJaume I) The southwest side
of Plaça del Rei is taken up by the Palau
del Lloctinent, built in the 1550s as the
residence of the Spanish viceroy of Catalonia and now home to part of the Arxiu de
la Corona d'Aragón. This unique archive
houses documents, from the 12th century
onwards, detailing the history of the Crown
of Aragón and Catalonia. Some of them appear in temporary exhibitions.

Museu Frederic Marès   MUSEUM

(Map p234; www.museumares.bcn.es; Plaça de
Sant Iu 5-6; ◎closed for renovation until 2011;
MJaume I) A short distance north of Plaça
del Rei is the Museu Frederic Marès, in another part of the Palau Reial Major. Marès
was a rich 20th-century Catalan sculptor and collector. He specialised in medieval Spanish sculpture, huge quantities of
which are displayed. In addition, there is a
mind-boggling array of other Marès knick-
knacks, from toy soldiers and cribs to scis-
sors and tarot cards, along with some of
his own sculptures. The shady courtyard
houses a pleasant summer cafe, Cafè de
l'Estiu (◎Apr-Oct), and a series of interactive screens that allow visitors to get an
idea of the collection while the museum
remains closed.

Roman Walls   ANCIENT WALLS

(Map p234) From Plaça del Rei it's worth
a detour to see the two best surviving
stretches of Barcelona's Roman walls. One
section is on the southeast side of Plaça de
Ramon Berenguer el Gran, with the Capella
Reial de Santa Àgata on top. The other is
further south, by the north end of Carrer
del Sots-tinent Navarro. They date from the
3rd and 4th centuries, when the Romans
rebuilt their walls after the first attacks by
Germanic tribes from the north.

Plaça de Sant Josep Oriol & Around

SQUARE, CHURCH

This small plaza is the prettiest in the Barri
Gòtic. Its bars and cafes attract buskers and
artists, and make it a lively place to hang out
for a while. It's surrounded by quaint streets,
many of them dotted with appealing cafes, timeless restaurants and cavernous old
shops. The Gothic Església de Santa Maria
del Pi (Map p234; ◎9.30am-1pm & 5-8.30pm;
MLiceu), completed in the 16th century,

BARCELONA SIGHTS

> **WANT MORE?**
>
> For in-depth information, reviews and
> recommendations at your fingertips,
> head to the Apple App Store to pur-
> chase Lonely Planet's *Barcelona City
> Guide* iPhone app.
>   Alternatively, head to Lonely
> Planet (www.lonelyplanet.com/Spain/
> Barcelona) for planning advice, author
> recommendations, traveller reviews
> and insider tips.

TOP FIVE FOR ART LOVERS

» Museu Nacional d'Art de Catalunya (p261)

» Museu Picasso (p241)

» Fundació Joan Miró (p263)

» Museu d'Art Contemporani de Barcelona (p238)

» Fundació Antoni Tàpies (p255)

dominates the square. The beautiful rose window above its entrance on Plaça del Pi is reputedly the world's biggest. Anarchists' fire gutted the church's interior in 1936 and most of the stained glass is modern.

Sinagoga Major
SYNAGOGUE

(Main Synagogue; Map p234; www.calldebarce lona.org; Carrer de Marlet 5; admission €2 donation; ⊙10.30am-6pm Mon-Fri, 10.30am-3pm Sat & Sun; ⓂLiceu) The area between Carrer dels Banys Nous, to the east of the Església de Santa Maria del Pi, and Plaça de Sant Jaume is known as the Call, and was Barcelona's **Jewish quarter** – and centre of learning – from at least the 11th century until anti-Semitism saw the Jews expelled from it in 1424. Here the sparse remains of what is purported to be the medieval Sinagoga Major have been revealed and returned to occasional use as a functioning temple. Remnants of medieval and Roman-era walls remain, suggesting (given their orientation towards Jerusalem) that there may have been a Jewish place of worship here in Roman times.

Plaça Reial & Around
SQUARE

Just south of Carrer de Ferran, Plaça Reial (Map p234) is an elegant shady square surrounded by eateries, nightspots and budget accommodation. Its 19th-century neoclassical architecture (which replaced a centuries-old monastery) would be at home in some Parisian quarter (although the palm trees wouldn't). The lamp posts next to the central fountain are Gaudí's first known works in the city.

Until 1990 the square and surrounding streets had long been a den of poverty, drug abuse and prostitution. A whiff of its dodgy past remains, in the form of a few down-and-outs and the occasional pickpocket. Today mostly locals and tourists fill the square's bars and restaurants with chatter and laughter, while coppers look on.

EL RAVAL

West of La Rambla, Ciutat Vella spreads to Ronda de Sant Antoni, Ronda de Sant Pau and Avinguda del Paral.lel, which together trace the line of Barcelona's 14th-century walls. Known as El Raval, the area contains what remains of one of the city's slums, the dwindling but still seedy red-light zone and drug abusers' haunt of the Barri Xinès, at its south end. It's not nearly as tricky as it once was, but watch your pockets nonetheless.

Museu d'Art Contemporani de Barcelona
MUSEUM

(Macba; Map p240; www.macba.cat; Plaça dels Àngels 1; adult/concession €7.50/6; ⊙11am-8pm Mon & Wed, 11am-midnight Thu-Fri, 10am-8pm Sat, 10am-3pm Sun & holidays; ⓂUniversitat) The vast, white Museu d'Art Contemporani de Barcelona is a temple to contemporary art. Artists frequently on show include Antoni Tàpies, Miquel Barceló and a host of 'very now' installation artists. Several temporary exhibitions are always going on at once in this busy gallery, the most important of its kind in the city.

On the south side of the square is the Gothic shell of the 16th-century Convent dels Àngels, now known as the Capella Macba, where part of the Macba's permanent exhibition is shown.

Centre de Cultura Contemporània de Barcelona

(CCCB; Map p240; www.cccb.org; Carrer de Montalegre 5; adult/senior & student €4.50/3.40; ⊙11am-8pm Tue-Wed & Fri-Sun, 11am-10pm Thu; ⓂUniversitat) Behind Macba, the Centre de Cultura Contemporània de Barcelona is a complex of auditoriums and exhibition halls created in the early 1990s from an 18th-century hospice. The big courtyard, with a vast glass wall on one side, is spectacular. Exhibitions are held here regularly. Admission is free from 8pm Thursdays and from 3pm Sundays and on the first Wednesday of the month.

FREE **Antic Hospital de la Santa Creu**
LIBRARY

(Map p240; www.bnc.cat; Carrer de l'Hospital 56; ⊙library 9am-8pm Mon-Fri, 9am-2pm Sat) Two blocks southeast of Plaça dels Àngels is an architectural masterpiece from another age. Founded in the early 15th century as the city's main hospital, the Antic Hospital de la Santa Creu today houses the **Biblioteca de Catalunya** (Catalonia's national

BARCELONA

library). Take a look inside to admire some fine Catalan Gothic construction. The adjacent **Institut d'Estudis Catalans** was, in the 17th century, a house of convalescence. The tile-decorated main cloister is well worth a peek if it's open.

FREE **La Capella** (www.bcn.cat/lacapella; ☉noon-2pm & 4-8pm Tue-Sat, 11am-2pm Sun & holidays), the former hospital's now rather bare one-time chapel, is used for temporary exhibitions.

FREE **Palau Güell** MODERNISTA MANSION (Map p240; www.palauguell.cat; Carrer Nou de la Rambla 3-5; ☉10am-2.30pm Tue-Sat; MDrassanes) Gaudí's Palau Güell is the only major Modernista building in Ciutat Vella. Gaudí built it in the late 1880s for his most constant patron, the industrialist Eusebi Güell. It lacks some of Gaudí's later playfulness but is still a characteristic riot of styles – art nouveau, Gothic, Islamic – and materials. After the civil war, police took it over and tortured political prisoners in the basement.

Features to look out for include the carved wooden ceilings and fireplace, the stonework, the use of mirrors, stained glass and wrought iron, and the main hall with its dome reaching right up to the roof. The roof is a weird world of fantastically shaped and polychrome-tiled chimney pots. At the time of writing, only the ground floor and basement could be visited due to ongoing restoration.

Església de Sant Pau CHURCH (Map p240; Carrer de Sant Pau 101; ☉cloister 10am-1pm & 4-7pm Mon-Sat; MParal.lel) The best example of Romanesque architecture in the city is the dainty little cloister of this church. Set in a somewhat dusty garden, the 12th-century church also boasts some Visigothic sculptural detail on the main entrance.

Museu Marítim MUSEUM (Map p240; www.mmb.cat; Avinguda de les Drassanes; adult/senior & student €2.50/1.25; ☉10am-8pm; MDrassanes) The once mighty Reials Drassanes (Royal Shipyards) are now home to the Museu Marítim, a rare work of civil Gothic architecture that was once the launch pad for medieval fleets. The museum, together with its setting, forms a fascinating tribute to the seafaring that shaped much of Barcelona's history. You can take a load off afterwards in the pleasant restaurant-cafe.

The shipyards, first built in the 13th century, gained their present form (a series of long bays divided by stone arches) a century later. Extensions in the 17th century made them big enough to handle the construction of 30 galleons at any one time. In their shipbuilding days (up to the 18th century), the sea came right up to them.

The centre of the shipyards is dominated by a full-sized replica (made in the 1970s) of Don Juan of Austria's flagship. A clever audiovisual display aboard the vessel brings to life the ghastly existence of the slaves, prisoners and volunteers (!) who at full steam could haul this vessel along at nine knots. The museum was being largely overhauled at the time of writing, so only part of the display was on show. It's free on Sundays after 3pm.

LA RIBERA

La Ribera is cut off from the Barri Gòtic by noisy Via Laietana, which was driven through the city in 1908. La Ribera, whose name refers to the waterfront that once lay much further inland, was the pumping commercial heart of medieval Barcelona. Its intriguing, narrow streets house major sights, and good bars and restaurants, mainly in the too-cool-for-school El Born area around Passeig del Born.

Palau de la Música Catalana
MODERNISTA THEATRE (Palace of Catalan Music; ☎902 47 54 85; www.palaumusica.org; Carrer de Sant Francesc de Paula 2; adult/student & EU senior €12/10; ☉10am-3.30pm; MUrquinaona) The Palau de la Música Catalana is a Modernista high point and World Heritage Site. It's not exactly a symphony, more a series of crescendos in tile, brick, sculpted stone and stained glass. Built between 1905 and 1908 by Lluís Domènech i Montaner for the Orfeo Català musical society, it was conceived as a temple for the Catalan Renaixença, the cultural Renaissance of the late 19th century.

You can see some of its splendours – such as the main facade with its mosaics, floral capitals and sculpture cluster representing Catalan popular music – from the outside and wander into the foyer to admire the lovely tiled pillars and decor of the cafe and ticket-office area.

Best of all, however, is the richly coloured auditorium upstairs, with its ceiling of blue-and-gold stained glass and, above

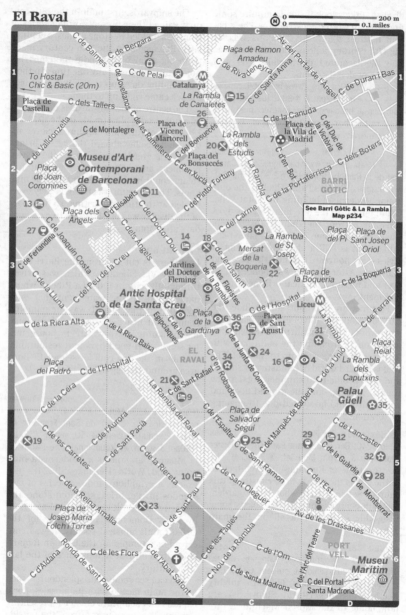

See Barri Gòtic & La Rambla Map p234

a bust of Beethoven, a towering sculpture of Wagner's Valkyrie (Wagner was number one on the Renaixença charts). To see this, you need to attend a concert or join a guided tour (which last 50 minutes and start on the hour).

To get to the Palau, turn left off Via Laietana into Carrer de Sant Francesc de Paula or Carrer de Sant Pere més Alt, a short way south of Plaça de Urquinaona.

Museu Picasso   MUSEUM
(Map p242; www.museupicasso.bcn.es; Carrer de Montcada 15-23; adult/student €9/6; ☺10am-8pm Tue-Sun & holidays; Ⓜ Jaume I) Barcelona's most visited museum occupies five of the many fine medieval stone mansions (worth wandering into for their courtyards and galleries) on narrow Carrer de Montcada. This collection is uniquely fascinating, concentrating on Picasso's formative years and several specific moments in his later life, but those interested primarily in cubism may not be satisfied. There are additional charges for special exhibitions; entry is free from 3pm Sundays and all day the first Sunday of the month. Allow two hours.

The museum's permanent collection is housed in the first three houses, the **Palau Aguilar**, **Palau del Baró de Castellet** and the **Palau Meca**, all dating to the 14th century. The 18th-century **Casa Mauri**, built over some medieval remains (even some Roman leftovers have been identified), and the adjacent 14th-century **Palau Finestres** accommodate temporary exhibitions.

A visit starts, naturally enough, at the beginning, with sketches, oils and doodling from Picasso's earliest years in Málaga and La Coruña – most of it done between 1893 and 1895. Some of his self-portraits, and the portraits of his father, which date from 1896, are evidence enough of his precocious talent. The enormous *Ciència i Caritat* (Science and Charity) is proof to anyone that, had he wanted, Picasso would have made a fine conventional artist. His first consciously thematic adventure, the Blue Period, is well covered. His nocturnal blue-tinted views of *Terrats de Barcelona* (Rooftops of Barcelona) and *El Foll* (The Madman) are cold and cheerless, yet somehow spectrally alive.

Among the later works, done in Cannes in 1957, *Las Meninas* is a complex technical series of studies on Diego Velázquez' masterpiece of the same name (which hangs in the Prado in Madrid).

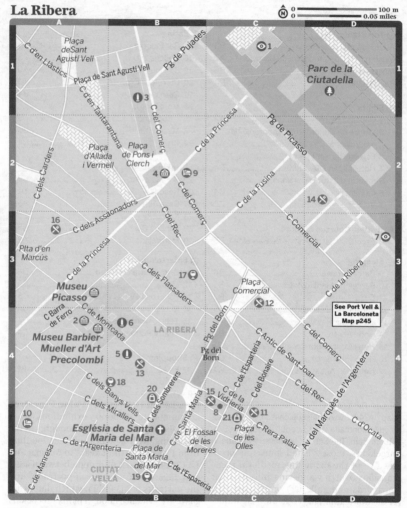

Museu Barbier-Mueller d'Art Precolombí MUSEUM

(Map p242; www.barbier-mueller.ch; Carrer de Montcada 14; adult/senior & student €3/1.50; ☺11am-7pm Tue-Fri, 10am-7pm Sat, 10am-3pm Sun & holidays; MJaumeI) Occupying Palau Nadal, this museum holds part of one of the world's most prestigious collections of pre-Colombian art, including gold jewellery, ceramics, statues and textiles. The artefacts from indigenous South American cultures come from the collections of the Swiss businessman Josef Mueller (1887–1977) and his son-in-law Jean-Paul Barbier, who directs

the Musée Barbier-Mueller in Geneva. The museum is small but the pieces are outstanding and often rotated, so that the exhibition is never quite the same on return visits. Admission is free on the first Sunday of the month.

Disseny Hub MUSEUM

(Map p242; www.dhub-bcn.cat; Carrer de Montcada 12; adult/senior & student €5/3; ☺11am-7pm Tue-Sat, 11am-8pm Sun, 11am-3pm holidays; MJaumeI)

The 13th-century Palau dels Marquesos de Lió is temporary home to part of the city's Disseny (Design) Hub collection of applied

BARCELONA SIGHTS

arts, which will eventually come together in the centre being built at Plaça de les Glòries (due to open in 2011). This building is used for temporary exhibitions. The building's courtyard, with its cafe-restaurant, makes a delightful stop. Admission includes entrance to the Palau Reial de Pedralbes branch (p260); entrance is free from 3pm Sundays.

Carrer de Montcada   MEDIEVAL STREET
Several other mansions on this street, once home to Barcelona's wealthy merchant barons, are now commercial art galleries, where you're welcome to browse. The 16th-century Palau dels Cervelló, for instance, houses the Galeria Maeght (Map p242; Carrer de Montcada 25), a branch of the renowned Paris gallery. The baroque courtyard of the originally medieval Palau de Dalmases (Map p242; Carrer de Montcada 20) is one of the finest on the strip and home to a rather over-the-top, rococo bar.

Església de Santa Maria del Mar CHURCH
(Map p242; Plaça de Santa Maria del Mar; ⊙9am-1.30pm & 4.30-8pm; ⓜJaume I) Carrer de Montcada opens at its southeast end into Passeig del Born, a plaza that once rang to the cheers and jeers of medieval jousting tournaments, today replaced at night by animated carousing. At its southwest tip rises Barcelona's finest Gothic church,

the Església de Santa Maria del Mar. Built in the 14th century, Santa Maria was lacking in superfluous decoration even before anarchists gutted it in 1909 and 1936. This only serves to highlight its fine proportions, purity of line and sense of space. You may occasionally catch an evening recital of baroque music.

Mercat de Santa Caterina   MARKET
(www.mercatsantacaterina.net, in Catalan; Avinguda de Francesc Cambó 16; ⊙7.30am-2pm Mon, 7.30am-3.30pm Tue, Wed & Sat, 7.30am-8.30pm Thu & Fri; ⓜJaume I) A 19th-century market, built on the site of a 15th-century monastery, made way in 2005 for this original, colourful version designed by the adventurous Catalan architect Enric Miralles. The outstanding element is the bright, ceramic-covered, wavy roof – a splash of pastel loopiness. Out the back, remnants of the monastery, known as the Espai Santa Caterina (admission free; ⊙8.30am-2pm Mon-Wed & Sat, 8.30am-8pm Thu & Fri), uncovered during excavations, are on public show with explanatory panels. Heading towards the waterfront along Via Laietana, the market is off to the left on Avinguda de Francesc Cambó.

Museu de la Xocolata   MUSEUM
(Chocolate Museum; Map p242; http://pastisseria.com; Plaça de Pons i Clerch; adult/senior & student €4.30/3.65; ⊙10am-7pm Mon-Sat, 10am-3pm Sun & holidays; ⓜJaume I) In the Museu de

TOP FIVE MUSEUMS

» CosmoCaixa (p258)

» Museu Marítim (p239)

» Museu d'Història de Barcelona (p236)

» Museu Barbier-Mueller d'Art Preco-lombí (p242)

» Palau Reial de Pedralbes (p260)

la Xocolata, you can trace the origins of this fundamental foodstuff and admire (but not chomp into!) somewhat cheesy chocolate models of things like La Sagrada Família. The museum is housed in part of the one-time **Convent de Sant Agustí**, which boasts a pleasant bar in what remains of the cloister at Carrer del Comerç 36.

Arxiu Fotogràfic de Barcelona

(www.bcn.cat/arxiu/fotografic; ⊙10am-7pm Mon-Sat) Upstairs from the Museu de la Xocolata, the Arxiu Fotogràfic de Barcelona has modest photo exhibitions on subjects connected to the city.

Museu del Rei de la Màgia   MUSEUM

(Map p234; ✆93 319 73 93; www.elreydelamagia.com; Carrer de l'Oli 6; admission without/with show €3/8; ⊙6-8pm Thu, shows 6pm Sat & noon Sun; Ⓜ Jaume I) This museum is a timeless curio. Run by a magician couple who have a 19th-century magic shop at Carrer de la Princesa 11, it is the scene of magic shows and home to a fascinating collection of magicians' paraphernalia dating back more than a century.

Parc de la Ciutadella   PARK

(Map p242; ⊙8am-9pm; Ⓜ Arc de Triomf) East of La Ribera and north of La Barceloneta, the gentle Parc de la Ciutadella makes a fine antidote to the noise and bustle of the city.

After the War of the Spanish Succession, Felipe V built a huge fort (La Ciutadella) to keep watch over Barcelona. Only in 1869 did the government allow its demolition, after which the site was turned into a park and used to host the Universal Exhibition of 1888.

The monumental **Cascada** near the Passeig de les Pujades entrance was created between 1875 and 1881 by Josep Fontsère, with the help of a young Antoni Gaudí. It's a dramatic combination of classical statuary, rugged rocks, greenery and thundering water.

Northwest of the park is the imposing Modernista **Arc de Triomf** (Passeig de Lluís Companys), with unusual, Islamic-style brickwork.

Castell dels Tres Dragons

Along the Passeig de Picasso side of the park are several buildings created for the Universal Exhibition. These include two arboretums and the Castell dels Tres Dragons (Three Dragons Castle), which until 2010 housed a zoology museum. It is a whimsical effort by Lluís Domènech i Montaner, who added medieval-castle trimmings on a pioneering steel frame. Designed as a temporary cafe to be knocked down after the exhibition, it has stood the test of time.

Parlament de Catalunya

(www.parlament.cat; ⊙10am-7pm Sat, 10am-2pm Sun & holidays) Southeast, in the fort's former arsenal, is the regional Parlament de Catalunya. Head up the sweeping **Escala d'Honor** (Stairway of Honour) and through several solemn halls to the **Saló de Sessions**, the semicircular auditorium where parliament sits. You can join free guided tours. It also opens on the first Friday of the month and on 11 and 12 September.

Zoo de Barcelona

(Map p245; www.zoobarcelona.com; Passeig de Picasso & Carrer de Wellington; adult/child €16/9.60; ⊙10am-7pm; Ⓜ Barceloneta) The south end of the park is occupied by the Zoo de Barcelona, which holds about 7500 living thingies, from gorillas to insects.

PORT VELL

Barcelona's old port at the bottom of La Rambla, to the west of La Barceloneta, was transformed in the 1990s to become a popular leisure zone.

Moll de la Fusta   PROMENADE

Northeast from the quay stretches the promenade Moll de la Fusta. Usually the **Pailebot de Santa Eulàlia** (adult/senior & student €2.50/1.25; ⊙noon-7.30pm Tue-Fri, 10am-7pm Sat, Sun & holidays; Ⓜ Drassanes), a fully functioning 1918 schooner restored by the Museu Marítim, is moored here for visits, although sometimes it's off on the high seas; admission is free with a Museu Marítim ticket.

Moll d'Espanya   PROMENADE

The heart of the redeveloped harbour is Moll d'Espanya, a former wharf linked to Moll de la Fusta by a wave-shaped footbridge,

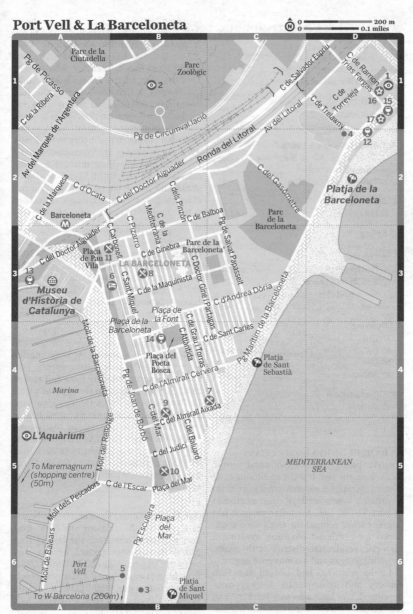

Rambla de Mar, which rotates to let boats enter the marina behind it. At the end of Moll d'Espanya is the glossy **Maremàgnum** shopping and eating complex, but the major attraction is **L'Aquàrium** (Map p245; www. aquariumbcn.com; Moll d'Espanya; adult/child €17.50/12.50; ⊗9.30am-9.30pm; Ⓜ Drassanes), with its 80m-long shark tunnel. Short of diving among them (which can be arranged here too), this is as close as you can get to a set of shark teeth without being bitten. Beyond L'Aquàrium is the big-screen **Imax cinema**.

Port Vell & La Barceloneta

LA BARCELONETA & THE COAST

It used to be said that Barcelona had 'turned its back on the sea', but the ambitious 1992 Olympics-inspired redevelopment program returned a long stretch of coast northeast of Port Vell to life. A similar process has largely turned around the city's once abandoned far northeast coastline, creating a high-rise residential district with parks, swimming areas and a conference centre.

La Barceloneta, laid out in the 18th century and subsequently heavily overdeveloped, was long a factory workers' and fishermen's quarter. It retains a gritty flavour, although the factories are a distant memory and there are unmistakable signs of gentrification. Some fishing families remain and the area is laced with seafood restaurants. Barcelona's small fishing fleet ties up along the Moll del Rellotge, south of the Museu d'Història de Catalunya.

Museu d'Història de Catalunya   MUSEUM

(Map p245; www.mhcat.net; Plaça de Pau Vila 3; permanent exhibition adult/student €4/3; ☉10am-7pm Tue & Thu-Sat, 10am-8pm Wed, 10am-2.30pm Sun & holidays; Ⓜ Barceloneta) This museum, in the Palau de Mar building (former warehouses) facing the harbour, incorporates lots of audiovisuals and interactive information points in a series of colourful displays recounting Catalonia's tumultuous past from prehistory to the 1980s. All sorts of scenes are re-created, from a Pyrenean cave dwelling through to a Roman house and a Spanish Civil War air-raid shelter. It's a little cheesy and short on real artefacts, but engaging enough. Admission is free on the first Sunday of the month.

Passeig Marítim de la Barceloneta
PROMENADE

On La Barceloneta's seaward side are the first of Barcelona's beaches, which are popular on summer weekends. The pleasant Passeig Marítim de la Barceloneta, a 1.25km promenade from La Barceloneta to Port Olímpic, is a haunt for strollers and rollers, so bring your rollerblades.

Port Olímpic   MARINA

(Ⓜ Ciutadella Vila Olímpica) A busy marina built for the Olympic sailing events, Port Olímpic is surrounded by bars and restaurants. An eye-catcher on the approach from La Barceloneta is Frank Gehry's giant copper *Peix* (Fish) sculpture. The area behind Port Olímpic, dominated by twin-tower blocks (the luxury Hotel Arts Barcelona and the Torre Mapfre office block), is the former Vila Olímpica living quarters for the Olympic competitors, which was later sold off as apartments.

El Fòrum   DEVELOPMENT PROJECT

(Ⓜ El Maresme-Fòrum) More and better beaches stretch northeast along the coast from Port Olímpic. They reach the largely completed development project known variously as Diagonal Mar and El Fòrum. Aside from high-rise hotels and apartment blocks looking out to sea, highlights include the protected swimming area, a marina, kids' playgrounds, good spots for rollerblading and skating, and the weird, triangular Edifici Fòrum building by Swiss architects Herzog & de Meuron. The navy blue raised facades look like sheer cliff faces, with angular crags cut into them as if by divine laser. It is being transformed into the Espai Blau (Blue Space), a modern showcase for

the Museu de Ciències Naturals (www.bcn.
es/museuciencies), which will be installed in
2011. Eventually the city zoo will be relocated to a waterfront position here too.

L'EIXAMPLE

Stretching north, east and west of Plaça de
Catalunya, L'Eixample (the Extension) was
Barcelona's 19th-century answer to overcrowding in the medieval city.

Work on it began in 1869, following a design by architect Ildefons Cerdà, who specified a grid of wide streets with plazas that
were formed by their cut-off corners. Cerdà
also planned numerous public green spaces, but few survived the ensuing scramble
for real estate. Only now are some being
recreated in the interior of some blocks.

L'Eixample was inhabited from the start
by the city's middle classes and that remains broadly the case. The development of
L'Eixample coincided with the city's Modernisme period and so it's home to many Modernista creations. These constitute the area's
main sightseeing attractions and, apart
from La Sagrada Família, the principal ones
are clustered on or near L'Eixample's main
avenue, Passeig de Gràcia.

Along the area's grid of straight streets
are the majority of the city's most expensive
shops and hotels, plus a range of eateries,
bars and clubs.

La Sagrada Família   CHURCH
(Temple Expiatori de la Sagrada Família; www.sa
gradafamilia.org; Carrer de Mallorca 401; adult/
senior & student €12/10; ⊙9am-8pm; MSagrada
Família) If you only have time for one sightseeing outing, this should be it. La Sagrada
Família inspires awe with its sheer verticality and, in the true manner of the great
medieval cathedrals it emulates, it's still not
finished after more than 100 years. Work is
proceeding apace, however, and it might be
done between the 2020s and 2040s. If the
work should be carried on is the subject of
controversy, but Spain's most visited monument was consecrated by Pope Benedict
XVI in late 2010. The main nave is now open
for daily mass. Feathers were much ruffled
by the high-speed train tunnel project, on
which work began in 2010, that will pass in
front of the church under Carrer de Mallorca. Church authorities fear that the tunnelling could damage the church's foundations.

You could spend a couple of hours in
here – the more you scrutinize decorative
details, the more you see.

The church was the project to which
Antoni Gaudí dedicated the latter part of
his life. He stuck to a basic Gothic crossshaped ground plan, but devised a temple
95m long and 60m wide, with capacity for
13,000 people. The completed sections and
museum can be explored at leisure. Up
to four daily guided tours (€4), lasting 50
minutes, are offered. You can enter from
Carrer de Sardenya and Carrer de la Marina. Audioguides (€4) are available and it
costs a further €2.50 per ride on the lifts
that take you up inside one of the towers on
each side of the church. Combined tickets
with Casa-Museu Gaudí in Park Güell are
available.

Nativity Facade

The northeast Nativity Facade is the Sagrada Família's artistic pinnacle and was partly completed under Gaudí's personal supervision. You can climb high up inside some
of the four towers by a combination of lifts
and narrow spiral staircases – a vertiginous
experience. The towers are destined to hold
tubular bells capable of playing complicated music at great volume. Beneath the towers is a tall, three-part portal on the theme
of Christ's birth and childhood. It seems to
lean outwards as you stand beneath, looking up. Gaudí used real people and animals
as models for many of the sculptures, along
with the occasional corpse from the local
morgue! The three sections of the portal
represent, from left to right, Hope, Charity
and Faith. Among the forest of sculpture on
the Charity portal, you can make out, low
down, the manger surrounded by an ox, an
ass, the shepherds and kings, with angel
musicians above.

Passion Facade

The southwest Passion Facade, which has
the theme of Christ's last days and death,
has been constructed since the 1950s with,
like the Nativity Facade, four needling towers and a large, sculpture-bedecked portal.
The sculptor, Josep Subirachs, worked on
its decoration from 1986 to 2006. He did
not attempt to imitate Gaudí, rather producing angular, controversial images that
people tend to love or loathe. The main series of sculptures, on three levels, are in an
S-shaped sequence starting with the Last
Supper at the bottom left and ending with
Christ's burial at the top right.

(Continued on page 252)

La Sagrada Família

A TIMELINE

1882 Francesc del Villar is commissioned to construct a neo-Gothic church.

1883 Antoni Gaudí takes over as chief architect, and plans a far more ambitious church to hold 13,000 faithful.

1926 Death of Gaudí; work continues under Domènec Sugrañes. Much of the apse **1** and Nativity Facade **2** is complete.

1930 Bell towers **3** of the Nativity Facade completed.

1936 Construction is interrupted by Spanish Civil War; anarchists destroy Gaudí's plans.

1939-40 Architect Francesc de Paula Quintana i Vidal restores the crypt and meticulously reassembles many of Gaudí's lost models, some of which can be seen in the museum **4**.

1976 Completion of Passion Facade **5**.

1986-2006 Sculptor Josep Subirachs adds sculptural details to the Passion Facade including the panels telling the story of Christ's last days, amid much criticism for employing a style far removed from what was thought typical of Gaudí.

2000 Central nave vault **6** completed.

2010 Church completely roofed over; Pope Benedict XVI consecrates the church; work begins on a high-speed rail tunnel that will pass beneath the church's Glory Facade **7**.

2020-2040 Projected completion date.

KRZYSZTOF DYDYNSKI

TOP TIPS

» **Light** The best light through the stained-glass windows of the Passion Facade bursts through into the heart of the church in the late afternoon.

» **Time** Visit at opening time on weekdays to avoid the worst of the crowds.

» **Views** Head up the Nativity façade bell towers for the views, as long as queues generally await at the Passion Facade towers.

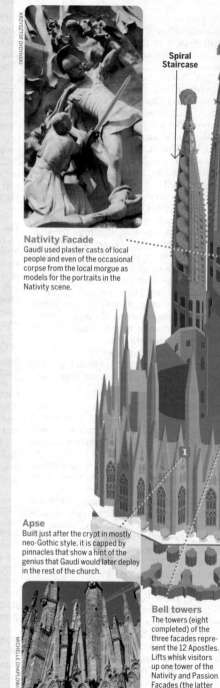

Spiral Staircase

Nativity Facade
Gaudí used plaster casts of local people and even of the occasional corpse from the local morgue as models for the portraits in the Nativity scene.

Apse
Built just after the crypt in mostly neo-Gothic style, it is capped by pinnacles that show a hint of the genius that Gaudí would later deploy in the rest of the church.

Bell towers
The towers (eight completed) of the three facades represent the 12 Apostles. Lifts whisk visitors up one tower of the Nativity and Passion Facades (the latter gets longer queues) for fine views.

MICHELLE CHAPLOW/ALAMY

Passion Facade
See the story of Christ's last days from Last Supper to burial in an S-shaped sequence from bottom to top of the facade. Check out the cryptogram in which the numbers always add up to 33, Christ's age.

STEPHEN SAAS

Completed church
Along with the Glory Facade and its four towers, six other towers remain to the completed. They will represent the four Evangelists, the Virgin Mary and, soaring above them all over the transept, a 170m colossus symbolising Christ.

Crypt
The first part of the church built, the crypt is in largely neo-Gothic style and lies under the transept. Gaudí's burial place here can be seen from the Museu Gaudí.

Escoles de Gaudi

Museu Gaudí
Jammed with old photos, drawings and restored plaster models that bring Gaudí's ambitions to life, the museum also houses an extraordinarily complex plumb-line device he used to calculate his constructions.

MANUEL COHEN/GETTY IMAGES

Glory Facade
This will be the most fanciful facade of all, with a narthex boasting 16 hyperboloid lanterns topped by cones that will look something like an organ made of melting ice cream.

Gaudí Genius

The name Gaudí has become a byword for Barcelona and, through his unique architectural wonders, one of the principal magnets for visitors to the city.

Born in Reus and initially trained in metalwork, Antoni Gaudí i Cornet (1852–1926) personifies, and largely transcends, the Modernisme movement that brought a thunderclap of innovative greatness to turn-of-the-century Barcelona. A devout Catholic and Catalan nationalist, his creations were a conscious expression of Catalan identity and, in some cases, of great piety.

He devoted much of the latter part of his life to what remains Barcelona's call sign: the unfinished Sagrada Família. His inspiration in the first instance was Gothic, but he also sought to emulate the harmony he observed in nature, eschewing the straight line and favouring curvaceous forms.

Gaudí used complex string models weighted with plumb lines to make his calculations. You can see examples in the upstairs mini-museum in La Pedrera.

The architect's work is an earthy appeal to sinewy movement, but often with a dreamlike or surreal quality. The private apartment house Casa Batlló is a fine example in which all appears a riot of the unnaturally natural – or the naturally unnatural. Not only are straight lines eliminated, but the lines between real and unreal, sober and dream-drunk, good sense and play are all blurred. Depending on how you look at the facade, you might see St George defeating a dragon, or a series of fleshless sea monsters straining out of the wall.

He seems to have particularly enjoyed himself with rooftops. At La Pedrera and Palau Güell in particular, he created all sorts of fantastical, multicoloured tile figures as chimney pots, looking like anything from *Alice in Wonderland* mushrooms to *Star Wars* imperial troopers.

KRZYSZTOF DYDYNSKI

Much like his work in progress, La Sagrada Família, Gaudí's story is far from over. In March 2000 the Vatican decided to proceed with the examination of the case for canonising him and pilgrims already stop by the crypt to pay him homage. One of the key sculptors at work on the church, the Japanese Etsuro Sotoo, converted to Catholicism because of his passion for Gaudí.

GAUDÍ'S BEST

» La Sagrada Família (p247), a symphony of religious devotion
» La Pedrera (p255), dubbed 'the Quarry' because of its flowing facade
» Casa Batlló (p254), a fairy-tale dragon
» Park Güell (p257), a park full of Modernista twists
» Palau Güell (p239), one of Gaudí's earliest commissions

Clockwise from top left
1. Casa Batlló (p254) 2. La Pedrera (p255) 3. Palau Güell (p239)

KIMBERLEY COOLE

(Continued from page 247)

Apse

The semicircular apse was the first part to be finished (in 1894). The interior of the church remains a building site but it was roofed over in 2010. A forest of extraordinary angled pillars soars up and branches out to support the roof. The image of the tree canopy, pierced by shafts of light tinted by the stained glass windows, was part of Gaudí's vision.

L'Eixample

Glory Facade

The Glory Facade is under construction and will, like the others, be crowned by four towers – the total of 12 representing the 12 apostles. Further decoration will make the whole building a microcosmic symbol of the Christian church, with Christ represented by a massive 170m central tower above the transept, and the five remaining planned towers symbolising the Virgin Mary and the four evangelists.

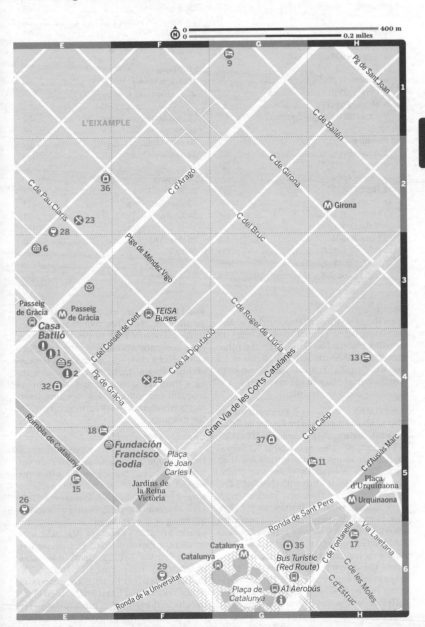

L'Eixample

Museu Gaudí

Open the same times as the church, the Museu Gaudí, below ground level, includes interesting material on Gaudí's life and other works, as well as models and photos of La Sagrada Família. You can look down onto Gaudí's burial place in the crypt below the museum (under the transept).

Casa Batlló — MODERNISTA MANSION

(Map p252; www.casabatllo.es; Passeig de Gràcia 43; adult/student, child & senior €17.80/14.25; ⏰9am-8pm; Ⓜ Passeig de Gràcia) If La Sagrada Família is his master symphony, then Casa Batlló is Gaudí's whimsical waltz. The facade, sprinkled with bits of blue, mauve and green tiles, and studded with wave-shaped window frames and balconies, rises to an uneven blue-tiled roof with a solitary tower. The roof represents Sant Jordi (St George) and the dragon, and if you stare long enough at the building, it almost seems like a living being. Inside the main salon overlooking Passeig de Gràcia everything swirls. The ceiling is twisted into a vortex around a sun-like lamp. The doors, windows and skylights are dreamy waves of wood and coloured glass. The same themes continue in the other rooms and covered terrace. The roof, with its twisting chimney pots, is equally astonishing, and provides a chance for a close-up look at the St George-and-the-dragon motif that dominates the view from the street. Queues to get in are frequent and, on occasion, opening hours can be shortened, so try turning up early in the morning.

Casa Lleó Morera & Casa Amatller — MODERNISTA MANSIONS

On the same block as Casa Batlló are two utterly different houses by the other two senior figures of Modernista architecture: Lluís Domènech i Montaner's Casa Lleó Morera (Map p252; Passeig de Gràcia 35; Ⓜ Passeig de Gràcia), which is closed to the public; and Casa Amatller (Map p252; www.amatller.org; Passeig de Gràcia 41; admission free; ⏰10am-8pm Mon-Sat, 10am-3pm Sun; Ⓜ Passeig de Gràcia) by Josep Puig i Cadafalch. The former is swathed in art nouveau carving on the outside and has a bright, tiled lobby, in which floral motifs predominate. The latter is altogether different, with Gothic-style window frames, a stepped gable borrowed from the urban architecture of the Netherlands, and all sorts of unlikely sculptures and busts jutting out. The pillared foyer and the staircase lit by stained glass are like the inside of some romantic castle. The building was renovated in 1900 for the chocolate baron and philanthropist Antoni Amatller (1851–1910) and is partly open to the public. Renovation due for completion in 2012 will see the 1st (main) floor converted into a museum with period pieces.

Museu del Perfum MUSEUM

(Map p252; www.museudelperfum.com; Passeig de Gràcia 39; adult/student & senior €5/3; ⊙10.30am-1.30pm & 4.30-8pm Mon-Fri, 11am-2pm Sat; MPasseig de Gràcia) The Museu del Perfum, in the Regia store between Casa Lleó Morera and Casa Amatller, contains everything from ancient scent receptacles to classic eau-de-cologne bottles.

La Pedrera MODERNISTA MANSION

(The Quarry; Map p252; www.fundaciocaixacata lunya.es; Carrer de Provença 261-265; adult/student & EU senior €10/6; ⊙9am-8pm; MDiagonal) Built between 1905 and 1910 as a combined apartment and office block, this is one of Gaudí's undisputed masterpieces. Formally called the Casa Milà, after the businessman who commissioned it, it's better known as La Pedrera because of its uneven grey-stone facade, which ripples around the corner of Carrer de Provença. The wave effect is emphasised by elaborate wrought-iron balconies. Queues are frequent, so early morning is the best time to try to get in.

Visit the lavish top-floor flat, attic and roof, together known as the **Espai Gaudí** (Gaudí Space). The roof is the most extraordinary element, with its giant chimney pots looking like multicoloured sci-fi versions of medieval knights. In the attic, where you can appreciate Gaudí's gracious parabolic arches, is a modest museum dedicated to his work. Models and videos bring to life explanations of each of his buildings.

Downstairs on the next floor the apartment (El Pis de la Pedrera) spreads out. It is fascinating to wander around this elegantly furnished home, done up in the style a well-to-do family might have enjoyed in the early 20th century. Don't be surprised if you feel like moving in.

Some of the lower floors of the building, especially the grand 1st floor, often host temporary expositions. On hot August eve-nings, La Pedrera usually stages a series of brief concerts on the roof.

Fundació Antoni Tàpies MUSEUM

(Map p252; www.fundaciotapies.org; Carrer d'Aragó 255; adult/child €7/5.60; ⊙10am-8pm Tue-Sun; MPasseig de Gràcia) Around the corner from Casa Batlló, the Fundació is a pioneering Modernista building of the early 1880s, as well as a homage to, and by, the elder statesman of contemporary Catalan art, Antoni Tàpies. The collection spans the arc of his creations (with more than 800 works) but only a fraction of these is ever on show, always in conjunction with other temporary exhibitions. In the main exhibition area (level 1, upstairs), you can see an ever-changing selection of around 20 of Tàpies's works, from early self-portraits of the 1940s to grand items like *Jersei Negre* (Black Jumper; 2008), in which the outline of a man with a hard-on is topped with a pasted-on black sweater. Level 2 hosts a small space for temporary exhibitions. Rotating exhibitions take place in the basement levels.

Museu del Modernisme Català MUSEUM

(Map p252; www.mmcat.cat; Carrer de Balmes 48; adult/child €10/5; ⊙10am-8pm Mon-Sat, 10am-3pm Sun; MPasseig de Gràcia) Housed in a Modernista building, the ground floor of this museum seems like a big Modernista furniture showroom. Several items by Antoni Gaudí, including chairs from Casa Batlló and a mirror from Casa Calvet, are supplemented by a host of items by his lesser-known contemporaries, including some typically whimsical, mock-medieval pieces by Josep Puig i

APPLE OF DISCORD

Casa Batlló is the centrepiece of the so-called Manzana de la Discordia (Apple of Discord – in a play on words, *manzana* means both city block and apple), along with Casa Lleó Morera and Casa Amatller, on the western side of Passeig de Gràcia between Carrer del Consell de Cent and Carrer d'Aragó. All three buildings were completed between 1898 and 1906. According to Greek myth, the original Apple of Discord was tossed onto Mt Olympus by Eris (Discord) with orders that it be given to the most beautiful goddess, sparking jealousies that helped start the Trojan War.

THE MODERNISTAS' MISSION

Antoni Gaudí (1852–1926), known above all for La Sagrada Família, was just one, albeit the most imaginative, of a generation of inventive architects who left an indelible mark on Barcelona between 1880 and the 1920s. They were called the Modernistas.

The local offshoot of the Europe-wide phenomenon of art nouveau, Modernisme was characterised by its taste for sinuous, flowing lines and (for the time) adventurous combinations of materials like tile, glass, brick, iron and steel. But Barcelona's Modernistas were also inspired by an astonishing variety of other styles too: Gothic and Islamic, Renaissance and Romanesque, Byzantine and baroque.

Gaudí and co were trying to create a specifically Catalan architecture, often looking back to Catalonia's medieval golden age for inspiration. It is no coincidence that Gaudí and the two other leading Modernista architects, Lluís Domènech i Montaner (1850–1923) and Josep Puig i Cadafalch (1867–1957), were prominent Catalan nationalists.

L'Eixample, where most of Barcelona's new building was happening at the time, is home to the bulk of the Modernistas' creations. Others in the city include Gaudí's **Palau Güell** (p239) and **Park Güell** (p257); Domènech i Montaner's **Palau de la Música Catalana** (p239), **Castell dels Tres Dragons** (p244) and the Hotel España restaurant (Carrer de Sant Pau 9-11, El Raval); and Puig i Cadafalch's Els Quatre Gats restaurant (Carrer de Montsió 3bis, Barri Gòtic).

Cadafalch. The basement is lined with Modernista art, including paintings by Ramon Casas and Santiago Rusiñol, and statues by Josep Llimona and Eusebi Arnau.

FREE **Palau del Baró Quadras & Casa de les Punxes**
MODERNISTA BUILDINGS

(Map p252; www.casaasia.es; Avinguda Diagonal 373; ☉10am-8pm Tue-Sat, 10am-2pm Sun; ⓜDiagonal) Puig i Cadafalch built Palau del Baró Quadras between 1902 and 1904, festooning the fantastical facade with neo-Gothic carvings and a fine stained-glass gallery. It houses **Casa Asia**, an Asia-Pacific cultural centre. Visiting the varied temporary exhibitions allows you to get a peek at the inside of this intriguing building, which is full of surprising oriental themes.

Nearby Casa Terrades, by the same architect, is better known as Casa de les Punxes (House of Spikes; Avinguda Diagonal 420) because of its pointed, witch's-hat turrets. This apartment block (1903–05) looks more like a fairy-tale castle.

Hospital de la Santa Creu i de Sant Pau
MODERNISTA HOSPITAL

(Hospital of the Sacred Cross & St Paul; www. rutadelmodernisme.com, www.santpau.es; Carrer de Cartagena 167; ⓜHospital de Sant Pau) Domènech i Montaner excelled himself as architect and philanthropist with this Modernista masterpiece, long one of the city's most important hospitals. The whole complex (a World Heritage Site), including 16 pavilions, is lavishly decorated and each pavilion is unique. Among the many artists who contributed statuary, ceramics and artwork was the prolific Eusebi Arnau.

The hospital facilities have been moved to modern buildings and the historic site is slowly being restored. At the time of writing, the only way to visit the Modernista hospital was by a 1¼-hour guided tour (adult/senior & student €10/5; ☉in English 10am, 11am, noon & 1pm), also available in Catalan, French and Spanish. Restoration work may mean these tours are not always held. On the other hand, the site is occasionally unlocked to the public on open days. To reach the former hospital, head north of La Sagrada Família to the end of Avinguda de Gaudí.

Torre Agbar
TOWER

(www.torreagbar.com; Avinguda Diagonal 225; ⓜGlòries) This glimmering cucumber-shaped tower by Jean Nouvel has come to share the skyline limelight with La Sagrada Família and it is now the most visible landmark in the city. You can generally get inside the foyer, where temporary exhibitions are sometimes staged. It is best viewed at night, when its carapace is lit up in reds, purples and blues. It's right by the Glòries metro station.

Fundación Francisco Godia
MUSEUM

(Map p252; www.fundacionfgodia.org; Carrer de la Diputació 250; adult/student €5/3.50; ☉10am-8pm Wed-Mon; ⓜPasseig de Gràcia) Francisco Godia (1921–90), head of one of Barcelona's great establishment families, liked fast cars (he came sixth in the 1956 Grand Prix season driving Maseratis) and fine art. An intriguing mix of medieval art, ceramics and modern paintings make up this varied private collection, housed in Casa Garriga Nogués, a carefully restored and stunning Modernista residence originally built for a rich banking family by Enric Sagnier in 1902–05. The art is spread over the 1st floor, ranging from brightly coloured Roman-esque wooden statues of the Virgin and Child, through classic Spanish ceramics to samples by Modernista painter Ramon Ca-sas and Valencia's Joaquim Sorolla.

Museu Egipci MUSEUM
(Map p252; www.museuegipci.com; Carrer de València 284; adult/senior & student €11/8; ⊙10am-8pm Mon-Sat, 10am-2pm Sun; MPas-seig de Gràcia) Hotel magnate Jordi Clos has spent much of his life collecting an-cient Egyptian artefacts, brought together in this private museum. It's divided into thematic areas (the Pharaoh, religion, fu-nerary practices, mummification, crafts etc) and boasts a pleasing variety of statu-ary, funereal implements and containers, jewellery (including a fabulous golden ring from around the 7th century BC), ce-ramics and even a bed made of wood and leather.

Fundació Suñol MUSEUM
(Map p252; www.fundaciosunol.org; Passeig de Gràcia 98; adult/concession €5/3; ⊙4-8pm Mon-Sat; MDiagonal) Rotating exhibitions of portions of this private collection of mostly 20th-century art (some 1200 works in total) offer the visitor anything from the photog-raphy of Man Ray to sculptures by Alberto Giacometti, and a hefty band of Spanish artists, from Picasso to Plensa.

GRÀCIA
Gràcia lies north of L'Eixample. Once a separate village and, in the 19th century, an industrial district famous for its Repub-lican and liberal ideas, it became fashion-able among radical and Bohemian types in the 1960s and '70s. Now more sedate and gentrified, it retains a slightly rebellious air (witness all the Catalan nationalist youth graffiti and the occasional surviving squat), a mixed-class population (with a high rate of students, both local and from abroad) and a very Catalan feel. Gràcia's interest lies in the atmosphere of its narrow streets, small plazas and the multitude of bars and restaurants.

The liveliest plazas are Plaça del Sol, Plaça de la Vila de Gràcia with its clock tower (a favourite meeting place) and Plaça de la Virreina with the 17th-century **Esglé-sia de Sant Joan** (Map p258). Three blocks northeast of Plaça de la Vila de Gràcia, there's a big covered market, the **Mercat de l'Abaceria** (Map p258). West of Gràcia's main street, Carrer Gran de Gràcia, seek out an early Gaudí house, the turreted, vaguely Mudéjar **Casa Vicens** (Carrer de les Carolines 22); it's not open to the public.

FREE **Park Güell** PARK
(Map p230; Carrer d'Olot 7; ⊙10am-9pm; MLesseps or Vallcarca, 24) North of Gràcia, Park Güell is where Gaudí turned his hand to landscape gardening and the artificial al-most seems more natural than the natural.

Park Güell originated in 1900 when Count Eusebi Güell bought a hillside property (then outside Barcelona) and hired Gaudí to cre-ate a miniature garden city of houses for the wealthy. The project was abandoned in 1914, but not before Gaudí had created 3km of roads and walks, steps and a plaza in his in-imitable manner, plus the two Hansel-and-Gretel-style gatehouses on Carrer d'Olot.

Try coming to the park early on a week-day. On summer weekends it can be un-pleasantly packed. Bus 24 drops you at an entrance near the top of the park.

Pavelló de Consergeria
Just inside the main entrance on Carrer d'Olot, the Pavelló de Consergeria is the typi-cally curvaceous, Gaudían former porter's home that hosts a display on Gaudí's build-ing methods and the history of the park. There are nice views from the top floor. At the time of writing, it was being refurbished.

DEADLY SERIOUS

Museu de Carrosses Fúnebres (Carrer de Sancho d'Àvila 2; ⊙10am-1pm & 4-6pm Mon-Fri, 10am-1pm Sat, Sun & holidays; MMarina) is probably the weirdest museum in town. This base-ment hearse museum is the place to come if you want to see how the great and good have been transported to their final resting places in Barce-lona since the 18th century. Solemn, wigged mannequins and life-size model horses accompany a series of dark hearses.

BARCELONA SIGHTS

Sala Hipóstila

The steps up from the entrance, which is guarded by a mosaic dragon-lizard, lead to the Sala Hipóstila, a forest of 88 stone columns (some of them leaning at an angle), intended as a market. On top of the Sala Hipóstila is a broad open space; its highlight is the **Banc de Trencadís**, a tiled bench curving sinuously around its perimeter and designed by Gaudí's right-hand man, Josep Maria Jujol (1879–1949).

Casa-Museu Gaudí

(www.casamuseugaudi.org; adult/senior & student €5.50/4.50; ⊙10am-8pm) The spired house to the right is the Casa-Museu Gaudí, where Gaudí lived for most of his last 20 years (1906–26). It contains furniture by him and other memorabilia.

TIBIDABO

Tibidabo (512m) is the highest hill in the wooded range that forms the back- drop to Barcelona and is a good place for some fresh air and fine views. It gets its name from the devil, who, trying to tempt Christ, took him to a high place and said, in the Latin version: *'Haec omnia tibi dabo si cadens adoraberis me.'* ('All this I will give you, if you will fall down and worship me.')

CosmoCaixa MUSEUM
(Museu de la Ciència; www.fundacio.lacaixa.es, in Catalan & Spanish; Carrer de Teodor Roviralta 47-51; adult/student €3/2; ⊙10am-8pm Tue-Sun & holidays; 🚌60, 🚃FGC Avinguda de Tibidabo) Located in a transformed Modernista building, this science museum is a giant interactive paradise with knobs, buttons, levers and lots more besides. Among the star attractions are the planetarium and the recreation over 1 sq km of a chunk of flooded Amazon rainforest *(Bosc Inundat)*, with more than 100 species of Amazon flora and fauna (including anacondas and poisonous frogs). It has become one of the city's big draws and is perfect for kids of all ages.

Parc d'Atraccions AMUSEMENT PARK
(www.tibidabo.es; Plaça de Tibidabo 3-4; adult/ senior & child €25/9; ⊙noon-10pm Wed-Sun, closed Jan & Feb) *Barcelonins* converge here

for stomach-churning and scream-inducing rides. El Pndol is a giant arm holding four passengers, which drops them at a speed that reaches 100km/h in less than three seconds (a force of 4g) before swinging outward. La Muntanya Russa is a massive new big dipper and Hurakan tosses its passengers about with sudden drops and 360-degree turns. A curious sideline is the Museu d'Autòmats, with around 50 automated puppets that go back as far as 1880 and are part of the original amusement park; you can still see some of these gizmos go.

Temple del Sagrat Cor   CHURCH
(Plaça de Tibidabo; ⊘8am-7pm) The Church of the Sacred Heart, looming above the top funicular station, is meant to be Barcelona's answer to Paris' Sacré Cœur. It's certainly equally as visible and even more vilified by aesthetes (perhaps with good reason). It's actually two churches, one on top of the other. The top one is surmounted by a giant Christ and has a lift to the roof (tickets €2; ⊘10am-7pm).

Jardins del Laberint d'Horta   GARDENS
(Carrer dels Germans Desvalls; adult/student €2.20/1.40, free Wed & Sun; ⊘10am-sunset; MMundet) Laid out in the twilight years of the 18th century by Antoni Desvalls, Marquès d'Alfarras i de Llupià, this carefully manicured park remained a private family idyll until the 1970s, when it was opened to the public. Many a fine party and theatrical performance was held here over the years, but now it serves as a kind of museum-

park. The gardens take their name from a maze (which is very easy to get lost in!) in their centre, but other paths take you past a pleasant artificial lake *(estany)*, waterfalls, a neoclassical pavilion and a false cemetery. The last was inspired by 19th-century romanticism, often characterised by an obsession with a swooning, anaemic (some might say plain silly) vision of death. At Mundet metro station, take the right exit upstairs; on emerging, turn right and then left along the main road (with football fields on your left) and then the first left uphill to the gardens (about five minutes).

COLLSEROLA
Parc de Collserola   PARK
(www.parccollserola.net; Carretera de l'Església 92; ⊘Centre d'Interpretació 9.30am-3pm) Stretching over 80 sq km, this park makes an ideal escape hatch from the city, with ample walking and mountain-biking possibilities.

To get to the park, take the FGC train from Plaça de Catalunya to Peu de Funicular and then the funicular to Baixador de Vallvidrera.

Museu-Casa Verdaguer
(www.museuhistoria.bcn.cat; Villa Joana, Carretera de l'Església 104; ⊘10am-2pm Sat, Sun & holidays Sep-Jul) Aside from nature, the principal point of interest in Parc de Collserola is the sprawling Museu-Casa Verdaguer, 100m from the park information centre and a short walk from the train station. Catalonia's revered and reverend writer, Jacint

---

GETTING TO TIBIDABO

Take one of the frequent Ferrocarrils de la Generalitat de Catalunya (FGC) trains to Avinguda de Tibidabo from Catalunya station on Plaça de Catalunya (€1.40, 10 minutes). Outside Avinguda de Tibidabo station, hop on the *tramvia blau* (one way/return €2.80/4.30, 15 minutes, every 15 or 30 minutes 10am to 6pm Saturdays, Sundays and holidays), Barcelona's last surviving old-style tram. It runs between fancy Modernista mansions – of particular note is Casa Roviralta (Avinguda de Tibidabo 31), now home to a well-known grill restaurant – and Plaça del Doctor Andreu and has been doing so since 1901. When the tram isn't in operation, a bus serves the route (€1.40).

From Plaça del Doctor Andreu, the Tibidabo funicular railway climbs through the woods to Plaça de Tibidabo at the top of the hill (one way/return €2.50/4, five minutes). Departures start at 10.45am and continue until shortly after the park's closing time.

An alternative is bus T2, the 'Tibibús', from Plaça de Catalunya to Plaça de Tibidabo (€2.60, 30 minutes). It runs every 30 to 50 minutes on Saturday, Sunday and holidays; purchase tickets on the bus. The last bus down leaves Tibidabo 30 minutes after the Parc d'Atraccions closes. You can also buy a combined ticket that includes the bus and entry to the Parc d'Atraccions (€25).

Verdaguer, spent his last days in this late-18th-century country house, before dying on 10 July 1902.

Torre de Collserola TOWER

(www.torredecollserola.com; Carretera de Vallvidrera al Tibidabo; adult/child & senior €5/3; ⏰11am-2pm & 3.30-8pm Sat, Sun & holidays) The 288m Torre de Collserola telecommunications tower was completed by Norman Foster in 1992. An external glass lift whisks you up 115m to the visitors' observation area, from where you can see for 70km on a clear day. Take bus 111 from Funicular de Vallvidrera.

PEDRALBES

A wealthy residential area north of the Zona Universitària, Pedrables is named after the eponymous convent that is a key attraction in the area. The real estate is as expensive as it comes in Barcelona, with generous houses and gardens lending it a sense of the 'burbs that appeals to locals for the peace and quiet it offers – a rare commodity in this noisy city.

Palau Reial de Pedralbes MUSEUM

(Avinguda Diagonal 686; adult/student & senior €5/3; ⏰palace 10am-6pm Tue-Sun, 10am-3pm holidays, park 10am-6pm daily; MPalau Reial) Across Avinguda Diagonal from the main campus of the Universitat de Barcelona, set in a lush, green park, is the 20th-century Palau Reial de Pedralbes, which belonged to the family of Eusebi Güell (Gaudí's patron) until they handed it over to the city in 1926. Then it served as a royal residence – King Alfonso XIII, the president of Catalonia and General Franco, among others, have been its guests. Admission is free from 3pm Sundays and on the first Sunday of the month.

Today the palace houses two museums. The **Museu de Ceràmica** (www.museu ceramica.bcn.es) has a fine collection of Spanish ceramics from the 13th to 19th centuries, plus work by Picasso and Miró. The **Disseny Hub** (Design Hub; www.dhub-bcn. cat) is itself the fusion of two collections (Museu de les Arts Decoratives and Museu Tèxtil i d'Indumentària), and also has a space for temporary exhibitions in La Ribera (see p242). The **Museu de les Arts Decoratives** brings together an eclectic assortment of furnishings, ornaments and knick-knacks dating as far back as the Romanesque period, while the **Museu Tèxtil i d'Indumentària** (www.museutextil.bcn.es) contains some 4000 items that range from 4th-century Coptic textiles to 20th-century local embroidery, with an emphasis on fashion from the 16th century to the 1930s.

Pavellons Güell

(www.rutadelmodernisme.com; guided tour adult/ senior & child €6/3; ⏰tours 10.15am & 12.15pm in English, 11.15am in Catalan & 1.15pm in Spanish Fri-Mon) Over by Avinguda de Pedralbes on the palace grounds are the Gaudí-designed stables and porter's lodge for the Finca Güell, as the Güell estate here was called. They were built in the mid-1880s, when Gaudí was strongly impressed by Islamic architecture. Outside visiting hours, there is nothing to stop you admiring Gaudí's wrought-iron dragon gate from the outside.

Museu-Monestir de Pedralbes MONASTERY

(www.museuhistoria.bcn.cat; Baixada del Monestir 9; adult/senior & student €7/5; ⏰10am-5pm Tue-Sat, 10am-8pm Sun, 10am-3pm holidays; FGC Reina Elisenda, 22, 63, 64 or 75) This peaceful old convent, founded in 1326 and now a museum of monastic life, stands at the top of Avinguda de Pedralbes in a divinely quiet corner of Barcelona. Displays are distributed in the cells around the elegant, three-storey cloister, a jewel of early-14th-century Catalan Gothic. Upstairs is a grand hall that was once the **dormidor** (sleeping quarters). It was lined by tiny night cells, but they were removed long ago. A modest collection of the monastery's art, especially Gothic devotional works, and furniture grace this space today.

Camp Nou FOOTBALL STADIUM

(www.fcbarcelona.com; Carrer d'Aristides Maillol; adult/senior & child €17/14; ⏰10am-8pm Mon-Sat, 10am-2.30pm Sun & holidays; MPalau Reial) Football fans flock to FC Barcelona's giant Camp Nou stadium, if not to see a match (see p289), then at least to visit the **Museu del Futbol Club Barcelona** next door. Barça is one of Europe's top football clubs and its museum is a hit with fans the world over.

The best bits of the museum itself are the photo section, the goal videos and the views out over the stadium. Among the quirkier paraphernalia are old sports board games, the life-sized diorama of old-time dressing rooms, posters and magazines from way back and the *futbolín* (table football) collection. You can admire the (in at least one case literally) golden boots of great goal scorers of the past and stacks of trophies. High-tech multimedia displays project great moments in Barça history. Sound installations include the club's anthem and match-day sounds from the stadium.

The guided tour of the stadium takes in the team's dressing rooms, heads out through the tunnel on to the pitch and winds up in the presidential box.

Plan about 2½ hours for the whole visit.

EL POBLE SEC

Draped on the eastern slopes of Montjuïc down to Avinguda del Paral.lel, working-class El Poble Sec (the Dry Village) is short on sights but hides several interesting bars and eateries. Until the 1960s the avenue was the centre of Barcelona nightlife, crammed with theatres and cabarets. A handful of them survives and one, the Sala Apolo (p286), converted itself successfully into a club.

Refugi 307   AIR-RAID SHELTER
(Map p262; www.museuhistoria.bcn.cat; Carrer Nou de la Rambla 169; admission €3; ⊙tours 11am-2pm Sat & Sun; Ⓜ Paral.lel) This air-raid shelter was one of more than 1300 across the city during the civil war. The narrow and winding tunnels were slowly dug to a total of 200m over two years from March 1937 and had a theoretical capacity for 2000 people. The half-hour tours (generally in Spanish or Catalan, but you can book ahead for English or French) provide some fascinating insights into life in wartime Barcelona. Just being inside here and imagining bombs dropping outside is enough to give you the heebie-jeebies.

MONTJUÏC

Montjuïc, the hill overlooking the city centre from the southwest, is dotted with museums, soothing gardens and the main group of 1992 Olympic sites, along with a handful of theatres and clubs. It's worth at least a day of your time.

The name Montjuïc (Jewish Mountain) indicates there was once a Jewish cemetery, and possibly settlement, here. Montjuïc also has a darker history: its castle was used as a political prison and execution site by various governments, including the Republicans during the civil war and Franco thereafter.

The first main burst of building on Montjuïc came in the 1920s, when it was chosen as the stage for Barcelona's 1929 World Exhibition. The Estadi Olímpic, the Poble Espanyol and some museums all date from this time. Montjuïc got a facelift and more new buildings for the 1992 Olympics, and further cosmetic surgery on the gar-

dens since the late 1990s has made them beautiful and soothing places to walk, contemplate or just lie down and snooze.

Abundant roads and paths, with occasional escalators, plus buses and a chairlift, allow you to visit Montjuïc's sights in any order you choose. The main attractions – the Museu Nacional d'Art de Catalunya, CaixaForum, the Poble Espanyol, the Pavelló Mies van der Rohe, the Fundació Joan Miró, the Estadi Olímpic and the views from the castle – make for a full couple of days' sightseeing.

Centre Gestor del Parc de Montjuïc
INFORMATION CENTRE
(Map p262; Passeig de Santa Madrona 28; ⊙10am-8pm) For information on the park, head for the Centre Gestor del Parc de Montjuïc in the Font del Gat building, a short walk off Passeig de Santa Madrona, east of the Museu Etnològic. It also has a pleasant bar-restaurant. A handful of other information offices are scattered about the park, including at the castle.

Plaça d'Espanya   PLAZA
The approach to Montjuïc from Plaça d'Espanya gives you the full benefit of the landscaping on the hill's northern side and allows Montjuïc to unfold for you from the bottom up. On Plaça d'Espanya's northern side is the former **Plaça de Braus Les Arenes bullring**, built in 1900 and slowly being converted into a shopping and leisure centre by Sir Richard Rogers.

Behind the bullring is **Parc Joan Miró**, created in the 1980s, and worth a quick detour for Miró's giant, highly phallic sculpture *Dona i Ocell* (Woman and Bird) in the northwest corner.

TOP CHOICE Museu Nacional d'Art de Catalunya   MUSEUM
(Map p262; www.mnac.cat; Mirador del Palau Nacional; adult/student €8.50/6, free on 1st Sun of month; ⊙10am-7pm Tue-Sat, 10am-2.30pm Sun & holidays; Ⓜ Espanya) The pompous-looking **Palau Nacional**, built in the 1920s for World Exhibition displays and designed to be a temporary structure, houses one of the city's most important museums, a veritable compendium of art in Catalonia down the centuries.

The star collection is the Romanesque art but the extensive Gothic art section also contains interesting material, such as works by Catalan painters Bernat Martorell and Jaume Huguet. From the Gothic section, you pass through two eclectic private

Montjuïc & Poble Sec

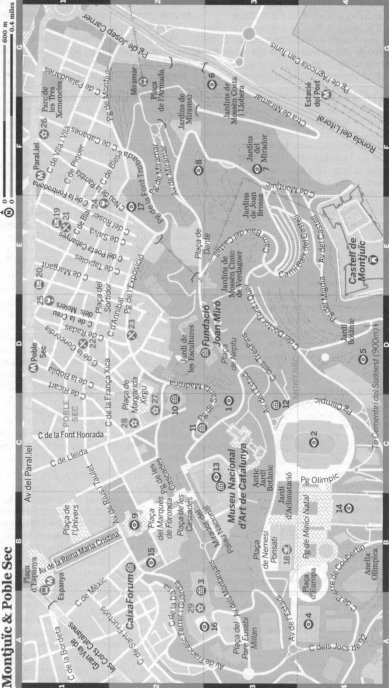

BARCELONA

600 m
0.4 miles

collections, the Cambò bequest and works from the Thyssen-Bornemisza collections. Works by the Venetian Renaissance masters Veronese (1528–88), Titian (1490–1557) and Canaletto (1697–1768), along with Rubens (1577–1640) and even England's Gainsborough (1727–88), feature.

Upstairs, after a series of minor works by a variety of 17th-century Spanish Old Masters, the collection turns to modern Catalan art. It is an uneven affair, but it is worth looking out for Modernista painters Ramon Casas and Santiago Rusiñol.

The photography section encompasses work from mostly Catalan snappers from the mid-19th century on. The Gabinet Numismàtic de Catalunya contains coins ranging from Roman Spain and medieval Catalonia to some engaging notes from civil war days.

Fundació Joan Miró   MUSEUM

(Map p262; www.bcn.fjmiro.es; Plaça de Neptu; adult/senior & child €8.50/6; ⊙10am-8pm Tue, Wed, Fri & Sat, 10am-9.30pm Thu, 10am-2.30pm Sun & holidays; ☒50, 55, 193 or funicular) Dedicated to one of the greatest artists to emerge in Barcelona in the 20th century, Joan Miró, this is a must-see gallery.

The foundation holds the greatest single collection of the artist's work, comprising around 220 of his paintings, 180 sculptures, some textiles and more than 8000 drawings spanning his entire life. Only a smallish portion is ever on display. The displays tend to concentrate on Miró's more settled last 20 years, but there are some important exceptions. The Sala Joan Prats and Sala Pilar Juncosa show work by the younger Miró that traces him slowly moving away from a relative realism towards his own signature style. Transitional works from the 1930s and '40s are especially intriguing. *Homenatge a Joan Miró* (Homage to Joan Miró), with photos of the artist, a 15-minute video on his life and a series of works from some of his contemporaries, like Henry Moore, Antoni Tàpies, Eduardo Chillida, Yves Tanguy, Fernand Léger and others, is a display spread across basement rooms.

Reckon on a couple of hours to take in the permanent and temporary exhibitions.

FREE Castell de Montjuïc

FORTRESS & GARDENS

(Map p262) The southeast of Montjuïc is dominated by the castle, which for most of its existence has been used to watch over

Montjuïc

A DAY ITINERARY

Possibly the site of ancient pre-Roman settlements, Montjuïc today is a hilltop green lung looking over city and sea. Interspersed across varied gardens are major art collections, a fortress, Olympic Stadium and more. A solid one-day itinerary can take in the key spots.

Alight at Espanya metro stop and make for CaixaForum **1**, always host to three or four free top-class exhibitions. The Pavelló Mies van der Rohe **2** across the road is an intriguing look at 1920s futurist housing by one of the 20th century's greatest architects. Uphill, the Romanesque art collection in the Museu Nacional d'Art de Catalunya **3** should not be missed. The restaurant here makes a pleasant lunch stop. Escalators lead further up the hill towards the Estadi Olímpic **4**, scene of the 1992 Olympic Games. The road leads east to the Fundació Joan Miró **5**, a shrine to the surrealist artist's creativity. Relax in the Jardins de Mossèn Cinto Verdaguer **6**, the prettiest on the hill, before taking the cable car to the Castell de Montjuïc **7**. If you pick the right day, you can round off by contemplating the gorgeously kitsch La Font Màgica **8** sound and light show.

TOP TIPS

» **Moving views** Take the Transbordador Aeri from La Barceloneta for a bird's eye approach to Montjuïc. Or use the Teleféric de Montjuïc cable car to the Castell for more aerial views.

» **Summer fun** The Castell de Montjuïc is the scene for outdoor summer cinema and concerts (see http://salamontjuic.org).

» **Beautiful bloomers** Bursting with colour and serenity, the Jardins de Mossèn Cinto Verdaguer are exquisitely laid out with bulbs, especially tulips, and aquatic flowers.

JEAN-PIERRE LESCOURRET

CaixaForum
This former factory and barracks designed by Josep Puig i Cadafalch is an outstanding work of Modernista architecture; like a Lego fantasy in brick.

Olympic Needle

Piscines Bernat Picornell

Poble Espanyol
Amid the rich variety of traditional Spanish architecture created in replica for the 1929 Barcelona World Exhibition, seek out the art on show in the Fundació Fran Daurel.

NEIL SETCHFIELD

Pavelló Mies van der Rohe
Admire the inventiveness of the great German architect Ludwig Mies van der Rohe in this recreation of his avant garde German pavillion for the 1929 World Exhibition.

La Font Màgica
Take a summer evening to behold the Magic Fountain come to life in a unique 15-minute sound and light performance, when the water looks like a mystical cauldron of colour.

8

Museu Nacional d'Art de Catalunya
Make a beeline for the Romanesque art selection and the 12th-century polychrome image of Christ in majesty recovered from the apse of a country chapel in northwest Catalonia.

3

Museu Etnològic

Teatre Grec

5

6

Museu Olímpic i de l'Esport

4

Estadi Olímpic

Jardí Botànic

7

Jardins de Mossèn Cinto Verdaguer

Castell de Montjuïc
Enjoy the sweeping views of the sea and city from atop this 17th-century fortress, once a political prison and long a symbol of oppression.

Fundació Joan Miró
Take in some of Joan Miró's giant bright canvases, and discover little-known works of his early years in the Sala Joan Prats and Sala Pilar Juncosa.

Museu d'Arqueologia de Catalunya
Seek out the Roman mosaic depicting the Three Graces, one of the most beautiful items in this museum, dedicated to the ancient past of Catalonia and neighbouring parts of Spain.

DON'T MISS

ROMANESQUE TREASURES IN THE MUSEU NACIONAL D'ART DE CATALUNYA

The Romanesque art section in the Museu Nacional d'Art de Catalunya (p261) constitutes one of Europe's greatest such collections and is an absolute must for lovers of medieval art – and an excellent place to learn about it for those who have had few previous opportunities. The collection consists mainly of 11th- and 12th-century murals, woodcarvings and altar frontals – painted, bas-relief wooden panels that were forerunners of the elaborate *retablos* (altarpieces) that adorned later churches. Gathered from decaying rural churches in northern Catalonia early last century, they are a surprising treasure of vivid colour, discrediting the idea that medieval churches were bereft of decoration. The two outstanding items are an image of Christ in Majesty, done around 1123 and taken from the apse of the Església de Sant Climent de Taüll in northwest Catalonia, and an apse image of the Virgin Mary and Christ Child from the nearby Església de Santa Maria de Taüll.

the city and as a political prison and killing ground. From the 1960s it housed a military museum.

In the coming years, it is planned to establish an international peace centre in the castle, as well as a display on its history. There will also be an interpretation centre dedicated to Montjuïc. While waiting for this to happen, a modest temporary exhibition has been established in one of the castle's bastions, on the right as soon as you enter. Called **Barcelona Té Castell** (Barcelona has a Castle), it explains something of the place's history as well as detailing plans for its future. Best of all are the views from the castle ramparts of the port and city below. Make the charming walk along the base of the seaward walls along the Camí del Mar (a dirt trail), drinking in views of the city and the sea. On weekends a popular, chilled **bar** opens at the end of this trail.

FREE Jardins   GARDENS
Towards the foot of the fortress, above the main road to Tarragona, the **Jardins de Mossèn Costa i Llobera** (Map p262; ☉10am-sunset) have a good collection of tropical and desert plants – including a veritable forest of cacti. Near the Estació Parc Montjuïc (funicular station) are the ornamental **Jardins de Mossèn Cinto Verdaguer** (Map p262; ☉10am-sunset), full of beautiful bulbs and aquatic plants. East across the road are the landscaped **Jardins Joan Brossa** (Map p262; ☉10am-sunset), set on the site of a former amusement park. These gardens contain many Mediterranean species, from cypresses to pines and a few palms. From the **Jardins del Mirador** (Map p262),

opposite the Estació Mirador, you have fine views over the port of Barcelona.

Poble Espanyol   THEME PARK
(Map p262; www.poble-espanyol.com; Avinguda de Francesc Ferrer i Guàrdia; adult/child €8.50/5.50; ☉9am-8pm Mon, 9am-2am Tue-Thu, 9am-4am Fri, 9am-5am Sat, 9am-midnight Sun; MEspanya, ☐50, 61 or 193) The so-called Spanish Village, Poble Espanyol is both a cheesy souvenir-hunters' haunt and an intriguing scrapbook of Spanish architecture. Built for the Spanish crafts section of the 1929 exhibition, it is composed of plazas and streets lined with surprisingly good copies of characteristic buildings from across the country's regions.

You enter through a towered medieval gate from Ávila. Inside, to the right, is an information office with free maps. Straight ahead from the gate is a *plaza mayor* (town square), surrounded by mainly Castilian and Aragonese buildings. This is often the scene of concerts. Elsewhere you'll find an Andalucian *barrio* (district), a Basque street, Galician and Catalan quarters, and even – at the eastern end – a small Dominican monastery. The buildings house dozens of moderate-to-expensive restaurants, cafes, bars, craft shops and workshops, and a few souvenir stores.

FREE Fundació Fran Daurel
(Map p262; www.fundaciofrandaurel.com; ☉10am-7pm) The Fundació Fran Daurel (in Poble Espanyol) is an eclectic collection of 300 works of art including sculptures, prints, ceramics and tapestries by modern artists ranging from Picasso and Miró to more contemporary figures, including

Miquel Barceló. The foundation also has a sculpture garden, boasting 27 pieces, nearby the Fundació and within the grounds of Poble Espanyol (look for the Montblanc gate).

FREE **La Font Màgica** FOUNTAIN
(Map p262; Avinguda de la Reina Maria Cristina; ⊘every 30min 7-9pm Fri & Sat Oct-late Jun, 9-11.30pm Thu-Sun late Jun-Sep; Mi Espanya) Avinguda de la Reina Maria Cristina, lined with exhibition and congress halls, leads from Plaça d'Espanya towards Montjuïc. On the hill ahead of you is the Palau Nacional de Montjuïc, and stretching up a series of terraces below it are Montjuïc's fountains, starting with the biggest, La Font Màgica, which comes alive with a 15-minute lights, water and music show repeated several times per evening.

Pavelló Mies van der Rohe PAVILION
(Map p262; www.miesbcn.com; Avinguda de Francesc Ferrer i Guàrdia; adult/student €4.50/2.30; ⊘10am-8pm; Mi Espanya) Just to the west of La Font Màgica is the strange Pavelló Mies van der Rohe. Architect Ludwig Mies van der Rohe erected the Pavelló Alemany (German Pavilion) for the 1929 World Exhibition. It was a startling modern experiment. What you see now is a replica erected by an association of his fans in the 1980s.

FREE **CaixaForum** ART GALLERY
(Map p262; www.fundacio.lacaixa.es, in Catalan & Spanish; Avinguda de Francesc Ferrer i Guàrdia 6-8; ⊘10am-8pm Tue-Fri & Sun, 10am-10pm Sat; Mi Espanya) Part of the Caixa bank's extensive collection of modern art from around the globe is housed in a remarkable former Modernista factory designed by Puig i Cadafalch. Constantly changing exhibitions are generally top quality and the elegant brick building itself warrants a wander even if the current exhibitions don't ring your bell.

Museu Etnològic MUSEUM
(Ethnology Museum; Map p262; www.museuetnologic.bcn.cat, in Catalan; Passeig de Santa Madrona 16-22; adult/senior & student €3.50/1.75; ⊘noon-8pm Tue-Sat, 11am-3pm Sun; ⌷55) The Museu Etnològic presents a wide-ranging, three-part exhibition with all sorts of traditional objects collected across Spain and around the world. Collections take in Japan, Nuristan (an area straddling Pakistan and Afghanistan), Morocco, Ethiopia, Australia, Papua New Guinea and the Americas (in particular Ecuador's Amazon region).

Admission is free on the first Sunday of the month.

Museu d'Arqueologia de Catalunya
MUSEUM
(Archaeology Museum; Map p262; www.mac.cat; Passeig de Santa Madrona 39-41; adult/student €3/2.10; ⊘9.30am-7pm Tue-Sat, 10am-2.30pm Sun; ⌷55 or 193) The Museu d'Arqueologia de Catalunya covers Catalonia and neighbouring areas in Spain. Items range from copies of pre-Neanderthal skulls to Carthaginian necklaces and Visigothic crosses. There's good material on the Balearic Islands, the ancient city of Empúries, and Roman finds dug up in Barcelona. You will find some rooms shut as the museum is slowly being overhauled.

Anella Olímpica OLYMPIC SITE
The 'Olympic Ring' is the group of sports installations where the main events of the 1992 Olympics were held. Westernmost is the **Institut Nacional d'Educació Física de Catalunya** (INEFC; Map p262), a kind of sports university, designed by one of Catalonia's best-known contemporary architects, Ricardo Bofill. Past a circular arena, Plaça d'Europa, with the Torre Calatrava telecommunications tower behind it, is the **Piscines Bernat Picornell** (Map p262), where swimming and diving events were held. For details on swimming here, see p269.

Estadi Olímpic
(Map p262; Avinguda de l'Estadi; ⊘10am-8pm; ⌷50, 61 or PM) Next comes a pleasant park, the Jardí d'Aclimatació, followed by the Estadi Olímpic, the main stadium of the games (enter at the north end). If you saw the Olympics on TV, the 65,000-capacity stadium may seem surprisingly small. So might the Olympic flame holder into which an archer spectacularly fired a flaming arrow during the opening ceremony. The stadium was opened in 1929 and restored for 1992.

Museu Olímpic i de l'Esport
(Map p262; www.fundaciobarcelonaolimpica.es; Avinguda de l'Estadi 60; adult/student €4/2.50; ⊘10am-8pm; ⌷50, 61 or 193) Across the road from the stadium is the Museu Olímpic i de l'Esport, an information-packed interactive museum dedicated to the history of sport and the Olympic Games. After picking up tickets, you wander down a ramp that snakes below ground level and is lined with displays on the history of sport, starting with the ancients.

You *could* walk from Ciutat Vella (the foot of La Rambla is 700m from the eastern end of Montjuïc). Escalators run up to the Palau Nacional from Avinguda de Rius i Taulet and Passeig de les Cascades. They continue as far as Avinguda de l'Estadi.

Bus

Several buses make their way up here, including buses 50, 55 and 61. Local bus 193 does a circle trip from Plaça d'Espanya to the castle.

Metro & Funicular

Take the metro (lines 2 and 3) to Paral.lel station and get on the **funicular railway** (⊙9am-10pm) from there to Estació Parc Montjuïc.

Telefèric de Montjuïc

From Estació Parc Montjuïc, this **cable car** (adult/child one way €6.30/4.80; ⊙10am-9pm) carries you to the Castell de Montjuïc via the *mirador* (lookout point).

Transbordador Aeri

To get to the mountain from the beach, take the Transbordador Aeri (*telefèric;* cable car). It runs between Torre de Sant Sebastiá in La Barceloneta and the Miramar stop on Montjuïc.

Palau Sant Jordi

(Map p262) West of the stadium is the Palau Sant Jordi, a 17,000-capacity indoor sports, concert and exhibition hall designed by the Japanese architect Arata Isozaki.

Jardí Botànic   BOTANICAL GARDEN
(Map p262; www.jardibotanic.bcn.es; Carrer del Doctor Font i Quer 2; adult/student €3.50/1.70; ⊙10am-8pm; ᄆ50, 61 or 193) South across the road from the Estadi, this botanic garden was created atop an old municipal dump. The theme is Mediterranean flora and the collection includes some 1500 species (40,000 plants) thriving in areas with a climate similar to that of the Mediterranean, such as the Eastern Med, Spain (including the Balearic and Canary Islands), North Africa, Australia, California, Chile and South Africa. Admission is free on the last Sunday of the month.

Cementiri del Sud-Oest   CEMETERY
(⊙8am-6pm; ᄆ193) On the hill south of the Anella Olímpica you can see the top of a huge cemetery, the Cementiri del Sud-Oest, which extends right down the south side of the hill. It was opened in 1883 and is an odd combination of elaborate architect-designed tombs for rich families and small niches for the rest. It contains the graves of numerous Catalan artists and politicians, including Joan Miró, Carmen Amaya (the flamenco star from La Barceloneta) and

Lluís Companys (a Nationalist president of Catalonia, who was executed by Franco's henchmen in the nearby Montjuïc castle in 1940).

 Activities

Cycle lanes have been laid out along many main arteries across the city, although the network is far from complete – cyclists are often obliged to challenge the traffic or break the law by dodging (often rightly indignant) pedestrians. Montjuïc and the Parc de Collserola are both hilly but *much* less stressful than the rest of the city in terms of traffic. Indeed the latter is ideal for a little mountain-bike training. Central Barcelona is swarming in bicycle rental outlets.

Runners converge on Barcelona annually to participate in the city's spring **marathon** (www.barcelonamarato.es); it usually starts and finishes at Plaça d'Espanya, passing Camp Nou, La Pedrera, La Sagrada Família, Torre Agbar, El Fòrum, Parc de la Ciutadella, Plaça de Catalunya and La Rambla.

The most popular parts of town for a gentle rollerblade are the esplanade along La Barceloneta beach and around Port Olímpic. Fitter types head up to Montjuïc.

Base Nautica Municipal
SAILING, WINDSURFING
(www.basenautica.org; Avinguda de Litoral; Ⓜ Poblenou) Just back from Platja de la Mar Bel-

la, head here for courses in pleasure-boat handling, kayaking or windsurfing (€185 for 10 hours' tuition).

Club Natació Atlètic-Barcelona
SWIMMING
(Map p245; www.cnab.org; Plaça del Mar; adult/child €10.55/6.13; ☺6.30am-11pm Mon-Sat, 8am-8pm Sun & holidays; Ⓜ Barceloneta, 🚍17, 39, 57, 64) Down by La Barceloneta, this has one indoor and two outdoor pools, a gym and private beach access.

Golondrina
EXCURSION BOAT
(www.lasgolondrinas.com; Moll de les Drassanes; adult/child €13.50/5; Ⓜ Drassanes) For a view of the harbour from the water, you can take a *golondrina* from in front of the Mirador a Colom. The one-hour round trip takes you to Port Olímpic, El Fòrum and back again. The number of departures depends largely on season and demand. As a rule, trips are only done between March and November. If you just want to discover the area around the port, you can opt for a 35-minute excursion to the breakwater and back (€6.50/2.60 per adult/child).

Piscines Bernat Picornell
SWIMMING
(Map p262; www.picornell.cat, in Catalan; Avinguda de l'Estadi 30-38; adult/child €9.65/5.95; ☺6.45am-midnight Mon-Fri, 7am-9pm Sat, 7.30am-4pm Sun; 🚍50, 61 or 193) Included in the standard price to Barcelona's Olympic pool is use of the gym, saunas and spa bath.

Poliesportiu Marítim
SWIMMING
(Map p245; www.claror.cat, in Catalan; Passeig Marítim de la Barceloneta 33-35; general admission Mon-Fri €15, Sat, Sun & holidays €17.80; ☺7am-midnight Mon-Fri, 8am-9pm Sat, 8am-4pm Sun & holidays; Ⓜ Ciutadella Vila Olímpica) Water babies will adore this thalassotherapeutic sports centre. Apart from the smallish training pool, the centre is a minor labyrinth of spa pools that are hot, warm and freezing cold, along with waterfalls for massage relief. When you're sufficiently relaxed, you can stumble outside and flop on to the beach.

Transbordador Aeri
CABLE CAR
(Passeig Escullera; one-way/return €9/12.50; ☺11am-8pm; Ⓜ Barceloneta, 🚍17, 39 or 64) The Transbordador Aeri, a cable car strung across the harbour to Montjuïc, provides a seagull's view of the city. Get tickets at Miramar (Map p262) in Montjuïc and the Torre de Sant Sebastià (Map p245) in La Barceloneta.

Courses
Barcelona is bristling with schools offering Spanish- and Catalan-language courses. You can learn lots more in Barcelona, too, such as salsa and sauces.

Antilla BCN Escuela de Baile
DANCE
(☎93 451 45 64, 610 900558; www.antillasalsa.com; Carrer d'Aragó 141; 10 1hr classes €120) The place to learn salsa and other Caribbean dance.

WORTH A TRIP

COLÒNIA GÜELL

Apart from La Sagrada Família, Gaudí's last big project was the creation of a utopian textile workers' complex, the **Colònia Güell** (www.coloniaguell.net; Carrer de Claudi Güell 6, Santa Coloma de Cervelló; adult/student & senior €5/3.50; ☺10am-2pm & 3-7pm Mon-Fri, 10am-3pm Sat, Sun & holidays; 🚉FGC lines S4, S7, S8 or S33), built for his magnate patron Eusebi Güell outside Barcelona at Santa Coloma de Cervelló. Gaudí's main role was to erect the colony's church. Work began in 1908 but the idea fizzled eight years later and Gaudí only finished the crypt, which still serves as a working church.

This structure is a key to understanding what the master had in mind for his magnum opus, La Sagrada Família. The mostly brick-clad columns that support the ribbed vaults in the ceiling are inclined at all angles in much the way you might expect trees in a forest to lean. That effect was deliberate, but also grounded in physics. Gaudí worked out the angles so that their load would be transmitted from the ceiling to the earth without the help of extra buttressing.

Near the church spread the cute brick houses designed for the factory workers and still inhabited today. In a five-room display with audiovisual and interactive material, the history and life of the industrial colony and the story of Gaudí's church are told in colourful fashion. Audioguides (€2) are available for visiting the site.

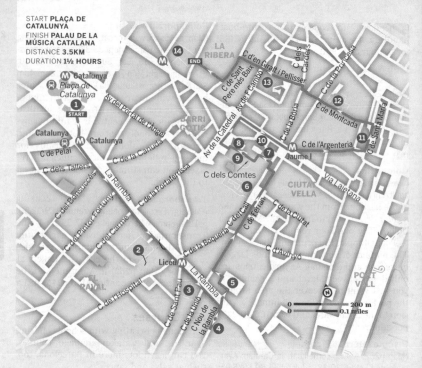

Walking Tour
Old Town

❯ A great deal of what makes Barcelona fascinating is crowded into a relatively compact space, making an introductory strolling tour a great way to make the city's acquaintance. There's nothing wrong with following the crowds to start off with, so wander down La Rambla from ❶ **Plaça de Catalunya**. Along the way, sniff around the ❷ **Mercat de la Boqueria**, one of Europe's most colourful and well-stocked produce markets. Pop into the ❸ **Gran Teatre del Liceu**, the city's main opera house, and then visit one of Gaudí's earlier efforts, the ❹ **Palau Güell**. From here, cross La Rambla and busy ❺ **Plaça Reial** and make for ❻ **Plaça de Sant Jaume**, at the core of the Barri Gòtic and the political heart of the city for 2000 years. You can examine the city's Roman origins in the nearby ❼ **Museu d'Història de Barcelona**, which also leads you to a fine Catalan Gothic hall and medieval chapel. From the complex of buildings huddled around the museum and Plaça del Rei, you pass the ❽ **Museu**

Frederic Marès en route for the main facade of the ❾ **Catedral** – make time to spend inside and to head up to the roof for bird's-eye views of the medieval city. From there, make the loop down Via Laietana to admire what remains of the ❿ **Roman walls**, and then branch off along Carrer de l'Argenteria (once home to Barcelona's silversmiths) to reach the splendid Gothic ⓫ **Església de Santa Maria del Mar**, a striking symbol of Catalan identity. Circle around it and up noble Carrer de Montcada, home to fine centuries-old mansions of which several house museums – including the ⓬ **Museu Picasso**. Proceed north past the ⓭ **Mercat de Santa Caterina**, a daring 21st-century reincarnation of a grand 19th-century produce market on the site of a medieval monastery; and then dogleg on to the stunning Modernista ⓮ **Palau de la Música Catalana**, best visited for a performance of anything from flamenco to Portuguese fado.

Cook and Taste COOKING
(Map p234; ☑93 302 13 20; www.cookandtaste.
net; Carrer del Paradís 3; half-day workshop €60)
Learn to whip up a paella or stir a gazpacho in this Spanish cookery school.

Escola Oficial d'Idiomes de Barcelona
SPANISH, CATALAN
(Map p240; ☑93 324 93 30; www.eoibd.es, in
Spanish; Avinguda de les Drassanes; ⓂDras-
sanes) Offers part-time courses (around 10
hours per week) in Spanish and Catalan
(€185.65 per semester). Because of the
high demand for Spanish, there is no
guarantee of a place.

International House SPANISH
(☑93 268 45 11; www.ihes.com/bcn; Carrer
de Trafalgar 14; ⓂArc de Triomf) Intensive
courses from around €410 for two weeks.
Staff can also organise accommodation.

Universitat de Barcelona SPANISH, CATALAN
Catalan (Map p252; ☑93 403 54 77; www.
ub.edu/slc; Carrer de Melcior de Palau 140;
ⓂSants) Spanish (☑93 403 55 19; www.eh.ub.
es; Gran Via de les Corts Catalanes 585;
ⓂUniversitat) Intensive courses (40 hours'
tuition over periods ranging from two
weeks to a month; €426) in Spanish are
held year-round. Longer Spanish and
Catalan courses are also available.

☞ Tours

A number of tour options present themselves if you want a hand getting around
the sights.

Barcelona Walking Tours WALKING
(☑93 285 38 34; Plaça de Catalunya 17-S) The
Oficina d'Informació de Turisme de Barcelona organises guided walking tours. One
explores the Barri Gòtic (adult/child €12.50/5;
⊙in English 10am daily, in Spanish & Catalan noon
Sat); another follows in the footsteps of Picasso (adult/child €19/7; ⊙in English 4pm Tue,
Thu & Sun, in Spanish & Catalan 4pm Sat) and
winds up at the Museu Picasso, entry to
which is included in the price; and a third
takes in the main jewels of Modernisme
(adult/child €12.50/5; ⊙in English 4pm Fri & Sat,
in Spanish 4pm Sat). Also offered is a gourmet
tour (adult/child €19/7; ⊙in English 10am Fri &
Sat, in Spanish & Catalan 10.30am Sat) of traditional purveyors of fine foodstuffs across
the old city; it includes a couple of chances
to taste some of the products. All tours last
two hours and start at the tourist office.
All tours are available in both English and
Spanish at 6pm from June to September.

BICYCLE TOURS

Barcelona is awash with companies
offering bicycle tours. Tours typically
take two to four hours and generally stick to the old city, the Sagrada
Família and the beaches. Operators
include Barcelona By Bike (☑93
268 81 07; www.barcelonabybike.com),
whose meeting point is on Carrer
de la Marina, near the casino at Port
Olímpic; BarcelonaBiking.com (Map
p234; ☑656 356300; www.barce
lonabiking.com; Baixada de Sant Miquel
6); Bike Tours Barcelona (Map p242;
☑93 268 21 05; www.biketoursbarce-
lona.com; Carrer de l'Esparteria 3); and
Fat Tire Bike Tours (Map p234; ☑93
301 36 12; www.fattirebiketoursbarce
lona.com; Carrer dels Escudellers 48).

Bus Turístic BUS
(☑010; www.tmb.net; day ticket adult/child €22/14;
⊙9am-7.30pm) This hop-on, hop-off service
covers three circuits (44 stops) linking virtually all the major tourist sights. Tourist
offices, TMB transport authority offices and
many hotels have leaflets explaining the
system. Each of the two main circuits takes
approximately two hours. The third circuit,
from Port Olímpic to El Fòrum, runs from
April to September and is less interesting.

Catalunya Bus Turístic BUS
(☑93 285 38 32; www.tmb.net) Routes include
a day in Vic (€35), north of Barcelona, visiting the old town and huge weekly market;
Girona and Figueres (€71); a Penedès wine
and cava (sparkling wine) jaunt with three
winery tours and lunch (€59); Montserrat
and Sitges (€69). All tours leave at 8.30am
from late March to October from Plaça de
Catalunya.

Barcelona Scooter SCOOTER TOURS
(☑93 285 38 32; tour €50; ⊙10.30am Sat,
3.30pm Thu) Run by Cooltra (see p293),
Barcelona Scooter offers a three-hour tour
by scooter around the city in conjunction
with the city tourism office. Departure is
from the Cooltra rental outlet.

BCN Skytour HELICOPTER
(☑93 224 07 10; www.cathelicopters.com; Heliport, Passeig de l'Escullera; tour per person €80;
⊙10am-7pm) A 10-minute thrill 800m up in
a helicopter will give a real bird's-eye view
of the city. Take a taxi to the heliport.

BARCELONA FOR CHILDREN

There's plenty to interest kids, from street theatre on La Rambla to the beaches. Transport is good, many attractions are huddled fairly close together and children are generally welcome in restaurants and cafes.

An initial stroll along La Rambla is full of potential distractions and wonders, from the bird stands to the living statues and buskers. The **Museu de Cera** (Wax Museum; p233) is a classic diversion.

At the bottom end of La Rambla, more options present themselves: a ride up to the top of the **Mirador a Colom** (p233) or seeing sharks at **L'Aquàrium** (p244).

The **Transbordador Aeri** (p269), strung across the harbour between La Barceloneta and Montjuïc, is an irresistible ride. Or scare the willies out of them with hair-raising rides at Tibidabo's **Parc d'Atraccions** (p258) amusement park.

Of the city's museums, those most likely to capture children's imaginations as much as that of their adult companions are the **Museu Marítim** (p239), the **Museu de la Xocolata** (p243) and the popular interactive **CosmoCaixa** (p258) science museum.

In the summer months you will doubtless be rewarded by squeals of delight if you take the bairns to one of the city's **swimming pools** (p268) or the **beach**. In cooler weather, parks can be a good choice. A walk in the gardens of Montjuïc, including some exploration of **Castell De Montjuïc** (p263), will appeal to everyone. Adults find the maze of the **Jardins del Laberint d'Horta** (p259) hard to work out, too. Another old favourite with most children is a visit to see the animals at the **Zoo de Barcelona** (p244).

Gocar   MOPED
(☑902 301333; www.gocartours.es; Carrer de Freixures 23bis; per hr/day €35/€99; ⊙9am-9pm) These GPS-guided 'cars' (really two-seat, three-wheel mopeds) allow you to tour around town and listen to commentaries on major sights as you go.

My Favourite Things   ACTIVITIES
(☑637 265405; www.myft.net; tours €26-32) Offers tours (with no more than 10 participants) based on numerous themes: anything from design to food and rollerblading to sailing. Some of the more unusual activities cost more and times vary.

✨ Festivals & Events

Reis/Reyes   EPIPHANY
Epifanía (the Epiphany) on 6 January is also known as the Dia dels Reis Mags/Día de los Reyes Magos (Three Kings' Day). The night before, children delight in the Cavalcada dels Reis Mags (Parade of the Three Kings), a colourful parade of floats and music during which tons of sweets are thrown into the crowd of eager kids (and not a few adults!).

Dia de Sant Jordi   SAINT GEORGE
This is the day of Catalonia's patron saint (George) and also the Day of the Book: men give women a rose, women give men a book,

publishers launch new titles. La Rambla and Plaça de Sant Jaume and other central city streets and squares are filled with book and flower stalls. Celebrated on 23 April.

Pride Barcelona   GAY PRIDE
(www.pridebarcelona.org) The Barcelona gaypride festival is a week of celebrations held towards the end of June with a crammed program of culture and concerts, along with the gay-pride march on the last Sunday of the month.

Festes de la Mercè   CITY FESTIVAL
(www.bcn.cat/merce) The city's biggest party involves four days of concerts, dancing, *castellers* (human-castle builders), a fireworks display synchronised with the Montjuïc fountains, dances of giants on the Saturday, and *correfocs* – a parade of fireworks-spitting monsters and demons who run with the crowd – spitting dragons and devils from all over Catalonia, on the Sunday. Held around 24 September.

Sónar   ELECTRONIC MUSIC
(www.sonar.es) Barcelona's celebration of electronic music is said to be Europe's biggest such event. Locations and dates change each year.

Primavera Sound   MUSIC
(www.primaverasound.com) For three days in late May or early June, the Auditori

Fòrum and other locations around town become the combined stage for a host of international DJs and musicians.

Dia de Sant Joan
MIDSUMMER

This is a colourful midsummer celebration on 24 June with bonfires, even in the squares of L'Eixample, and fireworks marking the evening that precedes this holiday.

Festival del Grec
MUSIC, THEATRE

(www.barcelonafestival.com) Held from late June to August, this festival involves music, dance and theatre at many locations across the city.

Festa Major de Gràcia
GRÀCIA

(www.festamajordegracia.org, in Catalan) This is a madcap local festival held in Gràcia around 15 August, with decorated streets, dancing and concerts.

La Diada
CATALONIA

Catalonia's national day on 11 September, marking the fall of Barcelona in 1714, is a fairly solemn holiday in Barcelona.

🛏 Sleeping

There is no shortage of hotels in Barcelona, but its continuing status as one of Europe's city-break-getaway flavours of the month and its busy trade-fair calendar mean that it is often a good idea to book in advance.

Those looking for cheaper accommodation close to the action should check out the Barri Gòtic and El Raval. Some good lower-end *pensiones* (small private hotels) are also scattered about L'Eixample. A range of boutique-style hotels with real charm in all categories has enriched the offerings in the past few years. Many midrange and top-end places are spread across L'Eixample, most of them in easy striking distance of the old town. Several fine hotels are located on the fringes of the busy Born area of La Ribera and a there's a handful of options near the beaches at La Barceloneta.

LA RAMBLA

Hotel Continental
HOTEL €€

(Map p240; ☎93 301 25 70; www.hotelconti nental.com; La Rambla 138; s/d €87/97; ❄@; ⓂCatalunya) Rooms in this classic old Barcelona hotel (where George Orwell stayed during the civil war) are spare but have old-time touches such as ceiling fans. Try for a double with balcony over La Rambla (for which you pay €20 extra). You can have breakfast in your room or head for the 24-hour breakfast buffet.

BARRI GÒTIC

Alberg Hostel Itaca
HOSTEL €

(Map p234; ☎93 301 97 51; www.itacahostel. com; Carrer de Ripoll 21; dm €14-20, d €55; @❄; ⓂJaume I) A bright, quiet hostel near the Catedral, Itaca has spacious dorms (sleeping six, eight or 12 people), with parquet floors, spring colours and a couple of doubles with private bathroom. It also has a couple of nearby apartments for six people (€120 per night).

Hostal Campi
HOSTAL €

(☎93 301 35 45; www.hostalcampi.com; Carrer de la Canuda 4; s/d without bathroom €34/57; ⓂCatalunya) An excellent bottom-end deal. The best rooms are the doubles with their own loo and shower. Although basic, they are extremely roomy and bright.

Hotel Neri
DESIGN HOTEL €€€

(Map p234; ☎93 304 06 55; www.hotelneri.com; Carrer de Sant Sever 5; d from €235; ❄@❄; ⓂLiceu) Occupying a beautifully adapted, centuries-old building, this stunningly renovated medieval mansion combines historic stone walls with sexy plasma TVs. Downstairs is a fine restaurant and you can take a drink and catch some rays on the roof deck.

Hotel California
HOTEL €€

(Map p234; ☎93 317 77 66; www.hotelcalifornia bcn.com; Carrer d'en Rauric 14; s/d €80/115; ❄@❄; ⓂLiceu) A classic, central, gay-friendly establishment, the California offers 31 simple but spotlessly kept rooms in light, neutral colours, with good-sized beds, plasma-screen TVs and a bustling breakfast room. Room service operates 24 hours.

Hotel Jardí
HOTEL €€

(Map p234; ☎93 301 59 00; www.hoteljardi-bar celona.com; Plaça de Sant Josep Oriol 1; d €65-95; ❄; ⓂLiceu) The best rooms in this attractively located spot are the doubles with a balcony over one of the prettiest squares in the city. The rest are dull.

EL RAVAL

Hotel San Agustín
HOTEL €€

(Map p240; ☎93 318 16 58; www.hotelsa.com; Plaça de Sant Agustí 3; s €123-144, d €171; ❄@❄; ⓂLiceu) Once an 18th-century monastery, this hotel opened in 1840, making it the city's oldest. The location is perfect: a quick stroll off La Rambla on a curious square. Rooms sparkle, are mostly spacious and light and have parquet floors. Consider an attic double (€134), with a sloping ceiling and bird's-eye views.

Hostal Gat Raval HOSTEL €€

(Map p240; ☑93 481 66 70; www.gataccom modation.com; Carrer de Joaquín Costa 44; s/d without bathroom €58/74; ✴@ 令; MUniversitat) There's a pea-green and lemon-lime colour scheme in this hip, young, 2nd-floor hostel-style lodgings deep in El Raval. Rooms are pleasant, secure and each is behind a green door, but only some have private bathroom. Across the road you have a choice of busy bars in which to while away the evenings.

Barceló Raval DESIGN HOTEL €€

(Map p240; ☑93 320 14 90; www.barceloraval. com; La Rambla del Raval 17-21; d €150-210; ✴@令≋; MLiceu) The rooftop terrace at this oval-shaped newcomer offers fabulous views and the B-Lounge bar-restaurant is the toast of the town for meals and cocktails. Three classes of room all offer slick appearance (lots of white and contrasting lime-green or ruby-red splashes of colour), Nespresso machine and iPod docks.

Casa Camper DESIGN HOTEL €€€

(Map p240; ☑93 342 62 80; www.casacamper. com; Carrer d'Elisabets 11; s/d €228/255; ⊜✴@; MLiceu) Run by the Mallorcan shoe people in the better end of El Raval, these designer digs offer rooms with a few surprises, like the Vinçon furniture. Across the corridor from each room is a separate, private sitting room, with balcony, TV and hammock.

Hotel Aneto HOTEL €

(Map p240; ☑93 301 99 89; www.hotelaneto.com; Carrer del Carme 38; s/d €45/65; ✴; MLiceu) Nestled in a lively street in one of the nicer parts of El Raval, the Aneto is a good-value, simple base to range out from. The best rooms are the doubles with the shuttered street-side balconies.

Hotel Peninsular HOTEL €€

(Map p240; ☑93 302 31 38; www.hpeninsular. com; Carrer de Sant Pau 34; s/d €55/78; ✴@令; MLiceu) The star attraction of this one-time convent is the plant-draped atrium extending the full height of the hotel, at the bottom of which you take breakfast in the morning. Rooms are simple, clean and (mostly) spacious.

Barcelona Mar Hostel HOSTEL €

(Map p240; ☑93 324 85 30; www.barcelonamar. com; Carrer de Sant Pau 80; dm €18-22, d €60; ✴@令; MParal.lel) Bunk down in no-nonsense double rooms or dorms for six to 16 people. You are within stumbling distance of plenty of bars on La Rambla del Raval. It's open 24 hours and there's free access to internet, lockers, kitchen and luggage storage.

LA RIBERA

TOP CHOICE ⟍ **Hotel Banys Orientals**

BOUTIQUE HOTEL €€

(Map p242; ☑93 268 84 60; www.hotelbanysori entals.com; Carrer de l'Argenteria 37; s/d €93/107; ✴@; MJaume I) Cool blues and aquamarines combine with dark-hued parquet floors to lend this boutique beauty an understated charm. All rooms – admittedly on the small side but impeccably presented – look onto the street or back lanes. It has more spacious suites in two other nearby buildings.

Chic & Basic DESIGN HOTEL €€

(Map p242; ☑93 295 46 52; www.chicandbasic. com; Carrer de la Princesa 50; s €96, d €132-171; ✴@; MJaume I) In a completely renovated building are 31 spotlessly white rooms. They have high ceilings, enormous beds (room types are classed as M, L and XL!) and lots of detailed touches (LED lighting, LCD TV screens and the retention of many beautiful old features of the original building, such as the marble staircase). Have a drink in its ground-floor White Bar, which is exactly as its name suggests. Chic & Basic also runs a *hostal* in El Raval.

Pensió 2000 PENSIÓN €

(☑93 310 74 66; www.pensio2000.com; Carrer de Sant Pere més Alt 6; s/d with bathroom €52/65; @; MUrquinaona) Sitting in front of the Modernista chocolate box that is the Palau de la Música Catalana (p239), this cheerful *pensión*, with its seven canary-yellow rooms, is a conveniently placed option. Two rooms (the pick) have their own bathroom. You can also take time out on the little terrace.

PORT VELL & LA BARCELONETA

W Barcelona HOTEL €€€

(☑93 295 28 00; www.w-barcelona.com; Plaça de la Rosa dels Vents 1; r €283-385; P✴@≋; MBarceloneta, ☐17, 39, 57 or 64) In an admirable location at the end of a beach, this spinnaker-shaped glass tower offers all sorts of rooms. Guests flit between the gym, infinity pool (with bar) and Bliss@spa. There's avant-garde dining on the 2nd floor in the Bravo restaurant and hip cocktail sipping with stunning views in the Eclipse bar.

Hotel 54 HOTEL €€

(Map p245; ☑93 225 00 54; www.hotel54bar celoneta.com; Passeig de Joan de Borbó 54;

An alternative accommodation option can be apartment rental. Typical short-term prices are around €80 to €100 for two people per night. For four people you might be looking at an average of €160 a night. If you want to do a short-term house swap, check out the ads on www.loquo.com.

There are scores of rental services: Aparteasy (Map p252; ☑93 451 67 66; www.aparteasy.com; Plaça del Doctor Letamendi 10); Feelathomebarcelona.com (Map p240; ☑651 894141; www.feelathomebarcelona.com; Carrer Nou de la Rambla 15); Barcelona On Line (Map p252; ☑902 887017, 93 343 79 93; www.barcelona-on-line.es; Carrer de València 352); Friendly Rentals (☑93 268 80 51; www.friendlyrentals.com; Passatge de Sert 4); Lodging Barcelona (Map p252; ☑93 458 77 58; www.lodgingbarcelona.com; Carrer de Balmes 62); and Rent a Flat in Barcelona (Map p252; ☑93 342 73 00; www.rentaflatin barcelona.com; Carrer de Fontanella 18).

If your budget is especially tight, look at the economical options on Barcelona30. com (☑902 585680; www.barcelona30.com).

The Universitat de Barcelona (Map p252; ☑93 402 11 00; Gran Via de les Corts Catalanes 585), the British Council (☑93 241 99 77; Carrer d' Amigó 83) and International House (☑93 268 45 11; Carrer de Trafalgar 14) have noticeboards with ads for flat shares.

The free English-language monthly *Barcelona Metropolitan,* found in bars, some hotels and, occasionally, tourist offices, carries rental classifieds in English, as does another monthly freebie, *Catalunya Classified.* Count on rent of €350 a month or more. To this, you need to add your share of bills (gas, electricity, water, phone and *comunidad* – building maintenance).

s/d €130/140; ❄ @; ⓜBarceloneta) Modern rooms, with dark tile floors, designer bathrooms and LCD TVs, are sought after for the marina and sunset views. Other rooms look out over the lanes of La Barceloneta and are cheaper. For those harbour views, you can also sit on the roof terrace.

Hotel del Mar
HOTEL €€

(☑93 319 33 02; www.gargallohotels.es; Pla del Palau 19; s/d €139/171; ❄ @; ⓜBarceloneta) The 'Sea Hotel' is neatly placed between Port Vell and El Born. Some of the rooms in this heritage building have balconies with waterfront views. It's no more than 10 minutes' walk from the beaches and seafood of La Barceloneta and the bars of El Born.

L'EIXAMPLE
Hostal Goya
HOSTAL €€

(Map p252; ☑93 302 25 65; www.hostalgoya. com; Carrer de Pau Claris 74; s €70, d €96-113; ❄; ⓜPasseig de Gràcia) The Goya is a gem of a spot on the chichi side of L'Eixample and a short stroll from Plaça de Catalunya. Rooms have parquet floors and a light colour scheme that varies from room to room. In the bathrooms, the original mosaic floors have largely been retained, combined with contemporary design features.

Hotel Axel
HOTEL €€

(Map p252; ☑93 323 93 93; www.axelhotels.com; Carrer d'Aribau 33; r from €142; ⊜❄@☀☎; ⓜUniversitat) Fashion- and gay-friendly, the sleek-lined, corner-block Axel offers modern touches in its designer rooms. Plasma-screen TVs and (in the double rooms) king-size beds are just some of the pluses. Take a break in the rooftop pool, the Finnish sauna or the hot tub. Or sip a cocktail at the summertime Skybar. The hotel was completely overhauled in 2010.

Hotel Praktik
HOTEL €€

(Map p252; ☑93 343 66 90; www.hotelpraktik rambla.com; Rambla de Catalunya 27; s €69, d €99-129; ❄@☀; ⓜPasseig de Gràcia) The original high ceilings and tile floors have been maintained in this one-time *hostal,* and daring ceramic touches, spot lighting, contemporary art, a chilled reading area and deck-style lounge terrace have been added.

Hotel d'Uxelles
HOTEL €€

(☑93 265 25 60; www.hotelduxelles.com; Gran Via de les Corts Catalanes 688; s/d €90/109; ❄@; ⓜTetuan) Wrought-iron bedsteads are overshadowed by flowing drapes in rooms that all have their own personal decor (from blues and whites to beige-and-cream combos). Bathrooms exude a vaguely Andalucian flavour. Some have little terraces. Get a back room, as Gran Via is incredibly noisy.

Hotel Constanza
BOUTIQUE HOTEL €€

(Map p252; ☑93 270 19 10; www.hotelconstanza. com; Carrer del Bruc 33; s/d €110/130; ✳@; ⓂGirona or Urquinaona) Constanza is a boutique belle that has stolen the heart of many a visitor to Barcelona. Even smaller singles are made to feel special with broad mirrors and strong colours (reds and yellows, with black furniture). Suites and studios are further options. The terrace is a nice spot to relax for a while, looking over the rooftops of L'Eixample.

Hostal Girona
HOSTAL €€

(☑93 265 02 59; www.hostalgirona.com; Carrer de Girona 24; s/d €70/85; ⓂGirona) A 2nd-floor, family-run *hostal*, the Girona is a basic but clean and friendly spot. The atmosphere is Catalan and somewhat frozen in time but good value. Rooms range from poky singles with communal bathroom to airy doubles with balcony (beware of traffic noise in summer, when you'll have to keep the windows open).

Hotel Omm
DESIGN HOTEL €€€

(Map p252; ☑93 445 40 00; www.hotelomm.es; Carrer de Rosselló 265; d from €345; P✳@✲; ⓂDiagonal) The balconies look like strips of metallic skin peeled back from the shiny surface of the hotel – the sort of idea a latter-day Modernista might have had! Light, clear tones dominate in the ultramodern rooms, and the sprawling foyer bar is a popular evening meeting point for guests and outsiders alike.

Fashion House
B&B €€

(☑637 904044; www.bcnfashionhouse.com; Carrer de Bruc 13; s/d/tr without bathroom €55/80/110; ✳@�ⓦ; ⓂUrquinaona) The name is a little silly but this typical, broad 1st-floor Eixample flat contains eight rooms of varying size done in tasteful style, with 4.5m-high ceilings, parquet floors and, in some cases, a little gallery onto the street. Bathrooms are located along the broad corridor, one for every two rooms. Breakfast is served in the main dining room or in the garden out back.

Market Hotel
BOUTIQUE HOTEL €€

(☑93 325 12 05; www.markethotel.com.es; Passatge de Sant Antoni Abad 10; s/ste €105/140, d €115-125; ✳@; ⓂSant Antoni) Attractively located in a renovated building along a narrow lane just north of the grand old Sant Antoni market (which unfortunately is shut for much-needed renovations), this place has an air of simple chic. Room decor is a pleasing combination of white, dark nut-browns, light timber and reds. Downstairs is a busy restaurant serving up Catalan and Med cuisine.

Somnio Hostel
HOSTEL €€

(Map p252; ☑93 272 53 08; www.somniohostels.com; Carrer de la Diputació 251; dm €25, s/d without bathroom €40/72; ◗✳@ⓦ; ⓂPasseig de Gràcia) A crisp, tranquil hostel with 10 rooms (two of them six-bed dorms and all with a simple white and light-blue paint job), Somnio is nicely located in the thick of things in L'Eixample. Rain showers and thick flex mattresses are nice features in this 2nd-floor digs.

Hostal Aribau
HOSTAL €

(Map p252; ☑93 453 11 06; www.hostalaribau. com; Carrer d'Aribau 37; s/d/tr with bathroom €60/65/80; ✳; ⓂUniversitat) Handily located within brisk walking distance of Ciutat

---

CAMPING

The nearest camping grounds to Barcelona lie some way out of town. A couple are on the main coast road heading for Sitges.

Some 11km northeast of the city and only 200m from El Masnou train station (reached by *rodalies* trains from Catalunya station on Plaça de Catalunya), **Camping Masnou** (☑93 555 15 03; Camí Fabra 33, El Masnou; 2-person site with car €34.25; ⊙year-round; P✲) offers some shade, is near the beach and is reasonable value.

Camping Tres Estrellas (☑93 633 06 37; www.camping3estrellas.com; Carretera C31, Km186.2, Viladecans; 2-person site with car €34; ⊙mid-Mar–mid-Oct; P@✲) is one of several camping grounds located on a stretch of beach starting about 12km southwest of Barcelona. It has shops, restaurants, bars, several pools and laundry facilities. There's a play area for kids and a basketball court. It's a comparatively green spot under shady pines. Bus L95 runs from the corner of Ronda de la Universitat and Rambla de Catalunya.

Vella and in a busy part of L'Eixample, this is a straightforward family-run *hostal* with smallish but clean rooms.

GRÀCIA

Hotel Casa Fuster
MODERNISTA HOTEL €€€
(Map p258; ☎932553000, 902202345; www.hotel casafuster.com; Passeig de Gràcia 132; s/d from €294/321; P ➲ ✳ @ ✉ ✸; MDiagonal) It is hard to believe the wrecking ball once threatened this Modernista mansion turned luxury hotel. Standard rooms are plush if smallish. Period features have been lovingly restored and complemented with hydromassage tubs and king-sized beds. Try for a room with a balcony looking down Passeig de Gràcia.

TIBIDABO

Alberg Mare de Déu de Montserrat
HOSTEL €
(☎93 210 51 51; www.xanascat.cat; Passeig de la Mare de Déu del Coll 41-51; dm under/over 26yr €21.55/25.95; P @; MVallcarca then ⬜28 or 92) Four kilometres north of the city centre, this hostel's main building is a magnificent former mansion with a Mudéjar-style lobby. Most rooms sleep six. Sitting outside on balmy summer nights makes a pleasant alternative to a trip into town. ISIC cardholders pay the under-26 price.

EL POBLE SEC

TOP CHOICE Hostel Mambo Tango
HOSTEL €
(Map p262; ☎93 442 51 64; www.hostel mambotango.com; Carrer del Poeta Cabanyes 23; dm €26; @ ✸; MParal.lel) A fun, international hostel to hang out in, the Mambo Tango has basic dorms (from six to 10 people) and a welcoming, somewhat chaotic atmosphere, which is reflected in the kooky colour scheme in the bathrooms. Advice on what to do and where to go out is always on hand.

Melon District
HOSTEL €
(Map p262; ☎93 329 96 67; www.melondistrict. com; Avinguda del Paral.lel 101; s €45-55, d €50-60; P ✳ @ ✸; MParal.lel) Whiter than white seems to be the policy in this student residence, where you can stay the night or book in for a year. Erasmus folks and an international student set are attracted to this hostel-style spot, where the only objects in the rooms that aren't white are the green plastic chairs.

✗ Eating

Barcelona is something of a foodies' paradise on earth, combining rich Catalan cooking traditions with a new wave of cutting-edge grub cooked by chefs at the vanguard of what has been dubbed *nueva cocina española*.

Traditional restaurants, often not too demanding fiscally speaking, are scattered across the Barri Gòtic and El Raval, where you'll also find plenty of hip little places. The El Born area of La Ribera teems with eateries, ranging from high-end experimental through many atmospheric spots in centuries-old buildings to the occasional knockabout joint.

Gràcia is full of tempting eateries, among them a legion of Middle Eastern and Greek joints.

Across the broad expanse of L'Eixample, the Zona Alta and further outlying districts, you'll find all sorts, from Chinese-run sushi bars to top-end dining experiences. You need to know where you are going, however, as wandering about aimlessly and picking whatever takes your fancy is not as feasible as in the old city.

Cartas (menus) may be in Catalan, Spanish or both; quite a few establishments also have foreign-language menus.

BARRI GÒTIC

Bar Celta
GALICIAN TAPAS €€
(Map p234; Carrer de la Mercè 16; meals €20-25; ⊙noon-midnight Tue-Sun; MDrassanes) Bar Celta specialises in *pulpo* (octopus) and other seaside delights from Galicia. The waiters waste no time in serving up bottles of crisp white Ribeiro wine to wash down the *raciones* (large servings of tapas).

Agut
CATALAN €€
(Map p234; Carrer d'en Gignàs 16; meals €35; ⊙lunch & dinner Tue-Sat, lunch Sun; ➲; MDrassanes) Contemporary paintings contrast with the fine traditional Catalan dishes offered in this timeless restaurant. You might start with something like the *bouillabaisse con cigalitas de playa* (fish stew with little seawater crayfish) for €11 and follow with an oak-grilled meat dish.

Milk
BRUNCH €
(Map p234; www.milkbarcelona.com; Carrer d'en Gignàs 21; meals €15-20; ⊙brunch 11am-4pm Thu-Sun; MJaume I) Known to many as a cool cocktail spot, the Irish-run Milk's key role for Barcelona night owls is providing morning-after brunches. Avoid direct sunlight and tuck into pancakes, salmon eggs Benedict and other hangover dishes in the penumbra. Anyone for a triple-whammy hamburger or a Milk's fry-up?

Pla

MODERN €€

(Map p234; ☎93 412 65 52; www.pla-repla.com; Carrer de la Bellafila 5; meals €45-50; ☺dinner daily; ☺; MJaume I) In this modern den of inventive cooking, with music worthy of a club, the chefs present deliciously strange combinations such as *bacallà amb salsa de pomes verdes* (cod in a green apple sauce). Exotic meats like kangaroo turn up on the menu, too.

Can Conesa

SNACKS €

(Map p234; Baixada de la Libreteria 1; rolls €3-5; ☺Mon-Sat; MJaume I) This place has been doling out delicious *entrepans* (bread rolls with filling), hot dogs and toasted sandwiches for more than 50 years – *barcelonins* swear by it and queue up for them.

EL RAVAL

Bar Pinotxo

TAPAS €€

(Map p240; Mercat de la Boqueria; meals €20; ☺6am-5pm Mon-Sat Sep-Jul; MLiceu) Of the half-dozen or so tapas bars and informal eateries within the market, this one near the Rambla entrance is about the most popular. Roll up to the bar and enjoy the people watching as you munch on tapas assembled from the products on sale at the stalls around you.

Can Lluís

CATALAN €€

(Map p240; Carrer de la Cera 49; meals €30-35; ☺Mon-Sat Sep-Jul; MSant Antoni) Three generations have kept this spick and span old-time classic in business since 1929. Beneath the olive-green beams in the back dining room, you can see the spot where an anarchist's bomb went off in 1946, killing the then owner. Expect fresh fish and seafood. The *llenguado* (sole) is oven-cooked in whisky and raisins.

Bodega 1800

WINE, SNACKS €€

(Map p240; http://bodega1800.com; Carrer del Carme 31; meals €25-30; MLiceu) This old wine store has been transformed into a charming wine bar. Linger at the casks inside this little bottle-lined establishment or in the adjacent arcade and be guided through snack and wine suggestions. Wine, no matter which one you want, goes for €2.50 a glass and snacks €3.50 a pop.

Casa Leopoldo

CATALAN €€

(Map p240; ☎93 441 30 14; www.casaleopoldo. com; Carrer de Sant Rafael 24; meals €50; ☺lunch & dinner Tue-Sat, lunch Sun Sep-Jul; ☺; MLiceu) Several rambling dining areas with magnificent tiled walls and exposed timber-beam ceilings make this a fine option. The seafood menu is extensive and the local wine list strong. This is an old-town classic beloved of writers and artists down the decades.

Organic

VEGETARIAN €

(Map p240; www.antoniaorganickitchen.com, in Spanish; Carrer de la Junta de Comerç 11; meals €15-20; ☺12.45pm-midnight; ☺; MLiceu) As you wander into this sprawling vegetarian spot, to the left is the open kitchen, where you choose from a limited range of options that change from day to day. Servings are generous and imaginative. The salad buffet is copious and desserts are good. The set lunch costs €9.50 plus drinks.

Mesón David

SPANISH €

(Map p240; Carrer de les Carretes 63; meals €15-20, menú del día €8.50; ☺Tue-Sun; MParal.lel) With its smoky timber ceiling, excitable waiting staff and generally chaotic feel, this tavern is a slice of the old Spain. Plonk yourself down on a bench for gregarious dining, such as house specialities *caldo gallego* (a sausage broth) and *lechazo al horno* (a great clump of oven-roasted suckling lamb for €8.90).

LA RIBERA

Cal Pep

TAPAS €€

(Map p242; ☎93 310 79 61; www.calpep.com; Plaça de les Olles 8; meals €45-50; ☺lunch Tue-Sat, dinner Mon-Fri Sep-Jul; ☺; MBarceloneta) It's getting a foot in the door here that's the problem. If you want one of the five tables out the back, you'll need to call ahead. Most people are happy elbowing their way to the bar for some of the tastiest gourmet seafood tapas in town. Pep recommends *cloïsses amb pernil* (clams and ham – seriously!) or the *trifàsic* (combo of calamari, whitebait and prawns).

Les Cuines de Santa Caterina

INTERNATIONAL €€

(www.cuinessantacaterina.com; Mercat de Santa Caterina; meals €25-30; ☺; MJaume I) Peck at the sushi bar, tuck into classic rice dishes or go vegetarian in this busy market restaurant in the Mercat de Santa Caterina. A drawback is the speed with which they whisk barely finished plates away from you but the range of dishes and bustling atmosphere are fun. They don't take reservations, so it's first come first served.

La Llavor dels Orígens

CATALAN €

(Map p242; www.lallavordelsorigens.com; Carrer de la Vidrieria 6-8; meals €15-20; ☺12.30pm-

12.30am; 🚇; Ⓜ Jaume I) In this treasure chest of Catalan regional products, the shop shelves groan under the weight of bottles and packets of goodies. It also has a long menu of smallish dishes, such as *sopa de carbassa i castanyes* (pumpkin and chestnut soup) or *mandonguilles amb albergínies* (rissoles with aubergine), that you can mix and match over wine by the glass.

Ikibana   JAPANESE FUSION €€

(Map p242; www.ikibana.es; Passeig de Picasso 32; meals €25-30; Ⓜ Barceloneta) It feels like you are walking on water as you enter this Japanese fusion lounge affair. A broad selection of makis, tempuras, sushi and more are served at high tables with leather-backed stools. The widescreen TV switches from chilled music clips to live shots of the kitchen. The set lunch is €12.

Pla de la Garsa   CATALAN €€

(Map p242; Carrer dels Assaonadors 13; meals €25; ⊘ dinner; 🚇; Ⓜ Jaume I) This 17th-century house is ideal for a romantic dinner. Timber beams, anarchically scattered tables and soft ambient music combine to make an enchanting setting over two floors for traditional, hearty Catalan cooking, with dishes such as *timbal de botifarra negra* (black pudding with mushrooms).

Casa Delfín   SPANISH €

(Map p242; Passeig del Born 36; meals €15-20; ⊘ noon-1am daily; Ⓜ Barceloneta) Under siege from triremes of ultra avant-garde cookeries, the 'Dolphin House' continues to do what it has always done best – a bountiful lunch from an extensive menu of Spanish favourites. No frills, just good tucker amid all the fancy folk. Sit outside.

El Xampanyet   TAPAS €

(Map p242; Carrer de Montcada 22; meals €15-20; ⊘ lunch & dinner Tue-Sat, lunch Sun; Ⓜ Jaume I) Nothing much has changed in this, one of the city's best-known *cava* bars. Plant yourself at the bar or seek out a table jammed up against the old-style tiled walls for a glass or three of *cava* and an assortment of tapas, such as the tangy *boquerons en vinagre* (white anchovies in vinegar).

LA BARCELONETA & THE COAST

TOP CHOICE Xiringuito d'Escribà

SEAFOOD, RICE DISHES €€

(☑ 93 221 07 29; www.escriba.es; Ronda Litoral 42, Platja de Bogatell; meals €40-50; ⊘ lunch daily; Ⓜ Llacuna) The Barcelona pastry family serves up top-quality seafood at this popular waterfront eatery. This is one of the few places where one person can order from their selection of paella and *fideuá* (vermicelli noodle dish prepared in similar fashion to paella; normally a minimum of two people).

Suquet de l'Almirall   SEAFOOD €€

(Map p245; ☑ 93 221 62 33; Passeig de Joan de Borbó 65; meals €45-50; ⊘ lunch & dinner Tue-Sat, lunch Sun; 🚇; Ⓜ Barceloneta or 🚌 17, 39, 57 or 64) At this family business run by one of the acolytes of Ferran Adrià's El Bulli restaurant, the order of the day is top-class seafood. A good option is the *pica pica marinera* (seafood mix; €38) or you could opt for the tasting menu (€44).

Vaso de Oro   TAPAS €€

(Map p245; Carrer de Balboa 6; meals €20-25; 🚇; Ⓜ Barceloneta) This must be one of the world's narrowest bars. Fast-talking waiters will serve up a few quick quips with your tapas of grilled *gambes* or *solomillo* (sirloin) chunks. Want something a little different to drink? Ask for a *flauta cincuenta* – half lager and half dark beer.

Can Maño   SPANISH €

(Map p245; Carrer del Baluard 12; meals €15-20; ⊘ Mon-Sat; Ⓜ Barceloneta) You'll need to be prepared to wait before being squeezed in at a packed table for a raucous night of *raciones* (posted on a board at the back) over a bottle of *turbio* – a cloudy white plonk. You can breakfast on *gambes* (prawns), too.

Can Ros 1911   SEAFOOD €€

(Map p245; Carrer del Almirall Aixada 7; meals €30-35; ⊘ Thu-Tue; 🚇; Ⓜ Barceloneta or 🚌 45, 57, 59, 64 or 157) Little has changed over the decades in this seafood fave. In a restaurant where the decor is a reminder of simpler times, a simple rule guides: serve up succulent fresh fish cooked with a light touch. It also does a rich *arròs a la marinera* (seafood rice), a generous *suquet* (fish stew) and a mixed seafood platter for two.

Can Majó   SEAFOOD €€

(Map p245; Carrer del Almirall Aixada 23; meals €30-40; ⊘ lunch & dinner Tue-Sat, lunch Sun; Ⓜ Barceloneta or 🚌 45, 57, 59, 64 or 157) Virtually on the beach (with tables outside in summer), Can Majó has a long and steady reputation for fine seafood, particularly its rice dishes (€15 to €22) and cornucopian *suquets*. The *bollabessa de peix i marisc* (fish and seafood bouillabaisse) is succulent.

SELF-CATERING

Shop in the **Mercat de la Boqueria** (Map p240; La Rambla de Sant Josep; ☺8am-8pm Mon-Sat), one of the world's great produce markets, and complement with any other necessities from a local supermarket. Handy ones include **Carrefour Express** (Map p240; La Rambla dels Estudis 113; ☺10am-10pm Mon-Sat; ⒨Catalunya), near the northern end of La Rambla; and **Superservis** (Map p234; Carrer d'Avinyó 13; ☺8.45am-2pm & 5-8.30pm Mon-Thu & Sat, 8.45am-8.30pm Fri; ⒨Liceu) in the heart of Barri Gòtic.

For freshly baked bread, head for a *forn* or *panadería*. For a gourmet touch, the food sections of El Corte Inglés department stores (p289) have some tempting local and imported goodies.

Torre d'Alta Mar   MEDITERRANEAN €€€
(Map p245; ☏93 221 00 07; www.torredealtamar.com; Torre de Sant Sebastiá, Passeig de Joan de Borbó 88; meals €70-80; ☺lunch & dinner Tue-Sat, dinner Sun & Mon; ⊖; ⒨Barceloneta or ⊟17, 39, 57 or 64) Head up to the top of the Torre de Sant Sebastiá and take a ringside seat for the best views of the city and seafood like the *Gall de Sant Pere amb salsa de garotes* (John Dory with sea-urchin sauce). The setting alone makes this ideal for impressing a date.

L'EIXAMPLE

TOP CHOICE Tapaç 24   TAPAS €€
(Map p252; www.carlesabellan.com; Carrer de la Diputació 269; meals €30-35; ☺9am-midnight Mon-Sat; ⒨Passeig de Gràcia) Specials in this basement tapas temple include the *bikini* (toasted ham and cheese sandwich – the ham is cured and the truffle makes all the difference), a thick black *arròs negre de sípia* (squid ink black rice) and, for dessert, *xocolata amb pa, sal i oli* (delicious balls of chocolate in olive oil with a touch of salt and wafer).

Amaltea   VEGETARIAN €
(www.amalteaygovinda.com; Carrer de la Diputació 164; meals €10-15; ☺Mon-Sat; ⊖⊘; ⒨Urgell) The weekday set lunch (€10.50) offers a series of dishes that change frequently with the seasons. At night, the set two-course dinner (€15) offers good value. The homemade desserts are tempting.

Cerveseria Brasseria Gallega   TAPAS €€
(☏93 439 41 28; Carrer de Casanova 238; meals €30; ☺Mon-Sat; ⒨Hospital Clínic) This traditional Galician eatery fills with locals surrounded by plates of abundant classics from Galicia. The fresh *pulpo a la gallega* (spicy octopus chunks with potatoes) as starter confirms this place as a cut above the competition.

Koyuki   JAPANESE €€
(Map p252; Carrer de Còrsega 242; meals €25-30; ☺lunch & dinner Tue-Sat, dinner Sun; ⒨Diagonal) Take a seat at one of the long tables in this basement Japanese eatery that is as popular with Japanese visitors as it is with Catalans in the know. The variety of *sashimi moriawase* is mixed, generous and constantly fresh. The *tempura udon* is a particularly hearty noodle option. Splash it all down with Sapporo beer.

Restaurant Me   PAN-ASIAN €€
(☏93 419 49 33; www.catarsiscuisine.com; Carrer de París 162; meals €25-30; ☺lunch & dinner Tue-Sat, dinner Sun; ⒨Diagonal) The chefs here create superb Asian dishes with the occasional New Orleans and international intrusion. Some vegetarian options, like the *banh xeo* (Vietnamese pancake filled with bamboo, *seitan* and mushrooms), accompany such self-indulgent choices as stuffed New Orleans prawns with tartare sauce.

Inopia   TAPAS €€
(www.barinopia.com; Carrer de Tamarit 104; meals €25-30; ☺lunch & dinner Tue-Fri, lunch Sat; ⒨Rocafort) Albert Adrià, brother of star chef Ferran, has his hands full with this constantly busy gourmet-tapas temple. Select a *pintxo de cuixa de pollastre a l'ast* (chunk of rotisserie chicken thigh) or the lightly fried, tempura-style vegetables. Wash down with house red or Moritz beer.

Relais de Venise   MEAT €€
(Map p252; Carrer de Pau Claris 142; meals €35; ☺Sep-Jul; ⊖; ⒨Passeig de Gràcia) There's just one dish, a succulent beef entrecôte with a secret 'sauce Porte-Maillot' (named after the location of the original restaurant in Paris), chips and salad. It is served in slices and in two waves so that it doesn't go cold.

Cata 1.81   GOURMET TAPAS €€
(Map p252; ☏93 323 68 18; www.cata181.com; Carrer de València 181; meals €50; ☺dinner Mon-Sat Sep-Jul; ⒨Passeig de Gràcia) Call ahead

for the back room behind the kitchen. Surrounded by shelves of fine wines, you will be treated to a series of dainty gourmet dishes, such as *truita de patates i tòfona negre* (thick potato tortilla with a delicate trace of black truffle).

Taktika Berri BASQUE €€
(Map p252; Carrer de València 169; meals €45-50; ⊘lunch & dinner Mon-Fri, lunch Sat; ☺; MHospital Clínic) Get in early as the bar teems with punters from far and wide, anxious to wrap their mouths around some of the best Basque tapas in town. The hot morsels are all snapped up as soon as they arrive from the kitchen, so keep your eyes peeled.

Casa Darío GALICIAN €€€
(Map p252; ☑93 453 31 35; www.casadario.com, in Spanish; Carrer del Consell de Cent 256; meals €50-60; ⊘Mon-Sat Sep-Jul; ☺; M Passeig de Gràcia) Step into the timeless world of old-time silver service and ample helpings of the gifts of the sea. Opt for one of the set-menu feasts (€50) and you will be served endless rounds of seafood wonders. Meat eaters are catered for too and you can even order takeaway.

Cosmo CAFE €
(Map p252; www.galeriacosmo.com; Carrer d'Enric Granados 3; ⊘10am-10pm Mon-Thu, noon-2am Fri & Sat, noon-10pm Sun; ☎; MUniversitat) This groovy space has psychedelic colouring in the tables and bar stools and high white walls out back for exhibitions. With a nice selection of teas, pastries and snacks and set on a pleasant pedestrian strip, it's perfect for a morning Facebook session on your laptop or a civilised evening tipple while admiring the art.

GRÀCIA
Envalira CATALAN €€
(Map p258; Plaça del Sol 13; meals €30; ⊘lunch & dinner Tue-Sat, lunch Sun; MFontana) An inconspicuous, old-time stalwart, Envalira specialises in fish and rice dishes, from *arròs a la milanesa* (a savoury rice dish with chicken, pork and a cheese gratin) to *bullit de lluç* (a slice of white hake boiled with herb-laced rice and clams).

Ipar-Txoko BASQUE €€
(Map p258; ☑93 218 19 54; Carrer de Mozart 22; meals €40-50; ⊘Tue-Sat Sep-Jul; MDiagonal) Inside this Basque eatery, the atmosphere is warm and traditional. Getxo-born Mikel turns out traditional cooking from north-

ern Spain, including a sumptuous *chuletón* (T-bone steak for two). Then there are curiosities, like *kokotxas de merluza,* heart-shaped cuts from the hake's throat. Mikel is on hand to explain everything – in English too.

O'Gràcia! MEDITERRANEAN €€
(Map p258; Plaça de la Revolució de Setembre de 1868 15; meals €30-35; ⊘Tue-Sat; ☺; MFontana) This is an especially popular lunch option, with the *menú del día* outstanding value at €10.50. The *arròs negre de sípia* makes a good first course, followed by a limited set of meat and fish options with vegetable sides. Serves are decent, presentation careful and service attentive. There's a more elaborate tasting menu at €24.50.

Bilbao SPANISH €€
(Map p258; ☑93 458 96 24; Carrer del Perill 33; meals €40; ⊘Mon-Sat; MDiagonal) Bilbao is a timeless classic and will especially appeal to carnivores. The back dining room has bottle-lined walls, stout timber tables and a yellowing light evocative of distant country taverns. Opt for a *chuletón* and wash it down with a good Spanish red.

A Casa Portuguesa PORTUGUESE €
(Map p258; www.acasaportuguesa.com; Carrer de Verdi 58; meals €20; ⊘dinner Tue-Fri, lunch & dinner Sat, Sun & holidays; MFontana) As well as being a convivial halt for a glass or two of fine wine (ask waiters for advice) or a simple *vinho verde* ('green wine', a typical, simple Portuguese white wine), it is a good spot to fill up on snacks (cheeses, little pies and pastries), all in the name of getting to know our Iberian friends better. Sample the classic Portuguese pastry *pastel de Belem*.

MONTJUÏC & POBLE SEC
Quimet i Quimet GOURMET TAPAS €€
(Map p262; Carrer del Poeta Cabanyes 25; meals €25-30; ⊘lunch & dinner Mon-Fri, noon-6pm Sat; ☺; MParal.lel) Quimet i Quimet is proof that good things come in small packages. Cram into this bottle-lined quad for gourmet tapas, fine wine and even a specially made dark Belgian beer.

Xemei VENETIAN €€
(Map p262; ☑93 553 51 40; Passeig de l'Exposició 85; meals €45; ⊘Wed-Mon; ☺; MParal.lel) To an accompaniment of gentle jazz, you might be served a starter of mixed *cicheti* (Venetian seafood tapas), followed by *bigoi in salsa veneziana* (thick spaghetti in an anchovy

GAY & LESBIAN BARCELONA

The city's tourist board publishes *Barcelona – The Official Gay and Lesbian Tourist Guide* biannually. A couple of informative free magazines are in circulation in gay bookshops and bars. One is the biweekly *Shanguide*. It is jammed with listings and contact ads and aimed principally at readers in Barcelona and Madrid.

Barcelona has a fairly busy gay scene, much of it concentrated in the 'Gaixample', between Carrer de Muntaner and Carrer de Balmes, around Carrer del Consell de Cent.

Popular with a young, cruisy gay crowd, **Arena Madre** (Map p252; www.arenadisco. com, in Spanish; Carrer de Balmes 32; admission €6-12; 12.30-5.30am; Passeig de Gràcia) is one of the top gay clubs in town. Keep an eye on Wednesday's drag shows.

Every bear needs a cave and **Bacon Bear** (Carrer de Casanova 64; 6pm-2.30am; Urgell) is a friendly one. It's really just a big bar for burly gay folk.

At **Dietrich Gay Teatro Café** (Map p252; Carrer del Consell de Cent 255; 10.30pm-3am; Universitat), it's show time at 1am, with at least one drag-queen gala per night at this cabaret-style locale dedicated to Marlene.

Metro (www.metrodiscobcn.com; Carrer de Sepúlveda 185; 1-5am Mon, midnight-5am Sun & Tue-Thu, midnight-6am Fri & Sat; Universitat) attracts a casual crowd with its two dance floors, three bars and very dark room.

and onion sauce). The *suprema de San Pedro* (tender white John Dory) is a fine fish choice.

Taverna Can Margarit
CATALAN €€

(Map p262; Carrer de la Concòrdia 21; meals €25-30; dinner Mon-Sat; Poble Sec) Once a wine store, this tavern has for years attracted sometimes raucous dinner groups around its rough benches for dishes like *conejo a la jumillana* (fried rabbit served with garlic and various herbs).

Drinking

Barcelona's bars run the gamut from wood-panelled wine cellars to bright waterfront places and trendy designer bars. Most are at their liveliest from about 10pm to 2am or 3am (later opening on Friday and Saturday), especially from Thursday to Saturday, as people get into their night-time stride.

The old town is jammed with venues. The hippest area since the late 1990s has been El Born, in the lower end of La Ribera, but there is an impressive scattering of bars across the lower half of the Barri Gòtic and in El Raval too. The last especially is home to some fine old drinking institutions as well as a new wave of funky, inner-city locales.

A word of warning on La Rambla: while it can be pleasant enough to tipple here, few locals would even think about it and bar prices tend to be exorbitant – €25 for a carafe of sangria is not unheard of.

Elsewhere, a series of squares and some streets of Gràcia are loaded up with bars. In the broad expanse of L'Eixample you need to know where to go. The upper end of Carrer d'Aribau is the busiest area (late in the week), along with the area around its continuation northwest of Avinguda Diagonal.

Some useful sources of information on bars, clubs and gigs include **Lecool** (www. lecool.com), **Agentes de la Noche** (www. agentesdelanoche.com), **Barcelonarocks. com** (www.barcelonarocks.com), **Clubbingspain.com** (www.clubbingspain.com) and **LaNetro.com** (http://barcelona.lanetro.com).

BARRI GÒTIC

TOP CHOICE Soul Club
DANCE BAR

(Map p234; Carrer Nou de Sant Francesc 7; 10pm-2.30am Mon-Thu, 10pm-3am Fri & Sat, 8pm-2.30am Sun; Drassanes) Each night the DJs change the musical theme, which ranges from deep funk to Latin grooves. The tiny front bar is for drinking and chatting (get in early for a stool or the sole lounge). Out back is where the dancing is done.

Barcelona Pipa Club
BAR

(Map p234; www.bpipaclub.com; Plaça Reial 3; 10pm-4am Sun-Thu, 10pm-5am Fri & Sat; Liceu) This pipe smokers' club is like someone's flat, with all sorts of interconnecting rooms and knick-knacks – notably the pipes after which the place is named. You buzz at the door and head two floors up. It is for members only until 11pm.

Manchester
BAR

(Map p234; www.manchesterbar.com; Carrer de Milans 5; ☺7pm-2.30am Sun-Thu, 7pm-3am Fri & Sat; ⓂLiceu) Settle in for a beer and the sounds of great Manchester bands, from the Chemical Brothers to Oasis, but probably not the Hollies. It has a pleasing rough-and-tumble feel, with tables jammed in every which way. Cocktails cost €4 from 7pm to 10pm.

Marula Cafè
BAR

(Map p234; www.marulacafe.com; Carrer dels Escudellers 49; ☺11pm-5am Sun-Thu, 11pm-5.30am Fri & Sat; ⓂLiceu) A fantastic new find in the heart of the Barri Gòtic, Marula will transport you to the 1970s and the best in funk and soul. James Brown fans will think they've died and gone to heaven. It's not, however, a monothematic place and occasionally the DJs slip in other tunes, from breakbeats to house.

EL RAVAL

Bar Marsella
BAR

(Map p240; Carrer de Sant Pau 65; ☺10pm-2am Mon-Thu, 10pm-3am Fri & Sat; ⓂLiceu) In business since 1820, the Marsella specialises in *absenta* (absinthe), a beverage known for its supposed narcotic qualities. Nothing much has changed here since the 19th century and the local tipple certainly has a kick.

Boadas
COCKTAIL BAR

(Map p240; Carrer dels Tallers 1; ☺noon-2am Mon-Thu, noon-3am Fri & Sat; ⓂCatalunya) Inside the unprepossessing entrance is one of the city's oldest cocktail bars (famed for its daiquiris). The bow-tied waiters have been serving up their poison since 1933; Joan Miró and Hemingway tippled here.

Casa Almirall
BAR

(Map p240; Carrer de Joaquín Costa 33; ☺5.30pm-2.30am Sun-Thu, 7pm-3am Fri & Sat; ⓂUniversitat) In business since the 1860s, this unchanged corner bar is dark and intriguing, with Modernista decor and a mixed clientele. There are some great original pieces in here, like the marble counter and the cast-iron statue of the muse of the 1888 World Fair.

Kentucky
BAR

(Map p240; Carrer de l'Arc del Teatre 11; ☺10pm-3am Tue-Sat; ⓂLiceu) All sorts of odd bods from the *barri* (district) and beyond squeeze into this long, narrow bar late at night. Opening times (which can mean staying open until 5am) depend in part on the presence (or absence) of the law in the street.

London Bar
BAR

(Map p240; Carrer Nou de la Rambla 34-36; ☺7.30pm-4am Tue-Sun; ⓂLiceu) Open since 1909, this Modernista bar started as a hang-out for circus hands and was later frequented by the likes of Picasso, Miró and Hemingway (didn't they have any work to do?). Still as popular as it was in Picasso's time, this place fills to the brim with punters at the long front bar and rickety old tables.

Marmalade
BAR

(Map p240; www.marmaladebarcelona.com; Carrer de la Riera Alta 4-6; ☺7pm-3am; ⓂSant Antoni) From the street you can see the golden hues of the backlit bar way down the end of a lounge-lined long passageway. To the left of the bar, by a bare brick wall, is a pool table, popular but somehow out of place in this chic, ill-lit chill den (with attached restaurant).

LA RIBERA

Gimlet
COCKTAIL BAR

(Map p242; Carrer del Rec 24; cocktails €10; ☺10pm-3am; ⓂJaume I) White-jacketed bar staff with all the appropriate aplomb will whip you up a gimlet or any other classic cocktail your heart desires. Barcelona cocktail guru Javier Muelas is behind this and several other cocktail bars around the city, so you can be sure of excellent drinks, some with a creative twist.

La Fianna
BAR

(Map p242; www.lafianna.com; Carrer dels Banys Vells 15; ☺6pm-1.30am Sun-Wed, 6pm-2.30am Thu-Sat; ⓂJaume I) There is something medieval Asian about this bar, with its bare stone walls, forged-iron candelabras and cushion-covered lounges. This place heaves and, as the night wears on, it's elbow room only.

La Vinya del Senyor
WINE BAR

(Map p242; Plaça de Santa Maria del Mar 5; ☺noon-1am Tue-Sun; ⓂJaume I) The wine list is as long as *War & Peace* and the terrace lies in the shadow of Santa Maria del Mar. You can crowd inside the tiny wine bar itself or take a bottle upstairs.

PORT VELL & LA BARCELONETA

The Barcelona beach scene, apart from the roasting of countless bodies, warms up to dance sounds from Easter to early October. In addition to waterfront restaurants and bars (especially on and near Port Olímpic), a string of *chiringuitos* (provisional bars) sets up along the beaches. Most serve food and some turn into miniclubs on the sand from the afternoon until as late as 2am.

Mellow Beach Club
BEACH BAR

(www.mellowbeachclub.com; Passeig del Mare Nostrum 19-21; ☺8pm-3am Fri & Sat, 8pm-1am Tue-Thu & Sun; MBarceloneta) With design by the Barcelona fashion kings Custo (p290), this cool beach bar, with sun lounges and adjacent indoor eatery, is perfect for slipping into the balmy night. Club sounds waft from the pink bar out over the sand and water. Seemingly crouched below the glass tower of the W Barcelona hotel, it attracts a host of beautiful people.

CDLC
LOUNGE BAR

(Map p245; www.cdlcbarcelona.com; Passeig Marítim de la Barceloneta 32; ☺noon-3am; MCiutadella Vila Olímpica) Seize the night by the scruff at the Carpe Diem Lounge Club, the perfect place for your first drink lounging back in semi-oriental surrounds. You could choose to eat too, but tables are shuffled away about midnight. Ideal for a warm-up before heading to the nearby clubs.

Oke
BAR

(Map p245; Carrer del Baluard 54; ☺11am-2am; MBarceloneta) An eclectic and happy crowd hangs about this hippie-ish little bar near La Barceloneta's market. Lounges, tables and chairs seem to have been extracted willy-nilly from garage sales. Juices, cocktails and snacks are the main fair, along with animated conversation wafting out over the street.

Shôko
LOUNGE BAR

(Map p245; www.shoko.biz; Passeig Marítim de la Barceloneta 36; ☺8pm-3am Tue-Sun; MCiutadella Vila Olímpica) Wafting over your mixed Asian-Med food in this club-lounge-restaurant is an opiate mix of Shinto music and Japanese electro. As the food is cleared, it turns into a funky-beat kinda dance place.

Luz de Gas Port Vell
BAR

(Map p245; moored on Moll del Dipòsit; ☺noon-3am Mar-Nov; MBarceloneta) Sit on the top deck of this boat and let go of the day's cares. Sip wine or beer, nibble tapas and admire the yachts. On shore it plays some good dance music at night.

L'EIXAMPLE

There are three main concentrations for carousers in L'Eixample, although bars are dotted about all over. The top end of Carrer d'Aribau and the area where it crosses Avinguda Diagonal attract a heterogeneous but mostly local crowd to its many bars and clubs. Carrer de Balmes is lined with clubs for a mostly teen 'n' twenties crowd. The city's gay-and-lesbian circuit is concentrated around Carrer del Consell de Cent (see the boxed text, p282).

Berlin
BAR

(Carrer de Muntaner 240; ☺10am-2am Mon-Wed, 10pm-2.30am Thu, 10pm-3am Fri & Sat; MDiagonal or Hospital Clínic) This elegant corner bar attracts waves of night animals starting up for a long evening. In warmer weather you can sit outside on the footpath or head downstairs into the basement if the bar's too crowded.

Dry Martini
COCKTAIL BAR

(www.drymartinibcn.com; Carrer del Consell de Cent 247; ☺5pm-3am; ℞FGC Provença) Well-dressed waiters serve up the best dry martini in town, or whatever else your heart desires, in this classic cocktail lounge. Sink into a leather lounge and nurse a huge G&T.

Premier
BAR

(Map p252; Carrer de Provença 236; ☺6pm-2.30am Mon-Thu, 6pm-3am Fri & Sat; ℞FGC Provença) Relax at the bar or in a lounge in this funky little French-run wine bar. The rather short wine list is mostly French or you can opt for a Moritz beer or a *mojito*. Later in the evening, a DJ adds to the ambience.

Milano
COCKTAIL BAR

(Map p252; Ronda de la Universitat 35; www.cam parimilano.com; ☺noon-2.30am; MCatalunya) There is a slight conspiratorial feel about heading down into this cocktail den that is swept aside when you are confronted by its vastness and the happily imbibing crowds ensconced at tables or perched at the broad, curving bar to the right.

Les Gens Que J'Aime
BAR

(Map p252; Carrer de València 286; ☺6pm-2.30am Sun-Thu, 6pm-3am Fri & Sat; MPasseig de Gràcia) This intimate relic of the 1960s offers jazz music in the background and a cosy scattering of velvet-backed lounges around tiny dark tables.

Michael Collins Pub
PUB

(www.michaelcollinspubs.com; Plaça de la Sagrada Família 4; ☺noon-3am; MSagrada Família) To be sure of a little Catalan-Irish *craic*, this barn-sized and storming pub is just the ticket.

GRÀCIA
La Cigale
BAR

(Map p258; Carrer de Tordera 50; ⊙6pm-2.30am Sun-Thu, 6pm-3am Fri & Sat; MJoanic) A very civilised place for a cocktail (or two for €8 before 10pm). Prop up the zinc bar, sink into a secondhand lounge chair around a teeny table or head upstairs. Music is soothing and conversation lively.

Musical Maria
BAR

(Map p258; Carrer de Maria 5; ⊙9pm-3am; MDiagonal) Even the music hasn't changed since this place got going in the late 1970s. Lovers of rock 'n' roll will enjoy sinking beers here, perhaps over a game of pool.

La Baignoire
BAR

(Map p258; Carrer de Verdi 6; ⊙7pm-2.30am Sun-Thu, 7pm-3am Fri & Sat; MFontana) This inviting, tiny wine bar is always packed. Grab a stool and high table and order fine wines by the glass (beer and cocktails available, too). It's perfect before and after a movie at the nearby Verdi cinema.

Sabor a Cuba
BAR

(Map p258; Carrer de Francisco Giner 32; ⊙10pm-2.30am Mon-Thu, 10pm-3am Fri & Sat; MDiagonal) A mixed crowd of Cubans and fans of the Caribbean island come to drink mojitos and shake their stuff in this home of *ron y son* (rum and sound).

TIBIDABO
Mirablau
BAR

(Plaça del Doctor Andreu; ⊙11am-4.30am Sun-Thu, 11am-5am Fri & Sat) Wander downstairs after 11pm to join the beautiful people in the squeeze-me small dance space. The views over sparkling Barcelona are magic.

MONTJUÏC & POBLE SEC
Maumau Underground
BAR

(Map p262; www.maumaunderground.com; Carrer de la Fontrodona 35; ⊙11pm-2.30am Thu-Sat; MParal.lel) Funk, soul, hip hop and more are on the program in this Poble Sec music and dance haunt. Above the backlit bar a huge screen pours forth psychedelic images.

Tinta Roja
BAR

(Map p262; www.tintaroja.net, in Spanish; Carrer de la Creu dels Molers 17; ⊙8.30pm-2am Thu, 8.30pm-3am Fri & Sat; MPoble Sec) Sprinkled with an eclectic collection of furnishings, dimly lit in violets, reds and yellows, the 'Red Ink' is an intimate spot for a drink and the occasional show in the back.

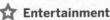 Entertainment

To keep up with what's on, pick up a copy of the weekly listings magazine, *Guía del Ocio* (€1) from news stands. The daily papers also have listings sections and the Palau de la Virreina (Map p240; ☏93 301 77 75; La Rambla de Sant Josep 99; ⊙10am-8pm; MLiceu) information office can clue you in to present and forthcoming events.

The easiest way to get hold of *entradas* (tickets) for most venues throughout the city is through the Caixa de Catalunya's Tel-Entrada (www.telentrada.com) service or Servi-Caixa (www.servicaixa.com). Another one to try for concerts is Ticketmaster (www.ticketmaster.es). There's a *venta de localidades* (ticket office) on the ground floor of the Plaça de Catalunya branch of **El Corte Inglés** (p289) and at some of its other branches around town; and at the **FNAC store** (p289) in the El Triangle shopping centre on the same square. You can also buy tickets through El Corte Inglés (☏902 400222; www.elcorteingles.es, in Spanish) by phone and online (click on *entradas*).

You can purchase some half-price tickets in person no more than three hours before the start of the show you wish to see at the Palau de la Virreina. The system is known as Tiquet-3.

Clubs
Barcelona's clubs are spread a little more thinly than bars across the city. They tend to open from around midnight until 6am.

TOP CHOICE **Elephant** MELLOW CLUB

(www.elephantbcn.com, in Spanish; Passeig dels Til.lers 1; admission Wed, Thu & Sun free, Fri & Sat €15; ⊙11.30pm-3am Wed, 11.30pm-5am Thu-Sun; MPalau Reial; P) Getting in here is like being invited to some Beverly Hills private party. Models and wannabes mix freely, as do the drinks. A big tent-like dance space is the focus, but there are various garden bars for mingling, too.

TOP CHOICE **Terrrazza** THE COOL CROWD

(Map p262; www.laterrrazza.com; Avinguda de Francesc Ferrer i Guàrdia; admission €10-20; ⊙midnight-5am Thu, midnight-6am Fri & Sat; MEspanya) One of the city's top summertime dance locations, Terrrazza attracts squadrons of beautiful people, locals and foreigners alike, for a full-on night of music and cocktails partly under the stars inside the Poble Espanyol complex.

BARCELONA ENTERTAINMENT

Catwalk

HOUSE

(Map p245; www.clubcatwalk.net; Carrer de Ramon Trias Fargas 2-4; admission €15; ☺midnight-6am Thu-Sun; MCiutadella Villa Olímpica) A well-dressed crowd piles in here for good house music, occasionally mellowed down with more body-hugging electro, R&B, hip hop and funk. Alternatively, you can sink into a fat lounge for a quiet tipple and whisper. Popular local DJ Jekey leads the way most nights.

Luz de Gas

30-SOMETHING SCENE

(www.luzdegas.com; Carrer de Muntaner 244-246; admission up to €20; ☺11.30pm-6am; MDiagonal then 🚌6, 7, 15, 27, 32, 33, 34, 58 or 64) Set in a grand theatre that is frequently the scene of live acts, this club attracts a crowd of smartly turned out clubbers, whose tastes in music vary according to the night. Next door, **Sala B** is a separate dedicated clubbers' room open on Fridays and Saturdays only.

Moog

TINY

(Map p240; www.masimas.com/moog; Carrer de l'Arc del Teatre 3; admission €10; ☺midnight-5am; MDrassanes) This fun, minuscule club is a downtown hit. In the main downstairs dance area, DJs dish out house, techno and electro, while upstairs you can groove to indie and occasional classic pop.

Otto Zutz

UPTOWN CLASSIC

(www.grupo-ottozutz.com; Carrer de Lincoln 15; admission €15; ☺midnight-5.30am Tue-Sat; ℝFGC Gràcia) Beautiful people only need apply for entry into this three-floor dance den. Head downstairs for house or upstairs for funk and soul. Wednesday and Thursday nights tend to be dominated by hip hop and R&B. On Friday and Saturday, the house shakes to house.

Sutton The Club

SELECT

(www.thesuttonclub.com; Carrer de Tuset 13; admission €15; ☺midnight-5.30am Thu, midnight-6am Fri & Sat, 6.30-11.30pm Sun; MDiagonal) A classic club with mainstream sounds, this place inevitably attracts just about everyone pouring in and out of the nearby bars at some stage in the evening – if the bouncers let them, that is.

Razzmatazz

5 CLUBS IN 1

(www.salarazzmatazz.com; Carrer dels Almogàvers 122 & Carrer de Pamplona 88; admission €15-30; ☺live music Wed-Sat, clubs 1-6am Fri & Sat; MMarina or Bogatell) A half-dozen blocks back from Port Olímpic is this

stalwart of Barcelona's club and concert scene, with five different clubs in one huge space.

Sala Apolo

RETRO CHIC

(Map p262; www.sala-apolo.com, in Catalan & Spanish; Carrer Nou de la Rambla 113; admission €6-12; ☺12.30-6am Fri & Sat, midnight-5am Sun-Thu; MParal.lel) This one-time theatre is now the setting for a great club and live-music venue. Nasty Mondays and Crappy Tuesdays (sic) are aimed at a diehard, we-never-stop-dancing crowd. Earlier in the evening, concerts generally take place. Tastes are as eclectic as possible, from local bands to name international acts.

Opium Mar

20-SOMETHINGS

(Map p245; www.opiummar.com; Passeig Marítim de la Barceloneta 34; ☺8pm-6am; MCiutadella Villa Olímpica) All whites, shimmering silver and dark contrasts mark the decor in this barn of a seaside dance place. Clubbers from around town pile in here for the thumping beat of house and techno from 3am. It's best in summer.

Karma

OLD TOWN FAVE

(Map p234; www.karmadisco.com, in Spanish; Plaça Reial 10; admission €8; ☺midnight-5.30am Tue-Sun; MLiceu) This basement place heaves to the sounds of indie, rock, punk and even '80s disco. Tunnel-shaped Karma is small and becomes quite packed.

Cinemas

Foreign films, shown with subtitles and their original soundtrack, rather than dubbed, are marked VO (*versión original*) in movie listings. A ticket usually costs €6.50 to €8.25, but most cinemas have a weekly *día del espectador* (viewer's day), often Monday or Wednesday, when they charge around €5 to €5.75. These cinemas show VO films:

Filmoteca

THEMATIC CINEMA CYCLES

(☎93 410 75 90; Avinguda de Sarrià 31-33; admission €2.70; MHospital Clínic) Specialises in film seasons that concentrate on particular directors, styles and eras of film.

Méliès Cinemes

OLD CLASSICS

(☎93 451 00 51; www.cinesmelies.net; Carrer de Villarroel 102; admission €3-5; MUrgell) Old classics in the original.

Renoir Floridablanca

CINEMA

(☎93 426 33 37; www.cinesrenoir.com, in Spanish; Carrer de Floridablanca 135; MSant Antoni) Art-house cinema on the edge of El Raval.

Verdi
CINEMA

(Map p258; ☎ 93 238 79 90; www.cines-verdi. com; Ⓜ Fontana) Verdi (Carrer de Verdi 32); Verdi Park (Carrer de Torrijos 49) One of the most popular art-house cinemas in town, located in the heart of Gràcia and surrounded by bars and eateries. There are two branches in parallel streets.

Yelmo Cines Icària
CINEMA

(☎ 93 221 75 85; www.yelmocineplex.es, in Spanish; Carrer de Salvador Espriu 61; Ⓜ Ciutadella Vila Olímpica) A massive complex where all the cinemas offer undubbed movies.

Theatre
Theatre is almost always performed in Catalan or Spanish. For more information on all that's happening in theatre, head for the information office at Palau de la Virreina, where you'll find leaflets and Teatre BCN, the monthly listings guide.

Teatre Lliure
CATALAN THEATRE

(Map p262; ☎ 93 289 27 70; www.teatrelliure. com; Plaça de Margarida Xirgu 1; admission €13-26; ◉ box office 5-8pm; Ⓜ Espanya) Consisting of two separate theatre spaces, the 'Free Theatre' puts on a variety of serious, quality drama pieces (pretty much exclusively in Catalan), contemporary dance and music.

Teatre Mercat de les Flors
CONTEMPORARY DANCE

(Map p262; ☎ 93 426 18 75; www.mercatflors. org; Carrer de Lleida 59; admission €15-20; ◉ box office 11am-2pm & 4-7pm Mon-Fri & 1hr before show; Ⓜ Espanya) At the foot of Montjuïc, this is an important venue for contemporary dance.

Teatre Nacional de Catalunya
CLASSIC PLAYS

(☎ 93 306 57 00; www.tnc.cat; Plaça de les Arts 1; admission €12-32; ◉ box office 3-7pm Wed-Fri, 3-8.30pm Sat, 3-5pm Sun & 1hr before show; Ⓜ Glòries or Monumental) Ricard Bofill's ultra-neoclassical theatre hosts a wide range of performances, principally drama but occasionally also dance and other performances.

Teatre Romea
AVANT-GARDE, CLASSICS

(Map p240; ☎ 93 301 55 04; www.teatreromea. com, in Catalan & Spanish; Carrer de l'Hospital 51; admission €17-28; ◉ box office 4.30pm till start of show Wed-Sun; Ⓜ Liceu) This theatre is a reference point for quality drama in Barcelona. It puts on a range of interesting plays – usually classics with a contemporary flavour.

Live Music
There's a good choice most nights of the week. Many venues double as bars and/or clubs. Starting time is rarely before 10pm. Admission charges range from nothing to €20 or more – the higher prices often include a drink. Note that some of the clubs previously mentioned, including Razzmatazz (p286), Sala Apolo (p286) and Luz de Gas (p286) often stage concerts. Keep an eye on listings.

Big-name acts, either Spanish or from abroad, often perform at venues such as the 17,000-capacity Palau Sant Jordi (p267) on Montjuïc or the Teatre Mercat de les Flors (p287).

Although numerous key flamenco artists grew up in the barris of Barcelona, opportunities for seeing good performances of this essentially Andalucian dance and music are limited. A few tablaos (tourist-oriented locales that stage flamenco performances) are scattered about.

Guía del Ocio has ample classical listings, but the monthly Informatiu Musical leaflet has the best coverage of classical music (as well as other genres). You can pick it up at tourist offices and the Palau de la Virreina.

Harlem Jazz Club
TOP CHOICE
MUSIC BAR

(Map p234; ☎ 93 310 07 55; www.harlem jazzclub.es; Carrer de la Comtessa de Sobradiel 8; admission up to €10; ◉ 8pm-4am Tue-Thu & Sun, 8pm-5am Fri & Sat; Ⓜ Drassanes) This narrow, smoky, old-town dive is one of the best spots in town for jazz. Every now and then it mixes it up with a little rock, Latin or blues. There are usually two sessions in an evening.

Bikini
MUSIC BAR

(☎ 93 322 08 00; www.bikinibcn.com; Carrer de Déu i Mata 105; admission €10-20; ◉ 10pm-6am Wed-Sun; Ⓜ Entença) This multihall dance space frequently stages quality acts ranging from funk guitar to rock, and from bossa nova to Latin. Performances generally start around 10pm and the club then swings into gear around midnight.

Jamboree
MUSIC BAR

(Map p234; ☎ 93 319 17 89; www.masimas. com/jamboree; Plaça Reial 17; admission €5-15; ◉ 9.30pm-6am; Ⓜ Liceu) Concerts start at 11pm and proceed until about 2am at the latest, at which point attentive jazz fans convert themselves into clubbers. Some of the great names of jazz and blues have filled the air with their sonorous contributions.

Jazz Sí Club MUSIC BAR
(☎93 329 00 20; www.tallerdemusics.com; Carrer de Requesens 2; admission €5-8; ⊙6-11pm; Ⓜ Sant Antoni) A cramped little bar run by the Taller de Músics (Musicians' Workshop) serves as the stage for a varied program of jazz through to some good flamenco (Friday nights). Thursday is Cuban night, Sunday is rock and the rest are devoted to jazz and/or blues sessions.

Monasterio MUSIC BAR
(☎616 287197; www.salamonasterio.com, in Spanish; Passeig d'Isabel II 4; ⊙9pm-2.30am Sun-Thu, 9.30pm-3am Fri & Sat; Ⓜ Barceloneta) Wander downstairs to the brick vaults of this jamming music den. There's a bit of everything, from jazz on Sundays, blues jams on Thursdays, rock 'n' roll on Tuesdays and up-and-coming singer-songwriters on Mondays.

Robadors 23 MUSIC BAR
(Map p240; Carrer d'En Robador 23; ⊙music from 8.30pm Wed; Ⓜ Liceu) On what remains a classic dodgy El Raval street, where a hardy band of streetwalkers, junkies and other misfits hangs out in spite of all the work being carried out to gentrify the area, a narrow little bar has made a name for itself with its Wednesday night gigs.

Sidecar Factory Club MUSIC BAR
(Map p234; ☎93 302 15 86; www.sidecarfactoryclub.com; Plaça Reial 7; admission €7-15; ⊙10pm-5am Mon-Thu, 10pm-6am Fri & Sat; Ⓜ Liceu) Downstairs from the bar and eatery are the red-tinged bowels of the club that opens for live music most nights. Just about anything goes, UK indie through to country punk, but rock and pop lead the way. Most shows start at 10pm (Thursday to Saturday).

Sala Tarantos MUSIC BAR, FLAMENCO
(Map p234; ☎93 319 17 89; www.masimas.net; Plaça Reial 17; admission from €7; ⊙performances 8.30pm, 9.30pm & 10.30pm daily; Ⓜ Liceu) This basement locale is the stage for some of the best flamenco to pass through Barcelona. You have to keep an eye out for quality acts, otherwise you can pop by for the more pedestrian regular performances. The place converts into a club later.

Tablao Cordobés FLAMENCO
(Map p240; ☎93 317 57 11; www.tablaocordobes.com; La Rambla 35; show €37, show & dinner €60-68; ⊙shows 8.15pm, 10pm & 11.30pm; Ⓜ Liceu) This long-standing *tablao* is typical of the genre. Generally people book for the dinner and show.

Tablao de Carmen FLAMENCO
(Map p262; ☎93 325 68 95; www.tablaodecarmen.com; Carrer dels Arcs 9, Poble Espanyol; show €35, show & tapas/dinner €45/69; ⊙shows 7.30pm & 10pm Tue-Sun; Ⓜ Espanya) Named after the great Barcelona *bailaora* (flamenco dancer) Carmen Amaya, the set-up at this establishment is similar to that at the Tablao Cordobés.

TOP CHOICE **Gran Teatre del Liceu** OPERA
(Map p234; ☎93 485 99 00; www.liceubarcelona.com; La Rambla dels Caputxins 51-59; ⊙box office 2-8.30pm Mon-Fri & 1hr before show Sat & Sun; Ⓜ Liceu) Barcelona's grand opera house, rebuilt after a fire in 1999, has world-class opera, dance and classical-music recitals. Tickets can cost anything from €7 for a cheap seat behind a pillar to €200 plus for a well-positioned night at the opera.

L'Auditori CLASSICAL MUSIC
(☎93 247 93 00; www.auditori.org; Carrer de Lepant 150; admission €10-60; ⊙box office 3-9pm Mon-Sat; Ⓜ Monumental) Barcelona's modern home for serious music lovers, L'Auditori puts on plenty of orchestral, chamber, religious and other music throughout the year.

Palau de la Música Catalana AUDITORIUM
(☎902 442882; www.palaumusica.org; Carrer de Sant Francesc de Paula 2; ⊙box office 10am-9pm Mon-Sat; Ⓜ Urquinaona) This Modernista delight is a traditional centre for classical and choral music, although nowadays you might see anything from South African dance to Portuguese fado.

Dance

The best chance you have of seeing people dancing the *sardana* (the Catalan folk dance) is at 7pm on Wednesday, 6.30pm on Saturday or noon on Sunday in front of the Catedral (p235). You can also see the dancers during some of the city's festivals. This dance in the round is intricate but hardly flamboyant.

Sport

Plaça de Braus Monumental BULLFIGHTING
(☎93 245 58 02; cnr Gran Via de les Corts Catalanes & Carrer de la Marina; ⊙ticket office 11am-2pm & 4-8pm Tue-Sun; Ⓜ Monumental) A decision by the regional Catalan parliament in July 2010 means the bullfight may be banned from January 2012, so aficionados need to get in a last look in the 2011 season. Fights are staged at around 6pm on Sunday afternoon in spring and sum-

mer. Tickets are available at the arena or through ServiCaixa (www.servicaixa.com). Prices range from €20 to €120. The higher-priced tickets are for the front row in the shade – any closer and you'd be fighting the bulls yourself.

Camp Nou
FOOTBALL

(☎902 189900; Carrer d'Aristides Maillol; ⊙box office 9am-1.30pm & 3.30-6pm Mon-Fri; ⓜPalau Reial or Collblanc) FC Barcelona (Barça for aficionados) has one of the best stadiums in Europe: the 99,000-capacity Camp Nou in the west of the city. Tickets for national-league games are available at the stadium, by phone or online. For the latter two options, nonmembers must book 15 days before the match. Tickets can cost anything from €31 to €225, depending on the seat and match.

Circuit de Catalunya
FORMULA ONE

(☎93 571 97 00; www.circuitcat.com) Formula One drivers come to Barcelona every April/ May to rip around the track at Montmeló, about a 30-minute drive north of the city. A seat for the Grand Prix race can cost anything from €110 to €435. On race days, the Sagalés bus company (☎902 130014; www.sagales.com) runs buses to the track from Passeig de Sant Joan 52 (€8 return), between Carrer de la Diputació and Carrer del Consell de Cent.

🛍 Shopping

All of Barcelona seems to be lined with unending ranks of fashion boutiques and design stores. Alongside the latest modes and big national and international names in fashion, an assortment of curious traditional shops offers everything from coffee and nuts to candles, and from sweets made in convents to amusing condoms.

Most of the mainstream fashion and design stores can be found on Plaça de Catalunya as it heads along Passeig de Gràcia, turning left into Avinguda Diagonal. From here as far as Plaça de la Reina Maria Cristina, the Diagonal is jammed with shopping options. There's plenty more in the streets around Passeig de Gràcia.

Fashion does not end in the chic streets of L'Eixample and Avinguda Diagonal. The El Born area in La Ribera, especially on and around Carrer del Rec, is awash with tiny boutiques, especially those purveying young, fun fashion. A bubbling fashion strip is the Barri Gòtic's Carrer d'Avinyó. For secondhand stuff, head for El Raval,

especially Carrer de la Riera Baixa. Carrer de Verdi in Gràcia is good for alternative shops too.

The single best-known department store is El Corte Inglés (www.elcorteingles.es) Plaça de Catalunya (Map p252; Plaça de Catalunya 14; ⊙10am-10pm Mon-Sat); Plaça de la Reina Maria Cristina (Avinguda Diagonal 617), with branches around town. FNAC (Map p240; www.fnac.es; Plaça de Catalunya 4; ⊙10am-10pm Mon-Sat), the French book, CD and electronics emporium, has a couple of branches around town. Bulevard Rosa (Map p252; www.bulevardrosa.com; Passeig de Gràcia 53; ⊙10.30am-9pm Mon-Sat) is one of the most interesting arcades, while the Maremagnum (www.maremagnum.es; Moll d'Espanya 5; ⊙10am-10pm) shopping centre can be a diversion when wandering around Port Vell.

Winter sales officially start on or around 10 January and their summer equivalents on or around 5 July.

Want some contemporary art? You'll find small galleries and designer stores around the Macba art museum (p238) on Carrer del Doctor Dou, Carrer d'Elisabets and Carrer dels Àngels. The classiest concentration of galleries is on and around the short stretch of Carrer del Consell de Cent between Rambla de Catalunya and Carrer de Balmes in L'Eixample.

POKING AROUND THE MARKETS

The sprawling Els Encants Vells (www.encantsbcn.com, in Catalan; Plaça de les Glòries Catalanes; ⊙7am-6pm Mon, Wed, Fri & Sat; ⓜGlòries), also known as the Fira de Bellcaire, is the city's principal flea market. There is an awful lot of junk, but you can turn up interesting items if you hunt around. The Barri Gòtic is enlivened by an art and crafts market (Plaça de Sant Josep Oriol; ⓜLiceu) on Saturday and Sunday, the antiques Mercat Gòtic (Plaça Nova; ⓜLiceu or Jaume I) on Thursday, and a coin and stamp collectors' market (Plaça Reial; ⓜLiceu) on Sunday morning. Just beyond the western edge of El Raval, the punters at the Mercat de Sant Antoni (⊙7am-8.30pm) dedicate Sunday morning to old maps, stamps, books and cards.

Altaïr
BOOKS

(www.altair.es; Gran Via de les Corts Catalanes 616; MUniversitat) This is an excellent travel bookshop with maps, guides and travel literature. There's a travellers' noticeboard and travel agency in here, too.

Laie
BOOKS

(Map p252; www.laie.es, in Catalan & Spanish; Carrer de Pau Claris 85; MCatalunya or Urquinaona) Novels and books on architecture, art and film, in English and French, and a fine cafe upstairs.

Antinous
BOOKS

(Map p234; www.antinouslibros.com, in Spanish; Carrer de Josep Anselm Clavé 6; MDrassanes) For a leisurely browse and coffee, this is about the best gay bookshop in town.

Antonio Miró
FASHION

(Map p252; www.antoniomiro.es, in Spanish; Carrer del Consell de Cent 349; ☺10am-8pm Mon-Sat; MPasseig de Gràcia) Mr Miró is one of Barcelona's haute-couture kings. He concentrates on light, natural fibres to produce smart, unpretentious men's and women's fashion. High-end evening dresses and shimmering, smart suits lead the way.

Custo Barcelona
FASHION

(Map p242; www.custo-barcelona.com; Plaça de les Olles 7; MJaume I) Custo bewitches people the world over with a youthful, psychedelic panoply of women's and men's fashion. It has several branches around town.

Red Market
FASHION

(Map p258; Carrer de Verdi 20; MFontana) Several funky fashion boutiques dot themselves along this street. Here you'll run into bright, uninhibited urban wear and accessories. Red dominates the decor more than the threads.

Urbana
FASHION

(Map p234; Carrer d'Avinyó 46; ☺11am-3pm & 4.30-9pm Mon-Sat; MLiceu) Colourful, fun city clothes, shoes and accessories await boys and girls in this easy-going store with Basque Country origins.

Casa Gispert
FOOD, DRINK

(Map p242; www.casagispert.com; Carrer dels Sombrerers 23; MJaume I) Prize-winning Casa Gispert has been toasting almonds and selling all manner of dried fruit since 1851. Pots and jars piled high on the shelves contain an unending variety of crunchy titbits.

Joan Murrià
FOOD, DRINK

(Map p252; www.murria.cat; Carrer de Roger de Llúria 85; MPasseig de Gràcia) Ramon Casas designed the Modernista shop-front ads for this delicious delicatessen, where the shelves groan under the weight of speciality food from around Catalonia and beyond.

Vila Viniteca
FOOD, DRINK

(www.vilaviniteca.es, in Spanish; Carrer dels Agullers 7; ☺8.30am-8.30pm Mon-Sat; MJaume I) One of the best wine stores in Barcelona (and, Lord knows, there are a few), this place has been searching out the best in local and imported wines since 1932.

Xampany
FOOD, DRINK

(Map p252; Carrer de València 200; ☺4.30-10pm Mon-Fri, 10am-2pm Sat; MPasseig de Gràcia) Since 1981 this 'Cathedral of Cava' has been a veritable Aladdin's cave of *cava,* with bottles of the stuff crammed high and into every possible chaotic corner of this dimly lit locale.

Vinçon
HOMEWARES

(Map p252; www.vincon.com; Passeig de Gràcia 96; ☺10am-8.30pm Mon-Sat; MDiagonal) Vinçon has the slickest designs in furniture and household goods, local and imported. The building once belonged to the Modernista artist Ramon Casas.

Camper
SHOES

(Map p252; www.camper.com; Carrer de València 249; MPasseig de Gràcia) This Mallorcan success story is the Clarks of Spain. Its shoes range from the eminently sensible to the stylishly fashionable. It has stores all over town.

❶ Information

Emergency

Tourists who want to report thefts need to go to the Catalan police, known as the **Mossos d'Esquadra** (☏088; Carrer Nou de la Rambla 80) or the **Guàrdia Urbana** (Local Police; ☏092; La Rambla 43).

Ambulance (☏061)

EU standard emergency number (☏112)

Fire brigade (Bombers; ☏080, 085)

Institut Català de la Dona (☏93 495 16 00; www.gencat.net/icdona; Plaça de Pere Coromines 1; MLiceu) For rape counselling.

Policía Nacional (☏091)

Internet Access

A growing number of hotels, restaurants, cafes, bars and other public locations offer wi-fi access.

Every year aggrieved readers write in with tales of woe from Barcelona. Petty crime and theft, with tourists as the prey of choice, are a problem, so you need to take a few common-sense precautions to avoid joining this regrettable list. Nine times out of 10 it is easy enough to avoid.

Thieves and pickpockets operate on airport trains and the metro, especially around stops popular with tourists (such as La Sagrada Família). The Old City (Ciutat Vella) is the pickpockets' and bag-snatchers' prime hunting ground. Take special care on and around La Rambla. Prostitutes working the lower (waterfront) end often do a double trade in wallet snatching. Also, stay well clear of the ball-and-three-cups (*trileros*) brigade on La Rambla. This is always a set-up and you will lose your money (and maybe have your pockets emptied as you watch the game).

Bornet (Carrer de Barra Ferro 3; per hr/10hr €2.80/20; ⏲10am-11pm Mon-Fri, 2pm-11pm Sat, Sun & holidays; Ⓜ Jaume I) A cool little internet centre and art gallery.

Media

El País includes a daily supplement devoted to Catalonia, but the region has a lively home-grown press, too. *La Vanguardia* and *El Periódico* are the main local Castilian-language dailies. The latter also publishes a Catalan version. *Avui* is the more conservative and Catalan-nationalist daily. *El Punt* concentrates on news in and around Barcelona.

Medical Services

Call ☑010 to find the nearest late-opening duty pharmacy. There are also several 24-hour pharmacies scattered across town.

Farmàcia Castells Soler (☑93 487 61 45; Passeig de Gràcia 90; Ⓜ Diagonal)

Farmàcia Clapés (☑93 301 28 43; La Rambla 98; Ⓜ Liceu)

Farmàcia Torres (☑93 453 92 20; www.farmaciaabierta24h.com; Carrer d'Aribau 62; ⒻFGC Provença)

Hospital Clínic i Provincial (☑93 227 54 00; Carrer de Villarroel 170; Ⓜ Hospital Clínic)

Hospital de la Santa Creu i de Sant Pau (☑93 291 90 00; Carrer de Sant Antoni Maria Claret 167; Ⓜ Hospital de Sant Pau)

Hospital Dos de Maig (☑93 507 27 00; Carrer del Dos de Maig 301; Ⓜ Hospital de Sant Pau)

Money

Banks abound in Barcelona, many with ATMs, including several around Plaça de Catalunya, on La Rambla and on Plaça de Sant Jaume in the Barri Gòtic.

The foreign-exchange offices that you see along La Rambla and elsewhere are open for longer hours than banks but generally offer poorer rates. **Interchange** (La Rambla dels Caputxins 74; ⏲9am-11pm; Ⓜ Liceu) represents American Express and will cash Amex travellers cheques, replace lost cheques and provide cash advances on Amex cards.

Post

The **main post office** (Plaça d'Antoni López; ⏲8.30am-9.30pm Mon-Fri, 8.30am-2pm Sat; Ⓜ Jaume I) is opposite the northeast end of Port Vell. There's a handy **branch** (Carrer d'Aragó 282; ⏲8.30am-8.30pm Mon-Fri, 9.30am-1pm Sat; Ⓜ Passeig de Gràcia) just off Passeig de Gràcia.

Tourist Information

A couple of general information lines worth bearing in mind are ☑010 and ☑012. The first is for Barcelona and the latter is for all of Catalonia (run by the Generalitat). You may sometimes strike English speakers but most operators are Catalan-Castilian bilingual only.

In addition to the following listed tourist offices, information booths operate at Estació Nord bus station, Plaça del Portal de la Pau and at the foot of the Mirador a Colom. At least three others are set up at various points around the city centre in summer.

Oficina d'Informació de Turisme de Barcelona (☑93 285 38 32; www.barcelonaturisme.com) Main Branch (Plaça de Catalunya 17-S underground; ⏲9am-9pm); Aeroport del Prat (terminals 1, 2B & 2A; ⏲9am-9pm); Estació Sants (⏲8am-8pm; Ⓜ Sants Estació); Town Hall (Carrer de la Ciutat 2; ⏲9am-8pm Mon-Fri, 10am-8pm Sat, 10am-2pm Sun & holidays; Ⓜ Jaume I) The main Barcelona tourist information office concentrates on city information and can help book accommodation. The branch in the airport's EU arrivals hall has information on all of Catalonia; a smaller office at the international arrivals hall opens the same hours. The train-station branch has limited city information. There's also a branch in the *ajuntament* (town hall).

Palau de la Virreina Arts Information Office (☑93 301 77 75; Rambla de Sant Josep 99; ⏲10am-8pm; Ⓜ Liceu) A useful office for events information and tickets.

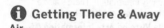

DISCOUNTS

Students generally pay a little over half of adult admission prices, as do children aged under 12 years and senior citizens (aged 65 and over) with appropriate ID. Several sights have free-entry days, often just once a month. For example, the Museu Picasso (p241) is free on the first Sunday of the month and the Museu Marítim (p239) on the first Saturday afternoon.

Possession of a Bus Turístic ticket (see p271) entitles you to discounts to some museums.

Articket (www.articketbcn.org) gives you admission to seven important art galleries for €22 and is valid for six months. The galleries are the Museu Picasso, Museu Nacional d'Art de Catalunya, the Museu d'Art Contemporani de Barcelona, the Fundació Antoni Tàpies, the Centre de Cultura Contemporània de Barcelona, the Fundació Joan Miró and La Pedrera. You can pick up the ticket through Tel-Entrada (☎902 101212; www.telentrada.com) and at the tourist offices on Plaça de Catalunya, Plaça de Sant Jaume and Sants train station.

Aficionados of Barcelona's Modernista heritage should consider the Ruta del Modernisme pack (www.rutadelmodernisme.com). For €12 you receive a guide to 115 Modernista buildings great and small, a map and discounts of up to 50% on the main Modernista sights in Barcelona, as well as some others around Catalonia. Pick it up at the tourist office at Plaça de Catalunya (p291).

Regional tourist office (☎93 238 80 91, outside Catalonia 902 400012; www.gencat. net/probert; Passeig de Gràcia 107; ⊙10am-7pm Mon-Sat, 10am-2.30pm Sun; ⓂDiagonal) Housed in the Palau Robert, it has a host of material on Catalonia.

Travel Agencies

Halcón Viatges (☎902 300600; www.halcon viajes.com, in Spanish; Carrer de Pau Claris 108; ⓂPasseig de Gràcia) Reliable chain of travel agents that sometimes has good deals. This is one of many branches around town.

Orixà (☎93 487 00 22; www.orixa.com; Carrer d'Aragó 227; ⓂPasseig de Gràcia) A good local independent travel agent.

Websites

www.barcelonaturisme.com The city's official tourism website.

www.barcelonareporter.com A portal that gathers news articles from and about Barcelona and Catalonia.

www.bcn.cat The City of Barcelona's municipal website, with many links.

www.lecool.com Subscribe for free to this site for weekly events listings.

www.rutadelmodernisme.com Web page of routes, monuments and events related to Modernisme.

Getting There & Away

Air

Aeroport del Prat (☎902 404704; www.aena. es) is 12km southwest of the centre at El Prat de Llobregat. Barcelona is a big international and

domestic destination, with direct flights from North America, as well as many European cities.

Several budget airlines, including Ryanair, use **Girona-Costa Brava airport**, 11km south of Girona and about 80km north of Barcelona. Buses connect with Barcelona's Estació del Nord bus station.

For general information on flights, see the Transport chapter (p891). See also Travel Agencies on p292.

Boat

BALEARIC ISLANDS

Regular passenger and vehicular ferries to/from the Balearic Islands, operated by **Acciona Trasmediterránea** (☎902 454645; www. trasmediterranea.es), dock along both sides of the Moll de Barcelona wharf in Port Vell. For more information, see p629.

ITALY

The Grimaldi group's **Grandi Navi Veloci** (☎in Italy 010 209 4591; www1.gnv.it; ⓂDrassanes) runs high-speed, luxury ferries three (sometimes more) days a week between Genoa and Barcelona. The journey takes 18 hours. Ticket prices vary wildly and depend on the season and how far in advance you purchase, starting at about €80 one way for an airline-style seat in summer. They can be bought online or at Acciona Trasmediterránea ticket windows. The same company runs a similar number of ferries between Barcelona and Tangiers, in Morocco (voyage time about 26 hours).

Grimaldi Ferries (☎902 531333, in Italy 081 496444; www.grimaldi-lines.com) operates similar services from Barcelona to Civitavecchia (near Rome; 20½ hours, six to seven times a week), Livorno (Tuscany; 19½ hours, three times a week) and Porto Torres (northwest Sardinia; 12 hours, daily). An economy-class airline-style seat costs from €29 in low season to €77 in high season on all routes.

Boats of both lines dock at Moll de Sant Bertran and all vessels take vehicles.

Bus

Long-distance buses for destinations throughout Spain leave from the **Estació del Nord** (☎902 260606; www.barcelonanord.com; Carrer d'Ali Bei 80; Ⓜ Arc de Triomf). A plethora of companies operates services to different parts of the country, although many come under the umbrella of **Alsa** (☎902 422242; www.alsa.es). There are frequent services to Madrid, Valencia and Zaragoza (20 or more a day) and several daily departures to such distant destinations as Burgos, Santiago de Compostela and Seville.

Eurolines (www.eurolines.com), in conjunction with local carriers all over Europe, is the main international carrier. It runs services across Europe and to Morocco, departing from Estació del Nord and **Estació d'Autobusos de Sants** (Carrer de Viriat), which is next to Estació Sants Barcelona. For information and tickets in Barcelona, contact Alsa. Another carrier is **Linebús** (www.linebus.com).

Within Catalonia, much of the Pyrenees and the entire Costa Brava are served only by buses, as train services are limited to important railheads such as Girona, Figueres, Lleida, Ripoll and Puigcerdà. If there is a train, take it – they're usually more convenient. For bus fares and journey times from Barcelona, see the appropriate destinations in the Catalonia chapter. Various bus companies operate across the region, mostly from Estació del Nord:

Alsina Graells (☎902 422242; www.alsa.es) A subsidiary of Alsa, it runs buses from Barcelona to destinations west and northwest, such as Vielha, La Seu d'Urgell and Lleida.

Barcelona Bus (☎902 130014; www.sagales.com, in Catalan & Spanish) Runs buses from Barcelona to Girona (and Girona to Costa Brava airport), Figueres, parts of the Costa Brava and northwest Catalonia.

Hispano-Igualadina (☎902 447726; www.igualadina.net; Estació Sants & Plaça de la Reina Maria Cristina) Serves central and southern Catalonia.

SARFA (☎902 302025; www.sarfa.com) The main operator on and around the Costa Brava.

TEISA (☎93 215 35 66; www.teisa-bus.com; Carrer de Pau Claris 117; Ⓜ Passeig de Gràcia) Covers a large part of the eastern Catalan Pyrenees from Girona and Figueres. From Barcelona, buses head for Camprodon via Ripoll and Olot via Besalú.

Departures from Estació del Nord include the following (where frequencies vary, the lowest figure is usually for Sunday; fares quoted are the lowest available):

DESTINA-TION	FREQUENCY (PER DAY)	DURATION (HR)	COST (ONE WAY, €)
Almería	4-5	11¼-14	62.42
Burgos	5-6	7½-8½	35.42
Granada	5-8	12½-14¼	68.65
Madrid	up to 16	7½-8	28.18
Seville	1-2	14¾	88.42
Valencia	up to 14	4-4½	25.34
Zaragoza	up to 22	3¾	13.71

Car & Motorcycle

Autopistas (tollways) head out of Barcelona in most directions, including the C31/C32 to the southern Costa Brava; the C32 to Sitges; the C16 to Manresa (with a turn-off for Montserrat); and the AP7 north to Girona, Figueres and France, and south to Tarragona and Valencia (turn off along the AP2 for Lleida, Zaragoza and Madrid). The toll-free alternatives, such as the A2 north to Girona, Figueres and France, and west to Lleida and beyond, or the A7 to Tarragona, tend to be busy and slow.

RENTAL

Avis, Europcar, Hertz and several other big companies have desks at the airport, Estació Sants train station and Estació del Nord bus terminus:

Avis (☎902 248824, 93 237 56 80; www.avis.com; Carrer de Còrsega 293-295; Ⓜ Diagonal)

Cooltra (☎93 221 40 70; www.cooltra.com; Passeig de Joan de Borbó 80-84; Ⓜ Barceloneta)

Europcar (☎93 302 05 43; www.europcar.com; Gran Via de les Corts Catalanes 680; Ⓜ Girona)

Hertz (☎93 419 61 56; www.hertz.com; Carrer del Viriat 45; Ⓜ Sants)

National/Atesa (☎902 100101, 93 323 07 01; www.atesa.es; Carrer de Muntaner 45; Ⓜ Universitat)

Pepecar (☎807 414243; www.pepecar.com; Plaça de Catalunya; Ⓜ Catalunya)

Train

The main international and domestic station is **Estació Sants** (Plaça dels Països Catalans), 2.5km west of La Rambla. Other stops on long-distance lines include **Catalunya** (Plaça de Catalunya) and **Passeig de Gràcia** (cnr Passeig de Gràcia & Carrer d'Aragó). Information windows operate at Estació Sants and Passeig de Gràcia station. Sants station has a **consigna** (left-luggage lockers; small/big locker per 24hr

€3/4.50; ⊙5.30am-11pm), a tourist office, a telephone and fax office, currency-exchange booths and ATMs.

INTERNATIONAL

For information on getting to Barcelona by rail from European cities, see the Transport chapter (p892).

One or two daily services connect Montpellier in France with Estació Sants (€59 each way in *turista* class, 4½ hours). A couple of other slower services (with a change of train at Portbou) also make this run. All stop in Perpignan.

From Estació Sants, up to eight trains daily run to Cerbère (from €10.60, 2½ hours), on the French side of the border, from where you can pick up trains to Paris via Montpellier.

DOMESTIC

Eighteen high-speed Tren de Alta Velocidad Española (AVE) trains between Madrid and Barcelona run daily in each direction, nine of them in under three hours. A typical one-way price is €114 but it comes down if you book a return or book well in advance on the website (which can bring the cost down to about €45). The line will eventually (perhaps by 2012) run right across Barcelona (via a controversial tunnel under construction) and north to the French frontier. France has promised that high-speed TGV trains will link Paris with Figueres by 2011. Some other popular runs include the following (fares represent range of lowest fares depending on type of train):

DESTINA-TION	FREQUENCY (PER DAY)	DURATION (HR)	COST (ONE WAY, €)
Alicante	up to 8	4¾-5½	49.90-54.80
Burgos	4	6-7	49-65.90
Valencia	up to 15	3-4½	38.50-43.10
Zaragoza	up to 35	1½-4¼	28.80-64.20

ⓘ Getting Around

The metro is the easiest way of getting around and reaches most places you're likely to visit (although not the airport). For some trips you need buses or FGC suburban trains. The tourist office gives out the comprehensive *Guia d'Autobusos Urbans de Barcelona*, which has a metro map and details all bus routes.

For public-transport information, call ✆010.

To/From the Airport

The **A1 Aerobús** (✆93 415 60 20; one way €5; 30-40min) runs from Terminal 1 to Plaça de Catalunya via Plaça d'Espanya, Gran Via de les Corts Catalanes (on the corner of Carrer del Comte d'Urgell) and Plaça de la Universitat (six to 15 minutes depending on the time of day) from 6.05am to 1.05am. A2 Aerobús does the same run from Terminal 2, from 6am to 12.30am. Buy tickets on the bus.

Renfe's R2 Nord train line runs between the airport and Passeig de Gràcia (via Estació Sants) in central Barcelona (about 35 minutes), before heading out of town. Tickets cost €3, unless you have a T-10 multitrip public-transport ticket. The service from the airport starts at 6.08am and ends at 11.38pm daily.

A taxi to/from the centre, about a half-hour ride depending on traffic, costs around €20 to €25.

Sagalés (✆902 130014; www.sagales.com) runs the **Barcelona Bus** (✆902 361550) service between Girona airport and Estació del Nord bus station in Barcelona (one way/return €12/21, 70 minutes).

Car & Motorcycle

An effective one-way system makes traffic flow fairly smoothly, but you'll often find yourself flowing the way you don't want to go, unless you happen to have an adept navigator and a map that shows one-way streets.

Limited parking in the Ciutat Vella is virtually all for residents only, with some metered parking. The narrow streets of Gràcia are not much better. The broad boulevards of L'Eixample are divided into blue and green zones. For nonresidents they mean the same thing: limited meter parking. Fees vary but tend to hover around €2.42 to €2.94 per hour. Parking stations are also scattered all over L'Eixample, with a few in the old centre too. Prices vary from around €3 to €4 per hour.

See p293 for car-rental outfits.

Public Transport

BUS

The city transport authority, **Transports Metropolitans de Barcelona** (TMB; ✆010; www.tmb.net), runs buses along most city routes every few minutes from 5am or 6am to 10pm or 11pm. Many routes pass through Plaça de Catalunya and/or Plaça de la Universitat. After 11pm, a reduced network of yellow *nitbusos* (night buses) runs until 3am or 5am. All *nitbus* routes pass through Plaça de Catalunya and most run about every 30 to 45 minutes.

METRO & FGC

The **TMB metro** has seven numbered and colour-coded lines. It runs from 5am to midnight Sunday to Thursday and holidays, from 5am to 2am on Friday and days immediately preceding holidays, and 24 hours on Saturday. Line 2 has access for people with disabilities and a growing number of stations on other lines also have lifts.

Suburban trains run by the **Ferrocarrils de la Generalitat de Catalunya** (FGC; ☎93 205 15 15; www.fgc.net) include a couple of useful city lines. One heads north from Plaça de Catalunya. A branch of it will get you to Tibidabo and another within spitting distance of the Monestir de Pedralbes. Some trains along this line run beyond Barcelona to Sant Cugat, Sabadell and Terrassa. The other FGC line heads to Manresa from Plaça d'Espanya and is handy for the trip to Montserrat (p298). These trains run from about 5am (with only one or two services before 6am) to 11pm or midnight (depending on the line) Sunday to Thursday, and from 5am to about 1am (or a little later, depending on the line and stop) on Friday and Saturday.

Three **tram** (☎902 193275; www.trambcn. com) lines run into the suburbs of greater Barcelona from Plaça de Francesc Macià and are of limited interest to visitors. Another line (T4) runs from behind the zoo near the Ciutadella Vila Olímpica metro stop to Sant Adrià via Fòrum. The T5 line runs from Glòries to Badalona. All standard transport passes are valid.

TICKETS & TARGETAS

The metro, FGC trains, *rodalies/cercanías* (Renfe-run local trains) and buses come under one zoned fare regime. Single-ride tickets on all standard transport within Zone 1 (which extends beyond the airport), except on Renfe trains, cost €1.40.

Targetes are multitrip transport tickets. They are sold at most city-centre metro stations. The prices given here are for travel in Zone 1. Children under four travel free.

Targeta T-10 (€7.85) Ten rides (each valid for 1¼ hours) on the metro, buses and FGC trains. You can change between metro, FGC, *rodalies* and buses.

Targeta T-DIA (€5.90) Unlimited travel on all transport for one day.

Targeta T-50/30 (€32.10) For 50 trips within 30 days.

Two-/three-/four-/five-day tickets (€11.20/15.90/20.40/24.10) These provide unlimited travel on all transport except the Aerobús; buy them at metro stations and tourist offices.

T-Mes (€48.85) For unlimited use of all public transport for a month.

Taxi

Taxis charge €2 flag fall plus meter charges of €0.86 per kilometre (€1.10 from 8pm to 8am and all day on weekends). A further €3.10 is added for all trips to/from the airport, and €1 for luggage bigger than 55cm by 35cm by 35cm. The trip from Estació Sants to Plaça de Catalunya, about 3km, costs about €10. You can call a **taxi** (☎93 225 00 00, 93 300 11 00, 93 303 30 33, 93 322 22 22) or flag them down in the streets. The call-out charge is €3.40 (€4.20 at night and on weekends). In many taxis it is possible to pay with credit card.

Taxi Amic (☎93 420 80 88; www.terra.es/ personal/taxiamic, in Spanish) is a special taxi service for people with disabilities or difficult situations (such as transport of big objects). Book at least 24 hours in advance if possible.

TRIXIS

These three-wheeled **cycle taxis** (☎93 310 13 79; www.trixi.info) operate along the waterfront and around much of the centre (noon to 8pm daily between March and November). They can take two passengers and cost €6/10/18 per quarter-hour/half-hour/hour. Children aged three to 12 pay half-price. You can find them near the Mirador a Colom and in front of the Catedral.

AROUND BARCELONA

Need a break from the hubbub? Several options within easy reach present themselves. Sitges is a pretty seaside town southwest of Barcelona with thumping nightlife. Wine lovers may want to explore the Penedès winemaking region, famous for its *cava*. From the hedonistic to the heavenly, head north for Catalonia's sacred mountain range, Montserrat. Closer to home, admire the genius of Gaudí at Colònia Güell.

Sitges

POP 27,700

Sitges attracts everyone from jet-setters to young travellers, honeymooners to weekending families, and from Barcelona's night owls to an international gay crowd. The beach is long and sandy, the nightlife thumps until breakfast and there are lots of groovy boutiques if you need to spruce up your wardrobe. In winter Sitges can be dead, but it wakes up with a vengeance for Carnaval, when the gay crowd puts on an outrageous show.

◉ Sights & Activities

Museu Romàntic   MUSEUM

(Carrer de Sant Gaudenci 1; adult/student €3.50/2; ◷9.30am-2pm & 4-7pm Tue-Sat, 10am-3pm Sun), Housed in late-18th-century Can Llopis mansion, the Museu Romàntic recreates with its furnishings and dioramas the lifestyle of a 19th-century Catalan landowning family. It also has a collection of several hundred antique dolls – and some of them are mighty ugly! Many of Sitges' grand old residences were built in the 19th century by locals who had made good (often in dubious businesses, such as cotton raising using slave labour) in South America and were commonly dubbed *Americanos* or *Indianos*.

Beaches   BEACHES
The main beach is divided by a series of breakwaters into sections with different names. A pedestrian promenade runs its whole length. In the height of summer, especially on Saturday and Sunday, the end nearest the Església de Sant Bartomeu i Santa Tecla gets jam-packed. Crowds thin out slightly towards the southwest end.

Museu Cau Ferrat   MUSEUM
(Carrer de Fonollar) Built in the 1890s as a house-cum-studio by artist Santiago Rusiñol, the house is full of his own art and that of his contemporaries. The interior, with its exquisitely tiled walls and lofty arches, is enchanting. Closed at the time of writing.

Museu Maricel del Mar   MUSEUM
(Carrer de Fonollar; adult/student €3.50/2; ⊗9.30am-2pm & 4-7pm Tue-Sat, 10am-3pm Sun) Next door to the Museu Cau Ferrat, with art and handicrafts from the Middle Ages to the 20th century.

✯ Festivals & Events

Carnaval   CARNIVAL
Carnaval in Sitges is a week-long riot made just for the extrovert, ambiguous and exhibitionist, capped by an extravagant gay parade that's held on the last night. To be held 3 to 9 March in 2011; dates change from year to year.

Festa Major   TOWN FESTIVAL
The town's Festa Major (Major Festival) over six days in late August features a huge fireworks display on the 23rd.

International Film Festival   FILM
(http://sitgesfilmfestival.com) Early October is the time for Sitges' International Film Festival.

🛏 Sleeping
Sitges has around 50 hotels and *hostales*, but many close from around October to April, then are full in July and August, when prices are at their highest and booking is advisable. Many, including the following, are gay-friendly without being exclusively so. Gay travellers looking for accommodation in Sitges can try Throb (www.throb.co.uk).

Romàntic Hotel   BOUTIQUE HOTEL €€
(☎93 894 83 75; www.hotelromantic.com; Carrer de Sant Isidre 33; s/d from €72/102; 🕸) These

Around Barcelona

COMBINED TICKET

A combined ticket (adult/student €6.50/3.50) is offered for Museu Romàntic, Museu Maricel del Mar and Museu Cau Ferrat. You can get it at any one of the museums concerned.

three adjoining 19th-century villas are presented in sensuous period style, with a leafy dining courtyard. If it has no rooms free, ask about its other charming boutique hotel, **Hotel La Renaixença** (Carrer d'Illa de Cuba 45), round the corner (the reception is at Romàntic Hotel). Indeed, it shares the street with several beautifully restored houses converted into enticing hotels.

Pensió Bonaire   PENSIÓN €€
(☑93 894 53 26; www.bonairehostalsitges.com; Carrer de Bonaire 31; d €65) Barely a stumble from the beach and with all sorts of fairly simple but perfectly comfortable rooms, this is a pretty decent budget option. Some rooms have balconies and all have their own bathroom. The singles, however, are very poky.

✗ Eating

Al Fresco   INTERNATIONAL €€
(Carrer de Pau Barrabeig 4; meals €30-40; ☺dinner Tue-Sat mid-Jan–mid-Dec; ☻) Hidden along a narrow stairway that masquerades as a street, it serves a varied array of food in a pleasant setting. You could try anything from an Indian-style chicken curry with green mango to a slab of Angus steak done in red wine and mustard and served with chips. One dish costs €22, or €34 for two (one of which will serve as a starter).

Costa Dorada   SEAFOOD €€
(Carrer del Port Alegre 27; meals €30; ☺lunch & dinner Fri-Tue, lunch Wed Jan-Nov) Old-world service with 1970s atmosphere (lots of tiles and bottles of wine on display) and reliable standards make the 'Gold Coast' a safe bet, especially for seafood, paella and *fideuá*.

La Nansa   SEAFOOD €€
(Carrer de la Carreta 24; meals €35; ☺Thu-Mon, closed Jan) Cast just back from the town's waterfront and up a little lane in a fine old house is this seafood specialist. It does a great line in paella and other rice dishes, including a local speciality, *cassola d'arròs a la sitgetana* (a brothy seafood rice dish).

Pic Nic   RICE, SEAFOOD €€
(www.restaurantpicnic.com; Passeig de la Ribera; meals €35-40; ☺lunch Sun-Thu, lunch & dinner Fri & Sat) With views straight out over the sea, this good-natured, rowdy seafood eatery is perfect for a group lunch. Fish and seafood rice dishes (paella and company) are the speciality here.

🍷 Drinking & Entertainment

Much of Sitges' nightlife happens on one short pedestrian strip packed with humanity right through the night in summer: Carrer 1er de Maig, Plaça de la Indústria and Carrer del Marqués de Montroig, all in a short line off the seafront. Carrer 1er de Maig – also known as Calle del Pecado (Sin Street) – vibrates to the volume of 10 or so disco-bars, all trying to outdo each other in decibels. You'll find more of the same, if slightly less intense, around the corner on Carrer de les Parellades, Carrer de Bonaire and Carrer de Sant Pere. That said, virtually all bars shut by 3.30am.

Bar Voramar   BAR
(www.pub-voramar.com; Carrer del Port Alegre 55) On Platja de Sant Sebastià, Bar Voramar is a 1960s throwback with nautical decoration and good music. Check it out for live jazz sessions.

L'Atlàntida Sitges   BAR
(www.clubatlantida.com; Platja Les Coves; ☺Wed-Sun Jun-Sep) Equally popular is the beachside L'Atlàntida Sitges, about 3.5km west of the centre. A shuttle bus runs here from Platja de Sant Sebastià on those nights it's open.

GAY & LESBIAN SITGES

Gay and gay-friendly bars abound. **El Horno** (www.sitges4men.com; Carrer de Joan Tarrida Ferratges 6; ☺5.30pm-2.30am) has a dark room to fumble about in and you can follow hirsute pursuits at **Bear's Bar** (www.bearsbarsitges.com; Carrer de Bonaire 17; ☺10pm-3.30am). For dancing late into the night, the **Organic Club** (Carrer de Bonaire 15; ☺midnight-6am) is a popular gay club, one of two in town. If you need any toys, head for the **Mask** (Carrer de Bonaire 22) erotic shop. For more on gay Sitges, check out www.gaysitgesguide.com.

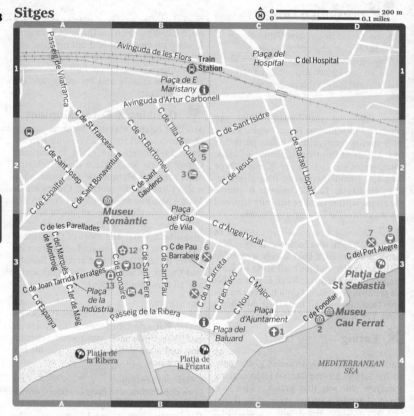

Sweet Pachá CLUB

(www.sweetpacha.com; Avinguda Port d'Aiguadolç 9) Clubbing near the waterfront. It's located just back from the Aiguadolç marina, 1.2km east along the coast from the Museu Maricel del Mar. The best bet is to get a cab.

Pachá CLUB

(www.pachasitges.com; Carrer de Sant Dídac, Vallpineda; ☺Sat & Sun) Clubbing north of the town centre.

🛈 Information

Main tourist office (☎93 894 50 04; www.sit gestur.com; Plaça de E Maristany 2; ☺9am-8pm)
Policia Local (☎704 10 10 92; Plaça d'Ajuntament)
Tourist office (☎93 811 06 11; Passeig de la Ribera; ☺10am-2pm & 4-8pm) A branch office.

🛈 Getting There & Away

Four *rodalies* trains an hour, from about 6am to 10pm, run from Barcelona's Passeig de Gràcia and Estació Sants to Sitges (€3, 38 to 46 min-utes depending on stops). The best road from Barcelona to Sitges is the C32 tollway. A direct bus run by Mon-Bus goes to Barcelona airport from Passeig de Vilanova.

Montserrat

Montserrat (Serrated Mountain), 50km northwest of Barcelona, is a 1236m-high mountain of truly weird rock pillars, shaped by wind, rain and frost from a conglomeration of limestone, pebbles and sand that once lay under the sea. With the historic Benedictine Monestir de Montserrat, one of Catalonia's most important shrines, cradled at 725m on its side, it makes a great outing from Barcelona. From the mountain, on a clear day, you can see as far as the Pyrenees and even, if you're lucky, Mallorca.

The *cremallera* (rack-and-pinion train) arrives on the mountainside, just below the monastery. From there, the main road

Sitges

curves (past a snack bar, cafeteria, information office and the Espai Audiovisual) up to the right, passing the blocks of Cel·les Abat Marcel, to enter Plaça de Santa Maria, at the centre of the monastery complex.

◎ Sights & Activities

Monestir de Montserrat — MONASTERY
(www.abadiamontserrat.net; ⊙9am-6pm) The monastery was founded in 1025 to commemorate a vision of the Virgin on the mountain. Wrecked by Napoleon's troops in 1811, then abandoned as a result of anticlerical legislation in the 1830s, it was rebuilt from 1858. Today a community of about 80 monks lives here. Pilgrims come from far and wide to venerate *La Moreneta* (The Black Virgin), a 12th-century Romanesque wooden sculpture of Mary with the infant Jesus, which has been Catalonia's patron since 1881.

Museu de Montserrat

(Plaça de Santa Maria; adult/student €6.50/5.50; ⊙10am-6pm) The two-part Museu de Montserrat has an excellent collection, ranging from an Egyptian mummy and Gothic altarpieces to art by El Greco, Monet, Degas and

Picasso. The Espai Audiovisual (adult/senior & student €2/1.50; ⊙9am-6pm), free with Museu de Montserrat entry, is a walk-through multimedia space (with images and sounds) that illustrates the daily life and activities of the monks and the history and spirituality of the monastery.

Basilica

(admission €5; ⊙7.30am-8pm) From Plaça de Santa Maria you enter the courtyard of the 16th-century basilica, the monastery's church. The basilica's facade, with its carvings of Christ and the 12 Apostles, dates from 1901, despite its 16th-century platteresque style. Follow the signs to the Cambril de la Mare de Déu (⊙8-10.30am & 12.15-6.30pm) to the right of the main basilica entrance to see the Black Virgin.

On your way out, have a look in the room across the courtyard from the basilica entrance, filled with gifts and thank-you messages to the Montserrat Virgin from people who give her the credit for all manner of happy events. The souvenirs range from plaster casts to wedding dresses.

Montserrat Boys' Choir

(Escolania; www.escolania.cat; ⊙performances 1pm & 6.45pm Mon-Thu, 1pm Fri, noon & 6.45pm Sun late Aug-late Jun) If you're around the basilica at the right time, you'll catch a brief performance by the Montserrat Boys' Choir, reckoned to be Europe's oldest music school.

Santa Cova Funicular

(one way/return €1.80/2.90; ⊙every 20min 10am-5.35pm) To see where the holy image of the Virgin was discovered, take the Santa Cova funicular down from the main area.

The Mountain — MOUNTAIN
You can explore the mountain above the monastery on a web of paths leading to some of the peaks and to 13 empty and rather dilapidated hermitages. The Funicular de Sant Joan (one way/return €4.50/7.20; ⊙every 20min 10am-5.40pm, closed Jan & Feb) will carry you up the first 250m from the monastery. If you prefer to walk, the road past the funicular's bottom station leads to its top station in about one hour (3km).

From the top station, it's a 20-minute stroll (signposted) to the **Sant Joan chapel**, with fine westward views. More exciting is the one-hour walk northwest, along a path marked with some blobs of yellow paint, to Montserrat's highest peak, **Sant Jeroni**, from where there's an awesome sheer drop on the north face. The walk takes you across the upper part of the mountain, with a close-up experience of some of the weird rock pillars. Many have names: on your way to Sant Jeroni look over to the right for **La Prenyada** (the Pregnant Woman), **La Mòmia** (the Mummy), **L'Elefant** (the Elephant) and **El Cap de Mort** (the Death's Head).

🛏 Sleeping & Eating

Cel.les Abat Marcel   STUDIOS **€€**
(📞93 877 77 01; 2-/4-person apt €97/173; P)
Here you will find comfortable apartments equipped with full bathroom and kitchenette. Smaller studios go for €56/81 for one/two people.

Hotel Abat Cisneros   HOTEL **€€**
(📞93 877 77 01; s/d €58/101; P❋) The only hotel in the monastery complex has modern, comfortable rooms, some of which look over Plaça de Santa Maria. It has a restaurant (meals €35), a cafeteria (meals €15 to €20) for lunch and a couple of cafes for breakfast.

ℹ Information

Information office (📞93 877 77 01; www.abadiamontserrat.net; ⏰9am-6pm) Located in the monastery, this has information on the complex and walking trails.

ℹ Getting There & Away

Bus
A daily bus from Barcelona with **Julià Tours** (📞93 317 64 54; Ronda de l'Universitat 5) to the monastery (€53) leaves at 9.30am (returning at 3pm). The price includes travel, all entry prices, use of funiculars at Montserrat and a meal at the cafeteria.

Car & Motorcycle
The most straightforward route from Barcelona is by Avinguda Diagonal, Via Augusta, the Túnel de Vallvidrera and the C16. Shortly after Terrassa, follow the exit signs to Montserrat, which will put you on the C58 road. Follow it northwest to the C55. Then head 2km south on this road to Monistrol de Montserrat, from where a road snakes 7km up the mountain. You could leave the car at the parking station in Monistrol Vila and take the *cremallera* up to the top.

Train & Cremallera
The R5 line trains operated by **FGC** (📞93 205 15 15) run from Plaça d'Espanya station in Barcelona to Monistrol de Montserrat up to 18 times daily starting at 5.16am. They connect with the rack-and-pinion train, the **cremallera** (📞902 312020; www.cremalleradmontserrat.com),

which takes 17 minutes to make the upwards journey and costs €5.15/8.20 one way/return. One way/return from Barcelona to Montserrat with the FGC train and *cremallera* costs €10.10/18.10. There is a also a cable-car option. For various all-in ticket options, check out the *cremallera* website or www.fgc.net.

Penedès Wine Country

Some of Spain's finest wines come from the Penedès plains southwest of Barcelona. Sant Sadurní d'Anoia, located about a half-hour train ride west of Barcelona, is the capital of *cava*. Vilafranca del Penedès, 12km further down the track, is the heart of the Penedès *Denominación de Origen* (DO; Denomination of Origin) region, which produces noteworthy light whites. Some reasonable reds also come out of the area. Visitors are welcomed on tours of several of the region's wineries; there'll often be a free glass along the way and plenty more for sale. Several companies offer package trips to Barcelona that include winery tours of the Penedès, although it is cheaper to do it on your own. One such option for luxury lovers, taking in the Penedès and other wine districts, is the one-week all-inclusive tour run by Cellar Tours (www.cellartours.com). Prices depend on the number of people on the tour and style of accommodation.

SANT SADURNÍ D'ANOIA
POP 12,200

One hundred or so wineries around Sant Sadurní produce 140 million bottles of *cava* a year – something like 85% of the entire national output. *Cava* is made by the same method as French Champagne. If you happen to be in town in October, you may catch the Mostra de Caves i Gastronomia, a *cava*- and food-tasting fest.

The best-known *cava* company, Freixenet (www.freixenet.es/web/eng; Carrer de Joan Sala 2; adult/child €6/2.20; ⏰1½hr tours 10am-1pm & 3-4.30pm Mon-Thu, 10am-1pm Fri-Sun) is right next to the train station.

Codorníu (www.codorniu.es; Avinguda de Jaume Codorníu; ⏰9am-5pm Mon-Fri, 9am-1pm Sat, Sun & holidays) is at Can Codorníu in a Modernista building at the entry to the town by road from Barcelona. Manuel Raventós, head of this firm back in 1872, was the first Spaniard to be successful in producing sparkling wine by the Champagne method.

You can simply turn up for tours at either of these establishments.

VILAFRANCA DEL PENEDÈS
POP 38,400

Vilafranca is larger and more interesting than Sant Sadurní.

◉ Sights

The mainly Gothic Basilica de Santa Maria (Plaça de Jaume I) stands at the heart of the old town. Begun in 1285, it has been much restored. It is possible to arrange visits of the bell tower in summer at around sunset. Ask at the tourist office.

The basilica faces the Vinseum (www.vinseum.cat; Plaça de Jaume I 5; adult/senior & student €5/3; ⊙10am-2pm & 4-7pm Tue-Sat, 10am-2pm Sun & holidays) across Plaça de Jaume I. Housed in a fine Gothic building, a combination of museums here cover local archaeology, art, geology and bird life, along with an excellent section on wine.

A statue on Plaça de Jaume I pays tribute to Vilafranca's famous *castellers,* who do their thing during Vilafranca's lively Festa Major (main annual festival) at the end of August.

Vilafranca's premier winery is Torres (www.torres.es; tours per person €6; ⊙9am-5pm Mon-Sat, 9am-1pm Sun & holidays), 3km northwest of the town centre on the BP2121 near Pacs del Penedès. The Torres family revolutionised Spanish winemaking in the 1960s by introducing new temperature-controlled, stainless-steel technology and French grape varieties.

✗ Eating

While there is no need to stay in Vilafranca and little attraction in doing so, eating is another story altogether. Cal Ton (Carrer Casal 8; meals €40; ⊙lunch & dinner Wed-Sat, lunch Tue & Sun) is one of several enticing options in town. Hidden away down a narrow side street, Cal Ton has crisp, modern decor and offers inventive Mediterranean cuisine – all washed down with local wines.

❶ Information

Tourist office (☏93 818 12 54; www.turismevilafranca.com; Carrer de la Cort 14; ⊙4-7pm Mon, 9am-1pm & 4-7pm Tue-Sat, 10am-1pm Sun) Can provide tips on visiting some of the smaller wineries in the area.

❶ Getting There & Away

Up to three *rodalies* trains per hour run from Estació Sants Barcelona to Sant Sadurní (€3, 45 minutes) and Vilafranca (€3.60, 55 minutes). By car, take the AP7 and follow the exit signs.

Catalonia

Best Places to Eat

» La Taula (p346)

» El Celler de Can Roca (boxed text, p321)

» Restaurant Txalaka (p315)

» Can Fabes (boxed text, p321)

» Sant Pau (boxed text, p321)

Best Places to Stay

» Hostal Sa Rascassa (p311)

» Hotel Mediterrani (p309)

» Hotel Llegendes de Girona (p314)

» Torre del Remei (p336)

» Mas del Tancat (p358)

Why Go?

From metropolitan Barcelona spreads a land of such diversity that you could spend weeks dissecting it. The stunning cove beaches of the Costa Brava are the jewel in the tourism crown, but for those who need more than a suntan and a lazy day, urban fun is to be found in the medieval city of Girona and in workaday Figueres, with its 'theatre-museum' to Salvador Dalí.

For something utterly different head north to where the Pyrenees rise up to mighty 3000m peaks from a series of green and often remote valleys littered with numerous hiking trails.

And if that weren't enough, there are the flamingo-tinted wetlands of the Ebro delta, the Roman city of Tarragona, and everywhere are medieval monasteries and remote hilltop villages.

Wherever you venture there is the undeniable sense that Catalonia (Catalunya in Catalan, Cataluña in Spanish) is different to the rest of Spain. It's a difference worth celebrating.

When to Go

Tarragona

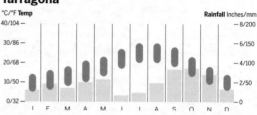

May Girona's in bloom during its flower festival and Costa Brava beaches are bloomin' gorgeous.

September The Catalan Pyrenees are aflame in autumnal colours and the hiking is perfect.

October/November The museums and galleries of the Dalí circuit are at their quietest and best.

COSTA BRAVA

Stretching from Blanes north all the way to the French border, the Costa Brava ranks with the Costa Blanca and Costa del Sol as one of Spain's three great holiday coasts. But alongside some occasionally awful concrete development, English breakfasts and *Konditoreien* (pastry shops), the 'Rugged Coast' has some of the most spectacular stretches of sand and sea in all of Spain.

Nestling in the hilly back country – green and covered in umbrella pine in the south; but barer and browner in the north – are scattered charming stone villages, the towering monastery of St Pere de Rodes and Salvador Dalí's fantasy castle home at Púbol. A little further inland are the bigger towns of Girona (or Gerona

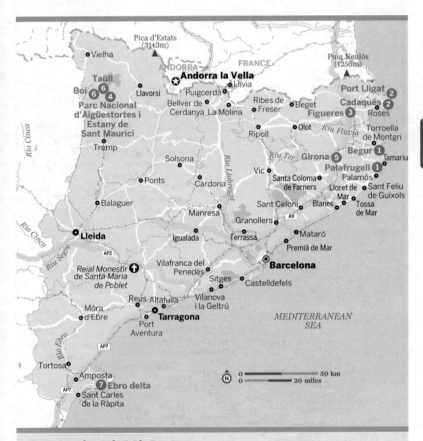

CATALONIA

Catalonia Highlights

① Chill out on Costa Brava coves and beaches near **Palafrugell** (p309) or **Begur** (p310)

② Discover the magical village of **Cadaqués** (p321) and nearby **Port Lligat** (p322), haunted by the memory of Salvador Dalí

③ Contemplate the absurd with a visit to the **Teatre-Museu Dalí** (p324) in Figueres

④ Conquer the trails of the **Parc Nacional d'Aigüestortes i Estany de Sant Maurici** (p340)

⑤ Explore the flower-bedecked medieval city centre of **Girona** (p312)

⑥ Seek out the Romanesque churches around **Boí** and **Taüll** (p340)

⑦ See the skies turn pink under flocks of flamingos in the **Ebro delta** (p357)

in Castilian), with its sizeable and strikingly well-preserved medieval centre, and Figueres (Figueras in Castilian), famous for its bizarre Teatre-Museu Dalí, the foremost of a series of sites associated with the famous eccentric surrealist artist Salvador Dalí.

The ruggedness of the Costa Brava continues under the sea, offering some of the best diving in Spain. Diving centres with certified instructors operate at a dozen or more places. The Illes Medes, off L'Estartit, are protected islets with probably the most diverse sea life along the Spanish coast.

Costa Brava

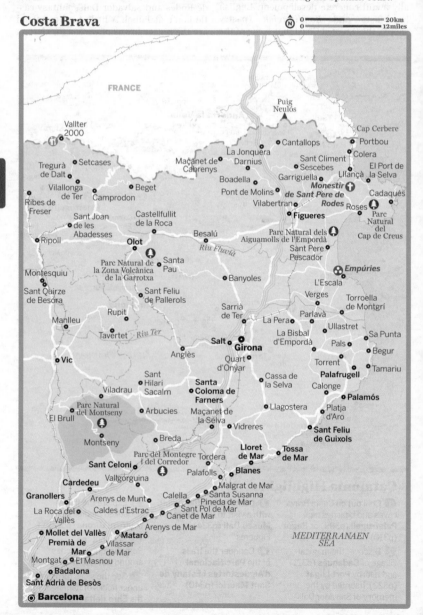

Catalan cooking nudges Basque cuisine for the title of Spain's best. Its essence lies in its sauces for meat and fish. There are five main types: *sofregit,* of fried onion, tomato and garlic; *samfaina, sofregit* plus red pepper and aubergine or zucchini (courgette); *picada,* based on ground almonds, usually with garlic, parsley, pine nuts or hazelnuts, and sometimes breadcrumbs; *alioli,* garlic pounded with olive oil, often with egg yolk added to make a mayonnaise; and *romesco,* an almond, tomato, olive oil, garlic and vinegar sauce, also used as a salad dressing.

Romesco is used above all, however, with *calçots,* which are a type of long spring onion, delicious as a starter with *romesco* sauce and only in season in late winter/ early spring. This is when Catalans get together for a *calçotada,* the local version of a barbecue. The *calçots* are the amusing part of the event, as the black ash in which they are grilled inevitably winds up on your hands and face! This is usually followed by an enormous meal with countless meat and sausage courses.

Catalans find it hard to understand why other people put mere butter on bread when *pa amb tomàquet,* bread slices rubbed with tomato, olive oil and garlic, is so easy. They eat it with almost everything.

Some typical Catalan dishes are listed below.

Starters

» *escalivada* – red peppers and aubergines (sometimes with onions and tomatoes), grilled, peeled, sliced and served lukewarm dressed with olive oil, salt and garlic

» *esqueixada* – salad of shredded salted cod (*bacallà*) with tomato, red pepper, onion, white beans, olives, olive oil and vinegar

Main Dishes

» *arròs a la cassola* or *arròs a la catalana* – Catalan paella, cooked in an earthenware pot, without saffron

» *arròs negre* – rice cooked in black cuttlefish ink; it sounds awful, but it's good

» *bacallà a la llauna* – salted cod baked in tomato, garlic, parsley, paprika and wine

» *botifarra amb mongetes* – pork sausage with fried white beans

» *cargols* – snails; a religion in parts of Catalonia

» *escudella* – a meat, sausage and vegetable stew

» *fideuá* – similar to paella, but using vermicelli noodles as the base

» *mandonguilles amb sipia* – meatballs with cuttlefish

» *sarsuela* (*zarzuela*) – mixed seafood cooked in *sofregit* with various seasonings

» *suquet* – a fish-and-potato hotpot, with generous clumps of both drenched in a tomato-based broth

ⓘ Getting There & Away

Direct buses from Barcelona go to most towns on or near the Costa Brava. The train line between Barcelona and the coastal border town of Portbou runs inland, through Girona and Figueres, most of the way. From Girona and Figueres there are fairly good bus services to the coast.

In summer, you could take an alternative approach to the southern Costa Brava from Barcelona by a combination of *rodalies* (local trains) and boat.

The AP7 *autopista* (tollway) and the toll-free NII highway both run from Barcelona via Girona and Figueres to the French border, a few kilometres north of La Jonquera. The C32 *autopista* follows the NII up the coast as far as Blanes.

Tossa de Mar

POP 5948

Curving around a boat-speckled bay and guarded by a headland crowned with defensive medieval walls and towers (from which you can enjoy marvellous sunsets), Tossa de Mar is a picturesque village of crooked, narrow streets onto which tourism has tacked a larger, modern extension. In July and August it's hard to reach the water's edge without tripping over oily limbs, but it is heaven compared with Lloret de Mar 12km southeast – a real concrete-and-neon jungle of Piccadilly pubs, *Bierkeller* and soccer chants.

Tossa was one of the first places on the Costa Brava to attract foreign visitors – a small colony of artists and writers gravitated towards what painter Marc Chagall dubbed 'Blue Paradise' in the 1930s. It retains much of that enchantment today, especially out of high season.

◎ Sights & Activities

Old Tossa   OLD TOWN

The deep-ochre, fairy-tale walls and towers on the pine-dotted headland, Mont Guardí, at the end of the main beach, were built between the 12th and 14th centuries. The area they girdle is known as the Vila Vella (Old Town). When wandering around Mont Guardí you will come across vestiges of a castle, and the Far de Tossa (lighthouse; adult/under 12yr €3/1.50; ⊙10am-10pm Tue-Sun mid-Jun–mid-Sep). Inside there is an imaginative 20-minute walk-through display on the history of lighthouses and life inside them. Next door is the groovy Bar Far de Tossa – perfect for a sundowner. In August, concerts are held on various nights by the light of the lighthouse.

Beaches & Boats   BEACHES

The main town beach, golden Platja Gran, is pretty but tends to be busy. Further north along the same bay are the quieter and smaller Platja del Reig and Platja Mar Menuda at the end of Avinguda de Sant Ramon Penyafort.

In summer (from Easter to September), glass-bottomed boats (adult/5-12yr €13/9) run hourly or half-hourly (10am to 5pm) to somewhat more tranquil beaches northeast of Platja Gran. You have the option of spending the day at Cala Giverola (a pleasant sandy cove with a couple of restaurants and bars) and returning on a later boat. The return trip is direct and takes 20 minutes.

Museu Municipal   MUSEUM

(Plaça de Roig i Soler 1; adult/child €3/free; ⊙10am-2pm & 4-8pm daily mid-Jun–mid-Sep, shorter hr rest of yr) In the lower part of Vila Vella, the Museu Municipal set in the 14th- and 15th-century Palau del Batlle, has mosaics and other finds from a Roman villa, off Avinguda del Pelegrí, and Tossa-related art including Chagall's *El Violinista*.

⌷ Sleeping

Tossa has around 60 hotels, *hostales* (budget hotels) and *pensiones* (small private hotels). You'll find all of them open from Semana Santa (Holy Week) to October, but only a handful outside those months.

TOP CHOICE Hostal Cap d'Or   HOTEL €€

(☑972 34 00 81; www.hotelcapdor.com; Passeig de la Vila Vella 1; s/d incl breakfast €53/96; ⓟ❋✿) Rub up against the town's history in this spot right in front of the walls. Rooms are lovingly decorated in sea-blues and whites and the best of them look straight onto the beach.

Hotel Sant March   HOTEL €€

(☑972 34 00 78; www.hotelsantmarch.com; Avendia Pelegrí 2; s/d €48/78; ⓟ❋✿✖) The large and immaculate rooms here don't overlook the beach but instead you can splash around in the swimming pool. Families will appreciate the kids' play area. It's located just beyond the general tourist pandemonium in a quieter residential area.

Hotel Canaima   HOTEL €€

(☑972 34 09 95; www.hotelcanaima.com; Avendia de la Palma 24; s/d incl breakfast €37/75; ❋✿) Surrounded by super-sized package-holiday hotels, this little family-run place offers something refreshingly different. Rooms are big and bright, with little balconies, and there's a laid-back cafe downstairs. It's an especially good deal for single travellers.

Hostal l'Alba   HOSTAL €

(☑972 34 08 59; www.hostalalba.es; Calle Giverola 3; s/d incl breakfast €40/60; ❋✿) This clean and friendly, family-run *pensión* above a

---

BEACHES NEAR TOSSA

The coast to the northeast and southwest of Tossa is dotted by rocky coves, some with charming little beaches. You can walk cross-country from Tossa to Cala Llevado and Cala d'En Carles beaches, 3km southwest, or the longer Platja de Llorell (3.5km away), or drive down to Platja de Llorell from the GI682. To the northeast, you can walk down from the GI682 to sandy coves such as Cala Pola (4km), Cala Giverola (5km), Cala Salions (8km) and Platja Vallpregona (11km).

neighbourhood bar offers a more genuine Spanish experience than the large international hotels on the seafront. However, it's often full so book ahead.

Hotel Diana HOTEL €€€
(☑972 34 18 86; www.hotelesdante.com; Plaça d'Espanya 6; d incl breakfast €140, with sea views €160-170; ☺Apr-Nov; ✴️🅿️🛜) Fronting Platja Gran, this artistic 1920s hotel has a Gaudí-built fireplace in the lounge and oozes Modernista decor and stained glass in the central covered courtyard. Half the rooms have beach views.

Camping Cala Llevadó CAMPING €
(☑972 34 03 14; www.calallevado.com; Cala Llevadó; sites per 2-person tent & car €39; ☺May-Sep; 🅿️🛇🐾) This ground stretches back from a cove 4km southwest of Tossa in the settlement of Santa Maria de Llorell. As well as its shady camping spots and prime location near a pretty beach, this high-quality facility offers tennis courts, a pool, a restaurant, shops and bars. It also has four-person bungalows from €93.

🍴 Eating & Drinking

Look out for a local speciality, *cimitomba*, fish prepared in a garlic sauce. There are hundreds of places to eat in Tossa, but many are little more than overpriced tourist traps. Of the numerous hotel restaurants, the one belonging to the Hostal Cap d'Or is worthy of mention for its €14.90 seafood-heavy set menu and its homemade cakes. Many of the old town's lively bars – most of which are pure 'Brits abroad' style places – are along and near Carrer de Sant Josep.

TOP CHOICE **La Cuina de Can Simon**
SEAFOOD €€€
(☑972 34 12 69; Carrer del Portal 24; mains €30-50; ☺lunch & dinner Wed-Sat & Mon, lunch Sun) Tossa's culinary star (Michelin says so!) nestles by the old walls in a former fisherman's stone house. It serves an imaginative array of Mediterranean cuisine mixed in with traditional Catalan seaside cooking such as the ever-appetising-sounding sea slug.

Castell Vell SEAFOOD €€
(Carrer del Abat Oliva 1; menus €20, mains €18-25; ☺lunch & dinner Tue-Sun, dinner Mon May-Oct) This rustic stone house lurks within the walls of the old town. Take your meal, which ranges from local cuisine to more international fare, out onto the terrace.

ℹ️ Information

The bus station is beside the GI682, which leads to Lloret de Mar. The main beach, Platja Gran, and the older part of town are a 10-minute walk southeast.

Tourist information office (☑972 34 01 08; www.infotossa.com; Avinguda del Pelegrí 25; ☺9am-9pm Mon-Sat, 10am-2pm & 5-8pm Sun Jul-Aug, shorter hr rest of yr) Next to the bus station.

ℹ️ Getting There & Away

Boat

From April to October **Dolfi-Jet** (www.dolfijetboats.com) is one of a couple of companies to run boats several times a day between Blanes, Lloret de Mar and Tossa de Mar (one to 1½ hours), with stops at a few points en route. You could catch one of the *rodalies* from Barcelona's Catalunya station to Blanes, then transfer to the boat. The trip to Tossa from Blanes costs €20 and from Lloret de Mer it's €15. In many places the boats simply pull up at the beach (in Tossa, at Platja Gran) and tickets are sold at a booth there.

Bus

Sarfa (www.sarfa.com) runs to/from Barcelona's Estació del Nord (€10.60, 1¼ hours) up to 11 times daily via Lloret de Mar (€1.50). Otherwise there is only a handful of summer connections to Girona and Sant Feliu de Guíxols.

Car & Motorcycle

From Barcelona, the C32 *autopista*, which takes you almost to Blanes, saves a weary trudge on the toll-free A2. To the north, the 23km stretch of the GI682 to Sant Feliu de Guíxols is a great drive, winding its way up, down and around picturesque bays.

Sant Feliu de Guíxols

POP 21,155

A snaking road hugs the spectacular ups and downs of the Costa Brava for the 23km from Tossa de Mar to Sant Feliu de Guíxols. On this road Rose Macaulay, author of *Fabled Shore* (1950), 'met only one mule cart, laden with pine boughs, and two very polite *guardias civiles*'. Along the way are several enticing inlets and largely hidden beaches, where the water is emerald-green. Easier ones to find include Cala Pola and Cala Giverola. About 7km further north, at Km35.1, you'll find parking for the cliff-backed 800m-long naturists' beach, Cala del Senyor Ramon.

Sant Feliu itself has an attractive waterside promenade and a handful of curious

OF RUNNING FIRE, GIANTS & BIG-HEADS

Catalans get up to unusual tricks at *festa* (festival) time. Fire and fireworks play a big part in many Spanish festivals, but Catalonia adds a special twist with the *correfoc* (fire-running), in which devil and dragon figures run through the streets spitting fireworks at the crowds. (Wear protective clothes if you intend to get close!)

Correfocs are often part of the *festa major*, a town or village's main annual festival, which usually takes place in July or August. Part of the *festa major* fun are the *sardana* (Catalonia's national folk dance) and *gegants*, splendidly attired 5m-high giants that parade through the streets or dance in the squares. Giants tend to come in male-and-female pairs, such as a medieval king and queen. Almost every town and village has its own pair, or up to six pairs, of giants. They're accompanied by grotesque 'dwarfs' (known as *capsgrossos*, or 'big-heads').

On La Nit de Sant Joan (23 June), big bonfires burn at crossroads and town squares in a combined midsummer and St John's Eve celebration, and fireworks explode all night. The supreme fire festival is the Patum in Berga. An evening of dancing and fireworks-spitting angels, devils, mulelike monsters, dwarfs, giants and men covered in grass culminates in a mass frenzy of fire and smoke. The 'real' Patum happens on Corpus Christi (the Thursday following the eighth Sunday after Easter Sunday), although there are simplified versions over the next two or three days. Unesco declared the Patum a World Heritage item in 2005.

leftovers from its long past, the most important being the so-called Porta Ferrada (Iron Gate): a wall and entrance, which is all that remains of a 10th-century monastery, the Monestir de Sant Benet. The gate lends its name to an annual music festival held here every July since 1962. With the help of a few local tips, you will discover some lovely beaches around here on either side of the town.

Sarfa buses call in here frequently (up to 12 from Easter to September) from Barcelona (€13.50, 1½ hours), on the way to Platja d'Aro or Palafrugell or both. They do *not* follow the coast road.

Platja d'Aro & Palamós

These spots mark the two ends of one of the Costa Brava's party spots. The beaches are OK, the high-rises are standard issue and the nightlife is busy. The area tends to attract more Spanish tourism than foreign. Around the main broad beaches and their resorts are some magnificent stretches of coast with enticing coves. Sarfa buses from Barcelona stop at both places (€13.95 and €14.95 respectively, 1½ hours to Platja d'Aro and 15 minutes more to Palamós).

The 2km-long Platja d'Aro beach is big and sandy, but for something more secluded you could head north along the GRS-92 coastal walking path, which winds along the high leafy coastline for about 4km to Sant Antoni de Calonge. The first beach you hit is Platja Rovira, and soon after, the smaller and more enchanting Platja Sa Cova. A little further on again are two small nudist coves, Platja d'en Ros and Platja d'es Canyers.

If you should end up in Palamós and wonder how it happened, all is not lost. Pick up the GRS-92 trail and head north for Platja del Castell, a virtually untouched strand. If you don't fancy the walk, drive out of Palamós heading for Palafrugell and look for signs that lead right to the beach. Two kilometres of partly unsealed road get you there. The northern end of the beach is capped by a high wooded promontory that hides the 'castle' (the remains of a 6th- to 1st-century-BC Iberian settlement) after which the beach is named.

Palafrugell & Around

North of Palamós begins one of the most beautiful stretches of the Costa Brava. The town of Palafrugell, 5km inland, is the main access point for a cluster of enticing beach spots. Calella de Palafrugell, Llafranc and Tamariu, one-time fishing villages squeezed into small bays, are three of the Costa Brava's most charming, low-key resorts.

Begur (p310), 7km northeast of Palafrugell, is a curious, tight-knit, castle-topped village with a cluster of less-developed beaches nearby (some of them splendid). Inland, seek out charming Pals and Peratallada.

PALAFRUGELL
POP 22,109

Palafrugell is the main transport, shopping and service hub for the area but is of little interest in itself. The C66 Palamós–Girona road passes through the western side of Palafrugell, a 10-minute walk from the main square, Plaça Nova. The tourist office ([J]972 30 02 28; www.turismepalafrugell.org; Carrer del Carrilet 2; ⊗9am-9pm Mon-Sat, 10am-1pm Sun Jul-Aug, 10am-1pm & 5-8pm Mon-Sat, 10am-1pm Sun May-Jun & Sep, shorter hr rest of yr) is beside the C66 Hwy. The bus station (Carrer de Torres Jonama 67-9) is a short walk from the tourist office.

Sarfa buses run to Palafrugell from Barcelona up to 16 times daily (€16.15, two hours). Many buses also run between Girona and Palafrugell (€5.45, one hour if you get the most direct service).

CALELLA DE PALAFRUGELL
POP 740

The low-slung buildings of Calella, the southernmost of Palafrugell's crown beach jewels, are strung Aegean-style around a bay of rocky points and small, pretty beaches, with a few fishing boats still hauled up on the sand. The seafront is lined with restaurants serving the fruits of the sea.

⊙ Sights & Activities

In addition to plonking on one of the beaches, you can stroll along pretty coastal footpaths northeast to Llafranc (20 or 30 minutes), or south to Platja del Golfet beach, close to Cap Roig (about 40 minutes).

Jardí Botànic de Cap Roig   GARDENS
(www.jardins.caproig.cat, in Spanish; adult/under 7yr €6/free; ⊗10am-8pm Apr-Sep, to 6pm Oct-Mar) Atop Cap Roig, the Jardí Botànic de Cap Roig is a beautiful garden of 500 Mediterranean species, set around the early-20th-century castle-palace of Nikolai Voevodsky. He was a tsarist colonel with expensive tastes, who fell out of grace in his homeland after the Russian Revolution.

🎪 Festivals & Events

Calella stages the Costa Brava's biggest summer cantada de havaneres. *Havaneres* are melancholy Caribbean sea shanties that became popular among Costa Brava sailors in the 19th century, when Catalonia main-

tained busy links with Cuba. These folksy concerts are traditionally accompanied by the drinking of *cremat* – a rum, coffee, sugar, lemon and cinnamon concoction that you set alight briefly before quaffing. Traditionally, Calella's *cantada* is held in August.

🛌 Sleeping

TOP CHOICE Hotel Mediterrani

BOUTIQUE HOTEL €€€
([J]972 61 45 00; www.hotelmediterrani.com; Francesc Estrabau 40; s incl breakfast €110, d incl breakfast €130-210; ⊗mid-May–Sep; [P][❋][🛜]) Swish, arty rooms with breathtaking views of a hidden sliver of sand and an aquamarine sea from some rooms make this hotel, at the southern end of town, very hard to beat.

Camping Moby Dick   CAMPING €
([J]972 61 43 07; www.campingmobydick.com; Carrer de la Costa Verde 16-28; sites per 2-person tent & car €24.20; ⊗Apr-Sep; [P][🛥]) Set in a pine-and-oak stand about 100m from the seaside, this camping ground is in an ideal location. It has tennis courts and offers the chance of diving and kayak excursions in the area.

ℹ Information

Tourist office ([J]972 61 44 75; Carrer de les Voltes 6; ⊗10am-8pm daily Jul-Aug, shorter hr rest of yr) Housed in a curious 19th-century house, La Perola, near the seafront.

ℹ Getting There & Away

Buses from Palafrugell run to Calella, then Llafranc, then back to Palafrugell (€1.40, 15 minutes). They leave every half-hour or so in July and August; the service is steadily reduced to three or four buses a day from November to February.

LLAFRANC
POP 330

Barely 2km northeast of Calella de Palafrugell, and now merging with it along the roads back from the rocky coast between them, Llafranc has a smaller bay but a longer stretch of sand, cupped on either side by pine-dotted craggy coast.

From the Far de Sant Sebastià (a lighthouse) and Ermita de Sant Sebastià (a chapel now incorporated into a luxury hotel), up on Cap de Sant Sebastià (east of the town), there are tremendous views in both directions along the coast. It's a 40-minute walk up: follow the steps from the harbour and the road up to the right. You can walk on to Tamariu.

Sleeping & Eating

Hostal Celimar   HOTEL €€
(☑972 30 13 74; www.hostalcelimar.com; Carrer de Carudo 12-14; s/d €53/79) This sunset-yellow *hostal* is barely a stumble from the beach and offers bright rooms, with differing colour schemes from room to room, and spotless bathrooms. One of the cheapest deals in town, it also happens to be one of the best.

Hotel Llevant   HOTEL €€€
(☑972 30 03 66; www.hotel-llevant.com; Francesc de Blanes 5; s/d from €140/160; P❄️☎️) In a stately old building, this whitewashed beachfront hotel has equally white and polished rooms, some with memorable sea views. Downstairs is a pleasant see-and-be-seen cafe and restaurant.

Chez Tomás   FRENCH CUISINE €€
(☑972 30 62 15; Carrer de Lluís Marqués Carbó 2; mains €12-19; ☉dinner daily Jun-Sep, lunch & dinner Fri-Sun Oct-May) As the name hints, the food here has a French flavour. Its strength is the use of fresh market produce to come up with such dishes as *filet de bou amb Torta de Casar trufada* (sirloin steak with a truffle-infused serving of a creamy cheese from Extremadura).

ℹ Information

Tourist office (☑972 30 50 08; Passeig Cypsela; ☉10am-8pm Jul-Aug, shorter hr rest of yr) A kiosk just back from the western end of the beach.

ℹ Getting There & Away

See Calella de Palafrugell for information on bus services. The Llafranc bus stop is on Carrer de la Sirena, up the hill on the Calella side of town.

TAMARIU
POP 270

About 3.5km north up the coast from Llafranc, as the crow flies, Tamariu is a small crescent-shaped cove surrounded by pine stands and other greenery. Its beach has some of the most translucent waters on Spain's Mediterranean coast.

Sleeping & Eating

The beachfront is lined with cafes and restaurants and although the quality is pretty good in all, you can't help but think that in all of them you're being seriously overcharged. There's very little accommodation in the village, which gives it an exclusive feel.

TOP CHOICE **Hotel Es Furió**   HOTEL €€
(☑972 62 00 36; www.esfurio.com; Carrer del Foraió 5-7; s/d incl breakfast €80/140;

❄️☎️) This one-time fishing family's house was converted into a hotel in 1934. Es Furió is set just back from the beach and has spacious, cheerfully decorated rooms, where pale oranges, aqua tints and other seaside hues hold sway. It has its own restaurant, which is half the price of those on the waterfront.

Hotel Tamariu   HOTEL €€€
(☑972 62 00 31; www.tamariu.com; Passeig del Mar 2; s/d incl breakfast €95/149; ❄️☎️) A more posh version of the neighbouring Hotel Es Furió, the Hotel Tamariu has marine-coloured rooms, stripy bedspreads and decent bathrooms, but it lacks the intimate character of its neighbour.

ℹ Information

Tourist office (☑972 62 01 93; Carrer de la Riera; ☉10am-1pm & 5-8pm Mon-Sat, 10am-1pm Sun Jun-Sep) In the middle of the village.

ℹ Getting There & Away

Sarfa buses from Palafrugell run to Tamariu (€1.40, 15 minutes) three or four times daily, from mid-June to mid-September only. Parking in the village is a nightmare in summer.

BEGUR
POP 4090

Attractive little Begur is dotted with tempting little bars and cafes and topped by a castell (castle), which dates to the 10th century and towers above the hill village. It's in much the same state in which it was left by the Spanish troops who wrecked it to impede the advance of Napoleon's army in 1810. Scattered around the village are six or so towers built for defence against 16th- and 17th-century pirates. It is an engaging little town and well worth a stopover.

There's a helpful tourist office (☑972 62 45 20; www.visitbegur.com; Avinguda del Onze de Setembre 5; ☉9am-2pm & 4-9pm Mon-Fri, 10am-2pm & 4-9pm Sat & Sun late Jun–mid-Sep, shorter hr rest of yr).

A few steps towards the castle from the central church is Hotel Rosa (☑972 62 30 15; www.hotel-rosa.com; Carrer de Pi i Ralló 19; s/d €80/103; ☉Mar-Nov; ❄️☎️), a little surprise package with well-kept, spacious rooms and bubbly staff. Eat at its Fonda Caner (meals €35; ☉dinner Mon-Fri, lunch & dinner Sat & Sun) at No 10.

Sarfa buses run up to four times a day from Barcelona (€18, two to 2¼ hours) via Palafrugell. On weekdays one Sarfa bus runs to Girona (€5.50, 1½ hours).

AROUND BEGUR

The sublime coastline around Begur, with its pocket-sized coves hemmed in by pine trees and subtropical flowers and lapped by azure water, is home to some of the most beautiful beaches in Spain, most of which, on account of their small size and difficult access, remain largely undeveloped. The whole area just shouts 'honeymoon'.

There are four main beaches here – all minuscule coves and utterly heavenly. The following starts with the southernmost, Aiguablava, and runs northward, ending at Aiguafreda.

AIGUABLAVA

Stunningly sited at the foot of forest-cloaked cliffs is Aiguablava, with its Parador Nacional de la Costa Brava (972 62 21 62; www.parador.es; d €171; ✳ P ⏚). This modern hotel has comfortable rooms with all the extras, but really you don't stay here for the rooms but rather for the views, which are so extraordinary that it was touch and go as to whether we would leave. Half-board is obligatory in July and August.

FORNELLS

Fornells sits just around the corner from Aiguablava and shares the same spectacular bay. With its rocky beach and transparent waters splashing against a tiny harbour, it's one of the most exclusive 'resorts' on the Costa Brava, and a world away from brash Lloret de Mar. In fact, so delightful is it that one look and you'll be tempted to stay forever. If you do, with its luxurious rooms and gobsmacking views, the Hotel Aigua Blava (972 62 20 58; www.aiguablava.com; s/d €156/193, d with sea view €258; ✳ P ⏚) should prove to be an adequate hideaway.

SA TUNA

Slightly more built-up, Sa Tuna sits on a quiet pebbly beach and is probably the most family-friendly of the beaches. You could stay in the beachfront Hostal Sa Tuna (972 62 21 98; d €160) and gobble down a paella (around €20) in its convivial seaside eatery.

AIGUAFREDA

The northernmost of Begur's liquid crown jewels is Aiguafreda, a rocky cove backed by pine-covered hills. There's nothing whatsoever here except for one shady five-room hotel, the Hostal Sa Rascassa (972 62 28 45; www.hostalsarascassa.com; s/d €84/105; ⏚Mar-Oct). A few years ago the Spanish media dubbed this one of the best-decorated hotels in Spain and a year or so later the UK's *Sunday Times* claimed that the cove it sits in was one of the best beaches in the world. Whilst we beg to differ with the *Times* – the beach is after all just a rocky landing strip for brightly painted wooden boats – we won't argue with the Spanish media. The hotel has delightful, earthy-toned rooms and an overriding sense of peace. Oh, and about that beach...well OK, as far as boat-landing strips go, this one is pretty special.

ⓘ Getting There & Away

A *bus platges* (beach bus) service runs from Plaça de Forgas in Begur between late June and mid-September.

PALS
POP 2540

About 6km inland from Begur (a five-minute ride on the Palafrugell bus, €1.40) is the pretty walled town of Pals. The main monument is the 15m Torre de les Hores (clock tower) but what makes the trip worthwhile is simply wandering around the uneven lanes and poking your nose into one medieval corner or another. From the Mirador del Pedró you can see northeast across the coastal plains to the sea, with the Illes Medes in the background. There are a number of *pensiones* and *casas rurales* (rural homes) in and around the town.

Up to four Sarfa buses come here from Barcelona (€17, 2¼ hours) on weekdays.

PERATALLADA
POP 152

The warm stone houses of Peratallada have made this village a favourite day trip for Catalans. Its beautifully preserved narrow streets, heavy stone arches, 12th-century Romanesque church and 11th-century castle-mansion (now a luxury hotel and restaurant) are supplemented by several places to stay, enticing restaurants and a sprinkling of low-key boutiques.

Hostal Miralluna (972 63 43 04; www.hostalmaralluna.com; Plaza del Oli 2; d incl breakfast from €180; ⏚Mar-Nov; ✳⏚) is a 17th-century village home, where the old stone-and-timber frame has been teamed with modern comforts to create an artistically rustic place to stay that offers a real pampering. An extra bonus is the exquisite hidden garden.

There are a number of other places to stay in the village including some cheaper *casas rurales*.

Buses from Begur run twice a day (€2.45) and to Girona once a day (€3.60).

Castell de Púbol

At La Pera, just south of the C66 and 22km northwest of Palafrugell, the Castell de Púbol (972 48 86 55; www.salvador-dali.org; La Pera; adult/under 9yr €7/free; 10am-8pm mid-Jun–mid-Sep, to sunset rest of yr, closed Jan–mid-Mar & Mon outside high season) forms the southernmost point of northeast Catalonia's 'Salvador Dalí triangle', other elements of which include the Teatre-Museu Dalí in Figueres, and the Cadaqués area.

In 1968 Dalí bought this Gothic and Renaissance mansion, which includes a 14th-century church, and gave it to his wife, Gala, who lived here until her death. Local lore has it that the notoriously promiscuous Gala was still sending for young village men almost right up to the time she died in 1982, aged 88.

The castle was renovated by Dalí in his inimitable style, with lions' heads staring from the tops of cupboards, statues of elephants with giraffes' legs in the garden, and a stuffed giraffe staring at Gala's tomb in the crypt. In the garage is the blue Cadillac in which Dalí took Gala for a last drive here – after she died in Port Lligat. He had her buried in a crypt here and spent the next two years in maudlin mourning.

Sarfa buses between Palafrugell and Girona run along the C66.

Girona

POP 95,000

A tight huddle of ancient arcaded houses, grand churches, climbing cobbled streets and medieval baths, all enclosed by defensive walls and a lazy river, constitute a powerful reason for visiting north Catalonia's largest city, Girona (Castilian: Gerona).

The Roman town of Gerunda lay on Via Augusta, the highway from Rome to Cádiz (Carrer de la Força in Girona's old town follows part of Via Augusta). Taken from the Muslims by the Franks in AD 797, Girona became capital of one of Catalonia's most important counties, falling under the sway of Barcelona in the late 9th century. Its wealth in medieval times produced many fine Romanesque and Gothic buildings that have survived repeated attacks and sieges through the centuries.

⊙ Sights

Catedral　　　　CATHEDRAL

The billowing baroque facade of the cathedral stands at the head of a majestic flight of

MUSEUM PASS

The Tiquet M5, available at all Girona's museums and the tourist office, is the most economical way of visiting the city's museums. You pay the full entrance fee at the first museum you visit and then get a 50% discount at the remainder. It's valid for six months.

steps rising from Plaça de la Catedral. Most of the building, however, is much older than its exterior. Repeatedly rebuilt and altered down the centuries, it has Europe's widest Gothic nave (23m). The cathedral's museum (www.catedralgirona.org; adult/under 7yr €5/free, Sun free; 10am-8pm Apr-Oct, to 7pm Nov-Mar, 10am-2pm Sun & holidays), through the door marked 'Claustre Tresor', contains the masterly Romanesque *Tapís de la Creació* (Tapestry of the Creation) and a Mozarabic illuminated *Beatus* manuscript, dating from 975. The Creation tapestry shows God at the epicentre and in the circle around him the creation of Adam, Eve, the animals, the sky, light and darkness.

The fee for the museum also admits you to the beautiful 12th-century Romanesque cloister, whose 112 stone columns display some fine, if weathered, carving. From the cloister you can see the 13th-century Torre de Carlemany bell tower.

TOP CHOICE　Passeig Arqueològic

　　　　　　　　　　　　GARDENS
Across the street from the Banys Àrabs (Arab Baths), steps lead up into some heavenly gardens where town and plants merge into one organic masterpiece. The gardens follow the city walls up to the 18th-century Portal de Sant Cristòfol gate, from where you can walk back down to the cathedral.

Museu d'Art　　　　ART GALLERY
(www.museuart.com; Plaça de la Catedral 12; admission €2; 10am-7pm Tue-Sat Mar-Sep, to 6pm Oct-Feb, 10am-2pm Sun & holidays) Next door to the cathedral, in the 12th- to 16th-century Palau Episcopal, the art museum collection, which consists of around 8500 pieces, ranges from Romanesque woodcarvings to early-20th-century paintings. All the art on display comes from the Girona region.

FREE　Església de Sant Feliu　　CHURCH
(Plaça de Sant Feliu; 9.30am-2pm & 4-7pm Mon-Sat, 10am-noon & 4-7pm Sun) Giro-

na's second great church is downhill from the cathedral. The 17th-century main facade, with its landmark single tower, is on Plaça de Sant Feliu, but the entrance is around the side. The nave has 13th-century Romanesque arches but 14th- to 16th-century Gothic upper levels. The northernmost of the chapels, at the far western end of the church, is graced by a masterly Catalan Gothic sculpture, Aloi de Montbrai's alabaster *Crist Jacent* (Recumbent Christ).

Banys Àrabs   ARAB BATHS
(www.banysarabs.org; Carrer de Ferran Catòlic; adult/child €2/1; ⊙10am-7pm Mon-Sat Apr-Sep, shorter hr rest of yr, 10am-2pm Sun & holidays) Although modelled on earlier Muslim and Roman bathhouses, the Banys Àrabs are a 12th-century Christian affair in Romanesque style. This is the only public bathhouse discovered from medieval Christian Spain, where, in reaction to the Muslim obsession with water and cleanliness (and a widely held view that water carried disease), washing almost came to be regarded as ungodly. The baths contain an *apodyterium* (changing room), followed by a *frigidarium* and *tepidarium* (with respectively cold and warm water) and a *caldarium* (a kind of sauna).

Monestir de Sant Pere de Galligants
                    MONASTERY, MUSEUM
Down across thin Riu Galligants, this 11th- and 12th-century Romanesque monastery has another lovely cloister with some marvellous animal and monster carvings on the capitals of its pillars. The monastery houses Girona's Museu Arqueològic (www.mac.cat; Carrer de Santa Llúcia; adult/senior & child €2.30/free; ⊙10.30am-1.30pm & 4-7pm Tue-Sat Jun-Sep, shorter hr rest of yr, 10am-2pm Sun & holidays), whose exhibits date from prehistoric to medieval times, and include Roman mosaics and some medieval Jewish tombstones.

The Call   JEWISH QUARTER
Until 1492 Girona was home to Catalonia's second-most important medieval Jewish community (after Barcelona), and its Jewish quarter, the Call, was centred on Carrer de la Força. For an idea of medieval Jewish life and culture, visit the Museu d'Història dels Jueus de Girona (Jewish History Museum; Carrer de la Força 8; adult/child €2/free; ⊙10am-8pm Mon-Sat Jun-Oct, shorter hr rest of yr, 10am-3pm Sun & holidays). Also known as the Centre Bonastruc Ça Porta, named after Jewish Girona's most illustrious figure, a 13th-century cabbalist philosopher and mystic, the centre – a warren of rooms and stairways around a courtyard – hosts temporary exhibitions and is a focal point for studies of Jewish Spain.

Museu d'Història de la Ciutat   MUSEUM
(www.girona.cat; Carrer de la Força 27; adult/child €3/free; ⊙10am-2pm & 5-7pm Tue-Sat, 10am-2pm Sun & holidays) The City History Museum has displays covering everything from the city's Roman origins, through the siege of the city by Napoleonic troops to the *sardana* (Catalonia's national folk dance) tradition.

Museu del Cinema   MUSEUM
(www.museudelcinema.org; Carrer de Sèquia 1; adult/child €5/free; ⊙10am-8pm Jul-Aug, shorter hr & closed Mon rest of yr) The Casa de les Aigües houses Spain's only cinema museum. The Collecció Tomàs Mallol includes not only displays tracing the history of cinema, but also a parade of hands-on items for indulging in shadow games, optical illusions and the like – it's great for kids.

SPRING IS IN THE AIR

Spring and early summer are wonderful times to be in Girona. The sky is fresh and blue, the mercury in thermometers rising but not yet overwhelming and the streets are ablaze in colourful flowers – literally! During Girona's *Temps de Flors* (Time of Flowers; www.gironatempsdeflors. net) in early May the city itself becomes one enormous flower arrangement as businesses, members of the public and public buildings attempt to outdo one another by decorating their homes, shop fronts and even churches in thousands of ornate flowers and works of art. Museums and other sights of interest, which also get in on the act, tend to open longer hours, private businesses open their doors for all to come and marvel at their flower arrangements, and a general air of romance seems to float over the city.

Note, however, that accommodation is stretched to the limit at this time of year – book ahead.

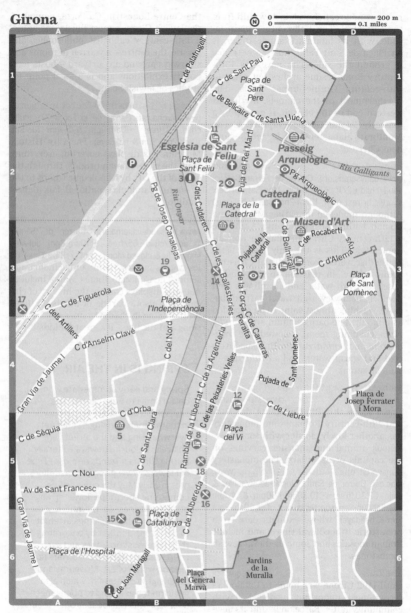

0 / 200 m
0 / 0.1 miles

CATALONIA COSTA BRAVA

Sleeping

TOP
CHOICE **Hotel Llegendes de Girona**

HOTEL €€€
(☎972 22 09 05; www.llegendeshotel.com; Portal de la Barca 4; d €123, 'Fountain of Lovers' room €288; P❀🕿) This new hotel has so many hi-tech gadgets it's like sleeping in the Space Shuttle. The rooms are supremely comfortable and the all-glass bathrooms with huge rain showers minimalist. One thing you possibly won't get at this hotel is a good night's sleep; in each room is a

little book detailing different tantric sex positions and three of the rooms have an 'Eros' sofa. Don't worry, it's not as seedy as it sounds!

Bed & Breakfast Bells Oficis   B&B €€
(☏972 22 81 70; www.bellsoficis.cat; Carrer dels Germans Busquets 2; r incl breakfast €35-85; ❄☏) Up the wobbly-winding staircase of an old building you'll discover six, very desirable, rooms. Some have unusual pebble art in the bathrooms, while others share bathrooms and some have views over the street. The biggest (€99) has ample room for four people.

Residència Bellmirall   BOUTIQUE HOTEL €€
(☏972 20 40 09; www.bellmirall.cat; Carrer de Bellmirall 3; s/d €40/75; ⊘closed Jan-Feb; ❄) Carved out of a 14th-century building in the heart of the old city, this 'residence' of heavy stone blocks and timber beams oozes character. Rooms with shared bathroom are marginally cheaper.

Gro Hostel Girona   HOSTEL €
(☏972 31 20 45; www.equity-point.com; Plaça de Catalunya 23; dm with/without bathroom & incl breakfast from €20/18; ❄☏@) One of a small chain of hostels (the others are in Barcelona and Madrid), this place offers not just the cheapest night's kip in Girona but is also a great-value, colourful and friendly hostel in its own right. From the kitchen access to internet and mounds of tourist info, it provides almost anything the passing traveller requires.

Hotel Històric   BOUTIQUE HOTEL €€
(☏972 22 35 83; www.hotelhistoric.com; Carrer de Bellmirall 4A; r €160/150; P❄☏) A bijou hotel in a historic building in old Girona, it has eight spacious rooms that are individually decorated. For a greater sense of home, you could opt for a small, self-contained apartment. If this place is full the owners can point you towards other rooms they have around town.

Pensió Viladomat   PENSIÓN €
(☏972 20 31 76; www.pensioviladomat.com; Carrer dels Ciutadans 5; s/d without bathroom €23/44, d with bathroom €60) This is one of the nicest of the cheaper *pensiones* scattered about the southern end of the old town. It has eight simple but well-maintained rooms.

✗ Eating

Restaurant Txalaka   BASQUE €€
TOP CHOICE (☏972 22 59 75; Carrer Bonastruc de Porta 4; menus €33, mains €15-20, pintxos €2.50-4; ⊘closed Sun) For sensational Basque cooking and *pintxos* (tapas) washed down with *txakoli* (the fizzy, white wine from the Basque coast) poured from a great height the way it's supposed to be, don't miss this popular place on the edge of the new town. The octopus dusted in paprika is the softest and most succulent we've ever had and the prawns in garlic and oil float our boat too.

L'Alqueria   CATALAN €€
(☏972 22 18 82; www.restaurantalqueria.com; Carrer Ginesta 8; mains €15-20; ⊘closed Sun &

KISS MY...

Girona is an addictive city and more than a few visitors promise themselves that they'll be back again soon. If you find yourself thinking this then the best way of ensuring that your wish comes true is to kiss the backside of the little lion statue that sits atop a plinth just after the bridge on Plaça de Sant Feliu. During the Swine Flu scare the local authorities removed the steps leading up to the lion's rear end, but it's now safe enough to pucker up to the King of the Jungle again.

Tue nights & all day Mon) This smart new restaurant serves the finest *arròs negre* (rice cooked in cuttlefish ink) and *arròs a la Catalan* in the city. If Valencia is more your thing, then there are various paellas. It's wise to book ahead.

Restaurant Albereda CATALAN €€
(☎972 22 60 02; www.restaurantalbereda.com; Carrer de l'Albereda 9; meals €40; ⏱lunch & dinner Tue-Sat, lunch Mon) Elegant Albereda, one of the town's top restaurants, dishes up stunning Catalan cuisine that you could be mistaken for thinking is art rather than mere food. The menu changes with the seasons.

La Terra INTERNATIONAL €
(☎972 21 92 54; Carrer de les Ballesteries 23; menus €6.90) Homemade burgers, quiches, cakes and enough tea to sate an Englishman go well with the wonderful river views and blue-and-white Andalucian-style tile work.

Xocolateria Antiga CAFE €
(Plaça del Vi 8; coffee & pastries €5-8; ⏱7am-9pm Mon-Sat) Modernista decor, frilly lace in the windows and hot, sticky cups of chocolate: time has stood still here. It's a great spot for breakfast.

Drinking & Entertainment

Students make the nightlife here, so in summer things calm down. Thursday is the big night of the week, as most people head for the coast on weekends. You can keep going until the wee hours near the river north of the old town, where you will find a string of bars (and restaurants) along Carrer de Palafrugell and Ronda de Pedret.

Café i Cu-cut BAR
(Plaça de l'Independència 10; ⏱10pm-3am) This is a local classic with a mixed crowd of students and 30-somethings all eager to get their bodies moving to anything from reggae through to pop, and even country.

Blau Club NIGHTCLUB
(www.blauclub.com; Camp de les Lloses 8; admission €12; ⏱11pm-5am Thu-Sun) This club is in the southern 'burbs of town. There are three dark spaces that pump out a mix of drum and bass, techno and hip hop. The DJs tend to be local talent.

Information

Parc Hospitalari Martí i Julià (Hospital; ☎972 18 25 00; Carrer del Doctor Castany)

Policía Nacional (☎972 48 60 01; Carrer de Sant Pau 2)

Tourist office (☎872 97 59 75; www.girona.cat/turisme; Joan Maragall 2; ⏱8am-8pm Mon-Fri, 8am-2pm & 4-8pm Sat, 9am-2pm Sun)

Turisme Imaginari (☎972 21 16 78; www.gironabooking.com; Punt de Benvinguda; ⏱9am-8pm Tue-Sun) Private tourist information office that assists with transport information and organises two-hour city tours (€10; 10.30am Tuesday to Sunday).

ℹ Getting There & Away

Air

Located 11km south of the centre is **Girona-Costa Brava airport**, and just off the AP7 and A2 is Ryanair's Spanish hub. **Sagalés** (www.sagales.com) operates hourly services from Girona-Costa Brava airport to Girona's main bus/train station (€2.15, 25 minutes) in connection with flights. See p294 for transport to/from Barcelona. Sarfa runs a couple of buses a day in summer, from the airport to coastal destinations, including Tossa de Mar (€8, 55 minutes) and, in season, Roses (€13, 1½ hours) and Figueres (€13, 55 minutes). A **taxi** (☎872 97 50 00) to/from the airport to central Girona costs around €22/25 day/night.

Bus

Teisa (www.teisa-bus.com in Catalan) runs up to eight services daily (four on Sunday) to Besalú (€3.55, 50 minutes) and Olot (€6.50, 1¼ hours). The bus station is behind the train station, about 400 metres west of the tourist office.

Train

Girona is on the train line between Barcelona, Figueres and Portbou on the French border. There are more than 20 trains per day to Figueres (€10.50 to €13.70, 30 to 40 minutes) and Barcelona (from €14.90, 1½ hours), and about

15 to Portbou or Cerbère (France) or both (from €12, 50 minutes to one hour). The train station is about 400 metres west of the tourist office.

Verges

POP 1116

About 15km northeast of Girona, the town of Verges has little to offer. But if you're in the area on Holy Thursday (Easter), make an effort to see the macabre evening procession of the Dansa de la Mort. People dressed as skeletons perform the Dance of Death through the streets as part of a much bigger procession enacting Christ's way to Calvary. The fun starts around 10pm.

Girona–Torroella buses pass through here.

Torroella de Montgrí

POP 11,598

On the Riu Ter, about 30km northeast of Girona and 15km north of Palafrugell, the agreeable old town of Torroella de Montgrí is the funnel through which travellers to L'Estartit must pass.

Overlooking the town from the top of the 300m limestone Montgrí hills to the north, the impressive but empty Castell de Montgrí was built between 1294 and 1301 for King Jaume II, during his efforts to bring to heel the disobedient counts of Empúries, to the north. There's no road, and by foot it's a 40-minute climb from Torroella. Head north from Plaça del Lledoner along Carrer de Fàtima, at the end of which is a sign pointing the way. In town, the Museu de la Mediterrània (www.museudelamediterrania. org; Carrer d'Ullà 31; admission free; ⊙10am-2pm & 6-9pm Mon-Sat, to 2pm Sun Jul-Aug, shorter hr rest of yr) is a local museum and cultural centre housed in the Can Quintana mansion. Ampsa (www.ampsa.org) runs buses about hourly (€1.40) to L'Estartit from June to September (half as often during the rest of the year). Sarfa has three or four daily buses to/from Barcelona (€18.95, three hours).

L'Estartit & the Illes Medes

POP 3571

L'Estartit, 6km east of Torroella de Montgrí, has a long, wide beach of fine sand but nothing over any other Costa Brava package resort – with the rather big exception of the Illes Medes (Islas Medes)! The group of rocky islets barely 1km offshore is home to some of the most abundant marine life on Spain's Mediterranean coast.

The main road in from Torroella de Montgrí is called Avinguda de Grècia as it approaches the beach; the beachfront road is Passeig Marítim.

🏃 Activities

Illes Medes   DIVING

The shores and waters around these seven islets, an offshore continuation of the limestone Montgrí hills, have been protected since 1985 as a *reserva natural submarina* (underwater nature reserve), which has brought a proliferation in their marine life and made them Spain's most popular destination for snorkellers and divers. Some 1345 plant and animal species have been identified here. There's a big bird population too; one of the Mediterranean's largest colonies of yellow-legged gulls (8000 pairs) breeds here between March and May.

Kiosks by the harbour, at the northern end of L'Estartit beach, offer snorkelling and glass-bottomed boat trips to the islands. Other glass-bottomed boat trips go to a series of caves along the coast to the north, or combine these with the Illes Medes.

🛏 Sleeping & Eating

Hostal Dalfó   HOSTAL €

(☑972 75 10 32; Carrer del Port 10; s/d €30/60; 🛜) Just back from the port, the small and simple white rooms here are as sparkling as the morning sun on the sea. Downstairs, Restaurant Can Dalfó (menus €16.20) stands out from the mass of nearby 'All-day English breakfast' places, and as would be expected in a port town, the menu is a big trawl of seafood.

Hotel Les Illes   HOTEL €€

(☑972 75 12 39; www.hotellesilles.com; Carrer de Les Illes 55; s/d incl breakfast €60/106) A decent, functional place with comfortable, if unspectacular, rooms, all with balconies. It is basically a divers' hang-out that's in a good spot back from the port. It has its own dive shop.

Les Medes   CAMPING €

(☑972 75 18 05; www.campinglesmedes.com; Paratge Camp de l'Arbre; sites per 2-person tent & car €34.90; ⊙Dec-Oct; 🅿🛜🏊🐾) Of the eight camping grounds in and around town, this child-friendly, activity-packed campsite is one of the best. It is set in a leafy location about 800m from the seaside and has

DIVING OFF THE COSTA BRAVA

The range of depths (down to 50m) and underwater cavities and tunnels around the Illes Medes contribute much to their attraction. On and around rocks near the surface are colourful algae and sponges, as well as octopuses, crabs and various fish. Below 10m or 15m, cavities and caves harbour lobsters, scorpion fish and large conger eels and groupers. Some groupers and perch may feed from the hand. With luck, you'll spot some huge wrasse. If you get down to the sea floor, you may see angler fish, thornback rays or marbled electric rays. Be aware that this area gets pretty busy with divers, especially on summer weekends.

Several outfits in L'Estartit can take you out scuba diving, at the Illes Medes or off the mainland coast; the tourist office has lists of them. If you're a qualified diver, a two-hour trip usually costs around €30 per person. Full gear rental can cost up to €45 a day. Night dives are possible (usually about €30 to €35). You generally pay extra to go with a guide and for insurance (if you don't have any). If you're a novice, do an introductory dive for around €60 or a full, five-day PADI Open Water Diver course for around €370.

a sauna as well as three pools. Bike rental and even massages are available. It doesn't accept credit cards.

Hostal Santa Clara HOTEL €
(972 75 17 67; www.hostalsantaclara.com; Passeig Marítim 18; s/d €31/62; P) On the waterfront and barely a 100-yard dash to the beach, this friendly, bustling spot with its own bar-restaurant has three floors of standard rooms with balconies looking out to sea.

The northern end of Passeig Marítim, by the roundabout, is swarming with eateries. These places are all pretty similar, presenting a mix of basic Spanish fare and chicken-and-chips-style meals.

ⓘ Information

Tourist office (☑972 75 19 10; www.visit estartit.com; Passeig Marítim; ◷9.30am-2pm & 4-8pm daily Jul-Sep, 9.30am-2pm & 4-7pm Mon-Sat, 10am-2pm Sun May-Jun & Oct, shorter hr rest of yr) At the northern end of Passeig Marítim.

ⓘ Getting There & Around

Sarfa buses run to and from Barcelona once or twice daily (€18.75, three hours) in summer. Otherwise change in Torroella de Montgrí.

L'Escala

POP 10,140

Travel back millennia in time to the ancient Greco-Roman site of Empúries (Castilian: Ampurias), set behind a near-virgin beach facing the Mediterranean. Its modern descendant, L'Escala, 11km north of

Torroella de Montgrí, is a sunny and pleasant medium-sized resort (a good deal more attractive than better-known Roses to the north) on the often windswept southern shore of the Golf de Roses. Birdwatchers flock to the Parc Natural dels Aiguamolls de l'Empordà, coastal wetlands that lie about 10km north of Empúries.

EMPÚRIES

Empúries was probably the first, and certainly one of the most important, Greek colonies on the Iberian Peninsula. Early Greek traders, pushing on from a trading post at Masilia (Marseille in France), set up a new post around 600 BC at what is now the charming village of Sant Martí d'Empúries, then an island. Soon afterwards they founded a mainland colony, Emporion (Market), which remained an important trading centre, and conduit of Greek culture to the Iberians, for centuries.

In 218 BC, Roman legions clanked ashore here to cut off Hannibal's supply lines in the Second Punic War. About 195 BC, they set up a military camp and, by 100 BC, had added a town. A century later it had merged with the Greek one. Emporiae, as the place was then known, was abandoned in the late 3rd century AD, after raids by Germanic tribes. Later, an early Christian basilica and a cemetery stood on the site of the Greek town, before the whole place, after over a millennium of use, disappeared altogether.

The Site ROMAN RUINS
(www.mac.cat; adult/child €3/free; ◷10am-8pm Jun-Sep, to 6pm Oct-May) The Greek town lies

in the lower part of the site, closer to the shore. Main points of interest include the thick southern defensive walls, the site of the Asklepion (a shrine to the god of medicine) with a copy of his statue found here, and the Agora (town square), with remnants of the early Christian basilica and the Greek *stoa* (market complex), beside it.

A museum (Barcelona's Museu d'Arqueologia de Catalunya, p267, has a bigger and better Empúries collection) separates the Greek town from the larger Roman town on the upper part of the site. The museum contains some stunning mosaics, statues and 2000-year-old drinking cups. Highlights of the Roman town include the mosaic floors of a 1st-century-BC house, the Forum and ancient walls. Outside the walls are the remains of an oval amphitheatre. A 2nd-century-AD bust in Carrara marble of the Roman god Bacchus was unearthed on the site in 2005.

A string of brown-sand beaches stretches along in front of the site. On one of the beaches, 1.2km from L'Escala, stands a Greek stone jetty.

Another few hundred metres north along the beaches from Empúries brings you to a gem, the 15th-century seaside hamlet of Sant Martí d'Empúries, all bright stone houses and cobbled lanes. On Plaça Major, several restaurant-bars compete for your attention under the watchful gaze of the strange, squat facade of the local church.

🛏 Sleeping & Eating

L'Escala is famous for its *anchoas* (anchovies) and fresh fish, both of which are likely to crop up on menus. Plenty of fairly expensive eateries are scattered along the waterfront parade of Port d'en Perris, as well as some more sleeping options. The town is essentially split into two-halves – the northern part is centred on the scrappy old town and is more popular with Spanish tourists; the hotels listed here are in this part. The southern half, which spreads along a big sandy bay, is more of an international holiday resort and lacks the character of the older part of town.

Hostal Casa Poch PENSIÓN €
(☎972 77 00 92; Carrer Grácia 10; s/d incl breakfast €25/40) Run by a friendly old couple, the rooms here, which are decorated in proper gran-and-grandad fashion, sit above a truly Spanish-flavoured local bar and offer exceptional value for money.

Hotel Empúries BOUTIQUE HOTEL €€€
(☎972 77 02 07; www.hostalempuries.com; Platja del Portitxol; d €130; P✷✷) A stylish hotel next to the Roman ruins and fronting a sandy splash of ocean. The rooms are as sandy coloured as the beach and the mosaic bathrooms clearly take their inspiration from the ruins.

Hotel Voramar HOTEL €€
(☎972 77 01 08; www.hotelvoramar.com; Passeig Lluís Albert 2; s/d incl breakfast from €75/118; P✷✷✷) Ignore the slightly shabby exterior, because inside this large package-holiday-style hotel you'll find good-sized, comfortable rooms, some of which have breathtaking sea views. In summer there's a private seawater swimming pool perched on the rocks just in front of the hotel.

ℹ Information

If you arrive by Sarfa bus, you'll alight on L'Escala's Plaça de les Escoles, where you'll find the **tourist office** (☎972 77 06 03; Plaça de les Escoles 1; ⊙9am-8pm daily mid-Jun–mid-Sep, shorter hr rest of yr). Empúries is 1km around the coast to the northwest of the town centre.

ℹ Getting There & Away

Sarfa has three daily buses from Barcelona (€18.95, three hours). Buses also run to and from Girona (€5.60, one hour).

Castelló d'Empúries

POP 12.111

This well-preserved ancient town feels far removed from the Costa Brava's typical cliChéd image of holiday high-rises and chaotic beaches. The town was once the capital of Empúries, a medieval Catalan county that maintained a large degree of independence up to the 14th century and today it makes a superb base for the nearby Parc Natural dels Aiguamolls de L'Empordá, as well as a number of wind-blown but peaceful beaches. Away from the feathered treats of the natural park, manmade beauty can be found in the town centre's Església de Santa Maria on Plaça de Jacint Verdaguer. It's a voluminous 13th- and 14th-century Gothic church with a sturdy Romanesque bell tower.

◉ Sights & Activities

Parc Natural dels Aiguamolls de l'Empordà BIRDWATCHING
(www.parcsdecatalunya.net, in Spanish; parking €2) The remnants of the mighty marshes

ℹ CATALONIA'S PARKS & RESERVES

Catalonia boasts 17 parks, nature reserves, a marine reserve and areas of special interest. For a complete run-down on all of them, check out www.parcsdecatalunya.net, a very handy website full of useful background information.

that once covered the whole coastal plain of the Golf de Roses are preserved in this natural park, which is a key site for migrating birds. Birdwatchers have spotted more than 100 species a day in the March–May and August–October migration periods, which bring big increases in the numbers of wading birds and even the occasional flamingo, glossy ibis, spoonbill or rare black stork. In all, in the migratory periods more than 300 species pass through (some 90 nest here). There are usually enough birds around to make a visit worthwhile at any time of year.

Head for the El Cortalet information centre (☺9.30am-2pm & 4.30-7pm Apr-Oct, shorter hr rest of yr), 1km east off the Sant Pere Pescador–Castelló d'Empúries road. Marked paths lead to a 2km stretch of beach and several *aguaits* (hides) with saltwater-marsh views. From the top of the Observatori Senillosa, a former silo, you can observe the whole park. The paths are always open, but morning and evening are the best times for birds (and mosquitoes!).

The nearest places to El Cortalet that can be reached by bus are Sant Pere Pescador, 6km south (served by four or five Sarfa buses daily from L'Escala and Figueres), and Castelló d'Empúries, 4km north.

🛏 Sleeping & Eating

There are a couple of great-value places to eat and drink in the town, as well as numerous *casas rurales* in the surrounding countryside.

Hotel de la Moneda   HOTEL €€
(☏972 15 86 02; www.hoteldelamoneda.com; Plaça de la Moneda 8-10; d incl breakfast €110-120; ☺closed 6 weeks Feb-Mar & 3 weeks Dec; P✳🛜🏊) This recently opened hotel inside a listed 18th-century building full of arches and domes is a great place to stay. Despite the historic background, it has been reno-

vated and decorated in an utterly modern style of lurid colours and zany works of art. Parking is €10.

Hotel Canet   HOTEL €€
(☏972 25 03 40; www.hotelcanet.com; Plaça del Joc de la Pilota 2; s/d from €55/80; P🛜✳🏊) This modernised 17th-century mansion in the town centre has elegant rooms, low-slung stone arches and a sun deck. A soothing swimming pool glistens within the stone walls of the interior courtyard. It also has a decent restaurant (mains around €15) offering mostly Catalan fare.

Taverna de les Cols   CATALAN €
(☏972 25 02 99; Plaça de les Cols 6; mains €10-15) This cheery restaurant, located in a sunny central plaza, serves a decent *arròs a la Catalan,* various paellas (for a minimum of two people), as well as many other saltwater delights.

ℹ Getting There & Away

Sarfa runs about 12 buses a day (fewer on Sunday, and up to 28 in July and August) from Figueres (€1.40, 15 minutes), five or six (more in July and August) from Cadaqués (€3.65, 50 minutes) and two from Barcelona's Estació del Nord (€18.10, two hours).

Roses & Around

POP 20,197

Some believe Roses is the site of an ancient Greek settlement, Rodes, although nothing remains to confirm the hypothesis. The town does boast the impressive seaward wall of its 16th-century citadel, but is an otherwise listless place whose melancholy main entrance road is lined by tacky water parks. Although this middling holiday town's beaches are OK (the tourist office has endless lists of accommodation), Roses is, above all, a handy base for going elsewhere.

With a vehicle you can get well beyond the crowds of Roses into the southern end of Parc Natural del Cap de Creus. About 6km east of Roses, a road runs up into the hills and along the rugged coast to Cala Montjoi.

Sarfa buses from Barcelona run two to four times a day to Roses, depending on the day and season (€19.45, 2¼ hours). Plenty run between Roses and Figueres (€2.75, 30 minutes).

Cadaqués & Around

POP 2860

If you have time for only one stop on the Costa Brava, you can hardly do better than Cadaqués. A whitewashed village around a rocky bay, it and the surrounding area have a special magic – a fusion of wind, sea, light and rock – that isn't dissipated even by the throngs of summer visitors.

A portion of that magic owes itself to Salvador Dalí, who spent family holidays in Cadaqués during his youth, and lived much of his later life at nearby Port Lligat. The empty moonscapes, odd-shaped rocks and barren shorelines that litter Dalí's famous paintings were not just a product of his fertile imagination. They are strewn all round the Cadaqués area in what Dalí described as a 'grandiose geological delirium'.

The country here is drier than further south. The sparseness continues to dramatic Cap de Creus, 8km northeast of Cadaqués, lending itself to coastscapes of almost surreal beauty.

Thanks to Dalí and other luminaries, Cadaqués pulled in a celebrity crowd for decades. One visit by the poet Paul Éluard and his Russian wife, Gala, in 1929 caused an earthquake in Dalí's life: he ran off to Paris with Gala (who was to become his lifelong obsession and, later, his wife) and joined the surrealist movement. In the 1950s the crowd he attracted was more jet-setting – Walt Disney, the Duke of Windsor and Greek shipowner Stavros Niarchos. In the 1970s Mick Jagger and Gabriel García Márquez popped by. Today the crowd is not quite as famous, and leans heavily to day-tripping French from across the border, but the enchantment of Cadaqués' atmosphere remains.

SEEING MICHELIN STARS

Once a simple bar and grill clutching on to a rocky perch high above the bare Mediterranean beach of Cala Montjoi and accessible only by dirt track from Roses, 6km to the west, **elBulli**, which has won a host of awards including three Michelin stars and the title 'Best Restaurant in the World' a record five times, became one of the world's most sought-after dining experiences thanks to star chef Ferran Adrià. In fact, so popular was the restaurant that all table bookings for the following year were taken on a single day and around two million people, each willing to pay €200 to €300 a head, would apply for one of the only 8000 eating slots available each year. But, to the shock of the gastronomic world, and no doubt to the relief of many chefs with their eyes on Adrià's crown, in early 2010 Adrià announced that he would be closing his restaurant for two years in order to 'experiment'. Then, just a fortnight later, he announced that elBulli would close permanently due to the restaurant making losses of around half a million euros a year. Instead Adrià will now concentrate his efforts on an academy for advanced cuisine.

But potential elBulli customers fret not. Catalonia has three other three-star Michelin eateries (in all of Spain, there are only six, excluding elBulli; the other three are in the Basque Country).

Can Fabes (☏93 867 28 51; www.canfabes.com; Carrer de Sant Joan 6, Sant Celoni; menus from €160; ☺Wed-Sat, lunch Sun, closed Jan) has long attracted a steady stream of gastronauts from Barcelona (53km to the south). Chef Santi Santamaria (the first Catalan chef ever awarded three Michelin stars) is a local boy who started up here in 1981. Dishes based on local products (seafood landed at Blanes, for example) are at the core of his cooking.

Barely 25km east, on the coast at Sant Pol de Mar, is another foodies' fave. **Sant Pau** (☏93 760 06 62; www.ruscalleda.com; Carrer Nou 10; menus €144; ☺lunch & dinner Tue-Wed, Fri & Sat, dinner Thu, closed most of May & Nov) is a beautifully presented mansion with a garden overlooking the Mediterranean. Carme Ruscalleda is the driving force here.

Finally, the new boy on the culinary scene is **El Celler de Can Roca** (☏972 22 21 57; www.cellercanroca.com; Carrer Can Sunyer 48, Girona; menus €95-145; ☺Tue-Sat), which received its third Michelin star in 2010. Housed in a modernised *masia* (country house), it offers thoroughly inventive and ever-changing takes on Mediterranean cooking. It's about 2km west of Girona (and is not the easiest place to find).

⊙ Sights

Beaches
BEACHES

Cadaqués' main beach, and several others along the nearby coast, are small, with more pebbles than sand, but their picturesqueness and beautiful blue waters make up for that. Overlooking Platja Llané, to the south of the town centre, is Dalí's parents' holiday home. Out the front is a statue by Josep Subirachs dedicated to Federico García Lorca and in memory of his 1920s stay. All the beaches around here suffer from strong winds that can make swimming, even in high summer, fun only for the thick-skinned.

Port Lligat & Casa Museu Dalí
MUSEUM

Port Lligat, a 1.25km walk from Cadaqués, is a tiny settlement around another lovely cove, with fishing boats pulled up on its beach. The **Casa Museu Dalí** (☏972 25 10 15; www.salvador-dali.org; Port Lligat; adult/child €10/free; ☺by advance reservation only) started life as a mere fisherman's hut, was steadily altered and enlarged by Dalí, who lived here from 1930 to 1982 (apart from a dozen or so years abroad during and around the Spanish Civil War), and is now a fascinating insight into the lives of the (excuse the pun) surreal couple. We probably don't need to tell you that it's the house with a lot of little white chimneypots and two egg-shaped towers, overlooking the western end of the beach. You must book ahead.

Cap de Creus
HEADLAND

Cap de Creus is the most easterly point of the Spanish mainland and is a place of sublime, rugged and very wind-battered beauty. In fact, so alien is the landscape here to almost anything else you might have seen in Spain that you could easily be forgiven for thinking you'd somehow fallen through a trapdoor and ended up in the Scottish Highlands or a high Norwegian plateau. With a steep, rocky coastline indented by dozens of turquoise-watered coves, it's an especially wonderful place to be at dawn or sunset. On top of the cape stand a lighthouse and the world's most unexpected **curry house** (☏972 19 90 05; mains €14-18; ☺daily), where you get all manner of homemade Indian tastes as well as cheesecake. You can also sleep over in one of a handful of rooms (which tend to be booked out months in advance in summer).

The Town
OLD TOWN

Cadaqués is perfect for wandering, either around the town or along the coast (in either direction). The 16th- and 17th-century **Església de Santa Maria**, with a gilded baroque *retablo* (altarpiece), is the focus of the oldest part of town, with its narrow, hilly streets. But strolling the little pedestrian-only lanes anywhere back from the waterfront is a delight.

Museu de Cadaqués
MUSEUM

(Carrer de Narcís Monturiol 15; ☺10am-1.30pm & 4-7pm Mon-Sat) Closed for renovations at the time of research; when it reopens it's likely that Dalí will continue to feature strongly in the works of art displayed here.

🏃 Activities

There are infinite possibilities for walking: out along the promontory between Cadaqués and Port Lligat; to Port Lligat and beyond; along the southern side of the Cadaqués bay to the Far de Cala Nans (lighthouse); or over the hills south of Cadaqués to the coast east of Roses.

Diving
DIVING

Clear waters plus a rocky, contorted coastline around Cadaqués equals great diving. the **Diving Centre Cadaqués** (☏652 31 77 97; www.divingccadaques.com; Carrer de la Miranda 8) can help beginners and experienced divers alike get under the waves. Equipment rental is €45 and courses start at €270.

🛏 Sleeping

Aside from one or two exceptions, the accommodation in Cadaqués is generally overpriced and staff are often lacking in customer-service abilities.

Hostal Vehí
TOP CHOICE
PENSIÓN €€

(☏972 25 84 70; www.hostalvehi.com; Carrer de l'Església 5; s/d without bathroom €30/55, d with bathroom €77; ❄) Near the church in the heart of the old town, this simple but engaging *pensión* with clean-as-a-whistle rooms tends to be booked up for July and August. Easily the cheapest deal in town, it's also about the best. In fact the only drawback we can come up with is that it's a pain to get to if you have a lot of luggage. Breakfast is €6 extra.

L'Hostalet de Cadaqués
HOTEL €€

(☏972 25 82 06; www.hostaletcadaques.com; Carrer Miquel Rosset 13; d €65; ❄☏) The rooms in this new hotel are tiny, but exceptionally well kept and hanging enticingly off the walls are pictures of the various beaches you will shortly be swimming off. It can suffer a little from noise from the nearby bars.

Hotel Llané Petit
HOTEL €€€

(972 25 10 20; www.llanepetit.com; Carrer del Dr Bartomeus 37; d with/without seaview €158/124; P✳🌐🛜) A four-storey place overlooking a pocket-sized cobbled beach, the hotel is perhaps not as 'petite' as all that (it has 35 rooms), but the location is splendid and all the rooms have a generous balcony to sit on. Otherwise, the rooms are decidedly straightforward in a somewhat passé style.

🍴 Eating

The seafront is lined with eateries, all of which have good food but are quite pricey. There's little to pick between most of them, but two value-for-money stand-out places are listed here.

Bar Lo Sai Si No Fos
SEAFOOD, PASTA €

(Plaça Dr Trempois 8; mains €5-12) This quaint blue-and-white restaurant, set inside a cellarlike room, offers real value with huge piles of prawns and garlic for €11, delicious fried balls of cod, lots of healthy salads and some tasty pasta dishes.

Casa Nun
SEAFOOD, VEGETARIAN €

(972 25 88 56; Plaça del Pianc Ditxos 6; menus €14-18) Head for the cute upstairs dining area or take one of the few tables outside overlooking the port. Everything is prepared with care, and, you guessed it, seafood predominates. There's usually a couple of vegetarian options too.

🍷 Drinking & Entertainment

Carrer Miquel Rosset is jam-packed with hole-in-the-wall bars that get messy on sultry summer nights.

L'Hostal
BAR

(Passeig; ⏰10pm-5am Sun-Thu, 10pm-6am Fri & Sat Apr-Oct) Facing the beachfront boulevard, this classic has live music on many nights (from midnight). One evening in the 1970s, an effusive Dalí called L'Hostal the *lugar más bonito del mundo* (most beautiful place on earth). Inside hang photos of the artist and hordes of other stars and starlets of times gone by.

Café de la Habana
LIVE MUSIC

(Carrer de Dr Bartomeus, Punta d'en Pampa; ⏰9pm-2.30am daily Easter-Oct, 9pm-2.30am Fri-

Sun Nov-Easter) One kilometre south of the town centre, this icon of Cadaqués' nightlife can get lively with Latin-music nights, art exhibitions and cool cocktails (not to mention the extensive range of Caribbean rums). There's live music most summer nights at 11pm. No under-18s.

ℹ️ Information

Centre de Salut (972 25 88 07; Carrer Nou 6-10)

Policía Local (972 15 93 43; Carrer de Carles Rahola 9) Out of town, off the road to Port Lligat.

Tourist office (972 25 83 15; Carrer del Cotxe 2; ⏰9am-9pm Mon-Sat, 10am-1pm & 5-8pm Sun Jun–mid-Sep, shorter hr rest of yr)

ℹ️ Getting There & Away

Sarfa buses to/from Barcelona (€21.35, 2¾ hours) leave twice daily (up to five daily in July and August). Buses also run to/from Figueres (€4.80, one hour) up to seven times daily (three in winter) via Castelló d'Empúries.

Cadaqués to the French Border

If you want to prolong the journey to France, El Port de la Selva and Llançà are pleasant, low-key beach resorts-cum-fishing towns. The former is backed by powerful mountains and filled with bobbing yachts, while the latter boasts a string of strands and coastal walking trail. Both have a range of accommodation. Portbou, on the French frontier, is rather less enticing. From El Port de la Selva you can undertake a wild and woolly walk high along the rugged coast. The trail, which is awkward at some points, leads east to Cap de Creus.

Monestir de Sant Pere de Rodes
MONASTERY

(adult/under 7yr €3.60/free, Tue free; ⏰10am-8pm Tue-Sun Jun-Sep, 10am-5.30pm Tue-Sun Oct-May) Combine all-encompassing views of a deep-blue Mediterranean and the (sometimes) snowy peaks of the nearby Pyrenees with a spectacular piece of Romanesque architecture and what you get is the Monestir de Sant Pere de Rodes, which sits 500m up in the hills southwest of El Port de la Selva. Founded in the 8th century, it later became the most powerful monastery between Figueres and Perpignan in France. The great triple-naved, barrel-vaulted basilica is

MOVING ON?

For tips, recommendations and reviews, head to shop.lonelyplanet.com to purchase a downloadable PDF of the Languedoc-Roussillon chapter from Lonely Planet's *France* guide.

flanked by the square Torre de Sant Miquel bell tower and a two-level cloister.

ⓘ Getting There & Away

The monastery is on a back road over the hills between Vilajuïga, 8km to its west, and El Port de la Selva, 5km northeast. Each town is served by Sarfa buses from Figueres, but there are no buses to the monastery. Vilajuïga is also on the train line between Figueres and Portbou.

Figueres

POP 43,330

Twelve kilometres inland from the Golf de Roses, Figueres (Castilian: Figueras) is a humdrum town with a single, unique and unmissable attraction: Salvador Dalí. In the 1960s and '70s Dalí created here, in the town of his birth, the extraordinary Teatre-Museu Dalí. Whatever your feelings about old Salvador, this is worth every cent and minute you can spare.

◎ Sights

Teatre-Museu Dalí   MUSEUM
(www.salvador-dali.org; Plaça de Gala i Salvador Dalí 5; admission incl Dalí Joies & Museu de l'Empordà adult/under 9yr €11/free; ⊙9am-8pm Jul-Sep, 9.30am-6pm Mar-Jun & Oct, shorter hr rest of yr, closed Mon Oct-Jun) A purple-pink building topped by giant boiled eggs and stylised Oscar statues? Smack in the middle of a dowdy provincial town? This can only mean one thing in these parts: Dalí!

Salvador Dalí was born in Figueres in 1904. Although his career took him to Madrid, Barcelona, Paris and the USA, he remained true to his roots and lived well over half his adult life at Port Lligat, east of Figueres on the coast. Between 1961 and 1974 Dalí converted Figueres' former municipal theatre, ruined by a fire at the end of the civil war in 1939, into the Teatre-Museu Dalí. 'Theatre-museum' is an apt label for this multidimensional trip through one of the most fertile (or disturbed) imaginations of the 20th century. It's full of surprises, tricks and illusions, and contains a substantial portion of Dalí's life's work.

Even outside, the building aims to surprise, from the collection of bizarre sculptures outside the entrance, on Plaça de Gala i Salvador Dalí, to the pink wall along Pujada del Castell, topped by a row of Dalí's trademark egg shapes and what appear to be sculptures of female gymnasts, and studded with what look like loaves of bread. The Torre Galatea, added in 1983, was where Dalí spent his final years.

Inside, the ground floor (1st level) includes a semicircular garden area on the site of the original theatre stalls. In its centre is a classic piece of weirdness called Taxi Plujós (Rainy Taxi), composed of an early Cadillac, which was said to have belonged to Al Capone, and a pile of tractor tyres; both are surmounted by statues, with a fishing boat balanced precariously above the tyres. Put a coin in the slot and water washes all over the inside of the car. The Sala de Peixateries (Fish Shop Room) off here holds a collection of Dalí oils, including the famous *Autoretrat Tou amb Tall de Bacon Fregit* (Soft Self-Portrait with Fried Bacon) and *Retrat de Picasso* (Portrait of Picasso). Beneath the former stage of the theatre is the crypt, with Dalí's plain tomb.

If proof were needed of Dalí's acute sense of the absurd, *Gala Mirando el Mar Mediterráneo* (Gala Looking at the Mediterranean Sea) on the 2nd level would be it. With the help of coin-operated viewfinders, the work appears, from the other end of the room, to be a portrait of Abraham Lincoln.

In August the museum opens at night (admission €12, 10pm to 1am) for a maximum of 500 people (booking essential). You are treated to a glass of *cava* (sparkling wine).

Dalí Joies

A separate entrance (same ticket and times) leads into the Owen Cheatham collection of 37 jewels, designed by Dalí, and called Dalí Joies (Dalí Jewels). Also on display are the designs themselves. Dalí did these on paper (his first commission was in 1941) and the jewellery was made by specialists in New York. Each piece, ranging from the disconcerting *Ull del Temps* (Eye of Time) through to the *Cor Reial* (Royal Heart), is unique.

Museu de l'Empordà
MUSEUM

(www.museuemporda.org; La Rambla 2; adult/child €2/free; ☉11am-8pm Tue-Sat, 11am-2pm Sun & holidays, May-Oct, shorter hr rest of yr) This local museum combines Greek, Roman and medieval archaeological finds with a sizeable collection of art, mainly by Catalan artists, but there are also some works on loan from the Prado in Madrid. Admission is free with a Teatre-Museu Dalí ticket.

Museu del Joguet
MUSEUM

(www.mjc.cat; Carrer de Sant Pere 1; adult/child €5/free; ☉10am-7pm Mon-Sat, 11am-6pm Sun Jun-Sep, shorter hr rest of yr) Spain's only toy museum has more than 3500 Catalonia- and Valencia-made toys from the pre–Barbie doll 19th and early 20th centuries. The Groucho Marx doll is an odd one!

Castell de Sant Ferran
CASTLE

(www.lesfortalesescatalanes.info, in Spanish; admission €5.50; ☉10.30am-8pm Easter & Jul–mid-Sep, 10.30am-3pm mid-Sep–Jun) The sprawling 18th-century fortress, which is billed as the largest in Europe, stands on a low hill 1km northwest of the centre. Built in 1750, it saw no action in the following centuries. After abandoning Barcelona, Spain's Republican government held its final meeting of the civil war (1 February 1939) in the dungeons. The admission fee is for a tour of the interior of the fortress. If you just want to stroll around the grounds, they're free and always open.

Museu de la Tècnica de l'Empordà
MUSEUM

(www.mte.cat; Carrer dels Fossos 12; adult/under 10yr €3/free; ☉10am-7pm Tue-Fri, 10am-1pm & 4-7pm Sat, 11am-2pm Sun & holidays) This technical museum is a treasure chest of old mechanical masterpieces, from typewriters and watches through to sewing machines, heaters and cash registers.

🛏 Sleeping & Eating

Most people treat Figueres as a day trip from the coast, and unless you're a diehard Dalí fan who really wants to get under the skin of the town to see if you can work out what made the man tick, we recommend you do the same. If you do choose to stay, there are around two dozen generally uninspiring but fair-priced places about town.

There are numerous cheerful places to get a meal throughout town, but the ones closest to the Teatre-Museu Dalí are little more than tourist traps.

Mas Pau
BOUTIQUE HOTEL €€

(☎972 54 61 54; www.maspau.com; Avinyonet de Puigventós; s/d €88/110; P ❋ 🖵) Four kilometres west of Figueres along the road to Besalú, Mas Pau is an enchanting country hotel-restaurant, created inside the rough-hewn stone of a 16th-century *masia,* and set amid soothing gardens. The Michelin-starred restaurant (meals €60 to €85; open Wednesday to Saturday, lunch only Sunday, dinner only Sunday in summer) has a great local reputation and offers elegant dishes based on local products and traditions.

Hotel Durán
HOTEL €€

(☎972 50 12 50; www.hotelduran.com; Carrer de Lasauca 5; d from €79; P ❋ 🖵) In business since the mid-19th century (on the site, it is said, of a wayside inn as far back as the 17th century), this hotel offers comfortable rooms with modern decorative touches (all soft beiges, browns and white), satellite TV and hairdryers in the bathroom. The dining room of the attached restaurant is like a royal banquet hall and the chairs like something from Alice in Wonderland, all of which helps make the €18 lunch menu well worth partaking in.

DEALING WITH DALÍ'S FANS

The Teatre-Museu Dalí is one of the busiest museums in Spain. Entrance queues can be well over an hour long and on busy days it's actually almost impossible to see any of the works of art – we've heard from people who've queued up for an hour to get in and then left after five minutes due to the claustrophobic nature of the heavy crowds in the narrow museum corridors. Spring and early summer are the worst times for this. In high season tour groups are banned, which goes a long way to keeping things manageable. If you really want to relax and appreciate the art, come in mid-winter.

On the same note, wheelchair access is restricted to the central courtyard, the treasure room and the ground floor.

Salvador Dalí at Home

Born in Figueres in 1904, Salvador Dalí was one of the leading lights of the surrealist movement. As well as painting, Dalí, who had a larger-than-life presence, also delved into the world of sculpture, film and photography.

Today, Dalí's presence remains everywhere on the northern Costa Brava, but there are some places where his spirit runs extra thick and colourful.

Dalí's goal in creating the Teatre-Museu Dalí (p324) in Figueres was to express his 'desires, enigmas, obsessions and passions' for everyone to see.

Figueres may have been his home town but Dalí's favourite place in Catalonia was whitewashed Cadaqués (p321), and its tiny neighbour of Port Lligat, where he lived and painted for the better part of 50 years.

Towards the end of his life, Dalí, and his muse (and wife), Gala, moved to the Castell de Púbol (p312) northeast of Girona, where Gala now lies in her crypt surrounded by giraffe-legged elephants.

ESSENTIAL DALÍ

Dalí created more than 1500 works in his lifetime. Some of his best known are:

» **The Persistence of Memory** (1931) Dalí's most famous work features the images of melting clocks, which symbolise the irrelevance of time.

» **Crucifixion (Corpus Hypercubus)** (1954) Jesus crucified on a net of hypercubes whilst Dalí's wife, Gala, looks on.

» **The Sacrament of the Last Supper** (1955) A classic Christian scene re-enacted through the eyes of a surrealist.

Clockwise from top left
1. Dalí statue, Cadaqués (p321) 2. & 3. Figueres Teatre-Museu Dalí (p324) 4. Gardens, Casa Museu Dalí (p322)

DENNIS JOHNSON

CHRISTOPHER GROENHOUT

ⓘ Information

Hospital (☎972 50 14 00; Ronda del Rector Aroles)

Policía Nacional (Carrer de Pep Ventura 8)

Tourist office (☎972 50 31 55; www.figueres ciutat.com, in Catalan; Plaça del Sol; ☺9am-8pm Mon-Sat, 10am-2pm Sun Jul-Sep, shorter hr rest of yr) Hours can be unpredictable.

ⓘ Getting There & Away

Sarfa buses serve Castelló d'Empúries (€1.40) 10 to 20 times daily and Cadaqués (€4.80, one hour) up to eight times daily.

Figueres is on the train line between Barcelona, Girona and Portbou on the French border, and there are regular connections to Girona (€3.90, 30 minutes) and Barcelona (from €9.40, 1¾ hours) and to Portbou and the French border (€2 to €2.30, 25 minutes).

Around Figueres

It is hard to imagine that, just a few kilometres outside Figueres, such pleasant countryside should soothe the eyes. Take the C252 road northeast of town for a refreshing excursion.

In Vilabertran, 2.5km from central Figueres, there is what started life as an Augustinian convent (Carrer de l'Abadia 4; admission €2.40, Tue free; ☺10am-1pm & 3-6.30pm Tue-Sun Jun-Sep, to 5.30pm rest of yr). The 11th-century Romanesque church, with its three naves and Lombard bell tower, is outstanding. Also of great charm is the cloister. This is the setting for an annual cycle of classical music by Schubert (www.schubertiadavi labertran.cat).

Five kilometres up the road, coquettish Peralada is known for the 16th-century Castell-Palau dels Rocabertí. The castle, with its round towers, has a rather French air and is given over to a casino and restaurant. The only way in, if you're not eating or gambling, is to turn up for a classical-music performance during the annual Festival del Castell de Peralada (www.festi valperalada.com; Carrer del Castell; ☺Jul-Aug) in summer.

Besalú

POP 2361

The tall, crooked 11th-century Pont Fortificat (Fortified Bridge) over Río Fluvià in medieval Besalú, with its two tower gates, looks like something Tolkien might have

invented. It is, however, quite real. As is the rest of this delightfully well-preserved town, which in the 10th and 11th centuries was the capital of an independent county that stretched as far west as Cerdanya before it came under Barcelona's control in 1111. The bridge is at the heart of a best-selling historical novel, *El Pont dels Jueus* (The Jews' Bridge), by local Martí Gironell.

⊙ Sights

Micromundi MUSEUM
(www.museuminiaturesbesalu.com; Plaça Prat de Sant Pere 15; adult/child €3.90/2.90; ☺10am-7pm Mon-Sat Mar-Sep, shorter hr rest of yr) At this curious museum dedicated to miniatures you can peer through microscopes and magnifying glasses to look at such oddities as the incredibly detailed representation of Pinocchio and Gepetto's workshop (inside a pistachio nut) or a remake of Paris' Eiffel Tower hundreds of thousands time smaller than the real thing.

ⓖ Tours

The tourist office offers guided visits to the Miqvé, a 12th-century Jewish ritual bath by the river around which remnants of the ancient synagogue were unearthed in excavations in 2005 (guided tours for a minimum of two people are €11.85 through the tourist office). There are also guided tours of the bridge and the Romanesque Església de Sant Vicenç. The church and Miqvé are otherwise normally closed. Have a look at the 11th-century Romanesque church of the Monestir de Sant Pere, with an unusual ambulatory (walkway) behind the altar, and the 12th-century Romanesque Casa Cornellà.

⌂ Sleeping & Eating

There are a couple of cheap *pensiones* in Besalú.

Els Jardins de la Martana BOUTIQUE HOTEL €€
(☎972 59 00 09; www.lamartana.com; Carrer del Pont 2; s/d €79/109; ⓟ❄ⓦ) This is a charming mansion set on the out-of-town end of the grand old bridge. It has well-appointed rooms, with tiled floors, high ceilings and elegant curtains. Most offer views from balconies across the bridge to the town, and you'll find comfortable sitting rooms and peaceful garden terraces.

Pont Vell CATALAN €€
(☎972 59 10 27; Pont Vell 26; meals €25-30; ☺lunch & dinner Wed-Sun, lunch Mon, closed

late Dec–late Jan & 1st week Jul) The views to the old bridge (after which the restaurant is named) are enough to tempt you to take a seat here, even without considering the wide-ranging, Michelin-approved menu full of locally sourced market produce.

ℹ️ Information

Tourist office (☑972 59 12 40; www.besalu. cat; Plaça de la Llibertat 1; ⏰10am-2pm & 4-7pm, closed 1st week Jan) On the arcaded central square.

ℹ️ Getting There & Away

The N260 road from Figueres to Olot meets the C66 from Girona at Besalú. See the Girona (p316) and Olot (p330) sections for information on Teisa bus services to Besalú.

THE PYRENEES

The Pyrenees in Catalonia encompass some awesomely beautiful mountains and valleys. Above all, the Parc Nacional d'Aigüestortes i Estany de Sant Maurici, in the northwest, is a jewel-like area of lakes and dramatic peaks. The area's highest mountain, the Pica d'Estats (3143m), is reached by a spectacular hike (suitable only for experienced hikers) past glittering glacial lakes. On arrival at the top, you enjoy a privileged point with 360-degree views over France and Spain.

As well as the natural beauty of the mountains, and the obvious attractions of walking, skiing and other sports, the Catalan Pyrenees and their foothills have a rich cultural heritage, notably the countless lovely Romanesque churches and monasteries, often tucked away in remote valleys. They are mainly the product of a time of prosperity and optimism in this region in the 11th and 12th centuries, after Catalonia had broken ties with France in 988 and as the Muslim threat from the south receded.

When looking for a place to kip, keep an eye out for *cases rurales* or *cases de pagès* (country houses converted into accommodation), usually set in old village houses and peppered across the Pyrenees. The annual *Guia d'Establiments de Turisme Rural* guide, published by the Generalitat (regional Catalan government), covers most of them.

Olot

POP 32,300 / ELEV 443M

The hills around Olot are little more than pimples, but pretty pimples indeed – the well-dormant volcanoes of the Parc Natural de la Zona Volcànica de la Garrotxa. The last time one burst was 11,500 years ago.

⊙ Sights

Museums MUSEUMS
(adult/child €3/free; ⏰11am-2pm & 4-7pm Mon-Sat, 11am-2pm Sun & holidays Jul-Sep, shorter hr rest of yr) The Museu Comarcal de la Garrotxa (Carrer de l'Hospici 8), in the same building as the tourist office, covers Olot's growth and development as an early textile centre and includes a collection of local 19th-century art. Found inside the pleasant Jardí Botànic, a botanical garden of Olot-area flora, is the interesting Museu dels Volcans, which covers local flora and fauna as well as volcanoes and earthquakes. Four volcanoes stand sentry on the fringes of Olot. To continue your education in volcanoes head for Volcà Montsacopa, 500m north of the centre, or Volcà La Garrinada, 1km northeast of the centre, both of which are volcanic craters.

Combined tickets for both these and other Olot museums are also available.

🛏️ Sleeping & Eating

Several simple eateries are clustered around Plaça Major but the best restaurants are out of the town centre.

TOP CHOICE **Can Blanc** CASA RURAL €€
(☑972 27 60 20; www.canblanc.es, in Spanish; Paratges de la Deu; s/d incl breakfast €61/100; P✳🌐🏊) A world away from the hustle of town, this place, which fills the gap between a hotel and a *casa rural*, sits on the southwestern edge of Olot, surrounded by parkland. Rooms come in a range of styles from classic colours to the well and truly mismatched. The pleasing gardens and pool will put a smile on your face on hot summer days and a great breakfast is thrown in. It's about 15 minutes' walk from the centre – ask for the next-door La Deu Restaurant – as people are more likely to know this.

Torre Malagrida HOSTEL €
(☑972 26 42 00; Passeig de Barcelona 15; dm student & under 26yr/26yr & over €18/22; ⏰closed Aug) This youth hostel is set in an unusual early-20th-century Modernista building

CATALONIA OLOT

surrounded by gardens. The accommodation is unadorned dorm-style and you can purchase meals and rent bicycles.

Pensió La Vila HOTEL €
(☎972 26 98 07; www.pensiolavila.com; Carrer de Sant Roc 1; s/d €25/42; ❄☎) Smack-bang in the middle of town and overlooking Plaça Major, this straightforward *pensión* has perfectly comfortable rooms over three floors with satellite TV.

Les Cols CATALAN €€€
(☎972 26 92 09; www.lescols.com; Carretera de la Canya; meals €35-45; ⏰lunch & dinner Wed-Sat, lunch only Tue) Set in a converted *masia*, more than 100 years old, Les Cols is about 4km north of central Olot. Inside, the decor has a 21st-century edge, with iron and glass walls, a chilled-out ambience and gourmet ambitions. Dishes with local products are prepared with a silken touch, from chicken and duck to wild boar.

La Deu Restaurant CATALAN €
(☎972 26 10 04; Carretera la Deu; menus from €10.84) Excellent-value meals in a lovely parkside setting.

❶ Information

Casal dels Volcans (☎972 26 62 02; Avinguda de Santa Coloma de Farners) For information about the Parc Natural de la Zona Volcànica de la Garrotxa. It's in the Jardí Botànic, 1km southwest of Plaça de Clarà.

Patronat Municipal de Turisme (☎972 26 01 41; http://areadepromocio.olot.cat; Carrer del Hospici 8; ⏰10am-8pm Mon-Sat, 10am-2pm Sun mid-Jul–mid-Sep, 10am-2pm & 4-7pm Mon-Sat, 11am-2pm Sun mid-Sep–mid-Jul). Near the bus station; has information about the Parc Natural.

❶ Getting There & Away

Teisa (www.teisa-bus.com) runs buses to/from Barcelona (via Banyoles) up to seven times a day (€14.35, two to 2¾ hours) and Girona via Banyoles and Besalú up to 15 times a day (€6.50, 1½ hours). The easiest approach by car from Barcelona is by the AP7 and C63.

Parc Natural de la Zona Volcànica de la Garrotxa

The park completely surrounds Olot but the most interesting area is between Olot and the village of Santa Pau, 10km southeast.

Volcanic eruptions began here about 350,000 years ago and the most recent one, at Volcà del Croscat, happened 11,500 years ago. In the park there are about 30 volcanic cones, up to 160m high and 1.5km wide. Together with the lush vegetation, a result of fertile soils and a damp climate, these create a landscape of unusual beauty. Between the woods are crop fields, a few hamlets and scattered old stone farmhouses.

The main park information office is the Casal dels Volcans in Olot. Another is the Centre d'Informació Can Serra beside the GI524 Olot–Banyoles road 4.5km from the centre of Olot. Have a look also at www.turismegarrotxa.com.

The old part of Santa Pau village, perched on a rocky outcrop, contains a porticoed plaza, the Romanesque Església de Santa Maria and a locked-up baronial castle. The village itself, which though very pretty is a little bit too twee, has a couple of places to stay including the great-value Can Menció (☎972 68 00 14; www.garrotxa.com/canmencio; Plaça Major 17; d €45), a cosy place on the main square.

Castellfollit de la Roca, on the N260 about 8km northeast of Olot, stands atop a crag composed of several layers of petrified lava – it's most easily viewed from the road north of the village.

Several good marked walks, which you can complete in less than a day, allow you to explore the park with ease. Inquire at the park information offices about routes.

Just off the GI524, and close to the most interesting parts of the park, are some pleasant, small country camping grounds. Wild camping is banned in the Garrotxa district, which stretches from east of Besalú to west of Olot, and from the French border to south of Sant Feliu de Pallerols.

Ripoll

POP 11,057 / ELEV 691M

One of Spain's finest pieces of Romanesque art, in the Monestir de Santa Maria, is to be found at the medieval heart of this otherwise somewhat shabby industrial town.

Thirty kilometres west of Olot, Ripoll can claim, with some justice, to be the birthplace of Catalonia. In the 9th century, Ripoll was the power base from which the local strongman, Guifré el Pilós (Wilfred the Hairy), succeeded in uniting several counties of the Frankish March along the southern side of the Pyrenees. Guifré went on to become the first Count (Comte) of Barcelona. To encourage repopulation of the

Pyrenees valleys, he founded the Monestir de Santa Maria, the most powerful monastery of medieval Catalonia.

There are numerous simple places to get a cheap and hearty Catalan meal in the town centre.

◉ Sights

Monestir de Santa Maria   MONASTERY
(adult/child €3/1; ⊘10am-1pm & 3-7pm Apr-Sep, to 6pm Oct-Mar) Following its founding in AD 879, the Monestir de Santa Maria grew rapidly rich, big and influential. From the mid-10th to mid-11th centuries it was Catalonia's spiritual and cultural heart. A five-naved basilica was built, and adorned in about 1100 with a stone portal that ranks among the high points of Romanesque art. Two fires had left the basilica in ruins by 1885, after which it was restored in a rather gloomy imitation of its former glory. The most interesting feature inside is the restored tomb of Guifré el Pilós.

You can visit the basilica and its great portal, now protected by a wall of glass. A chart near the portal (in Catalan) helps to decipher the feast of sculpture: a medieval vision of the universe, from God the Creator, in the centre at the top, to the month-by-month scenes of daily rural life on the innermost pillars.

Down a few steps, to the right of the doorway, is the monastery's beautiful claustre (cloister). It's a two-storey affair, created in the 12th to 15th centuries, close to the tourist office.

⊨ Sleeping

Hostal Paula   HOTEL €
(📞972 70 00 11; www.elripolles.com/calapaula; Carrer dels Pirineus 6; s/d €26/45) This friendly family establishment is barely a stone's throw from the Monestir de Santa Maria, but like the town itself there's nothing fancy whatsoever about the plain, but well-priced rooms.

ℹ Information

Tourist office (📞972 70 23 51; www.elripolles.com, www.ajripoll.org, both in Spanish; Plaça del Abat Oliba; ⊘9.30am-1.30pm & 4-7pm Mon-Sat, 10am-2pm Sun) By the Ribes de Freser–Sant Joan de les Abadesses road, which runs through the north of town. The Monestir de Santa Maria is virtually next door.

ℹ Getting There & Away

The bus and train stations are almost side by side on Carrer del Progrés, 600m southeast of the centre. Connections with Barcelona, Ribes de Freser and Puigcerdà are better by train. About 12 trains a day run to/from Barcelona (€6.50, about two hours), up to seven to Ribes de Freser (€1.60, 20 minutes) and six to Puigcerdà (€3.45, 1¼ hours).

Around Ripoll

A short way north of Ripoll, the GI401 branches west from Campdevànol, passes through Gombrèn and then proceeds in twisting and turning fashion on to La Pobla de Lillet, set a short way below the source of one of Catalonia's more important rivers, the Llobregat.

The grey stone village started life as a Roman outpost and grew to some importance as a local agricultural centre. People still cross its beautiful 12th-century Romanesque bridge and the town is also known for its delightful Jardins Artigas, a landscaped garden spread out along the river. Not any old landscaped garden, mind – but the handiwork of a certain Antoni Gaudí. You can sleep in one of the simple *pensiones*.

Follow the road up into the mountains from La Pobla de Lillet to the source of the Llobregat. Just 500m on and you reach the mountain hamlet of Castellar de n'Hug, over the shoulder from the La Molina ski resort (see p335). The hamlet was founded in the 13th century under the lords of Mataplana (based in Gombrèn). A tight web of alleys is bundled around the Romanesque Església de Santa Maria (much remodelled over the centuries), and from the square by the church you look north across a valley to the bare mountains beyond.

Six *pensiones* are gathered about the hamlet, three of them on Plaça Major. Most have a bar attached, where you can get something to eat.

One Transports Mir (www.autocarsmir.com) bus a day (except Sunday) runs between Ripoll and Bagà via Campdevànol, Gombrèn, Castellar de n'Hug and La Pobla de Lillet.

Vall Alto del Ter

This upper part of the Riu Ter valley reaches northeast from Ripoll to the pleasant towns of Sant Joan de les Abadesses and Camprodon, then northwest to the modest

The Catalan Pyrenees provide magnificent walking and trekking. You can undertake strolls of a few hours, or day walks that can be strung together into treks of several days. Nearly all can be done without camping gear, with nights spent in villages or *refugis* (mountain shelters).

Most of the *refugis* mentioned in this chapter are run by two Barcelona mountain clubs, the Federació d'Entitats Excursionistes de Catalunya (FEEC; www.feec.org, in Spanish) and the Centre Excursionista de Catalunya (CEC; www.cec.cat in Spanish). A night in a *refugi* costs around €12.50 to €18. Normally FEEC *refugis* allow you to cook; CEC ones don't. Moderately priced meals (around €15 to €17) are often available.

The coast-to-coast GR-11 long-distance path traverses the entire Pyrenees from Cap de Creus on the Costa Brava to Hondarribia on the Bay of Biscay. Its route across Catalonia goes by way of La Jonquera, Albanyà, Beget, Setcases, the Vall de Núria, Planoles, Puigcerdà, Andorra, south of Pica d'Estats (3143m), over to the Parc Nacional d'Aigüestortes i Estany de Sant Maurici, then on to the southern flank of the Val d'Aran and into Aragón.

The season for walking in the high Pyrenees is from late June to early October. Always be prepared for fast-changing conditions, no matter when you go.

Local advice from tourist offices, park rangers, mountain *refugis* and other walkers is invaluable. Dedicated hiking maps and guidebooks are essential. Lonely Planet's *Hiking in Spain* contains numerous options in the Catalan Pyrenees.

There's boundless scope for **climbing** – Pedraforca in the Serra del Cadí offers some of the most exciting ascents. For more information on walking in Spain, see p35.

Vallter 2000 ski centre (www.vallter2000.com; day lift pass €31), just below the French border and at 2150m. It has 13 pistes of all grades, nine lifts and a ski school, but snow can be unreliable (most is usually artificial). The area makes a more pleasant overnight stop than Ripoll, and from the upper reaches there are some excellent walks to the Vall de Núria. Get the Editorial Alpina *Puigmal* map guide.

The C38 road leaves the Ter valley at Camprodon to head over the 1513m Collado d'Ares into France.

SANT JOAN DE LES ABADESSES
POP 3590

Sant Joan de les Abadesses is an attractive little town with an extreme V-shaped and much-restored 12th-century bridge over the Ter. The Museu del Monestir (Plaça de l'Abadessa; admission €3; ☺10am-7pm Jul & Aug, 10am-2pm & 4-7pm May-Jun & Sep, shorter hr rest of yr) is a monastery founded by Guifré el Pilós, which began life as a nunnery – the nuns were expelled in 1017 for alleged licentious conduct. Its elegant 12th-century church contains the marvellous *Santíssim Misteri,* a 13th-century polychrome woodcarving of the descent from the cross, composed of seven life-sized figures. Also remarkable is the Gothic *retablo* of Santa Maria La Blanca,

carved in alabaster. The elegant 15th-century late-Gothic cloister is charming. Fonda Janpere (☎972 72 00 77; Carrer del Mestre Andreu 3; s/d per person €25) is a basic but pleasant enough hotel that is in fact the only place to stay in town. Teisa (www.teisa-bus.com) operates up to seven buses daily from Ripoll to Sant Joan de les Abadesses (€1.40, 15 minutes). One daily bus runs from Barcelona at 7.15pm (€9.20, two hours).

BEGET
Capping the end of a winding mountain lane that trails off here into a heavily wooded valley, this hamlet is a joy. The 12th-century Romanesque church is accompanied by an implausible array of roughly hewn houses, all scattered about stone-paved lanes. Through it gushes a mountain stream. Beget is on the GR-11 walking route.

There is no public transport to Beget.

Vall de Núria & Ribes de Freser

Around AD 700, the story goes, Sant Gil (St Giles) came from Nîmes in France to live in a cave in an isolated mountain valley 26km north of Ripoll, preaching the Gospel to shepherds. Before he left, four years later, apparently fleeing Visigothic persecution,

Sant Gil hurriedly hid away a wooden Virgin-and-child image he had carved, a cross, his cooking pot and the bell he had used to summon the shepherds. They stayed hidden until 1079, when an ox led some shepherds to the spot. The statuette, the *Mare de Déu de Núria*, became the patron of Pyrenean shepherds and Núria's future was assured. The first historical mention of a shrine was made in 1162.

Sant Gil would recoil in shock if he came back today. The large, grey sanctuary complex squatting at the heart of the valley is an eyesore and the crowds would make anyone with hermitic leanings run a mile. But otherwise Núria remains almost pristine, a wide, green, mountain-ringed bowl that is the starting point for numerous walks. Getting there is fun too, either on foot up the Gorges de Núria – the green, rocky valley of the thundering Riu Núria – or from Ribes de Freser town, by the little *cremallera* (rack-and-pinion railway), which rises over 1000m on its 12km journey up the same valley (there is no road to Núria, so you cannot drive there). Ribes de Freser, on the N152, is 14km north of Ripoll and the *cremallera* to Núria starts at the train station at the southern end of town. There's a road from Ribes to Queralbs, but from there on it's the *cremallera* or your feet.

◉ Sights

Santuari   PILGRIMAGE SITE
(www.valldenuria.com; ◷8.30am-5.45pm mid-Sep–mid-Jul, 8.30am-6.30pm mid-Jul–mid-Sep) As well as the Santuari de Núria and its sacred *símbols de Núria*, the large 19th- and 20th-century building that dominates the valley also contains a hotel, restaurants and exhibition halls. The Mare de Déu de Núria sits behind a glass screen above the altar and is in the Romanesque style of the 12th century, so either Sant Gil was centuries ahead of his time or this isn't his work! Steps lead up to the bell, cross and cooking pot (which all date from at least the 15th century). To have your prayer answered, put your head in the pot and ring the bell while you say it.

🏃 Activities

In winter, Núria is a small-scale ski resort with 10 short runs. A day lift pass costs €27.50.

Walkers should get Editorial Alpina's *Puigmal* map guide before coming to Núria. You can walk up the gorge to Núria but skip the first unexciting 6km from Ribes de Freser by taking the *cremallera* (or road) to Queralbs, thus saving your energies for the steepest and the most spectacular part of the approach, which is about three hours' walk up. Or take the *cremallera* up and walk down!

From the Vall de Núria, you can cap several 2700–2900m peaks on the main Pyrenees ridge in about 2½ to four hours' walking (one way) for each. The most popular is **Puigmal** (2909m).

🛏 Sleeping & Eating

Wild camping is banned in the whole Ribes de Freser–Núria area.

NÚRIA

Hotel Vall de Núria   HOTEL €€
(📞972 73 20 20; half-board per person for 2 nights up to €204) Housed in the sanctuary building, the hotel has comfortable rooms with bathroom and satellite TV. Apartments are also available most of the year. You'll find a couple of restaurants in the sanctuary building.

Alberg Pic de l'Àliga   HOSTEL €
(📞972 73 20 48; dm student & under 26yr/26yr & over incl breakfast €21/26) The youth hostel is at the top of the *telecabina* (cable car) on the eastern side of the valley. Dorm rooms sleep from four to 14. The cable car runs from 9am to 6pm daily (to 7pm mid-July to mid-September). On Friday evenings it also runs to meet the *cremallera* at around 7pm and 9pm.

RIBES DE FRESER

Hotel Els Caçadors   HOTEL €€
(📞972 72 70 06; www.hotelsderibes.com; Carrer de Balandrau 24; s/d from €39/78; 🛜) A family-run business, this small hotel offers simple rooms with bathroom and TV. The buffet breakfast (€7) is grand – loads of cold meats, cheeses, juice, cereal and sweet pastries. The downstairs restaurant is one of the most popular places to eat in town and does a filling lunch menu for €16.50.

QUERALBS

Nestled against a shaft of rock, the delightful hamlet of Queralbs feels like an eagle's nest balanced on a precipitous mountain slope. It makes for a much prettier base than Ribes de Freser.

There are lots of *casas rurales* in the vicinity.

Hôstal les Roquetes
HOTEL €

(☑972 72 73 69; www.hostalroquetes.com, in Spanish; Carretera de Ribes 15; s/d €36/60; P) At the entrance to the village, this great-value family-run hotel is the most reliable place to find a bed for the night. The attached restaurant has menus from €10.

ℹ️ Information
Núria's **tourist office** (☑972 73 20 20; www.valldenuria.com; ⊙8.30am-5.45pm mid-Sep–mid-Jul, 8.30am-6.30pm mid-Jul–mid-Sep) is in the sanctuary.

ℹ️ Getting There & Away
Transports Mir runs services between Ripoll and Ribes de Freser, with two or three buses a day Monday to Friday, and one on Saturday.

Up to seven trains a day run to Ribes-Enllaç from Ripoll (€1.60, 20 minutes) and Barcelona (€7.15, 2¼ hours).

The **cremallera** (☑972 73 02 02) is a narrow-gauge electric-powered rack-and-pinion railway that has been operating since 1931. It runs from Ribes-Enllaç station to Núria and back six to 12 times a day, depending on the season (adult one way/return €13.15/21, child one way/return €7.90/12.65, 65 minutes one way). All trains stop at Ribes-Vila and Queralbs (1200m). It's a spectacular trip, particularly after Queralbs, as the train winds up the Gorges de Núria. Some services connect with Renfe trains at Ribes-Enllaç.

Cerdanya
Cerdanya, along with French Cerdagne across the border, occupies a low-lying basin between the higher reaches of the Pyrenees to the east and west. Although Cerdanya and Cerdagne, once a single Catalan county, were divided by the Treaty of the Pyrenees in 1659, they still have a lot in common. Walkers should get a hold of Editorial Alpina's *Cerdanya* map and guide booklet (scaled at 1:50,000).

PUIGCERDÀ
POP 9022 / ELEV 1202M

Just 2km from the French border, Puigcerdà (puh-cher-*da*) is not much more than a way station, but it's a jolly one, particularly in summer and during the ski season. A dozen Spanish, Andorran and French ski resorts lie within 45km.

👁 Sights
The town was heavily damaged during the civil war and only the tower remains of the 17th-century Església de Santa Maria (Plaça de Santa Maria). The 13th-century Gothic Església de Sant Domènec (Passeig del 10 d'Abril) was also wrecked but later rebuilt. It contains 14th-century Gothic murals that somehow survived (opening times are erratic). The *estany* (lake) in the north of town is speckled with snow-white swans and has a backdrop of equally snow-white mountains. It was created back in 1380 for irrigation and is surrounded by turn-of-the-20th-century summer houses, built by wealthy Barcelona families.

🛏 Sleeping
The town and the surrounding area is home to a number of hotels, *pensiones* and *casas rurales*.

Hospes Villa Paüla
HISTORIC HOTEL €€€

(☑972 88 46 22; www.hospes.com; Avinguda Pons I Gasch 15; d incl breakfast from €165; P🛜❄) The town's most luxurious option has sublime modern rooms in a rusty-red manor house. Some of the rooms have views over the nearby snow-drenched peaks. Various massages are available for those with ski weary muscles.

Hotel del Lago
HOTEL €€

(☑972 88 10 00; www.hotellago.com; Avinguda del Dr Piguillem 7; s/d from €97/119; P@🛜❄) Near the *estany,* this resort-style hotel has well-laid-out rooms and a nice leafy garden. The rooms vary greatly: some have heavy timber beams, while corner ones have windows opening in several directions out to the leafy exterior. There's an in-house jacuzzi and massage centre.

Càmping Stel
CAMPING €

(☑972 88 23 61; www.stel.es; sites per 2-person tent & car €36.40; ⊙Apr-Sep P🛜❄) Out along the road to Llívia, this is the only nearby camping option, and a pleasant one, with a pool, basketball court and a football pitch.

🍴 Eating
The numerous French day trippers means restaurant prices are artificially high and quality sadly lacking. The adjoining squares of Plaça de Santa Maria and Plaça dels Herois are lined by cheerful bar-restaurants, some with unlikely names like Kennedy, and Bier Garden!

La Maison du Foie-Gras
FRENCH €

(☑972 88 11 22; Carrer Escoles 3; menus from €12.95; ⊙Mon-Sat) For a taste of France in

Spain (just) this busy place, decked out like a traditional French bistro, is a good bet. Customers fill their tummies with duck, steaks and, of course, delicious foie gras.

El Pati de la Tieta
INTERNATIONAL €

(☎972 88 01 56; Carrer dels Ferrers 20; pizzas €9-11, meals €35-45; ☺daily in high season, Thu-Sun Jul-May) One of the best choices, this understated restaurant offers a creative range of dishes, like the succulent *broquetes de cangur i verdures* (kangaroo on a skewer with vegetables).

❶ Information

Puigcerdà stands on a small hill, with the train station at the foot of its southwest side. A few minutes' climb up some flights of steps takes you to Plaça de l'Ajuntament, off which is the **tourist office** (☎972 88 05 42; Carrer de Querol 1; ☺10am-1pm & 4-7pm Mon-Fri, 10am-1pm & 4.30-7pm Sat, 10am-1pm Sun). There is also a **regional tourist office** (☎972 14 06 65; Carretera Nacional 152; ☺10am-1pm & 4-7pm Mon-Fri, 10am-1pm & 4.30-7pm Sat, 10am-1pm Sun) on the main road into town if coming from Barcelona.

❶ Getting There & Away

BUS

Alsina Graells runs four daily buses (one at weekends) from Barcelona (€17.80, three hours) via the 5km Túnel del Cadí and two or three to La Seu d'Urgell (€6, one hour). They stop at the train station.

CAR & MOTORCYCLE

From Barcelona, the C16 approaches Puigcerdà through the Túnel del Cadí. Bicycles are not allowed in the tunnel, which is a tollway.

The N152 from Ribes de Freser climbs west along the northern flank of the Rigard valley, with the pine-covered Serra de Mogrony rising to the south, to the 1800m Collado de Toses (pass), then winds down to Puigcerdà.

The main crossing into France is at Bourg-Madame, immediately east of Puigcerdà, from where roads head to Perpignan and Toulouse.

TRAIN

Six trains a day run from Barcelona to Puigcerdà (€9.40) via Ripoll and Ribes de Freser. Four in each direction make the seven-minute hop over the border to Latour-de-Carol in France, where they connect with trains from Toulouse or Paris, and with the narrow-gauge Train Jaune (yellow train) down the Têt Valley to Perpignan.

LLÍVIA
POP 1517 / ELEV 1224M

Six kilometres northeast of Puigcerdà, across flat farmland, Llívia is a piece of Spain within France. Under the 1659 Treaty of the Pyrenees, Spain ceded 33 villages to France, but Llívia was a 'town' and so, together with the 13 sq km of its municipality, remained a Spanish possession.

Surrounded as it is by France you might expect Llívia to feel more French than Spanish, but not a bit of it. As soon as you enter the town there's absolutely no mistaking where the town's loyalties lie. This is most notable in the early evening or on a Sunday, when the surrounding French villages are library-quiet and Llívia is boisterous with life. Aside from the novelty factor, the interest of Llívia lies in its tiny medieval nucleus, near the top of the town. The **Museu Municipal** (Carrer dels Forns 4) has been closed for apparently never-ending renovations for some years now, but the 15th-century Gothic **Església de Nostra Senyora dels Àngels**, just above the museum, is worth exploring. The museum is in what's claimed to be Europe's oldest pharmacy, the Farmacia Esteva, founded in 1415. From the church you can walk up to the ruined **Castell de Llívia** where, during the short-lived period of Islamic dominion in the Pyrenees, the Muslim governor Manussa enjoyed a secret dalliance with Lampègia, daughter of the Duke of Aquitaine (or so legend has it).

Dine on the balconies of **Restaurant Can Ventura** (☎972 89 61 78; Plaça Major 1; menus €21; ☺Wed-Sun), a ramshackle building dating from 1791. The food is delightful – traditional Catalan fare that comes from a discreetly hidden modern kitchen. Classics include local lamb slow-cooked in the oven for 12 hours.

Two or three buses a day run from Puigcerdà train station to Llívia.

LA MOLINA & MASELLA

These ski resorts lie either side of Tosa d'Alp (2537m), 15km south of Puigcerdà, and are linked by the Alp 2500 lift. The two resorts have a combined total of 101 runs (day lift pass for the whole area €38.50) of all grades at altitudes of 1600m to 2537m. Information, rental equipment and ski schools are available at both **resorts** (La Molina www.lamolina.com; Masella www.masella.com).

🛏 Sleeping

Many skiers choose to stay in Puigcerdà or further afield, but there are any number of resort-style hotels around the village – all of which are booked solid through the ski season.

HOSTEL €

(☎972 89 20 12; dm student & under 26yr/26yr & over €21/26; ⊗closed mid-Oct–Nov, 1 week mid-Apr; 🅿 @) At the bottom part of La Molina, near the train station, this is a handy youth hostel and is far and away the cheapest place to stay. Rooms range from doubles to eight-bed dorms. Many of the rooms have a bathroom.

❶ Getting There & Away

In the ski season there's a bus service from Puigcerdà. Most people come by car; the easiest route from Barcelona is by the C58 toll road and the C16 through the Túnel del Cadí. Roads also wind down to La Molina and Masella from the N152 west of the Collado de Toses.

NORTHERN CERDANYA

The N260 Hwy runs southwest from Puigcerdà along the Riu Segre valley towards La Seu d'Urgell. It cuts its path between the main Pyrenees chain to the north and the range made up mainly of the Serra del Cadí and Serra de Moixeró to the south. Up to three buses a day run along this valley between Puigcerdà and La Seu d'Urgell.

About 6km from Puigcerdà, Bolvir has a little Romanesque church and, more importantly, one of the most luxurious hotels in the entire Pyrenees.

Another kilometre on from Bolvir, take the Ger turn-off for an excursion into the mountains. A minor asphalted road winds its way west and north through the broad, arid Valltova valley to Meranges, a dishevelled, stone farming village that makes few concessions to the passing tourist trade.

🛏 Sleeping

If the Torre del Remei just isn't quite you, then you'll find several *casas rurales* nearby.

Torre del Remei   BOUTIQUE HOTEL €€€

(☎972 14 01 82; www.torredelremei.com; Camí Reial, Bolvir; d from €310; 🅿 ❄ ☲) This tastefully decorated Modernista mansion (which during the civil war was requisitioned as a school and later as a hospital by the Republican government) sits majestically amid tranquil gardens, and is a full-blown romantic dream fit for a king and queen. The rooms, exquisitely furnished and each one different, are superb and the dining is equally tempting (though very expensive – breakfast alone is €32 per person!).

Serra del Cadí

The N260 runs west along the wide Riu Segre valley from Puigcerdà to La Seu d'Urgell, with the Pyrenees climbing northwards towards Andorra, and the craggy pre-Pyrenees range of the Serra del Cadí rising steep and high along the southern flank. Calling these hills the mere 'pre-Pyrenees' does them a huge injustice. The sheer walls of rock here are every bit as spectacular as anything the Pyrenees themselves can raise up, and though popular with Catalans the area remains largely unknown to foreigners. Although this face of the Cadí – rocky and fissured by ravines known as *canales* – looks daunting enough, the range's most spectacular peak is Pedraforca (2497m), a southern offshoot with the most challenging rock climbing in Catalonia. Pedraforca and the main Cadí range also offer some excellent mountain walking for those suitably equipped and experienced.

The Pedraforca area is most easily reached from the C16, then along the B400, which heads west 1.5km south of Guardiola de Berguedà. Pedraforca looms mightily into view about halfway to the village of Saldes, which sits 1215m high at its foot, 15km from the C16. The main Cadí range runs east–west, about 5km north of Saldes. The Refugi Lluís Estasen nestles below the northern face of Pedraforca, 2.5km northwest of Saldes. You can reach it by footpath from Saldes or by a partly paved road that turns north off the B400 about 1km west of Saldes. Park at the Mirador de Gresolet (nice views), from where it's a 10-minute walk up to the refuge.

◉ Sights

The B400 runs from Saldes to the pretty stone village of Gósol, 6km further west. The original Gósol (Vila Vella), which dated back to at least the 9th century, is now abandoned on the hill south of the present village.

A road west from Gósol climbs the 1625m Coll de Josa pass, then descends past the picturesque hamlet of Josa del Cadí, an untouched place of brown stone houses cluttered around a brown stone church perched atop a lush green hill. There are no facilities of any sort. Next up is Tuixén (1206m), another attractive village on a small hill and sometimes written Tuixent. From Tuixén, scenic paved roads lead northwest to La Seu d'Urgell (36km) and

As late as the 1960s, Tuixén was known for its natural herbs and remedies and for the extraordinary women who would head off (often on foot) to sell them, the so-called Trementinaires (after *trementina*, or turpentine, one of their more popular items). From the late 19th century, these wandering saleswomen would leave for as long as four months and as far as Barcelona, leaving their menfolk behind to tend fields and animals, and only returned home when they had sold all their wares. Among the latter were *te de roca* ('rock tea' for upset tummies) and *orella d'ós* ('bear's ear' for coughs and colds). The women generally travelled in pairs, but even so, unaccompanied women travellers were otherwise virtually unheard of in Spain, much less from deep inland villages! The last Trementinaire, Sofia d'Ossera, undertook her final trip in 1982. Learn more in Tuixén's **Museu de les Trementinaires** (www.trementinaires.org, in Spanish; Plaça de la Serra del Cadí; admission free; ☺10am-2pm & 5-8pm Mon-Sat, 10am-2pm Sun Easter & Jul-Sep, shorter hr rest of yr).

south to Sant Llorenç de Morunys (28km), which is on a beautiful cross-country road from Berga to Organyà.

Activities

The name Pedraforca means 'stone fork' and the approach from the east makes it clear why. Popular with rock climbers, the two separate rocky peaks – the northern Pollegó Superior (2497m) and the southern Pollegó Inferior (2400m) – are divided by a saddle called L'Enforcadura. The northern face, rising near vertically for 600m, has some classic rock climbs; the southern has a wall that sends alpinists into raptures.

Pedraforca is also an option for walkers. From Refugi Lluís Estasen you can reach the Pollegó Superior summit in about three strenuous hours – either southward from the refuge, then up the middle of the fork from the southeast side (a path from Saldes joins this route); or westward up to the Collada del Verdet, then south and east to the summit. The latter route has some hairy precipices and requires a good head for heights. It's not suitable for coming down: you must use the first route.

Sleeping

SALDES & AROUND

There are at least four camping grounds along the B400 between the C16 and Saldes, some open year-round. In Saldes you'll find a handful of *pensiones* and a larger hotel.

Refugi Lluís Estasen   HOSTEL €
(☎608 315312; dm €15; ☺daily Jun-Sep, Sat, Sun & holidays rest of yr) Run by the FEEC and near the Mirador de Gresolet, this *refugi* has 87 places, meals and a warden in summer. In

winter it has about 30 places. When it's full you can sleep outside, but not in a tent.

GÓSOL & TUIXÉN

You'll find a handful of *casas rurales* in both villages, although some are rented out only on weekends or for a week at a time in summer. It's a good idea to reserve in advance as the village is packed on sunny weekends.

Cal Farragetes   CASA RURAL €
(☎973 37 00 34; www.calfarragetes.com; Carrer del Coll 7, Tuixén; d per person €25; P) A big, friendly stone place set over two floors around a sprawling courtyard, this country village house has smallish but immaculate rooms featuring iron bedsteads and wood panelling. The owners are obviously the village entrepreneurs as they also run an on-site shop, cafe and restaurant.

Information

The Parc Natural del Cadí-Moixeró's main **Centre d'Informació** (☎93 824 41 51; Carrer de la Vinya 1; ☺9am-1pm & 4-7pm Mon-Fri Jun-Sep, 8am-3pm Mon-Fri & 4-6.30pm Tue & Fri Oct-May, 9am-1pm & 4-6.30pm Sat, 9am-1pm Sun & holidays year-round) is in **Bagà**, a quiet village (walk down to the stone bridge that crosses the stream) 4km north of Guardiola de Berguedà on the C16.

In Saldes, the **Centre d'Informació Massís del Pedraforca** (☎93 825 80 46; ☺10am-2pm & 5.30-7.30pm Jul–mid-Sep, 11am-1pm mid-Sep–Jun) has information on the Saldes and Pedraforca area only.

Getting There & Around

You need your own vehicle to reach Saldes, Gósol or Tuixén.

CATALONIA SERRA DEL CADÍ

La Seu d'Urgell

POP 12,986 / ELEV 691M

The lively valley town of La Seu d'Urgell (la *se*-u dur-*zhey*) is Spain's gateway to Andorra, 10km to the north. It's an OK place to spend a night, with an admirable medieval cathedral, but as far as looks go this town really wasn't blessed. Accommodation is generally cheaper here than in Andorra.

When the Franks evicted the Muslims from this part of the Pyrenees, in the early 9th century, they made La Seu a bishopric and capital of the counts of Urgell. It has been an important market and cathedral town since the 11th century.

◎ Sights

FREE Catedral de Santa Maria   CATHEDRAL
(⊙10am-1pm & 4-7pm Mon-Sat Jun-Sep, shorter hr rest of yr) On the southern side of Plaça dels Oms, the 12th-century Catedral de Santa Maria & Museu Diocesà is one of Catalonia's outstanding Romanesque buildings despite various attempts at remodelling. It's one of more than a hundred Romanesque churches lining what has come to be known as the Ruta Románica, from Perpignan (France) to the Urgell district.

The fine western facade, through which you enter, is decorated in typical Lombard style. The inside is dark and plain but still impressive, with five apses, some murals in the southern transept, and a 13th-century Virgin-and-child sculpture in the central apse.

Museu Diocesà   MUSEUM
(www.museudiocesaurgell.org; adult/child €3/free; ⊙10am-1pm & 4-7pm Mon-Sat, 10am-1pm Sun Jun-Sep, shorter hr rest of yr) From next to the cathedral you can enter the Museu Diocesà, a superb museum that encompasses the fine cloister and the 12th-century Romanesque Església de Sant Miquel, as well as some good medieval Pyrenean church murals, sculptures and altarpieces.

⌖ Sleeping

Hotel El Castell   HISTORIC HOTEL €€€
(⌨973 35 00 00; www.hotelelcastell.com; Castellciutat; s/d from €180/225; P❋☀☁) Set in a castle in a hilltop jumble of lanes about 1.5km west of central La Seu, this spa hotel is a world of its own. Run by the Relais & Châteaux team, it is the classiest hotel for miles around, with soothing gardens, a gym, sauna and gourmet restaurant.

Hotel Andria   HISTORIC HOTEL €€
(⌨973 35 03 00; www.hotelandria.com; Passeig Joan Brudieu 24; s/d incl breakfast from €80/100; P☁) Easily the best town-centre option, this hotel, with its old knick-knacks on the walls and high, plant-bedecked arches and shady gardens, actually feels more like some old English colonial retreat in an Indian hill station than just another hotel in a less-than-salubrious Andorran border town.

Casa Rural La Vall del Cadí   CASA RURAL €
(⌨973 35 03 90; www.valldelcadi.com; Carretera de Tuixén; d €45-55; P❋☁) Barely a 1km walk south of the hospital and across the Segre River, you are in another, protected, bucolic world in this stone country house on a working farm. The cosy rooms, with terracotta floors, iron bedsteads and, in some cases, timber ceiling beams, have a nice winter detail – floor heating. Some rooms share bathrooms.

Hotel Nice   HOTEL €€
(⌨973 35 21 00; www.hotelnice.net; Avinguda de Pau Claris 4-6; s/d from €57/78; P☁) Of a couple of grotty options on the main street this one stands out for being the, excuse the pun, 'nicest' of the lot. A hefty breakfast is €8 extra.

✗ Eating

Ignasi   FRENCH €
(⌨973 35 49 49; Carrer de Capdevila 17; mains €5-9; ⊙Mon-Sat) The classiest, cosiest and most popular of several crêperies in town. It also does a fine line in pasta dishes. You may even have to reserve a table at weekends.

Restaurant Les Tres Portes   SPANISH €€
(⌨973 35 56 58; Carrer de Garriga i Massou 7; meals €30-35; ⊙Thu-Sun) This is a homely spot, where you can chow down on mixed Spanish cuisine in the peaceful garden. Inside, the decor is bright but warm, with orange walls and yellow-and-red table linen. It presents an even array of options taking in fish, seafood and meat mains. The *mitjana de cavall amb alls* (horsemeat prepared in garlic) is hearty at €18.

❶ Information

Tourist office (⌨973 35 15 11; www.turism eseu.com; Avinguda de les Valls d'Andorra 33; ⊙9am-8pm Mon-Fri, 10am-2pm & 4-8pm Sat, 10am-2pm Sun Jul-Aug, 10am-2pm & 4-6pm Mon-Sat Sep-Jun) At the northern entrance to town.

Getting There & Away

Bus

The bus station is on the northern edge of the old town. **ALSA** (www.alsa.es) runs five buses daily to Barcelona (€24.60, 3½ hours): two each via Solsona and Ponts, and one, which does not run on Sunday, via the Túnel del Cadí. There are also three to Puigcerdà (€6, one hour) and two to Lleida (€16.75, 2½ hours).

Car & Motorcycle

The N260 Hwy heads 6km southwest to Adrall, then turns off west over the hills to Sort. The C14 carries on south to Lleida, threading the towering Tresponts gorge about 13km beyond Adrall.

Vall de la Noguera Pallaresa

The Riu Noguera Pallaresa, running south through a dramatic valley about 50km west of La Seu d'Urgell, is Spain's best-known white-water river. The main centres for white-water sports are the town of Sort and the villages of Rialp and Llavorsí. You'll find companies to take you rafting, hydrospeeding, canoeing and kayaking or canyoning, climbing, mountain biking, horse riding and ponting (basically bungee jumping from bridges).

Activities

The Riu Noguera Pallaresa has no drops of more than grade 4 (on a scale of 1 to 6), but it's exciting enough to attract a constant stream of white-water fans between April and August. It's usually at its best in May and June.

The best stretch is the 14km or so from Llavorsí to Rialp, on which the standard raft outing lasts one to 1½ hours and costs around €35 per person. Longer rides to Sort and beyond will cost more.

At least one company, Yeti Emotions (www.yetiemotions.com; Carrer de Borda Era d'Alfons, Llavorsí), organises high-grade trips, for experienced rafters only, further upstream. It can also take you hiking, abseiling and, most bizarrely, on winter husky-sledge rides! Several other rafting companies operate from Llavorsí and other points like Sort. Canoeing trips on the same river start at €35.50 per hour.

You need to bring your own swimming costume, towel and a change of clothes. All other gear is usually provided.

Sleeping & Eating

Llavorsí is the most pleasant base, much more of a mountain village than Rialp or Sort, with a couple of camping grounds and four hotels. A couple of simple eateries can provide sustenance.

Hostal Noguera   HOTEL €€
(973 62 20 12; www.hostalnoguera.com; Carretera Vall d'Aran; s/d €27/52;) This stone building, on the southern edge of the village and overlooking the river, has well-kept, plain and tidy rooms that are a good deal. The downstairs restaurant does a tasty lunch menu for €16.

Camping Aigües Braves   CAMPING €
(973 62 21 53; sites per 2-person tent & car €20.40; mid-Mar–Aug;) About 1km north of Llavorsí proper, this pleasant riverside camping ground has a pool, restaurant and minimarket.

Information

The main **tourist office** (973 62 10 02; http:// turisme.pallarssobria.cat; Avinguda dels Comtes del Pallars 21; 9am-8pm Mon-Fri, 10am-2pm & 3-8pm Sat, 10am-1pm Sun Jul-Aug, 9am-3pm Mon-Thu, 9am-3pm & 4-6.30pm Fri, 10am-2.30pm Sat Sep-Jun) for the area is in Sort.

Getting There & Away

ALSA runs two daily buses from Barcelona to Sort, Rialp, Llavorsí (€28.10, 5½ hours) and Esterri d'Aneu (€31.20). From June to October it continues to Vielha (€36.90) and the Val d'Aran. The Barcelona–Vielha trip is shorter and cheaper via Lleida (€28.30, 5½ hours).

Northwest Valleys

North of the highway that leads northwest from Llavorsí towards the Port de Bonaigua pass stretches a series of verdant valleys leading up to some of the most beautiful sights in the Catalan Pyrenees.

The Vall de Cardòs and Vall Ferrera, heading back into the hills northeast of Llavorsí, lead to some remote and, in parts, tough mountain-walking country along and across the Andorran and French borders, including Pica d'Estats (3143m), the highest peak in Catalonia. Editorial Alpina's *Pica d'Estats* and *Montgarri* maps will help.

VALL DE CARDÒS

Heading north into the hills along the L504 road from Llavorsí, this pretty valley leads to challenging mountain-walking possibilities. Editorial Alpina's *Pica d'Estats* map guide is useful here. There is no public transport up the valley.

Lladrós and Lladorre, the latter graced with a charming Romanesque church, are pretty stone hamlets oozing bucolic charm. Tavascan marks the end of the asphalt road. It's a huddle of well-kept houses and a launch pad for numerous excursions. The most stunning piece of scenery is a crystal-blue glacial lake (the largest in the Pyrenees), Estany de Certascan, about 13km away along a tough road best negotiated by 4WD. Just out of view of the lake is the Refugi de Certascan (☎973 62 13 89; www. certascan.com, in Spanish; dm €15; ☉daily mid-Jun–mid-Sep, some weekends & holidays rest of yr), which has room for 40 people, showers and also offers meals. More trails and lakes await in this frontier mountain territory. The valley's towns are littered with charming *cases de pagès*, along with three hotels in Tavascan.

VALL FERRERA

Greener than the Vall de Cardòs and at the heart of the Parc Natural de l'Alt Pirineu (Catalonia's biggest nature reserve), this valley is another pleasant surprise, hiding several pretty villages and bringing even more good walking country within reach. The ascent of the Pica d'Estats (3143m), the region's highest peak, is generally undertaken from here. It's not for casual walkers. There is no public transport.

The prettiest hamlet, Àreu, is a popular base for walkers. It is divided into two separate settlements, each with a Romanesque church: Sant Climent is in the lower part and Sant Feliu de la Força is up the road.

VALLS D'ÀNEU

To proceed to the next valleys west, you return to Llavorsí and the C13 Hwy, along which you proceed north. After 12km you pass the turn-off on the left for Espot – this is the most popular way into the Parc Nacional d'Aigüestortes i Estany de Sant Maurici.

Six kilometres further on from the turn-off, after passing an artificial lake on the right where you can hire rowing boats and canoes to potter about in, you'll arrive at Esterri d'Àneu, a popular, if distant, base for the ski fields of Baqueira-Beret (p345) in the Val d'Aran. Of the various valleys that make up the Valls d'Àneu, the Vall d'Isil

is the most intriguing. Follow the C13 directly north through Esterri d'Àneu and it will lead you over a bridge across the Riu Noguera Pallaresa. You then follow this back road (the C147) up into a mountain valley, passing through the villages of Borén, Isil and the half-abandoned Alós d'Isil.

Parc Nacional d'Aigüestortes i Estany de Sant Maurici & Around

Catalonia's only national park extends 20km east to west, and only 9km from north to south. But the rugged terrain within this small area positively sparkles with more than two hundred small *estanys* and countless streams and waterfalls, combined with a backdrop of pine and fir forests, and open bush and grassland, bedecked with wildflowers in spring, to create a wilderness of rare splendour.

Created by glacial action over two million years, the park is essentially two east–west valleys at 1600m to 2000m altitude lined by jagged 2600m to 2900m peaks of granite and slate.

The national park, whose boundaries cover 141 sq km, lies at the core of a wider wilderness area, whose outer limit is known as the *zona perifèrica* and includes some magnificent high country to the north and south. The total area covered is 408 sq km and is monitored by park rangers.

The main approaches are via the village of Espot (1320m), 4km east of the park's eastern boundary, and Boí, 5.5km from the western side.

You can find information (in Spanish) at http://reddeparquesnacionales.mma.es/parques.

◎ Sights

You want more sights than just lofty mountains shimmering under crowns of snow and jewel-like necklaces of lakes? OK, we can do that too!

Vall de Boí   CHURCHES
(www.vallboi.com; admission €1.50 each or €6 for all 6 churches; ☉10am-2pm & 4-7pm) The Vall de Boí, southwest of the park, is dotted with some of Catalonia's loveliest little Romanesque churches, which together were declared a Unesco World Heritage site in 2000. Two of the finest are at Taüll, 3km east of Boí. Sant Climent de Taüll, at

CATALONIA

the entrance to the village, with its slender six-storey bell tower, is a gem, not only for its elegant, simple lines but also for the art that once graced its interior until the works were transferred to museums in the 20th century. The central apse contains a copy of a famous 1123 mural that now resides in Barcelona's Museu Nacional d'Art de Catalunya (see p261). At the church's centre is a *Pantocrator* (Christ figure), whose rich Mozarabic-influenced colours, and expressive but superhuman features, have become a virtual emblem of Catalan Romanesque art. Other art from this church has found its way to museums as far away as Boston in the USA.

Santa Maria de Taüll (◷10am-8pm), up in the old village centre and possessing a five-storey tower, is also well represented in the Barcelona museum but lacks the in situ copies that add to the interest of Sant Climent.

Other worthwhile Romanesque churches in the area are at Boí (Sant Joan), Barruera (Sant Feliu), Durro (Nativitat) and Erill la Vall (Santa Eulàlia). The latter has a slender six-storey tower to rival Sant Climent's and slopes upwards to the altar. Next door is the Centre d'Interpretació del Romànic (www. centreromanic.com; Carrer del Batalló 5; ◷9am-2pm & 5-7pm Mon-Sat, 10am-2pm Sun), which has a small Romanesque art collection; it's also where you can organise guided tours of the churches.

Activities

The park is criss-crossed by plenty of paths, ranging from well marked to unmarked, enabling you to pick suitable routes.

East–West Traverse

You can walk right across the park in one day. The full Espot–Boí (or vice versa) walk is about 25km and takes nine hours, but you can shorten this by using Jeep-taxis to/from

MAPS & GUIDES

Editorial Alpina's map guides are adequate, although they don't show every single trail. *Sant Maurici – Els Encantats* covers the eastern half of the park and its approaches; *Vall de Boí* covers the western half and its approaches; *Montsent de Pallars* covers the northern Vall Fosca; and *Val d'Aran*, naturally, covers the Val d'Aran. A better map of the whole area is the Institut Cartogràfic de Catalunya's *Parc Nacional d'Aigüestortes i Estany de Sant Maurici*, scaled at 1:25,000 – but even this is not perfect.

Lonely Planet's newly updated *Hiking in Spain* guide gives detailed route descriptions of several walks in and around the park.

The help of guides can be enlisted at the Espot and Boí information offices.

Estany de Sant Maurici or Aigüestortes (3km downstream from Estany Llong) or both. Espot (1300m) to Estany de Sant Maurici (1950m) is 8km (two hours). A path then climbs to the Portarró d'Espot pass (2423m), where there are fine views over both of the park's main valleys. From the pass you descend to Estany Llong and Aigüestortes (1820m; about 3½ hours from Estany de Sant Maurici). Then you have around 3.5km to the park entrance, 4km to the L500 and 2.5km south to Boí (1260m) – a total of about three hours. If attempting this route make sure you have the relevant maps and a compass as well as suitable clothing for a high mountain trek.

Shorter Walks

Numerous good walks of three to five hours' return will take you up into spectacular side valleys from Estany de Sant Maurici or Aigüestortes.

From the eastern end of Estany de Sant Maurici, one path heads south 2.5km up the Monastero valley to Estany de Monastero (2171m), passing Els Encantats on the left. Another goes 3km northwest up by Estany de Ratero to Estany Gran d'Amitges (2350m). From Planell Gran (1850m), 1km up the Sant Nicolau valley from Aigüestortes, a path climbs 2.5km southeast to Estany de Dellui (2370m). You can descend to Estany Llong (3km); it

takes about four hours from Aigüestortes to Estany Llong.

Sleeping

There are four similarly priced camping grounds in and around Espot. Serious walkers will want to take advantage of the network of six *refugis* in the park and nine more inside the *zona perifèrica*. They tend to be staffed from early or mid-June to September and for some weeks in the first half of the year for skiers. At other times several of them leave a section open where you can stay overnight; if you are unsure, call ahead or ask at the park information offices. Most charge €15 per person to stay overnight. See www.feec.org for more information.

The villages of Espot, Boí and Taüll have a range of accommodation options (including several midrange hotels in Espot). There are *hostales* and *cases de pagès* in Barruera, El Pont de Suert, Capdella and La Torre de Capdella.

Espot

Casa Palmira   CASA RURAL €
(☎973 62 40 72; d per person incl breakfast €28) There are a number of large and fairly soulless places in the village but this friendly, family-run place with immaculate rooms on a cobbled street just off the main square is our favourite. It is one of three country homestays here, all of which charge about the same.

Camping Vorapark   CAMPING €
(☎973 62 41 08; www.voraparc.com; Prat del Vedat; sites per 2-person tent & car €21.20; ☼Apr-Sep; P ⊞) This ground is about the best in Espot, around 1.5km out of town towards the park entrance. It has a pleasant swimming pool, as well as a pool hall, bar and minimarket.

Taüll

Three kilometres uphill from Boí, Taüll is by far the most picturesque place to stay on the west side of the park. It has nine *cases de pagès* and over a dozen hotels and *pensiones,* either in the village itself or in the surrounding area.

Pensión Santa Maria   BOUTIQUE HOTEL €€
(☎973 69 61 70; www.taull.com; Plaça Cap del Riu 3; d incl breakfast from €110; P ☻) Through a shady entrance a grand stone archway leads into the quiet courtyard of this rambling country haven, with rose-draped balcony. The rooms are tastefully furnished and the

building, all stonework with a timber-and-slate roof, oozes timeless character.

Eating

Note that throughout the area many places close midweek and in the low season. Most of the towns have one or two fairly basic restaurants.

Restaurant Juquim CATALAN €
(☑973 62 40 09; meals €20-25; ☺daily Jun–mid-Oct, Wed-Mon mid-Oct–May) This classic on Espot's main square has a varied menu concentrating largely on hearty country fare, with generous winter servings of *olla pallaresa* (steaming hotpot) or *civet de senglar* (wild boar stew).

❶ Information

Tourist Information

There are **national park information offices** (☺9am-1pm & 3.30-6.45pm daily Jun-Sep, 9am-2pm & 3.30-5.45pm Mon-Sat, 9am-2pm Sun Oct-May) in Espot (☑973 62 40 36) and Boí (☑973 69 61 89). The **tourist office** (☑973 69 40 00; ☺9am-2pm & 5-7pm Mon-Sat, 10am-2pm Sun) in Barruera, on the L500, 10km north from the N230, is a good source of information on the area around the west side of the park. A sub-branch is open at Taüll in Easter and June to September (same opening times). Offices south of the park are located in **El Pont de Suert** and **La Pobla de Segur**.

Park Rules

Private vehicles cannot enter the park. Wild camping is not allowed, nor are swimming or other 'aquatic activities' in the lakes and rivers. Hunting, fishing, mushroom-picking and just about every other kind of potentially harmful activity are banned.

❶ Getting There & Away

Daily buses from Barcelona, Lleida and La Pobla de Segur to Esterri d'Àneu (and in summer to the Val d'Aran) will stop at the Espot turn-off on the C13. From there you have an 8km uphill walk (or hitch) to Espot.

ALSA buses from Barcelona to La Pobla de Segur (€26.25, three to 4½ hours) run up to three times a day year-round. From July to mid-September a connecting bus runs daily from La Pobla de Segur to El Pont de Suert and from there to Barruera and the Boí turn-off (el Cruce de Boí) on the L500 (1km short of Boí).

❶ Getting Around

Once you're close to the park, the easiest way of getting inside it is by Jeep-taxi from Espot or Boí. There's a more or less continuous shuttle service between Espot and Estany de Sant Maurici, and between Boí and Aigüestortes, saving you, respectively, 8km and 10km. The return fare for either trip is €9.70 per person and the services run from outside the park information offices in Espot and Boí (from July to September 8am to 7pm, other months 9am to 6pm).

Val d'Aran

POP 9820

It wasn't all that long ago that the verdant Val d'Aran, Catalonia's northernmost outpost, was one of the remotest parts of Spain and it's only connection to the outside world was via a small pass leading into France. To reach the rest of Spain involved a hairy clamber over the spectacular surrounding 2000m-plus mountains. All this changed with the opening of a tunnel connecting the valley's capital, Vielha, with the rest of the country in the 1950s, which led to a surge of tourism development including the 1964 opening of the Baqueira-Beret ski resort. Despite all this, though, the valley feels like a secret world of cloud-scraping mountain peaks and tumbling valley slopes dotted with hill villages (many with exquisite little Romanesque churches – ask for a list in Vielha's tourist office) and is inspiringly beautiful when you get away from the tourist centres. From Aran's pretty side valleys, walkers can go over the mountains in any direction, notably southward to the Parc Nacional d'Aigüestortes i Estany de Sant Maurici.

Thanks in part to its geography, Aran's native language is not Catalan but Aranese *(aranés),* which is a dialect of Occitan or the *langue d'oc,* the old Romance language of southern France. Mind you, not even all the locals still speak it, as interviewees chatting in Catalan on Aranese radio attest!

Despite this northward orientation, Aran has been tied politically to Catalonia since 1175, when Alfonso II took it under his protection to forestall the designs of rival counts on both sides of the Pyrenees. A major hiccup came with the Napoleonic occupation from 1810 to 1815.

The Val d'Aran is some 35km long and is considered to have three parts: Naut Aran (Upper Aran), the eastern part, aligned east–west; Mijaran (Middle Aran) around Vielha; and Baish Aran (Lower Aran), where the Garona flows northeast to France.

VIELHA
POP 5239 / ELEV 974M

Vielha is Aran's junction capital, a barely controlled sprawl of holiday housing and apartments straggled along the valley and creeping up the sides. The tiny centre retains some charm but in general this is not the Val d'Aran's highlight. The Aranese spelling of Vielha's name is more common than the Catalan and Castilian version, Viella.

◎ Sights
The small old quarter is around Plaça dèra Glèisa and across little Riu Nere, just west of the square.

Glèisa de Sant Miquèu   CHURCH
(Plaça dèra Glèisa) The town's church displays a mix of 12th- to 18th-century styles, with a 13th-century main portal. It contains some notable medieval artwork, especially the 12th-century *Crist de Mijaran,* an almost life-sized wooden bust that is thought to have been part of a *Descent from the Cross* group.

Musèu dèra Val d'Aran   MUSEUM
(Carrèr Major 11; adult/senior & child €2/1; ◎10am-1pm & 5-8pm Tue-Sat, 11am-2pm Sun) This museum, housed in a turreted and somewhat decaying old mansion, tells the tale of Aran's history up to the present.

⛺ Sleeping
About a third of the Val d'Aran's hotels are in the capital. For some of the cheaper places, head down Passeig dèra Llibertat, north off Avenguda de Castièro. High season for most is Christmas to New Year, Easter and a handful of other peak holiday periods: high summer (July to August) and much of the ski season (January to February). At other times, prices can as much as halve.

Hostal El Ciervo   BOUTIQUE HOTEL €€
(☑973 64 01 65; www.hotelelciervo.net; Plaça de Sant Orenç 3; s/d €60/85; ◎closed Jun & Nov ⊛) With an exterior covered in paintings of trees and forest creatures, it's clear before you even pass through the doorway that this hotel has character, and true to initial appearances, each of its 20 rooms varies in style and feel. But all offer about the best deal money can buy in Vielha. Breakfast is €6.

Otel Ço de Pierra   HOTEL €€
TOP CHOICE (☑973 64 13 34; www.hotelpierra.com; Carrèr Major 26; s/d €47/62) In Betrén, a pretty village tacked on to the eastern end of Vielha's sprawl, seek out this new place

that respects the stone-and-slate pattern of traditional housing. The 10 rooms combine stone, timber and terracotta for warmth. What's fabulous is that you are in a timeless village about a 15-minute walk from the centre of Vielha.

✖ Eating
Quality dining is quite hard to come by in Vielha, but you will find no shortage of places serving average meals – many will dish up the local speciality, *olla aranesa* (a hearty hotpot).

Restaurant Gustavo (Era Mòla)
    FRENCH €€
(☑973 64 24 19; Carrèr de Marrèc 14; meals €30-35; ◎Thu-Tue mid-Jul–Sep & Dec-Apr) Located in a low-slung stone house in the heart of the old town, this is easily the best restaurant in town. Expect carefully prepared local cooking with a heavy French hand (you can't get more French than potted duck, ie rillettes). Savour the *solomillo de cerdo al Calvados* (pork fillet bathed in Calvados). The desserts rate a special mention.

ℹ Information
Mossos d'Esquadra (Catalan regional police; ☑973 35 72 85) Just north of the centre along the N230 to France.
Tourist office (☑973 64 01 10; www.torisme aran.org; Carrèr de Sarriulèra 10; ◎9am-9pm)

ARTIES
POP 490 / ELEV 1143M

Six kilometres east of Vielha, this village on the southern side of the highway sits astride the confluence of the Garona and Valarties rivers. Among its cheerful stone houses is the Romanesque Glèisa de Santa Maria, with its three-storey belfry and triple apse.

⛺ Sleeping
Aside from the two options listed below almost all other accommodation in the village closes up in May/June and October/November.

Hotel Edelmeiss   HOTEL €€
(☑973 64 09 02; s/d incl breakfast €56/96; ℙ⊛) There's nothing remotely fancy about this small, family-run hotel, but what you do get are the basics done very well and the result is a pleasant night's stay. Breakfast is served in the boisterous downstairs bar – a meeting point for the whole local community. Much of the electricity comes from the solar panels outside.

Parador Arties HISTORIC HOTEL €€€
(📞973 64 08 01; www.parador.es; d €149;
🅿️❄️📶) Occupying the grandest house in
the village, the palatial Parador Arties
has luxurious but fairly sterile rooms and
helpful staff.

SALARDÚ
POP 460 / ELEV 1267M

Three kilometres east of Arties, Salardú's
nucleus of old houses and narrow streets
has largely resisted the temptation to
sprawl. In the apse of the village's 12th- and
13th-century Sant Andreu church, you can
admire the 13th-century *Crist de Salardú*
crucifixion carving.

The town is a handy base for the Baqueira-
Beret ski resort, 4km from here.

🛏 Sleeping

There are plenty of places to stay in the village itself, but our favourite is to be found
in the tiny village of Bagergue, 2km north
of Salardú. Note, however, that in May/
June and October/November absolutely everything in and around Salardú goes into
hibernation.

Hotel Seixes HOTEL €€
(📞973 64 54 06; www.seixes.com; s/d incl breakfast €83/94; 🕐closed Jun; 🅿️📶) This hikers'
favourite has spacious and comfortable
rooms, some of which have huge views over
the valley and surrounding peaks. Whilst
you're tucking into a hearty breakfast the
staff will fill you in on all the local trekking
routes.

BAQUEIRA-BERET

Baqueira (Vaquèira, in Aranese), 3km east
of Salardú, and Beret, 8km north of Baqueira, form Catalonia's premier ski resort
(www.baqueira.es), favoured by the Spanish
royal family, no less! Its good lift system
gives access to 72 varied pistes totalling
104km (larger than any other Spanish resort), amid fine scenery at between 1500m
and 2510m.

There's nowhere cheap to stay in
Baqueira, and nowhere at all at Beret.
Many skiers stay down the valley in Salardú, Arties or Vielha. Out of season everything is closed.

NORTH OF VIELHA

The hills on either side of the highway up
to the French frontier hide some exquisite
countryside with fine walking trails and
an assortment of curious villages. Turn off

the highway at Eth Pònt d'Arròs and climb
a few kilometres into Arròs via Vila. This
and other sleepy villages around here are
full of charm with their stout old houses
and rambling lanes.

Another suggestion is to branch west,
off the main highway at Es Bòrdes, a typical Aranese village, and keep following the
road as it twists its way up into heavily
wooded countryside. The drive alone is a
real delight: follow the course of the Joèu
stream, as you gain altitude, to reach the
high mountain pastures of the Plan dera
Artiga de Lin plain. Walking trails lead
off into the tall forbidding mountains of
the Aragonese Pyrenees, capped by the Pic
d'Aneto (3404m).

❶ Getting There & Around

Bus

Two Alsa buses run daily between Barcelona
and Vielha (€30.05, 5½ hours) via Lleida and El
Pont de Suert. Lleida to Vielha (€12.05) takes
three hours.

A local bus service runs from four (at weekends) to nine times daily along the valley from
Baqueira to Les or Pontaut (for Eth Pont de Rei)
via Vielha and the intervening villages. Several
others run from Vielha either to Baqueira or to
Les/Pontaut. The trip from one end of the valley
to the other takes up to an hour.

Car & Motorcycle

The N230 Hwy from Lleida and El Pont de Suert
reaches Aran through the 5.25km Túnel de Vielha, then heads north from Vielha to the French
border at Eth Pont de Rei.

From the Vall de la Noguera Pallaresa, the C28
crosses the Port de la Bonaigua pass (2072m) –
which is sometimes closed in winter – into Naut
Aran, meeting the N230 Hwy at Vielha.

CENTRAL CATALONIA

Away from the beaches and mountains is a
host of little-visited gems splashed across
the Catalan hinterland. About halfway between Barcelona and the Pyrenees lies the
graceful town of Vic, with its grand Plaça
Major. Northwest of the capital, you can
strike out for Manresa (just beyond Montserrat), Cardona (with its windy castle
complex) and Solsona, en route to Lleida.
An alternative route to Lleida takes you
further south through the Conca de Barberà, which is littered with majestic medieval monasteries.

Vic

POP 38,320

With its enchanting old quarter crammed with Roman remnants, medieval leftovers, a grand Gothic cloister, an excellent art museum, some hectic markets and a glut of superb restaurants, Vic is one of the undiscovered tourist gems of Catalonia. Despite its resolutely Catalan political outlook, the town is very multicultural. Vic makes for a great day trip from Barcelona, but it's better to stay a little longer and wallow in the town's atmosphere.

◎ Sights

Old Town   OLD TOWN

Plaça Major, the largest of Catalonia's central squares, is lined with medieval, baroque and Modernista mansions. It's still the site of huge regular markets (◷Tue & Sat mornings) flogging everything from cabbages to slinky underwear and chickens to bunny rabbits – though not normally at the same stall! These markets have provided the square with an alternative name, Plaça del Mercadal. Around it swirl the serpentine streets of medieval Vic, lined by mansions, churches, chapels and an undeniably sunny southern atmosphere.

Catedral de Sant Pere   CATHEDRAL

(Plaça de la Catedral; adult/child €2/free; ◷10am-1pm & 4-7pm) The Catedral de Sant Pere is a neoclassical Goliath of gloomy taste, flanked by a Romanesque bell tower. Inside, the dark, square-based pillars are lightened by murals by Josep Maria Sert (he had to do them twice because the first set was destroyed by fire in 1936). The highlights of a visit are the Romanesque crypt, the treasury rooms and a wander through the stone lacework splendour of the Gothic cloister. Entrance to the cathedral itself is free – the above prices and times apply to the cloisters, treasury room and crypt.

Museu Episcopal   MUSEUM

(www.museuepiscopalvic.com; Plaça del Bisbe Oliba 3; adult/over 10yr €5/2.50; ◷10am-7pm Tue-Sat, 10am-2pm Sun Apr-Sep, shorter hr rest of yr) Around the corner from the cathedral, this museum holds a marvellous collection of Romanesque and Gothic art, second only to the Museu Nacional d'Art de Catalunya collection (p261) in Barcelona. The Romanesque collection includes the vivid *Davallament,* a scene depicting the taking down of Christ from the cross. The Gothic collection contains works by such key figures as Lluís Borrassà and Jaume Huguet.

★☆ Festivals & Events

Vic has a packed festival calendar. Some of the more important ones are listed here.

Palm Sunday   MARKETS

In the week running up to Palm Sunday, Plaça Major hosts the Mercat del Ram (Palm Market, a tradition that goes back to AD 875), selling palms and laurels. The Mercat del Ram is also the excuse for a major farm market, held out of the centre at the El Sucre trade fair (Carrer de la Llotja).

August   ANTIQUES

The trade fair grounds host the annual Fira d'Antiguitats de Vic (www.fav.cat), one of Spain's biggest antiques markets, for a week over mid to late August.

September   MUSIC

The city hosts the Mercat de Música Viva (www.mmvv.net), a big if somewhat chaotic event, over several days in which Catalan, national and foreign acts of various schools of Latin rock and pop get together to jam.

⌸ Sleeping & Eating

Vic is an easy day trip from Barcelona. The city is known for its disproportionate density of high-quality restaurants, and it's close enough to Barcelona for people from the big city to have an agreeable gourmet getaway.

Hostal Osona   HOSTAL €

(☑93 883 28 45; Carrer de Remei 3; s/d €20/36) If you need digs, this basic *hostal* has rooms with basin, and shared showers in the hall. It's a little to the south of the old town and has plenty of streetside parking.

Ciutat de Vic   HOTEL €€

(☑93 889 25 51; www.nh-hotels.com; Passatge can Mastrot; d €56-98; ❋🛜) Located just north of the old town, this standard chain hotel offers guests plenty of comfort, but little character. Customer service leaves much to be desired.

TOP CHOICE La Taula   CATALAN €€

(☑93 886 32 29, Plaça de Don Miguel de Clariana 4; menus from €16.90; ◷daily Jul-Aug, Tue-Sat & lunch only Sun Oct-Jun, closed Feb) In a town that bristles with superlative eateries, this one stands out as a bright star of traditional cooking, with fair prices and no pretensions (and considered by locals as one of the best in town).

Information

Tourist office (☎93 886 20 91; www.victur isme.cat; Carrer de la Ciutat 4; ◷10am-2pm & 4-8pm Mon-Fri, 10am-2pm & 4-7pm Sat, 10am-1.30pm Sun)

Getting There & Away

Regular *rodalies* (line C3) run from Barcelona (€5.70, up to 1½ hours).

Around Vic

RUPIT
POP 330

An enchanting excursion northeast of Vic takes you 31km along the C153 to Rupit, a splendid old village set amid rugged grazing country. You cross a suspension footbridge to reach the village, which is full of quaint 17th-century houses, a baroque church and tucked-away squares. Especially enticing is Carrer del Fossar, which climbs the spine of the hill, along which part of the village is spread-eagled. Rupit is a good base for rambles in the area.

Getting here without your own vehicle is problematic. Sagalés (www.sagales.com) buses leave Barcelona at 3pm and 6pm Monday to Friday and at 11.20am on Saturday. Change buses in Vic. The trip (€10.50) takes about 2½ hours from Barcelona.

Manresa

POP 76,558

A big commercial centre in the Catalan heartland, Manresa was the scene of the first assembly of the nationalist Unió Catalanista (1897), which published the *Bases de Manresa,* a political manifesto for an autonomous Catalan state.

Not a great deal of the old town remains, but you can't miss the great hulk that is the Basílica de Santa Maria, atop the Puig Cardener hill in the town centre. Its Gothic nave is second in size only to that of the cathedral in Girona. The unique Romanesque Pont Vell, whose eight arcs span the rather less-impressive Riu Cardener, was rebuilt after destruction in the civil war.

Cardona

POP 5187

Long before arrival, you spy in the distance the outline of the impregnable 18th-century fortress high above Cardona, which it-

self lies next to the Muntanya de Sal (Salt Mountain). Until 1990 the salt mines were an important source of income.

The castle (follow the signs uphill to the Parador Ducs de Cardona, a lovely place to stay overnight) was built over an older predecessor. The single most remarkable element of the buildings is the lofty and spare Romanesque Església de Sant Vicenç (adult/child €3/2; ◷10am-1pm & 3-6pm Tue-Sun Jun-Sep, shorter hr rest of yr). The bare stone walls were once covered in bright frescoes, some of which can be contemplated in the Museu Nacional d'Art de Catalunya (p261) in Barcelona.

Cardona is served by the ALSA Barcelona–Manresa–Solsona bus route. Up to four run daily from Barcelona (€12.85, two hours) and three or four from Manresa (€4.40, one hour). Up to four buses proceed to Solsona (€2.20, 25 minutes).

Solsona

POP 9000

They call the people of Solsona *matarucs* (donkey killers), which seems an odd tag until you hear what the townsfolk's favourite festive activity used to be. Every February the high point of Solsona's Carnaval fun was the hoisting of a donkey, by the neck, up the town bell tower (Torre de les Hores). The donkey, literally scared to death, not unreasonably, would defecate and urinate on its way up, much to the delight of the drink-addled crowd below. To be hit by a glob of either substance was, they say, a sign of good fortune for the coming year. Nowadays the donkey is a water-spraying fake.

The Catedral de Santa Maria on Plaça de la Catedral (admission free; ◷10am-1pm & 4-8pm) boasts Romanesque apses, a Gothic nave, a pretty cloister and the ghosts of a lot of pissed-off donkeys. Behind the cathedral is the neoclassical Palau Episcopal (Plaça del Palau; adult/senior & child €3/2; ◷10am-1pm & 4.30-7pm Tue-Sat, 10am-2pm Sun May-Sep, shorter hr rest of yr). Built in the 18th century, it houses a considerable collection of medieval art gathered from churches in the surrounding district.

Two to four Alsina Graells buses run daily from Barcelona (€15.30, two to 2½ hours) via Manresa (€6.65, 65 minutes) and Cardona to Solsona.

Conca de Barberà

This hilly, green, wine-making district comes as a refreshing surprise in the otherwise drab flatlands of southwest Catalonia and makes an alternative route from Barcelona (or Tarragona) to Lleida and beyond. Vineyards and woods succeed one another across rolling green hills, studded by occasional medieval villages and monasteries.

Getting to any of the following without your own set of wheels is a drag.

REIAL MONESTIR DE SANTA MARIA DE POBLET

The jewel in the crown of this rural region is doubtless this imposing fortified monastery (adult/child over 7yr €6/3.20; ⊙10am-12.45pm & 3-6pm Mon-Sat, 10am-12.30pm & 3-5.30pm Sun & holidays mid-Mar–mid-Oct, shorter hr rest of yr), founded by Cistercian monks from southern France in 1151.

The walls of this abbey devoted to Santa Maria (a Unesco World Heritage site) were a defensive measure and also symbolised the monks' isolation from the vanities of the outside world. A grand portal gives access to a long uneven square, the Plaça Major, flanked by several dependencies including the small Romanesque Capella de Santa Caterina. The nearby Porta Daurada is so called because its bronze panels were overlaid with gold to suitably impress the visiting emperor Felipe II in 1564.

Once inside the Porta Reial (Royal Gate), flanked by hefty octagonal towers, you will be led through a worn Romanesque entrance to the grand cloister, of Romanesque origins but largely Gothic in style. With its peaceful fountain and pavilion, the two-level cloister is a marvellous haven. You will be led from the cloister to the head of the church, itself a typically tall and austere Cistercian Gothic creation, to witness the sculptural glory in alabaster that is the *retablo* and Panteón de los Reyes (Kings' Pantheon). The raised alabaster coffins, restored by Frederic Marès (see p237), contain such greats as Jaume I (the conqueror of Mallorca and Valencia) and Pere III.

Hostal Fonoll (☑977 87 03 33; www.hostalfonoll.com; Plaça de Ramon Berenguer IV 2; s/d €40/70; P✳☎), opposite the monastery entrance, has simple but comfortable rooms. The dominating orange decor, especially in the bathrooms, is a little lurid! Or you can drop by for a coffee or food at the bar-restaurant downstairs. There's a Jacuzzi (€5) in the garden, access to a microwave and even a pool table.

AROUND REIAL MONESTIR DE SANTA MARIA DE POBLET

It is worth spending time exploring the vicinity. L'Espluga de Francolí, 2.5km away from the monastery along a pleasant tree-lined country road that makes walking tempting, is a bright town with several small hotels. Above all else, it is home to the Hostal del Senglar (☑977 87 04 11; www.hostaldelsenglar.com; Plaça de Montserrat Canals 1; meals €30-35), an excellent Catalan restaurant for meat lovers. The dining areas can be a little impersonal but the food and service are excellent. Kids can play in the gardens after lunch and the *hostal* also has 34 decent rooms if you need to stay overnight (single/double without breakfast €90/100).

More interesting still is Montblanc, 8km away. Surrounded by medieval battlements, this one-time royal residence is jammed with highlights, including a Gothic royal mansion and churches, as well as some vestiges of its Romanesque origins. The winding cross-country drive to Prades leads through lovely country.

MORE MONASTERIES

Two other fine Cistercian monasteries can be visited in the area. Following the AP7 motorway southwest from Vilafranca, take the AP2 fork about 18km west, then take exit 11 north for the medieval Reial Monestir de Santes Creus (Royal Monastery of the Holy Crosses; Plaça de Jaume el Just; adult/child €4.50/3, Tue free; ⊙10am-6.30pm Tue-Sun Jun-Oct, shorter hr rest of yr). Cistercian monks moved in here in 1168 and from then on the monastery developed as a major centre of learning and a launch pad for the repopulation of the surrounding territory. Behind the Romanesque and Gothic facade lies a glorious 14th-century sandstone cloister, chapter house and royal apartments where the *comtes-reis* (count-kings; rulers of the joint state of Catalonia and Aragón) often stayed when they popped by during Holy Week. The church, begun in the 12th century, is a lofty Gothic structure in the French tradition. It's about 28km east of Montblanc.

North from Montblanc (take the C14 and then branch west along the LP2335), country roads guide you up through tough countryside into the low hills of the Serra del Tallat and towards yet another Cister-

Avid tipplers will have come across a playful, relatively inexpensive bubbly called Freixenet. One of Spain's flagship exporters of *cava* (sparkling wine), Freixenet is based at the heart of Catalonia's Penedès wine region, which alone produces the bulk of Spain's sparkling white wines (see p300).

But Freixenet and bubbly are only the tip of the Catalan wineberg. Catalonia hosts 11 Denominación de Origen (DO) wine-producing zones and a remarkable variety of tipples. Less-well-known outside Spain than Rioja drops, Catalan wines are full of pleasant surprises. In 2000, the heavy, tannin-loaded, deep-coloured reds of El Priorat (www.doqpriorat.org) gained the much-desired Denominación de Origen Calificada (DOC) status long held only by Rioja wines. To further investigate El Priorat's wines, and wines from the adjacent Montsant DO region (which many in the know will tell you are just as good and much cheaper), head for the **tourist office** (📞 977 83 10 23; www.priorat.org; Carrer de Sant Marcel 2) in Falset for information on local wine cellars. Falset, the capital of the Priorat area, offers some fine restaurant options too.

Catalonia's other DO wines come from points all over the region, spread as far apart as the Empordà area around Figueres in the north, and the Terra Alta zone around Gandesa in the southwest. The Penedès region pumps out almost two million hectolitres a year and thus doubles the combined output of the remaining DO regions.

Most of the grapes grown in Catalonia are native to Spain and include the white macabeo, garnacha and xarel lo (for white wines), and the black garnacha, monastrell and ull de llebre (hare's eye) red varieties. Foreign varieties (such as chardonnay, riesling, chenin blanc, cabernet sauvignon, merlot and pinot noir) are also widespread.

Beyond the Penedès region, look out for Raïmat, in the Costers del Segre DO area in Lleida province, for fine reds and a couple of notable whites. Good fortified wines come from around Tarragona; some pleasing fresh wines are also produced in the Empordà area in the north.

cian complex, the **Reial Monestir de Santa Maria de Vallbona de les Monges** (Royal Monastery of St Mary of Vallbona of the Nuns; adult/child €2.50/2; ⏰10.30am-1.30pm & 4.30-6.45pm Tue-Sat, noon-1.30pm & 4.30-6.45pm Sun & holidays Mar-Oct, shorter hr rest of yr), founded in the 12th century and where around 20 nuns still live and pray. You will be taken on a guided tour, probably in Catalan, in which it will become clear that it has even today not yet fully recovered from civil war damage.

A combined ticket to all these and the Poblet monastery is available for €9. For more information on the area around the monasteries, check out the Ruta del Cister (Cistercian Route) website (www.larutadel cister.info).

Lleida

POP 135,920

The hot, dry inland provincial capital Lleida (Castilian: Lérida) can't be described as the most attractive city in Catalonia, but it's a friendly and lively place with just enough attractions to make a stopover worthwhile.

The old town is built around two hills, one topped by a mighty fortress-church and the other, a bit of a pimple by comparison, by another former fortress complex. The streets below offer a slightly decrepit, rough feel of a Spain of yesteryear and a noticeable African migrant presence that is very much part of Spain's present.

👁 Sights

La Seu Vella CATHEDRAL
(adult/under 7yr €3/free; ⏰10am-1.30pm & 4-7.30pm Tue-Sun Jun-Sep) Lleida's 'old cathedral', La Seu Vella towers above everything else in position and grandeur. It stands within a *recinte* (compound) of defensive walls erected between the 12th and 19th centuries.

The main entrance to the **recinte** (admission free; ⏰8am-9pm) is from Carrer de Monterey on its western side, but during the cathedral's opening hours you can use the extraordinarily ugly **ascensor** from above Plaça de Sant Joan.

The cathedral was built in sandy-coloured stone in the 13th to 15th centuries on the site of a former mosque (Lleida was under Islamic control from AD 719 to 1149). It's a masterpiece of the Transitional style, although it only recently recovered from 241 years' use as a barracks, which began as Felipe V's punishment for the city's opposition in the War of the Spanish Succession.

A 70m octagonal bell tower rises at the southwest end of the cloister, the windows of which are laced with exceptional Gothic tracery. The spacious if austere interior, used as stables and dormitories during the military occupation, has a veritable forest of slender columns with carved capitals.

Above the cathedral are remains of the Islamic fortress and residence of the Muslim governors, known as the Castell del Rei or La Suda.

Castell de Gardeny MONASTERY
(Turó de Gardeny; adult/child €2.5/free; ⊙10am-1.30pm & 4.30-7.30pm Tue-Sat, 10am-2pm Sun May-Oct, shorter hr rest of yr) The Knights Templar built a monastery complex here shortly after Lleida was taken from the Muslims in 1149. It was later expanded as a fortress in the 17th century. Today you can still see the original Romanesque Església de Santa Maria de Gardeny and a hefty tower. An imaginative display lends insight into the monastic life of the Knights Templar.

Museu de Lleida MUSEUM
(www.museudelleida.cat; Carrer de Sant Crist 1; adult/under 12yr €4/free; ⊙10am-2pm & 4-8pm Tue-Sat, 10am-2pm Sun Jun-Sep, shorter hr rest of yr) This swish museum brings under one roof collections of artefacts that reach back to the Stone Age, and passing through a handful of Roman leftovers, medieval art and on to the 19th century. Entrance is free on the first Tuesday of the month.

Carrer Major & Around OLD TOWN
A 13th-century Gothic mansion, La Paeria has housed the city government almost since its inception. The 18th-century neoclassical La Seu Nova on Plaça de la Catedral was built when La Seu Vella was turned into a barracks. Opposite is the Antic Hospital de Santa Maria (Plaça de la Catedral), with some Gothic elements and beautiful courtyard. You can wander into the courtyard any time the premises are open and sometimes visit temporary exhibitions.

The Museu d'Art Jaume Morera (Carrer Major 31; admission free; ⊙11am-2pm & 5-8pm Tue-Sat, 11am-2pm Sun) is a varied collection of work by Lleida-associated artists.

Dipósit del Pla de l'Aigua HISTORIC STRUCTURE
(Carrer de Múrcia 10; ⊙11am-2pm Sat, Sun & holidays) Lleida's 18th-century engineering wonder long stored and supplied the city's drinking water via five public fountains. With 25 imposing stone pillars, it could hold nine million litres of water. No wonder they called it the Water Cathedral!

FREE **Museu Roda-Roda** MUSEUM
(Carrer de Santa Cecília 22; admission free; ⊙10am-2pm & 4.30-8.30pm Tue-Sat, 11am-2pm Sun) *Chitty Chitty Bang Bang* nostalgics might want to pop by this modest collection of classic cars and motorcycles.

🛏 Sleeping & Eating

Lleida's total dearth of tourists is reflected in its total lack of inspiring hotels. On the plus side, though, you'll find no shortage of places to eat. And if you're going to have a meal here then take note of the fact that Lleida is Catalonia's snail *(cargol)*-eating capital. So many *cargols* are swallowed during the annual Aplec del Cargol (Snail Festival), held on a Sunday in early May, that some have to be imported.

Hotel Real HOTEL €
(☑973 23 94 05; www.hotelreallleida.com; Avinguda de Blondel 22; s/d from €49/51; 🅿🗶🛜) A modern mid-rise place, Hotel Real is aimed at business visitors and offers various classes of room. All are bright and clean, and the better ones have generous balconies. Avoid street-facing rooms, as there's no soundproofing – and listening in on the drunken conversations of passers-by at three in the morning gets a bit tedious. A couple of rooms have wheelchair access.

Restaurant Santbernat STEAKS €
(☑973 27 10 31; Carrer de Saracíbar; menus from €16.95; ⊙lunch & dinner Thu-Sun, lunch Mon-Wed; 🖼) You would hardly expect to find a hearty eatery like this up on the 1st floor of the rather dour bus station. The star attractions are chargrilled meat dishes, which are sizzled up on a big open grill before your eyes. There's a set meal for kids (€16.95) too.

El Celler del Roser SNAILS €
(☑973 23 90 70; Carrer dels Cavallers 24; menus from €11.80; ⊙lunch & dinner Mon-Sat, lunch Sun) While on the subject of snails, this classic specialises in the slithery delicacy (from €12.30), along with eight possible permutations of its award-winning *bacallà* (cod; from €17.20).

Information

Centre d'Informació i Reserves (☎902 25 00 50; http://turisme.paeria.es; Carrer Major 31bis; ⊙10am-2pm & 4-7pm Mon-Sat, 10am-1.30pm Sun & holidays) Turisme de Lleida provides information about the city.

Oficina Turisme de la Generalitat (☎973 24 88 40; Plaça de Ramon Berenguer IV; ⊙10am-2pm & 3.30-7.30pm Mon-Fri, 10am-2pm Sat) For tips on the rest of Lleida province.

Post office (Rambla de Ferran 16; ⊙8.30am-8.30pm Mon-Fri, 9.30am-2pm Sat)

Getting There & Away

Bus

Daily services by **ALSA** include up to 14 buses (three on Sunday) to Barcelona (€18, three hours); two to El Pont de Suert and Vielha (€12.15, 2½ hours); one (except Sunday) to La Pobla de Segur, Sort, Llavorsí and Esterri d'Àneu (€19.90, three hours); and two to La Seu d'Urgell (€16.90, 2½ hours).

Train

Lleida is on the Barcelona–Madrid line. Up to 34 trains, ranging from slow regionals (3½ hours) to the high-speed AVE, run daily to/from Barcelona, taking as little as one hour in the new Avant-class trains (which costs half the price as the AVE and is almost as fast). Fares range from €21.60 to €45.90. These same trains proceed to Madrid via Zaragoza.

Montsec

This hilly range 65km north of Lleida is the main stage for hang-gliders and ultralights in Catalonia. It is also a popular area for walking, caving and climbing.

The focal point is Àger, a village in the valley of the same name. If coming via Balaguer, you'll see it to the northeast as you reach the top of Coll d'Àger (912m). The village is draped like a mantle over a hill, protruding from the top of which is the intriguing ruin of the Església de Sant Pere.

Montsec has a half-dozen take-off points, including one at the Sant Alís peak (1678m), the highest in the range. Volàger (☎973 32 02 30; www.volager.com; Camí de Castellnou), based in Bellpuig, offers hang-gliding courses here and provides all the equipment. You can go hang-gliding with the school for a day (€80), while a full six-day course comes to €650.

A choice location for walkers and climbers is the stunning Congost de Mont-Rebei, a

narrow gorge of 80m-high rock walls at the western end of the Montsec range. The Riu Noguera Ribagorçana flows into the gorge from the north, along the border with Aragón. Caves along the foot of the gorge, and around the dam to the south, attract speleologists.

You can stay at one of a handful of *cases de pagès* or a *hostal*. About the only way to get into and around the area is with your own wheels.

COSTA DAURADA

South of Sitges (p295) stretches the Costa Daurada (Golden Coast), a series of mostly quiet resorts with unending broad beaches along a mainly flat coast, capped by the delta of the mighty Riu Ebre (Ebro), which protrudes 20km out into the Mediterranean. Along the way is the old Roman capital of Tarragona, and the modern extravaganza of Port Aventura – Catalonia's answer to EuroDisney.

Vilanova i la Geltrú

POP 61,427

Six minutes west of Sitges by train, Vilanova is home to the culinary delicacy of *xató* (an almond-and-hazelnut sauce used on various dishes, particularly seafood), the much-sought-after actor Sergi López, and an esplanade lined by a trio of beautiful broad beaches.

A few blocks inland from the beaches is Vilanova's main attraction, the Museu del Ferrocarril (Railway Museum; www.museudelferrocarril.org, in Spanish; Plaça d'Eduard Maristany; adult/child €5/4; ⊙10.30am-2.30pm & 5-8pm daily Aug, shorter hr rest of yr), housed in the 19th-century installations for the maintenance of steam trains, next to the train station. The collection of steam locomotives attracts kids of all ages.

Vilanova i la Geltrú stages a riotous Carnaval in February that lasts for 13 days. One of the high points is the Batalla de Caramels (Battle of the Sweets), when townsfolk in costume launch more than 100,000kg of sweeties at one another!

It's easy enough to pop down to Vilanova for the day from Barcelona or Sitges but there is one serious reason for hanging out a little longer...

Hotel Cèsar (93 815 11 25; www.hotel cesar.net; Carrer d'Isaac Peral 4-8; d €90-140; P❖🐾📶) is the town's top hotel. It's set in a leafy, tranquil part of town just back from the waterfront and offers a series of double rooms and suites in a variety of categories. The best rooms have their own computers with broadband internet access. Saunter to the sauna, or opt for a massage. The hotel is also home to La Fitorra (meals €35-40; Wed-Sun, dinner only Tue), one of the senior denizens of local cooking.

There's a tourist office (93 815 45 17; www.vilanovaturisme.net; Passeig del Carme; 10am-8pm Mon-Sat, 10am-2pm Sun) for information.

The town is just down the *rodalies* (line C2) from Sitges. From Barcelona the fare will set you back €2.90.

Altafulla

POP 3293

Roman citizens of Tarragona who used to holiday here would no doubt still be tempted. A cheekily pretty medieval core, all cream and whitewashed walls with rose-coloured stone portals and windows, is capped by a 13th-century castle. Just 10km east of Tarragona, Altafulla was converted into a fortified settlement in the wake of the Muslim invasion.

Altafulla's broad beach, which is sadly unimpressive (about 2km away on the other side of the freeway), is backed by a row of cheerful single-storey houses known as the Botigues de Mar (Sea Shops). Until well into the 19th century they served as warehouses but have since been converted into houses – many available for holiday let.

🛏 Sleeping & Eating

Gran Claustre Hotel   BOUTIQUE HOTEL €€€
(977 65 15 57; www.granclaustre.com; Carrer del Cup 2; d incl breakfast €170; P❖🐾📶) Situated inside a beautifully renovated building in the old town, the luxurious rooms here have stone-tiled rain showers, bright art-adorned walls and an overwhelming feeling of exclusivity. There's a divine wood-panelled pool in the courtyard.

Alberg Casa Gran   HOSTEL €
(977 65 07 79; Plaçeta 12; dm student & under 26yr/26yr & over €20/23) Occupying a fine old mansion in the old town, this is one of the region's more enchantingly placed youth hostels.

For food, two superb and utterly contrasting places in the old town are Restaurant Bruixes de Burriac (977 65 15 57; www.gran claustre.com; Carrer del Cup 2; menus from €30) at the Gran Claustre Hotel, with inspiring and imaginative regional dishes, and the much more simple Bar Balleste (977 65 28 39; Marqués de Tamarit 17; mains €10-15), on the main road running along the foot of the old town. The latter does a sensational lunch menu (€12) which, depending on the day, might include such unusual treats as chicken curry.

ℹ Getting There & Away

A couple of local trains per day run to Altafulla from Tarragona (€1.80, 10 minutes).

Tarragona

POP 140,323

The seemingly eternally sunny port city of Tarragona is a fascinating mix of Mediterranean beach life, Roman history and medieval alleyways. Easily Catalonia's most important Roman site, Tarragona's number-one attraction is its seaside-facing Roman amphitheatre. The town also has a delightful medieval core, dominated by a beautiful cathedral that's another trip on its own. And if the sense of history gets too much, just flop down onto one of the town beaches. Add into the mix plenty of tempting food options and an array of bars heaving into the wee hours and you get the most exciting urban centre in southern Catalonia.

History

Tarragona was first occupied by the Romans, who called it Tarraco, in 218 BC. In 27 BC Augustus made it the capital of his new Tarraconensis province (roughly all modern Spain) and stayed until 25 BC, directing campaigns in Cantabria and Asturias. Tarragona was abandoned when the Muslims arrived in AD 714, but reborn as the seat of a Christian archbishopric in 1089. Today its rich Roman remains and fine medieval cathedral make it an absorbing place.

◉ Sights & Activities

The tourist office dishes out three handy booklets detailing routes around the city taking in Roman, mediaeval and Modernista sites.

Museu d'Història de Tarragona
ROMAN RUINS

(MHT; www.museutgn.com; adult/child per site €3/free, incl all MHT elements €10/free; ⊙9am-9pm Mon-Sat, 9am-3pm Sun Easter-Oct, shorter hr rest of yr) To call the four sites that make up the Museu d'Història de Tarragona a museum is somewhat misleading, as they are in fact four separate Roman sites (which since 2000 together have constituted a Unesco World Heritage site) and a 14th-century noble mansion, which now serves as the Museu Casa Castellarnau (Carrer dels Cavallers 14).

Start exploring with the **Pretori i Circ Romans** (Plaça del Rei), which includes part of the vaults of the Roman circus, where chariot races were once held. The circus, 300m long, stretched from here to beyond Plaça de la Font to the west. Nearby Plaça del Fòrum was the location of the provincial forum and political heart of Tarraconensis province. Near the beach is the crown jewel of Tarragona's Roman sites, the well-preserved **Amfiteatre Romà** (Plaça d'Arce Ochotorena), where gladiators battled either each other or wild animals to the death. In its arena are the remains of 6th- and 12th-century churches built to commemorate the martyrdom of the Christian bishop Fructuosus and two deacons, who, they say, were burnt alive here in AD 259.

The remains of the **Fòrum Romà** (Carrer del Cardenal Cervantes) are dominated by several imposing columns. The northwest half of this site was occupied by a judicial basilica (where legal disputes were settled), from where the rest of the forum stretched downhill to the southwest. Linked to the site by a footbridge is another excavated area which includes a stretch of Roman street. This forum was the hub of public and religious life for the Roman town. The discovery in 2006 of remains of the foundations of a temple to Jupiter, Juno and Minerva (the major triumvirate of gods at the time of the Roman republic) suggests the forum was much bigger and more important than had previously been assumed.

The Passeig Arqueològic is a peaceful walk around part of the perimeter of the old town between two lines of city walls; the inner ones are mainly Roman, while the outer ones were put up by the British during the War of the Spanish Succession.

ℹ **TARRAGONA ALL IN ONE**

The Tarragona Card (€14 for 48 hours) gives you free entry to all museums and other sights in the city, free local buses and a host of discounts on anything from participating restaurants to taxis. You also receive a guidebook on the city. For the pass to be worth your while, you have to be pretty sure you want to visit virtually everything in town.

Museu Nacional Arqueològic de Tarragona
MUSEUM

(www.mnat.es; Plaça del Rei 5; adult/child €2.40/free; ⊙10am-8pm Tue-Sat, 10am-2pm Sun & holidays Jun-Sep, shorter hr rest of yr) This carefully presented museum gives further insight into Roman Tarraco. Exhibits include part of the Roman city walls, frescoes, sculpture and pottery. A highlight is the large, almost complete *Mosaic de Peixos de la Pineda,* showing fish and sea creatures. In the section on everyday arts you can admire ancient fertility aids, including an outsized stone penis, symbol of the god Priapus.

Admission entitles you to enter the museum at the Necròpolis Paleocristians (Avinguda de Ramón i Cajal 80; adult/child €2.40/free with Museu Nacional Arqueológic de Tarragona; ⊙10am-8pm Tue-Sat, 10am-2pm Sun Jul-Sep, shorter hr rest of yr). This large Christian cemetery of late-Roman and Visigothic times is on Passeig de la Independència on the western edge of town and boasts some surprisingly elaborate tombs. Unfortunately only its small museum is open.

Catedral
CATHEDRAL

(Pla de la Seu; adult/child €3.80/1.20; ⊙10am-7pm Mon-Sat, shorter hr rest of yr) Sitting grandly at the top of the old town, Tarragona's cathedral is undergoing a major facelift and much of it is largely closed (although it's scheduled to be finished long before you get your hands on this book). However, the cloisters and museum are open and continue to demand a solid chunk of your time. Built between 1171 and 1331 on the site of a Roman temple, it combines Romanesque and Gothic features, as typified by the main facade on Pla de la Seu. The entrance is by the cloister on the northwestern flank of the building.

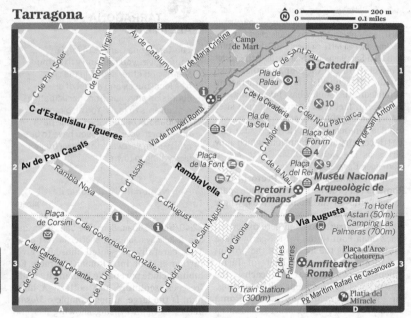

The cloister has Gothic vaulting and Romanesque carved capitals, one of which shows rats conducting what they imagine to be a cat's funeral...until the cat comes back to life! The rooms off the cloister house the **Museu Diocesà**, with an extensive collection extending from Roman hairpins to some lovely 12th- to 14th-century polychrome woodcarvings of a breastfeeding Virgin.

The interior of the cathedral, over 100m long, is Romanesque at the northeastern end and Gothic at the southwest. The aisles are lined with 14th- to 19th-century chapels and hung with 16th- and 17th-century tapestries from Brussels. The arm of St Thecla, Tarragona's patron saint, is normally kept in the **Capella de Santa Tecla** on the southeastern side. The choir in the centre of the nave has 15th-century carved walnut stalls. The marble main **altar** was carved in the 13th century with scenes from the life of St Thecla.

Beaches
BEACHES

The town beach, Platja del Miracle, is reasonably clean but can get terribly crowded. Platja Arrabassada, 1km northeast across the headland, is longer, and Platja Llarga, beginning 2km further out, stretches for about 3km. Buses 1 and 9 from the Balcó stop on Via Augusta go to both (€1.10). You can get the same buses from along Rambla Vella and Rambla Nova.

Museu del Port
MARITIME MUSEUM

(www.porttarragona.cat; Refugi 2 Moll de la Costa; adult/child €2/free; ⊙10am-2pm & 5-8pm Tue-Sat, 11am-2pm Sun & holidays Jun-Sep, shorter hr rest of yr) Down by the waterfront, this curious museum is housed in a dockside shed. There's not a lot to it; there are some displays tracing the history of the port from Roman times (in Catalan and Castilian only), a few model boats and one or two other seafaring items, but it will keep the children happy for a while.

FREE Pont del Diable
ROMAN RUIN

The so-called Devil's Bridge is actually the Aqüeducte Romà (⊙9am-dusk), yet another marvel left by the Romans. It sits, somewhat incongruously, in the leafy rough just off the AP7 freeway, which leads into Tarragona (near where it intersects with the N240). It is a fine stretch of two-tiered aqueduct (217m long and 27m high), along which you can totter to the other side. Bus 5 to Sant Salvador from Plaça Imperial de Tàrraco, running every 10 to 20 minutes, will take you to the vicinity, or park in one of the lay-bys marked on either

Tarragona

side of the AP7, just outside the freeway toll gates.

FREE **Museu d'Art Modern**   ART MUSEUM
(Carrer de Santa Anna 8; ⊘10am-8pm Tue-Fri, 10am-3pm & 5-8pm Sat, 11am-2pm Sun & holidays) This modest art gallery has some interesting temporary exhibitions as well as an impressive display of sculptures, bronzes and modern art.

🛏 Sleeping

Tarragona has about 25 hotels, most of them scattered about newer parts of town and nothing to write home about. There's a handful of good choices in or near the old town.

Pensió Forum   PENSIÓN €
(☑977 23 1718; Plaça de la Font 37; s/d €26/38) The small, but oh so colourful rooms at this helpful *pensión* perch above a restaurant and overlook the main square – views of which can be enjoyed from one of the rooms with a balcony. And the price...well, just look at it – how can you possibly find fault with this place when paying so little?

Hotel Astari   HOTEL €€
(☑977 23 69 00; www.hotelastari.com; Via Augusta 95-97; s/d €64/72; P❄🛜🏊) Of the town's several, largely uninspiring business hotels, this one five minutes' canter from

both the town centre and the beach offers probably the best value. Some of the plain rooms have balconies overlooking the sea and there's a really fantastic pool as well as good levels of service.

Hotel Plaça de la Font   HOTEL €€
(☑977 24 61 34; www.hotelpdelafont.com; Plaça de la Font 26; s/d €55/70; ❄) Rooms here, although a trifle cramped, have a pleasing modern look, with soft colours, sturdy beds and, in the case of half of the rooms, little balconies overlooking the square.

Camping Las Palmeras   CAMPING €
(☑977 20 80 81; www.laspalmeras.com; sites per 2-person tent & car €40-50; P🛜🏊) This cheerful camping ground lies at the far end of Platja Llarga (3km northeast of Tarragona) and is one of the better of eight camping grounds scattered behind the beaches northeast of the city. A big pool stretches out amid leafy parkland just back from the beach. The camping ground enjoys a 1.5km stretch of seaside frontage and untouched coastal woodland nearby. Windsurfing and kitesurfing classes are also on offer.

🍴 Eating

The quintessential Tarragona seafood experience can be had in Serrallo, the town's fishing port. About a dozen bars and restaurants here sell the day's catch, and on summer weekends in particular the place is packed. Most places close their kitchens by about 10.30pm. Two stand-outs here include L'Ancora (Carrer de Trafalgar 25; raciones €6-7; ⊘1pm-1am) and its sister establishment El Varadero (Carrer de Trafalgar 13; raciones €6-7), which brim with mouth-watering seafood and open late. Go for a selection of dishes, which might include *tigres* (stuffed, breaded and fried mussels), *ostrón* (fat oyster) and *cigalas a la plancha* (grilled crayfish). You can sit inside (head upstairs) or take a seat at one of the outdoor tables. Hour-long queues at midnight on summer weekends are not unheard of.

Aq   CATALAN €€
(☑977 21 59 54; Carrer de les Coques 7; mains around €15, menus from €18; ⊘Tue-Sat) This is a bubbly designer haunt with stark colour contrasts (black, lemon and cream linen), slick lines and intriguing international plays on traditional cooking, such as *garrí al forn amb timbal d'alberginia i tomaquet* (oven-cooked suckling pig with aubergine and tomato timbal).

Quim Quima INTERNATIONAL €€
(☏977 25 21 21; Carrer de les Coques 1bis; meals €35, menus from €19.90; ☉lunch Tue-Thu, lunch & dinner Fri & Sat) This renovated medieval mansion makes a marvellous setting for a meal. Huddle up to the bare stone wall or opt for the shady little courtyard. The playful menu is wide-ranging, including sausage-and-cheese crêpes and lasagne.

El Palau del Baró CATALAN €€
(☏977 24 14 64; www.palaudelbaro.com, in Spanish; Carrer de Santa Anna 3; meals €35-45, menus from €15-18; ☉lunch & dinner Tue-Sat, lunch Sun) The Baron's palace, a centuries-old mansion, provides a romantic, sumptuous 19th-century setting. Dishes are served with aplomb, and range from paella and *arròs negre* to various fish options.

Drinking & Entertainment

The bars and clubs along the waterfront at the Port Esportiu (marina), and in some of the streets in front of the train station, such as along Carrer de la Pau del Protectorat, are the main concentration of nightlife.

At the marina, head for Soho (admission free; ☉3pm-4am), which spins a chilled-out jazzy selection of tunes and is the in-spot of the moment.

Gioconda and New Brooklyn (admission €8; ☉10pm-5am Wed-Sun) are two of the more popular clubs at the marina, bursting with fevered dancers on weekends especially.

ⓘ Information

Hospital Joan XXIII (☏977 22 40 11; Carrer del Dr Mallafre Guasch 4)

Post office (Plaça de Corsini; ☉8.30am-8.30pm Mon-Fri, 9.30am-2pm Sat)

Regional tourist office (☏977 23 34 15; Carrer de Fortuny 4; ☉9am-2pm & 4-6.30pm Mon-Fri, 9am-2pm Sat)

Tarraconect@ (Carrer del Cós del Bou; per hr €1.50; ☉10.30am-2pm & 5-10.30pm Mon-Sat, 5-9pm Sun) Internet access.

Tourist office (☏977 25 07 95; www.tarragonaturisme.cat; Carrer Major 39; ☉10am-8pm Mon-Sat, 10am-2pm Sun Jul-Oct, 10am-2pm & 4-7pm Mon-Sat) There are a number of **information kiosks** scattered about town. Hours vary slightly, but in high-season are roughly around 10am to 8pm daily.

ⓘ Getting There & Away

Lying on main routes south from Barcelona, Tarragona is well connected.

Bus

Bus services run to Barcelona, Valencia, Zaragoza, Madrid, Alicante, Pamplona, the main Andalucian cities, Andorra and the north coast. The bus station is around 1.5km northwest of the old town.

Train

Tarragona has recently gained a swanky new train station, Camp de Tarragona, that's more like a state-of-the-art airport than a mere train station, but alas, although lots of money was pumped into its construction little thought was given to location and it's now an annoying 20-minute taxi ride out of the centre (around €24 in a taxi or €2.70 on one of the hourly buses from the bus station; the first bus departs at 6am and the last at 11.20pm). If you're just staying local, at least 16 regional trains per day run to/from Barcelona's Passeig de Gràcia via Sants. The cheapest fares (for regional and Catalunya Express trains) cost €13.80 to an average of €20 and the journey takes one to 1½ hours.

Port Aventura

One of Spain's most popular funfair adventure parks, Port Aventura (www.portaventura.es; adult/5-12yr €44/35; ☉10am-midnight Jul-Aug, shorter hr rest of yr) lies 7km west of Tarragona. The park has plenty of spine-tingling rides and other attractions, including 'fun' rides such as the Furius Baco (in which they claim you experience the fastest acceleration of any ride in the world).

In addition to the main area, Port Aventura Park, the complex includes Caribe Aquatic Park (adult/child €24/19; ☉10am-7pm Jul-Aug, shorter hr rest of yr), a waterworld with all sorts of wet rides, including some fear-inducing waterslides with more twists and turns than a Ken Follett mystery.

Trains run to Port Aventura's own station, about a 1km walk from the site, several times a day from Tarragona (€1.70 to €10.80, seven minutes) and Barcelona (from €7.10 to €18.40, around 1½ hours). By road, take exit 35 from the AP7, or the N340 from Tarragona.

Reus & Around

POP 107, 118

Reus was, for much of the second half of the 19th century, the second-most important city in Catalonia and a major export centre of textiles and brandy. Birthplace of Gaudí, it boasts a series of Modernista mansions. The tourist office (☏977 01 06 70; http://

turisme.reus.cat; Plaça Mercadal 3; ⊙10am-8pm Mon-Sat, 10am-2pm Sun) can provide a map guiding you to 30-odd Modernista mansions around the town centre. The tourist office organises guided visits (sometimes in English and French) to some of the most interesting of these houses, for which you need to book in advance. Regular trains connect Reus with Tarragona (€9.20, 15 to 20 minutes).

About 35km northwest of Reus, above the pretty mountain village of Siurana, stand the remains of one of the last Islamic castles to fall to the reconquering Christians. To its west rise the rocky walls of the Serra de Montsant range, and the area attracts rock climbers and walkers.

Tortosa

POP 34,832

Towering over this somewhat dusty inland town is a castle complex built by the Muslims when Tortosa, which was first settled by Iberian tribes more than 2000 years ago, was on the front line between the medieval Christian and Muslim Spain.

As well as the tourist office (⊘977 44 96 48; www.turismetortosa.com; Plaça del Carrilet 1; ⊙10am-1.30pm & 4.30-7.30pm Tue-Sat, 10am-1.30pm Sun May-Oct, 10am-1.30pm & 3.30-6.30pm Tue-Sat, 11am-1.30pm Sun), there is an information office with similar hours in the Jardins del Príncep.

The old town, concentrated at the western end of the city, north of the Ebro, is watched over by the imposing Castell de la Suda, where a small medieval Arab cemetery has been unearthed and in whose grounds there now stands a fine parador (⊘977 44 44 50; d from €138; P❀❄⊛). The Gothic cathedral (Seu; guided tours adult/10-12yr €3/1; ⊙10am-1.30pm & 4.30-7pm Mon-Sat, 12.30-2pm Sun) dates back to 1347 and contains a pleasant cloister and some baroque additions. Other attractions include the Palau Episcopal and the lovely Jardins del Príncep (adult/child €3/2; ⊙10am-1.30pm & 4.30-7.30pm Mon-Sat, 10am-1.30pm Sun), which is filled with sculptures and shady trees and makes a perfect place for a stroll (although the slopes are pretty steep!).

Hostal Virginia (⊘977 44 41 86; www.ho telvirginia.net; Avinguda de la Generalitat 139; s/d €34/45; P❀❄) is a cheerful, central stop, with modern if somewhat antiseptic rooms boasting good-sized beds and cool tile floors. There's a bar downstairs. If there's no room at this inn, you'll find several other, fairly antiseptic lower-midrange hotels elsewhere on the fringes of town. For food you could do worse than tuck into one of the lunch menus (€12) at the Restaurant Los Banys (⊘977 44 36 44; Pare Cirera 5).

The train and bus stations are opposite each other on Ronda dels Docs. Trains run to/from Barcelona, Lleida and Tarragona (€6.45, one hour 10 minutes). Two to four buses run into the Delta de l'Ebre area.

Ebro Delta

The delta of the Río Ebro (Catalan: Delta de l'Ebre), formed by silt brought down by the river, sticks out 20km into the Mediterranean near Catalonia's southern border. Dotted with reedy lagoons and fringed by dune-backed beaches, this flat and exposed wetland is northern Spain's most important water-bird habitat. The migration season (October and November) sees the bird population peak, with an average of 53,000 ducks and 15,000 coots, but they are also numerous in winter and spring: 10% of all water birds wintering on the Iberian Peninsula choose to park themselves here.

Even if you're not a twitcher a visit here is worthwhile for the surreal landscapes alone. Tiny whitewashed farmhouses seem to float on tiny islands among glowing green paddy fields (which in winter turn dry and barren). It's completely unlike anywhere else in Catalonia.

Nearly half of the delta's 320 sq km is given over to rice-growing. Some 77 sq km, mostly along the coasts and around the lagoons, form the Parc Natural Delta de l'Ebre.

MOSQUITOES

The hot and waterlogged Ebro delta doesn't just attract birds in their thousands. Mosquitoes are pretty fond of the place too and on a summer evening only a fool would dare step outside without a serious coating of repellent on them. Also make sure that anywhere you stay has mosquito-proof doors and windows (or at the very least mosquito nets). In the winter you needn't worry so much.

TAKING THE BULLS BY THE HORNS

Many Catalans advertise their loathing of bullfighting – and indeed that loathing will become official from 2012 when Catalonia will ban bullfighting altogether – but some may not be aware that in the southern corner of their region, locals have indulged in their own summer bovine torment. In Amposta and neighbouring towns, people celebrate *bous capllaçats* and *bous embolats*, the former a kind of tug-of-war between a bull with ropes tied to its horns and townsfolk, the latter involving bulls running around with flaming torches attached to their horns. Denounced by animal rights groups, they are allowed by the Catalan government, which recognises the right to hold these events because of their long history and the fact that the bulls are not killed. For more on bullfighting, see p865.

The town of Deltebre is the main centre in the delta and straggles about 5km along the northern bank of the river at the centre of the delta. Deltebre's western half is called Jesús i Maria and the eastern half La Cava. Facing Deltebre on the southern bank is Sant Jaume d'Enveja. Roads criss-cross the delta to Deltebre and beyond from the towns of L'Ampolla, Amposta and Sant Carles de la Ràpita, all on the N340. Three *transbordadors* (ferries), running from early morning until nightfall, link Deltebre to Sant Jaume d'Enveja (car and passengers €3), but their days might be numbered as a bridge running between Deltebre and Sant Jaume d'Enveja was under construction at the time of research.

Sights & Activities

Early morning and evening are the best times for birdwatching, and good areas include L'Encanyissada and La Tancada lagoons and Punta de la Banya, all in the south of the delta. L'Encanyissada has two observation towers and La Tancada one (others are marked on a map you can pick up at the Centre d'Informació). La Tancada and Punta de la Banya are generally the best places to see the greater flamingos, the delta's most spectacular birds. Almost 2000 of the birds nest here, and since 1992 the delta has been one of only five places in Europe where they reproduce. Punta de la Banya is joined to the delta by a 5km sand spit with the long, sandy, and often windy and rubbish-splattered Platja de l'Eucaliptus at its northern end.

Several companies based in Deltebre run identical daily tourist boat trips (€10 per person, 1½ hours) to the mouths of the Ebro and Illa de Buda at the delta's tip. The frequency of departures depends on the season (and whether or not there are enough takers).

In El Poblenou del Delta, visit Mas de la Cuixota (☏977 26 12 25; http://ebre.info/cuixota, in Spanish; Partida de l'Encanyissada). It rents out binoculars for birdwatching and runs organised trips along the delta canals in traditional, shallow-bottom boats, or *barques de perxar*.

Sleeping & Eating

Several camping grounds are scattered about Amposta, Deltebre and the surrounding countryside, along with a sprinkling of low-key hotels and a fair few *casas rurales*. There are a few places to stay in Sant Carles de la Ràpita, a pleasant fishing town with a marina. There are simple restaurants in all the main villages.

TOP CHOICE Mas del Tancat   CASA RURAL €
(☏656 901014; www.ebreguia.com/masdeltancat, in Spanish; Camí dels Panissos; d €55; P✳❂) A converted historic farmhouse, Mas del Tancat has just four rooms with iron bedsteads, terracotta floors and a warm welcome. Sitting by the waters of the delta, it is a tranquil escape. To help you get even more back to nature there are plenty of ducks, chickens, donkeys and goats hanging out in the grounds. Excellent home-cooked evening meals are available with notice for €15; breakfast is €6. Finding this place can be a bit problematic; it's between the town of Ampara and the village of Sant Jaume d'Enveja, but you might need to call ahead for directions.

Lo Segador   CASA RURAL €
(☏636 517755; www.losegador.com, in Spanish; Carrer Major 14, El Poblenou del Delta; d/tr €45/63; P✳) A family-run, six-room rural house with broad terraces, gardens and communal kitchen area, this spot offers

simple accommodation in a whitewashed village that feels like it's just blown in from the Sahara on a desert wind.

ℹ Information

The **Centre d'Informació** (☏977 48 96 79; Carrer de Martí Buera 22, Deltebre; ☉10am-2pm & 3-7pm Mon-Sat, 10am-2pm Sun May-Sep, shorter hr rest of yr) is combined with an **Eco-museu** (admission €1.20; ☉same as Centre d'Informació), with displays describing the delta environment and an aquarium-terrarium of delta species.

There's another **information office** (☏977 48 21 81; ☉same hr) with a permanent exposition (admission €1.20) on the delta's lagoons at La Casa de Fusta, beside L'Encanyissada lagoon, 10km southwest of Deltebre. Other offices are in Sant Carles de la Ràpita, Amposta and L'Ampolla.

ℹ Getting There & Away

The delta is easiest to get to and around with your own wheels, but it is possible to reach Tortosa by bus or a train/bus combination.

Autocars Hife (www.hife.es) runs buses to Jesús i Maria and La Cava from Tortosa (€2.95, 50 minutes) up to eight times daily (twice on Saturday, Sunday and holidays) and from Amposta (€2, 30 minutes) once daily.

Aragón

Best Places to Eat

» Tiempo de Ensueño
(p396)

» La Tasca de Ana (p376)

» Restaurante Callizo
(p382)

» Casa Pascualillo (p366)

» Bodegón de Mallacán
(p382)

Best Places to Stay

» Hotel los Siete Reyes
(p382)

» Parador de Sos del Rey
Católico (p371)

» Hotel Las Torres (p366)

» La Casa del Tío
Americano (p396)

» Hotel Barosse (p375)

Why Go?

Landlocked and little-known, Aragón is one of Spain's most surprising regions. It's in Aragón that the Pyrenees take on an epic quality, from shapely peaks to deep, deep valleys where quiet rivers meander through forests and past small hamlets that seem unchanged by the passing of time. Stone-built *pueblos* such as these are an Aragonese speciality: all across Aragón, you'll find numerous candidates for the title of Spain's most beautiful villages. Connections to the past also overflow from the cities, whether in Mudéjar Teruel or Zaragoza, a city bursting with sound and fury yet replete with soaring monuments to Roman, Islamic and Christian Spain. There are also world-class activities – hiking, canyoning and skiing – for those eager to explore the region under their own steam. But Aragón's calling card is its sense of timelessness, the sort of place where Old Spain lives and breathes.

When to Go

Zaragoza

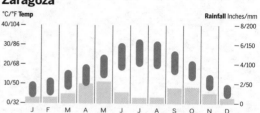

February Teruel's Fiesta Medieval returns you to the Middle Ages.	**Mid-June–early September** The best time to hike high into another world in the Aragonese Pyrenees.	**October** Zaragoza's Fiestas de Pilar combine the sacred with the city's famed love of revelry.

Zaragoza

POP 674,317

Zaragoza (Saragossa) rocks and rolls. The feisty citizens of this great city on the banks of the mighty Río Ebro make up over half of Aragón's population and they live a fairly hectic lifestyle with great tapas bars and raucous nightlife. But Zaragoza is so much more than just a city that loves to live the good life: there's also a host of historical sights spanning all the great civilisations (Roman, Islamic and Christian) that have left their indelible mark on the Spanish soul.

History

The Romans founded Caesaraugusta (from which 'Zaragoza' is derived – listen to it phonetically and you'll see what we

Aragón Highlights

❶ Hike the wilderness in the **Parque Nacional de Ordesa y Monte Perdido** (p377) in the Pyrenees

❷ Return to the medieval past in the stone-built villages of **Aínsa** (p381) and **Sos del Rey Católico** (p371) in the foothills of the Pyrenees

❸ Walk with wonder through the cobbled streets of **Albarracín** (p395) with its epic reminders of the Islamic past

❹ Hit the buzzing streets and bars of **Zaragoza** (p361) by night and visit its glorious monuments by day

❺ Savour the Mudéjar architecture and wafer-thin perfection of the best *jamón* (ham) from **Teruel** (p391)

❻ Go quietly through the beautiful Pyrenean valleys of **Echo** and **Ansó** (p372)

❼ Plunge down the canyons any way you can in **Alquézar** (p387)

ARAGÓN

mean) in 14 BC. As many as 25,000 people migrated to the city whose river traffic brought the known world to the banks of Río Ebro. The city prospered for almost three centuries, but its subsequent decline was confirmed in 472 when the city was overrun by the Visigoths. In Islamic times Zaragoza was capital of the Upper March, one of Al-Andalus' frontier territories. In 1118 it fell to Alfonso I 'El Batallador' (The Battler), ruler of the expanding Christian kingdom of Aragón, and immediately became its capital. In the centuries that followed, Zaragoza grew to become one of inland Spain's most important economic and cultural hubs and a city popular with Catholic pilgrims. Now Spain's fifth-largest city, Zaragoza's growing confidence was reflected in its successful staging of Expo 2008, which thrust the city well and truly into the international spotlight.

Sights

The great eras of the city's colourful history – Roman, Islamic and Christian – all left enduring monuments in Zaragoza. Outside high season, opening hours tend to be shorter than times listed here.

Christian Zaragoza

Basílica de Nuestra Señora del Pilar

CHURCH

(Plaza del Pilar; ☺7am-8.30pm) Brace yourself for the saintly and the solemn in this great baroque cavern of Catholicism. It was here on 2 January 40 that Santiago (St James the Apostle) is believed by the faithful to have seen the Virgin Mary descend atop a marble *pilar* (pillar). A chapel was built around the remaining pillar, followed by a series of ever-more-grandiose churches, culminating in the enormous basilica that you see today. Originally designed in 1681 by Felipe Sánchez y Herrera, it was greatly modified in the 18th century by the heavier hand of Ventura Rodríguez; the towers were not finished until the early 20th century. The exterior is another story altogether, its splendid main dome lording over a flurry of 10 minidomes, each encased in chunky blue, green, yellow and white tiles, creating a kind of rugged Byzantine effect.

The legendary **pilar** is hidden in the Capilla Santa, inside the east end of the basilica. A tiny oval-shaped portion of the *pilar* is exposed on the chapel's outer west side. A steady stream of people (with busloads of the faithful arriving at times) line up to brush lips with its polished and seamed cheek, which even popes have airkissed. Parents also line up from 1.30pm to 2pm and from 6.30pm to 7.30pm to have their babies blessed next to the Virgin. More than the architecture, these symbols of the sacred, and the devotion they inspire in the faithful, are what makes this cathedral special.

Hung from the northeast column of the Capilla Santa are two wickedly slim shells that were lobbed at the church during the civil war. They failed to explode. A miracle, said the faithful; typical Czech munitions, said the more cynical.

The basilica's finest artwork is a 16th-century alabaster altarpiece by Damián Forment. It stands at the outer west wall of the choir. Goya painted *La Reina de los Mártires* (Mary, Queen of Martyrs) in a cupola above the north aisle, outside the Sacristía de la Virgen.

A **lift** (admission €2; ⊙10am-1.30pm & 4-6.30pm Tue-Sun) whisks you most of the way up the north tower (Torre Pilar) from where you climb to a superb viewpoint over the domes and downtown Zaragoza.

La Seo
CATHEDRAL
(Plaza de la Seo; admission €4; ⊙10am-6pm Tue-Sun, closed lunchtime Sat & Sun) Dominating the eastern end of Plaza del Pilar is the Catedral de San Salvador, more popularly known as La Seo.

La Seo may lack the fame of the Basílica de Nuestra Señora del Pilar, but its interior is easily its architectural superior. Built between the 12th and 17th centuries, it displays a fabulous spread of architectural styles from Romanesque to baroque. It stands on the site of Islamic Zaragoza's main mosque (which in turn stood upon the temple of the Roman forum). The northwest facade is a Mudéjar masterpiece, deploying classic dark brickwork and colourful

If time's tight, there are four options for making the most of Zaragoza without empty-ing your wallet. Information on all of the following options is available from any of the tourist offices.

» **Zaragoza Card** (☎902 088908; www.zaragozacard.com; 24/48/72hr €15/20/24) Free entry to all sights, travel on the Tourist Bus and discounts on hotels, restaurants and car rental.

» **Tourist Bus** (Bus Turístico; ☎976 20 12 00; day/evening €7/10) Hop-on, hop-off sight-seeing bus that does two 75-minute city circuits daily in summer, less frequently the rest of the year.

» **Guided Tours** (Visitas Guíadas; ☎976 20 12 00; walking/bike tours €5/10) Book through the tourist office. Walking tours at 4pm or 6pm Saturday and bike tours at 10.30am Sunday.

» **BiziZaragoza** (☎902 319931; www.bizizaragoza.com; subscription €6) Public bicycle rental from numerous pick-up and drop-off points around town.

ceramic decoration in eye-pleasing geomet-ric patterns. All the chapels are framed by beautiful stonework and ring the changes from the eerie solemnity of the Capilla de San Marcos to the glorious Renaissance facade of the central Christ Chapel and the exquisite 15th-century high altarpiece in polychrome alabaster.

The admission price includes entry to La Seo's Museo de Tapices (☺10am-8.30pm Tue-Sun), which has an impressive collection of 14th- to 17th-century Flemish and French tapestries.

Iglesia de San Pablo   CHURCH
(cnr Calles de San Pablo & Miguel de Ara; ☺9am-1pm) This pretty church has a delicate 14th-century Mudéjar tower and an early-16th-century *retablo* (altarpiece) by Damián Forment. It's 200m west of Av de César Augusto.

Roman Zaragoza

The four museums dedicated to Zaragoza's Roman past form part of what's known as the Ruta de Caesaraugusta; a combined ticket costs €7.

Museo del Foro de Caesaraugusta
ROMAN MUSEUM
(Plaza de la Seo 2; admission €2.50; ☺9am-8.30pm Tue-Sat, 10am-2pm Sun) The trapezoid building on Plaza de la Seo is the entrance to an excellent reconstruction of part of Ro-man Caesaraugusta's forum, now well be-low ground level.

The remains of porticoes, shops, a great *cloaca* (sewer) system, and a limited collec-tion of artefacts dating from between 14 BC

and about AD 15 are on display. Sections of lead pipes used to channel water to the city demonstrate the Romans' genius for engi-neering. An interesting audiovisual show, presented on the hour in Spanish, breathes life into things, and audio guides (€2) are available.

Museo del Teatro de Caesaraugusta
ROMAN THEATRE, MUSEUM
(Calle de San Jorge 12; admission €3.50; ☺9am-8.30pm Tue-Sat, 9am-1.30pm Sun) Discovered during the excavation of a building site in 1972, the ruins of Zaragoza's Roman theatre are the focus of this interesting museum; the theatre once seated 6000 spectators. Great efforts have been made to help visi-tors reconstruct the edifice's former splen-dour, including evening projections of a virtual performance (admission €1; ☺10pm Fri & Sat) on the stage; get there early to en-sure a place. The exhibit culminates in a boardwalk tour through the theatre itself. The theatre is visible from the surrounding streets.

Other Roman Remains   ROMAN MUSEUMS
Just across Plaza de San Bruno from La Seo is the absorbing Museo del Puerto Fluvial (Plaza de San Bruno 8; admission €2.50; ☺9am-8.30pm Tue-Sat, 10am-2pm Sun), which displays the Roman city's river-port in-stallations. There's a quaint but enjoyable audiovisual program every half-hour. The Museo de las Termas Públicas (Calle San Juan y San Pedro 3-7; admission €2.50; ☺9am-8.30pm Tue-Sat, 10am-2pm Sun) houses the old Roman baths.

Islamic Zaragoza

Aljafería — ISLAMIC PALACE

(Calle de los Diputados; adult/under 12yr €3/free, free Sun; ☉10am-2pm Sat-Wed, 4.30-8pm Mon-Wed & Fri & Sat) La Aljafería is Spain's finest Islamic-era edifice outside Andalucía. It's not in the league of Granada's Alhambra or Córdoba's Mezquita, but it's nonetheless a glorious monument.

The Aljafería was built as a pleasure palace for Zaragoza's Islamic rulers, chiefly in the 11th century. After the city passed into Christian hands in 1118, Zaragoza's Christian rulers made alterations. In the 1490s the Reyes Católicos (Catholic Monarchs), Fernando and Isabel, tacked on their own palace, whereafter the Aljafería fell into decay. From the 1940s to 1990s restoration was carried out, and in 1987 Aragón's regional parliament, the Cortes de Aragón, was established here.

Inside the main gate, cross the rather dull introductory courtyard into a second, the **Patio de Santa Isabel**, once the central courtyard of the Islamic palace. Here you're confronted by the delicate interwoven arches typical of the geometric mastery of Islamic architecture. Opening off the stunning northern porch is a small, octagonal **oratorio** (prayer room), with a magnificent horseshoe-arched doorway leading into its *mihrab* (prayer niche indicating the direction of Mecca). The finely chiselled floral motifs, Arabic inscriptions from the Quran and a pleasingly simple cupola are fine examples of Islamic art.

Moving upstairs, you pass through rooms of the **Palacio Mudéjar**, added by Christian rulers in the 12th to 14th centuries, then to the Catholic Monarchs' **palace**, which, as though by way of riposte to the Islamic finery below, contains some exquisite Mudéjar coffered ceilings, especially in the lavish **Salón del Trono** (Throne Room).

Guided tours (☉in English 10am Jul & Aug, in Spanish 10.30am, 11.30am, 12.30pm, 4.30pm, 5.30pm & 6.30pm year-round) lasting 50 minutes run throughout the day and are included in the admission price.

Other Sights

FREE La Lonja — GALLERY

(Plaza del Pilar; ☉10am-1.30pm & 5-8.30pm Tue-Sat, 10am-1.30pm Sun) Now an exhibition hall, this finely proportioned Renaissance-style building, the second building east of the basilica, was constructed in the 16th century as a trading exchange. The coloured medallions on its exterior depict kings of Aragón, but the soaring columns rising to an extraordinary ceiling are the standout features. La Lonja is the site for a full calendar of temporary exhibitions.

FREE Museo de Zaragoza — MUSEUM

(Plaza de los Sitios 6; ☉10am-2pm & 5-8pm Tue-Sat, 10am-2pm Sun) Devoted to archaeology and fine arts, the city museum displays artefacts from prehistoric to Islamic times with some exceptional mosaics from Roman Cesaraugusta. The upper floor contains 15 paintings by Goya and more than two dozen of his etchings. It's 400m south of the Teatro Romano.

FREE Museo Camón Aznar — MUSEUM

(Calle de Espoz y Mina 23; ☉10am-2pm & 5-9pm Tue-Sat, 10am-2pm Sun) This eclectic collection of Spanish art through the ages features a room of Goya etchings (on the top floor) and half a dozen paintings attributed to El Greco. It spreads over the three storeys of the Palacio de los Pardo, a Renaissance mansion.

FREE Patio de la Infanta — ART GALLERY

(Calle San Ignacio de Loyola 16; ☉8.30am-2pm & 6-8.30pm Mon-Fri, from 11am Sat, 11am-1.30pm Sun) This exhibition space houses the Ibercaja bank's collection of paintings (with big names such as Goya regularly on show), displayed in a lovely plateresque (15th- and 16th-century Spanish baroque) courtyard. It's 600m south of Plaza de España.

Museo de Pablo Gargallo — ART GALLERY

(Plaza de San Felipe 3; admission €3.50; ☉9am-8.30pm Tue-Sat, 9am-2pm Sun) Within the wonderfully restored 17th-century Palacio Argillo is a representative display of sculptures by Pablo Gargallo (1881-1934), probably Aragón's most gifted artistic son after Goya.

★ Festivals & Events

Cincomarzada — HISTORY FIESTA

Every 5 March, Zaragozans commemorate the 1838 ousting of Carlist troops by a feisty populace. Thousands head for Parque Tio Jorge, north of the Ebro, for concerts, games, grilled sausages and wine.

Fiestas del Pilar — CITY FESTIVAL

Zaragoza's biggest event is a week of full-on celebrations (religious and otherwise) peaking on 12 October, the Día de Nuestra Señora del Pilar.

🛌 Sleeping

TOP CHOICE **Hotel Las Torres**　　　HOTEL €€
(Hotel Nastasi Basic ZGZ; ☎976 39 42 50; www.nastasibasiczgzhotel.com; Plaza del Pilar 11; s/d incl breakfast from €65/75; ❄️🖥️🛜) This is easily Zaragoza's best place to stay. The rooms are designer cool with dazzling white furnishings and daring wallpaper and they're not averse to the odd chandelier in the midst of all this modern chic. The bathrooms have hydromassage showers, and the views of the square and basilica from the balconies in most rooms are simply stunning. It also has a spa in the basement.

Hotel San Valero　　　HOTEL €
(☎976 29 86 21; www.hotelsanvalero.com; Calle de la Manifestación 27; d €40-48; ❄️🛜) It's difficult to believe the prices here. Centrally located, the rooms have a designer feel and while some could be larger, the value is unimpeachable. In short, it's a boutique hotel feel for *hostal* (budget hotel) prices.

Sabinas　　　APARTMENTS €
(☎976 20 47 10; www.sabina.es; Calle de Alfonso I 43; d/apt from €58/68; 🅿️❄️🛜) Apartments with a kitchen and sitting room styled with a contemporary look and a location a few steps off Plaza del Pilar make this a terrific option. The bathrooms are lovely and the price is extraordinarily good considering the location and size of the rooms. It also has standard doubles with a microwave.

Hostal el Descanso　　　HOSTAL €
(☎976 29 17 41; Calle de San Lorenzo 2; s/d without bathroom €20/30) This welcoming family-run place combines a terrific location overlooking a pretty plaza near the Roman theatre with simple, bright rooms with comfortable mattresses. It adds up to one of the best budget choices in town.

Hotel Sauce　　　HOTEL €€
(☎976 20 50 50; www.hotelsauce.com; Calle de Espoz y Mina 33; s/d €59/75; 🅿️❄️🛜) This small hotel has good rooms with a mix of styles from traditional and cosy to pastel tones and a modern, classy look. Bookings are advisable. Breakfast costs €7.50.

Albergue Juvenil de Zaragoza　　　HOSTEL €
(Zaragoza Hostel; ☎976 28 20 43; www.alberguezaragoza.com; Calle de los Predicadores 70; dm incl breakfast from €18, s/d €20/40; 🖥️) This dazzling new hostel opened in May 2008 and has super-new everything, save for some lovely original architectural features in the basement bar. Free breakfast, internet access and lockers are among the highlights. There's live flamenco most Thursday nights, live Jazz Sunday night and live acts most Friday and Saturday nights after 10pm.

Pensión Holgado　　　HOSTAL €
(☎976 43 20 74; www.pensionholgado.com, in Spanish; 3rd fl, Calle del Conde de Aranda 126; d with/without bathroom €39/33) Although slightly removed from the centre, this excellent *hostal* is handy for the Aljafería and the rooms are simple and well tended; the best are those with balconies on the 5th floor. Depending on who you get at reception, service is not Zaragoza's warmest. To get here, take bus 51 (€1) to Plaza del Portillo from the bus or train station.

Hotel Río Arga　　　HOTEL €€
(☎976 39 90 65; www.hotelrioarga.es, in Spanish; Calle Contamina 20; s/d from €43/60; 🅿️❄️🛜) In a quiet location, yet ideal for all central needs, there are comfy rooms here. Most of the rooms have been renovated with flat-screen TVs and a modern look.

🍴 Eating

The tangle of lanes in El Tubo, immediately north of Plaza de España, is home to one of Spain's richest gatherings of tapas bars. Other good areas to try include on or close to Plaza de Santa Marta and towards the southern end of Calle Heroísmo (located southeast of the city centre).

Casa Pascualillo　　　TAPAS €€
(Calle de la Libertad 5; meals €15-25; ⏲️Tue-Sat, lunch Sun) When *Metropoli,* the respected weekend magazine of *El Mundo* newspaper, set out to find the best 50 tapas bars in Spain, it's no surprise that Casa Pascualillo made the final cut. The bar groans under the weight of every tapas variety imaginable, with seafood and meat in abundance; the house speciality is El Pascualillo, a 'small' *bocadillo* (filled roll) of *jamón,* mushrooms and onion.

Taberna Doña Casta　　　TAPAS €€
(Calle Estébanes 6; meals €15-25; ⏲️Tue-Sun) If you like your tapas without too many frills, this enduringly popular and informal *taberna* (tavern) could become your culinary home in Zaragoza. The bottle of wine and six tapas for €23 is a terrific way to meet all your gastronomic needs at a reasonable price. Its specialities are *croquetas* (croquettes) and egg-based dishes.

Blasón del Tubo TAPAS €€
(Calle de Blasón Aragonés; meals €20-30; ⊗Wed-Sun, lunch Mon) Run by the same owners as Casa Pascualillo, Blasón del Tubo takes a more contemporary approach to tapas and there's a fine upstairs restaurant. There's a small selection of innovative tapas lined up along the bar, as well as a lengthy list of à la carte choices in the restaurant.

Casa Lac ARAGONESE, TAPAS €€
(☑976 29 90 25; Calle de los Mártires 12; meals €30-35; ⊗Wed-Mon) The grand old lady of the Zaragoza dining scene, Casa Lac pays homage to the 19th century (it opened in 1825) with its seigneurial decor and impeccable service. The food revolves around Aragonese staples, although the lamb carpaccio with foie gras shows it's not averse to a little experimentation. Dine upstairs with the who's who of Zaragoza society, or downstairs in the more informal tapas bar, where it also serves *raciones* (large tapas serving, €8 to €15).

La Miguería TAPAS €
(Calle Estébanes 4; migas €5-10, raciones €6-19; ⊗Mon-Sat) Who would have thought you could do so much with *migas* (breadcrumbs)... La Miguería serves this filling Aragonese quick-fix food in more than a dozen varieties, including drenched in olive oil, and topped with sardines and foie gras. It opens at 7.30pm, which may help those struggling to cope with late Spanish dinner times.

El Rincón de Aragón ARAGONESE €€
(☑976 20 11 63; Calle de Santiago 3-5; meals €20-35) The decor here is basic and the food stripped down to its essence, but the eating is top-notch and ideal for finding out why people get excited about Aragonese cooking. One house speciality is the *ternasco asado con patatas a la pobre* (roasted suckling lamb ribs with 'poor man's potatoes'). If you're feeling hungry, this and other local dishes usually appear on the four-course *menú Aragonés* (€19.90), which is a great order. The restaurant is in the covered lane between Calle de Santiago and Plaza del Pilar.

La Reserva MODERN SPANISH, TAPAS €€
(☑976 22 50 80; Calle de Cádiz 10; meals €15-30) Vying for attention with numerous international restaurants along Calle de Cádiz, La Reserva is always full and deservedly so. It serves tapas (from €3), *raciones* (€6.50 to €10), rice dishes (€15 to €20, minimum two

The kitchens and tables of Aragón are, like so many in inland Spain, dominated by meat. That's not to say you won't find fish, seafood and other Spanish staples. It's just that the *aragoneses* (people from Aragón) really get excited when offered *jamón de Teruel* (cured ham from Teruel province, especially around Calamocha), *jarretes* (hock of ham or shanks) and above all *ternasco* (suckling lamb, usually served as a steak or ribs with potatoes). The latter is so beloved that there's even a website (www.iloveternascodearagon.com, in Spanish) devoted to the dish with recipes and general adulation. Other popular dishes include *conejo a la montañesa* (rabbit mountain-style), *migas* (breadcrumbs, usually cooked with cured meats), *cardo* (cardoons) and *caracoles* (snails). Aragón also has five recognised wine-growing regions, the best-known of which is Somontano (see p388).

people) and warm salads (from €14.50). It's all very creative and contemporary, and the atmosphere informal. To get here, head south from Plaza de España for about 200m and turn right into Calle de Cádiz.

Churrería la Fama CHURROS €
(Calle Prudencio 25; 3 churros €2.50; ⊗8am-1pm & 5.30-9.30pm) La Fama, tucked away off Calle de Alfonso I, is a good spot for fresh *churros* (long, deep-fried doughnuts) and chocolate to go with morning coffee; if you've been out all night, being here when it opens is a great way to begin (or end) your day.

Casa Juanico TAPAS €
(Calle de Santa Cruz 21; tapas from €2.50) Everything from the best *jamón* to rice- or cod-based tapas.

Manjares TAPAS €
(Calle Estébanes 7; meals €15-20; ⊗Tue-Sun) Promises 'pleasures in miniature' and delivers *tostadas* (buttered toasts with a topping), *croquetas* and creative tapas.

La Calzorras TAPAS €
(Plaza de San Pedro Nolasco; meals €15-20) Plaza tables and tempting larger-than-tapas specialities for around €4.50.

Sagardi BASQUE TAPAS €
(Plaza de España 6; meals €15-20) *Pintxos* (Basque tapas; €2.50) line up along the bar San Sebastián–style with pleasant outdoor tables.

Drinking

Calle del Temple, southwest of Plaza del Pilar, is the spiritual home of Zaragoza's roaring nightlife. This is where the city's considerable student population heads out to drink and there are more bars lined up along this street than anywhere else in Aragón. It's the sort of street that you can wander down as late as 11pm and wonder if the action has moved elsewhere – no, it hasn't yet arrived and doesn't really get going until well after midnight. On this street, Bar Corto Maltés (Calle del Temple 23), El Jardín del Temple (Calle del Temple 18) and La Recogida (Calle del Temple 16) are always full and *probably* our favourites, while La Cucaracha (Calle del Temple 25) is great for well-priced cocktails.

Gran Café de Zaragoza CAFE
(Calle de Alfonso I 25; breakfasts from €2.50; ⊗8.30am-10pm Sun-Thu, 9am-2.30am Fri & Sat) This Zaragoza institution evokes the grand old cafes of Spain's past with a gold-plated facade and an old-style civility in the service. That said, it's a place to be seen by young and old alike and the elegant salon is a good place for morning coffee or breakfast.

Quo Vadis ROCK, LOUNGE BAR
(Plaza del Carmen 11; ⊗7am-1am Mon-Thu, 7am-3.30am Fri, 5pm-3.30am Sat, 5-11pm Sun) You don't need to be as sleek and cool as the bar staff or as shiny as the Modernista decor at this smart but easy-going bar to feel welcome here. There's a great friendly mood to go with the background music that ranges from 1970s and '80s to indie, but never too far from rock. It opens during the day for breakfast and snacks. To get here, walk southwest along Paseo de la Independencia, then turn right onto Calle de Cádiz and follow it to the end.

Rock & Blues Café MUSIC BAR
(Cuatro de Agosto 5-9; ⊗3pm-2.30am, later on weekends) Rock 'n' roll paraphernalia and homage to the likes of Jimi Hendrix set the tone for the music and style of this long-standing favourite. There's live pop, rock or blues on Thursdays at 10pm.

Zen Gong Café LOUNGE BAR
(Calle de Alfonso I 13; ⊗7am-2am Sun-Thu, 8am-4.30am Fri & Sat) This place wouldn't look out of place in Madrid or Barcelona, with stylish decor, weird-and-wonderful lighting and a breadth of atmospheres from breakfast cafe to lunchtime wine bar and then on into pop, house and even drag acts by night.

Café Praga CAFE
(Plaza de la Santa Cruz 13; ⊗9am-1am Mon-Thu, 10am-3am Sat & Sun) One of Zaragoza's favourite cafes, Praga has a front-row seat on one of the city's most agreeable plazas and there's occasional live music in the main bar.

☆ Entertainment

La Casa del Loco LIVE MUSIC
(www.lacasadelloco.com, in Spanish; Calle Mayor 10-12; live music free-€20; ⊗9pm-5.30am Thu-Sat) Hugely popular, especially when there's a live band playing. It's mostly rock with a mixed young-retro crowd. After the bands go home, DJs ensure that things get really lively until late.

Oasis NIGHTCLUB
(Calle de Boggiero 28; cover €10; ⊗from midnight Fri & Sat) A few streets west of the old centre, Oasis began life long ago as a variety theatre. It's currently going strong as a club with good techno house, but with a bit of 'anything goes'.

ⓘ Information

Municipal Tourist Office (www.zaragozaturismo.es) main office (☏976 20 12 00; Plaza del Pilar; ⊗9am-9pm mid-Jun–mid-Oct, 10am-8pm mid-Oct–mid-Jun); Torreón de la Zuda (Glorieta de Pío XII; ⊗10am-2pm & 4.30-8pm Mon-Sat, 10am-2pm Sun); Estación Intermodal Delicias (☏976 32 44 68; Avenida de Navarra; ⊗9am-9pm)

Oficina de Turismo de Aragón (☏976 28 21 81; www.turismodearagon.com; Avenida de César Augusto 25; ⊗9am-2pm & 5-8pm Mon-Fri, from 10am Sat & Sun) Around 500m southwest along Av de César Augusto from the western end of Plaza de César Augusto.

ⓘ Getting There & Away
Air

The **Zaragoza-Sanjurjo airport** (☏976 71 23 00), west of the city, has direct **Ryanair** (www.ryanair.com) flights to/from London (Stansted), Brussels (Charleroi), Paris (Beauvais), Dusseldorf (Weeze), Bologna, Rome (Ciampino), Milan, Málaga and Alicante. **Iberia** (www.iberia.es) and

Air Europa (www.aireuropa.com) also operate a small number of domestic and international routes.

Bus

Dozens of bus lines fan out across Spain from the bus station attached to the Estación Intermodal Delicias train station. The more useful companies include:

Alosa (⌖902 210700; www.alosa.es, in Spanish) Up to eight buses to/from Huesca (€6.30, 1½ hours) and Jaca (€13.15, 2¼ hours).

ALSA (⌖902 422242; www.alsa.es) Frequent daily buses to/from Madrid (from €14.47, 3¾ hours) and Barcelona (€13.71, 3¾ hours).

Train

Zaragoza's futuristic, if rather impersonal, **Estación Intermodal Delicias** (Calle Rioja 33) is connected by almost hourly high-speed AVE services to Madrid (€58.20, 1½ hours, approximately 10 daily) and Barcelona (€64.20, from 1½ hours). There are also services to Valencia (€28.60, 4½ hours, three daily), Huesca (from €5.70, one hour, nine daily), Jaca (€11.80, 3½ hours, three daily) and Teruel (€15.90, two hours, four daily).

❶ Getting Around

Airport Buses (⌖902 360065; €1.60) run to/from Paseo María Agustín 7 – which crosses Avenida de César Augusto around 500m southwest of Plaza de España – via the bus/train station every half hour (every hour on Sunday).

Buses 34 and 51 travel between the city centre and the Estación Intermodal Delicias; the former travels along the Avenida de César Augusto.

South of Zaragoza

The A23 south towards Teruel passes through Campo de Cariñena, one of Aragón's premier wine regions. Just off the motorway, the Ermita de la Fuente in Muel has some fine paintings of saints by the young Goya. If you take the slower but more tranquil N234 to Cariñena, bodegas (wine cellars) line the main road, and in Cariñena there's a good Museo del Vino (Wine Museum; Camino de la Platera 7; admission €2; ☉10am-2pm & 4-6pm, closed Sun afternoon & Mon).

Some 23km east of Cariñena along the A220 lies the small village of Fuendetodos, where Francisco José de Goya y Lucientes (Goya) began his days in 1746. The Casa Natal de Goya (Calle Zuloaga 3; incl Museo del Grabado de Goya €3; ☉11am-2pm & 4-7pm Tue-Sun) stayed in his family until the early 20th century, when renowned artist Ignacio Zu-

loaga bought it. Down the road, the Museo del Grabado de Goya (☉11am-2pm & 4-7pm Tue-Sun) contains an important collection of the artist's engravings. Up to four buses by Autocares Samar Buil (www.samar.es, in Spanish) daily head to Fuendetodos (€5.90, one hour) from Zaragoza's bus station.

A further 18km east, the twin towns of Belchite are an eloquent reminder of the destruction wrought in the Spanish Civil War. The ruins of the old town, which have been replaced by an adjacent new village, stand as a silent memorial to a brutal tug-of-war for possession of Aragón between Republican and Nationalist forces during the war. Buses (€4.75, 45 minutes) arrive from Zaragoza three times daily.

West of Zaragoza

TARAZONA
POP 11,211

The quiet, serpentine streets of Tarazona's old town are an evocative reminder of the layout of a medieval Spanish town. It has more than enough monuments to repay a stop.

◉ Sights

A signposted walking route takes you around the twisting cobbled ways of the medieval 'high part' of the town, north of Río Queiles, and meandering through these laneways is the undoubted highlight of Tarazona. Focal points for your wanderings include the extravagant facade of the Ayuntamiento and the slender Mudéjar tower of the Iglesia de Santa María Magdalena. There are splendid views from the church steps and the Palacio Episcopal (Bishop's Palace), next door, was a fortified Islamic palace. Tarazona's medieval judería (Jewish quarter) is also exceptionally well preserved. Throughout, the high balconied projections of the 'hanging houses' are remarkable.

In the lower town Tarazona's cathedral is a fetching concoction of Romanesque, Gothic, Mudéjar and Renaissance styles; it's currently closed to the public. Nearby, the octagonal Plaza de Toros Vieja (Old Bullring) is made up of 32 houses built in the 1790s complete with ringside window seats.

🛏 Sleeping & Eating

Hostal Santa Agueda   HOSTAL **€€**
(⌖976 64 00 54; www.santaagueda.com; Calle Visconti 26; s €37-48, d €59-70; ❋🔊) Just off Plaza San Francisco, this 200-year-old

home has lovely rooms with wooden beams and a charming proprietor. The little breakfast room is a glorious shrine to Raquel Meller, Aragón's queen of popular song during the early 20th century. Street-facing rooms cost the most and some have a sofa; breakfast costs €5.

Hotel Condes de Visconti   HOTEL €€
(☏976 64 49 08; www.condesdevisconti.com, in Spanish; Calle Visconti 15; d €68-89, ste €88-130; ✳@P) Beautiful rooms, mostly with colourful individual decor, plus a preserved Renaissance patio, make this 16th-century former palace a fine stopover. It also has a cafe and good old-fashioned service.

Hostal Palacete de los Arcedianos
HOSTEL €
(☏976 64 23 03; www.palacetearcedianos.com, in Spanish; Plaza de los Arcedianos 1; s/d €28/38) Up in the *judería,* this good budget choice offers unfussy, comfy rooms in a pleasant family-run place.

El Patio   TAPAS €
(Calle de Marrodán 16; meals €15-20; ☉10am-midnight) A local favourite, this tapas bar, behind the back wall of the Hostal Palacete de los Arcedianos, has loads of small dishes lined up along the bar.

ⓘ Information
Tourist office (☏976 64 00 74; www.tarazona.es, in Spanish; Plaza San Francisco 1; ☉9am-1.30pm & 4.30-7pm Mon-Fri, 10am-1.30pm & 4.30-7pm Sat & Sun) Organises Spanish-language guided tours of the city (one-/two-hour €3/5; 5pm Saturday, noon Sunday).

ⓘ Getting There & Away
Up to seven **Therpasa** (☏976 64 11 00; www.therpasa.es, in Spanish) buses run daily to/from Zaragoza's Estación Intermodal Delicias (€6.51, 1¼ hours) and Soria (€5.09, one hour).

AROUND TARAZONA
Backed by the often snowcapped Sierra del Moncayo, the fortified, Cistercian Monasterio de Veruela (admission €1.80; ☉10.30am-8.30pm), founded in the 12th century, looks more like a Castilian castle than a monastery. The rather stern Gothic church is flanked by a charming cloister, which has a lower Gothic level surmounted by a Renaissance upper gallery. There's a good wine museum within the complex. The monastery is 13km southeast of Tarazona and 1km from Vera de Moncayo. Two of Therpasa's daily Zaragoza–Tarazona buses stop in Vera itself (one on

Sunday); the others stop at the Vera turn-off on the N122, 4km from the monastery.

MONASTERIO DE PIEDRA
(☏902 196052; park & monastery adult/child €13/9.50, monastery adult €7.50; ☉park 9am-8pm, monastery 10.15am-1.15pm & 3.15-7.15pm) This one-time Cistercian monastery, 28km southwest of Calatayud, dates from the 13th century but was abandoned in the 1830s. Subsequent owners laid out the ground as a formal wooded park full of caves and waterfalls, the latter fed by Río Piedra. It's a wonderful place to spend a day with kids, although it has something of a theme park's crassness on summer weekends. Incorporated into the complex is the Hotel Monasterio de Piedra (☏976 84 90 11; www.monasteriopiedra.com; s/d from €73/113; ▣).

On Tuesday, Thursday, Saturday and Sunday (or daily in summer), Automóviles Zaragoza runs a 9am bus from Zaragoza to the monastery (€13, 2½ hours) via Calatayud, returning at 5pm.

THE NORTH (THE PYRENEES)

Leaving behind Zaragoza's parched flatlands, a hint of green tinges the landscape and there's a growing anticipation of very big mountains somewhere up ahead. And they are big. The Aragonese Pyrenees boast several peaks well over the 3000m mark and they're the most dramatic and rewarding on the Spanish side of the range. Viewed from the south their crenellated ridges fill the northern horizon wherever you turn and their valleys offer magnificent scenery, stunning stone-built villages, several decent ski resorts and great walking.

🏃 Activities
Some 6000km of trails, both long-distance trails (Grandes Recorridos; GR) and short-distance trails (Pequeños Recorridos; PR), are marked all across Aragón. The coast-to-coast GR11 traverses the most spectacular Aragón Pyrenees.

The optimum time for walking is mid-June to early September, though the more popular parks and paths can become crowded in midsummer. The weather can be unpredictable at any time of the year, so walkers should be prepared for extreme conditions at all times.

Aragón is one of Spain's premier ski destinations. The major ski stations are as follows:

» **Candanchú** (www.candanchu.com, in Spanish) 42km of widely varied pistes, 28km north of Jaca; was used for the 2007 European Youth Olympic Winter Sports Festival.

» **Astún** (www.astun.com, in Spanish) Also 42km of pistes mostly for experienced skiers, 3km east of Candanchú.

» **Panticosa** (www.panticosa-loslagos.com, in Spanish) At the confluence of two pretty valleys, the runs aren't Aragón's most challenging; the 2km-long Mazaranuala run is an exception; accessible from the A136 north of Sabiñago.

» **Formigal** (www.formigal.com) A regular host for ski competitions, Formigal has 57km of ski runs and 22 lifts; accessible from the A136 north of Sabiñago.

» **Cerler & Ampriu** (www.cerler.com, in Spanish) Cerler sits at 1500m 6km southeast of Benasque, while Ampriu is at 1900m 8km beyond Cerler; together they boast 45 runs totalling 52km. A bus service connects Benasque and the ski stations during ski season.

Dotted throughout the mountains are several mountain *refugios* (refuges). Some are staffed and serve meals, while others are empty shacks providing shelter only. At holiday times staffed *refugios* are often full, so unless you've booked ahead, be prepared to camp. The **Federación Aragonesa de Montañismo** (FAM; ☑976 22 79 71; www.fam.es, in Spanish; 4th fl, Calle Albareda 7, Zaragoza) in Zaragoza can provide information and a FAM card will get you substantial discounts on *refugio* stays. To make reservations in *refugios* and *albergues* (refuges), try www.alberguesyrefugiosdearagon.com (in Spanish).

The Aragonese publisher Prames produces the best maps for walkers.

Sos del Rey Católico

POP 690 / ELEV 625M

If Sos del Rey Católico were in Tuscany, it would be a world-famous hill town. Put simply, it's one of Aragón's most beautiful villages. Sos, as the village is universally known, lies 55km west of Jaca. Its old medieval town is a glorious maze of twisting, cobbled lanes that wriggle between dark stone houses with deeply overhung eaves.

Sos has historical significance to go with its beauty: born here in 1452 was the other half of one of the most formidable double acts in history, Fernando II of Aragón. He and his wife, Isabel I of Castilla, became known as the Reyes Católicos (Catholic Monarchs). Together they conquered the last Islamic kingdom of Granada and united Spain.

◉ Sights

The best way to experience Sos is to simply wander to get lost. The keep of the **Castillo de la Peña Feliciano** crowns the hilltop with fine views out over the rooftops and surrounding countryside, and the Gothic **Iglesia de San Esteban** (admission €2; ◷10am-1pm & 3.30-5.30pm) below it, with a weathered Romanesque portal, has a deliciously gloomy crypt with terrific frescoes and huge wooden birds as light-holders.

Fernando is said to have been born in the **Casa Palacio de Sada**, now containing an interpretive centre (adult/child €2.60/1.50, incl tour of village €4/2), with fine exhibits on the history of Sos and the life of the king.

🛌 Sleeping & Eating

Parador de Sos del Rey Católico

HOTEL €€

(☑948 88 80 11; www.parador.es; Calle Arquitecto Sainz de Vicuña 1; d €90-138; ◷closed Jan-mid-Feb; P❋🐾) A place that might just have pleased Los Reyes themselves, this grand building blends in perfectly with the stone-built buildings of Sos. The service is faultless and there's a terrific restaurant (set menus €25 to €50). Some rooms have fine village and mountain views.

El Peirón Hotel

HOTEL €€

(☑948 88 82 83; www.elpeiron.com, in Spanish; Calle Mayor 24; s/d incl breakfast from €70/80; ❋🐾) A welcome addition to Sos' already terrific accommodation scene, El Peirón occupies a lovely 17th-century Sos house and the rooms have exposed stone walls and are tastefully designed without being overdone; the bathrooms have hydromassage showers.

Ruta del Tiempo
HOTEL €€

(☏948 88 82 95; www.rutadeltiempo.es, in Spanish; Calle Larraldía 1; s incl breakfast €50, d €70-107; ※) This charming family-run place next to the central Plaza de la Villa has rooms on the 1st floor themed around three Aragonese kings, while the four 2nd-floor rooms have decorations dedicated to four different continents. They're all good but 'Asia' and 'Africa' are the largest and best rooms.

Albergue Juvenil
YOUTH HOSTEL €

(☏948 88 84 80; www.alberguedesos.com, in Spanish; Calle de las Encinas; dm under/over 26yr €15/17.50) Enjoy life in a restored medieval tower in superb modern conditions at this excellent hostel that has bright, stylish decor. Free bicycle rental is available and meals are served.

As Bruixas
GUEST HOUSE, ARAGONESE FUSION €€

(☏948 88 84 15; www.asbruixas.com, in Spanish; Calle Mayor 25; d/ste €60/70; ※) Named 'The Witches' by its charming management, this terrific place has three rooms offering a refreshing blend of vivid style and comfort, with plump mattresses, gleaming bathtubs and bohemian objects fished out of thrift shops. Its similarly postmodern dining room (meals €30 to €35) offers cuisine that gives traditional ingredients a fresh twist.

Hostal las Coronas
HOSTAL €€

(☏948 88 84 08; www.hostallascoronas.com, in Spanish; Calle Pons Sorolla 2; s/d from €48/60) Run by the friendly Fernando, this *hostal* has attractive rooms with the barest hints of character and those with balconies overlooking the plaza are lovely. The downstairs bar serves *bocadillos* (€5 to €7), tapas (€3) and *raciones* (from €7).

La Cocina del Principal
ARAGONESE €€

(☏948 88 83 48; Calle Mayor 17; meals €30-35; ☉Tue-Sat, lunch Sun) Outside of the hotel restaurants, this is the best restaurant in town, with carefully prepared local cooking, including snails and *jarretes* (hock of ham or shanks).

🛍 Shopping

Morrico Fino
DELICATESSEN

(Calle Mayor 14; ☉10.30am-2.30pm & 5-9pm) Tiny shops selling regional food products (especially wines, cheeses and cured meats) are found hidden in Sos' lanes and this place is a fine example of the genre.

ℹ Information

Tourist Office (☏948 88 85 24; Plaza Hispanidad; ☉10am-2pm & 4-8pm) Runs guided tours of the village on weekends.

ℹ Getting There & Away

A **Gómez** (☏976 67 55 29) bus departs Zaragoza (1½ hours, €9) for Sos at 7pm Monday to Friday. It returns from Sos at 7am.

Around Sos del Rey Católico

From just north of Sos, the engaging A1601 begins its 34km-long snaking journey west and then northwest en route to the N240. It passes the pretty villages of Navardún and Urriés, before climbing over the Sierra de Peña Musera and down to the gorgeous abandoned village of Ruesta. The final stretch traverses past some unusual rock formations and wheat fields with fine views of the hilltop village of Milanos away to the east.

Valles de Echo & Ansó

The verdant Echo and Ansó valleys are mountain magic at its best, beginning with gentle climbs through the valleys and the accumulating charms of old stone villages punctuating slopes of dense mixed woods of beech, pine, rowan, elm and hazel. As the valleys narrow to the north, 2000m-plus peaks rise triumphantly at their heads. Go quietly through these beautiful valleys; they encourage a gentle touch.

A bus to Jaca leaves Ansó at 6.30am, Siresa at 6.53am and Echo at 7am, Monday to Saturday, returning from Jaca at 6.50pm. A good road links Ansó and Echo, a distance of about 12km.

ECHO (HECHO)
POP 600 / ELEV 833M

Lovely Echo, the biggest village in the valley, is an attractive warren of solid stone houses with steep roofs and flower-decked balconies.

The helpful tourist office (☏974 37 55 05, 974 37 50 02; www.valledehecho.net, in Spanish; Carretera Oza; ☉10am-1.30pm & 5.30-7pm Fri & Sat, 10am-1pm Sun) also contains the small Museo de Arte Contemporáneo, a basement art gallery of changing exhibitions.

Alongside is the Museo de Escultura al Aire Libre, a hillside sculpture park. At the heart of the village is the endearing Museo Etnológico Casa Mazo (Calle Aire; admission €1.50; ⊙10.30am-1.30pm & 5-8pm), with a terrific display of photographs of villagers from the 1920s and 1930s.

South of town, Camping Valle de Hecho (✆974 37 53 61; www.campinghecho.com, in Spanish; sites per adult/tent/car €4.33/4.33/4.33; ☏☒) is a pleasant, well-kept camping ground.

The best place to stay in town is the charming Casa Blasquico (✆974 37 50 07; www.casablasquico.com; Plaza de la Fuente 1; d €49-53, tr €65; ⊙closed 1st half Sep), with six rooms. Breakfast costs €5.50. Downstairs in the same building, the much-lauded Restaurante Gaby (meals €25-30) is a delightful place to eat with an intimate wood-beamed dining room and an extensive wine list that includes 17 local wines; specialities include *ensalada de perdiz* (pheasant salad), *crepes de setas* (wild mushroom crepes) and *conejo a la casera* (home-style rabbit).

SIRESA & AROUND
POP 120 / ELEV 850M

A couple of kilometres north of Echo, Siresa is another charming village, although on a smaller scale. The beautiful 11th-century Iglesia de San Pedro (admission €1.50; ⊙11am-1pm & 5-7pm, closed Wed afternoon) is the town's centrepiece; it originally comprised part of one of Aragón's earliest monasteries.

Albergue Siresa (✆/fax 974 37 53 85; www.alberguesiresa.com, in Spanish & French; Calle Reclusa; dm incl breakfast €15, sheets €2) is a cheerful hostel providing bunk-and-breakfast accommodation in clean conditions, with other meals available. It also rents mountain bikes (€12 per day).

Hotel Castillo d'Acher (✆974 37 53 13; www.castillodacher.com; Plaza Mayor; d with/without bathroom €65/40) has a pleasant mix of rooms, some rather old-fashioned, others pine-clad and modern. It also has *casas rurales* (doubles €28) in the village. The big in-house restaurant does a good *menú del día* (set menu; €14).

There's perfect peace in fabulous surroundings at the outstanding Hotel Usón (✆974 37 53 58; www.hoteluson.com; s/d incl breakfast from €45/60, apt €65-125; ⊙Easter-Oct; P), high in the Echo valley, 5km north of Siresa on the road to the Selva de Oza.

Peace extends to the absence of TVs. The restaurant offers excellent home-cooked meals.

SELVA DE OZA
This top end of the Valle de Echo is particularly beautiful, the road running parallel to Río Aragón Subordán as it bubbles its way through thick woodlands. Around 7km beyond Siresa, the road squeezes through the Boca del Infierno (Hell's Mouth), while about 14km from Siresa the paved road ends, shortly after it connects with the GR11 path en route between Candanchú and Zuriza. At least half a dozen mountain peaks sit in an arc to the north for strenuous day ascents.

ANSÓ
POP 497 / ELEV 860M

Ansó takes you even further into a world of high places and harmony. The rough-hewn stone houses here are in grey stone, their roofs are of red tiles. Some walls are whitewashed, making a pleasing checkerboard pattern. Forested slopes climb ever upwards from where Ansó straggles along a low escarpment above a partly covered streambed. A grid of narrow streets surrounds the main square, Plaza Mayor.

PYRENEAN WILDLIFE

The most celebrated mammal in the Spanish Pyrenees is the brown bear (*oso pardo* in Spanish), of which an estimated 15 to 20 survive, distributed between Spain and France. However, only two of these, both males, are considered to be true Pyrenean bears, with the remainder introduced from Slovenia in order to ensure the survival of the species. Although the chances of seeing a bear are extremely slim, four are known to inhabit the upper reaches of the Valle de Ansó.

The Parque Nacional de Ordesa y Monte Perdido (p377) is home to at least 45 species of mammal and 130 bird species. Among the signature mammals is the chamois (*rebeco* in Spanish, *sarrio* in Aragonese), which wanders the park's upper reaches in herds of up to 50. Bird species include the rare and formidable lammergeier or *quebrantahuesos* (bearded vulture) and the ever-spectacular golden eagle.

Adjoining the rough-walled church, the delightful Posada Magoria (☎974 37 00 49; www.losposadamagoria.com, in Spanish; Calle Milagros 32; d €50-60) is crammed with character and lovingly kept by a family with lots of local knowledge. The kitchen *comedor* (dining room) serves up an excellent €12 *menú* of organically sourced vegetarian dishes; vegans are catered for too. At Casa Baretón (☎974 37 01 38; www.casabareton.com; Calle Pascual Altemir 16; s/d €35/49), the craftsman owner of this lovingly restored stone house has retained a number of old features to add to the comfort and charm of the rooms.

Bar Zuriza (Calle Mayor 71), near the top end of the village, serves decent tapas.

The tourist office (☎974 37 02 25; Plaza Mayor; ☻10am-2pm & 5-8pm Jul & Aug, weekends only Sep-Jun) offers free guided tours of the village.

VALLE DE ZURIZA
This narrow valley, which runs for 15km north of Ansó, follows the Rio Jeral and leads high into remote Pyrenean corners where raptors circle up among the snows and there's a good chance of seeing chamois. Where the paved road ends, wonderful walking trails such as the GR11 take over.

MONASTERIO DE SAN JUAN DE LA PEÑA
High in a mountain eyrie 21km southwest of Jaca, Monasterio de San Juan de la Peña is Aragón's most fascinating monastery. Gateway to the monastery is Santa Cruz de la Serós, a pretty village 4km south of the N240.

From Santa Cruz, a winding road climbs the Sierra de la Peña 7km to the stunning Monasterio Viejo (Old Monastery; www.monasteriosanjuan.com; ☻10am-8pm), tucked under an overhanging lip of rock at a bend in the road.

The rock shelter where the Monasterio Viejo is built, perhaps used by Christian hermits as early as the 8th century, became a monastery in the 10th century, when the Mozarabic lower church was constructed. The monastery emerged as the early spiritual and organisational centre of the medieval kingdom of Aragón. The highlight is the Romanesque cloister, with marvellous carved 12th- and 13th-century capitals depicting Genesis and the life of Christ. The first three kings of Aragón – Ramiro I (1036–64), Sancho Ramírez (1064–94) and

TICKETS & PARKING

Tickets to the two monasteries and to an audiovisual presentation on the Kingdom of Aragón are sold only at the Monasterio Nuevo. Tickets for one/two/three of these sights cost €6/9/12 for adults, students and seniors pay €5/7/10, while children between seven and 16 pay €3/4.50/6.

Except in winter, the only permissible parking is up the hill at the Monasterio Nuevo, from where a semiregular bus shuttles down to the Monasterio Viejo and back. In winter, you may be able to park around 200m down the hill from the Monasterio Viejo.

Pedro I (1094–1104) – are among those buried here.

A fire in 1675 led the monks to abandon the old monastery and build a new one in brick further up the hill: Monasterio Nuevo (New Monastery; ☻10am-8pm). It has a large visitors centre as well as the Monastery Interpretation Centre, which documents the archaeological history of the site, and the Kingdom of Aragón Interpretation Centre devoted to the kings of Aragón.

Unless you've a specialist interest, most visitors will be satisfied with the Monasterio Viejo.

🛏 Sleeping & Eating
Hostelería Santa Cruz   HOSTAL €
(☎974 36 19 75; www.santacruzdelaseros.com; Calle Ordana; s/d from €45/56) Near the church in Santa Cruz de la Serós, this is a beautiful place with friendly service and lovely rooms. Its restaurant serves a good *menú del día* (€12).

Hospedería Monasterio San Juan de la Peña   HOSPEDERÍA €€
(☎974 37 44 22; www.hospederiasdearagon.es; d €48-154; ❄🛜🐾) Part of the Monasterio Nuevo, this recently opened four-star hotel has supremely comfortable rooms, a spa complex and good restaurant. It's wheelchair accessible.

❶ Getting There & Away
There's no public transport to the monastery.

For walkers, a stiff 4km marked path (the GR65.3.2) leads up from Santa Cruz to the Monasterio Viejo in about 1½ hours, with an ascent of 350m.

Jaca

POP 13,396 / ELEV 820M

A gateway to the western valleys of the Aragonese Pyrenees and an agreeable town in its own right, Jaca has a pretty old town dotted with remnants of its past as the capital of the nascent 11th-century Aragón kingdom. These include an unusual fortress and some great places to eat. On winter weekends, après-ski funsters provide a lively soundtrack.

◎ Sights & Activities

Cathedral   CATHEDRAL
(◷11.30am-1.30pm & 4.15-8pm) Jaca's 11th-century cathedral is a powerful building, its imposing facade typical of the sturdy stone architecture of northern Aragón. It was once more gracefully French Romanesque in style, but a Gothic overhaul in the 16th century bequeathed a hybrid look. The interior retains some fine features, in particular the side chapel dedicated to Santa Orosia, the city's patron saint, whose martyrdom is depicted in a series of mysterious murals.

Ciudadela   CITADEL
(Citadel; www.ciudadeladejaca.es, in Spanish; adult/concession €10/5; ◷11am-2pm & 5-8pm Tue-Sun, closed second half Nov, last tickets sold at 1pm & 7pm) The star-shaped, 16th-century citadel is Spain's only extant pentagonal fortress (the one in Pamplona is not complete) and one of only two in Europe. It now houses an army academy, but visits are permitted, with 40-minute guided tours (in English, Spanish or French). In the citadel the Museo de Miniaturas Militares (Museum of Military Miniatures; www.museominiaturasjaca.es) is an extraordinary collection of models and dioramas of battles ancient and otherwise, with over 32,000 toy soldiers on show. Deer graze in the moat surrounding the citadel.

Old City   HISTORIC BUILDINGS
There are some lovely old buildings in the streets of the casco historico (old city) that fans out south of the cathedral, including the 15th-century Torre del Reloj (clock tower; Plaza del Marqués de la Cadena) and the charming little Ermita de Sarsa (Avenida Oroel).

Pista de Hielo   ICE-SKATING RINK
(Avenida del Perimetral) The town's state-of-the-art ice-skating rink opens most evenings – check with the tourist office for opening hours. It's opposite the southern end of Calle de Ramón y Cajal, around 400m south of Calle Mayor.

⚜ Festivals & Events

Festividad del Primer Viernes de Mayo
MEDIEVAL FESTIVAL
To see displays of medieval archery visit on the first Friday of May, when Jaca celebrates a Christian victory over the Muslims in 760.

Fiesta de Santa Orosia PATRON SAINT FESTIVAL
Jaca puts on its party gear for the weeklong Fiesta de Santa Orosia, which revolves round the saint's day of 25 June.

Festival Folklórico de los Pirineos
PYRENEAN FOLKLORE
The Festival Folklórico de los Pirineos, held in late July and early August, provides 1½ weeks of international music, dance, crafts and theatre. It's held in odd-numbered years.

🛏 Sleeping

It's worth booking ahead at weekends throughout the year, during the skiing season, and in July and August.

TOP CHOICE Hotel Barosse   GUEST HOUSE €€
(☎974 36 05 82; www.barosse.com, in Spanish; s incl breakfast €75-124, d incl breakfast €95-155; ※🐾) In the quiet hamlet of Barós, 2km south of Jaca, Hotel Barosse has six individually styled rooms with lovely attention to detail, from exposed stone walls, high ceilings and splashes of colour to fine bathroom packages of goodies. There's a reading room, garden, an on-site Jacuzzi and sauna, and fine views of the Pyrenees. Best of all, José and Gustavo are wonderful hosts. It's easily the best choice in Jaca.

Hostal París   HOSTAL €
(☎974 36 10 20; www.jaca.com/hostalparis, in Spanish; Plaza de San Pedro 5; s/d without bathroom from €30/40) Close to the cathedral, this friendly, central option has spotless, ample-sized rooms and smart shared bathrooms (seven bathrooms for 20 rooms) that you'd swear were recently renovated. Breakfast costs €3 and many rooms overlook the square.

La Casa del Arco   GUEST HOUSE €
(☎974 36 44 48; www.lacasadelarco.net, in Spanish; Calle de San Nicolás 4; s without bathroom €22, d with/without bathroom €55/40) Rooms at this fine all-round venue are cheerfully otherworldly, with a few bohemian touches.

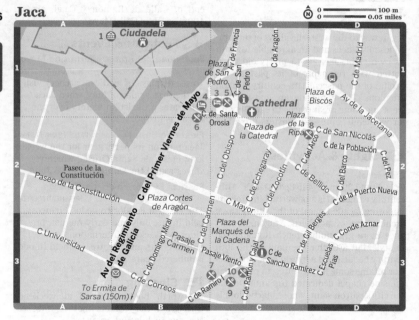

Hotel Mur
HOTEL €€

(☎974 36 01 00; www.hotelmur.com; Calle de Santa Orosia 1; s/d incl breakfast from €43/63) A pleasantly rambling place, this long-established hotel provides comfort and style, with light-filled rooms, some of which have views towards the citadel; those without exterior windows can be claustrophobic.

✕ Eating

TOP CHOICE La Tasca de Ana
TAPAS €

(Calle de Ramiro I 3; meals €15-20; ⏰7-11.30pm Mon-Fri, 12.30-3.30pm & 7-11.30pm Sat & Sun; 🛜) One of Aragón's best tapas bars, La Tasca de Ana has tempting options lined up along the bar, more choices cooked to order and a carefully chosen list of local wines. Check out its '*tapas mas solicitados*' (most popular orders) listed on the blackboard. When we were there, the 'Rodolfito' (prawn in sauce) had been top of the list for years, but there's so much here to get excited about. We especially like the toast with goat's cheese and blueberries.

La Casa del Arco
VEGETARIAN €

(☎974 36 44 48; www.lacasadelarco.net, in Spanish; Calle de San Nicolás 4; meals €15-20; 🍴) A haven of imaginative vegetarian food and with a delightfully alternative ambience, La Casa del Arco is terrific. Downstairs is a nice little bar, the Tetaría el Arco, which stages occasional music sessions and other events.

Restaurante El Portón
ARAGONESE €€

(☎974 35 58 54; Plaza del Marqués de la Cadena 1; meals €35-45) Located in a little tree-shaded plaza, this classy venue serves haute-cuisine versions of Aragonese fare. Reservations are a must. Highly recommended.

Crepería El Bretón
BRETON CRÊPES €

(☎974 35 63 76; Calle de Ramiro I 10; meals €15-20; ⏰Wed-Sun) Serving sweet and salty crêpes that are faithful to old Brittany recipes, this intimate French-run place is a fine alternative to Spanish cooking. It also serves salads, tapas, Brittany cider and an excellent *menú Bretón* for €10.50.

Bodegas Langa
DELICATESSEN, TAPAS €€

(Plaza de San Pedro 5; meals €15-25; ⏰Mon-Sat) Gourmet-food-store-cum-summer-tapas-bar.

Casa Martín
ARAGONESE €€

(☎974 35 69 04; Calle de Santa Orosia 2; meals €25-30) Try the *guisado de jabalí* (wild boar stew).

ℹ Information

Tourist office (☎974 36 00 98; Plaza de San Pedro 11-13; ⏰9am-1.30pm & 4.30-7.30pm Mon-Sat)

Jaca

ⓘ Getting There & Away

Five **Alosa** (www.alosa.es, in Spanish) buses go to Huesca (€6.85, 1¼ hours) and Zaragoza (€13.15, 2¼ hours) most days, and two go to Pamplona (€7.05, 1¾ hours) from the central **bus station** (☏974 35 50 60; Plaza de Biscós).

Around Jaca

VALLE DE CANFRANC

The N330 leads north from Jaca, via the pretty Río Aragón valley, to the Somport road tunnel into France, passing Canfranc-Estación after 25km. Opened in 1928, this enormous train station's distinctive architecture reflected the Modernista style. At the time it was Europe's second-largest station. The French unilaterally halted the service after an accident in 1970. Two trains a day from Zaragoza via Huesca and Jaca stop here.

Closer to Jaca, it's worth turning east off the N330 at Castiello de Jaca, and following the signs to tiny Villanovilla. The village came close to being abandoned, but has since been restored and hosts the terrific Restaurante La Garcipollera (☏974 34 81 83; www.turismoruralgarcipollera.es, in Spanish; meals €25-35; ☾lunch & dinner Sat, lunch Sun) which is at once a simple but well-turned-out *albergue* (single/double room from €35/50 including breakfast), and a terrific restaurant; specialities include snails in garlic mayonnaise and steaks. Further up

the valley, a 5km walk takes you to the peaceful Romanesque Ermita de Santa María de Iguacel; the dirt track is sometimes open to cars, but in terrible condition.

VALLE DE TENA

From the regional centre of Biescas, north of Sabiñánigo, the A136 climbs gently towards the French border.

Leading deep into the mountains, a narrow road runs 8km past the ski resort of Panticosa to the Panticosa Resort (☏974 48 71 61; www.panticosa.com, in Spanish), a stunning complex that includes the four-star Hotel Continental (d from €60); three restaurants including Restaurante del Lago (meals from €65), watched over by star chef Pedro Subijana; bars; a casino; and the Balneario (Termas de Tiberio), a luxurious spa complex recently remodelled by star architect Rafael Moneo. The setting is stunning, alongside a lake in an enclosed valley high in the Pyrenees.

Returning to the main A136, Sallent de Gállego, 3.5km north of the Panticosa turnoff, is a lovely stone village with a bubbling brook running through it.

From Jaca, one or two daily buses wind over to Panticosa and Formigal (€5.40, two hours). The N260 leaves the valley at Biescas and follows a pretty route to Torla and Aínsa.

Parque Nacional de Ordesa y Monte Perdido

This is where the Spanish Pyrenees really take your breath away. At the heart of it all is a dragon's back of limestone peaks skirting the French border, with a southeastward spur that includes Monte Perdido (3348m), the third-highest peak in the Pyrenees. Deep valleys slice down from the high ground. Most were carved by glaciers and at their heads lie bowl-like glacial *circos* (cirques) backed by spectacular curtain walls of rock. Chief among the valleys are Pineta (east), Escuaín (southeast), Bellos (south), Ordesa (southwest), Bujaruelo (west) and Gavarnie (north, in France).

🏃 Activities

For a range of walking options in the park, pick up a copy of the *Senderos* maps and route descriptions for the four sectors (Ordesa, Añisclo, Escuaín and Pineta) from any of the information offices.

Access Towns

The main entry point into the park is Torla (p380), 3km south of the southwest corner of the national park.

From Escalona, 11km north of Aínsa on the A138, a minor paved road heads northwest across to Sarvisé, a few kilometres south of Torla. This road crosses the park's southern tip, with a narrow, sinuous section winding up the dramatic Bellos valley and giving access to walks in the spectacular Cañón de Añisclo (the upper reaches of the Bellos valley).

From Bielsa a 12km paved road runs up the Valle de Pineta in the park's northeastern corner.

Information Centres

» **Centro de Visitantes de Torla** (☑974 48 64 72; ☺9am-2pm & 4-7pm) A good interpretation centre open from March to October, with the park's main information office open year-round; starting point for shuttle bus into the park.

» **Bielsa** (☑974 50 10 43; ☺9am-1.30pm & 3-6pm Easter-Oct, 8am-3pm Mon-Fri Nov-Easter)

» **Centro de Visitantes de Tella** (☺9am-1.30pm & 3-6pm Easter-Oct) In Tella in the Escuaín sector.

» **Escalona** (☑974 50 51 31; ☺9am-1.30pm & 3-6pm Easter-Oct, 8am-3pm Mon-Fri Nov-Easter)

Maps

Ordesa y Monte Perdido Parque Nacional (1:25,000), published by the Ministerio de Fomento in 2000, costs around €7 and comes with a booklet detailing 20 walks. It's available in Torla shops.

If you're keen to traverse the park along the GR11, look for the strip maps *Senda Pyrenaica*, produced by Prames. Another good reference is the guidebook *Through the Spanish Pyrenees: GR11 – A Trekking Guidebook* by Paul Lucia and available from Cicerone Press (www.cicerone.co.uk).

Rules & Regulations

Bivouacing is allowed only above certain altitudes (1800m to 2500m, depending on the sector); ask at one of the information centres for details. Swimming in rivers or lakes, mountain biking, fishing and fires are banned.

CIRCO DE SOASO

A classic day walk follows the Valle de Ordesa to Circo de Soaso, a rocky balcony whose centrepiece is the Cola de Caballo (Horsetail) waterfall. From the eastern end of the Pradera de Ordesa, cross Río Arazas and climb steeply up through woods on the valley's south side. This hardest part, called the Senda de los Cazadores (Hunters' Path), in which you ascend 600m, takes an hour. Then it's level or downhill all the way along the high Faja de Pelay path to the *circo*. Return by the path along the bottom of the valley, passing several waterfalls. The circuit takes about seven hours.

REFUGIO DE GÓRIZ & MONTE PERDIDO

Fit walkers can climb a series of steep switchbacks (part of the GR11) to Circo de Soaso and up to the Refugio de Góriz (☑974 34 12 01; dm €15), at 2200m. This 72-place refuge, attended and serving meals year-round, makes an obvious base for ascents of Monte Perdido. For July and August, book a month ahead. Monte Perdido is a serious undertaking that requires mountaineering skills, crampons and ice axes.

FAJA RACÓN, CIRCO DE COTATUERO & FAJA CANARELLOS

This walk takes you along spectacular high-level paths on the north flank of the Valle de Ordesa. It takes about five or six hours, an hour less if you omit Faja Canarellos. It shouldn't be attempted in winter and spring, when there's a high risk of ice, falling rocks and avalanches.

From Pradera de Ordesa head 600m west back along the paved road to Casa Oliván, and take the path signed 'Tozal del Mallo, Circo de Carriata'. About 1½ hours up this fairly steep, zigzag path, diverge eastward along the path signed 'Faja Racón': this high-level route of about 3km brings you out below the Circo de Cotatuero's impressive 200m waterfall. From here head downhill to a wooden shelter. Here you can either continue down the Cotatuero *circo* to a path junction 600m east of Pradera de Ordesa or, if you're still energetic, cross a bridge opposite the shelter to follow another high-level path of 3km to 4km, Faja Canarellos. This brings you down to the Valle de Ordesa at Bosque de las Hayas, from where it's 4km westward, gently downhill, to Pradera de Ordesa.

BRECHA DE ROLANDO
The cool-headed may climb part of the wall of the Circo de Cotatuero by the Clavijas de Cotatuero, a set of 32 iron pegs hammered into the rock; they follow more of a rising traverse than a vertical ladder. No special equipment is needed, but you need to be fit. From here you are about 2½ hours' march from the Brecha de Rolando (Roldán; 2807m), a dramatic, breezy gap in the mountain wall on the French frontier. You can also reach the Brecha by a 3½-hour path from Refugio de Góriz. From the Brecha it's a steep 500m descent to the French Refuge des Sarradets (☎ France 33-06 83 38 13 24).

PUERTO DE BUJARUELO
The GR11 describes a 6km arc up the very pretty Valle de Bujaruelo to San Nicolás de Bujaruelo. From there an east-northeast

Parque Nacional de Ordesa y Monte Perdido

path leads in about three hours (with a 950m ascent) up to the Puerto de Bujaruelo on the border with France. You're now in the French Parc National des Pyrénées, and in about two hours can descend to Gavarnie village. Alternatively you can head southeast and upwards for about 2½ hours to the Refuge des Sarradets and from there back into Spain via the Brecha de Rolando.

SOUTHERN GORGES
The Cañón de Añisclo is a gaping wound in the earth's fabric. Energetic walkers can start from the Refugio de Góriz and descend the gorge from the north; if you have a vehicle you can take a day walk from the southern end. Some 12km from Escalona on the road to Sarvisé, a broad path leads down to the dramatic Puente de San Úrbez, then up the canyon. You can walk as far north as La Ripareta and back in about five hours, or to Fuen Blanca and back in about eight hours.

The Gargantas de Escuaín is a smaller-scale but still-dramatic gorge on Río Yaga, further east. You can descend into the gorge in about an hour from the semi-abandoned hamlet of Escuaín, reached by a minor road off the Escalona–Sarvisé road.

BALCÓN DE PINETA
This challenging hike begins close to the Parador Nacional de Bielsa and, after the waterfalls of the Cascadas del Cinca, climbs via a series of steep switchbacks up to the 'Pineta Balcony' for stunning glacier and mountain views. The trek takes around five hours going up, around three on the way back.

 Getting There & Away

Bus

One daily bus operated by **Alosa** (☎902 21 07 00; www.alosa.es, in Spanish) connects Torla to Aínsa (€3.76, one hour) and Sabiñánigo (€3.40, one hour). In July and August one daily bus makes the Sabiñánigo–Sarvisé (but not Aínsa) run daily.

Park Access

Private vehicles may not drive from Torla to Pradera de Ordesa during Easter week and July to mid-September. During these periods a shuttle bus (€3/4.50 one way/return) runs between Torla's Centro de Visitantes and Pradera de Ordesa. A maximum of 1800 people are allowed in this sector of the park at any one time.

During the same periods, a one-way system is enforced on part of the Escalona–Sarvisé road. From the Puyarruego turn-off, 2km out of

Escalona, to a point about 1km after the road diverges from the Bellos valley, only northwestward traffic is allowed. Southeastward traffic uses an alternative, more southerly road.

Torla
POP 324

Torla is a lovely Alpine-style village of stone houses with slate roofs, although it does get overrun in July and August. Most people use Torla as a gateway to the national park, but it rewards those who linger overnight after the crowds have moved on. The setting is delightful, the houses clustered above Río Ara with a backdrop of the national park's mountains. In your ramblings around town, make for the 13th-century Iglesia de San Salvador; there are fine views from the small park on the church's northern side.

🛏 Sleeping

Reservations are essential during July and August. There are three camping grounds within 2km north of Torla (all closed from mid- or late October till Easter).

Hotel Villa de Torla　　　　　　HOTEL €€
(☎974 48 61 56; www.hotelvilladetorla.com, in Spanish; Plaza de Aragón 1; s €35-45, d €55-69; ☺mid-Mar–Dec; ▨) The rooms here are tidy – some are spacious and stylish, others have floral bedspreads and look a little tired. But the undoubted highlight is the swimming pool and the bar terrace, from where there are lovely views.

Hotel Villa Russell　　　　　　HOTEL €€
(☎974 48 67 70; www.hotelvillarussell.com; Calle de Capuvita; s €57-80, d €80-114; ▣⑤) Villa Russell has rooms that won't win a style contest, but they're enormous and come with sofas, microwave and hydromassage showers. On-site parking costs €6 and there's a Jaccuzzi and sauna.

Hotel Ballarín　　　　　HOTEL, HOSTEL €
(☎/fax 974 48 61 55; hotelballarin@terra.es; Calle de Capuvita 11; s €32-42, d €48-50) This place has well-kept rooms with superb views from the top rooms, but the welcome could be warmer. The owners also run the similarly well-tended Hostal Alto Aragón (☎/fax 974 48 61 72; Calle de Capuvita; s/d from €30/38) a few doors down.

There are also two French-run *refugios* in the centre of town:

Refugio Lucien Briet   REFUGIO €
(☎974 48 62 21; www.refugiolucienbriet.com, in
Spanish; Calle de Francia; dm/d €10/40)

L'Atalaya   REFUGIO €
(☎/fax 974 48 64 17; Calle de Francia; dm €11)

✖ Eating

All of the listed accommodation have restaurants with *menús* from €12 to €17.

Restaurante el Duende   ARAGONESE €€
(☎974 48 60 32; www.elduenderestaurante.com,
in Spanish; Calle de la Iglesia; meals €35-40) This
charming place is the best of many restaurants in town, with fine local cuisine, an extensive menu and eclectic decor in a lovely
19th-century building.

Around Torla

VALLE DE BUJARUELO
North of Torla and shadowing the eastern
boundary of the park, the pretty Valle de
Bujaruelo is another good base.

Camping Valle de Bujaruelo (☎974 48
63 48; www.campingvalledebujaruelo.com, in
Spanish; per person/tent/car €4.50/4.50/4.50,
r €37-57; ☻Easter–mid-Oct), located 3.5km
up the Valle de Bujaruelo, features a refuge with bunks, a restaurant and a supermarket. The setting's lovely and the facilities are well maintained.

Three kilometres further up the valley,
at San Nicolás, is an old hostelry called
Mesón de Bujaruelo (☎974 48 64 12; www.
mesondebujaruelo.com; dm/d €12/36, half-board
per person €28-37), which provides bunks
and meals in a pretty location by the Puerto
de Bujaruelo. Accommodation is too-cool-
for-style mountain basics, but it's all about
location here.

TORLA TO AÍNSA
The N260 from Torla to Aínsa runs for
44km through the lovely foothills of the
Pyrenees. At around the halfway point,
watch for the lookout over the Río Ara to
the evocative ruins of Jánovas, a village
abandoned in the 1970s. Nearby, in the
tiny village of San Martín de la Solana
(signposted north off the main road), Casa
de San Martín (☎974 50 31 05; www.casade
sanmartin.es; s/d from €128/160) is the ideal
rural retreat. The rooms are quite stunning, the setting tranquil and picturesque,
and the restaurant serves fine dinners (set
menus €37.50).

Aínsa

POP 2179

The beautiful hilltop village of medieval
Aínsa (L'Aínsa in the local dialect), which
stands above the modern town of the same
name, is one of Aragón's gems, a stunning
village hewn from uneven stone. From its
perch, you'll have commanding panoramic
views of the mountains, particularly of the
great rock bastion of La Peña Montañesa.

◉ Sights

Simply wander down through the village
along either Calle de Santa Cruz or Calle
Mayor, pausing in the handful of artsy
shops en route; note the drain pipes carved
into the shape of gargoyles.

Iglesia de Santa María   CHURCH
The restored Romanesque Iglesia de Santa
María, rising above the northeastern corner
of Plaza Mayor, lights up when you pop €1
into a box, with five minutes of Gregorian
chants thrown in. The crypt and Gothic
cloister are charming; you can also climb the
belfry (admission €1; ☻11am-1.30pm & 4-7pm Sat
& Sun, longer hr Jul & Aug) for glorious views of
the mountains to the north and down over
the terracotta rooftops of the old town.

Museo de Oficios y Artes Tradicionales
                                    MUSEUM
(admission €2.50; ☻10am-2pm & 4-8pm Fri-Sun)
Down on Plaza de San Salvador, this interesting museum has exhibits on local culture in one of the best-preserved old buildings in Aínsa.

Castle   CASTLE
The castle and fortifications off the western
end of the Plaza de San Salvador mostly
date from the 1600s, though the main tower
is 11th century; there are some reasonable
views from the wall. It contains an interesting ecomuseum (admission €4; ☻11am-2pm
Wed-Fri, 10am-2pm &4-7pm Sat & Sun Easter-Oct)
on Pyrenean fauna, and the Espacio del
Geoparque de Sobrarbe (www.geoparquepir
ineos.com; admission free; ☻10am-2pm & 4-7pm)
with displays on the region's intriguing geology, as well as good views from the tower.

✦ Festivals & Events

Festival Internacional de Música   MUSIC
(www.festivalcastillodeainsa.com, in Spanish) In
July, Aínsa hosts this month-long festival
with predominantly Spanish and a few
international music acts in the castle
grounds.

🛏 Sleeping

Booking ahead is always advisable, partly because demand is high but also because hotel receptions here are rarely staffed around the clock.

TOP CHOICE Hotel los Siete Reyes   HOTEL €€

(☎974 50 06 81; www.lossietereyes.com, in Spanish; Plaza Mayor; d incl breakfast €90-130; ❄🖨) Set in one of the most charming stone buildings overlooking Plaza Mayor, this temple of style has stunning bathrooms, polished floorboards, exposed stone walls, flat-screen TVs and some lovely period detail wedded to a contemporary designer look. The attic rooms are enormous, but all are spacious and some have lovely mountain views, while others look out over the Plaza Mayor. Simply outstanding.

TOP CHOICE Albergue Mora de Nuei   HOSTEL €

(☎974 51 06 14; www.alberguemorade nuei.com; Calle del Portal de Abajo 2; dm €15-17, d incl breakfast €50-60; 🖨) At the lower end of the old town, facing onto Plaza de San Salvador, this fine place is one of Aragón's best hostels. Rooms are colourful and lovingly maintained, and there's a roof terrace, an atmospheric basement bar, good food, and a semiregular calendar of live music and other cultural events. Highly recommended.

Hotel los Arcos   HOTEL €€

(☎974 50 00 16; www.hotellosarcosainsa.com, in Spanish; Plaza Mayor 23; d from €80; ❄🖨) In a fine position on Plaza Mayor, this lovely hotel has luxurious rooms with canopied beds and good-sized bathrooms. It doesn't quite scale the dizzy heights of its neighbour, Hotel los Siete Reyes, but it's still a wonderful place.

Other atmospheric places:

Hotel Villa Romanica   HOTEL €€

(☎974 50 07 50; www.hotelvillaromanica.com, in Spanish; Calle de Santa Cruz 21; s/d from €50/60; ❄)

Posada Real   POSADA €€

(☎974 50 09 77; www.posadareal.com; Plaza Mayor; d from €80; ❄)

Casa el Hospital   HOSTAL €

(☎/fax 974 50 07 50; www.casadelhospital.com; Calle del Arco del Hospital; s €25-29, d €39-55)

🍴 Eating

In summer, there are plenty of outdoor tables around Plaza Mayor, a delightful place to eat in the cool of a summer evening, although prices can be steep.

Restaurante Callizo   FUSION €€

(☎974 50 03 85; http://restcallizo.restaurant esok.com, in Spanish; Plaza Mayor; meals €30-40; ⊙closed Mon & dinner Sun Sep-Jun) This place is definitely something special, cleverly combining as it does traditional cuisine with gastronomic innovation on its constantly changing menu. The 'Village Scents' set menu (€25) is a gastronomic journey of the highest order, as is the 'Traditional & Vanguard' menu (€40); it also does a children's menu.

Bodegón de Mallacán   ARAGONESE €€

(www.posadareal.com, in Spanish; Plaza Mayor 6; meals €30-40) One of the most popular places on Plaza Mayor, this place has an extensive wine cellar, high-quality traditional local cooking and a number of pretty dining rooms. The duck in raspberry sauce is outstanding, but there's much to turn the head here. If you can't choose, try the 'Typical Aragón Menu' (€18).

L'Alfil   TAPAS €

(Calle Traversa; raciones €4.80-12, meals €15-20; ⊙Thu-Tue) A pretty little place with floral accompaniment to its outside tables, in a side street along from the church, this cafe-bar does a whole heap of *raciones* that are more creative than you'll find elsewhere, from ostrich chorizo, snails and deer sausage to wild boar paté and cured duck. It also serves good local wines.

Bodegas del Sobrarbe   ARAGONESE €€

(www.bodegasdelsobrarbe.com; Plaza Mayor 2; meals €25-35) This fine restaurant off the southeastern corner of Plaza Mayor offers meaty Aragonese fare with a few fish dishes. The wild boar with plum and green-apple purée is superb.

❶ Information

Municipal tourist office (☎974 50 07 67; www.ainsasobrarbe.net, in Spanish; Avenida Pirenáica 1; ⊙9am-9pm) Inconveniently in the new town down the hill, but with an outpost in the Museo de Oficios y Artes Tradicionales.

Regional tourist office (☎974 50 05 12; www.turismosobrarbe.com, in Spanish; Plaza del Castillo 1, Torre Nordeste; ⊙10am-2pm & 4-7pm) Extremely helpful; within the castle walls.

❶ Getting There & Away

Alosa (☎902 21 07 00; www.alosa.es, in Spanish) Daily buses to/from Barbastro (€5.07, one hour) and Torla (€3.76, one hour).

Autocares Bergua (📞974 50 06 01) Buses to/from Bielsa (€3.20, 45 minutes) between three and six times weekly.

Around Aínsa

Around 5km northeast of Aínsa, the quiet and uniformly stone-built hamlet of El Pueyo de Araguás is home to the Monasterio de San Victorián; although it was much modified in the 16th century, its Romanesque origins ensure that it lays claim to being the oldest monastery in Spain. Also in the village, the Casas Coronas date to 1519 and are among the oldest in the region.

Benasque

POP 2200 / ELEV 1140M

Aragón's northeastern corner is crammed with the highest and shapeliest peaks in the Pyrenees, and Benasque (Benás in the local dialect) is perfectly sited to serve as gateway to the highest valleys. Even in midsummer these epic mountains can be capped with snow and ice. The area, much of which is protected as the **Parque Natural Posets-Maladeta**, offers walkers almost limitless options and climbers a wide choice of peaks. Northeast of Benasque, the Pyrenees' highest peak, the **Pic d'Aneto** (3404m), towers above the massif.

🛏 Sleeping

During the ski season most offer packages with *media pensión* (half-board).

Hotel Aneto   HOTEL **€€€**
(📞974 55 10 61; www.hotelesvalero.com, in Spanish; Avenida de Francia 4; d from €130) A cut above the usual lodge-style accommodation that is a Benasque speciality, Hotel Aneto opened in 2008 with hardwood floors and a contemporary designer look.

Hotel Avenida   HOTEL **€€**
(📞974 55 11 26; www.h-avenida.com, in Spanish; Avenida de los Tilos 14; s €44-60, d €58-68) Rooms here are handsomely furnished and the service is friendly. There's a restaurant attached and cheaper room rates for longer stays.

Camping Aneto   CAMPSITE **€**
(📞974 55 11 41; www.campinganeto.com; per person/tent/car €6.25/6.25/6.25) The closest camping ground to town (3.5km away), Aneto is well equipped and has a shop and laundry.

> ### ℹ GETTING GEARED UP IN BENASQUE   383

Plenty of outfitters offer guides and instruction for climbing, skiing and other activities; most sell or rent clothing and equipment for the hills.

» **Barrabés** (www.barrabes.com, in Spanish; Avenida de Francia; ⏰10.30am-1.30pm & 4.30-9pm)

» **Casa de la Montaña** (📞974 55 20 94; Avenida de los Tilos)

» **Compañía de Guías Valle de Benasque** (www.guiasbenasque.com, in Spanish; Avenida Luchón 19)

🍴 Eating & Drinking

The best places are along Avenida de los Tilos and its continuation, Calle Mayor.

Taberna del Ixarso   TAPAS **€**
(Calle Mayor 12; meals €15-20) Meaty tapas such as chorizo and *salchichón* (sausage) help the drinks go down at this lively little bar, where local aficionados happily mix with tourists.

La Buhardilla   CRÊPES **€**
(Calle Mayor; meals €15-25) A plush crêperie at the heart of the old town, the 'attic's' sleek modern decor is softened by a big, open fire for chilly Pyrenean evenings. Sweet and savoury crêpes and fondues are what it's all about.

Restaurante el Fogaril   ARAGONESE **€€**
(📞974 55 16 12; Calle Mayor 5; meals €35-45) Treat yourself at this elegant country dining room, which serves outstanding Aragonese fare. Its specialities include young venison and stuffed partridge, *cozal* (small deer) and freshwater fish, all superbly prepared and presented.

ℹ Information

Tourist office (📞974 55 12 89; www.turismobenasque.com, in Spanish; Calle San Sebastián 5; ⏰9.30am-1pm & 4.30-8pm)

ℹ Getting There & Away

BUS Two buses operate Monday to Saturday, and one runs on Sunday, from Barbastro to Benasque (€7.55, two hours) and back.

CAR & MOTORCYCLE If you're driving, the approach from the south suddenly jumps out at you as the A139/N260 plunges through the Congosto de Ventamillo, a narrow defile carved

Villages of Aragón

Few regions can rival Aragón for its spread of charming villages. Most are built in the sturdy stone typical of the region, with terracotta and slate roofs. And their setting – against a backdrop of Pyrenean peaks or hidden in isolated corners of the south – is as beguiling as the architecture.

Aínsa

1 There's no more beautifully preserved village in Aragón after the sun sets, the crowds go home and silence reigns. Its stunning laneways, porticoed Plaza Mayor and views of the Pyrenees from the village's hilltop perch are simply wonderful.

Albarracín

2 One of Spain's most beautiful villages, Albarracín combines time-worn streets in shades of ochre with a dramatic setting. The views from the castle or the precipitous walls high on a ridge will stay with you long after you leave.

Sos del Rey Católico

3 Uniformly cobblestoned streets, the whiff of Spanish legend and a perch high above the madding crowd make Sos a memorable stop en route to or from the Pyrenees.

Daroca

4 Just when you think Aragón's southern badlands have little to offer, Daroca embraces you within its walls that encircle the town high on the ridgelines.

Alquézar

5 A centre for canyoning and other high-octane pursuits, Alquézar's alter ego is a tranquil village that, from above, resembles a Tuscan hill town.

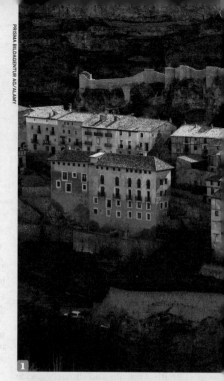

Clockwise from top left

by the crystalline Río Ésera. There's not much quarter given by traffic in either direction.

Around Benasque

South of Benasque, the village of Castejón de Sos is a paragliding centre with accommodation. For more information, try www.parapentepirineos.com (in Spanish) and www.volarencastejon.com.

From mid-June to mid-September, buses link Benasque with La Besurta, 16km north in the upper Ésera valley; and with the Refugio Pescadores in the Valle de Vallibierna, 11km northeast of Benasque. The buses stop at camping grounds on the A139 north of Benasque – you can use them to reach many of the walks mentioned in this section. Check current timetables at Benasque's tourist office.

VALLE DE VALLIBIERNA

This valley runs southeast up from the A139 about 5.5km north of Benasque. Take the track towards Camping Ixeia, which leaves the A139 just before the Puente de San Jaime (or Chaime) bridge, 3km from Benasque. You're now on the GR11 coast-to-coast trail, which after a couple more kilometres diverges into Valle de Vallibierna. It's then about a 6km (2½-hour) walk, ascending nearly 600m, to two small *refugios* (no facilities). Three groups of mountain lakes, the Lagos (or Ibons) de Coronas, Llosás and Vallibierna, can each be reached in under two hours from the refuges.

GR11 TO BIELSA

Westbound, the GR11 leaves the A139 just after the Puente de San Jaime. It's an easy three-hour walk (600m ascent) up the Valle de Estós to Refugio de Estós (☎974 55 14 83; dm adult/under 14yr €15/6.50), a good 115-bunk refuge (dinner €15) attended year-round. A further five hours bring you, via the 2592m Puerto de Gistaín (or Chistau) and some superb views of the Posets massif, to the excellent Refugio de Viadós (☎974 50 61 63; dm €10, half-board €25). It's staffed from June to September and Saturday and Sunday Easter to May. Viadós is a base for climbs on Posets (3369m), a serious undertaking that requires mountaineering skills and equipment and is a hard six hours-plus to the summit, with potential altitude effect. Route finding is not that easy. The GR11 continues some six hours west to the

hamlet of Parzán in the Bielsa valley, before heading into the Parque Nacional de Ordesa y Monte Perdido.

Autocares Bergua (☎974 50 00 18) runs a bus from Bielsa to Aínsa at 6am Monday, Wednesday and Friday (Monday to Saturday in July and August).

UPPER ÉSERA VALLEY & MALADETA MASSIF

North of Benasque, the A139 continues paved for about 12km. About 10km from Benasque, a side road leads 6km east along the pretty upper Ésera valley, ending at La Besurta, with a hut selling drinks and some food.

Hospital de Benasque (☎974 55 20 12; www.llanosdelhospital.com, in Spanish; dm €20-30, s/d incl breakfast from €67/82; P @), a little under halfway from the A139 to La Besurta, is a large mountain lodge in a beautiful location, surrounded by handsome peaks. There's a bar, restaurant, spa and wellness centre and a variety of accommodation ranging from bunks to semi-luxurious rooms.

An exacting trail from Llanos del Hospital, the ski station adjacent to the Hospital de Benasque, heads northeast and upwards to Peña Blanca, and from there winds steeply up to the 2445m Portillón de Benasque pass on the French frontier. This should take fit walkers about 2½ hours. You could return via the Puerto de la Picada, another pass to the east – or another 3½ hours north down past the Boums del Port lakes to the French town of Bagnères-de-Luchon.

South of La Besurta is the great Maladeta massif, a superb challenge for experienced climbers. This forbidding line of icy peaks, with glaciers suspended from the higher crests, culminates in Aneto (3404m), the highest peak in the Pyrenees.

Refugio de la Renclusa (☎974 55 21 06; dm €15, half-board €35), staffed and serving meals from about June to mid-October and weekends from March to June, is a 40-minute walk from La Besurta. Experienced and properly equipped climbers can reach the top of Aneto from here in a minimum of five hours.

The massif offers other peaks, including **Maladeta** (3308m). From La Besurta or La Renclusa, walkers can follow paths southeast beneath the Maladeta massif, leading into Catalonia.

Alquézar

POP 321 / ELEV 670M

Picturesque Alquézar, 20km northwest of Barbastro, means **canyoning** (*descenso de barrancos* in Spanish), which involves following canyons downstream by whatever means available – walking, abseiling, jumping, swimming, even diving. The Sierra de Guara, north of the Huesca–Barbastro road, is sliced through by more than 200 dramatic canyons of the Río Vero and other river systems; it is Europe's prime location for the sport, with the otherwise quiet village of Alquézar as its hub.

◉ Sights

Colegiata de Santa María
CASTLE-MONASTERY
(admission €2, incl Casa Fabián €3; ⊙11am-1.30pm & 4.30-7.30pm Wed-Mon) Alquézar is a beautiful stone village, draped along a ridgeline and crowned by the Colegiata de Santa María, a large castle-monastery. Originally built as an *alcázar* (fortress) by the Arabs in the 9th century, it was conquered around 1060 by Sancho Ramírez. Remnants of the Augustinian monastery he established here in 1099 are still visible. The columns within its delicate cloister are crowned by perfectly preserved carved capitals depicting biblical scenes, and the walls are covered with spellbinding murals. On the upper level is a museum of sacred art. Visits are by guided tour only. The door is locked while tours are in progress, so simply wait for the next tour.

Casa Fabián
MUSEUM
(☑974 31 89 13; Calle Baja 16; admission €1.50, incl Colegiata de Santa María €3; ⊙11am-2pm & 4-8pm Tue-Sun) The charming Casa Fabián, a folk museum in a 17th-century house, is full of intriguing artefacts of farming and domestic life and includes an old olive-oil press, dug out of the rocky foundations.

⚘ Activities

The main canyoning season is mid-June to mid-September and prices, which vary depending on the number of people and the graded difficulty of the trip, generally include gear, guide and insurance. Most of the agencies also offer rafting, trekking, mountain climbing and other activities. Recommended places include:

Avalancha
ACTIVITIES COMPANY
(☑974 31 82 99; www.avalancha.org; Calle Arrabal)

Guías Boira
ACTIVITIES COMPANY
(☑974 31 89 74; www.guiasboira.com; Paseo San Hipólito)

Vertientes
ACTIVITIES COMPANY
(☑974 31 83 54; www.vertientesaventura.com; Calle San Gregorio 5)

🛏 Sleeping & Eating

Hotel Maribel
BOUTIQUE HOTEL €€€
(☑974 31 89 79; www.hotelmaribel.es; Calle Arrabal; d from €125) This boutique hotel has plenty of charm and while the decor won't be to everyone's taste (following a wine theme and ranging from gorgeous to vaguely kitsch), every room is supremely comfortable.

Hotel Villa de Alquézar
HOTEL €€
(☑/fax 974 31 84 16; www.villadealquezar.com, in Spanish; Calle Pedro Arenal Cavero 12; s/d incl breakfast from €58/67; P🅿🛜) One of the best places in town, with a lot of style in its large airy rooms; several rooms have great balcony views and there are period touches throughout.

Albergue Rural de Guara
REFUGE €
(☑974 31 83 96; www.albergueruraldeguara.com, in Spanish; Calle Pilaseras; dm €13) This cheerfully run *albergue* is perched up above the village with fine views from the surrounds. Breakfast is €5.50.

Restaurants line up along the *mirador* (lookout) section of Calle Arrabal and you could pretty much take your pick with *menús* for €10 to €15.

Restaurante Casa Gervasio
ARAGONESE €€
(☑974 31 82 82; Calle Pedro Arnal Cavero; menú €25-30) Up in the old town, this is possibly Alquézar's best with an excellent *menu degustación* for €30.

❶ Information

Tourist office (☑974 31 89 40; www.alquezar.org, in Spanish; Calle Arrabal; ⊙10am-1.30pm & 4.30-7.30pm daily Jun-Oct, Sat, Sun & festivals only Nov-May) Runs guided tours three times daily in summer (prices vary from €1.20 to €8 depending on the number of people) and can arrange audio guides (€4).

❶ Getting There & Away

BUS Autocares Cortés (☑974 31 15 52) runs a bus to Alquézar from Barbastro (€1.75) daily except Sunday; check with the tourist office for times – it doubles as the local school bus and times change during holidays.

CAR & MOTORCYCLE North of Alquézar, the road through Colungo to Aínsa is a delightful drive through pre-Pyrenean canyon country.

Barbastro

POP 16,924

Barbastro had a 350-year spell as one of Islamic Spain's most northerly outposts. There are few traces today and it's a bit run-down, although its role as the capital of the Somontano wine region has breathed new life into the town. The area around Plaza del Mercado has some character and the 16th-century cathedral boasts a main altarpiece – an incomplete, yet still stunning, work by the Renaissance master Damián Forment. Espacio de Vino (☑974 31 30 31; www.dosomontano.com, in Spanish; ⊙9am-8pm Mon-Fri, 11am-8pm Sat) – a wine interpretation centre and wine shop (⊙10am-2pm & 4.30-7.30pm Tue-Sat Sep-Jun, daily Jul & Aug) – is devoted to the local Somontano vintages.

The central, wheelchair-accessible Hostal Pirineos (☑974 31 00 00; www.hostalpirineos.com; Calle General Ricardos 13; s/d €40/50; ᴘ❋) has bright decor and also runs the town's best cafe. For more comfort, the four-star Gran Hotel Ciudad de Barbastro (☑974 30 89 00; www.ghbarbastro.com; Plaza del Mercado 4; s/d €62/83; ᴘ❋❀) is right on Plaza del Mercado.

Barbastro's tourist office (☑974 30 83 50; Avenida de la Merced 64; ⊙10am-2pm & 4.30-7.30pm Tue-Sat Sep-Jun, daily Jul & Aug) has town maps and information on bodegas in the surrounding Somontano area.

From Barbastro's bus station (☑974 31 12 93), Alosa (www.alosa.es, in Spanish) operates buses to/from Huesca (from €4.05, 50 min-utes), Lleida (Lérida, €5.45, 1½ hours), Benasque (€7.55, two hours) and Aínsa (€5.07, one hour).

Huesca

POP 52,059

Huesca is a provincial capital in more than name, a village writ large that shutters down during the afternoon hours and only stirs to life in the evenings. That said, its old centre retains some appeal and its location in north-central Aragón can serve as a launch pad for the Aragonese high country.

◉ Sights

Plaza de la Catedral & Around

CATHEDRAL, MUSEUM

Sleepy Plaza de la Catedral, at the heart of the old town, is presided over by the venerable Gothic cathedral (⊙10.30am-2pm & 3.30-5.30pm). The richly carved main portal dates from 1300. The stately interior features an astonishing, 16th-century alabaster *retablo* by Damián Forment that betrays a mix of Gothic and Renaissance styles. The 16th-century ayuntamiento (town hall) across the square is a gem of Renaissance detail. A little way north, the octagonal Museo de Huesca (Plaza Universidad 1; admission free; ⊙10am-2pm & 5-8pm Tue-Sat, 10am-2pm Sun) contains a well-displayed collection (labels in Spanish only) covering the archaeology and art of Huesca province, including eight works by Goya (room 7).

Iglesia de San Pedro El Viejo   CHURCH
(Plaza de San Pedro; adult/concession €2/1; ⊙10am-1.30pm & 4-7.30pm, closed afternoons Oct-May) Another of the city's historical

---

SOMONTANO WINES

Somontano won the coveted Denominación de Origen (DO) status in 1984 and it has since become Aragón's most prestigious wine-growing region. Centred around Barbastro, Somontano's 33 vineyards produce reds, whites and rosés from 13 different types of foreign and local grape varieties (including chardonnay, cabernet sauvignon, syrah and pinot noir), often blending local grapes such as parreleta (a red grape indigenous to the Somontano region) with foreign varieties. Some of the better-known Somontano labels include Enate and Viñas del Vero.

The tourist office in Barbastro has brochures in Spanish, English and French outlining the various bodegas (wineries) that can be visited for sales and tasting. The Museo del Vino and interpretation centre attached to the tourist office also have audiovisual displays on Somontano wines, interactive grape-aroma displays and wine tastings (☑974 31 30 31; tastings €10; ⊙6-8pm Sat); reservations are essential. You should also check out www.rutadelvinosomontano.com, which maps out possible wine itineraries through the region.

and architectural landmarks, the church of San Pedro is 12th-century Romanesque. Its cloister is adorned with beautiful Romanesque capitals.

🛏 Sleeping

La Posada de la Luna POSADA €€€
(📞974 24 08 57; www.posadadelaluna.com; Calle Joaquin Costa 10; s/d from €95/130; P🌐🖥) Our favourite hotel in Huesca, this lovely boutique place incorporates some original features of old Huesca architecture with a whimsical but contemporary feel. It's a comfortable, charming place, but there are just eight rooms, so book ahead. The breakfast buffet costs an excessive €15.

Hostal Lizana/Hostal Lizana 2 HOSTAL €
(📞974 22 07 76; www.hostal-lizana.com; Plaza de Lizana 6; s €24-45, d €38-60; P🌐🖥) Facing each other across a pleasant little plaza are these two worthwhile places, both with decent rooms – the rooms in Lizana 2 are newer, the bathrooms generally larger and you've got a better chance of a balcony room here. Parking costs €10.

Camping San Jorge CAMPSITE €
(📞974 22 74 16; www.campingsanjorge.com, in Spanish; Calle de Ricardo del Arco; per person/tent/car €4/4/4; ☀Apr–mid-Oct) This well-run woodland site 1km west of the old town centre has good facilities. There's a restaurant offering everything from *bocadillos* to sit-down meals.

🍴 Eating

For the capital of a province that prides itself on its cuisine, Huesca has surprisingly few outstanding eateries. That doesn't, however, mean you'll leave hungry.

La Taberna del Pintxo TAPAS €
(Calle de San Orencio 7; meals €15-20; ☀9am-4pm & 7pm-1am) South of the old town centre, this engaging little bar has an eclectic menu that ranges from creative *bocadillos* (such as steak with Roquefort and walnuts), *pintxos*, *platos combinados* (all-in-one dish), *cazuelas* (meals cooked in ceramic pots) and a more traditional *menú del día* (€11).

Hervi ARAGONESE €€
(📞974 24 03 33; Calle Santa Paciencia 2; meals €25-35; ☀Fri-Wed; 🍴) A hugely popular lunchtime scene, Hervi offers a *menú del día* where the servings are enormous and, unusually for Aragón, there's a range of vegetarian options.

Taberna de Lillas Pastia ARAGONESE FUSION €€
(📞974 21 16 91; www.lillaspastia.es; Plaza de Navarra 4; meals €30-40) Dress up just a little for this classy eatery in the town's old casino. The food is excellent, with a gastronome's touch in both presentation and taste. Meat, fish and attentive service are recurring themes, with special desserts that change daily.

ℹ Information

Tourist office (📞974 29 21 70; www.huesca turismo.com; Plaza López Allué 1; ☀9am-8pm) Runs daily guided tours of the historic centre (adult/concession €2/1) from mid-June until mid-September, and daily bus tours (adult/concession €5/2.50, under 12 years free) during the same period to the Castillo de Loarre, Los Mallos and the Sierra de la Guara.

ℹ Getting There & Away

BUS Alosa (📞974 21 07 00; www.alosa.es, in Spanish) runs numerous daily buses to/from Zaragoza (€6.30, 1½ hours), Jaca (€6.85, 1¼ hours), Barbastro (from €4.05, 50 minutes), Lleida (Lérida; €9.50, 2½ hours) and Barcelona (€15, four hours), and a daily service to Benasque (€11.60, 2½ hours).

TRAIN Nine trains a day run to/from Zaragoza (from €5.70, one hour), including two high-speed AVE services (€15.40, 40 minutes). There are also AVE services to/from Madrid (€60.90, 2¼ hours, two daily), as well as services to Teruel (€22.30, three hours, one daily), Valencia (€35, 5¼ hours, one daily) and Jaca (€6.50, 2¼ hours).

Around Huesca

CASTILLO DE LOARRE

The evocative **Castillo de Loarre** (www.castillodeloarre.com, in Spanish; admission with/without tour €3.50/2; ☀10am-2pm & 4-8pm) broods above the southern plains across which Islamic raiders once rode. Raised in the 11th century by Sancho III of Navarra and Sancho Ramírez of Aragón, its resemblance to a crusader castle has considerable resonance with those times. Don't be surprised if it looks familiar – it starred in the 2005 Ridley Scott film *Kingdom of Heaven,* when the medieval fortress served as a backdrop for much of the action (though the film is set in 12th-century France). The banquet scenes were shot in the Iglesia de San Pedro. There's a labyrinth of dungeons, tunnels and towers and two towers offering magnificent views.

THE SPANISH LAS VEGAS?

Overdevelopment in pursuit of the tourist dollar has blighted many coastal regions of eastern Spain over the years, but plans for building Europe's largest casino complex in the dusty badlands southeast of Zaragoza may just be the country's most controversial megaproject yet. 'Gran Scala' is the brainchild of International Leisure Development, a British-based consortium with dreams of creating a 20-sq-km town of 100,000 inhabitants, sporting a whopping 32 casinos, 70 hotels, 232 restaurants and 500 shops by 2020. Mock Egyptian pyramids, Roman temples and even a replica of the Pentagon all form part of the €17-billion proposal for this project. When finished, its advocates promise, it will draw 25 million visitors a year. Although approved by Aragón's regional government, Gran Scala has drawn fierce opposition from environmental groups, who have pointed out that this is one of Spain's driest regions, which already suffers chronic water shortages.

The castle is a 5km drive or a 2km, one-hour, uphill walk by the PR-HU105 footpath, from the village of Loarre, 35km northwest of Huesca.

Camping Castillo de Loarre (☑974 38 27 22; www.campingloarre.com, in Spanish; per person/tent/car €4/4/4; @) is a good site located halfway between the village and the castle. **Hospedería de Loarre** (☑974 38 27 06; www.hospederiadeloarre.com; Plaza Miguel Moya; s/d incl breakfast from €63/78; ❄@) is a charming, small hotel occupying a converted 16th-century mansion on Loarre village square. Its restaurant offers medium-priced to expensive meals and the hotel is wheelchair accessible.

Daily buses run to Loarre village from Huesca (€2.62, 40 minutes) Monday to Saturday.

LOS MALLOS

After a rather unexciting patch along the Huesca–Pamplona road, you come to a dramatic area along Río Gállego north of Ayerbe. On the eastern bank, huge rock towers known as Los Mallos (Mallets) rise up – they wouldn't look out of place in the Grand Canyon and are popular with serious rock climbers. For a closer look, head for Riglos.

THE SOUTH

Don't be deceived by the monotony of the vast sweeps of countryside immediately south of Zaragoza. Head further south or southeast and the landscape takes on a certain drama and shelters some of inland Spain's most intriguing towns and villages.

Daroca

POP 2331

Daroca is one of southern Aragón's best-kept secrets, a sleepy medieval town, one-time Islamic stronghold and, later, a Christian fortress town in the early medieval wars against Castilla. Its well-preserved old quarter is laden with historic references and the crumbling old city walls encircle the hilltops; the walls once boasted 114 military towers. Coming from north or south, you slip quietly down off the N234 and enter Calle Mayor, the cobbled main street, through monumental gates and into another world.

◉ Sights & Activites

Iglesia Colegiata de Santa María   CHURCH
(☉11am-1pm & 5.30-7pm) The pretty Plaza de España, at the top of the village, is dominated by this Romanesque Mudéjar Renaissance-style church, which boasts a lavish interior and organ. It's one of Daroca's most appealing (and unexpected) gems.

Iglesia de San Miguel   CHURCH
Further up the hill to the west, this 12th-century church is an austerely beautiful masterpiece of Romanesque architecture, but its greatest treasures are the Gothic frescoes within. Sadly, the church is kept closed, except if you join one of the tourist office's guided tours or for concerts during the town's festivals.

Guided Tours   WALKING TOURS
The best of the self-guided walks offered by the tourist office is the 45-minute **Ruta Monumental**, which gives a wonderful feel for the town and is well signposted. The other is the two-hour **Ruta del Cas-**

tillo y **Las Murallas**, a far more strenuous undertaking that climbs up to and follows the walls; the reward being magnificent views over Daroca. The tourist office also organises free **guided tours**, each lasting 50 minutes, of the town on Saturday and Sunday mornings – but only if enough people show up.

✴ Festivals & Events

Feria Medieval   MIDDLE AGES
The best time to be in Daroca is during the last week of July, when Calle Mayor is closed to traffic, locals don their medieval finery and concerts mark the Medieval Festival.

Festival Internacional de Música Antigua   MEDIEVAL MUSIC
In the first two weeks of August, Daroca hosts the International Festival of Medieval Music with courses and concerts in the two main churches.

🛏 Sleeping & Eating

La Posada del Almudí   POSADA, HOTEL €€
(☎976 80 06 06; www.posadadelalmudi.es; Grajera 5; s/d incl breakfast €45/65; ✻🛜) A one-time 16th-century palace, this lovely old place has a charming personal touch. The rooms in the main building have been lovingly restored and are comfortable, although the larger duplexes with balcony (€120) are the nicest. Across the lane it also has a range of super-modern, smallish but comfortable rooms. The attached restaurant (*menú* €12) offers good traditional cuisine.

Hotel Cien Balcones   HOTEL €€
(☎976 54 50 71; www.cienbalcones.com, in Spanish; Calle Mayor 88; s/d incl breakfast from €55/70; P✻🛜) This stylish three-star hotel has large rooms with a minimalist designer flourish. There's a good restaurant (meals from €30) and a cafe that serves up cheap *bocadillos* and pizza.

ℹ Information
Tourist office (☎976 80 01 29; Plaza de España 4; ◷10.30am-2pm & 4.30-7.30pm) Offers maps for self-guided walks through town.

ℹ Getting There & Away
Buses stop outside the Mesón Félix bar, at Calle Mayor 104. Four daily buses run to Zaragoza and Teruel, Monday to Saturday.

Laguna de Gallocanta
Some 20km south of Daroca and a similar distance west of Calamocha on the N234, this is Spain's largest natural lake, with an area of about 15 sq km (though it can almost dry up in summer). It's a winter home for some 70,000 cranes and many other waterfowl. A Centro de Interpretación (◷10am-2pm & 4-8pm Sat & Sun, daily Nov & Feb), with information and exhibitions, is on the Tornos–Bello road near the southeast corner of the lake where the cranes gather. Take binoculars.

Teruel
POP 35,396 / ELEV 917M
One of Spain's most attractive provincial cities, Teruel is an open-air museum of ornate Mudéjar monuments. However, this is a living museum where the streets are filled with life – a reflection of a city reasserting itself with cultural attitude. For decades, Teruel had something of an image problem and an air of neglect, a place seemingly left behind by modern Spain's mainstream renaissance – '*Teruel existe!*' ('Teruel exists!') is still an oft-heard, only partly tongue-in-cheek refrain. But the city has pulled itself up by its boot-straps and it's well worth seeing what all the fuss is about. Be warned, though – in winter Teruel can be one of the coldest places in Spain, so come prepared.

DANCING IN THE DESERT

The rural town of Fraga in the relentless flatlands between Zaragoza and the Mediterranean coast is the unlikely locale for **Florida 135** (www.f135. com, in Spanish; Calle Sotet 2; admission €13; ◷from 11.30pm Sat), the temple of Spanish techno. The windowless 3000-sq-metre graffiti-strewn space is the most recent incarnation of a dance hall that's been going since 1942. Busloads of clubbers arrive for the club's main Saturday-night sessions. In mid-July, Fraga hosts the **Monegros Desert Festival** (www.monegrosfestival.com), formerly called the Groove Parade, attracting dozens of Spanish and internationally renowned DJs and bands.

◎ Sights

Most of Teruel's sights are close to Plaza del Torico (the name derived from a statue of what could be Spain's smallest bull), a lively focus of city life.

Cathedral   CATHEDRAL

(Plaza de la Catedral; adult/child €3/2; ◎11am-2pm & 4-8pm) Teruel's cathedral is a rich example of the Mudéjar imagination at work with its kaleidoscopic brickwork and colourful ceramic tiles. The superb 13th-century bell tower has hints of the Romanesque in its detail. Inside, the astounding Mudéjar ceiling of the nave is covered with paintings that add up to a medieval cosmography – from musical instruments and hunting scenes to coats of arms and Christ's crucifixion. Other highlights include the 16th-century wooden *retablo mayor* and the extraordinary 15th-century Gothic *retablo* in the Capilla de la Coronación.

Fundación Amantes   MUSEUM, CHURCH

(www.amantesdeteruel.es; Calle Matías Abad 3; Mausoleo/Iglesia de San Pedro & Torre de San Pedro €4/5, combined ticket €8; ◎10am-2pm & 4-8pm) The somewhat curious **Mausoleo de los Amantes** (Mausoleum of the Lovers) pulls out the stops on the city's famous legend of Isabel and Juan Diego (see the boxed text, p394). Here they lie in modern alabaster tombs, sculpted by Juan de Ávalos, with their heads tilted endearingly towards each other. Around this centrepiece has been shaped a remarkable audiovisual exhibition, featuring music and theatre. It skates very close to glorious kitsch, but is entirely persuasive. The Mausoleo is wheelchair accessible.

Attached to the complex is the 14th-century Iglesia de San Pedro, with a stunning ceiling, baroque high altar and simple cloisters, as well as the Torre de San Pedro (Torre Mudéjar), from where there are fine views over central Teruel.

Torre de El Salvador   TOWER, MUSEUM

(www.teruelmudejar.com, in Spanish; Calle El Salvador; adult/child €2.50/1.80; ◎10am-2pm & 4-8pm) The most impressive of Teruel's other Mudéjar monuments is the Torre de El Salvador, an early-14th-century extravaganza of brick and ceramics built around an older Islamic minaret. You climb the narrow stairways and passageways. Along the way, you'll find exhibits on Mudéjar art and architecture. The views from the summit are Teruel's best.

Torre de San Martín   TOWER

Although you can't climb it, Torre de San Martín, the northwestern gate of the old city, is almost as beautiful as the Torre de El Salvador. It was finished in 1316 and was incorporated into the city's walls in the 16th century.

FREE Museo Provincial   MUSEUM

(Plaza Polanco; ◎10am-2pm & 4-7pm Tue-Fri, 10am-2pm Sat & Sun) Teruel's Museo Provincial is housed in the 16th-century Casa de la Comunidad, a fine work of Renaissance architecture. The archaeological sections are a highlight, and there are changing exhibitions of contemporary art.

Aljibe Fondero   CISTERNS

(Calle Ramón y Cajal; adult/concession €1.20/0.80; ◎10am-2pm & 4-8pm Sep-Jul, 10am-8pm Aug) Off the southeastern corner of Plaza del Torico is the entrance to the Aljibe, a fascinating 14th-century underground water-storage facility. In addition to showcasing the extant remnants of the cisterns, there are interesting Spanish-language audiovisual presentations on medieval Teruel.

La Escalinata   STAIRCASE

The grand staircase that connects the Paseo del Óvalo on the old city's fringe to the train station, La Escalinata is a masterpiece of neo-Mudéjar monumental architecture. First built in 1920, it was painstakingly restored in the first years of the 21st century. Along with the redesigned Paseo del Óvalo, La Escalinata has won numerous awards for urban redesign. There's a lift back up to the Paseo.

Dinópolis   DINOSAUR THEME PARK

(www.dinopolis.com, in Spanish; adult/child €22/17; ◎10am-8pm) It's fun for all at this large, modern dinosaur theme park. It's 3km southwest of the town centre, well signposted just off the Valencia road. A highlight is 'El Ride', a motorised trip through time spiced up with animated dinosaur robots.

✮ Festivals & Events

Fiesta Medieval   MIDDLE AGES

On the weekend closest to 14 February, thousands of Teruel's inhabitants (and even more visitors from elsewhere) don medieval dress for the Fiesta Medieval. There are medieval markets and food stalls, but the centrepiece is the re-enactment of the Diego and Isabel legend (see the boxed text, p394).

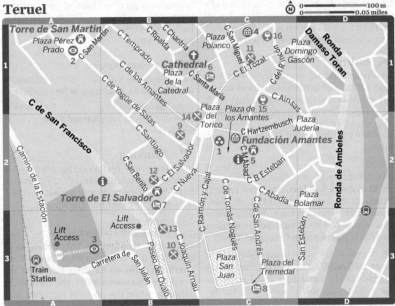

Teruel map showing street grid with labelled locations including Torre de San Martín, Plaza Pérez Prado, Cathedral, Plaza de la Catedral, Torre de El Salvador, Fundación Amantes, Plaza del Torico, Train Station, and numerous numbered points of interest.

Feria del Ángel   TERUEL

The **Día de San Cristóbal** (St Christopher's Day; 10 July) is the hub of the week-long Feria del Ángel, which commemorates Teruel's founding.

🛌 Sleeping

Hotel el Mudayyan   HOTEL €€

(☎978 62 30 42; www.elmudayyan.com, in Spanish; Calle Nueva 18; s €55-70, d €70-90; ❄️🖥️📶) Easily the most character-filled of Teruel's hotels, El Mudayyan has lovely rooms with polished wood floors, wooden beams and charming interior design that's different in every room. It also has a *tetería* (teahouse) in the basement and a curious subterranean passage that dates back to earliest Teruel.

Hostal Aragón   HOSTAL €

(☎978 60 13 87; www.hostalaragon.org; Calle Santa María 4; s with/without bathroom €25/21, d with/without bathroom €44/29) An unassuming place with well-kept wood-panelled rooms and on a narrow side street, this place drops its prices by a few euros midweek. We recommend booking at weekends and on holidays.

Hotel Plaza Boulevard   HOTEL €€

(☎978 60 86 55; www.plazaboulevard.sercotel. com, in Spanish; Plaza del Tremedal 3; s/d from

Teruel

◉ Top Sights

Cathedral	B1
Fundación Amantes	C2
Torre de El Salvador	B2
Torre de San Martín	A1

◉ Sights

1	Aljibe Fondero	C2
2	Iglesia de San Pedro	A1
3	La Escalinata	A3
4	Museo Provincial	C1
5	Torre de San Pedro	C2

🛌 Sleeping

6	Hostal Aragón	C1
7	Hotel El Mudayyan	B2
8	Hotel Plaza Boulevard	C3

🍽 Eating

9	Aqui Teruel!	B2
10	Bar Gregory	B3
11	La Taberna de Rokelin	C1
12	La Torre de Salavdor	B2
13	Mesón Óvalo	B3
14	Munöz	B2

🍷 Drinking

	Café-Pub La Torre	(see 12)
15	Flanagan's	C1
16	Fonda del Tozal	C1

€56/96; ✺🛜) Probably the pick of Teruel's other midrange hotels, Hotel Plaza Boulevard has a good location just off Plaza San Juan and comfortable modern rooms.

Eating

Landlocked Teruel is utterly devoted to meat eating and promotes its local *jamón* and other *embutidos* (cured meats) with enthusiasm. One local speciality you'll find everywhere is *las Delicias de Teruel* (local *jamón* with toasted bread and fresh tomato).

Muñoz   DELICATESSEN, CAFÉ €
(www.dulcesdeteruel.com; Plaza del Torico 23; ⏰9.30am-2pm & 5.30-9pm, closed Sun evening) Teruel's best place for breakfast or a deli snack in the early evening, Muñoz has a more classy feel to it (and better service) than other places around Plaza del Torico.

Bar Gregory   TAPAS BAR, ARAGONESE €
(Paseo del Óvalo 6; meals €15-20; ⏰closed Tue) The pick of the tapas bars lined up along Paseo del Óvalo, this place has all the local staples, outdoor tables at which to enjoy them and good service. There's also a decent restaurant, El Gregory Plus, attached.

La Torre de Salvador   ARAGONESE €€
(☑978 61 73 76; Calle El Salvador; meals €30-40; ⏰Tue-Sun) Right opposite the Torre de El Salvador, this smart restaurant raises the stakes with its *nouveau cuisine Aragonese*, with subtle dishes riffing on traditional themes, but plenty of local staples for those eager to get to the heart of Aragonese cooking.

Mesón Óvalo   ARAGONESE €€
(☑978 61 82 35; Paseo del Óvalo 8; meals €25-35; ⏰lunch & dinner Tue-Sat, lunch Sun) There's a strong emphasis on regional Aragonese cuisine at this pleasant place, with meat and game dishes to the fore. One fine local speciality is *jarretes* (hock of lamb stewed with wild mushrooms, a dish that dates back to the period when Muslims ruled this part of Spain).

Other temples to *jamón*:

La Taberna de Rokelin   TAPAS €
(Calle El Tozal 33; tapa/ración of ham €3/15)

Aqui Teruel!   TAPAS €
(Calle de Yagüe de Salas 4; tapa/ración €3.50/11)

Drinking

If you're fairly undiscerning about your night-time drinking holes, Plaza Bolamar has a bar on every doorstep with weekend crowds spilling over into the square.

Café-Pub La Torre   BAR
(Calle El Salvador 20; ⏰9am-1am Mon-Thu, noon-4am Fri & Sat, noon-1am Sun) This stylish place is our favourite bar in Teruel, as good for an afternoon drink as for lively late-night atmosphere. Its eastern wall is the Torre de El Salvador, while the upstairs bar often has contemporary art installations.

Fonda del Tozal   BAR
(Calle del Rincón 5; ⏰noon-late) The cavernous ground-floor bar is a rough-and-ready old place in which to unwind. It was formerly the stables of a very old inn and it's at its best when packed on weekend nights; on weekday afternoons, it can feel like the Wild West in a one-horse town.

Flanagan's   IRISH PUB
(Calle Ainsas 2; ⏰4pm-3.30am Sun-Thu, 5pm-4.30am Fri & Sat) We don't generally list Irish pubs, but this place rocks into the wee hours with the sort of music you're loathe to admit you like but dance to anyway.

THE LOVERS OF TERUEL

In the early 13th century Juan Diego de Marcilla and Isabel de Segura fell in love, but, in the manner of other star-crossed historical lovers, there was a catch: Isabel was the only daughter of a wealthy family, while poor old Juan Diego was, well, poor. Juan Diego convinced Isabel's reluctant father to postpone plans for Isabel's marriage to someone more appropriate for five years, during which time Juan Diego would seek his fortune. Not waiting a second longer than the five years, Isabel's father married off his daughter in 1217, only for Juan Diego to return, triumphant, immediately after the wedding. He begged Isabel for a kiss, which she refused, condemning Juan Diego to die of a broken heart. A final twist saw Isabel attend the funeral in mourning, whereupon she gave Juan Diego the kiss he had craved in life. Isabel promptly died and the two lovers were buried together.

ℹ Information

City tourist office (☑978 62 41 05; Plaza de los Amantes 6; ☉10am-2pm & 4-8pm Sep-Jul, 10am-8pm Aug) Ask here for audio guides (€2) to the old city.

Regional tourist office (☑978 64 14 61; Calle de San Francisco 1; ☉9am-2pm & 4.45-7.45pm)

ℹ Getting There & Away

From Teruel's **bus station** (☑978 61 07 89; www.estacionbus-teruel.com, in Spanish), **Autobuses Jiménez** (www.grupo-jimenez.com, in Spanish) runs regular buses to/from Zaragoza (€12.25, 2½ hours), Valencia (€11, 2¼ hours) and Madrid (€20.90, 4½ hours).

Teruel is on the railway between Zaragoza (€15.90, two hours) and Valencia (from €10.80, 2½ hours).

Albarracín

POP 1097 / ELEV 1180M

Albarracín is one of Spain's most beautiful villages. It takes time to get here, 38km west of Teruel, but it's worth it for the marvellous sense of timelessness that not even the modern onslaught of summer coach tours can erase. Ragged fortress walls rise up the surrounding slopes and the town's streets retain their mazelike charm, with centuries-old buildings leaning over them.

Built on a steep, rocky height carved out by a meander of Río Guadalaviar, Albarracín was, from 1012 to 1104, the seat of a tiny Islamic state ruled by the Berber Banu Razin dynasty with links to Córdoba. From 1170 to 1285 it was an independent Christian kingdom sandwiched between Castilla and Aragón.

◉ Sights

All across Albarracín, nearly every brick, stone, slab of concrete and slap of mortar is in some earthy shade of red or pink, creating wonderful plays of colour, particularly in the evening.

Cathedral   CATHEDRAL

(☉10.30am-2pm & 4-6pm, to 8pm Jul-Sep, closed Sun afternoon) With its cupola typical of the Spanish Levant, Albarracín's cathedral is one of the signature monuments of the village skyline; within, it has an elaborate gilded altarpiece. The Palacio Episcopal (Bishop's Palace) is attached to the cathedral.

Museo de Albarracín   ARCHAEOLOGICAL MUSEUM

(Calle San Juan; admission €2.50; ☉10.30am-1pm & 4.30-6pm, closed Sun afternoon) In the old

EL MAESTRAZGO

El Maestrazgo, a medieval knightly domain of wonderfully isolated valleys and rocky hills, spills over from Valencia province (see p572). **Cantavieja**, northeast of Teruel along the A226, is a dramatically sited ridge-top town that was reputedly founded by Hannibal and later became a seat of the Knights Templar. The best-preserved (and partly restored) part of town is the porticoed Plaza Cristo Rey. If you're heading for Morella in the Valencian Maestrazgo, the A226 northeast of Cantavieja will take you, snaking down past ragged cliffs and then via **Mirambel**, a fine example of a gently decaying, walled medieval town. One Monday-to-Friday bus runs from Teruel to Cantavieja (€8.50, 1½ hours).

city hospital, this interesting museum is devoted to the town's Islamic heritage, with numerous finds from the archaeological digs in the castle. Opposite the museum's entrance, the 17th-century **Ermita de San Juan** was built on the site of Albarracín's former synagogue.

Castle   CASTLE

(Castillo; admission €2.50; ☉guided tours noon, 1pm, 4.30pm & 5.30pm Mon-Fri, 11am & 6.30pm Sat, 11am, noon & 1pm Sun) Crowning the old town above the cathedral near the southern end of town, this fascinating castle, with 11 towers and an area of 3600 sq metres, dates from the 9th century when Albarracín was an important Islamic military post. In private hands until 2005, the archaeological digs have revealed fascinating insights into the town's history. All is explained on the hour-long Spanish-language tour (buy your tickets at the Museo de Albarracín); contact the Centro de Información to arrange English-language tours. Apart from anything else, the views from the ramparts are superb.

Muralla   CITY WALL

Albarracín's highest point, the **Torre del Andador** (Walkway Tower) dates from the 9th century; the surrounding walls are more recent and date from the 11th or 12th century. It's a stiff climb to the summit, but worth every gasp for the views down over the town.

Tours

El Andador WALKING TOUR
(☎978 70 03 81; www.elandador.es, in Spanish; Calle de la Catedral 4; tours €3.50) Twice daily 1½-hour walks through Albarracín.

Centro de Información WALKING TOUR
(☎978 70 40 35; www.albarracinespaciosyteso ros.com, in Spanish; Calle de la Catedral; tours €3.50) Organises 1½-hour guided walks up to four times daily.

Sleeping

La Casa del Tío Americano SMALL HOTEL €€
(☎978 71 01 25; www.lacasadeltioamericano. com; Calle Los Palacios 9; d €95; 🖲) A wonderful small hotel, 'The House of the American Uncle' boasts brightly painted rooms, some with exposed stone walls and special views and friendly, impeccable service. The views of the village from the breakfast terrace (and from rooms 2 and 3) are magnificent. A welcoming glass of champagne is a lovely touch.

Casa de Santiago SMALL HOTEL €€
(☎978 70 03 16; www.casadesantiago.net, in Spanish; Subida a las Torres 11; d/ste €70/95; 🖲) A beautiful place, with lots of exposed wood, tiled floors and with charming service to go with it, the Casa lies at the heart of the old town a few steps up from Plaza Mayor. You step off the street into an immediate comfort zone.

Habitaciones Los Palacios HOSTAL €
(☎978 70 03 27; www.montepalacios.com, in Spanish; Calle Los Palacios 21; s/d €28/45) This charming place has spotless rooms, some with balconies and gorgeous views. It's about 250m from Plaza Mayor, starting along Calle de Santiago and exiting through Portal de Molina.

Camping Ciudad de Albarracín
CAMPSITE €
(☎978 71 01 97; www.campingalbarracin.com; per person/tent/car €3.80/3.80/3.80; ⊙Apr-Oct) Pleasant, small and shaded, the camping ground is 2km from the heart of Albarracín, off the Bezas road. It also has timbered four-person chalets for €69.

Other stylish options:

Posada del Adarve SMALL HOTEL €
(☎978 70 03 04; www.posadadeladarve.com, in Spanish; Calle Portal de Molina 23; s €35, d €50-75; ⊚) An Albarracín town house lovingly

restored by the Portal de Molina (Molina Gateway).

Hotel Arabia HOTEL €€
(☎978 71 02 12; www.montesuniversales.com; Calle Bernardo Zapater 2; s €48-59, d €68-89, apt €77-194; 🖲) A 17th-century convent with good rooms and enormous apartments with terrific views.

La Casona del Ajimez SMALL HOTEL €€
(☎978 71 03 21; www.casonadelajimez.com, in Spanish; Calle de San Juan 2; d €76) Well-tended rooms at the southern end of town near the cathedral.

Eating

Tapas, *raciones* and hearty meals are available at all of the bars around town, with a particularly high concentration in the streets around the Plaza Mayor. Casa de Santiago hotel also has a good restaurant.

TOP CHOICE Tiempo de Ensueño
GOURMET FOOD €€
(☎978 70 40 70; www.tiempodeensuenyo.com; menú €38, meals €30; ⊙closed Wed) Every now and then, you stumble upon something special. This high-class restaurant has a sleek, light-filled dining room, attentive but discreet service and food that you'll remember long after you've left. Spanish nouvelle cuisine in all its innovative guises makes an appearance here with a changing menu, as well as a book-length wine list, mineral-water menu, choice of olive oils, welcome cocktail and, above all, exquisite tastes. There's a tempting *menu degustación* (€38) as well as à la carte choices.

ℹ Information

Centro de Información (☎978 70 40 35; Calle de la Catedral; ⊙10am-2pm & 4-6.30pm, closed Sun afternoon) Excellent, privately run information office.

Tourist office (☎978 71 02 62; Calle San Antonio; ⊙10am-2pm & 4-8pm Tue-Sun)

ℹ Getting There & Away

Buses travel once daily between Teruel and Albarracín (€3.80, 45 minutes).

Southeast of Teruel

The sparsely populated hills stretching east of Teruel into the Valencia region present a bleached maze of rocky peaks and dramat-

LUIS BUÑUEL & THE DRUMS OF CALANDA

Luis Buñuel's earliest memories were of the drums of Calanda. In the centuries-old ritual of the film director's birthplace, Good Friday noon marks the *rompida de la hora* (breaking of the hour). At that moment thousands commence banging on *tambores* (snare drums) and *bombos* (bass drums), together producing a thunderous din. The ceremony goes on for 24 hours, only ceasing for the passage of the standard Easter processions.

'The drums, that amazing, resounding, cosmic phenomenon that brushes the collective subconscious, causes the earth to tremble beneath our feet,' Buñuel recalls in his memoir, *Mi Ultimo Suspiro* (My Last Sigh). 'One has only to place his hand on the wall of a house to feel the vibrations... Anyone who manages to fall asleep, lulled by the banging, awakes with a start when the sound trails off. At dawn, the drum skins are stained with blood: hands bleed after so much banging. And these are the rough hands of peasants.'

This clamour worked its way into Buñuel's dreams and nightmares, and eventually into his surreal films; the drums left their imprint, along with a taste for ritual, costumes and disguises.

ic gorges inhabited by quiet, ancient stone *pueblos* (villages) well away from well-trodden tourist trails. Unless you have a lot of time, you'll need a vehicle; buses pass through daily at best.

A worthwhile route from Teruel for those with their own transport leads 43km southeast to Mora de Rubielos in the foothills of the Sierra de Gudar. A massive 14th-century castle (admission €1.50; ☺10am-2pm & 5-8pm Tue-Sun) towers over the village amid a sea of red and pink stone.

Another 14km southeast along the A232 is pretty Rubielos de Mora, a quiet web of narrow streets whose houses have typically small Aragonese balconies. The friendly Hotel Los Leones (☎978 80 44 77; www. losleones.info, in Spanish; Plaza Igual y Gil 3; s/d €75/110) has attractive period decor and comfortable rooms, and has a fine restaurant with a €30 *menú*.

Calanda

POP 3899

From Teruel the N420 heads north through mountainous terrain before descending to meet the east–west N211, which leads to Calanda. The chief (and, some would say, only) reason to visit Calanda is the Centro Buñuel Calanda (☎978 84 65 24; www. cbcvirtual.com, in Spanish; Calle Mayor 48; adult/concession €3.50/2.50; ☺10.30am-1.30pm & 4-8pm Tue-Sun), a museum devoted to the life and films of Luis Buñuel (1900–83). The museum tries to remain faithful to the surrealist spirit of the Calanda native, cleverly weaving images from his oeuvre into the tour. For true aficionados, a filmography room has computers with details of all 32 of Buñuel's films, accompanied by screenings of key scenes and commentary by the director.

Calanda is served by buses from Teruel.

Basque Country, Navarra & La Rioja

Best Places to Eat

» Arzak (p422)

» La Cuchara de San Telmo (p422)

» Rio-Oja (p406)

» Martín Berasategui Restaurant (p422)

» Mesón las Migas (p444)

Best Places to Stay

» Hotel Marqués de Riscal (p453)

» Pensión Bellas Artes (p420)

» Palacio Guendulain (p435)

» Hospederia las Pedrolas (p450)

» La Casa de los Arquillos (p430)

Why Go?

The jade hills and drizzle-filled skies of this pocket of Spain are quite a contrast to the popular image of the country. The Basques, the people who inhabit this corner, also consider themselves different. They claim to be the oldest Europeans and to speak the original European language. Whether or not this is actually the case remains unproven, but what is beyond doubt is that they live in a land of exceptional beauty and diversity. There are mountains watched over by almost-forgotten gods, cultural museums and art galleries, street parties a million people strong, and the best food in Spain.

Leave the rugged north behind and feel the temperature rise as you hit the open, classically Spanish plains south of Pamplona. Here you enter the world of Navarra and La Rioja. It's a region awash with glorious wine, sunburst colours, dreamy landscapes, medieval monasteries and enticing wine towns.

When to Go?

Bilbao

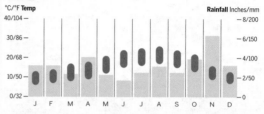

May–June Beat the crowds to the art galleries of Bilbao and the *pintxo* bars of San Sebastián.

6–14 July Run, very fast, away from a pack of marauding bulls in Pamplona.

September Hike the high passes of the Navarran Pyrenees and relish the autumnal colours.

BASQUE COUNTRY

No matter where you've just come from, be it the hot, southern plains of Spain or gentle and pristine France, the Basque Country is different. Known to Basques as Euskadi or Euskal Herria ('the land of Basque Speakers') and called El Pais Vasco in Spanish, this is where mountain peaks reach for the skies and sublime rocky coves are battered by mighty Atlantic swells. It's a place that demands exploration beyond the delightful and cosmopolitan main cities of Bilbao, Vitoria and San Sebastián. You travel through the Basque Country always curious, and always rewarded.

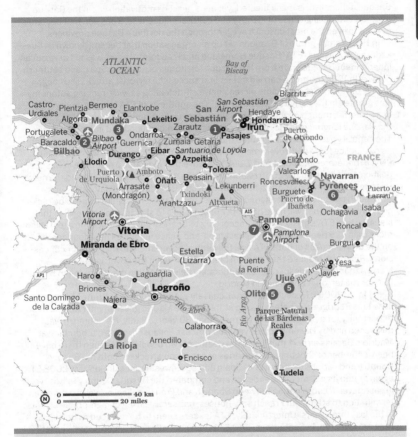

Basque Country, Navarra & La Rioja Highlights

❶ Play on a perfect beach, gorge on fabulous *pintxos* (Basque tapas), dance all night and dream of staying forever in stylish **San Sebastián** (p415), the food capital of the planet

❷ Wish that you too could paint like a genius in the galleries of **Bilbao** (p401)

❸ Get barrelled in the surf at **Mundaka** (p411) and recreate the Guggenheim in sandcastle form on a beautiful Basque **beach** (p414)

❹ Learn the secrets of a good drop in the museums and vineyards of **La Rioja** (p451)

❺ Roll back the years in the medieval fortress towns of **Olite** (p443) and **Ujué** (p444)

❻ Climb mist-shrouded slopes haunted by witches and vultures in the **Navarran Pyrenees** (p440)

❼ Pretend you're Hemingway during the Sanfermines week of debauchery in **Pamplona** (p436)

History

No one quite knows where the Basque people came from (they have no migration myth in their oral history), but their presence here is believed to predate even the earliest known migrations. The Romans left the hilly Basque Country more or less to itself, but the expansionist Castilian crown gained sovereignty over Basque territories during the Middle Ages (1000–1450),

BASQUE NATIONALISM

Basque nationalism is many faceted, yet at its heart its motivation lies in the Basque people's compelling sense of identity and cultural uniqueness, a passion that becomes evident to even the most casual traveller through the northern Basque provinces.

In 1959 a small group of Basques set up an organisation that became known as Euskadi Ta Askatasuna (ETA; Basque Homeland and Freedom). Its goal was to carve out an independent Basque state from the Basque territories of northern Spain and southern France. In 1968 the group carried out its first successful terrorist attack. Thus began a cycle of violence that became increasingly self-defeating as wide-ranging autonomy was granted in the early 1980s and 1990s. The antithesis of ETA was the emergence of a powerful, though peaceful, nationalism, especially among the young, that saw the Basque language as the most potent symbol of nationhood and independence. The central government has granted much autonomy to the Basque region, including its own police force and government. For around 30 years the region was run by the PNV, a moderate nationalist party, but, in a move that indicates a new page in Basque politics, the winner of the 2009 regional elections was the socialist party and the new Basque president, Patxi López, has vowed to fight ETA 'day in and day out'.

Though considerably weakened in the last few years, ETA is still a force to be reckoned with and López will have his work cut out if he's to stay true to his word. In the last 40 years ETA's grisly war has (according to Spanish government estimates) killed more than 825 people. Sporadic 'ceasefires' and peace initiatives have foundered on the unwillingness of both ETA and the central government to make major concessions. Relations reached their nadir in March 2004 when the government of José María Aznar made a desperate, and ultimately failed, election play by trying to blame ETA for the terrorist bombings in Madrid.

In March 2006 ETA declared its 'final' ceasefire. The response of Prime Minister José Luis Rodríguez Zapatero was to state that the Madrid government had 'the best opportunity for a peace process for more than 30 years'. Sadly, his optimism was misplaced and by December that year the process collapsed with a car bombing at Madrid's Barajas airport that led to the deaths of two people. Since then there have been a number of shootings and a series of car-bomb attacks in both the Basque Country and various other parts of Spain and southwest France. In January 2008 ETA again stated its call for independence and compared the Basque Country to Kosovo. A greater level of coordination between Spanish and French police, as well as more determination to stamp out French safe houses, has seen a string of high-profile arrests in the last three years. Unfortunately, ETA leaders seem to be replaced as quickly as they are arrested. In September 2010 ETA unexpectedly announced a total ceasefire and said that it would now look to achieve its goals through peaceful means. The Madrid government was quick to dismiss this announcement and, just 11 days later, a small bomb went off in an industrial part of Vitoria. Police blamed this on supporters of ETA rather than the group itself.

No one would claim that all Basques are passionate nationalists, but with expanded autonomy on the cards for Catalonia, the realisation of the peaceful aspirations of a large majority of Basques seems more promising than ever. Complex and conflicting issues remain, however, not least the vexed question of the Madrid government's policy of imprisoning outside the Basque Country those whom many Basques see as political prisoners. The 2003 banning of Basque political party Batasuna for its alleged relationship to ETA and widely condemned support for terrorism has further aggravated the situation. Resolving this would be a major step forward.

although with considerable difficulty; Navarra constituted a separate kingdom until 1512. Even when they came within the Castilian orbit, Navarra and the three other Basque provinces (Guipúzcoa, Vizcaya and Álava) extracted broad autonomy arrangements, known as the *fueros* (the ancient laws of the Basques).

After the Second Carlist War in 1876, all provinces except Navarra were stripped of their coveted *fueros,* thereby fuelling nascent Basque nationalism. Yet, although the Partido Nacionalista Vasco (PNV; Basque Nationalist Party) was established in 1894, support was never uniform as all Basque provinces included a considerable Castilian contingent.

When the Republican government in Madrid proposed the possibility of home rule (self-government) to the Basques in 1936, both Guipúzcoa and Vizcaya took up the offer. When the Spanish Civil War erupted, conservative rural Navarra and Álava supported Franco, while Vizcaya and Guipúzcoa sided with the Republicans, a decision they paid a high price for in the four decades that followed.

It was during the Franco days that Euskadi Ta Askatasuna (ETA; Basque Homeland and Freedom) was first born. It was originally set up to fight against the Franco regime, which suppressed the Basques through banning the language and almost all forms of Basque culture. After the overthrow of the dictator, ETA called for nothing less than total independence and continued its bloody fight against the Spanish government.

At the time of writing ETA had once again called a halt to armed attacks. Only time will tell if this ceasefire will last the distance.

Bilbao

POP 354,200

Bilbao (Bilbo in Basque) had a tough upbringing. Growing up in an environment of heavy industry and industrial wastelands, it was abused for years by those in power and had to work hard to get anywhere. But, like the kid from the estates who made it big, Bilbao's graft paid off when a few wise investments left it with a shimmering titanium fish called the Museo Guggenheim and a horde of arty groupies around the world.

The Bilbaocard (1-/2-/3-day pass €6/10/12) entitles the user to reduced rates on all city transport as well as reductions at many of the sights. It can be purchased from any of the tourist offices. **Creditrans** give significant discounts on the metro, tram and city-bus network. They are available in €5, €10 and €15 denominations from all metro and tram stations.

The Botxo (Hole), as it's fondly known to its inhabitants, has now matured into its role of major European art centre. However, in doing so, it hasn't gone all toffee-nosed and forgotten its past: at heart it remains a hard-working and, physically, rather ugly town, but it's one that has real character. It's this down-to-earth soul, rather than its plethora of art galleries, that is the real attraction of the vital, exciting and cultured city of Bilbao.

History

Bilbao was granted the title of *villa* (city-state) in 1300 and medieval *bilbaínos* went about their business in the bustle of Las Siete Calles, the original seven streets of the old town, and down on the wharves. The conquest of the Americas stimulated trade and Basque fishers, merchants and settlers soon built strong links to cities such as Boston. By the late 19th century the smokestacks of steelworks, shipbuilding yards and chemical plants dominated the area's skyline.

From the Carlist Wars through to the Spanish Civil War, Bilbao was always considered the greatest prize in the north, largely for its industrial value. Franco took the city in the spring of 1937 and reprisals against Basque nationalists were massive and long lasting. Yet during the Franco era, the city prospered as it fed Spanish industrial needs. This was followed by the seemingly terminal economic decline that has been so dynamically reversed in recent years.

◉ Sights

Museo Guggenheim　　　ART GALLERY
(www.guggenheim-bilbao.es; Avenida Abandoibarra 2; adult/child €13/free; ⊙10am-8pm Tue-Sun) Opened in September 1997, Bilbao's Museo Guggenheim lifted modern architecture and Bilbao into the 21st century –

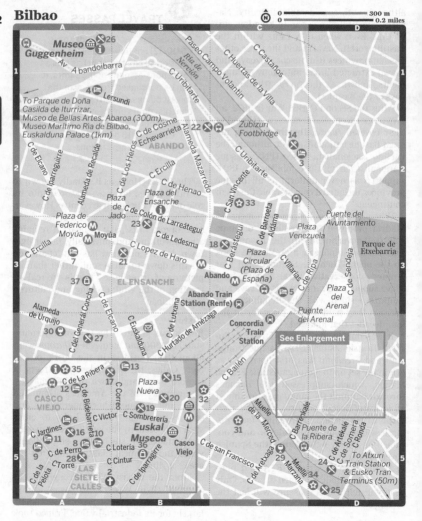

See Enlargement

with sensation. It boosted the city's already inspired regeneration, stimulated further development and placed Bilbao firmly in the world art and tourism spotlight.

Some might say, probably quite rightly, that structure overwhelms function here and that the Guggenheim is more famous for its architecture than its content. But Canadian architect Frank Gehry's inspired use of flowing canopies, cliffs, promontories, ship shapes, towers and flying fins is irresistible.

Like all great architects, Gehry designed the Guggenheim with historical and geo-graphical contexts in mind. The site was an industrial wasteland, part of Bilbao's wretched and decaying warehouse district on the banks of Ría de Bilbao. The city's historical industries of shipbuilding and fishing reflected Gehry's own interests, not least his engagement with industrial materials in previous works. The gleaming titanium tiles that sheathe most of the building like giant herring scales are said to have been inspired by the architect's childhood fascination with fish.

The interior of the Guggenheim is purposefully vast. The cathedral-like atrium is more than 45m high. Light pours in through the glass cliffs. Permanent exhibits fill the ground floor and include such wonders as mazes of metal and phrases of light reaching for the skies.

For most people, though, it is the temporary exhibitions that are the main attraction (check the website for upcoming shows). During our last visit, these included Robert Rauschenberg's fantastic recycled waste collections and a fabulous set of reality-distorting mirrors by Anish Kapoor.

Admission prices vary depending on special exhibitions; the last ticket sales are half an hour before closing. Free guided tours in English and French take place at 11am, 12.30pm, 4.30pm and 6.30pm; sign up half an hour before at the information desk. Groups are limited to 20, so get there early. Sign-language tours take place at 12.30pm on the last Sunday of each month. Excellent self-guided audio tours in various languages are free with admission. Entry queues can be horrendous, with wet summer days and Easter almost guaranteeing you a wait of over an hour. The museum is wheelchair accessible.

Museo de Bellas Artes ART GALLERY
(Fine Arts Museum; www.museobilbao.com; Plaza del Museo 2; adult/child €6/free, free Wed; ☺10am-8pm Tue-Sun) A mere five minutes from Museo Guggenheim is Bilbao's Museo de Bellas Artes. More than just a complement to the Guggenheim, it often seems to actually exceed its more famous cousin for content.

The museum houses a compelling collection that includes everything from Gothic sculptures to 20th-century pop art. There are three main subcollections: classical art, with works by Murillo, Zurbarán, El Greco, Goya and van Dyck; contemporary art, featuring works by Gauguin, Francis Bacon and Anthony Caro; and Basque art, with works of the great sculptors Jorge de Oteiza and Eduardo Chillida, and strong paintings by the likes of Ignacio Zuloaga and Juan de Echevarria. A useful audio guide costs €1. The museum is wheelchair accessible.

Casco Viejo OLD TOWN
The compact Casco Viejo, Bilbao's atmospheric old quarter, is full of charming streets, boisterous bars and plenty of quirky and independent shops. At the heart of the

Casco are Bilbao's original seven streets, Las Siete Calles, which date from the 1400s.

The 14th-century Gothic Catedral de Santiago (☻10am-1pm & 4-7pm Tue-Sat, 10.30am-1.30pm Sun) has a splendid Renaissance portico and pretty little cloister. Further north, the 19th-century arcaded Plaza Nueva is a rewarding *pintxo* (Basque tapas) haunt. There's a lively Sunday-morning flea market here, which is full of secondhand book and record stalls, and pet 'shops' selling chirpy birds (some kept in old-fashioned wooden cages), fluffy mice and tiny baby terrapins. Elsewhere in the market children and adults alike swap and barter football cards and old stamps from countries you've never heard of; in between weave street performers and waiters with trays piled high. A sweeter-smelling flower market takes place on Sunday mornings in the nearby Plaza del Arenal.

Euskal Museoa   MUSEUM

(Museo Vasco; www.euskal-museoa.org; Plaza Miguel Unamuno 4; adult/child €3/free, free Thu; ☻11am-5pm Tue-Sat, 11am-2pm Sun) This museum is probably the most complete museum of Basque culture and history in all the Basque regions. The story kicks off back in the days of prehistory and from this murky period the displays bound rapidly through to the modern age. The main problem with the museum is that, unless you speak Spanish (or perhaps you studied Euskara at school?), it's all a little meaningless as, amazingly, there are no English or French translations.

The museum is housed in a fine old building, at the centre of which is a peaceful cloister that was part of an original 17th-century Jesuit college. In the cloister is the **Mikeldi Idol**, a powerful pre-Christian, possibly Iron Age, symbolic figure.

The museum is wheelchair accessible.

Museo Marítimo Ría de Bilbao   MUSEUM

(www.museomaritimobilbao.org; Muelle Ramón de la Sota 1; adult/child €5/free; ☻10am-8pm Tue-Sun) The space-age Museo Marítimo Ría de Bilbao, appropriately sited down on the waterfront, uses bright and well-thought-out displays to bring the watery depths of Bilbao and Basque maritime history to life. There's an outdoor section where children (and nautically inclined grown-ups) can clamber about a range of boats pretending to be pirates and sailors.

Arkeologi Museo   MUSEUM

(www.bizkaia.net; Calzadas de Mallona 2; adult/child €3/free, free Fri; ☻10am-2pm & 4-7.30pm Tue-Sat, 10.30am-2pm Sun) A slick new museum that, through the use of numerous flashing lights, beeping things and a fair few spearheads and old pots, reinforces the point that the inhabitants of this corner of Spain have lived here for a very long time indeed. Labelling is in Spanish and Basque only.

Parque de Doña Casilda de Iturrizar

PARK

Floating on waves of peace and quiet just beyond the Museo de Bellas Artes is another work of fine art – the Parque de Doña Casilda de Iturrizar. The centrepiece of this whimsical park is the large pond filled with ornamental ducks and other waterfowl.

⭐ Festivals & Events

Bilbao has a packed festival calendar. The following are just the big daddies.

OPEN-AIR GALLERY

Part of the Guggenheim experience is a quiet wander around the outside of the building, appreciating the extraordinary imagination behind its design and catching the different colours reflected by the titanium tiles, limestone and glass.

Lying between the glass buttresses of the central atrium and Ría de Bilbao is a simple pool of water that emits at intervals a mist 'sculpture' by Fuyiko Nakaya. Nearby on the riverbank is a sculpture by Louise Bourgeois, a skeletal canopy representing a spider, entitled *Maman*, said to symbolise a protective embrace. In the open area to the west of the museum, a fountain sculpture randomly fires off jets of water into the air and youngsters leap to and fro across it. Beyond is a kids' playground.

On the Alameda Mazarredo, on the city side of the museum, is Jeff Koons' kitsch whimsy *Puppy*, a 12m-tall highland terrier made up of thousands of begonias. Bilbao has hung on to 'El Poop', who was supposed to be a passing attraction as part of a world tour. With the fond, deprecating humour of citizens of all tough cities, *bilbaínos* will tell you that El Poop came first – and then they had to build a kennel behind it.

Carnaval

FESTIVAL

Carnaval is celebrated with vigour in Bilbao in February.

Blues Music Festival

BLUES

In Getxo, 25km north of Bilbao, in June.

Bilbao BBK Live

MUSIC

(www.bilbaobbklive.com) Bilbao's biggest musical event is Bilbao BBK Live, which takes place over three days in early July.

International Jazz Festival

JAZZ

(www.jazzeuskadi.com in Spanish) In Getxo for a week in the middle of July.

Semana Grande

FESTIVAL

Bilbao's grandest fiesta begins on the first Saturday after 15 August. It has a full program of cultural events over 10 days.

Folk Music Festival

FOLK MUSIC

In the seaside suburb of Getxo in September.

🛏 Sleeping

Bilbao, like the Basque Country in general, is increasingly popular and it can be very hard to find decent accommodation (especially at weekends). You would be wise to book as far ahead as possible. The Bilbao tourism authority has a very useful **reservations department** (☑902 877298; www. bilbaoreservas.com).

TOP CHOICE Pensión Iturrienea Ostatua

BOUTIQUE HOTEL **€€**

(☑944 16 15 00; www.iturrieneaostatua.com; Calle de Santa María 14; d/tr €66/80; 🛜) Easily the most eccentric hotel in Bilbao, it's part farmyard, part old-fashioned toyshop, and a work of art in its own right. Try to get a double room on the 1st floor (singles don't come with quite as many frills and ribbons): they are so full of character that there'll be barely enough room for your own! If you do stay here, remember: whatever else you do, for goodness' sake don't let the sheep escape.

Hostal Begoña

BOUTIQUE HOTEL **€€**

(☑944 23 01 34; www.hostalbegona.com; Calle de la Amistad 2; s/d from €54/62.64; @🛜) The owners of this outstanding place don't need voguish labels for their very stylish and individual creation. Begoña speaks for itself with colourful rooms decorated with modern artworks, all with funky tiled bathrooms and wrought-iron beds. There's a car park nearby.

Barceló Nervión

CHAIN HOTEL **€**

(☑944 12 43 00; www.barcelonervion.com; Paseo Campo Volantin 11; s/d €42.50/59.50; 🅿✳@🛜)

OK, it's a chain hotel and, yes, whilst the rooms are cheap, they do charge over the odds for everything else. But let's be fair: hotels of this quality don't come much cheaper than this. The rooms are plain but spacious and they'll throw in a baby cot for no extra charge. The location, on the riverfront and equidistant to the old town and the Guggenheim, is ideal.

Gran Hotel Domine

DESIGN HOTEL **€€€**

(☑944 25 33 00; www.granhoteldominebil bao.com; Alameda Mazarredo 61; d from €140; 🅿✳@✳) Designer chic all the way, from the Javier Mariscal interiors to the Phillipe Starck and Arne Jacobsen fittings – and that's just in the loos. This stellar showpiece of the Silken chain has views of the Guggenheim from some of its pricier rooms and from the roof terrace. Booking online beforehand can lead to big discounts.

Petit Palace Arana

BOUTIQUE HOTEL **€€**

(☑944 15 64 11; www.hthoteles.com; Calle de Bidebarrieta 2; s/d from €70/75; 🛜) A funky hotel, which brings the style of today to a building of yesterday. Rooms have large, soft beds and great spotty tiled or zebra-striped bathrooms, and some come with river views. We have, however, received a few complaints about road noise.

Hotel Carlton

HISTORIC HOTEL **€€€**

(☑944 16 22 00; www.hotelcarlton.es; Plaza de Frederico Moyúa 2; r €200; 🅿✳@🛜) Style, class and sophistication: the reception area is overpoweringly ornate and the trend continues into the rooms, which are simply stunning. When James Bond came to Bilbao in *The World is Not Enough,* you can be absolutely sure that this is where he'd have stayed. Book online for occasional discounts of over 50%.

Pensión Gurea

PENSIÓN **€€**

(☑944 16 32 99; www.hostalgurea.com; Calle de Bidebarrieta 14; s/d €45/65; 🛜) It's a family affair at this jolly *pensión,* where husband and wife run around trying to please you and the kids just run around (don't worry: they're not noisy – normally!). It's well organised, with large rooms.

Hotel Bilbao Jardines

BOUTIQUE HOTEL **€€**

(☑944 79 42 10; www.hotelbilbaojardines.com; Calle Jardines 9; r €70; ✳🛜) A welcome change from Casco Viejo's dusty facades, the Jardines has fresh, green decor and rooms that lap up light like a sunbathing lizard. Good value for money.

Tryp Arenal
TRADITIONAL HOTEL €€

(944 15 31 00; www.solmelia.com; Calle los Fuegos 2; s/d €60/70; @) We could imagine a conservative banker from the 1920s choosing to stay here. Why? Because, although there's nothing daring or exciting about its rooms, it does offer sturdy, old-fashioned style and service and who can knock a 1920s banker for going with that?

Pensión Mardones
PENSIÓN €

(944 15 31 05; www.pensionmardones.com; Calle Jardines 4; s/d €34/48;) This well-kept number has nice carved wooden wardrobes in the rooms and lots of exposed wooden roof beams. The cheerful owner is very helpful and all up it offers great value.

Pensión Ladero
PENSIÓN €

(944 15 09 32; Calle Lotería 1; r €24-36) The no-fuss rooms here (all with shared bathrooms) are as cheap as Bilbao gets and represent good bang for your buck. After the mammoth climb up four storeys, you can treat yourself to a dessert. Rooms cannot be reserved in advance.

Camping Sopelana
CAMPING €

(946 76 21 20; www.campingsopelana.com; sites for 2 people & car €25.20;) This exposed site has a swimming pool and is within easy walking distance of Sopelana beach. It's on the metro line, 15km from Bilbao.

✕ Eating

In the world of trade and commerce, the Basques are an outward-looking lot, but when it comes to food they refuse to believe that any other people could possibly match their culinary skills (and they may well have a point). This means that eating out in Bilbao is generally a choice of Basque, Basque or Basque food. Still, life could be worse and there are some terrific places to stuff yourself.

The porticoed Plaza Nueva is a good spot for coffee and people watching, especially in summer.

TOP CHOICE | Rio-Oja
BASQUE €

(944 15 08 71; Calle de Perro 4; mains €9-12) An institution that shouldn't be missed. It specialises in light Basque seafood and heavy inland fare, but to most foreigners the sheep brains or squid floating in pools of its own ink are the makings of a culinary adventure story they'll be recounting for years. Don't worry, though: it really does taste much better than it sounds.

TOP CHOICE | Restaurante Guggenheim
GASTRONOMIC €€€

(944 23 93 33; www.restauranteguggenheim.com; bistro set menu €19.66, restaurant set menu €75, restaurant mains €30-35; closed Mon & Christmas period) El Goog's modernist, chic restaurant and cafe are under the direction of superchef Josean Martínez Alija. Needless to say, the *nueva cocina vasca* (Basque nouvelle cuisine) is breathtaking and the ever-changing menu includes such mouth waterers as Iberian pork meatballs with carrot juice and curry. Even the olives are vintage classics: all come from 1000-year-old olive trees! Reservations are essential in the evening, but at lunch it operates on a first-come, first-served basis from 1.30pm.

Mina Restaurante
GASTRONOMIC €€€

(944 79 59 38; www.restaurantemina.es; Muelle Marzana; menú del día €53.50) Offering unexpected sophistication and fine dining in an otherwise fairly grimy neighbourhood, this riverside, and appropriately fish-based, restaurant has recently been making waves in the Bilbao culinary world, with some critics citing it as the future numero uno of Basque cooking.

Café Iruña
BASQUE €

(944 23 70 21; cnr Calles de Colón de Larreátegui & Berástegui; menú del día €13.50) Moorish style and a century of gossip are the defining characteristics of this grande old dame. It's the perfect place to indulge in a bit of people watching and, while you're at it, you might as well also indulge in a meal or, in the evening, some *pinchos morunos* (spicy kebabs with bread; €2.20).

Larruzz Bilbao
MEDITERRANEAN €

(944 23 08 20; www.larruzzbilbao.com; Calle Uribitarte 24; mains €12-18) Set on the banks of the Nervión, this incredibly popular restaurant (book ahead) has a polished business exterior, but a stone-cottage country interior. Its real speciality is paella, but it also serves various meaty Mediterranean dishes. The attached cafe can fill those unlucky enough not to get a table with various tasty *pintxos*. It currently seems to be trading under two names.

Café Boulevard
CAFE €

(Calle del Arenal 3) A Bilbao institution since 1871, disaster struck around a year ago when it closed down. Now it's back in business with exactly the same dusty art-deco interior and old-fashioned service that we'd come to know and love. Bring a work of

Although it lacks San Sebastián's stellar reputation for *pintxos*, prices are generally slightly lower here and the quality is about equal. There are literally hundreds of *pintxo* bars throughout Bilbao, but the Plaza Nueva on the edge of the Casco Viejo offers especially rich pickings, as do Calle de Perro and Calle Jardines. Some of the city's long-time standouts (all charge from around €2.50 per *pintxo*) include **Bar Gure Toki** (Plaza Nueva 12), with a subtle but simple line in creative *pintxos;* **Café-Bar Bilbao** (Plaza Nueva 6), with cool blue southern tile work and warm northern atmosphere; **Casa Victor Montes** (p407), as well known for its *pintxos* as its full meals; and **Berton Sasibil** (Calle Jardines 8), where you can watch informative films on the crafting of the same superb *pintxos* that you're munching on.

Don't restrict your search for the perfect *pintxo* to the Casco Viejo: the El Ensanche area also has some good options. Two of the best are **El Globo** (Calle de Diputación 8), a popular bar with a terrific range of *pintxos modernos*, including favourites such as *txangurro gratinado* (spider crab); and **Los Candiles** (Calle de Diputación 1), a narrow, low-key little bar, with some subtle *pintxos* filled with the taste of the sea.

highbrow literature, sip a strong black coffee and enjoy the classiest cafe in town.

Abaroa
BASQUE €

(☎944 13 20 51; Paseo del Campo de Volantin 13; mains €8-13, menú del día €10.70) This intimate and brightly furnished restaurant is a big name with locals. It specialises in hearty countryside fare, but with a twist of today. The result is that black pudding and a bowl of beans have never been so well presented or tasted so good. There is a second, equally good branch on Plaza del Museo.

Casa Victor Montes
BASQUE €

(☎944 15 70 67; www.victormontesbilbao.com; Plaza Nueva 8; mains €15) Part bar, part shop, part restaurant, total work of art, the Victor Montes is quite touristy but locals also appreciate its over-the-top decoration, its good food and the 1000 or so bottles of wine lined up behind the bar. If you're stopping by for a full meal, book in advance and savour the house special, *bacalao* (dried cod).

Restaurante Vegetariano
VEGETARIAN €

(☎944 44 55 98; Alameda de Urquijo 33; mains €6-9; ☺lunch Mon-Sat; ☑) Full of beans, this little place is one of the Basque Country's all-too-rare vegetarian restaurants. It has crispy fresh salads, imaginative quiches and lots of bean-based meals. There's an excellent noticeboard covering everything and anything alternative taking place in the city.

Mercado de la Ribera
MARKET €

(Calle Ribera) For self-catering, try this market. Drifting round the fish section is a marvellous experience in itself.

Drinking

In the Casco Viejo, around Calles Barrenkale, Ronda and de Somera, there are plenty of terrific hole-in-the-wall, no-nonsense bars with a generally youngish crowd.

Across the river, in the web of streets around Muelle Marzana and Bilbao la Vieja, are scores of little bars and clubs. This is gritty Bilbao as it used to be in the days before the arty makeover. It's both a Basque heartland and the centre of the city's ethnic community. The many bars around here are normally welcoming, but one or two can be a bit seedy. It's not a great idea for a woman to walk here alone at night. Of the many bars in this neighbourhood, one very pleasant one for a sundowner over the river is **Marzana 16** (Calle de Marzana 16); its sandwiches are also worthy of praise.

Twiggy
BAR

(Alameda de Urquijo 35) Retro psychedelic! Happy post-hippie place with a cheerful mix of '60s kitsch for lovely people. Serves cheap snacks during the day.

Kamin
BAR

(Manuel Allende 8) Laid-back listening in rosy light among the Bilbao cognoscenti. The music trails sweetly through everything from rock and pop to alternative and fresh new sounds on the Basque scene. To get there head down Calle Ercilla from Plaza de Federico Moyua, turn right onto Alameda de Urquijo and it's three blocks down on the right.

BASQUE SIGNS

In many towns throughout the Basque region street names and signposts are changing from Castilian to Basque. Often this might be nothing more than Calle (street) becoming Kalea, with the actual name remaining unchanged, but not always. The problem is that not everyone uses these new names and many maps remain in Castilian. To make matters worse, it's often not the local council making these changes but people with aerosol cans. All this can make navigating a little confusing for tourists – San Sebastián and Bilbao are particularly hard. In this book we have attempted to stick with the most commonly used version or have included both Castilian and Basque. Below are some words that commonly appear on signs:

BASQUE	ENGLISH	SPANISH
aireportua	airport	aeropuerto
erdia	centre	centro
erdialdea	city centre	centro de la ciudad
jatetxea	restaurant	restaurante
kalea	street	calle
nagusía kalea	main street	calle mayor
komuna(k)	toilet(s)	servicios
kontuz	caution/beware	¡atención!
nekazal turismoas	village or farmstead accommodation	casas rurales
ongi etorri	welcome	bienvenido
turismo bulegoa	tourist office	oficina de turismo
turismoa/turismo	tourism	turismo

☆ Entertainment

There are plenty of clubs and live venues in Bilbao, and the vibe is friendly and generally easy-going. Venues' websites usually have details of upcoming gigs.

Bilbao offers regular performances of dance, opera and drama at the city's two principal theatres. Check the theatre websites for current information.

Kafe Antzokia LIVE MUSIC
(www.kafeantzokia.com; Calle San Vicente 2) This is the vibrant heart of contemporary Basque Bilbao, featuring international rock bands, blues and reggae, but also the cream of Basque rock-pop. Weekend concerts run from 10pm to 1am, followed by DJs until 5am. Cover charge for concerts can range from about €10 upwards. During the day it's a cafe, restaurant and cultural centre all rolled into one and has frequent exciting events on.

Teatro Arriaga THEATRE
(www.teatroarriaga.com; Plaza Arriaga) The baroque facade of this venue commands the open spaces of El Arenal between the Casco Viejo and the river.

Euskalduna Palace LIVE MUSIC
(www.euskalduna.net; Avenida Abandoibarra) About 600m downriver from the Guggenheim is another modernist gem, built on the riverbank in a style that echoes the great shipbuilding works of the 19th century. The Euskalduna houses the Bilbao Symphony Orchestra and the Basque Symphony Orchestra.

Conjunto Vacío NIGHTCLUB
(Muelle de La Merced 4; admission Fri & Sat €10) House is the spin here and there's a very style-conscious, confident, young, mixed gay-and-straight crowd.

Le Club NIGHTCLUB
(www.leclub.es; Muelle Marzana 4; admission €10) Three floors to twist, gyrate and then relax on. The 1st floor has rock and '80s pop, the 2nd has dance music and the 3rd is the chill-out lounge.

El Balcón de la Lola NIGHTCLUB
(www.musiclola.blogspot.com; Calle Bailén 10; admission Fri & Sat €10) One of Bilbao's most popular mixed gay-and-straight clubs, this is the place to come if you're looking for hip

industrial decor and a packed Saturday-night disco. It's located under the railway lines – look for the Betty Boo pictures.

Shopping

The old town is full of quirky fashion shops. News stands around Plaza de Federico Moyúa usually have a fair selection of foreign newspapers.

Elkar Megadenda BOOKS
(Calle de Iparragirre 26) Basque publications are strongly represented here. It also stocks books in Spanish and a few in English, and there's an excellent map and travel section.

Tintas BOOKS
(Calle del Generál Concha 10) Travel bookshop with a broad selection of travel books, road maps and topographical maps for trekkers.

Information

Emergency
Cruz Roja (944 43 47 92; Alameda de Urquijo 65) The Red Cross hospital.
Emergency (112)
Policía Municipal (944 20 50 00; Calle de Luís Briñas 14)

Internet Access & Telephone
L@zar (Calle de Sendeja 5; per hr €3.60; 10.30am-1am Mon-Fri, 11am-1am Sat & Sun) Also has cheap international phone rates.

Net House (Calle Villarías 6; per hr €3; 10am-2pm & 4.30-9pm Mon-Fri) Note that these hours seem a little flexible.

Medical Services
Hospital Civil de Basurto (944 00 60 00; Avenida Montevideo 18)

Money
There are numerous banks, most with ATMs, in Bilbao, particularly around Plaza Circular.

Post
Main post office (Alameda de Urquijo 19)

Tourist information
Tourist office (944 79 57 60; www.bilbao. net/bilbaoturismo) main office (Plaza del Ensanche 11; 9am-2pm & 4-7.30pm Mon-Fri); airport (944 71 03 01; 9am-9pm Mon-Sat, 9am-3pm Sun); Guggenheim (Avenida Abandoibarra 2; 10am-7pm Mon-Sat, 10am-6pm Sun); Teatro Arriaga (Plaza Arriaga; 9.30am-2pm & 4-7.30pm daily) Bilbao's friendly tourist-office staffers are extremely helpful, well informed and, above all, enthusiastic about their city. At all offices ask for the free bimonthly *Bilbao Guía*, with its entertainment listings plus tips on

restaurants, bars and nightlife. There is also a **call centre** (944 71 03 01; 9am-9pm Mon-Sat, 9am-3pm Sun), which is equally helpful.

Getting There & Away

Air
Bilbao's **airport** (902 404704; www.aena.es) is near Sondika, 12km northeast of the city. Services are excellent. There's a first-class tourist information office, a medical centre, ATMs, shops, cafes, a restaurant and car-hire offices. **EasyJet** (www. easyjet.com) has cheap flights between London and Bilbao and **Vueling** (www.vueling.com) buzzes between Bilbao and most major Spanish cities. For both, booking well ahead is advised.

Bus
Bilbao's main bus station, **Termibus** (San Ma-més), is west of the centre. There are regular services to the following destinations:

DESTINATION	FARE (€)	DURATION (HR)
Barcelona	41.90	7-8
Biarritz (France)	17.85	2¾
Durango	3.75	½
Elorrio	3.75	¾
Logroño	12.50	2
Madrid	27.17	4¾
Oñati	5.90	1¼
Pamplona	13.40	2
San Sebastián	9.85	1
Santander	from 6.71	1¼
Vitoria	5.65	1½

Bizkaibus travels to destinations throughout the rural Basque Country, including coastal communities such as Lekeitio (€3.20) and Bermeo (€2.40).

Train
The **Renfe** (www.renfe.es) Abando train station is just across the river from Plaza Arriaga and the Casco Viejo. There are frequent trains to the following destinations:

DESTINATION	FARE (€)	DURATION (HR)
Barcelona	62.30	6
Burgos	from 18.70	3
Madrid	from 48.60	5
Valladolid	from 25.70	4

Next door is the Concordia train station, with its handsome art-nouveau facade of wrought iron and tiles. It is used by the **FEVE** (www.feve.es, in Spanish) private rail company for running trains west into Cantabria. There are three daily trains to Santander (from €7.75, three hours) where you can change for stations in Asturias.

The Atxuri train station is about 1km upriver from Casco Viejo. From here, **Eusko Tren/Ferrocarril Vasco** (www.euskotren.es, in Spanish & Basque) operates services every half-hour to the following:

DESTINATION	FARE (€)	DURATION (HR)
Bermeo	2.40	1½
Guernica	2.40	1
Mundaka	2.40	1½

Hourly Eusko Tren trains go to San Sebastián (€6.50, 2¾ hours) via Durango, Zumaia and Zarautz, but the bus is much quicker.

ⓘ Getting Around

To/From the Airport

The **airport bus** (Bizkaibus A3247; €1.20, 30 minutes) departs from a stand on the extreme right as you leave arrivals. It runs through the northwestern section of the city, passing the Museo Guggenheim, stopping at Plaza de Federico Moyúa and terminating at the Termibus (bus station). It runs from the airport every 20 minutes from 6.20am to midnight. There is also a direct hourly bus from the airport to San Sebastián (€15.30, 1¼ hours), It runs from 7.45am to 11.45pm.

Taxis from the airport to the Casco Viejo cost about €25.

Metro

There are metro stations at all the main focal points of El Ensanche and at Casco Viejo. Tickets start at €1.40. The metro runs to the north coast from a number of stations on both sides of the river and makes it easy to get to the beaches closest to Bilbao.

Tram

Bilbao's Eusko Tran tramline is a boon to locals and visitors alike. It runs to and fro between Basurtu, in the southwest of the city, and the Atxuri train station. Stops include the Termibus station, the Guggenheim and Teatro Arriaga by the Casco Viejo. Tickets cost €1.40 and need to be validated in the machine next to the ticket dispenser before boarding.

Around Bilbao

BEACHES

Two reasonable beaches for swimming are Azkorri and Sopelana. The latter is the most consistent surf beach in the area. Better beaches can be found east of Plentzia. Also good is the sheltered beach at Gorliz, which has a pretty lighthouse and some fine views from the Astondo end of the beach. There are well-signposted tracks for walkers.

GUERNICA
POP 15,600

Guernica (Basque: Gernika) is a state of mind. At a glance it seems no more than a modern and ugly country town. Apparently, prior to the morning of 26 April 1937, Guernica wasn't quite so ugly, but the horrifying events of that day meant that the town was later reconstructed as fast as possible with little regard for aesthetics. Franco, who'd been having some problems with the Basques, decided to teach them a lesson by calling in his buddy Hitler. On that fateful morning planes from Hitler's Condor Legion flew backwards and forwards over the town demonstrating their new-found concept of saturation bombing. In the space of a few hours, the town was destroyed and 1654 civilians killed. What makes this even more shocking is that it wasn't the first time this had happened. Just days earlier, the nearby town of Durango suffered a similar fate, but that time the world had simply not believed what it was being told.

Franco chose Guernica for his 'lesson' because of its symbolic value to the Basques. It's the ancient seat of Basque democracy and the site at which the Basque parliament met beneath the branches of a sacred oak tree from medieval times until 1876. Today the original oak is nothing but a stump, but the Tree of Guernica lives on in the form of a young oak tree.

The tragedy of Guernica gained international resonance with Picasso's iconic painting *Guernica,* which has come to symbolise the violence of the 20th century. A copy of the painting now hangs in the entrance hall of the UN headquarters in New York, while the original hangs in the Centro de Arte Reina Sofía in Madrid. Many Basques had hoped that with the opening of the Guggenheim the painting would be moved to Bilbao, but this has never happened.

◉ Sights

Museo de la Paz de Gernika　　　MUSEUM
(Guernica Peace Museum; www.peacemuseum guernica.org; Plaza Foru 1; adult/child €4/free; ◷10am-8pm Tue-Sat, 10am-3pm Sun) Guernica's seminal experience is a visit to the museum, where audiovisual displays calmly reveal the horror of war and hatred, both in

PUENTE COLGANTE

A worthwhile stop en route to the beaches is the Unesco World Heritage–classed Puente Colgante, designed by Alberto Palacio, a disciple of Gustave Eiffel (he of Parisian tower fame). Opening in 1893, it was the world's first transporter bridge and links the suburbs of Getxo and Portugalete. A platform, suspended from the actual bridge high above, is loaded with up to six cars plus foot passengers; it then glides silently over Río Nervión to the other bank. Rides cost €0.30 one way per person. You can also take a lift up to the superstructure at 46m (€5) and walk across the river and back for some great views (not for those prone to vertigo). Another choice is to cross the river by small ferry boat (€0.30). The nearest metro stop from Bilbao is Areeta or Portugalete (both €1.40) and the nearest Renfe stop is in Portugalete (€1.40).

the Basque Country and around the world. Display panels are in Castilian and Basque, but translations are available. There are guided tours, in four languages, each day at noon and 5pm. The museum is wheelchair accessible. A couple of blocks north, on Calle Allende Salazar, is a ceramic-tile version of Picasso's *Guernica*.

Euskal Herriko Museoa MUSEUM
(Calle Allende Salazar; adult/child €3/1.50; ⊙10am-2pm & 4-7pm Tue-Sat, 10.30am-2.30pm Sun) Housed in the 18th-century Palacio de Montefuerte, this museum contains a comprehensive exhibition on Basque history and culture, with fine old maps, engravings and a range of other documents and portraits. The museum is wheelchair accessible.

Parque de los Pueblos de Europa
PARK, MONUMENT
The pleasant Parque de los Pueblos de Europa, behind the Euskal Herriko Museoa, contains a couple of typically curvaceous **sculptures** by Henry Moore and other works by Eduardo Chillida. The park leads to the attractive Casa de Juntas, where the provincial government has met since 1979. Nearby is the famous **Tree of Guernica**, now a mere stump, sheltered by a neoclassical gazebo. Another tree was recently planted in the rear courtyard.

🛏 Sleeping & Eating
The accommodation situation is in a pretty sorry state and most people sensibly visit as a day trip from Bilbao. There are several simple restaurants and bars scattered around the main square and surrounding streets.

ℹ Information
Tourist office (☑946 25 58 92; www.gernika -lumo.net; Artekalea 8; ⊙10am-2pm & 4-7pm Mon-Sat, 10am-2pm Sun) This helpful office

has friendly multilingual staff. It sells the Global Ticket (€5.25), a combined entry ticket for the town's sights.

ℹ Getting There & Away
Guernica is an easy day trip from Bilbao by ET/ FV train from Atxuri train station (€2.40, one hour). Trains run every half-hour.

MUNDAKA
POP 1800
Universally regarded as the home of the best wave in Europe, Mundaka is a name of legend for surfers across the world. The wave breaks on a perfectly tapering sandbar formed by the outflow of the Río Urdaibai and, on a good day, offers heavy, barrelling lefts that can reel off for hundreds of metres. Fantastic for experienced surfers, Mundaka is absolutely not a place for novices to take to the waves.

Despite all the focus being on the waves, Mundaka has done a sterling job of not turning itself into just another 'hey dude' surf town and remains a resolutely Basque port with a pretty main square and harbour area. There's a small tourist office (☑946 17 72 01; www.mundaka.org; Calle Kepa Deuna).

Those wishing to stay and practise their tube-riding skills should pull in at the Hotel Atalaya (☑946 17 70 00; www.atalayahotel. es; Kalea Itxaropena 1; s/d €86/108), which is in a lovely old building near the waterfront and has clean and reliable rooms – although, like everywhere in Mundaka, it's a little overpriced. If nights under canvas are more your thing, then Camping Portuondo (☑946 87 77 01; www.campingportu ondo.com; sites per person/tent €6.70/13.20, bungalows from €90.60; ▣), just to the south of town, should fit the bill. It has pleasant terraced grounds, a pool and a restaurant, but gets overrun in the summer.

Basque Culture

The Basques are different. They have inhabited their corner of Spain and France seemingly forever. Whilst much of their unique culture is hidden from prying eyes, the following are visible to any visitor.

Pelota

The national sport of the Basque country is *pelote basque* and every village in the region has its own court – normally backing up against the village church. Pelota originates from an ancient game called *jeu de paume* from which modern tennis also stems. Pelota can be played in several different ways – bare-handed, with small wooden rackets or, the version best known internationally, with a long hand-basket called a *chistera*, with which the player can throw the ball at speeds of up to 300km/h. It's possible to see pelota matches throughout the region during summer.

Lauburu

The most visible symbol of Basque culture is the *lauburu*, the Basque cross. The meaning of this ancient symbol is lost in the mists of time – some say it represents the four old regions of the Basque Country, others that it represents spirit, life, consciousness and form – but today most people regard it as a symbol of prosperity, hence its appearance in modern jewellery and above house doors. But it is also used to signify life and death and therefore is also common on old headstones.

Traditional Basque Games

Basque sports aren't just limited to pelota: there's also log cutting, stone lifting, bale tossing and tug of war. Most stemmed from the day-to-day activities of the region's farmers and fishermen. Although technology has replaced the need to use most of these skills on a daily basis, the sports are kept alive at numerous fiestas.

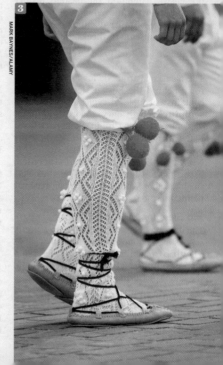

MARK BAYNES/ALAMY

Clockwise from top left
1. Log cutting 2. Watching pelota 3. Folk-dancing costume

Bulls & Fiestas

Although almost every town, village and city has its annual fiesta week, none are as famous, or perhaps infamous, as Sanfermines with its legendry *encierro* (bull run) in Pamplona. But how did the madness first begin? The purpose of the *encierro* is to transfer bulls from the corrals where they would have spent the night to the bullring where they would fight. Sometime in the 14th century one 'intelligent' guy worked out that the quickest and 'easiest' way to do this was to chase the bulls out of the corrals and into the ring. One thing led to another and the *encierro* went from being merely a way of moving bulls around to the full-blown carnage of Pamplona's Sanfermines.

Traditional Dress

The daylight hours of most Basque festivals are a good time to see traditional Basque dress and dance. It's said that there are around 400 different Basque dances, many of which have their own special kind of dress.

Basque Language

Victor Hugo described the Basque language as a 'country' and it would be a rare Basque who'd disagree with him. The language is the oldest in Europe and has no known connection to any Indo-European languages.

Buses and ET/FV trains between Bilbao and Bermeo stop here.

BERMEO
POP 17,000

Located just a few minutes to the north of Mundaka and on the open coast proper, this tough fishing port is refreshingly down to earth and hasn't lost its soul to tourism. Though there are no beaches here, it's an enjoyable place to while away a few hours watching the boats bustle in and out of the harbour.

There's a small tourist office (☑946 17 91 54; www.bermeo.org; Askatasun Bidea 2) on the waterfront. The absorbing Museo del Pescador (Plaza Torrontero 1; admission free; ☺10am-1.30pm & 4-7.30pm Tue-Sat, 10am-1.30pm Sun), in the handsome 15th-century Torre Ercilla, is steeply uphill from the tourist office.

A few kilometres beyond Bermeo, the Ermita de San Juan de Gaztelugatxe stands on an islet that is connected to the mainland by a bridge. It also has two natural arches on its seaward side. Built by the Knights Templars in the 10th century, it has also served as a handy shelter for shipwrecked sailors.

Half-hourly buses and ET/FV trains run from Bermeo to Bilbao (€2.40, 1¼ hours).

The Central Basque Coast

The coast road from Bilbao to San Sebastián is a glorious journey past spectacular seascapes, with cove after cove stretching east and verdant fields suddenly ending where cliffs plunge into the sea. *Casas rurales* (village or farmstead accommodation) and camping grounds are plentiful and well signposted.

ELANTXOBE
POP 444

The tiny hamlet of Elantxobe, with its colourful houses clasping like geckos to an almost sheer cliff face, is undeniably one of the most attractive spots along the entire coast. The difficulty of building here, and the lack of a beach, has meant that it has been saved from the worst of tourist-related development. Public-transport fans will be so excited by Elantxobe that the earth really will move for them – the streets are so narrow that buses don't have space to turn around, so the road spins around for them! See the Lekeitio section for bus connections.

LEKEITIO
POP 7300

Bustling Lekeitio has an attractive old core centred on the unnaturally large and slightly out-of-place-looking late-Gothic Iglesia de Santa María de la Asunción.

For most visitors, it's the two beaches that are the main draw. The one just east of the river, with a small rocky mound of an island just offshore, is one of the finest beaches in the Basque Country.

The 'highlight' of Lekeitio's annual Fiesta de San Antolín (5 September) involves a tug of war with a goose. The fun and games end when the goose's head falls off (nowadays they use a pre-killed goose).

Accommodation is scarce and pricey, but the tourist office (☑946 84 40 17; Plaza Independancia) can point you in the direction of private rooms. Otherwise the Aisia Lekeitio (☑946 84 26 55; www.aisiahoteles.com; Avenida Santa Elena; s/d €71.75/92), which in-

---

THE OLDEST LANGUAGE

'The Basque language is a country,' said Victor Hugo and the language certainly encapsulates all things Basque. Known as Euskara, the Basque language is thought to be one of Europe's oldest and most quixotic, with no known relationship to the Indo-European family of languages. Its earliest written elements were considered to be 13th-century manuscripts found at the Monasterio de Suso (p450) at San Millán de Cogolla in La Rioja province, but discoveries in 2006 at the archaeological site of Iruña-Veleia near Vitoria included inscriptions in Basque dating from the 3rd century AD.

Suppressed by Franco, Basque was subsequently recognised as one of Spain's official languages. Although Franco's repression meant that many older Basques are unable to speak their native tongue, it has now become the language of choice, and of identity, among a growing number of young Basques, fuelling a dynamic cultural renaissance and a nonviolent political awareness. There are now Basque-language radio and TV stations, and newspapers.

cludes a thalassotherapy centre, is the pick of the crop.

Bizkaibus A3513 (€3.10) leaves from Calle Hurtado de Amézaga, by Bilbao's Abando train station, about eight times a day (except Sunday) and goes via Guernica and Elantxobe. Fairly regular buses from Lekeitio run to San Sebastián (€7).

ZUMAIA
POP 8800

First impressions of Zumaia are not great, but struggle through the industrial zone that hems the town and you'll find an attractive centre. For beach lovers, further rewards await in the form of the Playa de Izturun, wedged in among slate cliffs, and the Playa de Santiago, a more traditional strand of soft sand a couple of kilometres east of the town centre. If you're more a culture vulture than a bronzed god or goddess, then the Museo de Zuloaga (☑943 86 23 41; admission €6; ⊙11am-2pm & 4-7pm Wed-Sun Apr-Dec), next to Playa de Santiago, should prove rewarding. It's housed in the one-time studio of Basque artist Ignacio Zuloaga (1870–1945) and contains some of his important works, as well as a handful by other headliners, including El Greco and Zurbarán. If you want to visit outside the April-to-December period, you can do so by appointment only.

For weary heads you'll find a couple of *casas rurales* in the hills behind Playa de Santiago. Of these, Karakas (☑943 86 17 36; www.nekatur.net; r €42.80), 1km inland and with gorgeous views over lush green fields down to the sea, has cheerful rooms and offers great value. It's on a working farm, which will doubtless keep any kids in tow happy.

GETARIA
POP 2525

The attractive medieval fishing settlement of Getaria is a world away from nearby cosmopolitan San Sebastián and is a much better place to get a feel for coastal Basque culture. The old village tilts gently downhill to a baby-sized harbour, at the end of which is a forested island known as El Ratón (the Mouse), on account of its similarity to a mouse (this similarity is easiest to see after several strong drinks!).

It might have been this giant mouse that first encouraged the town's most famous son, the sailor Juan Sebastián Elcano, to take to the ocean waves. His adventures eventually culminated in him becoming the first man to sail around the world, after the captain of his ship, Magellan, died halfway through the endeavour.

Just a couple of kilometres further east, along a coastal road that battles with cliffs, ocean waves and several cavelike tunnels, is Zarautz, the north coast's answer to the Costas of the Mediterranean. It's a built-up and ugly place but has a wonderful, long beach with some of the most consistent surfing conditions in the area.

Several harbour-front restaurants grill up the fresh catch of the day, which is washed down well with a glass of crisp, locally produced *txakoli* (white wine).

For accommodation, try one of the following. Getariano Pentsioa (☑943 14 05 67; www.pensiongetariano.es; Calle Herrieta 3; s/d €45/70; ◈) is a charming, mellow yellow building with flower-filled balconies and comfortable rooms. Right opposite the Getariano is the slightly more formal Hotel Itxas-Gain (☑943 14 10 35; www.hotelitxasgain. com; Roke Devnal; s/d €50/65; ◈), which has a mixture of room types: some have little balconies and whirlpool baths that overlook the whirlpool-like ocean. Finally, in nearby Zarautz, campers will find Gran Camping Zarautz (☑943 83 12 38; www.grancamping zarautz.com; sites for 2 people, tent & car €20.50), which has memorable views off the cliffs at the far eastern end of town.

San Sebastián
POP 183.300

It's said that nothing is impossible. This is wrong. It's impossible to lay eyes on San Sebastián (Basque: Donostia) and not fall madly in love. This stunning city is everything that grimy Bilbao is not: cool, svelte and flirtatious by night, charming and well mannered by day. Best of all is the summer fun on the beach. For it's setting, form and attitude, Playa de la Concha is the equal of any city beach in Europe. Then there's Playa de Gros, with its surfers and sultry beach goers. As the sun falls on another sweltering summer's day, you'll sit back with a drink and an artistic *pintxo* and realise that, yes, you too are in love with sexy San Sebastián.

San Sebastián has three main centres of action. The lively Parte Vieja (old town) lies across the neck of Monte Urgull, the bay's eastern headland, and is where the most popular *pintxo* bars and many of the cheap lodgings are to be found. South of the Parte Vieja

BASQUE COUNTRY, NAVARRA & LA RIOJA BASQUE COUNTRY

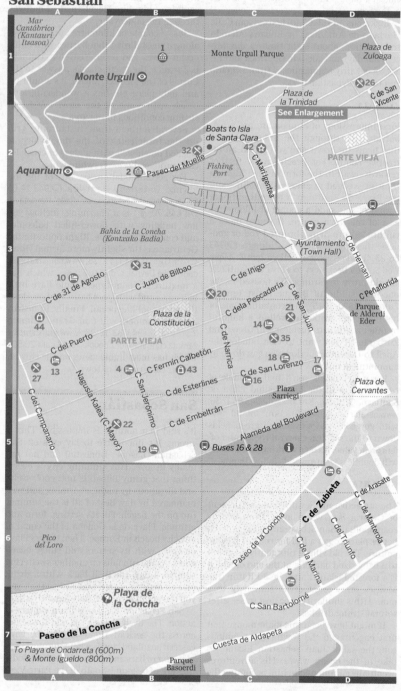

Mar Cantábrico (Kantauri Itsasoa)

Monte Urgull Parque

Plaza de Zuloaga

Monte Urgull

26

C de San Vicente

Plaza de la Trinidad

See Enlargement

PARTE VIEJA

Boats to Isla de Santa Clara

32

42

C Mari Igentea

Aquarium

2

Paseo del Muelle

Fishing Port

Bahía de la Concha (Kontxako Badia)

37

Ayuntamiento (Town Hall)

C de Hernani

10

31

C de 31 de Agosto

C Juan de Bilbao

C de Iñigo

C Peñaflorida

Parque de Alderdi Eder

44

20

C de la Pescadería

C del Puerto

Plaza de la Constitución

PARTE VIEJA

21

C de San Juan

14

C de Narrica

35

27

13

C Fermín Calbetón

4

C San Jerónimo

43

18

C de San Lorenzo

17

Plaza de Cervantes

Nagusia Kalea (C Mayor)

C de Esterlines

16

Plaza Sarriegi

C del Campanario

22

C de Embeltrán

Alameda del Boulevard

19

Buses 16 & 28

6

C de Arasate

Pico del Loro

Paseo de la Concha

C de Zubieta

C de Manterola

C de la Marina

C del Triunfo

Playa de la Concha

5

C San Bartolomé

Paseo de la Concha

To Playa de Ondarreta (600m) & Monte Igueldo (800m)

Cuesta de Aldapeta

Parque Basoerdi

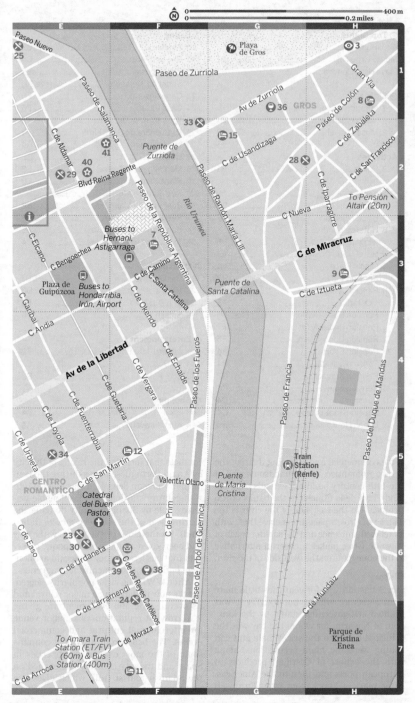

BASQUE COUNTRY, NAVARRA & LA RIOJA SAN SEBASTIÁN

is the commercial and shopping district, the Centro Romántico, whose handsome grid of late-19th-century buildings extends from behind Playa de la Concha to the banks of Río Urumea. On the east side of the river is the district of Gros, a pleasant enclave that, with its relaxed ambience and the surfing beach of Playa de Gros, makes a cheerful alternative to the honeypots on the west side of the river.

History
San Sebastián was for centuries little more than a fishing village, but by 1174 it was granted self-governing status by the kingdom of Navarra, for whom the bay was the principal outlet to the sea. Whale and cod fishing were the main occupations, along with the export of Castilian products to European ports and then to the Americas. After years of knockabout trans-European conflicts that included the razing of the city by Anglo-Portuguese forces during the Peninsular War, San Sebastián was hoisted into 19th-century stardom as a fashionable watering hole by Spanish royalty dodging the searing heat of the southern *meseta* (tableland). By the close of the century, the city had been given a superb belle-époque makeover that has left a legacy of elegant art-nouveau buildings and beachfront swagger.

After WWII the city's popularity sagged, but it's now undergoing a major revival and its overall style and excitement are giving it a growing reputation as a major venue for international cultural and commercial events. The beachfront area now contains some of the most expensive properties in Spain and the city is firmly entrenched on the Spanish tourist trail, which gives it a highly international feel.

◎ Sights

TOP CHOICE **Beaches & Isla de Santa Clara**

BEACHES

Fulfilling almost every idea of how a perfect city beach should be formed, **Playa de la Concha** and its westerly extension, **Playa de Ondarreta**, are easily among the best city beaches in Europe. Throughout the long summer months a fiesta atmosphere prevails, with thousands of tanned and toned bodies spread across the sands. The swimming is almost always safe. The **Isla de Santa Clara**, about 700m from the beach, is accessible by boats that run every half-hour from June to September from the fishing port. At low tide the island gains its own tiny beach.

Less popular, but just as showy, **Playa de Gros** (Playa de la Zurriola), east of Río Urumea, is the city's main surf beach. Though swimming here is more dangerous than at Playa de la Concha, it has more of a local vibe.

TOP CHOICE **Aquarium**

AQUARIUM

(www.aquariumss.com; Paseo del Muelle 34; adult/child €12/6; ⊙10am-8pm Mon-Fri, 10am-9pm Sat & Sun) In the city's excellent aquarium you'll fear for your life as huge sharks bear down on you and be tripped out by fancy fluoro jellyfish. The highlights of a visit are the cinema-screen-sized deep ocean and coral reef exhibits and the long tunnel, around which swim monsters of the deep. The aquarium has undergone a recent makeover and expansion, which has seen the opening of a maritime-museum section as well as a few more tanks full of fish. Allow at least an hour and a half for a visit.

Monte Igueldo

FUNFAIR

The views from the summit of Monte Igueldo, just west of town, will make you feel like a circling hawk staring over the vast panorama of the Bahía de la Concha and the surrounding coastline and mountains. The best way to get there is via the old-world **funicular railway** (return adult/child €2.60/1.90; ⊙10am-10pm) to the **Parque de Atracciones** (www.monteigueldo.es; admission €1.80; ⊙11am-9pm). Individual rides (which include roller coasters, boat rides, carousels and pony rides) cost between €1.80 and €2 extra. Trains on the funicular railway depart every 15 minutes.

Monte Urgull

CASTLE, MUSEUM

You can walk to the top of Monte Urgull, topped by low castle walls and a grand statue of Christ, by taking a path from Plaza de Zuloaga or from behind the aquarium. The

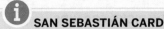

ⓘ SAN SEBASTIÁN CARD

419

The San Sebastián Card (€13) entitles users to free or reduced admission rates at many of the city's sights, free citywide transport, discounts in various shops and a free city tour. The card is valid for five days and available at the tourist office.

views are breathtaking. The castle houses the well-presented **Mirando a San Sebastián** (admission free; ⊙11am-8pm), a small museum focusing on the city's history.

Museo Naval

MUSEUM

(http://um.gipuzkoakultura.net, in Spanish & Basque; Paseo del Muelle 24; adult/child €1.20/free; ⊙10am-1.30pm & 4-7.30pm Tue-Sat, 11am-2pm Sun) This museum turns the pages of Basque seafaring and naval history. It's best appreciated by those with at least basic Spanish-language skills.

☞ Courses & Tours

Pintxo.Sanse

COOKING COURSES

(☏902 443442, from abroad +34 943 21 77 17; www.pintxosanse.com; €115) The food of San Sebastián is of a legendary status and it's those little parcels of delight, *pintxos,* that really set hearts aflutter. Just imagine how impressed your friends back home would be if the next time you throw a dinner party you whip out a few San Sebastián–style *pintxos.* In association with the tourist office, Pintxo.Sanse runs personalised three-hour courses (in Spanish, English and French) in creating your own culinary masterpiece.

San Sebastián Food

PINTXO TOURS, COOKING COURSES

(☏634 759503; www.sansebastianfood.com) San Sebastián Food runs an array of *pintxo* tasting tours (from €55) and cookery courses (from €85) in and around the city, as well as wine tastings at one of the most important private wine cellars in Spain (€65) and day-long wine-tasting tours to La Rioja (€185).

Sabores de San Sebastián

PINTXO TOURS

(Flavours of San Sebastián; tour €16; ⊙11.30am Tue & Thu Jul & Aug) The tourist office runs the Sabores de San Sebastián, a two-hour tour of the city's best *pintxo* haunts. For tours outside of high season, contact the tourist office.

TOP PICKS FOR KIDS

With all those tiring outdoor activities, the Basque Country, Navarra and La Rioja are great places for children. In no particular order, here are our top picks:

» Hunting for dinosaurs in Enciso (p449).

» Playing dungeons and dragons in the castles of Olite (p443) and Javier (p439).

» Gawping at Nemo and Jaws in San Sebastián's aquarium (p419).

» Sandcastle building for the tots and learning to surf for the big boys and girls almost anywhere along the Basque coast.

» For older children, playing Jack and Jill went up the (very big) hill in the Pyrenees (p440).

» Turning your little sister into a frog with the witches of Zugarramurdi (p440).

» Fiesta, fiesta! The daylight hours of almost every fiesta are tailor-made for children.

Pukas SURFING
(www.pukassurf.com, in Spanish; Paseo de Zurriola 24; ☺10am-1.30pm & 4-8pm Mon-Sat) Playa de Gros, with its generally mellow and easy waves, is a good place for learners to get to grips with surfing. Aspiring surfer wannabes should drop by Pukas, where surf lessons, and board and wetsuit hire are available. Prices vary depending on group size and lesson length, but start at €53 for a weekend course comprising a 1½-hour lesson each day.

🎇 Festivals & Events

San Sebastián has a busy festival calendar. The main events are the following:

Festividad de San Sebastián FESTIVAL
On 20 January, this is the city's main winter knees-up.

Carnaval FESTIVAL
In mid-February, Carnaval is a big event, but nearby Tolosa goes even more berserk.

International Jazz Festival JAZZ
(www.heinekenjazzaldia.com) Big-name acts converge in July for the International Jazz Festival.

Semana Grande FESTIVAL
In mid-August, Semana Grande is the big summer festival.

Regatta de Traineras ROWING
The Regatta de Traineras, a boat race in which local teams of rowers race out to sea, takes place on the first two Sundays in September.

Film Festival FILM
(www.sansebastianfestival.com) The world-renowned, two-week Film Festival has been an annual fixture in the second half of September since 1957.

🛏 Sleeping

Accommodation standards in San Sebastián are generally good, but prices are high and availability in high season is very tight. In fact, with the city's increasing popularity, many of the better places are booked up for July and August months in advance. If you do turn up without a booking, head to the tourist office, which keeps a list of available rooms.

TOP CHOICE **Pensión Bellas Artes**
BOUTIQUE HOTEL €€
(☎943 47 49 05; www.pension-bellasartes.com; Calle de Urbieta 64; s/d from €75/95; 🐾) To call this magnificent place a mere *pensión* is to do it something of a disservice. Its spacious rooms (some with glassed-in balconies), with their exposed stone walls and excellent bathrooms, should be the envy of many a more-expensive hotel. It also has to be the friendliest hotel in town – the staff seem to genuinely love their job and city and want to help you get the most out of your visit.

Pensión Aida BOUTIQUE HOTEL €€
(☎943 32 78 00; www.pensionesconencanto.com; Calle de Iztueta 9; s/d €59/82, studios €145; ✳@🐾) The owners of this excellent *pensión* read the rule book on what makes a good hotel and have complied exactly. The rooms are bright and bold, full of exposed stone and everything smells fresh and clean. The communal area, stuffed with soft sofas and mountains of information, is a big plus. They've recently added a handful of very slick studios that come with kitchenettes. For our money, we'd say this one is very hard to beat.

Pensión Amaiur Ostatua BOUTIQUE HOTEL €
(☎943 42 96 54; www.pensionamaiur.com; Calle de 31 de Agosto 44; s without bathroom €40-45, d without bathroom €50-65; @🖤) Sprawling over three floors of an old town house, this excellent *pensión* continues to improve. The rooms, all of which share bathrooms, are generally fairly small but have had a great deal of thought put into them and every room and every floor is different – maybe you'll get one with chintzy wallpaper or maybe you'll go for one with brazen primary colours. However, the best ones are those overlooking the street, where you can be completely enveloped in blushing red flowers. There's a kitchen on every floor for guest use. In high season you need to book well in advance.

Pensión Edorta BOUTIQUE HOTEL €€
(☎943 42 37 73; www.pensionedorta.com; Calle del Puerto 15; r without bathroom €60-70, r with bathroom €80-90; @) A fine *pensión* with rooms that are all tarted up in brash modern colours, but with a salute to the past in the stone walls and ceilings. It's very well cared for and well situated.

Pensión Altair BOUTIQUE PENSIÓN €€
(☎943 29 31 33; www.pension-altair.com; Calle Padre Larroca 3; s/d €60/84; ✳@🖤) This brand-new *pensión* might well be the future of the San Sebastián accommodation scene. It's in a beautifully restored town house, with unusual church-worthy arched windows and spacious minimalist rooms that are a world away from the fusty decor of the old-town *pensiones*. Reception is closed between 1.30pm and 5pm.

Pensión Kursaal BOUTIQUE HOTEL €€
(☎943 29 26 66; www.pensionesconencanto. com; Calle de Peña y Goñi 2; d €82-88; ✳@🖤) This excellent place, full of light and colour, has majestic rooms with a suitably refined edge, all of which help it feel more like a proper hotel than a *pensión*. It's virtually on Playa de Gros.

Pensión Donostiarra PENSIÓN €€
(☎943 42 61 67; www.pensiondonostiarra.com; Calle de San Martín 6; s/d €64/87; 🖤) This *pensión*, with its imposing old-fashioned stairway and clanking lift, is a charmer. The rooms are plush sky-blue affairs and some have wonderful stained-glass doors leading onto little balconies.

Olga's Place HOSTEL €
(☎943 32 67 25; Calle de Zabaleta 49; dm from €25; @🖤) What you get here is the basics done exceedingly well. The common areas are probably the best news – there are a couple of terraces to kick back on and a stack of DVDs to watch (should you somehow find yourself lost for things to do in San Sebastián), and there's also a kitchen for guest use. Rooms come in a mixture of styles – some with vertigo-inspiring bunks and others with more down-to-earth soft beds. It's booked up way ahead in season and there's a constant party atmosphere. It's currently the best hostel in town.

Hotel Maria Cristina HISTORIC HOTEL €€€
(☎943 43 76 00; www.starwoodhotels.com; Paseo de la República Argentina 4; s/d from €235/275; P✳@🖤) In case you're wondering what sort of hotels Lonely Planet authors normally stay in, the absolutely impeccable Maria Cristina, with its huge and luxurious rooms, is not one of them. However, don't be downhearted, because instead of hanging out with us, you'll get to mix with royalty and Hollywood stars. Yes, we know, it's disappointing.

Hostal Alemana BOUTIQUE HOTEL €€
(☎943 46 25 44; www.hostalalemana.com; Calle de San Martín 53; s/d €95/105; P🖤) With a great location just a sandy footstep from the beach, this smart hotel has opted for the white, minimalist look, countered with stylish B&W photos, all of which works very well and makes the rooms light and airy. Parking is €12.50 per day.

Hotel de Londres e Inglaterra
HISTORIC HOTEL €€€
(☎943 44 07 70; www.hlondres.com; Calle de Zubieta 2; s/d from €136/169; P✳🖤) Queen Isabel II set the tone for this hotel well over a century ago and things have stayed pretty regal ever since. It oozes class and some rooms have stunning views over Playa de la Concha.

Urban House HOSTEL €
(☎943 42 81 54; www.enjoyeu.com; Alameda del Boulevard 24; dm €27, r €60-80; 🖤) Loud, colourful rooms set the tone for this busy party house where summer fun rules supreme.

MOVING ON?

For tips, recommendations and reviews, head to shop.lonelyplanet.com to purchase a downloadable PDF of the French Basque Country chapter from Lonely Planet's *France* guide.

It's smack in the centre of the action and the young, multilingual staff will ensure you have a good time. They also organise a variety of city tours and surf lessons. During the high season it only offers beds in four-person dorms. The hostel also manages the bookings for several cheap and basic *pensiones* elsewhere in the old town – so if the main building is full, the staff can always find you a bed elsewhere.

Pensión Izar Bat   PENSIÓN €€
(☑943 42 15 73; www.pensionizarbat.com, in Spanish; Calle Fermín Calbetón; s €50-60, d €60-65; ⓐ) This sparkly, well-priced new venture has rooms covered in disco glitter paint, flaming orange walls and colour-clashing bed spreads. All rooms come with small private bathrooms.

Hospedaje Irune   PENSIÓN €€
(☑943 42 57 43; www.hospedajepensionirune. com; Calle San Jerónimo 17; s €45-50, d €65-70; ❋⟩) This cheerful place, with rooms that gather lots of sunlight and have good sound-proofing, is a great deal. Some rooms have little balconies and all have attached bathrooms, which is rare in this price category.

Pensión Santa Clara   PENSIÓN €€
(☑943 43 12 03; www.pensionsantaclara.com; Calle de San Lorenzo 6; s/d €57/67; ⟩) This cheerful *pensión* has just a handful of rainbow-bright rooms and the owner is a mine of information. Santa Clara's so central that the smell of *pintxos* will virtually permeate your sleep. There's also a useful book-swap service.

Pensión San Lorenzo   PENSIÓN €
(☑943 42 55 16; www.infonegocio.com/pension sanlorenzo; Calle de San Lorenzo 2; d €55; ⟩) The dandelion-yellow rooms here are some of the cheapest private bedrooms in the city. All rooms have bathrooms, but some share toilets.

Pensión Loinaz   PENSIÓN €€
(☑943 42 67 14; www.pensionloinaz.com; Calle de San Lorenzo 17; d €80; ⓐ) Modern, small and immaculate, Pensión Loinaz is a very pleasant place, with friendly English-speaking proprietors, spotless (shared) bathrooms and bright rooms.

Pensión Basic Confort   PENSIÓN €€
(☑943 42 25 81; www.basicconfort.com; Calle de Puerto 17; s/d €100/110; ⟩) Slightly overpriced but the handful of individually styled rooms here nevertheless provide a comfortable base for exploring the city.

We especially liked the 'Glasgow' room, all dressed up in tartan.

Camping Igueldo   CAMPING €
(☑943 21 45 02; www.campingigueldo.com; Paseo del Padra Orkolaga 69; sites for 2 people, car & tent or caravan €31.40; Ⓟ ⓐ⟩) This well-organised, tree-shaded camping ground, 5km west of the city, is served by bus 16 from Alameda del Boulevard (€1.36, 30 minutes).

✕ Eating

San Sebastián stands atop a pedestal as one of the culinary capitals of the planet. There are more Michelin stars per capita here than anywhere else on earth. As if that alone weren't enough, the city is overflowing with bars – almost all of which have bar tops weighed down under a mountain of *pintxo* excellence. These statistics alone make San Sebastián's CV look pretty impressive. But it's not just us who thinks this: a raft of the world's best chefs, including such luminaries as Catalan superchef Ferran Adriá, have said that San Sebastián is quite probably the best place on the entire planet to eat.

TOP CHOICE **La Cuchara de San Telmo**
                                        PINTXO BAR €
(Calle de 31 de Agosto 28) This unfussy, hidden-away (and hard to find) bar offers miniature *nueva cocina vasca* from a supremely creative kitchen. Chefs Alex Montiel and Iñaki Gulin conjure up such delights as *carrílera de ternera al vino tinto* (calf cheeks in red wine), with meat so tender it starts to dissolve almost before it's past your lips. A percentage of profits goes to the worthy Fundación Vicente Ferrer charity.

TOP CHOICE **Arzak**   GOURMET €€€
(☑943 27 84 65; www.arzak.info; Avenida Alcalde Jose Elosegui 273; meals €150; ☺closed Nov & late Jun) With three shining Michelin stars, acclaimed chef Juan Mari Arzak takes some beating when it comes to *nueva cocina vasca* and his restaurant is, not surprisingly, considered one of the best places to eat in Spain. Arzak is now assisted by his daughter Elena and they never cease to innovate. Reservations, well in advance, are obligatory. The restaurant is about 1.5km east of San Sebastián.

TOP CHOICE **Martín Berasategui Restaurant**
                                        GOURMET €€€
(☑943 36 64 71; www.martinberasategui.com; Calle Loidi 4, Lasarte-Oria; set menus from €94;

Just rolling the word *pintxo* around your tongue defines the essence of this cheerful, cheeky little slice of Basque cuisine. The perfect *pintxo* should have exquisite taste, texture and appearance and should be savoured in two elegant bites. The Basque version of a tapa, the *pintxo* transcends the commonplace by the sheer panache of its culinary campiness. In San Sebastián especially, Basque chefs have refined the *pintxo* to an art form.

Many *pintxos* are bedded on small pieces of bread or on tiny half-baguettes, upon which towering creations are constructed, often melded with flavoursome mayonnaise and then pinned in place by large toothpicks. Some bars specialise in seafood, with much use of marinated anchovies, prawns and strips of squid, all topped with anything from chopped crab to pâté. Others deal in pepper or mushroom delicacies, or simply offer a mix of everything. And the choice isn't normally limited to what's on the bar top in front of you: many of the best *pintxos* are the hot ones you need to order. These are normally chalked up on a blackboard on the wall somewhere.

Unfortunately such culinary brilliance no longer comes cheap, especially in San Sebastián. Expect to pay €2.50 to €3.50 for one *pintxo* and a glass of delicious *txakoli*, the young white wine of the Basque Country. Not so bad if you just take one, but is one ever enough!

⊘closed Dec–mid-Jan) With three Michelin stars and dozens of other awards, this superlative restaurant, about 9km southwest of San Sebastián, is considered by foodies to be one of the best restaurants in the world. The chef, Martín Berasategui, doesn't approach cooking in the same way as the rest of us. He approaches it as a science and the results are tastes you never knew existed. Reserve well ahead.

Astelena   PINTXO BAR €

TOP CHOICE (Calle de Iñigo 1) The *pintxos* draped across the counter in this bar, tucked into the corner of Plaza de la Constitución, stand out as some of the best in the city. Many of them are a fusion of Basque and Asian inspirations, but the best of all are perhaps the foie-gras-based treats.

Bodegón Alejandro   SEAFOOD €€
(☑943 42 71 58; Calle de Fermín Calbetón 4; menus €38.50, mains €15-18; ⊘closed Mon & dinner Sun) This highly regarded restaurant has a menu from which you can select such succulent treats as scallops and asparagus, baby tomatoes stuffed with squid or just plain old baked lobster. Oh, what choices!

Restaurante Ni Neu   GOURMET €€€
(☑943 00 31 62; www.restaurantenineu.com, in Spanish; Avenida de Zurriola 1; menus €24-57; ⊘lunch & dinner daily) The former Michelin-starred Kursaal has been rebranded as the Restaurante Ni Neu and, although the old chef and his star have gone, the menu, and meal quality, remains much the same. Anyway, who needs a Michelin star when you have a setting, inside the Kursaal Centre, with a view straight over Playa de Gros?

La Mejíllonera   PINTXO BAR €
(Calle del Puerto 15) If you thought mussels only came with garlic sauce, come here to discover mussels (from €3) by the thousand in all their glorious forms. Mussels not for you? Opt for the calamari and *patatas bravas* (fried potatoes with a spicy tomato and mayo sauce). We promise you won't regret it.

Bar Goiz-Argi   PINTXO BAR €
(Calle de Fermín Calbetón 4) *Gambas a la plancha* (prawns cooked on a hotplate) are the house speciality. Sounds simple, we know, but never have we tasted prawns cooked quite as perfectly as this.

Restaurante Alberto   SEAFOOD €
(☑943 42 88 84; Calle de 31 de Agosto 19; set menus €14; ⊘closed Tue) A charming old seafood restaurant with a fishmonger-style window display of the day's catch. It's small, dark and friendly, but much of the fish is sold by the kilo so bring a friend.

Kaskazuri   SEAFOOD €€
(☑943 42 08 94; Paseo de Salamanca 14; menus €20) Upmarket Basque seafood is all the rage in this flash restaurant, which is built on a raised platform allowing views of the former home of your dinner. It cooks up a storm with their €18 *menú del día*. Book in advance.

TXOKO

Peek through the keyholes of enough Basque doors and eventually you'll come across an unusual sight: a large room full of men, and only men, seated around a table bending under the weight of food and drink. This is *Txoko* (Basque Gastronomic Society) and it is an almost exclusively male preserve. The men who come here (who often wouldn't be seen dead in the kitchen at home) are normally highly accomplished amateur chefs who take turns cooking their own speciality for the critical consumption of the other members. It's often said that the best Basque food is to be found at the *Txoko*. Recently a few women have started to enter the *Txoko*, but only as guests and even then they are never allowed into the kitchen when the cooking is in process in case they distract the men. Women are, however, let into the kitchen afterwards – to do the washing up!

Restaurante Mariñela SEAFOOD €€
(☎943 42 73 83; Paseo del Muelle; mains €10-18) You pay for the fabulous harbour-front setting, but the location guarantees that the fish is so fresh it may well flop back off your plate and swim away. There are several similar neighbouring places.

La Zurri REGIONAL €
(☎943 29 38 86; Calle de Zabaleta 10; menus €10.30) Over the water in Gros, this ever-popular locals' restaurant has a menu as long as a conger eel and all of it is consistently good.

Casa Valles PINTXO BAR €
(Calle de los Reyes Católicos 10) With meaty *pintxos* beneath a forest of hung hams, this fine bar also does *raciones* (large tapas servings) and full meals (€13 to €30).

Bar Nagusía PINTXO BAR €
(Nagusía Kalea 4) This bar, reminiscent of old San Sebastián, has a counter that moans under the weight of its *pintxos*. You'll be moaning after a few as well – in sheer pleasure.

Txandorra Restaurante PINTXO BAR €
(Calle de Fermín Calbetón 7) *Pintxos* served in a gritty though memorable bar filled with one-armed bandits and other local characters. It also serves up full meals, with mains around €15.

Caravanserai INTERNATIONAL €
(☎943 47 54 18; cnr Calle San Bartolomé & Plaza del Buen Pastor; bocadillos from €4, meals from €8.50) Does tasty burgers, sandwiches and pasta.

Plaza Café CAFE €
(☎943 44 57 12; Plaza del Buen Pastor 14; breakfasts €3.50-7) In the cathedral plaza, the pleasant Plaza Café is a popular breakfast spot with locals.

San Martin Centre SUPERMARKET €
(Calle de Urbieta 9) At the heart of the Centro Romantíca, the smart San Martin Centre has a very big supermarket.

Mercado de la Bretxa SUPERMARKET €
On the east side of the Parte Vieja, Mercado de la Bretxa has an underground Lidl supermarket.

🍷 Drinking & Entertainment

It's said that San Sebastián's Parte Vieja contains more bars per square metre than anywhere else on Earth. Need we say more? It's hard to differentiate between most of these, as they all mutate through the day from calm morning-coffee hangouts to *pintxo*-laden delights before finally finishing up as noisy bars full of writhing, sweaty bodies. Nights in San Sebastián start late and go on until well into the wee hours.

Dioni's GAY BAR
(Calle Ijentea 2) More a spot for a black coffee in the early hours, this relaxed and very gay-friendly place has an '80s cocktail-bar ambience and is the perfect spot in which to watch the Eurovision Song Contest.

M.A.D BAR
(Calle de Larramendi 4) Musica, Arte and, well, we're not sure what the 'D' stands for, but otherwise it does what it says on the label. Alternative music blasts day and night, and photos and psychedelic art adorn the blood-red walls. There are a couple of similar places nearby.

Bar Ondarra BAR
(Avenida de Zurriola 16) Head over to Gros for this terrific bar that's just across the road from the beach. There's a great chilled-out

mixed crowd and, in the rockin' downstairs bar, every kind of sound gets aired.

Altxerri Jazz Bar
LIVE MUSIC

(www.altxerri.com; Blvd Reina Regente 2) This jazz and blues temple has regular live gigs by local and international stars. Jamming sessions take over on nights with no gig and there's an in-house art gallery.

Be Bop
BAR-CLUB

(Paseo de Salamanca 3) Grind your hips in this sultry bar-club, tricked out in bright red, green and cream and burnished by the evening sun. Cheesy pop anthems kick off the night, salsa turns things sexy later on and regular guest DJs add spice.

Etxe Kalte
JAZZ

(Calle Mari) A very-late-night jazz haunt near the harbour, it sometimes throws open its doors to all kinds of dance-music styles.

Splash
BAR

(Sánchez Toca 1) A brash, modern bar with outdoor seating and strong beats inside.

Shopping

The Parte Vieja is awash with small independent boutiques, whilst the Centro Romantíca has all your brand-name and chain-store favourites.

Elkar
BOOKS

(Calle de Fermín Calbetón 30) For a huge range of travel books and guides (including lots of Lonely Planet guides), maps and hiking books in English, Spanish and French, try this specialist travel bookshop. Almost opposite it is a bigger mainstream branch dealing in Spanish- and Basque-language books.

Kukuxumusu
CLOTHES

(Nagusía Kalea 15) The funkiest and best-known Basque clothing label has a whole wardrobe of original T-shirts and other clothing awaiting you here.

Information

Emergency
Emergency (☏112)

Internet access
Cibernetworld (Calle de Aldamar 3; per hr €3; ⊙9am-midnight) As well as internet, it also has luggage storage, general travel information and a foreign-language book exchange.

Zarranet (Calle de San Lorenzo 6; per hr €2; ⊙10.30am-2pm & 4-9pm Mon-Sat)

Medical Services
Casa de Socorro (Calle Bengoechea 4) Medical clinic.

Money
There are plenty of banks with ATMs throughout the city centre.

Post
Main post office (Calle de Urdaneta)

Tourist information
Oficina de Turismo (☏943 48 11 66; www.sansebastianturismo.com; Alameda del Boulevard 8; ⊙9am-8pm Mon-Sat, 10am-7pm Sun) This friendly office offers comprehensive information on the city and the Basque Country in general.

Getting There & Away

Air
The city's **airport** (☏902 404704; www.aena.es) is 22km out of town, near Hondarribia. There are regular flights to Madrid and occasional charters to other major European cities. Biarritz, just over the border in France, is served by Ryanair and EasyJet, among various other budget airlines, and is generally much cheaper to fly into.

Bus
The main bus station is a 20-minute walk south of the Parte Vieja, between Plaza de Pío XII and the river. Local bus 28 and 26 connects the bus station with Alameda del Boulevard (€1.35, 10 minutes). Note that the bus station will (supposedly!) be moving during the lifetime of this book to a new station on Paseo de Francia, next to the train station.

There are daily bus services to the following:

DESTINATION	FARE (€)	DURATION (HR)
Biarritz (France)	8.50	1¼
Bilbao	7.06-14	1
Bilbao airport	15.40	1¼
Madrid	from 31.99	5
Pamplona	6.88	1
Vitoria	5.68	1½

Car
Several major car-hire companies are represented by agencies in San Sebastián, including **Avis** (www.avis.com; Calle del Triunfo 2) and **Europcar** (www.europcar.com; Renfe train station). Further offices can be found at the airport.

Train
The main **Renfe train station** (Paseo de Francia) is just across Río Urumea, on a line linking Paris to Madrid. There are several services daily

to **Madrid** (from €52.60, five hours) and two to **Barcelona** (from €36.90, eight hours).

There's only one direct train to Paris, but there are plenty more from the Spanish/French border town of Irún (or sometimes Hendaye; €1.80, 25 minutes), which is also served by **Eusko Tren/Ferrocarril Vasco** (www.euskotren.es, in Spanish & Basque) on a railway line nicknamed 'El Topo' (the Mole). Trains depart every half-hour from Amara train station, about 1km south of the city centre, and also stop in Pasajes (€1.30, 12 minutes) and Irún/Hendaye (€1.50, 25 minutes). Another ET/FV railway line heads west to Bilbao via Zarautz, Zumaia and Durango, but it's painfully slow (like half-a-day slow), so the bus is a much better plan.

ℹ Getting Around

Buses to Hondarribia (€1.90, 45 minutes) and the airport (€1.90, 45 minutes) depart from Plaza de Guipúzcoa.

East of San Sebastián

PASAJES
POP 16,100

Pasajes (Basque: Pasaia), where Río Oiartzun meets the Atlantic, is the largest port in the province of Guipúzcoa. The main street and the area immediately around the central square are lined with pretty houses and colourful balconies, and are well worth a half-day's exploration. Highlights are the great seafood restaurants, the short ferry ride over the river and the spectacular entrance to the port, through a keyhole-like split in the cliff face – even more impressive when a huge container ship passes through it.

Nowadays Pasajes is virtually a suburb of San Sebastián and there are numerous buses plying the route between them.

HONDARRIBIA
POP 16,100

Lethargic Hondarribia (Castilian: Fuenterrabía), staring across the estuary to France, has a heavy Gallic fragrance and a charming Casco Antiguo (Old City), which makes it an excellent first or last port of call.

You enter the *casco* through an archway at the top of Calle San Compostela to reach the pretty Plaza de Gipuzkoa. Head straight on to Calle San Nicolás and go left to reach the bigger Plaza de Armas and the Gothic Iglesia de Santa María de la Asunción.

For La Marina, head the other way from the archway. This is Hondarribia's most picturesque quarter. Its main street, Calle San Pedro, is flanked by typical fishermen's houses, with facades painted bright green or blue and wooden balconies gaily decorated with flower boxes.

There are several places to stay, ranging from a campsite with right royal views to a castle converted into a luxury *parador* (state-owned hotel), and a number of great places to eat.

South of San Sebastián

The hills rising to the south between San Sebastián and Bilbao offer a number of appealing towns. There are plenty of *nekazal turismoas* (*casas rurales;* family homes in rural areas with rooms to rent).

MUSEO CHILLIDA LEKU

This open-air museum (www.museochillidaleku.com; adult/child €8.50/free; ⊙10.30am-8pm Mon-Sat, 10.30am-3pm Sun) is the most engaging museum in rural Basque Country. Amid the beech, oak and magnolia trees, you'll find 40 sculptures of granite and iron created by the renowned Basque sculptor Eduardo Chillida. Many more of Chillida's works appear inside the renovated 16th-century farmhouse.

To get here, take the G2 bus (€1.35) for Hernani from Calle de Okendo in San Sebastián and get off at Zabalaga. If you're driving, take the A1 south from San Sebastián. After 7km, take the turn-off southwest for Hernani (GI3132). The museum is 600m along on your left.

SANTUARIO DE LOYOLA

Just outside Azpeitia (12km south of the A8 motorway along the GI631) lies the portentous Santuario de Loyola (www.santuariodeloyola.org; ⊙10am-noon & 4-7pm), dedicated to St Ignatius, the founder of the Jesuit order. The dark, sooty basilica laden with grey marble and plenty of carved ornamentation is monstrous rather than attractive. The house where the saint was born in 1490 is preserved in one of the two wings of the sanctuary. Weekends are the most interesting times to come, as the sanctuary fills up with pilgrims.

OÑATI
POP 10,500

With a flurry of magnificent architecture and a number of interesting sites scattered through the surrounding green hills, the small, and resolutely Basque, town of Oñati is a great place to get to know the rural Basque heartland.

The tourist office (☎943 78 34 53; Calle San Juan 14; ⊘10am-2pm & 3.30-7.30pm Mon-Fri, 10am-2pm & 4.30-6.30pm Sat, 10am-2pm Sun) is just opposite the Universidad de Sancti Spiritus.

There are daily buses to/from San Sebastián, Vitoria and Bilbao.

◎ Sights

Universidad de Sancti Spiritus
HISTORIC BUILDING

Oñati's number-one attraction is the Renaissance treasure of the Universidad de Sancti Spiritus. Built in the 16th century, it was the first university in the Basque Country and, until its closure in 1902, alumni here were schooled in philosophy, law and medicine. Today it's been taken over as local council offices, but you can still enter the Mudéjar courtyard (⊘9am-2pm & 3-4.30pm Mon-Thu, 9am-2pm Fri) and admire its plateresque facade. The tourist office can organise guided tours (from €6) with a few hours' notice. Near the Universidad and also well worth a peek is the Iglesia de San Miguel, a late-Gothic confection whose cloister was built over the river. The church faces onto the main square, Foruen Enparantza, dominated by the eye-catching baroque ayuntamiento (town hall).

🛏 Sleeping

Oñati doesn't get a lot of tourists staying overnight, a fact that is reflected by the relative dearth of accommodation.

Arregi
CASA RURAL €

(☎943 78 08 24, 943 78 36 57; www.nekatur.net/arregi; Garagaltza 21; d €42) This is a splendid agritourism home 2km south of town. The nicely restored farmhouse sits in a green valley full of brown cows with big eyelashes, and has sheer views of bold mountainsides. The rooms themselves are spacious and nicely decorated, and there's a kitchen for guest use and a sitting room with a big log fire.

Ongi Ostatua
TRADITIONAL HOTEL €

(☎943 71 82 85; Calle Zaharra 19; s/d €30/42) A central place, which has cheap but dated rooms.

SANTUARIO DE ARANTZAZU & ARRIKRUTZ CAVES

About 10km south of Oñati is the love-it-or-loathe-it pilgrimage site of Santuario de Arantzazu (www.arantzazukosantutegia.org), a fabulous conflation of piety with avant-garde art. The sanctuary was built in the 1950s on the site where, in 1468, a shepherd found a statue of the Virgin under a hawthorn bush – on which the sanctuary's design is supposed to be based. The overwhelming impression of the building is of spiky towers and hollow halls guarded by 14 strange-looking, chiselled apostles and, in the crypt, a devil-red Christ – all of which caused a bit of a headache for the Vatican.

The road up and the setting are worth the trip in themselves, and the whole area lends itself to excellent walking – the Oñati tourist office has information on routes. If you do go for a walk around here, be a little careful, because there's more to these spectacular hills than meets the eye (see boxed text).

There's a cavern system a couple of kilometres back down the road towards Oñati. The Arrikrutz caves (adult/child €8/6; ⊘10am-2pm & 3-7pm Tue-Sun) have numerous slow-growing stalagmites and stalactites.

> ## THE THUNDER GODDESS
>
> It's said that one of the numerous caves on the slopes of the wild hills around Oñati is the home of Mari, the pre-Christian goddess of the Basques, who is said to control the weather. If you get lost while out walking, just shout out her name three times and she'll appear in the skies above you to guide you in the right direction. If, however, you stumble upon her cave home, then leave as fast as possible because she'll get very angry and, trust us, you really don't want to see what an angry Basque goddess looks like!

Vitoria

POP 235,600 / ELEV 512M

Vitoria (Basque: Gasteiz) has a habit of falling off the radar, yet it's actually the capital of not just the southern Basque province of Álava (Basque: Araba) but also the entire Basque Country. Maybe it was given this honour precisely because it is so forgotten, but, if that's the case, then prepare for some big changes. With an art gallery whose contents frequently supersede those of the more famous Bilbao galleries, a delightful old quarter, dozens of great *pintxo* bars and restaurants, a large student contingent and a friendly local population, you have the makings of a perfect city – it surely won't be long until the world catches on!

History

Vitoria's name may well derive from the Basque word *beturia,* meaning height, a reference to the hill on which the old town stands. It was so named by the Visigoths. Sancho VI of Navarra settled things by founding a 'New Vitoria' in the 12th century. Thereafter, Vitoria bounced to and fro between the Castilian and Navarran crowns. The economic advances of the late 19th century triggered Vitoria's expansion, which carried over into the 20th century. The city's historic and well-preserved nature made it a good choice for capital of the Basque autonomous government in 1981. The University of the Basque Country also has its base here.

◉ Sights

Artium ART GALLERY
(www.artium.org; Calle de Francia 24; admission by donation; ◷11am-2pm & 5-8pm Tue-Thu, 11am-2pm & 4-9pm Fri-Sun, closed Sep) Unlike some famous Basque art galleries, Vitoria's palace of modern art, the Artium, doesn't need to dress to impress and knows that it's what's on the inside that really counts. Compared to the Guggenheim, its lesser status allows it to be daring, eccentric and challenging in a way El Goog could never get away with. The large subterranean galleries are filled with engrossing works by Basque, Spanish and international artists, displaying some fairly intense modernist work. For example, at the time of research the collection included exhibitions on death and aging, as well as numerous sexual images such as plastic penises and photos of people having sex. Guided tours, in Spanish, run several times a day. After digesting the art, it's worth digesting some food at the much-praised **Cube Café** (menú del día €15), inside the museum. The gallery is wheelchair accessible.

FREE **Museo de Bellas Artes** ART GALLERY
(Paseo de Fray Francisco de Vitoria; ◷10am-2pm & 4-6.30pm Tue-Fri, 10am-2pm & 5-8pm Sat, 11am-2pm Sun & holidays) Housed in an astoundingly ornate building, the absorbing Museo de Bellas Artes has Basque paintings and sculpture from the 18th and 19th centuries. The works of local son Fernando de Amaríca are given good space and reflect an engaging romanticism that manages to mix drama with great warmth of colour and composition.

Catedral de María Inmaculada CATHEDRAL
(Cadena y Eleta; ◷10am-2pm & 4-6.30pm Tue-Fri, 10am-2pm Sat, 11am-2pm Sun) Vitoria's cathedral might look old but in fact it only dates from the early 1970s. There are some impressive, fairly adventurous stained-glass windows and a neck-stretching high nave. More interesting, though, is the attached museum of sacred art, which contains some early Christian stone carvings and Basque crosses, detailed paintings of biblical scenes and a glittering ensemble of crucifixes and ceremonial crosses – all of which come from the Basque Country.

FREE **Museo de Armería** ARMOUR MUSEUM
(Paseo de Fray Francisco de Vitoria; ◷10am-2pm & 4-6.30pm Tue-Fri, 10am-2pm Sat, 11am-2pm Sun) Any damsels in distress reading this ought to head to this museum where your knight in shining armour awaits. This collection of armour through the ages is surprisingly absorbing and begs the question of how on earth gallant men wearing all this lot even managed to move let alone rescue damsels from the clutches of fire-breathing dragons. Signage is in Basque and Spanish only.

FREE **Museo de Ciencias Naturales**
  NATURAL HISTORY MUSEUM
(Calle de las Siervas de Jesús 24; ◷10am-2pm & 4-6.30pm Tue-Fri, 10am-2pm Sat, 11am-2pm Sun) Inside this museum, housed in the impressive Torre de Doña Oxtanda, you can be dazzled by the collection of minerals, marvel at a mantis caught in amber, learn about the local wildlife and stare slack-jawed at a dinosaur jaw. Signage is in Basque and Spanish only.

Churches CHURCHES
At the base of Vitoria's medieval Casco Viejo is the delightful **Plaza de la Virgen Blanca**. It's lorded over by the 14th-century Iglesia de San Miguel, whose statue of the Virgen Blanca, the city's patron saint, lends its name to the plaza below.

The 14th-century Iglesia de San Pedro (Calle Herrería) is the city's oldest church and has a fabulous Gothic frontispiece on its eastern facade.

At the summit of the old town and dominating its skyline is the medieval Catedral de Santa María (☎945 12 21 60; www.catedral vitoria.com; ◷11am-2pm & 5-8pm). The cathedral is undergoing a lengthy, but much-praised, restoration project that's unlikely to be completed for some years yet. There

Vitoria

Top Sights

Artium	D1
Catedral de Maria Inmaculada	A3
Museo de Armería	A4
Museo de Bellas Artes	A4

Sights

1 Bibat	C1
2 Catedral de Santa María	C1
3 Iglesia de San Miguel	B2
4 Iglesia de San Pedro	B2
5 Museo de Ciencias Naturales	B1

Sleeping

6 Hotel Almoneda	B3
7 Hotel Amárica	B3
8 Hotel Dato	B3
9 Hotel Dato 28	B3
10 La Casa de los Arquillos	C2

Eating

11 Arkupe	C2
12 Asador Sagartoki	B2
13 Bar Deportivo Alaves	B2
14 Café Moderno	C2
15 Cube Café	D1
16 La Taberna de los Mundos	C3
17 Noventa y Siete	B2
18 Querida María Restaurante	C1
19 Salburua	C3
20 Virgen Blanca	B2

Drinking

21 El Parral	C2
22 Gora	C1

are excellent guided tours (€5) that give an insight into the excitement of restoration and discovery, as well as providing some contact with the cathedral's interior. You must book in advance either by telephone or via the website.

FREE **Bibat** MUSEUM
(Calle de la Cuchillería/Aiztogile Kalea 54; ⊙10am-2pm & 4-6.30pm Tue-Fri, 10am-2pm Sat, 11am-2pm Sun) Other museums worth perusing are the Museo de Arqueología and the Museo Fournier de Naipes, combined in Bibat. The Museo de Arqueología has giant TV screens that bring the dim and distant past to life. The eccentric Museo Fournier de Naipes, housed in the same complex as the Museo de Arqueología, has an impressive collection of historic presses and playing cards, including some of the oldest European decks. In both of these museums, signage is in Spanish and Basque only.

Festivals & Events

Fiestas de la Virgen Blanca FESTIVAL
The calm sophistication of Vitoria takes a back seat during the boisterous Fiestas de la Virgen Blanca, held from 4 to 9 August, with a range of fireworks, bullfights, concerts and street dancing. All of this is preceded by the symbolic descent of Celedón, a Basque effigy that flies down on strings from the Iglesia de San Miguel into the plaza below.

Azkena Rock Festival ROCK MUSIC
(www.azkenarockfestival.com) A fairly new gig is the Azkena Rock Festival held at the end of June. In 2010 headliners included Kiss, Bob Dylan, The Hives and Gov't Mule.

Jazz Festival JAZZ
(www.jazzvitoria.com) A jazz festival is held in mid-July that attracts numerous big national and international acts.

Sleeping

TOP CHOICE **La Casa de los Arquillos** B&B €€
(945 15 12 59; www.lacasadelosarquillos.com; Paseo Los Arquillos 1; d €69;) This new B&B is the most exciting thing to have happened to the Vitoria hotel scene in years. Located inside a beautiful old building in a prime location above the main square, the eight immaculate rooms take their young and funky inspiration from the artwork in the Artium. Every room is individually decorated in a highly original style – one has

tape measures above the bed and another has a doll sprouting limbs from its head! A hearty breakfast is thrown in. Note that the enthusiastic staff aren't always around, so it's best to call in advance and let them know what time you're arriving.

Hotel Dato & Hotel Dato 28
TRADITIONAL HOTEL €
(945 14 72 30; www.hoteldato.com; Calle de Eduardo Dato 28; s/d €37/52;) Two twin hotels on parallel streets. It's hard to know if the extravagant art-deco style, full of semi-naked nymphs, Roman pots and frilly fittings is tacky or classy. Either way it works well and the whole ensemble produces an exceptionally good-value and memorable hotel. Reception for both hotels is at Hotel Dato.

Hotel Almoneda TRADITIONAL HOTEL €€
(945 15 40 84; www.hotelalmoneda.com; Calle de la Florida 7; s/d incl breakfast €63/105;) This confident business-level hotel is a smidgen overpriced but otherwise decent enough. The rooms have creaky, polished wooden floors and beds as soft as a cloud, but the bathrooms are cramped to the extreme. A percentage of profits goes to Amnesty International.

Hotel América TRADITIONAL HOTEL €
(945 13 05 06; Calle de la Florida 11; s/d €37/55;) Functional, user-friendly rooms and the strategically positioned Buddhas help to keep your karma in check. The receptionist is often hanging out over the road, so you might have to wait a minute or two for him to turn up.

Eating

Head for the west sides of Plaza de España and the adjacent Plaza de la Virgen Blanca for breakfast and morning coffee in the bright light of day. Switch to the east sides for afternoon sun and stronger drinks.

Asador Sagartoki SIDRERÍA €
(Calle del Prado 18; mains €18) A marvellous *sidrería* (cider house) that has one of the most creative menus around and an atmosphere to go with it. The dining room stretches way beyond the busy front bar and the *pintxos* are sublime award winners. Marvel as the bar staff, arms flailing like birds wings, orchestrate jets of cider from the big barrels to the glasses in their outstretched hands; then try it yourself in the restaurant. Like most *sidrerías,* this is a place to come with friends.

Arkupe BASQUE €€
(☑945 23 00 80; Calle Mateo Benigno de Moraza 13; mains from €18, menus from €33) For divine Basque cooking, check out this place. The rough wooden exterior belies a formal and slightly chic atmosphere. There's an extensive wine list, with all the offerings racked up against the back wall. Reserve in advance.

La Taberna de los Mundos MODERN BASQUE €
(www.delosmundos.com; Calle Independencia 14; menus €11.50) A warm and inviting place in which to indulge in some superb-value set lunch menus, including vegetarian options. As the name implies, the decor is inspired by the wider world and includes frequent photo exhibitions of faraway locales. Despite such worldly backdrops, most of the food stays much closer to home, albeit with a few exotic Asian-inspired twists.

Querida María Restaurante
MODERN BASQUE €
(Plaza de Santa María; mains €12-18, menus €18) Facing the cathedral in the prettiest part of the old town, this informal and stylish poppy-red restaurant serves quality local dishes, including delights such as squid cooked in its ink with rice and a tamarind sauce.

Salburua PINTXO BAR €
(Calle de los Fueros 19; pintxos €2-3) In the new town, Salburua has picked up several awards for its *pintxos* and has an old-Basque-bar feel with *jamones* (hams) swinging from hooks behind a bar covered in flower-like edible delicacies.

Virgen Blanca BASQUE €
(menus €14) Virgen Blanca conjures up a perfectly formed Basque lunch *menú* that is particularly recommended.

Of the numerous restaurants and *pintxo* bars lining these adjoining squares, the current pick of the bunch are the Bar Deportivo Alaves and Noventa y Siete for their *pintxos*, and Café Moderno for a caffeine boost.

Drinking
There's a strong politico-arty vibe in the Casco Viejo, where a lively student cadre keeps things swerving with creative street posters and action. The main action is at Calle de la Cuchillería/Aiztogile Kalea and neighbouring Cantón de San Francísco Javier, both of which are packed with messy bars such as Gora and El Parral. There is a heavy Basque nationalist atmosphere in some bars.

ℹ Information
Emergency (☑112)
Hospital de Santiago (☑945 00 76 00; cnr Calles de la Paz & de Olaguíbel)
Main post office (Calle de las Postas)
Policía Nacional (☑091) Near the Hospital de Santiago.
Tourist office (☑945 16 15 98; www.vitoria -gasteiz.org/turismo; Plaza General Loma 1; ☺9.30am-7.30pm) Opposite the Basque parliament building.

ℹ Getting There & Away
Vitoria's **airport** (☑945 16 35 91) is at Foronda, about 9km northwest of the city, with connections to Madrid and Barcelona. There are car-hire offices and an ATM at the airport. Buses (€3) to town meet flights; taxis to town cost €15/20 during the day/night.

There are car parks by the train station, by the Artium and just east of the cathedral.

Vitoria's **bus station** (Calle de los Herrán) has regular services to the following:

DESTINATION	FARE (€)	DURATION (HR)
Barcelona	37.65	7
Bilbao	5.65	1¼
Madrid	23.98	4½
Pamplona	7.79	1¾
San Sebastián	9.85	2¼

Trains go to the following:

DESTINA-TION	FARE (€)	DURA-TION (HR)	FRE-QUENCY
Barcelona	from 59.30	5	1 daily
Madrid	from 33.70	4-6	5 daily
Pamplona	4.85	1	4 daily
San Sebastián	from 9.75	1¾	up to 10 daily

NAVARRA

Several Spains intersect in Navarra (Basque: Nafarroa). The soft greens and bracing climate of the Navarran Pyrenees lie like a cool compress across the sunstruck brow of the south, which is all stark plains, cereal crops and vineyards, sliced by high sierras with cockscombs of raw limestone. Navarra is also pilgrim territory: for centuries the faithful have used the pass at Roncesvalles to cross from France on their

BASQUE COUNTRY, NAVARRA & LA RIOJA VITORIA

At the gates of Spain, Navarra is the first Spanish leg of the journey to Santiago de Compostela for walkers on the Camino Francés route. The opening section, which crosses over the Pyrenees, is also one of the most spectacular parts of the entire Camino.

Roncesvalles to Pamplona

Just north of Roncesvalles at **Puerto de Ibañeta**, the Camino dramatically enters Spain and drops down to **Roncesvalles**. Dominated by its great, imposing abbey and embraced by soaring beech forest and green pastures dotted with sheep, Roncesvalles admirably sets the tone for this extraordinary route. Inside the heavily restored 13th-century Gothic church, you'll find the first statue of Santiago dressed as a pilgrim (with scallop shells and staff) and a finely sculpted 14th-century silver-encased Virgin and Child.

The Camino trail then traverses dense mixed forests, rural farmland and picturesque villages (especially **Burguete** and **Espinal**) on its route to Pamplona.

Pamplona (p432) became an official stop along the Camino in the 11th century, cementing its prosperity. Just inside the cathedral's bland neoclassical facade are the pure, soaring lines of the 14th-century Gothic interior. The 15th-century alabaster tombs of Pamplona's 1423 uniter, the Navarran king Carlos III El Noble and his wife, Doña Leonor, are particularly fine.

Pamplona to Logroño & Beyond

Heading west out of Pamplona via Zariquiegui, the Sierra del Perdón, with its long line of electricity-producing windmills, looms ahead. The sierra's pass reveals a bird's-eye view of the long valley leading to **Puente la Reina** (p445), where the Camino Aragonés, coming from the east, joins up with the Camino Francés. Nestled below in the patchwork quilt of wheat, white asparagus, grapes and olive trees, Eunate is a stunning 12th-century octagonal chapel, silently reigning over a desolate wheat field. Of probable Templars origin, the chapel once served as a pilgrim's graveyard.

The multistorey houses along Puente la Reina's main street have enormous wooden doors and finely carved eaves, lining the way to the town's striking 11th-century bridge. The diamond-shaped piers and hollows in the bridge's arches help reduce water resistance when the Río Arga rises during floods.

You'll find unusual Mudéjar-influenced Romanesque doorways, all with lobed arches, complicated knots and fascinating sculpture, in Puente la Reina's Iglesia de Santiago,

way to Santiago de Compostela (see Camino de Santiago, p37 and p432).

Navarra was historically the heartland of the Basques, but dynastic struggles and trimming due to reactionary politics, including Francoism, has left it as a semi-autonomous province, with the north being Basque by nature while the south leans towards Castilian Spain. The centre hangs somewhere in between and Navarra seems intrinsically uncommitted to the vision of a Basque future.

The Navarran capital, Pamplona, tends to grab the headlines with its world-famous running of the bulls, but the region's real charm is in its peppering of small towns and villages that seem to melt in with the landscape.

Pamplona

POP 195,800 / ELEV 456M

Senses are heightened in Pamplona (Basque: Iruña), capital of the fiercely independent Kingdom of Navarra, alert constantly to the fearful sound of thundering bulls clattering like tanks down cobbled streets and causing mayhem and bloodshed all the way. Of course, visit outside the eight days in July when the legendary festival of Sanfermines (see the boxed text, p436) takes over the minds and souls of a million people and the closest you'll come to a bloodthirsty bull is in a photograph. For those who do dare venture here outside fiesta time, despite the overriding feeling that you're the only one who missed the in picturesque hilltop Cirauqui's Iglesia de San Román, and in Iglesia de San Pedro de la Rúa in **Estella** (p445). In spring and early summer, enormous roses, geraniums and grapevines blanket the houses in these villages.

Estella contains exceptional monumental Romanesque architecture: the outstanding portal of the Iglesia de San Miguel; the cloister of the Iglesia de San Pedro de la Rúa; and the Palacio de los Reyes de Navarra. High up on the street-corner capital of the *palacio*, look for the vices of arrogance (a donkey playing a harp while a dog listens), lust (snakes sucking on the breasts of a woman) and avarice (naked people with money bags around their necks).

Outside Estella, evergreen oaks and wine groves fill undulating landscapes until a long, barren stretch leads through the sleepy towns of **Los Arcos**, **Sansol** and **Torres del Río**. In hillside Torres you'll find another remarkably intact eight-sided Romanesque chapel, the Iglesia del Santo Sepulcro. To see inside, which is complete with a rare 13th-century Christ figure (crucified with four nails), it's necessary to locate the local key lady. There's a sign on the door indicating her address, the hours of opening and requested donation.

The Camino heads through rolling, expansive stretches of Riojan wine and wheat fields, avoiding looming mountains to the south and north. At first urban and open, the constantly changing trail becomes rugged and wooded, eventually transforming into high, open tableland.

The great Río Ebro marks the entrance (once a major obstacle for pilgrims) to **Logroño** (p446) and explains its wealth and size. The dour Gothic Iglesia de Santiago houses a large Renaissance altarpiece depicting unusual scenes from the saint's life, including run-ins with the wicked necromancer Hermogenes. Michelangelo's crucifixion painting behind the main altar in the Catedral de Santa María de La Redonda is a must-see.

Nájera (p450) literally grew out of the town's red cliff wall when King Ramiro discovered a miraculous statue of the Virgin in one of the cliff's caves in the 11th century. He built the Monasterio de Santa María la Real around it and Nájera became Navarra's splendiferous capital. Look for the fine, flamboyant Gothic tombs of Navarra's early nobility.

Santo Domingo de la Calzada (p450) is one of the road's most captivating places. It is named for its energetic 11th-century founder, Santo Domingo, who cleared forests, built roadways, a bridge, a pilgrim's hospice and a church, and performed many wondrous miracles depicted masterfully in Hispano-Flemish paintings in the cathedral.

Camino in Navarra & La Rioja

BASQUE COUNTRY, NAVARRA & LA RIOJA NAVARRA

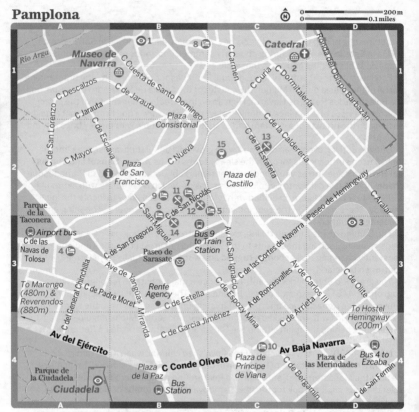

party, you will find Pamplona a fascinating place. And for those of you who come during fiesta week? Welcome to one of the biggest and most famous festivals in the world – if you hadn't drunk so much, it would have been a week you would remember forever!

History

The Romans called the city Pompaelo, after its founder Pompey the Great. They were succeeded by the Visigoths and then, briefly, by the Muslims. Navarra has been a melting pot of dynastic, political and cultural aspirations and tensions ever since Charlemagne rampaged across the Pyrenees from France in 778. The city achieved great things under Sancho III in the 11th century and its position on the Camino de Santiago ensured its prosperity. Twentieth-century affluence saw an expansion of the city.

⊙ Sights

Catedral CATHEDRAL
(Calle Dormitalería; guided tour per adult/child €4.40/2.60; ⊙10am-7pm Mon-Fri, 10am-2pm Sat) Pamplona's main cathedral stands on a rise just inside the city ramparts amid a dark thicket of narrow streets. The cathedral, which was undergoing a radical makeover at the time of research but was still open to the public, is a late-medieval Gothic gem spoiled only by its rather dull neoclassical facade, an 18th-century appendage. The vast interior reveals some fine artefacts, including a silver-plated Virgin and the splendid 15th-century tomb of Carlos III of Navarra and his wife Doña Leonor. The real joy is the Gothic cloister, where there is marvellous delicacy in the stonework. The Museo Diocesano occupies the former refectory and kitchen, and houses an assortment of religious art, including some fine Gothic woodcarvings. See the boxed text, p432), for more.

Pamplona

Museo de Navarra   MUSEUM
(www.cfnavarra.es/cultura/museo; Calle Cuesta
de Santo Domingo 47; adult €2, free Sat afternoon & Sun; ⊙9.30am-2pm & 5-7pm Tue-Sat,
11am-2pm Sun) Housed in a former medieval
hospital, this museum has an eclectic collection of archaeological finds (including a
Roman mosaic), as well as a selection of art
including Goya's *Marqués de San Adrián*.

Ciudadela & Parks   PARK
(Avenida del Ejército) The walls and bulwarks
of the grand fortified citadel, the star-
shaped Ciudadela, lurk amid the verdant
grass and trees in what is now a charming
park, the portal to three more parks that
unfold to the north and lend the city a beautiful green escape.

Museo Oteiza   MUSEUM
(www.museooteiza.org; Calle de la Cuesta 7, Alzuza;
adult €4, free Fri; ⊙11am-7pm Tue-Sat, 11am-3pm
Sun Jun-Sep) Around 9km northeast of Pamplona in the town of Alzuza, this impressive
museum contains almost 3000 pieces by the
renowned Navarran sculptor Jorge Oteiza.
As well as his workshop, this beautifully designed gallery incorporates the artist's former home in a lovely rural setting.

Three buses a day run to Alzuza from
Pamplona's bus station. If you're driving,
Alzuza is signposted north off the NA150,
just east of Huarte.

🛏 Sleeping

During Los Sanfermines, hotels raise their
rates mercilessly – all quadruple their normal rack rates and many increase them five-
fold – and it can be near impossible to get a
room without reserving between six months
and a year in advance. If you can't get a room,
then it's possible to sleep in almost any park
in the city (watch your belongings!) or you
may just find that a patch of rubbish-strewn
pavement suddenly looks like a very inviting
bed! The tourist office also maintains a list
of private houses with rooms to rent during this period and touts hang around the
bus and train stations offering rooms. With
numerous 'San Fermín' buses travelling up
from all nearby Spanish and French cities,
it's actually not a bad idea to stay in a different town altogether and catch a ride on
these party buses. Ask local tourist offices
for details of departure times and costs.

At any other time of year Pamplona is
packed with good-value accommodation
and it's rarely worth booking ahead. The
prices below are for high season but not
during San Fermín.

**TOP
CHOICE** **Palacio Guendulain**
                                HISTORIC HOTEL €€€
(☎948 22 55 22; www.palacioguendulain.com;
Calle Zapatería 53; d from €128; P❄🛜) To call
this stunning new hotel, inside the converted former home of the viceroy of New
Granada, sumptuous is an understatement.
On arrival, you're greeted by a museum-
piece 17th-century carriage decked in gold,
and a collection of classic cars lies scattered
about the courtyard under the watchful eye
of the viceroy's private chapel. The rooms
contain *Princess and the Pea*–soft beds,
enormous showers and regal armchairs.

Hotel Puerta del Camino
                                BOUTIQUE HOTEL €€
(☎948 22 66 88; www.hotelpuertadelcamino.com;
Calle Dos de Mayo 4; s/d €69.55/81.32; P❄@) A
very stylish new hotel inside a converted convent (clearly the nuns appreciated the finer
things in life!) beside the northern gates to
the old city. The functional rooms have clean,
modern lines and it's positioned in one of the
prettier, and quieter, parts of town. Some
rooms have views across the intricate city
walls and beyond to the soaring Pyrenees.

THE RUNNING OF THE BULLS

Liberated, obsessive or plain mad is how you might describe aficionados (and there are many) who regularly take part in Pamplona's Sanfermines (Fiesta de San Fermín), a nonstop cacophony of music, dance, fireworks and processions – and the small matter of running alongside a handful of agitated, horn-tossing *toros* (bulls) – that takes place from 6 to 14 July each year.

El encierro, the running of the bulls from their corrals to the bullring for the afternoon bullfight, takes place in Pamplona every morning during Sanfermines. Six bulls are let loose from the Coralillos de Santo Domingo to charge across the square of the same name (a good vantage point for observers). They continue up the street, veering onto Calle de los Mercaderes from Plaza Consistorial, and then sweep right onto Calle de la Estafeta for the final charge to the ring. Devotees, known as *mozos* (the brave or foolish, depending on your point of view), race madly with the bulls, aiming to keep close – but not too close. The total course is some 825m long and lasts little more than three minutes.

Since records began in 1924, 15 people have died during Pamplona's bull run. Many of those who run are full of bravado (and/or drink) and have little idea of what they're doing. Keeping ahead of the herd is the general rule. The greatest danger is getting trapped near a bull that has been separated from the herd – a lone, frightened 500kg bull surrounded by charging humans can be lethal. Needless to say this is not an activity to be recommended.

Participants enter the course before 7.30am from Plaza de Santo Domingo. At 8am two rockets are fired: the first announces that the bulls have been released from the corrals; the second lets participants know they're all out and running. The first danger point is where Calle de los Mercaderes leads into Calle de la Estafeta. Here many of the bulls skid into the barriers because of their headlong speed on the turn. They can become isolated from the herd and are then always dangerous. A very treacherous stretch comes towards the end, where Calle de la Estafeta slopes down into the final turn to Plaza de Toros.

Hostal Arriazu TRADITIONAL HOTEL €€
(☑948 21 02 02; www.hostalarriazu.com; Calle Comedias 14; s/d €51/60; 🗺) Falling somewhere between a budget *pensión* and a midrange hotel, there is superb value to be found in this former theatre. The rooms are plain but the bathrooms are as good as you'll find. There's a nice plant-packed glassed-in courtyard and a communal lounge area, in which, if running with bulls just isn't for you, a quiet evening can be spent reading the numerous scholarly looking books. Breakfast is €7.21 extra.

Habitaciones Mendi PENSIÓN €
(☑948 22 52 97; Calle de las Navas de Tolosa 9; s/d €30/45) Full of the spirits of Pamplona past, this charming little guesthouse is a real find. Creaky, wobbly, wooden staircases and equally creaky, chintzy rooms make it just like being at your gran's, and the woman running it will cluck over you as if she were your gran.

Hotel Castillo de Javier BOUTIQUE HOTEL €€
(☑948 20 30 40; www.hotelcastillodejavier.com; Calle de San Nicolás 50; s/d €45/63; 🗺🗺) On a street of cheap digs, this slick hotel shows a touch of class. The reception area is modern through and through, and the rooms are typical of a business-class hotel. Ask to see a few first as some are much more spacious than others.

Hostel Hemingway HOSTEL €
(☑948 98 38 84; www.hostelhemingway.com; Calle Amaya 26; dm €19-20, s/d from €22/44; 🗺) Bright, funky colours predominate at this well-run hostel a few minutes' walk from the old town. The dorms have four to six beds and share three bathrooms. There's a TV lounge and a kitchen for guest use. We don't have to tell you what a party it would be staying here during San Fermín. It's just off Avenida de Carlos III.

Hostal Don Lluis PENSIÓN €
(☑948 21 04 99; Calle de San Nicolás 24; s/d €35/40) This *pensión* has a price that's hard to beat and José, the owner, likes to make sure that all his guests are kept happy. Rooms are plain but spacious and some have small bathtubs you can make bubbles in.

A third rocket goes off when all the bulls have made it to the ring, and a final one when they have been rounded up in the stalls.

If you prefer to be a spectator rather than an action man (and we use the word man on purpose here as, technically, women are forbidden from running, although an increasing number are doing it anyway), then you need to have bagged your spot along the route early. By about 6am all the worthwhile vantage spots are gone. Even if you get yourself a space, don't expect an uninterrupted view because a second 'security' fence stands between the spectators and runners and, unfortunately, this blocks much of the view (only police, medical staff and other authorised people can enter the space between the two fences). Another option is to rent a space on one of the house balconies overlooking the course. Normally you'll only get onto one of these if you happen to be friends with the house owner, but some people are willing to accept paying guests onto their balconies (around €50). In order to find a balcony space, walk the route beforehand calling up to people on the balconies. Finally, you can watch the runners and bulls race out of the entrance tunnel and into the bullring by buying a ticket for a seat in the ring. These go on sale a few hours in advance and start at around €7.50. Whichever way you choose to watch the run, it'll all be over in a few blurred seconds.

Sanfermines winds up at midnight on 14 July with a candlelit procession, known as the Pobre de Mí (Poor Me), which starts from Plaza Consistorial.

Concern has grown about the high numbers of people taking part in recent *encierros*. The 2004 fiesta was considered to be one of the most dangerous in recent years, with dozens of injuries, but no deaths. For the 2005 fiesta, the authorities used a special antislip paint on the streets to cut down on bull skid, but there seemed to be just as many falls and there were several injuries, including four gorings. The 2008 event was also quite a bloody one, with 45 serious injuries (four of them due to gorings). For dedicated *encierro* news, check out www.sanfermin.com.

Pensión Arrieta
PENSIÓN €

(☎948 22 84 59; www.pensionarrieta.net; Calle de Arrieta 27; s/d €40/50) A homely and friendly *pensión*, with communal bathrooms and small rooms that smell of polished wooden floors. During Sanfermines, this is one of the cheapest places to stay as it only raises its prices to three times the normal rate.

Ezcaba
CAMPING €

(☎948 33 03 15; www.campingezcaba.com; sites per person/tent/car €5.20/5.60/5.20; P🛜💤🐾) On the banks of Río Ulzama, about 7km to the north on the N121, this is Pamplona's nearest camping ground. Bus 4 runs four times daily (more during Sanfermines) from Plaza de las Merindades by the BBVA bank. Prices double during Sanfermines.

✗ Eating

In the old town, both Calle de San Nicolás and Calle de la Estafeta are rammed with down-to-earth eating and drinking options. The following are just some of the best.

Baserri
BASQUE €

(☎948 22 20 21; Calle de San Nicolás 32; menú del día €14) This place has won enough *pintxo* awards that we could fill this entire book listing them. In fact, it's staggering to know that so many food awards actually exist! As you'd expect from such a certificate-studded bar, the *pintxos* are superb; sadly, the full meals play something of a second fiddle in comparison. Even so, locals still flock in for the €14 lunch menu.

Casa Otaño
BASQUE €

(☎948 22 50 95; Calle de San Nicolás 5; mains €15-18) A little pricier than many on this street but worth the extra. Its formal atmosphere is eased by the dazzling array of pink and red flowers spilling off the balcony. Great dishes range from the locally caught trout to heavenly duck dishes. The €17.80 *menú del día* is good value.

Sarasate
VEGETARIAN €

(☎948 22 57 27; Calle de San Nicolás 21; mains €8-15; ✗) This bright, uncluttered vegetarian restaurant on the 1st floor offers excellent veggie dishes and gluten-free options.

It's run by the same people as the Baserri, so the quality is undoubted. It's well worth getting stuck into one of its €10.50 *menús del día*.

Mesón Pirineo BASQUE €
(☎948 22 20 45; Calle de la Estafeta 41; mains €12-16) There's nothing fancy and modern about this place: it's just old Navarran style and superb *pintxos* all the way.

🍷 Drinking & Entertainment

Pamplona's resident student population ensures a lively after-dark scene year-round. There's a strong Basque vibe in the bars around Calle Carmen and Calle de la Calderería and up towards the cathedral. The area opposite the bullring on Paseo de Hemingway is also home to a few more bars and clubs. Larger nightclubs are found a walk or short taxi ride south and west of the old city centre, in the direction of the university. Doors at these places are usually open after 11pm Thursday to Saturday and the cover charge tends to be around €8 to €12, depending on the night. The most noteable are Reverendos (Calle de Monasterio de Velate 5) and Marengo (Avenida de Bayona 2).

Café Iruña HISTORIC CAFE
(Plaza del Castillo 44) Opened on the eve of Sanfermines in 1888, Café Iruña's dominant position, powerful sense of history and frilly belle-époque decor make this by far the most famous and popular watering hole in the city. As well as caffeine and alcohol, it also has a good range of *pintxos* and light meals.

ℹ Information

Emergency (☎112)

Hospital de Navarra (☎848 42 21 00; Calle de Irunlarrea 3)

Kuria.Net (Calle Curia 15; internet access per hr €2.50; ⊙10am-10pm Mon-Fri, 10am-2pm & 3-10pm Sat)

Main post office (☎948 20 68 40; cnr Paseo de Sarasate & Calle de Vínculo)

Policía Nacional (☎091; Calle del General Chinchilla 3)

Tourist office (☎848 42 04 20; www.turismo.navarra.es; Calle de Esclava 1; ⊙9am-8pm Mon-Sat, 9am-2pm Sun) This extremely well-organised office has plenty of information about the city and Navarra.

ℹ Getting There & Away

Air

Pamplona's **airport** (☎948 16 87 00), about 7km south of the city, has regular flights to Madrid and Barcelona. There's an ATM as well as car-rental desks. Bus 21 (€1.10) travels between the city (from the bus station and Calle de las Navas de Tolosa) and the airport. A taxi costs about €15.

Bus

From the **main bus station** (Calle Conde Oliveto 8), buses leave for most towns throughout Navarra, although service is restricted on Sunday.

Regular bus services travel to the following:

DESTINATION	FARE (€)	DURATION (HR)
Bilbao	13.40	2
Logroño	7.98	1¾
San Sebastián	6.88	1
Vitoria	7.79	1¾

Regional destinations include the followings:

DESTINA-TION	FARE (€)	DURATION (HR)	FRE-QUENCY
Estella	3.89	1	10 daily
Olite	3.13	¾	16 daily

Train

Pamplona's train station is linked to the city centre by bus 9 from Paseo de Sarasate every 15 minutes. Tickets are also sold at the **Renfe agency** (Calle de Estella 8; ⊙9am-1.30pm & 4.30-7.30pm Mon-Fri, 9am-1pm Sat).

Trains run to/from the following:

DESTINA-TION	FARE (€)	DURATION (HR)	FRE-QUENCY
Madrid	56	3	4 daily
San Sebastián	from 20.40	2	2 daily
Tudela	from 18.60	1	5 daily
Vitoria	4.85	1	4 daily

North of Pamplona

SIERRA DE ARALAR

One of Navarra's many natural parks, the scenic Sierra de Aralar offers pleasant walking. There's not much to Lekunberri, the area's main town, except a gaggle of solid Basque farmhouses in the old quarter and an ever-growing estate of soulless modern housing beyond. The tourist office (☑948 50 72 04; oit.lekunberri@cfnavarra.es; Calle de Plazaola 21, Lekunberri) here is very helpful and can advise on the numerous fantastic walks the area offers.

Most buses between Pamplona and San Sebastián stop in Lekunberri, but you'll need your own vehicle to explore the sierra.

◉ Sights

Santuario de San Miguel de Aralar CHURCH
(☉10am-2pm & 4-8pm Jun-Sep) For most people, the main reason for visiting Lekunberri is to travel the bendy back road NA1510, which leads southwest through a tasty tapestry of mixed deciduous and evergreen forests to culminate (after 21km) at the austere and very bleak 9th-century Santuario de San Miguel de Aralar, which lies in the shadow of Monte Altxueta (1343m). Despite its attractive naves and 800-year-old altarpiece, it isn't the sort of place you'd want to visit on a moonless night. There are some spectacular views down onto the plains to the south.

🛏 Sleeping & Eating

Lekunberri has a number of hotels and restaurants.

Hotel Ayestarán HISTORIC HOTEL €€
(☑948 50 41 27; www.hotelayestaran.com; Calle de Aralar 27, Lekunberri; d €91; 🅿🛜❄) Sleep with the memory of Hemingway at this beautiful hotel where the writer stayed en route to the Pamplona party. A signed photograph of him standing outside the hotel hangs on the wall. The attached restaurant is equally superb.

SIERRA DE ANDIA

Looking south from the Santuario de San Miguel de Aralar, it's impossible to miss the tempting massif rising up off the plains. This is the Sierra de Andia, and it, too, offers wonderful walking opportunities. To get there, take the very narrow, vertigo-inducing dirt road leading south from the *sanctuario* (do not attempt to drive this route in icy, foggy or very wet conditions) and then join the NA120, which runs, eventually, on to Estella via a laborious clamber up onto the sierra. The sheer mountainsides keep vultures and eagles hanging like mobiles on the thermals, and the limestone heights are a chaos of karst caves that once provided a home to witches. Once up on the plateau, things calm down considerably and you'll find a number of wild walks clearly signposted from the first car park you pass.

ℹ NAVARRA'S CASAS RURALES

Navarra has an excellent selection of *casas rurales* (village houses or farmsteads with rooms to let), which are often well-kept, beautiful houses in mountain villages. You can recognise *casas rurales* by one of two small plaques: one has 'CR' in white on a dark-green background; the more modern one, in brown, olive-green and white, displays the letter 'C' and the outline of a house.

A copy of the *Guía de Alojamientos* is available free from most tourist offices in Navarra. It lists all the private homes and farmsteads that rent out rooms. Reservations are recommended at peak periods.

East of Pamplona

JAVIER

POP 80 / ELEV 448M

Tiny Javier (Xavier), 11km northeast of Sangüesa, is a quiet rural village set in gentle green countryside. It's utterly dominated by a childhood-fantasy castle that is so perfectly preserved you half expect the drawbridge to come crashing down and a knight in armour to gallop out on a white steed. As well as being an inspiration for fairy-tale dreams, this is also the birthplace of the patron saint of Navarra, San Francisco Xavier, who was born in the village in 1506. Xavier spent much of his life travelling, preaching, teaching and healing in Asia. Today his body lies in a miraculous state of preservation in a cathedral in Goa, India. The **Castillo de Javier** (admission €2.50; ☉10am-1.30pm & 3.30-6.30pm Apr-Sep) houses a small museum dedicated to the life of the saint.

If you want to stay, the red-brick, ivy-clad **Hotel Xabier** (☑948 88 40 06; www.hotelxabier.com; d €70; 🅿🛜) has small rooms, from which you can peer out of your window on a moonlit night and look for ghosts flitting around the castle keep.

MONASTERIO DE LEYRE

Totally swamped with visitors on public holidays, the **Monasterio de Leyre** (adult €2.30; ☉10.15am-2pm & 3.30-7pm Mon-Fri, 10.15am-2pm & 4-7pm Sat & Sun Mar-Nov) is in an attractive setting in the shadow of the Sierra de Leyre, about 4km from Yesa on

There are numerous walking trails of mixed lengths and difficulties in the Pyrenees. It's even possible to follow high-altitude trails across the entire breadth of the range in around 45 days. If you are intending to do some proper walking, then keep in mind that the weather up here changes alarmingly fast. Even in August, a beautiful morning can quickly slide into an afternoon of violent storms. For even fairly moderate exploration, a two-season sleeping bag and all-weather gear are essential – even in summer.

Finding a suitable place to begin hiking can be a little confusing and, without a dedicated guidebook, a decent map and a compass, the most rewarding walks will elude you. Fortunately we can help you out here, too, with Lonely Planet's *Hiking in Spain* guide, which includes a number of walks in the Navarran Pyrenees and elsewhere in the Basque regions. Otherwise, almost every newsagent, bookshop and tourist office in the region has a full stock of locally produced hiking guides, but they are all in Spanish or French only and to understand the routes they describe you must speak one of these languages to a high level. Some of the shorter and more popular walks are more clearly signposted and accessible without knowledge of Spanish or French; otherwise tourist offices can sometimes supply basic maps of short walks.

We have not attempted to describe any walking routes here and have focused instead on mountain areas and villages accessible to visitors with their own car.

Further information (in Spanish) on these wonderful mountains can be obtained from the Federación Navarra de Deportes de Montaña y Escalada (in Pamplona 948 22 46 83, in San Sebastián 943 47 42 79; www.fedme.es, in Spanish).

---

the N240. The early Romanesque crypt has a three-nave structure with a low roof and the 12th-century main portal of the church is a fine example of Romanesque artistry.

Look down from the monastery, towards the main road, and you won't fail to notice the Embalse de Yesa, an enormous expanse of water that is perfect for swimming.

The Pyrenees

Awash in greens and often concealed in mists, the rolling hills, ribboned cliffs, clammy forests and snow-plastered mountains that make up the Navarran Pyrenees are a playground for outdoor enthusiasts and pilgrims on the Camino de Santiago. Despite being firmly Basque in history, culture and outlook, there is something of a different feeling to the tiny towns and villages that hug these slopes. Perhaps it's their proximity to France, but in general they seem somehow more prim and proper than many of the lowland towns. This only adds to the charm of exploring what are, without doubt, some of the most delightful and least exploited mountains in Europe.

Trekkers and skiers should be thoroughly equipped at any time of the year and note emergency numbers in case of difficulties: 112 in Navarra and 17 in Aquitaine (France).

VALLE DEL BAZTÁN

This is rural Basque Country at its most typical, a landscape of splotchy reds and greens. Minor roads take you in and out of charming little villages, such as Arraioz, known for the fortified Casa Jaureguizar; and Ziga, with its 16th-century church.

Just beyond Irurita on the N121B is the valley's biggest town, Elizondo, given a distinctly urban air by its tall half-timbered buildings. It's a good base for exploring the area. There's accommodation at the Antxitónea Hostal (948 58 18 07; www.antxitonea.com; Calle Braulío Iríarte 16; d from €72;), which has plain rooms with flower-coated balconies. The attached restaurant is worth frequenting.

Beyond Elizondo, the NA2600 road meanders dreamily about picturesque farms, villages and hills before climbing sharply to the French border pass of Puerto de Izpegui, where the world becomes a spectacular collision of crags, peaks and valleys. At the pass, you can stop for a short hike up to the top of Mt Izpegui. You'll find a good number of *casas rurales* throughout the area.

The N121B continues northwards to the Puerto de Otxondo and the border crossing into France at Dantxarinea. Just before the border, a minor road veers west to the almost overly pretty village of Zugarramurdi, home to the decidedly less pretty **Cuevas de Las Brujas** (adult/child €3.50/2; ☺10.30am-8pm). These caves were once, according to the Inquisition, the scene of evil debauchery. Having established this, the perverse masters of the Inquisition promptly tortured and burned scores of alleged witches. Playing on the flying-broomstick theme is the **Museo de las Brujas** (adult/child €4/2; ☺11am-7.30pm Tue-Sun), a fascinating dip into the mysterious cauldron of witchcraft in the Pyrenees.

Zugarramurdi has plenty of *casas rurales* but no public transport.

TO FRANCE VIA RONCESVALLES
As you bear northeast out of Pamplona on the N135 and ascend into the Pyrenees, the yellows, browns and olive greens of lower Navarra begin to give way to more-luxuriant vegetation before the mountains thunder up to great Pyrenean heights. It would be fair to say that this route, which follows the Camino de Santiago, is more culturally attractive than physically attractive.

BURGUETE
The main road runs tightly between neat, whitewashed houses with bare cornerstones at Burguete (Basque: Auritz), lending a more sober French air to things. Despite lacking the history, it actually makes a better night's halt than nearby Roncesvalles.

There are a sprinkling of *casas rurales* in the surrounding area. In the village itself you'll find **Don Jauregui de Burguete** (☎948 79 03 99; www.donjaureguideburguete. com; Calle de San Nicolás 32; d from €45), which has bright, youthful rooms and an excellent attached restaurant with a hearty €15.50 *menú del día*. Less rustic, but also less interesting than the Don Jauregui de Burguete, is **Hotel Loizu** (☎948 76 00 08; www.hotelloizu.com; Calle de San Nicolás 13; d €89; Apr-Dec; ☜), which is a proper hotel whose upper rooms have attractive beams and exposed stone walls. Campers will be happy at **Camping Urrobi** (☎948 76 02 00; www.campingurrobi.com; sites per person/tent/car €4.90/4.90/4.90, dm €9.25; ☺Apr-Nov; ☜), a few kilometres south of town. It also has a 42-bed hostel.

RONCESVALLES
History hangs heavily in the air of Roncesvalles (Basque: Orreaga). Legend has it that it was here that the armies of Charlemagne were defeated and Roland, commander of Charlemagne's rearguard, was killed by Basque tribes in 778. This is an event celebrated in the epic 11th-century poem *Chanson de Roland* (Song Of Roland) and a battle still talked about by today's Basques. In addition to violence and bloodshed, though, Roncesvalles has long been a key point on the road to Santiago de Compostela and today Camino pilgrims continue to give thanks at the famous monastery for a successful crossing of the Pyrenees, one of the hardest parts of the Camino de Santiago.

There's a **tourist office** (☎948 76 03 01; ☺10am-2pm & 4-7pm Mon-Sat, 10am-2pm Sun) at the entrance to the monastery complex. The main event here is the **monastery complex** (admission adult/child €4.10/1.70; ☺10am-2pm & 3.30-7pm), which contains a number of different buildings of interest. The 13th-century Gothic **Real Colegiata de Santa María** houses a much-revered, silver-covered statue of the Virgin beneath a modernist-looking canopy worthy of Frank Gehry. Also of interest is the cloister, which contains the tomb of King Sancho VII (El Fuerte) of Navarra, the apparently 2.25m-tall victor in the Battle of Las Navas de Tolosa, fought against the Muslims in 1212. See the boxed text, p432,for more. Nearby is the 12th-century **Capilla de Sancti Spiritus**.

If you just can't walk another step, you'll find a couple of places in town to stay, including the **Hostal Casa Sabina** (☎948 76 00 12; s/tw €36/50), where the rooms have twin beds only – possibly to stop any hanky-panky so close to a monastery? The bar and restaurant get more lively than the bedrooms. Another option, with simple rooms and gentle country charm, is **La Posada** (☎948 76 02 25; www.laposadaderon cesvalles.com; s/d €40/50).

A bus departs Roncesvalles at 9.20am every morning except Sundays for Pamplona (€6, 1¾ hours) via Burguete, and returns in the late afternoon.

PUERTO DE IBAÑETA & VALCARLOS
From Roncesvalles the road climbs to the Puerto de Ibañeta, from where you have magnificent views across the border and a number of memorable hiking routes. The last town before the frontier is Valcarlos (Basque: Luzaide). Built on the side of the slippery slope leading to France, this is a sleepy but pretty spot. Of the numerous *casas rurales* in town, the tree-framed **Casa Etxezuria** (☎948 79 00 11; www.etxezuria.com,

in Spanish; r €45), with mountain-flavoured rooms, is the most reliable – many of the others never seem to have anyone around to help you.

THE ROADS TO OCHAGAVÍA
Happy wanderers on wheels can drift around a network of quiet country roads, with pretty villages along the way, in the area east of the main Roncesvalles road. A couple of kilometres south of Burguete, the NA140 branches off east to Garralda. Push on to Arive, a charming hamlet, from where you could continue east to the Valle del Salazar, or go south along Río Irati past the fine Romanesque church near Nagore. Another option is to take a loop northeast through the beautiful Bosque de Irati forest, with its thousands of beech trees that turn the slopes a flaming orange every autumn and invite exploration on foot. Eventually this route will link you up with the Valle del Salazar at Ochagavía. If you stick to the NA140 between Arive and Ochagavía, Abaurregaina and Jaurrieta are particularly picturesque. Most villages along the route have *casas rurales*.

OCHAGAVÍA
This charming Pyrenean town lying astride narrow Río Zatoya sets itself quite apart from the villages further south. Grey stone, slate and cobblestones dominate the old centre, which straddles a bubbling stream crossed by a pleasant medieval bridge. The town's sober dignity is reinforced by the looming presence of the Iglesia de San Juan Evangelista.

This is a popular base for walkers and even skiers, so there are plenty of *casas rurales*. For a list of options and hiking opportunities in the region, visit the Centro de Interpretación de la Naturaleza (☑948 89 06 80; ☺10am-2pm & 4.30-8.30pm Mon-Sat, 10am-2pm Sun). Camping Osate (☑948 89 01 84; www.campingosate.net; sites per person/tent/car €4.30/4.20/4.30) also has two-person cabins from €43 and a hostel. The Hostal Auñamendi (☑948 89 01 89; www.hostalauniamendi.com; d €79) on the main square is the only official hotel in town.

To reach France, take the NA140 northeast from Ochagavía into the Sierra de Abodi and cross at the Puerto de Larrau (1585m), a majestically bleak pass. Four kilometres short of the border, there's a seasonal restaurant and bar for skiers.

VALLE DEL SALAZAR
If you've made your way to Ochagavía, a good choice for heading south is the Valle del Salazar, where many hamlets contain gems of medieval handiwork with quiet cobbled streets and little plazas. Esparza, with its mansions, medieval bridge and restored Iglesia de San Andrés, is particularly rewarding, while Ezcároz, Sarriés, Güesa and nearby Igal (off the main road) are also worth an amble. A daily bus runs the length of the Valle del Salazar between Pamplona and Ochagavía.

VALLE DEL RONCAL
Navarra's most spectacular mountain area is around Roncal and this easternmost valley is an alternative route for leaving or entering the Navarran Pyrenees. For details of *casas rurales* in the valley, visit the Roncal-Salazar (www.roncal-salazar.com) website.

BURGUI
The gateway to this part of the Pyrenees is Burgui – an enchanting huddle of stone houses built beside a clear, gushing stream (the Río Esca) bursting with frogs and fish and crossed via a humpbacked Roman bridge. You can swim from a small beach on the banks of the stream. The village is renowned for its almonds and on Almond Day (3 May) it even throws a little fiesta for them. Hostal El Almadiero (☑948 47 70 86; www.almadiero.com; Plaza Mayor; d incl half-board €124), in the heart of the village, has overpriced but otherwise bright and colourful rooms with 19th-century bathrooms (though with mod cons like hot water!).

RONCAL
The largest centre along this road, though still firmly a village, Roncal is a place of cobblestone alleyways that twist and turn between dark stone houses and meander down to a river full of trout. Roncal is renowned for its Queso de Roncal, a sheep's-milk cheese that's sold in the village.

Across the river on the southern exit from Roncal is Hostal Zaltua (☑948 47 50 08; www.zaltua.com; Calle de Castillo 23; d €45), which has cute rooms, some with river views. Outside of the high season, it's closed on Sundays.

The tourist office (☑948 47 52 56; www.vallederoncal.es), is on the main road towards the Isaba exit from town.

ISABA
Lording it over the other villages in the valley, lofty Isaba, lying above the conflu-

ence of Ríos Belagua and Uztárroz, is another popular base for walkers and skiers. The closest reliable cross-country skiing is about 12km away in Belagua.

There are plenty of sleeping places, but many are block-booked during the skiing season. A character-infused option is the Hostal Onki Xin (✆948 89 33 20; www.onkixin.com; d €55), housed inside a converted traditional house with fancily painted rooms and lots of wrinkly old wood and open stone walls. Camping Asolaze (✆948 89 30 34; www.campingasolaze.com; sites per person/tent/car €4.50/4/4.25, dm €9.75) is at Km6 on the road to France. It also has hostel-style accommodation.

South of Pamplona

Take the A15 south of Pamplona and you only have to drive for 15 minutes before you will enter an entirely new world. Within the space of just a few kilometres, the deep greens that you will have grown to love in the Basque regions and northern Navarra vanish and are replaced with a lighter and more Mediterranean ochre. As the sunlight becomes more dazzling (and more commonly seen!), the shark's-teeth hills of the north flatten into tranquil lowland plains, while the wet forests become scorched vineyards and olive groves, and even the people change – they're more gregarious and, as the graffiti ascertains, often fiercely anti-Basque. For the traveller it feels as though you are finally arriving in the Spain of the clichés.

OLITE
POP 3440 / ELEV 365M

Bursting off the pages of a fairy tale, the turrets and spires of Olite are filled with stories of kings and queens, brave knights and beautiful princesses. Though it might seem a little hard to believe today, this insignificant, honey-coloured village was once the home of the royal families of Navarra and the walled old quarter is crowded with their memories.

Founded by the Romans (parts of the town wall date back to Roman times), Olite first attracted the attention of royalty in 1276 but didn't really take off until it caught the fancy of King Carlos III (Carlos the Noble) in the 15th century who embarked on a series of daring building projects.

◎ Sights

Palacio Real   CASTLE
(Castillo de Olite; www.palaciorealdeolite.com; adult/child €3.50/2; ◎10am-8pm daily) It's Carlos that we must thank for the exceptional Palacio Real, which towers over the village. Back in Carlos' day, the inhabitants of the castle included not just princes and jesters but also lions, giraffes and other exotic pets, as well as Babylon-inspired hanging gardens. Today, though the princesses and lionesses are sadly missing, some of the hanging gardens remain. Integrated into the castle is the **Iglesia de Santa María la Real**, which has a superbly detailed Gothic portal. There are guided tours of the church; check with the tourist office for times.

Museo de la Viña y el Vino de Navarra
                                                   MUSEUM
(✆948 74 12 73; Plaza de los Teobaldos 10; adult/child €3.50/2; ◎10am-2pm & 4-7pm Mon-Sat, 10am-2pm Sun) Don't miss this museum, which is a fascinating journey through wine and wine culture. Everything is well labelled and laid out and some fascinating facts are revealed. For instance, did you know that Noah (the one of the Ark fame) was apparently the first human ever to get drunk? There's a €1 discount with a Palacio Real ticket.

Galerías Subterráneas   MUSEUM
(Plaza Carlos III; adult/child €1.50/1; ◎11am-1pm Tue-Fri, 11am-2pm & 5-7pm Sat, Sun & public holidays) At the other end of the medieval-luxury scale to the castle is this series of underground galleries, whose origin and use remain something of a mystery. Today they contain a small museum explaining the town's medieval life (in Spanish), which basically illustrates that, if you had blue blood or were rich, then life was one jolly round of wine, food and things that your mother wouldn't approve of and, if you weren't, well, life sucked.

🛏 Sleeping & Eating

Hotel el Juglar   BOUTIQUE HOTEL €€€
(✆948 74 18 55; Rúa Romana 39; s/d €100/120; P✳🕸🅿) A few minutes' walk into the new suburbs, this is the best deal in town. The handful of rooms are all slightly different from one another – some have big round whirlpool baths, some old-fashioned stone baths, and others elaborate walk-in showers. All have four-poster beds and lots of fancy decorations.

LAGUNA DE PITILLAS

The lakes and marshes that make up the Laguna de Pitillas are one of the top birding sites in Navarra – a region already renowned for its variety of feathered friends. Now a protected Ramsar wetland site of international importance, the Laguna de Pitillas provides a home for around 160 permanent and migratory species, including marsh harriers, great bitterns and even ospreys. To get there, take the N121 south of Olite and then turn off down the NA5330.

Principe de Viana   HISTORIC HOTEL €€€
(✆948 74 00 00; www.parador.es; Plaza de los Teobaldos 2; s/d incl breakfast from €138/184; ✳@) Situated in a wing of the castle (though some of the cheaper rooms are in a newer extension), this offering from the Parador chain is in a sumptuous, atmospheric class of its own. Though there might be good rooms available elsewhere in town for considerably fewer euros, they don't come with a castle attached.

Hotel Merindad de Olite HISTORIC HOTEL €€
(✆948 74 07 35; www.hotel-merindaddeolite. com; Rúa de la Judería 11; s/d from €78/88; ✳🤶) Built almost into the old town walls, this charming place has small but comfortable rooms and masses of period style. Get in fast because it fills quickly.

Hostal Rural Villa Vieja   BOUTIQUE HOTEL €€
(✆948 74 17 00; www.hostalvillavieja.com; Calle Villaveija 11; s/d €60/75; 🤶) Doing away with all the twee old-world decoration that is so common elsewhere in Olite, the slick rooms in this new hotel stick firmly with the 21st century thanks to the ample use of bright colours and pop art.

Hotel Casa Zanito   TRADITIONAL HOTEL €€
(✆948 74 00 02; www.casazanito.com; Rúa Mayor 10; s/d €57/67) This central hotel isn't very inspiring, but you can't knock the price. It also has a recommended restaurant with mains for around €12 to €23.

Restaurante Gambarte   BASQUE €€
(✆948 74 01 39; Calle Rúa del Seco 15; set menus from €20) Inside the cosy confines of this restaurant, which is widely regarded as the best in town, you can fill your belly with delights such as octopus with garlic and peppers.

ℹ Information
Olite has a friendly and helpful **tourist office** (✆948 74 17 03; Plaza de los Teobaldos 10; ⊙10am-2pm & 4-7pm Mon-Sat, 10am-2pm Sun), in the same building as the wine museum.

ℹ Getting There & Away
Up to nine buses a day run between Olite and Pamplona (€3.13, 40 minutes to one hour).

UJUÉ
Balancing atop a hill criss-crossed with terraced fields, the tiny village of Ujué, some 18km east of Olite and overlooking the plains of southern Navarra, is a perfect example of a fortified medieval village. Today the almost immaculately preserved village is sleepy and pretty, with steep, narrow streets tumbling down the hillside, but what gives it something special is the hybrid Iglesia de Santa María, a fortified church of mixed Romanesque-Gothic style. The church contains a rare statue of the Black Virgin, which is said to have been discovered by a shepherd who was led to the statue by a dove. In addition to the Virgin, the church also contains the heart of Carlos II.

The village plays host to a fascinating *romería* (pilgrimage) on the first Sunday after St Mark's Day (25 April), when hundreds of people walk through the night from Tudela to celebrate Mass in the village church.

Unfortunately, there is no formal accommodation in the village, but it makes a great lunch stop. Mesón las Migas (✆948 73 90 44; Calle Jesús Echauri; mains €12-18, menú del día €26), which serves traditional south Navarran food, is the best place to eat. Try the hunks of meat cooked over an open wood fire and don't miss the house special, *migas de pastor* (fried breadcrumbs with herbs and chorizo). On Sundays it often only serves the set menu.

MONASTERIO DE LA OLIVA
The 12th-century Monasterio de la Oliva (✆948 72 50 06; guided tours €2; ⊙9am-12.30pm & 3.30-6pm Mon-Sat, 9-11.45am & 4-6.15pm Sun), 2km from Carcastillo, was founded by Cistercian monks and is still functioning as a community. Its austere church gives onto a peaceful Gothic cloister. The monks are dressed in exotic white hooded robes.

PARQUE NATURAL DE LAS BÁRDENAS REALES

In a region largely dominated by wet mountain slopes, the last thing you'd expect to find is a sunburnt desert, but, in the Parque Natural de las Bárdenas Reales, a desert is exactly what you'll find. Established as a natural park in 1999 and as a UN Biosphere Reserve in 2000, the Bárdenas Reales is a desiccated landscape of blank tabletop hills, open gravel plains and snakelike gorges covering over 410 sq km of southeastern Navarra. As well as spectacular scenery, the park plays host to numerous birds and animals, including the great bustard, golden eagles, Egyptian and griffon vultures, numerous reptiles, mountain cats and wild boar. This may look like an almost pristine wilderness, but it is, in fact, totally artificial. Where now there is desert there was once forest, but man, being quite dumb, chopped it all down, let his livestock eat all the lower growth and suddenly found himself living in a desert. There are a couple of dirt motor tracks and numerous hiking and cycling trails, all of which are only vaguely signposted. The tourist offices in Olite and Tudela are the best places to pick up reliable information and maps.

TUDELA
POP 34,717 / ELEV 243M

The outskirts of Tudela are depressing indeed and almost enough to make you turn around. But persevere: thanks to Islam, things do improve! Tudela was in Muslim hands for some 400 years and the Islamic genius for serpentine street creation makes the old quarter a pleasure to wander through.

◉ Sights

Old Town   OLD TOWN

Slinking around the old quarter is a delight, with numerous little back lanes leading to interesting buildings or bars. Some goals worth seeking out include the brightly decorated, 17th-century Plaza de los Fueros, which has coloured panels high on its walls, depicting coats of arms and bullfighting scenes from the days when the square was used as a bullring. Today plenty of cheerful cafes encircle the plaza. In former incarnations, the 16th-century Iglesia de Santa María was both a mosque and a synagogue.

A short distance away is the cathedral, a sombre 12th-century Gothic pile. The western Puerta del Juicio is particularly striking, with its many sculpted figures looking decidedly uneasy about their participation in the Last Judgment and positively agonised on the right-hand side, where little devils are boiling them in oil. Take time to wander the streets, as there are some fine old mansions, many with Aragonese-style *aleros* (awnings) jutting out from the roof.

Museo Muñoz Sola   ART GALLERY
(www.museomunozsola.com; Plaza Vieja 2; admission €1; ⊙10am-1.30pm & 4-7pm Mon-Fri, 10am-1.30pm Sat & Sun) In the core of the old town, this museum displays the work of both local boy Cesar Muñoz Sola and a number of international artists.

⊨ Sleeping

Hostal Remigio   HOTEL €
(☑948 82 08 50; www.hostalremigio.com; Calle de Gaztambide 4; s/d €32/52) Just off Plaza de los Fueros, this very standard hotel has plenty of sturdy, good-value rooms.

❶ Information

There's an excellent **tourist office** (☑948 84 80 58; oit.tudela@navarra.es; Calle de Juicio 4; ⊙9.30am-2pm & 4-8pm Mon-Fri, 10am-2pm & 4-8pm Sat, 10am-2pm Sun) opposite the cathedral.

❶ Getting There & Away

Around six or seven trains run daily to/from Pamplona (from €18.60, one hour). Buses to Pamplona (€7.11, 1¼ hours, eight daily) operate from next to the train station, southeast of the town centre.

West of Pamplona

PUENTE LA REINA
POP 2670 / ELEV 421M

The spectacular six-arched medieval bridge at Puente la Reina (Basque: Gares), 22km southwest of Pamplona on the A12, throngs with the ghosts of a multitude of pilgrims. Over the centuries, they approached from Roncesvalles to the north and Aragón to the east and then united to take the one main route west to Santiago de Compostela. Their first stop here was at the late-Romanesque Iglesia del Crucifijo, erected by the Knights Templars and still containing one of the finest Gothic crucifixes in existence.

ESTELLA
POP 14,000 / ELEV 483M

Estella (Basque: Lizarra) was known as 'La Bella' in medieval times because of the splendour of its monuments and buildings, and though the old dear has lost some of its beauty to modern suburbs, it's not without charms. During the 11th century, Estella became a main reception point for the growing flood of pilgrims along the Camino de Santiago (see the boxed text, p432). Today most visitors are continuing that same plodding tradition.

The **tourist office** (☎948 55 63 01; Calle de San Nicolás 1; ⏰10am-2pm & 4-7pm Mon-Sat, 10am-2pm Sun) is on the western bank of the river below the 12th-century **Iglesia de San Pedro de la Rúa**, the most important monument in Estella. Adjacent to the tourist office is the **Palacio de los Reyes** (www.museogustavodemaeztu.com; Calle de San Nicolás 2; admission free; ⏰11am-1pm & 5-7pm Tue-Sat, 11am-1.30pm Sun), a rare example of Romanesque civil construction. It houses an intriguing collection of paintings by Gustavo de Maeztu y Whitney (1887–1947), who was of Cuban-English parentage but emphatically Basque in upbringing and identity. Landscapes, portraits and full-bodied nudes reflect Maeztu's engaging sensual romanticism. Across the river and overlooking the town is the **Iglesia de San Miguel**, with a fine Romanesque north door.

Every year from 31 July to 8 August, Estella hosts a **feria** (fair) with its own **encierro** (running of the bulls).

The **Hotel Yerri** (☎948 54 60 34; www.hotelyerri.es; Avenida de Yerri 35; s €40-45, d €62-67; P 📶) is a large place a few minutes' walk from the old centre with comfortable, though not terribly interesting, rooms.

On the main square, **Astarriaga Asador** (☎948 55 08 02; Plaza de Los Fueros 12; mains €10-15) is a very popular restaurant with Galicia-bound pilgrims on account of its energy-enhancing steak selections – some are almost the size of a cow.

About 10 buses leave from the **bus station** (Plaza Coronación) for Pamplona (€5, one hour) Monday to Friday, and six on Saturday and Sunday.

AROUND ESTELLA

The countryside around Estella is littered with monasteries. One of the best is the **Monasterio de Irache** (admission free; ⏰9am-1.30pm Tue, 9am-1.30pm & 5-7pm Wed-Fri, 9am-1.30pm & 4-7pm Sat & Sun, closed 15 Dec-31 Jan), 3km southwest of Estella, near Ayegui. This ancient Benedictine monastery has a lovely 16th-century plateresque cloister and its **Puerta Especiosa** is decorated with delicate sculptures.

About 10km north of Estella, near Abárzuza, is the **Monasterio de Iranzu** (www.monasterio-iranzu.com; adult/child €2.50/1.50; ⏰10am-2pm & 4-8pm). Originally founded way back in the 11th century, but recently restored, this sandy-coloured monastery with beautiful cloisters is so calm and tranquil that it could inspire religious meditation in Lucifer himself.

LA RIOJA

Get out the *copas* (glasses) for La Rioja and some of the best red wines produced in the country. Wine goes well with the region's ochre earth and vast blue skies, which seem far more Mediterranean than the Basque greens further north. In fact, it's hard not to feel as if you're in a different country altogether. The bulk of the vineyards line Río Ebro around the town of Haro, but extend into neighbouring Navarra and the Basque province of Álava. This diverse region offers more than just the pleasures of the grape, though, and a few days here can see you mixing it up in lively towns and quiet pilgrim churches, and even hunting for the remains of giant reptiles.

Logroño

POP 147,100

Logroño doesn't feel the need to be loud and brash. Instead it's a stately town with a heart of tree-studded squares, narrow streets and hidden corners. There are few monuments, but there are some fine restaurants and plenty of tapas/*pintxos* bars, while the citizens are unfailingly friendly. It's the sort of place that you cannot help but feel contented in – and it's not just the wine.

Sights

A stroll around the old town and down to the river is a pleasant diversion.

Catedral de Santa María de la Redonda CATHEDRAL

(Calle de Portales; ⏰8am-1pm & 6-8.45pm Mon-Sat, 9am-2pm & 6.30-8.45pm Sun) The Catedral de Santa María de la Redonda started life as a Gothic church before maturing into a full-blown cathedral. Inside you'll find it a little dark and overpowering. Outside it seems lighter and friendlier, thanks, no doubt, to the huge square it sits proudly in.

Iglesia de San Bartolomé
CHURCH

(Calle de Rodríguez Paterna) The impressive main entrance to the 13th-century Iglesia de San Bartolomé has a splendid portico of deeply receding borders and an expressive collection of statuary.

✦ Festivals & Events

Fiesta de San Mateo
GRAPE HARVEST

Logroño's week-long Fiesta de San Mateo starts on 21 September and doubles as a harvest festival, during which all of La Rioja comes to town to watch the grape-crushing ceremonies in the Espolón and to drink ample quantities of wine.

Actual
CULTURE

Actual, a program of cultural, musical and artistic events, is a much more sober festival that takes place through the first week of January.

Feast of San Bernabé
FEAST DAY

The Feast of San Bernabé is held on 11 June and commemorates the French siege of Logroño in 1521.

🛏 Sleeping

Logroño doesn't receive all that many tourists and this shows in the relative lack of hotels. However, what there is tends to be good value. Aside from those listed below, Logroño is also home to a number of comfortable but sterile business-class hotels, most of which are scattered around the fringes of the new town.

Hotel Marqués de Vallejo
DESIGN HOTEL €€

(✆941 24 83 33; www.hotelmarquesdevallejo. com; Calle del Marqués de Vallejo 8; s/d €71/86; P❄🛜) From the driftwood art in the communal spaces to the lollipops and raunchy red pouffes in the rooms, a huge amount of thought and effort has gone into the design of this stylish, modern and very well-priced hotel.

Hostal La Numantina
PENSIÓN €

(✆941 25 14 11; http://hostalnumantina.com, in Spanish; Calle de Sagasta 4; s/d €35/58) This professional operation caters perfectly to the traveller's needs. The rooms are comfortable and homely, with crazy patterned wardrobes and pool-sized baths. The best aspects, though, are the communal TV room and the ample tourist info.

Hostal Niza
PENSIÓN €€

(✆941 20 60 44; www.hostalniza.com, in Spanish; Calle de Capitán Gallarza 13; s/d from €40/60) Simple and smart rooms, each of which varies in style and character from the fairly plain and boring to the almost modern and exciting; all have tea- and coffee-making facilities. Right in the heart of the action.

Pensión La Bilbaina
PENSIÓN €

(✆941 25 42 26; Calle de Capitán Gallarza 10; s €25-30, d €36-40) A cute little place, with clean and pleasing rooms and an old-fashioned vibe. The grand entrance is an impressive mess of tile work.

Hotel Portales
BUSINESS HOTEL €€

(✆941 50 27 94; www.hotelportales.es; Calle Portales 85; d €74; P❄🛜) Sitting pretty on the edge of the old town, this is a modern business-class hotel for a price that in some other towns would only get you the skankiest of *pensiones*.

🍴 Eating

Logroño is a *pintxo* lover's delight, where *pintxos* cost around €2 to €4 each. The tourist office dishes out a leaflet detailing a *pintxo* crawl around the old town. Most of the action takes place on Calle Laurel and Calle de San Juan, where, among the dozens of possibilities, you will find these standouts:

Bar Soriano
TAPAS €

(Travesía de Laurel 2) The smell of frying food will suck you into this bar, which has been serving up the same delicious mushroom tapa, topped with a shrimp, for more than 30 years.

La Taberna de Baco
TAPAS €

(Calle de San Agustín 10) This place has a cracking list of around 40 different *pintxos*, including *bombitas* (potatoes stuffed with mushrooms) and *rabas de pollo* (fried chicken slices marinated in spices and lemon juice). You'll also find some delicious casseroles and salads.

Lorenzo
TAPAS €

(Calle del Laurel 4-6) This old-fashioned place serves the delicious *tío agus* (roasted pork in a secret sauce).

Bar Charly
PINTXO BAR

(Travesía de Laurel 2) Renowned for its *pimientos rellenos* (spicy red peppers stuffed full of meat), it's open in the evenings only.

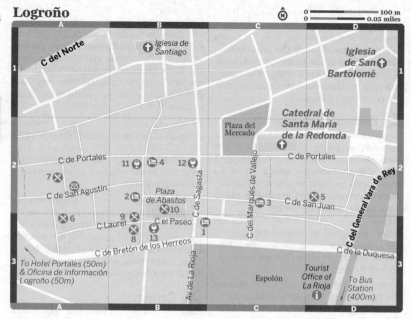

map: Logroño

La Taberna del Laurel PINTXO BAR
(Calle Laurel 7) The speciality at La Taberna del Laurel is *patatas bravas* (potatoes in a spicy tomato sauce). They're not just good: they're damn near divine.

Bar A Tu Gusto PINTXO BAR
(Calle de San Juan 21) Serves delicious shellfish and calamari in an Andalucian-flavoured bar.

Mercado de Abastos MARKET
(Plaza de Abastos) For self-catering there's the Mercado de Abastos, with a fish-and-meat section and superb fruit-and-veg shops.

Drinking

The bars along Calle Laurel are great places to start your evening as most offer good local wines for bargain prices.

Steel BAR
(Calle de Portales 49) This all-glass bar is something of a fashion emporium, with city style and a young vibe.

Noche y Día CAFE-BAR
(Calle de Portales 63) This popular coffee and drinks place lives up to its name, at least until 1am (fairly late for La Rioja). The clientele is older and tamer than at the others.

Vinos El Peso WINE SHOP
(Calle el Peso 1; ⊗9am-9pm Mon-Fri, 9am-4pm Sat, 9am-2pm Sun) There are countless wine outlets in town, but one excellent shop is Vinos El Peso.

ℹ Information

There are two tourist offices in Logroño: a regional office and a relatively new office run by the town council.

Main post office (Plaza de San Agustín 1) In the old town.

Oficina de Información Logroño (☑941 27 33 53; www.logroturismo.org; Calle de Portales 50; ⊗9.30am-2.30pm & 5-8pm Mon-Fri, 10am-2pm & 5-8pm Sat, 10am-2pm Sun) The town office.

Tourist Office of La Rioja (☑902 277200; www.lariojaturismo.com; Paseo del Espolón; ⊗10am-2pm & 4-7pm Mon-Fri, 10am-2pm & 5-8pm Sat, 10am-2pm & 5-7pm Sun) The regional office.

ℹ Getting There & Away

If you arrive at the train or bus station, first head up Avenida de España and then Calle del General Vara de Rey until you reach the Espolón, a large, park-like square lavished with plane trees. The Casco Viejo starts just to the north.

Logroño

⊙ Top Sights
Catedral de Santa María de la Redonda	C2
Iglesia de San Bartolomé	D1

⊜ Sleeping
1	Hostal La Numantina	B3
2	Hostal Niza	B2
3	Hotel Marqués de Vallejo	C2
4	Pensión La Bilbaina	B2

⊗ Eating
5	Bar A Tu Gusto	D2
	Bar Charly	(see 6)
6	Bar Soriano	A3
7	La Taberna de Baco	A2
8	La Taberna del Laurel	B3
9	Lorenzo	B3
10	Mercado de Abastos	B2

⊙ Drinking
11	Noche y Día	B2
12	Steel	B2
13	Vinos El Peso	B3

Buses, most operated by **Autobuses Jimenez** (www.autobusesjimenez.com, in Spanish), bounce off to the following:

DESTINATION	FARE (€)	DURATION (HR)
Bilbao	12.50	2
Burgos	8.07	2½
Haro	2.81	1
Pamplona	7.98	1¾
Santo Domingo de la Calzada	2.91	1

By train, Logroño is regularly connected to the following:

DESTINATION	FARE (€)	DURATION (HR)
Bilbao	12.80-21.40	2½
Burgos	15.10-34.90	1¾
Madrid	33.90	3½
Zaragoza	12.35-35.10	2½

South of Logroño

For those with their own transport, heading south for Soria leads through some stunning countryside. One route, which takes in shades of the Arab world and reminders of

the prehistoric, heads southeast of Logroño on the N232 past the large town of Calahorra with the twisted, bendy streets of an old quarter straight out of North Africa. From here head southwest, via Arnedo, to perfect Arnedillo.

ARNEDILLO & AROUND
The delightful spa village of Arnedillo, surrounded by slowly eroding hills, terraced in olive groves and watched over by circling hawks and vultures, is an ideal place to spend a peaceful day or two walking and dinosaur hunting. Just beyond Arnedillo is the hamlet of Peroblasco, confidently perched on a defensive posture on the crown of a hill and well worth a wander.

⊙ Sights
Centro Paleontológico de Enciso

DINOSAURS

(www.dinosaurios-larioja.org, in Spanish; adult/child €3/1.50; ⊙11am-2pm & 5-8pm) Never mind dodging crazy truck drivers: if you had been driving around these parts some 120 million years ago, it would have been crazy tyrannosauruses that you would have been dodging. Perhaps a little disappointingly, the dinosaurs are long gone, but, if you know where to look, you can still find clues to their passing. In the small and pretty hill village of Enciso, 10km or so further down the road from Arnedillo, dinosaur fever reaches a peak at the excellent Centro Paleontológico de Enciso, where both children and children at heart will enjoy checking their stats against those of a brontosaurus. Displays are in Spanish only.

After you've done your homework in the museum, head out to see what's left of the real thing in the form of dozens of dinosaur footprints scattered across former mudflats (now rock slopes) in the surrounding countryside. You can pick up a map indicating the location of the best dino prints from the museum or any nearby tourist office. With map in hand, take the southern exit from the village and the turn-off to the left over a small bridge. This is where the dino route starts, but the closest footprints (around 3km from the village) are found by turning left at the junction after the bridge and looking for the tyrannosaurus standing guard on the hill (be careful – he comes alive at night!).

Sleeping & Eating

For accommodation, the tourist office can supply details of nearby *casas rurales*. The following are all to be found in Arendillo.

Hospederia Las Pedrolas
TOP CHOICE

CASA RURAL €€

(☎941 39 44 01; Plaza Felix Merino 16; s/d incl breakfast €70/95; ❄❀) In Arnedillo centre this is an immaculately restored house full of tasteful furnishings and crooked roof beams. Comfortable rooms splashed in glaring whitewash leave you feeling as if you're sleeping inside a Mr Whippy ice cream and it's run with the kind of care and service you'd normally expect of a five-star hotel.

Casa Rural La Fuente
CASA RURAL €

(☎941 39 41 38; casarurallafuentearnedillo@hot mail.es; r €45) A couple of doors down from the Pedrolas at this funky *casa rural,* you get an art-stuffed room, kitchen use and a primitive sitting room.

Bodega la Petra
REGIONAL CUISINE €

(☎941 39 40 23; mains €10-15) You won't have failed to notice the now largely disused cave houses burrowed deeply into the sunburst red gorges throughout this area. Well, in this welcoming, village-centre restaurant, you finally get the chance to take a look inside one of these caves and live out any caveman fantasies you might be harbouring. In addition, you can get a meal that's probably much better than any a caveman got to eat.

ⓘ Information

Tourist office (☎941 39 42 26; www.valcida cos.es; ☺10am-2pm Tue-Thu & Sun, 10am-2pm & 4.30-6.30pm Fri & Sat) In the same building as the Centro Paleonotolgico de Ensico.

West of Logroño

NÁJERA
POP 8100 / ELEV 506M

The main attraction of this otherwise unexciting town is the Gothic Monasterio de Santa María la Real (admission €3; ☺10am-1pm & 4-7pm Mon-Sat, 10am-12.30pm & 4-6pm Sun), in particular its fragile-looking, early-16th-century cloisters. Along the edge of the old town are a series of rusty cliffs full of 6th-century cave houses. Unfortunately they've been closed to the public for many years. Buses between Logroño and Santo Domingo de la Calzada stop in Nájera.

SAN MILLÁN DE COGOLLA
POP 270 / ELEV 733M

About 16km southwest of Nájera are two remarkable monasteries in the hamlet of San Millán de Cogolla, framed by a beautiful valley.

The Monasterio de Yuso (www.monas teriodeyuso.org, in Spanish; adult/child €4/1.50; ☺10am-1.30pm & 4-6.30pm Tue-Sun), sometimes presumptuously called El Escorial de La Rioja, contains numerous treasures in its museum. You can only visit as part of a guided tour (in Spanish only; non-Spanish speakers will be given an information sheet in English and French). Tours last 50 minutes and run every half-hour or so. In August it's also open on Mondays.

A short distance away is the Monasterio de Suso (admission €3; ☺9.30am-1.30pm & 3.30-6.30pm Tue-Sun). Built above the caves where San Millán once lived, it was consecrated in the 10th century. It's believed that in the 13th century a monk named Gonzalo de Berceo wrote the first Castilian words here, although recent discoveries suggest otherwise (see the boxed text, p414). Again, it can only be visited on a guided tour. Tickets, which must be bought in advance and include a short bus ride up to the monastery, can be reserved by calling ☎941 37 30 82 or can be picked up at the very helpful tourist office at the Monasterio de Yuso. Maps detailing short walks in the region can also be obtained at the tourist office.

SANTO DOMINGO DE LA CALZADA
POP 6260 / ELEV 630M

Santo Domingo is small-town Spain at its very best. A large number of the inhabitants continue to live in the partially walled old quarter, a labyrinth of medieval streets where the past is alive and the sense of community is strong. It's the kind of place where you can be certain that the baker knows all his customers by name and that everyone will turn up for María's christening. Santiago-bound pilgrims have long been a part of the fabric of this town and that tradition continues to this day, with most visitors being foot-weary pilgrims. All this helps to make Santo Domingo one of the most enjoyable places in La Rioja.

The morose, monumental cathedral and its attached museum (admission €3.50, free Sun; ☺10am-7.30pm Mon-Sat, 10am-noon & 2-7.30pm Sun) glitter with gold that attests to the great wealth the Camino (see the boxed text, p432) has bestowed on otherwise backwater towns. The cathedral's most eccentric feature is the Disneyesque white rooster and hen that forage in a glass-fronted cage opposite the entrance to the crypt. These two celebrate a long-standing legend, the *Miracle of the Rooster*, which tells of a young man who was unfairly executed only to recover miraculously, while the broiled cock and hen on the plate of his judge suddenly leapt up and chickened off, fully fledged.

The Hostal R Pedro (☏941 34 11 60; www.hostalpedroprimero.es; Calle San Roque 9; s/d €50/61; 🛜) is a carefully renovated town house with superb-value, terracotta-coloured rooms, wooden roof beams and entirely modern bathrooms. If your idea of a religious-run hotel includes lumpy beds, 5am prayers and severe sisters, then forget it, because the Hospedería Sta Teresita (☏941 34 07 00; www.cister-lacalzada.com, in Spanish; Calle Pinar 2; s/d €37/56; 🛜) is much more about elevators, swipe cards and business-standard rooms. The Parador Santo Domingo Bernado de Fresneda (☏941 34 11 50; www.parador.es; Plaza de San Francisco 1; r from €138; P🛜) is the antithesis of the town's general air of piety. Occupying a former monastery, this palatial hotel offers anything but a frugal, monk-like existence.

There are a few lacklustre cafes and bars in the modern centre of town by the bus stop, but Restaurante Río (☏941 34 02 77; Calle Alberto Etchegoyen 2; mains €10) is a suitably small-town-Spain eating experience, with old men drinking wine before 10am and fussing family owners.

Buses run to Logroño (€2.91, one hour via Nájera, up to 13 daily on weekdays, fewer on weekends).

Wine Region

La Rioja wine rolls on and off the tongue with ease, by name as well as by taste. All wine fanciers know the famous wines of La Rioja, where the vine has been cultivated since Roman times. The region is classic vine country and vineyards cover the hinterland of Río Ebro. On the river's north bank, the region is part of the Basque Country and is known as La Rioja Alavesa.

HARO
POP 11,500 / ELEV 426M

Despite its fame in the wine world, there's not much of a heady bouquet to Haro, the capital of La Rioja's wine-producing region.

But the town has a cheerful pace and the compact old quarter, leading off Plaza de la Paz, has some intriguing alleyways with bars and wine shops aplenty. Keep an eye peeled for the huge stork's nest perched on the roof of the tourist office – if you have arrived here from the north, then this is about the first place where you'll start to see these wonderful birds.

👁 Sights

The Museo del Vino (☏941 31 05 47; Avenida Breton de los Herreros 4; adult/child €3/free, free Wed; ☺10am-2.30pm & 3.30-7pm Tue-Fri, 10am-7pm Sat, 10am-1.30pm Sun), near the bus station, houses a detailed display on how wine is made and has helpful information in Spanish, French and English.

The winery Bodegas Muga (☏941 30 60 60; www.bodegasmuga.com), just after the railway bridge on the way out of town, gives daily guided tours and tastings in Spanish and, although technically you should book in advance in high season, you can often just turn up and tack onto the back of a tour. For an English-language tour, it's essential to book several days ahead.

🎊 Festivals & Events

Batalla del Vino   WINE FESTIVAL
On 29 June the otherwise mild-mannered citizens of Haro go temporarily berserk during the Batalla del Vino (Wine Battle), squirting and chucking wine all over each other in the name of San Juan, San Felices and San Pedro. Plenty of it goes down the right way, too.

🛏 Sleeping & Eating

There are plenty of cafes and bars around Plaza de la Paz and the surrounding streets.

Casa de Legarda   CASA RURAL €€
(☏605 600646; www.casadelegarda.com; Calle Real 11; d €59-70; P🛜) In the small village of Briñas, 4km northeast of Haro, this gorgeous *casa rural* is housed inside a honey-coloured building dating back to 1634. Whilst the common areas are smothered in equally old-fashioned style, the room decoration is all bright theatrical paint jobs that are very much up to date. Try and get the 'Ventilla' room – it's like something from a surreal doll's house. There's a minimum stay of three nights in August.

Los Agustinos   HISTORIC HOTEL €€€
(☏941 31 13 08; www.hotellosagustinos.com; Calle San Agustín 2; s/d from €99/124; P✳🛜) History hangs in the air of this luxurious hotel.

IN SEARCH OF THE FINEST DROP

La Rioja is as much about serious wine drinking as it is holidaying. Well, there's a downside to everything!

Such research should be conducted only after proper training, so we recommend you begin at one or all of the region's wine museums. In Navarra, there is the exceptional **Museo de la Viña y el Vino de Navarra** (p443) in Olite, and Quaderna Via (www.quadernavia.com; admission free; ⊙8am-2pm & 4-7pm Mon-Fri, 10am-2pm Sat & Sun), around 4km west of Estella, near Igúzquiza. In La Rioja proper is Haro's excellent **Museo del Vino** (p451) and, finally, the big daddy of them all, **Dinastía Vivanco** (p452).

After all that history, you'll be needing a drink. What will it be? Wine categories in La Rioja are termed Young, Crianza, Reserva and Gran Reserva. Young wines are in their first or second year and are inevitably a touch 'fresh'. Crianzas must have matured into their third year and have spent at least one year in the cask, followed by a few months resting in the bottle. Reservas pay homage to the best vintages and must mature for at least three full years in cask and bottle, with at least one year in the cask. Gran Reservas depend on the very best vintages and are matured for at least two years in the cask followed by three years in the bottle. These are the 'velvet' wines.

Experts have developed a classification system for the years in which the wine was particularly good. Five stars (the maximum) were awarded in 1982, 1994, 1995, 2001 and 2004. Four-star years include 1981, 1987, 1991, 1996 and 1998.

The tourist offices in Haro, Laguardia and Logroño have lists of bodegas that can be visited throughout the region, although it usually requires ringing in advance to arrange a time.

The rooms are lovely although they've possibly gone a little overboard on the flowery bedspreads, but it's the stunning covered courtyard of this former monastery that steals the show. What really lets it down, though, are the staff who are as snooty as you would expect of a posh address in a wine town!

Restaurante Beethoven I & II

REGIONAL RESTAURANT €

(☑941 31 11 81; Calle de Santo Tomás 5 & 10; menus from €16) The best places to fill hungry tummies in Haro are these two restaurants facing each other across the narrow street. Number II is more formal, but both offer excellent La Riojan cuisine, all of it complemented by the very best local wines.

Hostal La Peña PENSIÓN €

(☑941 31 00 22; Calle La Vega 1; s/d €30/40) Just off Plaza de la Paz is this family-run, slightly old-fashioned place tiled in bold blue and white. Singles have shared bathrooms only.

ⓘ Information

Tourist office (☑941 30 33 66; Plaza de Florentino Rodríguez; ⊙10am-2pm & 4.30-7.30pm Mon-Sat, 10am-2pm Sun) A couple of hundred metres along the road from Plaza de la Paz, it has plenty of excellent information, including a list of wineries open to the public.

ⓘ Getting There & Away

Regular trains connect Haro with Logroño (€8.30 to €12, 40 minutes). Buses additionally serve Vitoria, Bilbao, Santo Domingo de la Calzada and Laguardia.

BRIONES

POP 900 / ELEV 501M

One man's dream is putting the small, obscenely quaint village of Briones firmly on the Spanish wine and tourism map. The sunset-gold village crawls gently up a hillside and offers commanding views over the surrounding vine-carpeted plains, where you will find the fantastic Dinastía Vivanco (Museo de la Cultura del Vino; www.dinastiavivanco.com; adult/child €7.50/free; ⊙10am-6pm Tue-Thu & Sun, 10am-8pm Fri & Sat). This space-age museum is the creation of Pedro Vivanco Paracuello. As he relates in the introductory film, he wanted to leave a legacy to the land that has provided for his family for generations. This museum is that legacy and it truly is an incredible one. There can be few more advanced private museums in the country. Over several floors and numerous rooms, you will learn all about the history and culture of wine and the various processes that go into its production. All of this is done through interesting displays brought to life with the latest in computer technology. The treasures on display include Picasso-designed wine jugs; Roman and Byzantine mosaics; gold-draped, wine-inspired religious artefacts; and the world's largest collection of corkscrews, including several in the shape of amusingly large penises (yes, we're easily entertained). At the end of the tour, you can enjoy some wine tasting and, by booking in advance, you can join a tour of the winery (€6.50 or €12 including museum entry; in Spanish only).

The village itself is also worth exploring, with the 16th-century Iglesia de Santa María de la Asunción, which contains a magnificent organ, an equally impressive altar, and a side chapel painted from head to toe with the great and good of the local Christian world. At the far end of the village are the very battered remains of an 11th-century castle, which now hide a small garden.

Currently the only place to rest wine-heavy heads is Los Calaos de Briones (☎941 32 21 31; www.loscalaosdebriones.com; Calle San Juan 13; r €58), which has pleasant rooms in shades of peach and sky blue. Some have suitably romantic four-posters. The attached restaurant is stuffed with excellent locally inspired cuisine (mains €12 to €15).

The village is several kilometres southeast of Haro and a couple of buses a day trundle out here.

THE NEW GUGGENHEIM(S)

'If Bilbao has one, we want one too', scream the villages of rural La Rioja. Impressed by the effect El Goog had on Bilbao's international standing and apparently unconcerned by the size and wealth difference between the big industrial city and their small farming communities, two villages have got themselves a Guggenheim lookalike.

When the owner of the Bodegas Marqués de Riscal, in the village of Elciego, decided he wanted to create something special, he certainly didn't hold back. The result is the spectacular Frank Gehry–designed Hotel Marqués de Riscal (☎945 18 08 80; www.starwoodhotels.com/luxury; r from €750; P❈☎). Costing around €85 million to construct and now managed by the Starwood chain, the building is a flamboyant wave of multicoloured titanium sheets that stands in utter contrast to the creaky old village behind it. Like the Guggenheim, this building is having a radical effect on the surrounding countryside and has led to more tourists, more jobs, more wine sales and more money appearing in the hands of locals. Casual visitors are not, however, welcome at the hotel. If you want a closer look, you have three options. The easiest is to join one of the bodega's wine tours (☎945 18 08 88; www.marquesderiscal.com; tour €10) – it's necessary to book in advance. You won't get inside the building, but you will get to see its exterior from some distance. A much closer look can be obtained by reserving a table at the Michelin-approved restaurant (☎945 18 08 80; menú from €80) or the bistro (☎945 18 08 80; menú from €50). (Be sure to dress smartly if eating at the restaurant.) But for the most intimate look at the building, you'll need to reserve a room for the night, but be prepared to part with some serious cash!

But what one Riojan bodega can do, another can do better and just a couple of kilometres to the north of Laguardia is the Bodegas Ysios (www.ysios.com; Camino de la Hoya, Laguarida). Designed by Santiago Calatrava as a 'temple dedicated to wine', it's wave-like roof made of aluminium and cedar wood matches the flow of the rocky mountains behind it. However, it looks its best at night when pools of light flow out of it. Daily tours (☎945 60 06 40; per person €5) of the bodega are by appointment only.

There are several other, somewhat less architecturally challenging, wine cellars around Laguarida that can be visited, often with advance notice only – contact the tourist office in Laguardia for details. Bodegas Palacio (☎945 60 01 51; www.bode gaspalacio.com; Carretera de Elciego; tour €5), only 1km from Laguardia on the Elciego road, is one of the most receptive to visitors. Its tours run several times daily Monday to Saturday in Spanish, English and German. Reservations on the above number are not essential but are a good idea (especially out of season). The same bodega also runs excellent **wine courses**. The beginners' wine-tasting course (€30) runs monthly throughout the year. Advance reservations are essential. It also does an advanced course (€40; minimum eight people), but these only run when requested in advance.

LAGUARDIA
POP 1490 / ELEV 557M

It's easy to spin back the wheels of time in the medieval fortress town of Laguardia, or the 'Guard of Navarra' as it was once appropriately known, sitting proudly on its rocky hilltop. The walled old quarter, which makes up most of the town, is virtually traffic-free and is a sheer joy to wander around. As well as memories of long-lost yesterdays, the town further entices visitors with its wine-producing present.

◉ Sights
Maybe the most impressive feature of the town is the castle-like Puerta de San Juan, one of the most stunning city gates in Spain. Equally impressive is the Iglesia de Santa María de los Reyes (guided tours €2), which has a breathtaking late-14th-century Gothic doorway thronged with beautiful sculptures of the disciples and other motifs. The statue of Santa María de los Reyes has the looks of a heartbreaker. Just alongside the entrance to the church is a little plaza with a metal sculpture, a delightful collection of casually displayed bags and boots, by the Vitoria artist Koko Rico.

For details of visits to some of the many bodegas in the area, see the boxed text, p453.

🛏 Sleeping & Eating
Laguardia has only a few places to stay, so, if you are determined to stay here, it may be wise to book ahead, especially at weekends and during holidays.

TOP CHOICE Casa Rural Legado de Ugarte
CASA RURAL €€
(☑945 60 01 14; www.legadougarte.com; Calle Mayor 17; r incl breakfast €75; 🐾) This is one that you're going to either love or hate – we love it. Inside a tenderly renovated house in the heart of the old town, the entrance and reception have more of the same old-world flavour you'll be starting to get bored of, but the bright and very comfortable rooms are an arresting mix of purple, silver and gold pomp. If that sounds a little too much, it also has a more classic blue-and-white room. The gregarious host is charming.

Posada Mayor de Migueloa
HISTORIC HOTEL €€
(☑945 62 11 75; www.mayordemigueloa.com; Mayor de Migueloa 20; s €72-90, d €93-115; P🐾🐾) For the ultimate in gracious La Rioja living, this old mansion-hotel is simply irresistible. Couples will be delighted to know that guests are supplied with a full range of massage oils and instructions on how to use them! The in-house restaurant offers original twists on local cuisine with meals starting at about €20.

Restaurante Hostal Biazteri
TRADITIONAL HOTEL €
(☑945 60 00 26; www.biazteri.com; cnr Calles Mayor & Berberana; d €35-53.50) The calm rooms found here are the cheapest and simplest in town. The attached restaurant is about the most popular place to eat.

ⓘ Information
There are several ATMs around the town.

Tourist office (☑945 60 08 45; www.laguardia-alava.com; Plaza de San Juan; ◷10am-2pm & 4-7pm Mon-Fri, 10am-2pm & 5-7pm Sat, 10.45am-2pm Sun) Has a list of bodegas that can be visited in the local area.

ⓘ Getting There & Away
Six slow daily buses connecting Vitoria and Logroño pass through Laguardia.

Cantabria & Asturias

Best Places to Eat

» Restaurante Cares
(p496)
» La Puerta Nueva (p474)
» El Molín de la Pedrera
(p494)
» Mesón Rampalay (p461)
» Real Balneario de Salinas
(p484)

Best Places to Stay

» Hotel Marina de Campíos
(p469)
» Posada San Pelayo
(p498)
» Hotel del Oso (p498)
» La Casa del Organista
(p466)
» Casa Cayo (p498)

Why Go?

You can traverse either of these two small regions from north to south in little more than an hour. But don't. Most of the coastline is a sequence of sheer cliffs, beautiful beaches and small fishing ports. Behind it, gorgeously green valleys dotted with stone-built villages rise to the 2000m-plus mountain wall of the Cordillera Cantábrica, which reaches majestic heights in the Picos de Europa. The damp climate makes sure you eat and drink well here too: as well as the fruits of the sea, local cheeses, quality meat, and cider from Asturias' apple orchards are on offer. And travellers with a feel for history will be in their element: early humans painted some of the world's most wonderful prehistoric art at Altamira and elsewhere, and it was at Covadonga in Asturias that the seed of the Spanish nation first sprouted 1300 years ago.

When to Go

Oviedo

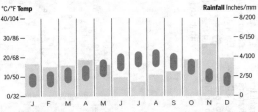

June & September Temperatures up, rainfall down, crowds away – best time for almost everything.

Early August Descenso Internacional del Sella – canoe mania from Arriondas to Ribadesella.

Late August Join thousands of tipplers at Gijón's Fiesta de la Sidra Natural (Natural Cider Festival).

Cantabria & Asturias Highlights

① Marvel at the prehistoric artistic genius of **Altamira** (p467), Puente Viesgo's **Cueva de El Castillo** (p463) and Ribadesella's **Cueva de Tito Bustillo** (p482)

② Walk the **Garganta del Cares** (p496) in the Picos de Europa

③ Let medieval **Santillana del Mar** (p466) bewitch you with its charms

④ Ride the scary **Teleférico de Fuente Dé** (p499) to the superb heights of the Picos de Europa

⑤ Explore the mountain passes and superb scenery

of the **Cordillera Cantábrica** (p487, p488 and boxed texts, p464, p470)

⑥ Delight in the grace of the pre-Romanesque buildings of **Oviedo** (p471)

⑦ Sidle up for cider poured in Asturias' convivial **sidrerías** (cider houses; p476)

⑧ Bathe at secluded **Playa del Silencio** (p484)

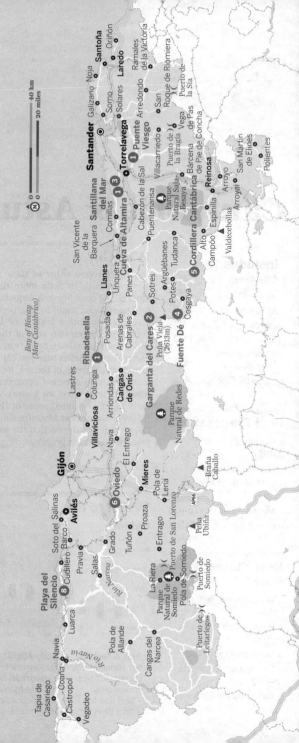

CANTABRIA

It's no wonder both Romans and Visigoths had a hard time subduing the Cantabrian clans. The lushness of the vegetation belies the difficulty of much of Cantabria's terrain. Sliced up by deep, multi-branched mountain valleys connected only by steep passes, until recently the region remained virtually untouched by the modern legions of visitors that flock to Spain each year.

It offers a little of everything for the traveller. Some pretty beaches make summer seaside days quite possible (unreliable weather permitting), while the inland valleys, sprinkled with quiet towns and villages, are a feast of beauty for the eyes, whether you choose to drive the country roads or walk the trails. The rugged ranges culminate in the west in the abrupt mountain walls of the Picos de Europa.

The capital, Santander, offers a slice of urban life with its bustling bodegas and handful of sights. The towns of Santillana del Mar and Comillas entice with their medieval and Modernista trappings. The prehistoric art of the Cueva de Altamira, Cueva de El Castillo and Cueva de Covalanas is some of the very best in the world.

The Romans finally carried the day against the proud Cantabrians and pacified the area by around 19 BC. The Visigoths only managed to secure the area shortly before they were themselves eclipsed by the Moors in AD 711, after which Cantabria quickly became part of the nascent Christian Kingdom of Asturias. In more recent centuries, Cantabria was long regarded simply as a coastal extension of Castilla and its gateway to what was confidently known as the Mar de Castilla (Castilian Sea). Cantabria became a separate region under Spain's 1978 constitution. Its people are known as *montañeses* as they were perceived by Castilians to hail from the mountains of the Cordillera Cantábrica.

Santander

POP 143,100

The belle-époque elegance of El Sardinero apart, modern Santander is not the most beautiful of cities. A huge fire raged through the city centre back in 1941, leaving little that's old or quaint. But Cantabria's capital makes the most of its setting along the northern side of the handsome Bahía de Santander, and it's a lively place to

---

ⓘ CANTABRIA WEBSITES

» **www.turismodecantabria.com** Encyclopedic official tourism site.

» **www.culturadecantabria.com** (in Spanish) Good source of wide-ranging information.

» **www.clubcalidadcantabriainfinita.es** Around 100 top-quality, characterful places to stay and eat.

» **www.turismoruralcantabria.com** Lists some of Cantabria's more than 400 often beautifully restored country-home lodgings.

---

spend a day or two, with bustling shopping streets, a heaving bar and restaurant scene, some good city beaches and a few museums and historic sights to leaven the mix.

The parklands of the Península de la Magdalena mark the eastern end of the bay. North of the peninsula, Playa del Sardinero, the main beach, faces the open sea.

History

When the Romans landed here in 21 BC, they named the place Portus Victoriae (Victory Harbour) and, indeed, within two years they had vanquished the Cantabrian tribes that had given them such strife. Santander prospered as a trading and fishing port from the 12th century, and emerged as Cantabria's main city in the 18th century. Its heyday came in the early 20th century when King Alfonso XIII (r 1902–30) made a habit of spending summer here and turned Santander, especially the Sardinero area, into a fashionable seaside resort.

⊙ Sights & Activities

Península de la Magdalena   PARK

(☉8am-10pm; ⊞) These parklands are perfect for a stroll and are popular with picnickers. Kids will enjoy the sea lions and the little train that choo-choos around the headland. The peninsula is crowned by the Palacio de la Magdalena, the former royal palace. It's an exuberant and eclectic pile, built between 1908 and 1912 as a gift from the city to the royal family, which used it every summer until 1930.

Beaches   SAND, SURF

Playa de los Peligros, Playa de la Magdalena and Playa de Bikinis, the beaches on the Bahía de Santander 1.5km to 2.5km east

Santander

CANTABRIA & ASTURIAS CANTABRIA

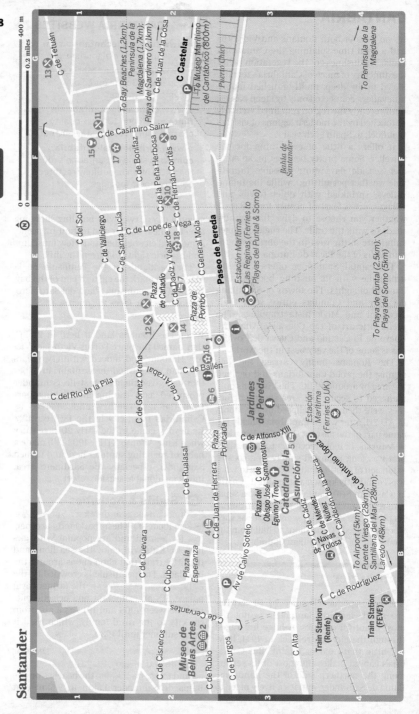

0 400 m
0 0.2 miles

To Bay Beaches (1.2km);
Peninsula de la
Magdalena (1.7km);
Playa del Sardinero (2.1km)

To Peninsula de la
Magdalena

C Castelar

To Museo Marítimo
del Cantábrico (800m)

Puerto Chico

13 C de Tetuán

11 C de Casimiro Sainz

15 17 C de Bonifaz

8 C de la Peña Herbosa

C de Hernán Cortés

10

C del Sol

C de Valliciergo

C de Santa Lucía

C de Lope de Vega

18 C de Daoiz y Velarde

C General Mola

Paseo de Pereda

Bahía de
Santander

Estación Marítima
Las Reginas (Ferries to
Playas del Puntal & Somo)

To Playa de Puntal (2.5km);
Playa del Somo (5km)

9 Plaza
de Cañadío

12

14

7

Plaza de
Pombo

C de Río de la Pila

C de Gómez Oreña

C del Arrabal

C de Bailén

16 1

6

Jardines
de Pereda

Plaza
Porticada

Plaza la
Esperanza

C de Guevara

C Cubo

C de Rualasal

C de Juan de Herrera

C de Alfonso XIII

Estación
Marítima
(Ferries to UK)

C de Antonio López

Catedral de la
Asunción

5

Plaza del
Obispo José
Eguino y Trecu

C de
Somorrostro

C de Cádiz

C de Méndez
Núñez

C Navas
de Tolosa

C Calderón de la Barca

To Airport (5km);
Puente Viesgo (28km);
Santillana del Mar (28km);
Laredo (48km)

Av de Calvo Sotelo

4

Museo de
Bellas Artes

2

C de Cisneros

C de Rubio

C de Burgos

C de Cervantes

C Alta

C de Rodríguez

Train Station
(Renfe)

Train Station
(FEVE)

Santander

of the centre, are more protected than the glorious 1.25km sweep of Playa del Sardinero. Surfers emerge in force along Sardinero when the waves are right, mainly in autumn and winter, when they can reach 1.5m. Sardinero is backed by some of Santander's most expensive real estate, including emblematic early-20th-century piles such as the Gran Casino. Buses 1, 2 and 3 (€1.10) run to Sardinero from outside the post office.

Playa del Puntal, a finger of sand jutting out from the eastern side of the bay roughly opposite Playa de la Magdalena, is idyllic on calm days (but beware the currents). Weather permitting, boats sail there every 30 minutes from 10.30am to 8pm, June to late September, from the Estación Marítima Los Reginas (€3.60 return).

From the same station there is a year-round passenger ferry (€4.30 return, every 30 or 60 minutes from 8.30am to 8.30pm) to Playa de Somo, just beyond Playa del Puntal. Somo has another sandy beach with, usually, bigger surf than Sardinero. This makes it a good and popular place to learn to surf from spring to autumn. Santander boasts several surf schools: the Escuela Cántabra de Surf (www.escuelacantabradesurf.com) at Playa de Somo is well recommended and has been doing the job for two decades. A two-/five-day course (two hours a day) costs €60/130, including board and wetsuit. You'll find several surf shops at Somo: board/wetsuit rental costs around €15/10 per half-day.

Catedral de la Asunción   CATHEDRAL

(Plaza del Obispo José Eguino y Trecu) Santander's cathedral is composed of two Gothic churches, one above the other. The 14th-century upper church (◎10am-1pm & 4.30-7pm Mon-Fri, 10am-1pm & 5-9pm Sun), off which is a 15th-century cloister, was extensively rebuilt after the 1941 fire. In the lower, 13th-century, Iglesia del Santísimo Cristo (◎8am-1pm & 4-8pm), glass panels reveal excavated bits of Roman Santander under the floor. Displayed nearby are silver vessels containing the skulls of the early Christian martyrs San Emeterio and San Celedonio, Santander's patron saints. The care of these holy relics, brought (according to legend) from La Rioja to escape the Muslim invasion, prompted the construction of the monastery that originally stood here.

Jardines & Paseo de Pereda
PARK, PROMENADE

Spreading east of the cathedral, these lovely gardens are named after the Cantabrian writer José María de Pereda, whose seminal work, *Escenas Montañesas,* is illustrated in bronze and stone here. You can't miss the 1875 Banco de Santander building, with the grand arch in the middle, across the road here. Its facade is crowned by statues representing the arts, culture, commerce and navigation. The Santander is now Spain's biggest bank and is a significant world player, so the architectural grandiloquence is not entirely misplaced.

The bayfront promenade fronting the Jardines de Pereda continues east to the Puerto Chico (Little Port) marina. Half the city seems to stroll here on summer evenings. The former ferry station, the Palacete del Embarcadero, was raised in 1932 and recalls another era and even another place, with a touch of Brighton about it.

It's now used for temporary exhibitions. Both Paseo de Pereda and Calle Castelar, opposite Puerto Chico, are dotted with appealing cafes and lined with opulent buildings characterised by their glassed-in balconies, the fruit of early-20th-century boom times.

Museo Marítimo del Cantábrico MUSEUM
(www.museosdecantabria.com, in Spanish; Calle San Martín de Bajamar; adult/child €6/4; ⊙10am-7.30pm) If seafaring is your thing, visit the maritime museum near the bay beaches. The four floors cover all facets of Cantabria's relationship with the sea, and include an aquarium. The displays range from marine biology to maritime history, which is perhaps the most interesting, dealing, for example, with Portus Victoriae, the Roman port town from which Santander later grew. The 60-tonne whale skeleton is a star attraction.

Plazas SQUARES
One block north of the Jardines de Pereda is the stately Plaza Porticada, surrounded by 64 porticoes. It was created after the disastrous fire of 1941. A short walk east are the more spacious Plaza de Pombo and lively Plaza de Cañadío, which brims with bars and can get quite boisterous at night.

FREE **Museo de Bellas Artes** MUSEUM
(☎942 20 31 20; Calle de Rubio 6; ⊙10.30am-1pm & 6-9pm Tue-Sat, 11am-1.30pm Sun) Santander's extensive Fine Arts Museum offers an eclectic collection spanning the 16th to 20th centuries. Much of it is secondary Spanish art, though you'll find the odd curio, such as Goya's portrait of King Fernando VII. In an equally portentous building at the same address is the Biblioteca de Menéndez Pelayo (☎942 23 45 34; admission free; ⊙9-11.30am Mon-Fri), a vast old library that belonged to local intellectual giant Marcelino Menéndez Pelayo (1856–1912), a teacher, philosopher and poet who left the city his precious collection of 41,500 volumes. Next door stands his family home, the Casa Museo de Menéndez Pelayo (☎942 23 44 93; admission free; ⊙10.30am-1pm & 6.30-8pm Mon-Fri, 10.30am-1pm Sat).

✴ Festivals & Events

Semana Grande is Santander's big summer fiesta, a week of fun around 25 July. Preceding this, in the middle of the month, is the Baños de Ola, which relives the arrival of the first tourists to bathe in the waves at El Sardinero in the mid-19th century. Right through summer, the Palacio de la Magdalena hosts the Universidad Internacional Menéndez Pelayo (www.uimp.es), a global get-together for specialists in all sorts of disciplines. The Festival Internacional de Santander (www.festivalsantander.com) is a sweeping musical review throughout August, covering everything from jazz to opera.

🛏 Sleeping

The city centre, where most of the action is, has plenty of options in all price ranges. There are also some good midrange and top-end digs over by Playa del Sardinero, though some close from about October to mid-May, when that area has a dreary out-of-season air. Most rates dip sharply outside the July/August high season, but overall, accommodation in Santander is not great value for what you pay.

Hostal La Mexicana HOSTAL €€
(☎942 22 23 50; www.hostallamexicana.com; Calle de Juan de Herrera 3; s/d €46/64; ⊕🛜) A very well-kept and well-run 38-room *hostal* (budget hotel) on a mostly traffic-free shopping street. Rooms have solid, old-fashioned-style wooden furniture and in most cases bathtubs. There's a room to park bicycles in.

Hotel Central HOTEL €€€
(☎942 22 24 00; www.elcentral.com; Calle General Mola 5; s/d €96/148; ✳@🛜) A remodelled century-old hotel of a startling blue hue, the Central is indeed smack in the heart of the city. Rooms are colourfully and originally decorated (the unfinished paintwork on the doors is apparently part of the concept), but the place is surely due for a spruce-up. Singles are smallish.

Casa del Surf HOSTAL €€
(☎616 382534; www.casadelsurf.es, in Spanish; El Regunil 40, Somo; s/d €36/66; P⊕🛜) The beach village of Somo, across the bay from Santander, has a touch of surf culture, and the Casa del Surf is a nice hang-out for anyone who likes a laid-back vibe. It has eight clean, bright rooms, and a sociable bar and garden area where you can get breakfast and light meals. It's easy to organise surfing classes and other activities here.

Pensión La Corza PENSIÓN €
(☎942 21 29 50; Calle de Hernán Cortés 25; r with/without bathroom €55/42) One of the best deals around, La Corza is on pleasant Plaza de Pombo. It has high-ceilinged, handsome-

ly furnished rooms up on the 3rd floor, some with balconies overlooking the square.

Hotel París
HOTEL €€€

(☎942 27 23 50; www.hotelparissantander.es, in Spanish; Avenida de los Hoteles 6; s/d €94/140; ☺Jul-Sep; P🚭) This Sardinero charmer in off-white boasts rooms dominated by the same colour theme. Otherwise they are quite different from one another, but the overall effect is a lingering sensation of the late 19th century. Parquet floors, spare but elegant furnishings and a few nice architectural touches make this an attractive choice.

Hotel Bahía
HOTEL €€€

(☎942 20 50 00; www.grupo sardinero.com; Calle de Alfonso XIII 6; s/d €181/227; P🚭@🚭) Downtown Santander's top hotel, opposite the UK ferry port, has been completely renovated and offers super-comfortable rooms, many with great views, plus an elegant restaurant and spacious, tastefully outfitted common areas.

Hostal Carlos III
HOSTAL €€

(☎/fax 942 27 16 16; Avenida de la Reina Victoria 135; s/d €58/78; ☺Easter-Oct) Painted mouldings adorn the good-sized rooms in this vintage, somewhat worn, turreted structure in Sardinero. Many rooms have balcony or terrace; some are in an ugly front building but have sea views.

✖ Eating

Central Santander is thronged with great food options. You can push in for a few scrumptious snacks in a tapas bar, dig into hearty local food in a no-nonsense bodega or head upmarket in any number of restaurants. The bayfront promenades brim with cafes and pavement tables.

Mesón Rampalay
TAPAS €€

(Calle de Daoíz y Velarde 9; tapas €1.40-2.10, raciones €5-13) The packed Rampalay is a don't-miss Santander classic. It has a particularly tempting array of tapas, from pheasant breast or sirloin in wine to eggs scrambled with shrimps and asparagus.

La Conveniente
TAPAS, TABLAS €€

(Calle de Gómez Oreña 9; raciones €5-15; ☺dinner Mon-Sat; 🍴) This cavernous bodega has high stone walls, wooden pillars and beams, and more wine bottles than you may ever have seen in one place. Squeeze into the tramlike enclosure at the front or line up for a seat out back (or just snack at the bar). The food

> ## WHAT'S COOKING IN CANTABRIA?
>
> Cantabria's eating habits vary considerably from the coast to the interior. *Sorropotún*, a tuna (*bonito*)-and-potato-based stew that fishermen used to take with them on long Atlantic fishing expeditions, is nowadays a speciality of San Vicente de la Barquera. Santander is perhaps the best place for fresh seafood, while the rivers inland are the source of trout and salmon. The classic country dish is *cocido montañés*, a hearty stew of white beans, cabbage, potato, chorizo, black pudding and sometimes port. Cantabria's green cattle pastures yield an array of tasty cheeses: lovers of smelly cheese should seek *queso picón* (a mix of cow's, sheep's and goat's milk), made in the Picos de Europa villages of Tresviso and Beges. *Embutidos* (sausages) and *cecinas* (dried meats) made from venison and wild boar are other local favourites.

offerings are fairly straightforward – *tablas* (platters) of cheese, *embutidos* (sausages), ham, pâtés – and servings are generous.

El Serbal
CREATIVE SPANISH €€

(☎942 22 25 15; Calle de Andrés del Río 7; meals €40-70; ☺lunch & dinner Tue-Sat, lunch Sun) Probably the best restaurant in town, Serbal is an elegantly understated place beneath a brick apartment block. It offers imaginative twists on essentially typical northern Spanish food – like serving loin of beef with ham-and-truffle ravioli and potatoes cooked in clay. You could let rip with a tasting menu (€56).

Cañadío
CREATIVE SPANISH €€

(☎942 31 41 49; Calle de Gómez Oreña 15; meals €35-55; ☺Mon-Sat) A tastefully modernised place with art on the red walls, high-backed chairs, fine linen and timber floors, Cañadío offers creative cooking with local inspiration. Hake is prepared every which way. Or you can join the crowds in the front bar for ultra-tempting tapas.

días desur
TAPAS €

(Calle de Hernán Cortés 47; tapas €1.50-2; ☺9am-2am) The white brick walls, black-and-white photos and space to sit and converse augur something out of the ordinary, and the tapas meet that challenge with their mix of Cantabrian, Andalucian and international flavours. Try a mini chicken tandoori brochette or a quesadilla with ibérico ham and cream cheese, along with a glass of one of the lyrically described wines.

Bar Del Puerto SEAFOOD €€
(☎942 21 30 01; Calle de Hernán Cortés 63; meals €40-50; ☺lunch Tue-Sun, dinner Tue-Sat) With its grand windows looking out towards the waterfront of the Puerto Chico, this is the perfect spot for damn-near-perfect seafood. Your choice of critter will have a huge influence on the fiscal outlay.

La Flor de Tetuán SEAFOOD €€
(☎942 21 83 53; Calle de Tetuán 25; meals €40-50; ☺Mon-Sat) A simple seafood delight, offering anything from a crayfish-filled salad to a slab of catch-of-the-day lightly grilled. Most shellfish are sold by weight. It's the best of a strip of four small, packed seafood eateries on this street.

Drinking & Entertainment

Plaza de Cañadío is home to several *bares de copas,* where you can enjoy an outdoor beer in the evening as well as cocktails, spirits and wine till the early hours. These and numerous similar establishments along Calles de Daoíz y Velarde and Hernán Cortés generally go on well after midnight.

The neighbourhood of Calle de Santa Lucía, Calle del Sol and Calle del Río de la Pila teems with a more bohemian and teenage bevy of bars, most staying open until 3am or 4am. Wander around and you'll likely run across a couple with music and atmosphere to your liking.

La Floridita PUB, NIGHTCLUB
(Calle de Bailén 4; ☺6.30pm-3.30am; ☏) This Cuban-themed pub-cum-nightspot attracts a broad age group. Among its many features, Floridita boasts a luminous green bar and big cocktails. It opens good and early.

Cool MUSIC BAR
(Calle de San Emeterio 3; ☺from 7pm) Despite beyond-capacity crowds, this small hash-infused bar stays pretty relaxed, with everyone getting their dose of funky music and pungent fumes.

Rocambole MUSIC BAR
(Calle de Hernán Cortés 37; ☺from 9pm) The action often goes on till dawn at this large but dimly lit bar, which often hosts live bands. Make for the jazz jam sessions from 10pm on Thursday.

Montrëal Lounge NIGHTCLUB
(www.montrealsantander.com, in Spanish; Calle de Santa Lucía 48; ☺midnight-6am Thu-Sat) For post-pub clubbing (around 3.30am or 4am), this inner-city house hang-out attracts a boisterous and fairly young crowd.

ℹ Information

Cyberlocutorio (FEVE train station, Calle de Rodríguez; internet per hr €1; ☺10am-10pm Mon-Sat, 12.30-10pm Sun)

Municipal tourist office (☎942 20 30 00; www.santander.es, in Spanish; Jardines de Pereda; ☺9am-9pm) A branch office in El Sardinero, opposite Plaza de Italia, operates in summer.

Post office (Plaza Alfonso XIII)

Regional tourist office (☎901 111112, 942 31 07 08; www.turismodecantabria.com; Calle de Hernán Cortés 4; ☺9am-9pm) Inside the Mercado del Este.

ℹ Getting There & Around

Air

The airport is 5km south of town at Parayas. Buses run to/from Santander bus station (€1.60) about every half-hour, 6.30am to 10.30pm (fewer at weekends). Flights:

Iberia (www.iberia.com) Madrid and Barcelona several daily; Seville, Valencia and Palma de Mallorca a few per week.

Ryanair (www.ryanair.com) London (Stansted), Madrid and Barcelona daily; Alicante, Brussels (Charleroi), Dublin, Düsseldorf (Weeze), Frankfurt (Hahn), Málaga, Milan (Bergamo), Pisa and Rome (Ciampino) up to four weekly.

Boat

Brittany Ferries (www.brittany-ferries.co.uk) Three weekly car ferries from Portsmouth, UK (24 hours) and one from Plymouth, UK (20 to 24 hours), mid-March to mid-November. Fares can vary enormously: a two-week return trip for two adults and a car, from either UK port, booked in July, might cost UK£972 for August travel or UK£478 for October/November, with interior cabins.

Bus

Transporte de Cantabria (www.transportede cantabria.es) is a useful source for schedules.
ALSA (www.alsa.es) is the major company operating from the **bus station** (☎942 21 19 95; Calle Navas de Tolosa), with services to many Cantabrian and other destinations including the following:

Bilbao (€6.70 to €12.80, 1¼ to two hours, 19 or more daily)

Burgos (€11.20 to €19.50, 2½ to 3½ hours, six daily)

Madrid (€27.50 to €42, 5¼ to six hours, six or more daily)

Oviedo (€13.19 to €23.64, 2¼ to 3¼ hours, nine or more daily)

San Sebastián (€13 to €25, 2½ to four hours, eight or more daily)

Train

There are two train stations, next door to each other on Calle de Rodríguez:

Renfe (www.renfe.com) Two or three long-distance trains daily to Madrid (€47.90, 4½ hours) via Palencia and Valladolid; two daily regional trains as far as Valladolid (€16.60, four hours).

FEVE (✆942 20 95 22; www.feve.es) Two daily trains to San Vicente de la Barquera, Llanes, Ribadesella, Arriondas and Oviedo (€14.15, 4½ hours); three to Bilbao (€7.75, 2¾ hours).

Around Santander

PUENTE VIESGO & AROUND

POP (PUENTE VIESGO) 550

The valley town of Puente Viesgo, 25km south of Santander on the N623 towards Burgos, lies at the foot of the conical Monte Castillo. About 2km up this hill are the Cuevas de Monte Castillo, a series of caves frequented by humans since 150,000 years ago. Four of the caves are World Heritage-listed for their top-rank cave art and two of these, the **Cuevas de El Castillo y Las Monedas** (✆942 59 84 25; per cave adult/child €3/1.50; ⌚9.30am-2.30pm & 3.30-7.30pm), are open for guided visits (45 minutes each). El Castillo is the more spectacular: here, you penetrate 760m into the cave where the art is almost as breathtaking as that at the Cueva de Altamira. The 275 paintings and engravings of deer, bison, horses, goats, aurochs, mammoths, handprints and mysterious symbols and signs date from 26,000 to 11,000 BC – and unlike those at Altamira, these are the genuine article rather than a replica. Las Monedas has less art (animals painted in black outline, from around 10,000 BC) but also contains a labyrinth of stalactites and stalagmites in an astounding array of shapes. Booking ahead is highly advisable, especially for El Castillo. You can do so by phone or online at http://cuevas.culturadecantabria.com. After the caves you might like to take a half-hour trot up Monte Castillo, where you will find the minor remains of a medieval castle.

Seven buses run to Puente Viesgo from Santander Monday to Friday (€2.05, 40 minutes), with three or four on weekends.

Those with a vehicle should head about 3km northeast from Puente Viesgo to admire the 12th-century **Colegiata de Santa Cruz de Castañeda** in the village of Socobio – one of the finest Romanesque churches in Cantabria.

LANGRE

About 20km east of Santander by car (follow the signs for Somo and then proceed towards Galizano) are the wild beaches of Langre, backed by cliffs topped with green fields. Most people head for Langre Grande (car park €3), although nearby Langre Pequeña is more protected.

PARQUE DE LA NATURALEZA CABÁRCENO

This open-air **zoo** (✆902 210112; www.parquedecabarceno.com; adult/child €20.20/12.15; ⌚9.30am-6pm; 👪), 17km south of Santander, is a curious but successful experiment, a free-range home on the site of former open-cut mines for everything from rhinos to wallabies and gorillas to dromedaries. You need a car to tour its 20km of roadways. Access is from Obregón on the CA262.

Eastern Cantabria

The 95km stretch of coast between Santander and Bilbao offers citizens of both cities several seaside bolt holes. While the towns here are less appealing than those on Cantabria's western coast, some of the beaches are top-drawer, and the valleys and hills inland are gorgeously picturesque.

SANTOÑA

The fishing port of Santoña is dominated by two fortresses, the **Fuerte de San Martín** and, further east, the abandoned **Fuerte de San Carlos**. You can take a pleasant walk around both, or take the shuttle ferry (€1.80) across the estuary to the western end of the long, sandy Laredo beach. You can also head off for a hike in the **Parque Cultural Monte Buciero** east of the town centre. Otherwise, go north along the C141 to **Playa Berria**, a magnificent sweep of sand on the open sea, linked to Santoña by frequent buses (€1.35). Here, **Hotel Juan de la Cosa** (✆942 66 12 38; www.hoteljuandelacosa.com; Avenida de Berria

WORTH A TRIP

CANTABRIA'S EASTERN VALLEYS

Rich in unspoiled rural splendour, the little-visited valleys of eastern Cantabria are ripe for exploration. Plenty of routes suggest themselves: what follows is but a sample.

From El Soto, on the N623 just south of Puente Viesgo, take the CA270 southeast towards Vega de Pas, the 'capital' of the Valles Pasiegos (the valleys of the Pas, Pisueña and Miera rivers; www.vallespasiegos.org), one of Cantabria's most traditional rural areas. From Vega de Pas continue southeast – the views from the **Puerto de la Braguía pass** are stunning – into Castilla y León, before turning north again near Las Nieves to follow the BU571 up over the Puerto de la Sía pass towards Arredondo in the Alto Asón district (the southeastern corner of Cantabria; www.citason.com, in Spanish). The road is full of switchbacks, has a couple of mountain passes and passes the 50m waterfall that constitutes the **Nacimiento (Source) del Río Asón**.

Alto Asón claims more than half of the 9000 known caves in Cantabria, and from Arredondo you can go east to Ramales de la Victoria, a valley town with the two outstanding visitable caves. The **Cueva de Cullalvera** (☎942 59 84 25; adult/child €6/4; ⏲9.30am-2.30pm & 3.30-7.30pm) is an impressively vast cavity with some signs of prehistoric art. The **Cueva de Covalanas** (☎942 59 84 25; adult/child €3/1.50; ⏲9.30am-2.30pm & 3.30-7.30pm), 3km up the N629 south from Ramales, then 650m up a footpath, is World Heritage–listed for its numerous excellent animal paintings from around 18,000 BC, done in an unusual dot-painting technique. Guided visits to either cave last 45 minutes and it's advisable to book ahead by phone or at http://cuevas.culturadecantabria.com.

If you're up for a more adventurous style of caving, the **Red de Cuevas de Alto Asón** (☎667 701623, 942 64 65 04; www.decuevas.es, in Spanish) offers a variety of guided trips from Ramales, ranging from easy, flat underground walks to serious 18-hour traverses. Prices start at a reasonable €25 for a two-hour outing.

Ramales is served by 11 daily Turytrans buses from Laredo (€1.65, 35 minutes). South of Ramales the N629 climbs to the 920m Alto de los Tornos lookout, with spectacular panoramas, before continuing towards Burgos in Castilla y León.

14; s €90-98, d €119-131; P ⊜ @ ᯤ) may be in a brutish-looking building, but inside the blue-hued rooms are spacious and about two-thirds of them have beach views. There's a good restaurant with a seafood emphasis, too.

Fourteen buses run Monday to Saturday (seven on Sunday) to Santoña from Santander (€3.95, one hour). From July to September there's also a half-hourly passenger ferry to central Laredo (€3).

LAREDO

Tacked on to one end of a long sandy beach, the compact, cobblestoned *puebla vieja* (old town) of Laredo makes for a pleasant stroll. For an abundant *arroz con bogavante* (lobster and seafood rice) for two (€45), call in at the stone-walled **Restaurante La Abadía** (Rua Mayor 18; meals €35-50; ⏲Thu-Tue).

Plenty of buses from Santander (€3.75, 40 minutes) call in here.

PLAYAS DE ORIÑÓN & SONABIA

One of the most popular beaches along this coast is at Oriñón, just off the *autovía* (toll-free highway) 14km east of Laredo. The broad sandy strip is set deep behind protective headlands, making the water calm and *comparatively* warm. The settlement itself is made up of drab holiday flats and caravan parks. For a smaller but wilder sandy beach, continue 1.7km past Oriñón to Playa de Sonabia, set in a rock-lined inlet beneath high crags from which a colony of huge griffon vultures circles the skies above you. An up-and-down walking trail of 10km, taking around 3½ hours, links Oriñón with Laredo via Playa de Sonabia and another, even more isolated beach, Playa de San Julián.

CASTRO URDIALES

POP 25,300

The haughty Gothic jumble that is the **Iglesia de Santa María de la Asunción** (⏲10am-1.30pm & 4-7.30 Tue-Sun) stands out above the harbour and the tangle of narrow lanes that make up the medieval centre of Castro Urdiales. It could be a seaside set for *The Name of the Rose*. The church shares its little headland with the ruins of what was for centuries the town's defensive bastion, now supporting a lighthouse.

Of the two beaches, the northern Playa de Ostende is the more attractive. High above and all around the old town rise the serried ranks of high-density housing (mostly aimed at commuters to Bilbao) that have gone up since the late 1990s, blighting various parts of the Cantabrian coast. Find out about other area beaches at the tourist office (942 87 15 12; Avenida de la Constitución 1; 9.30am-1.30pm & 4-7pm), by the fishing port in the heart of the town.

Several inexpensive places to stay are scattered about the old centre. Pensión La Mar (942 87 05 24; www.lamarcastro.es; Calle de la Mar 27; s/d €36/55;) is one of the best. It's one block from the waterfront and has crisp and functional, if unexciting, rooms, some of which look onto the narrow pedestrian street. Top digs are at Hotel Las Rocas (942 86 04 00; www.lasrocashotel.com; Calle Flavióbriga 1; s/d €110/140; P), just behind the southern Playa de Brazomar. The contemporary-style rooms are adorned with a touch of colourful art and most have large glassed-in galleries and beach views.

Traditional fare, such as *sopa de pescado* (fish soup) and *pudín de cabracho* (scorpion-fish pâté), abounds in *mesones* (old-style eateries) and *tabernas* (taverns) along Calle de la Mar and Calle de Ardigales, and in front of the fishing boats at Plaza del Ayuntamiento.

ALSA (Calle de Leonardo Rucabado 42) runs at least 11 buses daily to Santander (€5.65, one hour). Buses to Bilbao (€3.30, one hour) go every half-hour, making various stops in town, including in front of La Barrera flower shop at Calle La Ronda 52, half a block from the seafront.

Southern Cantabria

Fine panoramas of high peaks and deep river valleys flanked by patchwork quilts of green await the traveller penetrating the Cantabrian interior. Every imaginable shade of green seems to have been employed to set this stage, strewn with warm stone villages and held together by a network of narrow country roads.

From industrial Torrelavega, the A67 road winds south along the Besaya valley, a time-honoured route between Cantabria's coast and Castilla. A Roman road ran along it, and you can walk its best-preserved stretch, 5km between Pie de Concha and Pesquera (both with Renfe train stations), in under two hours.

Other curiosities on the way south to Reinosa include the Palacio de Hornillos in Las Fraguas, built by an English gent in the 19th century and indeed looking very much like an English country seat. A few kilometres further south, in Helguera, is a rare 10th-century Mozarabic church.

Reinosa (population 10,300), southern Cantabria's main town, is an unexceptional place, but its tourist office (942 75 52 15; http://turismoreinosa.es, in Spanish; Avenida del Puente de Carlos III 23; 9.30am-2.30pm & 5-8pm Mon-Fri, 9.30am-2.30pm Sat & Sun, closed Sun Oct-Jun) can inform you about plenty of curiosities in the area. These include the Colegiata de San Pedro in Cervatos, 5km south, one of Cantabria's finest Romanesque churches, with a rare array of erotic carvings. At Retortillo, 5km east of Reinosa, the Museo Domus (626 325927; adult/child €3/1.50; 10.30am-1.30pm & 4-7pm Wed-Sun) is a full-scale recreation of a Roman house, almost next door to the ruins of Cantabria's most significant Roman town, Julióbriga (admission free; 10.30am-1.30pm & 4-7pm Wed-Sun). The Domus ticket also gives entry to the Centro de Interpretación del Rupestre at Santa María del Valverde (see p468).

Reinosa has a half-dozen sleeping options. Set in a charmingly restored, turn-of-the-20th-century Modernista building, the Villa Rosa (902 930374; www.villarosa. com, in Spanish; Calle de los Héroes de la Guardia Civil 4; s/d incl breakfast €53.50/90.95;) is what it says it is – pink. It looks more like something you'd expect in central Europe and most of the 12 very comfy rooms have an inviting period feel as well as good, up-to-date installations. It's handily close to the train and bus stations.

Seven or eight Renfe *cercanías* (suburban trains; €4.10, 1¾ hours) and three or four regional and long-distance trains head from Santander to Reinosa daily. There are at least six buses (€5.75, 1½ hours) too. A few daily trains and buses head south to Palencia, Valladolid, Salamanca and Madrid.

Western Cantabria

SANTILLANA DEL MAR
POP 1080

They say this is the city of the three lies, since it is not holy *(santi)*, flat *(llana)* or by the sea *(del mar)*! Some good-looking liar! This medieval jewel is in such a perfect state of preservation, with its bright cobbled streets and tanned stone and brick buildings huddling in a muddle of centuries of history, that it seems too good to be true. Surely it's a film set! Well, no. People still live here, passing their precious houses down from generation to generation.

Strict town planning rules were first introduced back in 1575, and today they include the stipulation that only residents or guests in hotels with garages may bring in their vehicles. Other hotel guests may drive to unload luggage and must then return to the car park at the town entrance.

Santillana is a bijou in its own right, but makes an obvious base for visiting the nearby Cueva de Altamira too.

◎ Sights

Colegiata de Santa Juliana   CHURCH
(admission €3; ⊙10am-1.30pm & 4-7.30pm Tue-Sun) A stroll along the cobbled main street, past solemn nobles' houses dating from the 15th to 18th centuries, leads you to this lovely 12th-century Romanesque former monastery. The big drawcard is the cloister, a formidable storehouse of Romanesque handiwork, with the capitals of its columns carved into a huge variety of figures. The sepulchre of Santa Juliana, a 3rd-century Christian martyr from Turkey (and the real source of the name Santillana), stands in the centre of the church. The monastery and town grew up around the saint's relics, which were brought here after her death.

Museo Diocesano   MUSEUM
(www.santillanamuseodiocesano.com, in Spanish; Calle del Cruce; ⊙10am-1.30pm & 4-6.30pm, closed Mon Oct-May) Just south of the main road running through town, a former Dominican monastery contains a fascinating collection of 'popular' polychrome wooden statuary, some of it quite bizarre.

Museo de Tortura   MUSEUM
(Calle del Escultor Jesús Otero 1; adult/student/child €3.60/2.40/free; ⊙10am-9pm) This exhibition displays more than 70 grim instruments of torture used by the Inquisition in its unremitting battle against heresy. You may not want to bring kids in here even though they don't pay!

Torre del Merino   TOWER
(Plaza de Ramón Pelayo) This emblematic 14th-century tower on the main square is sometimes used for temporary exhibitions.

⨇ Sleeping

There are dozens of places to stay, many of them in atmospheric historic buildings converted for your comfort and pleasure. They are scattered about the old part of town, and around Campo del Revolgo south of the main road, as well as along the roads towards the Cueva de Altamira, Comillas and Santander. Some close from about November to February.

La Casa del Organista   HOTEL €€
(☎942 84 03 52; www.casadelorganista.com; Camino de Los Hornos 4; s/d €75/91; 🅿😊🛜) Rooms at this elegant 18th-century house, once home to the *colegiata*'s organist, are particularly attractive, with plush rugs, antique furniture and plenty of exposed heavy beams and stonework. Some have wood-rail balconies looking across fields towards the *colegiata*.

Posada Santa Juliana   POSADA €€
(☎942 84 01 06; Calle Carrera 19; d €61; ⊙Apr-Sep; 🛜) A short walk in from the main road, this is a charming medieval house with six smallish but tastefully restored doubles with creaking timber floors and wooden furniture. Inquire with the friendly folk at Los Nobles restaurant opposite.

Casa del Marqués   HISTORIC HOTEL €€€
(☎942 81 88 88; www.turismosantillanadelmar.com; Calle del Cantón 26; s/d incl breakfast €187/209; ⊙Mar-early Dec; 🅿😊❄@🛜) Feel like the lord or lady of the manor in this 15th-century Gothic mansion, once home to the Marquis of Santillana. Exposed timber beams, thick stone walls and cool terracotta floors contribute to the atmosphere of the 15 all-different rooms. They're proud of their banister, 700 years old and made from a single tree.

Hotel Siglo XVIII   HOTEL €€
(☎942 84 02 10; www.hotelsigloxviii.com, in Spanish; Calle de Revolgo 38; d €85; 🅿🛜🏊) This has to be one of the better deals in Santillana. Surrounded by a garden and green fields, this stone mansion, although quite new, is faithful to the town's style. Rooms are inviting, with antique furniture, and access to a pool at these prices is a bonus.

Posada de la Abadía
POSADA €

(☎942 84 03 04; www.posadadelabadia.com, in Spanish; Calle de Revolgo 26; s/d €47/59; P❖@🛜) A small family-run hotel in a traditional Cantabrian-style house, south of the main road. It's clean and friendly, and the 10 pretty, if not exactly inspired, rooms all have bathtub. Rates almost halve in winter.

✖ Eating

Santillana has many humdrum eateries catering to the passing tourist trade, and you should be able to get a full meal at most for around €20 to €25. There are some better options, however.

Restaurante Gran Duque
TRADITIONAL CANTABRIAN €€

(www.granduque.com; Calle del Escultor Jesús Otero 5; meals €25-45; ❖closed Sun dinner, Mon lunch & Jan) The food is high-quality local fare and what sets it apart is the setting, a grand stone house with noble trappings and nice decorative touches such as the exposed brick and beams. There is a reasonable balance of surf or turf options, but the latter are better. *Menús* (set menus) go for €18, or €46 or €60 for two.

La Villa
CANTABRIAN €€

(Plaza de la Gándara; meals €25-35; ❖Thu-Tue) Wander through the great timber doors into the courtyard. To your left is a bar with benches; to the right and upstairs is the dining area. They're brought together as though under a big top of heavy, dark timber beams. The meat dishes, such as the *solomillo con salsa de queso* (sirloin in cheese sauce), are its strong suit.

Casa Uzquiza
CANTABRIAN €€

(Calle del Escultor Jesús Otero 11; menús €10; meals €25-40; ❖closed Feb & Tue Sep-May) This two-floor restaurant overlooking countryside, with some garden tables too, offers many of the usual local suspects, such as *cocido montañés* (a hearty stew of white beans, cabbage, potato, chorizo, black pudding and sometimes port), and surprises with an elegant touch, such as *lomos de bacalao en pil-pil de erizo* (soft steamed cod drenched in a thick yellow sea urchin sauce).

❶ Information

Tourist office (☎942 81 88 12; Calle del Escultor Jesús Otero 20; ❖9am-9pm) At the main car park.

❶ Getting There & Away

Autobuses La Cantábrica (☎942 34 27 01) Runs three or four daily buses from Santander

to Santillana (€2.25, 40 minutes), and on to Comillas and San Vicente de la Barquera. They stop by Campo del Revolgo.

MUSEO & CUEVA DE ALTAMIRA

Spain's finest prehistoric art, in the Cueva de Altamira, 2km southwest of Santillana, was discovered in 1879 by Cantabrian historian and scientist Marcelino Sanz de Sautuola and his eight-year-old daughter María Justina. It took more than 20 years, after further discoveries of cave art in France, before scientists accepted that these wonderful paintings of bison, horses and other animals really were the handiwork of primitive people many thousands of years ago. By 2002 Altamira had attracted so many visitors that the cave was closed to prevent deterioration of the paintings.

The nearby Museo de Altamira (☎942 81 80 05; http://museodealtamira.mcu.es; adult/ under 18yr, EU senior or student €3/free, Sun & from 2.30pm Sat free; ❖9.30am-8pm Tue-Sat, 9.30am-3pm Sun & holidays) enables everyone to view the inspired, 14,500-year-old paintings in replica form in a dazzling, full-sized recreation of the cave's most interesting chamber, the Sala de Polícromos (Polychrome Hall). The viewing is enhanced by the museum's excellent other displays, in English and Spanish, on prehistoric humanity and cave art around the world, from Altamira to Australia.

You can visit the replica cave, called the Neocueva, with or without a Spanish-language guide: if you choose to enter without a guide, you receive a moderately useful self-guiding leaflet. In either case you will be assigned a Neocueva entry time with your ticket.

For Easter week and July, August and September it's worth purchasing tickets in advance, through the website or branches of Banco Santander (www.bancosantander. es, in Spanish); on the website type 'Altamira' in the search box.

Those without vehicles must walk or take a taxi to Altamira from Santillana del Mar.

There are plans to reopen the real cave for very limited numbers of visitors, with Barack Obama pencilled in as the first invitee.

COMILLAS
POP 1870

Sixteen kilometres west from Santillana through verdant countryside, Comillas has a golden beach and a tiny fishing port, but there is much more: a pleasant, cobbled old

ALONG THE RÍO EBRO

Spain's most voluminous river, the Ebro (whence 'Iberia' stems), rises at Fontibre about 6km west of Reinosa, fills the Embalse del Ebro reservoir and then meanders south and east into Castilla y León. You can follow its course along the GR-99 long-distance footpath or, if you're not quite that energetic, in a vehicle along minor roads out of Reinosa.

Head first east along the CA730 to Bolmir, from which the road follows the southern shore of the reservoir towards Arroyo. Just before Arroyo, turn right (south). Along this exceedingly narrow route, you encounter the Monasterio de Montesclaros, with a history going back to the 12th century. Next, descend to Arroyal and work your way south to eventually hit a T-junction where the CA272 meets the CA273. Just downstream from here the Ebro turns east along the pretty Valderredible valley. About 13km east along the CA272 is Polientes, where you'll find banks, a petrol station and four places to stay. Along or just off the road you can visit several remarkable chapels hewn from the rock between the 6th and 10th centuries, when Christian missionaries were trying to make headway with the none-too-receptive Cantabrians. The best example, the Iglesia de Santa María de Valverde, with two naves and three apses cut from the rock, and a later bell tower built above-ground, is actually about 10km west of the T-junction. Beside it you'll find the excellent Centro de Interpretación del Rupestre (✆626 325927; ◷9.30am-2.30pm & 3.30-7.30pm mid-Jun–mid-Sep, closed Mon-Fri rest of year), telling the story of this curious cave-church phenomenon. Eastward, there are chapels at Puente del Valle, Campo de Ebro and, beyond Polientes, Cadalso and Arroyuelos.

Across the Ebro from Arroyuelos, San Martín de Elines is worth a detour for its fine Romanesque church.

centre, and hilltops crowned by some of the most original buildings in Cantabria. For the latter, Comillas is indebted to the first Marqués de Comillas, who was born here as plain Antonio López, made a fortune in Cuba as a tobacco planter, shipowner, banker and slave trader, and then returned to commission leading Catalan Modernista architects to jazz up his home town in the late 19th century. This in turn attracted other bourgeoisie to construct quirky mansions here.

◉ Sights

Capricho de Gaudí   GAUDÍ SUMMERHOUSE
Antoni Gaudí left few reminders of his genius beyond Catalonia, but of those that he did, the 1885 Gaudí Caprice in Comillas is easily the most flamboyant. The brick building, originally a summer playpad for the Marqués de Comillas' wife's brother-in-law, is liberally striped with ceramic bands of alternating sunflowers and green leaves. The building is on a rise southwest of the town centre; it's now a top-end restaurant that gathers mixed reviews and you can only go inside if you're eating there.

Palacio de Sobrellano   STATELY HOME
Just above the Capricho de Gaudí, in the same hillside parklands, stand the Marquis' wonderful neo-Gothic Palacio de Sobrellano (✆942 72 03 39; admission €3; ◷9.30am-2.30pm & 3.30-7pm, closed Mon & Tue Sep-Jun) and his ornate family tomb, the Capilla Panteón de los Marqueses de Comillas (admission €3; ◷10.30am-1.30pm & 4-7pm, closed Mon & Tue Sep-Jun), both designed by Joan Martorell. With the *palacio*, Martorell truly managed to out-Gothic real Gothic. Visits to both buildings are by guided tour.

Town Centre   PLAZAS, CHURCH
Comillas' compact medieval centre is built around several cobbled plazas, with a vernacular architecture of solid sandstone houses with wooden balconies or glassed-in galleries. The main church, the Iglesia de San Cristóbal, was constructed in the 17th century from the townspeople's own pockets after they took umbrage at the Duque de Infantado's retinue refusing to share a pew with common folk in the old church.

Universidad Pontificia   MODERNISTA SEMINARY
Joan Martorell also had a hand in this former seminary on the hill opposite the Palacio de

Sobrellano, but Lluís Domènech i Montaner, another Catalan Modernista, contributed the medieval flavour to this elaborate building. It's now being converted from pontifical university into an international Spanish-language-and-culture study centre, the **Centro Internacional de Estudios Superiores de Español** (www.fundacioncomillas.es). The grounds may open by 2011.

Cemetery MODERNISTA GRAVEYARD

The old parish church, in ruins, now forms part of the town cemetery down towards the beach. Domènech i Montaner revamped the ensemble, which is topped by a white marble Guardian Angel statue by Jose Llimona. It has a distinctly spooky aura when floodlit at night.

Playa de Oyambre BEACH

Of several beaches around Comillas, the long, sandy Playa de Oyambre, 5km west, is decidedly superior. Two year-round camping grounds operate behind it.

Sleeping

TOP CHOICE Hotel Marina de Campíos HOTEL €€€

(☎942 72 27 54; www.marinadecampios.com; Calle del General Piélagos 14; r incl breakfast €110-150; ⊙closed Mon-Thu mid-Sep–mid-Jul; 📶) This 19th-century Comillas house, a few steps from the central Corro de Campíos plaza, has been revamped into a stylish and comfy contemporary hotel with 20 or so all-different rooms, sporting four-poster beds and bold colour schemes. There's a lovely inner patio with the piano bar opening on to it.

Hostal Esmeralda HOSTAL €€

(☎942 72 00 97; www.hostalesmeralda.com, in Spanish; Calle de Antonio López 7; s/d €60/80; 🚭📶) Just a short distance east of the town centre, Esmeralda is a handsomely restored old stone building with large, old-fashioned rooms, lots of character and dashes of colourful decor. It's well looked-after and well run. Rates come down by at least a quarter outside August.

Eating

Plenty of restaurants and cafes around the central squares provide straightforward seafood and meat *raciones* (large tapas servings; €7 to €15), *menús* (€12 to €15) and *platos combinados* (basically, meat-and-three-veg dishes; €7). **Restaurante Tulipanes** (Calle de los Arzobispos 12; ⊙8am-1am) has a strong local flavour, decked with black-and-white photos of old Comillas.

Restaurante Gurea CANTABRIAN, BASQUE €€

(Calle Ignacio Fernández de Castro 11; meals €25-45; ⊙closed Mon Oct-May) Behind Hostal Esmeralda in a backstreet, this elegant restaurant dishes up Basque and Cantabrian fare. The €50 *menú* for two is a good bet – or you could just go for *cocido montañés* with bread, wine and dessert for €12.50.

Information

Tourist office (☎942 72 25 91; www.comillas.es; Plaza de Joaquín del Piélago; ⊙9am-9pm) In the town hall building.

Getting There & Away

Comillas is served by the same buses as Santillana del Mar (€3.50, one hour from Santander). The main stop is on Calle del Marqués de Comillas, near the driveway to the Capricho de Gaudí.

SAN VICENTE DE LA BARQUERA

POP 3440

As you approach from a height on the CA131, 10km west of Comillas past the green and humid estuary land of the Parque Natural de Oyambre, you see how a broad swath of seawater has cut a gash through the coast at San Vicente de la Barquera. The main estuary is spanned by the long, low-slung, 15th-century Puente de la Maza. To the east, out of view of the main road, runs the 3km-long golden strand of **Playa del Rosal** and the wilder, clothing-optional **Playa de Merón** (heed the warning signs about currents at these beaches). The town huddles between the bridge and another narrow inlet on the western side.

San Vicente was an important port in the Middle Ages and ranked as one of the Cuatro Villas de la Costa, a federation of dominant fishing and trading towns that was converted by Carlos III into the province of Cantabria in 1779.

The old part of town is topped by a 13th-century **castle** (adult/child €1.40/0.70; ⊙11am-2pm & 5-8pm Tue-Sun) and some remnants of the old city walls, but its outstanding monument is the largely 13th-century **Iglesia de Santa María de los Ángeles** (⊙10am-1.30pm & 4-7.30pm Tue-Sun), further inland. Although Gothic, it sports a pair of impressive Romanesque doorways. Inside, the lifelike statue of 16th-century Inquisitor Antonio del Corro (reclining on one elbow, reading) is deemed the best piece of Renaissance funerary art in Spain.

Beside the central Plaza de José Antonio, **Hotel Luzón** (☎942 71 00 50; www.hotelluzon.net; Calle de Miramar 1; s/d €45/70; 📶) is

CANTABRIA'S WESTERN VALLEYS

Generally ignored by holidaymakers, who concentrate their attention on the Picos de Europa further west, the valleys of the Río Saja and, next west, the Río Nansa, make a soft contrast to the craggy majesty of the Picos.

A beautiful drive starting from the Picos de Europa is the CA282, which snakes up high and eastwards from La Hermida on Río Deva. The village of Puentenansa forms a crossroads. Fifteen kilometres north (turn east at Rábago and climb 7km) is El Soplao (☎902 820282; www.elsoplao.es; adult/senior, student & child €7/7.50; ⌚10am-9pm, closed Mon Oct-Jun), a 14km stretch of caves full of stalactites and stalagmites, and before 1979 a lead and zinc mine. The one-hour visit travels 400m into the cave in a mine train then continues a little further on foot. A separate adventure tour going 3km into the caves (€30, 2½ hours) opens up an extraordinary subterranean world.

The CA281 south from Puentenansa follows the Río Nansa upstream. Along the way, a short detour east leads to the attractive hamlet of Tudanca, dominated by the Casona de Tudanca (www.museosdecantabria.com, in Spanish; adult/child €3/1.50; ⌚11am-2pm & 4-6.15pm, to 5.30pm Sun, closed mid-Dec–end Jan & Mon Oct-Apr), a white, 18th-century rural mansion. Guided visits last 45 minutes. The house was built by an *indiano* – that is, someone who had made a fortune in Spain's Latin American colonies (in this case Peru) and returned. Inside you'll see all sorts of centuries-old furniture and diverse objects. The house also contains the 18,000-volume library of writer José María de Cossío, to whom it belonged in the 20th century.

The CA281 eventually meets the CL627, on which you can head south to Cervera de Pisuerga in Castilla y León or turn northwest back to the Picos.

Proceeding east from Puentenansa takes you through Carmona, with many fine stone mansions. When you reach the village of Valle de Cabuérniga and the Río Saja, head south on the CA280 towards Reinosa. The views are magnificent. The hamlet of Bárcena Mayor, about 9km east of the main road, is a popular spot with a couple of *casas rurales* (rural homes) to stay in and great *mesones* (taverns), where you should try the *cocido montañés* (a hearty stew of white beans, cabbage, potato, chorizo, black pudding and sometimes port). It's a good base for walks in the dense beech forests, valleys and hills of the Parque Natural Saja-Besaya, which surrounds it. The park's Centro de Interpretación (☎608 455873; ⌚10am-7.30pm Tue-Sun, closed Tue & Wed Oct-Jun) is 6km beyond the Bárcena Mayor turn-off on the CA280.

a stately looking, stone-fronted home possessing an air of older times with its high ceilings and quiet drawing rooms. Rooms are plain but most have a sense of space and many have broad views over town and water.

El Pescador (Avenida del Generalísimo 26; meals €20-30; ⌚closed Tue & Mon dinner Sep-May) is the liveliest of the mainly seafood-dominated restaurants that line Avenida del Generalísimo, which leads off Plaza de José Antonio. Stand around in the good-natured bar area knocking back tapas, or make your way out back to the dining area overlooking the estuary.

The tourist office (☎942 71 07 97; www. sanvicentedelabarquera.org; Avenida del Generalísimo 20; ⌚10am-1.30pm & 4.30-7pm Mon-Sat, 10am-2pm Sun) doubles as an agent for *casas rurales* (rural homes) in the area.

San Vicente bus station, by the Puente de la Maza, is served by at least seven daily buses to Santander (€4.55, 1¼ hours, some via Comillas and Santillana del Mar), six to Oviedo (€9.27, two hours, some stopping at Llanes, Ribadesella and Arriondas), and one or more to Potes (€3.30, 1½ hours). Two slower FEVE trains stop daily en route between Santander and Oviedo.

ASTURIAS

'Ser español es un orgullo', the saying goes, *'ser asturiano es un título'*. 'If being Spanish is a matter of pride, to be Asturian is a title', or so some of the locals would have you think.

Asturias has many similarities with neighbouring Cantabria and its scenic beauty is, if anything, even greater. The coast is a little wilder and more dramatic, and strung with even more beaches (it's said there are more than 600), always with rolling green countryside behind. Inland, the mountains are generally higher, the valleys deeper (though equally green) and the villages a mite more rustic. Much of the Picos de Europa are on Asturian territory, and fishing villages such as Llanes and Cudillero make great bases for exploring the lovely coast, dotted with picture-postcard coves and inlets. For the architecture buff, Asturias is the land of the pre-Romanesque – modest but unique survivors of early medieval building and decoration. The region's cultured capital, Oviedo, is both historic and contemporary, with its old centre and fine restaurants.

Asturias also has its gritty industrial side. The Oviedo-Gijón-Avilés triangle is the heart of industrial Asturias and mines still operate in various spots, especially in the southwest.

Like neighbouring Galicia, Asturias was Celtic territory before the arrival of the Romans (and it's bagpipe territory today!). It's also the sole patch of Spain never completely conquered by the Muslims. King Pelayo warded them off in the Battle of Covadonga in AD 722, laying the foundations of the Kingdom of Asturias from which modern Spain grew. Asturias, its trumpeters say, is the real Spain; the rest is simply *tierra de reconquista* (reconquered land).

The Reconquista's southward progress left Asturias increasingly a backwater. As a concession, Juan I of Castilla y León made Asturias a *principado* (principality) in 1388, and to this day the heir to the Spanish throne holds the title Príncipe de Asturias (just as Prince Charles is the Prince of Wales). Annual awards handed out by the prince to personalities of distinction in Oviedo's Teatro Campoamor every October are Spain's equivalent of the Nobel prizes.

Asturias of the 20th century was at once rural backwater and industrial hotbed. A miners' revolt in 1934 was crushed by a certain General Franco, who two years later launched the civil war.

Oviedo

POP 208,000 / ELEV 232M

The compact but characterful and historic *casco antiguo* (old town) of Asturias' civilised capital is agreeably offset by elegant parks (notably the lovely, leafy Campo de San Francisco) and modern shopping streets to its west and north. Out on the periphery, the hum and heave of factories is a strong reminder that Oviedo is a key producer of textiles, weapons and food.

History

When Asturian king Alfonso II El Casto (the Chaste; AD 791–842) defeated a Muslim detachment that had practically razed the settlement of Oviedo, he was sufficiently impressed by the site to rebuild and expand it, and move his court there from Pravia. Oviedo remained the kingdom's capital until 910, when it moved to León and the kingdom became the Kingdom of León. Oviedo's university was founded around 1600, and industry took off in the 19th century. The 1934 miners' revolt and a nasty siege in the first months of the Spanish Civil War led to the destruction of much of the old town.

◉ Sights

Catedral de San Salvador   CATHEDRAL

(☑985 20 31 17; admission cathedral free, Cámara Santa, museum & cloister €3.50, free Thu afternoon; ◷10.15am-7.15pm Mon-Fri, 10.15am-5.15pm Sat) The cathedral's origins lie in the Cámara Santa, a chapel built by Alfonso II to house holy relics. The chapel is now a small part of a much bigger complex, which was built piecemeal over many years, chiefly in Gothic and baroque styles between the 13th and 18th centuries.

Inside the Capilla del Rey Casto, a baroque chapel entered from the cathedral's north transept, the **Panteón Real** is believed to hold the tombs of most of the Asturian monarchs, including Alfonso II himself.

ℹ **ASTURIAS WEBSITES**

» www.infoasturias.com Excellent, comprehensive site of Asturias' regional tourism office.

» www.casasdealdea.com Search the *casas rurales* (rural homes) that pepper the countryside and small towns.

» www.casonasasturianas.com (in Spanish) Around 60 of the best country-house hotels.

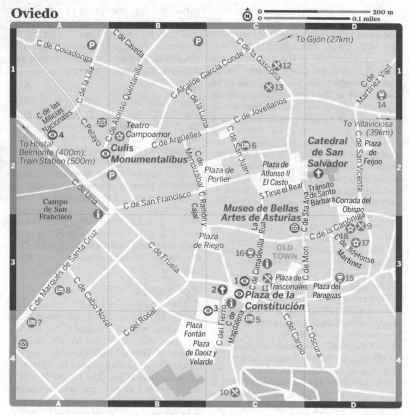

You enter the Cámara Santa, cloister and museum from the southern transept. The pre-Romanesque Cámara Santa contains some key symbols of medieval Spanish Christianity. Alfonso II presented the Cruz de los Ángeles (Cross of the Angels) to the cathedral in 808, and it's still Oviedo's city emblem. A century later Alfonso III donated the Cruz de la Victoria (Cross of Victory), which in turn became the sign of Asturias. Behind the Cruz de los Ángeles is the Santo Sudario, a cloth said to have covered Christ's face. These items are viewed from the Sala Apostolar, whose remarkable Romanesque sculptures of the apostles are in the style of Maestro Mateo, creator of the Pórtico de la Gloria in Santiago de Compostela's cathedral. Turning to leave, you'll see three heads sculpted from a single block of stone above the doorway. This strikingly simple work depicts, from left to right, the Virgin Mary, Christ and St John on Calvary.

Their bodies were originally painted on the wall below.

The cloister is pure 14th-century Gothic, rare enough in Asturias. The pre-Romanesque Torre Vieja (Old Tower), from the late 9th century, rises above its northwestern corner (best viewed from the street Tránsito de Santa Bárbara).

Around the Cathedral MUSEUM, MANSIONS
Plaza de Alfonso II El Casto and neighbouring Plaza de Porlier are fronted by elegant mansions dating from the 17th and 18th centuries. The nearby Museo de Bellas Artes de Asturias (www.museobbaa.com, in Spanish; Calle de Santa Ana 1; admission free; ⏱10.30am-2pm & 4-8pm Tue-Sat, 10.30am-2.30pm Sun), housed in two buildings dating to the 17th and 18th centuries, rewards a visit. Its collection includes paintings by Goya, El Greco, Zurbarán and other Spanish greats, and plenty by Asturians, such as Evaristo Valle.

Oviedo

Plazas & Statues   QUAINT NOOKS

Explore the old town's nooks and crannies. **Plaza de la Constitución** occupies a barely perceptible rise close to the heart of old Oviedo, capped at one end by the **Iglesia de San Isidoro**, and lined on one side by the 17th-century **ayuntamiento** (town hall). To the south, past the **Mercado El Fontán** food market, arcaded **Plaza Fontán** is equipped with a couple of *sidrerías* (cider houses) and has passages leading under the pretty houses to surrounding streets.

Other little squares include **Plaza de Trascorrales**, **Plaza de Riego** and **Plaza del Paraguas**. The latter got its name from its inverted-umbrella design, which once accommodated an open-air market. Today it sports a big concrete umbrella to protect people from the elements.

Wandering around central Oviedo, you'll run into an array of striking modern open-

air sculptures, such as Eduardo Úrculo's **Culis Monumentalibus** on Calle Pelayo and a **statue of Woody Allen** (minus glasses, which some vandal has removed) on Calle de las Milicias Nacionales. Allen expressed a particular affection for Oviedo when filming scenes here for his 2008 flick *Vicky Cristina Barcelona*.

Palacio de Exposiciones y Congresos
CONTEMPORARY ARCHITECTURE

(www.pec-oviedo.com; Calle de Arturo Álvarez Buyila) Star Spanish architect Santiago Calatrava's Palace of Congresses and Exhibitions (due for 2011) will be a dashing addition to Oviedo, a startling complex that, from the front, looks like a white praying mantis. It's 1km west of the centre.

🎉 Festivals & Events

Oviedo's biggest fiesta is that of **San Mateo**, celebrated in the third week of September and climaxing around 21 September.

🛏 Sleeping

The busy boulevard, Calle de Uría, from the train station to the old town is a gallery of inexpensive, and in some cases very pleasant, lodgings.

Hotel Libretto   HOTEL €€€

(☑985 20 20 04; www.librettohotel.com; Calle de Marqués de Santa Cruz 12; s/d €160/171; P❄@🖥) Music lovers will appreciate this opera-inspired hotel in a Modernista-style building facing Campo de San Francisco. Phone or check the website for frequent special offers. Many of the 15 sleekly decorated rooms feature giant photos of opera singers in their bathrooms. You can choose from a menu of pillows, and there are bikes to rent too.

Hotel de la Reconquista   HOTEL €€€

(☑985 24 11 00; www.hoteldelareconquista.com; Calle de Gil de Jaz 16; s/d from €131/157; P❄✳@🖥) The city's top lodgings, two blocks northwest of Campo de San Francisco, started life as an 18th-century hospice. Rooms come in different shapes and sizes, with timber furniture, floor-to-ceiling windows, and gentle ochre-and-white colour schemes.

Hotel Santa Cruz   HOTEL €€

(☑985 22 37 11; www.santacruzoviedo.com; Calle de Marqués de Santa Cruz 6; s/d €50/65; P❄🖥) Only a couple of rooms overlook the lovely big green park across the street, and there's nothing inspired about the decor. But with well-sized, spotless rooms, friendly reception and a central location, this amounts to decent value.

Hostal Belmonte
HOSTAL €

(☎985 24 10 20; www.hostalbelmonte.com, in Spanish; Calle de Uría 31; s/d €37/49; ❀🛜) A quick stroll from the train station, this charming 3rd-floor lodging (there's a lift) offers cosy rooms with timber floors and an at-home feel. Three cheaper rooms with shared bathroom are also available.

Casa Camila
RURAL HOTEL €€

(☎985 11 48 22; www.casacamila.com; Calle de Fitoria 29; s/d €78/107; 🅿🛜) Family-run Camila has just seven rooms (including one single and one great double with private terrace and Jacuzzi for €130) and is a charmer. It's in Fitoria, 4km northeast of the centre, and offers wonderful views over the city. Rooms are spacious, with an old-world rustic flavour.

Hostal Arcos
HOSTAL €

(☎985 21 47 73; www.hostal-arcos.com, in Spanish; Calle de Magdalena 3; s €45-48, d €50-58; ❀🛜) The only lodging actually in the old town is a modern brick building with 10 simple, clean rooms, some quite cheery and colourful.

Hotel El Ovetense
HOTEL €

(☎985 22 08 40; www.hotelovetense.com, in Spanish; Calle de San Juan 6; s/d €37/53; ❀🛜) A stone's throw from the cathedral, with 17 functional but clean rooms spread over four floors, and a lively *sidrería* downstairs.

✖ Eating

Oviedo's *sidrería* rules include getting good grub at reasonable prices. To sample the experience head for Calle de la Gascona, which is lined with boisterous *sidrerías*, most serving *raciones* from €8 to €18. Two or three constitute a full meal. Elsewhere, Oviedo also boasts some of northern Spain's most sophisticated eateries.

TOP CHOICE **La Puerta Nueva**
NORTHERN/MEDITERRANEAN €€

(☎985 22 52 27; Calle de Leopoldo Alas 2; meals €40-60; ⊙closed Sun-Wed dinner; ❀) A gourmet experience, mixing northern Spanish with Mediterranean cooking in a homey, welcoming atmosphere. The best option is to tackle one of the tasting menus. Market supplies largely determine what appears on the menu.

Tierra Astur
CIDER, GRILLED MEATS €

(☎985 20 25 02; Calle de la Gascona 1; meals €20-30) A particularly atmospheric *sidrería*/restaurant, Tierra Astur is famed for its grilled meats and prize-winning cider. Folks queue for tables, or give up and settle for tapas at the bar. Some just buy typical local products in the shop area to the right and go home. Platters of Asturian sausage, cheese or ham are a good starter option.

La Corrada del Obispo
ASTURIAN €€

(☎985 22 00 48; Calle de la Canóniga 18; meals €40-60; ⊙closed Sun dinner, Mon) Modern decor combines with the exposed stone walls of this 18th-century house to provide a welcoming setting for fine local cooking. It does a succulent grilled *mero* (grouper) with red-pepper risotto, and you might be able to snare a table in the upstairs gallery. Woody Allen shot some scenes for *Vicky Cristina Barcelona* here.

Sidrería Pigüeña
CIDER, SEAFOOD €€

(Calle de la Gascona 2; meals €40-50; ⊙Thu-Tue) A boisterous Gascona cider bar and restaurant, the Pigüeña is jammed most nights, especially weekends, with a broad mix of locals, from labourers to lovers, hoeing into seafood and *rollitos de verdura con marisco* (seafood-stuffed vegetable tubes), and slurping bottles of cider. Let the waiters serve the cider though!

La Taberna del Zurdo
FUSION €€

(☎985 96 30 96; Calle de Cervantes 27; meals €30-60; ⊙8.30am-4pm & 8am-11.30pm Mon-Fri, 1-4pm & 8pm-midnight Sat, 1-4pm Sun Sep-Jul) A mix of tradition and innovation, where you might start with a salad of prawns, parmesan and walnuts and follow it by sirloin with goat's cheese, bacon and potato cakes. Or you can drop by for beautifully presented gourmet tapas, which have won numerous national prizes. It's 300m northwest of Campo de San Francisco.

 Bocamar
SEAFOOD €€

(☎985 23 70 92; Calle del Marqués de Pidal 20; meals €40-65; ⊙closed Sun dinner) Woody Allen dined at Bocamar, 200m north of Campo de San Francisco, a sober-enough-looking place from the outside and with a decidedly maritime air. This is probably the best seafood restaurant in town, where all items (fresh from the sea to the north) are prepared with a lightness of touch that makes all the difference.

Largely cut off from the rest of Christian Europe by the Muslim invasion, the tough and tiny kingdom that emerged in 8th-century Asturias gave rise to a unique style of art and architecture known as pre-Romanesque.

The 14 buildings, mostly churches (and collectively a World Heritage Site), that survive from the two centuries of the Asturian kingdom take some inspiration from Roman, Visigothic and possibly Carolingian French buildings, but have no real siblings. Typical are the straight lines of their profiles and floor plans, semicircular arches in the Roman style, and a triple-naved plan for the churches. In many cases the bases and capitals of columns, with their Corinthian or floral motifs, were simply cannibalised from earlier structures. The use of lattice windows as a design effect owes something to developments in Muslim Spain.

Some of the best of the genre is found in and near Oviedo, including the cathedral's Cámara Santa. The Iglesia de San Julián de los Prados (Iglesia de Santullano; adult/child €1.20/0.60, Mon free; ⊙10am-12.30pm Mon, 10am-12.30pm & 4-5.30pm Tue-Fri, 9.30am-noon & 3.30-5pm Sat), 1.2km northeast of Campo de San Francisco, just above the road to Gijón, is the largest remaining pre-Romanesque church, and one of the oldest, built in the early 9th century under Alfonso II. It is flanked by two porches – another Asturian touch – and the inside is covered with frescoes. On the slopes of Monte Naranco, 3km northwest of central Oviedo, the tall, narrow Palacio de Santa María del Naranco and the Iglesia de San Miguel de Lillo (admission to both adult/child €3/2, Mon free; ⊙9.30am-1pm Sun & Mon, 9.30am-1pm & 3.30-7pm Tue-Sat) were built by Ramiro I (842–50), Alfonso II's successor, and mark an advance in Asturian art. An outstanding decorative feature of the beautifully proportioned Santa María (which may have been a royal hunting lodge) is the *sogueado*, the sculptural motif imitating rope used in its columns. Some of the medallions are copies of ancient Iranian motifs, known here through Roman contact. Only about one-third of San Miguel remains – the rest collapsed centuries ago – but what's left has a singularly pleasing form. Also here, the Centro de Interpretación de Prerrománico (⏿985 11 49 01; ⊙10am-1.25pm & 4-7.25pm) has informative displays and models in English, Spanish and French. To get here take bus 10, hourly from about 9.10am to 9.10pm, northwest on Calle de Uría near the train station.

Visits to San Julián, Santa María and San Miguel are guided (in Spanish) except on Monday.

Restaurante El Raitán VARIED €€
(Plaza de Trascorrales 6; meals €30-50; ⊙closed Tue & Wed dinner; ⏿) Dark timber dominates several labyrinthine dining areas. The menu is extensive and there are also set menus (€15 to €36) on Asturian, vegetarian, sea and forest themes. The *medallones de solomillo* (sirloin medallions) are melt-in-the-mouth tender and the salads enormous.

🍷 **Drinking & Entertainment**

The narrow pedestrian streets of the old town are thronged with people having a great time inside and outside dozens of bars on weekends. The main axis is Calle de Mon, with wall-to-wall bars, and its extension, the slightly less manic and aptly named Calle Oscura ('Dark Street'). During the week, bars are generally open 11pm to 3.30am and can be quiet. On Friday and Saturday they mostly stay open until 5.30am and are jammed. For bars with live music, head to Calle de Martínez Vigil, where you might hear anything from blues to Celtic to Spanish indie rock to Beatles covers, starting any time from 8pm to 11pm.

El Mateín del Paraguas BAR
(Plaza del Paraguas; ⊙8pm-2am) A good place to start an evening, with a convivial mixed crowd and tasty tapas to accompany your cider, beer or whatever. Teenagers assemble with their bottles under the giant concrete umbrella in the square outside.

Ca Beleño CELTIC MUSIC
(Calle de Martínez Vigil 4; http://cabeleno.com; ⊙from 5pm) This is a well-established venue for Celtic music, whether of Asturian, Galician or Irish extraction. It usually has live groups from 10pm on Thursday.

Morgana Le Fay MUSIC BAR

(Calle de Cimadevilla 15; ⊗11pm-3.30am or later
Thu-Sat) A long bar with multicoloured
lighting and mainstream dance tunes (it
even has a doorman, although this ain't a
club), this place fills with a mixed, eclectic crowd.

Swing Jazz JAZZ BAR

(Calle de la Canóniga 14; ⊗from 9pm) With
low lighting and loud jazz, this New
York–style bar gets going early, and usually hosts bands Friday and Saturday at
11.45pm.

Salsipuedes PUB, NIGHTCLUB

(www.salsipuedes.es; Calle de Ildefonso Martínez
7; ⊗midnight-5am Fri & Sat) A place to go if
you're looking to party on around 3am,
blue-lit Salsipuedes has several bars and
dance floors on three levels of an old-
town house.

 Information

Post office (Calle de Santa Susana 18) The
most central office while the main one at Calle
de Alonso Quintanilla 1 is under renovation.

Oficina Municipal de Turismo (http://turismo.
ayto-oviedo.es, in Spanish) Old Town (✆984 08
60 60; Plaza de la Constitución 4; ⊗9.30am-
7.30pm); Campo de San Francisco (✆985 22 75
86; Calle de Marqués de Santa Cruz; ⊗9.30am-
2pm & 4.30-7.30pm); Bus Station (✆985 11 70
50; ⊗9.30am-2pm & 4.30-7.30pm)

Regional tourist office (✆902 300202;
www.infoasturias.com; Calle de Cimadevilla 4;
⊗10am-8pm Mon-Fri, 10am-7pm Sat & Sun,
closed Sun mid-Sep-Jun)

ⓘ Getting There & Around

Air

The **Aeropuerto de Asturias** (✆902 404704) is
at Santiago del Monte, 47km northwest of Oviedo and 40km west of Gijón. Buses run hourly
to/from Oviedo's ALSA bus station (€6.35, 45
minutes).

Airlines and destinations:

Air Berlin (www.airberlin.com) Destinations in
Germany

Air Europa (www.aireuropa.com) Madrid, Paris

Air France (www.airfrance.com) Paris

easyJet (www.easyjet.com) London (Stansted),
Geneva

Iberia (www.iberia.com) Madrid, Barcelona,
Seville, Valencia, Málaga, Brussels, Lisbon

Spanair (www.spanair.es) Barcelona

Vueling Airlines (www.vueling.com) Barcelona

Bus

From the **ALSA bus station** (✆902 422242;
Calle de Pepe Cosmen), 300m northeast of the
train station, direct services head up the motorway to Gijón (€2.15, 30 minutes) every 10 or 15
minutes from 6.30am to 10.30pm. Other daily
buses head to Asturian towns, Galicia, Cantabria
and elsewhere, including these:

Cangas de Onís (€6.10, 1½ hours, eight or
more daily)

Madrid (€30.10 to €49.69, 5¼ to 6½ hours,
15 daily)

Ribadesella (€7, 1¼ hours, four or more daily)

Santander (€13.19 to €23.64, 2¼ to 3¼ hours,
12 daily)

Santiago de Compostela (€26.31 to €42.90,
4¾ to 5½ hours, three or four daily)

SAMPLING CIDER

Ancient documents show that Asturians were sipping cider as far back as the 8th
century! The region churns out 80% of Spanish cider (the rest is made in Galicia, the
Basque Country and Navarra): anything up to 30 million litres a year, depending on
the apple harvest. Apples are reaped in autumn and crushed to a pulp (about three-
quarters of the apple winds up as apple juice). A mix of bitter, sour and sweet apples
is used. The cider is fermented in *pipes* (barrels) kept in *llagares* (the places where the
cider is made) over winter. It takes about 800kg of apples to fill a 450-litre *pipa*, which
makes 600 bottles.

Traditionally, the *pipes* were transported to *chigres* (cider taverns) all over Asturias,
and punters would be served direct from the *pipa*. The *chigre* is dying out, though, and
most cider is now served in bottles in *sidrerías* (cider houses), usually with food. The
cider is served *escanciada*, that is, poured from the bottle held high overhead into a
glass held low. This gives it some fizz. Such a shot of cider – about one-fifth of a glass
– is known as a *culete* or *culín* and should be knocked back in one (leaving a tiny bit in
the bottom of the glass) before the fizz fizzles out.

The main cider-producing region is east of Oviedo: find out more at Comarca de la
Sidra (www.comarcadelasidra.com).

Train

One **station** (Avenida de Santander) serves both train companies, Renfe and FEVE, the latter located on the upper level. **Renfe** (www.renfe.com) runs trains to León, Madrid and Barcelona at least once daily. For Gijón, Renfe *cercanías* (€2.75, 35 minutes), go once or twice an hour until after 10pm.

FEVE (☑985 98 23 81; www.feve.es) runs four or five daily trains to Arriondas (€4.50, 1½ hours), Ribadesella (€5.80, two hours) and Llanes (€7.45, 2½ hours), with two continuing to Santander (€14.15, 4½ hours) and one to Bilbao. Westbound, FEVE has three direct trains daily to Cudillero (€2.85, 1¼ hours), and two to Luarca (€6.45, 2¼ hours), which continue into Galicia as far as Ferrol.

Around Oviedo

EL ENTREGO

Asturias has a proud mining history, an industry that promoted the arrival of the railways and metal industries and opened the region up to the rest of the country. You can plunge into that history at the Museo de la Minería y de la Industria (☑985 66 31 33; www.mumi.es, in Spanish; Calle El Trabanquín; adult/child €5/2.50; ☺10am-8pm Tue-Sat, to 2pm Sun) in El Entrego, 25km east of Oviedo. The displays, full-scale machinery models, and a replica of a mineshaft and tunnel, bring to life the tough story of mining.

Hourly Renfe *cercanías* from Oviedo call at El Entrego (€2.15, 40 minutes).

NAVA

This nondescript railway town 33km east of Oviedo also happens to be Asturias' biggest cider production centre. The Museo de la Sidra (Cider Museum; www.museodelasidra.com; Plaza del Príncipe de Asturias; adult/child €3.50/2.50, Tue free; ☺11am-2pm & 4-8pm Wed-Sat, noon-2pm & 4-8pm Tue & Sun, closed Sun evening mid-Sep–mid-Jun; ☑), with beautiful old timber presses, explanatory films and the chance to crush your own apple, is an entertaining display on the history of cider. Kids will like the virtual game of Asturian bowling and the *juego de la rana,* an ancestral Asturian pastime in which you try to throw metal disks into the mouth of a metal frog. You finish the tour with a fresh glass of cider. Navas' Festival de la Sidra Natural, around 11 July, includes plenty of free cider and an international pouring contest. At least eight ALSA buses (€2.55, 40 minutes) and seven FEVE trains (€2.20, 45 minutes) run to Nava from Oviedo.

WORTH A TRIP

PARQUE NATURAL DE REDES

Drivers looking for a treat should head southeast from El Entrego along the AS117 up the Nalón valley towards the 1490m Puerto de la Tarna pass on the Castilla y León border. The latter part of the route is a paradise of green, crossing the Parque Natural de Redes, with plenty of walking routes, a range of accommodation, and a Centro de Interpretación (☑985 60 80 22; www.parquenaturalderedes.es; ☺10am-2pm & 4-8pm) at Campo de Caso.

Gijón

POP 264,000

Bigger, grittier and gutsier than Oviedo, Gijón (khi-*hon*) produces iron, steel and chemicals, and is the main loading terminal for Asturian coal. But Gijón is emerging like a phoenix from its industrial setting, having given itself a facelift with pedestrianised streets, parks, seafront walks and cultural attractions. It's a party town too, and in summer puts on a vast entertainment program.

◉ Sights & Activities

Cimadevilla   OLD TOWN

The ancient core of Gijón is concentrated on the headland known as Cimadevilla. At the top of this, what was once a fortified military zone has been converted into an attractive park. At the north edge of the promontory stands the Elogio del Horizonte, a monumental concrete sculpture by Basque artist Eduardo Chillida that has become a symbol of the city.

Wrapped around the landward side of Cimadevilla is an enticing web of narrow lanes and small squares. Plaza de Jovellanos is dominated by the home of 18th-century Enlightenment politician Gaspar Melchor de Jovellanos, now housing the Museo Casa Natal de Jovellanos (☑985 18 51 52; admission free; ☺10am-2pm & 5-7.30pm Tue-Sun), devoted mainly to Asturian art and Jovellanos himself.

To the east, underneath Campo Valdés, are the town's Termas Romanas (Roman Baths; adult/senior, student & child €2.40/1.40, Sun free; ☺10am-2pm & 5-7.30pm Tue-Sun), built in the 1st to 4th centuries AD.

CANTABRIA & ASTURIAS AROUND OVIEDO

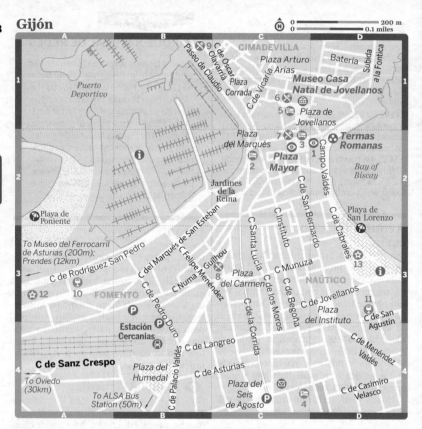

West of the baths spreads the harmonious Plaza Mayor, with porticoes on two sides and the casa consistorial (town hall) on a third.

Museo del Ferrocarril de Asturias
RAILWAY MUSEUM
(☑985 30 85 75; Plaza de la Estación del Norte; adult/senior, student & child €2.40/1.40, Sun free; ◔10am-2pm & 5-7.30pm Tue-Sun; ④) Gijón's excellent railway museum explores the important role of trains in Asturian history, with 50 locomotives and carriages, and plenty of choo-choo paraphernalia. It's housed in the 19th-century Renfe train station, a few minutes' walk west of the city centre.

Acuario
AQUARIUM
(☑958 18 52 20; www.acuariodegijon.com; adult/child €12/6; ◔10am-10pm; ④) On Playa de Poniente, a little beyond the Museo del Ferrocarril, this singular aquarium has 4000 specimens, from otters to sharks and penguins, in 50 tanks ranging over 12 separate underwater environments, from tropical oceans to the Bay of Biscay and an Asturian river environment with trout and salmon.

Museo del Pueblo de Asturias
ETHNOGRAPHIC MUSEUM
(☑985 18 29 60; Paseo del Dr Fleming 877, La Huelga; adult/senior & student €2.40/1.40, free Sun; ◔10am-2pm & 5-7.30pm Tue-Sun) This museum, on a large woodland site 2km east of the city centre, is devoted to traditional Asturian culture, with several typical buildings including grain stores, houses, a bowling alley and some quirky shepherds' shelters, plus exhibits of bagpipes, cooking, carriages and more. Take bus 4 from Calle de Capua to the Grupo Cultura Covadonga stop, about 400m from the museum.

Laboral Ciudad de la Cultura
ARTS CENTRE
(☑902 306600; www.laboralciudaddelacultura.com; Calle de Luis Moya Blanco 261; ◔10am-9pm)

Gijón

Constructed in the 1940s as a Jesuit-run *universidad laboral* (vocational training centre), the austerely grand 'Laboral', 4km southeast of the centre, has been reborn as a dynamic arts and education centre. It now houses part of Oviedo University, a conservatory, drama college, broadcasting studios and performance and exhibition spaces. Comprehensive Spanish-language tours and trips up the 130m tower cost €4.20 and €1.60 respectively. You can visit the impressive main courtyard and oval-shaped church (now a gallery) for free. Take bus 1 from Calle de Palacio Valdés.

Jardín Botánico Atlántico

BOTANICAL GARDEN

(☎985 13 07 13; www.botanicoatlantico.com; adult/senior & under 26yr €5.70/2.80; ☺10am-9pm Tue-Sun) Across the road from the Laboral, this verdant garden provides an excellent introduction to the flora of Spain's north coast and other territories fringing the Atlantic Ocean.

Beaches

BEACHES

For swimming, Playa de San Lorenzo is a surprisingly good, clean city beach, but

virtually disappears when the tide comes in. Playa de Poniente, west of the Puerto Deportivo (marina), has imported sand and is much broader.

★★ Festivals & Events

Throughout the summer, Gijón finds some excuse for a fiesta almost every week, from the Semana Negra (Black Week) arts festival in early July, focusing on detective novels, to the Fiesta de la Sidra Natural (Natural Cider Festival) in late August, which includes an annual attempt on the world record for the number of people simultaneously pouring cider. Varied musical programs and plenty of partying accompany all these events. The biggest week of all is Semana Grande (early to mid-August).

⌖ Sleeping

Getting a room in August can be a challenge, so try to book ahead. Prices tumble outside summer.

La Casona de Jovellanos HOTEL €€

(☎985 34 20 24; www.lacasonadejovellanos.com; Plaza de Jovellanos 1; s/d €62/81; ☜) This antique-furnished 16th-century house is one of only two hotels in the old heart of town. It's on one of Cimadevilla's nicest squares, and there's a lively *chigre* (cider tavern) downstairs.

Hotel Asturias HOTEL €€

(☎985 35 06 00; www.hotelasturiasgijon.es, in Spanish; Plaza Mayor 11; s/d €64/86; ❄☜) Touched with elegance, the Asturias' spacious, parquet-floored rooms overlook Cimadevilla's main square, and some have sea glimpses. The hotel has bikes for rent at €2 per four hours.

Parador de Gijón Molino Viejo

PARADOR €€€

(☎985 37 05 11; www.parador.es; Parque de Isabel la Católica; r from €110; ℗❄☜) In a building that spreads out discreetly at one end of the city's most pleasing park, 2km southeast of the centre, these are the nicest top-end digs. Rooms are modern and comfortable; those with park views cost another €24.

Hostal Manjón HOSTAL €

(☎985 35 23 78; Plaza del Marqués 1; s/d €36/50; ☺) Though basic and in a rather ugly high-rise (1st floor), this place is clean, friendly and in a handy location. Rooms are bright and big enough, and all except one overlook the marina or Palacio de Revillagigedo.

Hotel Hernán Cortés
HOTEL €€

(☎985 34 60 00; www.hotelhernancortes.es; Calle de Fernández Vallín 5; s/d from €85/110; ✳@☎) Good, large, modern rooms and efficient service at a medium-sized hotel in the heart of town.

✖ Eating

The most atmospheric area is Cimadevilla, though the newer part of the city centre also offers many options. Pedestrianised Calle de la Corrida is lined with cafes, some serving *platos combinados*.

Casa Zabala
SEAFOOD €€

(☎985 34 17 31; Calle del Vizconde de Campo Grande 2; meals €40-60; ⊗closed Sun dinner, Mon) Nestled among the many estimable *sidrerías* around Cimadevilla, Casa Zabala is good for seafood and fish of a more sophisticated ilk than you generally encounter hereabouts. The old-time looks have been maintained, and it's not everywhere you'll be served monkfish with scallops, guacamole and anchovy oil.

El Candil
ASTURIAN, BASQUE €€

(☎985 35 30 38; www.elcandilgijon.es, in Spanish; Calle Numa Guilhou 1; meals €40-60; ⊗Mon-Sat) A mix of local and Basque cooking is served up in this warm little eatery, in a neighbourhood with some of Gijón's more upmarket restaurants. Paintings of fish and copper pans decorate the yellow walls. Start with *fabas con almejas* (clams and beans) and follow with the catch of the day.

Casa Gerardo
ASTURIAN €€€

(☎985 88 77 97; Carretera AS19, Prendes; meals €45-70; ⊗1-4pm Tue-Sun, 9-11pm Fri & Sat) About 12km west of Gijón, this stone-fronted house has been serving up good local cooking since 1882. Five generations of the Morán family have refined their art to the point of snagging a Michelin star. Fare is chiefly fish and shellfish, but there's also a local *fabada* (bean-based casserole), and some creative desserts. ALSA buses make the 20-minute run (€1.30) here every two hours.

El Centenario
CIDER, SEAFOOD €

(Plaza Mayor 7; raciones €5-15; ⊗closed Mon) Lower Cimadevilla is packed with busy *sidrerías*-cum-seafood houses and this is one of the best. Among more exotic local specialities are *oricios* (sea urchins) and *centollos* (spider crabs). Cider goes for €2.50 per bottle.

Restaurante Mercante
SEAFOOD €€

(Cuesta del Cholo 2; meals €25-50) For views of the port while you munch on your fish and seafood, this is a great spot. On warm days, grab a table on the cobbled terrace, otherwise head upstairs. It's a bit of a knockabout place, full of atmosphere and always busy.

♟ Drinking & Entertainment

Normal bars shut by 1.30am Sunday to Thursday and 3.30am on weekends. Those licensed to have bands and DJs (many fall into this category) can remain open two hours more. Clubs disgorge their punters at 7.30am. The folks here really are deprived!

The *sidrerías* in Cimadevilla and around town are a fun way to start the night (and inject some food), and further up in Cimadevilla, a student/teenage music-bar scene flourishes around Plaza Corrada and down Calle de la Vicaría. The Naútico area near Playa de San Lorenzo harbours a whole assortment of locales from funky little bars to big, glittery nightclubs.

La Galana
SIDRERÍA

(Plaza Mayor 10; ⊗noon-4pm & 7pm-1.30am) A boisterous traditional *sidrería* where you can nibble on tapas to accompany the torrents of cider that bar staff pour into your glass.

Café Dam
GALLERY, MUSIC BAR

(www.cafedam.net, in Spanish; Calle de San Agustín 14; ⊗5.30pm-1am Sun-Thu, 5.30pm-3am Fri, 5.30pm-5am Sat) Amsterdam-inspired, this is a gallery, chill bar and a great den for varied live music and DJs on Friday and Saturday from 11pm.

Otto
NIGHTCLUB

(Jardines del Naútico; ⊗2am-5am Thu, 2am-7.30am Fri & Sat) Salsa-oriented club on the San Lorenzo waterfront for those who want to dance, dance, dance!

Maluka Club
UNDERGROUND CLUB

(Calle de Capua 6; ⊗midnight-3.30am Thu, midnight-5.30am Fri & Sat) The best house DJs in town, in Naútico.

A more mature crowd descends on the string of bars and clubs in the Fomento area near Playa de Poniente, ranging from salsa den La Bodeguita del Medio (www.labodeguitadelmedio-gijon.com; Calle de Rodríguez San Pedro 43; ⊗from 6pm Mon-Sat) to Ca Beleño (http://cabeleno.com; Calle de Rodríguez San Pedro 39; ⊗noon-1.30am Mon-Wed, 5pm-2.30am Thu-Sat; ☎), a jazz and Celtic-music bar.

ⓘ Information

Municipal tourist office (☎985 34 17 71, 902 013500; www.gijon.info; Espigón Central de Fomento; ☉10am-8pm) On a pier of the Puerto Deportivo; other information booths open at Playa de San Lorenzo and elsewhere in summer.

ⓘ Getting There & Around

Bus

Buses fan out across Asturias and beyond from the **ALSA bus station** (☎902 422242; Calle de Magnus Blikstad), including to Asturias airport (€6.35, 35 minutes, hourly 6am to 8pm & 10pm), Oviedo (€2.15, 30 minutes, every 10 to 15 minutes, 6.30am to 10.30pm) and Santander (€14.36 to €26.04, 2¾ to 3¾ hours, 11 daily).

Train

The main station is **Estación Cercanías** (Plaza del Humedal), also called Estación FEVE, although it is used by long-distance trains as well as *cercanías* and by Renfe as well as FEVE! Renfe also uses Estación Jovellanos, 600m west. See p477 for trains between Oviedo and Gijón.

FEVE (www.feve.es), using Estación Cercanías only, runs direct *cercanías* to Cudillero (€2.85, 1¾ hours, five to 12 daily). For most FEVE destinations you have to change at Pravia or Oviedo.

East Coast

Mostly Spanish holidaymakers seek out a summer spot on the beaches and coves along the coast east of Gijón, backed by the Picos de Europa, which rise only 15km inland.

VILLAVICIOSA & AROUND
POP (VILLAVICIOSA) 6050

Apart from the Romanesque Iglesia de Santa María, Villaviciosa's pretty little centre is mostly a child of the 18th century. Villaviciosa rivals Nava as Asturias' cider capital and at El Gaitero (www.gaitero.com; ☉10am-1.30pm &4-6.30pm Mon-Fri, 10am-1.30pm Sat, closed mid-Sep–mid-May), on the N632 about 1km from the centre, you can tour both the company's cider-brewing bodegas (admission free) and its museum (admission €1.50).

The surrounding area is sprinkled with often diminutive and ancient churches. Don't miss the Iglesia de San Salvador de Valdediós (☎985 89 23 24; admission €1.25; ☉11am-1pm & 4.30-6.30pm Tue-Sun, closed Tue-Fri afternoons Oct-Mar), about 9km southwest, off the AS267 to Pola de Siero. This triple-naved pre-Romanesque church was built in AD 893 as part of a palace complex for Alfonso III in what Asturians dubbed 'God's Valley' (though archaeologists have failed

to find any remnant beyond this simple church). ALSA buses between Oviedo and Villaviciosa (four or more each way daily) will drop you at San Pedro de Ambás, a 2km walk from the site.

Another fine Romanesque church is the Iglesia de San Juan de Amandi (☉11.30am-1.30pm & 5.30-7.30pm Tue-Sun, closed afternoons Oct-Jun), 1.5km south of Villaviciosa in Amandi.

In Villaviciosa itself, which you could easily leave off your itinerary, there are around 14 hotels and *pensiones* (small private hotels). But the most attractive lodgings in the area are at La Casona de Amandi (☎985 89 01 30; Calle de San Juan 6; www.lacasonadeamandi.com, in Spanish; s/d incl breakfast €80/90; P ☺), a 19th-century farmhouse with ample gardens, in Amandi. Rooms, all of which ooze their own character and vary in size, contain Isabelline furnishings.

Facing the sea on the western side of the Ría de Villaviciosa is the minute port of Tazones, where Carlos I supposedly first landed in Spain in 1517. It's a popular spot with a cluster of seafood restaurants and the twin small portside hotel-restaurants Hotel Imperial (☎985 89 71 16; www.hoteltazones.com) and Hotel El Pescador (☎985 89 70 77; www.hotelpescadortazones.com). In either a straightforward room will cost €55 in August. The best restaurant is the portside Restaurante Rompeolas (☎985 89 70 13; Calle de San Miguel 21; meals €30-50; ☉Wed-Mon), serving fresh local seafood – go for the monkfish and fried potatoes!

The eastern side of the estuary is covered by the broad golden sands of the 1km-long Playa de Rodiles. Surfers might catch a wave here in late summer.

ⓘ Getting There & Away

ALSA provides nine or more buses daily to Oviedo (€3.70, 35 minutes to one hour) and Ribadesella (€3.45, 30 minutes to one hour), and 14 or more to Gijón (€2.60, 45 minutes). Three or more daily buses run from Villaviciosa to Tazones (€1.35, 15 minutes).

VILLAVICIOSA TO RIBADESELLA

Colunga, 18km east of Villaviciosa, is home to the popular Museo del Jurásico de Asturias (MUJA; www.museojurasicoasturias.com; Rasa de San Telmo; adult/senior & child €6.60/4.40; ☉10.30am-2.30pm & 4-8pm, closed Mon & Tue mid-Sep–mid-Jun; ⓘ), which takes us through 185 million years of prehistory with dinosaur footprints, fossils and bones (which are plentiful along this part of the Asturian coast) and 20 giant dinosaur replicas. The pair of mating tyrannosaurus is over 12m high. Of several sandy beaches on this stretch of coast, one of the less busy in summer is 770m-long **Playa de Caravia**, backed by green slopes, near Prado.

RIBADESELLA
POP 3150

Unless you've booked in advance, it's best to stay away from Ribadesella on the first weekend after 2 August, when the place goes mad for the Descenso Internacional del Sella, a canoeing festival. Otherwise, Ribadesella is a low-key fishing town and resort. Its two halves, split by the Río Sella's estuary, are joined by a long, low bridge. The western half has a good, expansive beach, Playa de Santa Marina, while the older part of town and fishing harbour are on the eastern side.

Sights & Activities

TOP CHOICE **Cueva de Tito Bustillo** CAVE ART
(985 86 11 20; adult/senior, student & child €4/2, Wed free; 10am-5pm Wed-Sun Apr-Sep) To see some of Spain's best cave art, including superb horse paintings probably done around 13,000 to 12,000 BC, plan on visiting this World Heritage–listed cave. There's a daily limit of 360 visitors and reservations are highly advisable, by phone or online at www.tematico.asturias.es/cultura/yacimientos (in Spanish). The cave is a short distance south of the western end of the Sella bridge. The hour-long tour includes some slippery stretches, and is not recommended for children under 11. Also here are a worthwhile **interpretation centre** and a separate large cave (without art), **La Cuevona** (admission to both free; 10am-4.20pm Wed-Sun), both open all year. A replica of the Tito Bustillo cave is being built just along the road; when it opens, the real cave is likely to be closed to most visitors.

Sleeping

Hotel Ribadesella Playa HOTEL €€
(985 86 07 15; www.hotelribadesellaplaya.com; Calle de Ricardo Cangas 3; s/d incl breakfast €90/116; P) Most hotels are in the western part of town and this one fronts Playa de Santa Marina in a quaint turreted 1900s mansion. Rooms are nice and tasteful in blues and greens, with carpets and full-length mirror-wardrobes. Depending on business, it may close from about November to February.

Hotel Covadonga HOTEL €
(985 86 01 11; Calle de Manuel Caso de la Villa 6; r €55;) About 100m back from the port in the older part of town, the Covadonga is a step back in time, a little dusty but full of character and generally booked in August.

Eating

The busy waterfront *sidrerías* on the eastern side of the river are a good bet for seafood.

Casa Gaspar CIDER €€
(Calle de López Muñiz 6; dishes €6-18; Fri-Wed) If waves of fish leave you nauseous, you could opt for grilled meats, *revueltos* (scrambled-egg dishes) or other *raciones*, and cider in copious quantities, at Casa Gaspar, in the heart of the old town. On summer nights especially it gets rollickingly busy.

Casa Tista SEAFOOD €€
(meals €30-60) For the best in fresh fish (grilled or lightly baked) or shellfish (mostly sold by weight) head for Casa Tista, 5km east of Ribadesella along the AS263, just after the hamlet of Toriello. Sit inside or under the leafy pergola.

Information

Tourist office (985 86 00 38; www.ribadesella.es; Paseo Princesa Letizia; 10am-9pm, closed Mon Oct-Jun) At the eastern end of the Sella bridge.

Getting There & Away

The **bus station** (985 86 13 03; Avenida del Palacio Valdés) is about 300m south of the bridge. Destinations include Oviedo (€7, one to 1¾ hours, six to nine daily), Gijón (€5.95 to €6.87, 1½ to 1¾ hours, nine to 12 daily), Llanes (€2.40, 30 to 40 minutes, nine to 11 daily) and Santander (€8.10, 1½ or 2½ hours, two daily).

FEVE trains run at least five times daily to Llanes, Arriondas and Oviedo, and twice to Santander.

RIBADESELLA TO LLANES

More than 20 little beaches and coves await discovery between Ribadesella and Llanes by those with transport and time, and plenty of country hotels and *casas rurales* lie on or near the AS263 between the two towns. About 12km short of Llanes, **Playa de San Antolín** is a vast, unprotected beach where surfers might pick up the odd wave. A couple of kilometres further on, turn off the AS263 at Posada to reach Niembro, from which tracks access **Playa de Torimbia**, a beautiful, golden crescent where some bathers shed all, and the more family-oriented Playa de Toranda, both backed by green hills.

La Montaña Mágica (☑985 92 51 76; www.lamontanamagica.com; s/d €65/80; P) at El Allende de Vibaño, 7km inland from Posada, is a charming converted farmstead in a particularly gorgeous foothill setting with views of the Picos de Europa.

LLANES

POP 5340

Inhabited since ancient times, Llanes was for a long period an independent-minded town and whaling port with its own charter awarded by Alfonso IX of León in 1206. Today, with a small medieval core and bustling harbour, it's one of northern Spain's more popular holiday destinations – a handy base for some very pretty beaches and with the Picos de Europa close at hand.

Strewn alongside the far end of the pier like a set of children's blocks are the Cubes of Memory, painter Agustín Ibarrola's playful public artwork using the port's breakwater as his canvas. La Basílica (Plaza de Cristo Rey), the town's main, mostly Gothic church, was begun in 1240 and is worth a quick inspection if you find it open. Of the three town beaches, Playa de Toró to the east, its limpid waters dotted with jutting pillars of rock, is easily the best.

Llanes and its surrounding area have plenty of accommodation, but from June to mid-September booking is virtually essential if you want to stay in the town, especially at weekends. The spick-and-span Pensión La Guía (☑985 40 25 77; www.pensionlaguia.com; Plaza de Parres Sobrino 1; s/d €40/65; ☻☎), in a 300-year-old house just west of the river, is a charming web of dark timber beams and terracotta floors; the rooms are plain but bright, with glassed-in balconies overlooking a plaza.

Plenty of lively marisquerías (seafood eateries) and sidrerías line Calles Mayor and de Manuel Cué, so stoking up on sea critters and washing them down with cascades of cider is an easy task.

The tourist office (☑985 40 01 64; www.llanes.com; Calle de Alfonso IX; ☺10am-2pm & 5-9pm) is in La Torre, a tower left over from Llanes' 13th-century defences, and can tell you about the area's various walking routes, including the GR-E9 along the coast.

The bus station (Calle La Bolera) is east of the river. Seven daily ALSA buses stop in Llanes between Gijón (€8.28, 1¼ to two hours) and Santander (€6.20, 1¼ to two hours). At least 13 run to Oviedo (€9.35, 1¼ to 2¼ hours).

Four or more FEVE trains come here daily from Oviedo, Arriondas and Ribadesella, two of them continuing to Santander.

EAST OF LLANES

The 350m-long Playa La Ballota is a particularly attractive beach a few kilometres east of Llanes, hemmed in by green cliffs and accessible by dirt track. Part of it is for nudists. On the coast by Vidiago, search out Los Bufones de Arenillas, geiser-style jets of seawater pumped up rhythmically by the sea through a tunnel in the limestone. Playa de la Franca, further towards Cantabria, is also nice and has a summer camping ground. Two kilometres from Pimiango (past a spectacular coastal lookout), the World Heritage–listed Cueva del Pindal (☑608 175284; adult/senior & child €3/1.50; ☺10am-2pm & 3.30-4.30pm Wed-Sun) contains 31 Palaeolithic paintings and engravings of animals, including rare depictions of a mammoth and a fish. It's not in the same league as Altamira or Tito Bustillo, but its setting, in a recess in

---

WHAT'S COOKING IN ASTURIAS?

Traditional Asturian food is simple peasant fare. Best known is the fabada asturiana, a hearty bean dish jazzed up with meat and sausage. A broth version that goes lighter on the beans is pote asturiano. Cachopo (breaded veal stuffed with ham, cheese and vegetables) is a carnivore's dream, with vegetables to boot! As in Cantabria, the rivers of Asturias provide trout, salmon and eels.

The region is also famed for its cheeses, especially the powerful bluey-green queso de Cabrales from the foothills of the Picos de Europa. The basic raw material of Cabrales is untreated cow's-milk cheese, sometimes mixed with small quantities of goat's and/or sheep's milk. The cheese is matured in mountain caves and all Cabrales is strong, and odorous, stuff.

Cider is the Asturian tipple of preference, but some young red and white wine is made around Cangas del Narcea in the west.

wooded coastal cliffs, with a 16th-century chapel, a ruined Romanesque monastery and an interpretation centre also visitable close by, makes for an appealing visit. You can reserve cave visits by phone; otherwise try to get there for 10am in summer, as a maximum of eight groups of 25 are taken in each day.

West Coast

The cliffs of Cabo Peñas, 17km northeast of Avilés, mark the start of the western half of Asturias' coast as well as its most northerly and highest (almost 100m) points.

AVILÉS
POP 79,300

From the 1950s to 1980s, with mining and large-scale steel, glass and other industries in full swing, the old estuary port of Avilés was one of the most polluted cities in Europe. Since then its industries have been scaled back and the air, the Ría de Avilés estuary and the compact old town have been cleaned up, and Avilés is looking to a more tech-based future. The old centre, a stark contrast to the outlying 20th-century wasteland, makes for an attractive few hours' strolling, especially along colonnaded streets like Calles Ferrería, San Francisco and Galiana. Plaza de España is fronted by two elegant 17th-century buildings, one of which is home to the town hall.

The key symbol of Avilés' regeneration is the Centro Niemeyer (www.niemeyer center.org), an extraordinary gift from Brazilian architect Oscar Niemeyer (the creator of Brasilia), which is due to open its doors by 2011 on once-industrial land, just across the river from the city centre. This multifaceted international cultural centre, which is shaping to become a rival to Bilbao's Museo Guggenheim, had already organised numerous big-name events in Avilés even before its buildings were completed.

You'll find everything up to a five-star historic-building hotel among Avilés' 16 hotels and *pensiones*. Hotel Don Pedro (☑985 51 22 88; www.hdonpedro.com; Calle de La Fruta 22; s/d €55/65; 🅿😊❄️🛜) has attractive, comfy rooms with exposed stone or brick, and rugs on wooden floors. Central streets such as San Francisco, and Plaza de Carbayedo at the end of it, have a good assortment of eating options, but seafood

lovers should make for Salinas, a coastal suburb, and the Real Balneario de Salinas (☑985 51 86 13; www.restaurantebalneario.com; Avenida de Juan Sitges 3; meals €45-75; ⊙closed Sun dinner, Mon & early Jan–early Feb). Opened as a bathing and social centre right on the beach by King Alfonso XIII in 1916, it's a top seafood restaurant today. Ask for the day's catch and salivate! Afterwards (or before) take a walk along to the rocky cape La Peñona.

The tourist office (☑985 54 43 25; Calle de Ruiz Gómez 21; ⊙10am-8pm, closed Sat & Sun afternoon mid-Sep–Jun) can give you a nice walking-tour booklet in English.

ALSA buses run every half-hour to Gijón (€2.10, 30 minutes). There are also lots to Oviedo (€2.20, 30 to 60 minutes). FEVE trains connect with both cities too.

CUDILLERO
POP 1620

Cudillero is the most picturesque fishing village on the Asturian coast, and it knows it. The houses, painted in varying pastel shades, cascade down to a tiny port on a narrow inlet. Despite its touristy feel, Cudillero is cute and remains reasonably relaxed, even in mid-August when almost every room in town is occupied.

The main activity in town is watching the fishing boats come in (between 5pm and 8pm) and unload their catch, then sampling fish, molluscs and urchins at the *sidrerías*. You can also head along well-made paths to several lookouts, including La Garita La Atalaya perched high above the harbour. The former *lonja* (fish market) is now a minor but interesting fishing museum, Los Pixuetos y la Mar (admission €1; ⊙10.30am-1.30pm & 3-8pm Tue-Sun), in Spanish only.

🏃 Activities

The coast around here is an appealing sequence of cliffs and beaches. The nearest beach is the fine, sandy Playa de Aguilar, a 3km drive or walk east. Those to the west include Playa Concha de Artedo (4km) and the pretty Playa de San Pedro (10km).

TOP CHOICE Playa del Silencio   BEACH

Also called El Gavieiru, this is one of Spain's most beautiful beaches: a long sandy cove backed by a natural rock amphitheatre. It's 15km west of Cudillero: take the exit for Novellana and follow signs to Castañeras.

Sleeping & Eating

Accommodation in Cudillero itself is limited, especially during the low season, when some places shut down. The cheaper places are back up the main street, away from the port. Plenty of hotels, *casas de aldea* (village houses), *pensiones* and apartments are scattered around the countryside within a few kilometres. There's no shortage of eateries down towards the port. A meal with drinks is likely to cost you €25 to €35 in most places.

La Casona de Pío   HOTEL €€
(✉985 59 15 12; www.lacasonadepio.com; Calle del Ríofrío; s/d €73/92; ☺❀) Just back from the port area is this charming stone house, featuring 11 very comfortable rooms with a rustic touch, and a good restaurant.

Hotel Casa Prendes   HOTEL €€
(✉985 59 15 00; www.hotelprendes.com, in Spanish; Calle San José 4; s/d €82/88; ☺❀) This blue-fronted stop is a nicely maintained port hotel with stone-walled rooms. Rates drop dramatically outside August. The owners also rent apartments.

El Faro   SEAFOOD €€
(Calle del Ríofrío; meals €40-50; ☺closed Wed) An attractive eatery hidden one street back from the port. Stone, timber and blue decor create a welcoming atmosphere in which to dig into an *arroz caldoso* (seafood and rice stew).

Restaurante El Patrón   CIDER €
(Calle de Suárez Inclán 2; meals €30-50) Back up the road a bit from the port, this down-to-earth *sidrería* is where many locals hang out for *raciones* of seafood, cheese, sausage, ham or pâtés.

ⓘ Information

Tourist office (✉985 59 13 77; www.cudillero. org; ☺10am-9pm, closed Sun afternoon Oct-Jun) By the port, which is also the only place to park.

ⓘ Getting There & Away

From the bus station, at the top of the hill 800m from the port, three or more daily buses go to Gijón (€4.85, 1¼ hours,) and six or more to Avilés (€2.80, 45 minutes), where you can connect for Oviedo. The FEVE train station is 1km further inland: trains to Gijón (€2.85, 1¾ hours) run about hourly (fewer at weekends); for Oviedo (€2.85, 1¼ to two hours) you must usually change at Pravia.

More dishevelled than Cudillero, Luarca has a similar setting in a deep valley running down to a larger harbour full of small fishing boats. It's a base for some good nearby beaches. Find your way up to the town's **Atalaya lookout**, with its small church, surprisingly elaborate cemetery and dramatic coastal views. Luarca's mariners' guild met for centuries at the nearby Mesa de Mareantes, where the town's history is now told in colourful tiles. The **Museo del Calamar Gigante** (www.cepesma.com), a large new museum devoted to the giant squid, should have opened beside the harbour by the time you get there. It's run by Cepesma, a local marine environmentalist organisation.

⚡ Activities

Sandy, 600m-long **Playa de Cueva**, 7km east of Luarca on the old coast road (N634), is one of the best beaches in the district, with cliffs, caves, a river and occasional decent surf. Five kilometres further on, **Cabo Busto** will give you some sense of the Asturian coast's wildness as waves crash onto the jagged, rocky cliffs. **Playa de Otur** (also called Villar), 8km west of Luarca, and **Playa de Barayo**, 1km further, are good sandy beaches in pretty bays. Barayo, popular with nudists, is a protected natural reserve at the mouth of a river winding through wetlands and dunes. To reach it, turn off the N634 to Puerto de Vega and head for the village of Vigo, then follow signs (which are painted on the road) for the beach. From the car park, the beach is accessible by a well-marked 30-minute nature hike.

Sleeping & Eating

At least seven hotels and *hostales* are on or just off the central Plaza de Alfonso X, including three cheapies in Calle Crucero. Seafood eateries dot the waterfront.

Hotel Villa La Argentina   HOTEL €€
(✉985 64 01 02; www.villalaargentina.com; r €95-103; ☺closed early Jan–mid-Mar; 🅿❀) This 1899 *casa de indianos* was built by a Spaniard who got rich in Latin America. It is now a comfy 12-room hotel amid lovely gardens. It drips with belle époque elegance: antique furniture brings warmth to the rooms, with their high ceilings, chandeliers and understated decoration. It's in the Villar district about 1.5km southeast (uphill) from Luarca.

AUTOMÓVILES LUARCA

Seasoned bus travellers should know that the name of Spain's biggest bus company, ALSA, stands for Automóviles Luarca Sociedad Anónima (Luarca Automobiles Company Limited). ALSA began life as Luarca Automóviles de Viajeros back in the 1890s, when its new steam-driven coaches reduced the Luarca–Oviedo journey to just seven hours, from the 15 hours previously taken by stagecoaches.

Hotel La Colmena   HOTEL €€
(☑985 64 02 78; Calle de Uría 2; s/d €45/65; ☎) Rooms in this comfortable hotel are nicer than the rather gloomy exterior suggests. It has some nice touches, such as the dark parquet floors, high ceilings and tall windows, though the showers are a bit of a squeeze. It's on a corner of Plaza de Alfonso X.

Restaurante Sport   SEAFOOD €€
(Calle de Rivero 9; meals €30-60; ⊘closed Wed & Sun dinner) This family seafood restaurant, facing the river a few steps back from the harbour, has been pleasing customers with its local fish and shellfish since the early 1950s. Slurp a half-dozen oysters (€9) as a starter. The *rollo de bonito al estilo de Luarca* (delicious patties of northern tuna mixed with vegetables and drowned in fresh tomato sauce) is a traditional local dish. *Percebes* (goose barnacles), a northwest-Spain delicacy, are sold at €7 per 100g. Anything *'del pincho'* has been caught with a rod and line.

ⓘ Information
Tourist office (☑985 64 00 83; www.turismo luarcavaldes.com, in Spanish; Calle Caleros 11; ⊘10.30am-2pm & 4.30-8pm Mon-Sat, noon-2pm & 4.30-6.30pm Sun) Facing Plaza de Alfonso X.

ⓘ Getting There & Away
At least four daily ALSA buses run to Oviedo (€8.65, 1½ hours) and west along the coast as far as Ribadeo (€6.05, 1½ hours) in Galicia. The FEVE train station is 800m south of the town centre. Two trains run daily east to Cudillero and Oviedo, and west to Castropol and as far as Ferrol (Galicia).

COAÑA & RÍO NAVIA
The small town of Coaña lies about 4km inland of the port of Navia, west of Luarca. A couple of kilometres beyond is the **Castro de Coaña** (☑985 97 84 01; adult/child €3/1.50, Wed free; ⊘11am-2pm & 4-7pm Tue-Sun, closed afternoons Oct-Mar), one of the best-preserved Celtic settlements in northern Spain and well worth visiting.

From the *castro* (Celtic fortified village), a road snakes its way high above the cobalt-blue Río Navia, through classic Asturian countryside – meadows alternating with rocky precipices – to Lugo in Galicia, crossing some of Galicia's least-visited and wildest territory, around the town of **Fonsagrada**.

TAPIA DE CASARIEGO
POP 2370
This welcoming fishing haven makes a pleasant lunch stop if you're driving, and if you get stuck here, you'll find a half-dozen options for stopping overnight. Beaches along the next few kilometres west, such as **Playa Anguileiro**, **Playa La Paloma**, **Playa de Santa Gadea** and **Playa de Peñarronda**, all boast surfable waves, and there are several surf shops in Tapia.

CASTROPOL & AROUND
The Ría de Ribadeo marks the frontier between Asturias and Galicia. Spanning the broad mouth of this, the first of the many grand estuaries that slice into Galicia's coast, is the Puente de los Santos.

Whitewashed Castropol village (population 550), on a rise a few kilometres up the eastern side of the *ría* (estuary), is a tranquil alternative to Ribadeo, Galicia, the town on the other side. From Castropol, the N640 southwest to Lugo forms a little-travelled back route into Galicia. At the northern entrance into Castropol, **Hotel Casa Vicente** (☑985 63 50 51; Carretera General; s/d incl breakfast €37/55; P☎) has 14 pleasant rooms (eight with matchless views of the *ría*) and a good **restaurant** (meals €40-60; ⊘closed Tue) specialising in day-fresh local seafood and meat.

Like a haughty countess, the early-20th-century mansion complex **Palacete Peñalba** (☑985 63 61 25; www.hotelpalacete penalba.com; Calle Granda; d €139-161; P✳@☎) stands amid almost 18,000 sq metres of sculpted gardens studded with palms, magnolias and statues, in **Figueras del Mar**, a fishing and minor shipbuilding village 4km north of Castropol. A total of 20 luxurious, unique rooms are spread over two buildings, one of them a Modernista gem.

Inland Western Asturias

Although it's mostly inconvenient to reach unless you're driving, there's some gorgeous country in southwest Asturias. Even just passing through on alternative routes into Castilla y León can be rewarding, such as the AS228 via the 1587m Puerto Ventana, the AS227 via the beautiful 1486m Puerto de Somiedo, or the AS213 via the 1525m Puerto de Leitariegos.

SENDA DEL OSO

TOP CHOICE Senda del Oso (Path of the Bear) is the name of a 20km walking and cycling path that follows the course of a former mine railway between the villages of Tuñón and Entrago, southwest of Oviedo. It also offers the near certainty of seeing Cantabrian brown bears in semiliberty and it's a fun outing, especially with children, on its own or as part of a longer trip encompassing the Parque Natural de Somiedo. There are many *casas rurales* and village hotels in the area. A good source of further information (including on numerous other walking trails) is www.caminorealdelamesa.es.

With easy gradients, the Senda del Oso runs through increasingly spectacular valley scenery into deep, narrow canyons, with several bridges and tunnels. You can rent mountain bikes for €9/10 per half-/full day at Tuñón's Centro BTT Valle del Oso (985 76 11 77, 659 209383; www.vallesdeloso. es, in Spanish) or from Deporventura (666 557630; www.deporventura.es, in Spanish) at the Área Recreativa Buyera, beside the AS228 Tuñón–Entrago road 5km further south. They typically open on Saturday and Sunday from April to October (daily in July and August, when it's advisable to reserve bikes at least 24 hours ahead).

About 5km south of Tuñón (or a 1.1km walk from the Área Recreativa Buyera), the Senda del Oso passes the Cercado Osero, a 40,000-sq-metre compound where Paca and Tola, two female bears orphaned by a hunter in 1992, live in semiliberty. Each day around noon, except during their hibernation from about December to February, the bears are fed at a spot beside the path and you stand a very good chance of seeing them. During the mating season from about April to June you may find the sisters in another compound just below the path at the same spot, where in recent years a male has been brought from captivity in the hope they would reproduce (no baby bears

as of 2010, though not for lack of trying on Tola's part).

Fundación Oso de Asturias (www. osodeasturias.es, in Spanish) runs the Paca-Tola project. Its headquarters, the Casa del Oso (985 96 30 60; admission free; ☉10am-2pm & 4-6pm) – in Proaza, 1km south of the Área Recreativa Buyera – has exhibits in Spanish on Spanish brown bears.

Four kilometres beyond Entrago (the southern end of the Senda del Oso), the Parque de la Prehistoria (902 306600; www.parquedelaprehistoria.es; Hwy AS228, San Salvador de Alesga; adult/senior & child €5.50/3.30; ☉10.30am-2.30pm & 4-8pm, closed Mon & Tue mid-Sep–Mar, Wed Dec-Feb) provides an excellent introduction to Spanish and European cave art and is well worth the trip. It includes replicas of Asturias' World Heritage–listed Tito Bustillo and Candamo caves and France's Niaux cave, and has a very good museum-gallery that explains much of the what, when, who, how and why of Europe's Palaeolithic cave art phenomenon.

Getting There & Away

Pullmans Llaneza (985 46 58 78) runs three or four daily buses from Oviedo's ALSA bus station to Tuñón, Proaza and Entrago (one hour), terminating at San Martín, 1km beyond Entrago and 3km before the Parque de la Prehistoria.

PARQUE NATURAL DE SOMIEDO

If you fancy exploring beautiful mountain country that few foreigners know, head for this 292-sq-km protected area on the northern flank of the Cordillera Cantábrica. Composed chiefly of five valleys descending from the Cordillera's 2000m-plus heights, the park is characterised by lush woodlands, dramatic rocky mountains and high pastures dotted with *brañas,* groups of (now largely abandoned) thatched herders' shelters (*cabanas de teito*). It's also the main habitat of Spain's brown bear population. Useful websites are www.somiedo.es and www.parquenaturalsomiedo.com (in Spanish).

Each of the valleys has a number of marked walking trails, which you can find out about at the park's excellent Centro de Recepción (985 76 37 58; ☉10am-2pm & 4-9pm) in the centre of the unremarkable village of Pola de Somiedo. Pola also has a bank, ATM, supermarket and around 15 places to stay including the gorgeous Palacio de Florez Estrada (985 76 37 09, 607 752324; www.florezestrada.com, in Spanish; s/d incl breakfast €80/110; ☺closed mid-Dec–end Jan; ℗@☒), an olde-worlde riverside mansion in lovely gardens, and nearby Auriz (☑985 76 37 54, 629 130007; www.auriz.es; apt for 2/4 €100/130; ℗), with comfy, modern, two-floor, two-bedroom apartments.

One of the best (and most popular) walking areas is the Valle del Lago, whose upper reaches contain glacial lakes and high summer pastures. You must leave vehicles in Valle del Lago hamlet, a wonderful 8km drive southeast of Pola de Somiedo that winds and climbs to about 1300m. Among several places to stay and eat here is Braña La Code (☑985 76 37 76; www.lacode.es; cabins for 2/4/6 €86/134/162; ℗), with half a dozen quaint *cabanas de teito,* built with traditional materials but with considerably more comfort than the real thing (including kitchenettes and bathrooms)! La Code adjoins the agreeably rustic Camping Lagos de Somiedo (☑985 76 37 76; www.camping lagosdesomiedo.com; sites per 2 people, car & tent €20; ☺Jun-Sep; ℗), and the two share a bar-restaurant serving simple meals.

Other good walks include the La Peral-Villar de Vildas route in the upper Pigüeña valley, which takes you to one of the largest and best-preserved *brañas,* La Pornacal; and the ascent of the park's highest peak, Cornón (2194m).

One or two daily buses run between Oviedo and Pola de Somiedo (€7.55, 1¾ hours). From the Senda del Oso area, with your own wheels, you can approach by the spectacular AS265 west from San Martín, which enters the Somiedo park at the Puerto de San Lorenzo pass (1894m, often snowed under in winter) and reaches the AS227 at La Riera, 8km north of Pola de Somiedo. At the Puerto de San Lorenzo the AS265 crosses the Camín Real de la Mesa, an ancient track linking Astorga (Castilla y León) with the Asturian coast that is now a long-distance footpath, the GR-101.

PICOS DE EUROPA

These jagged, deeply fissured mountains straddling southeast Asturias, southwest Cantabria and northern Castilla y León amount to some of the finest walking country, and some of the most spectacular country of any kind, in Spain. The Picos comprise three limestone massifs: the eastern Macizo Andara, with a summit of 2444m; the western Macizo El Cornión, rising to 2596m; and the particularly rocky Macizo Central or Macizo Los Urrieles, reaching 2648m. The 647-sq-km Parque Nacional de los Picos de Europa covers all three massifs and is Spain's second-biggest national park.

Virtually deserted in winter, the area is bursting in August and you should always try to book ahead, whether you are heading for a hotel or a mountain *refugio* (shelter). July is not far behind. June and September are more tranquil and just as likely to be sunny as August.

THERE'S A BEAR IN THERE

The wild mountain area of southwest Asturias and northern Castilla y León is the main remaining bastion of the Cantabrian version of the brown bear *(oso pardo),* of which an estimated 130 remain (about 100 here and the rest in an easterly area straddling southeast Asturias, southwest Cantabria and northern Castilla y León). Loved by ecologists and loathed by farmers, this lumbering beast can reach 250kg and live 25 to 30 years. The bear population, though it has increased from 70 in the 1990s and is rarely hunted nowadays, is not out of the woods. Bears now occasionally pop up in villages and on farms, attacking honeycombs, livestock and rubbish containers. Part of the reason seems to be the reduction of blueberries in the forests – due, it is thought, to global warming – which is pushing the almost wholly vegetarian bears to look for other sources of food. Conservationists fear for the bears if they come to depend on humans for food. Unregulated tours through the Parque Natural de Somiedo in search of bears could make things worse, especially if organisers leave food out to attract the bears.

Fundación Oso Pardo (www.fundacionosopardo.org, in Spanish) runs the Centro de Información del Oso (☑985 76 34 06; ☺5.30-9.30pm Jul & Aug) in Pola de Somiedo, which organises bear-themed hikes (half-/full day adult €11/19, child €6/3) through the Somiedo park. They are not specifically aimed at spotting bears, though you might get lucky.

ℹ Information

The national park has four main information centres:

Centro de Información Casa Dago (☎985 84 86 14; Avenida de Covadonga 43, Cangas de Onís; ☺9am-2pm)

Oficina de Información Posada de Valdeón (☎987 74 05 49; El Ferial, Posada de Valdeón; ☺8am-22.30pm Mon-Fri, 9am-2pm & 4-7pm Sat & Sun, closed Sat & Sun Oct-Jun)

Centro de Visitantes Sotama (☎942 73 81 09; ☺9am-8pm Jul-Sep, 9am-6pm Oct-Jun) On the N621 in Tama, 2km north of Potes.

Centro de Visitantes Pedro Pidal (☺10am-6pm mid-Mar–early Dec) At the Lagos de Covadonga.

Other information points open at strategic points around the national park from 1 July to 15 September and during other major national holidays. Basic information on walks and accommodation is available at all these offices. Local tourist offices provide information too.

Cangas de Onís and Potes are the best places to buy outdoor equipment. Wild camping is not permitted within the national park.

Websites worth checking out include www. picosdeeuropa.com, www.reddeparquesnacionales.mma.es and, for the eastern Picos, www. liebanaypicosdeeuropa.com.

Maps

The best maps of the Picos, sold in shops in Cangas de Onís, Potes and elsewhere for €4 to €5 each, are Adrados Ediciones' *Picos de Europa* (1:80,000), *Picos de Europa Macizos Central y Oriental* (1:25,000) and *Picos de Europa Macizo Occidental* (1:25,000).

ℹ Getting There & Around

The main access towns for the Picos are Cangas de Onís in the northwest, Arenas de Cabrales in the central north and Potes in the southeast. Paved roads lead from Cangas southeast up to Covadonga, Lago de Enol and (almost) Lago de la Ercina; from Arenas south up to Poncebos then east up to Sotres and Tresviso; and from Potes west to Fuente Dé.

Trying to taste the main delights of the Picos by public transport can be frustrating. Just a few bus services – mostly summer-only – will get you into the hills from the surrounding towns. An alternative to buses is taxis.

Bus & Train

Details of the following services change from time to time, but their broad outlines are likely to be maintained.

OVIEDO TO ARRIONDAS, CANGAS DE ONÍS, ARENAS DE CABRALES & PANES From Oviedo, ALSA runs at least seven buses daily to Arriondas (€5.45, one to 1¼ hours) and Cangas de Onís (€6.10, 1½ hours). Buses to Arenas de

Picos de Europa

The mountains of the Cordillera Cantábrica, striding east–west along the southern boundaries of Cantabria and Asturias, reach their greatest, and most spectacular, heights in the subrange called the Picos de Europa.

Rising up only 15km from the Bay of Biscay, and stretching little more than 40km from east to west and 25km north to south, the Picos still encompass enough awesome mountain and gorge scenery to make them arguably the finest hill-walking country in Spain. They offer plentiful short and long outings for striders of all levels, plus lots of scope for climbers and cavers, too.

The Picos' three limestone massifs are divided by deep, north–south-running valleys, one of which, the stunning Garganta del Cares (Cares Gorge), forms the most popular mountain walk in the country. Elsewhere you can ramble past high-level lakes and across alpine meadows dotted with grazing cattle, peer over kilometre-high precipices and traverse rocky wildernesses spotting chamois skipping around dramatic crags. At the heart of the Picos rises the iconic El Naranjo de Bulnes, a huge tower of rock that presents a classic challenge for serious climbers.

Nor are the Picos just about energetic outdoor pursuits. You can enjoy them without moving a foot (almost). A couple of roads, a cable car and a funicular railway all climb to some very spectacular places.

Right
1. Garganta del Cares (Cares Gorge; p496) 2. El Naranjo de Bulnes (Pico Urriello; p497)

Cave Art

Humanity's first accomplished art was painted, drawn and engraved on the walls of European caves by Palaeolithic (Old Stone Age) hunter-gatherers between about 35,000 and 10,000 BC. The greatest concentration of this art, and its greatest artistic heights, are found in northern Spain and southern France.

Most of the images depict wild animals such as horses, deer, bison, wild boar and mammoths, and in the best examples the fluidity of the drawing, the skilful employment of colour and relief, and the lifelike animal representations, attain the level of artistic genius. Getting a close-up view of this work, created by hunter-gatherers living an arduous existence during the last Ice Age – probably as some form of homage or worship – is truly awe-inspiring.

The world-famous bison and other beasts of the Cueva de Altamira (p467; now viewable in replica form only) have been on the World Heritage list since 1985, and in 2008 a further 17 Palaeolithic art caves in northern Spain were added to the list. In addition to Altamira, any of the following will be a highlight of your trip:

» Cueva de Tito Bustillo (p482)
» Cueva de El Castillo (p463)
» Cueva de Covalanas (boxed text, p464)

Also well worth is a visit is Asturias' Parque de la Prehistoria (p487), which has three spectacular replica caves and an excellent museum.

For more on cave art check out http://cuevas.culturadecantabria.com and www.infoasturias.com.

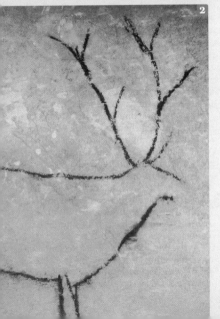

Left
1. Museo de Altamira (p467) 2. Puente Viesgo cave (p463)

WARNING

Picos weather is notoriously changeable, and mist, rain, cold and snow are common problems. When the summer sun shines, you need protection from that too. Higher up, few trails are marked and water sources are rare. Paying insufficient attention to these details has cost several lives over the years.

Cabrales, Niserias and Panes run from Arriondas (three or more daily) and Cangas (one or more). At Panes you can switch to buses running between Santander and Potes (the last one to Potes leaves Panes at 7.25pm Monday to Friday, 5.40pm other days).

Arriondas is also on the FEVE railway between Oviedo, Ribadesella, Llanes and Santander.

CANGAS DE ONÍS TO COVADONGA Three or more ALSA buses daily run from Cangas de Onís to Covadonga (€1.35, 15 minutes). The last bus down from Covadonga is at 8pm in July and August, and as early as 5.15pm at other times.

CANGAS DE ONÍS TO LAGO DE ENOL To avoid traffic chaos, the road from Covadonga to Lago de Enol is closed to private vehicles from about 8.30am to 8pm from late July to early September and for a few days during Semana Santa and some other major holidays. During these times a shuttle bus service (day ticket adult/child €7/3) operates to Covadonga and Lago de Enol from four car parks (per vehicle €2) in Cangas de Onís and along the road between there and Covadonga.

CANGAS DE ONÍS TO OSEJA DE SAJAMBRE One bus a day, Monday to Friday from early September to late June only, links these two spots (€2.75, one hour).

ARRIONDAS TO RIBADESELLA & LLANES Arriondas is linked with the two coastal towns by three or more buses (€1.60, 25 minutes to Ribadesella; €3.70, one hour to Llanes) and six FEVE trains daily.

PONCEBOS & GARGANTA DEL CARES For some weeks during the summer high season (dates vary) an ALSA bus runs in the morning from Oviedo to Cangas de Onís and Posada de Valdeón, then in the afternoon/evening from Poncebos back to Cangas and Oviedo. The idea is that you walk the 8km road along the Cares valley from Posada to Caín, then along the Garganta del Cares gorge to Poncebos, and are picked up at the end. In the same period up to three buses a day also run between Arenas de Cabrales and Poncebos.

ARENAS DE CABRALES TO LLANES Two buses daily, except Saturday, link Arenas with

Llanes (€2.95, one hour, or €5.60, two hours, depending on the route).

SANTANDER & LEÓN TO EASTERN PICOS From Santander, **Autobuses Palomera** (☎942 88 06 11) travels via San Vicente de la Barquera to Panes, Urdón, La Hermida, Lebeña and Potes (€7.40, 2½ hours), and returns, one to three times daily. A connecting service between Potes and Espinama runs once or twice daily Monday to Friday, and in July and August this is sometimes extended to Fuente Dé (about 50 minutes from Potes), with daily services.

ALSA runs one daily bus from León to Potes (€7, three hours) and on to Santander, and vice-versa.

Taxi

As well as regular taxis that stick to the better roads, such as **Taxitur** (☎608 781143) in Cangas, there are 4WD taxi services that can manage some of the mountain tracks. One of the latter is operated by Casa Cipriano in Sotres. A regular taxi costs €28 from Cangas de Onís to the Lagos de Covadonga, and about €20 from Arenas de Cabrales to Sotres, or Potes to Fuente Dé.

Western Picos

ARRIONDAS
POP 2600

Arriondas is the starting point for easy and popular canoe trips down the pretty Río Sella to various end points between Toraño and Llovio (7km to 16km). That is about the limit of the interest in this otherwise dreary provincial town.

A dozen agencies in town will rent you a canoe, paddle, life jacket and waterproof container, show you how to paddle and bring you back to Arriondas at the end. This stretch of the Sella has a few entertaining minor rapids, but it's not a serious whitewater affair, and anyone from about eight years old can enjoy the outing. The standard charge, including a picnic lunch, is €25 per person. Starting time is normally from 11am to 1pm. Bring a change of clothes. Agencies in Cangas de Onís and nearby coastal towns offer much the same deal, including transport to Arriondas and return.

The river is at its busiest on the first Saturday after 2 August, when 1500 canoes head downriver to Ribadesella, in the Descenso Internacional del Sella (www.descensodelsella.com), an international canoeing event.

Arriondas has a range of accommodation, including Hotel La Estrada (☎985 84 07 67; www.laestradahotel.com; Calle Inocencio del Valle 1; s/d incl breakfast €45/80; ☑closed

Nov-Feb; P🖂), a bright and comfortable modern place in *indiano* style. The most original place for a feed is the 'nouveau Asturian' El Corral del Indianu (☎985 84 10 72; www.elcorraldelindianu.com; Avenida de Europa 14; meals €50-70; ☺Fri-Wed Feb-Dec, closed Sun & Wed dinner). The garden is beautiful for summertime meals. Inside, the decor is startling, with bare stone and contemporary art. You might start with a *sopa de navajas, regaliz y pistachos* (razor clam soup with liquorice and pistachios) and follow with fish of the day.

CANGAS DE ONÍS
POP 4500

Good King Pelayo, after his victory at Covadonga, moved about 12km down the hill to settle the base of his nascent Asturian kingdom at Cangas in AD 722. Cangas' big moment in history lasted 70 years or so, until the capital was moved elsewhere. Its second boom time arrived in the late 20th century with the invasion of Picos de Europa tourists. In August especially, the largely modern and rather drab town is bursting with trekkers, campers and holidaymakers, many searching for rooms – a common story throughout eastern Asturias in high summer.

◉ Sights

Puente Romano   BRIDGE
The so-called Roman Bridge spanning the Río Sella, which arches like a cat in fright, was actually built in the 13th century, but is no less beautiful for the mistaken identity. From it hangs a copy of the Cruz de la Victoria, the symbol of Asturias, which resides in Oviedo's cathedral.

Capilla de Santa Cruz   CHAPEL
(Avenida Contranquil; ☺11am-2pm & 4-7pm Tue-Sat) This tiny chapel was built in 1943 to replace an 8th-century predecessor (erected by Pelayo's daughter Favila) that was destroyed during the Spanish Civil War. The 1940s rebuilders discovered that the mound the chapel sits on was an artificial one containing a megalithic tomb 6000 years old, which can now be seen beneath the chapel's floor.

Parque de la Naturaleza La Grandera ZOO
(☎985 94 00 17; adult/child €9/6; ☺11am-8pm; 🚸) On the Covadonga road at Soto de Cangas, 3km east of Cangas, La Grandera has 400 mainly European creatures, including bears, wolves, birds of prey and other Span-

ish wildlife that you would be pretty lucky to see on the trail. Trained raptors fly at noon and 5pm.

🏃 Activities

Many agencies offer a range of activities, including canoeing on the Río Sella (around €28 per person), horse riding (€15 per hour), canyoning (€36 for two to three hours) and caving (€22 to €25 for two to three hours). Cangas Aventura (☎985 84 92 61; www.cangasaventura.com, in Spanish;Avenida de Covadonga 17) is a well-established agency.

🛏 Sleeping

Cangas has loads of hotels and a few *pensiones,* many of which almost halve their high-season rates from about mid-September to June. There are plenty more places, including numerous *casas rurales,* in nearby villages. Soto de Cangas, Mestas de Con and Benia de Onís, along the road towards Arenas de Cabrales, all have several options. Most places in town can also inform you of rental apartments.

Hotel Puente Romano   HOTEL €€
(☎985 84 93 39; www.hotelimperion.com/puenteromano; Calle del Puente Romano; d €80; P🖂☺🖂) An 1880s Asturian mansion, much remodelled inside (including a glass lift and soundproofing from the road outside) but still with a good deal of original stone and wood, this is one of Cangas' more characterful hotels. Rooms are attractive and good-sized and those on the 1st and 2nd floors are bright. Some have views of the bridge. Single rates available outside August.

La Cepada   HOTEL €€€
(☎985 84 94 45; www.hotellacepada.com; Avenida Contranquil; s €135, d €140-169; P🖂@🖂) On an elevated perch 1.5km south of the centre, it's an eyesore of a building but all 20 spacious, bright, modern rooms, as well as the cafe terrace, have fine views over the town and distant Picos. Some have four-poster beds and there's a good restaurant too.

Hostal de Fermín   HOSTAL €
(☎985 94 75 62, 676 015377; www.casafermin. net, in Spanish; Paseo de Contranquil 3; d incl breakfast €60; P) In a vaguely bucolic setting 500m past the Capilla de Santa Cruz, this brick structure has bright, clean, simple rooms and a popular summer *sidrería.* Single rates are usually available. From the bus station, just walk 300m along the road to the right.

🍴 Eating

For typical *sidrerías* head to Calle de Ángel Tarano, a short street between Avenida de Covadonga and Cangas' second river, the Río Güeña.

TOP CHOICE El Molín de la Pedrera

MODERN ASTURIAN €€

(☑985 84 91 09; www.elmolin.com; Calle del Río Güeña 2; meals €30-50; ⊗closed Tue dinner, Wed; ☻) This stone-and brick-walled eatery overlooking the Río Güeña wins with both its traditional Asturian dishes like *fabada* or *tortu de maíz* (maize cakes) and more creative efforts like the brochette of monkfish, prawns and *jamón bellota* (ham from acorn-fed pigs). Many dishes are available as tapas too.

Mesón Puente Romano
ASTURIAN €

(menús del día €10-13) The terrace is just below the bridge, or you could opt for the lugubrious cellarlike dining room. The set lunch could be *fabada* (a hefty Asturian bean stew) followed by trout with ham or beef medallions in a Cabrales cheese sauce. Servings are generous.

ℹ Information

Tourist office (☑985 84 80 05; www.cangas deonis.com; Avenida de Covadonga 1; ⊗9am-9pm) On the main street.

ℹ Getting There & Away

The bus station is in the Barrio La Pedrera on the northern side of the Río Güeña, linked by a footbridge to the town centre.

COVADONGA

The importance of Covadonga, 12km southeast of Cangas de Onís, lies in what it represents rather than what it is. Somewhere hereabouts, in approximately AD 722, the Muslims received their first defeat in Spain at the hands of King Pelayo, who set up the Asturian kingdom, which is considered to be the beginning of the Reconquista – a mere 800-year project.

The place is an object of pilgrimage, for in a cave here, the Santa Cueva, the Virgin supposedly appeared to Pelayo's warriors before the battle. On weekends and in summer the queues at the cave, now with a chapel installed, are matched only by the line of cars crawling past towards the Lagos de Covadonga. The Fuente de Siete Caños spring, by the pool below the cave, is supposed to ensure marriage within one year to women who drink from it.

Landslides destroyed much of Covadonga in the 19th century and the main church here now, the Basílica de Covadonga, is a neo-Romanesque affair built between 1877 and 1901. About 100m from the basilica is the Museo de Covadonga (adult/child €3/2; ⊗10.30am-2pm & 4-7pm), filled with all sorts of items, mostly donations by the illustrious faithful.

LAGOS DE COVADONGA

Don't let summer traffic queues deter you from continuing the 10km uphill from Covadonga to these two beautiful little lakes. Most of the day trippers don't get past patting a few cows' noses near the lakes, so walking here is as nice as anywhere else in the Picos. At peak visitor periods the road from Covadonga to the lakes is closed to private vehicles, but a shuttle bus runs from Cangas de Onís – see p492 for details.

Lago de Enol is the first lake you reach, with the main car park just past it. It's linked to Lago de la Ercina, 1km away, not only by the paved road but also by a footpath via the Centro de Visitantes Pedro Pidal (⊗10am-6pm mid-Mar–early Dec), which has displays on Picos flora and fauna. There are rustic restaurants near both lakes, closed in winter. Bathing in the lakes is banned.

When mist descends, the lakes, surrounded by the green pasture and bald rock that characterise this part of the Picos, take on an eerie appearance.

Walks from the Lakes

Two marked circuit walks, the *itinerario corto* (about one hour) and the *itinerario largo* (PR-PNPE2; 2½ hours), take in the two lakes, the visitors centre and old mine, the Minas de Buferrera. Two other relatively easy trails will take you a bit further afield. The first (PR-PNPE4) leads about 5km southeast, with an ascent of 600m, from Lago de la Ercina to the Vega de Arío, where the Refugio Vega de Arío (Refugio Marqués de Villaviciosa; ☑649 721971; dm €10) has sleeping space for 40 people, and is attended with meal service from June to October. The reward for about 2½ hours' effort in getting there is magnificent views across the Garganta del Cares (Cares Gorge) to the Macizo Central of the Picos.

The alternative walk (PR-PNPE5) takes you roughly south from Lago de Enol to the Refugio de Vegarredonda (☑985 92 29 52; www.vegarredonda.com; dm €10) and on to the Mirador de Ordiales, a lookout point over a 1km sheer drop into the Valle de Angón. It's about a 3½-hour walk (one way) – relatively easy along a mule track as far as the *refugio,* then a little more challenging on up to the mirador. Drivers can cut about 40 minutes off the walk by driving as far as the Pandecarmen car park, 2km from Lago de Enol. The 68-place *refugio* is attended, with meal service, from March to November.

DESFILADERO DE LOS BEYOS
The N625 south from Cangas de Onís follows the Río Sella upstream through one of the most extraordinary defiles in Europe. The road through the Desfiladero de los Beyos gorge is a remarkable feat of engineering. Towards the southern end of the defile, you cross from Asturias into Castilla y León.

Hotel Puente Vidosa (☎985 94 47 35; www.puentevidosa.com, in Spanish; s/d €65/79; P☒), gloriously perched on a bend in the Sella by a waterfall, is 20km south of Cangas. The converted stone house contains 19 lovely rustic rooms with gorge(ous) views and wood panelling. A pool, sauna and Jacuzzi add to the value.

SOTO DE SAJAMBRE
POP 70 / ELEV 930M
Just inside Castilla y León and 4km north off the N625, this pretty village by a freshwater stream is a great base for hikers. Walks from Soto de Sajambre include La Senda del Arcediano (GR-201), a very scenic trip of five or six hours north to Amieva, manageable by most walkers, and a more difficult trail east to Posada de Valdeón. There is a handful of sleeping options here.

Central Picos

A star attraction of the Picos' central massif is the gorge that divides it from the western Macizo El Cornión. The popular Garganta del Cares (Cares Gorge) trail can be busy in summer, but the walk is worthwhile. This part of the Picos also has plenty of less heavily tramped paths and climbing challenges once you've 'done' the Cares. Arenas de Cabrales and Poncebos are obvious bases.

ARENAS DE CABRALES
POP 830
Arenas de Cabrales lies at the confluence of Ríos Cares and Casaño, 30km east of Cangas de Onís. The busy main road is lined with hotels, restaurants and bars, and just

PICOS WILDLIFE

Although some wolves and the odd brown bear still survive in the Picos, you're unlikely to see either. Far more common is the *rebeco* (chamois). Around 6000 of them skip around the rocks and steep slopes. Deer, badgers, wild boar, squirrels and martens, in various quantities, inhabit wooded areas.

A variety of eagles, hawks and other raptors soar in the Picos' skies. Keep your eyes peeled for the majestic *águila real* (golden eagle) and the huge scavenging *buitre leonado* (griffon vulture). Choughs, with their unmistakable caws, accompany walkers at high altitudes.

off it lies a little tangle of quiet squares and back lanes.

On the second-last or last Sunday in August, the **Certamen del Queso** (Cheese Festival) is held in this home of the fine smelly Cabrales cheese. Thousands come to enjoy the exhibitions, processions, cheese-making demonstrations and tastings. At other times you can learn all about Cabrales cheese at Arenas' **Cueva El Cares** (☎985 84 67 02; adult/child €4.50/3; ⊙10am-2pm & 4-8pm, closed Mon-Fri Oct-Mar), a cheese-cave museum on the Poncebos road.

Arenas has a camping ground and about 10 other accommodation options, as well as holiday apartments.

Hotel Rural El Torrejón (☎985 84 64 11; www.eltorrejon.com, in Spanish; r incl breakfast €57; P☏), located in a bright-red country house, welcomes the weary traveller with tastefully decorated rooms in a rural style with lots of fragrant wood. It's good value and the setting is idyllic, beside the Río Casaño, a couple of minutes' walk from the village centre.

Hostal Naturaleza (☎985 84 64 87; d €40; P), about 800m from the centre of Arenas along the road to Poncebos, is a quiet little house with a series of smallish but well-scrubbed rooms. The owner, Fina, also has a couple of houses for rent in Arenas.

Camping Naranjo de Bulnes (☎985 84 65 78; sites per 2 people, car & tent €24; ⊙closed Nov-mid-Mar) is a large and efficiently run camping ground within a chestnut grove, 1.5km east of the town centre on the Panes road.

TOP CHOICE **Restaurante Cares** (menús €14-15; ⊘closed Mon Oct-May), beside the Poncebos junction on the main road, is one of the best restaurants for miles around. Happily for those who don't always want to eat their main meal at lunchtime, it does a great-value *menú de noche* as well as a *menú del día*, plus *platos combinados* and à la carte fish and meat dishes. Dig into a hearty *cachopo* and finish with *delicias de limón* (between lemon mousse and yoghurt).

Buses stop next to the **tourist office** (☑985 84 64 84; www.cabrales.org; ⊘10am-2pm & 4-8pm Tue-Sun, closed Oct-Jun), a kiosk in the middle of town at the junction of the Poncebos road.

GARGANTA DEL CARES

Nine kilometres of well-maintained path (the PR-PNPE3) high above the Río Cares between Poncebos and Caín constitute, perhaps unfortunately, the most popular mountain walk in Spain; in August the experience is akin to London's Oxford St on a Saturday morning. If you do arrive with the holiday rush, try not to be put off – the walk is a spectacular excursion between two of the Picos' three massifs. If you're feeling fit (or need to get back to your car), it's quite possible to walk the whole 9km and return as a (somewhat tiring) day's outing; it takes about seven hours plus stops. A number of agencies in Arriondas, Cangas de Onís and Potes will transport you to either end of the walk and pick you up at the other end, usually for €35 to €50 per person.

Poncebos & Funicular de Bulnes

Poncebos, a straggle of buildings at the northern end of the gorge, set amid already spectacular scenery, is exclusively dedicated to Picos tourism. A road turning uphill just above the Pensión Garganta del Cares leads 1.5km up to the hamlet of **Camarmeña**, where there's a lookout with views to El Naranjo de Bulnes in the Macizo Central.

A few metres up the Sotres road, just below Poncebos, is the lower end of the **Funicular de Bulnes** (☑985 84 68 00; adult/child return €19.70/5.90; ⊘10am-8pm Easter & Jul-Sep, 10am-12.30pm & 2-6pm rest of year), a tunnel railway that climbs 2km inside the mountain to the hamlet of Bulnes, which is inaccessible by road. The funicular makes the seven-minute trip every half-hour in either direction.

At Poncebos, the eight-room **Hotel Garganta del Cares** (☑985 84 64 63; www.hotelgargantadelcares.com, in Spanish; s/d incl breakfast €38/62; ⊘closed early Dec–end Jan; **P**🐾🖥) offers the beds and meals (*menú del día* €9.50) that are the closest to the Garganta del Cares trail. Rooms are plain and well cared-for. The classier **Hotel Mirador de Cabrales** (☑985 84 66 73; www.arceahoteles.com; s/d incl breakfast €92/110; ⊘closed Oct-Feb; **P**🐾) stands next door.

Garganta del Cares Walk

By doing the walk from north to south, you save the best till last. Follow the 'Ruta de Cares' sign pointing uphill about 700m along the road from the top end of Poncebos. The beginning involves a steady climb upwards in the wide and mostly bare early stages of the gorge. After about 3km you'll reach some abandoned houses. A little further and you're over the highest point of the walk. You should encounter a couple of drink stands along the way (the stuff is transported by horse).

As you approach the regional boundary with Castilla y León, the gorge becomes narrower and its walls thick with vegetation, creating greater contrast with the alpine heights above. The last stages of the walk are possibly the prettiest, and as you descend nearer the valley floor, you pass through a series of low, wet tunnels to emerge at the end of the gorge among the meadows of Caín.

Caín

If you're coming from the south, the trailhead of the walk is at Caín, where the rickety (and picturesque) road from Posada de Valdeón comes to an end.

Casa Cuevas (☑987 74 05 00; www.casacuevas.es, in Spanish; d €40) has basic but decent rooms. There are at least two fancier places to stay, plus a couple of bars and restaurants. More lodgings are in the villages south of Caín, including Cordiñanes and the rather drab Posada de Valdeón.

SOTRES

A side road heads up 11km from Poncebos to Sotres, the highest village in the Picos at 1045m and the starting point for a number of good walks. There are half a dozen places to stay, most with their own restaurants.

Casa Cipriano (☑985 94 50 24; www.casacipriano.com, in Spanish; s/d €30/50; 🖥) is a favourite haunt of mountain aficionados. Aside from the 14 simple but cheerful rooms, the staff offers a professional mountain-and-caving guide service and simple restaurant.

Hotel Peña Castil (☑985 94 50 80; www.hotel.penacastil.com, in Spanish; s/d incl breakfast €40/60; ☎) offers 10 impeccable if smallish rooms in a renovated stone house. The rooms have graciously tiled floors, some wood panelling and fine showers, and some have perky balconies.

Walks around Sotres

A popular route goes east to the village of **Tresviso** and on to **Urdón**, on the Potes–Panes road. As far as Tresviso (10km) it's a paved road, but the final 6km is a dramatic walking trail, the **Ruta de Tresviso** (PR-PNPE30), snaking 850m down to the Desfiladero de la Hermida gorge. Doing this in the upward direction, starting from Urdón, is at least as popular. An alternative track (part of the PR-PNPE28) winds off the Sotres–Tresviso road and down via the hamlet of Beges to La Hermida, also in the Desfiladero de la Hermida.

Many walkers head west from Sotres to the **Collado de Pandébano**, about 90 minutes' walk away up on the far side of the Duje valley. From Pandébano it's possible to see the 2519m rock finger called **El Naranjo de Bulnes** (Pico Urriello), an emblem of the Picos de Europa and a classic challenge for climbers.

Few walkers can resist the temptation to get even closer to El Naranjo. It's possible to walk in around three hours, along the PR-PNPE21 trail, from Pandébano to the **Vega de Urriellu**, at the foot of the northwestern face of the mountain, where the 96-bunk **Refugio Vega de Urriellu** (☑985 92 52 00; www.picuurriellu.com; dm €10) is attended, with meal service, year-round.

Otherwise, you can descend for about an hour west to **Bulnes**. Bulnes is divided into two parts, the upper Barrio del Castillo and the lower La Villa. All amenities are in La Villa, including an attractive six-room *casa rural*, **La Casa del Chiflón** (☑985 84 59 43; www.casadelchiflon.com, in Spanish; s/d/tr/q incl breakfast €45/60/75/90; ☉closed Dec-Feb) and **Bar Bulnes** (☑985 84 59 34; raciones €4-11; ☉10am-8pm Easter & Jul-Sep, 10am-6pm rest of year, closed Mon-Fri 5 Jan–2 weeks before Easter), with good home cooking. You can also get to Bulnes from Poncebos by walking about two hours uphill, or taking the Funicular de Bulnes.

Eastern Picos

The northern gateway to the eastern part of the Picos is the humdrum town of **Panes**, where the AS114 from Cangas and Arenas meets the N621 running from the coast south to Potes. The N621 south from Panes follows the Río Deva and enters the impressive **Desfiladero de la Hermida** gorge. You cross into Cantabria here at Urdón, at the bottom end of the Ruta de Tresviso path, about 2km before the hamlet of **La Hermida**. There's not much at La Hermida but the bubbling Río Deva, the Picos looming to the west and a couple of *pensiones*.

LEBEÑA

About 8.5km south of La Hermida is a spot that warrants visiting. A kilometre east of the N621 stands the fascinating little **Iglesia de Santa María de Lebeña** (admission €1; ☉10am-1.30pm & 4.30-7.30pm Tue-Sun), built in the 9th or 10th century. The horseshoe arches in the church are a telltale sign of its Mozarabic style – rarely seen this far north in Spain. The floral motifs on the columns are Visigothic, while below the main *retablo* (altarpiece) stands a Celtic stone engraving. They say the yew tree outside (recently reduced to a sad stump) was planted 1000 years ago.

POTES

POP 1520 / ELEV 291M

Overrun in peak periods, but with some charm in the old centre (restored in attractive traditional stone and slate after considerable damage during the civil war), Potes is a popular staging post on the southeastern edge of the Picos, with the Macizo Andara rising close at hand. The Río Quiviesa, which is spanned by the medieval San Cayetano bridge, joins the Río Deva at the heart of the village. Beside the bridge, the squat **Torre del Infantado** was built as a defensive tower in the 15th century and is now the town hall, having long served as a prison. A short distance up the Deva, the 14th-century **Iglesia de San Vicente**, deconsecrated in the 19th century, is a nice example of rustic Gothic architecture.

🛏 Sleeping, Eating & Drinking

Potes' dozen hotels, *hostales* and *pensiones* are mostly simple, straightforward places, clustered fairly close to one another.

TOP CHOICE **Casa Cayo** HOSTAL €
(☎942 73 01 50; www.casacayo.com, in Spanish; Calle Cántabra 6; s/d €35/50; ✉📶) This is the pick of the bunch, with helpful service and attractive, comfy, wood-beamed rooms. Open the timber window shutters early in the morning to listen to the nearby burbling river. You can eat well in the excellent restaurant for about €20. Try the *cocido lebaniego completo* (€14), a feast that starts with unlimited noodle soup followed by a plate loaded with meat, sausage, chickpeas, potato, cabbage and spinach.

Tasca Cántabra RURAL CANTABRIAN €€
(Calle Cimavilla; meals €20-35; ⊙Thu-Tue) For a cheerful meal try this old-town eatery; try local fave *cocido lebaniego* or the speciality, *chorizo de jabalí* (wild-boar suasage).

Casa Camacho BAR €
(Plaza Llano; ⊙9am-midnight) For a taste of real local flavour duck into this shabby but friendly establishment for a shot or two of the *orujo* – a liquor made from grape pressings (similar to Italian grappa) that is found throughout northwest Spain and is something of a Potes speciality. The family here makes several varieties, including one flavoured with honey from their own bees.

ℹ Information

Tourist office (☎942 73 07 87; Plaza de la Serna; ⊙10am-2pm & 4-7pm) Shares a building with the bus station on the western side of town. Inquire here about the various adventure outfits operating from Potes and offering everything from horse riding and 4WD excursions to canoeing and canyoning.

Centro de Visitantes Sotama (☎942 73 81 09; ⊙9am-8pm Jul-Sep, 9am-6pm Oct-Jun) On the N621 in Tama, 2km north of Potes, with interesting displays on Picos de Europa geology, mining, rivers and wildlife, Romanesque architecture and Beato de Liébana.

MONASTERIO DE SANTO TORIBIO DE LIÉBANA

The Valle de Liébana, of which Potes is in a sense the 'capital', lies between the southeast side of the Picos de Europa and the main spine of the Cordillera Cantábrica. Christian refugees from Muslim-occupied Spain fled to this frontline valley in the 8th century. The settlers brought with them the Lígnum Crucis, purportedly the single biggest chunk of Christ's cross, which had supposedly been transported from Jerusalem by Bishop Toribio of Astorga in the 4th century. The holy relic has been housed ever since in the **Santo Toribio Monastery** (admission free; ⊙10am-1pm & 4-7pm Tue-Sun), 3km west of Potes (signposted off the Fuente Dé road).

The relic, which according to tradition features the hole made by the nail that passed through Christ's left hand, is an extraordinary magnet for the faithful. It's kept inside a crucifix of gold-plated silver, which is housed in a lavish 18th-century baroque chapel off the monastery's austere Gothic church (dating from 1256).

Head of the monastery in the latter half of the 8th century was Beato de Liébana, who won fame in medieval Europe for his beautifully illustrated *Commentary on the Apocalypse*. Copies of this tome were distributed throughout Europe and came to be known as Beatos. Around 25 survive today, scattered across Europe, but the original was lost.

About 500m past the monastery is the tiny **Ermita de San Miguel**, a chapel with great valley views.

POTES TO FUENTE DÉ

The 23km CA185 from Potes to Fuente Dé is a beautiful trip, with several places to stay (including three camping grounds) along the way. At **San Pelayo**, 5km from Potes (the turn-off is actually signposted 'Lon'), **Posada San Pelayo** (☎942 73 32 10; www. posadasanpelayo.com, in Spanish; s/d €65/81; ℗✉📶) is a friendly, family-run *casa rural*, of recent construction but in traditional country style, with spacious rooms in cheerful colours, ample, comfortable common areas and a lovely garden with great mountain views. **Cosgaya**, 13km southwest of Potes, is home to the majestic twin stone townhouses of the **Hotel del Oso** (☎942 73 30 18; www.hoteldeloso.com; s/d €66/83; ℗▧), which face each other across the Río Deva and the road. Spacious rooms with timber floors and finishings are very inviting, and the restaurant is one of the area's best.

The last stop of any significance before Fuente Dé is **Espinama**, from which a 4WD track leads about 7km north and uphill to the Hotel Áliva and on to Sotres. The village has a choice of decent places to stay, all with restaurants. Family-run **Hostal Remoña** (☎942 73 66 05; s/d €23/45; ✉@📶; ⊙closed Wed Oct-Jun) has large rooms, some with balconies overlooking the little Río Nevandi, and serves up venison as well as beef from the owners' own farm.

POTES TO POSADA DE VALDEÓN

Drivers will be rewarded by a trip from Potes around to the southern approaches to the Picos. Take the N621 (direction Riaño) south of Potes and you are soon on a narrow road winding through the verdant Valle de Liébana. After about 8km, you reach the cute crossroads hamlet of La Vega de Liébana (ALSA buses call in here), with a handful of places to stay. Branch 12km south to Cucayo, a lovely trip that rises to about 900m. Cucayo is the end of the road. Around you are scarred mountain peaks and green fields below. Stay at the marvellous Posada de Cucayo (☎942 73 62 46; www.laposadadecucayo.com; d incl breakfast €56-65; P), where nine of the 10 spacious, tasteful doubles enjoy sweeping views. The owners will also have you making bread, jams and cheese and milking cows if you truly want a taste of rural bliss!

Back in La Vega, the road southwest quickly penetrates a gorge before rising to the often fog-bound Puerto de San Glorio pass (1609m). It then drops down quickly on the Castilian side of the frontier. At Portilla de la Reina, take the narrow and still pretty country lane across the Puerto de Pandetrave northwest to Posada de Valdeón, where you are at the southern gateway to the Picos.

FUENTE DÉ & THE TELEFÉRICO

At 1078m, Fuente Dé lies at the foot of the stark southern wall of the Macizo Central. In four minutes the dramatic Teleférico (Cable Car) de Fuente Dé (☎942 73 66 10; www.cantur.com; adult/child return €15/5; ☺9am-8pm Easter & Jul–mid-Sep, 10am-6pm rest of year, closed early Jan–end Feb) whisks people 753m up to the top of that wall, from where walkers and climbers can make their way deeper into the central massif.

Be warned that during the high season (especially August) you can wait for hours at the bottom to get a seat. Coming down, you simply join the queue and wait – a little tedious if the queue is long.

🏃 Activities

It's a walk of 3.5km from the top of the *teleférico* to the Hotel Áliva. From the hotel, two 4WD tracks descend into the valley that separates the central massif from its eastern cousin. The first winds its way some 7km south down to Espinama, while the other will take you north to Sotres via Vegas de Sotres.

Other possibilities for the suitably prepared include making your way across the massif to El Naranjo de Bulnes or climbing Peña Vieja (2613m). These require proper equipment and experience – Peña Vieja has claimed more climbers' lives than any other mountain in the Picos. Less exacting is the PR-PNPE23, a route of about 5.5km northwest from the *teleférico,* passing below Peña Vieja by marked trails to the foot of the Horcados Rojos crags, with an ascent of 500m. It takes about 4½ hours there and back.

🛏 Sleeping & Eating

Fuente Dé has a camping ground and two hotels including an ugly *parador* (luxurious state-owned hotel), both of which offer 4WD trips into the mountains.

Hotel Rebeco HOTEL €€
(☎942 73 66 01; www.hotelrebeco.com, in Spanish; s/d incl breakfast €54/70; P☺🐾) This handsome stone lodge is the better-value option (over the *parador*) at Fuente Dé. Many of the 30 rooms have mountain views and 11 (most with rear view) include loft levels that are suitable for kids. It has a good, reasonably priced restaurant and you can't help but admire owner Conchi Cuesta's tapestries!

Hotel Áliva HOTEL €€
(☎942 73 09 99; www.cantur.com; s/d €47/75; ☺Jun–mid-Oct) Set 1700m high, this modern 27-room hotel features a cafe as well as a sun deck. It's 3.5km by 4WD track from the top of the *teleférico:* if you're staying, they'll drive you for free.

Santiago de Compostela & Galicia

Best Places to Eat

» A Curtidoría (p508)

» Adega O Bebedeiro
(p516)

» Restaurante Ó Dezaseis
(p508)

» O Fragón (p523)

» Casa Verdún (p529)

Best Places to Stay

» Parador de Santo Estevo
(p539)

» Casa de Trillo (p523)

» Hospedería Cordobelas
(p520)

» Pazo A Capitana (p526)

» Casa-Hotel As Artes
(p507)

Why Go?

Galicia's spiritual, cultural and official capital is Santiago de Compostela, the destination of tens of thousands of pilgrims who set out every year on the famous Camino de Santiago. This magical medieval city still has a palpable aura of the middle ages.

But Galicia, a unique region with its own language and distinctive culture, is much more than Santiago. The wild coastline is frayed up and down its 1200km by majestic *rías* (inlets or estuaries) and strung with cliffs, sandy beaches, islands and fishing ports that bring in indisputably the best seafood in Spain. Then there's the interior, a labyrinth of valleys and hills, green as Ireland and dotted with half-forgotten villages, twisting country lanes and aged stone monasteries. Galicia isn't all lost in the past either. Buzzing cities like A Coruña, Vigo and Lugo are contemporary cultural and commercial hubs with nocturnal lives as heady as anywhere in the country.

When to Go?
Santiago de Compostela

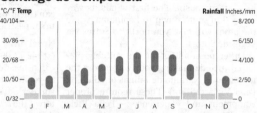

June & September No peak-season crowds, lower room prices and (hopefully) decent weather

2nd Weekend in July Dance a jig at the Festival Ortigueira, Spain's biggest Celtic music festival

24 July Spectacular fireworks end Santiago de Compostela's celebration for the Día de Santiago

History

Early Galicians built many dolmens (megalithic tombs) and later, in the Iron Age, *castros* (protected settlements of circular stone huts). Several examples of both types of these ancient monuments have been excavated and can be visited today. Most Galicians say the *castro*-builders were Celts, though sceptics claim Celtic origins are exaggerations of Galicia's romantic nationalists.

The Romans united 'Gallaecia' in the first century BC, founding cities like Lucus Augusti (Lugo). The region was ruled by the Germanic Suevi for most of the 5th and 6th centuries AD, before the Visigoths asserted themselves. After the Muslim invasion of 711, Galicia fell under the Christian

Santiago de Compostela & Galicia Highlights

1 Savour the unique atmosphere and history of Santiago de Compostela's **cathedral** (p503)

2 Gaze towards America at Spain's 'Land's End', **Cabo Fisterra** (p522)

3 Feast on freshly caught seafood, anywhere near the coast

4 Seek out remote beaches on rugged coasts like **Area de Trece** (p524) on the Costa da Morte or the Rías Altas' **Praia de Picón** (p521)

5 Get lost in the beautiful arcaded streets of **Santiago de Compostela** (p502)

6 Stand atop southern Europe's highest sea-cliffs at the **Garita de Herbeira** (p520)

7 Sail out to the pristine beaches and walking trails of the spectacular, traffic-free **Illas Cíes** (p534)

8 Follow the Camino de Santiago down from the heights of **O Cebreiro** to the monastery at **Samos** (p540)

GALICIA WEBSITES

Galicia's official tourism website, www.turgalicia.es, available in nine languages, is an encyclopedic reference for visitors. Among other things it offers an online booking service for many of the region's attractive rural accommodation options – as does www.turismoruralgalicia.com.

kingdom of Asturias within a few decades. It remained within the Asturian kingdom and its successors, León and Castilla, thereafter, apart from a couple of brief periods as an independent kingdom in the 10th and 11th centuries.

The big event in the area's medieval history was the 'rediscovery' of the grave of Santiago Apóstol (St James the Apostle) in 813, at what would become Santiago de Compostela. The site grew into a rallying symbol for the Christian Reconquista of Spain, and pilgrims from all over Europe began trekking to Santiago, which came to rival Rome and even Jerusalem as a pilgrimage site. For more, see p37.

But by the time the Reconquista was completed in 1492, Galicia had become an impoverished backwater in which Spain's centralist-minded Reyes Católicos (Catholic Monarchs), Isabel and Fernando, had already begun to supplant the local tongue and traditions with Castilian methods and language. The Rexurdimento, an awakening of Galician national consciousness, did not surface until late in the 19th century, and then suffered a 40-year interruption during the Franco era. In the 19th and 20th centuries, hundreds of thousands of impoverished Galicians departed on transatlantic ships in search of a better life in Latin America.

Things have looked up since democracy returned to Spain in the 1970s. Galicia today is an important fishing, shipbuilding and agricultural centre. It has more ports than any other region of the European Union, and a measure of industry, commerce and (mainly domestic) tourism, though pockets of poverty remain, especially in the deep countryside. Galicia's extremely indented coastline also, incidentally, serves as a major entry point into Europe for South American cocaine.

Thanks to their distinctive culture and history of isolation from the centre, most Galicians today see their region as somewhat apart from the rest of Spain, though only a tiny minority actually want independence.

Climate
You can't get away from the fact that Galicia is wet. Swept by one rainy front after another, blowing in from the Atlantic, Galicia has twice as much rain overall as the Spanish national average. June to August are the least rainy months, but even in these months you've got to be prepared for rainy days.

Language
Long suppressed during the Franco years (strange, since Franco was born in Galicia), though widely spoken and seen now, the Galician language (Galego or, in Castilian, Gallego) is a Romance language that is close to Portuguese and slightly less so to Castilian. In this chapter we use the names you're likely to encounter during your travels. By and large, this means Galician spellings for towns, villages and geographical features.

Santiago de Compostela
POP 79,000 / ELEV 260M

Locals say the arcaded, stone streets of Santiago de Compostela are at their most beautiful in the rain, when the old city glistens. Most would agree, however, that it's hard to catch the Galician capital in a bad pose. Whether you're wandering the pedestrianised medieval streets of the old city, nibbling on tapas in the taverns along Rúa do Franco, or gazing down at the rooftops from atop the cathedral, Santiago seduces.

The faithful believe that Santiago Apóstol (St James the Apostle) preached in Galicia and, after his death in Palestine, was brought back by stone boat and buried here. The tomb was supposedly rediscovered in 813 by a religious hermit who followed a guiding star (hence, it's thought, 'Compostela' – from the Latin *campus stellae*, field of the star). The grave became a rallying symbol for Christian Spain, the Asturian king Alfonso II turned up to have a church erected above the holy remains, pilgrims began flocking to it and the rest is history. For more on the Camino de Santiago pilgrim trail, see p37.

The biggest numbers of pilgrims and tourists hit the city in July and August, but Santiago has a festive atmosphere throughout the warmer half of the year. Early-bird pilgrims start arriving in serious numbers in April. If you'd like to enjoy the place less than jam-packed, May, June and September are good months to come.

Praza de Galicia marks the boundary between the old town and the Ensanche (Extension), the 20th-century shopping and residential area are to its south.

History

By the 11th century the pilgrimage was becoming a major European phenomenon. The Romanesque cathedral was begun in 1075. Bishop Gelmírez obtained archbishopric status for Santiago in 1100 and added numerous churches in the 12th century, when enthusiasm for the pilgrimage peaked, bringing a flood of funds into the city. The following centuries were marked by squabbling between rival nobles, dampened down by Isabel and Fernando after the Reconquista. After misguidedly siding with the Carlists in the 1830s, Santiago slipped into the background. Only since the 1980s, as capital of the autonomous region of Galicia and a rediscovered tourist and pilgrimage site, has the city been revitalised. Each year some 150,000 pilgrims make the journey here.

◉ Sights

Among Santiago's greatest pleasures are simply wandering its arcaded streets and drifting in and out of the tapas bars along the Rúas Franco and Raíña.

Catedral de Santiago de Compostela
CATHEDRAL

(Praza do Obradoiro; www.catedraldesantiago.es; ⏰7am-9pm) The grand heart of Santiago, the cathedral soars above the city centre in a splendid jumble of moss-covered spires and statues. Though Galicia's grandest monument was built piecemeal through the centuries, its beauty is only enhanced by the mix of Romanesque, baroque and Gothic flourishes. What you see today is actually the fourth church to stand on this spot. The bulk of it was built between 1075 and 1211, in Romanesque style, with a traditional Latin-cross layout and three naves. Much of the 'bunting' (the domes, statues and endless trimmings) came later. The cathedral's artistic and architectural riches fill guidebooks of their own (a worthwhile investment at around €7 if you want to delve into the detail of this amazing building).

Outside the Catedral
The main entrance is via the lavish staircase and facade on the Praza do Obradoiro, but owing to restoration work inside, this is likely to be closed most of the time until 2012. Until then, you will probably enter through the south door on Praza das Praterías (beneath the only facade that conserves its original Romanesque structure).

The baroque Obradoiro facade was erected in the 18th century partly to protect the cathedral's original entrance.

Inside the Catedral
The artistically unparalleled **Pórtico de la Gloria** (Galician: Porta da Gloria) features 200 Romanesque sculptures by Maestro Mateo, who was placed in charge of the cathedral-building program in the late 12th century by Fernando II of León. You may find the Pórtico partly shrouded in scaffolding until restoration works are completed.

A throned Christ is the main figure in the portico's central archway, as depicted in Revelations, surrounded by the four Evangelists plus angels and symbols of Jesus' passion. In an arc above are the 24 musicians said

THE BOTAFUMEIRO

The use of a large censer or *botafumeiro* (loosely 'smoke spitter') in the Catedral de Santiago dates from the 13th century, at which time covering up the odours of road-weary pilgrims who slept and cooked inside was more than a mere ceremonial act. The *botafumeiro* in use today was made in the 1850s, weighs in at 62kg and reaches a speed of 68km/h as it swings high over the centre of the cathedral. It misses hitting the north and south transept vaults by only 51cm while reaching an angle of 82 degrees. The *botafumeiro* has fallen only twice, in 1499 and 1622, and is a perfect, gigantic pendulum conceived three centuries before pendulum physics was officially worked out.

These days it only swings on certain feast days or if a pilgrimage group donates €300. When not in action, it's kept in the Museo da Catedral.

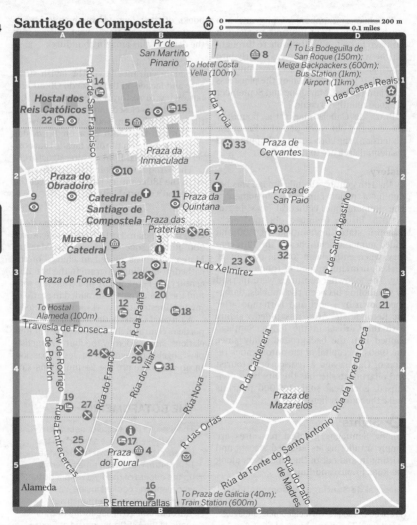

in the Apocalypse to sit around the heavenly throne. Below Christ's feet is Santiago, and below him Hercules (holding open the mouths of two lions). On the other side of the central pillar is Maestro Mateo. For centuries, tradition called for visitors to bump heads with the maestro to acquire some of his genius. But countless knocks led to Mateo's notably flat nose, and he is now blocked off behind a metal barrier. Another tradition called for a brief prayer as visitors placed their fingers in the five holes above Hercules' head, created by the repetition of this very act by millions of faithful over the centuries. It too is now blocked off.

The remarkably lifelike figures on the right side of the portico are apostles, while those to the left represent Old Testament prophets. The only female statue depicts Queen Esther, the inspiration, according to local lore, for Galicia's iconic *tetilla* cheese ('titty cheese'). Supposedly, her stone breasts were originally much larger. When local leaders deemed them inappropriate and filed them down, townspeople responded by creating the cone-shaped *tetilla* cheese in Esther's honour.

Santiago de Compostela

Towards the far (west) end of the cathedral's main nave, to the right of the Churrigueresque **Altar Mayor** (Main Altar), a small staircase leads up, above the altar, to a 13th-century **statue of Santiago**, which the faithful queue up to embrace. From here you emerge on the left side, then descend some steps to contemplate what you are assured is Santiago's **tomb**. Behind the Altar Mayor is the **Puerta Santa** (Holy Door), which opens onto the Praza da Quintana and is cracked open only in holy years (next in 2021).

A special pilgrims' Mass is celebrated at noon daily. Other high-altar Masses take place at 10am, 6pm and (except Sunday) 7.30pm.

Tours

For an unforgettable bird's-eye view of the city, take the **cathedral rooftop tour** (✆981 55 29 85; www.santiagoturismo.com; per person €10; ◷10am-2pm & 4-8pm), starting in the Pazo de Xelmírez to the left of the cathedral's Obradoiro facade. This is also the only way to visit the **Pazo de Xelmírez** itself, dating from 1120, where the main banquet hall is adorned with exquisite little wall busts depicting feasters, musicians,

kings and jugglers. The tours are popular so it's worth going beforehand to reserve a time slot.

Museo da Catedral　　　　　MUSEUM
(Cathedral Museum; www.catedraldesantiago.es; Praza do Obradoiro; adult/child €5/free; ◷10am-2pm & 4-8pm, closed Sun afternoon) The many-roomed Museo da Catedral, entered to the right of the cathedral's Obradoiro facade, spreads over four floors and includes the cathedral's large 16th-century, Gothic/plateresque cloister. You'll see Maestro Mateo's original stone choir (destroyed in 1603 but recently pieced back together), rooms of tapestries including a set from designs by Goya, an impressive collection of religious art (including the *botafumeiro,* in the second-floor library), the lavishly decorated 18th-century *sala capitular* (chapter house), and, off the cloister, the treasury and the Panteón de Reyes, which contains tombs of kings of medieval León. The museum ticket also covers the crypt beneath the Pórtico de la Gloria, entered at the foot of the Obradoiro facade steps, which is notable for its 12th-century architecture and rich decoration.

The cathedral is surrounded by handsome plazas that invite you to wander through them. The grand Praza do Obradoiro (Workshop Plaza), to which most arriving Camino pilgrims instinctively find their way, earned its name from the stonemasons' workshops set up here while the cathedral was being built. At its northern end, the Renaissance Hostal dos Reis Católicos was built in the early 16th century by order of the Catholic Monarchs, Isabel and Fernando, as a refuge for pilgrims and the sick and a symbol of the crown's power in this ecclesiastical city. Today it shelters well-off travellers instead, as a luxurious *parador*. Along the western side of the square is the elegant 18th-century Pazo de Raxoi, now the city hall.

South of the cathedral, stop in cafe-lined Praza de Fonseca to peek into the Colexio de Fonseca (admission free; ⊘11am-2pm & 5-8.30pm Tue-Sat, 11am-2pm Sun), with a beautiful Renaissance courtyard and exhibition gallery; it was the original seat of Santiago's university (founded in 1495).

Around the corner, Praza das Praterías (Silversmiths' Square) is marked with the Fuente de los Caballos (1829) fountain, with the cathedral's south facade at the top of the steps. Curiously, the Casa do Cabildo, facing it on the lower side of the square, is no more than a 3m-deep facade, erected in 1758 to embellish the plaza.

Following the cathedral walls, you enter Praza da Quintana. Across the plaza is the long, stark wall of the Mosteiro de San Paio de Antealtares, founded by Alfonso II for Benedictine monks to look after St James' relics; it was converted to a nunnery in 1499. Climbing the steps at the top of the plaza you'll find the entrance to the convent. Inside, the Museo de Arte Sacra (Vía Sacra 5; admission €1.50; ⊘10.30am-1.30pm & 4-7pm Mon-Sat Apr-Dec) contains the original altar raised over the Santiago relics. The church itself is of relatively simple design, with the exception of its main altar, a frenzy of gilded baroque. You can stop by in the evening to hear the nuns singing vespers (⊘8pm Mon-Fri, 7.30pm Sat & Sun).

Keep following the cathedral walls northwards to reach Praza da Inmaculada, known for its *azabache* (jet) shops – souvenirs made from this hard, black mineral have been a Santiago craft since the middle ages. This is also where pilgrims arriving in Santiago via the Camino Francés (French Route) first set eyes on the cathedral. Opposite looms the huge Benedictine Mosteiro de San Martiño Pinario, an austere baroque seminary that also functions as a *hospedería* (budget hotel). Galicia Dixital (http://galicia digital.xunta.es; admission free; ⊘10.30am-2pm & 5-8.30pm Mon-Sat; ⊞) occupies the left flank of the monastery and is full of interactive audiovisual fun like a simulated roller-coaster ride over Santiago's rooftops and an underwater adventure off the Galician coast.

FREE | Museo do Pobo Galego   FOLK MUSEUM
(Galician Folk Museum; www.museodo pobo.es, in Galician & Spanish; Rúa San Domingos de Bonaval; ⊘10am-2pm & 4-8pm Tue-Sat, 11am-2pm Sun) A short walk northeast of the old town, the former Convento de San Domingo de Bonaval houses exhibits on Galician life and arts ranging from the fishing industry to music and traditional costumes.

Alameda   PARK
The largest of several verdant parks just outside the city's medieval core is the Alameda, which sprawls southwest from the old town in a tidy grid of tree-lined promenades, with some peerless views of the cathedral towers.

Ciudad de la Cultura   CULTURAL CENTRE
(City of Culture; www.cidadedacultura.org) This vast and ambitious 21st-century cultural centre is being constructed atop Monte Gaiás, about 1.5km southeast of the old city, to the designs of American Peter Eisenman. The first sections, the Library and Archive of Galicia, were expected to open in late 2010, with the Museum of Galicia following in 2011.

FREE | Museo das Peregrinacións
PILGRIMAGE MUSEUM (www.mdperegrina cions.com; Rúa de San Miguel 4; ⊘10am-8pm Tue-Fri, 10.30am-1.30pm & 5-8pm Sat, 10.30am-1.30pm Sun) Eight rooms explore the Camino de Santiago phenomenon over the centuries.

Fundación Eugenio Granell   ART MUSEUM
(www.fundacion-granell.org; Praza do Toural; adult/senior & child €2/free; ⊘11am-2pm & 4-9pm Tue-Sat, 11am-2pm Sun) Includes much of Galician surrealist Granell's own body of work as well as his collections of surrealist and ethnic art.

⟡ Tours

Compostur   WALKING TOURS
(☏902 190160; www.santiagoreservas.com) The city's official tour operator offers a range

of two-hour walking tours in English and/or Spanish that give a fascinating glimpse into the stories behind Santiago's old stone walls. Get information on current offerings at the city's tourist office, where the walks start. A general old-town tour in English (adult/child €10/5) leaves at 1pm Tuesday and Saturday from June to October and 1pm Sunday in other months. Other options include a gastronomic tour, a convents tour and a nocturnal tour.

✦ Festivals & Events

July is Santiago's busiest month. The **Día de Santiago** (Feast of Saint James) is on 25 July, which is simultaneously Galicia's 'national' day. Two weeks of festivities surround the festival, which culminates in a spectacular fireworks display on 24 July.

🛏 Sleeping

From cheap *hostales* to chic hotels, Santiago has hundreds of lodgings at all price levels. In summer, especially July and August, the best-value places may fill up weeks ahead. Book in advance if you can. High season tends to last longer here than elsewhere in Galicia, so you'll be lucky to get any discounts between Easter and October.

Casa-Hotel As Artes　　　HOTEL €€
(✆981 55 52 54; www.asartes.com; Travesía de Dos Puertas 2; r €102-130; ☎) On a quiet street close to the cathedral, As Artes' lovely stone-walled rooms exude a romantic rustic air. Breakfast (€10.80) is served in a homey dining room overlooking the street.

Parador Hostal dos Reis Católicos
　　　　　　　　　　　　　　HOTEL €€€
(✆981 58 22 00; www.parador.es; Praza do Obradoiro 1; r incl breakfast from €190; P✲@☎) Opened in 1509, and rubbing shoulders with the cathedral, this palatial *parador* is Santiago's top hotel. Even if you don't book one of its regal rooms, stop in for tea at the elegant cafe.

Hotel Costa Vella　　　HOTEL €€
(✆981 56 95 30; www.costavella.com; Rúa da Porta da Pena 17; s €59, d €81-97; ⊜✲☎) The tranquil, thoughtfully designed rooms (some with galleries) and a lovely garden cafe (open 8am to 11pm) make this a wonderful option. Even if you don't stay, it's an ideal spot for breakfast or coffee.

Hotel Airas Nunes　　　HOTEL €€
(✆981 56 93 50; www.pousadasdecompostela.com; Rúa do Vilar 17; d €97; ✲@☎) For laid-back elegance, this is a great choice, though it can be hard to get a room. The spiralling granite staircase leads to 10 appealing rooms with garnet-and-green colour schemes, buttery yellow walls, warm wooden furniture and wood-beam ceilings.

Meiga Backpackers　　　HOSTEL €
(✆981 57 08 46; www.meiga-backpackers.es; Rúa dos Basquiños 67; dm incl breakfast €18; ⊜@☎) Clean, colourful, friendly, and handily placed between the bus station and city centre, Meiga has spacious bunk dorms, a kitchen, a garden and no curfew. It's the only place you need consider if you're on the budget backpacking trail – unless you want a private room, in which case, **Meiga Backpackers Pension** (✆981 59 64 01; www.meiga-backpackers.es; Rúa da República del Salvador 32; d €36-42; ⊜☎), in the new town, could fit the bill nicely.

Hostal Alameda　　　HOSTAL €
(✆981 58 81 00; www.alameda32.com in Spanish; Rúa de San Clemente 32; s/d €41/54, with shared bathroom €25/34; ⊜☎) Great value, with good-sized, recently decorated rooms, this *hostal*, run by a friendly family, sits opposite the Alameda park on the edge of the old town.

Barbantes Libredón　　　HOSTAL €€
(✆981 57 65 20; www.libredonbarbantes.com; Praza de Fonseca; s/d €48/68; ☎) This is actually two *hostales* under the same management on opposite sides of the same lively little square, a stone's throw from the cathedral. Rooms in both are simple but bright and fresh-feeling. Those in the Barbantes, on the south side of the square, are mostly newer and have a touch more contemporary pizzazz – and in many cases small balconies with cathedral views. Bathrooms are a bit cramped and there are no lifts. Reception for both is in the Libredón, on the north side of the plaza.

Hotel Rúa Villar　　　HOTEL €€€
(✆981 51 98 58; www.hotelruavillar.com; Rúa do Vilar 8-10; s €97, d €130-162; ✲☎) Rúa Villar is in an artfully restored 18th-century building whose focal point is a central sitting area capped with a splendid stained-glass skylight. Service is attentive and the 16 rooms, with soft beds and original elements like stone walls, are cosy and inviting, if not spacious. Interesting original modern art adorns the walls, and the classy **restaurant** (mains €19-34) specialises in daily fresh seafood.

Hotel Entrecercas HOTEL €€
(☎981 57 11 51; www.hotelentrecercas.es, in Spanish; Ruela Entrecercas 11; s/d incl breakfast €70/98; ☻✳@☏) A homey, family-run place, the Entrecercas inhabits a restored 600-year-old house near the Praza da Galicia. Exposed stone walls and flowered curtains lend the comfy rooms a rustic touch.

Hostal Suso HOSTAL €
(☎981 58 66 11; Rúa do Vilar 65; r €50; ☏) Stacked above a cafe, this family-run *hostal* is one of the best deals in town. Immaculate, recently wallpapered rooms with spic-and-span bathrooms have firm beds and modern wood furniture.

Hostal Mapoula HOSTAL €
(☎981 58 01 24; www.mapoula.com; Rúa Entremurallas 10; s/d €36/49; ☻@☏) Rooms at this stylish and friendly 3rd-floor *hostal* are reasonably sized and decorated with flair in a sunny orange-and-rust-red colour scheme. The bathrooms are a tight squeeze but clean.

Hospedería Seminario Mayor MONASTERY €€
(☎981 56 02 82; www.sanmartinpinario.eu; Praza da Inmaculada 5; s/d incl breakfast €52/70; ☻) Rooms are basic, but have recently been upgraded with wrought-iron furnishings – this establishment does offer the rare experience of staying inside a Benedictine monastery. With over 100 rooms it often has vacancies when other places don't.

Hotel Virxe da Cerca HOTEL €€€
(☎981 56 93 50; www.pousadasdecompostela. com; Rúa da Virxe da Cerca 27; s €97-108, d €130-146; P✳@☏) Backed by tranquil gardens where breakfast is served, this elegant hotel at the edge of the old quarter was an 18th-century Jesuit residence.

✗ Eating

Central Santiago is packed with eateries, especially along Rúa do Franco (named for the French, not the dictator) and the parallel Rúa da Raíña. Most do their job pretty well. Rúa da Troia is another fruitful grazing ground, with half a dozen places serving inexpensive seafood and grilled meat indoors and outdoors. Don't leave Santiago without trying a *tarta de Santiago,* an iconic almond cake.

A Curtidoría CREATIVE GALICIAN €€
(☎981 55 43 42; Rúa da Conga 2-3; meals €25-50; ☻closed dinner Sun; ♪) Understatedly styl-

ish and a favourite lunch spot with locals, A Curtidoría overlooks four streets from its two dining rooms and specialises in inventive but uncomplicated fish, meat and rice dishes like crab-stuffed peppers, grilled turbot with glazed vegies or entrecote with wild mushroom sauce. It offers a number of vegetarian dishes and a menu for celiacs, and the good *menú del día* (€12) is also available Monday to Wednesday evenings.

Restaurante Ó Dezaseis GALICIAN €
(☎981 56 48 80; Rúa de San Pedro 16; raciones & mains €6-14, menú €12; closed Sun) Wood-beam ceilings and exposed stone walls give an invitingly rustic air to this popular cellar tavern just beyond the northeast edge of the old town. The mixed crowd tucks into specialities like *caldeirada de rape y rodaballo* (monkfish and turbot casserole) and *lacón con grelos* (ham with greens).

Mesón Ó 42 RACIONES €€
(☎981 58 10 09; Rúa do Franco 42; raciones €5-18) With a solid list of favourite local *raciones* like *empanadas* (pies), shellfish, octopus and tortillas, as well as fish, meat and rice dishes, this popular place stands out from the crowd with its well-prepared food and good service.

Casa Rosalía TAPAS, RACIONES €
(Rúa do Franco 10; raciones €4-16) With a more contemporary style than other nearby bars, Rosalía draws crowds for tapas and *raciones* like scallop-and-monkfish brochette or Galician cheese salad. A selection of tempting snacks (€1.10-€1.60) ranges along the bar.

O Beiro TAPAS, RACIONES €€
(Rúa da Raíña 3; raciones €8-20; closed Mon) The house speciality is *tablas* (trays) of delectable cheeses and sausages, but you can also get other *raciones* and tapas at this friendly two-storey tavern and *vinoteca* (wine bar).

El Pasaje SEAFOOD €€
(☎981 55 70 81; Rúa do Franco 54; meals €30-60; closed dinner Sun) For a special meal, this classic spot offers melt-in-your-mouth Galician fish, shellfish and steaks. A series of intimate dining rooms scattered over several floors ensures a tranquil setting.

La Bodeguilla de San Roque ECLECTIC €
(☎981 56 43 79; Rúa de San Roque 13; raciones & mains €4-14; ☻9am-12.30am, closed 4-7pm Sun) Just northeast of the old town, this busy two-storey restaurant serves an eclectic range of excellent dishes ranging from

CRACKIN' GOOD SHELLFISH

Galician seafood is plentiful, fresh, and may well be the best you have ever tasted. The region's signature dish is *pulpo á galega*, tender slides of octopus tentacle sprinkled with olive oil and paprika (*pulpo á feira* has chunks of potato added). Mollusc mavens will enjoy the variety of *ameixas* (clams) and *mexillons* (mussels). Special shellfish of the region include *vieiras* and *zamburiñas* (types of scallop), *berberechos* (cockles), *navajas* (razor clams) and the tiny, much-prized goose barnacles known as *percebes*, which bear a curious resemblance to fingernails. Other delicacies include various crabs, from little *nécoras* and *santiaguiños* to *centollos* (spider crabs) and the great big *buey del mar* ('ox of the sea'). Also keep an eye open for the *bogavante* or *lubrigante,* a large, lobster-like creature with two enormous claws. Shellfish are often priced by weight and the most expensive can go for over €100 per kg: around 300g is a typical main-course-size serving.

Amid the crustacean fever, don't forget that many Galician restaurants also serve market-fresh fish and some top-class meat from the lush inland pastures.

---

salads and scrambled eggs to Galician veal fillet or plates of cheeses, sausages or ham.

O Gato Negro TAPAS, RACIONES €
(Rúa da Raíña; raciones €3-25; ☺) Marked by a green door and a black cat, this old-town haunt serves plates of seafood, ham, cheeses or peppers on five sought-after tables.

La Crepe CREPERIE €
(Praza da Quintana 1; crepes & salads €7-10; ✍) A dozen different salads and a wide range of sweet and savoury crepes make this spot a hit with vegetarians, though meaty options are served as well.

🍷 Drinking & Entertainment
The old town is packed with bars and cafes. On summer evenings every streetside nook is filled with people relaxing over tapas and beer or wine. For cafes, head for Praza da Quintana and Rúa do Vilar. The liveliest bar area lies east of Praza da Quintana, especially along Rúa de San Paio de Antealtares. Things get lively after dinner, especially Thursday to Sunday, when Santiago's large student population comes out in full force. In the new town south of Praza de Galicia, people gravitate towards clubs along Rúas da República Arxentina and Nova de Abaixo.

A busy agenda of concerts, theatre and exhibitions goes on year-round. For details, pick up *Culturall* or find the cultural guide on www.santiagoturismo.com.

TOP CHOICE **A Casa das Crechas** CELTIC MUSIC
(www.casadascrechas.com in Galician; Vía Sacra 3; ☺from 6pm) There's no better place for Celtic music. Head to the tightly packed downstairs bar from 10.30pm most

Tuesdays, Wednesdays and Thursdays for jam sessions and concerts.

Borriquita de Belém JAZZ BAR
(Rúa de San Paio de Antealtares 22; ☺from 8pm) Just south of Praza de San Paio, this inviting, tightly packed little bar serves mojitos and wine from the barrel and has live jazz or flamenco from around 10.30pm some nights, most often Monday and Wednesday.

Café Casino CLASSIC CAFE
(Rúa do Vilar 35; ☺10am-1am; ☺🛜) This long, wood-panelled hall with art nouveau carvings is the most elegant spot for a cake and coffee, tea or alcoholic beverage. Piano players entertain in the evenings.

Ultramarinos LIVE MUSIC
(www.ultramarinos.org in Galician; Rúa das Casa Reais 34; ☺9pm-4am; 🛜) A great two-level venue with a chill cafe upstairs and dancing and music (frequently live, of almost all types you can think of) downstairs.

Modus Vivendi MUSIC BAR
(Praza de Feixóo 1; ☺6.30pm-3am or later) A Santiago classic, this atmospheric pub in the stables of an 18th-century mansion attracts all types and hosts occasional DJs, live music and exhibitions. It's reckoned to be Galicia's oldest 'pub' (since 1972).

🔒 Shopping
The old town is littered with enticing boutiques and other shops purveying jewellery (including pieces made from Santiago's traditional jet), books, original art, Galician wine and *tetilla* cheese, and Galician craft specialities such as Camariñas lace and Sargadelos pottery. Great for a browse.

Santiago de Compostela

Built on the belief that the apostle St James the Greater (Santiago in Spanish) lies buried here, Santiago de Compostela became one of medieval Christendom's three most important pilgrimage centres, along with Jerusalem and Rome.

The faithful flocked from all over Europe along the various Caminos de Santiago (Santiago Routes) for contact with the sacred relics and the salvation this could bring. In his guise as Santiago Matamoros (St James the Moor-Slayer), the saint became the patron and inspiration of the Christian Reconquista of Spain. A magnificent stone cathedral was built over the burial site, and the flood of money the pilgrims brought to Santiago helped create a magnificent stone city around the cathedral.

The pilgrimage faded in importance after the 13th century but the cathedral and city remained, a centre of learning and Catholic culture in a remote corner of northwest Spain. With the amazing revival of the Camino since the 1990s, Santiago is today again abuzz with the chatter of many tongues, while its ancient stone streets and buildings still retain their medieval aura. It's also a 21st-century university town, with an equally buzzing contemporary cultural and entertainment scene. There's nowhere quite like it.

ESSENTIAL SANTIAGO

» **Cathedral** (p503)
» **Praza do Obradoiro** (p506)
» **Museo da Catedral** (p505)
» **Feasting on Galician seafood** (p509)
» **Celtic Music at A Casa das Crechas** (p509)

Right
1. Praza das Praterías (p506) 2. Pórtico de la Gloria, Catedral de Santiago de Compostela (p503)

The Coast of Galicia

Deeply indented by over a dozen long estuaries, Galicia's coastline twists and turns for 1200km over a straight-line distance of little more than 350km. Along the way it encompasses hundreds of mainly sandy beaches, awesome cliffs, dozens of islands and a succession of fishing ports large and tiny.

Cabo Fisterra

1 Spain's 'Land's End' (p522), this dramatic, lighthouse-topped, rocky cape juts into the Atlantic on the beautiful, remote Costa da Morte. There's nothing between here and America except ocean.

Illas Cíes

2 Part of Galicia's Islas Atlánticas national park, the three Cíes islands (p534) in the mouth of the Ría de Vigo combine spectacular cliffs and lookouts with pristine beaches. They're traffic-free and the only accommodation is a summer campground.

Torre de Hércules

3 A Coruña's lighthouse (p513) has an 18th-century shell but the interior is pure Roman, placed on a windy headland in the 1st centuryAD to mark the edge of the civilised world for legions sailing north to Brittany.

Praia A Lanzada

4 Dune-backed A Lanzada (p526) sweeps a magnificent 2.3km along the ocean side of an isthmus near O Grove. It's understandably one of the most popular of Galicia's 772 beaches. Even in August, many of the others are empty by comparison.

Fruits of the Sea

5 Galicia's ocean-fresh seafood (p509), from *pulpo á gallega* (tender, spicy octopus slices) to melt-in-mouth *lubiña* (sea bass), is a reason in itself to come here. In any coastal town or village (and many inland) you can get a meal to remember.

Left
1. Scallops 2. View from Torre de Hércules (p513)

ℹ Information

Biblioteca Pública Ánxel Casal (Avenida de Xoan XXIII; internet free; ⊙8.30am-9pm Mon-Fri, 10am-2pm Sat) Just north of the old town: take your passport number. Free.

City tourist office (☑981 55 51 29; www.santiagoturismo.com; Rúa do Vilar 63; ⊙9am-9pm)

Cyber Nova 50 (Rúa Nova 50; internet per hr €2; ⊙9am-midnight)

Hospital Clínico Universitario (☑981 95 00 00; http://chusantiago.sergas.es; Travesa da Choupana)

Pilgrims' Reception Office (Oficina de Acogida de Peregrinos; ☑981 56 88 46; www.peregrinossantiago.es; Rúa do Vilar 1; ⊙9am-8pm) People who have covered at least the last 100km of the Camino de Santiago on foot or horseback, or the last 200km by bicycle, with spiritual or religious motives, can obtain their 'Compostela' certificate to prove it here.

Policía Nacional (☑981 55 11 00; Avenida de Rodrigo de Padrón 3)

Post office (Rúa das Orfas 17; ⊙8.30am-8.30pm Mon-Fri, 9.30am-2pm Sat)

Regional tourist office (☑981 58 40 81, 902 332010; www.turgalicia.es; Rúa do Vilar 30-32; ⊙10am-8pm Mon-Fri, 11am-2pm & 5-7pm Sat, 11am-2pm Sun)

ℹ Getting There & Away

Air

The **Lavacolla airport** (☑981 54 75 00; www.aena.es) is 11km east of the city.

Air Europa (www.aireuropa.com) Madrid, Canary Islands

Aer Lingus (www.aerlingus.com) Dublin

Flights Iberia (www.iberia.com) Madrid and Barcelona daily; also Bilbao, Geneva, Seville, Valencia

Ryanair (www.ryanair.com) Madrid and Barcelona daily; London (Stansted), Málaga, Frankfurt and Rome several days a week

Spanair (www.spanair.es) Barcelona, Madrid

Vueling Airlines (www.vueling.com) Barcelona, Málaga, Zürich

Bus

The **bus station** (☑981 54 24 16; www.tussa.org in Spanish; Praza de Camilo Díaz Baliño) is about a 20-minute walk northeast of the centre.

Castromil-Monbus runs to many places in Galicia, with services to A Coruña (€5.95 to €6.95, 50 to 90 minutes, 17 or more daily), Pontevedra (€5.80, 50 to 90 minutes, 10 or more daily), Ourense (€10.35, two hours, five or more daily) and elsewhere. Empresa Freire heads to Lugo (€8.25, two hours, five or more daily).

ℹ GALICIA BUS & TRAIN COMPANIES

Contact details for the main bus companies serving Galician cities and towns:

» **ALSA** (☑902 422242; www.alsa.es)

» **Arriva** (☑902 277482; www.arriva.es)

» **Autocares Vázquez** (☑981 14 84 70; www.autocaresvazquez.net in Spanish)

» **Autores & Avanza** (www.avanzabus.com in Spanish)

» **Castromil-Monbus** (☑902 292900; www.monbus.es in Spanish)

» **Empresa Freire** (☑981 58 81 11; www.empresafreire.com)

» **Rialsa** (☑981 37 20 01; www.rialsa.com in Spanish)

Most trains are run by **Renfe** (☑902 240202; www.renfe.com), but a second company, **FEVE** (www.feve.es), operates a line running east from Ferrol to Ribadeo and on across Asturias and Cantabria to Bilbao.

All the above websites give timetable information and in some cases online ticketing.

ALSA operates further afield, including services at least once daily to Oviedo (€26 to €43, 4¾ to 5½ hours), Santander (€44, 10 hours), San Sebastián (€58, 12½ to 13½ hours), León (€23 to €27, six hours) and Madrid (€42 to €60, eight to 9¾ hours). ALSA also has direct daily services to Porto (€29, three hours) and Lisbon (€50, seven to nine hours) and (with transfers) to places like Paris, London and Amsterdam.

Further daily services head to the Costa da Morte and Rías Baixas.

Train

The **train station** (Avenida de Lugo) is about a 15-minute walk south from the old town. Regional trains run roughly every hour up and down the coast, linking Santiago with Vigo (€7.50 to €8.90, 1½ to two hours), Pontevedra (€4.90 to €5.90, 50 to 70 minutes) and A Coruña (€4.90 to €5.90, 40 minutes). A daytime Talgo and an overnight Trenhotel head to Madrid (€49.50, nine hours).

ℹ Getting Around

Private vehicles are barred from the old town from about 10am to dusk for most of the summer, so you have to park around its fringes, where several underground car parks generally charge around €16 per 24 hours.

Santiago is walkable, although it's a bit of a hike from the train and bus stations to the centre of town.

Up to 36 Empresa Freire buses (€1.80) run daily between Lavacolla airport and Rúa do Doutor Teixeiro, in the new town southwest of Praza de Galicia, via the bus station. Taxis charge around €18.

City bus 6 runs every 20 to 30 minutes from Rúa do Hórreo near the train station to Rúa da Virxe da Cerca on the eastern edge of the old town. Bus 5 runs every 15 to 30 minutes between the bus station, Rúa da Virxe da Cerca and Praza de Galicia. Tickets cost €0.90.

A CORUÑA & THE RÍAS ALTAS

In few places do land and sea meet in such abrupt beauty. The striking scenery of the Rías Altas, with their untamed beaches, towering sea cliffs and powerful waves, is certainly more dramatic than the landscapes of the Rías Baixas. Combine that with the allure of cultured, maritime A Coruña and the lively little resort hubs along the eastern and northern shores, and you'll be wondering why more visitors don't journey north.

A Coruña

POP 222,000

A Coruña (Castilian: La Coruña) is a port city and a beachy hot spot; a busy commercial centre and a cultural enclave; a historic city and a buzzing modern metropolis with a thriving nightlife – all in all, it's an intriguing place to wander as one distinctive neighbourhood gives way rapidly to another.

Britain looms large on A Coruña's horizon. In 1588 the ill-fated Spanish Armada weighed anchor here, and the following year Sir Francis Drake tried to occupy the city but was seen off by María Pita, a heroine whose name lives on in the city's main square. In 1809, during the Peninsular War, a British army sent to help Spain resist the invading French was forced into a Dunkirk-style evacuation here, losing its leader Sir John Moore in the Battle of Elviña just south of the city. In the 19th and 20th centuries A Coruña's port was the gateway through which hundreds of thousands of Galician emigrants left for new lives in the Americas. Today this is Galicia's wealthiest city, home to, among other things, the world's biggest textile company (by turnover), Inditex.

Downtown A Coruña lies along a northeast-pointing isthmus which is straddled by the port and the main beaches. A mushroom-shaped headland extends 2km north from the isthmus, with a wonderful broad pedestrian walkway circling its entire perimeter.

◉ Sights & Activities

Torre de Hércules ROMAN LIGHTHOUSE
(www.torredeherculesacoruna.com; Avenida de Navarra; adult/senior & child €2.50/1.50, Mon free; ⊙10am-8.45pm Sun-Thu, 10am-11.45pm Fri & Sat, earlier closing Sep-Jun) A city symbol that achieved Unesco World Heritage listing in 2009, the 'Tower of Hercules' sits near the windy northern tip of the headland. Legend attributes its construction to one of the labours of Hercules, but it was actually the Romans who built a lighthouse here in the 1st century AD – a beacon on the edge of the civilised world. The 50m-high, square stone tower we see today was erected in 1790, but inside, apart from the staircase and cupola, it is original Roman. Climb the 234 steps to the top for views of the city, coast and the intriguing sculptures of the surrounding Parque Escultórico (Sculpture Park).

To get here, take bus 3 or 3A from Paseo de la Dársena near Plaza de María Pita, or the Paseo Marítimo tram.

Ciudad Vieja OLD CITY
Shady plazas, charming old churches and hilly cobbled lanes fill A Coruña's compact old town, making it an enjoyable place for a stroll. To get here, cross the stately Plaza de María Pita, rimmed with cafes and dominated by the early-20th-century Ayuntamiento (city hall) and a monument to the eponymous heroine.

The 12th-century Iglesia de Santiago (Calle de Santiago), with three Romanesque apses backing on to pretty little Plaza de la Constitución, is the city's oldest church. A short walk through the labyrinth brings you to the Xardín de San Carlos, where General Sir John Moore (a British general killed in the nearby Battle of Elviña in 1809) lies buried. Charles Wolfe's famous poem on Moore's burial is inscribed on a plaque. Across the street, the Museo Militar (☏981 20 53 00; Plaza de Carlos I; admission free;

A Coruña

300 m
0.2 miles

Ensenada del Orzán

Playa del Orzán

To Aquarium Finisterrae (1.4km); Torre de Hércules (2.5km)

To Playa de Riazor (300m); Discoteca Playa Club (1km)

To Hotel Zenit Coruña (300m)

Av de Pedro Barrié de la Maza

Ría Nueva

Calle Cancela

Calle de la Cordelería

13

Calle de General Mola

Calle de los Olmos

Jardines de Méndez Núñez

Calle Estrella

4

Calle de la Galera

Calle San Andrés

Calle del Orzán

C del Sol

5

Calle Canalejo

Calle Ciega

Calle de Zalaeta

2

Calle del Hospital San Roque

6

Calle Real

Avenida de la Marina

To Fundación Caixa Galicia (50m); Fundación Barrié de la Maza (100m); Train Station (2km); Bus Station (2km); Airport (8km)

C Luchana

C de la Franja

8

Calle de la Trompeta

C de la Florida

Calle de Riego de Agua

Calle de San Agustín

Plaza del Humor

Plaza de España

Calle de la Torre

Travesía de la Torre

14

To Torre de Hércules (1.7km)

Ayuntamiento

Plaza de María Pita

7   11   9

1

Puerta Real

Paseo de la Dársena

Dársena de la Marina

Puerto de A Coruña

To Castillo de San Antón (400m)

Iglesia de Santiago

CIUDAD VIEJA

Plaza del General Azcárraga

Calle de la Maestranza

Calle Zapatería

Xardín de San Carlos

3

Ría de A Coruña

12

Calle de la Galera

A Coruña

◎ Top Sights
Ayuntamiento D3
Iglesia de Santiago E4
Xardín de San Carlos...........................F4

◎ Sights
1 Galerías D3
2 Museo de Bellas Artes B2
3 Museo Militar...................................F4

🛏 Sleeping
4 Hostal La Provinciana A4
5 Hotel Sol...B3
6 Pensión Hotil B3

🍴 Eating
7 Chocolatería Valor D3
8 Mesón do Pulpo D3
9 Pablo Gallego Restaurante................D3
10 Restaurante Bania A3
11 Taberna Da Penela D3
12 Tapa Negra C3

⚙ Entertainment
13 A Cova Céltica A3
14 Sala Mardigras C1

⊙10am-2pm & 4-7pm Mon-Sat, 10am-2pm Sun) showcases a surprising assembly of arms, uniforms, banners and other military gear from the 18th to 20th centuries.

Standing proud at the entrance to the port, the 16th-century **Castillo de San Antón** houses the **Museo Arqueológico e Histórico** (☑981 18 98 50; Paseo Marítimo 2; adult/senior & child €2/1; ⊙10am-9pm Tue-Sat, 10am-3pm Sun), an interesting collection on the area's prehistoric and Roman times.

On your way back to the centre, stop by the **Plaza del Humor**, decked with caricatures of famous laughter-makers from Cervantes to the Pink Panther – so what is Dostoevsky doing here?

Art
GALLERIES

A Coruña is an art hub. Works by masters like Goya, Rubens and Sorolla, and a fine collection of 19th-century Galician Sargadelos ceramics, are among the highlights of the sleek **Museo de Bellas Artes** (☑981 22 37 23; Calle de Zalaeta; admission €2.40, Sat afternoon & Sun free; ⊙10am-8pm Tue-Fri, 10am-2pm & 4.30-8pm Sat, 10am-2pm Sun). The **Fundación Caixa Galicia** (www.fundacioncaixa galicia.org; Cantón Grande 21-24) and **Fundación Barrié de la Maza** (www.fbarrie.org;

Cantón Grande 9), both just southwest of the centre, stage interesting contemporary art and other exhibitions.

Galerías
TYPICAL ARCHITECTURE

The expanse of classic late-19th-century Galician *galerías* (glassed-in balconies) fronting Avenida de la Marina is an iconic A Coruña sight and the origin of its label 'the city of glass'.

Aquarium Finisterrae
SHARKS, SEALS

(☑981 18 98 42; www.casaciencias.org, in Spanish; adult/senior & child €10/4; Paseo Marítimo 34; ⊙10am-9pm; 🚸) Kids love the seal colony and the underwater Nautilus room (surrounded by sharks, rays and 50 other species) at this aquarium, west of the Torre de Hércules.

Beaches
SAND, SEA

A Coruña's city beach is a glorious 1.4km long protected sweep of sand. Named **Playa del Orzán** at its east end and **Playa de Riazor** at the west, it gets busy in summer.

👉 Tours

From May to December the municipal tourist office gives free weekly 1½-hour tours, available in English, of the Torre de Hércules and the Parque Escultórico and the Ciudad Vieja by night. Check with the office for current times and starting points.

🎉 Festivals & Events

A Coruña really lets its hair down for the **Fiestas de María Pita** in August, a month-long festival with concerts, street fairs and more.

🛏 Sleeping

Central lodging options are mostly straitjacket business hotels or modest *hostales,* but there are a few places that escape the mould.

Hotel Sol
HOTEL €€

(☑981 21 03 62; www.hotelsolcoruna.com; Calle del Sol 10; r €70; P🐕@🛜) A friendly, family-run place with 10 stylish, modernised rooms and 30 older but still comfortable ones, the Sol is a good deal, especially outside August, when rates tumble. Parking is free. The street can get noisy on weekend nights, so request an inside room if you bed down early.

Hotel Zenit Coruña
HOTEL €€

(☑981 21 84 84; www.zenithoteles.com; Calle Comandante Fontanes 19; s €79-105, d €99-125;

P⊖✳@🛜) The sunny, stylishly minimalist, all-exterior rooms have glass wardrobe doors and washbasins, tasteful modern art, marble bathrooms and enormous TVs, and it's all just a block from Playa del Orzán.

Pensión Hotil · HOSTAL €
(📞981 97 63 02; www.hostalhotil.com, in Spanish; Calle de la Galera 26-28; s €25-35, d €40-90; ⊖🛜) This sparkling new *hostal* sports a lift and 30 shiny rooms with big windows, wrought-iron lamps and interesting touches like stone walling and bits of art. They're cosy, though modestly sized.

Hostal La Provinciana · HOSTAL €
(📞981 22 04 00; www.laprovinciana.net, in Spanish; Rúa Nueva 9; s/d/tr €43/56/76; @🛜) The 20 all-exterior rooms here are bright and squeaky clean, with generous-sized bathrooms and hardwood floors. The style is retro-frilly, and the staff amiable.

✖ Eating

For tapas, *raciones,* wine and cheap lunch *menúes,* hit the Zona de Vinos – the narrow lanes west of Plaza de María Pita, especially Calle de la Franja. Here, there are plenty of straightforward, lively *mesones* (old-style eateries) and *tabernas* (taverns), such as the octopus specialist **Mesón do Pulpo** (Calle de la Franja 9; ⊘closed Sun). They serve up *raciones* of seafood (€6-14), grilled meats and fish, or two-person *mariscadas* (shellfish platters) or *parrilladas* (fish mixed grills).

Adega O Bebedeiro · GALICIAN €
(📞981 21 06 09; Calle de Ángel Rebollo 34; meals €20-30; closed dinner Sun & lunch Mon) It's in a humble street 500m northwest of Plaza de España and it looks a dump from outside, but the inside is rustically neat with stone walls and a conversation-inspiring assortment of Galician bric-a-brac. The food is something else – home-style cooking with a few inventive touches, like crab-stuffed peppers in cheese sauce, oxtail with fried potatoes, or scallop-stuffed sea bass in puff pastry, all in generous quantities. Packed at weekends.

Taberna Da Penela · GALICIAN €€
(📞981 20 19 69; Plaza de María Pita 9; meals €25-45; ⊘closed Mon; ⊖) Get tasty Galician favourites like octopus, *caldo gallego* (a soup of beans, cabbage, potatoes and bits of meat), hake and monkfish at this popular plaza-side spot. It does a great *tortilla de Betanzos* (a gooey potato omelette) too, and has a varied wine list.

Tapa Negra · CREATIVE TAPAS
(Calle de Barrera 32; tapas €1.50-2.20; ⊘closed Mon) Stone walls and a black, white and red decor bespeak something different, and this popular, contemporary tapas bar delivers with tasty, adventurous combinations like *filloa de mariscos* (seafood crepe) and *fajita árabe* (spicy chicken in pita bread).

Pablo Gallego Restaurante
CREATIVE GALICIAN €€€
(📞981 20 88 88; Plaza de María Pita 11; meals €35-80; ⊘closed Sun) The classiest choice on the plaza, this serene, stone-walled dining room prepares 21st-century updates on traditional Galician ingredients. Try goose-barnacle-and-seaweed croquettes, grilled *lubrigante* or a monkfish-and-prawn brochette.

Chocolatería Valor · CAFE €
(Plaza de María Pita 5; breakfast €2-5; ⊘9am-1pm & 5-10pm; ⊖) With lusciously thick chocolate with *churros,* indulgent ice creams, milkshakes and great coffee, Valor is ideal for breakfast or an afternoon pick-me-up.

Restaurante Bania · VEGETARIAN €
(📞981 22 13 01; Calle de Cordelería 7; mains €4-15, menú €9.25, closed Sun & dinner Mon; 📋) Interesting salads, tofu dishes and vegetable ensembles are the heart of this classy all-vegetarian eatery.

⚫ Drinking & Entertainment

At night, A Coruña buzzes with taverns, bars and clubs. Before midnight, navigate the Zona de Vinos or head to Plaza de María Pita for low-key drinks and people-watching. Dozens of pubs and music bars on Calle del Sol, Calle de Canalejo and other streets behind Playa del Orzán party on from around midnight till 3am or 4am at weekends. Calle del Orzán, known as Soho, is a quirky cohabitation of local bars, trendy cafes, bohemian dives and ordinary small businesses with graffiti-messed walls.

Sala Mardigras · LIVE BANDS
(www.salamardigras.com in Spanish; Travesía de la Torre 8; admission free-€5; ⊘from 10pm Thu-Sat) Crowds pack this funky little music den to hear bands play blues, rock, pop, metal or indie.

A Cova Céltica · FOLK
(Calle del Orzán 82; ⊘closed Sun; 🛜) Galician folk music, often live from around 10pm Fridays, sets the tone at this popular tavern.

Discoteca Playa Club VANGUARD DISCO
(www.playaclub.net in Spanish; Playa de Riazor;
admission incl 1 drink €7-8; ⏰from 3am Thu-Sat)
As the pubs close, the discos start to fill.
This ever-popular spot boasts views over
the bay and a dance-inducing musical
mix of alternative pop, Nu Jazz, funk and
electronica.

ℹ️ Information

Municipal tourist office (☎981 92 30 93;
www.turismocoruna.com; Plaza de María Pita
6; ⏰9am-8.30pm Mon-Fri, 10am-2pm & 4-8pm
Sat, 10am-3pm Sun)

Regional tourist office (☎981 22 18 22;
Dársena de la Marina; ⏰10am-2pm & 4-7pm
Mon-Fri, 11am-2pm & 4-7pm Sat, 11am-2pm
Sun)

ℹ️ Getting There & Away

Air

From A Coruña's **Alvedro airport** (☎981 18 72
00), 8km south of the centre, Iberia (at least
four times daily), Spanair and Air Europa fly to
Madrid; and Vueling Airlines, Spanair and Air
Europa fly to Barcelona. Vueling also flies daily to
London (Heathrow), five times weekly to Seville
and three times to Amsterdam.

Bus

From the **bus station** (☎981 18 43 35; Calle
de Caballeros 21), 2km south of the centre,
Castromil-Monbus heads south to Santiago de
Compostela (€6.95, 50 to 90 minutes, 15 or
more daily) and beyond. Arriva serves the Rías
Altas, Lugo and Ourense; Autocares Vázquez
serves the Costa da Morte; and ALSA heads
further afield to destinations including Madrid
(€41 to €60, 6¾ to 8¾ hours, six or more daily)
and towns along Spain's north coast.

Train

The **train station** (Plaza de San Cristóbal) is
2km south of the centre. Renfe heads south
about hourly, stopping in Santiago de Compostela (€5.90, 40 minutes), Pontevedra (€12.90,
1½ to two hours) and Vigo (€14.50, two to 2½
hours). Up to five daily trains head to Lugo
(€15.80, 1½ to two hours) and León (€36, 6¼
hours), and two to Madrid (€52, 7¾ to 10¼
hours). Trains along Spain's north coast are
operated by FEVE and start from Ferrol, which is
served by four or five daily RENFE trains (€4.90,
1¼ hours) from A Coruña.

ℹ️ Getting Around

Buses (€1.20) run every half-hour from 7.15am
until 9.45pm (hourly from 9am or 10am at
weekends) between the airport and Puerta Real
in the centre.

THE FIRST ZARA

Fashion fans may want to make the
pilgrimage to the original Zara (cnr
Calle de Juan Flórez & Avenida de Arteixo; ⏰10am-2pm & 5-9pm Mon-Sat),
in A Coruña's main shopping area at
the southwest end of the isthmus.
Opened in 1975, it today looks much
like the other 1400 Zara shops around
the world. This was the small beginning for Galician Amancio Ortega's
mega-successful Inditex group,
which has since launched Pull&Bear,
Bershka, Stradivarius and other international brands but still has its headquarters in Arteixo on A Coruña's
outskirts.

Local buses 5 and 11 link the train station with
central A Coruña. Buses 1, 1A, 2 and 4 stop outside the bus station en route to the city centre.
Rides cost €1.10.

Every 20 to 30 minutes from noon to 9pm mid-
June to mid-October and hourly on weekends
until 6.30pm the rest of the year, trams (€2) run
along Paseo Marítimo from near the Castillo de
San Antón right round the headland to the Torre
de Hércules and Playa de Riazor.

Rías Altas

If you're seeking dramatic scenery, look no
further than the Rías Altas. Here, towering forests open to views of sheer sea cliffs,
sweeping beaches and vivid green fields
studded with farmhouses. Add in medieval towns like Betanzos and Pontedeume
and the constant roar of the Atlantic, and
it's easy to argue that the Rías Altas form
Galicia's most beautiful area. The beaches
here are far less crowded than in the Rías
Baixas, making this an ideal destination for
travellers who are yearning to get off the
beaten path.

BETANZOS
POP 10,700

The medieval town of Betanzos straddles
the Ríos Mendo and Mandeo, which meet
here to flow north into the Ría de Betanzos.
Once a thriving port rivalling A Coruña,
Betanzos still has a well-preserved old town
and is renowned for its welcoming taverns
with local wines and good food.

DON'T MISS

TOP FIVE BEACHES

Of the 772 beaches along Galicia's 1200km of coastline, these five stand out from the crowd.

» **Illas Cíes** (p534) For strolling.

» **Praia A Lanzada** (p526) For swimming.

» **Praia As Catedrais** (p522) For stellar picnics.

» **Area de Trece** (p524) For seclusion.

» **Praia de Picón** (p521) For stunning scenery.

◉ Sights

Praza dos Irmáns García Naveira   PLAZA
The sprawling main square is named after two local brothers who made a fortune in Argentina then returned to do good works in Betanzos in the late 19th century. Its houses are glassed in by classic *galerías*. Around 50,000 people cram into the square at midnight on 16 August to witness the release of an enormous paper hot-air balloon from the tower of Santo Domingo church in the **Fiesta de San Roque**.

Museo das Mariñas   MUSEUM
(☑981 77 19 46; adult/child €1.20/free; ☺10am-2pm & 4-8pm Mon-Fri, 10.30am-1pm Sat) Just around the corner from the main square, this museum, housed in a 16th-century convent, peers into traditional Galician life with exhibits ranging from the mundane (old coffee mugs) to the culturally significant (typical costumes), plus archaeology and art.

Old Town   CHURCHES
Take Rúa Castro up into the oldest part of town. Praza da Constitución is flanked by a couple of appealing cafes along with the neoclassical **Casa do Concello** and Romanesque/Gothic **Igrexa de Santiago**. A short stroll northeast, two beautiful Gothic churches, **Santa María do Azougue** and **San Francisco**, stand almost side by side. The latter is full of fine stone carving including many sepulchres of 14th- and 15th-century Galician nobility – notably that of Fernán Pérez de Andrade 'O Boo' (The Good), the powerful knight who had all three of these Gothic churches built along with a slew of other works. O Boo's sepulchre rests on a stone bear and boar (the latter being the Andrade family emblem). Spot the Galician bagpiper amid the Last Judgment carvings above the altar.

Riverside Walk   STROLL
For a dose of natural beauty, take the riverside walk that begins at the end of Rúa Ánxeles and leads 3km (about 45 minutes) to **Os Caneiros**, the destination of a popular summertime *romería* (pilgrimage).

⌖ Sleeping & Eating

The **Complejo San Roque** (☑981 77 55 55; www.complejosanroque.es; Estrada de Castilla 38; s/d €81/91; Ⓟ❄@), 500m southeast of the main square, is a Modernista poorhouse converted into a sleek hotel, with sunny rooms that have a vaguely maritime air. The cream facade is unmissable from the main road.

In town, **Hotel Garelos** (☑981 77 59 30; www.hotelgarelos.com; Calle Alfonso IX 8; s/d €65/86; ❄❄☎) has spic-and-span rooms with parquet floors and marble bathrooms, and is hung with 60 attractive original watercolours.

A string of terrace cafes flanks Praza Irmáns García Naviera. Amid the sidewalk tables dart two narrow alleyways, Venela Campo and Travesia do Progreso. The taverns down here are popular for drinks, tapas (€1.50 to €2.50) and *raciones* (€5 to €12). Be sure to try *tortilla de Betanzos*. **O Pote** (Travesia do Progreso 9) does some of the best food and its terrific €15 *menú del día* includes said *tortilla*.

ⓘ Information

Tourist office (☑981 77 66 66; www.betanzos. es; Praza da Galicia 1; ☺10am-2pm & 5-8pm, closed Sat afternoon & Sun Oct-May). On an extension of Praza dos Irmáns García Naveira.

ⓘ Getting There & Away

Arriva buses to/from A Coruña (€2.20, 40 minutes, every half-hour Monday to Friday, hourly Saturday and Sunday) stop in Praza dos Irmáns García Naveira. Seven or more Arriva buses head to Pontedeume (€1.95, 30 minutes) and a few to Lugo, Ortigueira, Viveiro and Ribadeo.

Betanzos Cidade train station is northwest of the old town, across the Río Mendo. Four or five trains go daily to/from A Coruña (€3.30, 40 minutes).

PONTEDEUME
POP 4650

This hillside town overlooks the Eume estuary, where fishing boats bob. The old town is an appealing combination of handsome galleried houses, narrow cobbled streets and occasional open plazas, liberally sprinkled with taverns and tapas bars. Several parallel narrow streets climb up from the main road, the central one being the porticoed Rúa Real. Down near the waterfront rises the stout Torreón dos Andrade, once the castle keep of the local feudal lords, the Andrades. It houses a tourist office (981 43 02 70; 10.30am-2pm & 5-8pm Tue-Sat, 11am-2pm Sun), which includes an Andrade Interpretation Centre!

Pontedeume has a few OK *hostales,* such as Hostal Allegue (981 43 00 35; Calle del Chafaris 1; d €41), but the area's best sleeping options are rural hotels like the enchanting Casa do Castelo de Andrade (981 43 38 39; www.casteloandrade.com; Lugar Castelo de Andrade; d €100-122), 7km from town. It's a pretty stone farmhouse near the Parque Natural Fragas do Eume, with 10 immaculate rooms.

A fine place to eat in town is Restaurante Luis (Calle San Agustín 12; meals €15-35; closed dinner Sun;), with a full range of Galician hunger-killers from fried squid to a 400g *chuletón* (giant beef chop).

PARQUE NATURAL FRAGAS DO EUME
East of Pontedeume, the 91-sq-km Fragas do Eume park runs up the valley of the Río Eume, home to the best-preserved Atlantic coastal forest in Europe, with mixed deciduous woodlands and several species of rare relict ferns that have survived here for many millions of years. The Centro de Interpretación (981 43 25 28; 9am-2pm & 4-8pm) is 6km from Pontedeume on the Caaveiro road (no public transport comes here). Next door, Restaurante Andarubel (981 43 39 69; mains €8-20) rents **bikes** for €5/8/12 per one/two/four hours. From here, you can cycle or drive a paved road up through the thickly forested, fairly flat (but steep-sided) valley, or walk a footpath along the opposite bank, for 7.5km. Here the road ends and a 500m path leads up to the Mosteiro de Caaveiro (10am-2pm

& 4.30-8.30pm, reduced hr & closed Mon-Fri approx Oct-May), which dates back to the 9th century and is visitable by free hourly guided tours. Over Easter and from mid-June to the end of September, the road from the Centro de Interpretación is closed to cars, but is covered by a half-hourly free bus.

Until other access routes are developed further, this is the only part of the park most visitors see, though there are several walking trails further east. A visitors centre is also being built near the Mosteiro de Monfero on the south side of the park.

Eumeturismo (www.eumeturismo.org) is a useful web source for information on the area.

CEDEIRA & AROUND
POP (CEDEIRA) 4850

Heading north, the coast is studded with small maritime towns and pretty beaches worth exploring. The Rías Altas' largest hub is the naval port of Ferrol, 17km north of Pontedeume. It's the western terminus of the FEVE railway from the Basque Country and was the birthplace of General Franco, but it has little to detain you. Continuing north, you'll come to Valdoviño, with the beautiful Praia Frouxeira. Just beyond Valdoviño, Praia de Pantín has a great right-hander for surfers and hosts an international surfing competition in early September.

Some 38km from Ferrol is the fishing port and very low-key resort of Cedeira. The cute, little old town, with narrow streets and white-painted, galleried houses, sits on the west bank of the Río Condomiñas, while popular Praia da Magdalena fronts the modern, eastern side of town. Around the headland to the south is the more appealing Praia de Vilarrube, a protected dunes and wetlands area.

For a nice hour or two's stroll, walk oceanward along the waterfront to the fishing port, climb up beside the old fort above it and then walk out onto the headland overlooking the mouth of the Ría de Cedeira. The rocky coast around here produces rich harvests of *percebes* (goose barnacles), a much-coveted delicacy.

Sleeping & Eating
Cedeira is full of bars and cafes. This is especially the case around the river mouth and just east of it on Praza Sagrado Corazón.

Hospedería Cordobelas

COUNTRY GUESTHOUSE **€€**

(☑981 48 06 07; www.cordobelas.com in Spanish; Rúa Cordobelas 29; s/d €60/75; ⊙closed mid-Dec–mid-Jan; P⑂) About 300m off the main road, 1km before Cedeira as you approach from the south, this really charming stone-built property comprises four converted century-old village houses with comfortable, spacious, rustic-style rooms, and a fabulous garden.

Hotel Herbeira

CONTEMPORARY HOTEL **€€€**

(☑981 49 21 67; www.hotelherbeira.com; Rúa Cordobelas; s/d €107/130; ⊙closed mid-Dec–mid-Jan; P❄@⑂▤) As sleek as Galicia gets, this family-run hotel, just off the main road 1km outside Cedeira, boasts 16 minimalist rooms in muted tones, with glassed-in galleries and stunning views over the *ría*.

Pensión Chelsea

HOSTAL **€**

(☑981 48 23 40; Plaza Sagrado Corazón 15; r €45; ⊜) In the heart of town, the Chelsea offers well-kept, good-sized rooms decorated in a cheerful seaside-ish manner.

Mesón Muiño Kilowatio

TAPAS **€**

(Rúa do Mariñeiro 11; tapas €4-8; ⊙closed Tue) This tiny bar packs 'em in for generous servings of *marraxo* (a type of shark), *raxo* and *zorza* (types of chopped grilled pork) and other Galician delights.

El Náutico

SEAFOOD **€€**

(☑981 48 00 11; Rúa do Mariñeiro 7; meals €20-40) Succulent shellfish – most notably *percebes* – and tuna top the menu at this justifiably popular seafood restaurant facing the river.

❶ Information

Cedeira's **tourist office** (☑981 48 21 87; Avenida de Castelao 18; ⊙10.30am-2pm & 4.30-7.30pm Mon-Fri, 10.30am-2pm Sat) is in the new town.

❶ Getting There & Away

By bus from the south, you'll need to change in Ferrol, from where Rialsa runs up to seven buses daily to Cedeira (€2.75, 45 minutes). Arriva runs one or two daily buses to Cariño (€2.60, 50 minutes).

SERRA DA CAPELADA

The wild, rugged coastline that the Rías Altas are famous for begins above Cedeira. If you have your own car (and, even better, time for some walks), Galicia's northwestern corner is a captivating place to explore, with lush forests, vertigo-inducing cliffs and stunning oceanscapes.

In summer, busloads of tourists descend on the hamlet of **San Andrés de Teixido** (12km past Cedeira), a jumble of stone houses renowned as a sanctuary of relics of St Andrew. You might skip San Andrés and head on up the winding CP2205 for incredible views; it's a lovely road that runs northeast towards Cariño. Six kilometres beyond San Andrés is the must-see **Garita de Herbeira lookout**, 600m above sea level. This is the best place to be wowed over southern Europe's highest sea cliffs. Further on, make a 9km detour to the **Mirador A Miranda**, a sublime vantage point over the Estaca de Bares that's only slightly marred by the presence of two communications towers.

Four kilometres north of the workaday town of **Cariño** looms the mother of Spanish capes, **Cabo Ortegal**, where the Atlantic Ocean meets the Bay of Biscay. Great stone shafts drop sheer into the ocean from such a height that the waves crashing on the rocks below seem pitifully benign. Just offshore, **Os Tres Aguillóns**, three islets, provide a home to hundreds of marine birds like yellow-leg seagulls and storm petrels. With binoculars, you may spot dolphins or whales near the cape.

There are some lovely walks out here. On the road from Cariño, stop at the first mirador to take the 3.2km/30-minute clifftop trail to the **San Xiáo de Trebo** chapel. This well-marked path traverses a forest, crosses the Río Soutullo and affords grand views.

Rural hotels are the way to go in the area. Charming **Muiño das Cañotas** (☑981 42 01 81; www.muinodascanotas.com in Spanish; A Ortigueira 10, A Pedra; r incl breakfast €65-80; P⊜⑂), in a pretty little valley 200m off the main DP6121, 2km south of Cariño, has five beautiful rooms in a recently converted 14th-century watermill.

CARIÑO TO VIVEIRO

From Cariño, the road south heads round the Ría de Ortigueira to the fishing port of **Ortigueira**. Further on, a short detour off the AC862 leads to the small but lovely **Praia de Santo António** in Porto de Espasante. For a chill base overlooking this beach, book a room at the aged but well-kept **Hotel Orillamar** (☑981 40 80 14; s/d incl breakfast €55/75; P@), whose panoramic restaurant (meals €25 to €50) serves excellent seafood and meat.

Between here and the Bares peninsula to the east, the coast is strung with some

Galician folk music has much in common with other Celtic traditions in Brittany, Ireland and Scotland, and the sounds of the *gaita* (bagpipe), violin, *bombo* (a big drum) and accordion-like *zanfona* provide the soundtrack to many events. Several Celtic music festivals liven up the summer months. The biggest and best is the Festival Ortigueira (www.festivaldeortigueira.com) at Ortigueira in the Rías Altas in July. Other festivals worth seeking out include the Interceltico (www.festivalinterceltico.com) in Moaña (Ría de Vigo) and the Festa da Carballeira (www.festadacarballeira.com) in Zas (Costa da Morte) – both are held on the last weekend of July or the first weekend of August.

Leading *gaiteros* (bagpipers) and other folkies are popular heroes in Galicia. If you fancy tuning into this quintessentially Galician cultural genre, look out for gigs by pipers Carlos Núñez, Xosé Manuel Budiño or Susana Seivane, piper/singer Mercedes Peón, singer Uxía, or groups Luar Na Lubre, Berrogüetto or Milladoiro.

of the most dramatic and least-known beaches in Spain, at the foot of the spectacular Acantilados de Loiba cliffs. Easiest to reach is Praia de Picón: take the signposted turning at Km 63 of the AC682 in Loiba, and follow the DP6104 to Picón village, where a sharp left turn leads to a small picnic area, from which a path with a wooden handrail heads down to the beach.

O Barqueiro, on the Ría del Barqueiro, is a storybook Galician fishing village where slate-roofed, white houses cascade down to the port. There's little to do but stroll along the coast and watch the day's catch come in. A few daily FEVE trains and Arriva buses on Ferrol–Viveiro routes serve the town.

For an even quieter base, push north up the Bares peninsula to Porto de Bares/Vares, little more than a beach with a few boats belly-up in the sand. For a treat, book a room in the signalling-station-turned-contemporary-hotel Semáforo de Bares (☑981 41 71 47; www.hotelsemaforodebares.com; Estaca de Bares; s €65, d €90-150; P❄), where six rooms (the best are quite indulgent) sit 3km above the village on a panoramic hilltop. In the village and overlooking the beach, Restaurante La Marina (meals €10-40) does great seafood paellas (€32 or €48 for two).

The Bares peninsula is a hot spot for migrating birds in late summer and early autumn, and has several good walking trails. From the lighthouse near the peninsula's tip, a trail follows the spine of a serpentine rock outcrop almost to its end. This is the Punta da Estaca de Bares – Spain's most northerly point.

VIVEIRO
POP 7300

This town at the mouth of the Río Landro has a well-preserved historic quarter, where outward appearances haven't changed a great deal since Viveiro was rebuilt after a 1540 fire. It's famous for its elaborate Easter-week celebrations, when the town fills with processions and decorations.

Hotel Vila (☑982 56 13 31; www.hotel-vila.net; Avenida Nicolás Cora Montenegro 57; s/d €43/53.50; ☎), just down from FEVE's Viveiro Apeadero station, is a well-kept and well-run one-star with bright, yellow-walled rooms and up-to-date furnishings. The Pazo da Trave (☑982 59 81 63; www.pazodatrave.com; Galdo; r €82-158; P❄❄), 3km inland (off the LU540 south of Viveiro), is a converted centuries-old manor house where original artwork adds flair to the rustic-chic rooms. In town, you can eat good fish, steak or salads at the slightly frilly O' Asador (☑982 56 06 88; Rúa Melitón Cortiñas 15; meals €30-60; ❄). Don't be in a hurry though!

FEVE trains between Ferrol and Oviedo stop in and a few Arriva buses fan out to Lugo and along the Rías Altas, though there are no buses to Ribadeo at weekends.

RIBADEO
POP 6400

This lively port town is a sun-seeker magnet in summer. It sits on the west side of the Ría de Ribadeo, which separates Galicia from Asturias. Though Ribadeo itself is beachless, it's surrounded by incredible shoreline.

The old town is an attractive mix of maritime charm and eclectic 20th-century architecture. The tranquil, palm-studded central square, Praza de España, is highlighted by the Modernista Torre de los Moreno, with a glazed ceramic dome. For sea and sand you'll have to head out of town, but you won't be disappointed with the spectacular beaches, especially Praia As Catedrais (Cathedrals Beach). The 1.5km sandy stretch is home to awesome Gothic-looking rock arches, creations best seen at low tide.

This area has plenty of camping grounds, beachy *hostales* and appealing hotels. One of the best is A Cortiña (☑982 13 01 87; www. cantalarrana.com, in Spanish; Calle Paco Lanza, Grañol; r €74; Ⓟ), an adorable country house in the town (a short stroll from the FEVE train station). It has loads of charm (think quilts, gingham curtains and antique furniture). Just up from the leisure port, you can get fine seafood, grilled meats and pasta dishes in the cosy upstairs dining room at Solana (Rúa de Antonio Otero 41; meals €20-45). The smoky tavern downstairs serves tapas, *raciones* and *bocadillos*.

Get the scoop on everything else at the tourist office (☑982 12 86 89; www.ribadeo. org; Praza de España 7; ☉10.30am-2pm & 4-8pm, closed Sun afternoon Jul-Sep, Sun Oct-Jun).

Multi-stop FEVE trains operate to/from Oviedo (€10.75, 3½ hours, two daily) and Ferrol (€9.75, three hours, four daily). Four or more daily buses head to Luarca, Oviedo, Lugo and (except weekends) Viveiro, and two go daily to Santiago de Compostela.

COSTA DA MORTE

Rocky headlands, winding inlets, small fishing towns, narrow coves, wide sweeping bays and many a remote, sandy beach – this is the eerily beautiful 'Coast of Death'. For some the most enchanting part of all Galicia, this relatively isolated and unspoilt shore runs from Muros, at the mouth of the Ría de Muros, round to Caión, just before A Coruña. It's a coast of legends, like the one about villagers who put out lamps to lure passing ships to their doom on deadly rocks. This treacherous coast has certainly seen more than its share of shipwrecks, and the idyllic landscape can undergo a rapid transformation when ocean mists blow in.

If you're looking for a quiet base to explore the region, consider staying in a rural hotel. Many are listed at the very useful www.turismocostadamorte.com.

Some buses run from Santiago de Compostela and A Coruña to many places on the Costa da Morte, but having your own wheels makes it far easier to get about. The area's sinuous highways aren't the easiest to navigate, but it's a marvellous area to explore.

Muros & Carnota

The Costa da Morte starts in the municipality of Muros, long an important port for Santiago de Compostela. These days, the town is best known as a quiet spot for a seaside meal after a morning spent sunbathing on one of the area's beaches. At Pachanga (Avenida Castelao 29; raciones €4-11), on the waterfront, crowds wash down plates of octopus with glasses of light Albariño wine.

At Monte Louro, the coast turns north and you immediately encounter a series of long, sweeping, sandy beaches facing the open Atlantic, most notably the incredible 7km curve of Praia de Carnota. When the wind is up, Carnota can get rough: the most protected sections are at the south end, signposted (all with separate names) from the village of Lira. The village of Carnota is renowned as home to Galicia's largest *hórreo* (traditional stone grain store typical of Galicia). Exactly 34.5m long, it was built late in the 18th century. The villages of Caldebarcos, at the north end of the Carnota bay, and O Pindo, a few kilometres further on, are starting points for walking routes in the amazingly eroded granite hills above the coast here. From O Pindo the road continues round the beautiful Ría de Corcubión towards Fisterra.

Fisterra & Around

POP (FISTERRA) 3000

Cabo Fisterra (Castilian: Cabo Finisterre) is the western edge of Spain, at least in popular imagination. The real westernmost point is Cabo de la Nave, 5km north, but that doesn't keep throngs of people from heading out to this beautiful, windswept cape, which is also kilometre 0 of the 86km Fisterra variant of the Camino de Santiago. Pilgrims ending their journeys here ritually burn smelly socks, T-shirts etc on the rocks just past the lighthouse.

The cape is a 3.5km drive past the town of Fisterra: on the way out is the 12th-century Igrexa de Santa María das Areas, a mix of Romanesque, Gothic and baroque. Some 600m past the church, a track up to the right to Monte Facho and Monte de San Guillerme provides a more challenging but more tranquil alternative walking route to the cape. The area is laced with myth and superstition, and they say childless couples used to come up here to improve their chances of conception.

Fisterra itself is a small, moderately attractive port and tourist destination, with a picturesque harbour. Enticing area beaches include Praia da Mar de Fora, over on the ocean side of the promontory from town.

Of a dozen places to stay, the best is Hotel Rústico Ínsula Finisterrae (✆981 71 22 11; www.insulafinisterrae.com in Spanish; A Insua 76; r incl breakfast €84-99; P☺🤍🛜🗶), a century-old converted farmhouse at the top of the town. The spacious, sunny rooms have brass beds, fresh white linen and stone walls, and some have fantastic views. In town, Hostal Mariquito (✆981 74 00 44; Rúa de Santa Catalina 44; s/d €30/42; @) has spacious, clean rooms (though some saggy beds) just above the waterfront.

The recently spruced-up waterfront is studded with seafood eateries. A lot of them cater to an undiscriminating market but neat, contemporary O Fragón (✆981 74 04 29; Praza da Cerca 8; meals €40-70, menú €24; ☺closed Wed-Sun dinner Sep-Jun) provides some original dishes prepared with care, such as wild turbot with sautéd vegies and dried fruits. It's just round the corner, past the main restaurant drag.

Monbus runs one or two daily buses to/from Santiago de Compostela (€14, three hours) via Muros and Carnota, and others with a transfer at Cee. Autocares Vázquez runs two or three buses to/from A Coruña (€13.20, 2½ hours).

Muxía & Around
POP (MUXÍA) 1640

The route north from Fisterra to Muxía passes along enchanting lanes through thick woodlands; along the way is a nice detour to picturesque Cabo Touriñán. Just south of Muxía, Praia de Lourido is an unspoilt stretch of sand in a sheltered bay perfect for a sunny day.

Muxía itself is a photogenic little fishing port with a handful of cosy bars. Follow the 'Santuario da Barca' signs along the waterfront to reach one of Galicia's most beloved pilgrimage points: Punta da Barca, where the baroque Santuario da Virxe da Barca marks the spot where legend attests that the Virgin Mary arrived in a stone boat and appeared to St James. The boat's hull and sail are supposedly here, among the rocks strewn below the chapel.

Just outside town on the Santiago road, you can get both a fabulous seafood meal and a good bed at Tira da Barca (✆981 74 23 23; www.tiradabarca.com; r €60; P), a seven-room hotel whose high-end restaurant, with menúes from €25 to €48, plus drinks, draws local executive types for top-quality shellfish.

TOP CHOICE Casa de Trillo (✆981 72 77 78; www.casadetrillo.com; r incl breakfast €70-90; P@) offers even more charm, deep in typically Galician countryside about 8km south of Muxía, at Santa Mariña. This hospitable 16th-century manor house has a lot of history, lovely gardens and cosy, well-appointed rooms, and is a great base for exploring the area.

Heading on from Muxía towards Camariñas, take the road via Leis, an idyllic hamlet studded with *hórreos* and farmhouses, and the pretty riverside village of Cereixo. Along this enchanting route you can stop at the inviting Praia do Lago.

Two or three daily buses link Muxía with Santiago, Cee, Camariñas and A Coruña.

Camariñas to Camelle

The fishing village of Camariñas is known for its women's traditional *encaixe* (lacework). Several shops specialise in lace and there's an interesting Museo do Encaixe (Lace Museum; Praza Insuela; admission €2; ☺11am-2pm & 5-8pm Tue-Sun) in front of the town hall.

The best spot to lay your head is Hotel Puerto Arnela (✆981 70 54 77; www.puertoarnela.es in Spanish; Plaza del Carmen 20; r incl breakfast €45-80; 🛜), facing the harbour. A stone manor house with delightfully rustic rooms, it also has a simple restaurant (meals €17 to €30; closed dinner Sunday) serving good basics like grilled seafood and chicken.

Camariñas has at least one daily bus service to/from Santiago, Cee, Muxía and A Coruña, some involving connections en route.

TOP FIVE VILLAGES

There's steep competition in Galicia for the title of prettiest village, but if you're yearning for old-world charm, there's no beating the following:

» **Muxía** (p523) A lovely, laid-back fishing port.

» **Cambados** (p526) A taste of Galician wine country.

» **Combarro** (p530) Great seafood in a picture-perfect setting.

» **Castro Caldelas** (p539) Story-book charm nestled in the hills.

» **O Cebreiro** (p540) The hilltop hamlet where the Camino de Santiago enters Galicia.

The rugged coast between Camariñas and Camelle is one of the most beautiful stretches of the Costa da Morte. You can walk, bike or drive the **coastal road** (part paved, part smooth dirt/gravel) from Camariñas northwest to the Cabo Vilán lighthouse (5km), then northeast and east to Camelle, a further 22km. The road winds above secluded beaches (like Area de Trece), across windswept hillsides and past weathered rock formations; it's guaranteed to keep your camera clicking. There are many places to stop along the way, such as the Cemiterio dos Ingleses (English Cemetery), the sad burial ground from an 1890 British shipwreck.

The sleepy fishing village of Camelle has no great charm, but it does have the quirky Museo do Alemán, an open-air sculpture garden made by 'Man', an eccentric longtime German resident, from rocks and ocean bric-a-brac. The sculptor died in 2002, after being devastated by the *Prestige* oil spill, which splotched his fanciful figures black. The museum (now oil-free) stands beside the end of the pier: you can no longer go in, but can examine it from the pier. Praia de Traba, a little-frequented 2.5km stretch of sand with dunes and a lagoon, is a nice 4km walk east along the coast from Camelle. Café Bar Molinera (981 71 02 38; Rúa Principal 79; apt €40) has four good apartments for up to four people.

Laxe & Around

POP (LAXE) 1900

A sweeping bay beach runs right along the waterfront of Laxe, and the 15th-century Gothic church of Santa María da Atalaia stands guard over the harbour. The lively waterfront makes this a good base for exploring the coast. The sleek Playa de Laxe Hotel (981 73 90 00; www.playadelaxe.com; Avenida Cesáreo Pondal 27; s €76, d €87-108) just off the beach towards the south end of town, has 40 rooms with parquet floors and clean-lined decor. It's worth paying a bit extra for the rooms with ocean views and more space. There are several inviting places for tapas, *raciones* and drinks along the main waterfront street, Rúa Rosalía de Castro. Best for a proper meal is Mesón O Salvavidas (meals €30-50) with tempting grilled seafood and meats, right next door to the Playa de Laxe Hotel.

Much of this area's appeal lies beyond its towns. Laxe's tourist office (981 70 69 03; Avenida Cesáreo Pondal 27; 9.30am-2.30pm & 5.30-8pm Tue-Thu, 9.30am-2.30pm Mon & Fri), and an information kiosk (open daily from mid-June to mid-October) on Rúa Rosalía de Castro have a booklet on area **walks**, including the PR-G70 loop (4.6km, two hours) around the Monte da Insua peninsula, and a longer coastal walk west to Praia de Traba via the surf beach Praia de Soesto.

Drive inland past Canduas, then south on the AC430 to find the turn-off to the Castro A Cidá de Borneiro, a pre-Roman *castro* amid thick woodlands.

Laxe is linked to A Coruña by two or more daily Vázquez buses (€8.45, 1¾ hours).

RÍAS BAIXAS

Wide beaches and relatively calm, warm waters have made the Rías Baixas (Castilian: Rías Bajas) Galicia's best-known tourist area. It boasts way more towns, villages, hotels, rental apartments and restaurants than other stretches of the Galician coast, which obscures some of its natural beauty. Still, the mix of pretty villages, sandy beaches and good eating options keep most people happy. Throw in the Illas Cíes, lovely old Pontevedra and bustling Vigo, and you have a tempting travel cocktail.

The following sections start at the inland end of each *ría* and work outwards, but if you have a vehicle and plenty of time you could simply follow the coast around from one *ría* to the next. That would be some 250km from Muros to Nigrán – a straight-line distance of just 72km!

Get lots of information about the area, including links to rural hotels, online at www.riasbaixas.depo.es.

Ría de Muros y Noia

NOIA
POP 8300

This beachless town was Santiago de Compostela's de facto port for centuries. Now, the crooked streets of its historic centre make a pleasing place for a stroll.

Two must-see monuments are the Gothic Igrexa de San Martiño (⊙8.30am-noon & 4.30-9pm), dominating the old town's Praza do Tapal, with wonderful sculptures of the apostles, Christ and archangels on its western facade, and the Igrexa de Santa María A Nova (Carreiriña do Escultor Ferreiro; ⊙10.30am-1.30pm & 4-6pm, closed Sat & Sun afternoon). Both are classics of the Galician 'sailors' Gothic' style, typified by a single very wide nave. Santa María is surrounded by a pretty cemetery and contains a collection of tombstones from members of medieval guilds, many of them showing the tools of their trades such as an anchor, knives (for butchers) or a pair of soles (for shoemakers).

Noia has a lively tapas scene. Just north of the Igrexa de San Martiño, Tasca Típica (Rúa Cantón 15; raciones €3.50-12) is a dark, stone-walled tavern in the stables of the 14th-century Pazo Dacosta. It's great for a drink, snacks or even a sit-down meal; there are a handful of tables in the candle-lit dining room.

SOUTH SHORE

The coast here isn't completely unspoilt, but it's pleasantly low-key. In Porto do Son, a busy port, a small beach and diminutive old town jumble together by the *ría,* and you'll find several good tapas bars and informal restaurants. Hotel Villa del Son (✆981 85 30 49; www.hotelvilladelson.es; Rúa de Trincherpe 11, Porto do Son; s/d €40/58; ☎) has tidy rooms with cool tile floors, bright bathrooms and cheery country-cottage-type de-

cor. For the local speciality, *arroz con bogavante* (a paella-like dish made with a type of lobster) or fair-priced grilled fish and meat dishes (or pizzas!), try popular Hórreo (Rúa de Felipe III 25; meals €18-30).

Two kilometres past Porto do Son you'll reach the turn-off for the spectacular Castro de Baroña prehistoric settlement. Park by the cafe and take the rocky path down to the ruins. Galicia's ancients sure knew how to choose real estate: the settlement is poised majestically on a wind-blasted headland overlooking the crashing waves of the Atlantic. Stretching south from the *castro,* Praia Area Longa is the first of a small string of surfing beaches down this side of the *ría.*

Drivers could detour to the Dolmen de Axeitos, a well-preserved megalithic monument, signposted between Xuño and Ribeira; or up to the 600m-high Mirador A Curota, where on a really good day you can see all the way from Cabo Fisterra to

Rías Baixas

the Monte de Santa Trega; or to Corrubedo at the tip of the peninsula, with beaches either side of town, a lighthouse at the end of the road and a few relaxed bars around its small harbour.

Ría de Arousa

PADRÓN
POP 3000

As the story goes, this is where Santiago's corpse landed in Galicia in its stone boat. These days, Padrón is best known for its tiny green peppers, *pimientos de padrón*, which were imported from Mexico by 16th-century Franciscan friars and are now grown all around town. When fried up and sprinkled with coarse salt, they're one of Spain's favourite tapas. Just beware of the odd spicy one.

Padrón produced both Galicia's 'national poet' Rosalía de Castro (1837–85) and Nobel prize–winning novelist Camilo José Cela (1916–2002). The poet's pretty stone house, opposite the train station, is now the Casa-Museo Rosalía de Castro (www.rosaliadecastro.org, in Galician & Spanish); Cela's life is documented at the Fundación Camilo José Cela (www.fundacioncela.com), in Iria Flavia, 1km north of central Padrón.

There are a couple of tempting restaurants. A Casa dos Martínez (✑981 81 05 77; Rúa Longa 7; meals €40-50, menú €27.50; ⊘2-3.30pm Tue-Sun, 9.30-11pm Fri & Sat), on a pedestrian street in the old heart of town, serves up great creative *cocina de mercado* (with meat, seafood, vegies and other ingredients fresh from the market).

Castromil buses run several times daily from Padrón to Santiago de Compostela (€1.90, 30 minutes) and Pontevedra (€3.80, one hour), and a few travel daily to Noia, Cambados and O Grove.

CAMBADOS
POP 6700

The capital of the Albariño wine country, famed for its fruity whites, Cambados is a pretty little seaside town founded by the Visigoths, with a compact core of old streets lined with stone architecture. You can visit a handful of wineries in and around town, and a popular **wine festival** takes place at the end of July.

Though better-known wineries lie outside Cambados itself, the most accessible are two small establishments in the handsome, 17th-century Pazo de Fefiñáns, on broad Praza de Fefiñáns at the northern end of town. They are Bodegas del Palacio de Fefinañes (www.fefinanes.com; tour with/without tasting €4/2; ⊘10am-2pm & 4-8pm Mon-Sat) and Gil Armada (www.pazodefefinans.com; exhibition with/without tasting €4/2; ⊘10am-2pm & 5-8pm Mon-Fri).

Galicia's best-known winery, Martín Códax (www.martincodax.com; Rúa Burgáns 91, Vilariño; admission free; ⊘11am-1pm & 5-7pm Mon-Fri, 11am-1pm Sat, closed Sat Oct-May) is only a short drive from town. Tours start hourly and include an optional free tasting. You can get more details on Rías Baixas wine routes at www.rutadelvinoriasbaixas.com.

Cambados has five museums (joint admission €3; ⊘10am-2pm & 4.30-7.30pm Tue-Sun), mainly devoted to wine and fishing, but there's also one preserving a quaint old tide-operated cereal mill.

A lovely sleeping option is Pazo A Capitana (✑986 52 05 13; www.pazoacapitana.com in Spanish; Rúa Sabugueiro 46; s/d incl breakfast €75/97; closed mid-Dec–mid-Jan; [P][⊛][❀][◎]), a 17th-century country house on the edge of town with stately rooms, beautiful, expansive gardens and an on-site winery. A good budget choice is the almost new Hotel O' Lagar (✑986 52 08 07; www.hotelolagar.com, in Spanish; Rúa Pontevedra 14; s/d €40/50; [◎]), run by an amiable mother-and-son team, with sparkling clean rooms and its own cafe.

Pedestrian-friendly Rúa Príncipe, Rúa Real and Praza de Fefiñáns have plenty of rather touristy eateries and some characterful bars like Bar Laya (Praza de Fefiñáns), which makes its own wine, but one of the best feeds is at A Traiña (Ribeira de Fefiñáns; meals €30-60), facing the waterfront. It does good fish *guisos* (casseroles) and *arroz con bogavante*.

The helpful tourist office (✑986 52 07 86; www.cambados.es in Spanish; Avenida de Galicia; ⊘10am-2pm & 4.30-7.30pm) is a few steps from the bus station.

Cambados is linked by bus to Santiago de Compostela, Pontevedra and O Grove.

O GROVE
POP 7400

More than two dozen sandy beaches around O Grove, including the spectacular Praia a Lanzada, have made this seaside town and the relatively unspoilt peninsula surrounding it a buzzing summer destination. Dune-backed A Lanzada sweeps 2.3km along the west side of the isthmus leading to the peninsula: it's enticingly natural, but not exactly deserted, as the mammoth car park attests.

Approaching O Grove proper, you could cross the bridge leading to the Illa A Toxa, a manicured island known for its spas, golf course and swanky hotels. Take a stroll in the gardens surrounding the Capilla de las Conchas, a church completely plastered with *vieira* (clam) shells.

In fine weather from April to November, several companies depart from the harbour on *ría* cruises, chiefly to look at the **bateas** – platforms where mussels, oysters and scallops are cultivated. Tours, including mussel tastings, cost €13/6 per adult/child and last 75 minutes. An interesting summer destination is Illa de Sálvora, one of the small islands that make up Galicia's Islas Atlánticas national park. Sálvora has a mainly rocky coast, a lighthouse, an abandoned village, and an old fish-salting plant that was converted to a mansion by its former owners. Daily four-hour trips (adult/child €20/10) from July to September with Cruceros do Ulla (☑986 73 18 18) or Cruceros Rías Baixas (www.crucerosrias baixas.com, in Spanish) include a guided walk and a little beach time.

To learn more about Galician marine life, visit Acquariumgalicia (www.acquariumgali cia.com; adult/child €10/6.50; �l11am-2pm & 4.30-7.30pm Tue-Sun; ☝) at Punta Moreiras on the northwest side of the O Grove peninsula, where some 95 mostly Galician species are showcased.

Several marked **walking trails** ramble around the western part of the O Grove peninsula. For wonderful views, and birdwatching, head up to the Mirador A Siradella, sitting 159m above O Grove and signposted from town.

Nine camping grounds are scattered around the west side of the peninsula. In town, accommodation is mostly spread along Rúa Castelao, running between the centre and the A Toxa bridge. A spectacular option outside town is Hotel Samar (☑986 73 83 78; www.samarhotel.com, in Spanish; d €130-170; ☒☺✳), which looks right along Praia A Lanzada from its perch at the beach's north end. The 14 rooms all have their own terraces and many enjoy beach views.

O Grove is famous for its shellfish – sample delicacies like *berberechos* (cockles) and *centollo* (spider crab) in restaurants. In mid-October the town hosts the **Festa do Marisco** shellfish festival. Of the slew of large seafood houses facing the water, one good option is the two-floor Restaurante Xantar da Ría (Rúa Beiramar; 34; meals €20-45; ☺☏). It serves up reasonably priced *guisos*, *arroces* (rice-based dishes), *mariscadas* and *parrilladas*.

The tourist office (☑986 73 14 15; www.tur ismogrove.com in Spanish; Praza do Corgo; ☺10am-8pm Mon-Sat, 11am-2pm Sun) is near the fishing harbour, in the heart of O Grove.

The bus station (☑986 73 03 55) is on Rúa Beiramar, by the port. Monbus runs at least nine buses daily to Pontevedra (€3.75, one hour), and three to Santiago de Compostela (€5.50, 2¼ hours) via Cambados.

Pontevedra

POP 60,200

Galicia's smallest provincial capital may have a story-book old quarter, but it's no sleepy museum city. The interlocking lanes and plazas of the compact centre are abuzz with shops, markets, cafes and tapas bars. In the 16th century Pontevedra was the biggest city in Galicia and an important port. Columbus' flagship, the *Santa María,* was built here. In the 17th century it began to decline in the face of growing competition in the *ría* and the silting up of its port. Today it's an inviting riverside city that combines history, culture and style into a lively base for exploring the Rías Baixas.

◉ Sights

The pedestrianised historic centre of Pontevedra was once enclosed behind medieval walls, though remnants are scarce. More than a dozen plazas dot the old quarter – the liveliest are the Prazas da Verdura, do Teucro, da Leña and da Ferrería.

At the southeastern edge of the old town, you can't miss the distinctive curved facade of the Santuario da Virxe Peregrina, an almost circular 18th-century caprice with a distinctly Portuguese flavour. Set back from the broad Praza da Ferrería is the 14th-century Igrexa de San Francisco (☺7.30am-12.45pm & 5.30-9pm), said to have been founded by St Francis of Assisi when on pilgrimage to Santiago de Compostela. What was the adjacent convent is now the local tax office.

Head down Rúa da Pasantería to Praza da Leña, an enchanting niche, partly colonnaded and with a *cruceiro* (stone crucifix, a traditional Galician art form) in the

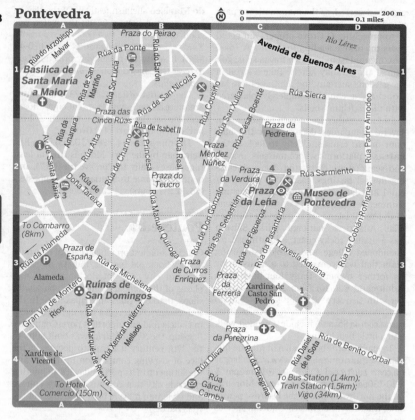

Pontevedra

middle. Just off it is the main entrance to the **Museo de Pontevedra** (☏986 85 14 55; Rúa da Pasantería 2-12; admission free; ⊙10am-2pm & 4.30-8.30pm Tue-Sat, 11am-2pm Sun), a highly eclectic collection scattered over six centre-city buildings. The displays in this main section (with labelling in Spanish and Galician) run from Galician archaeology to a captain's cabin of a 19th-century warship. Another part of the museum, the **Ruínas de San Domingos** (Gran Vía de Montero Ríos; admission free; ⊙10am-9pm Tue-Sat, 11am-2pm Sun), harbours an intriguing assemblage of heraldic shields, sepulchres and other medieval carvings in the remains of a 14th-century church.

Up Rúa de Isabel II stands the **Basílica de Santa María a Maior** (⊙10am-1pm & 5.30-8.30pm Mon-Sat, 10am-2pm & 6-9pm Sun), an impressive, mainly Gothic church built by Pontevedra's sailors' guild with a whiff of plateresque and Portuguese Manueline influences. Busts of Columbus and that other great Spanish empire-builder, Hernán Cortés, flank the rosette window on the western facade.

Festivals & Events

For a week in mid-August, the **Festas da Peregrina** feature a big funfair on the Alameda and concerts in Praza da Ferrería. In late July the Festival Internacional de Jazz e Blues (www.jazzpontevedra.com) attracts top-notch musicians from around the world.

Sleeping

Hotel Rúas HOTEL €€
(986 84 64 16; www.hotelruas.net; Rúa Figueroa 35; s/d €43/70; ❂❃@❆) Surprisingly classy one-star rooms, most with idyllic plaza views, have shiny wooden floors, unfussy furnishings and large bathrooms. The restaurant does a very good set lunch for €12 Monday to Friday.

Dabarca APARTMENT HOTEL €€
(986 86 97 23; www.hoteldabarca.com; Calle Palamios 2; s/d €102/108; ❂❃❆@❆) Run like a hotel but offering apartments instead of standard rooms, this sleek spot is ideal for families (there's a small surcharge per child in double rooms). Apartments are fitted with a small kitchenette, washing machine and beige, Ikea-inspired furniture. It's just beyond the Alameda gardens.

Parador Casa del Barón PARADOR HOTEL €€€
(986 85 58 00; www.parador.es; Rúa do Barón 19; r €160; ❂❃❆) A refurbished 16th-century Renaissance palace, this elegant hotel is decorated with period furniture and has a lovely garden.

Casa Maruja PENSIÓN €
(986 85 49 01; Avenida de Santa María 12; s €15-25, d €38) Though some beds might be lumpy, this clean and friendly budget option has several bright rooms with sublime views onto a quiet plaza.

Hotel Comercio HOTEL €
(986 85 12 17; www.hcomercio.com in Spanish; Rúa Augusto González Besada 5; s/d €41/55; ❆) A sound fall-back when other central budget options are full (a frequent occurrence).

Eating

You'll be pleasantly surprised how little it costs to eat well here. Virtually all the old town's plazas are ringed with restaurants

doing good-value set lunches by day and tapas and *raciones* by evening.

Casa Verdún TAPAS, RACIONES €
(Rúa Real 46; raciones €6-12; ❂closed Sun) A superior tapas-and-*raciones* spot with an interior patio as well as a busy bar area. Multifarious tempting options range from monkfish brochette or inventive salads to entrecote steak in Valdeón cheese.

O Rianxo HOME-STYLE GALICIAN €
(Praza da Leña 6; meals €16-25) One of several good places on this attractive plaza, Rianxo serves top local favourites like *caldeirada de raya* (a piquant fish-and-potato hotpot), either out on the plaza or in the upstairs dining room.

Bar 5 Calles TAPAS, RACIONES €
(Praza das Cinco Rúas; raciones €3-6) Sit at the solid wooden tables here for drinks and all sorts of very Galician, very good snacks such as octopus, *empanada de maíz con berberechos* (cockle pie), or *calamares a la romana* (fried, breaded squid), freshly sizzled up in the busy kitchen.

La Tienda de Clara GRILL €
(986 10 23 10; Calle García Sánchez 15; meals €15-30; ❂noon-midnight) Just south of the old town, this refreshingly bright spot, decked out with contemporary art, grills anything from fish to quail to rabbit to steak to vegetables. Eat on high stools at long tables in front of the open kitchen, in the interior dining room or outside.

Drinking & Entertainment

It's hard to find a bar-less street in the old town. For coffee, laid-back drinks and people-watching, you have several atmospheric squares to choose from, like Praza da Verdura, Praza do Teucro, Praza da Leña or Praza de Curros Enríquez. From there you can head to the pocket of bars on Rúa do Barón and then, for some heftier *marcha* (action), up the road to the thumping music bars of Rúa de Charino.

❶ Information

Municipal tourist information kiosk (Praza de Ourense; ❂10am-2pm & 4.45-6.30pm Mon-Sat, 10.30am-2pm Sun)

Turismo Rías Baixas (986 84 26 90; www.riasbaixas.depo.es; Praza de Santa María; ❂9am-8pm Mon-Fri, 10am-2pm Sat & Sun) Information on all Pontevedra province.

ⓘ Getting There & Around

The **bus station** (☑986 85 24 08; www.auto busespontevedra.com; Rúa da Estación) is about 1.5km southeast of the town centre. Castromil-Monbus goes at least 26 times daily to Vigo (€2.65, 30 minutes), 13 times to Santiago (€5.70, one hour) and seven times to Ourense (€10, two hours). Buses also run to Sanxenxo, O Grove, Cambados, Tui and far-off cities like Lugo and Madrid.

Pontevedra's **train station** (☑986 85 13 13), across the street from the bus station, is on the Vigo–Santiago de Compostela line, with almost hourly train services to those cities and A Coruña.

City buses run between the bus station and Praza de España, on the edge of the old town, every half-hour.

Ría de Pontevedra

COMBARRO
POP 1260

Near Pontevedra on the *ría's* north shore, the postcard-perfect village of Combarro unfurls around a tidy bay. With a jumble of seaside *hórreos,* a historic quarter that looks like it was plucked straight out of the Middle Ages, and crooked lanes (some of them hewn directly out of the rock bed) dotted with *cruceiros* and wonderful little restaurants, this is some people's favourite stop in the Rías Baixas. It can get extremely busy in high summer, though.

The main activity here is eating, and you have several excellent choices. Savour excellent fish, rice and meat dishes and cheaper *raciones* at spots like Taberna O Peirao (Rúa do Mar 6; meals €35-55), featuring a waterside terrace among the *hórreos.*

Just beyond Combarro, veer down towards tranquil Praia de Covelo to find the humble-looking but locally revered El Caracol (Rúa Peirao do Covelo 14; meals €40-70), a tavern with a porch-like terrace overlooking the water. The house speciality is baked fish, but it's also known for its rice dishes.

Monbus buses between Pontevedra and Sanxenxo stop at Combarro.

SANXENXO
POP 2340

Sanxenxo (Castilian: Sangenjo) has been dubbed the 'Marbella of Galicia' and, though almost deserted for at least half the year, it does have a thing or two in common with Spain's Mediterranean resorts in the summer season: a busy leisure port, some

good beaches, a long buzzing waterfront, and streets packed with eateries and tourist accommodation. The tourism here however is almost exclusively Spanish.

Praia de Silgar is a fine, sandy and busy beach. West, towards Portonovo, dune-backed Praia de Baltar is a bit quieter. Beyond Sanxenxo, a road parallels the wave-battered shore at the tip of the *ría,* although sand-and-sea views are limited because of the nonstop parade of hotels, *hostales* and general tourist sprawl.

For a seafront location, stylish and comfortable Hotel Rotilio (☑986 72 02 00; www.hotelrotilio.com; Avenida do Porto 7; s €76, d €119-173; P ❀) overlooks both Praia de Silgar and the marina. All 40 rooms are exterior and most have balconies. Its restaurant, La Taberna de Rotilio (meals €40-60; ⊙closed Mon & Sun dinner Oct-Jun), serves up terrific Galician seafood and meat with a creative touch. Portonovo, 2km west, has many tapas bars and seafood eateries.

There's a tourist office (☑986 72 02 85; www.sanxenxo.es in Spanish; Porto Juan Carlos I; ⊙9am-9pm, closed Sun & Mon mid-Oct–mid-Jun), plus a large car park, in the shiny marina development immediately east of Praia de Silgar.

Buses between Pontevedra and O Grove (over 20 a day in summer) stop in Sanxenxo.

SOUTH SHORE

From Marín, you can head a few kilometres inland up to the Mirador de Cotorredondo, a lookout commanding magical views over the Rías de Pontevedra and Vigo. Otherwise, zip past the sprawl surrounding Marín to discover the quiet appeal of the *ría's* southern shore, where you can stop at beaches like wide Praia de Lapamán or in maritime towns like Bueu, with its pretty beach and busy waterfront. Venture past the fishing hamlet of Beluso towards Cabo de Udra, where the jagged shoreline is adorned with a backdrop of the Illa de Ons and there are several secluded (though not secret) beaches like the clear-watered Praia Mourisca.

Ría de Vigo

The AP9 motorway's Puente de Rande suspension bridge brings the *ría's* northern shore into easy reach of the city. At the far tip of the *ría,* the peaceful village of Hío draws visitors who want a glimpse of

ILLA DE ONS

In summer you can hop on a boat out to vehicle-free Ons island, part of the Islas Atlánticas national park, with its sandy beaches, cliffs, ruins, walking trails and rich bird life. Campers wanting to pitch at the island's camping area (free of charge) must make a reservation when they book their boat ticket, or beforehand online at www.iatlanticas.es (in Spanish).

Weather permitting, Naviera Mar de Ons (www.mardeons.com, in Spanish) and Cruceros Rías Baixas (www.crucerosriasbaixas.com, in Spanish) sail to Illa de Ons several times daily from Sanxenxo and Portonovo from 1 July to late September (round trip adult/child €14/7).

Galicia's most famous **cruceiro**, a small but elaborate cross that stands outside the San Andrés de Hío church. Sculpted during the 19th century from a single block of stone, it narrates key passages of Christian teaching, from Adam and Eve to the taking down of Christ from the cross.

Numerous sandy beaches are signposted in the area. About 2.5km north of Hío by paved road is the tranquil, sandy Praia Areabrava.

Continue west through the hamlet of Donón and towards windswept Cabo de Home, a rocky cape with an archaeological site, views of the Illas Cíes and several walking trails.

Near the beach and the famous *cruceiro*, Hotel Doade (☑986 32 83 02; www.hotel doade.com; Bajada Praia de Arneles 1, Hío; s/d €64/75; P☀) has spacious, spic-and-span rooms with peach-coloured walls and fresh, white linen. The restaurant specialises in *ría*-fresh seafood.

Vigo

POP 208,000

Depending on where you aim your view-finder, Vigo is a gritty port city, a cosmopolitan art centre, or a noble and historic capital. Home to Europe's largest fishing fleet, this is an axis of trade and commerce in northern Spain. Yet it is also walkable and compact, and it boasts some of the best seafood in the world.

People started to notice Vigo in the Middle Ages when it began to overtake Baiona as a major port. The first industries started up here in the 18th century, but Vigo's major development was in the 20th century, during which its population grew 15-fold. Today its port is a stop for many cruise ships.

The Casco Vello (Old Town) climbs uphill from the port; the heart of the modern town spreads east from here, between Rúa do Príncipe and the waterfront.

◎ Sights & Activities

Vigo's greatest charms are its simplest: navigating the steep, jumbled lanes of the Casco Vello; watching the boats come and go in the harbour; slurping oysters on lively Rúa Pescadería; and window-shopping along the busy Rúa do Príncipe (an outdoor mall of sorts).

Casco Vello   OLD TOWN
The heart of the old town is the elegant Praza da Constitución, a perfect spot for a drink. Head north down Rúa dos Cesteiros, famous for its wicker shops, and you'll come upon the Igrexa de Santa María, built in 1816 – long after its Romanesque predecessor had been burnt down by Sir Francis Drake.

Parque do Castro   PARK
Directly south (and uphill) of the old town you can wander in the verdant Parque do Castro, where you can inspect a castro dating to the 3rd century BC and poke around the medieval ruins of the Castelo do Castro, which formed part of the city's defences built under Felipe IV.

Praia de Samil   BEACH
A long swath of sandy beaches stretches southwest of the city. The best is Praia de Samil (1.2km long), backed by a long seaside promenade and with great views of the Illas Cíes. Buses 10 (daily) and C15B (not Sundays) go to Samil from the harbourfront Rúa Cánovas del Castillo.

Museo do Mar   MUSEUM
(www.museodomar.com/gl, in Spanish; Avenida Atlántida 160; adult/child €3/1.50; ⊗11am-2pm &

5-9.30pm Tue-Fri, 11am-10pm Sat & Sun; 🚹) On the way out to Praia de Samil, this museum features innovative exhibits on Galicia's relationship with the sea, encompassing among other things a lighthouse, an aquarium and a 19th-century submarine. The museum is served by the same buses as Praia de Samil.

FREE **Museo de Arte Contemporánea de Vigo** MUSEUM

(Marco; www.marcovigo.com; Rúa do Príncipe 54; ⊙11am-9pm Tue-Sat, 11am-3pm Sun) Vigo has a well-earned reputation as an art centre, and there are several top-line museums and galleries to prove it. Pick up *Guía del Ocio* (in Spanish) at a tourist office for full exhibit listings. If you have time for just one artistic stop, make it here, the prime venue for exhibitions ranging from painting and sculpture to cinema, fashion and design.

FREE **Museo Quiñones de León** MUSEUM

(✆986 29 50 70; ⊙10am-1.30pm & 5-8pm Tue, Thu & Fri, 10am-8pm Wed, 5-8pm Sat, 10am-1.30pm Sun) Set amid the gardens of the **Parque de Castrelos**, 3km south of the city centre, this 17th-century palace has a worthwhile art, archaeological and historical collections.

🛏 Sleeping

It's worth booking ahead in July and August.

Hotel América HOTEL €€

(✆986 43 89 22; www.hotelamerica-vigo.com; Rúa de Pablo Morillo 6; s/d incl breakfast €69/102; 🅿✳@🛜) As stylish as Vigo gets, the América gets two thumbs up for its contemporary feel (well-equipped, spacious rooms; tasteful modern art; elegantly muted colour schemes), friendly, efficient staff and quiet side-street location near the waterfront. The breakfast is a good buffet-style affair, served on the roof terrace in summer. Discounts often available Friday to Sunday nights.

Hotel Puerta del Sol HOTEL €€

(✆986 22 23 64; www.alojamientosvigo.com; Porta do Sol 14; s/d €55/70; 🖨🛜) With its central location overlooking two Casco Vello plazas and attractive rustic-chic rooms, it's no wonder this bright little hotel fills up fast. Extras include in-room CD players. It also offers three-person apartments across the street, with kitchen, for €95.

Hotel AC Palacio Universal HOTEL €€

(✆986 44 92 50; www.ac-hotels.com; Rúa de Cánovas del Castillo 28; r from €119; 🅿🖨✳🛜)

Vigo's last word in luxury, this swanky hotel is a stylish, contemporary revamp of a lovely 19th-century palace overlooking the harbour club. The 69 rooms are sober but sophisticated, with soothing beige decor. Check the website for discount offers.

Hotel Náutico HOTEL €

(✆986 12 24 40; www.hotelnautico.net, in Spanish; Rúa de Luis Taboada 28; s/d incl breakfast €37/53; 🛜) With clean, crisp style and a pleasant nautical look, this contemporary hotel near the Praza de Compostela park is a solid bet. Rooms are small but cosy, with perks like heated towel rails.

Hotel Princesa HOTEL €€

(✆986 44 20 13; hotelprincesa@gmail.com; Rúa de Fermín Penzol 14; s/d incl breakfast €35/60; @) Another solid bet, on the eastern edge of the Casco Vello: the clean, carpeted rooms are quite bright, and there's a neat breakfast cafe.

🍴 Eating

For tapas bars and informal cafes, head to the narrow lanes and pretty plazas of the old town, especially around Praza da Constitución. There's also a lively tapas scene along Rúa de Rosalía de Castro, about 800m east. Rúa Pescadería, in the lower part of the old town, is a short block jammed with people tucking into fresh seafood. From 9.30am until 3.30pm you can buy oysters for around €12 per dozen from the *ostreras* (shuckers) at the west end of the street. Sit down to eat them with a drink at one of the neighbouring restaurants. Oysters and Albariño wine are Vigo's traditional Sunday-morning hangover cure.

A'Curuxa ECLECTIC €€

(✆986 43 88 57; Rúa dos Cesteiros 7; menú €8.50, meals €20-40; ⊙closed Tue) This delightful stone tavern just off Praza da Constitución mixes the traditional and contemporary in decor and menu. Try Galician favourites like *arroces* and *cocidos* (stews), or opt for a creative salad or seafood tapas. Great atmosphere, though service can be slow.

Casa Esperanza TRADITIONAL GALICIAN €€

(Rúa de Luis Taboada 28; menú €27, meals €35-50; ⊙closed sun & 2nd half of Aug) Serving up traditional, fresh Galician fare since 1949, stone-walled Esperanza is equally great for meats (with or without cheese sauces) or any type of fish prepared almost any way you want it.

El Capitán SEAFOOD €€
(☏986 22 09 40; Rúa do Triunfo 5; meals €30-60)
With only half a dozen tables and an open
kitchen, this simple but special old-town
spot prepares top-quality fish, *arroces* and
octopus.

Restaurant Ébano CONTEMPORARY GALICIAN €€
(Rúa de Luis Taboada 27; meals €30-50) Across
the street from Casa Esperanza, the Ébano
provides a more contemporary twist in
both decor and cuisine, with dishes like
duck magret in a fruit and port sauce.

Restaurante Cúrcuma VEGETARIAN €
(Rúa do Brasil 4; meals €15-25; ⊙closed Sun; ☏)
Deservedly popular, this bright restaurant a
couple of blocks uphill from the train station does well-prepared vegetarian dishes
like tofu brochettes or vegie moussaka, plus
daily specials such as lentil soup and crepes.

🍸 Drinking & Entertainment

Vigo's nightlife is hopping. Start off slow at
one of several enticing cafe-bars around Praza da Constitución in the old town, or Praza
de Compostela or Rúa de Montero Ríos (opposite the waterfront) to the east.

Estrella de Galicia (Praza da Compostela
17) has Galicia's favourite beer (Estrella)
sitting in big copper vats by the entrance.
From around 10pm to 1am, the bars along
Rúa de Rosalía de Castro, such as Tudo
Brasil, with cocktails and tropical ambience, or the packed pub Van Gogh Café,
are at their peak.

The real *zona de marcha* for the 20s
crowd, from around midnight, is about 1km
southeast of the old town in the Churruca
district just above Praza do Portugal. You
might start at the retro lounge-style Black
Ball (Rúa de Churruca 8), then stop into La
Fábrica de Chocolate Club (Rúa de Rogelio
Abalde 22), which hosts a live band or guest
DJ or two each week. Especially bohemian
haunts are found along Rúa dos Irmandi-
ños and Rúa de Iglesia Espondas.

Faro de Vigo newspaper and free booklet
Go! have what's-on listings.

Mondo Club CLUB
(www.myspace.com/mondoclubvigo in Spanish;
Rúa de Joaquín Loriga 3; ⊙1-6.30am Thu-Sat
nights) The huge, 1000-plus-capacity club
has resident DJs spinning a rock/pop/
electro/indie/'80s/'90s mix and frequent
Spanish and international touring bands.

Centro Cultural Caixanova CULTURAL CENTRE
(www.obrasocialcaixanova.com in Spanish; Rúa

de Policarpo Sanz 13) This centre has a busy
program of concerts, dance and theatre.

ℹ️ Information

SereoCiber (Praza da Princesa 3; internet
per hr €1.80; ⊙9am-midnight Mon-Fri, 11am-
midnight Sat & Sun)

Municipal tourist office (☏986 22 47 57;
www.turismodevigo.org; Rúa de Teófilo Llorente
5; ⊙10am-2pm & 4-7pm, closed Sun approx
Oct-Jun)

Regional tourist office (☏986 43 05 77;
oficina.turismo.vigo@xunta.es; Rúa Cánovas
del Castillo 22; ⊙9.30am-2pm & 4.30-6.30pm
Mon-Sat, closed Sat afternoon approx mid-
Sep–mid-Jun)

ℹ️ Getting There & Away

Air

Vigo's **Peinador airport** (☏986 26 82 00) is
about 9km east of the centre. Iberia flies to/
from Madrid, Barcelona, Bilbao, Valencia and
Málaga; Spanair serves Barcelona and Madrid.
Air France and Air Europa fly to/from Paris.

Bus

The **bus station** (☏986 37 34 11; www.vigobus.
com, in Spanish; Avenida de Madrid 57) is 2km
southeast of the old city. Autores heads to
Madrid (€38 to €52, 7¼ to nine hours, at least
six daily), Castromil-Monbus makes several
trips daily to all major Galician cities, including
Pontevedra (€2.65, 30 minutes), Santiago de
Compostela (€8.40, 1½ hours), Ourense (€10,
1½ hours) and the coastal resorts.

Autna (www.autna.com, in Spanish) runs
four times daily Monday to Friday (once daily
on weekends) to/from Porto, Portugal (€10, 2½
hours), with connections there for Lisbon.

Other buses, many run by ALSA, head for
Oviedo, Santander, Bilbao, Barcelona, Seville
and elsewhere.

Train

The train station is 1km southeast of the old
centre. Renfe runs approximately hourly to Pontevedra (€2 to €3, 30 minutes) and Santiago de
Compostela (€7.50 to €8.50, 1½ to two hours),
and eight times daily to Ourense (€9.90 to
€19.20, 1½ to two hours). There are twice-daily
trains to Madrid and Barcelona.

ℹ️ Getting Around

Vitrasa (☏986 29 16 00; www.vitrasa.es, in
Spanish; per ride €1.17) runs city buses. Bus
C9A runs between the central Porta do Sol and
the airport; buses C2 and C4C link the centre
and the bus station; and lines C4, C9 and 11 join
the centre with Rúa do Urzáiz close to the train
station.

Illas Cíes

Illas Cíes, three spectacular islands that form a beautiful bird sanctuary and are home to some of Galicia's most privileged beaches, are a 45-minute ferry ride from Vigo. Sitting 14km offshore, this small archipelago is the main attraction of the Parque Nacional de las Islas Atlánticas de Galicia (http://reddeparquesnacionales.mma.es, in Spanish), a national park that also includes the Ons, Sálvora and Cortegada archipelagos further north.

The three Cíes islands (Illa de Monteagudo and Illa do Faro, which are joined by a sandy isthmus, and the southern Illa do San Martiño) form a 6km breakwater that protects Vigo and its *ría* from the Atlantic's fury. This is an ideal spot for swimming and lolling on pristine beaches, birdwatching, or walking the trails along the shores or to the spectacular high lookouts.

You can only visit the Illas Cíes during Semana Santa, on weekends from then to the end of May, or daily from June to early September. To stay overnight you must camp at Camping Illas Cíes (www.campingislascies.com; sites per 2 adults & tent €24.15, 2-person tent rental per night €45 with 2-night minimum). For camping from June to September you must book in advance, online or at the camping office (☺8.30am-1.30pm & 2.30-7pm) at the Illas Cíes ferry terminal in Vigo; if you are sailing from Vigo you must obtain a camping permit at the office there. The campground has a restaurant and supermarket, and a capacity of 800 people – often filled in August.

Boats to the islands are run, weather permitting, by Naviera Mar de Ons (☎986 22 52 72; www.mardeons.com, in Spanish), with up to eight trips daily (round trip adult/child €18.50/6) from Vigo, and four daily from Baiona and Cangas, for the same price, in July and August.

THE SOUTHWEST

From Vigo, the PO552 highway runs southwest along the *ría* to Baiona, then dives south, skimming a rocky coast that, while beautiful, has resisted excessive tourist development because it has fewer sandy beaches.

Baiona

POP 3000

Crowned with a spectacular seaside fortress, Baiona (Castilian: Bayona) is a popular resort that balances coast and culture. Its shining moment came on 1 March 1493, when one of Columbus' small fleet, the *Pinta,* stopped in for supplies, bearing the remarkable news that the explorer had made it to the Indies (in fact, the West Indies). Then an important trading port, Baiona was later eclipsed by Vigo. These days, you can visit a replica of the Pinta (admission €1; ☺10am-7.30pm), which sits moored in Baiona's harbour.

A tangle of inviting lanes makes up Baiona's casco histórico (historic centre). There are a handful of 16th- and 17th-century houses and chapels, with cafes, restaurants and artisans' shops scattered about.

You can't miss the pine-covered promontory Monte Boi, dominated by the Fortaleza de Monterreal (pedestrian/car €1/5; ☺10am-10pm). The fortress, erected between the 11th and 17th centuries, is protected by an impenetrable 3km circle of walls. An enticing 40-minute walking trail loops the promontory's rocky shoreline, which is broken up by a few small beaches. Also within the precinct today is a luxurious *parador* hotel – have a drink on its cafe terrace, with fabulous views across the bay.

For better beaches, take the seaside promenade towards the Praia Ladeira, 1.5km east of the centre. Some 2.5km further on is the magnificent sweep of Praia América at Nigrán. Most buses between Baiona and Vigo stop at these beaches.

◉ Sleeping & Eating

Many of Baiona's hotels are clustered near the harbour-front road, and the cobbled lanes in the centre of town are full of restaurants, tapas bars and watering holes.

Hotel Anunciada   HOTEL €€
(☎986 35 60 18; www.hotel-anunciada.com; Rúa Elduayen 16; s €49, d €65-86; ☻☏) Well run, this hotel has some inviting contemporary-styled rooms with bay views, and other smaller rooms, also pleasant, with flowery prints.

Parador de Baiona   HOTEL, RESTAURANT €€€
(☎986 35 50 00; www.parador.es; r incl breakfast from €238; P☻❊☏☲) This privileged *parador* stands in the centre of Monte Boi. The grandiose rooms boast canopied beds and wonderful views, while the sophisticated

restaurant (meals €30 to €70) offers a sampling of local specialities like *vieiras asadas al horno* (oven-roasted scallops).

Jaqueyvi
RESTAURANT €€

(Rúa do Reloxo 2; meals €25-50; ☺closed mid-Jan–mid-Feb, Wed Oct-May) A fine choice, with some tables out on its pedestrian street, it does excellent grilled meats as well as all the Galician seafood favourites.

❶ Information

Get maps and more at the **tourist office** (☎986 68 70 67; www.baiona.org; Paseo da Ribeira; ☺10am-3pm & 4-9pm) on the approach to Monte Boi.

❶ Getting There & Away

ATSA (☎986 35 53 30) buses run north to Vigo (€2.30) every 30 minutes till 9pm most days, but just a couple a day go south to A Guarda. In summer, boats sail to the Illas Cíes.

A Guarda

POP 6200

A fishing port just north of where the Río Miño spills into the Atlantic, A Guarda (Castilian: La Guardia) is a ho-hum town with a pretty harbour and some good seafood restaurants. Its big draw is beautiful Monte de Santa Trega (admission in vehicle per person Tue-Sun Feb-Dec €0.80, other times free), the hill rising high above the town.

Drive (4km) or take the 45-minute trail walk from the base of the Monte up to its summit. On the way up, poke around the Iron Age Castro de Santa Tegra. At the top of the mount, you'll find a 16th-century chapel, an interesting small archaeological museum (admission free; ☺10am-8pm Tue-Sun) on *castro* culture, and a couple of cafes. The beauty of the place is slightly marred by cheesy souvenir shops and the odd tour bus, but the views up the Miño, across to Portugal and out over the Atlantic are too marvellous to miss (especially at sunset).

It's also nice to take the 3km **walking path** south from A Guarda's harbour along the coast to the heads of the Miño.

A real treat, Hotel Convento de San Benito (☎986 61 11 66; www.hotelsanbenito.es; Praza de San Bieito; s €57, d €83-104; ⓟ❁❋❀) is housed in a 16th-century convent down by the harbour. Its 24 elegant rooms are romantic and individually decorated, with period furniture and original architectural elements like exposed stone walls.

A Guarda is famed for its *arroz con bogavante* and more than a dozen eateries line up in front of the harbour. At one end sits the humble Porto Guardés (Rúa do Porto 1; fish dishes €6-12; ☺6pm-midnight), where grilled swordfish, tuna, hake, sole and other seafood are served in a tavern-like atmosphere. Head to the far end of the strip for upscale seafood at Marisquería Anduriña (Rúa do Porto 58; fish dishes €15-24; arroz con bogavante for 2 €54; closed Nov, dinner Sun Sep-Jul), where tanks of live *bogavante* tempt.

ATSA buses run to/from Vigo (€5.50, 80 minutes) approximately half-hourly. Most go via Tui, but a few go via Baiona. Service is reduced at weekends. A ferry (vehicle & driver/passenger €2.49/0.60; ☺hourly 9.30am-10.30pm to 8.30pm Sep-Jun) crosses the Miño from Camposancos, 2km south of A Guarda, to Caminha, Portugal.

Tui

POP 6100

Sitting above the banks of the majestic Miño River, the border town of Tui (Castilian: Tuy) draws Portuguese and Spanish day trippers with its lively cafe scene, tightly packed medieval centre and magnificent cathedral. Just across the bridge is Portugal's equally appealing Valença.

◉ Sights

Heading towards the old town, you'll come first to the plaza-like Paseo Calvo Sotelo first, better known as the Corredoira. From here, enter the historic district via the Porta da Pía, a gate in the 12th-century defensive wall.

The highlight of the old town is the fortress-like Catedral de Santa Maria (admission €2; ☺9.30am-1.30pm & 4-8pm), which reigns over Praza de San Fernando. Begun in the 12th century, it reflects a stoic Romanesque style in most of its construction, although the portal is ornate Gothic. It was much altered in the 15th century and extra stone bracing was added after the Lisbon earthquake in 1755. You can visit the main nave and chapels for free, but it's well worth the ticket price to see the Gothic cloister, Romanesque chapter house, cathedral museum, tower and gardens with views over the river, and the Museo Diocesano (☺Easter–mid-Oct, closed Mon-Thu to end May), across the street, with its archaeology and art collection.

🛏 Sleeping & Eating

There are several inviting places to eat near the cathedral. On Friday to Sunday nights, Entrefornos and other quaint cobbled streets behind the cathedral are the scene of some major partying.

O Novo Cabalo Furado   GUEST HOUSE €€
(☎986 60 44 45; www.cabalofurado.com; Rúa Seijas 3; s/d/apt €35/60/75; ❄🛜) In the heart of the old town, the rooms and apartments at this intimate guest house are simple but inviting, with all-wood furnishings and sparkly new bathrooms.

Quinta do Ramo   COUNTRY HOTEL €€
(☎986 62 28 84; www.quintadoramo.com, in Spanish; Lugar de Ramo 5, Forcadela, Tomiño; d incl breakfast €70; 🅿) An exquisite garden alive with fruit trees and flowery bushes surrounds this elegant rural hotel 10km west of Tui towards A Guarda. The 19th-century stone house has 10 cosy, country-style rooms and an upscale restaurant (meals €30 to €60) serving excellent meat and fish dishes like grilled sole and Galician-style hake.

O Vello Cabalo Furado   GALICIAN €
(Rúa Seijas 2; menú €9.50, meals €20-40; ⏰closed Sun Jul & Aug, dinner Tue & Sun Sep-Jun; 🌿) This large inviting dining hall serves hearty specialities such as *cocido gallego*, *chuletón de ternera* (giant beef chop) and a long list of local fish dishes.

ℹ Information

There's a **municipal tourist kiosk** (⏰10am-7.30pm, closed Christmas-late Apr) on the Corredoira, and a **regional tourist office** (☎986 60 17 89; Rúa Colón 2; ⏰9.30am-1.30pm & 4.30-6.30pm) 400m from the Corredoira.

ℹ Getting There & Away

ATSA buses to both Vigo and A Guarda (both €2.95, 40 minutes, approximately every half-hour) stop on Paseo de Calvo Sotelo, opposite Librería Byblos. Service is considerably reduced at weekends.

THE EAST

Although often overshadowed by the glorious coastline and the better-known attractions in Santiago de Compostela and A Coruña, eastern Galicia is a treasure-trove of enticing provincial cities, spectacular natural landscapes and old-fashioned rural enclaves. Every valley is another world and you may start to understand why stories of witchcraft abound in Galicia. This is perfect territory for travellers who like digging out their own gems.

Ourense

POP 101,000

Galicia's third-largest city has a spruced-up labyrinth of a historic quarter, a lively tapas scene and tempting thermal baths. Ourense (Castilian: Orense) first came into its own as a Castilian trading centre in the 11th century. The broad Río Miño runs east–west across the city, crossed by several bridges, including the medieval Ponte Vella. The compact old town, full of fine old architecture thanks in large part to Ourense's long ecclesiastical tradition, rises to the south of the river.

⊙ Sights & Activities

The old town unfolds around the crucifix-shaped, 12th-century **Catedral do San Martiño** (Rúa de Juan de Austria; admission free; ⏰11.30am-1.30pm & 4-7.30pm, closed to tourist visits Sun morning). The cathedral's artistic highlight is the gilded Santo Cristo chapel, near the northern entrance. At the west end is the Pórtico do Paraíso, a coloured (and less inspired) Gothic copy of Santiago de Compostela's Pórtico de la Gloria.

Radiating around the cathedral is a maze of narrow streets begging to be explored. Intriguing churches like the concave-facaded **Santa Eufemia**, the 12th-century **Trinidade** and the baroque **Santa María la Madre** and **Santo Domingo** dot the centre and are accompanied by well-kept gardens and beguiling squares. The largest square is sloping Praza Maior, rimmed by cafes and with the **Casa do Concello** (City Hall) at its foot. Climb up to what remains of the 14th-century **Convento de San Francisco** (Rúa de Emilia Pardo Bazán; admission free; ⏰9.30am-2.30pm & 4-9pm, closed Sun afternoon & Mon) to walk round its beautiful Gothic cloister, with 63 arches resting on all-different capitals.

Ourense's original raison d'être is the hot springs, **As Burgas** (Rúa As Burgas); gushing out 67°C waters with therapeutic properties, they have been used since Roman times. Just out of the centre, along the north bank of the Río Miño, is a string of other **natural hot springs** that have been beautifully landscaped and provide the perfect spot to unwind (take swimming gear). Three sets of open pools are free and open 24 hours daily. There are also two privately run sets of pools: closest to the centre are the Termas Chavasqueira (www.termaschavasqueira.com, in Spanish; admission €3.80; ☺9am-11.30pm Sun & Tue-Thu, 9am-3am Fri & Sat), with four warm pools and one cold one, plus a Japanese sauna and a cafe. You can walk there from the old town in 20 to 30 minutes or take the Tren de la Termas (tickets €0.70; ☺hourly 10am-1pm & 4-8pm), a mini-train, from Praza Maior.

🛏 Sleeping

Ourense's hotels are a bit of a letdown given the city's cultural flavour.

Hotel Zarampallo   HOTEL €
(☑988 23 00 08; www.zarampallo.com, in Spanish; Rúa dos Irmáns Villar 19; s/d €35/50; ☺☺☺) With a great city-centre location, this contemporary family-run hotel has modern rooms with peach-coloured walls, narrow balconies overlooking a pedestrian street, clean white bathrooms, and local art hanging on the walls.

Hotel Princess   HOTEL €€
(☑988 26 95 38; www.hotelprincess.net, in Spanish; Avenida de la Habana 45; s/d €72/95; ☺❋☺) Just north of the old town, the Princess is efficiently run and comfortable, in a staid provincial way, with flower-print bedspreads in the carpeted rooms.

🍴 Eating

Ir de tapeo ('going for tapas') is a way of life in Ourense, and central streets like Fornos, Paz, Lepanto, Viriato, San Miguel and Praza do Ferro brim with taverns where having to push and shove your way to the bar is seen as a sign of quality. Tapas begin at €1 and are nearly always washed down with a glass of local wine.

Mesón Porta da Aira   TAPAS, RACIONES €
(Rúa dos Fornos 2; tapas €2-7, dishes €9-24) This tiny eatery has locals flocking in for the generous platters of *huevos rotos:* lightly fried eggs over a bed of thinly sliced potatoes, to which you can add various sausages and meats.

Restaurante San Miguel   SEAFOOD, MEAT €€
(Rúa San Miguel 12; meals €30-60, menú €33; ☺) Specialising in seafood (as the gurgling lobster tanks attest), this is the kind of

place where bow-tied waiters sweep breadcrumbs off the table and even the water is served in goblets. There's also a good selection of Galician meats for carnivores.

Lizarran   TAPAS, RACIONES €€
(Rúa Lepanto 29; raciones €6-16) Well positioned overlooking Praza do Ferro, Lizarran is good for grilled meats and fish or lighter *raciones* such as salads or wild mushrooms in garlic. Or you can just snack on the *pinchos* (€1) that they bring round on plates.

🍷 Drinking & Entertainment

Ourense is packed with intimate pubs and tapas bars that easily make the transition into night-time. Stroll the streets around the cathedral for a host of options. For live music, head to downtown Praza Eufemia, where Miudiño sometimes hosts groups playing Celtic music, and Café Latino has a fabulous corner stage for groups playing jazz and other styles.

ℹ Information

Municipal tourist office (☑988 36 60 64; www.turismodeourense.com, in Spanish; Calle Isabel La Católica 2; ☺9am-2pm & 3-8pm Mon-Fri, 11am-2pm Sat & Sun) Underneath the Xardinillos Padre Feijóo park, just off pedestrianised Rúa do Paseo.

Regional tourist office (☑988 37 20 20; ☺9am-2pm & 4.30-8.30pm Mon-Sat) On the Ponte Vella.

ℹ Getting There & Away

Ourense's **bus station** (☑988 21 60 27; Carretera de Vigo 1), 2km northwest of the centre, has services throughout Ourense province and to Galicia's main cities. Monbus runs to Santiago (€10.35, two hours, four or more daily), Vigo (€10, 1½ hours, five or more daily), Lugo (€8, 1¾ hours, four or more daily) and elsewhere. Avanza journeys to Madrid (€32 to €46, six to seven hours, five or more daily).

The **train station** (Rúa de Eulogio Gómez Franqueira) is 500m north of the Río Miño. Renfe runs to Santiago (€8 to €19, 1½ to two hours, six daily), Vigo (€10 to €19, two hours, eight daily), León (€20 to €29, four hours, four daily), Madrid (€44, 5½ to 7½ hours, two daily) and elsewhere.

ℹ Getting Around

Local buses 1, 3, 6A and 6B run between the train station and Parque de San Lázaro in the city centre. The 6A and 6B also serve the bus station. Bus 12 also connects the bus station with Parque San Lázaro.

Ribadavia

The headquarters of the Ribeiro wine region, where some of Galicia's best whites are made, Ribadavia sits on the Río Avia in a verdant valley. Its little historic centre is an enticing maze of narrow stone streets lined with heavy stone arcades and broken up by diminutive plazas; within this in medieval times was Galicia's largest Jewish quarter.

Upstairs from the tourist office is the **Museo Sefardí de Galicia** (Praza Maior 7; admission €1; ☉9.30am-2pm Tue-Sun), with exhibits, in Galician, on the Jews of Galicia.

The heart of the medieval **Barrio Xudío** (Jewish Quarter) was Rúa Merelles Caulla, running from Praza Maior to Praza Madalena. The **Casa da Inquisición** fronts Praza García Boente, two blocks down Rúa San Martiño. The **Museo Etnolóxico** (Rúa Santiago 10; admission free; ☉10am-2.30pm & 5-9pm Tue-Fri, 11am-2.30pm Sat & Sun, closed Sat & Sun mid-Sep–mid-Jun), with its Galician folk history collection, is worth a look, too – it's just down the street from the Romanesque **Igrexa de Santiago**. The large **Castelo do Sarmento** (Rúa Progreso), where the Counts of Ribadavia lived before moving to Praza Maior in the 17th century, is likely to open for visits by 2011 after restoration.

Relax with a stroll along the 5km-long **riverside path** that runs by the gurgling Río Avia: you can access it by steps down from Praza Buxán, next to Praza Madalena.

In early July, Ribadavia stages Galicia's biggest wine festival, the **Feria del Vino del Ribeiro**.

Pensión Plaza (☎988 47 05 76; s/d €27.50/37.50; ☁) has 12 simple but correct rooms. There are several wonderful rural hotels in the area: a 10-minute drive east of town, you can kill several birds with one stone at the **Casal de Armán** (☎699 060464; www.casaldearman.net in Spanish; O Cotiño, San Andrés; r incl breakfast €70-90; ℗☺☏), a dignified stone house that serves as a rural hotel, restaurant (meals €30 to 45) and winery rolled into one. Traditional Galician fare is served with style in its rustic-chic dining room, while the six rooms overlook the countryside.

For food, head to Praza Maior, which is ringed by cafes and restaurants such as **Restaurante Plaza** (Praza Maior; menú €9-12, meals €15-30), where you can get good, straightforward fish, meat and shellfish.

The **tourist office** (☎988 47 12 75; www.ribadavia.com; Praza Maior 7; ☉9.30am-2.30pm & 4-8pm, closed Sun afternoon) is in the former mansion of the Counts of Ribadavia on the lovely main square.

At least three buses and four trains run daily to Ourense and Vigo from stations in the east of town, just over the Río Avia.

Ribeira Sacra & Cañón do Sil

Northeast of Ourense, along the Sil and Miño Rivers, unfolds the unique natural beauty and cultural heritage of the Ribeira Sacra ('Sacred Riverbank'), named for the abundance of monasteries in the area. From the 6th century or even earlier, Christian hermits and monks were drawn to this remote but beautiful and fertile area, and at least 18 monasteries grew up here in medieval times. This still rural area is poorly served by public transport, but if you have a vehicle, a good map, and a dose of wanderlust, it makes for a marvellous road trip. The following sections detail a possible day or two-day route through the area, focusing on the magnificent Cañón do Sil (Sil Canyon), surrounded by steep hills and dense woodlands. For more information see www.ribeirasacra.org.

OURENSE TO PARADA DE SIL

Take the wide OU536 highway about 15km east from Ourense to Tarreirigo, then head north on the OU0509, a winding country lane that meanders through moss-laden forests. Veer right at the sign for Luintra and after 1km take a narrow road down to the right to the **Mosteiro de San Pedro de Rocas**, founded in 573, made up of three cave chapels carved into the rock of the hillside. You can't enter the chapels, but the wide gates let you see inside. Also at this enchanting spot is a **Centro de Interpretación** (admission free; ☉10.30am-1.45pm & 4-7.45pm Tue-Sun), with interesting exhibits on the Ribeira Sacra. You can also take a beautiful walk round the **Camino Real** (PR-G4), a 9km circuit that loops through this area of dense woodlands and jagged rocky hills.

Back on the OU0509, continue to Luintra then head east along the OU0508 and follow signs to the **Mosteiro de San Estevo**. The existing mammoth construction dates to the 12th century, after pilgrims started arriving to pray at the tombs of nine bishops who retreated here in the preceding centuries. Much modified over the years, San Estevo has three magnificent cloisters (one Romanesque, two Renaissance), an originally Romanesque church and an 18th-century baroque facade. Abandoned in the 19th century, it was restored and opened as a *parador* hotel in 2004. Nonguests are free to enter the church and wander round the cloisters and eat in the cafe or restaurant.

Continue along the OU0508 to Loureiro. From here, a scenic and sinuous road leads 4km down to the Río Sil at the foot of the canyon, where you can take a 1½-hour cruise with Viajes Pardo ([☎]902 21 51 00; www.riosil.com, in Spanish; adult/child €14/11; ⊙daily Aug, Sat & Sun mid-Mar–early Dec). Schedules are variable so check first if you're keen on the idea.

The river canyon is perhaps even more beautiful from above. Continue along the OU0508 as it winds its way through moss-drenched forests and along a ridge high above the gorge to Parada de Sil. Entering this village, turn left towards the Mosteiro Santa Cristina. In 4.5km you'll reach the ruins of this medieval monastery with its 12th-century Romanesque church, hidden among the trees above the canyon and looking romantically forlorn. You can freely explore it inside and out. From Parada de Sil you can also reach the Balcón de Madrid lookout (1km from the village), with spectacular views of the canyon 500m below.

CASTRO CALDELAS
POP 700

The OU0605 continues along another dreamy stretch of highway, passing waterfalls, farm plots divided by crumbling stone walls, story-book villages and occasional jaw-dropping vistas of the gorge below. At a crossroads with multiple signposts, go left along the OU0606 to A Teixeira, and then follow the signs to Castro Caldelas, a delightful village with the requisite cobblestone streets, glassed-in Galician balconies and well-tended flower boxes. Explore the old quarter at the top of the village, crowned by the 16th-century Igrexa Santa Isabel and a 14th-century castle which affords great views. The tourist office ([☎]988 20 46 30; ⊙10am-2pm & 5-8pm), just outside the castle, has information about the whole Ribeira Sacra area.

CASTRO CALDELAS TO MONFORTE DE LEMOS

From Castro Caldelas, the OU903 winds down to the Sil canyon, then becomes the LU903 as it climbs the north side of the gorge and cuts across some of the impossibly steep vineyards that characterise the area. At Doade, a few kilometres up the hill, you can visit and taste at several wineries, including Regina Viarum ([☎]619 009777; www.reginaviarum.es in Galician; ⊙10am-2pm & 4-8pm, closed Mon & Tue Oct-Mar).

About 15km further on, you enter the historic crossroads town of Monforte de Lemos. Once an important rail junction, Monforte is neither as compact nor as pristine as other stops on the route, but its cultural monuments make it well worth a visit. The 16th-century Ponte Vella (Old Bridge) spanning the Río Cabe is one of the prettiest sights. Most important on the list of things to see in the area is the hill Monte de San Vicente, where the Pazo Condal, formerly the residence of the counts of Lemos, is now a *parador* hotel. Flanking the *pazo* are the Renaissance church facade of the Mosteiro de San Vicente and the medieval Torre da Homenaxe (tours €1.50; ⊙11am & 4pm Tue-Sun), a defensive tower left as the last vestige of the castle that once stood here. The Colexio dos Escolapios (tours €3; ⊙noon & 4pm Tue-Sat), a large and austere Renaissance monastery beside the tourist office ([☎]982 40 47 15; www.concellodemonforte.com; Campo da Compañía; ⊙10am-2pm & 4-7pm), has two El Grecos in its small art gallery. The tourist office has masses of information on things to see and do in the town and area.

[🛏] Sleeping & Eating

Parador de Santo Estevo

PARADOR HOTEL €€€

([☎]988 01 01 10; www.parador.es; Nogueira de Ramuín; s/d €136/170; [P❋@✿≋]) The Ribeira Sacra's best-known monastery is also an indulgent hotel with all the comforts and a wonderful setting above the river canyon, which is overlooked by many of the rooms. Its excellent restaurant (*menú* €31 to 35, mains €19 to 25) serves local specialities like *caldo gallego* as well as special options for vegetarians and celiacs.

Casa Grande Cristosende

RURAL HOTEL €

([☎]988 20 75 29; www.casagrandecristosende.es; Cristosende, Teixeira; r €49-80; [✿]) A charming 500-year-old manor house in a tiny village 2km from A Teixeira, this rural hotel has

CAMINOS OF GALICIA

All of the Caminos de Santiago converge in Galicia, their shared goal. About 80% of pilgrims arrive by the Camino Francés (Map p37), breasting the hills on the border of Castilla y León, then striding west for the final 154km across welcome green countryside to Santiago de Compostela. But plenty also reach Santiago by the Camino Portugués (crossing the border at Tui), Camino Inglés (from A Coruña or Ferrol) and Camino Primitivo (from Oviedo via Lugo).

Tiny O Cebreiro, where the Camino Francés enters Galicia, is 1300m above sea level and marks the top of the longest, hardest climb on the route. It also features several *pallozas* (circular, thatched dwellings of a type known in rural Galicia since pre-Roman times) dotted among its stone houses. About half the buildings are bars (many doing cheap *menúes del día*) or hostels – the nicest accommodation is at Hotel Cebreiro (982 36 71 82; www.hotelcebreiro.com in Spanish; r €40-60).

In Triacastela, 19km downhill from O Cebreiro, the Camino diverges, with both paths reuniting later in Sarria. The more beautiful and interesting option is the longer (25km) southern route via Samos, a lovely village built around the very fine Benedictine Mosteiro de Samos (tours €3; every 30min 10am-12.30pm & 4.30-6.30pm), founded in the 6th century. The monastery has two lovely big cloisters (one Gothic, with distinctly unmonastic Greek nymphs adorning its fountain, the other neoclassical and filled with roses). Upstairs are four walls of murals detailing St Benedict's life, painted in the 1950s after a horrendous fire that burned almost everything in the monastery except for the contents of the church and sacristy. Samos has several refuges and *hostales,* but much nicer is Casa Díaz (982 54 70 70; www.casadediaz.com; s €31, d €39-69; P), an 18th-century farmhouse-turned-rural-hotel at Vilachá, 3.5km beyond Samos.

People undertaking just the last 100km of the Camino usually start in Sarria, which has a charmless centre but a more pleasant *casco antiguo* on the hill above. The Camino winds through village after village, across forests and fields, then descends steeply to Portomarín, above the Río Miño. Further on, the stretch from Palas de Rei to Melide follows some lovely rural lanes. From Melide, 53km remain through woodlands, villages, countryside and, at the end, city streets. The Camino approaches the centre of Santiago de Compostela along Rúa de San Pedro and arrives in Praza da Inmaculada on the northern side of the cathedral. Many pilgrims take a few more steps down through the tunnel at the foot of this plaza to emerge on magnificent Praza do Obradoiro, in front of the cathedral's famous western facade.

If you're touring Galicia rather than pilgriming it, the 30km from O Cebreiro to Samos make a marvellous side trip. Drivers entering Galicia along the A6 from Madrid and Astorga can turn off into Pedrafita do Cebreiro, then follow the LU633 4km south to O Cebreiro. The road from there to Samos winds down through green countryside with great long-distance views, frequently criss-crossing the Camino.

Monday to Friday at 5.30pm, a bus departs Lugo bus station for Pedrafita do Cebreiro (€9, two hours) via Sarria, Samos and O Cebreiro. The return service starts from Pedrafita at 6.45am Monday to Friday.

eight large, inviting rooms with modern furnishings but an almost monastic simplicity. The restaurant (*menú* €16) serves hearty Galician fare.

Pousada Vicente Risco GUEST HOUSE €
(988 20 33 60; www.pousadavicenterisco.com in Spanish; Rúa Grande 4, Castro Caldelas; s/d incl breakfast €35/45) One of three charming guest houses in the old upper part of Castro Caldelas, this quaint spot has eight

well-kept rooms with classic-style furniture and some rustic touches, like exposed stone walls, plus a good little restaurant.

Hotel Puente Romano HOTEL €
(982 41 11 67; www.hpuenteromano.com, in Spanish; Paseo del Malecón, Monforte de Lemos; s/d €29/44;) In the heart of Monforte, overlooking the Ponte Vella, this humble hotel has 33 bright, clean, good-sized rooms. Hostal Puente Romano next door,

under the same management, has mostly smaller rooms, all with river views, for very reasonable rates (single/double €18/28).

Restaurante O Grelo   GALICIAN €€
(982 40 47 01; Campo de la Virgen, Monforte de Lemos; meals €35-50; closed dinner Sun) In a rustic stone building on the road that climbs Monforte's Monte de San Vicente, this character-filled place specialises in grilled meats, seafood, and venison in wine, plus traditional Galician favourites like *lacón con grelos* (ham with greens).

Restaurante Polar   ECLECTIC €
(Rúa Cardenal Rodrigo de Castro 13, Monforte de Lemos; menú €11-12, à la carte meals €15-35;) With three eating areas, there is a huge choice, including pizzas, tapas, pasta, salads, grilled meats and fish, that pleases everyone.

❶ Getting There & Away

From Monforte, the wide N120 highway zips back to Ourense. Monbus buses (€5.50, one hour, three daily) and Renfe trains (€4 to €13.50, 40 minutes, six daily) also link the two places. A few buses head from Monforte to Lugo, Santiago de Compostela and León. Trains between León and Vigo also call in. Both stations are north of the Monte de San Vicente.

Lugo

POP 88,000 / ELEV 475M

The grand Roman walls encircling old Lugo are considered the world's best preserved and are the number one reason visitors land here. Yet within the fortress is a beautifully preserved labyrinth of streets and squares, most of them traffic-free and ideal for strolling. First established over an ancient *castro* in 15 BC, Lugo was a major town of Roman Gallaecia and today is a quiet but very engaging city. The main plazas and most interesting streets, plus the large cathedral, are mostly concentrated in the southwest quarter of the old city.

⊙ Sights

Roman Remains   WALLS, EXCAVATIONS
The path running right round the top of the World Heritage–listed **Roman walls** is to Lugo what a maritime promenade is to a seaside resort: a place to jog, take an evening stroll, see and be seen. Several staircases and a ramp access the walkway; one is by the **Porta de Santiago** (Santiago Gate) near the cathedral.

The walls, which make a 2.2km loop around the old city, rise 15m high, are studded with 85 stout towers and represent 18 centuries of history. First erected in the 3rd century, the walls were improved through the years, although they were never very successful at protecting the city. Lugo fell to the Suevi in 460 and the Muslims 300 years later. Until well into the 19th century the city gates were closed at night and tolls were charged to bring in goods from outside.

The **Centro de Interpretación de la Muralla** (Praza do Campo 11; adult/senior, student & child €3/1.50; 10.30am-2pm & 4.30-8pm), a block north of the cathedral, gives interesting background on the Roman walls, with three videos and free audioguides, all available in English.

Video is also used to help re-create the Roman house whose underground ruins form the basis of the Museo Casa dos Mosaicos (Rúa de Doctor Castro 20; admission €2; ☺11am-2pm & 5-7pm Tue-Sun).

A 1km downhill walk southwest from the centre, the Ponte Romana (Roman Bridge) spanning the Río Miño is actually medieval, though a Roman one did once stand here. Nearby are the Termas Romanas (Hotel Balneario de Lugo; admission free; ☺8.30am-8.30pm), where you can inspect the dressing rooms, 44°C sulphurous spring and part of the swimming pool of Lugo's Roman baths, all within the modern installations of a spa hotel that utilises the same waters.

Catedral de Santa María   CATHEDRAL

(Praza Pio XII; ☺8.30am-8.30pm) The cathedral, inspired by Santiago's grand cathedral, was begun in 1129, though work continued for centuries, resulting in an aesthetic mix that includes dashes of styles ranging from Romanesque (as in the transepts) to neoclassical (as in the main facade). It's a serene building that merits a close look. Behind the high altar, an ultra-ornate baroque chapel surrounds the beautiful Gothic image of Nosa Señora dos Ollos Grandes (Our Lady of the Big Eyes), the city's Christian patroness. The cathedral's superb original main altarpiece, carved with scenes from the life of Christ by Cornelis de Holanda in the 1530s, now stands in two parts in the two transepts. Outside, just above the north doorway, the sculpture of Christ in majesty is one of the finest pieces of Spanish Romanesque stone carving.

FREE Museo Provincial   MUSEUM

(www.museolugo.org in Spanish; Praza da Soidade; ☺11am-2pm & 5-8pm Mon-Sat, 11am-2pm Sun, closed Sat afternoon & Sun Jul & Aug) Lugo's museum includes what remains of the Convento de San Francisco – a Gothic cloister and the convent kitchen and refectory. It's one of Galicia's best and biggest museums, with collections ranging from pre-Roman gold jewellery and Roman mosaics to Galician Sargadelos ceramics and Galician art from the 15th to 20th centuries.

🛏 Sleeping

Orbán e Sangro   BOUTIQUE HOTEL €€

(☎982 24 02 17; www.pazodeorban.es; Travesía do Miño; s €65-108, d €86-130; ❀✳@☎) The 12 rooms of this welcoming boutique hotel

(opened in 2008 in an 18th-century mansion just inside the city walls) are regal, with rich linen, antique furnishings, designer bathrooms and huge 2.15m beds. It has its own tavern in a curious early-20th-century style.

Hotel Méndez Núñez   HOTEL €€

(☎982 23 07 11; www.hotelmendeznunez.com; Rúa da Raíña 1; s/d €54/65; ❀✳@☎) This century-old hotel has been completely remodelled and offers bright, spacious quarters, gleaming bathrooms and good views, though the beds can be too soft.

Hotel España   HOTEL €

(☎982 23 15 40; Rúa Vilalba 2; s €24-32, d €42; ❀) Outside the Porta do Bispo Aguirre, this absolutely-no-frills hotel offers small, spick-and-span rooms with comfortable beds. Some are sunny, with Roman-wall views.

🍴 Eating

Rúa da Cruz, Rúa Nova and Praza do Campo, north of the cathedral, are packed with tempting restaurants and tapas bars. Many of the latter offer not just one but two free tapas with a drink: one will be offered to you on a plate, and for the other you have to try to pick from a list that bar staff recite at high speed.

A Nosa Terra   TAPAS, RACIONES €

(Rúa Nova 8; raciones €8-18) An inviting classic on the Rúa Nova tapas trail, with a long by-the-glass wine list. Stand in the narrow bar area or sit at tables in the back for raciones of *pulpo á feira* or *lacón con grelos*.

Mesón de Alberto   GALICIAN €€

(☎982 22 83 10; Rúa da Cruz 4; tapas menú €13, meals €35-60; ☺closed Sun, dinner Tue) Alberto serves very well prepared traditional meat, fish and shellfish – meals in the main dining room, tapas downstairs. The tapas tasting *menú* is a good bet if your appetite is medium.

A Taberna do España   GALICIAN €

(Rúa Castelao 4; dishes €5-15, menú €12; ☺closed Sun; ❀☎) Just outside the eastern walls, this bright, contemporary spot offers plenty of traditional Galician favourites like *pulpo á feira* and roast *jarrete de ternera* (hock of beef) but also more imaginative concoctions like seafood-stuffed peppers. The *menú*, also available at dinner Monday to Thursday, is a good deal.

ANCARES & COUREL

Southeast of Lugo, close to the border of Castilla y León, the Serra dos Ancares and Serra do Courel are remote mountain areas with high ridges and peaks, beautiful forests and rustic villages. They are crossed by long- and short-distance hiking trails and will reward anyone who fancies getting to know the deepest of deep Galicia. There's a scattering of country guest houses and hotels. Main access towns are Pedrafita do Cebreiro, Becerreá, Seoane do Courel, Folgoso do Courel and Quiroga. For more information, go to www.turgalicia.es, www.turismoruralgalicia.com or www.lugotur.com (in Spanish) – or obtain Lonely Planet's *Hiking in Spain*.

🍷 Drinking & Entertainment

Weekend nights, things get lively in the old town. Start with tapas and drinks along Rúa Nova, Praza do Campo, Rúa da Cruz or Rúa Bispo Basulto, north of the cathedral, or Praza do Campo Castelo (east of Praza Maior), then hit the music bars around the cathedral or the *chundas* (electronica dance clubs) along Rúa Mariña Española, south of the walls.

The old-timey Café del Centro (Praza Maior 9; ⊙7am-2am) is a great breakfast and coffee spot by day, but from around midnight on Friday and Saturday, low-key jazz, classical or easy-listening music makes this a chill hang-out.

ℹ Information

Municipal tourist office (☏982 25 16 58; www.lugoturismo.com; Praza do Campo 11; ⊙10.30am-2pm & 4.30-8pm) In the Centro de Interpretación de la Muralla.

Regional tourist office (☏982 23 13 61; Rúa do Miño 12; ⊙10am-2pm & 4-7pm Mon-Sat, 10am-2pm Sun, closed Sun Sep-Jun) A stone's throw from the municipal office.

ℹ Getting There & Away

From the **bus station** (☏982 22 39 85; Praza da Constitución), Empresa Freire runs to Santiago de Compostela (€8.25, 1½ to two hours, six or more daily), and Arriva offers direct services to A Coruña (€9.45, 1¼ hours, five or more daily). Several daily buses head to Monforte de Lemos, Ourense, Pontevedra, Viveiro, Ribadeo and Ponferrada. ALSA serves León and Madrid, as well as Asturias and beyond.

Four or more daily Renfe trains head to A Coruña (€8.30 to €15.70, two hours) and Monforte de Lemos (€4.90 to €12.60, one hour). One overnight train goes to Madrid (€51, nine hours).

Valencia & the Costa Blanca

Best Places to Eat

» Tridente (p561)

» Desierto de las Palmas (p569)

» Piripi (p585)

» Rincón de Capis (p587)

» Canela y Clavo (p589)

Best Places to Stay

» Ad Hoc (p558)

» Hotel Chamarel (p576)

» Villa Venecia (p580)

» Hostal Les Monges Palace (p583)

» Cases Noves (p590)

Why Go?

Those 5.5 million overseas visitors to the Comunidad Valenciana (Valencia region) each year can't be wrong. So many confine themselves to the coastal playgrounds, summer nightlife and splendid beaches of the aptly named Costa Blanca (White Coast) in the south or the lower-key resorts of the north's Costa del Azahar (Orange Blossom Coast). But rent a bike or car, leave behind the hedonism of the thin coastal strip and you'll savour the region's rich interior where mountains buckle, castles crown hilltops, and villages – many dating back to Muslim times – slumber on.

Valencia city, the region's capital and Spain's third city, exudes a new urban confidence and makes a great short-break venue. Come for its nightlife, its quality museums, great restaurants and the stunning contemporary architecture of the City of Arts & Sciences.

When to Go?
Valencia

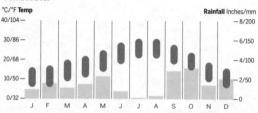

15–19 March Las Fallas, Valencia city's wild spring festival, brings some two million visitors to town

22–24 April At Alcoy's Moros y Cristianos fiesta, warriors engage in mock battle

August & September Inland Maestrazgo is at its best for walking and exploring

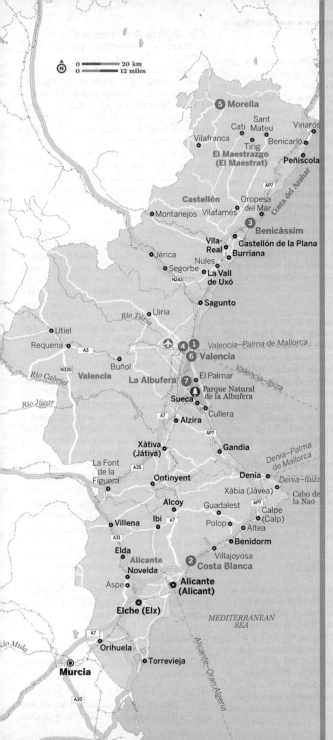

Valencia & the Costa Blanca Highlights

❶ Fling fireworks and suffer serious sleep deprivation at **Las Fallas** (p556), Europe's wildest spring festival

❷ Sway on the smart tram that follows the spectacular **Costa Blanca coastline** (p575) between Alicante and Benidorm

❸ Shake your booty at **Festival Internacional de Benicàssim** (p570), Benicàssim's outdoor international music festival

❹ Gasp at the daring architecture of the **Ciudad de las Artes y las Ciencias** (p546) in Valencia city

❺ Savour your first glimpse of the medieval fortress town of **Morella** (p573) from afar

❻ Stake out the savannah and visit Madagascar at Valencia city's ecofriendly **Bioparc** (p546)

❼ Take a sunset boat ride on the lake of **La Albufera** (p565)

Valencia City

POP 814,000

Valencia, Spain's third-largest city, for ages languished in the long shadows cast by Madrid, Spain's political capital, and Barcelona, the country's cultural and economic powerhouse. No longer. Stunning public buildings have changed the city's skyline – Sir Norman Foster's Palacio de Congresos, David Chipperfield's award-winning Veles i Vents structure beside the inner port, and, on the grandest scale of all, the Ciudad de las Artes y las Ciencas, designed in the main by Santiago Calatrava, local boy made good.

An increasingly popular short-break venue, Valencia is where paella first simmered over a wood fire. It's a vibrant, friendly, mildly chaotic place with two outstanding fine-arts museums, an accessible old quarter, Europe's newest cultural and scientific complex – and one of Spain's most exciting nightlife scenes.

History

Pensioned-off Roman legionaries founded 'Valentia' on the banks of Río Turia in 138 BC. The Arabs made Valencia an agricultural and industrial centre, establishing ceramics, paper, silk and leather industries and extending the network of irrigation canals in the rich agricultural hinterland.

Muslim rule was briefly interrupted in 1094 by the triumphant rampage of the legendary Castilian knight El Cid (p180). Much later, the Christian forces of Jaime I definitively retook the city in 1238.

Valencia's golden age was the 15th century and into the 16th, when it was one of the Mediterranean's strongest trading centres. There followed a gradual decline, relieved in the 19th century by industrialisation and the development of a lucrative citrus trade to northern Europe.

CREEPING CATALAN

More and more town halls are replacing street signs in Spanish with the Valenciano/Catalan equivalent. While the difference between the two versions is often minimal, this can sometimes be confusing for visitors. Occasionally we use the Valenciano form where it's clearly the dominant one. But since Spanish is the version every local understands and the majority uses, we've elected to stick with it in most cases.

⊙ Sights & Activities

CIUDAD DE LAS ARTES Y LAS CIENCIAS

The aesthetically stunning City of Arts & Sciences (Map p550; ☎reservations 902 10 00 31 or book online; www.cac.es; combined ticket for all 3 attractions adult/child €31.50/24) occupies a massive 350,000-sq-metre swath of the old Turia riverbed. It's mostly the work of local architect Santiago Calatrava, designer of, among many other exciting creations around the world, the transport terminal for the new World Trade Center site in New York.

Take bus 35 from Plaza del Ayuntamiento or bus 95 from Torres de Serranos or Plaza de América.

Oceanogràfic AQUARIUM
(Map p550; adult/child €24/18; ⊙10am-6pm or 8pm). This will probably be the highlight of the complex, especially if you have young children. The aquariums of this watery world have sufficient water sloshing around to fill 15 Olympic-sized swimming pools. There are also polar zones, a dolphinarium, a Red Sea aquarium, a Mediterranean seascape – and a couple of underwater tunnels, one 70m long, where the fish have the chance to gawp at visitors.

Palau de les Arts Reina Sofía CONCERT HALL
(Map p550; www.lesarts.com; Autovía a El Saler) Brooding over the riverbed like a giant beetle, its shell shimmering with translucent mosaic tiles, it has four auditoriums. With seating for 4400, it's exceeded in capacity only by the Sydney Opera House.

Hemisfèric IMAX CINEMA
(Map p550; adult/child €7.50/5.80) The unblinking heavy-lidded eye of the Hemisfèric is at once planetarium, IMAX cinema and laser show. Optional English commentary.

Museo de las Ciencias Príncipe Felipe
SCIENCE MUSEUM
(Map p550; adult/child €7.50/6; ⊙10am-7pm or 9pm) This interactive science museum has plenty of touchy-feely things for children and machines and displays for all ages. Each section has a pamphlet in English summarising its contents.

WESTERN VALENCIA

For both of Western Valencia's sights, take bus 7, 81 or 95 or get off at the Nou d'Octubre metro stop.

TOP CHOICE Bioparc ANIMAL PARK
(Map p550; www.bioparcvalencia.es; Avenida Pio Baroja 3; adult/child €21/15.50; ⊙10am-

Beaches, of course. The nearest is the combined beach of Malvarrosa and Las Arenas (the latter meaning 'sand'), a shortish bus or tram ride from the centre. The high-speed tram itself is fun: feel the G-force as it surges along.

The other great playground, year-round, is the diverted Río Turia's former 9km riverbed. Of its formal playgrounds, the giant Gulliver, in the Jardines del Turia, just asks to be clambered all over.

The Jardín Botánico is altogether more peaceful; mind the cacti and feral cats, play hide-and-seek among the trees, and keep an eye out for frogs in the fountain.

Of the Ciudad de las Artes y las Ciencias' diversions, the Oceanogràfic, with more than 45,000 aquatic beasts and plants, has something for all ages. The science museum, reasonably documented in English, is more for over-12s (we've seen primary-school kids innocently and casually wrecking the hands-on exhibits), while the IMAX cinema offers thrills for all. The fun is far from free, however, so do research the range of family and combined tickets.

dusk) 'Zoo' is far too old-fashioned and in-apt a term for this wonderful, innovative, ecofriendly and gently educational space where wild animals apparently (fear not: only apparently) roam free as you wander from savannah to Equatorial Africa and Madagascar, where large-eyed lemurs gambol around your ankles.

Museo de Historia de Valencia MUSEUM
(Map p550; Calle Valencia 42; www.mhv.com.es in Spanish; adult/child €2/1; ⊙10am-2pm & 4.30-8.30pm Tue-Sat, 10am-3pm Sun) Above the riverbed Parque de Cabecera, the Museo de Historia de Valencia plots more than 2000 years of the city's history. Hands-on and with lots of film and video, it's great fun. Ask to borrow the museum's informative folder in English.

PLAZA DE LA VIRGEN & AROUND
This busy plaza, ringed by cafes and imposing public buildings, was once the forum of Roman Valencia, the axis where its main north–south and east–west highways met.

Central Fountain FOUNTAIN
The handsome reclining figure in Plaza de la Reina's central fountain represents Río Turia, while the eight maidens with their gushing pots symbolise the main irrigation canals flowing from it.

Catedral CATHEDRAL
(Map p554; adult/child incl audioguide €4/2.70; ⊙10am-5.30pm or 6.30pm Mon-Sat, 2-5.30pm Sun) Valencia's cathedral is a microcosm of the city's architectural history: the Puerta del Palau on the eastern side is pure Romanesque; the dome, tower and Puerta

de los Apóstoles on Plaza de la Virgen are Gothic; the presbytery and main entrance on Plaza de la Reina are baroque.

Don't miss the rich, recently revealed Italianate frescoes above the main altarpiece. In the flamboyant Gothic Capilla del Santo Cáliz, right of the main entrance, is what's claimed to be the Holy Grail, the chalice from which Christ sipped during the Supper. The next chapel north, La Capilla de San Francisco de Borja, has a pair of particularly sensitive Goyas.

Left of the main portal is the entrance to the Miguelete bell tower (Map p554; adult/child €2/1; ⊙10am-7pm). Climb the 207 steps of its spiral staircase for terrific 360-degree city-and-skyline views.

As for over a thousand years, the Tribunal de las Aguas (Water Court) meets every Thursday exactly at noon outside the cathedral's Puerta de los Apóstoles. Here, local farmers' irrigation disputes are settled in Valenciano.

La Almoina ARCHAEOLOGICAL SITE
(Map p554; adult/child €2/1; ⊙10am-2pm & 4.30-8.30pm Tue-Sat, 10am-3pm Sun) Beneath the adjacent, interconnecting square, the archaeological remains of the kernel of Roman, Visigoth and Islamic Valencia shimmer through a water-covered glass canopy. Guided tours explore this underground area, leaving approximately every half-hour. Phone to book one in English.

Cripta de la Cárcel de San Vicente Mártir MULTIMEDIA DISPLAY
(Map p554; ✆96 394 14 17; Plaza del Arzobispo 1; adult/child €2/1; ⊙10am-2pm & 4.30-8.30pm Tue-Sat, 9.30am-2pm Sun). The crypt of this

Space-Age Splendour

Rising from the former river bed and extending over 2km, the giant structures of the Ciudad de las Artes y las Ciencias (City of Arts & Sciences; p546) define contemporary Valencia.

Oceanogràfic

1 Fish and marine animals from the seven seas live within this watery world, largest of its kind in Europe. Watch the fish watch you as you walk its underwater tunnels.

Hemisfèric

2 Seen from outside, the daringly designed Hemisfèric broods like a huge, heavy-lidded eye over the shallow lake that laps around it. Within, it's both IMAX cinema and planetarium.

Palau de les Arts

3 Darth Vader's helmet? A giant extra-terrestrial carapace? Perhaps a supine armadillo? Or simply the world's largest opera auditorium, Sydney's excepted. Shimmering with *trencadis* – bright, white slivers of broken-tile mosaic – it broods over the former riverbed.

Restaurante Submarino

4 For a great gastronomic experience in original surroundings, drop down beneath wide mock-lilypads to where, instead of wallpaper, more than 1000 silvery bream slowly gyrate around you, mournfully eyeing your plate and their erstwhile brothers and sisters.

L'Umbracle

5 Diaphonous, feathery arches, albeit in concrete, recall the ribs of a palm frond and curve above this 320m-long walkway. Here in summer, Valencia's most-beautiful people will sip cocktails before dropping to the *discoteca* beneath.

DAVID TOMLINSON

GREG ELMS

Clockwise from top left
1. Palau de les Arts Reina Sofía (p546) 2. L'Umbracle
3. Oceanogràfic (p546)

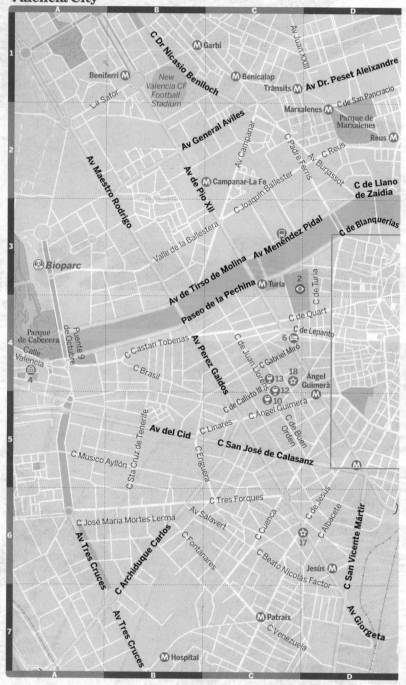

VALENCIA & THE COSTA BLANCA

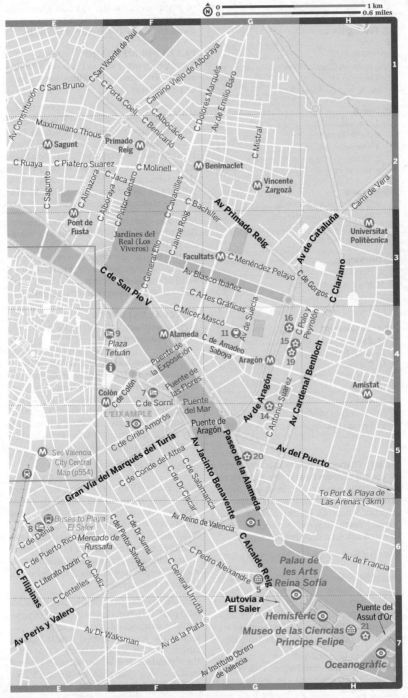

N 0 — 1 km
0 — 0.6 miles

C Constitución
C San Bruno
C San Vicente de Paul
C Porta Coeli
Camino Viejo de Alboraya
C Dolores Marqués
Av de Emilio Baro

Maximiliano Thous
C Albocácer
C Benicarló
C Mistral

Ⓜ Sagunt
Primado Reig Ⓜ
Ⓜ Benimaclet

C Ruaya
C Piatero Suarez
C Molinell
Vincente Zargozá
Camí de Vera

C Sagunto
C Almazora
C Jaca
Cami de Vera

Ⓜ Pont de Fusta
C Alboraya
C Pintor Genaro
C Cavanilles
Av Primado Reig
Av de Cataluña
Ⓜ Universitat Politècnica

Jardines del Real (Los Viveros)
C Bachiller
C Jaime Roig
Facultats Ⓜ C Menéndez Pelayo
C de Gorgos
C Clariano

C de San Pio V
C General Elío
Av Blasco Ibáñez
C Artes Gráficas
C Micer Mascó
Av de Suecia
16 ☆ C Polo y Peyrolón
15 ☆

🏢 9
Plaza Tetuán
ⓘ
Ⓜ Alameda
11 🚇 C de Amadeo Saboya
Aragón Ⓜ
19 ☆

Colón
Puente de la Exposición
Puente de las Flores
Amistat Ⓜ

Ⓜ Colón
7 🏢
C de Sorní
Puente del Mar
Av de Aragón
14 ☆
C Antonio Suárez
Av Cardenal Benlloch

L'EIXAMPLE
3 ☉
C de Cirilo Amorós
Puente de Aragón

Ⓜ
See Valencia City Central Map (p554)
Gran Via del Marqués del Turia
C de Conde del Altea
Av Jacinto Benavente
Paseo de la Alameda
20 ☆
Av del Puerto

To Port & Playa de Las Arenas (3km)

8 🚌
Buses to Playa El Saler
C de Denia
C del Pintor Salvador
C de Salamanca
C de Dr Ciscar
Av Reino de Valencia
C Alcalde Reig
☉ 1

C Filipinas
C de Puerto Rico
Mercado de Russafa
C de Dr Sumsi
C Pedro Aleixandre
Palau de les Arts Reina Sofia
Av de Francia

C Literato Azorín
C de Cádiz
C Centelles
C General Urrutia
5 🏛
☉

Autovía a El Saler
Hemisfèric ☉
Puente del Assut d'Or

Av Peris y Valero
Av Dr Waksman
Av de la Plata
Museo de las Ciencias Príncipe Felipe 🏛
21 ☆

Av Instituto Obrero de Valencia
Oceanogràfic ☉

Valencia City

Visigoth chapel, reputedly used as a prison for the 4th-century martyr San Vicente, isn't particularly memorable in itself. What's worthwhile is the multimedia show that presents Valencia's history and the saint's life and death. Reserve by phone or on the spot and ask for a showing in English.

Nuestra Señora de los Desamparados
CHURCH
(Map p554; ◎7am-2pm & 4.30-9pm) Above the altar is a highly venerated statue of the Virgin, patron of the city. If you come after hours, peer in through the grilles, worn smooth over the years by thousands of supplicants, on the southern, cathedral side.

Palau de la Generalitat
PALACE
(Map p554) This handsome 15th-century Gothic – much amended – palace is the seat of government for the Valencia region. Its symmetry is recent: the original renaissance tower received its twin only in the 1950s.

PLAZA DEL MERCADO
Facing each other across Plaza del Mercado are two emblematic buildings, each a masterpiece of its era.

FREE **La Lonja**
HISTORIC BUILDING
(Map p554; ◎10am-2pm & 4.30-8.30pm Mon-Sat, 10am-3pm Sun) This splendid late-15th-century building, a Unesco World Heritage Site, was originally Valencia's silk and commodity exchange. Highlights are the colonnaded hall with its twisted Gothic pillars and the 1st-floor Consulado del Mar with its stunning coffered ceiling.

Mercado Central
MODERNISTA MARKET
(Map p554; ◎7.30am-2.30pm Mon-Sat) Valencia's Modernista covered market, recently scrubbed and glowing as new, was constructed in 1928. With over 900 stalls, it's a swirl of smells, movement and colour. Don't miss the fish, seafood and offal annexe.

CENTRAL VALENCIA
TOP CHOICE **Instituto Valenciano de Arte Moderno (IVAM)**
CONTEMPORARY ART GALLERY
(Map p554; www.ivam.es; Calle Guillem de Castro 118; adult/child €2/1; ◎10am-8pm or 9pm Tue-Sun) IVAM (pronounced 'ee-bam') hosts excellent temporary exhibitions and houses an impressive permanent collection of 20th-century Spanish art, including a whole gallery of spiky, abstract creations in metal by the Catalan sculptor Julio Gonzalez.

FREE **Museo de Bellas Artes**
FINE ARTS MUSEUM
(Map p554; Calle San Pío V 9; ◎10am-8pm Tue-Sun) Bright and spacious, the Museo de Bellas Artes ranks among Spain's best. Highlights include the grandiose Roman *Mosaic of the Nine Muses*, a collection of magnificent late-medieval altarpieces and works by El Greco, Goya, Velázquez, Murillo, Ribalta and artists such as Sorolla and Pinazo of the Valencian Impressionist school.

Palacio del Marqués de Dos Aguas PALACE
(Map p554; Calle Poeta Querol 2) A pair of wonderfully extravagant rococo caryatids (pillars in the form of draped female figures) curl around the main entrance of this over-the-top palace. Inside, the **Museo Nacional de Cerámica** (Map p554; adult/child €3/1.50, ◎10am-2pm & 4-8pm Tue-Sat, 10am-2pm Sun)

displays ceramics from around the world – and especially of the renowned local production centres of Manises, Alcora and Paterna.

Torres de Serranos   TOWERS
(Map p554; Plaza de los Fueros; adult/child €2/1 ⊙10am-2pm & 4.30-8.30pm Tue-Sat, 10am-3pm Sun) Two imposing, twin-towered stone gates are all that remain of Valencia's old city walls. Once the main exit to Barcelona and the north, the 14th-century Torres de Serranos overlook the former bed of Río Turia.

FREE Torres de Quart   TOWERS
(Map p554; Calle Guillem de Castro ⊙10am-2pm & 4.30-8.30pm Tue-Sat, 10am-3pm Sun) You can also clamber to the top of the 15th-century Torres de Quart, which face towards Madrid and the setting sun. Up high, you can still see the pockmarks caused by French cannonballs during the 19th-century Napoleonic invasion.

Estación del Norte   TRAIN STATION
(Map p554; Calle Xàtiva) Trains first chugged into this richly adorned Modernista terminal in 1917. Its main foyer is decorated with ceramic mosaics and murals – and mosaic 'bon voyage' wishes in major European languages.

Museo del Patriarca   FINE-ART GALLERY
(Map p554; Calle la Nave 1; admission €2; ⊙11am-1.30pm) This bijou gallery is a must if you're interested in ecclesiastical art. It's particularly strong on Spanish and Flemish Renaissance painting, with several canvases by Juan de Juanes, Ribalta and El Greco.

Museo Fallero   FALLAS MUSEUM
(Map p550; Plaza Monteolivete 4; adult/child €2/1; ⊙10am-2pm & 4.30-8pm Tue-Sat, 10am-3pm Sun) Each Fallas festival, only one of the thousands of *ninots*, near-life-sized figurines that strut and pose at the base of each *falla* (huge statues of papier-mâché and polystyrene), is saved from the flames by popular vote. Those reprieved over the years are displayed here.

Mercado de Colón   MODERNISTA MARKET
(Map p550; Calle Cirilo Amorós) This magnificent Modernista building, now colonised by boutiques and cafes, was a market in its time, built in the 19th century to serve the rising bourgeoisie (or rather their servants) of the new suburb of L'Eixample.

Plaza Redonda   SMALL SQUARE
(Map p554) Again trim and smart after an elaborate makeover, this small, circular space – which was once the market's ab-

attoir – is ringed by stalls selling bits and bobs, buttons and bows, clothes and locally made crafts and ceramics.

FREE Museo de Prehistoria & Museo de Etnología   MUSEUM
(Map p554; Calle Corona 36; ⊙10am-8pm or 9pm Tue-Sun) Sharing premises usually called La Beneficencia, is a history museum with finds from the Palaeolithic period, plus Roman and Iberian artefacts, and a folk museum displaying photographs and household items from the city's more recent past.

FREE Museo Taurino   BULLFIGHTING MUSEUM
(Map p554; Pasaje Doctor Serra 10 ⊙10am-8pm Tue-Sun) This small museum holds a collection of bullfighting memorabilia. It's right beside Plaza de Toros; after visiting the museum, you're allowed to strut in the sand of the bullring and dream.

L'Iber (Museo de Soldaditos de Plomo)   TOY SOLDIERS
(Map p554; Calle Caballeros 20-22; admission €4; ⊙11am-2pm & 4-7pm Wed-Sun) L'Iber claims to be the world's largest collection of toy soldiers. The 4.7m x 2.8m set piece of the Battle of Almansa (1707) has over 9000 combatants and cases teem with rank upon rank, battalion following battalion, of toy soldiers.

FREE Baños del Almirante   BATH HOUSE
(Map p554; Calle Baños del Almirante 3-5; ⊙10am-2pm & 6-8pm Tue-Sat, 10am-2pm Sun) These Arab-style baths, constructed in 1313, functioned continuously as public bathing facilities until 1959. There's an excellent audiovisual presentation with optional English commentary every half-hour.

Iglesia de Santa Catalina   CHURCH
(Map p554) Its striking 18th-century baroque belfry is one of the city's best-known landmarks.

FUN FOR FREE

The following museums and sites, normally paying, don't charge visitors on Saturday and Sunday.

» Museo Nacional de Cerámica
» Museo Fallero
» Museo de Historia de Valencia
» La Almoina
» Torres de Serranos
» Cripta de la Cárcel de San Vicente Mártir

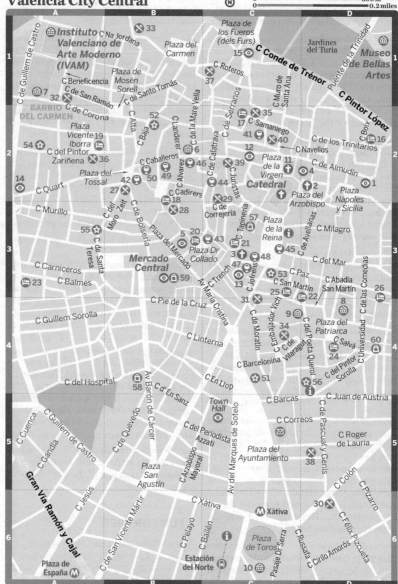

PARKS & GARDENS

Jardines del Turia   FORMER RIVERBED

(Map p554) Stretching the length of Río Turia's former course, this 9km-long lung of green is a mix of playing fields, cycling, jogging and walking paths, fountains, lawns and playgrounds. See Lilliputian kids scrambling over a magnificent, ever-patient Gulliver east of the Palau de la Música.

Jardín Botánico   BOTANICAL GARDENS

(Map p550; Calle Quart 80; admission €1; ⊙10am-dusk Tue-Sun) Established in 1802, this was

Spain's first botanic garden. With mature trees and plants, an extensive cactus garden and a wary colony of feral cats, it's a shady, tranquil place to relax.

Jardines del Real PARK
(Map p550) Reaching down to the riverbed are the Royal Gardens, another lovely spot for a stroll. Once the grounds of a palace, they're usually called Los Viveros.

Parque de Cabecera RIVERBED PARK
(Map p550; Paseo de la Pechina) This public park at the western extremity of the riverbed has a mini lake where you can hire swan-shaped pedalos. Climb the man-made hillock for a special panorama of Valencia.

BEACHES
Playa de la Malvarrosa runs into Playa de las Arenas. Each is bordered by the Paseo

Marítimo promenade and a string of restaurants. One block back, lively bars and discos thump out the beat in summer.

Playa El Salér, 10km south, is backed by shady pine woods. **Autocares Herca** (☎96 349 12 50; www.autocaresherca.com, in Spanish) buses run between Valencia and Perelló hourly (half-hourly in summer), calling by El Salér village. They stop (look for the Herca sign) at the junction of Gran Vía de las Germanias and Calle Sueca, beside Plaza de Cánovas and in front of the Ciudad de las Artes y Las Ciencias.

☞ Tours

Hire a horse-drawn carriage in Plaza de la Reina and clip-clop around the Centro Histórico, lording it over the pedestrians below. A 40-minute trip costs €30 for up to five passengers.

Valencia Guías   BICYCLE TOUR
(☎96 385 17 40; www.valenciaguias.com; Paseo de la Pechina 32) Daily 3½-hour guided bicycle tours in English (€25 including rental; minimum two persons). Also two-hour walking tours in Spanish and English (adult/child €15/7.50), leaving Plaza de la Reina tourist office at 10am each Saturday.

Art Valencia   WALKING TOUR
(☎96 310 61 93; www.artvalencia.com) Two-hour walking tours (€14) in English and Spanish departing 11am Friday from Plaza de la Reina tourist office.

✯✯ Festivals & Events

February

Valencia Escena Oberta   STREET THEATRE
(www.festivalveo.com, in Spanish) Valencia Open Stage offers 10 days of Spanish and European street theatre, dance and startling contemporary art.

March & April

Las Fallas   PARADES, FIREWORKS
See the boxed text.

Semana Santa   HOLY WEEK
Elaborate Easter Holy Week processions in the seaside district of La Malvarrosa.

Fiesta de San Vicente Ferrer
                                  PARADES, PLAYS
Colourful parades and miracle plays performed around town on the Sunday after Easter.

May

Fiesta de la Virgen   EFFIGY PROCESSION
The effigy of the Virgen de los Desamparados (Valencia's patron saint), hemmed in by fervent believers struggling to touch her, makes the short journey across Plaza de la Virgen to the cathedral on the second Sunday of May.

Danza Valencia   CONTEMPORARY DANCE
Strictly contemporary dancing by Spanish and international dance troupes during two weeks spanning late April and early May.

LAS FALLAS

The exuberant, anarchic swirl of **Las Fallas de San José** – fireworks, music, festive bonfires and all-night partying – is a must if you (together with some two million other visitors) are in Spain between 12 and 19 March.

The *fallas* themselves are huge sculptures of papier mâché on wood (with, increasingly, environmentally damaging polystyrene), built by teams of local artists. In 2009 the combined cost of their construction was more than €10 million. Each neighbourhood sponsors its own *falla*, and when the town wakes after the *plantà* (overnight construction of the *fallas*) on the morning of 16 March, more than 350 have been erected. Reaching up to 15m in height, with the most expensive costing in 2009 €900,000 (oh yes, we've got those euro zeros right!), these grotesque, colourful effigies satirise celebrities, current affairs and local customs.

Around-the-clock festivities include street parties, paella-cooking competitions, parades, open-air concerts, bullfights and nightly free firework displays. Valencia considers itself the pyrotechnic capital of the world and each day at 2pm from 1 to 19 March a *mascletà* (over five minutes of deafening thumps and explosions) shakes the window panes of Plaza del Ayuntamiento.

At the end of each festival the best *falla* is voted upon and the winner placed in the Museo Fallero.

After midnight on the final day the remaining *fallas* go up in flames – backed by yet more fireworks.

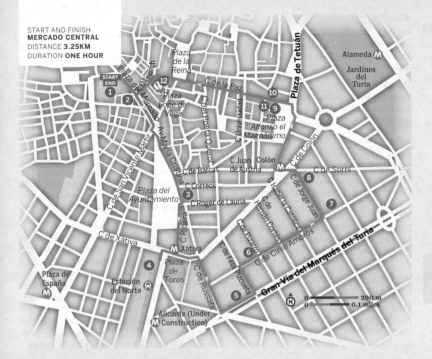

Walking Tour
Modernismo Meander

> This walk takes in Valencia's main Modernista (art nouveau) buildings.

After sniffing around ① **Mercado Central**, take in the elaborate stucco facade of ② **Calle Ramilletes 1**, on the corner where it meets Plaza del Mercado. Follow Avenida María Cristina to Plaza del Ayuntamiento, site of the resplendent ③ **Central Post Office**. Drop in and raise your eyes to savour its magnificent leaded-glass dome. Valencia's biggest concentration of flower stalls fringe this open square, where the strictly neoclassical Town Hall stares across at its Modernista rival.

At the end of Calle Ribera, detour briefly to ④ **Estación del Norte** and its Modernista booking hall of dark wood. Take Calle Russafa, then turn left for ⑤ **Casa Ortega** (Gran Vía 9) with its elaborate floral decoration. Go left along Calle Félix Pizcueta, then first right, stopping at ⑥ **Casa Ferrer** (Calle Cirilo Amorós 29), garlanded with stucco roses and ceramic tiling. Continue

northwards to the resplendent ⑦ **Mercado de Colón**, a good spot for a drink, then head west to ⑧ **Casa del Dragón** (Calle Jorge Juan 3), named for its dragon motifs.

Cross Calle Colón, turn right along Calle Poeta Quintana and pass the mounted statue of a haughty King Jaime I to join Calle de la Paz. Back in the 19th century, ⑨ **Hotel Vincci Palace**, restored and re-vamped, was known as the Palace Hotel, in its time Valencia's finest. Both it and ⑩ **No 31** have elaborate, decorated miradores (corner balconies), while ⑪ **Red Nest Hostel** (No 36) has delicate, leafy iron railings.

At the end of Calle de la Paz, continue straight – maybe calling in for an *horchata* at ⑫ **Horchatería Santa Catalina**. Then, at Plaza Lope de Vega, turn left into Calle Trench to return to the Mercado Central.

June

Corpus Christi
PROCESSION, PLAYS

Celebrated with an elaborate procession and mystery plays on the ninth Sunday after Easter.

Día de San Juan
BEACH BONFIRES

From 23 to 24 June, Midsummer's Day is celebrated; thousands mark the longest day with bonfires on the beach.

July

Feria de Julio
FAIR

Performing arts, brass-band competitions, bullfights, fireworks and a 'battle of the flowers' in the second half of July.

October

Día de la Comunidad
REGIONAL DAY

Commemorates the city's 1238 liberation from the Arabs on 9 October.

Mostra de Valencia
CINEMA FESTIVAL

Week-long film festival.

Valencia Bienial
VISUAL ARTS

Held in October to November in odd-numbered years, a festival of modern visual arts with exhibitions all over town.

HOSTELS

Valencia has plenty of cheerful, modern, great-value hostels.

Center Valencia (Map p554; ☎963 91 49 15; www.center-valencia.com; Calle Samaniego 18)

Hilux Hostal (Map p554; ☎963 91 46 91; www.feetuphostels.com; Calle Cadirers 11)

Hôme Backpackers (Map p554; ☎963 91 37 97; www.likeathome.net; Calle Santa Cristina)

Hôme Youth Hostel (Map p554; ☎963 91 62 29; www.likeathome.net; Calle Lonja 4)

Indigo Youth Hostel (Map p554; ☎963 15 39 88; www.indigohostel.com; Calle Guillem de Castro 64)

Purple Nest Hostel (Map p550; ☎963 53 25 61; www.nesthostelsvalencia.com; Plaza Tetuan 5)

Red Nest Hostel (Map p554; ☎963 42 71 68; www.nesthostelsvalencia.com; Calle Paz 36)

🛏 Sleeping

Since Valencia is a business centre, big hotels struggle to fill rooms at weekends and most offer fat weekend and high-summer discounts.

TOP CHOICE Ad Hoc
HOTEL €€

(Map p554; ☎96 391 91 40; www.adhoc hoteles.com; Calle Boix 4; s €65-101, d €76-125; ❈🐾) Friendly, welcoming Ad Hoc offers comfort and charm deep within the old quarter and also runs a splendid small restaurant (Monday to Friday and lunch Saturday). The late-19th-century building has been restored to its former splendour with great sensitivity, revealing original ceilings, mellow brickwork and solid wooden beams.

Chill Art Jardín Botánico
BOUTIQUE HOTEL €€

(Map p550; ☎96 315 40 12; www.hoteljardinbotan ico.com; Calle Doctor Peset Cervera 6; s €94-133, d €94-149; ❈🐾🐾) Welcoming and megacool, this intimate – only 16 rooms – hotel is furnished with great flair. Candles flicker in the lounge and each bedroom has original artwork. Understandably, the Instituto Valenciano de Arte Moderno (IVAM), an easy walk away, regularly selects it as a venue for its guests.

TOP CHOICE Petit Palace Bristol
BOUTIQUE HOTEL €€

(Map p554; ☎96 394 51 00; www.hthoteles.com; Calle Abadía San Martín 3; r €60-130; ❈@🐾) Hip and minimalist, this lovely boutique hotel, a comprehensively made-over 19th-century mansion, retains the best of its past and does a particularly scrumptious buffet breakfast. Invest €10 extra for one of the superior doubles on the top floor, with its broad wooden terrace giving panoramic views over the city. Free bikes for guests.

Petit Palace Germánias
BOUTIQUE HOTEL €€

(Map p550; ☎96 351 36 38; www.hthotels.com; Calle Sueca 14; r €65-120; ❈@🐾) Younger sister to Petit Palace Bristol, this equally attractive boutique hotel, just that little bit further from the centre, has its own seductive charms. Guests can borrow bikes for free.

Neptuno
HOTEL €€€

(☎96 356 77 77; www.hotelneptunovalencia.com; Paseo de Neptuno 2; s €115-135, d €128-148; ❈🐾) Neptuno, ultramodern and ultracool, overlooks the leisure port and beach of Las Arenas. It's ideal for mixing cultural tourism with a little beach frolicking. Its restaurant, Tridente, is one of Valencia's finest.

Hospes Palau de la Mar HOTEL €€€
(Map p550; ☎96 316 28 84; www.hospes.es; Calle Navarro Reverter 14; d €115-175; ❈ ✦ ♥) Created by the merging of two elegant 19th-century mansions (plus 18 very similar modern rooms surrounding a tranquil internal garden), this boutique hotel, all black, white, soft fuscous and beige, is cool, confident and contemporary plus. There's a sauna, jacuzzi – and a pool scarcely bigger than your bathtub.

Hostal Antigua Morellana HOSTAL €
(Map p554; ☎96 391 57 73; www.hostalam.com; Calle En Bou 2; s €45-55, d €55-65; ❈) The friendly, family-run 18-room Hostal Antigua Morellana is tucked away near the central market. Occupying a renovated 18th-century *posada* (a place where wealthier merchants bringing their produce to the nearby food market could spend the night), it has cosy, good-sized rooms, most with balconies.

Pensión París PENSIÓN €
(Map p554; ☎96 352 67 66; www.pensionparis. com; 1st & 3rd fl, Calle Salvá 12; s €23, d €34-42) Welcoming, with spotless rooms – most with corridor bathrooms, some with en suite facilities – this family-run option on a quiet street is the antithesis of the crowded, pack-'em-in hostel.

SH Inglés HOTEL €€
(Map p554; ☎96 351 64 26; www.hotelinglesva lencia.com; Calle Marqués de Dos Aguas 6; r €90; ❈ @ ♥) In a stylishly renovated, much-modified 18th-century palace, the Hotel Inglés has 63 rooms, each with parquet floor, dark, stained-wood bedhead and a large glass-topped working table. Its congenial cafe and some of its bedrooms overlook the glorious rococo main entrance to the Palacio del Marqués de Dos Aguas.

Acta Atarazanas HOTEL €€
(☎96 320 30 10; www.actahoteles.com; Plaza Tribunal de las Aguas 5; r €60-100; ❈ ♥) The cream walls and fabrics of each bedroom contrast with the dark, stained woodwork. Sybaritic bathrooms have deep tubs with hydromassage and the broad showerhead is as big as a discus. From the breezy rooftop terrace there's a magnificent wraparound view of sea and city. It's located near the beach and port.

✗ Eating
Valencia is the capital of La Huerta, a fertile coastal agricultural plain that supplies the city with delightfully fresh fruit and vegetables.

For independence and your own accommodation, from one night to long stay, consult the following websites:
www.roomsdeluxe.com
www.valenciaflats.com
www.accommodation-valencia.com

CENTRO HISTÓRICO

TOP CHOICE **Carosel** MEDITERRANEAN €€
(Map p554; ☎96 113 28 73; Calle Taula de Canvis 6; lunch/dinner menus €15/22; ☺lunch & dinner Tue-Sat, lunch Sun) Jordi, ex-chef of Seu-Xerea, and his partner Carol run this delightful small restaurant with its minimalist, bright white on dark-brown decor. After a trio of tasty lunchtime starters, attractively presented on a single platter, comes a rice dish of just the right consistency, then a choice of rich desserts. The evening *menú* follows the same pattern but with more of all. Warmly recommended.

Bar Pilar TAPAS €
(Map p554; ☎96 391 04 97; C del Moro Zeit 13; ☺noon-midnight) Cramped, earthy Bar Pilar is great for hearty tapas and *clóchinas* (small, juicy local mussels), available between May and August. For the rest of the year it serves *mejillones,* altogether fatter if less tasty. Ask for an *entero,* a platterful in a spicy broth that you scoop up with a spare shell. At the bar, etiquette demands that you dump your empty shells in the plastic trough at your feet.

Seu-Xerea FUSION, MEDITERRANEAN €€
(Map p554; ☎96 392 40 00; www.seuxerea.com; Calle Conde Almodóvar 4; mains €16-19, menus €22-50; ☺lunch & dinner Mon-Fri, dinner Sat) This welcoming restaurant is favourably quoted in almost every English-language press article about Valencia city. Its creative, regularly changing à la carte menu features dishes both international and rooted in Spain. Wines, selected by the owner, a qualified sommelier, are uniformly excellent.

L'Hamadríada MEDITERRANEAN €€
(Map p554; ☎96 326 08 91; www.hamadriada. com, in Spanish; Plaza Vicente Iborra; lunch menu €13, menus €18-22, mains €12.50-16; ☺lunch Sun-Tue, lunch & dinner Wed-Sat) Staff are well informed and attentive at the Wood Nymph, a local favourite. Down a short,

blind alley, this slim white rectangle of a place does an innovative midday *menú*, perfectly simmered rice dishes, and grills where the meat, like the vegetables, is of prime quality.

Mattilda
MEDITERRANEAN €€
(Map p554; ☎96 382 31 68; Calle Roteros 21; menus €11-13, mains €11-17; ☺lunch Mon & Tue, lunch & dinner Wed-Sat) The decor is stylish, modern and unpretentious – just like Francisco Borell and his cheery young team, who offer friendly service, an imaginative à la carte selection and a particularly good value lunch *menú*.

Ginger Loft Café
BAR, CAFE €
(Map p554; ☎96 352 32 43; www.thegingerloft. com; C de Vitoria 4; mains €7.50, menus €12; ☺lunch & dinner Tue-Fri & Sun, dinner Sat) Mike from Scotland and his Peruvian-Japanese partner, Santiago, run this delightful small cafe. Select wines are all from the Valencia region. There's a pageful of sexy cocktails and the largest selection of gin bottles you've ever seen. Snack from their great selection of Spanish hams and cheeses, or choose a dish from the international range of mains.

La Tastaolletes
VEGETARIAN €
(Map p554; ☎96 392 18 62; www.latastaolletes. com, in Spanish; Calle Salvador Giner 6; tapas & salads €6-9.50, mains €8-11; ☺lunch & dinner Tue-Sat, lunch Sun; ☑) La Tastaolletes does a creative range of vegetarian tapas and mains. Pleasantly informal, it's worth visiting for the friendly atmosphere and good, wholesome food created from quality prime ingredients. Salads are large and leafy and desserts (indulge in the cheesecake with stewed fruits) are a dream.

Espai Visor
VEGETARIAN €€
(Map p554; ☎96 392 23 99; www.espaivisor.com; C de Correjería 40; menus €18, mains around €12; ☺dinner Tue-Sat; ☎☑) In a city with few vegetarian options, this tiny restaurant and photographic gallery stands out. Dishes are enticingly illustrated (no surprise that owner Pep Benlloch is a professional photographer) and the menu is innovative. Free wi-fi too.

Palacio de la Bellota
SEAFOOD €€€
(Map p554; ☎96 351 53 61; www.palaciodelabello ta.es; C de Mosén Femades 7; ☺Mon-Sat) Palacio de la Bellota is one of a handful of superb upmarket seafood restaurants flanking this pedestrianised street. Shellfish are hauled fresh from the Mediterranean and the fish selection is also excellent. Ham as well, legs of it dangling in profusion from the ceiling. Eat inside or on its street terrace.

La Lluna
VEGETARIAN €
(Map p554; ☎96 392 21 46; Calle San Ramón 23; meals around €15; ☺Mon-Sat; ☑) Friendly and full of regulars, with walls of clashing tilework, La Lluna has been serving quality, reasonably priced vegetarian fare (including a superb-value four-course lunch *menú* at €7.20) for over 25 years.

Fresc Co
BUFFET €
(Map p554; ☎96 310 63 88; Calle Felix Pizcueta 6; buffet lunches under €10) Fresc Co's all-you-can-eat buffet offers a veritable kitchen garden of salad items and a choice of pasta or pizza. With its bare, mellow brickwork, it's an agreeable, excellent-value place, though you're not encouraged to linger once dessert's over. Three other branches around town.

La Utielana
VALENCIAN €
(Map p554; ☎96 352 94 14; Plaza Picadero dos Aguas 3; menus €10, mains €15; ☺lunch & dinner Mon-Fri, lunch Sat) Tucked away off Calle Prócida and not easy to track down, La Utielana well merits a minute or two of sleuthing. Very Valencian, it packs in the crowds, drawn by the wholesome fare and exceptional value for money. Arrive early as it doesn't take reservations – if you have to wait, grab a numbered ticket from the dispenser.

Las Cuevas
TAPAS €
(Map p554; ☎96 391 71 96; Plaza Cisneros 2; tapas €4.50-11; ☺lunch & dinner Mon-Fri, dinner Sat) 'The Caves', recently installed in a new premises, is vast, full of nooks and crannies and aptly named. Its bar groans with a huge range of freshly made tapas.

Pepita Pulgarcita
TAPAS €€
(Map p554; ☎96 391 46 08; C Caballeros 19; tapas €6-11.50; ☺1pm-1.30am Tue-Sun, 7pm-1.30am Mon) With wines stacked high behind the bar and subtle, inventive tapas, tastefully presented, tiny Pepita Pulgarcita is great for a snack, meal or simply a *copa*.

LAS ARENAS
At weekends, locals in their hundreds head for Las Arenas, just north of the port, where a long line of restaurants overlooking the beach all serve up authentic paella in a three-course meal costing less than €20.

Arroz (rice) underwrites much of Valencian cuisine – such as paella, first simmered here and exported to the world. For a more original experience, try alternatives such as *arroz a banda* (simmered in a fish stock); *arroz negro* (with squid, including its ink); *arroz al horno* (baked in the oven). For *fideuá*, Valencian cooks simply substitute noodles for rice.

Other regional specialities include *horchata*, an opaque sugary drink made from pressed *chufas* (tiger nuts), into which you dip large finger-shaped buns called *fartons*. Finally, despite its name, *Agua de Valencia* couldn't be further from water. The local take on Buck's Fizz, it mixes *cava* (sparkling Champagne-method wine), orange juice, gin and vodka.

TOP CHOICE **Tridente**   GOURMET FUSION **€€€**
(☑96 371 03 66; Paseo Neptuno; menus €45-65, mains €22-30; ⊙lunch & dinner Tue-Sat, lunch Sun) Begin with an aperitif on the broad beachfront terrace of Tridente, restaurant of Neptuno hotel, then move inside, where filtered sunlight bathes its soothing cream decor. There's an ample à la carte selection but you won't find details of the day's *menús* in front of you – they're delivered orally by the maître d', who speaks good English. Dishes with their combinations of colours and blending of sweet and savoury are creative and delightfully presented and portions are generous.

Lonja del Pescado   FISH **€**
(☑96 355 35 35; Calle Eugenia Viñes 243; meals around €20; ⊙lunch Sat & Sun, dinner Tue-Sun Mar-Oct, lunch Sat & Sun, dinner Fri & Sat Nov-Feb) One block back from the beach at Malvarrosa, this busy, informal place in what's little more than an adorned tin shack offers unbeatable value for fresh fish. Grab an order form as you enter and fill it in at your table.

La Pepica   FISH, SEAFOOD **€€**
(☑96 371 03 66; Paseo Neptuno 6; meals around €25; ⊙lunch & dinner Mon-Sat, lunch Sun) More expensive than its competitors, La Pepica is renowned for its rice dishes and seafood. Here, Ernest Hemingway, among many other luminaries, once strutted. Between courses, browse through the photos and tributes that plaster the walls.

🍸 Drinking

Fuelled by a large student population, Valencia's nightlife has a justified reputation way beyond its borders.

The Barrio del Carmen has both the grungiest and grooviest collection of bars. The other major area is around the university; Avenidas de Aragón and Blasco Ibáñez and surrounding streets have enough bars and *discotecas* (clubs) to keep you busy beyond sunrise.

Another zone well worth checking out is around the Mercado de Abastos, while in summer the new port area and Malvarrosa leap to life.

CENTRO HISTÓRICO
El Carmé has everything from designer pubs to rough thrash-metal haunts. On weekends, Calle Caballeros, the main street, seethes with punters seeking *la marcha* (the action). **Plaza del Tossal** is rimmed by sophisticated bars, and **Calle Caballeros** has a couple of bars for beautiful people.

Cafe-Bar Negrito   CAFE BAR
(Map p554; Plaza del Negrito, El Carmé) Recently re-designed, it traditionally attracts a more left-wing, intellectual clientele.

Café Lisboa   CAFE BAR
(Map p554; Plaza del Doctor Collado 9, El Carmé) Another lively, student-oriented bar with a large, street-side terrace. The bulletin board is a palimpsest of small ads for apartment shares and language tuition.

Café Infanta   CAFE BAR
(Map p554; Plaza del Tossal) The interior is a clutter of cinema memorabilia, while its external terrace is great for people-watching.

TOP CHOICE **Sant Jaume**   CAFE BAR
(Map p554; Plaza del Tossal) A converted pharmacy, its 1st floor is all quiet crannies and poky passageways.

Johnny Maracas   SALSA BAR
(Map p554; 39 Calle Caballeros) A suave salsa place with fish tanks on the bar.

MANOLO EL DEL BOMBO

If you watched a Spain game in the last World Cup – or indeed any football international in which Spain features – you'll probably have seen a guy in a beret broader than a dinner plate, whacking the hell out of a giant bass drum to rouse the fans. He's Manolo the Drum, one of Valencia's most famous citizens.

When not beating his drum, Manolo runs a bar in the shadow of Valencia football club's old Mestalla stadium. A place of pilgrimage for serious footy fans, his **bar** (Map p550; www.mano-loeldelbombo.com, in Spanish; Plaza del Valencia Club de Fútbol 5; ⊘noon-10pm Tue-Sun) is plastered with photos and mementoes – and there's his drum, dangling from the ceiling.

Fox Congo   BAR
(Map p554; 35 Calle Caballeros) Also great for dancing, it has a cool backlit alabaster bar and walls clad in leather and sheet-metal.

Three friendly bars each have their own distinct character.

Café de las Horas   COCKTAIL BAR
(Map p554; Calle Conde de Almodóvar 1) Offers high baroque, tapestries, music of all genres, candelabras and a long list of exotic cocktails.

Finnegan's   BAR
(Map p554; Plaza de la Reina) The longest established of Valencia's several Irish bars and a popular meeting place for English speakers.

Two traditional places to sample *horchata* in the heart of town are **Horchatería de Santa Catalina** (Map p554) and **Horchatería el Siglo** (Map p554), facing each other in eternal rivalry on Plaza Santa Catalina.

OTHER AREAS
Near the Mercado de Abastos, just west of the town centre, **Calle Juan Lloréns** and surrounding streets are another hip area where bars abound.

Café Carioca   MUSIC BAR
(Map p550; Calle Juan Lloréns 52) Cavelike with funky mosaic walls, Café Carioca has three bars. The tempo of the music increases as

the night wears on; expect dance, hip hop, soul and house – and plenty of dancing.

Peatonal   MUSIC BAR
(Map p550; Calle Juan Lloréns 39) Peatonal, like Café Carioca just opposite, is a long-established stayer in a zone where bars come and go. The music's disco, mainly Spanish pop and commercial, and there's a DJ on Thursday. Drinks are two for the price of one until 1am.

Tango y Truco   BAR
(Map p550; Calle Calixto III 10) Posters and photos of Maradona, Eva Perón and other icons, Argentinian and international, plaster the walls of this cosy corner of Buenos Aires in downtown Valencia.

☆ Entertainment
Longest established of several online 'what's on' guides is www.thisisvalencia. com. *La Turia* is a detailed weekly guide in Spanish on sale at kiosks and newsagents. *Hello Valencia* (Spanish and English) and *24-7 Valencia* (in English) are free monthlies. Both are available in tourist offices and selected bars and clubs.

Most clubs have cover charges (€10 to €20), so keep an eye out for discounted passes, carried by many local bars.

Dance Clubs & Discotecas
Terraza Umbracle   LOUNGE BAR
(Map p550; ⊘midnight-6.30am Thu-Sat mid-May–mid-Oct) At the southern end of the Umbracle walkway within the City of Arts and Sciences, this a cool, sophisticated spot to spend a hot summer night. Catch the evening breeze under the stars on the terrace, then drop below to **M.Y.A.**, a top-of-the-line club with an awesome sound system. Admission (€20 including first drink) covers both venues.

Radio City   CLUB
(Map p554; www.radiocityvalencia.com, in Spanish; Calle Santa Teresa 19; ⊘10pm-3.30am) Almost as much mini-cultural centre as club, Radio City, always seething, knows how to pull in the punters with activities including cinema, flamenco (11pm Tuesday) and dancing to an eclectic mix. Pick up a flyer here for its younger sister, Music Box.

Music Box   CLUB
(Map p554; Calle Pintor Zariñena 16; ⊘midnight-7am Tue-Sat) At this smaller, younger sibling of Radio City, the music's eclectic with something for everyone. Entry is free except

after 3am on Friday and Saturday, when there's a €10 cover charge.

Mosquito
MUSIC BAR

(Map p550; Calle Polo y Peyrolón 11) DJs at this tiny box of a place dispense classic soul, R&B and a leavening of hip hop. However many shots you knock back, you'll know you're in the right place by the giant papier mâché mosquito hovering above its circular bar.

Dub Club
CLUB

(Map p550; Calle Jesús 91; ⊘Thu-Sun) 'We play music not noise' is the slogan of this funky dive with its long, narrow bar giving onto a packed dance floor. And it indeed offers great music and great variety, including live jazz jamming, reggae, dub, drum 'n' bass, funk, breakbeat and more.

Bananas
DISCOTECA

(www.bananasworldmusic.com, in Spanish; Carretera Valencia-Alicante, El Romani; ⊘from midnight Fri & Sat) Just about the maxiest maxidisco you'll ever party at, Bananas packs in dancers by the thousand, playing techno with a dash of house. Forget taxi lines: take the special train that leaves Estación del Norte at 1.15am, go Bananas and return on the early bird at 6.15am. Warning: Bananas can be quite druggy.

Caribbean's
DANCE BAR

(Map p550; Calle Bélgica 5; ⊘Tue-Sat) Drinks (try the mojitos) are decently priced at this small, below-ground and usually jam-packed dance bar that blends house, hip hop and R&B. Wednesday night is student night.

La Claca
CLUB

(Map p554; www.laclaca.com, in Spanish; Calle San Vicente Mártir 3; ⊘7pm-3.30am) La Claca, central and popular, has nightly DJs playing funk, hip hop and indie music. Earmark Sunday evening at 8.30pm for some of the best live flamenco in town.

Live Music

Black Note
LIVE JAZZ

(Map p550; Calle Polo y Peyrolón 15) Valencia city's most active jazz venue, Black Note has live music Monday to Thursday and good canned jazz, blues and soul on Friday and Saturday. Admission, including first drink, costs from €6 to €15 depending on who's grooving.

Jimmy Glass
JAZZ BAR

(Map p554; www.jimmyglassjazz.net, in Spanish; Calle Baja 28) Playing jazz from the owner's vast CD collection, Jimmy Glass also sometimes has live performances. It's just what a jazz bar should be – dim, smoky and serving jumbo measures of creative cocktails.

El Loco
LIVE MUSIC

(Map p550; www.lococlub.org, in Spanish; Calle Erudito Orellena 12) This popular, long established venue puts on groups and solo acts from Wednesday to Saturday.

Football

Valencia Club de Fútbol (www.valenciacf.com) is the city's major football team. You can pick up a scarf, woolly hat, shirt or other memento from its club shop (p568).

Valencia's other professional club, Levante (www.levanteud.com), a minnow by comparison, bounces in and out of La Liga, the Spanish first division. Do take in a game – these guys, newly promoted and on a high as we write, need all the support they can get.

Cinemas

Filmoteca
ARTHOUSE CINEMA

(Map p554; www.ivac-lafilmoteca.es, in Spanish; Plaza del Ayuntamiento; admission €1.50) This cinema, on the 4th floor of the Teatro Rialto building, screens undubbed classic and arthouse films – and hasn't raised its admission price in over 20 years!

Babel
ARTHOUSE CINEMA

(Map p550; www.cinesalbatrosbabel.com, in Spanish; Calle Vicente Sancho Tello 10) Multi-screen, shows exclusively undubbed films. Admission prices are lower on Monday.

Theatre & Opera

Teatro Principal
THEATRE

(Map p554; ☑96 353 92 00; Calle Barcas 15) Valencia's main venue for theatre.

Palau de la Música
CONCERT HALL

(Map p550; ☑96 337 50 20; www.palaudevalencia.com, in Spanish; Paseo de la Alameda 30) Hosts mainly classical music recitals.

Palau de les Arts Reina Sofía
OPERA HOUSE

(Map p550; ☑902 10 00 31; www.lesarts.com; Autovía a El Saler) With its four auditoriums, it's a spectacular arts venue offering mostly opera.

🛍 Shopping

Librería Patagonia
TRAVEL BOOKSHOP

(Map p554; www.libreriapatagonia.com, in Spanish; Calle Hospital 1) Excellent travel bookshop and travel agency with some guides in English and lots of Lonely Planet titles.

Mercado Central FOOD MARKET

(Map p554; Plaza del Mercado; ⊙7.30am-2.30pm Mon-Sat) A visit to Valencia's magnificent covered market is a must, even if you only browse.

Kanda Books SECONDHAND BOOKSHOP

(Map p554; www.kandabooks.es; Calle Tapinería 18) Friendly, well-stocked secondhand bookstore with many titles in English.

Valencia Club de Fútbol Shop (Map p554;
Calle Pintor Sorolla 24) Souvenirs, scarfs and hats for the city's major football club.

❶ Information

Call ☏902 12 32 12 throughout the region for tourist information (at premium rates).

Regional tourist office (☏96 398 64 22; www.comunitatvalenciana.com; Calle Paz 48; ⊙9am-8pm Mon-Sat, 10am-2pm Sun)

Restobar Rivendel (Calle del Hospital 18; internet access per hr €2, wi-fi free; ⊙8.30am-midnight Mon-Sat, to 4pm Sun) Cool bar with internet access.

Turismo Valencia (VLC) tourist office (Map p554; ☏96 315 39 31; www.turisvalencia.es; Plaza de la Reina 19; ⊙9am-7pm Mon-Sat, 10am-2pm Sun) Has several other branches, including train station and airport arrivals area.

❶ Getting There & Away

Air

Valencia's **Aeropuerto de Manises** (☏96 159 85 00) is 10km west of the city centre along the A3, direction Madrid. It's served by metro lines 3 and 5.

Budget flights serve major European destinations such as Paris, Milan, Geneva, Amsterdam and Brussels. Flights to/from Ireland and the UK include:

EasyJet Bristol and London (Gatwick)

Ryanair Year round: London (Stansted). Summer only: Bournemouth, Bristol, Dublin, East Midlands.

Boat

Acciona Trasmediterránea (www.acciona-trasmediterranea.es) operates car and passenger ferries to Ibiza, Mallorca and Menorca.

Bus

Valencia's **bus station** (☏96 346 62 66) is beside the riverbed on Avenida Menéndez Pidal. Bus 8 connects it to Plaza del Ayuntamiento.

Avanza (www.avanzabus.com) operates hourly bus services to/from Madrid (€18 to €27, four hours).

ALSA (www.alsa.es) has up to 10 daily buses to/from Barcelona (€26 to €30, 4½ hours) and over 10 to Alicante (€21, 2½ hours), most passing by Benidorm (€14.50, 1¾ hours).

Train

From Valencia's Estación del Norte, major destinations include:

DESTINATION	PRICE (€)	DURATION (HR)	DAILY
Alicante	29	1¾	8
Barcelona	39-43	3 to 3½	at least 12
Madrid	47.50	3¾	up to 10
Madrid*	around €75	1½	up to 12

* On the AVE high-speed train.

Trains run every half-hour to Castellón (€4.50, up to one hour) via Sagunto (€3, 30 minutes).

❶ Getting Around

Valencia has an integrated bus, tram and metro network.

Tourist offices of Turismo Valencia (VLC) sell the **Valencia Tourist Card** (€10/16/20 per one/two/three days), entitling you to free urban travel and discounts at participating sights, shops and restaurants.

To/From the Airport

Metro lines 3 and 5 connect airport, downtown and port. A taxi into the centre costs around €17 (there's a supplement of €2.50 above the metered fee for journeys originating at the airport).

Bicycle Hire

Do You Bike (☏96 315 55 51; www.doyoubike.com; Plaza Horno San Nicolás)

Orange Bikes (☏96 391 75 51; www.orangebikes.net; Calle Editor Manuel Aguilar 1)

Solution Bike (☏96 110 36 95; www.solutionbike.com; Calle Embajador Vich 11)

Valencia Guías (☏96 385 17 40; www.valenciaguias.com; Paseo de la Pechina 32)

Car & Motorcycle

Street parking is a pain. There are large underground car parks beneath Plazas de la Reina and Alfonso el Magnánimo and, biggest of all, near the train station, covering the area between Calle Xàtiva and the Gran Vía.

Reliable local car rental companies operating from Valencia airport, which are usually substantially less expensive than the multinationals, include:

Javea Cars (☏96 579 3312; www.javeacars.com)

Solmar (☏96 153 90 42; www.solmar.es)

Victoria Cars (☎96 583 02 54; www.victoria cars.com).

Public Transport

Most buses run until about 10pm, with seven night services continuing until around 1am. Buy a **Móbilis**, a touch-sensitive, rechargeable card (€2), sold at major metro stations, most tobacconists and some newspaper kiosks

The high-speed tram is a pleasant way to get to the beach port. Pick it up at Pont de Fusta or where it intersects with the metro at Benimaclet.

Metro (www.metrovalencia.es) lines cross town and serve the outer suburbs. The closest stations to the centre are Ángel Guimerá, Xàtiva (for the train station), Colón and Pont de Fusta.

Taxi

Call **Radio-Taxi** (☎96 370 33 33) or **Valencia Taxi** (☎96 357 13 13).

Around Valencia City

LA ALBUFERA

About 15km south of Valencia, La Albufera is a huge freshwater lagoon separated from the sea by La Devesa, a narrow strip of sand dunes and pine forests. The lake and its shores are a breeding ground and sanctuary for migrating and indigenous birds. Keen birdwatchers flock to the Parque Natural de la Albufera, where around 90 species regularly nest while more than 250 others use it as a staging post on their migrations.

Sunsets can be spectacular. You can take a boat trip out on the lagoon, joining the local fisherfolk, who use flat-bottomed boats and nets to harvest fish and eels from the shallow waters.

Surrounded by rice fields, La Albufera was the birthplace of paella. Every second house in the villages of El Palmar and El Perellonet is a restaurant, often run by exor part-time fisherfolk and serving paella and other rice and seafood dishes.

Autocares Herca buses for Playa El Salér are also good for La Albufera, and go on to either El Palmar (six daily) or El Perello (hourly or half-hourly), further down the coast.

SAGUNTO
POP 66,100

You come to Sagunto (Valenciano: Sagunt), 25km north of Valencia, primarily to enjoy the spectacular panorama of the town, coast and green sea of orange groves from its hilltop castle complex. It's usually vis-

To speed around town, take advantage of Valencia's brand new, splendidly practical bike-hire scheme (☎902 006598; www.valenbisi.es). Simply insert your credit card at any one of the projected 275 points to get a card (€10), valid for a week, that you can top up, if need be. The first half-hour of any journey comes free. Hop on, cycle off, then leave the bike at any of the many bike stations around town that are already functioning.

ited as a day or half-day excursion from Valencia.

Sagunto was once a thriving Iberian community (called – infelicitously, with hindsight – Arse) that traded with Greeks and Phoenicians. In 219 BC Hannibal besieged and destroyed the town, sparking the Second Punic War between Carthage and Rome. Rome won, named the town Saguntum and set about rebuilding it.

From the train station it's a 15-minute walk to the tourist office (☎96 265 58 59; Plaza Cronista Chabret; ⊙9am-2pm & 4-6.30pm Mon-Fri, 9am-2pm Sat & Sun). A further 10-minute uphill walk – detour into the small *judería*, the former Jewish quarter – brings you to the Roman theatre. Its modern 'restoration' is controversial but the acoustics remain outstanding and it's the main venue for Sagunto's three-week, open-air August **arts festival**.

Higher up, the stone walls of the castle complex (admission free; ⊙10am-dusk Tue-Sat, 10am-2pm Sun) girdle the hilltop for almost a kilometre. Mostly in ruins, its seven rambling sections each speak of a different period in Sagunto's long history.

There are frequent trains between Valencia and Sagunto (one-way/return €2.90/4.70) and AVSA (☎96 267 14 16) runs a service (€2.30, half-hourly) from Valencia's bus station.

SEGORBE
POP 9250 / ELEV 395M

Segorbe, 33km northwest of Sagunto and 56km from Valencia, has a substantial baroque cathedral. Within its more delicate Gothic cloister is a fine ecclesiastical museum (adult/child €3/2; ⊙11am-1.30pm & 5-7pm

Tue-Sun) with a sculpture of the Virgin and Child by Donatello and several colourful altarpieces.

TOP CHOICE Museo del Aceite (☑96 471 20 45; Plaza Belluga 3; adult/child €2/free; ☉11am-1.30pm & 5-8pm), in a former olive mill, is a highly recommended multimedia tribute to the area's staple crop, olives. Its shop is the place to pick up local hams, sausages, wines and, of course, virgin olive oil. Above the museum are six attractive furnished apartments (www.labelluga.com, in Spanish), which can be rented by the day.

At the western corner of the old town is a pair of cylindrical towers (guided visit adult/under 12yr €2/free; ☉noon Tue-Sun). The Torre de la Carcel for a time served as the town's lock-up while the town executioner, for those whose fate was even worse, lived nearby in the Torre del Verdugo.

Segorbe's medieval aqueduct, of which a healthy hunk remains, brought water from the fountain of **La Esperanza** (Hope), from where it still springs eternal.

The town's major fiesta is its **Entrada de Toros y Caballos** (Entry of Bulls and Horses). Prompt at 2pm for seven days in the first half of September, skilled horsemen guide and prod the bulls down Calle Colón between two human walls of spectators. The Centro de Interpretación de la Entrada de Toros y Caballos (adult/child €2/free) is a thrilling multilingual evocation of this rumbustious spectacle. It shares premises with the tourist office (☑964 71 32 54; Calle Marcelino Blasco 3; ☉9am-2pm & 4-6pm or 5-7pm Mon-Sat, 10.30am-1.30pm Sun).

REQUENA
POP 21,950 / ELEV 690M

From the heart of Requena, 65km west of Valencia, rears La Villa, its medieval nucleus, jumbled and irregular with twisting streets and blind alleys. Requena's former wealth came from silk; at one time it had about 800 active looms, making this tiny town Spain's fourth-biggest producer. Nowadays it's primarily wine and livestock country, producing robust reds, sparkling *cavas* and rich hunks of sausage and spicy meats.

The first or second weekend in February marks the **Muestra del Embutido**, the Sausage Show; when an estimated 10,000kg of sausage and 25,000 servings of roast pork are gobbled up. In late August/early September, Requena's **Fiesta de la Vendimia** is 12 days of hearty bacchanal, celebrating the end of the grape harvest.

◉ Sights

Enter the old quarter from its northern side, passing by the largely 15th-century, originally Islamic Torre del Homenaje. Within the town walls are the Gothic Santa María and San Salvador churches, each with a magnificent if much weathered main portal, and sturdy noblemen's mansions such as the Casa-Museo del Arte Mayor de la Seda (Silk Guild House).

Museo del Vino   WINE MUSEUM
(Calle Somera) This tribute to the Requena region's greatest product was about to open

LA TOMATINA

Buñol? It'll make you see red.

The last or penultimate Wednesday in August (the date varies) marks Spain's messiest festival. Held in Buñol, an otherwise drab industrial town 40km west of Valencia city, La Tomatina is a tomato-throwing orgy that attracts more than 40,000 visitors to a town of just 9000 inhabitants.

At precisely 11am a rocket swooshes skywards and over 100 tonnes of ripe, squishy tomatoes are tipped from trucks to the waiting crowd. For precisely one hour, until a second rocket is fired, everyone joins in a frenzied, cheerful, anarchic tomato battle. After being pounded with pulp, expect to be sluiced down with hoses by the local fire brigade.

The mayhem takes place on the town's main square and Calle del Cid. Most people come for the day, arriving on the morning train from Valencia and heading back in the afternoon. Don't forget a set of fresh clothes and perhaps a pair of goggles to protect the eyes.

Alternatively, you can watch the spectacle in dry comfort on Canal 9, Valencia's local TV channel. For more background, log on to www.latomatina.es.

when we last visited town. Items range from 5th-century-BC Iberian amphoras – proving that wine was fermented here even in those distant days – to wine presses, both automatic and manual. In the old quarter, the museum sits handsomely within the equally attractive 15th-century Palacio del Cid.

Plaza de la Villa   SQUARE
Also called Plaza Albornoz, this plaza hides in its intestines a network of interlinked cellars, once used as storerooms and, during strife, hideouts. Guided visits (adult/ child €4/3; ☺3-6 times daily Tue-Sun) descend from the entrance on the eastern side of the old quarter's main square. Ask at the tourist office for times.

FREE **Ferevin**   WINE SHOWROOM
(www.ferevin.com in Spanish; Cuesta de las Carnicerías; ☺11am-2pm Tue-Sun plus 5-7pm Sat) A showroom for Utiel-Requena's association of wine producers, it carries a good selection of the region's best vintages and has free sampling, each week highlighting a different bodega.

Museo Municipal   MUSEUM
(Calle Carmen; adult/child €4/3; ☺11am-2pm Tue-Sun) The museum has a rich collection of traditional costumes, re-creations of a bourgeois town house and country dwellings and exhibits illustrating Requena's silk weaving past.

Museo de Arte Contemporáneo
                                      ART MUSEUM
(☎96 230 30 32; Cuesta del Ángel 2; adult/child €4/3; ☺11am-2pm & 6-9 Tue-Sat, 11am-2pm Sun) Requena's contemporary art museum has canvases mainly by Spanish artists, including Picasso, Miró, Sempere, Tàpies and Dalí.

🛏 **Sleeping & Eating**
On the old town's main square are two attractive sleeping options, each with a good restaurant.

TOP CHOICE **Mesón del Vino**   BAR, RESTAURANT €
(☎96 230 00 01; Avenida Arrabal 11; ☺lunch & dinner Wed-Sun, lunch Mon) Down on the main street, drop in here for a drink or a full-scale meal at this splendidly democratic spot, tiled floor to ceiling. A huge stuffed bull's head greets everyone from local intellectuals to blue collar workers as they enter.

Mesón La Villa   RESTAURANT €€
(☎96 230 21 32; Plaza Albornoz 13; mains €8-14.50) If you can't visit Requena's cellars,

The Valencia to Barcelona train line follows the coast and regional trains stop at all main towns. From Valencia, trains run every half-hour to Castellón de la Plana. At least six trains daily call at Benicàssim, Oropesa, Benicarló/ Peñíscola and Vinaròs train stations.

dine here and ask your hosts to let you see theirs (admission €1), briefly used by the local branch of the Inquisition (see the Papal coat of arms on the facade) to turn the screws on heretics.

Hôtel La Villa   HOTEL €
(☎96 230 03 74; www.hotellavillarestaurante. com, in Spanish; Plaza Albornoz 8; s/d €36/55; ❄) Until recently this hotel was a family home; now it offers 18 attractive rooms and a couple of suites, all furnished in rustic style.

Hôtel Doña Anita   HOTEL €€
(☎96 230 53 47; www.tubal.net, in Spanish; Plaza Albornoz 15; s/d €48/75) Across the square, in a new building despite its antique air, Doña Anita offers greater luxury. It also organises wine tastings and tours of Requena-Utiel bodegas.

ⓘ **Information**
The **tourist office** (☎96 230 38 51; www.req uena.es; Calle García Montés; ☺9.30am-2pm Tue-Sun plus 4-7pm Sat & Sun) is below the main entrance to the old town. Ask for the English version of its *Sensaciones por Descubrir,* a helpful guide to La Villa.

ⓘ **Getting There & Away**
Up to 12 buses (€4.50, one hour) and seven trains (€4.40, 1½ hours) run daily to/from Valencia.

COSTA DEL AZAHAR

All along the Costa del Azahar (Orange Blossom Coast) spread citrus groves, from whose headily scented flowers the region takes its name. The busy, developed – not always harmoniously – seaside resorts are enticing if you're after sun and sand. By contrast, the high hinterland, especially the wild, sparsely populated lands of the Maestrazgo, offer great walking, solitude and hearty mountain cooking.

Castellón de la Plana

POP 180,000

The outskirts of Castellón de la Plana are grim, industrial and rambling, but if you penetrate to the beating heart of this commercial town, you're in for a pleasant surprise. Plaza Mayor and, just to its south, Plaza Santa Clara form the nucleus of what matters to the visitor.

⊙ Sights

El Grau de Castellón, Castellón's port, is 4km east of the centre and serves the region's exports as well as the local fishing fleet. The beaches start north of here.

FREE **Museo de Bellas Artes**

FINE-ARTS MUSEUM

(Avenida Hermanos Bou 28; ⊙10am-8pm Mon-Sat, 10am-2pm Sun) Highlights in this striking award-winning contemporary building are its large ceramics section, reflecting the region's major industry, two superbly wrought silver crosses and a set of 10 magnificent canvases by Zurbarán.

Galleries

ART GALLERIES

Two other galleries that show temporary exhibitions also impress by their architecture. The **Espai d'Art Contemporani** (Calle Prim) is a dazzling piece of contemporary design. By contrast, the freshly and sensitively restored **Llotja del Cánem** (Calle Caballeros 1), in the shadow of the cathedral, brings new life to what was originally Castellón's hemp exchange.

Concatedral de Santa María

CATHEDRAL

From Plaza Mayor, bordered by the early 18th-century town hall and busy covered market, thrusts the long finger of **El Fadrí** (1604), an octagonal bell tower and symbol of the city. Beside the tower is the reconstructed Concatedral de Santa María, shattered in the civil war and now restored to its original state.

🛏 Sleeping & Eating

Hotel Intur Castellón

HOTEL €€

(☑964 22 50 00; www.intur.com, in Spanish; Calle Herrero 20; r €60-75; ❄@🗑) Although stark from the outside, there's a bright, spacious central atrium within, overlooked by each of the 120 rooms. Weekend rates and summer tariffs are particular bargains.

La Casita de Gredos

RESTAURANT €€

(☑964 22 09 33; Calle Gracia 26; menus €21, mains €10-19; ⊙lunch Mon-Sat, dinner Fri & Sat)

With an enticing lunch *menú* that changes daily and creative fish and meat dishes based upon fresh local produce, this long, low, welcoming place is renowned for its *bacalao* (dried and salted cod) dishes and select wine list. Reservations essential.

Julivert

CAFE, RESTAURANT €

(☑964 23 52 72; Calle Caballeros 41; menus €10; ⊙lunch Mon-Thu, lunch & dinner Fri & Sat; ☑) This tiny place does a good three-course *menú* finishing with a homemade dessert and always offering a vegetarian option.

La Cambra dels Vins

GOURMET FOOD

(Calle Caballeros 24; ⊙Mon-Fri & morning Sat) Carries a carefully chosen selection of Spanish wines – malt whiskies too – plus exotic cans and jars of picnic enhancers.

Carnicería Charcutería Miguel

GOURMET FOOD

(73 Calle Navarra) A treasure chest of wines, honeys, pâtés and (rare in Spain) vintage cheeses.

🍷 Drinking

Casa Ripo

WINE BAR

(www.casaripo.com in Spanish; Calle Ximénez 11; ⊙Mon-Sat) Walking around Castellón, you'll probably have come across the fleshy-lipped, ample-haunched sculptures of esteemed local sculptor Juan Ripollés. This suave wine bar, which serves delightful tapas and snacks and carries a good wine list, seems too smart a haunt for a self-proclaimed bohemian. But all around the walls, as proof, are his quirky canvases and sketches.

ℹ Information

Main tourist office (☑964 35 86 88; Plaza María Agustina 5; ⊙9am-7pm Mon-Fri, 10am-2pm Sat) Ask for its free brochure, *A Cultural Experience in Castellón de la Plana*.

ℹ Getting There & Away

Castellón has a combined bus and train station, about 1km northwest of the centre. Long-distance buses use the **bus station** (☑964 24 07 78). For both Valencia and resorts to the north (except for Benicàssim, for which frequent buses leave from Plaza Fadrell), trains are swifter and more frequent.

During the lifespan of this edition, it's probable that the near-complete **Castellón airport** (www.aerocas.com in Spanish), long in gestation, will be receiving flights from European destinations.

Around Castellón de la Plana

VILAFAMÉS
POP 2000

What draws visitors to Vilafamés, a hillside village 26km north of Castellón, is its excellent **Museo de Arte Contemporáneo** (Calle Diputació 20; adult/child €2/free; ⏱10am-1.30pm & 4-7pm Tue-Sun). Within the 15th-century Palacio de la Bailía, worth a visit in its own right, is a wonderful, highly eclectic collection of contemporary paintings and sculpture.

The village is an agreeable clutter of whitewashed houses and civic buildings in rust-red stone. From Plaza de la Sangre, steep steps take you up to the ruined **castle** and a sensational panorama.

The 11 rooms of **L'Antic Portal** (☑964 32 93 84; www.hotelvilafames.com in Spanish; Calle de la Fuente 6; r €70-80; ❄🛜) are pleasingly contemporary in design. Within the shell of an antique building (a huge hunk of original rock contributes to one of the walls), each room has a small balcony. It belongs to neighbouring **Hotel El Rullo** (☑964 32 93 84; Calle de la Fuente 2; s/d €22/42), a modest family hotel that offers cheaper, simpler rooms and does an economical *menú*.

Vilafamés' **tourist office** (☑964 32 99 70; Plaza del Ayuntamiento 2) is beside the town hall.

MONTANEJOS
POP 600 / ELEV 460M

It's a spectacular drive along the CV20 from Castellón up the gorges of Río Mijares to this resort, spa village and rock-climbing base at the heart of the Sierra de Espadán. Surrounded by craggy, pine-clad mountains, its fresh mountain air attracts summer visitors in plenty and there's bathing for free in the 25°C waters of **Fuente de los Baños**, 1km north.

Drawing its waters from the natural springs of Fuente de los Baños, the **Balneario** (Spa; www.balneario.com/montanejos, in Spanish) has a huge range of watery health-inducing treatments.

Geoextrem.com (www.geoextrem.com, in Spanish) offers outdoor thrills including, kayaking, canyon descents, rock climbing and caving. Operating year-round, it has a base at Fuente de los Baños in summer.

Most hotels open only in summer and at weekends. An exception is **Hotel Rosaleda del Mijares** (☑964 13 10 79; www.hoteles rosaleda.com; Carretera Tales 28; incl breakfast s €56-70, d €72-140; ⏱Feb–mid-Dec; ❄🛜), which lays on a filling *menú* (€15) in its vast dining room. The 81 rooms are attractive and comfortable, with large beds. The hotel has its own pool and gym and also offers a fistful of spa packages.

The **tourist office** (☑964 13 11 53; www.montanejos.com, in Spanish; Carretera Tales) is within the *balneario*.

GRUTA DE SAN JOSÉ

Gruta de San José (Valenciano: Coves de Sant Josep; www.riosubterraneo.com, in Spanish; adult/child €9.50/4.50; ⏱11am-1.15pm & 3.30-5.45pm or 6.30pm) is a winding tunnel, scoured naturally through the karst. On the outskirts of La Vall d'Uixó, 35km southwest of Castellón, it bores into the hillside for 2.75km. Boats glide through the first subtly lit 800m, followed by a walk through limestone grottos.

Benicàssim

POP 18.100

Benicàssim, scarcely a couple of blocks wide, stretches for 6km along the coast. It has been a popular resort since the 19th century, when wealthy Valencian families built summer residences here. To this day, over 75% of summer visitors are Spanish and many people from Madrid, Valencia and nearby Castellón own summer apartments.

⊙ Sights & Activities

Those 6km of broad beach are the main attraction. Bordering the promenade at the northeastern end are **Las Villas**, exuberant, sometimes frivolous holiday homes built by wealthy *valencianos* at the end of the 19th century and into the 20th. Ask for the tourist office leaflet, *The Las Villas Path*.

TOP CHOICE **Desierto de las Palmas** INLAND HILLS The twisting, climbing CV147 leads after about 6km to this inland range – cooler than the coast, on occasion misty – with a Carmelite monastery (1697) and first-class restaurant at its heart. Nowadays a nature reserve and far from desert (for the monks it meant a place for mystic withdrawal), it's a green, outdoor activities area. From **Monte Bartolo** (728m), its highest point, there are staggering views.

Time your visit to coincide with lunch at Restaurante Desierto de las Palmas.

Aquarama   WATER PARK
(www.aquarama.net, in Spanish; adult/child half-day €9.30/13, day €13.50/19.50; ⊙11am-7pm mid-Jun–Aug) This vast water park is just south of town, off the N340.

✽ Festivals & Events

Festival Internacional de Benicàssim
                                           MUSIC
(FIB; www.fiberfib.com) In late July or early August, fans by the tens of thousands gather for this annual four-day festival, one of Europe's major outdoor music festivals. Top acts in 2010 included Lily Allen, Charlotte Gainsbourg, Dizzee Rascal and Vampire Weekend.

🛏 Sleeping

Hotel Avenida   HOTEL €€
(☎964 30 00 47; www.hotelecoavenida.com; Avenida Castellón 2; d €37-77; ⊙mid-Feb–Sep; ✳@⌘🐾🛰) This appealing family-owned hotel, just off the old town's main street, has a pool, jacuzzi and shady courtyard. Rooms are large, parking's free and it's excellent value. The entrance is on Calle Quatro Caminos.

TOP / CHOICE **Hotel Voramar**   BEACHSIDE HOTEL €€
(☎964 30 01 50; www.voramar.net, in Spanish; Paseo Marítimo Pilar Coloma 1; r incl breakfast €90-144; ✳@🛰) Venerable (it's been run by the same family for four generations) and blooded in battle (it functioned as a hospital in the Spanish Civil War), the Voramar has more character than most of Benicàssim's modern upstarts and is also the only hotel that faces directly onto the sands. The **restaurant**, where the cuisine is first class, has large windows overlooking the sea.

Benicàssim's five camping grounds are all within walking distance of the beaches.

Camping Azahar   CAMPING GROUND €
(www.campingazahar.es, in Spanish; per person/tent/car €4.25/14.45/4.20; ⊙year-round; 🐾🛰) Extensive sites are shaded by mature mulberry trees. There's a restaurant, a large pool and toilet blocks that are kept scrupulously clean.

🍴 Eating

Plenty of economical restaurants line Calle de Santo Tomás and Calle Castellón, the old town's main street.

Restaurante Desierto de las Palmas
                          MOUNTAIN RESTAURANT €€
(☎964 30 09 47; mains €15-24; ⊙lunch & dinner daily Jun-Sep, lunch Wed-Mon Oct-May) Families flock from miles around to this popular venue, famed for its rice and seafood dishes, in the hills behind Benicàssim. Lively, noisy and very Spanish, it sits on a spur close to the Carmelite monastery and offers heart-stopping views from its broad windows.

Torreón   RESTAURANT €€
(☎964 30 03 42; Avenida Ferrandis Salvador 2; mains €12-15) Overlooking the 16th-century Torre San Vicente watchtower that gives this cafe-restaurant its name, it's a great spot to catch the sea breezes while nibbling on a snack, sipping a drink or tucking into a full meal. If you're dining, book in advance to enjoy a place on the smaller, less crowded of its two terraces.

La Manduca   BAR RESTAURANT €€
(☎964 30 17 18; Calle Santo Tomás 69; mains €10.50-17) This contemporary bar and restaurant stretches between two streets. There's an ample selection of starters, pizzas and local specialities from the sea.

🍷 Drinking

In summer and at weekends, Benicàssim rocks. The eastern end of Calle de los Dolores in the old town is cheek-by-jowl bars. The town's biggest *discoteca*, Magic (☎617 30 02 76), faces Aquarama.

ℹ Information

Main tourist office (☎964 30 09 62; www.beni cassim.org; Calle Santo Tomás 74; ⊙9am-2pm & 4-7pm) One kilometre inland in the old town.

ℹ Getting There & Away

Buses run every half-hour (every 15 minutes in summer) to Castellón, from where train connections are much more plentiful.

Oropesa del Mar

It's a fine coastal scenic drive from Benicàssim to Oropesa (Valenciano: Orpesa) along a narrow road winding around the rocky coastline. Even more satisfying is the recently opened Via Verde, a 6km dedicated route for cyclists and walkers. Following a former railway track, it connects the two resorts and offers comparable views at a gentler pace.

Oropesa itself is expanding rapidly and none too prettily northwards, embracing the massive spa and resort of Marina d'Or.

Naturhiscope (964 31 30 26; Plaza de la Iglesia; admission €1.50; 10am-2pm & 4-7pm Mon-Sat) is a collection of photos and everyday objects, interpreting the town and its relationship with the sea in a high-tech context. Inspirational for some, pretentious flummery for others.

Two tiny museums, also in the old town, are each run by passionate, eccentric amateurs. The **Museo del Naipe** (Playing Card Museum; 626 564749; Calle Hospital 1; admission €2; 10am-1.30pm & 6-8pm) has over 5000 different packs and other memorabilia from around the world, explained with beguiling enthusiasm. Outside opening times, just knock; the owner lives above.

Luis Elvira, another collecting squirrel, has assembled a unique collection of cogs and grills, shields and other items in metal at the **Museo del Hierro** (Metalwork Museum; 964 31 07 51; Calle Ramón y Cajal 12; admission €3; 10am-2pm Mon-Fri).

Oropesa's main **tourist office** (964 31 23 20; www.oropesadelmar.es, in Spanish; Plaza París; 9.30am-2pm & 4.30-6.30pm or 5-8pm) is beside Playa de la Concha.

Peñíscola

POP 7900

Peñíscola's old town, all cobbled streets and whitewashed houses, huddles within stone walls that protect the rocky promontory jutting into the sea. It's pretty as a postcard – and just as commercial, with ranks of souvenir and ceramics shops (one prominent item: a pot with an – oh dear – stiff penis for a spout, a pun that doesn't even work in Spanish). By contrast, the high-rises sprouting northwards along the coast are mostly leaden and charmless. But the Paseo Marítimo promenade makes pleasant walking, and the beach, which extends as far as neighbouring Benicarló, is superb, sandy and over 5km long.

◉ Sights & Activities

Castle   CASTLE
(adult/child €3.50/free; 9.30am-5.30pm or 9.30pm) The rambling 14th-century castle was built by the Knights Templar on Arab foundations and later became home to Pedro de Luna ('Papa Luna', the deposed Pope Benedict XIII).

La Casa del Ayer   HISTORIC HOUSE
TOP CHOICE (www.lacasadelayer.es in Spanish; Calle Jaime Sanz Roca 20; adult/child €2/1.50; 10.30am-1.30pm & 4-7pm Fri-Wed) A lovingly restored and re-furnished early-19th-century house. Every item has been collected or cajoled by Regina del Val and her partner Felix. After Regina's exuberant introduction, wander at will among the rooms, then buy an item or two of local produce from the shop below.

Sierra de Irta   NATURE PARK
To escape the summer crowds, seek solitude in the Sierra de Irta. Running south from Peñíscola, it's both nature park and protected marine reserve. It's also one of the very last unspoilt stretches of Valencian coastline, best explored on foot or by mountain bike. You can attack the full 26km of the circular PR V-194 trail or slip in one or more shorter loops. Ask at the tourist office for its free *Paths Through Irta* brochure.

🛏 Sleeping & Eating

There are two great alternatives to the beachside concrete towers. Since they're small, do reserve.

Hotel-Restaurante Simó   HOTEL €€
(964 48 06 20; www.restaurantesimo.es, in Spanish; Calle Porteta 5; s €40-55, d €55-75; closed Jan) At the base of the castle pile and right beside the sea, the Simó has a restaurant (mains €13-25) with magnificent views across the bay. Seven of its nine simple, unfussy and relatively spacious rooms enjoy an equally impressive vista.

Hostería del Mar   HOTEL €€
(964 48 06 00; www.hosteriadelmar.net; Avenida Papa Luna 18; s €53-107, d €73-142;) Once, this four-star, family-owned place was the only hotel along the promenade. And it still preserves more character than most of its undistinguished multistorey neighbours. Nearly all rooms have balconies overlooking the beach and there's even a casino, should you fancy your chances of recovering your room cost.

Chiki Bar Restaurante   PENSIÓN €
(605 280295; Calle Mayor 3-5; r €40-50) High in the old town, Chiki Bar has, in addition to its engaging name, seven spotless, modern rooms with views. You might want your earplugs since the nearby parish church chimes tinnily, on the hour, every hour. From March to October, it runs an attractive restaurant (mains from €9; closed Tue)

with a great-value three-course *menú* (€11). Hours are unreliable, so do ring in advance.

Casa Jaime
FISH €€

(☎964 48 00 30; Avenida Papa Luna 5; mains €15.75-27.50; ☺daily mid-Jun–mid-Sep, closed Wed & dinner Sun mid-Sep–mid-Jun) Dine on the ample outside terrace or in the cosy dining room, where you can see mum and dad (once a fisherman who learnt his trade cooking for the crew) at work in the kitchen. They're renowned for their *suquet de peix* (fish stew; €23.50, minimum two people), and other rice and simmered fish dishes.

Hogar del Pescador
FISH €€

(☎964 48 95 88; Plaza Lonja Vieja; fish from €10) This popular fisherfolk's cafe by day is great value for everything from the sea. For the maximum taste sensation, a couple could share, for example, a *mariscada* (seafood special; €35), followed by a *combinado degustación* (€21), a magnificent platter of mixed fish and crustaceans.

❶ Information

Main tourist office (☎964 48 02 08; www.peni scola.es; ☺9.30am-1.30pm & 4-7pm Mon-Sat, 10am-1pm Sun) At the southern end of Paseo Marítimo. Pick up its free descriptive booklet, *The Old City*.

❶ Getting There & Around

Year-round, local buses run at least every half-hour between Peñíscola, Benicarló and Vinaròs. From July to mid-September there's an hourly run to Peñíscola/Benicarló train station.

Vinaròs

POP 28.300

Unlike its luxury-loving neighbours, Vinaròs is a working town, and a fairly grim one. Two redeeming features are its active fishing port, famous for *langostinos* (king prawns), and its splendid, wide, recently pedestrianised promenade that many a better endowed tourist resort should envy.

The Iglesia Arciprestal (Plaza del Ayuntamiento) is a stocky baroque fortified church with a tall bell tower and elaborate main doorway decorated with candy-twist columns. Opposite is the Modernista Casa Giner (1914), garnished with floral motifs and fine miradors (enclosed balconies). These days a Benetton shop, its original stained glass proclaims its earlier quaint function as *paquetería* and *mercería* (haberdasher and draper).

From here, pedestrianised Calle Mayor leads past the Modernista covered market (being gutted and restored when we last visited) to the promenade and beaches.

Vinaròs has two big annual bashes. Forty days before the privations of Lent, the town erupts with one of Spain's biggest and most exuberant **carnivals**, culminating in three days of intensive strutting and parading. From 10 to 13 August, the **Fiesta del Langostino** celebrates Vinaròs' prime catch with seaside samplings and lots of other outdoor fun.

You've plenty of eating choices on the waterfront, most specialising in seafood.

A well-lobbed *langostino* from the quayside fish market, Bar Puerto (☎964 45 56 72; Calle Costa Borrás 60; mains €9.50-16, mixed platters €8.50-12), small, friendly and informal, does a great range of tapas and fishy mains.

In more classic mode, La Cuina (☎964 45 47 36; Paseo Blasco Ibáñez 12; menus €18-37, mains €14-22; ☺closed dinner Sun), one of several enticing promenade restaurants, is bedecked with crisp white tablecloths and napkins. To enjoy the riches hauled from the Mediterranean, invest in the six-course fish and seafood *menú degustación* (€37; minimum two people).

Vinaròs' tourist office (☎964 45 33 34; www.turisme.vinaros.es; Plaza Jovellar 2; ☺10am-2pm & 5-7pm Tue-Sat, 11am-2pm Sun Oct-May) is round the corner from Iglesia Arciprestal.

EL MAESTRAZGO

Straddling northwestern Valencia and southeast Aragón, El Maestrazgo (Valenciano: El Maestrat) is a mountainous land, a world away from the coastal fleshpots. Here ancient *pueblos* (villages) huddle on rocky outcrops and ridges. One such place, Sant Mateu, was chosen in the 14th century by the maestro (hence the name El Maestrazgo) of the Montesa order of knights as his seat of power.

The Maestrazgo is great, wild, on-your-own trekking territory. *La Tinença de Benifassà* and *Els Ports*, two excellent 1:30,000 maps, designed for walkers and available from the Morella tourist office among other outlets, cover most of the area.

KING OF ALL THE PRAWNS

The *langostinos* (king prawns) that make it as far as Vinaròs' wholesale fish market (around 15 tonnes of them annually) have had a hard time of it. They hatch in the sandy beds of the Río Ebro delta, to the north, where the estuary's low salinity enhances their flavour and plumpness. Once mature, they leave its relative comfort to scrabble their way over rocky promontories and struggle against strong currents and waves, only to be scooped up and netted and find their way, sizzling and grilled or simply boiled, to your plate.

So prized is this delicacy with its reputedly aphrodisiac qualities that it's been designated as the town's official tourist emblem.

Sant Mateu

POP 2200 / ELEV 325M

A drive 5km south from the N232 along the CV132 brings you to Sant Mateu, once capital of the Maestrazgo. Its solid mansions and elaborate facades recall the town's more illustrious past and former wealth, based upon the wool trade.

From colonnaded Plaza Mayor, ringed with cafe terraces, signs point to four small municipal museums (each adult/child €1.50/free; ☺10am-noon & 4-6pm Tue-Sun): the Museo Paleontológico, Museo Arciprestal of religious art (in Casa Abadía, beside the parish church tower), Museo les Presons in the former jail and Museo Histórico Municipal, entered via the tourist office.

Radiating from the village are three signed circular walking trails of between 2½ and five hours that lead through the surrounding hills. Ask for the free tourist office pamphlet *Senderos de Sant Mateu* (in Spanish).

Family-run (see the photos of its three generations around the tiled dining room), Hotel-Restaurante La Perdi (☎964 41 60 82; laperdicb@hotmail.com; Calle Historiador Betí 9; s/d €24/36) is a bargain with five modern, comfortable rooms and a restaurant (mains €6-14.50) that does a bargain *menú* (€9). Room reservations are normally essential.

Follow signs from Plaza Mayor to the Ermita de la Mare de Déu dels Àngels, perched on a rocky hillside, a 2.5km drive or considerably shorter walk. A monastery until the Spanish Civil War (take a peep at its over-the-top baroque chapel), it's nowadays a quality restaurant (☎626 525219; menus €21-35; ☺lunch Wed-Sun, dinner Sat) offering incomparable views of the surrounding plain.

Sant Mateu's tourist office (☎964 41 66 58; www.santmateu.com in Spanish; Calle Historiador Betí 10; ☺10am-2pm & 4-6pm Tue-Sat, 10am-2pm Sun) is just off Plaza Mayor, in Palacio Borrull, a stalwart 15th-century building.

ⓘ Getting There & Away

Weekdays, **Autos Mediterráneo** (☎964 22 00 54) buses link Sant Mateu with the following destinations:

Vinaròs €2.50, 35 minutes, four daily

Castellón €4.80, 1½ hours, three daily

Morella €3, 45 minutes, two daily

On Saturday, one service runs from Castellón to Morella via Sant Mateu. The bus stop is in Plaza Llaurador, 100m east of Hotel Restaurante Montesa.

Around Sant Mateu

FREE Museo de Valltorta (☎964 76 10 25; ☺10am-2pm & 4-7pm or 5-8pm Tue-Sun) is a well-illustrated museum, 10km southwest of Sant Mateu in Tirig. It presents the Maestrazgo's rich heritage of rock paintings, recognised as a Unesco World Heritage treasure. From here guided walks to the clifftop overhangs and much-faded paintings leave four times daily.

Morella

POP 2800 / ELEV 1000M

Bitingly cold in winter and refreshingly cool in summer, Morella is the Maestrazgo's principal town. This outstanding example of a medieval fortress town is perched on a hilltop, crowned by a castle and girdled by an intact rampart wall over 2km long. It's the ancient capital of Els Ports, the 'mountain passes', a rugged region offering some outstanding scenic drives and strenuous cycling excursions, plus excellent possibilities for walkers.

◉ Sights & Activities

Morella is a pleasantly confusing, compact jumble of narrow streets, alleys and steep steps. Its main street, running between Puerta San Miguel and Puerta de los Estudios, is bordered by shops selling mountain honey, perfumes, cheeses, pickles and pâtés, skeins of sausages and fat hams.

Castle   CASTLE

(adult/child €2/1.50; ⊙11am-5pm or 7pm) Though badly knocked about, Morella's castle well merits the strenuous ascent to savour breathtaking views of the town and surrounding countryside. At its base is the bare church and cloister of the Convento de San Francisco, destined to become a *parador* hotel.

Basílica de Santa María la Mayor
CHURCH

(Plaza Arciprestal; ⊙11am-2pm & 4-6pm or 7pm) This imposing Gothic basilica has two elaborately sculpted doorways on its southern facade. A richly carved polychrome stone staircase leads to the elaborately sculpted overhead choir, while cherubs clamber and peek all over the gilded altarpiece. Its ecclesiastical treasure is kept within the Museo Arciprestal (admission €1.50).

Museo Tiempo de Dinosaurios
DINOSAUR MUSEUM

(adult/child €2/1.50; ⊙11am-2pm & 4-6pm or 7pm) Opposite the tourist office, the museum has dinosaur bones and fossils – the Maestrazgo's remote hills have been a treasure trove for palaeontologists – together with an informative video (in Spanish).

Museo del Sexenni   FIESTA MUSEUM

(adult/child €2/1.50; ⊙11am-2pm & 4-6pm Easter-October) In the former Church of Sant Nicolau, displays models, photos and items associated with the Sexenni, Morella's major fiesta.

On the outskirts of town stretch the arches of a handsome 13th-century aqueduct.

✦ Festivals & Events

Sexenni   TOWN FIESTA

Morella's major festival is the Sexenni, held during August every six years without interruption since 1673 (the next is in 2012) in honour of the town's patron, the Virgen de Vallivana. Visit the Museo del Sexenni to get the flavour of this major celebration with its tonnes of confetti and elaborate compositions in crêpe paper.

Festival de Música Barroca   MUSIC

Annually in August, there's a baroque music festival, starring the Basílica de Santa María la Mayor's huge organ.

🛏 Sleeping & Eating

Hotel El Cid   HOTEL €

(☎964 16 01 25; www.hotelelcidmorella.com; Puerta San Mateu 3; s/d €33/57; 📶) Beside the ramparts and above its popular bar and restaurant, Hotel El Cid has smart, attractively furnished modern rooms (204 and 304, at the same price, have a small salon attached). Most have balconies, offering magnificent views of the surrounding countryside.

Hotel del Pastor   HOTEL €€

(☎964 16 10 16; www.hoteldelpastor.com; Calle San Julián 12; incl breakfast s €48-55, d €59-73) Its 12 rooms, spread over four floors (there's no lift but that's the only downside of this attractive option), are traditionally furnished in warm ochre colours with plenty of polished wood. Bathrooms all have marble washstands and tub and large mirrors.

Daluan   CONTEMPORARY FUSION €€

(964 16 00 71; www.daluan.es, in Spanish; Callejón Cárcel 4; mains €12-15; lunch menus €14, menus €26-30; ⊙lunch Sun-Wed, lunch & dinner Fri & Sat) Run by Avelino Ramón, a cookery teacher by trade, and his wife Jovita, Daluan's small interior is satisfyingly contemporary. Its terrace, beside a quiet alley, is equally relaxing. Expect friendly service and a hugely creative menu that changes regularly with the seasons. In summer it does a magnificent value 12-course tapas *menú* for €25.

Restaurante Casa Roque
MOUNTAIN CUISINE €€

(☎964 16 03 36; Cuesta San Juan 1; mains €22-28; ⊙lunch & dinner Tue-Sat, lunch Sun) Within a vast 17th-century mansion, Casa Roque does a good-value weekday *menú* (€11) and rich mountain *menús* (€22 and €28) offering typical Els Ports dishes such as *conejo al Maestrazgo con caracoles* (rabbit with snails stewed in a tasty, herbed sauce).

Casa Masoveret   GOURMET FOOD €

(www.casamasoveret.com in Spanish; Segura Barreda 9) At this exceptionally friendly place, perch on a wooden bench and enjoy a glass of choice wine while nibbling on tapas of mountain cheeses and ham or scoffing a well-filled *bocadillo*. Scan the shelves too for gourmet produce.

Mesón del Pastor MOUNTAIN CUISINE €€
(964 16 02 49; www.hoteldelpastor.com, in Spanish; Cuesta Jovaní 5-7; mains €7-14, menus €14-24; ⊙lunch Thu-Tue, dinner Sat) Within the dining room, bedecked with the restaurant's trophies and diplomas, it's all about robust mountain cuisine: thick gruels in winter, rabbit, juicy sausages, partridge, wild boar and goat.

❶ Information

The **tourist office** (964 17 30 32; www. morella.net; Plaza San Miguel 3; ⊙10am-2pm & 4-6pm or 7pm Mon-Sat, 10am-2pm Sun daily Apr-Oct, closed Mon Nov-Mar) is just behind Torres de San Miguel, twin 14th-century towers flanking the main entrance gate.

❶ Getting There & Around

Morella is best reached via Castellón, which has good train connections. Two daily weekday buses (€9, 2¼ hours) and one Saturday service of **Autos Mediterráneo** (964 22 00 54) run to/from Castellón's train station.

Vilafranca

POP 2600

Vilafranca, like Morella 36km to its south, grew rich from wool. Sheep no longer graze in such numbers but their legacy lives on in the estimated 1000km of dry stone walls that stripe and criss-cross the land. Stone for walls, sheep pens, huts and houses are all illustrated in the excellent **Museo de Pedra en Sec** (Dry Stone Museum; 964 44 14 32; ⊙10am-1.30pm & 4-7pm Thu-Sat, 10.30am-1.30pm Sun). Documentation is only in *valenciano* but it's a very visual experience.

Call by the tourist office, just opposite, which holds the museum keys. Then, to stretch your legs and consolidate the museum experience, enjoy one of three one-hour country walks, supported by the tourist office's audioguide in English.

COSTA BLANCA

The long stripe of the Costa Blanca (White Coast) is one of Europe's most heavily visited areas. If you're after a secluded midsummer beach, stay away – or head inland to enjoy traditional villages and towns that have scarcely heard the word tourism. Then again, if you're looking for a lively social scene, good beaches and a suntan...

It isn't all concrete and package deals. Although the original fishing villages have long been engulfed by the sprawl of resorts, a few old town kernels, such as those of Xàbia (Jávea) and Altea, still survive.

In July and August it can be tough finding accommodation if you haven't booked. Out of season, those places remaining open usually charge far less than in high summer.

Most buses linking Valencia and Alicante head down the motorway, making a stop in Benidorm. A few, however, call by other intervening coastal towns. A smart new tram plies the scenic route between Alicante and Benidorm, from where a narrow-gauge train runs northwards to Denia. Both stop at *pueblos* en route. Renfe trains connect Valencia with Gandia.

Inland Trips from the Costa Blanca, by Derek Workman, describes 20 one-day car excursions into the interior in detail and with flair.

Gandia

POP 80,000

Gandia, 67km south of Valencia, is a tale of two cities. The main town, once home to a branch of the Borja dynasty (more familiar as the infamous Borgias), is a prosperous commercial centre.

◎ Sights & Activities

Palacio Ducal de los Borja PALACE
(www.palauducal.com; Calle Duc Alfons el Vell 1; guided tour adult/child €6/5; ⊙10am-1.30pm & 4-7.30pm Mon-Sat) Gandia's magnificent palace was the 15th-century home of Duque Francisco de Borja. Highlights include its finely carved *artesonado* ceilings and rich ceramic work – look out for the vivid *mapa universal* floor composition. One-hour guided tours in Spanish, with an accompanying leaflet in English, leave about every half-hour.

Playa de Gandia BEACH
Four kilometres away on the coast, Playa de Gandia has a long, broad beach of fine sand, groomed daily by a fleet of tractors. It's a popular and predominantly Spanish resort with a good summer and weekend nightlife.

🛏 Sleeping & Eating

Hotel Riviera HOTEL €€
(96 284 50 42; www.hotelesrh.com; Paseo Neptuno 28; half-board per person €39-90; ❉@🛜❄) It's well worth paying the few coppers extra

for half-board at this 72-room beachside hotel, one of Denia's earliest but comprehensively renovated over the years. Invest an extra €5.50 per person for one of the eight full-frontal seaview rooms.

Hostal El Nido
HOSTAL €€
(☎96 284 46 40; www.hostalelnido.com, in Spanish; Calle Alcoy 22; s €35-50, d €45-69; ☎) Its 10 rooms, equipped with standing fans in summer, are as cheerful as the owners at this modest place, a block back from the beach. Between June and September it also runs a small bar for guests.

Eating choices abound in Paseo Marítimo Neptuno. You'll also find a few longer-established places at the western end of the port and along Calle Verge.

Restaurante Emilio
TRADITIONAL €€
(☎96 284 07 61; www.restauranteemilio.es, in Spanish; Bloque F-5, Avenida Vicente Calderón; mains €15-22; ⊗closed Wed except Jul–mid-Sep) Despite a cupboardful of gastronomic accolades, Emilio, his wife and three children manage to preserve a family atmosphere in this traditionally furnished restaurant, set back from the beach, where you'll eat very well indeed.

Arrop
GOURMET €€€
(☎96 295 07 68; www.arrop.com, in Spanish; Calle Sant Joan de Ribera 20; menus €20-45, mains €26-30; ⊗closed Sun & dinner Tue) Inland in the main town, Arrop is a delight. Choose its *menú Ricard Camarena'* (€69), and let Arrop's master chef make the decisions as you savour his exciting, innovatory take on traditional *valenciano* cuisine.

Drinking
There's great summer and weekend nightlife at Playa de Gandia, with bars clustered around Plaza del Castell, barely 300m inland from the beach. After they close, head for one of the through-the-night discos such as Bacarrá (Calle Legazpi 7), two blocks from the beach, or La Diva (Cami Vell de Valencia), further inland.

ⓘ Information
Playa de Gandia tourist office (☎96 284 24 07; www.gandiaturismo.com; Paseo de Neptuna 45; ⊗9.30am-2pm & 4-7.30pm Mon-Fri, 9.30am-1.30pm Sat & Sun)
Town tourist office (☎96 287 77 88; ⊗similar hours) Opposite the bus/train station.

VALENCIA & THE COSTA BLANCA COSTA BLANCA

ⓘ Getting There & Around
Trains run between Gandia and Valencia (€4.40, one hour) every 30 minutes (hourly at weekends). The combined bus and train station is opposite the town tourist office. Stopping beside the office, La Marina Gandiense buses for Playa de Gandia run every 20 minutes.

Denia
POP 44,500
Denia, the Comunidad Valenciana's major passenger port, has the shortest sea crossings to the Balearic Islands. The beaches of La Marina, to its north, are good and sandy, while southwards the fretted coastline of Las Rotas and beyond offers less-frequented rocky coves.

◉ Sights & Activities
Castle
PANORAMA
(admission free; ⊗10am-1.30pm & 5pm-dusk) From Plaza de la Constitución, steps lead up to the ruins of Denia's castle from where there's a great overview of the town and coast.

Mundo Marino
BOAT TRIPS
(www.mundomarino.es) To catch the sea breezes, sign on with Mundo Marino which does return boat trips (adult/child €15/7.50; 45min) to/from Xàbia, some continuing to Calpe (€30/15) and Altea (€35/17.50).

Tururac
OUTDOOR ACTIVITIES
(www.tururac.com; Plaza Oculista Buigues 2) For more active fun, call by Tururac, which can take you caving, canyoning, mountain biking and more. Its HQ is barely 50m from the tourist office.

To be independent, cycle the circumference of the Parc Natural del Montgó, following a 26km signed route along traffic-free paths that links Denia and Xàbia, then return to Denia on the Mundo Marino boat.

Sleeping
TOP CHOICE **Hotel Chamarel** BOUTIQUE HOTEL €€
(☎96 643 50 07; www.hotelchamarel.com; Calle Cavallers 13; s/d incl breakfast from €75/85; ✽☎) This delightful hotel, tastefully furnished in period style by a pair of seasoned travellers, occupies an attractive 19th-century bourgeois mansion. Its 15 rooms surround a tranquil, plant-shaded internal patio. The vast internal salon with its correspondingly large marble-topped bar is equally relaxing. The whole is a capacious gallery for the paintings of artist and owner Mila Vidal-

lach, whose canvases decorate bedrooms and public areas. Ask for room 201, under the eaves, oriental in mood and positively breathing feng shui. Parking is €12.

Posada del Mar
HOTEL €€€

(☑96 643 29 66; www.laposadadelmar.com; Plaza Drassanes 2; s/d incl breakfast from €110/120; P✳@☎) This sensitively renovated hotel occupies a 13th-century building that last functioned as Denia's customs house. Each of its 25 rooms is individually decorated with a nautical theme and light streams through large windows that overlook the harbour. Parking is €16.

Costa Blanca
HOTEL €€

(☑96 578 03 36; www.hotelcostablanca.com, in Spanish; Calle Pintor Llorens 3; s/d from €42/59; ✳@☎) Beside the train station, this is an excellent-value option except in high summer, when prices rise to €92. Rooms are comfortable and cosily furnished, there's a small, well-stocked bar and the port is but a few steps away.

✗ Eating

There's a clutch of tempting restaurants, catering for all pockets, along harbour-facing Explanada Cervantes and Calle Bellavista, extending to Plaza del Raset. Many began life as simple bars for the fisherfolk from the old fish market, just across the road. Pedestrianised Calle Lepanto, which extends westwards from Hotel Chamarel, is flanked by tempting tapas bars.

Sal de Mar
GOURMET FOOD €€

(☑96 642 77 66; menus €20-40, mains €17-23; ☺Wed-Mon) Chef Federico Guajardo runs this, the gourmet restaurant of Hotel Posada del Mar. It's a splendid option, whether you choose to dine or simply *tapear* (eat tapas), either in its intimate interior or on the summertime terrace.

El Raset
RICE, FISH €€

(☑96 578 50 40; Calle Bellavista 7; menus €22, mains €17-24) Eat on the wide terrace or within the cool, air-conditioned interior of El Raset, reputed for its rice dishes. Its excellent four-course lunch *menú* includes, as starters, a variety of tapas such as baby cannelloni stuffed with seafood. Dishes are attractively presented and service is genial and helpful.

Asador del Puerto
GRILL €€

(☑96 642 34 82; Plaza del Raset 10-11; menus €27-38.50, mains €19-24) This is an excellent

choice for either meat, roasted in a wood-fired oven, or fish dishes. Try the *cochinillo* (suckling pig; €23.50), crispy on the outside, juicy within and roasted to a turn.

❶ Information

The **tourist office** (☑96 642 23 67; www.denia.net; Calle Manuel Lattur 1; ☺9.30am-2pm & 5-8pm) is near the waterfront. Both train station and ferry terminal are close by.

❶ Getting There & Away

From the station, hourly trains follow the scenic route southwards to Benidorm (€3.30, 1¼ hours), connecting with the tram for Alicante.

For the Balearic Islands, **Balearia Lines** (☑902 160180; www.balearia.com) runs ferries to/from Mallorca and Ibiza.

Xàbia

POP 31,600

With a third of its resident population and over two-thirds of its annual visitors non-Spanish (every second shop seems to be an estate agent/realtor), Xàbia (Spanish: Jávea) isn't the best place to meet the locals. That said, it's gentle, family-oriented and well worth a visit early in the season, when the sun shines but the masses have yet to arrive.

Xàbia comes in three flavours: the small old town 2km inland; El Puerto (the port), directly east of the old quarter; and the beach zone of El Arenal, a couple of km south of the harbour.

✺ Activities

In addition to sun fun on El Arenal's broad beach, the old town merits a brief wander. The tourist office carries a pack titled *Xàbia: Nature Areas Network,* containing five brochures, each describing a waymarked route in the area, including an ascent of Montgó, the craggy mountain that looms over the town. Year-round, the tourist office leads free guided walks at least twice weekly; for details, see its leaflet, *Rutas Senderismo.*

⌂ Sleeping

Hotel Miramar
HOTEL €€

(☑/fax 96 579 01 02; www.hotelmiramar.com.es; Plaza Almirante Bastarreche 12; s €30-40, d €55-70; ✳☎) This imposing family-run building, right beside the port, almost tumbles into the sea. Its 26 rooms, eight with balcony, are cosy; those overlooking the bay carry a €10 to €15 supplement. There's a bar and restaurant, too.

Pensión la Marina
PENSIÓN €

(☎96 579 31 39; www.lamarinapension.com; Av Marina Española 8; r €40-60; 🖥) This small, English-owned place has eight rooms plus a couple of family options, all with ceiling fans. Its huge plus is its position, right beside the pedestrianised promenade. For dinner, go no further than the restaurant below, which serves tasty Mediterranean food, and enjoy your 20% discount as a client of the *pensión*.

Parador de Jávea
PARADOR €€€

(☎96 579 02 00; www.paradores.es; Avenida del Mediterráneo 233; d €113-206) Architecturally, Xàbia's boxy, once-modern *parador* is unexciting but it enjoys a magnificent site, on a headland overlooking the bay of El Arenal, and has all the usual *parador* comforts.

✗ Eating & Drinking

The old town has several enticing tapas bars, while restaurants and bars flank Avenida de la Marina Española, the pedestrianised promenade south of the port. In El Arenal, cafes and restaurants hug the rim of beachside Paseo Marítimo.

Amarre 152
MODERN SPANISH €€

(☎96 579 06 29; Port de la Fontana; meals around €30) At the end of a backwater in El Arenal, this is a delightful retreat (just count your way along the moorings to number 152), with a designer interior and tiny quayside terrace. Great for rice dishes, and its fish is the freshest.

El Posito
MEDITERRANEAN €€

(☎96 579 30 63; Plaza Almirante Bastarreche 11; menu s€14, meals around €25) Sharing with the port tourist office what was once the fishermen's social centre, this pretty blue-and-white building has a terrace that's broader than most. El Posito does an excellent-value *menú*, makes a relaxing drinks stop and has a good range of tapas and sandwiches.

Bar Imperial
TAPAS

(☎96 646 11 81; Plaza de Baix 2) In the old town, full of atmosphere and well worth a visit, serves tapas and full meals.

La Rebotica
TAPAS

(☎96 646 13 18; Calle San Bartolomeo 6) At La Rebotica, too, inland and in the old town, you can either tuck into a full meal or nibble on tapas.

Temptacions
TAPAS BAR €

(☎96 579 29 20; Plaza de la Iglesia 10) Indeed a tempting place for tapas or a drink, this cosy place is adapted from two old houses (only their doorway arches, curving over the interior, still survive).

El Tropezón Valencian
REGIONAL CUISINE €€

(☎96 579 13 16; Calle Tossal de Dalt 3) Intimate, rectangular and within a typical renovated town house, this relatively new arrival with its bare stone walls and beams specialises in regional cuisine.

❶ Information

Connections (Calle Cristo del Mar 29, El Puerto; per hr €2.50; ⊙9.30am-2pm & 5-7pm Mon-Sat) Internet access.

Tourist offices (www.xabia.org; ⊙9am-1.30pm & 4-7.30pm or 4.30-8pm Mon-Fri, 10am-1.30pm Sat) El Arenal (☎96 646 06 05; Carretera Cabo de la Nao); Old Town (☎96 579 43 56; Plaza de la Iglesia); Port (☎96 579 07 36; Plaza Almirante Bastareche 11; ⊙also Sat afternoon & Sun morning)

❶ Getting There & Around

At least six buses run daily to both Valencia (€10) and Alicante (€8.50). They stop on Avenida Óndara, at Rotonda del Olivo, with a large olive tree at its heart.

You can rent a cycle at **Xàbia's Bike Centre** (www.xabiasbike.com, in Spanish; Avenida Lepanto 21; per day/week from €7/42) in the port area.

Calpe
POP 29,650

The Gibraltaresque Peñon de Ifach, a giant molar protruding from the sea, rears up from the seaside resort of Calpe (Valenciano: Calp).

Two large bays sprawl either side of the Peñon: Playa Arenal on the southern side is backed by the old town, while Playa Levante, to the north, has most of the more recent development.

From the Peñon's **Aula de Naturaleza** (Nature Centre) a fairly strenuous walking trail – allow 2½ hours for the round trip – climbs towards the 332m-high summit, offering great seascapes from its end point at the end of a dark tunnel. In July and August walkers depart every 15 minutes in batches of 20, so you may have a short wait.

🛏 Sleeping

Hostal Terra de Mar BOUTIQUE HOSTAL €€
(📞629 665124; www.hostalterrademar.com, in Spanish; Calle Paternina 31; s/d incl breakfast €70/95; ❄) You're greeted by a giant mural of bangled hands, from which rose petals flutter, and fresh flowers flourish in reception at this stylish option. Each floor has its own style (climb the stairs and you can travel from Japan to Morocco to Africa and Paris). The low-season tariff for its 12 rooms (single/double with breakfast €35/55 October to May) is an excellent deal.

Hotel Esmeralda HOTEL €€
(📞96 583 61 01; www.rocaesmeralda.com; Calle Ponent 1; r €84-195; ❄@🛜🛆) At the northern limit of Playa Levante, the huge Esmeralda, as much leisure complex as hotel, is particularly suited to families with children. If the sea fails to call, there are three outside pools and a heated indoor one too, plus a gym, a couple of restaurants and a cafe.

Pensión Centrica BUDGET PENSIÓN €
(📞96 583 55 28; mjpiffet@hotmail.com; Plaza de Ifach 5; basic s/d €13/28) This French-run place just off Avenida Gabriel Miró has 13 well-maintained rooms with ceiling fans and corridor bathrooms. With its welcoming, hostel-like atmosphere, it has a fridge, microwave and oven for guests' use. Look out for the giant iguana...

🍴 Eating

There are plenty of restaurants and bars around Plaza de la Constitución and along main Avenida de Gabriel Miró, plus a cluster of good fish places down by the port.

Los Zapatos MODERN EUROPEAN €€
(📞96 583 15 07; www.restauranteloszapatos. com; Calle Santa María 7; menus €16, mains €14.50-23; ⏰Thu-Mon) Highly recommended, this German-run restaurant has a short, specialised à la carte menu and a carefully selected wine list of mainly Spanish vintages. In season it does a tempting *menú caza y pescado* (hunting and fish *menú*) with wild boar and fish of the day.

La Cambra SPANISH €€
(📞96 583 06 05; Calle Delfín 2; mains €15-21; ⏰lunch Mon-Thu, lunch & dinner Fri & Sat) All antique wood and tiles, traditional La Cambra specialises in rice dishes (around €12) and also has a rich à la carte selection of Basque and Valencian dishes.

ℹ Information

Librería Europa (www.libreria-europa-calpe. com; Calle Oscar Esplá 2) Good stock of titles in English and other European languages.

Main tourist office (📞96 583 85 32; www. calpe.es; Plaza del Mosquit; ⏰9am-2.30pm & 4-7.30pm Mon-Fri, 10am-1.30pm Sat) In the old town.

ℹ Getting There & Away

BUS Connects Calpe with both Alicante (€6.50, 1½ hours, nine daily) and Valencia (€12, 3½ hours, six daily). The **bus station** (Avenida de la Generalitat Valenciana) is just off the ring road.
TRAIN Hourly narrow-gauge trains travel daily northwards to Denia (€2.25, 40 minutes) and south to Benidorm (€2, 30 minutes), connecting with the tram for Alicante.

Altea

POP 11.900
Altea, separated from Benidorm only by the thick wedge of the Sierra Helada, could be a couple of moons away. Altogether quieter, its beaches are mostly of pebbles. The modern part, extending along the coast, is a bog-standard coastal resort. By contrast, the whitewashed old town, perched on a hilltop overlooking the sea, is just about the prettiest *pueblo* in all the Comunidad Valenciana.

Aparthotel & Restaurante Venus Albir (📞96 686 48 20; www.venusalbir.com; Plaza Venus, Albir-Alfaz del Pi; d €47-90; tr €63-120; ❄🛜🛆), in Albir, a continuation of Altea southwards, is a particularly ecofriendly hotel. It has 24 comfortable apartments with mini-kitchen and balcony and you can indulge in a variety of healthy, de-stressing activities. At its **restaurant** (mains €13.50-23), open to all, ingredients are strictly organic. It does an excellent-value four-course lunch *menú* (€14.50, including a couple of glasses of wine) and the small shop sells organic products that feature in its cuisine.

Off Plaza de la Iglesia in Altea's old town, and especially down Calle Major, there's a profusion of cute little restaurants, many open for dinner only except in high summer.

Altea's **tourist office** (📞96 584 41 14; Calle San Pedro 9; ⏰10am-2pm & 5-7.30pm or 8pm Mon-Fri, 10am-1pm Sat) is on the beachfront.

Benidorm

POP 73,950

It's easy to be snobbish about Benidorm (indeed, one prominent guidebook series in English doesn't even mention the town). Yes, she long ago sold her birthright to mass package tourism. But the old girl, though violated most summer nights by louts from northern Europe, still retains a certain dignity. The foreshore is magnificent as the twin sweeps of Playa del Levante and the longer Playa del Poniente meet beneath Plaza del Castillo, where the land juts into the bay like a ship's prow.

In winter half of all visitors are over 60, mostly from northern Europe. During summer Benidorm is for all ages.

Sights & Activities

Terra Mítica   THEME PARK
(Mythical Land; www.terramiticapark.com; adult/child €35/26.50; ⏰10am to at least 8pm mid-Mar–Sep) Spain's biggest theme park is the Costa Blanca's answer to Disneyland. A fun day out, especially if you're with children, it's Mediterranean in theme, with plenty of scary rides, street entertainment and areas devoted to ancient Egypt, Greece, Rome, Iberia and the islands. Opening days are complex, so do check outside high season.

Terra Natura & Aqua Natura
                                   THEME PARK
(www.terranatura.com; adult/child €25/20; ⏰10am-dusk) At this rival theme park, over 1500 animals live in habitats approximat-

---

THE CHOCOLATE FACTORY

Even if your name's not Charlie and though you may be over 12 years old, you'll enjoy a tour of the Museo de Chocolate (Chocolate Museum; www.valor.es; Calle Pianista Gonzalo Soriano 13; admission free; ⏰10am-1pm & 4-7pm Mon-Fri, 10am-1pm Sat) in Villajoyosa, 14km south of Benidorm. This showcase of Valor, Spain's largest chocolate-making company, displays everything related to cocoa, chocolate and the transformation of one to another, has a gallery of sculptures in – yes – chocolate and includes a visit to the factory and shop, where you'll need all your willpower to resist such sweet temptation. Guided visits on the hour, every hour.

---

ing their natural environment. There's also a great water park (⏰Jun–mid-Sep; supplement €6) and, for the brave, the chance to swim with sharks (fairly small and benign, no visitors yet lost).

Aqualandia   WATER PARK
(www.aqualandia.net, in Spanish; adult/child €27/20; ⏰10am-dusk mid-May–mid-Oct) Aqualandia is Europe's largest water park. Beside it is Mundomar (☎96 586 01 00; www.mundomar.es, in Spanish; adult/child €24/18; ⏰10am-dusk), a marine and animal park with parrots, dolphins, sea lions, even bats. Each park (combined ticket adult/child €35/25) is worth a full day.

Excursiones Marítimas Benidorm
                                   BOAT TRIPS
(www.excursionesmaritimasbenidorm.es, in Spanish) Runs hourly boats (adult/child return €12.50/10) to the Isla de Benidorm, a cruise up the coast to Calpe (€20/13) and a full-day outing to the island of Tabarca (p587) for €25/16.

Sierra Helada   COASTAL WALKING
Should Benidorm's frenetic pace get you down, pick up a free copy of *Routes Across Sierra Helada* from the tourist office and stride out into the hills of the Sierra Helada, just north of Rincón de Loix, for superb bay views.

Sleeping

TOP CHOICE **Villa Venecia**   BOUTIQUE HOTEL €€€
(☎96 585 54 66; www.hotelvillavenecia. com; Plaza San Jaime 1; r from €185; ❅🖥🌊) Up high opposite the old town's church and lording it over the seething beach crowds below, this new five-star hotel has it all. Each of the 25 rooms has plunging sea views, an ultramodern bath tub, power showers, large flat-screen TV and Nespresso. As you lounge beside its puddle of a rooftop pool, perhaps after a session in the spa and wellness centre, you could be nautical miles away from Benidorm. Its bar and excellent Llum de Mar restaurant are open to allcomers.

Hotel La Santa Faç   HOTEL €€
(☎96 585 40 63; www.santafazhotel.com, in Spanish; Calle Santa Faç 18; s €35-50, d €55-85; ⏰May-Oct; ❅🖥) This long-established hotel, sandwiched between two streets in the old quarter, is friendly and full of character. All rooms have a balcony and there's a well-stocked bar with billiard table.

Hotel Colón
HOTEL €€

(☎96 585 04 12; www.hotelcolon.net; Paseo de Colón 3; s €43-69, d €55-96; ☺Apr-Oct; ❄️@🛜) Conveniently positioned where the old town meets Playa del Poniente, the Colón is great value outside high season. Half-board is only €4 more than B&B, though don't expect fine cuisine. West-facing rooms have great views of Playa del Poniente.

Hotel Iris
BUDGET HOTEL €

(☎96 586 52 51; www.iris-hotel.net; Calle Palma 47; s €25-50, d €25-65; ❄️@🛜) Here's a friendly budget choice on a fairly quiet street. Rooms that don't have air-con come with fans and most have a small balcony too. There's a cosy ground-floor bar with an internet terminal. If it's good enough for the mayor of Benidorm, who sleeps here during the town's fiesta, it's good enough for you…!

Gran Hotel Bali
HOTEL €€

(☎96 681 52 00; www.granhotelbali.com; Calle Luis Prendes; half-board per person €46.50-95; ❄️@🛜🏊) This mammoth complex, 186m high and as much space-age village as hotel, is Europe's tallest. Like a massive silver knife cleaving the sky, its vastness isn't to everyone's taste but, with 23 lifts/elevators (have fun riding one of the two external ones), 776 rooms and a pair of restaurants that can accommodate up to 1000 diners, it's superlative in many senses.

✖ Eating

For Benidorm's biggest concentration of restaurants and tapas bars serving decent Spanish fare, take your pick from those lining Calle Santo Domingo at the Plaza de la Constitución end.

⟨TOP CHOICE⟩ La Cava Aragonesa
TAPAS BAR €

(Plaza de la Constitución) What a magnificent selection of tapas, fat canapés and 20 different plates of cold cuts, all arrayed before you at the bar and labelled in both Spanish and English! Good wine by the glass too – a decent measure of standard Catalan bubbly is just €1. Next door is its sit-down **restaurant** (☎96 680 12 06; menus €10-13, mains €10-18), where you can select from 20 different wooden platters of mixed foods – and more than 600 varieties of wine.

Llum de Mar
MODERN MEDITERRANEAN €€

(☎96 585 54 66; Plaza San Jaime 1; rice dishes €12.50-15.50, mains €18-22) Light of the Sea, restaurant of Villa Venecia hotel and open to all, is an intimate place. With a capacity

ⓘ
ACCOMMODATION DISCOUNTS

Almost everyone's on a package deal in Benidorm, so accommodation can be expensive for the independent traveller. Book online through **Benidorm Spotlight** (www.benidorm-spotlight.com) for significant discounts.

for scarcely 30 (reservations essential), it offers splendid à la carte fare while a vast seascape spreads before you through its large picture windows.

Ulía
FISH, RICE €€€

(☎96 585 68 28; Calle Vicente Llorca Alós 15; ☺lunch & dinner Tue-Sat, dinner Sun) This vast restaurant overlooking Playa del Poniente is, locals will tell you, the best place in town for rice dishes and fish (try *chopitos frescos*, baby squid, deep fried and crispy). Its genial waiters bustle and hop and it also carries a great wine selection, fully on view, as are the beach and sea, directly across the corniche.

Restaurante Marisquería Club Naútico
MEDITERRANEAN €€

(☎96 585 54 25; Paseo de Colón; menus €24, mains €10-19) At this elegant restaurant beside the port, you can pick at tapas by the bar or have a full meal on the large terrace – where you can also simply enjoy a drink and the view over Benidorm's small port.

Casa de la Portuguesa
MEDITERRANEAN €€

(☎96 585 89 58; Calle San Vicente 39; mains €10-16) With its tables spilling onto the narrow street in summer, this restaurant, a favourite of Benidorm's movers and shakers, is nevertheless very reasonably priced. It's family-run and it owes its reputation to its great rice dishes and fresh fish.

La Rana
SPANISH €€

(☎96 586 81 20; Costero del Barco 6; mains €5.50-17.50) One of Benidorm's oldest restaurants (that aged cash register must have rung up the very first bills), The Frog (see the hundreds of model frogs, large and small, in a glass case) is family-run and something of a time warp, with the feel of a generation ago. It serves authentic Spanish cuisine, using the freshest of ingredients plucked from the giant fridge before you. Tucked away up a cobbled alley, it's well worth tracking down.

SUPERLATIVE BENIDORM

» In 2009 Benidorm registered nearly 10 million overnight stays.

» Around five million visitors arrive every year, including well over a million Brits.

» Its 155 skyscrapers are exceeded only by New York's.

» 127 hotels (let's not even consider the apartment blocks) provide nearly 40,000 beds. In Europe, only London and Paris have more.

» There's a full 6km of sandy beach.

🍷 Drinking & Entertainment

For a sophisticated drink in a town not noted for subtlety, park yourself on a stool at Fratelli (Calle Doctor Orts Llorca; ⊙1pm-5am), a cool designer cocktail place that styles itself 'Bar Fashion'.

At the western end of Playa del Levante, music spills out from three beachside bars (⊙10am-5pm) that each have mega *discotecas* on Avenida de la Comunidad Valenciana on the outskirts of town. Their *discotecas* and other similar giants open daily in July and August, and at weekends year-round. Back on the beach, Ku (www.kubenidorm.es), with its reproduction Hindu and Buddhist statues, plays the oriental card and has a cool rear chill-out zone. At its near neighbour KM (www.kmdisco.com), the music's eclectic until 6pm, when it's strictly house. Next door to KM, Beach Club Penelope (www.penelopebeach.com, in Spanish) is a small sibling of the Penelope brand, found all over Europe. All are laid-back cafes during the day, changing tempo once the sun sets.

ℹ Information

Main tourist office (☑96 585 13 11; Avenida Martínez Alejos 16; ⊙9am-9pm Mon-Fri, 10am-3pm Sat) Also kiosks at bus station, on Avenida de Europa and in Rincòn de Loix.

Vic Center (Calle Lepanto 9; per hr €2; ⊙9.30am-11pm) Internet access.

ℹ Getting There & Away

BUS From Benidorm's bus station (served by local bus 41 and 47), **ALSA** (☑96 680 39 55; www.alsa.es) runs to the following destinations:

Alicante €4, one hour, frequent

Alicante airport €8, 50 minutes, hourly

Valencia €15, 1¾ hours, 12 daily

Valencia airport €17.50, 2¼ hours, two daily

TRAM & TRAIN You can take the tram southwards to Alicante (€4.40, one hour, every 30 minutes) or the little train to Denia (€3.30, 1¼ hours, hourly).

ℹ Getting Around

BUS Bus 1 serves Terra Mítica and Terra Natura and also Mundomar and, beside it, Aqualandia.

CYCLE HIRE At the time of writing, Benidorm was about to introduce a hop on, hop off bike-hire scheme. Otherwise, call by **Marco Polo** (☑96 586 33 99; Avenida de Europa 5; half-/full day from €5/9).

TAXI ☑96 586 18 18.

Alicante

POP 335,000

Alicante (Valenciano: Alacant) lives for much more than tourism alone. It's a dynamic, attractive provincial town, the Valencia region's second largest. Around Catedral de San Nicolás are the narrow streets of El Barrio, the historic quarter. Try to fit in at least one overnight stay to experience its frenetic – and unmistakably Spanish – nightlife.

◎ Sights & Activities

FREE **Castillo de Santa Bárbara**   CASTLE
(⊙10am-10pm) There are sweeping views over the city from this 16th-century castle, which will soon house Museo de la Ciudad de Alicante (MUSA), a new museum recounting the history of the city. A lift/elevator, reached by a footbridge opposite Playa del Postiguet, rises through the bowels of the mountain. To return, it's a pleasant walk through Parque de la Ereta via Calle San Rafael to Plaza del Carmen.

TOP CHOICE **Museo de Arte Contémporaneo de Alicante (MACA)**   ART GALLERY
(Plaza Sta María 3; admission free) Closed for many years while its premises, the splendid 17th-century Casa de la Asegurada, was renovated and enlarged, this splendid museum was about to reopen at the time of writing. It has an excellent collection of 20th-century Spanish art, including works by Dalí, Miró, Chillida, Sempere, Tàpies and Picasso.

Museo Arqueológico Provincial (MARQ)
ARCHAEOLOGICAL MUSEUM
(www.marqalicante.com; Plaza Doctor Gómez Ulla; adult/child €3/free; ⊙10am-7pm Tue-Sat, 10am-

2pm Sun) Very visual and high-tech, this museum well merits a visit even though there's little information in English. It's an easy walk from the centre or hop on bus 2, 6, 9, 20 or 23.

FREE **Museu de Fogueres**   FOLK MUSEUM
(Spanish: Museo de las Hogueras; Rambla de Méndez Núñez 29; ☉10am-2pm & 5-8pm or 6-9pm Tue-Sat, 10am-2pm Sun) In addition to a wealth of photographs, costumes and *ninots* (small effigies saved from the flames) it has a great audiovisual presentation of what the Fiesta de Sant Joan, all fire and partying, means to *alicantinos*.

FREE **Museo de Bellas Artes Gravina (MUBAG)**   ART GALLERY
(Calle Gravina 13-15; ☉10am-2pm & 4-8pm or 5-9pm Mon-Sat, 10am-2pm Sun) Alicante's fine-arts museum, with canvases from the Middle Ages to the 1920s, is within the Palacio de Gravina, a stalwart 18th-century mansion. The setting and presentation are terrific – perhaps more so than the paintings themselves.

Panoramis   LEISURE COMPLEX
An area of shops, restaurants and hip bars on the western causeway. To get there, follow the curve of the port along pedestrianised Paseo Explanada de España or the waterfront promenade (separated only by a hideously busy road).

Basílica de Santa María   CHURCH
(☉10am-12.30pm & 6-8.30pm) The flamboyant, 18th-century facade and ornate, gilded altarpiece both contrast with the nave's Gothic simplicity.

Kon Tiki   BOAT TRIP
(☏96 521 63 96) Makes the 45-minute boat trip (€16 return) to the popular island of Tabarca (p587).

Icarus   SCULPTURE
This splendid waterside bronze figure of a pin-headed Icarus bearing a surfboard as he emerges from the water is by contemporary sculptor Esperanza d'Ors.

Beaches   BEACHES
Immediately north of the port is the sandy beach of Playa del Postiguet. Playa de San Juan, easily reached by the tram, is larger and usually less crowded.

⚜ Festivals & Events

Fiesta de Sant Joan   MIDSUMMER'S DAY
Alicante's major festival is the Fiesta de Sant Joan, spread either side of 24 June, the longest day, when the city stages its own version of Las Fallas (see the boxed text, p556), with fireworks and satirical effigies (Valenciano: *fogueres,* Spanish: *hogueras*) going up in smoke all over town.

🛏 Sleeping

Hotel Amérigo   HOTEL €€€
(☏96 514 65 70; www.hospes.es; Calle de Rafael Altamira 7; r from €122; ❄@☎⊠) Within an old Dominican convent, this glorious five-star choice harmoniously blends the traditional and ultramodern. Savour the cuisine in Monastrell, its gourmet restaurant, enjoy the views from the rooftop pool, itself a work of art, or build up a sweat in the fitness area – if you can tear yourself away from the comfort of your stunningly designed room.

TOP CHOICE **Hostal Les Monges Palace**   HOSTAL €
(☏96 521 50 46; www.lesmonges.net; Calle San Agustín 4; s €30-44, d €45-59; ❄@☎) This agreeably quirky place is a treasure with its winding corridors, tiles, mosaics and antique furniture. Each room is individually decorated and reception couldn't be more welcoming. To really pamper yourself, choose one of the two rooms with sauna and jacuzzi (€98). Look out for the small Dalí original beside the reception desk.

Guest House Antonio   BOUTIQUE HOSTAL €
(☏650 718353; www.guesthousealicante.com; Calle Segura 20; s €35-40, d €45-50; ❄☎) Here's a magnificent budget choice. Each of the eight large, tastefully decorated rooms has a safe, full-sized fridge and free beverage-making facilities. The five apartments (€70 to €80), two with their own patio, have a mini-kitchen and washing machine and are exceptional value. Antonio also has two other apartments, one nearby, the other handy for the bus station.

Abba Centrum   HOTEL €€
(☏96 513 04 40; www.abbahoteles.com, in Spanish; Calle del Pintor Lorenzo Casanova 31; r €77.50-125; ❄@☎) Abba Centrum is a hugely attractive option, right by the bus station and with the train station a short walk away. Popular with business visitors, its weekend rates (August too) drop to a bargain €65 per room. Mini-gym, sauna and hammam are all free to guests. Parking is €13.

Hotel Spa Porta Maris & Suites del Mar   HOTEL, APARTMENTS €€€
(☏96 514 70 21; www.hotelspaportamaris.com; Plaza Puerta del Mar 3; r €100-150; ❄@☎⊠)

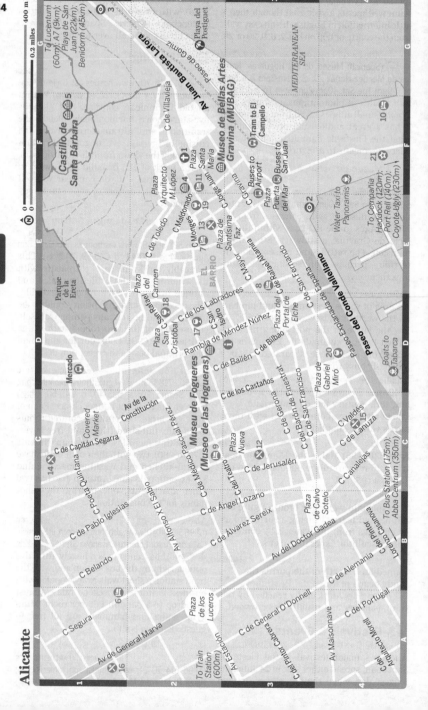

Alicante

Each of the 142 rooms and 39 suites has a balcony overlooking either beach or marina. Among the many facilities at this hyperhealthy four-star option are pools, gym and a wellness centre. Then again, no one will care if you simply slob around.

Hostal La Milagrosa   HOSTAL €
(☏96 521 69 18; www.hostallamilagrosa.com; Calle Villavieja 8; s/d €20/40, with bathroom €35/50; ✳@☏) The Miracle is another good central budget choice with simple rooms, a small guest kitchen, washing machine and roof terrace. It also has three apartments (€60) that can sleep up to six (per extra person €20).

Hotel San Remo   HOTEL €
(☏96 520 95 00; www.hotelsanremo.net; Calle Navas 30; s €35-40, d €45-55; ✳@☏) This friendly, family-run hotel has 27 spruce, well-maintained if smallish rooms. Although it doesn't offer breakfast, there's a coffee machine near reception that dispenses the real brew.

✖ Eating

TOP CHOICE **Piripi**   VALENCIAN CUISINE €€
(☏96 522 79 40; Avenida Oscar Esplá 30; mains €12-26) This highly regarded restaurant is strong on rice, seafood and fish, which arrives fresh and daily from the wholesale markets of Denia and Santa Pola. There's a huge variety of tapas (we counted 10 different cylinders of salami and sausage

arraigned on the bar and one of the jovial team of waiters is engaged constantly in cutting near-transparent slices of prime quality ham). There's a *valenciano* speciality that changes daily.

El Trellat   MODERN CREATIVE €
(☏965 20 62 75; Calle de Capitán Segarra 19; lunch menus €10, dinner menus €10-25; ☉lunch Mon-Sat, dinner Fri & Sat) Beside the covered market, this small, friendly place does exceptionally creative, flexible *menús:* first course a serve-yourself buffet, then an ample choice of inventive mains. For dessert, trust Manuel, the chef/owner; he previously worked in Alicante's premier cake shop.

Tabulé   VEGETARIAN €
(☏96 513 34 45; Avenida Pérez Galdós 52; menus €18; ☉lunch daily, dinner Wed-Sat; ☏) Service is swift and friendly at this vegetarian restaurant, where you take what's on offer on the day's *menú,* which includes a drink and coffee. You won't repeat yourself; it's original, inventive and changes weekly.

One One   MEDITERRANEAN €€
(☏96 520 63 99; Calle Valdés 9; meals around €25; ☉Tue-Sat) It's easier if you speak a little Spanish at this wonderfully eccentric place (pronounced 'on-eh, on-eh') with its faithful following of regulars but a touch of bravado will get you by (just ask your ebullient host about his travels to Peru). It's a true bistro,

the walls scarcely visible for photos and posters, and there's no menu. Just listen carefully as Bartólome intones...

Cantina Villahelmy   FUSION **€€**
(☎965 21 25 29; Calle Mayor 37; mains €8-17; ☉lunch & dinner Tue-Sat, lunch Sun) One wall's rough stone, another bright orange and navy blue, painted with skeletons, creepy-crawlies and a frieze of classical figures. Intimate, funky and popular, the Villahelmy has lots of snacks, excellent salads and a menu that features dishes from couscous to octopus.

Bíomenú   VEGETARIAN **€**
(☎96 521 31 44; Calle Navas 17; mains €4.60-7, salads €15; ☉9.30am-4.30pm Mon-Sat; ✍) This ultracheap option is both vegetarian restaurant (load your plate from its varied pay-by-weight salad bar) and shop specialising in organic produce.

Self-caterers will enjoy browsing around Alicante's huge, art nouveau twin-storey covered market (Avenida Alfonso X El Sabio).

🍷 Drinking
At La Bohemia (Calle Villavieja 1; ☉8am-1pm & from 5pm Tue-Sun; ☎), both cafe and cocktail bar, you'll be made welcome from breakfast until late. Penetrate to the chillout zone at the rear, where candles flicker in niches hacked into the rough-textured natural rock. There's live music each Friday and Saturday.

Wet your night-time whistle in some of the wall-to-wall bars of the **old quarter**, around Catedral de San Nicolás. Early opener Desdén Café Bar (Calle de los Labradores 22) is a friendly place to kick off the evening, while Desafinado (Santo Tomas 6) is a heaving dance bar with DJs that also offers good jazz. An easy walk away, Z Club (Calle Coloma; ☉Tue-Sun) is a smart *discoteca*. Don't turn up before 3am unless you want to dance alone.

Alternatively, head for the sea. **Paseo del Puerto**, tranquil by day, is a double-decker line of bars, cafes and night-time discos while **Semiramis**, a short ferry hop across the harbour's waters, competes for your attention. If you don't recognise Compañía Haddock by the din, you will from the image of Tintin's pipe-smoking companion. Sitting above it – and risking bringing the roof down on a good night – is Port Rell. A couple of doors along, Coyote Ugly usually packs a crowd and sometimes has live music.

☆ Entertainment
Casino   CASINO
(☉4pm-4am Mon-Sat) Alicante's newest and brashest attraction offers plenty of opportunities to fritter away your holiday money.

ℹ Information
Municipal tourist office (www.alicante turismo.com) Branches at bus station and train station.

Regional tourist office (☎96 520 00 00; Rambla de Méndez Núñez 23; ☉9am-8pm Mon-Sat, 10am-2pm Sun)

Xplorer Cyber Café (Calle de San Vicente 46; internet per hr €1.20; ☉9am-midnight)

ℹ Getting There & Away
AIR Alicante's El Altet airport, gateway to the Costa Blanca, is around 12km southwest of the centre. It's served by budget airlines, charters and scheduled flights from all over Europe.

BUS From the bus station destinations include the following:

DESTINA-TION	PRICE (€)	DURATION (HR)	DAILY FREQUENCY
Benidorm	4	1	frequent
Madrid	27.50	5¼	at least 10
Murcia	5.50	1	at least 7
Valencia	21	2½	at least 10

TRAIN Destinations from the main **Renfe Estación de Madrid** (Avenida de Salamanca) include the following:

Barcelona €55, five hours, eight daily

Madrid €45, 3¾ hours, seven daily

Murcia €4.50, 1¼ hours, hourly; via Orihuela and Elche

Valencia €29, 1¾ hours, 8 daily; via Villena and Xàtiva

TRAM (www.fgvalicante.com) Tram line 1 to Benidorm (€4.40, one hour, every 30 minutes) takes a coastal route that's scenically stunning at times. Catch it from the Mercado stop beside the covered market or from Puerto Plaza del Mar, changing at La Isleta or Lucentum.

ℹ Getting Around
AIRPORT BUS Bus C-6 (€2.60, 30 minutes, every 20 minutes) runs between Plaza Puerta del Mar and the airport, passing by the north side of the bus station.

CAR-RENTAL Reliable and economical local companies operating from the airport include the following:

Javea Cars (www.javeacars.com)

Solmar (www.solmar.es)

Victoria Cars (www.victoriacars.com)

TAXI ☑ 96 525 25 11.

WATER TAXI Buquebus (one-way/return €2/2.50; ⏰7pm-2am Mon-Fri, noon-2am Sat & Sun Jun-Sep) makes the 10-minute crossing from Paseo del Puerto to Panoramis.

Isla de Tabarca

A trip to Tabarca, around 20km south of Alicante as the seagull flies, makes for a pleasant day trip – as much for the boat ride itself as for the island, which heaves with tourists in summer. Pack your towel and face-mask. Most of the waters that lap this small island, 1800m long and 400m wide at its broadest point, are protected and no-go areas. But fish don't understand such boundaries and you'll enjoy some great underwater viewing in permitted areas.

In summer, daily boats visit the island from Alicante, Benidorm and Torrevieja, and there are less-regular sailings year-round.

Torrevieja

POP 101.800

Torrevieja, set on a wide coastal plain between two lagoons, one pink, one emerald, has good beaches. Sea salt production remains an important element of its economy.

◎ Sights & Activities

Vía Verde   WALKING, CYCLING
The Vía Verde is a 6km-long walking and cycling track that follows an old train line, down which the last train steamed over 50 years ago. Running beside the lagoon and through the salt pans, it makes for a great half-day outing.

Day Trip to Tabarca   BOAT TRIP
(www.maritimastorrevieja.com; return trip €21, child under 8yr free; ⏰mid-Mar–mid-Nov) Just to the south of the tourist office is a large **parking area** and the jetty from which boats of Marítimas Torrevieja leave for day trips to the island of Tabarca.

FREE **Museo del Mar y de la Sal**
                                           SALT MUSEUM
(Sea & Salt Museum; Calle Patricio Pérez 10; ⏰10am-1.30pm & 5-9pm Tue-Sat, 10am-1.30pm Sun) An appealing clutter of mementoes and bric-a-brac, it helps you appreciate why salt still means so much to *torreviejenses*.

FREE **Centro de Interpretación de la Industria Salinera**   SALT MUSEUM
(Avenida de la Estación; ⏰8.30am-2pm Mon-Fri) This centre is more didactic than the Salt Museum, yet with a lightness of touch. It's in Torrevieja's former train station.

Aquópolis   WATER PARK
(www.aquopolis.es/torrevieja; Av Delfina Viudes; adult/child €22/17; ⏰11am-6pm Jun–mid-Sep) Say it aloud and the pun will make you wince – is a fun water park on the outskirts of town.

FREE **El Delfín**   SUBMARINE
(⏰5-10pm Wed-Sun Jun-Sep, 9am-2pm Oct-May) A decommissioned navy submarine that you can prowl around.

⛏ Sleeping

Hotel Masa Internacional   HOTEL €€
(☑96 692 15 37; www.hotelmasa.com; Avenida Alfredo Nobel 150; s €60-93, d €83-111; ❈ ☎ ⏰) This smart clifftop hotel, 3.5km northeast of Torrevieja, is a lovely luxury choice, remote from all the downtown frenzy. Rooms overlooking the sea come at no extra cost. Parking is €6.

Hotel Madrid   HOTEL €€
(☑96 571 00 38; www.ansahotel.com, in Spanish; Calle Villa Madrid 15; incl breakfast s €46-60, d €67-92; ❈ @ ☎) The Madrid is a friendly, family-run option with 40 comfortable, fairly spacious rooms, one equipped for travellers with disabilities. There's also a top-floor jacuzzi and, just across the road, the hotel's swimming pool. Guests can hire a bike for a bargain €6 per day.

Hotel Cano   HOTEL €
(☑96 670 09 58; www.hotelcano.com; cnr Calle Zoa & Calle Antonio Machado; s €30-43, d €40-60; ☎ ❈) Five blocks west of the bus station, the Cano has 57 trim, modern rooms, many with balcony. Those in the newer wing have more modern furniture and plenty of pleasing woodwork.

✗ Eating

Plenty of restaurants around the waterfront offer cheap meals and international menus. On Plaza Isabel II, park yourself on a patio and enjoy great grilled fresh fish.

Rincón de Capis   GOURMET €€
(☑96 570 85 00; Calle San Gabriel 5; mains €15-20; ⏰lunch Wed-Mon, dinner Fri & Sat) Four siblings and a couple of in-laws run this splendid choice, where you can eat à la carte in the very *torreviejense* decor upstairs, enjoy the

bar lunch *menú* (€12) or treat yourself to their creative eight-course *menú de degustación* (€50 – or €60 with wines to match).

Mesón de la Costa   MEDITERRANEAN **€€**
(☑96 670 35 98; www.elmesondelacosta.com, in Spanish; Calle Ramón y Cajal 23; meals €20) Hams dangle from the ceiling of this low-beamed house of plenty. Greeting you as you enter are salvers and tureens of chicken, snails, grilled vegetables, fresh seafood on ice, and a cornucopia of fruit lies behind the glass doors of the refrigerator. Set one block back from the promenade, it's an authentically, enticingly Spanish restaurant that prides itself on the prime quality of its raw materials.

Restaurante Vegetariano   VEGETARIAN **€**
(☑96 670 66 83; Calle Pedro Lorca 13; salads €5.50-9.50, mains €10; ⏰Tue-Sun; ☑) Also one block back from the beachfront, this little vegetarian haven serving salads, sandwiches, pizzas, pastas, pâtés and tasty mains is run by a Spanish-Australian couple.

Mercado de Abastos   MARKET
(Plaza Isabel II) Torrevieja's covered market is a great basket-filler for self-caterers.

ℹ Information

The **main tourist office** (☑96 570 34 33; Plaza de Capdepont; ⏰8.30am-8.30pm Mon-Fri, 10am-2pm Sat) is near the waterfront.

ℹ Getting There & Away

From the **bus station** (Calle Antonio Machado), Autocares Costa Azul runs eight buses daily to Cartagena (€4.20, 1½ hours) and Alicante (€3.65, one hour).

INLAND FROM THE COSTA BLANCA

The borderline between the holiday *costa* and the interior is, perhaps appropriately, a motorway. Venture away from the Med, west of the AP7, to find yourself in a different, truly Spanish world. By far the easiest way to explore this hinterland is with your own transport.

Xàtiva

POP 28,600

Xàtiva (Spanish: Játiva) makes an easy and rewarding 50km day trip from Valencia. It has a small historic quarter and a mighty castle strung along the crest of the Serra Vernissa, at whose base the town snuggles.

The Muslims established Europe's first paper manufacturing plant in Xàtiva, which is also famous as the birthplace of the Borgia Popes Calixtus III and Alexander VI. The town's glory days ended in 1707 when Felipe V's troops torched most of the town.

◉ Sights & Activities

What's interesting lies south and uphill from the Alameda. Ask at the tourist office for its English brochure *Xàtiva: Monumental Town*.

Museo del Almudín   MUSEUM
(Calle Corretgería 46; adult/child €2.20/1.10; ⏰10am-2pm & 4-6pm Tue-Fri, 10am-2pm Sat & Sun; mornings only mid-Jun–mid-Sep) In this museum items of most interest, including a couple of fine portraits by Ribera, are up on the penultimate floor. You can't miss the portrait of Felipe V, hung upside down in retribution for his torching the town.

Colegiata Basílica   CHURCH
(Collegiate Church; ⏰10.30am-1pm) The 16th-century basilica impresses by its sheer size but little else. Outside are a couple of fine statues of Xàtiva's two Borgia Popes, while in a couple of side chapels are 20th-century portraits of clerics assassinated by the Republican side during the Spanish civil war.

Castle   CASTLE
(adult/child €2.10/1.10; ⏰10am-6pm or 7pm Tue-Sun) The climb to the castle is long, but the views are sensational. On the way up, on your left is the 18th-century **Ermita de San José** and, to the right, the lovely Romanesque **Iglesia de Sant Feliu** (1269), Xàtiva's oldest church. Alternatively, hop aboard the little tourist train (€4 return) that heads up from the tourist office at 12.30pm and 5.30pm (4.30pm mid-September to mid-June) or call a taxi (☑96 227 16 81) and stride back down.

🛏 Sleeping & Eating

Hostería Mont Sant   RURAL HOTEL **€€**
(☑96 227 50 81; www.mont-sant.com; s €90, d from €102; ❄🐾🛜) On the road to the castle, this place sits charmingly amid extensive groves of palm and orange. Stay in the main building, once a farm, or in one of the spacious modern wooden cabins. There's a splendid restaurant, divided into intimate crannies. Sip your sundowner beside the mirador with its plunging view of the plains.

Hotel Huerto Virgen de las Nieves
HOTEL €€
(☑96 228 70 58; www.huertodelavirgendelas
nieves.com, in Spanish; Avenida Ribera 6; s 60-
80, d €65-85; ❄@☎⊠) This intimate hotel
(it has only nine rooms), all warm brick,
woodwork and cobbled floors, gives onto a
secluded garden shaded by palm trees and
cypresses. Bedrooms are large (though the
well-equipped bathrooms are tiny), blending traditional furniture with bright, contemporary artwork.

Casa la Abuela   CLASSIC MEDITERRANEAN €€
(☑96 228 10 85; Calle de la Reina 17; mains €12-19,
menus €15-20) Renowned for its rice dishes,
'Grandmother's House' is equally strong on
meat options, such as its ultra-tender *media paletilla de cordero confitada a bajo
temperatura,* half a shoulder of lamb roasted for hours at low temperature.

TOP
CHOICE **Canela y Clavo**
MODERN MEDITERRANEAN €€
(☑96 228 24 26; www.canelayclavo.com; Alameda
Jaume I 64; mains €11-19) Staffed by black-clad
waiters, this contemporary place stands out
among the restaurants bordering Xàtiva's
broad, tree-lined main avenue. It does particularly creative mains, an excellent-value
four-course lunch *menú* (€16) and an equally innovative range of tapas, to be nibbled
in its bright, modern bar.

ℹ Information

Tourist office (☑96 227 33 46; www.xativa
turismo.com in Spanish; Alameda Jaime I 50;
⊙10am-2.30pm Tue-Sun mid-Jun–mid-Sep,
10am-1.30pm & 4-6pm Tue-Fri, 10am-1.30pm
Sat & Sun rest of year) On the Alameda, Xàtiva's
shady main avenue.

ℹ Getting There & Away

The train is by far your best bet. Frequent
regional trains connect Xàtiva with Valencia
(€3.45, 40 minutes, half-hourly) and most Valencia–Madrid trains stop here too. You can also
reach Alicante (€10-21.50, 1½ hours, six daily).

Villena

POP 35,200

Villena, on the N330 between Alicante and
Albacete, is the most attractive of the towns
along the corridor of the Val de Vinalopó.

Plaza de Santiago is at the heart of its old
quarter. Within the imposing 16th-century
Palacio Municipal (Plaza de Santiago 2) is Villena's Museo Arqueológico (admission free;
⊙10am-2pm Tue-Sun). Pride of its collection
are 60 gold artefacts weighing over 10kg,
dating from around 1000 BC and found
by chance in an old riverbed. Perched high
above the town, the 12th-century Castillo
de la Atalaya is splendidly lit at night. Free
guided visits, in Spanish with English sum-
mary, take place three times each morning,
Tuesday to Sunday.

Hotel Restaurante Salvadora (☑96
580 09 50; www.hotelsalvadora.com, in Spanish;
cnr Calles Luis García & Jacinto Benavente; s/d
€49/68; ❄☎) is the town's sole hotel, featuring simple, clean, well-priced rooms,
a popular bar with a great range of tapas,
and a gourmet restaurant (mains €8-15,
4-course menú degustación €25) that does a
mean *triguico picao* (€6.50), the local speciality – a thick gruel of wheat, beans, pork
and turnip.

The tourist office (☑96 615 02 36; www.
turismovillena.com; Plaza de Santiago 5; ⊙10am-
2pm Mon-Fri, 10.30am-1.30pm Sat & Sun) is on
the main square.

Elda

POP 55,200

Elda vies with Elche for the title of shoe-
making capital of Spain. Foot fetishists
shouldn't miss the Museo del Calzado
(Shoe Museum; www.museocalzado.com; Avenida
Chapí 32; adult/child €2.40/1.20; ⊙10am-2pm &
4-8pm Tue-Sat, 11am-2pm Sun Sep-Jul, 10am-2pm
Tue-Fri Aug). Above the mezzanine floor with
its rows of Heath Robinson drills, stamps
and sewing machines, it's wall-to-wall footwear: boots through the ages; shoes from
around the world; fanciful designs that
must have been agony to wear; and donated
cast-offs from matadors, flamenco dancers,
King Juan Carlos, Queen Sofia, Rafa Nadal, Fernando Alonso and other well-shod
greats.

Novelda

POP 27,150

Novelda was once an affluent town that derived its wealth from the saffron trade. Just
25km from Alicante, it's rich in Modernista
sights.

FREE Casa-Museo Modernista (☑96
560 02 37; Calle Mayor 24; ⊙guided
visits on the hr 9am-2pm & 4-7pm) is a bourgeois
mansion completed in 1903. Its stained
glass, soft shapes in wood, period furniture

and magnificent spiralling wrought-iron staircase take the breath away.

Novelda's tourist office (☑96 560 92 28; www.novelda.es; Calle Mayor 6; ☺9am-2pm & 4.30-6pm Mon-Fri, 10am-2pm Sat) is within the town's Centro Cultural, itself a lovely Modernista building. Admire too the fine facade of Casa Bonmati (Plaza de España 9) and make the smallest of detours to take in the glorious Santuario de Santa María Magdalena (☺10am-2pm & 5-8pm), the carefully crafted equivalent, on a doll's-house scale, of Gaudí's famous Sagrada Família in Barcelona.

Alcoy

POP 61,500 / ELEV 565M

The industrial town of Alcoy (Valenciano: Alcoi), 54km north of Alicante, makes the most of its heritage and well merits your passing by. Ask at the tourist office for its brochure *Modernism in Alcoy* and explore its fine Modernista buildings.

Begin your visit with Explora (Calle Tints; adult/child €3/1.50; ☺10am-2pm & 4-7pm Tue-Sat, 11am-2pm Sun), a new, high-tech presentation of Alcoy from prehistoric times to the industrial age with additional sections on Modernismo and Moros and Cristianos fiestas.

Between 22 and 24 April, the town holds its rumbustious Moros y Cristianos festival (see the boxed text, p591). To get a feel for this exuberant fiesta, visit the Museo Alcoyano de la Fiesta (Calle Sant Miquel 60-62; adult/child €3/1.50; ☺10am-2pm & 4-7pm Tue-Sat, 11am-2pm Sun) with its posters, musical instruments, resplendent costumes and a stirring, noisily evocative 20-minute film of the action.

Roam the vast, evocative underground galleries of Refugio de Cervantes (Calle Els Alsamora 1; adult/child €2/1; ☺10am-2pm & 4-7pm Tue-Sat, 11am-2pm Sun), one of over 25 air raid shelters excavated beneath Alcoy during the Spanish Civil War and nowadays a small well-documented and illustrated museum.

The ultramodern Hotel AC Ciutat d'Alcoi (☑96 533 36 06; www.ac-hotels.com; Calle Colón 1; r €60-107; ✳@🌐) was once an electricity substation, though you'd never believe it. The black and chestnut brown of bedroom furnishings contrast pleasingly with crisp white sheets. It also runs a superlative restaurant, La Llum (☑96 533 45 40; menus €22.50, mains €10.50-16; ☺Mon-Sat). Parking is €10.50.

Immediately west of Plaza de España, Plaça de Dins, arcaded and more intimate, is packed with drinkers and diners on warm summer evenings.

Alcoy's tourist office (☑96 553 71 55; www.alcoiturisme.com; Calle San Lorenzo 2; ☺10am-2pm & 4-6pm Mon-Fri, 11am-2pm Sat & Sun) is just off the main Plaza de España.

Guadalest

POP 230

You'll be far from the first to discover the village of Guadalest; nowadays coaches, heading up from the Costa Blanca resorts, disgorge more than two million visitors every year. But get there early, or stay around after the last bus has pulled out, and the place will be almost your own.

Crowds come because Guadalest, reached by a natural tunnel and overlooked by the Castillo de San José, is indeed very pretty, and it's a joy to stroll through a traffic-free village.

Among the village's nine small museums of this and that, two stand out.

FREE Museo Etnológico (donations welcome; ☺10am-6.30pm daily Jun-Oct, Sun-Fri Nov-May) is a small, sensitive presentation of what life in Guadalest was like before the coach parties came along.

Call by the Museo de Saleros y Pimenteros (www.museodesalerosypimenteros. es, in Spanish; adult/child €3/free; ☺10.30am-7.30pm) for its sheer quirkiness. Beside the tourist office, its cabinets cascade with more than 20,000 salt and pepper pots of every imaginable shape and theme.

Sofía, born and brought up in Guadalest, and her husband Toni run a delightful, welcoming B&B, Cases Noves (☑076 01 01 71; www.casesnoves.es; incl breakfast s 45-55, d €75-85; ✳@🌐), in this large, thoughtfully renovated building. Both know the area intimately and readily give advice on local sights and the splendid opportunities for hill walking and cycling (they'll rent you a bike too). Bedrooms all have power showers, a safe, dvd player and fresh flowers. Breakfasts include fresh fruit and juices and quality coffee. Relax in the reading room, the TV room with over 300 feature films, or the adjacent music room with just as many CDs. In winter toast your toes by the open fireplace. In summer, savour the gorgeous terrace with its views of the distant sea and the village illuminated at night.

More than 80 towns and villages in the south of Valencia hold their own Fiesta de Moros y Cristianos (Moors and Christians festival) to celebrate the Reconquista, the region's liberation from Muslim rule.

Biggest and best known is Alcoy's (22 to 24 April), when hundreds of locals dress up in elaborate traditional costumes representing different 'factions' – Muslim and Christian soldiers, slaves, guild groups, town criers, heralds, bands – and march through the streets in colourful processions with mock battles.

Processions converge upon Alcoy's main plaza and its huge, temporary wooden fortress. It's an exhilarating spectacle of sights and sounds: soldiers in shining armour, white-cloaked Muslim warriors bearing scimitars and shields, turban-topped Arabs, scantily clad wenches, brass bands, exploding blunderbusses, firework displays and confetti showering down on the crowds.

Each town has its own variation on the format, steeped in traditions that allude to the events of the Reconquista. So, for example, Villena's festival (5 to 9 September) features midnight parades, while La Vila Joiosa (24 to 31 July), near Benidorm, re-enacts the landing of Muslim ships on the beaches.

Elche

POP 233,250

Precisely 23km southwest of Alicante, Elche (Valencian: Elx) is split by the channelled trickle of Río Vinalopó. It's a Unesco World Heritage site twice over: for the *Misteri d'Elx*, its annual mystery play, and for its extensive palm groves, Europe's largest, planted by the Phoenecians and extended by the Arabs. Islamic irrigation systems converted the region into a rich agricultural producer that still offers citrus fruit, figs, almonds, dates and 85% of Spain's pomegranates.

Though its suburbs are soulless, Elche's heart is green and open, with parks, date groves and public gardens. Its sights are comprehensively signed in English.

◉ Sights & Activities

Around 200,000 palm trees, some shaggy and in need of a haircut, most trim and clipped, each with a lifespan of some 250 years, make the heart of this busy industrial town a veritable oasis. A signed 2.5km **walking trail** (ask at the tourist office for its leaflet *Historic Palm Groves Route*) leads from the Museu del Palmerar through the groves.

Huerto del Cura   GARDENS
(Porta de la Morera 49; adult/child €5/2.50, audioguide €2; ☉10am-sunset) Opposite the hotel of the same name, this lovely private garden has tended lawns, colourful flowerbeds, cacti – and, of course, ranks of palm trees.

Museu del Palmerar   PALM MUSEUM
(Porta de la Morera 12; adult/child €1/0.50; ☉10am-1.30pm & 4.30-8pm Tue-Sat, 10.30am-1.30pm

Sun) In a former farmhouse, this museum is all about the date palm and the intricate blanched, woven fronds used throughout Spain in Palm Sunday rites. Wander through the delightful adjacent palm grove and orchard with its gurgling irrigation channels and typical fruit trees of the *huerta*.

Museo Arqueológico y de Historia de Elche   ARCHAEOLOGICAL MUSEUM
(MAHE; Diagonal del Palau 7; adult/child €3/1; ☉10am-1.30pm & 4.30-8pm Tue-Sat, 10.30am-1.30pm Sun), well signed in Spanish and English, recounts Elche's history through selected artefacts, touch screens and giant computer animations.

Centro de Visitantes   AUDIOVISUAL SHOW
(admission free; ☉10am-7pm Mon-Sat, 10am-2pm Sun) For an alternative overview of the town, call by the Centro de Visitantes. Every half-hour, at this Arab-style building, in the park behind the tourist office, there's an evocative 10-minute audiovisual presentation.

Baños Árabes   ARAB BATHS
(Arab Baths; ☑96 545 28 87; Passeig de les Eres de Santa Lucía 13; adult/child €1/0.50; ☉10am-1.30pm & 4.30-8pm Tue-Sat, 10.30am-1.30pm Sun) At these 12th-century baths you can also watch an enjoyable audiovisual presentation with optional English soundtrack.

Basílica de Santa María   CHURCH
(☉7am-1pm & 5.30-9pm) This vast baroque church is used for performances of the *Misteri d'Elx*. Climb up its tower (adult/child €2/1; ☉11am-6pm or 7pm) for a sweeping, pigeon's-eye view over the palms.

Alcúdia
ARCHAEOLOGICAL SITE

The well-documented site is 3.5km south of the town centre. Here was unearthed the Dama de Elche, a masterpiece of Iberian art that's now in Madrid's Museo Arqueológico Nacional collection (see p76). Visit the site's excellent **Museo Arqueológico** (www.laalcudia.ua.es in Spanish; adult/child €3/1; ⊙10am-5pm or 8pm Tue-Sat, 10am-3pm Sun). The museum displays the rich findings from a settlement that was occupied continuously from Neolithic to late-Visigoth times.

Sleeping

Hotel Huerto del Cura
HOTEL €€

(☑96 661 00 11; www.huertodelcura.com; Porta de la Morera 14; r Mon-Thu €112, Fri-Sun €102-132; P✳@☀) Accommodation is in trim bungalows within lush, palm-shaded gardens. It's a family-friendly place with playground, large pool and babysitting service. Complete the cosseting at Elche's longest-standing luxury hotel by dining in **Els Capellans**, its renowned restaurant. Parking is €12.

Pensión Faro
PENSIÓN €

(☑96 546 62 63; Camí dels Magros 24; basic s/d €15/30) West of Río Vinalopó and an easy walk from the historic centre, this friendly, family-run place is a little gem. Its nine rooms, all with corridor bathroom, are simple, spotless and equipped with ceiling fans.

✗ Eating

Carrer Mare de Déu del Carmé (Calle Nuestra Señora del Carmen) has a cluster of cheap and cheerful eateries. On summer evenings almost the whole length of this short street is set with tables.

Restaurante Dátil de Oro
MEDITERRANEAN €€

(☑96 545 34 15; www.datildeoro.com, in Spanish; mains €12-20, menus €16-25) Within the municipal park, the Golden Date is a vast emporium to eating that can accommodate almost 800 diners. Even so, the cuisine is far from institutional and it's one of the best places in town to sample local dishes, such as *arroz con costra* (rice with a crusty egg topping); also date flan and even date ice cream.

El Granaíno
SPANISH €€

(☑96 666 40 80; Calle Josep María Buck 40; mains around €18; ⊙Mon-Sat) The tiled exterior of this long-established favourite hints at the classic, quintessentially Spanish cuisine of this family-run restaurant with its impressively long bar and bodega of more than 7000 bottles.

❶ Information

The **tourist office** (☑96 665 81 96; www.turismedelx.com; ⊙9am-7pm Mon-Fri, 10am-7pm Sat, 10am-2pm Sun) is at the southeast corner of Parque Municipal (Town Park).

❶ Getting There & Around

Train and bus stations are beside each other on Avenida de la Libertad (also called Avenida del Ferrocarril).

MISTERI D'ELX

The *Misteri d'Elx*, a two-act lyric drama dating from the Middle Ages, is performed annually in Elche's Basílica de Santa María.

One distant day, according to legend, a casket was washed up on Elche's Mediterranean shore. Inside were a statue of the Virgin and the *Consueta*, the music and libretto of a mystery play describing Our Lady's death, assumption into heaven and coronation.

The story tells how the Virgin, realising that death is near, asks God to allow her to see the apostles one last time. They arrive one by one from distant lands and, in their company, she dies at peace. Once received into paradise, she is crowned Queen of Heaven and Earth to swelling music, the ringing of bells, cheers all round and – hey, we're in the Valencia region – spectacular fireworks.

The mystery's two acts, *La Vespra* (the eve of her death) and *La Festa* (the celebration of her assumption and coronation), are performed in Valenciano by the people of Elche themselves on 14 and 15 August respectively (with public rehearsals on the three previous days).

You can see a multimedia presentation – complete with virtual apostle – in the **Museu de la Festa** (☑96 545 34 64; Carrer Major de la Vila 25; adult/child €3/1; ⊙10am-1.30pm & 4.30-8pm Tue-Sat, 10.30am-1.30pm Sun), about a block west of the basilica. The show lasts 35 minutes and is repeated several times daily, with optional English commentary.

BUS

Alicante €1.90, 35 minutes, every half-hour

Valencia €11.75, 2½ hours, four to six daily

Murcia €3.95, 45 minutes, four to six daily

TRAIN Elche is on the Alicante–Murcia train line. About 20 trains daily rattle through, bound for Alicante (€2.10) or Murcia (€2.95) via Orihuela (€2.10).

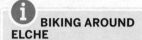

BIKING AROUND ELCHE

To take advantage of Elche's brand-new **bike-hire scheme** (www.bicielx. es in Spanish; per day €3), call by the kiosk at the bus station and you're launched. It's the ideal way to explore the palm groves and visit Alcudia.

Orihuela

POP 86,200

Beside Río Segura and flush with the base of a barren mountain of rock, the historical heart of Orihuela with its Gothic, Renaissance and, especially, baroque buildings well merits a short detour.

◉ Sights

Museo de la Muralla MUSEUM
(✆96 530 46 98; Calle del Río; admission free; ☺10am-2pm & 4-7pm or 5-8pm Tue-Sat, 10am-2pm Sun) Access to this museum is through the main door to the Universidad Miguel Hernandez. A 20-minute guided tour in Spanish (ask for the English leaflet) leads you through the vast underground remains of the city walls, Arab baths, domestic buildings and a Gothic palace.

Convento de Santo Domingo CONVENT
(Calle Adolfo Claravana; ☺9.30am-1.30pm & 4-7pm or 5-8pm Tue-Sat, 10am-2pm Sun) A 16th-century convent with two fine Renaissance cloisters and a refectory clad in 18th-century tilework.

Catedral de San Salvador CHURCH
(Calle Doctor Sarget; ☺10.30am-2pm & 4-6.30pm Tue-Fri, 10.30am-2pm Sat) Another of the town's splendid ecclesiastical buildings is this 14th-century Catalan Gothic cathedral, with its three finely carved portals and a lovely little cloister.

Iglesia de las Santas Justa y Rufina CHURCH
(Plaza Salesas 1; ☺as cathedral) Worth admiring is the church's Renaissance facade and its Gothic tower graced with gargoyles.

Palacio Episcopal PALACE, MUSEUM
(Calle Ramón y Cajal) Behind the sober baroque facade the palace is undergoing renovations to become the **Museo Diocesano**, whose rich collection includes Velázquez' *Temptation of St Thomas*.

Also noteworthy in town are the mainly 14th-century **Iglesia de Santiago Após-** tol (Plaza de Santiago 2), and, crowning the mountain, the ruins of a **castle** originally constructed by the Muslims.

🛏 Sleeping & Eating

Hotel Melia Palacio de Tudemir HOTEL €€
(✆96 673 80 10; www.solmelia.com; Calle Alfonso XIII 1; r €89; ❄) Palace is indeed the word for this tastefully renovated 18th-century building. There's a pleasant cafe (open 8am to midnight) offering plenty of tasty tapas and a restaurant (*menús* €16, mains €18 to €21; open lunch only) that stands out among Orihuela's limited dining options.

Hostal Rey Teodomiro HOSTAL €
(✆/fax 96 674 33 48; 1st fl, Avenida Rey Teodomiro 10; s/d €32/53.50; ❅❄) In the modern part of town and handy for bus and train stations, this is an excellent-value budget option, with air-con in all 23 rooms. Those facing the grassy square have balconies.

Barra Restaurante Joaquín
MEDITERRANEAN €€
(✆96 674 34 15; Avenida Rey Teodomiro 18; mains €15-21; ☺closed Sun & dinner Wed) For food that is grilled, roasted, or at most garnished with a simple sauce meunière. The Joaquin's reputation rests upon the superb quality of its fresh meat, fish and seafood, served unadorned and without fancy sauces. Dine in the convivial bar or in the more restrained surroundings of the rear restaurant.

❶ Information

Orihuela's **tourist office** (✆96 530 46 45; www. orihuelaturistica.es, in Spanish) is on Plaza Marqués de Rafal.

❶ Getting There & Away

Bus and train stations are combined at the Intermodal, an airy structure at the end of Avenida de Teodomiro. Orihuela is on the Alicante–Murcia train line and has frequent services to both places, calling by Elche.

Mallorca, Menorca & Ibiza

Best Places to Eat

» Cas Ferrer de Sa Font (p640)

» Mesón El Gallo (p637)

» Simply Fosh (p601)

» Restaurant Es Mirador (p617)

» Comidas Bar San Juan (p617)

Best Places to Stay

» Es Petit Hotel (p605)

» Hotel Casal d'Artà (p612)

» Casa Alberti (p633)

» Fornalutx Petit Hotel (p607)

» Hotel Born (p600)

Why Go?

'Come to savour the splendid walking and cycling of the Tramontana and my northern coast', Mallorca will exhort. Menorca will cite her profusion of prehistoric sites and the forts her conquerors built and left behind. Unless she's still sleeping off her latest excess, in-your-face Ibiza will brag of her megaclubs, boutiques and oh-so-cool vibes. Tiny Formentera, for her part, will pipe up to remind you of her traffic-light country roads and white sands.

All four will protest vigorously and rightfully that they suffer from a bad press. 'Yes,' the two big sisters will ruefully confess, 'patches have their share of mass tourism at its worst.' 'But', all four will chorus, 'you must meet us halfway.' So, take advantage of the islands' good public transport system or hire a car to seek out an infinity of small coves, fishing villages, sandy beaches, endless olive and almond groves and citrus orchards.

When to Go

Palma de Mallorca

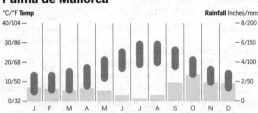

March & April Spring flowers brush your boots as you walk Mallorca's Serra de Tramuntana

June–September Beach by day, clubbing through the night, raving round the Ibiza clock

July & August Torchlit re-enactments at Maó's two historical forts on Menorca

❶ Getting There & Around

AIR

In summer, masses of charter and regular flights converge on Palma de Mallorca and Ibiza from all over Europe. Major operators from the Spanish mainland include **Iberia** (www.iberia.es), **Air Europa** (www.aireuropa.com), **Spanair** (www.spanair.com), **Air Berlin** (www.airberlin.com) and **Vueling** (www.vueling.com).

Tariffs for inter-island flights, with a flying time of less than 30 minutes, vary hugely. A trip from Palma de Mallorca to Maó or Ibiza costs anything from €30 to €170.

BOAT

Compare prices and look for deals at **Direct Ferries** (www.directferries.es).

The following serve the Balearic Islands:

Acciona Trasmediterránea (☏902 454645; www.trasmediterranea.es)

Baleària (☏902 160180; www.balearia.com)

Cala Ratjada Tours (☏902 100444; www.calaratjadatours.es, in Spanish)

Iscomar (☏902 119128; www.iscomar.com)

Ferry routes to the mainland:

Ibiza (Ibiza City) To/from Barcelona (Acciona Trasmediterránea, Baleària), Valencia (Acciona Trasmediterránea).

Ibiza (Sant Antoni) To/from Denia and Barcelona (Baleària), Valencia (Acciona Trasmediterránea, Baleària).

Mallorca (Palma de Mallorca) To/from Barcelona and Valencia (Acciona Trasmediterránea, Baleària), Denia (Baleària).

Menorca (Maó) To/from Barcelona and Valencia (Acciona Trasmediterránea, Baleària).

Inter-island ferry routes:

Ibiza (Ibiza City) To/from Palma de Mallorca (Acciona Trasmediterránea, Baleària).

Mallorca, Menorca & Ibiza Highlights

❶ Admire the Gothic splendour of the cathedral in **Palma de Mallorca** (p638)

❷ Take a hike in Mallorca's **Serra de Tramuntana** (p604)

❸ Join the party that sets the Mediterranean on fire in the amazing clubs of **Ibiza** (p621)

❹ Chill out at Formentera's sunset parties at the Blue Bar on **Platja de Migjorn** (p629)

❺ Enjoy scented strolls in villages like **Fornalutx** (p607) in Mallorca's northwest

❻ Gasp at the turquoise hues of the sea around the promontory of **Cap de Formentor** (p609)

❼ Peer into prehistory at Naveta des Tudons and the other ancient monuments around **Ciutadella** (p636)

❽ Slip into Menorca's limpid waters at **Cala Macarelleta** and **Cala en Turqueta** (p642)

❾ Say three Hail Marys before winding along the spectacular 12km route to **Sa Calobra** (p608)

WEBSITES

Consult these pan-Balearics websites:

www.illesbalears.es Official tourism website for all the islands.

www.platgesdebalears.com The low-down on every beach.

www.balearsculturaltour.com Handicrafts, cultural events, scenic splendours and more.

Mallorca (Cala Ratjada) To/from Ciutadella (Cala Ratjada Tours).

Mallorca (Palma de Mallorca) To/from Ibiza City (Acciona Trasmediterránea and Baleària) and Maó (Acciona Trasmediterránea, Baleària).

Mallorca (Port d'Alcúdia) To/from Ciutadella (Iscomar).

Menorca (Ciutadella) To/from Cala Ratjada (Cala Ratjada Tours) and Port d'Alcúdia (Iscomar).

Menorca (Maó) To/from Palma de Mallorca (Acciona Trasmediterránea, Baleària).

For ferries between Ibiza and Formentera, see p629.

MALLORCA

In 1950 the first charter flight landed on a small airstrip on Mallorca, which, at 3620 sq km, is the largest of the Balearic Islands. Today annual visitors hover around 10 million, most in search of the three *s*'s: sun, sand and sea – and swamping the local island populace of some 845,000 people (around half of whom live in the capital, Palma de Mallorca).

But there's much more to Mallorca than the beach. Palma de Mallorca (or, simply, Palma) is the main centre and a charming stop (it can be, er, insular: locals, who call their island *Sa Roqueta* (the Little Rock), refer to what lies beyond Palma as the *part forana*, the 'outside part'). The northwest, dominated by the Serra de Tramuntana mountain range, is a beautiful region of olive groves, pine forests and ochre villages, with a spectacularly rugged coastline.

Most of Mallorca's best beaches are on the north and east coasts. Although many have been encircled by insensitive tourist development, you can still seek out an exception or two. There's also a scattering of fine beaches along parts of the south coast.

Getting Around

BOAT Palma and the major resorts and beaches around the island are connected by boat tours and water-taxi services. Most feature in the tourist office brochure, *Excursions En Barca*, available in English.

BUS Most of the island is accessible by bus from Palma. All buses depart from or near the **bus station** (Carrer d'Eusebi Estada). For information, contact **Transport de les Illes Balears** (TIB; ✆971 17 77 77; http://tib.caib.es, in Spanish). One-way fares from Palma include Cala Ratjada (€6), Ca'n Picafort (€4.25), Port de Pollença (€4.55) and Port d'Andratx (€3.60).

CAR & MOTORCYCLE You can rent cars and bikes, and often scooters too, in even smallest resort. Palma alone has over 30 agencies. The big league has representatives at the airport and along Passeig Marítim, along with several cheaper companies. One of the best deals is **Hasso** (✆902 203012; www.hasso -rentacar.com).

TAXI You can get around the island by taxi, but it's costly. Prices are posted at central points in many towns. You're looking at around €90 from the airport to Cala Ratjada or €34 from Palma to Sóller.

TRAIN Two train lines run from Plaça d'Espanya in Palma de Mallorca. The popular, old train runs to Sóller and is a pretty ride. A standard train line runs inland to Inca (€1.80, 40 minutes, every half-hour), where the line splits with a branch to Sa Pobla (€2.40, one hour, hourly) and another to Manacor (€2.40, 1¼ hours, hourly).

Palma de Mallorca

POP 401,000

Palma de Mallorca is the island's only true city. Its old quarter is an enchanting blend of tree-lined boulevards and cobbled laneways, Gothic churches and baroque palaces, and private patios and designer bars.

MALLORCA WEBSITES

www.informamallorca.net Official Mallorca tourism website.

www.abc-mallorca.com Privately run and in the know.

www.mallorcahotelguide.com Website of the Mallorca hoteliers' association.

http://tib.caib.es Bus timetables throughout the island (in Spanish).

⊙ Sights

CENTRAL PALMA DE MALLORCA

Central Palma is known especially for the elegant courtyards, called *patis,* of its many noble houses and mansions. Most are in private hands, but you can often peek into a *pati* through its wrought-iron grill.

Catedral
CATHEDRAL

(La Seu; Carrer del Palau Reial 9; adult/child €4/3; ⊙10am-5.15pm Mon-Fri, 10am-3pm Sat) Palma's vast cathedral is often likened to a huge ship moored at the city's edge. Construction on what had been the site of the main mosque started in 1300 but wasn't completed until 1601. This awesome structure is predominantly Gothic, apart from the main facade (replaced after an earthquake in 1851) and parts of the interior (renovated in Modernista style by Antoni Gaudí at the beginning of the 20th century).

Entry is via a small, three-room **museum**, which holds a collection of religious artwork and precious gold and silver effects. The cathedral's interior is stunning, with ranks of slender columns supporting the soaring ceiling and framing three levels of elaborate stained-glass windows. The front altar's centrepiece, a light, twisting wrought-iron sculpture suspended from the ceiling, is one of Gaudí's more eccentric creations. For once, however, Gaudí is upstaged by the island's top contemporary artist, Miquel Barceló, who reworked the **Capella del Santíssim i Sant Pere**, at the head of the south aisle, in a dream-fantasy, swirling ceramic rendition of the miracle of the loaves and fishes.

Palau de l'Almudaina
PALACE

(Carrer del Palau Reial; adult/child €3.20/2.30, audioguide €2.50; ⊙10am-5.45pm Mon-Fri, 10am-1.15pm Sat) Originally an Islamic fort, this mighty construction was converted

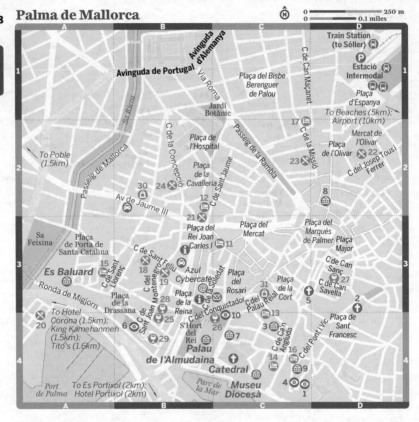

into a residence for the Mallorcan monarchs at the end of the 13th century. It is still occasionally used for official functions when King Juan Carlos is in town. At other times you can wander through a series of cavernous and austere stone-walled rooms, a chapel with a rare Romanesque entrance, and upstairs royal apartments adorned with Flemish tapestries and period furniture.

Museu Diocesà ECCLESIASTICAL MUSEUM

(Carrer del Mirador 5; adult/child €3/2; ☺10am-2pm Mon-Sat). From the cathedral's exit, walk around the east end to the Palau Episcopal (bishop's residence) and, within it, to this rich collection. After the cathedral's seething crowds, it's a tranquil and fascinating excursion into Mallorca's Christian art history. Items, garnered from all over the island, are particularly well displayed and illuminated.

Es Baluard ART MUSEUM

(Museu d'Art Modern i Contemporani; www.esbaluard.org, in Spanish; Porta de Santa Catalina 10; permanent exhibition adult/child €6/4.50, temporary exhibitions €4/3; ☺10am-8pm Tue-Sun) This 21st-century concrete complex nests within Palma's grand Renaissance-era seaward fortifications. A playful game of light, surfaces and perspective, it makes the perfect framework for the works within. These start with Catalan and other landscape artists at work in Mallorca in the 19th and 20th centuries and continue with a revolving display of 20th-century greats – you might see works by anyone from Oskar Kokoschka to Amedeo Modigliani. The views from the ramparts and cafe are splendid.

Palau March ART MUSEUM

(www.fundbmarch.es; Carrer de Palau Reial 18; adult/child €3.60/free; ☺10am-6pm Mon-Fri, 10am-2pm Sat) This house, palatial by any definition, was one of several residences of the phenomenally wealthy March family. Sculptures by 20th-century greats, such as Henry Moore, Auguste Rodin, Barbara Hepworth and Eduardo Chillida, grace the outdoor terrace. Within is a vast 18th-century Neapolitan nativity scene, alive with expressive folk figures, and a set of Salvador Dalí prints.

FREE **Museu d'Art Espanyol
Contemporani** ART MUSEUM
(Museu Fundació Juan March; www.march.es/arte/palma; Carrer de Sant Miquel 11; ⊙10am-6.30pm Mon-Fri, 10.30am-2pm Sat) On permanent display within this 18th-century mansion are some 70 pieces held by the Fundación Juan March. Together they constitute a veritable who's who of mostly 20th-century artists, including Picasso, Miró, Juan Gris (of cubism fame), Dalí and the sculptor Julio González.

Can Marquès HISTORIC HOUSE
(Carrer de Ca'n Angluda 2A; adult/child €6/5; ⊙10am-3pm Mon-Fri, 11am-2pm Sat) This exquisitely furnished mansion, the only one of its kind in Palma open to visitors, retains elements dating to the 14th century. It gives a fascinating insight into how the well-to-do lived around the turn of the

20th century. The building shows elements of Gothic, baroque and even Modernista influences.

Basílica de Sant Francesc CHURCH
(Plaça de Sant Francesc 7; admission €1; ⊙9.30am-12.30pm & 3.30-6pm Mon-Sat, 9.30am-12.30pm Sun) One of Palma's oldest churches, Basílica de Sant Francesc was begun in 1281 in Gothic style; its baroque facade was added in 1700. You enter by the beautiful, two-tiered, trapezoidal cloister. Inside is the **tomb** of, and **monument** to, the 13th-century scholar Ramon Llull.

Casa-Museu Joaquim Torrents Lladó
HISTORIC HOUSE
(Carrer de la Portella 9; adult/child €4/2.50; ⊙10.30am-2.30pm Tue-Sat) Once home of the eponymous Catalan artist (1946–93), this is another fine mansion, with a timber gallery overlooking a courtyard. Displaying many of his works, it has been largely preserved as he left it.

Banys Àrabs BATHHOUSE
(Carrer de Serra 7; adult/child €12/free; ⊙9am-7.30pm) These modest remains of Arab baths are one of the few reminders of Muslim domination of the island. All that

survives are two small underground chambers, one with a domed ceiling supported by a dozen columns, some of whose capitals were recycled from demolished Roman buildings.

Museu de Mallorca
MUSEUM

(Carrer de la Portella 5) Well worth a visit, but will remain closed for extensive renovations until at least 2012.

La Llotja
ART MUSEUM

(Plaça de la Llotja; ☺11am-1.45pm & 5-8.45pm Tue-Sat, 11am-1.45pm Sun) This gorgeous Gothic structure, opposite the waterfront, was built as a merchants' stock exchange and is used for temporary exhibitions.

Museo de Muñecas
MUSEUM

(Carrer del Palau Reial 27; adult/child €3.50/2.50; ☺10am-6pm Tue-Sun) Near the cathedral, this shop-cum-museum is dedicated to old dolls.

Església de Santa Eulàlia
CHURCH

(Plaça de Santa Eulàlia 2; ☺11am-1pm & 6-7.45pm Mon-Fri) This soaring Gothic pile, with a colossal free-standing baroque altarpiece, is one of Palma's oldest churches.

WESTERN PALMA

Castell de Bellver
CASTLE

(adult/child €2.50/1; ☺8.30am-8.30pm Mon-Sat, 10am-6.30pm Sun) South of the Poble Espanyol, this unusual, circular 14th-century castle (with a unique round tower) is set atop a pleasant park. It's the setting for a July classical music festival.

Fundació Pilar i Joan Miró
ART MUSEUM

(http://miro.palmademallorca.es; Carrer de Saridakis 29; adult/child €6/3; ☺10am-7pm Tue-Sat, 10am-3pm Sun) In Cala Major (about 4km southwest of the city centre), this museum is housed in a modern complex on the site of Joan Miró's former studios. On show is a rotating collection of the works stored here at the time of his death. Take bus 3 or 46 from Plaça d'Espanya.

Poble Espanyol
REPLICA BUILDINGS

(Carrer del Poble Espanyol 55; adult/child €8/5; ☺9am-7.30pm) A copy of the village of the same name in Barcelona, it contains replicas of famous monuments and other buildings representative of a variety of Spanish architectural styles – not to mention souvenir shops galore.

🛏 Sleeping

There *are* budget places around but, in general, you'll be paying rather more if you want an alternative to unexceptional but good-value package-tour hotels.

TOP CHOICE Hotel Santa Clara
BOUTIQUE HOTEL €€€

(☎971 72 92 31; www.santaclarahotel.es; Carrer de Sant Alonso 16; s/d from 155/210; ❄@⊛) Boutique meets antique in this historic mansion, converted with respect, where subdued greys, steely silvers and cream blend harmoniously with the warm stone walls, ample spaces and high ceilings of the original structure. There's a small, decked roof terrace, ideal for a sunbathe or a sundowner, and a spa with free facilities for guests.

Misión de San Miguel
BOUTIQUE HOTEL €€€

(☎971 21 48 48; www.urbanrustichotels.com; Carrer de Can Maçanet 1; r from €150; ❄@⊛) The hotel is on a side alley off Carrer Oms. Its 32 spacious rooms are quiet, with firm mattresses and rain showers. The restaurant serves a fabulous made-to-order breakfast (€11) and the patio area is romantic and relaxing.

Hotel Born
HISTORIC HOTEL €€

(☎971 71 29 42; www.hotelborn.com; Carrer de Sant Jaume 3; incl breakfast s €52, incl breakfast d €76-97; ❄@⊛) A superb place in the heart of the city, this hotel is housed in an 18th-century palace. Rooms combine elegance and history with all mod cons. The best have an engaging view onto the palm-shaded patio.

Hotel San Lorenzo
HISTORIC HOTEL €€€

(☎971 72 82 00; www.hotelsanlorenzo.com; Carrer de Sant Llorenç 14; s/d from €145/155; ❄⊛⊠) Tucked away inside the old quarter, this hotel is in a beautifully restored 17th-century building. It has a marvellous Mallorcan courtyard, its own bar, dining room and lovely small garden with swimming pool.

Hostal Corona
CLASSIC HOTEL €

(☎971 73 19 35; www.hostal-corona.com; Carrer de Josep Villalonga 22; s €30, d €45-60) With its palm trees and cornucopia of plants, the generous courtyard garden of this little hotel (the house was once a private villa) has a faraway feel. Rooms are simple, with timber furnishings and old tiled floors. In the evening, the courtyard turns into a popular, chilled-out bar. The nearest bus stop is at

Avinguda de Joan Miró 24 (take bus 3 or 46 from Plaça d'Espanya).

Hotel Dalt Murada
HISTORIC HOTEL **€€€**

(☎971 42 53 00; www.daltmurada.com; Carrer de la Almudaina 6; d from €148) Gathered around a medieval courtyard, this carefully restored old town house with 14 rooms is a gorgeous option, with antique furnishings and art work, many belonging to the friendly family who still own and run the place. The decidedly 21st-century penthouse suite has incomparable views of the cathedral.

Hostal Brondo
FAMILY HOTEL **€€**

(☎971 71 90 43; www.hostalbrondo.net; Carrer de Ca'n Brondo 1; d with bathroom €70, s/d without bathroom €40/55; ☜) Climb the courtyard stairs to arrive in a cosy sitting room overlooking the narrow lane. Six of the 10 high-ceilinged rooms (room 6 has a pair of glassed-in balconies) have private bathrooms and all are furnished individually in varying styles, from Mallorcan to vaguely Moroccan.

Hotel Palacio Ca Sa Galesa
HISTORIC HOTEL **€€€**

(☎971 71 54 00; www.palaciocasagalesa.com; Carrer del Miramar 8; s/d €261/332; ❋@☜☒) Welcome to the classiest act in town. Rooms in this enchanting 16th-century mansion are arranged around a cool patio garden. A genteel air wafts through the elegant bedrooms, each named after a famous composer and furnished with antiques, artwork and silk bed throws. There are free bicycles for guest use.

✖ Eating

Plenty of eateries and bars cater to Palma's visitors in the maze of streets between Plaça de la Reina and the port. The seaside Es Molinar area around Es Portixol has cheerful seafood eateries and laid-back bars.

[TOP CHOICE] Simply Fosh
INTERNATIONAL **€€**

(☎971 72 01 14; www.simplyfosh.com; Carrer de la Missió 7A; mains €14-26, dinner menúes €52; ☺Mon-Sat) It's great gourmet cuisine at the restaurant of Michelin-starred British chef Marc Fosh. Quality is sustained right down to the cheese board, with its selection of the very best that Spain offers. The decor, all white, black and chestnut brown with fresh plants on every table, is just as satisfying.

FINDING A BED

The Balearics in high summer (roughly, late June to mid-September) can be incredibly busy. Palma de Mallorca alone turns around some 40 inbound and outbound flights a day. Most of the millions of visitors have pre-booked package accommodation and the strain on local infrastructure can make it tricky for the independent traveller. Book at least the first couple of nights around this time to avoid an uncomfortable start. In July and August hotel prices are at their highest. This chapter reflects such high-season maxima. In most places you can expect to pay considerably less in quieter times. Check hotel websites for special offers and promotions.

La Bodeguilla
SPANISH **€€**

(☎971 71 82 74; www.la-bodeguilla.com; Carrer de Sant Jaume 3; mains €17.50-19.50; ☺Mon-Sat) This gourmet restaurant does creative interpretations of dishes from across Spain (such as *cochinillo,* suckling pig, from Segovia; and *lechazo,* young lamb, baked Córdoba-style in rosemary).

Bon Lloc
VEGETARIAN **€**

(☎971 71 86 17; www.bonllocrestaurant.com, in Spanish; Carrer de Sant Feliu 7; menúes €13.50; ☺lunch Mon-Sat; ✎) This 100% vegetarian place, where all produce is organic, is light, open and airy. There are no agonising decisions – just a satisfying, take-it-or-leave-it four-course *menú*. It's hugely popular, so do ring to reserve.

Ca n'Eduardo
FISH **€€€**

(☎971 72 11 82; www.caneduardo.com, in Spanish; Es Mollet; mains €22.50-28.50) What better place to sample fish than here, right above the fish market? With its bright, contemporary decor and picture windows overlooking the fishing port, Ca n'Eduardo has been serving satisfying meals since the 1940s.

13%
TAPAS **€**

(☎971 42 51 87; www.13porciento.com; Carrer de Sant Feliu 13A; meals around €15; ✎) At the quieter end of the old town, this L-shaped barn of a place is both wine and tapas bar. Most items are organic and there's plenty of choice for vegetarians. Wines are displayed on racks (both bar and takeaway prices are quoted, so you know the exact mark-up).

Taberna El Burladero TAPAS €

(☎971 71 34 59; Carrer de la Concepció 3B; www.tabernaelburladero.com; tapas €3.50-4.50, dishes €5.50-12.50; ☺Mon-Sat) Disregard the hackneyed blow-ups of bullrings and matadors that fill the walls. And ignore that stuffed bull's head staring down. Despite initial appearances, this ultramodern place serves delightful, original tapas at competitive prices.

Mercat de l'Olivar FOOD MARKET €

The town market is the place for self-caterers to stock up.

🍷 Drinking & Entertainment

The old quarter is the city's most vibrant nightlife zone. Particularly along the narrow streets between Plaça de la Reina and Plaça de la Drassana, you'll find an enormous selection of bars, pubs and bodegas. Look around the Santa Catalina (especially Carrer de Sant Magí) and Es Molinar districts too. About 2km west of the old quarter along and behind Passeig Marítim (aka Avinguda de Gabriel Roca) is a concentration of taverns, girlie bars and clubs – El Garito, King Kamehameha and Tito's are the favourites. According to a much-flouted law, bars should shut by 1am Sunday to Thursday, and 3am Friday and Saturday.

S'Arenal and Magaluf, the seaside resorts east and west of Palma respectively, are full of bars and discos filled to bursting with mainly package tourists.

Vamos 365 (www.vamosmallorca365.com), a monthly freebie, has its finger on Palma's night-time pulse.

⟨TOP CHOICE⟩ Puro Beach DESIGNER BAR

(www.purobeach.com; ☺11am-2am Apr-Oct) This laid-back, sunset chill lounge has a tapering outdoor promontory with an all-white bar that's perfect for sunset cocktails, DJ sessions and fusion food escapes. Blend in with the monochrome decor and wear white, emphasising your designer tan. It is just a two-minute walk east of Cala Estancia (itself just east of Ca'n Pastilla).

Ca'n Joan de S'Aigo CAFE

(Carrer de Can Sanç 10; ☺8am-9pm Wed-Mon) Dating from 1700, this is *the* place for a hot chocolate (€1.40) in what can only be described as an antique-filled milk bar. The house speciality is *quart,* a feather-soft sponge cake that children love, with almond-flavoured ice cream.

Café Cappuccino CAFE

(www.grupocappuccino.com; Carrer del Conquistador 13) You'll pay more for your coffee fix here. But what coffee! And what style! And such breakfasts (€7 to €13), from feather light to filling every last cranny. This is one of nearly a dozen hyper-hip coffee houses belonging to Cappuccino, a Mallorcan chain.

Abaco DESIGNER BAR

(www.bar-abaco.com, in Spanish; Carrer de Sant Joan 1; ☺from 9pm) Behind a set of ancient timber doors is the bar of your wildest dreams. Inside, a typical Mallorcan patio and candle-lit courtyard are crammed with elaborate floral arrangements, cascading towers of fresh fruit and bizarre artworks.

Jazz Voyeur Club MUSIC BAR

(www.jazzvoyeur.com; Carrer dels Apuntadors 5; ☺from 10pm) A tiny club no bigger than most people's living rooms, Voyeur hosts live jazz bands nightly. Red candles burn on the tables and a few plush chairs are scattered about – get here early if you want to grab one.

Neo Cultural COCKTAIL BAR

(☎971 72 89 94; Carrer Boteria 8; ☺from 7pm) Neo Cultural, a more than worthwhile place to dine or pick at tapas (tapas €4.50 to €9.50; *menúes* €16.50 to €18.50), especially merits a visit for its great range of cocktails and congenial bar staff – movers and shakers who are adept at creating their own concoctions.

El Garito MUSIC BAR

(www.garitocafe.com; Dàrsena de Can Barberà; ☺7pm-4.30am). DJs and live performers, doing anything from jazz rock to disco classics and electro beats, heat up the scene from around 10pm. Admission is generally free.

King Kamehameha CLUB

(Passeig Marítim 29) Pulsating with up-to-the-minute electronic tracks and a young, international crowd.

Tito's CLUB

(Passeig Marítim 33) Another classic club, it's only open Thursday to Sunday in the low season (October to May).

Shopping

Camper SHOES

(Avinguda de Jaume III 16) Best known of Mallorca's famed shoe brands, funky, eco-chic Campers are now trendy worldwide.

Vidrierias Gordiola GLASSWARE
(Carrer de la Victoria 8; ⊘closed Sat afternoon)
Mallorca's best-known glassmakers offer
everything from traditional goblets and
vases to decidedly modern works of art.

ℹ Information

Airport tourist office (☏971 78 95 56;
⊘8am-8pm Mon-Sat, 9am-1.30pm Sun) Tourist
information.

Azul Cybercafé (Carrer de la Soledat 4;
internet access per hr €2.90; ⊘9am-1.30pm &
3-7pm Mon-Fri, noon-4pm Sat)

Consell de Mallorca tourist office (☏971 71 22
16; www.infomallorca.net; Plaça de la Reina 2;
⊘8am-8pm Mon-Fri, 9am-2pm Sat) Covers the
whole island. For cultural and sporting events,
consult *On Anar*, its free quarterly what's-hap-
pening guide with a version in English.

Municipal tourist office (☏902 10 23 65;
Casal Solleric, Passeig d'es Born 27; ⊘9am-
8pm Mon-Sat) Also has a branch in the train
station.

Visit Palma (www.visit-palma.com) Palma's
hotel association's website.

ℹ Getting Around

Sant Joan airport is about 10km east of Palma.
For trains and buses to other parts of the island,
see p603.

TO/FROM THE AIRPORT Bus 1 runs every 15
minutes between Sant Joan airport and Plaça
d'Espanya in central Palma and on to the ferry
terminal. A taxi costs €15 to €20.

BUS There are 25 local bus services around
Palma and its bay suburbs with **EMT** (☏971 21
44 44; www.emtpalma.es). Single-trip tickets
cost €1.10 or you can buy a 10-trip card for €8.
For the beaches at S'Arenal, take bus 15 from
Plaça d'Espanya.

TAXI For a taxi, call ☏971 75 54 40.

Southwest Coast

A freeway skirts around the Badia de Palma
towards Mallorca's southwest coast. Along
the way you'll pass the resorts of Cala Major, Ses Illetes (lovely little beaches), Palma
Nova and Magaluf (nice long beaches and
mass British tourism), all basically a continuation of Palma's urban sprawl. From Andratx
(worth a stop for a taste of an inland Mallorca town, especially busy in the early evening
when people sit around for drinks at terraces
on Plaça d'Espanya and Plaça des Pou), two
turn-offs lead down to the coast: one goes to
Port d'Andratx and the other to Sant Elm.

WORTH A TRIP

A SLOW CHUG NORTH TO SÓLLER

A delightful journey into the past is
also a pleasing way to head north
from Palma de Mallorca for Sóller.
Since 1912, a narrow-gauge train with
timber-panelled carriages has trun-
dled along this winding 27km route
from Plaça de l'Estació (one-way/
return €10/17, 1¼ hours, up to seven
times daily). You pass through ever-
changing countryside that becomes
dramatic in the north as it crosses the
Serra de Alfàbia, offering fabulous
views over Sóller and the sea on the
final descent into town.

PORT D'ANDRATX

Port d'Andratx spreads around low hills surrounding a narrow bay, where yachties hang
out. A couple of dive schools are based here.

Two hundred metres back from the harbour, Hostal-Residencia Catalina Vera
(☏971 67 19 18; www.hostalcatalinavera.es;
Carrer Isaac Peral 63; s/d €44/68) is a lovely
guest-house retreat, with rooms set around
a tranquil garden courtyard. The best
doubles have balconies and prices haven't
budged in years.

A couple of blocks inland from the waterfront, Restaurante La Gallega (☏971 67 13
38; Carrer Isaac Peral 52; meals €30; ⊘Tue-Sun,
closed Nov) is a popular local seafood restaurant overlooked by many visitors, enticed
by the pricier waterfront alternatives.

SANT ELM

The seaside hamlet of Sant Elm is popular for day trips from Palma. The last part
of the drive across from Andratx via the
sleepy village of S'Arracó is a spectacular,
7km winding route through leafy hills. If
you'd rather walk this section, take a regular bus from Palma to Andratx (€4, 30 minutes, 20 daily).

Sant Elm's sandy beach is pleasant, but
can get crowded. Just offshore is a small
rocky islet – within swimming distance for
the fit. Further north is a small dock from
where you can join a **glass-bottomed boat
tour** or take a 15-minute **boat trip** (€10, five
daily February to November) to the imposing, uninhabited Illa Sa Dragonera, which
is criss-crossed with good walking trails.

A PLACE IN THE SUN OR RURAL GETAWAY

Renting apartments, studios, bungalows and villas has long been a popular way to stay on the islands. Rural accommodation, often in stylishly transformed tranquil country retreats (almost always with a pool), has become especially popular. Mallorca leads the way with some truly beautiful, bucolic options. We note some in the course of this chapter. A great deal more can be found in Lonely Planet's *Mallorca*. Otherwise, these websites will get you started:

» www.fincas4you.com

» www.fincasinmallorca.com

» www.mallorca.co.uk

» www.rusticrent.com

» www.topfincas.com

Trails lead northwest out of the village to La Trapa, a former monastery, and pebbly Cala d'En Basset cove. Reckon on an hour each way for each.

Northwest Coast & Serra de Tramuntana

Dominated by the rugged Serra de Tramuntana range, Mallorca's northwest coast and its hinterland make up 'the other Mallorca'. There are no sandy beach resorts here. The coastline is rocky and largely inaccessible and villages are mostly built of local stone. The mountainous interior is much loved by walkers for its stirring landscapes of pine forests, olive groves and spring wildflowers. Beautiful in summer, it's a peaceful, virtually year-round destination for walkers.

The main road through the mountains (the Ma10) runs roughly parallel to the coast between Andratx and Pollença. It's a stunning, scenic drive and hugely popular bicycling route, especially during spring, when the muted mountain backdrop of browns, greys and greens is splashed with the bright colours of yellow wattles, blood-red poppies and garish cycling vests. There are plenty of well-sited miradors to punctuate your trip.

ESTELLENCS

POP 390

Estellencs is a pretty village of stone buildings scattered around rolling hills below the Puig Galatzó (1025m) peak. It's a popular base for walkers and cyclists. A rugged walk of about 1km leads down to a cove with crystal-clear water.

The higgledy-piggledy, stone Petit Hotel Sa Plana (☎971 61 86 66; www.saplana.com; Carrer de Eusebi Pascual; s €75, d €90-110; ❄📶🏊), with its tousled garden, is family owned and particularly welcoming. Each of its five rooms is distinctive and tastefully decorated with period furnishings.

BANYALBUFAR

POP 600

Eight kilometres northeast of Estellencs, Banyalbufar is similarly positioned high above the coast. Surrounded by steep, stone-walled farming terraces carved into the hillside, the village has a cluster of bars and cafes, plus three hotels.

The four guest rooms of charming stone Ca Madò Paula (☎971 14 87 17; www.camadopaula.com; Carrer de la Constitució 11; d up to €110; ❄@📶) are decorated simply with a few antique touches and a couple have sea views. The small dining room could be that of your Mallorcan granny.

The Palma–Estellencs bus passes through Banyalbufar four to nine times daily.

VALLDEMOSSA

POP 2000

Valldemossa is an attractive blend of tree-lined streets, old stone houses and impressive new villas. The ailing composer Frédéric Chopin and his lover, writer George Sand, spent their 'winter of discontent' here in 1838–39.

Sights & Activities

Real Cartuja de Valldemossa MONASTERY

(adult/child €8.50/4; ⌚9.30am-4.30pm Mon-Sat, 10am-1pm Sun) The lovers stayed in this grand monastery that had been turned into rental accommodation after its monks were expelled in 1835. Their stay wasn't entirely happy and Sand later wrote *Un Hiver à Mallorque* (A Winter in Mallorca), which, if nothing else, made her perennially unpopular with Mallorcans.

Tour buses arrive in droves to visit the monastery, a beautiful building with lovely gardens and fine views. In the couple's former quarters are Chopin's piano (which, due to shipping delays, arrived only three weeks before their departure), his death mask and several original manuscripts. Entry includes a 15-minute piano recital (up to eight times daily) and entry to the adjacent 14th-century Palau del Rei Sanxo (King Sancho's Palace) and local museum.

Costa Nord MULTIMEDIA DISPLAY
(Avenida de Palma 6; adult/child €5/free; ☺9.30am-5pm Mon-Fri, 9am-1.30pm Sat & Sun) After a 15-minute three-screen evocation of the history of Valldemossa, narrated by Michael Douglas (who has a villa outside Port de Valldemossa), test your sea legs with a virtual trip aboard Nixe, the yacht of Archduke Luis Salvador.

Camino del Archiduque WALK
More actively, stretch those legs by walking this 3½-hour circular route from Valldemossa that offers dizzyingly spectacular coastal views and seascapes.

Port de Valldemossa WALK/DRIVE
From Valldemossa, a tortuous 7km road leads down to this rocky cove with a dozen or so buildings.

🛏 Sleeping & Eating

TOP CHOICE **Es Petit Hotel** BOUTIQUE HOTEL €€€
(📞971 61 24 79; www.espetithotel-valldemossa.com; Carrer d'Uetam 1; d from €125; ❄) This friendly family home (the owners still live here) has been converted into an enticing boutique hotel. In the shady garden and on the terrace with a countryside view where humanity scarcely intrudes, you could be an island away from the flow of Cartuja visitors that streams by the front door (which they lock at peak times to keep the hordes at bay!). Everything is done with an eye to detail and comfort and the ample buffet breakfast bursts with variety.

Restaurant Es Port SPANISH €€
(📞971 61 61 94; meals €30-35; ☺Feb-Nov) This popular restaurant is located on the seafront in Port de Valldemossa.

❶ Getting There & Away
Bus 210 from Palma to Valldemossa runs five to 12 times daily.

MIRAMAR & CAN MARROIG
Miramar (www.sonmarroig.com, in Spanish; adult/child €4/free; ☺9am-4.45pm), 5km north of Valldemossa on the road to Deià, is one of Habsburg Archduke Luis Salvador's former residences, built on the site of a 13th-century monastery, of which only a small part of the cloister remains.

Can Marroig (admission €4; ☺9.30am-7.30pm Mon-Sat), 2km further on, is another of the archduke's residences. Altogether more opulent, it's a delightful, rambling mansion, crammed with furniture and period items. The views are the stuff of dreams. Wander 3km down to the coast and Foradada, a high hole in the rock where the sea peeks through.

DEIÀ
POP 750
Deià is perhaps Mallorca's most famous village. Its setting is idyllic, with a cluster of stone buildings cowering beneath steep hillsides terraced with vegetable gardens, vineyards and fruit orchards.

Such beauty has always been a drawcard and Deià was once second home to an international colony of writers, actors and musicians. The most famous member was the English writer Robert Graves, who died here in 1985 and is buried in the town's hillside cemetery.

◉ Sights & Activities
The Ma10 passes though the village centre, where it becomes the main street. Several pricey artists' workshops and galleries sell locally produced work.

❶ BUSSING AROUND THE NORTHWEST

Between April and October, two daily buses leave Ca'n Picafort and Port de Sóller simultaneously at 9am and 3pm. Though very few passengers make the whole journey, the service is particularly popular with walkers. The following list shows the duration of the bus trip between each stop.

Port de Sóller–Sóller 10 minutes

Sóller–Monasteri de Lluc one hour

Monasteri de Lluc–Cala Sant Vicenç 30 minutes

Cala Sant Vicenç–Port de Pollença 15 minutes

Port de Pollença–Alcúdia 15 minutes

Alcúdia–Port d'Alcúdia 15 minutes

Port d'Alcúdia–Ca'n Picafort 30 minutes

WORTH A TRIP

RUTA DE PEDRA EN SEC

A week's walk would see you traverse the Serra de Tramuntana from Port d'Andratx to Pollença, mostly following old mule trails that are often cobbled. You'd be following the partially completed 135km GR221 long-distance trail, aka the Ruta de Pedra en Sec (Dry Stone Route). The 'dry stone' refers to an age-old building method throughout the island. In the mountains you'd see farming terraces, houses, walls and more built of stone without mortar. Eventually the signed trail will have eight stages, with a *refugi* (mountain hostel) waiting for you at the end of each day. For a detailed guide to the route so far, pick up *GR221: Mallorca's Dry Stone Way* by Charles Davis. Also check out www.conselldemallorca.net/mediambient/pedra.

Casa Robert Graves   HISTORIC BUILDING
(www.fundaciorobertgraves.com; Ca N'Alluny; adult/child €5/2.50; ⊙10am-4.15pm Mon-Fri, 10am-2pm Sat) Graves moved to Deià in 1929 and had his house built here. A five-minute walk out along the road to Sóller, Casa Robert Graves is a fascinating tribute to the writer, furnished as if he'd just stepped out for a stroll. Begin with the evocative audiovisual presentation, roam through the house and savour its lovely garden.

Cala Deià   BEACH
This shingled beach is a popular swimming spot with a couple of busy summertime bar-restaurants. The steep walking track from town takes about half an hour. You can also drive down (3km from central Deià), but competition for a parking spot (€5 for the day) can be intense.

Deià Coastal Path   WALK
Some fine walks criss-cross the area, such as this gentle path to the pleasant hamlet of Lluc Alcari (three hours return). Another nearby option is the old mule trail between Deià and Sóller (two hours each way).

Parish Church   CHURCH
The village's steep cobbled lanes lead to the parish church, which has an attached museum.

🛏 Sleeping

Hostal Miramar   FAMILY HOTEL €€
(☎971 63 90 84; www.pensionmiramar.com; Carrer de Ca'n Oliver; r incl breakfast with/without bathroom €84/75; ⊙Mar–mid-Nov) Hidden within the lush vegetation above the main road and with views across to Deià's hillside church and the sea beyond, this 19th-century stone house with gardens is a shady retreat with nine rooms. Various artists (you can scarcely see the breakfast room walls for canvases) have stayed here over the years.

S'Hotel des Puig   HOTEL €€€
(☎971 63 94 09; www.hoteldespuig.com; Carrer des Puig 4; s/d incl breakfast €90/145; ⊙Feb-Nov; ❄🛜🏊) The eight rooms of this gem in the middle of the old town reflect a muted modern taste within ancient stone walls. At the rear of the hotel on the hill are a cool pool and quiet terrace.

Hotel Costa d'Or   HOTEL €€€
(☎971 63 90 25; www.hoposa.com; s/d incl breakfast from €99/171; ⊙Apr-Oct; ❄@🛜🏊) This secluded spot is on the coast 3km north of Deià, in the hamlet of Lluc Alcari. Designer rooms are in a stone building that backs on to woods high above the Med. Rooms with sea views cost considerably more, but you get the same views from the restaurant, terrace and pool. A 15-minute walk through pine forest takes you down to a little pebbly beach with crystal-clear water.

🍴 Eating

El Barrigón de Xelini   TAPAS €
(Avinguda del Arxiduc Lluís Salvador 19; meals €20; ⊙Tue-Sun) You never quite know what to expect here, but tapas, more than 50 kinds drawn from all over Spain, are at the core. It has a penchant for lamb mains, too. On summer weekends, there's live jazz on offer.

Sebastian   MEDITERRANEAN €€
(☎971 63 94 17; Carrer de Felip Bauzà 2; mains €23-27; ⊙dinner Thu-Tue) With its bare stone walls and crisp white linen, Sebastian offers a refined dining environment. The menu is short and subtle with three fish mains and three meat choices, each enhanced with a delicate sauce or purée.

❶ Information

Deià Mallorca (www.deia.info) Check out this website for information about the town.

SÓLLER
POP 13,950

The shady ochre town of Sóller is set amid citrus orchards in a broad valley. Behind it rise the stone walls of the Serra de Tramuntana. It makes a fine base for exploration of the northwest, whether on foot or by vehicle.

The main square, Plaça de la Constitució, is 100m downhill from the train station, which also hosts a couple of intriguing art exhibitions (⊙10am-6.30pm) of Spanish masters – the Sala Picasso (ceramics) and Sala Miró (prints). Around the square are bars and restaurants, the town hall and the large, mainly baroque Església de San Bartolomé (⊙11am-1.15pm & 3-5.15pm Mon-Thu, 11am-1.15pm Fri & Sat). Its Modernista facade was designed by a student of Antoni Gaudí, who is also responsible for the even more strikingly Modernista frontage of the Banco de Sóller (nowadays Banco de Santander), right beside the church.

A 1km stroll west of the square leads to the Jardí Botànic (www.jardibotanicdesoller. org; adult/child €5/free; ⊙10am-6pm Tue-Sat, 10am-2pm Sun), a peaceful botanical garden that showcases flowers and other plants native to the islands.

Do jump aboard one of Sóller's open-sided, vintage wooden **trams** (€4), which rattle 2km down to Port de Sóller on the coast. They depart from the train station every 30 minutes between 7am and 8.30pm.

The Sóller area has plenty of boutique hotels in historic buildings and country houses; many are listed on www.sollernet. com. Right beside the train station, family-run Hotel El Guía (☑971 63 02 27; www. sollernet.com/elguia; Carrer del Castanyer 2; s/d €53/84) is a good place to meet fellow walkers. Its bright, simple rooms feature timber trims and modern bathrooms and it runs a creditable restaurant.

In a former cart workshop, Ca's Carreter (☑971 63 51 33; Carrer del Cetre 9; menúes €12, mains around €16; ⊙lunch & dinner Tue-Sat, lunch Sun) is a welcoming spot that serves modest Mallorcan cooking, including fresh local fish and other mainly local ingredients.

Among the 40 or so trays of locally made ice creams at Sa Fabrica de Gelats (www. gelatsoller.com; Plaça del Mercat), those concocted from fresh orange or lemon juice are outstanding. To take away, or lick or savour slowly in the peaceful patio.

Sóller's tourist office (☑971 63 80 08; www.sollernet.com; ⊙9.45am-2pm & 3.15-5pm Mon-Fri, 9.15am-3pm Sat) is in an old train carriage beside the station. For planning walks around and beyond the Sóller basin, pick up the tourist office's pamphlet Sóller Bon Dia Senderismo. Lonely Planet's Walking in Spain describes three splendid day walks that set out from the village.

BINIARAIX & FORNALUTX

From Sóller it's a pleasant 2km drive, pedal or stroll through narrow laneways up to the hamlet of Biniaraix. From there, a classic walk ascends the Barranc de Biniaraix, following part of the old pilgrim route from Sóller to the Monestir de Lluc.

Climbing northwards, the narrow, twisting scenic road climbs to Fornalutx, through terraced citrus groves.

Fornalutx is a pretty village of distinctive stone houses with green shutters, colourful flower boxes and well-kept gardens, many now owned by expats.

Fornalutx Petit Hotel (☑971 63 19 97; www.fornalutxpetithotel.com; Carrer de l'Alba 22; s/d €80/145; ⊙mid-Feb–mid-Nov; ❄@🖙🐾), a tastefully converted former convent just below the main square, is as much art gallery as boutique hotel. Each of the eight rooms is named after a contemporary Mallorcan painter and displays their canvases, all of which are for sale. The former chapel, converted into a suite (€240), is especially pleasing. There's a free guest sauna and hot tub and a wonderful terrace with views over the fertile valley. Should you want to exchange travel anecdotes, the couple who owns it spent three years sailing around the world.

MOORS & CHRISTIANS IN IMMORTAL COMBAT

Every second weekend in May, Sóller is invaded by a motley crew of Muslim pirates. Es Firó, involving over 1000 townsfolk, is a good-natured mock battle between pagesos (locals) and moros (Moors). Soller's take on Moros i Cristians (Moors and Christians) celebrates the repelling of a Moorish raiding party on 11 May 1561. Locals dress up and black up as scimitar-waving Moorish pirates, pitched against pole-toting defenders in a series of mock engagements, to the thunder of drums and blunderbusses.

WORTH A TRIP

CALA TUENT

If you have wheels, you can skip the crowd scenes of Sa Calobra. Around 2km before the tiny port, follow a turn-off west for Cala Tuent, a tranquil emerald-green inlet with a pebble beach in the shadow of Puig Major.

You'll eat like royalty at Ca N'Antuna (971 63 30 68; Carrer de Arbona Colom 14; mains around €15; lunch & dinner Tue-Sat, lunch Sun), a restaurant overlooking the village, from which it's 500m northeast on the Ma2121. As indeed did Queen Sofía of Spain when she lunched here. It's locally famous for its meat dishes, such as *lechona asada* (crispy roast pork) and *conejo con cebolla* (rabbit with onions).

SA CALOBRA

The 12km road between the Ma10 and the small port of Sa Calobra is a spectacular drive. Carved through weird mountainous rock formations, it skirts narrow ridges and twists down to the coast in an endless series of hairpin bends. You won't be alone in Sa Calobra. Armies of buses and fleets of pleasure boats disgorge battalion after battalion of visitors. A short trail through a rock tunnel leads to a small cove with some fabulous but often crowded swimming spots and, upstream, a spectacular river gorge, the Torrent de Pareis.

Boats make spectacular excursions beneath the cliffs from Port de Sóller to Sa Calobra, some calling by Cala Tuent.

MONESTIR DE LLUC

Legend has it that, some time in the 13th century, a shepherd boy and a monk stumbled across a small statue of the Virgin Mary beside a stream and took it to the parish church. The next day, it had vanished and reappeared on the stream bank. After this happened twice more, the villagers got the message and built a chapel to shelter the sacred statue where it was originally found.

A monastery was established shortly thereafter. Since then thousands of pilgrims come every year to pay homage to the statue of the Virgin of Lluc, known as *La Moreneta* (The Little Dark One). At 11.15am and 4.45pm Monday to Friday and 11am on Sunday, *Els Blauets,* the famed boys' choir, sings. Founded nearly 500 years ago, they're called The Blues for the colour of their cassocks.

The present monastery (www.lluc.net; admission free; 8.30am-8pm) is a huge, austere complex, dating from the 18th century. Off the central courtyard is the entrance to the Basílica de la Mare de Déu; the statue of the Virgin is in the ambulatory behind its main altar. There's also a museum (admission €4; 10am-2pm Sun-Fri) of local archaeological finds and a modest art collection.

The monastery's vast accommodation section, Santuari de Lluc (971 87 15 25; s/d €35/40), is popular with school groups, walkers and pilgrims. Downstairs rooms are dark and best avoided. Be prepared to make your own bed. There are also some apartments with cooking facilities (€48). Around the complex are several restaurants and cafes.

POLLENÇA
POP 17,260

Next stop on the Mallorcan pilgrimage is this attractive inland town. The devout climb up Calvari (Calvary), 365 stone steps leading to a hilltop chapel. The views from the top are well worth the effort. Central Plaça Major is a good place to relax; its cafes and restaurants (including the venerable Club Pollença, which recently celebrated its first century) have broad terraces.

If you're around on 2 August and notice a bunch of wild buccaneers disembarking, don't worry. It's just Pollença enjoying its **Festes de la Patrona**, celebrating the whupping of Muslim invaders back in 1550.

A 1.5km road, best attacked on foot, ascends south of the town up to the former monastery of Santuari de la Mare de Déu des Puig (971 18 41 32; d €22), where you can stay in basic former cells. Booking is mandatory. Even if you don't fancy such an ascetic experience, it's worth the climb for a superb wraparound panorama.

Restaurant Eu Centro (971 53 50 82; Carrer del Temple 3; mains €9-13; Thu-Tue), just north of Plaça Major, offers Mallorcan cooking and tapas, with favourites such as *tumbet* (layered mixed-vegetable bake) and *frit mallorquí* (lamb offal and vegetable fry-up).

CALA SANT VICENÇ

A series of four jewel-like coves, this is a tranquil resort in a magnificent setting.

Yes, there are plenty of English breakfasts and German bratwurst, but the impact's minimal compared with the big beaches further southeast. And the water is so limpid you feel you could see to the centre of the world.

Set back from the road between Cala Molins and Cala Carbo, **Hostal los Pinos** (☎971 53 12 10; www.hostal-lospinos.com; s/d incl breakfast €44/70; ☺May–mid-Oct; ☀) has two gleaming white villas sitting on a leafy hillside. Superior doubles have partial sea views, plus separate sleeping and lounge areas and balconies. It's relaxed and peaceful, yet only a short walk from the beachside action.

PORT DE POLLENÇA
On the north shore of the Badia de Pollença, this resort is popular with British families on package breaks. Sailboards and yachts can be hired on the beaches. South of town, the bay's shore line becomes quite rocky and the beaches are less attractive.

CAP DE FORMENTOR
A splendid drive leads from Port de Pollença out high along this rocky promontory. Stop at the **Mirador de Sa Creueta** (232m), 3km out of Port de Pollença, for a dramatic view. Midway along the promontory is the historic **Hotel Formentor**, a jewel of pre-WWII days, and the nearby shady strand of **Platja de Formentor** (aka Platja del Pi). Another spectacular 11km bring you to the lighthouse on the cape that marks Mallorca's northernmost tip.

Badia d'Alcúdia
The long beaches of this bay fringe Mallorca's northeast coast, its broad sweeps of sand stretching from Port d'Alcúdia to Ca'n Picafort.

ALCÚDIA
POP 19,100
Wedged between the Badia de Pollença and Badia d'Alcúdia, busy Alcúdia was once a Roman settlement. Remnants of the Roman theatre survive and the old town is still partly protected by largely rebuilt medieval walls. Wander through the Roman ruins of **Pollentia** (www.pollentia.net; adult/child €3/2; ☺9.30am-8pm Tue-Sun), just outside the ramparts. The pleasant town centre is worth a look, too.

Fonda Llabres (☎971 54 50 00; www.fondallabres.com; Plaça de sa Constitució 6; s/d €30/36; ☀) offers cheap yet comfortable beds. It occupies a pair of buildings (one was the former telephone exchange) in the heart of the village. Even less expensive rooms without private bathrooms are also available.

Bus 351 from Palma (€4.60, one hour) calls at Alcúdia hourly.

PORT D'ALCÚDIA
A lovely stretch of sand arcs southwards from the large harbour, from where boat trips leave daily to destinations such as **Platja de Formentor**. Nearby **Cap des Pinar** is a pretty peninsula that lends itself to cycling and hiking.

Parc Natural de S'Albufera (☺9am-5pm), a protected wetland just south of Port d'Alcúdia, is a birdwatchers' paradise, where more than 300 species have been spotted. Leaving the main Ma12, it's a pleasant 1km canalside and duckboard walk to the visitors centre. From here you can follow three short, signed walks of about 750m, each with hides and observation platforms.

The 17 doubles of tidy, friendly **Hostal Vista Alegre** (☎971 54 73 47; www.hvista-alegre.com; Passeig Marítim 10; s/d €20/35; ☀) face inland and have air-con (€5 extra). Exceptions are three large triples, which face the port and have a small balcony: no air-con here – but who needs it with the sea breezes puffing in?

CA'N PICAFORT & AROUND
A smaller version of Port d'Alcúdia, Ca'n Picafort is a package-tour frontier town. It's somewhat raw and soulless, but the beaches are pretty good. About 5km further south along the coast is Son Serra de Marina, whose southeast edge is capped by a fine 2km-long beach favoured by windsurfers.

Set back from the Ma12 south of Ca'n Picafort at the Km17.7 milepost, Can Sol is a complex of former farm buildings. From them, three signed trails (2km to 3.5km one way) lead down to **Son Real** (☺10am-4pm) nature park and Mallorca's largest necropolis. Within the main building is a highly recommended, sensitively conceived **multimedia display** (adult/child €5/2.50) illustrating traditional Mallorcan rural life.

HOLGER LEUE

JON DAVISON

1

1. D'Alt Vila, Ibiza City (p614)

D'Alt Vila's 16th-century walls were raised by Felipe II; the town is a Unesco World Heritage Site.

2. Cala Sant Vicenç (p608)

A tranquil resort in a magnificent setting in a series of four jewel-like coves.

3. Castell de Bellver (p600)

An unusual, circular 14th-century castle (with a unique round tower) set atop a pleasant park.

2

4. Palma de Mallorca (p596)

Mallorca's only true city contains an enchanting blend of tree-lined boulevards, Gothic churches and designer bars.

5. Menorca's prehistoric sites (p636)

Taulas (horseshoe-shaped sanctuaries with tall T-shaped pillars at their heart) are unique to Menorca.

HOLGER LEUE

East Coast

Many of the fine beaches along Mallorca's east coast have succumbed to the ravages of mass tourism. Beside much of its northern half stretch a series of concrete jungles that rivals the worst excesses of the Costa del Sol on the Spanish mainland. Further south the coastline is corrugated with a series of smaller coves and ports, saving it from the same fate.

ARTÀ
POP 7400

Watching over the quiet inland town of Artà is a 14th-century hilltop fortress and **Església de San Salvador**, from where you have a wonderful panorama across the rooftops, countryside and out to sea.

On the coast, 11km southeast of Artà at the limit of the Ma4042, the **Coves d'Artà** (www.cuevasdearta.com; admission €10.50; ⏱10am-5pm), sunken into the cliffs, are a less-visited rival to Porto Cristo's Coves del Drac. Tours of the caves leave every 30 minutes.

TOP CHOICE **Hotel Casal d'Artà** (☎971 82 91 63; www.casaldarta.de; Carrer de Rafael Blanes 19; s/d incl breakfast €55/91; ❄🛜) is a wonderful old mansion in the heart of town. You'll find fresh fruit in your room on arrival and fresh flowers on your breakfast table. There's a flower-filled roof terrace, with a bubbling fountain and incomparable views over the village and – just – the sea. Beside reception is a small self-service honesty bar (drop your money in the piggy bank). Ask for room 4 or 8; both have sybaritic baths sunken into a tiny alcove.

CALA RATJADA
POP 6000

The main streets in this busy but not unattractive resort are wall-to-wall souvenir shops, and the pretty sands are filled with slabs of sizzling flesh. Head for beaches out of town, like **Cala Mesquida**.

Three kilometres inland, the intact **Castell de Capdepera** (adult/child €3/free, audioguide €2; ⏱9am-5pm) rears above the village of the same name. You can walk the battlements and visit its small museum of palmfibre basket weaving, once the mainstay of the village economy. Leave your car below and walk the last, steep stretch.

You can reserve accommodation online at the local hotel association's site, **First Sun Mallorca** (www.firstsunmallorca.com).

DON'T MISS

MALLORCA'S TOP FIVE BEACHES

» **Platja de Formentor** (p609)
» **Cala Llombards** (p613)
» **Cala Sant Vicenç** (p608)
» **Cala Deià** (p606)
» **Es Trenc** (p613)

Bus 411 links Palma de Mallorca and Cala Ratjada (€10, 1¾ hours, five daily), via Artà. In summer, boats run to Ciutadella in Menorca (see p629).

COVES DEL DRAC & PORTO CRISTO

These spectacular and much visited **caves** (Dragon's Caves; www.cuevasdeldrach.com; adult/child €11.50/free; ⏱10am-5pm) are on the southern side of town. A 1km shuffle with the crowd, accompanied by a multilingual commentary, leads to a vast amphitheatre and lake, where you'll enjoy a brief classical music recital. One-hour tours of the caves leave on the hour. Credit cards aren't accepted.

PORTOCOLOM

A tranquil village set on a generous harbour, Portocolom has managed to resist the tourist onslaught with dignity. Within a couple of kilometres are some fine beaches, such as the immaculate cove of **Cala Marçal**.

Right on the waterfront, **Hostal Porto Colom** (☎971 82 53 23; www.hostalportocolom. com; Carrer d'en Cristòfol Colom 5; s/d €55/90, mains €15-20; ❄) has breezy rooms with parquet floors, big beds and sunny decor. Downstairs, there's a cool restaurant and lounge bar.

Buses 490 and 491 run daily to/from Palma via Felanitx (€5.50, 1¾ hours, eight daily).

CALA D'OR TO CALA MONDRAGÓ

Once a quaint fishing village, Cala d'Or is now an overblown big-dollar resort. Its sleek marina is lined with glistening megayachts and blindingly whitewashed villas crowd the surrounding hills.

Immediately south of Cala d'Or (and virtually joined to it by urban sprawl) is the smaller and more tranquil **Portopetro**. Centred on a boat-lined inlet and surrounded by residential estates, it has a cluster of harbourside bars and restaurants, and a couple of small beaches nearby.

Two kilometres south of Portopetro, Cala Mondragó is one of the most attractive coves on the east coast. Sheltered by large rocky outcrops and fringed by pine trees, it has a string of three protected sandy beaches connected by coastal footpaths.

With a full five storeys, Hotel Playa Mondragó (971 65 77 52; www.playamondrago.com; Cala Mondragó; s/d incl breakfast €63/96; Easter-Oct;) is barely 50m back from the most accessible beach. It's a tranquil option, where the better rooms have balconies and fine sea views.

CALA FIGUERA

The fisherfolk here really still fish, threading their way down the winding inlet before dawn, while tourists sleep off the previous night's food and drink. What has probably kept the place in one piece is the fact that the nearest beach, pretty Cala Santanyí, is a few kilometres drive southwest.

Nicer still is Cala Llombards, which you can walk to (scaling endless stairs) from Cala Santanyí or drive to via Santanyí (follow signs to Llombards, then Cala Llombards).

Barely 300m from the port of Cala Figuera, Hostal Mar Blau (971 64 52 27; www.marblau.eu; s €29-37, d €38-46; Apr-Oct;) is a friendly, particularly well-priced option. Rooms (the more expensive ones have air-con and a fridge) are clean as a new pin. For greater independence, go for one of the fully equipped apartments (€46 to €80, minimum stay three days), some of which have sea views.

Bus 502 makes the trip from Palma (€6.50, 1¾ hours) via Colònia de Sant Jordi twice a day.

COLÒNIA DE SANT JORDI

On the southeast coast, the resort town of Colònia de Sant Jordi is unexciting. Some good beaches lurk nearby, however, particularly Ses Arenes and Es Trenc (with a nudist strip), both a few kilometres up the coast towards Palma.

On the former prison island of Cabrera, 18km offshore, more than 5000 French soldiers died after being abandoned in 1809 by their Spanish captors towards the end of the Peninsular War. It and the surrounding islets form the protected Parc Nacional Arxipèlag de Cabrera.

Excursions A Cabrera (971 64 90 34; www.excursionsacabrera.com, in Spanish; adult/child €38/20; Apr-Oct) does full-day boat trips to the island, while Marcabrera (622 574806; www.marcabrera.com; adult/child €38/30) offers two-hour speedboat trips around the archipelago, including time ashore.

The Interior

East of the Serra de Tramuntana, Mallorca's interior is a largely flat and fertile plain. Occupied by partly abandoned farmland and often fairly unremarkable agricultural townships, it marks its own time and holds various low-key gems.

Several of the island's larger inland towns are well known for their specialised products. Binissalem is a major centre of the island's wine industry (which produces small quantities of, at times, great whites and reds), while Felanitx is at the heart of another wine-producing area; the latter also has a name for ceramics. Inca is the seat of much of Spain's leather and shoe production, and it has plenty of outlets and shops – check out Gran Via de Colom and Avinguda del General Luque. Industrial and melancholy, Manacor is known for furniture-making and manufactured pearls – the main Majorica factory has a huge shop just inside town on the road in from Palma. It's also the birthplace of tennis megastar Rafael Nadal.

Just 6km east of Felanitx and atop a 510m hill, the fortresslike Santuari de Sant Salvador broods over the landscape. The monks are long since gone from Petit Hotel San Salvador (971 51 52 60; www.santsalvadorhotel.com; s/d €45/68, buffet dinner €15), but their former cells have been converted into simple, spruce rooms, each with an outstanding panoramic view and private bathroom. The hotel runs a great little cafe (not to be confused with the grim alternative within the monastery itself).

IBIZA

For many, Ibiza (Eivissa in Catalan) means endless partying in Mediterranean macroclubs. There is, however, another side to the island. The Greeks called Ibiza and Formentera the Islas Pitiusas (Islands of Pine Trees). The landscape is harsh and rocky. Alongside hardy pines, the most common crops are olives, figs and almonds. Surprisingly, about half the island (especially the

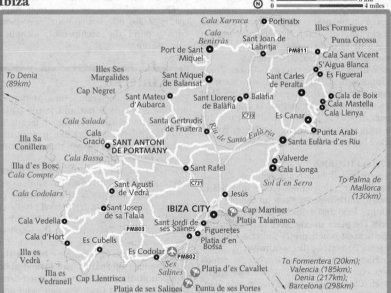

MALLORCA, MENORCA & IBIZA IBIZA

comparatively unspoilt northeast) remains covered by thick woods.

In 1956 the island boasted 12 cars and in the 1960s the first hippies from mainland Europe began to discover its idyllic beaches. A mixed World Heritage Site because of Ibiza City's architecture and the island's rich sea life, Ibiza soon latched on to the money-spinner of bulk tourism. Today the resident populace of 117,700 watches on as millions (more than four million passengers annually pass through its airport) visit S'Illa Blanca (The White Island) each year.

Birthplace of the rave, Ibiza has some of Spain's most (in)famous clubs and plenty of bars. But coastal walking trails, woods and quiet (if not deserted) beaches allow you to elude Ministry of Sound–style madness, too.

ⓘ Getting Around

TO/FROM THE AIRPORT Bus 9 goes to the airport from Sant Antoni every 1½ hours; bus 10 from Ibiza City every 20 minutes; and bus 24 from Es Canar via Santa Eulària every two hours.

BUS Fares don't exceed €3 for the longest journey. Tourist offices carry the free *Ibiza's Public Transport Guide,* which gives details of bus routes and times throughout the island. Online, check out www.eivissabus.info.

CAR & MOTORCYCLE The big boys have car-hire desks at the airport and in Ibiza City. Local (and often cheaper) outfits are scattered around the island. The bulk of those in Ibiza City gather around Carrer de Felipe II and Carrer de Carles III, just west of the port.

Ibiza City

POP 44,800

Ibiza's capital is a vivacious, enchanting town with a captivating old quarter. It's also a focal point for some of the island's best nightlife.

⊙ Sights

D'ALT VILA & AROUND

From Sa Penya wander up into D'Alt Vila, the old walled town (and a Unesco World Heritage Site). The Romans were the first to fortify this hilltop, whose existing walls were raised by Felipe II in the 16th century to protect against invasion by French and Turkish forces.

Ramparts   CITY WALLS

A ramp leads from Plaça de Sa Font in Sa Penya up to the **Portal de ses Taules** gateway, the main entrance. Above it hangs a commemorative plaque bearing Felipe II's coat of arms and an inscription recording the 1585 completion date of the fortification – seven artillery bastions joined by thick protective walls up to 22m in height. You can walk the entire perimeter of these impressive Renaissance-era walls, designed to withstand heavy artillery, and enjoy great views along the way.

Catedral
CATHEDRAL

Ibiza's cathedral elegantly combines several styles: the original 14th-century structure is Catalan Gothic but the sacristy was added in 1592 and a major baroque renovation took place in the 18th century. Inside, the Museu Diocesà (admission €1.50; ☺9.30am-1.30pm Tue-Sun, closed Dec-Feb) contains centuries of religious art.

Bastions
FORTIFIED TOWERS

(adult/child €2/1.50; ☺10am-2pm & 6-8pm Tue-Sat, 10am-2pm Sun) In the Baluard de Sant Jaume, an exhibition of military paraphernalia includes soldiers' cuirasses that you can try for size (and weight!) and cannonballs to heave. An exhibition within the Baluard de Sant Pere, the next bastion northwards, demonstrates the tricks of artillery warfare and how to mount a cannon and has an AV illustration of how the city walls were constructed.

Centre d'Interpretació Madina Yabisa
MUSEUM

(Carrer Major 2; adult/child €2/1.50; ☺10am-2pm & 6-8pm Tue-Sat, 10am-2pm Sun) This small display replicates the medieval Muslim city of Madina Yabisa (Ibiza City) prior to the island's fall to Christian forces in 1235. Artefacts, audiovisuals and maps help transport you to those times. The centre is housed in what was, from the 16th century, the Casa de la Cúria (law courts), parts of whose walls were the original Islamic-era defensive walls. Much of the display was inspired by excavations done along Carrer de Santa Maria in the early 2000s.

FREE Necròpolis del Puig des Molins
BURIAL GROUND

(Carrer de la Via Romana 31; ☺10am-2pm & 6-8pm Tue-Sat, 10am-2pm Sun) The earliest tombs within this ancient burial ground date from the 7th century BC and Phoenician times. Follow the path around and peer into the burial caverns, oriented north to south, cut deep into the hill. You can descend into one interlocking series of these *hypogea* (burial caverns). The site museum displays finds such as amulets and terracotta figurines discovered within the more than 3000 tombs that honeycomb the hillside. Both museum and site were closed for restoration work at the time of writing

Museu Arqueològic
MUSEUM

(Plaça de la Catedral 3; adult/child €2.40/free; ☺10am-2pm & 6-8pm Tue-Sat, 10am-2pm Sun) Contains an important collection of artefacts from the Phoenician and Carthaginian periods, plus a few pieces from Roman and Islamic times.

FREE Museu d'Art Contemporani
MUSEUM

(Ronda de Narcís Puget; ☺10am-1.30pm & 4-6pm Tue-Fri, 10am-1.30pm Sat & Sun) Its normal home is within an 18th-century powder store and armoury. While it undergoes lengthy refurbishing, elements of the collection are on show in the Casa Consistorial (Town Hall) on Plaça d'Espanya.

FREE Museu Puget
MUSEUM

(Carrer de Sant Ciriac 18; ☺10am-1.30pm & 5-8pm Tue-Fri, 10am-1.30pm Sat & Sun) A historic mansion with typical late-Gothic courtyard and stairs to the upper floor houses 130 paintings by Ibizan artist Narcís Puget Viñas (1874–1960) and his son, Narcís Puget Riquer (1916–83).

SA PENYA

There's always something going on portside. People-watchers will be right at home – this pocket must have one of the highest concentrations of exhibitionists and weirdos in Spain.

IBIZA WEBSITES

www.ibiza.travel Official Ibiza tourism website.

www.eivissaweb.com Multilingual Ibiza search engine.

www.ibiza-online.com Another general search engine.

www.ibizahotelsguide.com Official website of Ibiza's hoteliers' association.

www.ibizaholidays.com, www.ibiza-spotlight.com Good for accommodation and general island information.

www.casasruralesibiza.com, www.ibizaruralvillas.com For rural villas and houses (both in Spanish).

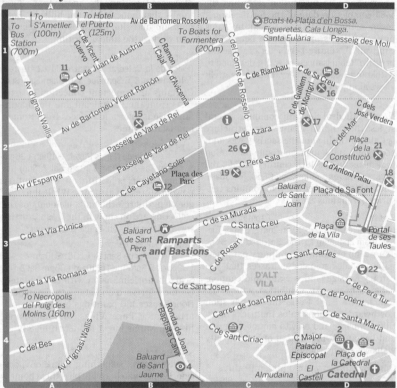

Sa Penya bursts with funky and trashy **clothing boutiques**. The so-called **hippie markets**, street stalls along Carrer d'Enmig and the adjoining streets, sell everything under the sun.

🛏 Sleeping

Hotel Mirador de Dalt Vila

BOUTIQUE HOTEL **€€€**

(☎971 30 30 45; www.hotelmiradoribiza.com; Plaça d'Espanya 4; s €305, d from €450; ⊗Easter-Dec; ❋@🏠🏊) This rose-hued mansion is the Fajarnés family home. The 13 rooms are delightfully furnished. At every turn, public areas display paintings and exquisite objets d'art, all from the family's private collection. The spa-pool has a counter-current swim jet for the active and the restaurant is a gourmet's delight.

Hotel La Ventana

HISTORIC HOTEL **€€€**

(☎971 30 35 37; www.laventanaibiza.com; Carrer de Sa Carrossa 13; d from €165; ❋🏠) This charming 15th-century mansion is set on a little tree-shaded square in the old town. Some rooms come with stylish four-poster beds and mosquito nets. The rooftop terrace, trim gardens and restaurant are welcome extras.

Hostal La Marina

PORTSIDE ACCOMMODATION **€€**

(☎971 31 01 72; www.hostal-lamarina.com; Carrer de Barcelona 7; r €68-125; ❋) Looking onto both the waterfront and bar-lined Carrer de Barcelona, this mid-19th-century building has all sorts of brightly coloured rooms. A handful of singles and some doubles look onto the street (with the predictable noise problem), but you can opt for pricier doubles and attics with terraces and panoramic port and/or town views. The same people run other lodging options along the street.

Hostal-Residencia Parque

SMALL HOTEL **€€**

(☎971 30 13 58; www.hostalparque.com; Carrer de Vicent Cuervo 3; s €80, d €110-170) The

the advantage, in some cases, of balconies overlooking the animated street. It also runs Hostal Juanito (d €50), sans balconies, across the road at No 19.

Casa de Huéspedes Navarro

BUDGET HOTEL €

(🕿971 31 07 71; Carrer de Sa Creu 20; s/d without bathroom €28/55; ⊙May-Oct) Right in the thick of things, this simple option has eight rooms at the top of a long flight of stairs. The front rooms have harbour views, interior ones are quite dark (but cool in summer) and there's a sunny rooftop terrace. Bathrooms are shared but spotless.

🍴 Eating

TOP CHOICE Comidas Bar San Juan

MEDITERRANEAN €

(🕿971 31 16 03; Carrer de Guillem de Montgri 8; meals €15-20; ⊙Mon-Sat) A family-run operation with two small dining rooms, this simple eatery offers outstanding value, with fish dishes for around €10 and many small mains for €6 or less. It doesn't take reservations, so arrive early.

Restaurant Es Mirador

GOURMET €€

(🕿971 30 30 45; Plaça d'Espanya 4; menú €45, mains €26-30; ⊙Easter-Dec) At this intimate – do reserve – restaurant with its painted barrel ceiling and original canvases around the walls, you'll dine magnificently. Service is discreet yet friendly, and dishes are creative, colourful and delightfully presented. Do allow time to sip an *aperitivo* in the equally cosy bar; at your feet is an underfloor display of antiquities recovered from the sea.

Can Costa

IBIZAN €

(🕿971 31 08 65; Carrer de Sa Creu 19; menú €10, mains €6.50-12.50; ⊙Mon-Sat) Amid Ibiza's posing and pretension, it's a joy to find this simple, no-fuss Spanish eatery, with its plastic check tablecloths and artificial flowers, Grandmother busy in the back and Dad taking orders, a towel slung over his shoulders. Begin with their thick, deeply satisfying *potaje de la casa* (house soup), select one of the exceptionally well-priced, ample mains and finish with a homemade dessert, such as the egg-rich *flan de coco* (coconut caramel custard).

Ca n'Alfredo

IBIZAN €€

(🕿971 31 12 74; Passeig de Vara de Rei 16; menú €30, mains €18-30; ⊙lunch & dinner Tue-Sat, lunch Sun) Locals have been flocking to Alfredo's since 1934. It's great place for the

best doubles here overlook pleasant Plaça des Parc from above the eponymous cafe. Doubles are comfortable but singles are predictably poky. Best are the three attic rooms (€130 to €170), with their own terrace and views of the old town.

Hotel El Puerto

HOTEL, APARTMENTS €€

(🕿971 31 38 12; www.ibizaelpuerto.com; Carrer de Carles III 22; s/d €90/140; ❂@🛜🏊) The hotel offers more than 90 rooms and a similar number of apartments (€150 for two people). Just outside the old town, it's handy for the Formentera ferry. Rooms are fairly standard, but some are generous in size and the pool is a plus.

Hostal Las Nieves

HOTEL €€

(🕿971 19 03 19; www.hostalibiza.com; Carrer de Juan de Austria 18; d with bathroom €75, s/d without bathroom €30/60) One of several simple *hostales* in the El Pratet area, this place offers fairly spartan rooms but with

Ibiza City

freshest of seafood and other island cuisine that's so good it's essential to book. Try the *filetes de gallo de San Pedro en salsa de almendras* (John Dory fillets in almond sauce).

S'Ametller IBIZAN €€
(☎971 31 17 80; www.restaurantsametller.com; Carrer de Pere Francesc 12; menú €19.50, meals €30-35; ☉lunch Mon-Thu, lunch & dinner Fri & Sat) The 'Almond Tree' offers local cooking based upon fresh market produce. The daily *menú* (for dessert, choose the house *flaó*, a mint-flavoured variant on cheesecake and a Balearic Islands speciality) is inventive and superb value. As an indication of its credentials, S'Ametller also offers cookery courses – including one that imparts the secrets of that *flaó*.

La Scala INTERNATIONAL €€
(☎971 30 03 83; www.la-scala.com; Plaça de sa Carrossa 7; meals €40; ☉dinner Wed-Sun) This candle-lit place serves international cuisine with a central-European bent. A highlight is its meat dishes. The interior's attractive enough but more appealing is the pretty, floral open-air terrace.

La Brasa GRILLED MEATS €€
(☎971 30 12 02; Carrer Pere Sala 3; menú €10.50, mains €15-20) La Brasa's forte is its quality fish and meat, sizzled over charcoal. An-

other strong feature is its garden, shaded by vines, palms and banana trees and adorned with bursts of bougainvillea.

Croissant Show CAFE €
(☎971 31 76 65; Plaça de la Constitució; ☉6am-11pm) Opposite the food market, this is where *everyone* goes for an impressive range of pastries and other post-partying breakfast goodies. It is quite a scene all on its own.

Mercat de Verdures FOOD MARKET €
(Plaça de la Constitució; ☉7am-7pm Mon-Sat) Buy fresh fruit and vegies from this open-air market, opposite the entrance to D'Alt Vila.

🍸 Drinking & Entertainment

Sa Penya is the nightlife centre. Dozens of bars keep the port area jumping from sunset until the early hours. Alternatively, various bars at Platja d'en Bossa combine sounds, sand and sea with sangria and other tipples. After they wind down, you can continue at one of the island's world-famous discos.

Discobus (www.discobus.es; €3; midnight-6am Jun-Sep) runs around the major discos, bars and hotels in Ibiza City, Platja d'en Bossa, Sant Rafel, Es Canar, Santa Eulària and Sant Antoni.

Bars

Carrer de Barcelona, which runs parallel with the harbour, is lined with high-energy bars. Most have tall tables on the street and pump out loud music. Touts do their damnedest to 'invite' passers-by to join them for a drink, sometimes with the lure of discounted passes to the clubs. All open nightly from early evening until 3am or 4am May to September. Those along Carrer de Garijo Cipriano are a little less in your face.

KM5
CHILL-OUT BAR
(www.km5-lounge.com; Carretera de Sant Josep Km5.6; ⊙8pm-4am May-Sep) This bar, named after its highway location, is where you go to glam it up. Head out of town towards Sant Josep and dance in the gardens as you gear up for the clubs. Lounging is the second major activity and there are plenty of pillows strewn about the tents.

Teatro Pereyra
MUSIC BAR
(📋971 30 44 32; www.teatropereyra.com; Carrer del Comte de Rosselló 3; ⊙8am-4am) Away from the waterfront hubbub, this hugely atmospheric place, all stained wood and iron girders, was once the foyer of the long-abandoned 1893 theatre at its rear. It's packed most nights with a more eclectic crowd than the standard preclubbing bunch, and it offers nightly live music sessions. By day, it's a stylish place for a drink or snack.

Lola's Club
CLASSIC BAR
(C Alfonso XII 10; ⊙1-6am) Anyone who remembers Ibiza in the '80s will have fond memories of Lola's Club, one of the first on the island. It's still a hip miniclub, nowadays with a gay leaning. Right beside it, Lolita (⊙7pm-3am), a sparky little terrace in its own right, is a great spot for a drink before climbing the stairs to join her bigger sister.

Blu
MUSIC BAR
(www.blu-ibiza.com; Carrer de Navarra 27, Figueretes; ⊙10pm-4am) A one-time strip joint, Blu works with some of the island's top promoters to bring good DJ sets to the dance floor. It is also at the lower price end – you can frequently get in for €15 (including first drink). It's in Figueretes one block south of Avinguda d'Espanya, down Carrer del País Basc.

DON'T MISS

IBIZA'S TOP FIVE BEACHES
» **Cala Benirràs** (p623)
» **Cala Mastella** (p622)
» **Cala de Boix** (p622)
» **Cala Xarraca** (p623)
» **Cala Codolars** (p625)

Bora Bora Beach Club
BEACH BAR
(noon-4am May-Sep) At Platja d'en Bossa, about 2km from the old town, this is *the* place – a long beachside bar where sun and fun worshippers work off hangovers and prepare new ones. Entry's free and the ambience is chilled, with low-key club sounds wafting over the sand. From midnight, everyone crowds inside. It's off Carrer del Fumarell.

Zoo Ibiza
BAR
(www.zooibiza.com; Plaça d'Antoni Riquer) A popular option on Carrer de Barcelona.

Gay & Lesbian Venues

The gay scene is based towards the east end of Sa Penya, particularly along the far end of Carrer de la Mare de Déu and around Carrer de Santa Llúcia. Many of the big clubs have special gay nights. Check out www.gayibiza.net.

Anfora
GAY CLUB
(Carrer Sant Carles 7; www.disco-anfora.com; admission €12-17; ⊙Apr-Oct) Seemingly dug out of walls of rock, this is a favourite gay dance haunt high up D'Alt Vila. Heteros are welcome to hang about too.

Angelo
GAY BAR
(Carrer de Santa Llúcia 12) In the shadow of the old city walls, Angelo is a busy gay bar with several levels. The atmosphere is relaxed and heteros wind up here too. Nearby are a handful of other gay-leaning bars, such as the slicker Soap.

ℹ Information

Tourist offices Ibiza City (📋971 39 92 32; www.eivissa.es; Plaça de la Catedral; ⊙10am-2pm & 5-9pm Mon-Sat, 10am-2pm Sun); island-wide office (📋971 30 19 00; www.ibiza. travel; Passeig de Vara de Rei 1; ⊙9am-8pm Mon-Sat, 9am-3pm Sun); port (Carrer Antoni Riquer 2; ⊙9.30am-6pm Mon-Sat, 10am-1pm Sun) Loans free audioguides to the city; bring your passport or identity document.

ⓘ **CYCLING IBIZA**

Tourist offices carry a terrific little free wallet that describes 23 cycle routes around the island. Varying from easy to tough and in time from 45 minutes to eight hours, they'll inspire both easy riders and heads-down hurtlers.

ⓘ Getting There & Away

AIR Ibiza's airport (Aeroport d'Eivissa), just 7km southwest of Ibiza City, receives direct flights from mainland Spanish cities and a host of UK and other European centres.

BOAT Formentera ferries leave from a separate terminal 300m north of the centre.

Aquabus Hourly ferries (one-way/return €3.50/6) to/from Playa d'en Bossa and Figueretes, May to October.

Cruceros Santa Eulalia (www.ferrysanta eulalia.com) Boats to Cala Llonga, Santa Eulària d'es Riu and Es Canar; up to six times daily (all €13 return), May to mid-October.

BUS Buses to other parts of the island depart from the new bus station (nearing completion when we last visited) on Avenida de la Pau, northwest of the town centre.

ⓘ Getting Around

Bus 10 (€3, every 20 minutes) runs from the airport to the central port area via Platja d'en Bossa. There's also an **airport taxi** (☏971 39 84 83; around €15).

Around Ibiza City

Platja de ses Salines and, just over the bluff, Platja d'es Cavallet, at the southernmost tip of the island, are the best beaches within easy striking distance of Ibiza City. The area takes its name from the salt pans exploited here since Carthaginian times – big business until tourism came along.

Across the dunes arcs a long crescent-shaped bay with a broad sandy beach, broken by rocky slabs. The beach, with its scatter of open-air beach bars, is popular with Ibiza's party-hard crowd. Sa Trinxa, at the eastern end of the beach, remains the coolest of the Ses Salines bars. It serves snacks, salads and fruit smoothies – stronger drinks, too – and, when the DJ gets into gear (from 2pm), the temperature rapidly rises.

Platja d'es Cavallet, the next bay around to the east, is Ibiza's official nudist beach, to which you can also drive.

Bus 11 runs eight to 10 times daily to Ses Salines from Ibiza City. A taxi costs around €15.

East Coast

A busy highway (C733) speeds you north out of Ibiza City towards Santa Eulària d'es Riu on the east coast. More scenic is the slower coastal road via Cala Llonga, which winds through low hills and olive groves, with detours along the way to several beaches. To follow it, take the turn-off to Jesús a couple of kilometres northwest of Ibiza City.

Cala Llonga is set on an attractive bay with high rocky cliffs sheltering a lovely sandy beach, but the town itself is blighted by high-rise hotels.

SANTA EULÀRIA D'ES RIU
POP 31,300

Ibiza's third-largest town is a bustling place, with a couple of child-friendly, gently sloping beaches, a large harbour and plenty of 20th-century tourist-resort architecture.

◉ Sights

The hillock of Puig de Missa, a world away from the beaches, is the core of the original town. As well as the pleasant 16th-century church, the Església de Santa Eulària, you'll find the Museu Barrau (◷9.30am-1.30pm Tue-Sat), a white house with blue shutters dedicated to local artist Laureà Barrau; and the Museu Etnogràfic (☏971 33 28 45; adult/child €3/free; ◷10am-2pm Mon-Sat, 11am-1.30pm Sun), which displays farming and household instruments.

⬛ Sleeping & Eating

Modern hotels and apartments crowd the Santa Eulària beachfront. You'll find a cluster of affordable *hostales* a couple of blocks inland.

Most restaurants and cafes along the beachfront are tacky and overpriced. Four blocks back, there are several decent eateries along Carrer de Sant Vicent.

Ca's Català HOTEL €€
(☏971 33 10 06; www.cascatala.com; Carrer del Sol; s €55, d €80-118; ❋�🐟⬚) This cheerful British-run option has the feel of a private villa. The majority of its 12 particularly large rooms overlook a garden courtyard and pool with bar. Most bedrooms have ceiling fans and a few come with air-con.

Doubles, all with four-poster bed, are in attractive, gleaming white.

Hostal-Residencia Sa Rota HOTEL **€€**
(☏971 33 00 22; www.ibiza-hotels.com/sarota; Carrer de Sant Vincent 59; s/d €45/75; ☎) A good-value *hostal,* open year-round, this place features bright, generous rooms (the doubles in particular), with modern bath or shower. The downstairs cafe has a relaxing outdoor extension with an ivy-shaded pergola.

CLUBBING ON IBIZA

From late May to the end of September, the west of the island is one big, continuous dance party from sunset to sunrise and back again. Entrepreneurs have built an amazing collection of clubs here – huge, throbbing temples to which thousands of disciples flock to pay homage to the gods of hedonism. In 2009 the International Dance Music Awards quoted two Ibiza clubs, Pacha and Space, among their worldwide top five.

The major clubs operate nightly from around 1am to 6am. Each has something different to offer. Theme nights, fancy-dress parties and foam parties are regular features. Some places go a step or two further, with go-go girls (and boys), striptease acts and even live sex as the (ahem) climax.

Entertainment Ibiza-style doesn't come cheaply. Admission can cost anything from €25 to €60 (mixed drinks and cocktails then go for around €10 to €15). If you hang out around the right bars in Sa Penya, you might score a flier that entitles you to discounted admission handed out by sometimes scantily clad club promoters and touts – if they think you've got the look.

Different DJ teams make the rounds of the big clubs. One of the best known in Ibiza, Manumission (www.manumission.com), is famous for its sexy acts and has a popular morning slot at least one day a week at Space.

Space CLUB
(www.space-ibiza.es; ⊗Jun–mid-Oct) In Platja d'en Bossa, aptly named Space can pack in as many as 40 DJs and up to 12,000 clubbers. Action here starts mid-afternoon and regular daytime boats make the trip between Platja d'en Bossa and Ibiza City (€6 return).

Pacha CLUB
(www.pacha.com; ⊗nightly Jun-Sep, Fri & Sat Oct-May) In business on the northern side of Ibiza City's port since 1973, Pacha has 15 bars (!) and various dance spaces that can hold 3000 people. The main dance floor, a sea of colour, mirror balls and veils draped from the ceiling, heaves to deep techno. On the terrace, sounds are more gentle and relaxing.

Amnesia CLUB
(www.amnesia.es; ⊗early Jun-Sep) Four kilometres out on the road to Sant Rafel, it has a sound system that seems to give your body a massage. A huge glasshouse-like internal terrace, filled with palms and bars, surrounds the central dance area, a seething mass of mostly tireless 20-something dancers. It gets heated in here, so every now and then icy air is pumped through.

Es Paradis CLUB
(www.esparadis.com; Carrer de Salvador Espriu 2, Sant Antoni; ⊗mid-May–Sep) This club boasts an equally amazing sound system, fountains and an outdoor feel (there's no roof, but then it doesn't rain in summer anyway). It's one of the prettiest of the macroclubs, with loads of marble, a glass pyramid and plenty of greenery. Queues can be enormous, so get there early. Es Paradis is known for its water parties, when the dance floor is flooded.

Privilege CLUB
(www.privilegeibiza.com) One kilometre from Amnesia, this club, with its 20 bars, interior pool and capacity for 10,000 clubbers, claims to be the world's largest. The main domed dance temple is an enormous, pulsating area, where the DJ's cabin is suspended above the pool.

ⓘ SAILINGS FROM SANTA EULÀRIA

In summer, Cruceros Santa Eulària (www.ferrysantaeulalia.com) runs boats to several destinations, including the following:

DESTINATION	BOATS PER DAY	ADULT/ CHILD
Cala Llonga	9	€10/5
Ibiza	6	€15/7.50
Formentera	1	€28/14

El Naranjo   FISH €€

(☎971 33 03 24; Carrer de Sant Josep 31; menú €15, mains €19-23; ☉dinner Tue-Sun) Enjoy fish, always fresh and cooked to retain all its juices, in the shady garden of 'The Orange Tree'. This very Spanish gourmet option is especially popular with locals seeking somewhere special.

☆ Entertainment

Guarana   CLUB

(www.guaranaibiza.com; Passeig Marítim; ☉8pm-6am) By the marina, this is a cool club away from the Ibiza–Sant Rafel–Sant Antoni circuit.

ⓘ Information

Tourist office (☎971 33 07 28; www.santa eulariadesriu.com; Carrer Marià Riquer Wallis 4; ☉9.30am-1.30pm & 5-7.30pm Mon-Fri, 9.30am-1pm Sat) Just off the main street.

ⓘ Getting There & Away

Regular buses connect Santa Eulària with Ibiza City, Sant Antoni and the northern beaches.

SANTA EULÀRIA TO S'AIGUA BLANCA
◉ Sights & Activities

Sant Carles de Peralta   VILLAGE

This sleepy village sits on the main road northwest of Santa Eulària. Just outside the village, at Km12, is the Las Dalias alternative market (www.lasdalias.es, in Spanish; ☉10am-8pm Sat & 8pm-1.30am Mon Jun-Sep).

Cala Llenya & Cala Mastella   BEACHES

A side road leads to Cala Llenya, a pleasant little pine-fringed cove with a deep, sandy beach, and the even tinier, just as pretty, Cala Mastella beach. At the latter, scramble around the rocks at the eastern end along a much crumbled concrete path to reach one of Ibiza's most authentic restaurants.

Cala de Boix, Es Figueral & S'Aigua Blanca   BEACHES

The road to Cala Mastella continues a couple of kilometres to the curl of Cala de Boix and its tempting waters.

Back on the main road, the next turn-off leads to the low-key resort area of Es Figueral, with a golden sand beach and turquoise water. A little further on, a turn-off takes you to the still lovelier beaches of S'Aigua Blanca, where clothing is optional.

On weekends and from July to August, all these beaches can be very, very busy.

🛏 Sleeping & Eating

Hostal Restaurante Es Alocs
BEACHSIDE HOTEL €€

(☎971 33 50 79; www.hostalalocs.com; s/d €35/65; ☉May-Oct) This very friendly choice sits right on the beach at Platja Es Figueral. Rooms occupy two floors and most have a small fridge and balcony. The bar-restaurant has a wonderful terrace, deeply shaded with tangled juniper and chaste trees.

Can Curreu   COUNTRY VILLA €€€

(☎971 33 52 80; www.cancurreu.com; Carretera de Sant Carles Km12; d incl breakfast from €275; ❋ 🛜 🏊) Above terracing of almond and other fruit trees and amid close-clipped lawns bordered by a kaleidoscope of roses, this much modified Ibizan farmstead has 17 exquisitely decorated and furnished rooms. Room rates include access to the relaxing spa with its multiple facilities. Signed 'Casa Rural', the hotel's a short drive through fields from the Km12 marker, 1.5km south of Sant Carles.

Hostal Cala Boix   HOTEL €€

(☎971 33 52 24; www.hostalcalaboix.com; d incl breakfast €80; ☉May-Oct; ❋) Set uphill and back from the Cala de Boix, this option couldn't be further from Ibiza madness. All rooms have a balcony and many have sea views. At S'Arribiada, its hearty restaurant, Thursday is barbecue day, while each Tuesday fresh sardines sizzle on the grill.

Es Bigotes   FISH €€

(meals €25; ☉lunch Easter-Oct). Offering *bullit de peix* (whatever fish was caught that morning simmered with herbs, mixed vegetables and potatoes in a huge vat), followed by *arròs caldós* (saffron rice cooked in the broth of the *bullit de peix*), this simple shack is known far and wide. Finish off with *café de caleta* (coffee prepared with lemon zest, cinnamon and flamed brandy). No phone, no reservations; in July and August, you need to turn up in person at least the day before to book a spot. During other months, arrival by 1pm should get you a table. To arrive by car, take the last turning left before Cala Mastella.

Bar Anita BAR-RESTAURANT €
(✆971 33 50 90; mains €8-16) A timeless tavern opposite the village church of Sant Carles de Peralta, this restaurant and bar has been attracting all sorts from around the island for decades. They come to enjoy pizza, pasta and a hearty meal – or simply to drink and chat.

CALA SANT VICENT
The package-tour resort of Cala Sant Vicent extends around the shores of a protected bay on the northeast coast. Its long stretch of sandy beach is backed by a string of modern midrise hotels. A 2.5km drive northwards winds through a leafy residential area high up to Punta Grossa, with spectacular views over the coast and east out to sea.

North Coast & Interior
The north of Ibiza has some of the island's most attractive landscapes. Its winding back roads, coastal hills and inland mountains are popular with both walkers and cyclists.

PORTINATX
Portinatx is the north coast's major tourist resort. Busy, yes, but a good spot for families and positively underpopulated when set against the megaresorts around Ibiza town. Its three adjoining beaches – S'Arenal Petit, S'Arenal Gran and Platja Es Port – are each beautiful but often crowded.

Cala Xarraca, west of Portinatx, is a picturesque, partly protected bay with a rocky shoreline and dark-sand beach. Development is limited to a solitary bar-restaurant and a couple of private houses.

SANT MIQUEL DE BALANSAT & AROUND
One of the largest inland villages, Sant Miquel is overlooked by its shimmering white, boxlike 14th-century church (✆9.30am-1.30pm & 4.30-7.30pm Tue-Fri, 9.30am-12.30pm Sat). The restored early-17th-century frescoes in the Capella de Benirràs are a swirl of flowers and twisting

vines. Each Thursday from June to September, there's traditional island dancing on the pretty patio at 6.15pm.

The country mansion of Can Planells (✆971 33 49 24; www.canplanells.com; Carrer de Venda Rubió 2; d incl breakfast from €185; ✼☎✆), just 1.5km outside Sant Miquel on the road to Sant Mateu d'Aubarca, exudes relaxed rural luxury in its handful of tastefully arranged doubles and suites. The best suites have private terraces, and the house is set amid delightful gardens and fruit-tree groves.

The fine beaches of the busy resort of Port de Sant Miquel are dominated by the huge concrete honeycomb of Hotel Club San Miguel. In this attractive, deep-sunk bay, you can **waterski**, **canoe** and hire **snorkelling** gear to explore the rocky shore line.

A turn-off to the right just before Port de Sant Miquel takes you around a headland to the Cova de Can Marçà (✆971 33 47 76; www.covadecanmarsa.com; adult/child €8.50/4.50; ☉10.30am-7.30pm), underground caverns spectacularly lit by coloured lights. Tours in various languages take around 30 to 40 minutes. After resurfacing, pause for a drink on its terrace and savour the panorama of sheer cliffs and deep blue water.

Beyond the caves, an unsealed road continues 4km around the coast to the unspoiled bay of Cala Benirràs (with less bump and bounce, a sealed road from the Sant Joan–Sant Miquel road brings you there too), with high, forested cliffs and a couple of bar-restaurants that back onto the beach. At dusk on Sunday you may well encounter hippies with bongos banging out a greeting to the sunset, something they have been doing for decades.

SANT LLORENÇ DE BALÀFIA & AROUND
Overlooking this quiet hamlet is a brilliant-white Ibizan, 18th-century fortress-church, from when attacks by Moorish pirates were the scourge of the island. From Sant Llorenç head 500m east to the C733 road and turn north. Take a lane called the C733 beside the restaurant Balafía to reach the minuscule, once-fortified hamlet of Balàfia, with two towers, flowers and lots of *privado* signs around its half-dozen houses – but don't let these deter you from exploring its couple of lanes.

A few kilometres north along the C733, a signed turn-off just after Km17 leads to Can Gall (✆971 33 70 31; www.agrocangall. com; r €215-255; ☉closed Dec; ✼☎✆), once a farmhouse and nowadays a tranquil rural paradise set amid citrus groves. The nine bedrooms are each a delight to linger in, but tear yourself away to wallow in the infinity pool or savour the breeze from its chill-out terrace.

TOP CHOICE La Paloma (☎971 32 55 43; mains €16-26; dinner Tue-Sun mid-Mar–Nov), located in Sant Llorenç 100m downhill from the church, is an ecofriendly option. It offers creative Mediterranean, especially Italian, cuisine (hams and salamis come fresh from Tuscany) and sources vegetables from its own kitchen garden.

Below La Paloma, Paloma Café (meals €15-20; ⏰9am-4pm, Mon-Sat; 🍴🚸) is a delightful, laid-back place where you can snack on anything from quiche to carrot cake in the shade of its overgrown terrace. Much of its produce is organic and locally sourced and the friendly young team will do you a picnic basket on request.

For a slap-up grill over a wood fire, stop by Balafia (☎971 32 50 19; meals €25-30; ⏰dinner Mon-Sat mid-May–Oct, lunch Mon-Sat Nov–mid-May), set back from the C733 just beyond the junction with the road from Sant Llorenç and recognisable by its bright red and yellow sunset sign.

SANTA GERTRUDIS DE FRUITERA
If you blinked at the wrong time, you might miss tiny Santa Gertrudis, south of Sant Miquel. Clustered around the central, pedestrianised Plaça de l'Església, you'll find art-and-craft galleries, antique and bric-a-brac shops, plus several good bars, especially Bar Costa (Plaça de l'Església 11), with original paintings plastered on every wall of its cavernous interior.

For over 10 years, Anne, originally from France, aided by her daughter and grandson, has run Casi Todo (☎971 19 75 23; Plaça de l'Església 20; mains €11-15; ⏰dinner Sun-Fri Jun-Oct, lunch Mon-Fri Nov-May), where she rustles up simple, tasty mains and a glorious selection of homemade desserts.

West Coast

SANT ANTONI DE PORTMANY
POP 21,850

Sant Antoni (San Antonio in Spanish), widely known as 'San An', is about as Spanish as bangers and mash. It's the perfect destination if you've come in search of booze-ups, brawls and hangovers. The bulk of punters are young and from the UK.

About the only sight in town is the pretty, mainly 17th-century Església de Sant Antoni (Plaça de l'Església), a couple of blocks in from the marina.

Not far north of Sant Antoni are several undeveloped beaches, such as Cala Salada, a wide bay with sandy shores backed by pine forest. Closer to Sant Antoni are the pretty inlet beaches of Cala Gració and Cala Gracioneta, separated by a small rocky promontory.

🛏 Sleeping & Eating

Hostal la Torre   CLIFFTOP HOTEL €€
(☎971 34 22 71; www.hostallatorre.com; incl breakfast s €75, incl breakfast d €90-130; ⏰Easter-October) Though barely 2km north of Sant Antoni on the headland of Cap Negret, it's a world away from the town's bustle. Sea views from the bar-restaurant terrace are magnificent – even more so from the upper area, exclusive to hotel guests – and most of the 18 rooms have been recently and radically upgraded.

Villa Mercedes   FUSION RESTAURANT €€
(☎971 34 85 43; www.villamercedesibiza.com; Molls dels Pescadors; mains €13.50-23; ⏰7pm-3am; 🍴) This traditional Ibizan bourgeois mansion stands out among the sometimes horrendous muddle of Sant Antoni. It looks over the marina and offers eclectic cooking, from wok-fried vegetables through rice and noodle dishes to the local catch of the day.

🍷 Drinking
From the port, head for the small rock-and-sand strip on the north shore to join hundreds of others for sunset drinks at a string of chilled bars. All serve food too.

Café del Mar (www.cafedelmar.es; ⏰4pm-1am) is an Ibiza institution that celebrated its 30th anniversary in 2010. Others include Café Mambo (www.cafemamboibiza.com; ⏰1pm-2am) and Savannah (www.savannahibiza.com; ⏰2pm-2am).

They face stiff competition from another set of stylish lounge bars about 300m further north along the pedestrian walkway. Places such as Coastline, Sun Sea Bar, Kasbah and Kanya all have pools and attract plenty of punters. Between June and September, once the sun goes down, all turn up the rhythmic heat and pound on until late.

WHAT'S COOKING IN THE BALEARIC ISLANDS?

Fish and seafood are the lead items in many a Balearic kitchen. In the marshlands of S'Albufera, in eastern Mallorca, rice and eels are traditional mainstays. The former is used in many dishes, while the latter mostly pop up in *espinagada*, an eel-and-spinach pie. Valldemossa is famous for its versions of *coca*, a pizza-like snack that you will find around the islands, particularly around Mallorca. One of the local specialities is the potato version, *coca de patata*. Menorca is especially known for its cheeses and *caldereta de llagosta*, a juicy lobster stew. A favourite in Ibiza is *frito de pulpo* (a baked dish of octopus, potatoes, paprika and herbs). Another is *bullit de peix*, a fresh fish and potato stew.

The interior of Mallorca is serious wine country, with two Denominación de Orígen (DO) areas, Binissalem and Pla i Llevant (roughly the southeast sector of the island). Limited quantities of wine (some very good) are also made in Menorca, Ibiza and Formentera (try the whites here).

Around the other side of the bay at Cala de Bou, you can eat, drink and soak up the final rays of the day at Kumharas (www.kumharas.org; Carrer de Lugo 2). Sunday night is best, with live performances (especially fire dancers). Look for the Rodeo Vaca Loca sign on the main road and turn down Carrer de Lugo towards the sea.

ⓘ Information

Tourist office (☑971 34 33 63; Passeig de Ses Fonts; ☻9.30am-8.30pm Mon-Fri, 9.30am-1pm Sat & Sun) Beside the harbour.

ⓘ Getting There & Away

BOAT Cruceros Portmany (www.cruceros portmany.com; adult/child €9/4.50) boats depart around every half-hour to Cala Bassa (20 minutes) and Cala Compte (30 minutes).

BUS Bus 3 runs every 15 to 30 minutes to Ibiza City (40 minutes). Bus 8 (eight daily June to October) serves Cala Bassa.

CALA BASSA TO CALA D'HORT

Heading west and south from Sant Antoni, you'll come to the popular bay of Cala Bassa. Walk in beyond the rocks to this lovely, sandy horseshoe bay. The next few coves around the coast hide some extremely pretty beaches including Cala Compte, with its translucent water, and tiny Cala Codolars. All are accessible by local bus and/or boat from Sant Antoni. Further south, Cala Vedella is a modest resort, with a fine beach in the centre of town.

A gorgeous drive through scented pine trees brings you to the bijou bay of Cala d'Hort, overlooked by the towering mass of the islet of Es Vedrà. The water here is an inviting shade of blue and the beach, a long arc of sand sprinkled with pebbles and

rocks. Sip a drink, ideally at sunset, on the terrace of El Carmen (☑971 18 74 49; r €75; ☻mid-Mar–Oct). This friendly bar-restaurant-hotel, from where you tumble onto the beach, has seven rooms, all with fridge and dramatic sea views and all except one with a deep, spacious balcony.

FORMENTERA

A short boat ride south of Ibiza, Formentera is less than 20km across from east to west. It's the smallest and least-developed of the four main Balearic Islands, with a population of 9500. Visitors come to enjoy its sandy beaches and short walking and cycling trails. It's a popular day trip from Ibiza and gets crowded in midsummer (especially with the Italian contingent, for whom Formentera is what Bali is to Australians), but most of the time it is still possible to find yourself a strip of sand out of sight and earshot of others.

Formentera's predominantly flat landscape is rugged and, at times, bleak. The coast is alternately fringed with jagged cliffs and beaches backed by low dunes. A handful of farmers scrape a living from the land in the centre and east, but elsewhere the island is a patchwork of pine plantations, sun-bleached salt beds, low stone walls and mostly untilled fields.

◉ Sights & Activities

Apart from walking, cycling and lying on beaches, activities are limited. Points of interest include a series of crumbling stone watchtowers along the coastline, traces of a ruined Roman fortress (Fortificació Romà)

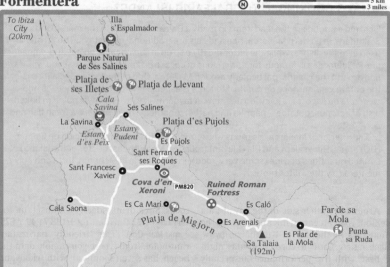

on the south coast, and 40 minor archaeological sites (most signposted in distinctive pink off the main roads).

Divers could approach Diving Center Formentera (www.blue-adventure.com; La Savina; dive with rental gear €45), one of a handful of island dive centres. Wet4Fun (☑670 366314; www.wet4fun.com; ☺Jun-Sep), with its main base in Es Pujols, offers the chance to learn windsurfing and kitesurfing, as well as sailing, canoeing and kayaking.

PARQUE NATURAL DE SES SALINES

The Ses Salines nature park, a protected area, begins just north of Estany Pudent (the aptly named 'Smelly Lake'). It extends along the slim finger of land that pokes northwards towards Ibiza and across the narrow intervening strait to also embrace Ses Salines, the salt pans of Ibiza's southern tip. Platja de Llevant and Platja de ses Illetes, a pair of beautiful strips of white sand, line the promontory. A 3km partly dirt road (toll for cars/motorbikes €4/2) heads north from the La Savina–Es Pujols road.

A 4km **walking trail** leads from the La Savina–Es Pujols road to the far end of the promontory, from where you could wade across the narrow strait to Illa s'Espalmador, a tiny uninhabited islet with beautiful, quiet beaches (especially S'Alga, on the southeast side) and mud baths. Be careful when wading out – you can easily be caught by incoming tides. The Barca Bahia boat (€15 return) runs up to three times daily from La Savina ferry port to the island, calling at Platja de ses Illetes.

SANT FRANCESC XAVIER

Formentera's capital and biggest population centre, Sant Francesc Xavier is an attractive whitewashed village, with some good cafes overlooking small, sunny plazas. The town's older buildings include a 14th-century chapel, an 18th-century fortress and the Museu Etnològic (☑971 32 26 70; Carrer de Jaume I 17; admission free; ☺10am-2pm & 5-7pm Mon-Fri), a modest ethnological museum illustrating Formentera's agricultural and fishing heritage.

CALA SAONA

On the road south of Sant Francesc Xavier, a third of the way to Cap de Barbaria, turn west to the delectable cove of Cala Saona. Although not even 150m long, the beach is one of the island's best, with just one big hotel, a couple of bar-restaurants overlooking the aqua-and-blue-black waters, and a discreet smattering of houses.

CAP DE BARBARIA

A narrow sealed road heads south out of the capital through stone-walled farmlands to Cap de Barbaria, the island's southernmost point. It's a pleasant ride to the lonely white lighthouse at the road's end, although there's little to do once you get there, except gaze out to sea. From the *far* (lighthouse) a 10-minute walk eastwards along a track leads to the Torre d'es Cap de Barbaria, an 18th-century watchtower.

ES PUJOLS

Once a sleepy fishing village, Es Pujols has been transformed by tourism. Rows of sun-bleached timber boat shelters still line the beachfront, overshadowed by modern hotels, apartments and restaurants. If the beaches are too crowded for your liking, more-secluded options lie within easy striking distance (keep walking northwest towards Platja de Llevant).

COVA D'EN XERONI

On the main road east of Sant Ferran just beyond Km6, turn right at the Spar supermarket for the Cova d'en Xeroni (☎971 32 82 14; adult/child €4/2.50; ⊙10am-1.30pm & 5-8pm Mon-Sat May-Oct). This underground cavern rich in stalactites and stalagmites was revealed in 1975 when the landowner was digging a well. It's a one-man band, so treat opening times with a grain of salt. How many visits are organised each day (the most likely times are 1pm and 6pm) depends on demand and whether or not the discoverer's son is around.

PLATJA DE MIGJORN

East of Sant Ferran towards Es Caló, a series of bumpy tracks leads from the main road to the south-coast beaches, known collectively as Platja de Migjorn. The best are at the eastern end around Es Arenals. Most of these beach settlements are no more than a handful of houses and apartments, a couple of bar-restaurants and the odd *hostal*.

EASTERN END

The fishing settlement of Es Caló is on a tiny rocky cove ringed by faded timber boat shelters. The coastline is jagged, but immediately west of Es Caló you'll find some good swimming holes and rock pools with small patches of sand.

From Es Caló, the road twists up to the island's highest point. Close to the top,

FORMENTERA'S TOP BEACHES

» **Platja de Migjorn**
» **Cala Saona)**
» **Platja de Ses Illetes**
» **Platja de Llevant**

beside Restaurante El Mirador, there are spectacular views along the length of the island, whose eastern extremity is an elevated limestone plateau. Most of the coastline is only accessible by boat. A road runs arrow-straight to the island's eastern tip, passing through Es Pilar de la Mola, which comes alive for hippie markets, which are held from 4pm to 9pm each Wednesday and Sunday. At the end of the road are the Far de sa Mola lighthouse, a monument to Jules Verne (who used this setting in one of his novels), a bar and spectacular seascapes.

🛏 Sleeping

Camping is prohibited. Most accommodation caters to package-tour agencies, so is overpriced and/or booked out in midsummer. Rental apartments (a better deal for stays of a week or more) are more common than *hostales* and hotels (of which there are just over 50). Check out www.formentera hotelsguide.com and www.guiaformentera. com.

Astbury Formentera (www.formentera. co.uk) is a UK-based specialist in house and apartment rentals in Formentera.

SANT FRANCESC XAVIER

Several *hostales* are scattered about this pleasant town and prices are more realistic than at some of the beach locations.

Casa Rafal (☎971 32 22 05; Carrer d'Isidoro Macabich 12; d incl breakfast €70; ⊙closed Dec & Jan), just off sleepy Plaça de sa Constitució, is a friendly, modest two-storey spot that offers good, clean rooms with ceiling fans. There's a bar-restaurant downstairs with a pleasant terrace.

CALA SAONA

A white behemoth of a building overlooking the beach, Hotel Cala Saona (☎971 32 20 30; www.hotelcalasaona.com; s/d €160/180; ⊙May-Oct; ❈@🕏🏊) offers 116 rooms, a pool, tennis courts and a restaurant. From the best rooms, the view is straight across the beach and out to sea. Its beach bar-restaurant is perfect for a sunset sangria. Prices halve in low season.

ES PUJOLS

Ochre fronted and about 100m inland from the beach, **Hostal Voramar** (🖉971 32 81 19; www.hostalvoramar.com; Av Miramar 25-33; s/d incl breakfast €115/150; ☺May-Oct; 🕸@🛜🌊) has comfortable rooms, most with balcony. For night owls, breakfast is served from 8.30am until noon. Have a workout in the small gym. The same people own the simpler, adjacent **Fonda Pinatar** (s/d €88/112).

SANT FERRAN DE SES ROQUES

A classic for decades, **Hostal Pepe** (🖉971 32 80 33; Carrer Major 68; s/d incl breakfast €45/65; ☺May–mid-Oct; 🌊) sits on the pleasant (and, on summer nights, lively) main street near the village's old sandstone church. White-washed with flashes of blue, it has 45 simply furnished, breezy rooms, all with balcony.

PLATJA DE MIGJORN

There's a sprinkling of *hostales* and apartments along Formentera's south beach, but most only deal with tour operators.

At **Hostal Ca Marí** (🖉971 32 81 80; Es Ca Marí; s/d €80/125; 🕸🌊), rooms and apartments all share gardens, a central bar, a restaurant, a pool and a grocery shop in the little settlement of the same name. The beach, where the *hostal* has its own bar-restaurant, is barely 100m away.

ES CALÓ

In a diminutive fishing hamlet overlooking a small rocky harbour, **Hostal Rafalet** (🖉971 32 70 16; s/d €75/105) is a welcoming *hostal*, where many of the spacious rooms have sea views. Downstairs, there's a popular bar and seafood restaurant with portside terrace.

 Eating

Most waterfront eateries offer a standard range of seafood and paella-style options. All those recommended here open from May to October only unless otherwise indicated.

ES PUJOLS

El Caminito (🖉971 32 81 06; Carretera La Savina-Es Pujols; meals €40-50; ☺dinner Apr-Nov) brings a touch of the Pampa to the Med.

MAYONNAISE

Menorcans claim to have given the world the name 'mayonnaise', arguing that the term is derived from *salsa mahonesa*, meaning 'sauce of Mahón (Maó)'. The French, too, claim it as their own, but the islanders argue that it was originally brought to the mainland by the troops of the Duc de Richelieu after they defeated the British in 1756. A plausible story (in fact, it's widely used all around the northern Mediterranean), but perhaps best taken with a small pinch of salt – like the best mayonnaise.

This Argentine grill, one of the best restaurants on the island, serves juicy slabs of meat. It's 1km outside Es Pujols on the road to La Savina.

SANT FERRAN DE SES ROQUES

Pedestrianised Carrer Major has a string of summertime eateries.

Family-run **Can Forn** (🖉971 32 81 55; Carrer Major 39; meals €30-35; ☺closed lunch Sun) specialises in island cuisine, offering dishes such as *calamar a la bruta* ('dirty calamari', with potato, Mallorcan sausage and squid ink). It's at the northern limit of the main street.

PLATJA DE SES ILLETES

In a tastefully renovated mill, **Es Molí de Sal** (🖉971 18 74 91; meals €40-50) boasts a lovely terrace and magnificent sea views. It serves some of Formentera's finest seafood. Try one of the rice dishes or the house speciality, *caldereta de llagosta* (lobster stew).

PLATJA DE MIGJORN

Set amid a greenery-filled dune, **Vogamari** (🖉971 32 90 53; meals €30-35; ☺closed dinner Tue) is a simple island eatery with a broad veranda. It's great for fresh fish, paella or solid meat dishes. Turn off the PM820 at Km9.5.

Sa Platgeta (🖉971 18 76 14; Platja de Migjorn, Es Ca Marí; meals €35; ☺Mon-Sat) is, according to some locals, one of the best spots on the island for fresh fish. Planted amid pines just back from a narrow, rock-studded beach, this simple bar-restaurant has a pleasant shady terrace. It's 500m west of Es Ca Marí (follow the signs through the backstreets or take the waterfront boardwalk).

At the eastern extremity of the beach, **Restaurante Es Cupiná** (☑971 32 72 21; Plajta de Migjorn; meals around €35) is a big name on the island. In business for nearly 40 years, this breezy restaurant is noted for its freshly cooked fish of the day.

ES CALÓ

S'Eufabi (☑971 32 70 56; Km12.5; mains €10-18, menú €11; ☉daily) dishes up some of the best paella and *fideuá* (a fine noodle variant) on Formentera at a reasonable price. This shady eatery is about 1km east of Es Caló, on the left as you begin the gentle ascent towards Es Pilar de la Mola.

ES PILAR DE LA MOLA

Pequeña Isla (☑971 32 70 68; www.pequena isla.com; Avinguda del Pilar 101; meals €30-35), the 'Little Island', has a shady roadside terrace and serves up hearty meat items, fresh grilled fish, paella and other rice dishes, as well as various island specialities, including simmered lamb and fried octopus.

⭐ Entertainment

ES PUJOLS

In summer Es Pujols gets lively. Its intense tangle of intertwined bars along or just off Carrer d'Espardell (just back from the waterfront) stay open until 3am or 4am. Customers are 90% Italian – indeed you'd hardly know you were in Spain! A favourite since 1994 is the red and rocking **Indiana Café**, with its high tables and stools. Next door, **Neroopaco** is all black and white, low seating and deep house. Nearby Carrer de Roca Plana also has a few bars, of which boisterous **Pachanka** is a good one to keep in mind for later in the evening.

Vivi Club (Avinguda Miramar) is a pleasant music bar with pine trees in the garden. The purple lighting tinges everything, even your cocktails.

SANT FERRAN DE SES ROQUES

An island classic, **Fonda Pepe** (Carrer Major 55; ☉May-Oct) is a knockabout bar connected with the *hostal* across the street of the same name. It has been serving *pomadas* (shots of gin and lemon) for decades and attracts a lively crowd of locals and foreigners of all ages and persuasions.

PLATJA DE SES ILLETES

Bigsurlife (☉10.30am-sunset May-Oct) attracts a good-natured and beautiful Italian crowd. The daily event is drinks (huge glass steins of mojito) on the beach for sunset. About 20m before the turn-off for Platja de ses Illetes from the La Savina–Es Pujols road, a parking area is signposted to the left. Another 30m brings you to the beach and bar.

Tiburón (☉10am-sunset May-Oct), about 200m further along the strand, is an equally fun beach tavern that tends to attract more locals for fish, salads, sangria and, of course, sunsets.

PLATJA DE MIGJORN

Above the long strand, the scattering of bars range from sophisticated (often Italian-run) chill-out scenes for sipping cocktails to more rough-and-ready affairs.

TOP / CHOICE **Blue Bar** (www.bluebarformentera. com; ☉noon-4am Apr-Oct) is a long-established Formentera favourite that offers good seafood, rice dishes and spadefuls of *buen rollito* (good vibes). At the south's chill-out bar par excellence, everything is blue – seats, sunshades, tables, loos and walls. Why, they even mix a blue Curacao-based cocktail! Take the sandy track at Km8.

Milan meets the sea at **10.7** (www.10punto7. com; meals around €30; ☉May-Sep; 🔊), an Italian-owned bar-restaurant with an international wine list. Sushi is the speciality. The rolling waves below, mellow black-and-white decor and relaxed vibe are perfect for lingering. Take the dirt track at, specifically, Km10.7.

Xiringuito Bartolo (☉May-Oct), at the eastern extremity of the beach, must be the world's tiniest beach bar, much loved by islanders. Sitting cheerfully on stilts, it hosts two longish tables. Bartolo serves up drinks and snacks to wander away with if there's nowhere to sit.

ℹ Information

Formentera's main **tourist office** (☑971 32 20 57; www.formentera.es; ☉10am-8pm Mon-Fri, 10am-3pm Sat & Sun) is beside the ferry landing point in La Savina. There are smaller branches in Es Pujols and opposite the church in Sant Francesc Xavier.

ℹ Getting There & Around

BOAT Regular passenger ferries (single/return adult €25/45, child €15/30; 25 to 35 minutes each way) run between Ibiza City and La Savina.

MALLORCA, MENORCA & IBIZA MENORCA

ℹ MENORCA WEBSITES

www.menorca.es Official Menorca tourism website.

www.visitmenorca.com Website of the hoteliers' association.

www.menorcamonumental.org Excellent presentation of Menorca's monuments and historical sites.

www.tmsa.es Bus timetables throughout the island.

Baleària-Trasmapi (www.balearia.com, www.trasmapi.com) Over 10 daily. Small car costs €78 one way; motorcycle, €32; bicycle, free.

Mediterranea-Pitiusa (www.medpitiusa.net) Passengers only; six fast ferries daily.

BUS Autocares Paya (☎971 32 31 81; www.autocarespaya.com, in Spanish) runs a regular bus service connecting the main villages, but you're much more flexible on a scooter or bicycle.

CAR & BICYCLE Kiosk after kiosk offering car, scooter and bicycle hire greet you on arrival at La Savina's harbour. Daily rates are around €7 for a town bike, €10 for a mountain bike, €25 for a motor scooter and up to €55 for a motorcycle. A car is superfluous on this tiny island, but they are available for rent, starting at around €35 per day.

TAXI ☎971 32 23 42.

MENORCA

Menorca (population 90,240) is the least overrun and most tranquil of the Balearic Islands. In 1993 Unesco declared it a Biosphere Reserve, aiming to preserve environmental areas, such as the Parc Natural S'Albufera d'es Grau wetlands, and the island's unique archaeological sites.

Its 216km coastline is fretted with relatively untouched beaches, coves and ravines. Inland, criss-crossing its fields and green, rolling hills are an estimated 70,000km of dry stone walls.

Some say the island owes much to Franco for not being overrun with tourist development. While neighbouring Mallorca went over to the Nationalists almost at the outset of the civil war, Menorca resisted. Franco later 'rewarded' Mallorca with a construction free-for-all and penalised Menorca by blocking development.

The second-largest and northernmost of the Balearics, Menorca has a wetter climate and is usually a few degrees cooler than the other islands. Particularly in the low season, the 'windy island' is buffeted by *tramuntana* winds from the north.

Getting Around

TO/FROM THE AIRPORT Bus 10 (€1.60) runs between Menorca's airport, 7km southwest of Maó, and the city's bus station every half-hour. A taxi costs around €15.

BUS You can get to most destinations from Maó, but, with a few exceptions, services are infrequent and sluggish.

CAR & MOTORCYCLE Daily hire costs €35 to €45 for a modest sedan. All the big operators have representatives at the airport. In Maó, try the following:

Autos Mahon Rent (☎971 36 56 66; www.autosmahonrent.com; Moll de Llevant 35-36)

Autos Valls (☎971 35 42 44; www.autosvalls.com; Plaça d'Espanya 13)

Maó

POP 29,100

The British have invaded Menorca four times (if you count the latest, modest campaign that began with the first charter flight from London in 1953). As a result Maó (Mahón in Spanish), the capital, is an unusual blend of Anglo and Spanish characteristics.

The British made it the capital of Menorca in 1713 and the influence of their almost 100-year presence (the island reverted to Spanish rule in 1802) is still evident in the town's architecture, traditions and culture. Even today the majority of Maó's overseas visitors come from Britain.

Maó's harbour, a full 5km long, is the second-largest natural haven in the world after Pearl Harbour. This strategic shelter, where Mediterranean seaways crossed, led to its possession and repossession by the Spanish, French and British. Nowadays, the deep, well-protected waters handle everything from small fishing boats to tankers. The town is built atop the cliffs that line the harbour's southern shore. Although some older buildings still remain, the majority of the architecture is in the restrained 18th-century Georgian style (note the sash windows and, as the Menorcans say to this day, *boíners* – bow windows).

◉ Sights & Activities

Maó's main plaza is the large Plaça de s'Esplanada, originally a parade ground,

Menorca

10 km
6 miles

To Barcelona
(256km)

To Palma de
Mallorca (187km);
Ibiza (282km);
Valencia (417km)

Cap de Favàritx
Cala Presili
Platja d'en Tortuga
Illa d'en Colom
Es Grau
Sa Mesquida
Golden Farm Cap Negre
Collingwood House
Es Freus
Fortalesa de la Mola
Castell San Felipe
Es Castell
Cala de
Sant Esteve
Fort
Marlborough
ME6
Maó
Torello
Sant
Lluís
Platja de
Punta Prima
Binibèquer
Cap
d'en
Font
Cala de
Binidalí

Parc Natural
S'Albufera
d'es Grau

ME7
Rafal
Rubí
ME5
Talati
de Dalt
ME1
Sant
Climent
Aeropuerto
de Menorca
Llucmaçanes
Es Canutells
Cala'n
Porter Cova
d'en
Xoroi

Far de Cavalleria
Ecomuseu Cap de Cavalleria
Platges de Fornells
Fornells

Cap de
Cavalleria
Cala
Pregonda
Platja
Cavalleria

Cala en
Calderer

Cala
Morell

Cap
Gros
Algaiarens
La Vall

Naveta des
Tudons

Son
Catlar

Ciutadella
Santandria
Cala Blanca
Cap
d'Artrux
Platja de
Son Xoriguer

Cala en
Bosc
Arenal
de Son
Saura

Cala en
Turqueta
Cala es
Talaier

Cala
Macarella
Cala
Macarelleta

Santa
Galdana
ME22

Ferreries

ME1

Es Mercadal
Monte
El Toro
(357m)
ME15
ME16
ME18
Es Migjorn
Gran
ME20

Alaior
Torralba
d'en Salord
Torre d'en
Galmes
Cales
Coves
Son Bou

To Cala Ratjada (41km);
Port d'Alcúdia (63km)

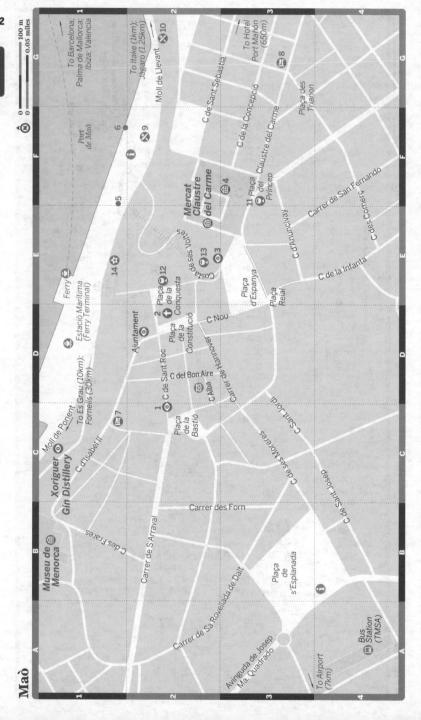

Maò

To Barcelona; Palma de Mallorca; Ibiza; Valencia

To Itake (1km); Jagaro (1.25km) ✕ 10

Moll de Llevant

To Hotel Port Mahón (650m)

Plaça des Trianon

C de Sant Sebastià

C de la Concepció

Carrer de San Fernando

C des Comer

C del Claustre del Carme

Port de Maò

✕ 9

6

🛈

5

Mercat Claustre del Carme 🏛

11 Plaça del Princep

4 🏛

C d'Anuncivay

C de la Infanta

Plaça d'Espanya

Plaça Reial

Costa de ses Voltes

13

3

Ferry 🛥

14 ★

2 Plaça de la Conquesta 12

Plaça de la Constitució

C Nou

Estació Marítima (Ferry Terminal)

Ajuntament

Carrer de Hannover

C de Sant Roc

C del Bon Aire

C Alba

C Sant Jordi

Plaça d'Espanya

To Es Grau (10km); Fornells (30km)

1 C de Sant Roc

Plaça de la Bastió

7 🏛

Moll de Ponent

Xoriguer Gin Distillery 🏛

C d'Isabel II

C des Frares

Museu de Menorca 🏛

Carrer de S'Arraval

Carrer des Forn

Carrer de Sa Rovellada de Dalt

C des Moreras

C de Sant Josep

Plaça de s'Esplanada

🛈

Bus Station (TMSA) 🚌

Avinguda de Josep Ma. Quadrado

To Airport (7km)

N ⊕ 0 — 100 m
0 — 0.05 miles

Maó

laid out by the British. There's a craft and clothing market here every Tuesday and Saturday.

The narrow streets to the east are Maó's oldest. The **Arc de Sant Roc**, a 16th-century archway straddling Carrer de Sant Roc, is the only remaining relic of the medieval walls that once surrounded the old city.

The **Església de Santa Maria la Major** (Plaça de la Constitució), further east, was completed in 1287 but rebuilt during the 18th century. It houses a massive organ, built in Barcelona and shipped across in 1810. At the northern end of this plaza is the neoclassical **ajuntament** (town hall).

Plaça d'Espanya   SQUARE
Just above Plaça d'Espanya is the **Mercat Claustre del Carme**, where former church cloisters have been imaginatively converted into a buzzing market and shopping centre. Upstairs, enjoy temporary art exhibitions and the modest **Museu Hernández Sanz Hernández Mora** (⏷971 35 05 97; admission

free; ⏷10am-1pm Mon-Sat), devoted to Menorcan themes, illustrated by artworks, maps and decorative items dating back to the 18th century. In the square itself, explore the pungent **fish market** (⏷to 1pm Tue-Sat), housed in an attractive olive-green wooden building.

Museu de Menorca   MUSEUM
(Plaça de Sant Francesc; adult/child €2.40/free; ⏷9.30am-2pm & 6-8.30pm Tue-Sat, 10am-2pm Sun) This 15th-century former Franciscan monastery has been in its time a nautical school, a public library, a high school and a children's home. Well documented and presented in Catalan, Spanish and English, its collection covers the earliest history of the island, the Roman and Byzantine eras, and Islamic Menorca, and includes paintings, some fascinating early maps and other material from more recent times, too.

Xoriguer Gin Distillery   DISTILLERY
(Moll de Ponent 93; ⏷8am-7pm Mon-Fri, 9am-1pm Sat) At this showroom, you can taste and buy the distinctively aromatic Menorcan gin. From the range of sample liqueurs, try a shot of camomile-based Hierba de Menorca, Palo with its bitter gentian flavour or Calent, cinnamon-scented and traditionally served hot.

Harbour Cruises   BOAT TOURS
A cluster of operators do one-hour **glass-bottomed boat cruises** (€10/5 per adult/child) around the harbour. The underwater perspective, though interesting enough, is outclassed by the stunning views of both banks.

Beaches   BEACHES
The closest decent beaches to the capital are **Es Grau**, 10km to the north, and **Platja de Punta Prima**, 8km to the south. Both are connected to Maó by local bus.

🛏 Sleeping

To sleep steeped in history, stay at Collingwood House, the former residence of British Admiral Collingwood, Lord Nelson's right hand man; for details, see p634.

TOP CHOICE **Casa Alberti**   HISTORIC HOTEL €€€
(⏷971 35 42 10; www.casalberti.com; Carrer d'Isabel II 9; s/d incl breakfast €122/145; ⏷Easter-Oct) Climb the central stairs with striking wrought-iron banisters to your vast room with white walls and whitest-of-white sheets. Each of the six bedrooms within this 18th-century mansion is furnished with

FORTS & MANSIONS

Great Britain occupied Menorca principally to gain possession of Maó's deep natural harbour. It built **Fort Marlborough** (adult/child €3/1.80; 9.30am-2.30pm Sun Easter–mid-Dec) to defend the sound and protect Castell San Filipe, which it had also overrun. Most of the fortress is excavated into the rock beside the charming emerald-green inlet, Cala de Sant Esteve (2.5km beyond Es Castell – known historically as Georgetown to the Brits). A short video sets the historical background to a walk through the tunnels, elivened by figurines, explosions and a well-produced recorded commentary (including an English version). From the central hillock there's a fine view of Cala de Sant Esteve, the scant above-ground remains of Castell San Felipe and, to the south, the circular Torre d'en Penjat (Torre Stuart).

Across the inlet, **Castell San Felipe** (www.museomilitarmenorca.com; adult/child €5/2.50), originally constructed in the 16th century, became, under British control, one of the largest fortresses in Europe. When Spain recovered the island, King Carlos III had the fort largely destroyed. However, its labyrinth of underground tunnels has remained more or less intact. Occasional guided visits are possible – call or check the website for latest times (usually once or twice a week). Night-time **torchlit tours** (adult/child €20/10; in Spanish 8.30pm-11pm Sat, in English 8.30pm-11pm Sun mid-Jun–mid-Sep), complete with actors playing soldiers and the acrid whiff of gunpowder, take you into the bowels of this once-mighty fortress.

To immerse yourself more fully in the area's British colonial past, stop at **Collingwood House** (Hotel del Almirante; 971 36 27 00; www.hoteldelalmirante.com; s/d incl breakfast €80/105;), which was once the residence of Admiral Cuthbert Collingwood, Nelson's fellow commander-at-sea. It's now a charming hotel, replete with maritime reminiscences, pool, terrace, bar and wonderful views over the harbour from its tiled restaurant. With its heavy carpets, dark-timber doors and furniture, and countless paintings and sketches of great vessels and their commanders, you could almost be in a minor museum. If you stay, ask for a room in the main, historic building. The hotel is located on the main road about halfway between Maó and Es Castell.

In the 19th century Queen Isabel II ordered the construction of a new fortress. The extensive **Fortalesa de la Mola** (www.fortalesalamola.com; adult/child €7/4.75, audioguide €2; 10am-8pm), built between 1848 and 1875, sprawls over the promontory of the same name on the northern shore of the bay. It's about a 12km drive from Maó, so you'll want to set aside a couple of hours for the visit. You will go rambling through galleries, gun emplacements and barracks. A guided tour in Spanish and English (prior reservation recommended) sets out at 10.30am. Twice a month in July and August staff organise torchlit night tours. The only way here is by car, unless you want to call a **water taxi** (616 428891, return per person €10). It will pick up at various points in Maó and Es Castell and makes for a scenic journey in its own right.

On the way back towards Maó, you'll notice a rose-coloured stately home surrounded by gardens. At **Golden Farm** (Granja Dorada; closed to the public), they say, Nelson and his lover Lady Hamilton enjoyed a tryst in 1799.

---

traditional items, while bathrooms are designer cool and contemporary. There's an intimate dinner-only Japanese restaurant (reservations essential). Rates drop substantially outside high season.

Hostal-Residencia La Isla   FAMILY HOTEL €
(971 36 64 92; www.hostal-laisla.com, in Spanish; Carrer de Santa Caterina 4; s/d incl breakfast €35/58;) This large, family-run *hostal*

is excellent value. Its small rooms all come with their own bathroom and a few have air-con. The decor is uninspiring, but the folks are friendly and run a bustling workers' bar-restaurant downstairs.

Hotel Port Mahón   MODERN HOTEL €€€
(971 36 26 00; www.sethotels.com; Avinguda del Port de Maó; s/d from €143/196;) This fine four-star hotel has 73 nicely turned-out

rooms, a pool, pleasant gardens and a couple of restaurants. It also has eight luxurious suites. Rooms with balcony (€230) offer a grand view over the port. Decor varies from room to room.

✕ Eating

You're almost guaranteed to eat well at any of the harbourside fish restaurants. Also worth investigating are many waterfront eateries in Cales Fonts, just 3km away in Es Castell.

Itake   BASQUE €
(✆971 35 45 70; Moll de Llevant 317; lunch/dinner menúes €16/19; ☺lunch & dinner Tue-Sat, dinner Sun; ❋) The lamps above each table don't match. Nor do the glasses. Or the tables themselves. And it doesn't matter a jot. The dinner menu in particular is a delight, with plenty of choice, including an especially long and tempting dessert card. And the accompanying sauces – port-based, for example, with the *pato Itake* (duck Itake style); enhanced by local cheese upon the *filete de cerdo ibérico con queso de Menorca* (fillet of pork) – are smooth and creamy.

El Varadero   HARBOURSIDE €€
(✆971 35 20 74; Moll de Llevant 4; mains €11.50-17; ☺Easter-Nov) With such a splendid vista from the harbourside terrace, it must be tempting to simply sit on your laurels. But El Varadero doesn't. There's a range of tempting rice dishes and a short, select choice of fish and meat mains. If a full meal is too much, drop by for a tapa or two with a glass of wine and savour the view.

La Minerva   FISH €€
(✆971 35 19 95; www.restaurantelaminerva.com, in Spanish; Moll de Llevant 87; mains €15.50-42) Dine in the air-conditioned interior, with its tastefully nautical theme (no cheap swags of net or glass marker balls here), or, more romantically, on its pontoon, moored to the quayside. Wherever you dine, the food is just as delectable. The €15 *menú*, offered at both lunch and dinner, is excellent value.

Jàgaro   SEAFOOD €€€
(✆971 36 23 90; Moll de Llevant 334; meals €60) Here at the last in the long line of eateries fronting the harbour, rice dishes, fish and, especially, other seafood are the order of the day. The adventurous can try *ortiga de mar* (sea anemone) or *morena mansa* (sea cucumber).

🍷 Drinking & Entertainment

Nightlife in Maó is low-key compared with Mallorca or Ibiza. Most of the action is on the waterfront.

Mirador Café   MUSIC BAR
(www.miradorcafe.com, in Spanish; Plaça d'Espanya 2; ☺10am-2am Mon-Sat) Inside this small, popular music bar, your host's collection of exotic masks leers down at you. Best of all, take a ringside seat outside and drink in the port views with your beer. The cafe's beside a short cul-de-sac at the top of Costa de ses Voltes.

Ars Café   CAFE-RESTAURANT
(www.arscafe.info, in Spanish; Plaça del Príncep 12; mains €7-12; ☺Mon-Sat) Arty and Boho at the edges (despite the suave, ultramodern toilets, with their vast, full length mirrors), this is a friendly, relaxing place to drink or eat. For maximum atmosphere, choose the front, main bar – except after midnight on Friday and Saturday, when you need to head down to the cellar bar, with its DJ and live music.

Akelarre   JAZZ CLUB
(Moll de Ponent 41-43; ☺3pm-4am) Ambient and jazz dance music trill during the wee hours in this place, made welcoming by the warm, stone interior. Live music frequently enlivens proceedings earlier in the evening (starting around 11pm and costing €10 cover charge). Thursday night is blues jam night.

Corto Maltés   TERRACE BAR
(Plaça de la Conquesta 5; ☺10am-11.30pm Mon-Sat) Owner and comics fanatic Pol will serve you a tasty tapa with one of his range of bottled beers. Sit back on this broad square

---

MENORCAN GIN

Although no document attests this, local lore has it that gin was first distilled on the island in the 18th century to slake the thirst of British and Dutch soldiers. You can drink it the usual way, long with tonic. Or do as the Menorcans do and ask for a *gin con limonada* (called locally a *pomada*), a shot of gin in a small glass, topped up with real lemonade. If you like your drink strong, order a *saliveta* (literally 'little spit') for a shot of neat gin, graced with a green olive.

beneath the censorious eye of King Alfonso III, whose statue rears before you.

Information

Tourist office town (☑971 36 74 15; Plaça S'Esplanada; ◷9am-1.30pm & 5-7.30pm Mon-Fri, 9am-2pm Sat); airport (◷7.30am-10pm); port (Moll de Llevant 2; ◷8am-8.30pm Tue-Sun, 8am-1pm Mon) Opening hours from November to April are much reduced.

Getting There & Around

BUS TMSA (www.tmsa.es) runs hourly express buses (45 minutes) between Maó and Ciutadella. In summer there are also at least eight stopping services to Ciutadella via Alaior, Es Mercadal and Ferreries; regular buses to south-coast beaches; and a handful to Santa Galdana (one hour).

Five **Autos Fornells** (www.autosfornells.com) buses run daily between Maó and Fornells (30 minutes).

WORTH A TRIP

MENORCA'S PREHISTORIC MYSTERIES

As long ago as 2000 BC, the islanders were constructing sturdy stone edifices. Menorca's interior remains sprinkled with reminders of those times. Many of the most significant sites are open to the public. In winter, sites are unattended and can be visited freely (and free of charge).

The monuments are linked to three main periods: the Pre-Talayotic (or cave era) from 2000 BC to 1300 BC; the Talayotic (Bronze Age) from 1300 BC to 800 BC; and the Post-Talayotic (Iron Age) from 800 BC to around 100 BC. Similarly, there are three general types of structures: *navetas*, *talayots* and *taulas*.

Navetas, built from large rocks in the shape of upturned boat hulls, are thought to have been used as tombs or meeting places – perhaps both. *Talayots*, large stone mounds found all over the island (and elsewhere in the Balearics), were used as watchtowers or to exert power over the surrounding region. Unique to Menorca, *taulas* are horseshoe-shaped sanctuaries with tall T-shaped pillars at their heart. These could have been used as sacrificial altars, but nobody is sure how such enormous stone slabs were moved or what they signify.

South of Ciutadella (from the *ronda* – ring road – follow the road for Cala Macarella and after 2.8km veer right), Son Catlar (admission free; ◷10am-sunset) is the largest Talayotic settlement in the Balearic Islands. Its five *talayots* and the remains of its dwellings cover around six hectares. East of Ciutadella (near the Km40 road marker), the Naveta des Tudons (adult/child €2/1.20; ◷9.15am-8.30pm Tue-Sat, 9.30am-3pm Sun & Mon) is a stone burial chamber constructed around 1000 BC.

From Maó, all the following sites are well signed from the Me1 highway to Ciutadella.

At the Talayotic settlement of Talatí de Dalt (adult/child €4/free; ◷10am-sunset), 3km west of Maó, the roots of wild olive trees force apart the weathered stones of the large central *talayot*. There's also a particularly well-preserved *taula*.

About 4km further along on the north side of the road, a walk across the fields brings you to Rafal Rubí, a pair of well-preserved burial *navetas*.

Take a left turn from the Me1 after 5km more for Torralba d'en Salord (adult/child €3.50/free; ◷10am-8pm Mon-Sat), another Talayotic settlement whose outstanding feature is an impressive *taula*.

If you only visit one Talayotic site, let it be Torre d'en Galmés (adult/child €3/1.80; ◷9.15am-8pm Tue-Sat, 9.15am-3pm Sun & Mon), southwest of Alaior. Stop by the small information centre, which has an instructive 10-minute video presentation, then wander at will over the site with its three hilltop *talayots*, rambling circular dwellings, deep underground storage chambers and sophisticated water collection system.

Further south on the coast at Cales Coves, some 90 caves dug into the coastal cliffs were apparently used for ritual burials. More recently some of the caves have been homes to hippie colonies. Nearby, the large Cova d'en Xoroi (☑971 37 72 36; www.covadenxoroi.com, in Spanish; Cala'n Porter; adult/child €7/3.50; ◷11.30am-10pm Jun-Sep) can be visited as a sight by day or club by night. The sunset chill-out scene starts around 8pm and the disco gets into action from around midnight until 5am. Foreign DJs make regular summer appearances. Admission includes a drink.

In winter, these services drop or are much reduced.

CAR Autos Mahon Rent (☑971 36 56 66; www.autosmahonrent.com; Moll de Llevant 35-36) rents bikes (€15 per day), scooters and cars.

The Interior – Maó to Ciutadella

The Me1, Menorca's main road connecting Maó and Ciutadella, divides the island into north and south. It passes through Alaior, Es Mercadal and Ferreries. Along the way smaller roads branch off towards the beaches and resorts of the north and south coasts.

Many of Menorca's most significant archaeological sites are signposted off the main road.

ALAIOR

This tiny town is home to the local cheese and shoe industries. **Coinga** (www.coinga.com; Carretera Nova; ☺9am-1pm & 5-8pm Mon-Fri, 9am-1pm Sat), the main cheese manufacturer, has its showroom and outlet at the entry to town, coming from Maó. There are factory visits at 11.30am Tuesday and Thursday.

ES MERCADAL

Es Mercadal, one of the oldest villages on the island (a market has been held here since at least 1300), is at the turn-off north for Fornells. You also leave the Me1 here to get to **Monte El Toro** (all of a towering 357m), Menorca's highest point. A twisting road leads to the summit, which is shared by a 16th-century church and former Augustine monastery (now run by a handful of Franciscan nuns), a cluster of satellite dishes and radio towers, and a statue of Christ (built to honour the dead of the civil war). On a clear day you can see Mallorca.

Head up the graceful marble stairway to **Restaurant N'Aguedet** (☑971 37 53 91; Carrer de Lepanto 30; mains €11-25.50), an elegant den of island cooking that has the stamp of approval of Catalan megachef Ferran Adrià (see p321). Here you can dine on typical island meat dishes, such as the melt-in-your-mouth *lechón* (suckling pig) or *conejo con cebolla y alcaparras* (rabbit with onion and capers).

FERRERIES

Menorca's highest town is another centre of cheese, shoes and leather-goods pro-

DON'T MISS

MENORCA'S TOP FIVE BEACHES

» **Cala Macarelleta** (p642)
» **Cala en Turqueta** (p642)
» **Cala Pregonda** (p641)
» **Cala Presili** (p641)
» **Cala Morell** (p641)

duction. At its Saturday morning market, stallholders sell fresh produce, along with traditional Menorcan crafts and artworks. The turn-off to the resort of Santa Galdana is just west of town.

The beautiful, 200-year-old rambling whitewashed house and pretty garden of **Mesón El Gallo** (☑971 37 30 39; www.mesonelgallo.com; mains €9-21; ☺lunch Tue-Thu & Sun, lunch & dinner Fri & Sat Feb-Jun & Sep-Nov, dinner Tue-Fri, lunch & dinner Sat & Sun Jul & Aug) merit a visit for their own sake. Enjoy meat dishes, grilled just as you wish them, on the vine-clad terrace or in the rustic interior with its beams and terracotta floor. From Ferreries, head down the Santa Galdana turn-off for 1.5km.

Ciutadella

POP 29,150

Founded by Carthaginians and known to the Muslims as Medina Minurqa, Ciutadella was almost destroyed following the 1558 Turkish invasion and much of the city was subsequently rebuilt in the 17th century. It was Menorca's capital until the British arrived.

Known as Vella i Bella ('Old and Beautiful'), Ciutadella is an attractive, distinctly Spanish city with a picturesque port and an engaging old quarter. Its character is quite distinct from that of Maó, and its historic centre is far more appealing.

◉ Sights

The glory of central Ciutadella is that it's almost entirely traffic free.

Plaça d'es Born   CENTRAL SQUARE
Around Ciutadella's main square are gracious 19th-century buildings, including the **Ajuntament** (town hall) and **Palau Torresaura**. The **obelisk** at the centre was raised to commemorate those townsfolk who died trying to ward off the Turks on 9 July

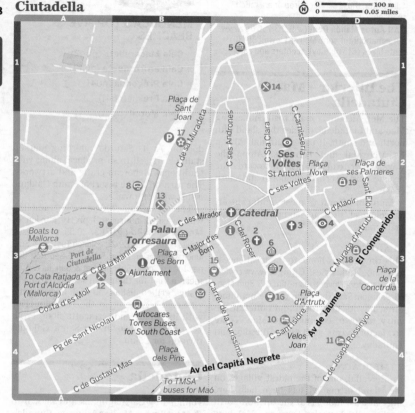

Boats to
Mallorca
Port de
Ciutadella
To Cala Ratjada &
Port d'Alcúdia
(Mallorca)
Costa d'es Moll

Plaça de
Sant
Joan

Plaça de
Sant
Joan

Palau
Torresaura

Plaça
d'es Born

Ajuntament

Autocares
Torres Buses
for South Coast

Plaça
dels Pins

Pg de Sant Nicolau

C de Gustavo Mas

To TMSA
buses for Maó

Av del Capitá Negrete

Ses
Voltes
St Antoni
Plaça
Nova
Plaça de
ses Palmeres

Catedral

El Conqueridor

Plaça
de la
Conctrdia

Plaça
d'Artrutx

Av de Jaume I

Velos
Joan

1558. For the finest view of the port and the town's remaining bastions and bulwarks, sneak behind the town hall and up to the **Bastió d'Es Governador** (⊙9am-1pm Mon-Fri). Nearby Plaça dels Pins, more relaxed and shaded by mature pine trees, has a children's playground and trim track (exercise trail with bars and planks for push-ups and stretches).

Old Ciutadella HISTORIC QUARTER
The narrow cobbled lanes and streets between Plaça d'es Born and Plaça de ses Palmeres (Plaça d'Alfons III) hold plenty of interest, with simple whitewashed buildings abutting ornate churches and elegant palaces. Attractively arcaded **Carrer ses Voltes** (The Arches) is lined with smart shops, restaurants and bars. The town's small **fish market** (⊙7am-1pm Tue-Sat) is in a pleasing Modernista tiled building, constructed in 1895.

Catedral & Churches
ECCLESIASTICAL ARCHITECTURE
The 14th-century **cathedral** (Plaça de la Catedral; ⊙10.30am-1.30pm & 4-7pm Mon-Sat) was built in Catalan Gothic style (although with a baroque facade) on the site of Medina Minurqa's central mosque.

Old Ciutadella also has a pair of fine baroque 17th-century churches. **Església del Roser** (Carrer del Roser) is now used as an occasional exhibition gallery. **Església dels Socors** (Carrer del Seminari 9) is home to the **Museu Diocesà** (adult/child €3/free; ⊙10.30am-1.30pm Tue-Sat May-Oct), a fine little museum, secular as much as religious, that complements the Museu Municipal.

Noble Mansions SECULAR ARCHITECTURE
Noble mansions, such as **Palau Martorell** (Carrer del Santíssim 7) and **Palau Saura** (Carrer del Santíssim 2), are used for temporary exhibitions. Even if you can't get inside, their facades impress.

Ciutadella

Museu Municipal   MUSEUM
(🖉971 38 02 97; Bastió de sa Font; adult/child €2.25/free; ⊙10am-2pm & 6-9pm Tue-Sat) The single, vaulted gallery of the town museum mostly displays Talayotic and Roman finds from the area. Ask to borrow its comprehensive documentation in English.

Castell de Sant Nicolau
                              HISTORIC WATCHTOWER
(Plaça del Almirante Ferragut; adult/child €1.50/free; ⊙5pm-sunset Jun-Aug) West of the town centre, this stout little 17th-century watchtower stands guard at the southern head of the port entrance. Views over the waters to Mallorca and southwards along the coast are stunning.

Menorca Blava   BOAT TRIPS
(www.menorcablava.com; boat trip adult/child €40/20) Runs boat trips to the beaches of the southern coast, departing at 10am, returning at 5pm and including a paella lunch.

Diving Centre Ciutadella   DIVE CENTRE
(🖉971 38 60 30; www.menorcatech.com; Plaça de Sant Joan 10; per dive €45; ⊙May-Oct) One of three dive centres in and around Ciutadella, it's handily located in the port.

🎉 Festivals & Events

The **Festes de Sant Joan** are held in Ciutadella in the days around 23 June, the high point and eve of the saint's feast day. One of Spain's best-known and most traditional festivals, they feature busy processions, prancing horses (Menorcans pride themselves on their riding skills), performances of traditional music and dancing, and plenty of partying.

🛏 Sleeping

Hotel Sant Ignasi   COUNTRY MANSION €€€
(🖉971 38 55 75; www.santignasi.com; Carretera de Cala Morell; s/d incl breakfast €170/275; ❉🛜🏊) This venerable 18th-century mansion, planted solidly in grounds shaded by mature wild olive trees, is in open country, a mere 3km outside Ciutadella. Each of the 20 serene rooms has its own individual style and there's a first-class restaurant. Prices more than halve over winter months. From the Cala Morell road, take a narrow lane signed 'Hotel Rural' for 1.6km.

Hotel Gèminis   HOTEL €€
(🖉971 38 46 44; www.hotelgeminismenorca.com; Carrer de Josepa Rossinyol 4; s/d €65/96; ❉🛜🏊) A friendly, stylish two-star place on a backstreet, this graceful, three-storey, rose-and-white lodging offers comfortable if somewhat neutral rooms just a short walk away from the city centre. The best rooms have a sizeable balcony.

Hostal-Residencia Oasis
                        BUDGET ACCOMMODATION €
(🖉971 38 21 97; Carrer de Sant Isidre 33; s/d €35/45) Run by a delightful elderly couple, this quiet place is close to the heart of the old quarter. Rooms, mostly with bathroom, are set beside a spacious garden courtyard. Their furnishings, though still trim, are from deep into the last century.

🍴 Eating

Ciutadella's small port teems with restaurants and cafes, many of which are set in the old city walls or carved out of the cliffs that line the waterfront.

TOP CHOICE Cas Ferrer de sa Font

MENORCAN €€

(☎971 48 07 84; www.casferrer.com; Carrer del Portal de sa Font 16; meals €35; ⊗Tue-Sun) Nowhere on the island will you find more authentic Menorcan cuisine based upon meats and vegetables from the owner's organic farm. Dine on the delightful interior patio of this charming 18th-century building or inside, below beams and soft curves, in what was once a blacksmith's forge.

Café Balear

SEAFOOD €€

(☎971 38 00 05; www.cafe-balear.com; Plaça de Sant Joan 15; meals €25-30; ⊗Tue-Sun) Sometimes the old-timers are the best. Set apart from the town's more frenetic restaurant activity, this remains one of Ciutadella's classic seafood stops. You can eat outside and admire the old quarter towering before you while tucking into local prawns, *navajas* (razor shells) or fresh fish, caught from Café Balear's own boat.

Bar Triton

SEAFOOD, MEDITERRANEAN €

(☎971 38 00 02; Carrer de la Marina 55; mains €11-15.50) Join local fishermen and other folks as they hang out here and down generous servings of seafood and such house specialities as *pilotes* (small meatballs in tomato sauce).

🍷 Drinking & Entertainment

The bulk of the town's nightlife is concentrated along the waterfront and, in particular, around both sides of Plaça de Sant Joan.

Café des Museu

COCKTAIL BAR

(Carreró d'es Palau 4; ⊗10pm-3.30am) In the old town, this charming cocktail bar tucked away down a tight lane occasionally hosts live gigs – anything from acid jazz to bossa nova.

Jazzbah

LIVE MUSIC

(Plaça de San Joan 3; admission €10; ⊗11pm-5am) This venue is worth watching for its live concerts, happening house nights and chill-out sessions. The latter take place on the terrace.

La Margarete

BAR

(Carrer de Sant Joan 6; ⊗10pm-3.30am) Tucked away down a side street, this is a stylish option. The interior is slick with a modern, arty decor. On warmer nights, enjoy its pleasant cropped lawn.

🛍 Shopping

Ciutadella has two magnificent, long-established delicatessens.

El Paladar

GOURMET FOOD

(Camí de Maó; www.elpaladar.es, in Spanish) Penetrate deep into this boutique for wines, pickles, pâtés and ripe local cheeses. There are pig products too: in 2010 the owner was the Spanish ham-slicing champion.

Ca Na Fayas

GOURMET FOOD

(www.canafayas.es; Carrer Murada d'Artrutx 32 & Avinguda de Jaume I El Conqueridor 47) This is a similar richly scented gourmet emporium with entrances on two streets. Whole cheeses, shelf upon shelf of them, fill the shop window.

ℹ️ Information

Tourist office (☎971 38 26 93; Plaça de la Catedral 5; ⊗8.30am-3pm & 5-9pm) Has an all-Mallorca remit.

ℹ️ Getting There & Away

BOAT Ferries for Mallorca (Port d'Alcúdia and Cala Ratjada) leave from the northern side of the Port de Ciutadella, pending completion of a new port in Son Oleo, just south of town. For more detail, see p629.

BUS TMSA (www.tmsa.es) runs hourly express buses (45 minutes) between Ciutadella and Maó, departing from Plaça Menorca. Autocares Torres buses serve the coast south of Ciutadella as far as Son Xoriguer, departing from Plaça dels Pins.

FANCY FOOTWORK

Mallorca is better known for its shoe-making tradition (especially with the international success of the Camper company), but Menorca, too, has long had its share of cobblers. The best-loved local product is the *avarca* (*abarca* in Spanish), a loose, comfortable slip-on sandal that covers the front of the foot and straps around the heel. Sometimes with soles fashioned from recycled car tyres, they make great summer shoes. Shops sell them all over the island (and indeed all over the Balearics).

ⓘ Getting Around

Autos Ciutadella (☎971 48 00 24; www.autosciutadella.com; Avinguda del Capità Negrete) Local car rental agency offering competitive prices.
Velos Joan (☎971 38 15 76; www.velosjoan.com; Carrer de Sant Isidre 30) Bike rental (€10 per day).

Around Ciutadella

North of Ciutadella, Cala Morell is a low-key development of whitewashed villas. Steep steps lead to the small port and beach, backed by a couple of bar-restaurants. More intriguing is the Cala Morell Necropolis, prehistoric burial caves hacked into the coastal cliffs, along a track just south of the housing complex.

Before reaching Cala Morell, a right turn to Algaiarens leads, after about 6km, to a privately owned car park, a 500m walk short of a pair of crescent-shaped, white-sand beaches.

North Coast

Menorca's north coast is rugged and rocky, punctured by small, scenic coves. It's less developed than the south and, with your own transport and a bit of footwork, you'll discover some of the Balearics' best off-the-beaten-track beaches.

ES GRAU

This spruce, whitewashed hamlet sits beside an open bay. Here, you can rent a kayak or bike from Menorca en Kayak (☎669 097977; www.menorcaenkayak.com; ⊗Easter-Oct) and explore the Parc Natural S'Albufera d'es Grau from sea or land. The beach's shallow waters are ideal for young families.

Bar Es Moll (Carrer d'es Pescadors 17; meals €15-20; ⊗Apr-Oct), a basic place with plastic tables and chairs, serves tapas and portions of fresh sardines, mussels and prawns. Its charm is its position, above the jetty where local fishing boats dock.

PARC NATURAL S'ALBUFERA D'ES GRAU

Inland from Es Grau and separated from the coast by a barrier of high sand dunes is S'Albufera, the largest freshwater lagoon in the Balearics. Home to many species of wetland birds, it's also an important stopover for migrating species. The lagoon and its

CAMÍ DE CAVALLS

This signed walking trail, the GR223, revives an 18th-century defensive route that linked coastal watch towers, fortresses and artillery batteries. Well signed (look for the horseshoe symbol), it snakes around the coastline for 184km, with occasional forays inland, and can be walked in easy sections. Most stretches are attackable by mountain bike, too. Ask for details at tourist offices or buy *Guide of Camí de Cavalls: 20 Itineraries for Discovering Mallorca* (€21).

shores form the 'nucleus zone' of Menorca's Biosphere Reserve, a natural park protected from the threat of development. Borrow a pair of binoculars from the park's information office (⊗9am-3pm) and follow one of two easy trails, each lasting under an hour. Illa d'en Colom, a couple of hundred metres offshore, is also within the protected park.

CAP DE FAVÁRITX

The drive up to this narrow rocky cape at the northern extremity of the Parc is a treat. The last leg is across a lunar landscape of black slate. At the end of the road (on the way, ignore the *propriedad privada* – private property – sign; it's public access), a lighthouse stands watch as the sea pounds relentlessly against the impassive cliffs. South of the cape stretch some fine remote sandy bays and beaches, including Cala Presili and Platja d'en Tortuga, both reachable only on foot.

CAP DE CAVALLERIA & AROUND

Three kilometres south of Fornells, turn west and follow signs for 7km to reach a parking area for the stunning little double-crescent, golden beach of Platja Cavalleria (a 10-minute walk from the car park).

Ecomuseu Cap de Cavalleria (www.ecomuseudecavalleria.com; adult/child €3/free; ⊗10am-7pm Apr-Oct) is a small, private museum 1km north of Platja Cavalleria's car park. Panels and videos illustrate the north coast, its fauna, the lighthouse, ancient inhabitants and Roman occupation. Borrow the booklet with full English translations of the captions. The museum's *Les 7 Rutes* is a detailed multilingual map showing every feature of the peninsula.

A further spectacular 2km drive north brings you to the tip of Cap de Cavalleria, abrupt cliffs, Far de Cavalleria (Spain's oldest lighthouse) and a series of crumbling civil war Republican gun emplacements. Returning southwards, a side road leads after about 3km to Cala Binimella, an OK beach with a nearby bar-restaurant. You can walk from there to the much prettier Cala Pregonda.

FORNELLS
POP 950

This picturesque whitewashed village is on a large, shallow bay popular with windsurfers. Fornells is renowned for its waterfront seafood restaurants, most of which serve up the local, decidedly pricey speciality, *caldereta de llagosta* (lobster stew).

Sights & Activities

The sheltered, unruffled waters of the long slim bay are ideal for novice windsurfers. Wind Fornells (www.windfornells.com; per 2/3/4 2hr sessions €130/180/224) offers courses at all levels from mid-May to October.

If the sight of fishing boats bobbing in the bay stirs the sea wolf in your soul, embark on a three- to four-hour catamaran trip with Catamaran Charter (www.catamarancharter. net; Passeig Marítim 69; adult/child €60/35). Also trading as Katayak (www.katayak.net, in Spanish), it hires out kayaks and bicycles. For underwater fun, check out Catamaran Charter's neighbour, Diving Center Fornells (www.divingfornells.com; Passeig Marítim 68). All three operate from April to October.

Watching over the bay at the northern limit of town, the Torre de Fornells (adult/child €2.40/1.45; ⊙10am-3pm Tue-Sun Easter-Oct), a squat, round defensive tower, was built by the British in 1801. Clamber up to its topmost point for great views.

JOINING AN ARCHAEOLOGICAL DIG

The Ecomuseu Cap de Cavalleria team are excavating the remains of the nearby Roman settlement of Sanisera. Each year the museum runs several three-week residential excavation campaigns, open to students and amateurs who wish to learn about archaeology in practice. Instruction is in both English and Spanish. For details, check its website, www.ecomuseudecavalleria.com.

Sleeping & Eating

A pair of friendly bar-*hostales* with pools sit side by side on Plaça S'Algaret. Except for August (when rooms cost €90 to €100), they offer exceptional value.

Hostal La Palma   HOTEL €
(☎971 37 66 34; s/d €25/50; ⊙Easter-Oct; ❄@≋) Behind this busy bar-restaurant are cheerful rooms with bathrooms, balconies and views of the surrounding countryside. Singles aren't available in August.

Hostal S'Algaret   HOTEL €
(☎971 37 65 52; www.hostal-salgaret.com; s/d €25/50; ⊙May-Oct; ❄@≋) In business since the 1950s, this pleasant, simple *hostal* has crisp, clean rooms with balconies. Its restaurant is a bustling spot for your seafood hit.

Es Port   SEAFOOD €€
(☎971 37 64 03; Passeig Marítim 5; meals €30-35; ⊙Sat-Thu Easter-Oct) Some fine fresh fish and other seafood are done here. Of course, it does *caldereta de llagosta* (€64), but less financial outlay goes into a sizzling *paella de llomanto* (lobster paella; €35).

S'Ancora   SEAFOOD €€
(☎971 37 66 70; Passeig Marítim 7-8; menúes €11-17, mains €12-23) 'The Anchor' enjoys a more upmarket setting, next door to Es Port. All dark-brown wicker chairs on the terrace and olive-green decor within, it offers much the same basic fruits of the sea with a slicker presentation of dishes.

South Coast

Menorca's southern flank tends to have the better beaches – and thus the greater concentration of development. The jagged coastline is occasionally interrupted by a small inlet with a sandy beach, backed by a cluster of gleaming-white villas, largely small-scale and in the Moorish Mediterranean style.

CIUTADELLA TO SON BOU

The rugged coastline south of Ciutadella gives way to a couple of smallish beaches at the resorts of Santandria and Cala Blanca. On the island's southwest corner looms the large resort of Cala en Bosc, a busy boating and diving centre. Not far east are the popular beaches of Platja de Son Xoriguer, connected to Ciutadella by frequent buses.

Between Son Xoriguer and Santa Galdana lie some of the island's least-accessible

WORTH A TRIP

PEDRERES DE S'HOSTAL

You'll get butterflies simply gazing down into the depths of these vast stone quarries (www.lithica.es; Camí Vell; adult/child €4/free; ☺9.30am-2.30pm & 4.30pm-sunset Mon-Sat, 9.30am-2.30pm Sun), exploited until 1994. The bleached *marés*, a variety of sandstone extracted here and in other quarries around the island, has historically been Menorca's main building material. Over decades, powerful machines gouged out huge hollow, inverted cubes. In these deep pits with their superb acoustics, concerts are sometimes organised. In an earlier age, human muscle and sinew hacked away the rock, leaving bizarre shapes and formations. Here, in the older quarry, where nature has resumed possession, Lithica, the association of volunteers that has recovered this monument to human endeavour, maintains a botanical garden of endemic Menorcan species and a charming medieval garden with a fountain at its heart.

Allow at least 45 minutes to ramble through the quarries, which are off the old road to Maó. Take the Ronda Sur ring road to the Puerta del Mar roundabout with its large rectangular sculpture. They're well signed from here.

coves. A narrow country road leads south of Ciutadella (follow the 'Platjes' sign from the *ronda* – ring road) and then forks twice to (almost) reach the unspoiled beaches (from west to east) of Arenal de Son Saura, Cala Es Talaier, Cala en Turqueta, Cala Macarelleta and Cala Macarella.

For Cala Macarella, for instance, you arrive at a car park and must walk 15 minutes to the beach (which has a restaurant). You can walk or swim around to the still prettier Cala Macarelleta. The walk between Cala Macarella and Cala en Turqueta takes an hour.

Southwest of Ferreries is Santa Galdana, just the place if karaoke, English pubs and minigolf are your idea of fun. In fairness, the beach is beautiful and the tack mild. A walking track leads west along the coast to Cala Macarella (30 minutes). To the east of Santa Galdana, Cala Mitjana is another enticing strand.

Pleasant Camping S'Atalaia (☎971 37 42 32; www.campingsatalaia.com, in Spanish; site per person/tent/car €7.50/10/3; ✸), shaded by pine trees, is two-thirds of the way down the Ferreries–Santa Galdana road.

The resort of Son Bou, southwest of Alaior, boasts the island's longest beach and most depressing development. Just back from the beach are the remains of a 5th-century Christian basilica.

SOUTH OF MAÓ

The coast south of Maó is more intensively developed.

Sant Lluís, a bright, white, grid-pattern inland town, was built by the French during their brief occupation of the island be-

tween 1756 and 1763. It's worth a short stop to visit the Molí de Dalt (☎971 15 10 84; adult/child €1.20/0.60; ☺10am-2pm Mon-Sat), the island's last surviving working windmill, constructed during the French era. Within it, there's a small **museum** of rural implements and tools.

In Sant Lluís, Hotel Biniarroca (☎971 15 00 59; www.biniarroca.com; r incl breakfast €160-295; ☺Easter-Nov; ☎✸) is a cosy, welcoming, rambling rural retreat. Furnished for comfort and ease, it's run with panache by a pair of British lady artists and designers. Ducks peck and sheep graze just beyond the fence of their lovely garden, at once formal and pleasantly rumpled. Their gourmet restaurant (☺dinner only) is open to all comers. Rates are much lower outside high summer.

Platja de Punta Prima is a small holiday resort with a pleasant 200m-long beach. Although it's protected by the low expanse of Illa de l'Aire, you can still catch the occasional wave. Regular buses run here from Maó.

Westwards along the coast, Binibèquer (aka Binibeca) has all the appearance of a charming old fishing village; in fact, it was designed as a single unit and constructed in the early 1970s. Gleaming white and something of a tourist beehive, the curious houses, tight alleys and narrow cove with its transparent water are delightful, whatever their genesis.

Cala de Binidalí, a few kilometres further west, straggles without focus and its beach is tiny. But the water is so enticingly azure it makes you want to dive in and swim out to open sea.

Murcia

Includes »

Best Places to Stay

» Hotel Casa Emilio (p647)
» Arco de San Juan (p647)
» Hotel Los Habaneros (p651)

Best Places to Eat

» Figón de Alfaro (p648)
» La Tartana (p652)
» Restaurante Juan de Toledo (p655)

Why Go?

Situated with the modesty of a maiden aunt between the boisterous resorts of Valencia's Costa Blanca to the north and the popular beaches of Almería to the south, Murcia province is one of the least-visited corners of Spain and yet is home to absorbing sights, lively workaday towns and the sizzling Costa Cálida (Hot Coast) with its steamy annual average of 3000 hours of sunshine.

Unsurprisingly, the economy here is primarily based on agriculture, with the main crops of citrus fruits and grapes watered by an irrigation system comprising waterwheels, aqueducts and canals dating back to the 11th century.

Explore the busy capital with its splendid cathedral and superb tapas bars. Cartagena also has plenty of appeal and is busy excavating, digging deep to reveal its rich classical heritage; inland, pretty Lorca is famous for its Easter processions. Nature-lovers should head for the dramatic unspoilt beauty of the natural parks.

When to Go
Murcia

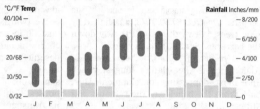

March & April Catch the extraordinary Easter Week processions in Lorca, famed throughout Spain

May & June Head for the beaches on the Costa Cálida before the crowds (and the centigrade) peak

September Get into the historical spirit of Cartagena during the annual *Carthagineses y Romanos* festival

Murcia City

POP 434,000

Officially twinned with Miami, Murcia is the antithesis of the city of vice; it's a laid-back provincial capital that comes alive during the weekend *paseo* (stroll). Bypassed by most tourists and treated as a country cousin by too many Spaniards, the city nevertheless merits a visit. Head for the river, the cathedral and the surrounding pedestrian streets.

In AD 825 Muslims moved into the former Roman colony and renamed it 'Mursiya'. The town was reconquered in 1243

Murcia Highlights

❶ Sip a drink at sundown in Murcia's Plaza del Cardenal Belluga overlooked by the magnificent **cathedral** (p646)

❷ Marvel at the pageantry of Lorca's spectacular **Semana Santa processions** (p654)

❸ Explore Cartagena's fascinating **Roman and Carthaginian sites** (p650)

❹ Lace up those hiking boots and explore the unspoilt beauty of the **Parque Natural de Sierra Espuña** (p655)

❺ Wonder at the luxurious ornamentation of the Patio Arabe at Murcia's **Real Casino** (p646)

❻ Indulge in a therapeutic (and free) **mud treatment** (p653) at Lo Pagán in the

natural saltwater lagoon of Mar Menor

❼ Eat **tapas** (p652) that are innovative, unusual and extremely moreish

❽ Chill out while checking out the extraordinary **pozos de la nieve** (ice houses, p655) in the Parque Natural de Sierra Espuña

N 0 ——— 250 m
0 ——— 0.1 miles

by Alfonso X of Castilla y León and it's said his shrivelled heart is preserved within the cathedral's altar. Enriched by silk and agriculture, the city was at its grandest in the 18th century, from when the cathedral's magnificent baroque facade dates.

Looted by Napoleonic troops in 1810, and then overcome by plague and cholera, the city fell into decline. A century later, during the Spanish Civil War, Murcia was the scene of bitter fighting and many churches were destroyed. Thankfully, the cathedral survived.

◉ Sights

TOP CHOICE **Real Casino de Murcia**

HISTORICAL BUILDING

(www.casinodemurcia.com; Calle Trapería 18; admission €5; ◷11.30am-9pm) Murcia's resplendent casino first opened as a gentlemen's club in 1847. Painstakingly restored to its original glory, it was reopened by King Juan Carlos in November 2009. The building is a fabulous combination of historical design and opulence, providing an evocative glimpse of bygone aristocratic grandeur. Beyond the decorative facade are a dazzling Moorish-style patio; a classic English-style library with 20,000 books, some dating from the 17th century; a magnificent ballroom with glittering chandeliers; and a compelling *tocador* (ladies powder room) with a ceiling fresco of cherubs, angels and an alarming winged woman in flames. There is also the neoclassical *Patio Pompeyano* and the classic wood-panelled *sala de billar* (billiards room).

Catedral de Santa María   CATHEDRAL

(Plaza del Cardinal Belluga; ◷7am-1pm & 5-8pm) Murcia's cathedral was built in 1394 on the site of a mosque. The initial Gothic architecture was given a playful baroque facelift in 1748. The 15th-century Capilla de los Vélez is a highlight; the chapel's flutes and

Murcia City

curls resemble piped icing. The **Museo de la Catedral** (admission free; ☺10am-12.30pm & 5-8pm Tue-Sat, 10am-2pm Sun) displays religious artefacts, but is most striking for the excavations on display: the remains of an 11th-century Moorish dwelling and of a small *mezquita* (mosque), visible below a glass walkway.

FREE **Museo de Bellas Artes** ART GALLERY
(Calle del Obispo Frutos 12; ☺10am-8.30pm Tue-Sat, 10am-2pm Sun) An inviting, light gallery devoted to Spanish artists. The 2nd- floor Siglo de Oro gallery includes canvases by Murillo, Zurbarán and by 'Lo Spagnoletto', José (Jusepe) de Ribera. For a break from all that religious piety, don't miss the superbly kitsch dazzle of glamorous *señoritas* on the 3rd floor.

Museo Salzillo SCULPTURE MUSEUM
(www.museosalzillo.es, in Spanish; Plaza de San Agustín 1-3; admission €5; ☺10am-2pm & 5-8pm Tue-Fri, 10am-2pm Sat) Located in the baroque chapel of Ermita de Jesús and devoted to Murcian sculptor Francisco Salzillo (1707–83). The highlights are his exquisite *pasos* (figures carried in Semana Santa processions) and carved-wood nativity figurines. To get here head west from Gran Via del Escultor Francsico Salzillo along Calle Santa Teresa.

Museo de la Ciencia y del Agua SCIENCE MUSEUM
(Plaza de la Ciencia 1; adult/child €1.20/free; ☺10am-2pm & 5-8pm Tue-Sat, 11am-2pm Sun; 🖲) Beside the river and one for the children. Although everything's in Spanish, this small hands-on science museum has plenty of buttons to press and knobs to twirl, plus fish tanks and a small planetarium.

FREE **Museo Arqueológico** ARCHAEOLOGICAL MUSEUM
(www.museoarqueologicomurcia.com; Avenida Alfonso X El Sabio 7; ☺10am-8.30pm Tue-Sat, 10am-2pm Sun) Has exceptionally well laid out and documented exhibits spread over two floors that start with Palaeolithic times and include audiovisual displays.

✯ Festivals & Events

Semana Santa EASTER WEEK
The city's Easter processions rival Lorca's in their fervour.

Bando de la Huerta SPRING FESTIVAL
Two days after Easter Sunday, the mood changes as the city celebrates this annual spring festival with parades, food stalls, folklore and carafe-fulls of fiesta spirit.

🛏 Sleeping

TOP CHOICE **Hotel Casa Emilio** MODERN HOTEL €
(☏968 22 06 31; www.hotelcasaemilio. com; Alameda de Colón 9; s/d €45/50; P ❀ ☎) Across from the Floridablanca gardens, near the river, this is an attractively designed and well-maintained hotel with spacious, brightly lit rooms, large bathrooms and good firm mattresses. Parking costs €9.

Arco de San Juan HISTORIC HOTEL €€
(☏968 21 04 55; www.arcosanjuan.com, in Spanish; Plaza de Ceballos 10; s/d €75/130; P ❀ ☎) This four-star hotel in a former 18th-century palace hints at its palatial past with a massive 5m-high original door and some

hefty repro columns. The rooms are classic and comfortable, with hardwood details and classy fabrics. Parking here costs €15.75.

Hotel Hispano II
MODERN HOTEL €€
(☏968 21 61 52; www.hotelhispano.net, in Spanish; Calle Radio Murcia 3; s/d incl breakfast €48/58; P❄@) Hotel Hispano II and Pensión Hispano I, around the corner (closed for refurbishment until early 2011) share a garage (parking €13). The trim, modern Hispano II is famous for its excellent restaurant (Restaurante Hispano), and is popular with business travellers. The traditional rooms have shiny dark-wood furnishings and plush fabrics.

Hotel Rincón de Pepe
MODERN HOTEL €€
(☏968 21 22 39; www.nh-hotels.com; Calle de los Apóstoles 34; r €95-126; P❄@) Acres of marble lobby greet guests at this corporate-style hotel. Rooms have glossy parquet floors and large luxurious bathrooms. The hotel restaurant promises a gourmet dining experience. There's a small casino here, as well.

El Churra
MODERN HOTEL €€
(☏968 23 84 00; www.elchurra.net; Avenida Marqués de los Vélez 12; s/d €54/75; P❄@) A slickly run hotel with stylish rooms. Head north on Calle de la Puerta Nueva.

Pensión Segura
BUDGET HOTEL €
(☏968 21 12 81; Plaza de Camachos 14; s/d €36/44; ❄@) Small rooms with yellow-and-white paintwork, sparkling floor tiles and slimline wardrobes and bathrooms.

ℹ️ **TOURIST TICKETS & INFORMATION**

The tourist office has two handy services to save money and time: **Puerto de Culturas** (www.cartagenapuertodeculturas.com) offers four different combined tickets (€11 to €20) covering Murcia's sights and tours. Tickets are available at each venue or at the tourist office. Access city information via your mobile phone, including special events, itineraries and activities taking place during your proposed stay. Just send a text message with the word TOURISM to mobile number ☏609 031060 or complete a form via the tourism webpage (www.cartagenaturismo.es).

🍴 Eating

Murcia has some outstanding restaurants. For the highest concentration, head for Plaza San Juan and Plaza Romea. Tapas bars are prolific around Plaza de las Flores and Plaza Santa Catalina.

Figón de Alfaro
INNOVATIVE TAPAS €
(Calle Alfaro 7; meals €12-15; ⊙lunch & dinner Mon-Sat, lunch Sun) Popular with all ages and budgets, Figón de Alfaro offers a chaotic bar area or a more sedate interconnecting dining room. Choose from full meals, a range of juicy *montaditos* (mini-rolls) or innovative one-offs such as *pastel de berejena con salsa de calabacín* (aubergine pie with a courgette sauce).

La Parranda
MEDITERRANEAN €€
(Calle San José 1; meals €15-20; ⊙lunch & dinner Thu-Tue) This *taberna* has an upbeat contemporary vibe with its light wood-panelled dining space and menu of traditional and modern tapas, *raciones* (large tapas servings) and more substantial meals. In a hurry? Go for the *brocheta de langostinas* (prawn skewer). In not so much of a hurry...follow this with a creamy *panacotta*. The sister La Parranda restaurant is situated on the nearby foodie square, Plaza San Juan.

Los Zagales
HOMESTYLE COOKING €
(Calle Polo Medina 4; meals €10-15) Lying within confessional distance of the cathedral (since 1926), Los Zagales dishes up superb, inexpensive tapas, *raciones, platos combinados* (mixed platters), home-made desserts (and home-made chips). This is where the locals eat, so you may have to wait for a table. It's worth it.

Restaurante Hispano
INNOVATIVE SPANISH €€
(Calle Arquitecto Cerdán; raciones €7, meals €20-25; ⊙lunch & dinner Mon-Sat, lunch Sun) The warm and inviting bar area here has inventive *raciones*, such as baby broad beans sautéed with artichokes and onion. The smarter restaurant beyond serves more traditional dishes.

Los Arroces del Romea
RICE DISHES €€
(Plaza Romea; meals €20-25; ✍) Watch the speciality paella-style rice dishes being prepared in cartwheel-sized pans over the flames while you munch on circular *murciano* bread drizzled with olive oil. There are five rice dishes to choose from, including vegetarian.

Alborado
SOPHISTICATED MODERN €€

(Calle Andrés Baquero 15; meals €20-25; ☻)
Dishes up gourmet variations on traditional specialities.

Las Cadenas
TRADITIONAL MURCIAN €€

(☎968 22 09 24; Calle de los Apóstoles 10; meals €20-28; ☺ Mon-Sat) Has an elegant dress-for-dinner feel and traditional menu. Reservations recommended.

Drinking & Entertainment

Most through-the-night-life buzzes around the university. There are some vibrant bars and clubs here, including Sala Revolver (Calle Victorio), with its emphasis on Latin and Spanish rock, and, a few doors away, Mestizo (Calle Victorio; ☺10pm-late Thu-Sun), a pulsating student bar. For a classier atmosphere, head to La Muralla (Calle de los Apóstoles 34; ☺10.30pm-late), located in the bowels of Hotel Rincón de Pepe, with a cocktail bar snuggled against the original city walls. Nearby, Fitzpatrick (Plaza Cetina; ☺3pm-3am) has suitably blarney atmosphere and all the predictable ales on tap.

Shopping

For local handicrafts try Centro para la Artesanía (Calle Francisco Rabal 8), which is both an exhibition space and sales outlet, located just west of Plaza de la Fuensanta, and Paparajote (Calle de los Apóstoles 14), which also sells gourmet goodies.

ℹ Information

The regional tourist authority website is www.murciaturistica.es.

Locutorio Viajacom (Plaza de Camachos; per hr €1; ☺10am-2pm & 4.30-10pm) Internet access.

Tourist kiosk (Calle de Santa Clara; ☺10am-2pm & 5-8pm Mon-Sat, 10am-2pm Sun) Only open in summer.

Tourist office (☎968 35 87 49; www.murcia ciudad.com; Plaza del Cardenal Belluga; ☺10am-2pm & 5-9pm Mon-Sat, 10am-2pm Sun)

ℹ Getting There & Away

AIR Murcia's San Javier airport is situated beside the Mar Menor, closer to Cartagena than Murcia city. Connections to the UK include the following:

easyJet (www.easyjet.com) London (Gatwick), Birmingham, Bristol and Newcastle.

Jet2.com (www.jet2.com) Blackpool, Edinburgh, Leeds, Manchester and Newcastle.

CITY PARKS

If you are visiting midsummer, escape the blazing heat by visiting one of Murcia's lovely parks. The classic, small but beautiful Jardín Floridablanca has several magnificent banyan trees distinctive for their massive spread of thick woody roots, as well as jacarandas, Cyprus trees, palms, rose bushes and shady benches, plenty of them, for contemplating the view. A larger park and botanical garden, Murcia Parque lies just west of the Puente del Malecón footbridge and is similarly replete with leafy splendour.

Ryanair (www.ryanair.com) London (Luton and Stansted), Dublin, Leeds, Glasgow, East Midlands and Liverpool.

BUS At least 10 buses run daily to both Cartagena (€3.95, one hour) and Lorca (€5.35, 1½ hours).

TRAIN Up to five trains travel daily to/from Madrid (€44.60, 4¼ hours). Hourly trains operate to/from Lorca (€15.60, one hour).

ℹ Getting Around

BUS From the bus station, take bus 3 into town; from the train station, hop aboard bus 9 or 39.

CAR & MOTORCYCLE There's a handy car park at Jardín San Esteban, north of the centre.

TAXI A taxi between the airport and Murcia city costs around €40.

MURCIA REGION

The Murcia region offers a tantalising choice of landscapes, ranging from the chill-out beaches of the Costa Cálida to the medieval magic of its towns. To appreciate fully the unspoiled hinterland, you will need your own wheels.

Cartagena
POP 211,000

This is a city where you should walk with your eyes raised to the skyline: the Modernista buildings, with their domes, swirly decorations and pastel colours, add a sumptuous quality to the architecture. The city is equally laden with archaeological sites, as well as excellent restaurants and bars.

The city has a chequered economic history. The mining boom of the late 19th century all but ceased by the late 1920s, while the naval presence of dollar-rich sailors on

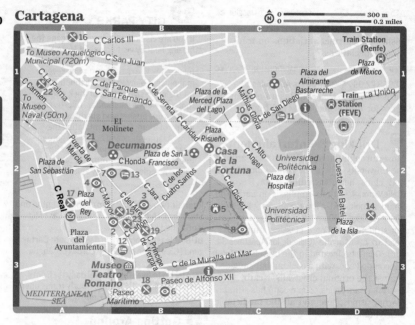

MURCIA MURCIA REGION

R&R also waned. Cartagena's closed shops and dilapidated buildings all spoke of recession.

But the town is picking itself up while digging deep into the past: excavations are stripping back more and more of its old quarter to reveal a long-buried – and fascinating – Roman and Carthaginian heritage.

History

In 223 BC Hasdrubal marched his invading army into the Iberian settlement of Mastia, renaming it Carthago Nova. The town prospered during Roman occupation and, under Muslim rule, became the independent emirate of Cartajana. The Arabs improved agriculture and established the town's reputation for building warships before being expelled by the Catholics in 1242. The defensive walls were raised in the 18th century. Although the city was badly bombed in the civil war, industry and the population flourished during the 1950s and '60s.

⊙ Sights & Activities

TOP CHOICE **Museo Teatro Romano**

THEATRE MUSEUM
(Plaza del Ayuntamiento 9; adult/child €5/2; ⊙10am-8pm Tue-Sat, 10am-2pm Sun) The city's latest museum was designed by Pritzker

Prize–winning architect Rafael Moneo. The tour transports visitors from the initial museum on Plaza del Ayuntamiento, via escalators and an underground passage beneath the ruined cathedral, to the magnificent, recently restored Roman theatre dating from the 1st century BC. The tour and layout of the museum is designed to reflect Cartagena's fascinating layers of urban history and includes Roman statues and artefacts, excavated from the site, as well as the cathedral's crypt and remains of an original Moorish dwelling. Explanatory plaques are in Spanish and English.

Roman Cartagena ARCHAEOLOGICAL SITES
Other Roman sites include the Augusteum (Calle Caballero; adult/child €2.50/free; ⊙4-7.30pm Tue-Sun), which has an exhibition on the Roman Forum. The Decumanos (Calle Honda; adult/child €2/free; ⊙10am-2.30pm Tue-Sun) has evocative remains of one of the town's main Roman streets linking the port with the forum, and including an arcade and thermal baths. The Casa de la Fortuna (Plaza Risueño; adult/child €2.50/free; ⊙10am-2.30pm Tue-Sun) consists of fascinating remains of an aristocratic Roman villa dating back to the 2nd and 3rd centuries, complete with murals and mosaics, and part of an excavated road. Finally, the Mu-

ralla Púnica (Calle de San Diego; adult/child €3.50/free; ⊙10am-2.30pm & 4-7.30pm), built around a section of the old Punic wall, concentrates on the town's Carthaginian and Roman legacy.

Modernista Cartagena

MODERNISTA ARCHITECTURE

Cartagena is rich in Modernista buildings; several of the best now house banks (no surprise there). Particularly magnificent are Casa Cervantes (Calle Mayor 11); Casa Llagostera (Calle Mayor 25); the zinc-domed Gran Hotel (Calle del Aire); the strawberries-and-cream confection of Casa Clares (Calle del Aire 4); and the splendid Palacio Aguirre (Plaza de la Merced), now an exhibition space for modern art (known as MURAM).

Castillo de la Concepción   CASTLE

For a sweeping panoramic view, stride up to Castillo de la Concepción, or hop on the lift (€1). Within the castle's gardens, decorated by strutting peacocks, the Centro de Interpretación de la Historia de Cartagena (adult/child €3.50/free; ⊙10am-2.30pm & 4-8.30pm) offers a mid-tech potted history of Cartagena through the centuries via audio screens and a 10-minute film (in English and Spanish).

FREE Museo Arqueológico Municipal

ARCHAEOLOGICAL MUSEUM

(Calle Ramón y Cajal 45; ⊙10am-2pm & 5-8pm Tue-Fri, 11am-2pm Sat & Sun) Built above a late-Roman cemetery with a rich display of Carthaginian, Roman, Visigoth and Islamic artefacts. To get here, head northwest of the centre, via Calle La Palma.

FREE Museo Naval   NAVAL MUSEUM

(Calle Menéndez Pelayo 8; ⊙10am-1.30pm Tue-Sun; ⛨) Has a great collection of naval maps and charts, plus replicas of boats big and small. Located northwest of the centre via Calle Real.

★ Festivals & Events

Semana Santa   EASTER WEEK

Cartagena's haunting processions are as elaborate as anything Andalucía can offer.

La Mar de Músicas   WORLD MUSIC

Bringing the best of world music to Cartagena, this annual festival is held in the castle's auditorium throughout July.

Carthagineses y Romanos

HISTORICAL FESTIVAL

(www.cartaginesesyromanos.es) For 10 days during the second half of September, locals play war games in a colourful fiesta that re-enacts the battles between rival Carthaginian and Roman occupiers during the second Punic War.

🛏 Sleeping

Hotel Los Habaneros   MODERN HOTEL €€

(☎968 50 52 50; www.hotelhabaneros.com, in Spanish; Calle de San Diego 60; s/d €55/68; ▣✳@🛜❄) Located across from the Murcia Púnica tourist office, this shiny modern hotel has good-sized rooms decorated

DON'T MISS

GO THE TAPAS ROUTE

Murcia is excellent for tapas with plenty of variety, generous portions and a considerable vegetarian choice for non-carnivorous folk. Most of the restaurants listed in this chapter are fronted by tapas bars or serve *raciones* (large tapas serving), which are great for sharing. Overall, Murciano tapas are more inventive than the norm and reflect the province's comprehensive agriculture with its use of fresh seasonal ingredients.

in cream and burgundy. Features include hairdryers, satellite TV and large tubs with showers. Parking costs €10.60.

Pensión Oriente   BUDGET HOTEL €
(☑968 50 24 69; 2nd fl, Calle Jara 27; s/d without bathroom €25/34) The Oriente has 12 old-fashioned rooms with high ceilings, dark furniture and fans. A couple also sport fridges and/or balconies. The one spacious en suite (€38) is worth the extra euros.

Hotel NH Cartagena   MODERN HOTEL €€
(☑968 12 09 08; www.nh-hotels.com; Calle Real 2; d €100; P ❄ @ ☎) Occupying the former port offices, the bland concrete facade jars somewhat with its neoclassical town hall neighbour. The rooms are NH formula (modern and stylish); however, the upper floors have bay views and there are little extras such as electric kettles.

✗ Eating

There are plenty of bars and restaurants around Plaza del Ayuntamiento and the side streets off Calle Mayor. Cartagena has a handy covered market that is good for self-caterers.

TOP CHOICE La Tartana   TAPAS €
(Puerta de Murcia 14; tapas €1.50, raciones €4-8) In a charming Modernista building on this wide pedestrian shopping street, this is the best place in town to come for tapas, *montaditos* and *raciones*. The selection includes classy numbers such as triangles of fried cheese with raspberry sauce. Typically packed with gossiping locals, La Tartana's atmosphere and service are tops. The same owners also run **La Tapería** (Calle del Parque 2), which offers similar food in more upmarket surroundings.

Restaurante Azafrán   SOPHISTICATED MODERN €€
(☑968 52 31 72; www.restauranteazafran.com; Calle La Palma 3; meals €35; ☺Mon-Sat; ☎) Despite the residential location, the Saffron has a far-from-pedestrian feel with its dramatic display of photos, background jazz and shady terrace. Fronted by a sophisticated tapas bar, main dishes feature traditional and modern recipes. Reservations recommended.

La Tagliatella   ITALIAN €
(Calle Cañon 4; pizzas €11, pasta €13; ☺lunch & dinner Tue-Sat, lunch Mon; ☑) A step up from other Italian restaurants in the area, this is a welcoming eatery, good for sharing pizza and pasta with sauces including lobster and cream, and pesto with walnuts and gorgonzola. The pizzas are crispy-based with robust toppings.

Rincón Gallego   SEAFOOD €€
(Calle Cañon 13; meals €15-25; ☺Mon-Sat) This extensive menu of fish dishes includes several ways of preparing the speciality – octopus – including the deliciously simple grilled octopus with fresh lemons. Other dishes include that fail-safe favourite: fish and chips.

La Patacha   SEAFOOD €€
(☑968 10 39 71; Paseo de Alfonso XII; meals €25-38) This permanently moored boat has a wide choice of (obviously) seafood and fish. Reservations recommended.

Columbus   TRADITIONAL MURCIAN €€
(Calle Mayor 18; meals €20-25) Great bustling location, across from the magnificent Casa Cervantes, serving local dishes.

Casa del Pescador   SEAFOOD €€
(Plaza de la Isla; meals €20-35; ☺lunch daily, dinner Tue-Sat year-round, closed Tue Aug) Renowned for its seafood.

Jie Ichiban   JAPANESE €€
(☑968 50 87 40; Plaza del Rey 6; meals €15-20) Good Japanese restaurant.

CUT-PRICE CAVIAR

A locally produced variant of caviar (*huevas de mújol*) is produced on the Mar Menor. It's available in jars in most local supermarkets at a very reasonable price compared to the real thing, but tastes surprisingly authentic – and good.

ℹ Information

Exit (Plaza del Rey 5; per hr €2; ☺noon-midnight Mon-Sat, 4pm-midnight Sun) Internet access.

Tourist kiosk (Paseo de Alfonso XII; ☺10am-2pm & 4-6pm Mon-Fri, 10am-1pm Sat & Sun)

Tourist office (☎968 50 64 83; www.cartagena.es; Plaza del Almirante Bastarreche; ☺10am-2pm & 4-6pm Mon-Fri, 10am-1pm Sat) Plenty of excellent information.

ℹ Getting There & Away

BUS Buses run eight times daily to Alicante (€7.25, two hours), 10 times to Murcia (€3.95, one hour) and to La Manga (€3.45 to €4.25, one hour).

TAXI A taxi to or from San Javier airport will cost you approximately €40.

TRAIN For Renfe train destinations, change in Murcia (€4.85, 50 minutes, four to seven daily). Beware: take the local train as the Talgo express alternative costs a hefty €16. Local FEVE trains make the short run to Los Nietos (€2.25, 30 minutes, every 40 minutes) on the Mar Menor.

Costa Cálida

With more than 300 days of annual sunshine and an average temperature of 18°C, the Hot Coast is aptly named.

MAR MENOR

The Mar Menor is a 170-sq-km saltwater lagoon. Its waters are a good 5°C warmer than the open sea and excellent for water sports, including jet-skiing, kayaking and waterskiing. Check the Sports category on the comprehensive www.marmenor.net website for more information. The lagoon is separated from the sea by La Manga (The Sleeve), a 22km sliver of land overdeveloped with close-packed high-rise accommodation; the world would lose little if it one day cut loose and drifted away.

Cabo de Palos, at the peninsula's southern limit, has a small harbour filled with pleasure boats and is surrounded by low-rise restaurants and holiday apartments. The waters around the tiny offshore (and protected) Islas Hormigas (Ant Islands) are great for scuba diving. Atura-Sub (www.aturasub.com; La Bocana 28) and nearby BuceaYa (www.buceaya.com, in Spanish), located beside the marina, offer dives, including all equipment, from €45. Both offices are staffed sporadically; book through the websites.

FREE MUD TREATMENTS

In Lo Pagán there is the added attraction (for some) of natural mud treatments. Head north of the promenade where a 2km walkway juts out into the lagoon, with a number of short wooden jetties. Have a dip on the west side of the path and coat yourself in mud. Be careful: *el lodo*, the squelchy, inky goo, retains the heat. Let it dry, wash it off, then to really tone yourself up take a dip in the saltwater lagoon opposite. Great fun and therapeutic too, given the mud's high salt and iodine content.

At the northern end of the lagoon, Lo Pagán is a mellow, low-rise resort with a long promenade, pleasant beach and plenty of bars and restaurants. Avoid the crowds of July and August.

Just east of Lo Pagán lie the Salinas de San Pedro (salt pans) where you can follow a well-signposted *senda verde* (footpath). This relatively easy walk of just over 4km passes by several lagoons favoured by flocks of pink flamingos trawling for small fry.

During June, July and August San Javier, located around 5km southwest of the salt pans, plays host to the Festival Internacional de Jazz (International Jazz Festival; www.jazzsanjavier.es).

GOLFO DE MAZARRÓN

The rugged coast west of Cartagena is fretted with small coves and unspoilt beaches, best reached by car. Inland, where agricultural business prevails, the shimmering silver lakes turn out to be entire valleys sheathed in plastic where vegetables are force-grown in greenhouses for local and export markets.

If speed matters, take the AP7 toll motorway. Otherwise, opt for the more picturesque N332, which swoops and snakes through the coastal mountains. Both bring you to Puerto de Mazarrón, a bustling, likeable resort with shops and restaurants. Head west of the centre for the best beaches. At Playa La Ermita, the beachfront Centro de Buceo del Sureste (www.buceosureste.com) offers dives from €36. Five kilometres further west, tiny Bolnuevo has surreal sandstone-sculptured rocks that eroded over millions of years: the Gredos de

ADDING COLOUR TO SEMANA SANTA

In Lorca you'll find issues are clearly blue and white – the colours of the two major brotherhoods that have competed every year since 1855 to see who can stage the most lavish Semana Santa display.

Lorca's Easter parades beat to a different rhythm, distinct from the slow, sombre processions elsewhere in Murcia. While still deeply reverential, they're full of colour and vitality, mixing Old and New Testament legend with the Passion story.

If you hail from Lorca, you're passionately Blanco (White) or Azul (Blue). Each brotherhood has a statue of the Virgin (one draped in a blue mantle, the other in white, naturally), a banner and a spectacular museum. The result of this intense and mostly genial year-round rivalry is just about the most dramatic Semana Santa you'll see anywhere in Spain.

Bolnuevo (Bolnuevo Rocks). It's well signposted. The beach opposite is long and sandy with a reputable seafood restaurant, **La Siesta** (meals €20-25; ⊗Fri-Wed). Just 1km further west, a cove for naturists is appropriately well secluded. Continuing on another 30km, **Águilas**, with its coves and beaches flanking the town, is similarly good for getting sand between the toes.

Lorca

POP 89,900 / ELEV 330M

This appealing market town is the site of some of Spain's most flamboyant Semana Santa (Holy Week) celebrations, which may be appreciated via various museums, if you can't make the dates. Well worth a stopover, the old quarter is partly pedestrianised with some fine baroque buildings, crowned by a 13th-century castle.

Lorca's economy is primarily based on the export of pork products and textiles, although tourists dip in regularly from the holiday resorts and the town fills its coffers at Easter time.

◉ Sights

The **Centro de Visitantes** sells various combined tickets (€12 to €24) to the sights. A **tourist train** (adult/child €3/2.30) provides a painless chug up to the castle. You can pick it up at various sights throughout town.

Semana Santa Museums MUSEUMS
Peculiar to Lorca are two small museums exhibiting the magnificent Semana Santa costumes. Some cloaks are up to 5m in length and all are elaborately hand-embroidered in silk, depicting colourful religious and historical scenes. The **Museo de Bordados del Paso Azul** (Calle Nogalte 7; adult/child €3/free; ⊗10am-2pm & 5-7.30pm Tue-Sat, 10am-2pm Sun) competes in splendour with the **Museo de Bordados del Paso Blanco** (Calle Santo Domingo 8; adult/child €3/free; ⊗10am-2pm & 5-7.30pm Tue-Sat, 10am-2pm Sun), annexed to the church of Santo Domingo. For more on Semana Santa, see the boxed text.

Casa de Guevara PALACE
(Calle Lope Gisbert; adult/child €3/2.50) Behind the baroque facade of the 17th-century Casa de Guevara is a fascinating palace that includes a harmonious patio, a (transplanted) late-19th-century pharmacy (complete with bottles of medicinal potions, including cocaine), and plush rooms with fine paintings, furniture and artefacts.

Plaza de España BAROQUE BUILDINGS
You'll find more splendid baroque buildings around Plaza de España, including the **Pósito**, a 16th-century former granary; the 18th-century **Casa del Corregidor**; and the town hall. Lording over the square is the golden limestone **Colegiata de San Patricio** (⊗11am-1pm & 4.30-6pm), a church with a handsome baroque facade and predominantly Renaissance interior.

La Fortaleza del Sol CASTLE
(adult/child €10/free; ⊗10.30am-6.30pm Tue-Sun, closed Jan-Mar; ⊞) The town's castle has been transformed into a veritable theme park – La Fortaleza del Sol offers dioramas, actors in costume and various gadgetry. While children will probably enjoy all the jollity, adults may ponder the days when visiting the castle was a less-contrived, more contemplative experience.

Museo Arqueológico MUSEUM
(Plaza de Juan Moreno; adult/child €2/free; ⊗10am-2pm & 5-7.30pm Tue-Sat, 10am-2pm

Sun) Lorca's Museo Arqueológico, set in the grand 16th-century Casa de los Salazar, provides an insight into the city's ancient history, which dates back to the mid-Palaeolithic period.

🛏 Sleeping & Eating

Pensión del Carmen BUDGET HOTEL €

(☎968 46 64 59; Rincón de los Valientes 3; s/d €18/36; ❋) A great budget choice. Cheerful and family-run, Carmen has seven doubles and seven singles, all spotless. You'll find it in a tiny square just off Calle Nogalte.

Hotel Alameda HOTEL €€

(☎968 40 66 00; www.hotel-alameda.com; 1st fl, Calle Musso Valiente 8; s/d €35/55; P❋🛜) Look beyond the insipid marble-chip flooring and dated floral fabrics, as the rooms here are large and good value, and the hotel is excellently located. Add a zero to the price during Easter week, in return for front row seats.

Restaurante Juan de Toledo

MURCIAN FOOD €€

(☎968 47 02 15; Calle Juan de Toledo 14; meals €25; ⏲lunch & dinner Tue-Sat, lunch Sun) Situated within an atmospheric old building usually decorated with upstairs' daily wash, the *menú* (set menu) here is meatily uncomplicated. Choose from dishes such as *rabo de toro estofado* (oxtail stew) and *solomillo a la brasa* (grilled fillet steak). Lightweights can opt for a bowl of *gazpacho* with all the trimmings.

Jardines de Lorca MODERN HOTEL €€€

(☎968 47 05 99; www.sercotelhoteles.com; Alameda de Rafael Méndez; s/d €140/165; P❋@🖵🛜) This angular, red-brick hotel has slick, corporate-style rooms with excellent facilities, including a spa.

Almond Tree Villa GUEST HOUSE €€

(☎606 203963; www.almondtreevilla.com; s/d €35/50) Twenty-seven kilometres south-west of Lorca, this gay-friendly country villa nestles in almond groves and is ideal if you are seeking a stress-free break in bucolic surroundings.

🛍 Shopping

The cavernous Centro de Artesanía (Calle Lope Gisbert), beside the tourist office, sells local traditional crafts.

ℹ Information

Centro de Visitantes (visitors centre; ☎902 40 00 47; www.lorcatallerdeltiempo.com; ⏲9.30am-2pm & 4-7pm Tue-Sun) Located in a former convent and has a multimedia exhibition (adult/child €3/free) illustrating Lorca's long history.

Tourist office (☎968 46 61 57; www.lorca.es; Calle Lope Gisbert 10; ⏲9.30am-2pm & 5.30-7.30pm Mon-Sat, 10am-3pm Sun) Can provide a map and plenty of city information.

ℹ Getting There & Around

BUS & TRAIN Hourly buses (€5.35, 1½ hours) and trains (€15.60, one hour) run between Lorca and Murcia.

CAR & MOTORCYCLE There's a large underground **car park** (Plaza Colón) 200m west of the tourist office.

Parque Natural de Sierra Espuña

This park is a 40-minute drive southwest of Murcia towards Lorca. Just north of the N340, it has more than 250 sq km of unspoilt highlands covered with trails and popular with walkers and climbers.

Limestone formations tower above the sprawling forests. In the northwest of the park are 26 *pozos de la nieve* (ice houses) where, until the arrival of industrial refrigeration, snow was compressed into ice, then taken to nearby towns in summer.

WORTH A TRIP

ARTISTIC CENTRE IN FORMER CANNERY

Art is not a new concept in these parts where the rich cultural heritage ranges from the Neolithic cave paintings found in Cueva de los Letreros (just over the Andalucía border near Vélez Rubio) to Cartagena's stunning Roman mosaics. Located in the tiny village of Ceutí, La Conservera Centro de Arte Contemporáneo (http://laconservera.org/; ⏲10am-2pm & 5-9pm Tue-Sat), 24km northwest of Murcia, opened in May 2009 as an artistic centre showcasing well-known international contemporary artists and sculptors whose work shares a common concept. The exhibition centre is housed in a converted cannery stripped of machinery. The result is vast spaces covering 4800 sq m, ideal for these spacious, light-filled galleries.

Access to the park is best via Alhama de Murcia. Visit the informative Ricardo Codorniu Visitors Centre (☎968 42 54 55; www.sierraespuna.com; ☺10am-2pm & 5-7pm Mon-Sat, 10am-2pm Sun) located in a traditional country house in the heart of the park.

The nearby village of El Berro has a couple of restaurants and the friendly Camping Sierra Espuña (☎968 66 80 38; www.campingsierraespuna.com; sites per person/tent/car €4/4/4, 4-/6-person bungalow €75/84; ☒), with superb facilities, including barbecue pits, swimming pool, minigolf and cafeteria.

Andalucía

Includes »

Best Places to Eat

» Catalina (p674)

» Restaurante Arrayanes (p757)

» Restaurante Virgen del Carmen (p698)

» El Jardín de la Califa (p708)

Best Places to Stay

» Hotel Costasol (p778)

» Hotel Hacienda Posada de Vallina (p743)

» Casa Morisca Hotel (p755)

Why Go?

Picture the scenes...

Seville, 8am: the ornate Giralda shimmers above the Río Guadalquivir, a tardy shop-worker hurries across the San Telmo Bridge, and two attractive señoritas in polka-dot dresses stagger back from last night's feria.

Ronda, 3pm: a waiter pulls down the shutters in a deserted cafe, a lean cat slinks down a blinding whitewashed street; nothing else moves – it's too damned hot.

Cádiz, 1am: waves crash outside a paint-peeled flamenco club; inside, a singer strikes an anguished note and summons up something deep, dark and soulful.

Images of Andalucía are so potent – so quintessentially Spanish – that you sometimes feel a sense of déjà vu, as if you've already been there in your dreams: a solemn Easter parade, an ebullient spring festival, exotic nights in the Alhambra. In the stark light of day the picture is no less compelling. Here in the arid landscapes of southern Iberia, amazing experiences await.

When to Go

Seville

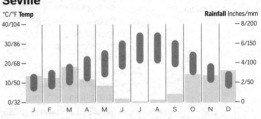

April Sombre Semana Santa processions are followed by the exuberance of the spring fairs.

May The weather's still relatively cool, plus many towns and villages celebrate *romerías* (pilgrimages).

Late September The heat diminishes, the crowds go home – but it's still warm enough for the beach.

SHERRY

To appreciate sherry, take a bodega tour in one of the three historic 'sherry triangle' towns of Jerez de la Frontera (p699), El Puerto de Santa María (p697) and Sanlúcar de Barrameda (p697).

Fast Facts

» Population: 8.2 million

» Area: 87,268 sq km

» Number of Visitors (2009): 14.7 million

» Annual Income: €15,000

Planning Your Trip

» Book your accommodation at http://hotels.lonelyplanet.com.

» Andalucía is a region of festivals – research what's on and try to incorporate one or two.

» Check train timetables on www.renfe.es and bus timetables on www.movielia.es.

Resources

» www.andalucia.com

» www.andalucia.org

Romerías

The Spanish word *romería* means 'pilgrimage' or 'trip'. In the traditional folklore of Anadalucía it is intrinsically linked to the Romería del Rocío, the self-proclaimed mother of all pilgrimages. Every year in May up to one million people converge on a large stretch of marshland in Huelva province to venerate a tiny image of the Virgin. The origins of this festival are primarily religious, though the realities of the modern-day activities are a little less sanctimonious. Throughout the months of May and June almost every village in Andalucía replicates the wild hysteria of El Rocío, with colourful processions to similar religious sites acting as a prelude to music, drinking, debauchery, family reunions and spontaneous outbreaks of flamenco. They're classic spectacles.

FEDERICO GARCÍA LORCA

It is debatable whether you can truly understand modern Anadalucía without at least an inkling of Spain's greatest poet and playwright, Federico García Lorca. Lorca epitomised many of Andalucía's potent hallmarks – passion, ambiguity, exuberance and innovation – and he brought them skilfully to life in a litany of precocious works, including the play *Blood Wedding* and the poem *Romancero Gitano*. Granada produced, inspired and ultimately destroyed Lorca, and it is here that his legacy remains most evident. But, keep your ear to the ground, and you'll feel his influence almost everywhere. Catch a live performance of his work, visit his birth house in Fuente Vaqueros (p761) or just wander the streets and fields of Granada and the Vega and compose your own poetic itinerary.

Top Five Flamenco Places

» Peña Flamenca La Perla (p694), Cádiz – Listen out for *alegrías* (upbeat flamenco songs) performed by equally upbeat *gaditanos* (residents of Cádiz).

» Casa Anselma (p677), Seville – *Sevillanas* (a folklore flamenco song and dance) and spontaneous dancing mixed with the occasional soul-searching *soleá* (sad flamenco lament).

» El Lagá Tio Parrilla (p701), Jerez – In true Jerez fashion, shows invariably end with a rousing, fast-paced *bulería* (upbeat flamenco song).

» Peña de La Platería (p759), Granada – Listen out for home-grown, highly ornamental *granaínas* (flamenco song from Granada) in Spain's oldest *peña flamenca* (flamenco club).

» Peña El Taranto (p779), Almería – The fount of the *taranto*, a distinctive eastern take on the traditional fandango.

History

Around 1000 or 900 BC, Andalucía's agricultural and mining wealth attracted Phoenician trading colonies to coastal sites such as Cádiz, Huelva and Málaga. In the 8th and 7th centuries BC, Phoenician influence gave rise to the mysterious, legendarily wealthy Tartessos civilisation somewhere in western Andalucía. From the 3rd century BC to the 5th century AD, Andalucía, governed from Córdoba, was one of the most civilised and wealthiest areas of the Roman Empire.

Andalucía was the obvious base for the Muslim invaders who surged onto the Iberian Peninsula from Africa in 711 under Arab general Tariq ibn Ziyad, who landed at Gibraltar with around 10,000 men, mostly Berbers (indigenous North Africans). Until the 11th century Córdoba was the leading city of Islamic Spain, followed by Seville until the 13th century, and finally Granada until the 15th. At its peak in the 10th century, Córdoba was the most dazzling city in Western Europe, famed for its 'three cultures' coexistence of Muslims, Jews and Christians. Islamic civilisation lasted longer in Andalucía than anywhere else on the Iberian Peninsula, and it's from the medieval name for the Muslim areas of the peninsula, Al-Andalus, that the name Andalucía comes.

The Emirate of Granada, the last bastion of Al-Andalus, finally fell to the Reyes Católicos (Catholic Monarchs), Ferdinand and Isabella, in 1492. Columbus' landing in the Americas the same year brought great wealth to Seville and later Cádiz, the Andalucian ports through which Spain's trade with the Americas was conducted. But the Castilian conquerors killed off Andalucía's deeper prosperity by handing out great swaths of territory to their nobles, who set sheep to run on former food-growing lands.

By the late 19th century rural Andalucía was a hotbed of anarchist unrest. During the civil war Andalucía split along class lines and savage atrocities were committed by both sides. Spain's subsequent 'hungry years' were particularly hungry here in the south, and between 1950 and 1970 some 1.5 million Andalucians left to find work in the industrial cities of northern Spain and other European countries.

But tourism, industrial growth and massive European Union (EU) subsidies for agriculture have made a big difference since the 1960s. The left-of-centre Partido Socialista Obrero Español (PSOE; Spanish Socialist Workers' Party) has controlled Andalucía's regional government in Seville since 1982. The worst of Andalucian poverty has been eradicated by welfare provision and economic improvement. Education and health care have steadily improved, and the PSOE has given Andalucía Spain's biggest network of environmentally protected areas (though only in the last couple of years has it begun to tackle the rampant overdevelopment of many coastal areas).

Andalucía has been badly affected by the economic meltdown that followed the 2008/09 banking crisis. Figures released in May 2010 put the region's unemployment rate at a whopping 27% percent, well above the (already poor) national average (close to 20%). Rates in provinces such as Cádiz and Málaga were over 30%. Another hard-hit group was Andalucía's army of expats – mostly situated on the Costa del Sol – many of whom were forced to pack up and head home.

Seville

POP 703,000

Some cities have beauty. Others have soul. A few have both. Seville falls into the last category; it's a feisty assortment of matadors and *cantadors* (flamenco singers), oranges and opera, gargantuan Gothic and magnificent Mudéjar. Though there's solemnity here (hear the bitingly sad flamenco laments), there's also exuberance (hit the riotous spring fair). But it's Seville's capriciousness that leaves the heaviest impression. Come here in April and watch as haunting Semana Santa (Holy Week) metamorphoses into the cacophony of Feria de Abril (p671) and you'll wonder whether Bizet's *Carmen* wasn't more real than imagined.

Furnished with monuments, fine art, endless festivals, and the world's greatest Gothic cathedral, Seville was responsible for hooking some of the world's first 'tourists' – Richard Ford and Lord Byron among them. The palatial buildings are little changed since the 19th century, though recent upgrades to infrastructure including a new tram/metro line, a car-free city centre, and an Amsterdam level of bike provision have made viewing them a whole lot more pleasurable.

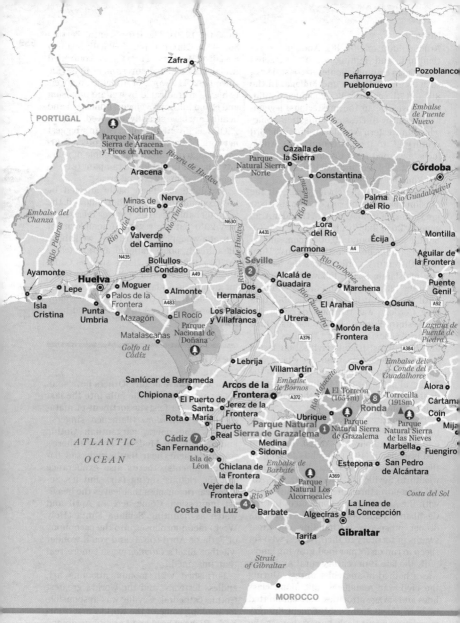

Andalucía Highlights

❶ Watch eagles hovering over the crags and castles of **Parque Natural Sierra de Grazalema** (p703)

❷ Climb the Giralda and contemplate the scale of Seville's **cathedral** (p663)

❸ Slip under the radar on the tapas trail in little-visited **Jaén** (p769)

❹ Feel the wind in your hair at one of the long, wide, deserted beaches on the **Costa de la Luz** (p708)

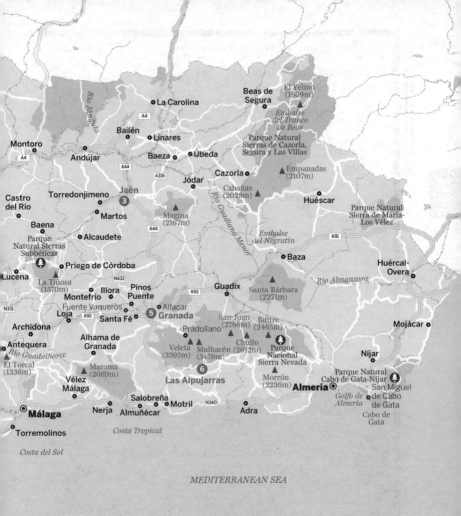
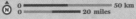

5 Go to **Granada** (p758) and watch a Lorca play in the Alhambra's Generalife gardens

6 Enter the ethereal world of the valleys of **Las Alpujarras** (p766) on foot

7 View an unforgettable flamenco show amid the peeling paint and crashing surf of the city of **Cádiz** (p688)

8 Hire a bike and take a ride through the white towns around **Ronda** (p706)

Seville

ANDALUCÍA

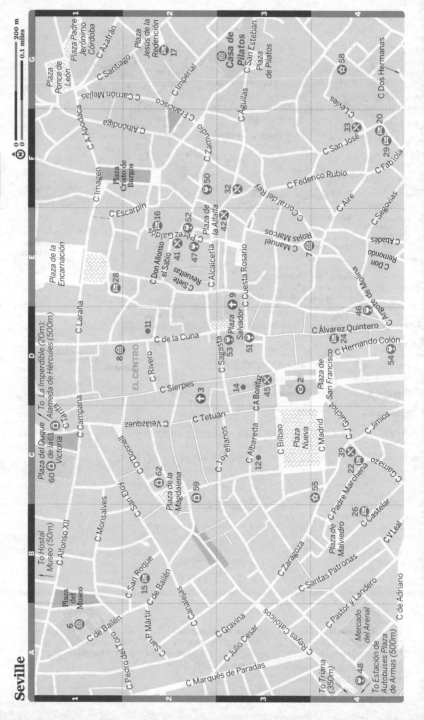

0 200 m
0 0.1 miles

Plaza del Museo
Plaza Padre Jerónimo Córdoba
Plaza Jesús de la Redención
Casa de Pilatos
Plaza de Pilatos
Plaza de San Esteban

EL CENTRO

History

Roman Seville, named Hispalis, was a significant port on the Río Guadalquivir, which is navigable to the Atlantic Ocean 100km away. Muslim Seville, called Ishbiliya, became the most powerful of the *taifas* (small kingdoms) into which Islamic Spain split after the Córdoba caliphate collapsed in 1031. In the 12th century a strict Islamic sect from Morocco, the Almohads, took over Muslim Spain and made Seville capital of their whole realm, building a great mosque where the cathedral now stands. Almohad power eventually crumbled and Seville fell to Fernando III (El Santo, the Saint) of Castilla in 1248.

By the 14th century, Seville was the most important Castilian city, and was in sole control of trade with the American colonies from 1503. It rapidly became one of the most cosmopolitan cities on earth. However, over the next 300 years, both plague and the silting up of the river contributed to Seville's long decline. Seville fell very quickly to the Nationalists at the start of the Spanish Civil War in 1936. Things looked up a few decades later in the 1980s when Seville was named capital of the new autonomous Andalucía within democratic Spain, and *sevillano* (resident of Seville) Felipe González became Spain's prime minister. The Expo 92 international exhibition (1992) brought to the city millions of visitors, eight new bridges across the Guadalquivir, and the speedy AVE rail link to Madrid. And in the new century, where less is more, Seville is already experimenting with green initiatives, including trams, a metro and bikes that glide quietly alongside antique monuments to past glory.

◎ Sights

Seville's major monuments – the cathedral, the Giralda and the Alcázar complex – are all just east of Avenida de la Constitución and south of the city's true centre (El Centro). But there's plenty more to see and do in El Centro and around.

Catedral & Giralda CATHEDRAL
(adult/under 16yr €8/free; ⊘11am-5.30pm Mon-Sat, 2.30-6.30pm Sun Sep-Jun) After Seville fell to the Christians in 1248 its main mosque was used as a church until 1401, when it was knocked down to make way for what would become one of the world's largest cathedrals and an icon of Gothic architecture. The building wasn't completed until 1507.

Seville

The original mosque's beautiful minaret, La Giralda, still stands on its eastern side. There is wheelchair access to the cathedral complex.

Sala del Pabellón

Selected treasures from the cathedral's art collection are exhibited in this first room after the ticket office.

Cathedral Chapels & Stained Glass

The sheer size of the broad, five-naved cathedral is obscured by a welter of interior decoration typical of Spanish cathedrals. Near the western end of the northern side is the **Capilla de San Antonio**, with Murillo's large 1666 canvas depicting the vision of St Anthony of Padua; thieves excised the kneeling saint in 1874 but he was found in New York and put back.

Columbus' Tomb

Inside the cathedral's southern door stands the elaborate tomb of Christopher Columbus, dating from 1902. However, the remains within the tomb are the subject of heated debate, with some arguing that the explorer is (mainly) buried in the Dominican Republic.

Capilla Mayor

Towards the eastern end of the main nave is the Capilla Mayor; its Gothic altarpiece is the jewel of the cathedral and reckoned to be the biggest altarpiece in the world. Begun by Flemish sculptor Pieter Dancart in 1482 and completed by others by 1564, this sea of gilded and polychromed wood holds more than 1000 carved biblical figures.

Sacristies & Chapter House

South of the Capilla Mayor you'll find rooms containing many of the cathedral's art treasures. The westernmost of these is the **Sacristía de los Cálices** (Sacristy of the Chalices), where Goya's 1817 painting of the Seville martyrs, *Santas Justa y Rufina* (potter sisters who died at the hands of the Romans in AD 287), hangs above the altar. A lion licks Rufina's feet, as reputedly happened when she was thrown to the said beasts during her travails. The room's centrepiece is the **Custodia de Juan de Arfe**, a huge 475kg silver monstrance made in the 1580s by Renaissance metal smith Juan de

Arfe. Displayed in a glass case are the city keys handed to the conquering Fernando III in 1248.

The beautifully domed **cabildo** (chapter house), in the southeastern corner of the cathedral, was built between 1558 and 1592 to the designs of Hernán Ruiz, architect of the Giralda belfry. High above the archbishop's throne at the southern end is a Murillo masterpiece, *La Inmaculada*. Eight Murillo saints adorn the dome.

Giralda

In the northeastern corner of the cathedral interior you'll find the passage for the climb up the Giralda. The ascent is quite easy, as a series of ramps – built so that the guards could ride up on horseback – goes all the way up. The climb affords great views.

Over 90m high, La Giralda was the minaret of the mosque that stood on the site before the cathedral; it was constructed in brick by Almohad caliph Yusuf Yacub al-Mansur between 1184 and 1198. Its proportions, decoration and colour make it perhaps Spain's most perfect Islamic building. The topmost parts (from the bell level up) were added in the 16th century. At the very top is **El Giraldillo**, a 16th-century bronze weathervane, which represents Faith and is a symbol of Seville.

Patio de los Naranjos

Planted with over 60 orange trees, this was originally the courtyard where Muslims

---

SEVILLE IN...

Two Days

Kick off day one with a visit to the **Alcázar** then wander through the **Barrio de Santa Cruz** and enjoy lunch at the **Corral del Agua**. In the afternoon head over towards the Río Guadalquivir and visit the **Museo de Bellas Artes**. Spend the evening sniffing out the tapas bars in the vicinity of Plaza de la Alfalfa. Stick around later for some late-night bars.

Devote the morning of day two to the **cathedral** and **Giralda** before heading up to El Centro to visit the **Palacio de la Condesa de Lebrija** and some city-centre shops. In the evening cross over the river to Triana and sample fried fish in Calle del Betis. Line up at midnight for the weird and wonderful flamenco happenings at **Casa Anselma**.

Four Days

The late night will necessitate a late breakfast – the waiters at **Horno de San Buenadventura** will oblige. Spend a lazy day relaxing in leafy **Parque de María Luisa**, where you can negotiate its two museums if you have the energy. Dodge the tapas and treat yourself to a classy dinner at **Restaurante Egaña Oriza**. On day four pop into the **Museo del Baile Flamenco** and/or the **Casa de Pilatos**. Grab a snack at **Extraverde** and order dinner at **Restaurante La Cueva** before enjoying the night-time shenanigans in **Alameda de Hércules**.

Seville Cathedral

WHAT TO LOOK FOR

'We're going to construct a church so large, future generations will think we were mad' declared the inspired architects of Seville in 1402 at the beginning of one of the most grandiose building projects in medieval history. Just over a century later their madness was triumphantly confirmed.

To avoid getting lost, orientate yourself by the main highlights. Directly inside the southern (main) entrance is the grand mausoleum of Christopher Columbus **1**. Turn right here and head into the south-eastern corner to uncover some major art treasures: a Goya in the Sacristía de los Cálices, a Zurbarán in the Sacristía Mayor **2**, and Murillo's shining Immaculada in the Sala Capitular. Skirt the cathedral's eastern wall taking a look inside the Capilla Real **3** with its important royal tombs. By now it's impossible to avoid the lure of Capilla Mayor **4** with its fantastical altarpiece. Hidden over in the northwest corner is the Capilla de San Antonio **5** with a legendary Murillo. That huge doorway almost in front of you is rarely opened Puerta de la Asunción **6**. Make for the Giralda **7** next, stealing admiring looks at the high, vaulted ceiling on the way. After looking down on the cathedral's immense footprint, descend and depart via the Patio de los Naranjos **8**.

TIPS BOX

» **Queue-dodge** Reserve tickets online at www.servicaixa.com for an extra €1 up to six weeks in advance.

» **Pace yourself** Don't visit the Alcazar and Cathedral on the same day. There is far too much to take in.

» **Viewpoints** Take time to admire the cathedral from the outside. It's particularly stunning at night from the Plaza Virgen de los Reyes, and from across the river in Triana.

Capilla Mayor
Behold! The cathedral's main focal point contains its greatest treasure, a magnificent gold-plated altarpiece depicting various scenes in the life of Christ. It constitutes the life's work of one man, Flemish artist Pieter Dancart.

Patio de los Naranjos
Inhale the perfume of 60 Sevillan orange trees in a cool patio bordered by fortress-like walls – a surviving remnant of the original 12th-century mosque. Exit is gained via the horseshoe-shaped Puerta del Perdón.

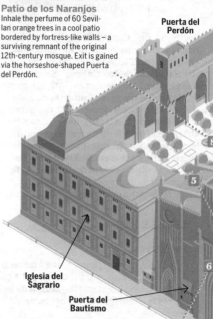

Puerta del Perdón

Iglesia del Sagrario

Puerta del Bautismo

Puerta de la Asunción
Located on the western side of the cathedral and also known as the Puerta Mayor, these huge, rarely opened doors are pushed back during Semana Santa to allow solemn processions of Catholic *hermanadades* (brotherhoods) to pass through.

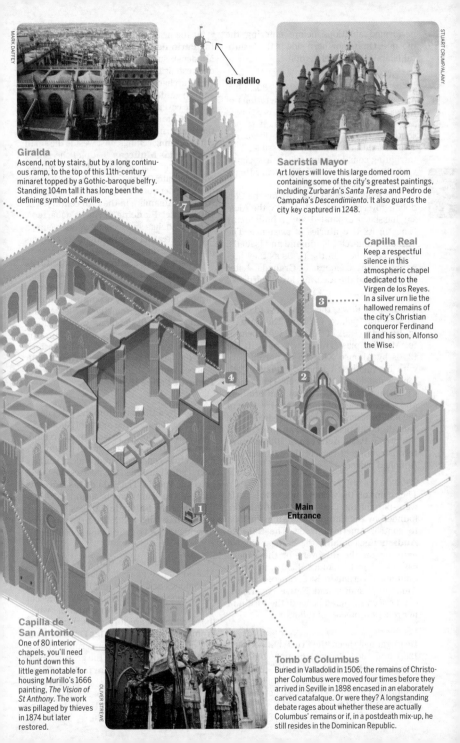

Giraldillo

Giralda
Ascend, not by stairs, but by a long continuous ramp, to the top of this 11th-century minaret topped by a Gothic-baroque belfry. Standing 104m tall it has long been the defining symbol of Seville.

Sacristía Mayor
Art lovers will love this large domed room containing some of the city's greatest paintings, including Zurbarán's *Santa Teresa* and Pedro de Campaña's *Descendimiento*. It also guards the city key captured in 1248.

Capilla Real
Keep a respectful silence in this atmospheric chapel dedicated to the Virgen de los Reyes. In a silver urn lie the hallowed remains of the city's Christian conqueror Ferdinand III and his son, Alfonso the Wise.

Main Entrance

Capilla de San Antonio
One of 80 interior chapels, you'll need to hunt down this little gem notable for housing Murillo's 1666 painting, *The Vision of St Anthony*. The work was pillaged by thieves in 1874 but later restored.

Tomb of Columbus
Buried in Valladolid in 1506, the remains of Christopher Columbus were moved four times before they arrived in Seville in 1898 encased in an elaborately carved catafalque. Or were they? A longstanding debate rages about whether these are actually Columbus' remains or if, in a postdeath mix-up, he still resides in the Dominican Republic.

MARK DAFFEY

STUART CRUMP/ALAMY

OLIVER STREWE

performed ablutions before entering the mosque. On its northern side is the beautiful Islamic Puerta del Perdón.

TOP CHOICE **Alcázar** CASTLE
(adult/child €7.50/free; ⊘9.30am-7pm Apr-Sep) Residence of many generations of kings and caliphs, the Alcázar is Seville's answer to Granada's Alhambra. It stands south of the cathedral across Plaza del Triunfo and is wheelchair accessible. This intriguing complex is intimately associated with the life and loves of the extraordinary Pedro I of Castilla (1350–69).

Originally founded as a fort for the Cordoban governors of Seville in 913, the Alcázar has been expanded and rebuilt many times in its 11 centuries of existence. The Catholic Monarchs, Ferdinand and Isabella, set up court here in the 1480s as they prepared for the conquest of Granada. Later rulers created the Alcázar's lovely gardens.

Patio del León

The Lion Patio was the garrison yard of the Al-Muwarak palace. Off here, the **Sala de la Justicia** (Hall of Justice), with beautiful Mudéjar plasterwork, was built in the 1340s by Alfonso XI, who disported here with his mistress Leonor de Guzmán. Alfonso's dalliances left his heir Pedro I (El Cruel/Justiciero) with five half-brothers and a severe case of sibling rivalry. One of the half-brothers, Don Fadrique, died in the Sala de la Justicia. The room gives on to the pretty **Patio del Yeso**, a 19th-century reconstruction of part of the 12th-century Almohad palace.

Patio de la Montería

The rooms on the western side of this patio were part of the Casa de la Contratación, founded by the Catholic Monarchs in 1503 to control American trade. The **Sala de Audiencias** contains the earliest known painting on the discovery of the Americas (by Alejo Fernández, 1530s), in which Columbus, Fernando El Católico, Carlos I, Amerigo Vespucci and Native Americans can be seen sheltered beneath the Virgin in her role as protector of sailors.

Palacio de Don Pedro (Mudéjar Palace)

He might have been 'the Cruel', but between 1360 and 1364 Pedro I humbly built his exquisite palace in 'perishable' ceramics, plaster and wood, obedient to the Quran's prohibition against 'eternal' structures, reserved for the Creator.

At the heart of the palace is the wonderful **Patio de las Doncellas** (Patio of the Maidens), surrounded by beautiful arches and exquisite plasterwork and tiling. In 2004, archaeologists uncovered its original sunken garden from beneath a 16th-century marble covering.

The **Cámara Regia** (King's Quarters) on the northern side of the patio has two rooms with stunning ceilings. Just west is the small **Patio de las Muñecas** (Patio of the Dolls), the heart of the palace's private quarters, with delicate Granada-style decoration; indeed, plasterwork was actually brought here from the Alhambra in the 19th century. The **Cuarto del Príncipe** (Prince's Quarters), to its north, has an excellent wooden cupola ceiling recreating a starlit night sky and was probably the queen's bedroom.

The spectacular **Salón de Embajadores** (Hall of Ambassadors), off the western end of the Patio de las Doncellas, was Pedro I's throne room and incorporates caliphal-style door arches from the earlier Al-Muwarak palace. Its fabulous wooden dome of multiple star patterns, symbolising the universe, was added in 1427. On its western side, the beautiful **Arco de Pavones**, with peacock motifs, leads into the **Salón del Techo de Felipe II**.

Salones de Carlos V

Reached by a staircase from the Patio de las Doncellas, these are the rooms of Alfonso X's 13th-century Gothic palace, much remodelled since then. It was here that Alfonso's intellectual court gathered and, a century later, Pedro I installed the mistress he loved, María de Padilla. The **Sala de las Bóvedas** (Hall of the Vault) has beautiful 1570s tiling, while the **Salón de Tapices** (Tapestry Room) has huge 18th-century tapestries showing Carlos I's 1535 conquest of Tunis.

Gardens & Exit

From the Salones de Carlos V, enter the Alcázar's large gardens. Those in front of the Salones de Carlos V and Palacio de Don Pedro were mostly brought to their present form in the 16th and 17th centuries, while those to the east are 20th-century creations. From the little **Jardín de las Danzas** (Garden of the Dances) a passage runs beneath the Salones de Carlos V to the grotto known as the **Baños de Doña María de Padilla**.

From the new gardens you can leave the Alcázar via the **Apeadero**, a 17th-century entrance hall, and the **Patio de las Banderas** (Patio of the Banners).

FREE **Archivo de Indias** MUSEUM
(Calle Santo Tomás; ☺10am-4pm Mon-Sat, 10am-2pm Sun & holidays) On the western side of Plaza del Triunfo, the Archivo de Indias is the main archive on Spain's American empire, with 80 million pages of documents dating from 1492 through to the end of the empire in the 19th century: a most effective statement of Spain's power and influence during its Golden Age.

BARRIO DE SANTA CRUZ

Seville's medieval *judería* (Jewish quarter), east of the cathedral and Alcázar, is today a tangle of atmospheric, winding streets and lovely plant-decked plazas perfumed with orange blossom. Among its most characteristic plazas is Plaza de Santa Cruz, which gives the *barrio* (district) its name. Plaza de Doña Elvira is another romantic perch, especially in the evening.

Hospital de los Venerables Sacerdotes
ART GALLERY
(Plaza de los Venerables 8; adult/child €4.75/free, Sun afternoon free; ☺10am-1.30pm & 4-7.30pm) Once a residence for aged priests, this 17th-century building now holds roving art exhibitions and has a lovely central courtyard.

EL CENTRO

The real centre of Seville is the densely packed zone of narrow streets north of the cathedral.

Plaza de San Francisco & Calle Sierpes
SQUARE
Plaza de San Francisco has been Seville's main public square since the 16th century. The southern end of the ayuntamiento (town hall) here is encrusted with lovely Renaissance carving from the 1520s and '30s.

Pedestrianised Calle Sierpes, heading north from the plaza, and the parallel Calle Tetuán/Velázquez are the hub of Seville's fanciest shopping zone. Between the two streets is the 18th-century Capilla de San José (Calle Jovellanos; ☺8am-12.30pm & 6.30-8.30pm), with breathtakingly intense baroque ornamentation.

The Palacio de la Condesa de Lebrija (Calle de la Cuna 8; admission whole bldg/ground fl only €8/4, ground fl admission 9am-noon Wed free; ☺10.30am-7.30pm Mon-Fri, 10am-2pm & 4-6pm Sat), a block east of Calle Sierpes, is a 16th-century noble mansion remodelled in 1914 by traveller and art connoisseur Doña Regla Manjón, Countess of Lebrija.

Plaza Salvador SQUARE
This plaza, which has a few popular bars, was once the forum of Roman Hispalis. It's dominated by the Parroquia del Divino Salvador, a big baroque church built between 1674 and 1712 on the site of Muslim Ishbiliya's main mosque. The interior reveals a fantastic richness of carving and gilding. At sunset, colour from stained-glass windows plays on the carvings to enhance their surreal beauty.

Casa de Pilatos MUSEUM
(Calle Águilas; admission whole house/lower fl only €8/5, EU citizen 1-5pm & 3-7pm Wed free; ☺9am-7pm Apr-Oct) Another of the city's finest noble mansions, 500m northeast of the cathedral, is still occupied by the ducal Medinaceli family. This extensive and splendid 16th-century building is a mixture of diverse architectural styles.

EL ARENAL

A short walk west from Avenida de la Constitución brings you to the bank of the Río Guadalquivir, lined by a pleasant footpath. The nearby district of El Arenal is home to some of Seville's most interesting sights.

Torre del Oro MUSEUM
(adult/student & senior €2/1; ☺10am-1.30pm Tue-Fri, 10.30am-1.30pm Sat & Sun, closed Mon, holidays & Aug) This 13th-century riverbank Islamic watchtower supposedly had a dome covered in golden tiles, hence its name, 'Tower of Gold'. It has long been one of the most recognisable architectural symbols of Seville. Inside is a small maritime museum.

Museo del Baile Flamenco MUSEUM
(www.museoflamenco.com; Calle Manuel Rojas Marcos 3; adult/child €10/6; ☺9.30am-7pm daily) The brainchild of *sevillana* flamenco dancer, Cristina Hoyos, this is Seville's newest museum. It's spread over three floors of an 18th-century palace, although at €10 a pop it is more than a little overpriced. Exhibits include sketches, paintings, photos of erstwhile (and contemporary) flamenco greats, plus a collection of dresses and shawls. Performances, classes and workshops are regular occurrences here, and there's the obligatory shop.

Hospital de la Caridad ART GALLERY
(Calle Temprado 3; admission incl audioguide €5, Sun & holidays free for EU citizens; ☺9am-1.30pm & 3.30-7.30pm Mon-Sat, to 1pm Sun & holidays) A marvellous sample of Sevillean golden-age art adorns the church in this charity hospice a block from the river. It was founded

ANDALUCÍA

in the 17th century by Miguel de Mañara, a legendary libertine who changed his ways after experiencing a vision in his own funeral procession. Seventeenth-century masterpieces include Valdés Leal's frightening *In Ictu Oculi* (In the Blink of an Eye) and *Finis Gloriae Mundi* (The End of Earthly Glory).

Plaza de Toros de la Real Maestranza
BULLRING, MUSEUM

(☎954 22 45 77; www.realmaestranza.es; Paseo de Cristóbal Colón 12; tours adult/over 65yr/under 12yr €6/4/2.50; ☺half-hourly 9.30am-8pm, 9.30am-3pm bullfight days) Seville's bullring is one of the most handsome in Spain, and probably the oldest (building began in 1758). It was here, and in the ring at Ronda, that bullfighting on foot (instead of horseback) began in the 18th century. Unfortunately, the obligatory guided tours are a little robotic.

Museo de Bellas Artes
ART GALLERY

(Plaza del Museo 9; adult/EU citizen, retired, student €1.50/free; ☺9am-8.30pm Tue-Sat, to 2.30pm Sun, closed Mon) Set in a beautiful former convent, Seville's fine-arts museum does full justice to Seville's leading role in Spain's artistic golden age. The museum is wheelchair accessible.

SOUTH OF THE CENTRE
Heading south you enter a leafy domain of romantic parks and monuments built for the 1929 World's Fair.

FREE Antigua Fábrica de Tabacos
UNIVERSITY

(Calle San Fernando; ☺8am-9.30pm Mon-Fri, to 2pm Sat) Seville's massive former tobacco factory – workplace of Bizet's passionate operatic heroine, Carmen – was built in the 18th century and is the second-largest building in Spain after El Escorial. It's now the university and is wheelchair accessible.

Hotel Alfonso XIII
HISTORIC HOTEL

(Calle San Fernando 2) As much a monument as an accommodation option, and certainly more affordable if you come for a cup of coffee as opposed to a room, this striking hotel – conceived as the most luxurious in Europe when it was built in 1928 – was constructed in tandem with the Plaza de España for the 1929 world fair. The style is classic neo-Mudéjar with glazed tiles and terracotta bricks.

Parque de María Luisa & Plaza de España
PARK

(☺8am-10pm) A large area south of the former tobacco factory was transformed for Seville's 1929 international fair, the Exposición Iberoamericana, when architects adorned it with fantastical buildings, many of them harking back to Seville's past glory or imitating the native styles of Spain's former colonies. In its midst you'll find the large Parque de María Luisa, a living expression of Seville's Moorish and Christian past.

Plaza de España, one of the city's favourite relaxation spots, faces the park across Avenida de Isabel la Católica. Around it is the most grandiose of the 1929 buildings, a semicircular brick-and-tile confection featuring Seville tile work at its gaudiest.

On Plaza de América, at the southern end of the park, is Seville's **Museo Arqueológico** (adult/EU citizen, under 16yr & senior €1.50/free; ☺9am-8.30pm Tue-Sat, to 2.30pm Sun & holidays), with plenty to interest. Facing it is the **Museo de Artes y Costumbres Populares** (adult/EU citizen €1.50/free; ☺9am-8.30pm Tue-Sat, to 2.30pm Sun & holidays). Both are wheelchair accessible.

NORTH OF THE CENTRE
Most head north after dark for the nightlife in the Alameda de Hércules, but in the daytime it's worth bringing the kids.

Isla Mágica
AMUSEMENT PARK

(☎902 16 17 16; www.islamagica.es; all-day ticket adult/child €28/20; ☺11am-11pm Mon-Fri & Sun, to midnight Sat, closed Nov-Mar) This Disneygoes-Spanish-colonial amusement park provides a great day out for kids and all lovers of white-knuckle rides. Confirm times before going; hours vary by season – see website. Both buses C1 and C2 run to Isla Mágica.

Courses
Seville has many dance and flamenco schools; tourist offices and *El Giraldillo* (see Information, p678) have information on options. It is also one of the most popular cities in Spain to study Spanish. The best schools offer both short- and long-term courses at a variety of levels.

Sevilla Dance Centre
FLAMENCO, DANCE

(☎954 38 39 02; Calle Miguel Cid 67; ☺5.30-9pm) The Centre's focus is on hip hop and contemporary/jazz dance teaching and performance.

Espacio Meteora
FLAMENCO, DANCE

(☎954 90 41 83; Calle Duque Cornejo 16A) Innovative arts centre.

Fundación Cristina Heeren de Arte Flamenco
FLAMENCO, DANCE

(☎954 21 70 58; www.flamencoheeren.com; Avenida de Jerez 2) Long-term courses in all flamenco arts; also one-month intensive summer courses.

Giralda Center
SPANISH LANGUAGE

(☎954 22 13 46, 954 21 31 65; www.giralda center.com; Calle Mateos Gago 17)

Carpe Diem
SPANISH LANGUAGE

(☎954 21 85 15; www.carpediemsevilla.com; Calle de la Cuna 13)

Lenguaviva
SPANISH LANGUAGE

(☎954 90 51 31; www.lenguaviva.net; Calle Viriato 24)

LINC
SPANISH LANGUAGE

(☎954 50 04 59; www.linc.es; Calle General Polavieja 13)

CLIC
SPANISH LANGUAGE

(☎954 50 21 31; www.clic.es; Calle Albareda 19)

👉 Tours

Horse-drawn carriages wait near the cathedral, Plaza de España and Puerta de Jerez, charging a hefty €50 for up to four people for a one-hour trot around the Barrio de Santa Cruz and Parque de María Luisa areas.

Sevilla Tour
BUS TOUR

(☎902 10 10 81; www.citysightseeing-spain.com) Open-topped double-decker buses and converted trams make one-hour city tours, with earphone commentary in a choice of languages. The €16 ticket is valid for 24 hours, and you can hop on or off near the Torre del Oro, Avenida de Portugal behind Plaza de España or the Isla de La Cartuja. Buses typically leave every 30 minutes between 7am and 8pm.

Cruceros Turísticos Torre del Oro
RIVER CRUISES

(☎954 56 16 92; adult/under 14yr €17/free) One-hour sightseeing river cruises from the Torre del Oro, every half-hour from 11am; last departure can range from 6pm in winter to 9pm in summer.

Sevilla Walking Tours
GUIDED WALKS

(☎902 15 82 26; www.sevillawalkingtours. com) English-language tours of the main monumental area, at 10.30am Monday to Saturday, lasting about two hours for €12. Meet in Plaza Nueva. The same group also offers tours of the cathedral and Alcázar.

SEVILLE FOR CHILDREN

Many of Seville's adult attractions will appeal to kids on a different level, including the cathedral and the Alcázar, the latter of which has a dedicated booklet for kids, available in most newsagents. The city abounds in open spaces and parks (often with special kids sections); head for the banks of the Guadalquivir, Parque de María Luisa (p670) and the Jardines de Murrillo. Ice-cream and churros (long, deep-fried doughnuts) cafes are also ubiquitous. If the tapas get too sophisticated, try a good Italian restaurant such as Cosa Nostra (p676). Isla Mágica (p670) is specifically targeted at kids, particularly those aged 10 or above. Tours by boat, open-top double-decker bus or horse-drawn carriage also prove popular with kids.

🎉 Festivals & Events

Seville's Semana Santa processions and its Feria de Abril, a week or two later, are worth travelling a long way for, as is the Bienal de Flamenco.

Semana Santa
HOLY WEEK

(www.semana-santa.org, in Spanish) Every day from Palm Sunday to Easter Sunday, large, life-sized *pasos* (sculptural representations of events from Christ's Passion) are carried from Seville's churches through the streets to the cathedral, accompanied by processions that may take more than an hour to pass. The processions are organised by over 50 different *hermandades* or *cofradías* (brotherhoods, some of which include women). The climax of the week is the *madrugada* (early hours) of Good Friday, when some of the most-respected brotherhoods file through the city. The costume worn by the marching penitents consists of a full robe and a conical hat with slits cut for the eyes. The regalia was incongruously copied by America's Ku Klux Klan.

Procession schedules are widely available during Semana Santa; or see the Semana Santa website. Arrive near the cathedral early evening for a better view.

Feria de Abril
SPRING FAIR

The April Fair in the second half of the month is the joyful celebration after the solemnity of Semana Santa. The biggest and most colourful of all Andalucía's ferias, it takes place on a special site, El Real de la Feria, in the Los Remedios area southwest of the city centre. The ceremonial lighting of the feria grounds on the Monday night is the starting gun for six nights of partying. Much of the site is occupied by private *casetas* (enclosures), but there are also public ones. There's also a huge fairground.

During the afternoon, from around 1pm, those with horses and carriages parade about the feria grounds in their finery (horses are dressed up, too). It is also during the feria that Seville's major bullfighting season takes place.

Bienal de Flamenco FLAMENCO FESTIVAL
(www.bienal-flamenco.org) Spain's biggest flamenco festival is staged for a month in September of even-numbered years (it alternates with Málaga), and brings together the best of classical and experimental music and dance.

Sleeping

There's a good range of places to stay in all three of the most attractive areas – Barrio de Santa Cruz (close to the Alcázar and within walking distance of Prado de San Sebastián bus station), El Arenal (convenient for Plaza de Armas bus station) and El Centro.

Room rates in this section are for each establishment's high season – typically from March to June and again from September to October. During Semana Santa and the Feria de Abril rates are invariably doubled and sell out completely. Book ahead at this time.

Renting a tourist apartment here can be good value: typically costing under €100 a night for four people, or between €30 and €70 for two. Try **Apartamentos Embrujo de Sevilla** (627 569919; www.embrujodesevilla.com), which specialises in historic town mansion apartments, or **Sevilla5.com** (637 011091, 954 22 62 87; www.sevilla5.com).

BARRIO DE SANTA CRUZ
This old Jewish labyrinth is stuffed with majestic mansions, hidden patios and some very atmospheric accommodation.

Un Patio en Santa Cruz HOTEL €€€
(954 53 94 13; www.patiosantacruz.com; Calle Doncellas 15; s/d €78/128;) This two-star hotel gives you super-clean rooms, fresh-smelling linens, wi-fi in rooms, and a pot of morning coffee (in the lobby). The setting in

Santa Cruz is handy if a little noisy at night. Service is friendly and efficient.

Hotel Amadeus HOTEL €€
(954 50 14 43; www.hotelamadeussevilla.com; Calle Farnesio 6; s/d €85/95;) This musician family converted their 18th-century mansion into a stylish hotel with 14 elegant rooms of which Mozart would have been proud. A couple of the newer rooms have been soundproofed for piano or violin practice.

Las Casas de la Judería HOTEL €€€
(954 41 51 50; www.casasypalacios.com; Callejón Dos Hermanas 7; s/d from €140/175;) At last a five-star that might actually be worth it. Countless patios and corridors link this veritable palace that was once 18 different houses situated on the cusp of the Santa Cruz quarter. The decor is exquisite, from the trickling fountains to the antique furniture and paintings. Fork out €140 and you could be living like a Moorish prince.

Hotel Puerta de Sevilla HOTEL €€
(954 98 72 70; www.hotelpuertadesevilla.com; Calle Puerta de la Carne 2; s/d €66/86;) A small shiny hotel in a great location, the Puerta de Sevilla has azulejos tiles, flower-pattern textiles and wrought-iron beds all for one star. An extra bonus is the first-class but friendly service.

Hotel Alcántara HOTEL €€
(954 50 05 95; www.hotelalcantara.net; Calle Ximénez de Enciso 28; s/d €68/89;) This small, friendly hotel on a pedestrian street punches above its weight with sparkling modern bathrooms, windows on to the hotel's patio, and pretty floral curtains. It's next door to the Casa de la Memoria Al-Andalus (p677).

Pensión San Pancracio PENSIÓN €
(954 41 31 04; Plaza de las Cruces 9; s/d without bathroom €25/35, d with bathroom €50) An ideal budget option in Santa Cruz, this old rambling family house has plenty of different room options (all cheap) and a pleasant flower-bedizened patio/lobby. Friendliness makes up for the lack of luxury.

Hostería del Laurel HOTEL €€
(954 22 02 95; www.hosteriadellaurel.com; Plaza de los Venerables 5; s/d incl breakfast €75/105;) Above a characterful old bar of the same name on a small Santa Cruz plaza, one of the city's prettiest plazas, the Laurel has spacious if uninspired rooms and good-sized bathrooms.

Pensión Córdoba PENSIÓN €€
(☎954 22 74 98; www.pensioncordoba.com; Calle Farnesio 12; s/d without bathroom €45/65, with bathroom €55/75; ✱) Run by a friendly older couple for the past 30 years, this place is located on a quiet pedestrian street. Rooms are basic but spotless.

Hotel Goya HOTEL €
(☎954 21 11 70 www.hotelgoyasevilla.com; Calle Mateos Gago 31; s/d €40/60; ✱@☎) The gleaming Goya is more popular than ever. Pets are welcome. Book ahead.

EL ARENAL

A central location and a good mix of accommodation budgets make this river-side neighbourhood worth contemplating as a base.

Hotel Simón HOTEL €€
(☎954 22 66 60; www.hotelsimonsevilla.com; Calle García de Vinuesa 19; s €60-70, d €95-110; ✱) A typically grand 18th-century Sevillan house, with an ornate patio and spotless and comfortable rooms, this place gleams way above its two-star rating. Some of the rooms are embellished with rich azulejos tile work.

Hotel Vincci La Rábida HOTEL €€€
(☎954 50 12 80; www.vinccihoteles.com; Calle Castelar 24; s/d €159/195; P✱@☎) A beautiful four-storey columned atrium-lounge greets you in this converted 18th-century palace. Despite being part of the mainly Spanish-based Vincci chain, the hotel retains its history and originality.

Hostal Museo HOTEL €
(☎954 91 55 26; www.hostalmuseo.com; Calle Abad Gordillo 17; s/d €40/60; ✱@☎) The immaculate rooms here are endowed with solid wooden furniture and comfortable beds.

B&B Naranjo HOTEL €€
(☎954 22 58 40; Calle San Roque 11; s/d €45/65; ✱@) Homely pine furniture and restful colours add a touch of warmth.

Hotel Maestranza HOTEL €€
(☎954 56 10 70; www.hotel-maestranza.es; Calle Gamazo 12; s/d €53/87; ✱@☎) A small, friendly hotel on a quietish street, the Maestranza has spotless, plain rooms.

EL CENTRO

Handily situated for everywhere, El Centro mixes hotel glitter with some real bargains.

Hospas Casas del Rey de Baeza HOTEL €€€
(☎954 56 14 96; www.hospes.es; Plaza Jesús de la Redención 2; r from €136; P✱@☎☎) This expertly run and marvellously designed hotel off Calle Santiago occupies former communal housing patios dating from the 18th century. The large rooms boast attractive modern art, CD player, DVD and wi-fi. Public areas include a lounge and a gorgeous pool.

Oasis Backpackers' Hostel HOSTEL €
(☎954 29 37 77; www.oasissevilla.com; Plaza de la Encarnación 29, dm/d incl breakfast €15/50; ✱@☎) Seville's offbeat, buzzing backpacker central offers 24-hour free internet access. The new location is in Plaza Encarnación, a narrow street behind the Church of the Anunciación. Each dorm bed has a personal safe, and there is a small rooftop pool. There's no curfew; this is Spain!

Casa Sol y Luna HOTEL €
(☎954 21 06 82; www.casasolyluna1.com; Calle Pérez Galdós 1A; d with bathroom €45, s/d/tr without bathroom €22/38/60) This is a first-rate *hostal* (budget hotel) in a beautifully decorated house dating from 1911 (with embroidered white linen), which lies close to the congenial Plaza de la Alfalfa. Pay special attention to the 24-hour booking confirmation policy.

Hotel San Francisco HOTEL €€
(☎/fax 954 50 15 41; www.sanfranciscoh.com; Calle Álvarez Quintero 38; s/d €55/68; ⊙closed Aug; ✱@☎) A well-positioned place on a pedestrianised street close to the cathedral, the San Francisco is definitely one-star territory, with variable service, dark, but clean rooms and wi-fi in the reception only.

NORTH OF THE CENTRE

Located on the wrong side for most of the sights, you'll need to find a real corker to stay here.

Hotel San Gil HOTEL €€€
(☎954 90 68 11; www.hotelsangil.com; Calle Parras 28; s/d €141/176; P✱@☎☎) Around the corner from the Basílica de la Macarena, this renovated early-20th-century building focuses on the Moorish concept of keeping the beauty within. While it's plain on the outside, the inner reception and courtyard are beautiful. The slightly out-of-centre location is made up for by the hushed interiors and spacious rooms decorated in relaxing neutrals.

LOCAL KNOWLEDGE

TONI VILCHEZ: MANAGER 'EXTRAVERDE'

Tony Vilchez is manager of the newly inaugurated Extraverde (p674). Here are his four 'best of Seville province' recommendations.

Best Olive Oil

Of Seville's many fine olive oils, one in particular stands out: Basilippo Extra Virgin, a gourmet oil harvested early and with limited production. Aromatic, fruity, smooth and heavy with the flavour of almonds, in 2009 it was voted second best olive oil in the world by the Comité Oleícola Internacional (COI).

Best Wine

Seville isn't strongly associated with wine production. However, of the few wines produced in the province, the most well known is Fragata, a sweet white with a low grade best enjoyed with seafood, ham and sausages.

Best Cheese

Produced in Castilblanco de los Arroyos, a small town in the Sierra Norte de Sevilla, Mare Nostrum is arguably the province's tastiest cheese. Aromatic, intense and pungent, its quality is ensured by artisanal production techniques, a small-scale dairy-farm culture and use of the finest goat's milk.

Best Ham

Jamón ibérico is one of Spain's most celebrated gastronomic exports, the so-called caviar of hams. Four key factors determine the ham's continued high quality: ancient traditions, a unique dehesa (oak pasture) ecology, an exceptional breed of pig, and working processes that have been passed down from generation to generation. These four conditions combined produce 'Jamones Sierra de Sevilla'.

✗ Eating

In the competition to produce Andalucía's most inventive tapas Seville wins – hands down. Most tapas bars open at lunchtime as well as in the evening.

For a sit-down meal, restaurants preparing Spanish food open late: ie at 9pm, or nearer 10pm in summer. But with a surfeit of tourists, Seville has plenty of earlier options.

BARRIO DE SANTA CRUZ & AROUND
Good tapas bars are everywhere in this compact quarter. Wander the narrow streets and allow the atmosphere to draw you in.

TOP CHOICE Catalina   TAPAS €
(Paseo Catalina de Ribera 4; raciones €10) If your view of tapas is 'glorified bar snacks', then your ideas could be blown out of the water here, with a creative mix of just about every ingredient known to Iberian cooking. Start with the goat's cheese, aubergine and paprika special.

Bodega Santa Cruz   TAPAS €
(Calle Mateos Gago; tapas €1.50-2) Forever crowded and with a mountain of paper

on the floor, this place is usually standing room only, with tapas and drinks enjoyed alfresco as you dodge the marching army of tourists squeezing through Santa Cruz's narrow streets.

Extraverde   TAPAS €
(☎954 21 84 17; Plaza de Doña Elvira 8; tapas €2.50-4; ⊙10.30am-11.30pm) New on the scene, Extraverde (see also p674) is a unique bar–shop specialising in Andalucian products such as olive oil, cheese and wine. You can taste free samples standing up, or sit down inside and order a full tapa.

Restaurant La Cueva   TRADITIONAL €€
(☎954 21 31 43; Calle Rodrigo Caro 18 & Plaza de Doña Elvira, 1; mains €11-24, menús €16) Slightly frosty service is made up for with excellent paella and a storming fish zarzuela (casserole; €30 for two people). The interior is roomy, while the alfresco tables overlook dreamy Plaza de Doña Elvira.

Restaurante Egaña Oriza
                                 MODERN SPANISH €€€
(☎954 22 72 11; Calle San Fernando 41; mains €22-32; ⊙closed Sat lunch & Sun) Regarded as one

of the city's best restaurants, Egaña Oriza also knocks up creative tapas. It's situated opposite the bus station, so this could be your first (and best) culinary treat in Seville.

Café Bar Las Teresas
TAPAS €

(Calle Santa Teresa 2; tapas €2.20-4) Always busy, an inviting cool, tiled inner decor, and a location at the nexus of the Santa Cruz district; all this bodes well for the hard-to-miss Las Teresas. The tapas aren't bad either.

Corral del Agua
ANDALUCIAN €€€

(954 22 48 41; Callejón del Agua 6; mains €16.50-22; lunch & dinner Mon-Sat) Inventive Al-Andalus and traditional dishes are served in a semitropical courtyard under a twining canopy of vines and jacaranda.

Cervecería Giralda
TAPAS €

(Calle Mateos Gago 1; tapas €3.50-5) Exotic tapas variations are merged with traditional dishes in this one-time Muslim bathhouse.

EL ARENAL

Surprisingly lively at night, El Arenal has some good tapas places where most people seem to congregate in the street.

Mesón Cinco Jotas
TAPAS €

(Calle Castelar 1; tapas/media raciones €3.80/9.45) Try some of the best *jamón* in town here and move on to the *solomillo ibérico* (Iberian pork sirloin) in sweet Pedro Ximénez wine for the peak of porcine flavour.

Enrique Becerra
ANDALUCIAN €€€

(954 21 30 49; Calle Gamazo 2; mains €16.50-24; closed Sat & Sun) Adding a smart touch to El Arenal, Enrique Becerra cooks up hearty Andalucian dishes. The lamb drenched in honey sauce and stuffed with spinach and pine nuts is delectable.

EL CENTRO

Plaza de la Alfalfa wears many hats. It is the hub of the tapas scene in the day, a stopping-off point for boisterous families in the early evening, and a fount of late-night bars and clubs after darkness falls. There are a couple of decent Italian restaurants on or around the square if you need a break from the usual Spanish suspects.

Robles Laredo
MODERN SPANISH €€

(Plaza de San Francisco; raciones €9-12) This small Italianite cafe–restaurant is fairly dwarfed by its two huge chandeliers and a vast collection of delicate desserts dis-

played in glass cases. The tapas are equally refined. Try the foie gras, beefburgers with truffle sauce, or oysters and whitebait.

Bar Alfalfa
TAPAS €

(Cnr Calles Alfalfa & Candilejo; tapas €2-3) It's amazing how many people, hams, wine bottles and other knick-knacks you can stuff into such a small space. No matter – order through the window when the going gets crowded. You won't forget the tomato-tinged magnificence of the Italy-meets-Iberia *salmorejo* bruschetta.

Horno de San Buenadventura
COFFEE, SNACKS €

(Plaza de la Alfalfa 10; snacks €6-10) There are actually two of these gilded pastry/coffee/snack bars in Seville, one here in Plaza de Alfalfa and the other opposite the cathedral. All kinds of fare are on show, though it's probably best enjoyed for its lazy continental breakfasts (yes, the service can be slow) or a spontaneous late-night cake fix.

Bar Levíes
INTERNATIONAL €

(Calle San José 15; tapas €2-5) The ultimate student tapas haunt (read: cheap), crowded Levíes is actually two bars in one, serving a mixture of *raciones* (large tapas servings), beer, pizzas and desserts. The food's average, but the atmosphere's electric.

Habanita
ANDALUCIAN, CUBAN €€

(606 716456; Calle Golfo 3; raciones €8-15; closed Sun evening;) This top restaurant serves a winning variety of Cuban (in the pre-rationing days!), Andalucian and vegetarian food. Try the fried yucca and stewed meat.

ALAMEDA DE HÉRCULES

Seville's trendiest nightlife quarter also has some decent eating places overlooking the main pedestrianised park.

Antigua Abacería de San Lorenzo
DELI, TAPAS €

(954 38 00 67; www.antiguaabaceriadesan lorenzo.com; Calle Teodosio 53; tapas €1-5; 9.30am-midnight, closed 5-8pm Sat & Sun Jun-Sep) A traditional combination of provisions store, deli, tapas bar and prepared-food takeaway in a cleverly restored 17th-century house.

TRIANA

The riverside restaurants along riverfront Calle del Betis are at their best around 11pm. Sit outside and enjoy fried seafood with the Torre del Oro reflecting on the river.

Ristorante Cosa Nostra ITALIAN €

(Calle del Betis 52; pizzas €8.50-12; ☺closed Mon)
Forget the Mafiosi nameplate; this is the
best Italian food in Seville and well worth
crossing the river for. The pizzas are spun
in front of your eyes and the rich creamy
risottos ought to have every paella chef in
the city looking over their shoulder.

Casa Cuesta MODERN SPANISH €

(☏954 33 33 37; Calle de Castilla 3-5; mains €9-
10) Something about the carefully buffed
wooden bar and gleaming beer pumps suggests the owners are proud of Casa Cuesta.
They should be; it's a real find for food and
wine lovers alike.

 ## Drinking

Bars usually open 6pm to 2am weekdays,
8pm till 3am at the weekend. Drinking and
partying really get going around midnight
on Friday and Saturday (daily when it's hot).
In summer, dozens of open-air late-night
bars *(terrazas de verano)* spring up along
both banks of the river.

BARRIO DE SANTA CRUZ

The Barrio has the most-concentrated strip
of drinking nooks in the city; ideal for bar-
hopping.

P Flaherty Irish Pub PUB

(Calle Alemanes 7) Its location right next to
the cathedral makes this one of the busiest – and biggest – bars around. If there's a
football game on, the atmosphere here revs
up a notch.

Antigüedades BAR

(Calle Argote de Molina 40) This place blends
mellow beats with offbeat decor. The tiled
window seats with a view of the busy street
are the best place to nurse your drink.

EL ARENAL

El Arenal is buoyant after dark, when the
streets are choked with bevies of alfresco
drinkers enjoying the breeze off the river.

Casa Morales BAR

(Garcia de Vinuesa 11) Founded in 1850, not
much has changed in this defiantly old-
world bar, with charming anachronisms
wherever you look. Towering clay *tinajas*
(wine storage jars) carry the chalked-up
tapas choices of the day. Locals sweat it out
on summer nights like true *sevillanos*.

El Capote BAR

(Calle de Arjona) A beachside ambience complete with palm trees makes for relaxed alfresco drinking right next to Puente de Triana. There's a tempting *churrería* (*churros*
cafe) that catches the morning hangover
crowd on the bridge nearby.

Café Isbiliyya BAR

(Paseo de Cristóbal Colón 2) Cupid welcomes
you to this gay music bar, which puts on
extravagant drag shows on Thursday and
Sunday nights.

EL CENTRO

Plaza del Salvador is brimful with drinkers from mid-evening to 1am. Grab a drink
from La Antigua Bodeguita or La Sa-
potales next door and sit on the steps of
the Parroquia del Salvador.

Calle Pérez Galdós, off Plaza de la Alfalfa,
is frequented for its hole-in-the-wall places
including the tiny Cabo Loco (Calle Pérez
Galdós 26), with plenty of cheap shots, and
the '80s-themed La Rebótica (Calle Pérez
Galdós 11), with another 50 or so alcohol-
infused concoctions to choose from.

El Garlochi BAR

(Calle Boteros 4) Named after the *gitano*
(Roma) word for 'heart', this deeply camp
bar hits you with its Semana Santa iconography: clouds of incense, Jesus and Virgin
images, and potent cocktails with names
like Sangre de Cristo (Blood of Christ).

ALAMEDA DE HÉRCULES

In terms of hipness and trendy places to go
out, the slightly shabby Alameda is where it's
at, and it's also the heartbeat of gay Seville.

Bulebar Café BAR

(Alameda de Hércules 83; ☺4pm-late) This
place gets pretty *caliente* (hot) at night,
but is pleasantly chilled in the early evening, with friendly staff.

Café Central BAR

(Alameda de Hércules 64) One of the oldest
and most popular places along the street,
Central has yellow bar lights, wooden
flea-market chairs and a massive crowd
that gathers at weekends.

TRIANA

If you want a change from the slicker watering holes of the city proper, try the raff-
ish, ripe-for-development Triana riverfront.
The wall overlooking the river along Calle
del Betis forms a makeshift bar. Carry your
drink out from one of the following places:
Alambique, Big Ben, Sirocca and Muí
d'Aquí. They're all clustered at Calle del Betis 54 and open from 9pm.

☆ Entertainment

Seville is reborn after dark, with live music, experimental theatre and exciting flamenco.

Clubs

Clubs in Seville come and go fast but a few stand the test of time. The partying starts at a fashionably late 2am to 3am at the weekend. Dress smarter (ie no sportswear) at the weekend, as clubs become pickier about their punters.

Bestiario   NIGHTCLUB
(www.bestiario.net; Calle Zaragoza 33; admission varies; ☺11pm-late Thu-Sat) In the revolving merry-go-round of Seville clubs, Bestiario makes claims to be the funkiest. The cafe-bar keeps going till sunrise and has a penchant for retro '80s sounds. It's right next to Plaza Nueva.

Boss   NIGHTCLUB
(Calle del Betis 67; admission free with flyer; ☺8pm-7am Tue-Sun) Make it past the two gruff bouncers and you'll find Boss a top dance spot, and relatively posh for Triana. The music is highly varied.

Live Music

Seville has Andalucía's most-varied music scene, with big-name pop acts and a much-celebrated flamenco scene.

La Imperdible   BAR
(☑954 38 82 19; www.imperdible.org; Plaza del Duque de la Victoria; adult/child €12/5) This epicentre of experimental arts stages lots of contemporary dance, theatre and flamenco, usually around 9pm. The bar here also hosts varied music events from around 11pm Thursday to Saturday.

Fun Club   BAR
(Alameda de Hércules 86; admission live-band nights €3-6, other nights free; ☺11.30pm-late Thu-Sun, from 9.30pm live-band nights) With funk, Latino, hip hop and jazz bands taking the stage, Fun Club is home to a nocturnal alternative crowd living it large in Alameda de Hércules.

Flamenco

Soleares, Flamenco's truest *cante jondo* (deep song; an anguished instrument of expression for a group on the margins of society) was first concocted in Triana; head here to find some of the more authentic clubs. Elsewhere, the city puts on nightly *tablaos* (flamenco shows) at about half a dozen different venues.

DON'T MISS

677

CASA DE LA MEMORIA DE AL-ANDALUS

This **flamenco tablao** (flamenco show; ☑954 56 06 70; Calle Ximénez de Enciso 28; tickets €15; ☺9pm) in Santa Cruz is probably the most intimate and authentic nightly flamenco show, offering a wide variety of flamenco styles in a room of shifting shadows. Space is limited to 100, so reserve tickets in advance.

TOP CHOICE **La Carbonería**   BAR
(Calle Levíes 18; ☺about 8pm-4am) During the day there is no indication that this happening place is anything but a large garage. But, come after 8pm and this converted coal yard in the Barrio de Santa Cruz reveals two large bars, and nightly live flamenco (11pm and midnight) for no extra charge.

Casa Anselma   FLAMENCO BAR
(Pagés de Corro 49; ☺midnight to close, Mon-Sat) If you can squeeze in past the foreboding form of Anselma (a celebrated Triana flamenco dancer) at the door you'll quickly realise that anything can happen in here. Casa Anselma (beware: there's no sign, just a doorway embellished with azulejos tiles) is the antithesis of a tourist flamenco *tablao,* with cheek-to-jowl crowds, thick cigarette smoke, zero amplification and spontaneous outbreaks of dexterous dancing. Pure magic. Anselma is in Triana on the corner of Calle Alfarería about 200m from the western side of the Puente de Isabel.

Bullfights

Whether you appreciate this as sport for the brave or view it is a form of animal cruelty is a matter for debate. Either way, it is certainly an important aspect of Spanish tradition. Fights at Seville's ancient, elegant, 14,000-seat **Plaza de Toros de la Real Maestranza** (Paseo de Cristóbal Colón 12; www.realmaestranza.com) are among the biggest in Spain. Seville's crowds are some of the most knowledgeable in the bullfighting world. The season runs from Easter Sunday to early October, with fights every Sunday, usually at 7pm, and every day during the Feria de Abril and the week before it.

From the start of the season until late June/early July, nearly all the fights are by fully fledged matadors. Seats cost €32.50 to €110 but only cheap *sol* seats (those in the sun at the start of proceedings) may be available to those who don't hold season tickets. Most of the rest of the season, *novilleras* (novice bullfights) are held, with tickets costing €5 to €30. Tickets are sold in advance at Empresa Pagés (954 50 13 82; Calle de Adriano 37) and from 4.30pm on fight days at the bullring itself.

For more information on bullfighting, see p865.

 Shopping

The craft shops in the Barrio de Santa Cruz are inevitably tourist oriented, but many sell attractive ceramic tiles and poster art.

Shoe fetishists beware: Seville has possibly the densest quota of shoe shops on the planet, primarily focused in El Centro around the pedestrianised shopping streets of Calles Sierpes, de la Cuna, Velázquez and Tetuán. Head to Calle Feria, located a couple of blocks to the north of Plaza de la Encarnación, to look for your handmade flamenco guitar. El Corte Inglés department store occupies four separate buildings a little west, on Plaza de la Magdalena and Plaza del Duque de la Victoria. Further north, Calle Amor de Dios and Calle Doctor Letamendi have more alternative shops. In the traditional tile-making area of Triana, a dozen shops and workshops still offer charming, artful ceramics around the junction of Calles Alfarería and Antillano Campos.

LTC   MAPS
(Avenida Menéndez Pelayo 46; closed Sat) Andalucía's top map shop; handy if you're plotting a regionwide tour. From Plaza San Sebastián head northeast up Avenida Menéndez Pelayo for 600m.

Mercadillo   FLEA MARKET
(Calle Feria; Thu) This large flea market near Alameda de Hércules is worth a visit.

 Information

Emergency
Ambulance (061)
Emergency (112)
Policía Local (092)
Policía Nacional (091)

Internet Access
Ciber Alcázar (Calle San Fernando 35; 10am-11pm Mon-Fri, noon-11pm Sat & Sun) Offers inexpensive international calls (as well as several internet booths).

Internetia (Avenida Menéndez Pelayo 45; per hr €2; 10am-11pm)

Media
El Giraldillo Andalucía-wide what's-on mag, free at tourist offices and some hotels, with a strong Seville emphasis.

Tourist Free mag for tourists, with worthwhile information.

Welcome & Olé Another free mag, containing tourist info and event listings.

Medical Services
Centro de Salud El Porvenir (954 71 23 23; cnr Avenidas Menéndez y Pelayo & de Cádiz) Public clinic with emergency service.

Hospital Virgen del Rocío (955 01 20 00; Avenida de Manuel Siurot) The main general hospital, 1km south of Parque de María Luisa.

Money
There's no shortage of banks and ATMs in the central area. Santa Justa train station, the airport and both bus stations have ATMs.

Post
Post office (Avenida de la Constitución 32)

Telephone
Ciber Alcázar (Calle San Fernando 35; 10am-11pm Mon-Fri, noon-11pm Sat & Sun) Offers inexpensive international calls.

Tourist Information
Regional tourist offices Avenida de la Constitución 21 (9am-7pm Mon-Fri, 10am-2pm & 3-7pm Sat, 10am-2pm Sun, closed holidays); Estación Santa Justa (9am-8pm Mon-Fri, 10am-2pm Sat & Sun, closed holidays).

Turismo Sevilla (www.turismosevilla.org; Plaza del Triunfo 1; 10.30am-7pm Mon-Fri)

Websites
Discover Sevilla (www.discoversevilla.com) An excellent, comprehensive site.

Explore Seville (www.exploreseville.com)

Seville Tourism (www.turismo.sevilla.org) The city's informative official tourism site.

 Getting There & Away

Air
Seville's **Aeropuerto San Pablo** (24hr) has a fair range of international and domestic flights. **Iberia** (www.iberia.com) flies direct to Barcelona, Madrid and half a dozen other Spanish cities, as well as to London and Paris. **Spanair** (www.spanair.com) also flies to Madrid and, along with **Air Europa** (www.air-europa.com) and **Vueling** (www.vueling.com), to Barcelona.

Vueling also covers Paris, Rome, Amsterdam and Brussels to Seville.

From the British Isles there are flights with **British Airways** (www.ba.com) from London Gatwick. **Ryanair** (www.ryanair.com) flies from Liverpool, Bristol, London Stansted, Rome and various Italian destinations and, more recently, Marrakech. **Air-Berlin** (www.airberlin.com) flies to several major German, Swiss and Austrian cities from Seville. **Transavia** (www.transavia. com) comes from Paris and **SN Brussels Airlines** (www.flysn.com) from Brussels. Carrier and schedule information changes frequently, so it's best to check with specific airlines or major online bookers.

Bus

From the **Estación de Autobuses Prado de San Sebastián** (Plaza San Sebastián), there are 12 or more buses daily to/from Cádiz (€11.50, 1¾ hours), Córdoba (€10, two hours), Granada (€19, 3½ hours), Jerez de la Frontera (€8, 1¼ hours), Ronda (€11, 2½ hours, five or more daily) and Málaga (€15.75, 2¾ hours). This is also the station for other towns in Cádiz province, the east of Seville province, and destinations along the Mediterranean coast from the Costa del Sol to Barcelona.

From the **Estación de Autobuses Plaza de Armas** (Avenida del Cristo de la Expiración), destinations include Madrid (€18.65, six hours, 14 daily), El Rocío (€5.10, 1½ hours, three to five daily), Aracena (€5.67, 1¼ hours, two daily) and other places in Huelva province, Mérida (€13, three hours, 12 daily), Cáceres (€15, four hours, six daily) and northwestern Spain. This is also the station for buses to Portugal. **ALSA** (www. alsa.es) runs two daily buses to Lisbon (€35, seven hours daily), one via Badajoz and Évora, the other (overnight) via Faro. **Casal** (www.auto carescasal.com) and **Damas** (www.damas-sa.es) do similar Portuguese runs to Lisbon and Lagos respectively. Finally, **Eurolines** (www.eurolines. es) will take you to Germany, Belgium, France, Holland and Sofia, capital of Bulgaria.

Train

The modern, efficient **Estación de Santa Justa** (Avenida Kansas City) is 1.5km northeast of the city centre. There's also a city-centre **Renfe ticket office** (Calle Zaragoza 29).

Twenty or more superfast AVE trains, reaching speeds of 280km/h, whiz daily to/from Madrid (€80.70, 2½ hours). There are cheaper 'Altaria' services (€63.30, 3½ hours). Other destinations include Barcelona (€61 to €88, 10½ to 13 hours, three daily) and the AVE (€130, 6½ hours, one daily), Cádiz (€12.75, 1¾ hours, 13 daily), Córdoba (€16 to €32, 40 minutes to 1½ hours, 21 or more daily), Granada (€24, three hours, four daily), Huelva (€9.65, 1½ hours, three daily), Jerez de la Frontera (€8.80, 1¼ hours,

SEVILLE GOES GREEN

Where cars once angrily honked, bikes and pedestrians (and the odd noise-less tram) now roam. Welcome to the new Seville, a cleaner, greener more breathable metropolis that has bidden *¡Adiós!* to the organised urban chaos so familiar in other Mediterranean cities. Since 2006 Seville has instituted multiple clean-up measures including an electric tram, a comprehensive bike-borrowing system, a new underground metro train line (with three more in the offing) and the pedestrianisation of several arterial city-centre streets. The result is more redolent of Amsterdam than Andalucía, but no one's complaining. Noise levels have dropped, pollution has plummeted, important historic buildings (including the cathedral) are free of grime, and people have switched from using cars to public transport or – even better – bikes. Leave your car on the city limits and join them.

nine daily), Málaga (€19.10 to €36.40, two to 2½ hours, five daily) and Mérida (€14, five hours, one daily).

ⓘ Getting Around

To/From the Airport

The airport is 7km east of the city centre on the A4 Córdoba road. **Los Amarillos** (www.los amarillos.es) runs buses between the airport and the Avenida del Cid near the San Sebastián bus station (€2.20 to €2.50, at 15 and 45 minutes past the hour, 5.45am-00.45am; less frequent on Sundays). A taxi costs about €20.

Bicycle

SeVici (☎902 01 10 32; www.sevici.es; ⊗7am-9pm) is a bright, green idea from Seville's urban authority: a cycle-hire network comprising almost 200 fully automated pick-up/drop-off points dotted all over the city (clearly shown on a nifty folding pocket map); you can pick up from one location and drop off at another. A one-week subscription costs €5. Your first 30 minutes' cycling is free, the next hour costs €1, second and subsequent hours are €2 per hour. Alternatively, you can pay €10 and sign up for a year (forms available at tourist information offices or online). In that case, your first hour will cost €0.50 and subsequent hours €1. A clear, compact cycle-route map of the city is available from tourist information centres.

Quieter, cleaner and infinitely more stylish than fuming amid traffic fumes, the SeVici cycle network is an idea all Spanish cities would do well to follow. The only possible drawback is the €150 deposit for both long- and short-term hires; use a credit card, which 'freezes' the deduction, instead of a debit card.

Bus

Run by Seville's urban transport authority **Tussam** (www.tussam.es), buses C1, C2, C3 and C4 do useful circular routes linking the main transport terminals and the city centre. The C1, from in front of Estación de Santa Justa, follows a clockwise route via Avenida de Carlos V (close to Prado de San Sebastián bus station and the Barrio de Santa Cruz), Avenida de María Luisa, Triana, Isla Mágica and Calle de Resolana. The C2, heading west from in front of Estación de Santa Justa, follows the same route in reverse. Bus 32, also from outside Santa Justa, runs to/from Plaza de la Encarnación in El Centro.

The clockwise number C3 will take you from Puerta Carmona (near Prado de San Sebastián bus station and the Barrio de Santa Cruz) to Puerta La Carne and Puerto Jerez. The C4 does the same circuit anticlockwise except that from Estación de Autobuses Plaza de Armas it heads south along Calle de Arjona and Paseo de Cristóbal Colón, instead of crossing the river to Triana.

Bus rides cost €1.20.

Car & Motorcycle

Hotels with parking usually charge you €12 to €18 a day for the privilege – no cheaper than some public car parks but at least your vehicle will be close at hand. **Parking Paseo de Colón** (cnr Paseo de Cristóbal Colón & Calle Adriano; per hr up to 10hr €1.20, 10-24hr €13.50) is a relatively inexpensive underground car park.

Metro

Seville's long-awaited light **metro** (www.sevilla21.com/metro, in Spanish), touted since the 1970s, finally opened in April 2009. Line 1 (three future lines are projected) runs from the west to the south, from Ciudad Expo to Olivar de Quinto (in the suburb of Dos Hermanas), covering 18km and taking in 22 stations. Tickets cost €1.30/1.55/1.75 for zones 1/2/3 or you can buy a day pass for €4.50.

Tram

Tranvia (www.tussam.es, in Spanish), the city's sleek, environmentally sustainable tram service, was launched by Tussam in 2007. Lines T1 and T4 swish 1.4km back and forth between the Plaza Nueva (near the *ayuntamiento*) and along Avenida de la Constitución to the Archivo de Indias and Puerta de Jerez, then down San Fernando to the bus station at Prado de San Sebastián. Individual rides cost €1.20, or you can buy a

Bono (travel pass offering five rides for €5) from many newspaper stands and tobacconists.

Around Seville

Seville province invites day trips. You'll find Andalucía's best Roman ruins at Itálica. On the rolling agricultural plains east of Seville, fascinating old towns such as Carmona and Osuna bespeak many epochs of history.

CARMONA
POP 27,950 / ELEV 250M

Long-civilised Carmona, continuously inhabited since the Neolithic era and fortified since the 8th century BC, perches on a low hill dotted with venerable palaces and impressive monuments 38km east of Seville off the A4 to Córdoba.

☉ Sights

The tourist office in the Puerta de Sevilla, the impressive fortified main gate of the old town, sells tickets (adults/students and seniors, €2/1) for the gate's interesting upper levels.

The Puerta de Córdoba, in Calle Dolores Quintanilla at the end of the street passing the Iglesia Priorial de Santa María, is an original Roman gate in marvellous repair, framing the fertile Seville countryside that unfolds like a precious, faded rug. South of here is the stark, ruined Alcázar, an Almohad fort that Pedro I turned into a country palace. It was brought down by earthquakes in 1504 and 1755, and part of it is now the site of a luxurious *parador* (state-owned hotel).

Iglesia Priorial de Santa María   CHURCH
(Calle Martín López de Córdoba; admission €3; ☉10am-2pm & 5-7pm Mon-Fri, to 2pm Sat) This splendid church was built mainly in the 15th and 16th centuries. But its **Patio de los Naranjos** was originally a mosque's courtyard and has a Visigothic calendar carved into one of its pillars. Particularly beautiful is the embossed and inlaid pair of bible covers from around 1400.

FREE **Roman Necropolis**   ROMAN RUINS
(Avenida de Jorge Bonsor; ☉9am-2pm Tue-Sat 15 Jun–14 Sep, to 5pm Tue-Fri, closed holidays 1 Jul–31 Aug) Just over 1km southwest of the Puerta de Sevilla is Carmona's impressive Roman necropolis. You can look down into a dozen family tombs, hewn from the rock.

DON'T MISS

ITÁLICA

Situated in the suburban settlement of Santiponce, 8km northwest of Seville, **Itálica** (adult/EU citizen €1.50/free; ⏲8.30am-8.30pm Tue-Sat, 9am-3pm Sun Apr-Sep) was the first Roman town in Spain. Founded in 206 BC, it was also the birthplace and home of the 2nd-century-AD Roman emperors Trajan and Hadrian. The partly reconstructed ruins include one of the biggest of all the Roman amphitheatres, broad paved streets, ruins of several houses with beautiful mosaics, and a theatre.

Buses run to Santiponce (€1.30, 40 minutes) from Seville's Plaza de Armas bus station, at least twice an hour from 6.35am to 11pm Monday to Friday, and a little less often at weekends. They stop right outside the Itálica entrance.

FREE **Ayuntamiento** TOWN HALL
(Calle El Salvador; ⏲8am-3pm Mon-Fri) Contains a large, very fine **Roman mosaic** of the Gorgon Medusa.

Museo de la Ciudad MUSEUM
(City History Museum; Calle San Ildefonso 1; admission €3, Tue free; ⏲11am-7pm Tue-Sun, 11am-2pm Mon) Behind Iglesia Prioral de Santa María, this museum will give you the equivalent of a minor history credit and lays out everything sequentially in historical eras.

Sleeping & Eating

TOP CHOICE **Posada San Fernando** HOTEL €€
(☎954 14 14 08; www.posadasanfernando.com; Plaza de San Fernando 6; s/d/tr €60/65/100; ❄📶) Recently opened and furnished with *mucho amor* (and attention to historical detail), this *posada* (rural home) is a giveaway for the price. The 18 rooms have plenty of atmosphere and antiques, plus complimentary tea and coffee (unusual in Spain).

Parador Alcázar del Rey Don Pedro HISTORIC HOTEL €€€
(☎954 14 10 10; www.parador.es; r €160-171; P❄@📶🏊) Carmona's luxuriously equipped *parador* feels even more luxurious for the ruined Alcázar in its grounds. The beautiful dining room (*menú del día* – daily set menu – €32) overlooks a jaw-dropping (and unexpected) view of the surrounding Vega roasting under the Sevillian sun.

Casa de Carmona HOTEL €€€
(☎954 19 10 00; www.casadecarmona.com; Plaza de Lasso 1; s/d/ste incl breakfast €155/160/225; P❄📶🏊) A superluxurious hotel in a beautiful 16th-century palace, the Casa de Carmona feels like the aristocratic home that it used to be. Its elegant restaurant (mains €18 to €25) serves haute cuisine with an *andaluz* (Andalucian) touch.

Hospedería Palacio Marques de las Torres HOTEL, HOSTEL €
(☎954 19 62 48; www.hospederiamarquesdelastorres.com; Calle Fermin Molpeceres 2; dm/s/d incl breakfast €20/40/50; ❄📶🏊) Modern comforts amid 18th-century graciousness make for a handsome mix. Two four-person dorm cabins rub shoulders with comfortable hotel rooms containing plush beds in a converted *palacio*. Plus there's a fabulous turquoise pool in the sunny garden.

Carmona has a particularly big tapas scene for such a small place and the tourist office offers its very own 'tapas tour' map. Start at cool but friendly **Bar Goya** (Calle Prim 2; tapas/raciones €2/8) just off Plaza San Fernando, where Seville quality is maintained without the Seville clamour. From here you can work your way around approximately 20 featured bars if you have the stomach!

Information

Tourist office (www.turismo.carmona.org; ⏲10am-3pm & 4.30-6pm Mon-Sat, 10am-3pm Sun & holidays) Helpful tourist office, in the Puerta de Sevilla at the main entrance to the old part of town.

Getting There & Away

Buses from Seville leave from Avenida de Portugal close to the Prado de San Sebastián bus station (€2.55, 45 minutes, 20 per day Monday to Friday, 10 on Saturday, seven on Sunday) and on Paseo del Estatuto in Carmona (300m west of the old-town entrance).

OSUNA

POP 18,000 / ELEV 330M

Just off the A92 towards Granada, 91km from Seville, Osuna is the loveliest of Seville province's country towns, with beautifully preserved baroque mansions and an amazing Spanish Renaissance monastery. Several of the most impressive buildings were created by its ducal family, one of Spain's richest since the 16th century.

☉ Sights

The massive buildings on the hill overlooking the centre graphically symbolise the weight of various kinds of authority in old Spain. Behind the town hall, the Palacio de los Cepeda (Calle de la Huerta) has rows of dramatic columns embellished with the Cepeda family coat of arms. Nearby, the Cilla del Cabildo Colegial (Calle San Pedro 16) bears a sculpted representation of Seville's Giralda.

Colegiata de Santa María de la Asunción   ART GALLERY
(☑954 81 04 44; Plaza de la Encarnación; admission by guided tour only €2.50; ☉10am-1.30pm & 4-7pm Tue-Sun May-Sep) Encased in a 16th-century collegiate church, this gallery contains a wealth of sacred art collected by the Dukes of Osuna, including several paintings by José de Ribera. The visit includes the lugubrious **Sepulcro Ducal**, the Osuna family vault.

Monasterio de la Encarnación   MUSEUM
(admission €2; ☉10am-1.30pm & 4-7pm Tue-Sun May-Sep) Opposite the Colegiata, this former monastery is now Osuna's museum of religious art, with beautiful tile work and a rich collection of baroque art. Just down the road, the pointy blue-and-white-tiled towers of the Antigua Universidad fascinate like illustrations in a sinister fairy tale.

🛏 Sleeping

Hotel Palacio Marqués de la Gomera
                              HISTORIC HOTEL €€
(☑954 81 22 23; www.hotelpalaciodelmarques.com; Calle San Pedro 20; s/d €94/115; P❋@🛜) This luxury hotel occupies one of Osuna's finest baroque mansions. It is exceptionally handsome, with rooms of princely proportions and quiet luxury. It even boasts its own ornate private chapel, well-upholstered library and billiards room.

Hostal Esmeralda   HOTEL €
(☑955 82 10 73; Calle Tesorero 7; s/d €32/58; P❋) Central and well-maintained, with a downstairs bar and patio, the family-run Esmeralda ticks all the budget boxes and offers a little more beside: an underlying air of cheerfulness, for example.

ℹ Information

Oficina Municipal de Turismo (Calle Carrera 82; ☉9.30am-1.30pm & 4-6pm Tue-Sat,

9.30am-1.30pm Sun) All the info you will need on the town, including some useful guides.

ℹ Getting There & Away

The **bus station** (Avenida de la Constitución) is 500m southeast of Plaza Mayor. Up to 11 daily buses run to Seville (Prado de San Sebastián, €6.65, 1½ hours). The **train station** (Avenida de la Estación) is 1km southwest of the centre, with six trains per day to Seville (€8.80, one hour).

HUELVA PROVINCE

To fly-by-nighters, Huelva province is that nodule of land 'on the way to Portugal'. To those willing to drag their heels a little, it's home to the region's best cured ham, its most evocative fandangos, and Spain's largest and most ebullient *romería*. Throw in some British-influenced mining heritage, Christopher Columbus memorabilia, and what is possibly Spain's most revered national park, and you've got the makings of an Andalucian break well outside the standard mould.

Huelva

POP 148,000

Blemished by factories and with its historical heritage smashed to pieces in the 1755 Lisbon earthquake (and not rebuilt), Huelva is never going to win any beauty contests. If you're passing through, there's a clutch of journeyman hotels, and some low-key but poignant Columbus memorabilia to ponder (yes, the great explorer first sailed from here). Alternatively, you can tackle Huelva province's sights on day trips from Seville or from the more salubrious small town of Aracena (p687) 100km to the north.

☉ Sights

Huelva's sights don't really merit a plural.

FREE **Museo Provincial**   MUSEUM
(Alameda Sundheim 13; ☉2.30-8pm Tue, 9am-8pm Wed-Sat & Sun) Once you've contemplated the art pieces and artefacts dug up from archaeological digs, you can be on your way.

🛏 Sleeping & Eating

NH Luz Huelva   HOTEL €€€
(☑959 25 00 11; www.nh-hotels.com; Alameda Sundheim 26; s/d €140/156; P❋@🛜) This is supposedly Huelva's best hotel, though it's a little utilitarian for its advertised four stars,

with plain but spacious rooms overlooking other apartment blocks, and a lack of any hidden extras (you only get 30 minutes' free wi-fi). Rates can drop significantly in low season.

Albergue Juvenil de Huelva HOSTEL €
(☎959 65 00 10; www.inturjoven.com; Avenida Marchena Colombo 14; per person incl breakfast €20-25; ✳@) This is a good, modern, wheelchair-accessible youth hostel, where all rooms have a bathroom and absolutely no frills. It's 2km north of the bus station: city bus 6 from there stops just around the corner from the hostel, on Calle JS Elcano.

Hotel Los Condes HOTEL €€
(☎959 28 24 00; Alameda Sundheim 14; s/d incl breakfast €59/71; P✳@?) Large, bright, modern rooms, with orange bathrooms, plus funkily decorated reception, free internet and breakfast included, add up to a good-value hotel.

Mesón El Pozo TAPAS €€
(Calle Alonso Śanchez 14; tapas €2.50, raciones from €12; ⊙closed Sun & Aug) Locally popular backstreet bar with a fish-biased menu befitting of an oceanside city.

Trattoria Fuentevieja ITALIAN €
(Avenida Martín Alonso Pinzón; mains €6-11; ⊙closed Sun dinner) This ultrapopular Italian spot serves a good range of salads, as well as pizza, pasta and meat dishes. It's just off the main square.

❶ Information

Regional tourist office (Plaza Alcalde Coto Mora 2; ⊙9am-7.30pm Mon-Fri, 10am-2pm Sat & Sun) Outstandingly well informed and helpful.

❶ Getting There & Away

From the **bus station** (☎959 25 69 00) at least 18 daily buses head to Seville (€7.14, 1¼ hours) and four to Madrid (€21.80, seven hours) operated by **Damas** (www.damas-sa.es). Two (except Saturday, Sunday and holidays from October to May) head for Lagos (€13 to €14, four hours) in Portugal via Faro and Albufeira. From the **train station** (☎902 24 02 02) three daily trains head to Seville (€9.65, 1½ hours).

Lugares Colombinos

The Lugares Colombinos (Columbus Sites) are the three townships of La Rábida, Palos de la Frontera and Moguer, along the eastern bank of the Tinto estuary east of Huelva. All three played key roles in the discov-

ery of the Americas and can be combined in a single day trip from Huelva, the Doñana area or the nearby coast.

LA RÁBIDA
POP 600
In this pretty and peaceful town, don't miss the 14th-century Monasterio de La Rábida (admission €3; ⊙10am-1pm & 4-7pm Tue-Sun), visited several times by Columbus before his great voyage of discovery. On the waterfront below the monastery is the Muelle de las Carabelas (Wharf of the Caravels; admission €3.30; ⊙10am-2pm & 5-9pm Tue-Fri, 11am-8pm Sat, Sun & holidays Jun-Sep), where you can board replicas of Columbus' tiny three-ship fleet, crewed by ludicrous mannequins.

PALOS DE LA FRONTERA
POP 8500
In La Rábida's neighbouring town you'll find the Casa Museo Martín Alonso Pinzón (Calle Colón 24; admission free; ⊙10am-2pm Tue-Sat), once the home of the *Pinta*'s captain. Further along Calle Colón is the 15th-century Iglesia de San Jorge, where Columbus and his men took communion before embarking for their great voyage.

If you can't face staying in Huelva itself, try the Hotel La Pinta (☎959 53 05 11; Calle Rábida 79; s/d €41/67; P✳), which has a big bar, restaurant (with models of Columbus' ships) and decent-sized, clean rooms. Stop to take on supplies yourself at El Bodegón (Calle Rábida 46; mains €10-23; ⊙closed Tue), a noisy, atmospheric cavern of a restaurant that cooks up fish and meat on wood-fired grills.

MOGUER
POP 16.300
Sleepy Moguer provided many of Columbus' crew. The 14th-century Monasterio de Santa Clara (☎959 37 01 07; Plaza de las Monjas; guided tours €3; ⊙11am-2pm & 5-7pm Mon-Fri) is where Columbus kept a prayerful vigil the night after returning from his first voyage, in March 1493.

Mesón El Lobito (Calle Rábida 31; raciones €5-12; ⊙closed Wed), 'the Wolf', is a characterful place to sample good country cooking under the gaze of its snarling, stuffed namesake.

There's a helpful tourist office (Calle Castillo; ⊙10am-2pm & 5-7pm Mon-Sat, 10am-3pm Sun, Mon & holidays) a couple of blocks south of the central Plaza del Cabildo, in Moguer's castillo, a dramatic, bare-walled enclosure of Almohad origin, expanded in the 14th century.

❶ Getting There & Away

At least 10 buses a day leave Huelva for La Rábida (€1.31, 15 minutes), with half of them continuing to Palos de la Frontera (€1.31, 20 minutes) and Moguer (€1.31, 30 minutes). The others go on to Mazagón.

Parque Nacional de Doñana

Spain's most celebrated and in many ways most important wildlife refuge, the Doñana National Park, created in 1969, is one of Europe's last remaining great wetlands. Covering 542 sq km in the southeast of Huelva province and neighbouring Seville province, this World Heritage site is a vital refuge for such endangered species as the Spanish imperial eagle. It offers a unique combination of ecosystems and a place of haunting beauty that is well worth the effort of getting to. To visit the national park you must take a tour from the Centro de Visitantes El Acebuche on the western side of the park, or from El Rocío at the park's northwestern corner, or from Sanlúcar de Barrameda (p697) at its southeastern corner.

Half the park consists of *marismas* (wetlands) of the Guadalquivir delta, the largest area of wetlands in Europe. Almost dry from July to October, in autumn the *marismas* fill with water, attracting hundreds of thousands of wintering waterbirds from the north. As the waters sink in spring, other birds – greater flamingos, spoonbills, storks – arrive, many to nest. The park also has a 28km Atlantic beach, separated from the *marismas* by a band of sand dunes up to 5km wide; and 144 sq km of *coto* (woodland and scrub), which harbours many mammals, including deer, wild boar and semiwild horses.

Interesting areas surrounding the national park are included in the 540-sq-km Parque Natural de Doñana, a separate protected area comprising four distinct zones.

EL ROCÍO
POP 1200

The village of El Rocío overlooks a section of the Doñana *marismas* at the park's northwestern corner. The village's sandy streets bear as many hoofprints as tyre marks, and they are lined with rows of verandahed buildings that are empty most of the time. But this is no ghost town: most of the houses belong to the 90-odd *hermand-* *ades* of pilgrim-revellers and their families, who converge on El Rocío every year in the extraordinary Romería del Rocío. In fact, a party atmosphere pervades the village at most weekends as *hermandades* arrive to carry out lesser ceremonial acts.

◉ Sights & Activities

Deer and horses graze in the shallow water in front of the village, and you might see a flock of flamingos wheeling through the sky in a great pink cloud. The bridge over the river on the A483, 1km south of the village, is another good viewing spot.

Ermita del Rocío   CHURCH
(☺8am-10.30pm Apr-Sep, 8.30am-8pm Oct-Mar) The heart of the village, this church houses the celebrated Virgen del Rocío, a tiny wooden image in long, jewel-encrusted robes. Many come to pay their respects every day in this handsome white-walled church.

Centro de Visitantes José Antonio Valverde   VISITOR CENTRE
(☎671 564145; ☺10am-7pm, to 8pm or 9pm Apr-Aug) Several operators run tours along the northern fringe of the national park to this remote visitors centre overlooking a year-round lake. On these trips you have high chances of seeing deer and boar and will definitely see a great diversity of birds. January, April and May are the best months.

For recommended tour operators, see p685.

⌂ Sleeping & Eating

Don't bother even trying for a room at Romería del Rocío time.

Hotel & Restaurante Toruño   HOTEL €€
(☎959 44 23 23; Plaza Acebuchal 22; s/d incl breakfast €58/80; ❰❉@) An attractive villa overlooking the *marismas,* Toruño has 30 well-appointed rooms. Some have marsh views, so you can see the spoonbills having their breakfast when you wake. Across the road, the restaurant (mains €12 to €22) dishes up generous portions of well-prepared country and coastal fare. Served proudly on a plate, the red and fragrant *salmorejo* soup is surely the richest and thickest in all Andalucía.

Camping La Aldea   CAMPING GROUND €
(☎959 44 26 77; www.campinglaaldea.com; Carretera El Rocío Km25; sites per adult/tent/car €6.50/6.50/6.50, cabin or bungalow for 4 or 5 adults €100-180; ❰❉@❋) At the northern end of the village, well-equipped La Aldea

Every Pentecost (Whitsuntide), the seventh weekend after Easter, El Rocío is inundated with up to a million pilgrim-revellers from all corners of Spain in the Romería del Rocío (Pilgrimage to El Rocío). This vast cult festivity revolves around the tiny image of Nuestra Señora del Rocío, which was found here in a tree by a hunter from Almonte back in the 13th century. Carrying it home, the hunter stopped for a rest and the statue miraculously made its own way back to the tree. Before long a chapel was built where the tree had stood (now El Rocío) and pilgrims were making for it.

Today almost 100 *hermandades* from around and beyond Andalucía, some comprising several thousand men and women, travel to El Rocío each year on foot, on horseback and in gaily decorated covered wagons pulled by cattle or horses, using cross-country tracks.

Solemn is the last word you'd apply to this quintessentially Andalucian event. The 'pilgrims' dress in bright Andalucian costume and sing, dance, drink and romance their way to El Rocío.

Things reach an ecstatic climax in the early hours of the Monday. Members of the *hermandad* of Almonte, which claims the Virgin for its own, barge into the church and bear her out on a float. Chaotic struggles ensue as others battle with the Almonte lads for the honour of carrying La Blanca Paloma, but somehow good humour survives and the Virgin is carried round to each of the brotherhood buildings, finally returning to the Ermita in the afternoon.

has a range of cosy cabins and bungalows as well as over 250 camping spaces.

Pensión Cristina   HOTEL €
(☑959 44 24 13; Calle El Real 58; s/d €30/36) Just east of the Ermita, the Cristina provides reasonably comfortable budget rooms and a popular restaurant (mains €5 to €15) serving paella, venison, seafood and more.

Aires de Doñana   ANDALUCIAN €€
(Avenida de la Canaliega 1; mains €15-19; ⊙closed Mon) Aires de Doñana stands out among El Rocío eateries with its picture windows right over the *marismas,* polished service and successfully imaginative menu.

❶ Information

Tourist office (www.turismodedonana.com; Avenida de la Canaliega; ⊙9.30am-1.30pm & 3-5pm Mon-Fri) By the main road at the western end of the village. It can make reservations for park tours.

Centro de Información La Rocina (⊙9am-3pm & 4-7pm, to 8pm or 9pm Apr-Aug, to 3pm Sun 15 Jun–14 Sep) Located 1km south on the A483, this centre has national park information and paths to nearby birdwatching hides.

CENTRO DE VISITANTES EL ACEBUCHE

Twelve kilometres south of El Rocío on the A483, then 1.6km west, El Acebuche (☑959 43 96 29; ⊙8am-9pm May-Sep, to 7pm Oct-Apr)

is the national park's main visitor centre. It has an interactive exhibit on the park and paths to birdwatching hides, plus a film show of Iberian lynxes at El Acebuche – the closest visitors can get to them.

National Park Tours

Trips in 20-person all-terrain vehicles from El Acebuche are the only way for ordinary folk to get into the interior of the national park from the western side. Book ahead through **Cooperativa Marismas del Rocío** (☑959 43 04 32/51; www.donanavisitas.es; 4hr tour per person €26; ⊙8.30am & 3pm Tue-Sun mid-Sep–Apr, 8.30am & 5pm Mon-Sat May–mid-Sep). During spring, summer and holidays, book at least a month ahead, but otherwise a week is usually plenty of notice. Bring binoculars if you can, drinking water in summer and mosquito protection except in winter. Most guides speak Spanish only. The tour normally starts with a long beach drive, before moving inland. You can be pretty certain of seeing deer and boar, but ornithologists may be disappointed by the limited bird-observation opportunities.

For more specialist trips, try one of the following private operators:

Discovering Doñana   NATURALIST GUIDES
(☑959 44 24 66; www.discoveringdonana. com; Calle Águila Imperial 150, El Rocío; 6hr trip 1-4 people €120) Expert English-speaking guides; most trips are of broad interest,

and the website carries glowing testimonials to guides' enthusiasm and dedication.

Doñana Nature NATURALIST GUIDES
(☑959 44 21 60; www.donana-nature.com; Calle Las Carretas 10, El Rocío; half-day trips per person €25) The half-day trips (8am and 6pm daily, 3.30pm in winter) are of general interest; there are also specialised ornithological and photographic trips. English- and French-speaking guides are available.

Doñana Ecuestre HORSE-RIDING GUIDES
(☑959 44 24 74; www.donanaecuestre.com; Avenida de la Canaliega; per 1hr/2hr/half-day €20/30/40) Offers enjoyable guided horse rides through the woodlands west of El Rocío, some led by qualified biologists.

MATALASCAÑAS & MAZAGÓN

These two small resorts on the long, sandy beach running northwest from the national park provide alternative bases to El Rocío. Matalascañas town itself is a sad contrast to the adjacent wildernesses, but Mazagón, 28km up the coast, is more low-key. At **Cuesta de Maneli**, between the two, a 1.2km boardwalk leads across 100m-high dunes from a car park to the beach through glorious pines and junipers.

Both towns have large camping grounds and a range of hotels.

Hotel Albaida (☑959 37 60 29; www.hotelalbaida.com; Carretera Huelva-Matalascañas, Mazagón; s/d incl breakfast €55/75; **P**❄☎) has airy rooms and welcoming staff; among pines just off the highway and close to the beach. Book ahead for **Hotel Doñana Blues** (☑959 44 98 17; www.donanablues.com; Sector I, Parcela 129, Matalascañas; r from €65; ❄@☎), a small hotel in comfortable yet appealingly rustic style, set in pretty gardens.

The interior and exterior of the **Parador de Mazagón** (☑959 53 63 00; www.parador.es; Playa de Mazagón; r €160-171; **P**❄@☎≋), 6km east of central Mazagón, blend pleasingly with its splendid natural surroundings, and the luxurious rooms all have sea views.

ⓘ Getting There & Away

Three daily buses run between Seville (Plaza de Armas) and Matalascañas (€6.50, 1¾ hours) via El Rocío (€6, 1½ hours). One or two further services along the A483 between Almonte and Matalascañas also stop at El Rocío. All these buses will stop on request outside El Acebuche visitor centre.

From Huelva, buses go to Mazagón (€2.10, 35 minutes, up to 13 daily), with just two of these (Monday to Friday only) continuing to Matalascañas (€4.30, 50 minutes). Extra services may run in summer. You can travel between Huelva and El Rocío by changing buses at Almonte.

Minas de Riotinto

POP 6200 / ELEV 420M

Tucked away on the fringe of Huelva's northern hills is one of the world's oldest mining districts – an unearthly, sculpted and scarred landscape that makes a fascinating stop. Copper was being dug up here at least 4000 years ago, iron has been mined since at least Roman times, and in the 19th century the British-dominated Rio Tinto Company turned the area into one of the world's great copper-mining centres. The area was mined so intensively that it left much of the land looking more like the surface of Mars than Planet Earth. Whole villages were moved, mountains blasted and deep holes dug. The environmental impact was substantial, and mining operations ceased in 2001.

The area's hub is the town of Minas de Riotinto, 68km northeast of Huelva.

◉ Sights & Activities

The attractions are run by the **Parque Minero de Riotinto** (☑959 59 00 25; www.parquemineroderiotinto.com), headquartered at the well-signposted Museo Minero.

The Parque Minero is not running trips to the **Corta Atalaya**, 1km west of the town, but you can still get a peep at this awesome opencast mine, 1.2km long and 335m deep, if you follow the sign to it as you enter Minas de Riotinto from the southwest.

Museo Minero MUSEUM
(Plaza Ernest Lluch; adult/under 13yr €4/3; ◉10.30am-3pm & 4-7pm) This fascinating museum, which was the Riotinto company hospital between 1873 and 1954, takes you right through the Riotinto area's unique history from megalithic tombs to the Roman and British colonial eras and finally the closure of the mines in 2001. Its best features include a 200m-long recreation of a Roman mine, and the Vagón del Maharajah, a luxurious carriage used by Alfonso XIII to visit the mines.

Ferrocarril Turístico-Minero TOURIST RAILWAY
(adult/child €10/9) An easy and fun way to see the mining area, this 22km round trip

takes visitors through the surreal landscape in restored early-20th-century railway carriages. Trips start at Talleres Minas, 2.5km east of Minas de Riotinto. Check website for departure time, as they vary from once to twice a day (usually 1pm and 4:30pm) depending on the season; bookings essential.

Peña de Hierro   MINING SITE
(adult/child €8/7; ⊙noon-1.30pm & 5.30-7pm) Another trip is to these old copper and sulphur mines 9km from Minas de Riotinto. Here you see the source of Río Tinto, an 85m-deep open-cast mine, and are taken into a 200m-long underground mine gallery. It's essential to book ahead, and schedules may change.

❶ Getting There & Away
Up to six daily buses run from Huelva to Minas de Riotinto (€5.50, 1½ hours) and Nerva (€6, 1¾ hours) and vice versa. **Casal** (☑954 99 92 62) has three daily buses from Seville (Plaza de Armas) to Nerva (€4, 1½ hours) and Minas de Riotinto (€4.50, 1¾ hours).

Aracena & Around
POP 6300 / ELEV 730M
Who knew? The gently folded uplands of northern Huelva province offer yet another nuance to rural *andaluz* culture: pastoral, flower-bedecked hills and sheltered valleys replete with gnarly oak trees and foraging pigs that produce what many consider to be the finest cured ham in Spain – the legendary *jamón iberico*. You can dump your car here; the region's sleepy, half-forgotten villages are all linked by good footpaths that thread out from the regional nexus of Aracena, a whitewashed market town that is markedly different in character to the traditional *pueblos blancos* (white towns) further east. The 1840-sq-km **Parque Natural Sierra de Aracena y Picos de Aroche** comprises Andalucía's second-largest protected area.

◉ Sights & Activities
The **Cerro del Castillo** is where the old town originated. Climb to the top of the hill to view the 13th-century Portuguese-built **castillo** and the adjacent **Iglesia Prioral** (⊙9.30am-7pm). A little lower down in Plaza Alta there's an interesting **Centro de Visitantes** (⊙10am-2pm & 4-6pm), which showcases the highlights of the natural park.

Gruta de las Maravillas   CAVE
(Calle Pozo de la Nieve; tour adult/under 19yr €8.50/6; ⊙tours every hr or ½hr 10am-1.30pm & 3-6pm) Aracena's biggest tourist attraction, the 'Cave of Marvels' ranks among Spain's most picturesque cave systems, and is beautifully lit for maximum theatricality.

Linares de la Sierra   HIKING
Hikes in the Aracena area are legion and the trails are rarely crowded. If you're on a day trip from Seville try the undulating route to Linares de la Sierra and – time and energy permitting – continue onto **Alájar** (there's a return bus from Alájar to Aracena that leaves at 4pm connecting with the 5pm Aracena–Seville service). The signposted path is easy to find on the southwest side of Aracena approximately 500m past the municipal swimming pool. Follow the wide bucolic track as far as **Linares** (6km), a soporific village renowned for its *llanos* (front-patio mosaics). From here the path narrows and becomes a little trickier to navigate, though you'll spot plenty of snorting pigs and eye-catching wildflowers along the way. Just before the hamlet of Los Madroñeros, fork right on the 'Caracol' trail (signposted), which traverses an oak-sprinkled hillside into Alájar (total distance 12km).

You can stay over in Alájar at **La Posada** (☑959 12 57 12; www.laposadadealajar.com; Calle Médico Emilio González 2, Alájar; s/d incl breakfast €45/60), a very cosy inn whose English-speaking owners are keen walkers. Shop around in the village for the excellent local ham. Another walking path heads northwest to the next village, Castaño de Robledo.

⌂ Sleeping & Eating
Hospedería Reina de los Ángeles
                                HOTEL €
(☑959 12 83 67; www.hospederiareinadelosangeles; Avenida Reina de los Ángeles; s/d €30/50; @☎) On the edge of town, this former residence for school students certainly has the feel of an academic institution. Nonetheless, the 90 utilitarian rooms with phone and TV are spotless, and there's a convivial cafe-bar.

Molino del Bombo   HOTEL €
(☑959 12 84 78; www.molinodelbombo.com, in Spanish; Calle Ancha 4; s/d €30/60; ✷@☎) As rustic as a farmhouse fireside, the Molino stands near the top of the town and offers charming country-style rooms at extremely reasonable prices.

Café-Bar Manzano ANDALUCIAN €€
(Plaza del Marqués de Aracena; tapas €2-4, raciones €9-18; ⊗8am-8pm or later Wed-Sat & Mon, 10am-8pm Sun) This terrace cafe on the main plaza is a fine spot to watch Aracena go by and enjoy varied tapas and *raciones* that celebrate wild mushrooms and other regional fare.

Mesón Aracena Jabujo ANDALUCIAN €€
(Calle San Pedro 38) This is one of numerous bar–restaurants on the San Pedro strip on the western side of town that specialises in *jamón ibérico*. Not to be missed.

ℹ Information

Municipal tourist office (☑959 12 82 06; Calle Pozo de la Nieve; ⊗10am-2pm & 4-6.30pm) Faces the entrance to the Gruta de las Maravillas and sells some maps of the area.

ℹ Getting There & Away

The **bus station** (Avenida de Sevilla) is towards the southeast edge of town. Two daily buses come from Seville (Plaza de Armas; €5.67, 1¼ hours), one or two from Huelva (€6.75, 2¼ hours), and up to three from Minas de Riotinto (€2.30, one hour). A Casal bus leaves at 10.30am to the Portuguese border just beyond Rosal de la Frontera, where you can change to onward buses for Lisbon (€18.50, nine hours from Aracena).

CÁDIZ PROVINCE

If you're limited for time, and want to get the fullest and most candid idea of what Andalucía is all about, decamp to Cádiz province, where the region's 'greatest hits' are crammed into a triangle of land less than 100km north to south. Much of what today is considered to be definitively Andalucian was first hatched here in sherry bodegas, Roma neighbourhoods, grand bullrings and traditional tapas bars. Further back in history lie Moorish relics in Zahara de la Sierra, Roman ruins in Bolonia, and the beginnings of Europe's earliest civilisation in the mildewed but magnificent city of Cádiz, or Gadir as it was known to the Phoenicians of antiquity.

Cádiz's human history sits seamlessly next to its natural world, a distinctive rural landscape punctuated with numerous *pueblos blancos,* two extensive natural parks – Grazalema and Alcornocales – and one of the finest stretches of beach in Spain, the Costa de la Luz, which culminates in the dude-dominated surf town of Tarifa.

Cádiz's hidden apostrophe (though it's not technically in Spain) is the Rock of Gibraltar, a surreal bastion of stiff-upper-lip Britishness floating in the hot-blooded Mediterranean.

Cádiz

POP 128,600

You could write several weighty university theses about Cádiz and still fall a mile short of nailing its essence. Old age accounts for much of the complexity. Cádiz is generally considered to be the oldest continuously inhabited settlement in Europe. Now well into its fourth millennium, the ancient centre is as romantic as it is mysterious, an ocean settlement surrounded almost entirely by water where Atlantic waves crash against eroded sea walls, municipal beaches stretch for miles, and narrow streets echo with the sounds of cawing gulls and frying fish. Come here for the seafood, surfing, and cache of intriguing churches and museums that inflict little, if any, damage on your wallet. More importantly, come here for the *gaditanos* (residents of Cádiz), an upfront and gregarious populace who have made *alegrías* (upbeat flamenco songs) into an eloquent art form.

History

Cádiz is probably the oldest city in Europe. Historians date its founding to the arrival of Phoenician traders in 800 BC.

In less-distant times, Cádiz began to boom after Columbus' trips to the Americas. He sailed from here on his second and fourth voyages. Cádiz attracted Spain's enemies too: in 1587 England's Sir Francis Drake 'singed the king of Spain's beard' with a raid on the harbour, delaying the imminent Spanish Armada. In 1596, Anglo-Dutch attackers burnt almost the entire city.

Cádiz's golden age was the 18th century, when it enjoyed 75% of Spanish trade with the Americas. It grew into the richest and most cosmopolitan city in Spain and gave birth to the country's first progressive, liberal middle class. During the Napoleonic Wars, Cádiz held out under French siege from 1810 to 1812, when a national parliament meeting here adopted Spain's liberal 1812 constitution, proclaiming sovereignty of the people.

Cádiz Province

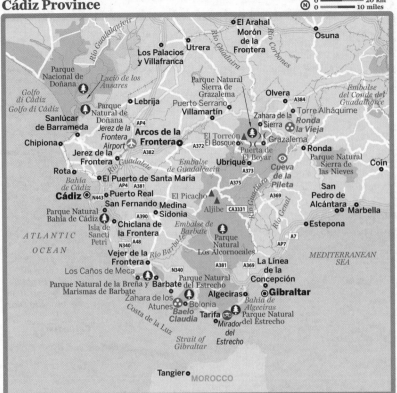

The loss of the American colonies in the 19th century plunged Cádiz into a decline from which it is only today recovering, with increased tourism playing a significant role.

The year 2012 looks set to be a big one for Cádiz, with the city dolling itself up for the 200th anniversary of La Pepa, Spain's (and the world's) first liberal constitution, signed in 1812. Look out for special concerts, an Ibero-American theatre festival, the Alcanes film festival, street markets, forums, exhibitions and more. For further information see www.bicentenariocadiz1812.es.

Sights & Activities

Barrios NEIGHBOURHOODS
To understand Cádiz you need to first become acquainted with its *barrios*. The old city can be split into classic quarters: **Barrio del Pópulo**, home of the cathedral, and nexus of the once prosperous medieval settlement; **Barrio de Santa María**, the old Roma

quarter and an important fount of flamenco; **Barrio de la Viña**, a former vineyard that became the city's main fishing quarter; and the **Barrio del Mentidero**, centre of Cádiz's modern nightlife and bar scene.

Plaza San Juan de Dios & Around SQUARE
Broad Plaza San Juan de Dios is lined with cafes and is dominated by the imposing neoclassical **ayuntamiento** built around 1800. Between here and the cathedral is the Barrio del Pópulo, the kernel of medieval Cádiz and a focus of the city's ongoing sprucing-up program. At the nearby **Roman Theatre** (Campo del Sur; admission free; ⊙10am-2.30pm & 5-7pm Wed-Mon) you can walk along a gallery beneath the tiers of seating. The theatre was discovered by chance in 1980.

Catedral CATHEDRAL
(Plaza de la Catedral; adult/student €5/3, 7-8pm Tue-Fri & 11am-1pm Sun free; ⊙10am-6.30pm Mon-Sat,

ANDALUCÍA CÁDIZ

ANDALUCÍA CÁDIZ PROVINCE

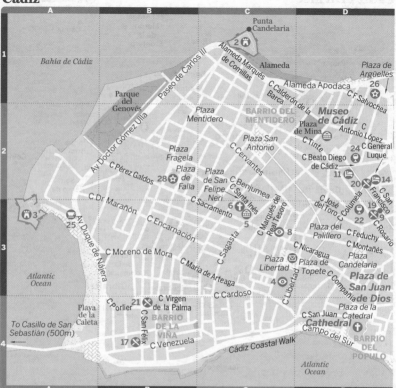

1.30-6.30pm Sun) Cádiz' yellow-domed cathedral is an impressively proportioned baroque–neoclassical construction, but by Spanish standards very sober in its decoration. It fronts a broad, traffic-free plaza where the cathedral's ground-plan is picked out in the paving stones. The decision to build the cathedral was taken in 1716 but the project wasn't finished until 1838, by which time neoclassical elements, such as the dome, towers and main facade, had diluted Vicente Acero's original baroque plan. From a separate entrance on Plaza de la Catedral, climb to the top of the **Torre de Poniente** (Western Tower; adult/child/senior €4/3/3; ⏲10am-6pm, to 8pm 15 Jun–15 Sep) for marvellous vistas.

Plaza de Topete & Around   SQUARE
A short walk northwest from the cathedral, this square is one of Cádiz's liveliest, bright with flower stalls and adjoining the large, lively **Mercado Central** (Central Market).

Nearby, the **Torre Tavira** (Calle Marqués del Real Tesoro 10; adult/student €4/3.30; ⏲10am-6pm, to 8pm 15 Jun–15 Sep) is the highest of Cádiz's old watchtowers (in the 18th century the city had no fewer than 160 of these, built so that citizens could observe the comings and goings of ships without leaving home). It provides great panoramas and has a **camera obscura** projecting live images of the city onto a screen.

The **Museo de las Cortes de Cádiz** (☎956 22 17 88; Calle Santa Inés 9; admission free; ⏲9am-1pm Tue-Sun, 5-7pm Tue-Fri Jun-Sep) is full of historical memorabilia focusing on the 1812 parliament, including a marvellous large 1770s model of Cádiz, made for King Carlos III. The museum was being renovated at the time of writing. Along the street is the **Oratorio de San Felipe Neri** (Plaza de San Felipe Neri; admission €2.50; ⏲10am-1.30pm Mon-Sat), the church where the Cortes de Cádiz met. This is one of Cádiz's finest ba-

Coastal Walk WALK

This airy 4.5km walk takes at least 1¼ hours. Go north from Plaza de Mina to the city's northern seafront, with views across the Bahía de Cádiz. Head west along the Alameda gardens to the Baluarte de la Candelaria, then turn southwest to the Parque del Genovés, a semitropical garden with waterfalls and quirkily clipped trees. Continue to the Castillo de Santa Catalina (admission free; ⊙10.30am-8.30pm, to 7.45pm Nov-Feb), built after the 1596 sacking; inside are an interesting historical exhibit on Cádiz and the sea, and a gallery for exhibitions. Sandy Playa de la Caleta (very crowded in summer) separates Santa Catalina from the 18th-century Castillo de San Sebastián. You can't enter San Sebastián, but do walk along the breezy 750m causeway to its gate. Finally, follow the broad promenade along Campo del Sur to the cathedral.

Playa de la Victoria BEACH

This lovely, wide ocean beach of fine Atlantic sand stretches about 4km along the peninsula from its beginning 1.5km beyond the Puertas de Tierra. At weekends in summer almost the whole city seems to be out here. Bus 1 (Plaza España-Cortadura) from Plaza de España will get you there.

🎎 Festivals & Events

Carnaval CARNIVAL

No other Spanish city celebrates its annual carnival with the enthusiasm and originality of Cádiz, where it turns into a 10-day party spanning two weekends. The fun, abetted by huge quantities of alcohol, is infectious. Groups called *murgas,* in fantastic costumes, tour the city on foot or on floats, singing witty satirical ditties, dancing or performing sketches. In addition to the 300 or so officially recognised *murgas,* judged by a panel in the Gran Teatro Falla, there are also the *ilegales* – any group that fancies taking to the streets and trying to play or sing.

Some of the liveliest scenes are in the working-class Barrio de la Viña and on Calles Ancha and Columela, where *ilegales* tend to congregate.

Rooms in Cádiz get booked months in advance for Carnaval, even though prices can be double their summer rates. If you don't manage to snatch one, you could just visit for the night from anywhere else within striking distance. Plenty of other people do this.

roque churches, with a beautiful dome, an unusual oval interior and a Murillo *Inmaculada* on the altarpiece.

Museo de Cádiz TOP CHOICE MUSEUM

(Plaza de Mina; EU citizen/other free/€1.50; ⊙2.30-8.30pm Tue, 9am-8.30pm Wed-Sat, 9.30am-2.30pm Sun) Cádiz's excellent major museum faces one of the city's largest and leafiest squares. The stars of the ground-floor archaeology section are two Phoenician marble sarcophagi, carved in human likeness, and a monumental statue of the Roman emperor Trajan, from Baelo Claudia (p711). The fine-arts collection upstairs has 21 superb canvases by Francisco de Zurbarán, and the painting that cost Murillo his life – the altarpiece from Cádiz's Convento de Capuchinas. The baroque maestro died from injuries received in a fall from scaffolding while working on this in 1682.

🛏 Sleeping

TOP CHOICE **Hotel Argantonio**   HOTEL €€

(☎956 21 16 40; www.hotelargantonio .com; Calle Argantonio 3; s/d incl breakfast €90/107; ❄@🤝) A very attractive small new hotel in the old city, with an appealing Mudéjar accent to its decor. Staff are welcoming, and the rooms are comfortable, with wi-fi access and flat-screen TVs.

Hospedería Las Cortes de Cádiz

HOTEL €€€

(☎956 21 26 68; www.hotellascortes.com; Calle San Francisco 9; s/d incl breakfast €107/148; P❄@🤝) This excellent hotel occupies a remodelled 1850s mansion. The 36 rooms, each themed around a figure, place or event associated with the Cortes de Cádiz, sport classical furnishings and modern comforts. The hotel also has a roof terrace, Jacuzzi and small gym.

Casa Caracol   HOSTEL €

(☎956 26 11 66; www.caracolcasa.com; Calle Suárez de Salazar 4; dm/hammock incl breakfast €16/10; @🤝) Casa Caracol is the only backpacker hostel in the old town. Friendly, as only Cádiz can be, it has bunk dorms for four and eight, a communal kitchen, and a roof terrace with hammocks. Green initiatives include recycling, water efficiency and plans for solar panels. It's advisable to book through www.hostel world.com or www.hostelbookers.com as the hostel often fills up.

Hostal Fantoni   HOTEL €€

(☎956 28 27 04; www.hostalfantoni.es; Calle Flamenco 5; s/d €45/65; ❄@) The Fantoni offers a dozen clean if rather cell-like rooms (there's a notable lack of windows). However, air-con units, an attractive tiled lobby and a breezy roof terrace do their best to make amends.

Hostal Bahía   HOTEL €€

(☎956 25 90 61; Calle Plocia 5; s/d €60/76; ❄@) All rooms here are exterior and impeccably looked after, with phone, TV and built-in wardrobes. They're plain and straightforward, but good value.

🍴 Eating

Cádiz's hallowed seafood street is Calle Virgen de la Palma in the Viña quarter. Good un-fancy restaurants are legion here. Try **El Faro** (Calle San Félix 15; mains €15-25), decorated with pretty ceramics, or the even grittier **Taberna El Albero** (Cnr Calles San Félix & Virgen de la Palma). In and around Plaza de San Juan de Díos is another good place to dine.

Arrocería La Pepa
RICE DISHES €€

(📞956 26 38 21; Paseo Maritimo 14; paella per person €12-17) To get a decent paella you have to leave the old town behind and head for a few kilometres southeast along Playa de la Victoria – a pleasant, appetite-inducing oceanside walk along a popular jogging route or a quick ride on the No 1 bus. Either method is worth it. The fish in La Pepa's seafood paella tastes as if it's just jumped the 100 or so metres from the Atlantic onto your plate.

El Fogón de Mariana
MEAT DISHES €€

(Calle Antulo 2; mains €11-19) Part of the small Montanera group (there's another one in San Fernando), this two-floored nonsmoking restaurant specialises in Iberian meats but doesn't miss the ball in other areas either. Its combination of creative food and friendly but efficient service could put it among the best in Cádiz.

Cafetería Las Nieves
COFFEE, SNACKS €

(Plaza Mendizábal 4; coffees & tostadas €2; ☉7.45am-10pm Mon-Fri, 9am-1.30pm Sat) Near Plaza San Juan de Dios, this friendly cafe with decor of brick, tile and prints guarantees a good simple breakfast. Take your toast with *mermalada* or – as the Spanish do – olive oil and tomatoes, and wash it down with a coffee or hot chocolate.

El Aljibe
TAPAS €€

(www.pablogrosso.com; Calle Plocia 25; tapas €2-3.50, mains €10-15) *Gaditano* chef Pablo Grosso concocts delicious combinations of the traditional and the adventurous. Try the pheasant breast stuffed with dates and the *solomillo ibérico* (Iberian pork sirloin) with Emmental cheese, ham and piquant peppers. You can enjoy his creations as tapas in the stone-walled downstairs bar.

La Gorda Te Da De Comer
TAPAS

(tapas €2-2.40, media raciones €6) Luque (Calle General Luque 1; ☉9-11.30pm Mon, 1.30-4pm & 9-11.30pm Tue-Sat); Rosario (cnr Calles Rosario & Marqués de Valdeiñigo; ☉1-4pm & 9-11.30pm Tue-Sat) Incredibly tasty food at low prices amid trendy pop design at both locations. Try the *solomillo* in creamy mushroom sauce or the curried chicken strips with Marie-Rose dip.

🍷 Drinking

In the old city, the Plaza de Mina–Plaza San Francisco–Plaza de España area is the main hub of the nocturnal bar scene; things get moving around midnight at most places, but can be quiet in the first half of the week.

Quilla
CAFE

(Playa de la Caleta; ☉10am-midnight; 📶) A bookish coffee bar overlooking Playa de la Caleta, with pastries, tapas, wine, art expos and free wi-fi – to say nothing of the gratis sunsets.

Nahu
BAR, CAFE

(www.nahucadiz.es; Calle Beato Diego 8; ☉from 5pm) An African-themed music cafe that's consistently popular. DJs spin different rhythms each night, from reggae or world to hip hop or chill-out.

Café de Levante
BAR

(www.cafelevante.com; Calle Rosario 35; ☉from 8pm) A cosy little bar with an artsy and student clientele, and walls adorned with all sorts of curious photos and posters.

El Teniente Seblon
BAR

(Calle Posadilla 4) This arty, gay-friendly bar is one of the liveliest evening spots in the Barrio del Pópulo.

The second hot spot is down Playa de la Victoria, along Paseo Marítimo and nearby in the Hotel Playa Victoria area, about 2.5km from the Puertas de Tierra. One of the hippest bars is glamorous Barabass (www.barabass.es; Calle General Muñoz Arenillas 4-6; admission incl 1 drink €8; ☉6pm-6am).

☆ Entertainment

Head out late, Thursday to Saturday nights, to Punta de San Felipe (known as La Punta) on the northern side of the harbour. Here, a line of disco bars and the big

---

CÁDIZ FOR NADA

One of the beauties of Cádiz (for there are many) is that the lion's share of its sights cost absolutely nothing. Stash your wallet in your hotel safety deposit box and go out and enjoy the following:

» Cathedral (free 7pm to 8pm Tuesday to Friday and during Sunday Mass)

» Coastal walk

» Mercado Central

» Beaches

» Museo de Cádiz (free to EU citizens)

» Museo de las Cortes de Cádiz (free to EU citizens)

» Castillo de Santa Catalina

» Peña Flamenca La Perla

disco Sala Anfiteátro (Paseo Pascual Pery; admission €6-8) pack with an 18-to-25 crowd from around 3am to 6am, while El Malecón (Paseo Pascual Pery; admission €8-10) is the place for salsa and gets going a bit earlier, with free salsa classes at midnight Saturday.

TOP CHOICE **Peña Flamenca La Perla**
FLAMENCO VENUE
(www.perladecadiz.com, in Spanish; Calle Carlos Ollero) The paint-peeled Peña La Perla set romantically next to the crashing Atlantic surf hosts flamenco nights at 10pm most Fridays, more so in spring and summer. Right beside the ocean just off Calle Concepción Arenal in the Barrio de Santa María, entry is free and the audience is stuffed with aficionados. It's an unforgettable experience.

Centro Municipal de Arte Flamenco 'La Merced'
FLAMENCO VENUE
(☎956 28 51 89; Plaza de la Merced; ☺10am-2pm, 6-9pm Mon-Sat) Less earthy than La Perla, this centre runs courses and holds regular performances. It's in the heart of Barrio de Santa María, the old Flamenco quarter.

The Gran Teatro Falla (☎956 22 08 34; Plaza de Falla) and the Central Lechera (☎956 22 06 28; Plaza de Argüelles) host busy and varied programs of theatre, dance and music.

ℹ Information

You'll find plenty of banks and ATMs along Calle Nueva and the parallel Avenida Ramón de Carranza.

Hospital Puerta del Mar (☎956 00 21 00; Avenida Ana de Viya 21) The main general hospital, 2km southeast of Puertas de Tierra.

Locutorio Telefónico (Calle Lázaro Dou 1; internet per hr €2; ☺10am-midnight) Has phone booths and sells discount phonecards.

Municipal tourist office (Paseo de Canalejas; ☺8.30am-6pm Mon-Fri, 9am-5pm Sat & Sun)

Regional tourist office (Avenida Ramón de Carranza; ☺9am-7.30pm Mon-Fri, 10am-2pm Sat, Sun & holidays)

ℹ Getting There & Around

Bicycle
Urban Bike (www.urbanbikecadiz.es; Calle Marques de Valderfigo 4; ☺10am-2pm & 5.30-9pm Mon-Fri, 10am-2pm Sat) Rents bikes for 1/12/24 hours (€3/10/14).

Boat
See p696 for details of the passenger ferries heading across the bay to El Puerto de Santa María.

Bus
Most buses are run by **Comes** (☎956 80 70 59; Plaza de la Hispanidad). Destinations include Seville (€11, 1¾ hours, 10 daily), El Puerto de Santa María (€2.10, 30 to 40 minutes, 19 or more daily), Jerez de la Frontera (€3, 40 minutes, nine or more daily), Tarifa (€8.46, two hours, five daily) and other places down the Cádiz coast, Arcos de la Frontera (€5.95, 1¼ hours, five daily Monday to Friday, two daily Saturday and Sunday), Ronda (€13, three hours, two daily), Málaga (€20, four hours, six daily), Olvera (€12.40, three hours) and Granada (€28, five hours, four daily).

Los Amarillos (www.losamarillos.es), from its stop by the southern end of Avenida Ramón de Carranza, operates up to four further daily buses to Arcos de la Frontera (€5.65, 1¼ hours) and up to 13 daily to Sanlúcar de Barrameda (€3.50, 1¼ hours). Some services go less often on Saturday and Sunday.

Car & Motorcycle
The AP4 motorway from Seville to Puerto Real on the eastern side of the Bahía de Cádiz carries a €5.50 toll. The toll-free A4 is slower.

There's a handily placed **underground car park** (Paseo de Canalejas; per 24hr €9) near the port area.

Train
From the **train station** (☎902 24 02 02) up to 36 trains run daily to El Puerto de Santa María (€3.90, 40 minutes) and Jerez de la Frontera (€4.80, 50 minutes), up to 15 to Seville (€12.75, two hours), three to Córdoba (€23.85 to €38.20, three hours) and two to Madrid (€70, five hours).

El Puerto de Santa María

POP 85,100

Stop two in the revered sherry triangle and second only to Ronda and Seville as a bull-fighting centre, El Puerto is also known for its gastronomy, spearheaded by fresh-from-the-ocean fish. A pleasant half-hour ferry ride from Cádiz across the bay, it also harbours a string of fine beaches and vibrates in summer with a series of colourful festivals when *sevillanos* and people from all round Cádiz province steam in for day- and night-time shenanigans.

◉ Sights & Activities

The four-spouted Fuente de las Galeras Reales (Fountain of the Royal Galleys), by the Muelle del Vapor, once supplied water to America-bound ships.

The nearest beach is pine-flanked Playa de la Puntilla, a half-hour walk from the centre – or take bus 26 (€1) along Avenida Aramburu de Mora. In high summer the beaches furthest out, such as Playa Fuenterrabía, reached by bus 35 from the centre, are least hectic.

Castillo de San Marcos
CASTLE

(956 85 17 51; Plaza Alfonso El Sabio 3; admission Tue/Thu & Sat free/€5; tours 11.30am, 12.30pm, 1.30pm Tue, 10.30am, 11.30am, 12.30pm, 1.30pm Thu & Sat) The castle is open for half-hour guided tours three days a week, with a sampling of Caballero sherry included (the company owns the castle). The highlight is the pre-13th-century mosque (now a church) preserved inside.

Fundación Rafael Alberti
MUSEUM

(www.rafaelalberti.es; Calle Santo Domingo 25; admission €5; 11am-2.30pm Tue-Sun) A few blocks further inland from the castle, this place has interesting exhibits on Rafael Alberti (1902–99), one of the great poets of Spain's 'Generation of 27', who grew up here. The exhibits are well displayed and audioguides in English, German or Spanish (€2) are available.

FREE Plaza de Toros
BULLRING

(956 54 15 78; Plaza Elías Ahuja; 11am-1.30pm & 5.30-7pm Tue-Sun) Four blocks southwest from the Iglesia Mayor Prioral, El Puerto's grand 19th-century bullring is one of the most celebrated in Spain. Top matadors fight here every Sunday in July and August: the ring is closed for visits the day before and after fights.

Sherry Bodegas
SHERRY BODEGAS

The best known of El Puerto's seven sherry wineries, Osborne (956 86 91 00; www. osborne.es; Calle Los Moros 7; tours in English/ Spanish/German €6; tours 10.30am, noon & 12.30pm Mon-Fri, Sat 11am & noon) and Terry (956 15 15 00; Calle Toneleros 1; tours in English & Spanish €8; tours 10.30am & 12.30pm Mon-Fri), offer weekday tours and sometimes add extra tours, including on Saturday, in summer. For Osborne you need to phone ahead; for Terry you don't.

Iglesia Mayor Prioral
CHURCH

(8.30am-12.45pm Mon-Fri, 8.30am-noon Sat, 8.30am-1.45pm Sun, 6-8.30pm daily) El Puerto's most splendid church, the 15th-to 18th-century Iglesia Mayor Prioral dominates nearby Plaza de España.

🛏 Sleeping

The tourist office's accommodation list and website helpfully highlight places with wheelchair access.

El Baobab Hostel
HOSTEL €

(956 54 21 23; www.casabaobab.es, in Spanish; Calle Pagador 37; s/d/tr incl breakfast €20/40/60; P🌐📶) Opposite the famous bullring, this small Argentine-run hostel (40 pax capacity) would seem more like an intimate hotel if it wasn't for the economical price. Throw in breakfast and free wi-fi and you've got the best cheap digs in town.

Hotel Monasterio San Miguel
HOTEL €€€

(956 54 04 40; www.hotelesjale.com; Calle Virgen de los Milagros 27; s/d €105/140; P🌐📶@🅿️) A gourmet restaurant, a pool in a semitropical garden, and classically elegant rooms await your pleasure at this luxurious converted 18th-century monastery.

🛏 Casa del Regidor Hotel
HISTORIC HOTEL €€

(956 87 73 33; www.hotelcasadelregidor.com; Ribera del Río 30; s/d €65/95; P🌐@📶) A converted 18th-century mansion with its original patio. The excellent rooms have all mod cons and solar-heated hot water.

Casa No 6
HOTEL €€

(956 87 70 84; www.casano6.com; Calle San Bartolomé 14; s/d/q incl breakfast €70/80/140; P) This beautifully renovated 19th-century house provides a friendly welcome and charming, spacious and spotless rooms. There's usually a three-night minimum stay in high summer.

✕ Eating

El Puerto has one of the best collections of tapas bars of any town of its size in Andalucía. The main streets to look in are the central Calle Luna; Calle Misericordia and Ribera del Marisco to its north; and Avenidas Bajamar and Aramburu de Mora to its south. Seafood is the speciality. For wonderful local cakes, including the speciality *carmelos*, try Cafetería La Merced (Calle Ganada 46).

Romerijo
SEAFOOD €

(Plaza de la Herrería; seafood per 250g from €4.50) A huge, always busy El Puerto institution, Romerijo has two buildings, one boiling the seafood, the other frying it. Choose from the displays and buy by the quarter-kilogram in paper cones to eat at the formica tables.

Casa Flores
SEAFOOD €€€

(☑956 54 35 12; www.casaflores.es; Ribera del Río 9; mains €20-30) For more formal dining, go for tile-bedecked Casa Flores. Fish and seafood are the specialities, but there are good choices for meat eaters too.

Casa Luís
TAPAS €

(Ribera del Marisco; tapas €3; ⊗closed Mon) This tightly packed den near the river favours meat over fish, with innovative concoctions like *paté de cabracho* (scorpion fish paté).

🍷 Drinking

Bodega Obregón
BAR €

(Calle Zarra 51; ⊗closed Mon) Think sherry's just a drink for grandmas? Come and have your illusions blown out of the water at this spit-and-sawdust-style bar where the sweet stuff is siphoned from woody barrels. Flamenco is supposed to happen Sundays between 12.30pm and 3pm.

ℹ️ Information

Tourist office (☑956 54 24 13; www.turismo elpuerto.com; Calle Luna 22; ⊗10am-2pm & 6-8pm May-Sep) This good tourist office is 2½ blocks straight ahead from the Muelle del Vapor.

ℹ️ Getting There & Away

Boat

The small ferry *Adriano III*, known as **El Vapor** (www.vapordeelpuerto.com), a decades-old symbol of El Puerto, sails to El Puerto (€5, 40 minutes) from Cádiz's Estación Marítima (Passenger Port) five or six times daily from early February to early December (except Monday from late September to late May). The faster catamaran (€1.95, 25 minutes), operated by the public **Consorcio de Transportes Bahía de Cádiz** (www.cmtbc.com), sails between Cádiz (Terminal Marítima, near the train station) and El Puerto 18 times a day Monday to Friday, six times on Saturday and five on Sunday and holidays. In El Puerto, the Catamarán docks on the river 400m southwest (downstream) from the Muelle del Vapor.

Bus

Buses run to Cádiz (€1.45, 30 to 40 minutes) from the Plaza de Toros about half-hourly. For Jerez de la Frontera (€1.10, 20 minutes) there are nine to 17 daily buses from the train station, plus six (Monday to Friday only) from the bullring. Buses for Sanlúcar de Barrameda (€2.05, 30 minutes, five to 13 daily) depart from the bullring. Buses to Seville (€8.85, 1½ hours, three daily) go from the train station.

Train

Up to 36 trains travel daily to Jerez de la Frontera (€2.10, 15 minutes) and Cádiz (€3.90, 40 minutes), and up to 15 daily to Seville (€10.65, 1½ hours).

Sanlúcar de Barrameda
POP 67,000

Sanlúcar is one of those lesser-known Andalucian cities that you'd do well to shoehorn into your itinerary. The reasons? Firstly, there's gastronomy. Sanlúcar cooks up some of the best seafood in the region on a hallowed waterside strip called Bajo de Guía. Secondly, Sanlúcar sits at the northern tip of the esteemed sherry triangle and the bodegas here, nestled in the somnolent old town, retain a less commercial, earthier quality. Thirdly, situated at the mouth of the Guadalquivir estuary, the city provides a quieter, less trammelled entry point into the ethereal Parque Nacional de Doñana, preferably via boat.

As if that wasn't enough, Sanlúcar harbours a proud nautical history: both Columbus (on his third sojourn) and Portuguese mariner Ferdinand Magellan struck out from here on their voyages of discovery.

With excellent transport links, Sanlúcar makes an easy day trip from Cádiz or Jerez.

◎ Sights

FREE Palacio de Orleans y Borbón
PALACE

(⊗10am-2.30pm Mon-Fri) From Plaza del Cabildo, cross Calle Ancha to Plaza San Roque and head up Calle Bretones, which becomes Calle Cuesta de Belén and doglegs up to this beautiful neo-Mudéjar palace that was built as a summer home for the aristocratic Montpensier family in the 19th century and is now Sanlúcar's town hall.

Iglesia de Nuestra Señora de la O
CHURCH

(⊗Mass 8pm Mon-Sat, 9am, noon & 8pm Sun) A block to the left from the palace, along Calle Caballeros, this medieval church stands out among Sanlúcar's churches for its beautiful Gothic Mudéjar main portal, created in the 1360s, and the richness of its interior decoration, including the Mudéjar *artesonado* ceilings.

Palacio de los Duques de Medina Sidonia
PALACE

(☑956 36 01 61; www.fcmedinasidonia.com; Plaza Condes de Niebla 1; tour €3; ⊗11am &

noon Mon-Sat) Next door to the Iglesia de Nuestra Señora de la O, this was the rambling home of the aristocratic family that once owned more of Spain than anyone else. The house, mostly dating to the 17th century, bursts with antiques, and paintings by Goya, Zurbarán and other famous Spanish artists.

Castillo de Santiago CASTLE
(📞956 08 83 29; Plaza del Castillo; tours €7; ⏰10am-1pm Tue-Sat) Located amid buildings of the Barbadillo sherry company, this restored 15th-century castle has great views from its hexagonal Torre del Homenaje (Keep). Entry to the Patio de Armas is free.

👉 Tours

Sherry Bodegas

Sanlúcar produces a distinctive sherrylike wine, manzanilla. Several bodegas give tours for which you don't need to book ahead, including these:

Barbadillo SHERRY BODEGA
(📞956 38 55 00; www.barbadillo.com; Calle Luis de Eguilaz 11; tours €3; ⏰in English 11am Tue-Sat, in Spanish noon & 1pm Tue-Sat) Near the castle, Barbadillo is the oldest and biggest manzanilla firm. There's also a good manzanilla museum (⏰10am-3pm Tue-Sat) here, which you can visit independently of the tour.

Hidalgo-La Gitana SHERRY BODEGA
(📞956 38 53 04; www.lagitana.es; Calzada del Ejército; tours in English & Spanish €5; ⏰11am & noon Mon-Fri, 11am Sat)

Pedro Romero SHERRY BODEGA
(📞956 36 07 36; Calle Trasbolsa 84; tours €6; ⏰in English & Spanish noon Mon-Sat, 5pm Tue-Fri, in German 11am Mon-Fri) This bodega also holds 2½-hour tasting sessions (€20 per person) at noon on Tuesday, Thursday and Saturday.

Parque Nacional de Doñana

Boat departures for the Parque Nacional de Doñana leave from Bajo de Guía, 750m northeast from La Calzada. Here, the Centro de Visitantes Fábrica de Hielo (📞956 38 65 77; www.parquenacionaldonana.es; ⏰9am-8pm) provides displays and information on the Parque Nacional de Doñana.

From Bajo de Guía, Viajes Doñana (📞956 36 25 40; Calle San Juan 20; tours per person €36; ⏰office 9am-2pm & 5-8.30pm Mon-Fri, 10am-1pm Sat) and Viajes Correcaminos

(📞956 38 20 40; Calle Ramón y Cajal 4) operate 3½-hour guided tours into the national park, at 8.30am and 2.30pm on Tuesday and Friday (the afternoon trips go at 4.30pm from May to mid-September). After the river crossing, the trip is by 20-person 4WD vehicle, visiting much the same spots as the tours from El Acebuche. On the trip, either take mosquito repellent or cover up.

⭐ Festivals & Events

The Sanlúcar summer gets going with the Feria de la Manzanilla, in late May or early June, and blossoms in July and August with jazz, flamenco and classical-music festivals, one-off concerts by top Spanish bands, and Sanlúcar's unique horse races, the Carreras de Caballo (www.carrerassanlucar.es), in which thoroughbred racehorses thunder along the beach during two three-day evening meetings during August.

🛏 Sleeping

Book well ahead at holiday times.

Hotel Posada de Palacio TOP CHOICE
HISTORIC HOTEL €€
(📞956 36 48 40; www.posadadepalacio.com; Calle Caballeros 11; s/d from €88/109; 🅿✳@🛜) Sanlúcar's most atmospheric lodging is this exquisite 18th-century mansion, stuffed with pretty patios and terraces, plenty of antiques, and rooms kitted out with period furnishings. It's regally romantic.

Hotel Barrameda HOTEL €€
(📞956 38 58 78; www.hotelbarrameda.com; Calle Ancha 10; s/d incl breakfast €54/81; ✳🛜) This 30-room hotel is bang in the centre. The ground-floor reception gives onto a patio; rooms have stylish modern furnishings, marble floors, framed art prints and wi-fi access, and there's a roof terrace too.

Tartaneros Hotel HOTEL €€
(📞956 38 53 93; www.hoteltartaneros.com; Calle Tartaneros 8; s/d from €85/100; 🅿✳) A century-old industrialist's mansion with assorted fin-de-siècle artefacts and comfortable rooms, at the inland end of Calzada del Ejército.

Hostal Blanca Paloma HOTEL €
(📞956 3636 44; Plaza San Roque 15; s/d/tr €18/30/45) This place is very basic but is ideally situated, in pretty Plaza San Roque. Ten clean rooms share two bathrooms. There's a decent cafe next door for breakfast.

Eating

Spain holds few dreamier dining experiences than tucking into ocean-fresh seafood while watching the sun go down over the Guadalquivir at Bajo de Guía, a strip of high-quality but easygoing fish restaurants overlooking the river estuary about 750m northeast of the town centre.

Cafes and bars, many of them serving manzanilla from the barrel, surround Plaza del Cabildo and Plaza San Roque behind it: Casa Balbino (Plaza del Cabildo 11; tapas €2-3) is a must for tapas. For some of the best ice cream in Andalucía don't miss Helados Artesanos Toni (Plaza de Cabildo 2; www.heladostoni.com), family run since 1896, with videos demonstrating the fine art of ice cream–making rolling behind the counter.

TOP CHOICE | Restaurante Virgen del Carmen

SEAFOOD €€

(Bajo de Guía; fish mains €9-15) In the dice-roll that is the Bajo de Guía, this is arguably the best restaurant. The huge *parrillada de pescado* (fish combo) plate – served either *plancha* (grilled) or *frito* (fried) – comes with an eye-boggling assortment of fish and is a bargain at €28 (serves two).

Cafetería Guzmán El Bueno

COFFEE, SNACKS €

(Plaza Condes de Niebla 1; dishes €3-8; ⊙8.30am-9pm, to early am Sat & Jul-Aug) Sink into plump cushions surrounded by antique furnishings at the cafe in the Palacio de los Duques de Medina Sidonia. Fare is simple – omelettes, cheese, ham – but the setting is uniquely atmospheric.

Casa Bigote

SEAFOOD €€

(Bajo de Guía 10; fish mains €7-14; ⊙closed Sun) The food here gets excellent reviews from everyone. Do try the house speciality – *hamburguesas de bacalao con salsa* (codburgers with sauce; €8.50).

Entertainment

There are some lively music bars on and around Calzada del Ejército and Plaza del Cabildo, and lots of concerts in summer.

Information

Tourist office (www.turismosanlucar.com, in Spanish; ⊙10am-2pm & 6-8pm Mon-Fri, 10am-12.45pm Sat & 10am-2pm Sun) Multilingual and very helpful; located on Calzada del Ejército.

Getting There & Away

Buses from Sanlúcar include services to El Puerto de Santa María (€2.05, 30 minutes, five to 12 daily), Cádiz (€3.50, 1¼ hours, five to 12 daily), Jerez de la Frontera (€1.68, 30 minutes, seven to 15 daily) and Seville (€7.55, 1½ hours, five to 10 daily).

Jerez de la Frontera

POP 202,700

Stand down all other claimants. Jerez, as most savvy Spain-o-philes know, *is* Andalucía. It just doesn't broadcast the fact in the way that Seville and Granada do. As a result, few people plan their trip around a visit here, preferring instead to jump-cut to the glories of the Giralda and the Alhambra. If only they knew. Jerez is the capital of *andaluz* horse culture, stop one on the famed sherry triangle and – cue the protestations from Cádiz and Seville – the cradle of Spanish flamenco. The *bulería,* Jerez's jokey, tongue-in-cheek antidote to Seville's tragic *soleá,* was first concocted in the legendary Roma *barrios* of Santiago and San Miguel. If you really want to unveil the eternal riddle that is Andalucía, start here.

Sights

Real Escuela Andaluza del Arte Ecuestre

EQUESTRIAN SHOWS

(☏956 31 80 08; www.realescuela.org; Avenida Duque de Abrantes; ♿) The famed Royal Andalucian School of Equestrian Art trains horses and riders in equestrian skills, and you can watch them going through their paces in training sessions (adult/child €10/6; ⊙11am-1pm Mon, Wed & Fri Sep-Jul, Mon & Wed Aug) and visit the Horse Carriage Museum, which includes an 18th-century Binder Hunting Break. The highlight for most is the official exhibición (show; adult/child €18/11.50, ⊙noon Tue & Thu Sep-Jul, noon Tue, Thu & Fri Aug), where the handsome white horses show off their tricks to classical music. You can book tickets online for this – advisable for the official shows, which can sell out.

Zoo Jerez

ZOO

(www.zoobotanicojerez.com; Calle Taxdirt; adult/child €9/6; ⊙10am-6pm Tue-Sun Oct-Apr, 10am-7pm Tue-Sun May-Sep; ♿) Coming to Jerez to go to the zoo is like going to the Serengeti to watch flamenco but, if the kids won't relent, the city harbours one of Andalucía's better wildlife arenas, housing 1300 beasts and a recuperation centre for wild animals. It's 1km north of the centre.

Old Quarter

Alcázar
FORTRESS
(Alameda Vieja; admission incl/excl camera obscura €5.40/3; ⊙10am-8pm Mon-Sat, 10am-3pm Sun) This 11th- or 12th-century Almohad fortress is the obvious place to start a tour of old Jerez. Inside, there's a beautiful **mezquita** (mosque), converted to a chapel by Alfonso X in 1264, an impressive set of **Baños Árabes** (Arab Baths) and the 18th-century **Palacio Villavicencio**. In the palace's tower a **camera obscura** provides a live panorama of Jerez, with multilingual commentary. Sessions begin every half-hour until 30 minutes before closing time.

Cathedral
CATHEDRAL
(⊙11.30am-1pm & 6.30-8pm Mon-Sat, Mass 11.30am, 1.30pm, 7.30pm & 9pm Sun) The orange-tree-lined promenade around the Alcázar overlooks the mainly 18th-century cathedral, built on the site of Scheris' main mosque.

A couple of blocks northeast of the cathedral is Plaza de la Asunción, with the handsome 16th-century Antiguo Cabildo (Old Town Hall) and lovely 15th-century Mudéjar Iglesia de San Dionisio.

TOP CHOICE Hammam Andalusi
HAMMAM
(☑956 34 90 66; www.hammamandalusi.com; Calle Salvador 6; baths €18, with 15min massage €28; ⊙10am-midnight) Although this is a slightly sanitised version of what you would get in Morocco, it has modern innovations such as a chocolate bath (€85). Reserve a day in advance.

Barrio de Santiago
NEIGHBOURHOOD
Northwest of Plaza de la Asunción, the Barrio de Santiago has a sizeable Roma population. The excellent Museo Arqueológico (☑956 35 01 33; Plaza del Mercado) here was still undergoing protracted renovations at the time of writing; it is expected to reopen soon. When it does its impressive collection of local finds includes a 7th-century-BC Greek helmet, found in Río Guadalete, among other highlights. Also in this area is the Centro Andaluz de Flamenco (Andalucian Flamenco Centre; http://caf.cica.es, in Spanish; Plaza San Juan 1; admission free; ⊙9am-2pm Mon-Fri). Jerez is at the heart of the Seville–Cádiz axis where flamenco originated. This centre is a kind of flamenco museum, library and school, with a different flamenco video screened each day.

Try not to miss what is arguably Jerez's loveliest church, the 15th-/16th-century Gothic Iglesia de San Miguel (Plaza San Miguel; ⊙Mass 8pm Mon-Sat, 9am, noon & 8pm Sun), just southeast of Plaza del Arenal.

Sherry Bodegas

Jerez is home to around 20 bodegas and most are open to visits, but they're scattered around town and many of them require you to call ahead. The tourist office has up-to-date information.

Bodegas González Byass
SHERRY BODEGA
(☑902 44 00 77; www.bodegastiopepe.com; Calle Manuel María González 12; tours €10; ⊙11am-6pm) Home of the Tio Pepe brand and one of the biggest sherry houses, handily located just west of the Alcázar. Six or seven tours each are given daily in English and Spanish, and a few in German and French. Reservations can be made online.

Bodegas Tradición
SHERRY BODEGA
(☑956 16 86 28; www.bodegastradicion.com; Plaza Cordobeses 3; ⊙9am-6.30pm Mon-Fri, 10am-2pm Sat Mar-Jun, 8am-3pm Sat Jul & Aug) Another interesting bodega, not only for its extra-aged sherries (20 or more years old), but because it houses the Colección Joaquín Rivera, a private Spanish art collection that includes important works by Goya, Velázquez and Zurbarán. Tours of the collection are given three or four times a day.

Sandeman
SHERRY BODEGA
(☑956 31 29 95; www.sandeman.eu; Calle Pizarro 10; tours €6; ⊙11am-2.15pm Mon, Wed & Fri, 10.15am-2.15pm Tue & Thu) Has three or four tours each in English, Spanish and German, one in French.

★ Festivals & Events

Jerez has a comprehensive calendar of festive events. These are the biggest highlights:

Motorcycle Grand Prix
MOTORCYCLES
Usually March, April or May – Jerez's Circuito Permanente de Velocidad (Racing Circuit; ☑956 15 11 00; www.circuitodejerez.com), on the A382 10km east of town, hosts several motorcycle- and car-racing events each year, including one of the Grand Prix races of the World Motorcycle Championship.

Festival de Jerez
FLAMENCO
(www.festivaldejerez.es) Late February/early March – Jerez's biggest celebration of flamenco.

Feria del Caballo HORSES

Late April or first half of May – Jerez's week-long Horse Fair is one of Andalucía's grandest festivals, with music, dance and bullfights as well as all kinds of equestrian competitions and parades.

🛏 Sleeping

Many places almost double their rates for the Motorcycle Grand Prix and Feria del Caballo, and you need to book ahead.

Nuevo Hotel HOTEL €

(📞956 33 16 00; www.nuevohotel.com; Calle Caballeros 23; s/d incl breakfast €35/50; ❋🛜) One of the most pleasant family-run hotels in Anadalucía, the Nuevo's comfortable rooms are complemented by spectacular *habitación* 208, replete with Islamic-style stuccowork and azulejos tiles. You'll wake up thinking you've taken up residence in the Alhambra.

🌿 Hotel Chancillería HOTEL €€

(📞956 30 10 38; www.hotelchancilleria. com; Calle Chancillería 21; s/d incl breakfast €80/120; ❋@🛜) This 14-room hotel in the atmospheric Barrio de Santiago is a great addition to Jerez's accommodation. Full of lovely original crafts, it has many ecofriendly touches including solar water heating and grey-water recycling. It's also extremely well set up for wheelchair users. The hotel's restaurant, Sabores (📞956 32 98 35), has an esteemed young chef.

Hotel Casa Grande HOTEL €€€

(📞956 34 50 70; www.casagrande.com.es; Plaza de las Angustias 3; s/d/ste €75/95/125; ❋@🛜) This hotel occupies a carefully restored and strikingly decorated 1920s mansion centred on a bright patio. Rooms vary in style, and there's a great roof terrace. The breakfasts (€10) are special too.

Hotel La Albarizuela HOTEL €€€

(📞956 34 68 62; www.hotelalbarizuela.com; Calle Honsario 6; s/d €99/139; P❋🛜) A contemporary place popular with an under-30s crowd, Albarizuela is bright, minimalist and rather funkier compared with its older opposition. Deep discounts (often around 60% from mid-October to mid-April) are frequently offered, so email or phone for the best deals.

Hotel Palacio Garvey HOTEL €€€

(📞956 32 67 00; www.sferahoteles.net; Calle Tornería 24; s/d €224/293; P❋@🛜❋) The Garvey is a sensational conversion of the 19th-century neoclassical palace of one of Jerez's sherry families. The 16 rooms are superluxurious.

Hostal/Pensión San Andrés HOTEL, PENSIÓN €

(📞956 34 09 83; www.hotelsanandres.es, in Spanish; Calle Moreno 12; s/d €26/40; ❋) The friendly San Andrés has three pretty, plant-filled patios and a range of rooms, including economical shared-bathroom options. The hotel section is cosier than the *pensión*.

Hostal Las Palomas HOTEL €

(📞956 34 37 73; www.hostal-las-palomas.com; Calle Higueras 17; s with/without bathroom €25/30, d with/without bathroom €25/35) A faint Moroccan theme, touches of art, earthy colours and a good roof terrace are among the pluses of this economical but well-presented *hostal*. Triple and quadruple rooms are available.

🍴 Eating

The sherry trade has introduced English and French accents into the local cuisine. Jerez also prizes its cured and grilled meats, and fish. Central Jerez is littered with great tapas bars. The pedestrian streets just north of Plaza del Arenal are a fine place to start. About 500m north, further brilliant tapas bars surround little Plaza Rafael Rivero. Head here at lunchtime or after 9.30pm.

TOP CHOICE Cruz Blanca TAPAS €

(Plaza de la Yerva; tapas €1.80/3) The Cruz whips up good seafood, egg, meat and salad offerings and has tables on a quiet little plaza. The marinated fish in a pesto-inflected sauce could steal the crown for Jerez's best meal.

La Carboná TRADITIONAL €€

(Calle San Francísco de Paula 2; mains €10-16; ⊙closed Tue) This popular, cavernous restaurant, with an eccentric menu and young waitstaff, occupies a wood-beamed former tavern. Specialities include charcoal-grilled Cantabrian meats and fresh fish, and there's plenty of sherry to keep things lively.

El Gallo Azul TRADITIONAL €€

(Calle Larga 2; raciones from €11.50) Housed in what has become Jerez's signature building, a circular facade emblazoned with a Sherry logo, El Gallo Azul (the Blue Cockerel) has a restaurant upstairs and tapas at street level. It's also an excellent perch on which to enjoy an afternoon coffee and a slice of cake as the city springs back to life after the siesta.

Bar Juanito
TAPAS €

(www.bar-juanito.com; Pescadería Vieja 8-10; tapas from €2.20, media-raciones €5-7) Competes with El Gallo Azul for the title of 'city institution' and has been in business for 60 years. With its village-in-the-city atmosphere and award-winning tapas (the artichokes in particular) it looks like it'll log a few more years yet.

Mesón del Asador
MEAT DISHES €

(Calle Remedios 2; tapas €2.15) This is the place for meat lovers to go in Jerez; the oxtail is phenomenal, to say nothing of the *solomillo, morcilla* (blood sausage), etc. Generous tapas are served at the bar only, or you can sit down with the locals for a full spread.

La Casa del Arroz
RICE DISHES €€

(Calle Francos 10; mains €9-14; ✍) This polished restaurant specialises in very well-prepared paella and other rice dishes, with some creative touches.

Mesón El Patio
TRADITIONAL ANDALUCIAN €€

(Calle San Francisco de Paula 7; mains €8-17; ☾closed Sun evening & Mon) Convivial yet a touch refined, El Patio serves excellent fish and meat dishes in a restored sherry warehouse.

🍸 Drinking

A few bars in the narrow streets north of Plaza del Arenal can get lively with an under-30 crowd: try beer bar Dos Deditos (Plaza Vargas 1) and wine bar La Carbonería (Calle Letrados 7). Northeast of the centre, La Plaza de Canterbury (cnr Calles Zaragoza & N de Cañas) has a couple of pubs (one English and one Irish) around a central courtyard that attract a 20s clientele, while music bars northeast on Avenida de Méjico are the late-night headquarters for the 18–25 crowd.

Damajuana
BAR

(www.damajuanacafebar.com; Calle Francos 18; ☾4.30pm-3am Tue-Sun) This is one of two historic bars on Calle Francos where flamenco singers and dancers have long met and drank; it has a studenty vibe, with exhibitions and occasional live music.

☆ Entertainment

The tourist office is very helpful with what's-on information; also visit www.turismo jerez.com and look out for posters. Several

peñas flamencas (flamenco clubs) welcome genuinely interested visitors: ask at the Centro Andaluz de Flamenco (p699) for a list. One place that is particularly helpful is Peña Flamenca Los Cernicalos (☏956 33 38 71; www.flamencodejerez.com; Calle Sancho Vizcaino 25). In addition to performances, ask about guitar or dance lessons here: one day/week €17/60.

TOP CHOICE El Lagá Tio Parrilla
FLAMENCO TABLAO

(Plaza del Mercado; show & 2 drinks €25; ☾10.30pm Mon-Sat) A high quota of Roma (both performers and clientele) ensures that this place wins most plaudits for its regular flamenco tablaos. Gutsy shows rarely end without rousing renditions of that old Jerez stalwart – the *bulería*.

Bereber
FLAMENCO TABLAO

(www.tablaodelbereber.com; Calle Cabezas 10; ☾4.30pm-late) An amazing reformed palace in the Barrio de San Mateo, mixing noble and Islamic style with several patios, rooms and bars, some open to the sky. The flamenco show at 9pm (€70) includes dinner and drinks.

Teatro Villamarta
THEATRE

(☏956 35 02 72; www.villamarta.com; Plaza Romero Martínez) Stages a busy program where you can pick up Bizet, Verdi, Mozart and – of course – a dash of flamenco.

Discoteca Oxi
NIGHTCLUB

(www.oxixerez.es; Calle Zaragoza 20; ☾9pm-late Wed-Sat) Jerez's newest disco has four different rooms and attracts a young crowd who dance till dawn (7am) at weekends. Theme nights are popular.

Sala Audrey
BAR

(www.salaaudrey.com; Calle Carmen 22; ☾10pm-late Wed-Sat) This hip little venue is dedicated to Audrey Hepburn, and has DJs spinning house, funk or reggae.

ℹ Information

Ciberjerez (Calle Santa María 3, internet per hr €1.80; ☾10am-2.30pm & 5.30-11pm Mon-Sat May-Sep, 5-10pm Sun)

Municipal tourist office (www.turismo jerez.com; Alameda Cristina; ☾9am-3pm & 5-6.30pm Mon-Fri, 9.30am-2.30pm Sat & Sun) Expert multilingual staff and comprehensive website.

Provincial tourist office (airport; ☾8.15am-2pm & 5-6.30pm Mon-Fri)

ⓘ Getting There & Around

Air

Jerez airport (☏956 15 00 00), 7km northeast of town on the NIV, is increasingly busy with flights from European cities and has at least six car-rental offices. **Ryanair** (☏956 15 01 52) flies here daily from London Stansted, Frankfurt and Madrid. A variety of other airlines come from Amsterdam, Brussels, Paris and several German airports. **Iberia** (☏902 40 05 00), **Vueling** (☏902 33 39 33) and **Spanair** (☏956 15 01 30) fly direct from Madrid and Barcelona.

Bus

A useful airport-bus service runs 16 times daily (six times on Saturday and Sunday) from the airport to Jerez bus station (€1, 30 minutes), with three services daily continuing to El Puerto de Santa María train station (from the airport €1.10, 50 minutes) and six or more to Cádiz's Comes bus station (€2.85, 1¼ hours).

Jerez's **bus station** (Plaza de la Estación) is 1.3km southeast of the centre. Destinations include Seville (€7.50, 1¼ hours, 11 or more daily), Sanlúcar de Barrameda (€1.68, 30 minutes, seven or more daily), El Puerto de Santa María (€1.10, 20 minutes, 15 or more daily), Cádiz (€2.85, 40 minutes, nine or more daily), Arcos de la Frontera (€2.48, 45 minutes, 13 or more daily) and Ronda (€19.50, 2½ hours, three daily).

Train

Jerez **train station** (Plaza de la Estación) is beside the bus station, with up to 36 daily trains to El Puerto de Santa María (€2.10, 15 minutes) and Cádiz (€4.80, 50 minutes), and 10 or more to Seville (€8.80, 1¼ hours).

Arcos de la Frontera

POP 29.900 / ELEV 185M

Choosing your favourite *pueblo blanco* is like choosing your favourite Beatles album; they're all so damned good, it's hard to make a definitive decision. Pressured for an answer many people single out Arcos, a larger-than-average white town thrillingly sited on a high, unassailable ridge with sheer precipices plummeting away on both sides. With the Sierra de Grazalema as a distant backdrop, Arcos possesses all the classic white-town calling cards: spectacular location, soporific old town, fancy *parador,* and volatile frontier history. The odd tour bus and foreign-owned homestay do little to dampen the drama.

For a brief period during the 11th century, Arcos was an independent Berber-ruled kingdom. In 1255 it was claimed by Christian King Alfonso X for Seville.

⊙ Sights

Along the streets east of Plaza del Cabildo, take time to seek out lovely buildings such as the Iglesia de San Pedro (Calle Núñez de Prado; admission €1; ⊙10am-1pm & 4-7pm Mon-Sat, to 1.30pm Sun), another Gothic baroque confection sporting what is perhaps one of the most magnificent small church interiors in Andalucía (and it's not depressingly dark, either). Nearby, the 17th-century Palacio Mayorazgo, now a community building, has a Renaissance facade and pretty patios. You're allowed to have a peek inside.

Plaza del Cabildo   SQUARE

The old town captures multiple historical eras evoking the ebb and flow of the once-disputed Christian-Moorish frontier. Plaza del Cabildo is the centre of this quarter. Close your eyes to the modern car park and focus instead on the fine surrounding buildings (all old) and a vertiginous mirador (lookout) with views over Río Guadalete. The 11th-century Castillo de los Duques is firmly closed to the public, but its outer walls frame classic Arcos views. On the plaza's northern side is the Gothic-cum-baroque Basíllica-Parroquia de Santa María sporting beautiful stone choir stalls and Isabelline ceiling tracery. On the eastern side, the Parador Casa del Corregidor hotel is a reconstruction of a 16th-century magistrate's house. If you think you've already seen every possible jaw-dropping vista in Andalucía, drink this one in – preferably over a *café con leche* (half coffee and half warm milk) and accompanying *torta* (piece of cake). Outside is an equally dramatic mirador at the far end of the plaza.

⊙ Tours

One-hour guided tours of the old town's monuments and pretty patios start from the tourist office at 11am Monday to Friday.

✶ Festivals & Events

Semana Santa   HOLY WEEK

Holy Week processions through the narrow old streets are dramatic; on Easter Sunday there's a hair-raising running of the bulls.

Fiesta de la Virgen de las Nieves

FLAMENCO

This three-day festival in early August includes a top-class flamenco night in Plaza del Cabildo.

Feria de San Miguel RELIGIOUS
Arcos celebrates its patron saint, San Miguel, with a four-day fair at the end of September.

🛏 Sleeping

TOP **Parador Casa del Corregidor**
CHOICE HISTORIC HOTEL **€€€**
(📞956 70 05 00; www.parador.es; Plaza del Cabildo; r from €155; ❄️@🛜) The highlight of this *parador* is the courtyard restaurant full of palm trees and tinkling water. Rooms are comfortable but not ostentatious. Views from the lounge and the pricier rooms are seemingly endless.

Hotel El Convento HOTEL **€€**
(📞956 70 23 33; www.hotelelconvento.es; Calle Maldonado 2; s/d incl breakfast from €55/70; ❄️@) The nuns who used to live in this beautiful, former 17th-century convent obviously appreciated a good view. Now it's been turned into a slightly chintzy hotel with an honoury Rick Steves room spelt out in azulejos tiles.

Hotel Marques de Torresoto HOTEL **€**
(📞956 70 07 17; www.hotelmarquesdetorresoto.com; Calle Marqués de Torresoto 4; s/d €35/50; ❄️🛜) The deal of the season is waiting in the junglelike inner courtyard of this Arcos gem. Beyond the grand entry the 15 rooms are a little plain with an odd layout, but at this price who's complaining?

Hotel Real de Veas HOTEL **€€**
(📞956 71 73 70; www.hotelrealdeveas.com; Calle Corredera 12; s/d incl breakfast €55/70; ❄️@🛜) A superb option inside a lovingly restored building. The dozen or so rooms are arranged around a glass-covered patio and are cool and comfortable. It's one of the few places that has easy car access.

Hostal San Marcos HOTEL **€**
(📞956 70 07 21; Calle Marqués de Torresoto 6; s/d €35/45; ❄️) A simple old-town *hostal,* there are four pretty rooms and a roof terrace. The attached restaurant is a delight of wrinkled old characters.

✗ Eating

TOP **La Taberna de Boabdil**
CHOICE MOROCCAN, INTERNATIONAL **€€**
(Paseo de los Boliches 35; tasting menus €18; ◷10am-midnight, closed Tue) Worth visiting Arcos for (like you needed an excuse), this atmospheric Moorish eating place is situated in an old cave, inhabited for aeons. The food is as eclectic as the decor and

the atmosphere improves as the night progresses.

Mesón Don Fernando ANADALUCIAN **€**
(Calle Boticas 5; mains €9-11, ◷closed Mon) Up in the old-town maze, Mesón Don Fernando has a lively Spanish atmosphere where you can enjoy treats like rabbit stew and deer steaks while sitting outside relishing the evening breeze. There's another good place next door.

ⓘ Information

The **tourist office** (Plaza del Cabildo; ◷10am-2.30pm & 5.30-8pm Mon-Fri, 10.30am-1.30pm & 5-7pm Sat, 10.30am-1.30pm Sun) is on the old town's main square. There's also a **tourist information kiosk** (Paseo de Andalucía).

Banks and ATMs are along Calle Debajo del Corral and Calle Corredera.

ⓘ Getting There & Away

Services from the **bus station** (Calle Corregidores) run to Jerez (€2.48, 45 minutes, 12 to 15 daily), Cádiz (€5.59, 1¼ hours, five daily), Ronda (€8.20, two hours, three daily) and Seville (€7.65, two hours, two daily). Frequencies to some destinations are reduced on Saturday and Sunday.

Parque Natural Sierra de Grazalema & Around

Of all Andalucía's protected areas, Parque Natural Sierra de Grazalema is the most accessible and best set up for lung-stretching sorties into the countryside. Though not as lofty as the Sierra Nevada, the park's rugged pillarlike peaks nonetheless rise abruptly off the plains northeast of Cádiz, revealing precipitous gorges, wild orchids and hefty rainfall (stand aside Galicia and Cantabria, this is the wettest part of Spain, logging an average 2000 millimetres annually). Grazalema is also fine walking country (the best months are May, June, September and October). For the more intrepid there are opportunities for climbing, caving, canyoning, kayaking and paragliding.

The park extends into northwestern Málaga province, where it includes the Cueva de la Pileta (p733). The Centro de Visitantes (📞956 72 70 29; www.cma.jnta.andalucia.es; Avenida de la Diputación; ◷10am-2pm & 6-8pm Mon-Sat, 9am-2pm Sun), with limited displays and information, is situated in the village of El Bosque, 20km east of Grazalema village.

GRAZALEMA
POP 2240 / ELEV 825M

For good reason Grazalema is the most popular travellers' base in the sierra: the red-roofed village, hunched up under an enormous shaft of rock, could have sprouted from Middle Earth. Local products include pure-wool blankets and rugs.

The village centre is the pretty Plaza de España, overlooked by the 18th-century Iglesia de la Aurora. Here you'll find the tourist office (☉10am-2pm & 4-9pm), with a shop selling local products. Two banks on Plaza de España have ATMs.

🏃 Activities

You're in walking country, so make the most of it. Good hiking info can be procured at the tourist office. Four of the park's best hikes (including the 12.5km El Pinsapar walk through Spain's best-preserved fir woodland) traverse restricted areas and must be booked ahead at the visitor centre in El Bosque. Of the free-access paths, the most dramatic is the 7.2km Sendero Salto del Cabrero between Grazalema village and Benaocaz via the Puerto del Boyar that traverses the western flanks of the Sierra del Endrinal. Look out for rare wild orchids along the way.

Horizon   ADVENTURE GUIDES
(☑956 13 23 63; www.horizonaventura.com; Calle Corrales Terceros 29) This highly experienced adventure firm will take you climbing, bungee jumping, canyoning, caving, paragliding or walking, with English-speaking guides. It also offers guided walks of El Pinsapar and other places.

🛏 Sleeping & Eating

La Mejorana   HOTEL €
(☑956 13 23 27; www.lamejorana.net; Calle Santa Clara 6; r incl breakfast €58; @☒) This is the sort of dreamy hotel you'd choose for a romantic weekend break. There are only five rooms, all of which are full of Spanish charm, and a very tempting pool hidden under a cover of shady green plants. It's tucked away at the top of the village.

Mesón El Simancón   ANDALUCIAN €
(Plaza Asomaderos; mains €6-15, menús €12.90; ☉closed Tue) There are plenty of places to eat and drink around Plaza de España and on Calle Agua. The Simancón, right by the car park, serves well-prepared ham, beef, quail, venison, wild boar and *revueltos* (scrambled egg dishes).

ZAHARA DE LA SIERRA
POP 1600 / ELEV 550M

Rugged Zahara, set around a vertiginous crag at the foot of the Sierra de Grazalema, hums with Moorish mystery. For over 150 years in the 14th and 15th centuries it stood on the old medieval frontier facing off against Christian Olvera, clearly visible in the distance. These days Zahara encapsulates all of the best elements of a classic white town and is popular as a result. Come during the afternoon siesta, however, and you can still hear a pin drop.

The precipitous road over the ultrasteep 1331m Puerto de los Palomas (Doves' Pass) links Zahara with Grazalema (18km) and is a spectacular ride full of white-knuckle switchbacks (try it on a bike!).

Zahara's streets invite investigation, with vistas framed by tall palms and hot-pink bougainvillea. To climb to the 12th-century castle keep, take the path almost opposite the Hotel Arco de la Villa – it's a steady 10- to 15-minute climb. The castle's recapture from the Christians by Abu al-Hasan of Granada, in a night raid in 1481, provoked the Catholic Monarchs to launch the last phase of the Reconquista, which ended with the fall of Granada.

Adventure-tourism firm Al-qutun (☑956 13 78 82; www.al-qutun.com; Calle Arrabalería, Algodonales), in Algodonales, 7km north of Zahara, organises canyoning, guided walks, kayaking, paragliding, caving and climbing. Get in touch for the schedule. Another memorable way of seeing the Sierra is from the saddle of a horse. Riders can arrange tours through Rutas a Caballo Santiago (☑608 840376; www.zaharadelaiser ra.info/caballos).

Accommodation options include Hostal Marqués de Zahara (☑/fax 956 12 30 61; www.marquesdezahara.com; Calle San Juan 3; r incl breakfast €50; ❄︎🛜), a rambling old place in the village centre whose rooms have seen better days. The 17 rooms at modern Hotel Arco de la Villa (☑956 12 32 30; www.tugasa. com; Paseo Nazarí; s/d €35/59; 🅿❄︎🛜), which is partially built into the rock face, have jaw-dropping views but little rural character.

Restaurante Los Naranjos (Calle San Juan 12; mains €8-12; ☉9am-11pm) serves hearty hill-country platefuls both indoors and outside under the orange trees and has saved many a hiker's/cyclist's legs.

Zahara village centres on Calle San Juan, where you'll find the natural park's helpful Punto de Información Zahara de la Sierra (Plaza del Rey 3; ☉9am-2pm & 4-7pm).

One of Spain's most prophetic environmental initiatives is the Vía Verdes, or greenways, which has transformed old railway lines into traffic-free thoroughfares for bikers, hikers, horse riders and wheelchair users. There are currently 12 of these greenways in Andalucía, but by popular consensus the Vía Verde de la Sierra between Olvera and Puerto Serrano is usually voted the most rewarding. Aside from wild, rugged scenery, the Olvera Vía Verde is notable for its four spectacular viaducts, 30 tunnels, and three old stations-turned-hotels that are spread over a 36km route. Ironically, the train line that the greenway follows was never actually completed. Constructed in the 1920s as part of the abortive Jerez to Almargen railway, the project sent its private backers bankrupt during the Great Depression and the line wasn't used. After languishing for decades, it was restored in the early 2000s.

The unique Hotel/Restaurant Estación Verde (☑661 463 207; s/d/apt €30/50/130; restaurant closed Mon) just outside Olvera is a great place to start the route. You can hire bikes here for €15 a day. Pay another €15 and the owners can organise a return taxi from Puerto Serrano at the other end.

A highlight of the Via Verde is the Peñon de Zaframagon, a distinctive crag that acts as a prime breeding ground for griffon vultures. A new interpretative centre (adult/child €2/1; ⊙10am-4pm) on the vía allows close up observations.

OLVERA

A bandit refuge until the mid-19th century, Olvera has come in from the cold and now supports more family-run farming co-ops than anywhere else in Spain. A white town par excellence, it is also renowned for its olive oil, renaissance church, and roller-coaster history that started with the Romans.

Built on top of an older church, the neoclassical Iglesia Parroquial Nuestra Señora de la Encarnación (Plaza de la Iglesia; ⊙Mass Sun) was commissioned by the Dukes of Osuna and completed in 1843. Perched above it is the 12th-century Nasrid Castillo Árabe (⊙9am-2pm Tue, Thu, Sat & Sun). Next door in La Cilla (⊙10.30am-2pm & 4-6pm Tue-Sun, to 7pm May-Sep), an old grain store of the Dukes of Osuna, you'll find the fascinating Museo 'La Frontera y los Castillos', the Vía Verde de la Sierra Interpretive Centre relating the natural history of the nearby bike path, and the tourist office. All share the same opening times.

For accommodation try the excellent Hotel/Restaurant Estación Verde. Bars and restaurants line Avenida Julian Besteiro.

SETENIL DE LAS BODEGAS

While most white towns sought protective status atop lofty crags, the people of Setenil did the opposite and burrowed into the dark caves beneath the steep cliffs of the River Trejo. The strategy clearly worked. It took the Christian armies a 15-day siege to dislodge the Moors from their well-defended positions in 1484. Many of the original cave-houses remain and some have been converted into bars and restaurants. Further afield, you can hike along a 6km path (the Ruta de los Molinos) past ancient mills to the next village of Alcalá del Valle.

Near the top of the town is the 12th-century castle (opening hours are sporadic; check at tourist office) captured by the Christians just eight years before the fall of Granada.

Setenil has some great tapas bars; an ideal pit stop while you study its unique urban framework. Start in Restaurante Palermo (Plaza de Andalucía) at the top of town and work your way down.

The tourist office (Calle Villa; ⊙10am-4pm Tue-Sun) is in the 16th-century Casa Consistorial, which exhibits a rare wooden Mudéjar ceiling.

① Getting There & Around

Los Amarillos (☑902 21 03 17) runs buses to El Bosque from Jerez (€5.75, two hours, six daily) and Arcos (€2.55, one hour, 11 daily). From El Bosque, buses leave for Grazalema (€2.10, 30 minutes) at 3.30pm Monday to Saturday. Grazalema to Ronda buses (€2.45, 45 minutes) depart at 8.15am and 4.15pm.

Setenil de las Bodegas is accessible by bus from Jerez (€8.88, 2½ hours, twice daily), Málaga (€9.16, 2½ hours, twice daily) and Olvera (€1.17, 25 minutes, three daily). The Jerez and Málaga buses also serve Olvera. There's no bus service between Zahara and Grazalema.

White Towns Tour

One-Day Drive or Two-to-Three-Day Bike Ride

Lying on the old Christian-Muslim fault-line, Andalucía's white towns are imbued with historical significance; this tour shows some of the famous and not-so-famous. It can be done by car or bike.

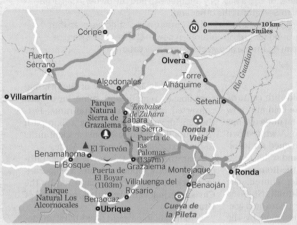

» Start in **Ronda** (p730), Andalucía's premier *pueblo blanco* (white town).

» Escape to **Setenil** (p705), a cave village set into the cliffs above the River Trejo. Stop for morning tapas and some spontaneous exploration.

» Continue north to **Torre Alháquime**, which remained Moorish a full 150 years longer than its close neighbour, Olvera. These days it's refreshingly soporific and well off the tourist route.

» Four kilometres further on is **Olvera** (p705), visible for miles around and famous for its fine Renaissance church and lofty Nasrid castle.

» By diverting onto the 36km Vía Verde de la Sierra, cyclists can travel cross-country to

Puerto Serrano (p705), a sparkling white town at the trail's western terminus.

» Heading southeast on asphalt you'll encounter **Algodonales**, notable for its hang-gliding opportunities, guitar factory and copious bird species.

» Visible to the south is **Zahara de la Sierra** (p704), perched above a sparkling reservoir and photographed more times than King Juan Carlos I.

» It's a steep climb up to natural-park HQ **Grazalema** (p703), a great place to stop for a hearty mountain dinner. From here it's mainly downhill back to Ronda.

Above
1. Grazalema (p704) 2. Ronda (p730)

Great Art

Take an underrated painter from Seville (Murillo) and a prodigious genius from Málaga (Picasso), add some Roman mosaics, a smattering of Velázquez, and a bullfighting aficionado named Goya. The result: a glorious and enormously influential artistic era that graphically defined Spanish and European culture for over two millennia.

Spain's world dominance in art was first established in the 16th century during El Siglo de Oro (the Golden Century), when Andalucía stood at the gateway of a resurgent Europe hungry for power and exploration. While the country's political influence began to wane in the 18th century, Iberian art retained its prominence, particularly in Andalucía, where Velázquez and Murillo provided a bridge to cubism and the revolutionary experimentalism of Picasso.

Although Madrid's Prado (p69) remains the undisputed high church of Spanish art, Andalucía's cultural cities play an integral supporting role.

SNAPSHOTS OF GENIUS

» Seville – showcasing multiple artistic eras, the **Museo de Bellas Artes** (p670) pays proud homage to talented local son Murillo.

» Málaga – Picasso's birthplace celebrates his early life in a couple of well-laid-out **museums** (p720).

» Ronda – the town's bullfighting museum contains numerous prints and sketches by **Goya** (p731).

» Cádiz – the fine-arts section of the **Museo de Cádiz** (p691) exhibits paintings by Zubarán, plus the work that cost Murillo his life.

Left
1. Museo de Bellas Artes (p670), Seville 2. Casa Natal de Picasso (p722), Málaga

Southern Costa de la Luz

Arriving on the Costa de la Luz from the Costa del Sol is like opening the window in a crowded room and gasping in the early-morning sunlight. Bereft of tacky resorts and unplanned development, suddenly you can breathe again. More to the point, you're unequivocally back in Spain; a world of flat-capped farmers and clacking dominoes, grazing cows and Sunday Mass followed by a furtive slug of dry sherry. Don't ask why these wide yellow sandy beaches and spectacularly located white towns are so deserted. Just get out and enjoy them while you still can.

VEJER DE LA FRONTERA
POP 12,800 / ELEV 190M

Vejer – the jaw drops, the eyes blink, the eloquent adjectives dry up. Looming moodily atop a rocky hill above the busy N340, 50km south of Cádiz, this placid, yet compact white town is something very special. Yes, there's a cool labyrinth of twisting streets, some serendipitous viewpoints, and a ruined castle. But, Vejer possesses something else – soulfulness, an air of mystery, an imperceptible touch of *duende,* perhaps (see p760).

◉ Sights

Plaza de España has a fantastical Seville-style terracotta and tiled fountain and is surrounded by some amazing eating nooks.

FREE Castle   CASTLE
(☉approx 10am-9pm Jun-Sep) Vejer's much-reworked castle has great views from its battlements. Its small museum with erratic opening hours preserves one of the black cloaks that Vejer women wore until just a couple of decades ago (covering everything but the eyes).

Casa de Mayorazgo   CASTLE
(Calléjon de la Villa; admission by donation) Of the town's many viewpoints, this place offers one of the best, from one of three towers. It also has a pretty patio.

🛏 Sleeping & Eating

Here are three more reasons to come to Vejer.

TOP
CHOICE Hotel La Casa del Califa
                          HOTEL, MOROCCAN €€
(☎956 44 77 30; www.lacasadelcalifa.com; Plaza de España 16; s/d incl breakfast €73/86; ❉@) Rambling over several floors, this gorgeous hotel oozes character. Rooms are peaceful

and very comfortable, with Islamic decorative touches. Special 'Emir' service (€43) also bags you fresh flowers, chocolates and champagne. Downstairs there's a superb Middle Eastern restaurant, El Jardín del Califa (mains €8-16; ☑).

La Botica de Vejer   HOTEL €€
(☎956 45 02 25, 617 477636; www.laboticade vejer.com; Calle Canalejas 13; s/d incl breakfast €80/90; ❉@☎) Open your bedroom shutters and behold. With a view like this the furnishings barely matter, but they're sparsely elegant anyway. Downstairs is a soulful patio where breakfast is taken and you can converse with the knowledgable owners.

Restaurante Trafalgar   ANDALUCIAN FOOD €€
(Plaza de España 31; mains €11-18) The Trafalgar has some tables outside on Vejer's happening plaza, and prepares typical Cádiz fish, seafood and meat with a contemporary flourish.

☆ Entertainment

Peña Cultural Flamenca 'El Aguilar de Vejer'   FLAMENCO BAR
(Calle Rosario 29; cover charge €3) Part of Vejer's magic is its genuine small-town flamenco scene best observed in this atmospheric old-town bar/performance space.

❶ Information

Buses stop beside the **tourist office** (www. turismovejer.com; Avenida Los Remedios 2; ☉10am-2pm daily, 6-8pm Mon-Sat approx May-Oct), about 500m below the town centre. Also here is a convenient large, free car park.

❶ Getting There & Away

From Avenida Los Remedios, buses run to Cádiz (€4.85, 50 minutes) five or six times a day. Buses for Tarifa (€3.71, 45 minutes, 10 daily), Algeciras (€5.84, 1¼ hours, 10 daily), Jerez de la Frontera (€5.88, 1½ hours, two daily), Málaga (€16, 2¾ hours, two daily) and Seville (€13.95, 2¼ hours, four daily) stop at La Barca de Vejer, on the N340 at the bottom of the hill. It's a steep 20-minute walk up to town from here or an equally steep €6 in a taxi.

LOS CAÑOS DE MECA
POP 200

The 'chilled' beach village of Los Caños straggles along a series of spectacular open beaches southwest of Vejer. Once a hippie hideaway, Los Caños still has a highly alternative, hedonistic scene, especially in summer with its nudist beaches and a strong gay following. Windsurfing, kitesurfing, surfing, horse riding and hikes in the nearby Parque Natural de la Breña y Marismas de Barbate are all among the activities you can pursue here.

At the western end of Los Caños a side road leads out to a lighthouse on an unremarkable spit of land with a famous name – **Cabo de Trafalgar**, which marks the site of the eponymous battle in 1805. The beach under the cliffs here – **Playa del Faro** – is a popular nudist spot.

Some 5km along the coast northwest of Los Caños, the long beach at **El Palmar** has Andalucía's best board-surfing waves from about October to May. Several places rent boards and give surfing classes: try **Escuela de Surf 9 Pies** (✆620 104241; www.9piesescueladesurf.com, in Spanish; board & wetsuit rental per 2/4hr €12/20, classes 2/4hr €27/52), open all year towards the north end of the beach. **Trafalgar Surf** (✆666 942849; www.trafalgarsurftrip.com; beginners' classes from 35€) offers classes in English at the area's best surfing beach on the day, with free pick-up anywhere along the coast from Los Caños to La Barrosa.

Sleeping & Eating

For further accommodation options check www.playasdetrafalgar.com or www.placerdetrafalgar.com.

Hostal Mini-Golf　　　HOTEL €€
(✆956 43 70 83; www.hostalminigolf.com; Avenida Trafalgar 251; s/d €50/70; P❋) This budget place opposite the Cabo de Trafalgar turn-off has fresh, clean rooms, with TV and winter heating, around a simple Spanish patio. There's a cafe and, yes, minigolf in the front garden.

Hotel Madreselva　　　HOTEL €€
(✆956 43 72 55; www.madreselvahotel.com; Avenida Trafalgar 102; s/d incl breakfast €80/98; ☾closed Nov-Feb; P❋☀) The 18 rooms at this artistically designed place have their own garden-patios. There's a good pool, and mountain biking, horse riding, massages and surfing can be arranged.

El Pirata　　　SEAFOOD €€
(Avenida Trafalgar 67; mains €9-13; ☾year-round) Enjoying a superb beachside position, this place seems to sum up Caños' hedonism. Enjoy the excellent seafood at lunchtime and come back in the evening for music and dancing that often drifts out onto the beach.

La Pequeña Lulu　　　CAFE, BAR €
(Avenida Trafalgar 2; dishes €6-15) This funky French-run cafe-bar at the far eastern end of the village serves excellent light meals from crêpes to couscous on a lovely terrace.

Drinking & Entertainment

Good bars include **Los Castillejos** (☾Easter-Oct) towards the eastern end of Avenida Trafalgar and super-relaxed **Las Dunas** (☾year-round) on the road out to Cabo de Trafalgar. Both host live music of various kinds from about midnight and stay open till 2 or 3am.

Getting There & Away

Monday to Friday, there are two Comes buses to/from Cádiz (€5, 1¼ hours) to El Palmar (€4.53, 1¼ hours) and Los Caños (€4.99, 1½ hours). There's also one morning bus, Monday to Friday, running between Vejer and both places. There may be extra services from Cádiz and even Seville from mid-June to early September.

ZAHARA DE LOS ATUNES
POP 1200

Sitting in the middle of a broad, 12km, sandy beach, Zahara is an elemental place. At its heart stands the crumbling old Castillo de las Almadrabas, once a refuge against pirate attacks and a depot for the local tuna fishers. Today the nearest tuna fleet is at Barbate, and Zahara has become a fashionable Spanish summer resort, with more of a family ambience than Los Caños de Meca. There's an old-fashioned core of narrow streets around the ruined castle. The southern end of town, known as Atlanterra, is being developed somewhat unsympathetically, but the pristine beaches and walking trails beyond Atlanterra are well worth exploring.

Sleeping & Eating

Most restaurants in the old part of town are on or near Plaza de Tamarón, near Hotel Doña Lola, and most offer similar *andaluz* fare.

Hotels Almadraba & Almadrabeta
　　　HOTEL €€
(✆956 43 92 74; www.hotelesalmadraba.es; Calle María Luisa 13 & 15; s/d Almadraba €65/80, Almadrabeta €45/70; P❋) These two neighbouring hotels, under one management, provide 25 simple but pleasing rooms with TV and winter heating. The restaurant here, specialising in fish and meat, is one of the best in town.

Camping Bahía de la Plata
CAMPING GROUND €
(☑956 43 90 40; www.campingbahiadelaplata.
com; Carretera de Atlanterra; sites per adult/
tent/car €7/8/4.50, bungalow €120) Good
tree-lined camping ground fronting the
beach at the southern end of Zahara.

Restaurante La Jabega SEAFOOD €€€
(Calle Tomillo 7; raciones €10-13, mains €9-30)
Just back from the beach north of the
Hotel Gran Sol, the Jabega is acclaimed
for its seafood, especially its enticing
albóndigas de choco (cuttlefish fishballs).

ⓘ Getting There & Away
Comes runs up to three daily buses to/from
Cádiz (€6.55, two hours) via Vejer de la Frontera
and Barbate, and one to/from Tarifa (€3.37, 40
minutes). There are usually extra services from
mid-June to September.

Tarifa
POP 17,200

Marking the southernmost point of the
Costa de la Luz, diminutive Tarifa provides
an ideal prelude to the beach nirvana located further north. Though it's no undiscovered Eden, visitors here are more
likely to be wielding surfboards than nine
irons, ensuring that the mood hangs a little
looser and the hotels and restaurants are
refreshingly easier on the wallet. Tarifa's
wind-lashed old town retains a whiff of
the Moroccan medina in its whitewashed
maze, while its beaches are to kitesurfers
what the Bernabéu is to Real Madrid fanat-
ics. Fifteen kilometres across the strait lies
exotic Africa, just 35 minutes away by boat
and doable as a short-but-sweet day trip (to
Tangier).

Tarifa takes its name from Tariq ibn Ma-
lik, who led a Muslim raid in 710, the year
before the main Islamic invasion of the peninsula.

◉ Sights

Old Town OLD TOWN
A wander round the old town's narrow
streets, which are of mainly Islamic origin,
is an appetiser for Morocco. The Mudéjar
Puerta de Jerez was built after the Reconquista. Look in at the small but action-
packed **market** (Calle Colón) before wending
your way to the mainly 15th-century **Iglesia de San Mateo** (Calle Sancho IV El Bravo;
◷9am-1pm & 5.30-8.30pm). South of the

church, the **Mirador El Estrecho**, atop
part of the castle walls, has spectacular
views across to Africa, located only 14km
away.

Castillo de Guzmán CASTLE
(Calle Guzmán El Bueno; admission €2; ◷11am-
4pm) Originally built in 960 on the orders
of Cordoban caliph Abd ar-Rahman III,
this fortress is named after the Reconquista hero Guzmán El Bueno. In 1294, when
threatened with the death of his captured
son unless he surrendered the castle to
attacking Islamic forces, El Bueno threw
down his own dagger for the deed to be
done. Guzmán's descendants later became
the Duques de Medina Sidonia, one of
Spain's most powerful families. You'll need
to buy tickets for the fortress at the tourist
office.

⚐ Activities

Beaches BEACHES
On the isthmus leading out to Isla de las
Palomas, tiny **Playa Chica** lives up to its
name. Spectacular **Playa de los Lances** is
a different matter, stretching northwest for
10km to the huge sand dune at **Ensenada
de Valdevaqueros**.

Kitesurfing & Windsurfing
KITESURFING, WINDSURFING
Most of the action occurs along the coast
between Tarifa and Punta Paloma, 11km
northwest. The best spots depend on the
day's winds and tides: El Porro on Ensenada de Valdevaqueros is one of the most
popular, with easy parking. Both wind- and
kitesurfing are practised year-round, but
the biggest season is from about April to
October.

Tarifa now has around 30 kitesurf and
windsurf schools, many of them with offices or shops along Calle Batalla del
Salado or on Calle Mar Adriático. Others
are based along the coast. Many rent and
sell equipment. It's essential for kitesurfing beginners to take classes. An eight-
hour beginners' course in groups of up to
four, usually over two days, costs around
€180 including equipment. Full equipment
rental is around €80 for one day. Two-hour
windsurfing classes in groups of up to
four are around €55; board-and-sail rental
for two/four hours is around €45/60, or
€60/75 if you need a wetsuit and harness
too. Some experienced, recommended
schools:

BAELO CLAUDIA

In the tiny village of Bolonia hidden on a beautiful bay about 20km up the coast from Tarifa, you'll find the ruins of the most complete Roman town yet uncovered in Spain, Baelo Claudia (956 10 67 97; adult/EU citizen €1.50/free; 10am-8pm Tue-Sat, 10am-2pm Sun & holidays). The site – which affords fine views across the water to Africa – includes a theatre where plays are still sometimes staged, a market, forum, temples, and workshops that turned out the products that made Baelo Claudia famous in the Roman world: salted fish and *garum*, a prized condiment made from fish entrails. There's a good recently opened museum too.

Baelo Claudia's zenith was in the 1st century AD during the reign of Emperor Claudius (AD 41–54).

A hilly 7km side road to Bolonia heads west off of the N340, 15km from Tarifa. A couple of local buses run daily from Tarifa to Bolonia in July and August only.

Spin Out/Adrenalin

WINDSURFING, KITESURFING

Valdevaqueros (956 23 63 52; www.tarifaspinout.com; El Porro Beach, Ensenada de Valdevaqueros, N340 Km75)

Club Mistral WINDSURFING, KITESURFING

(www.club-mistral.com) Hurricane (956 68 90 98; Hurricane Hotel, N340 Km78); Valdevaqueros (619 340913; Cortijo Valdevaqueros, Ensenada de Valdevaqueros, N340 Km75)

Tarifa Max KITESURFING

(696 558227; www.tarifamax.net) Town (O'Neill shop, Calle Tinto 1); N340 (Hotel Copacabana, N340 Km75)

Hot Stick WINDSURFING, KITESURFING

Town (956 68 04 19; www.hotsticktarifa.com; Calle Batalla del Salado 41) Offers one-/two-day courses for €70/130; windsurf classes too.

Horse Riding HORSE RIDING

On Playa de los Lances, Aventura Ecuestre (956 23 66 32; www.aventuraecuestre.com; Hotel Dos Mares, N340 Km79.5) and Hurricane Hípica (646 964279; Hurricane Hotel, N340 Km78) both rent well-kept horses with excellent guides. An hour's beach ride costs €30. Three- or four-hour inland rides are €70.

Whale-Watching WHALE-WATCHING

The Strait of Gibraltar is a top site for viewing whales and dolphins. Killer whales visit in July and August, huge sperm and fin whales lurk here from spring to autumn, and pilot whales and three types of dolphin stay all year. Several organisations in Tarifa run daily two- to 2½-hour boat trips to observe these marine mammals, and most offer a free second trip if you don't at least see dolphins. Most trips cost €30/20 for over/under 14 years; special 3½-hour killer-whale trips in July and August are around €40/25. At holiday times you may need to book two or three days ahead. If the strait is too rough, the boats may head for the Bahía de Algeciras with its groups of dolphins.

firmm WHALE-WATCHING

(956 62 70 08; www.firmm.org; Calle Pedro Cortés 4; Mar-Oct) Uses every trip to record data.

Turmares WHALE-WATCHING

(956 68 07 41; www.turmares.com; Avenida Alcalde Juan Núñez 3; Jan-Nov) Has the largest boats (one with a glass bottom), holding 40 and 60 people.

Whale Watch España WHALE-WATCHING

(956 62 70 13; www.whalewatchtarifa.net; Avenida de la Constitución 6; Apr-Oct)

Birdwatching BIRDWATCHING

From March to May and August to October, if the *levante* (easterly wind) is blowing or there's little wind, the Tarifa area, including the spectacular Mirador del Estrecho lookout point, is great for watching bird migrations across the Strait of Gibraltar. The volunteer-staffed Estación Ornitológica de Tarifa (639 859350; cocn.tarifainfo.com; N340 Km78.5; 5-9pm Tue-Sat, 10am-2pm Sun), 5km northwest of town, provides lots of information on the area's birds. Andalucian Guides (956 43 29 49; www.andalucianguides.com) leads recommended birdwatching day trips in the area from €135 for one to three people.

Sleeping

High season is typically from the beginning of July to mid-September, and it's essential to phone ahead in August.

ANDALUCÍA CÁDIZ PROVINCE

IN TOWN

Posada La Sacristía HISTORIC HOTEL €€€

(☎956 68 17 59; www.lasacristia.net; Calle San Donato 8; r incl breakfast €115-135) Tarifa's most elegant accommodation is in a beautifully renovated 17th-century town house with both Moorish and Thai Buddhist influences. The 10 white rooms have some lovely details. There's a new in-house massage and therapy centre too. It also offers 10 other rooms, suites and apartments scattered around the old town.

La Estrella de Tarifa HOTEL €€

(☎956 68 19 85; www.laestrelladetarifa.com; Calle San Rosendo 2; r incl breakfast €75-110, ste €120-145) Full of intriguing nooks and crannies, this comfortable small hotel in an old town house rambles up and down over four floors with Moroccan decor in soothing blue and white.

Melting Pot HOSTEL €

(☎956 68 29 06; www.meltingpothostels.com; Calle Turriano Gracil 5; dm/d incl breakfast €25/55; @🛜) The Melting Pot is a friendly, well-equipped hostel just off the Alameda. The five dorms, for five to eight people, have bunks, and there's one for women only. A good kitchen adjoins the cosy bar-lounge, and all guests get their own keys.

Hostal Africa HOTEL €

(☎956 68 02 20; Calle María Antonia Toledo 12; s with/without bathroom €50/35, d with/without bathroom €65/50; ⊙closed 24 Dec–31 Jan) The well-travelled owners of this revamped house know just what travellers need. Rooms are attractive and there's an expansive terrace with wonderful views. Short-term storage for boards, bicycles and baggage available.

Posada Vagamundos HOTEL €€

(☎956 68 15 13; www.posadavagamundos. com; Calle San Francisco 18; d/ste incl breakfast €105/125) Right in the centre in a carefully restored 18th-century convent building, Vagamundos has 11 exotic rooms with African-Asian-Islamic decor and a wi-fi-equipped cafe.

ALONG THE COAST

Six year-round camping grounds (www. campingsdetarifa.com, in Spanish), with room for more than 4000 campers, and several, mostly expensive, hotels are dotted along the beach and on and near the N340 within 10km northwest of Tarifa.

Arte Vida Hotel HOTEL €€€

(☎956 68 52 46; www.hotelartevidatarifa.com; N340 Km79.3; s/d incl breakfast €120/140; P) The stylish Arte Vida, located just over 5km from Tarifa's town centre, combines attractive, medium-sized rooms with an excellent restaurant that serves up stunning views. Its grassy garden opens right on to the beach.

Hurricane Hotel HOTEL €€€

(☎956 68 49 19; www.hotelhurricane.com; N340 Km78; r incl breakfast land-/oceanside €156/171; P✳🏊) This classy Moroccan-style hotel, 6km from Tarifa, is the place to go if you're feeling flush. Beautifully set in semitropical gardens, it has large rooms, two pools, two restaurants, on-site riding stables and a kitesurf and windsurf school. The buffet breakfast could well be the best you'll ever have.

Hotel Dos Mares HOTEL €€€

(☎956 68 40 35; www.dosmareshotel.com; N340 Km79.5; r or bungalow incl breakfast €195; P✳@🏊) On the beach about 4.5km from Tarifa, Islamic-themed Dos Mares offers rooms and bungalows outside. The bar, with views to Africa, is a popular hang-out, and there's a good beachside *chiringuito* (small, open-air bar) too. The hotel also boasts tennis and paddle courts, a gym and its own stables.

✖ Eating

Tarifa has some excellent breakfast joints and a couple of good Moroccan-Arabic-inspired restaurants. The most populous 'eat street' is Paseo de la Alameda, leading northwest from the port.

TOP CHOICE **Café Azul** BREAKFAST €

(Calle Batalla del Salado 8; breakfasts €3.50-5; ⊙9am-3pm) This little Italian-owned place packs 'em in every day for Tarifa's best breakfasts. The muesli, fruit salad and yoghurt is large and tasty, or choose one of the excellent crêpes. There's good coffee, juices and shakes, plus *bocadillos* (filled rolls) and cakes.

Bamboo BREAKFAST, BAR €

(Paseo de la Alameda 2; snacks from €4) The best of both worlds on the Alameda, Bamboo does great breakfasts plus shakes and smoothies in the morning, and hosts cocktails, music and DJs at night. Decor is Tarifa eclectic (sofas and pouffes) and clientele is surfer cool.

Restaurante La Olla SEAFOOD, PAELLA €
(Alcalde Juan Nuñez 7; paellas from €10) Set portside, La Olla is the place to come for paella and seafood (you can breathe it in through the door). Try the *arroz negro* (black rice) made with squid. There's also a breakfast buffet and wi-fi.

Chilimoso ARABIC €
(☑956 68 50 92; Calle Peso 6; dishes €4-6; ☑) This tiny place serves tasty vegan and vegetarian food with oriental leanings. Try the felafel with hummus, tzatziki and salad.

Mandrágora MOROCCAN, ARABIC €€
(☑956 68 12 91; Calle Independencia 3; mains €12-18; ☺from 8pm Mon-Sat) Follow the 'listed in Lonely Planet' sign to this intimate place with its Moroccan-Arabic-inspired menu. Try the fruity lamb tagine or monkfish in a wild mushroom sauce.

Bodega La Casa Amarilla TAPAS €€
(☑956 68 19 93; Calle Sancho IV El Bravo 9; mains €14-18) With an attractive, flowery patio, this is a top place in town for local grilled meats and fish, good *revueltos* and tapas.

☕ Drinking & Entertainment

A large ever-changing contingent of surfing and kiteboarding dudes ensures that Tarifa has a decent bar scene focused primarily on narrow Calle Santísima Trinidad and Calle San Francisco, just east of the Alameda.

Don't even bother going out before 11pm. The real dancing starts around 2.30am and ultimate endurance freaks keep bopping until 8am. Many places close on Sunday. Several bars line the southern end of the Alameda. Try **La Ruina**, with good electro dance music, or **Bistro Point** (cnr Calles Santísima Trinidad & San Francisco), with a friendly international crowd and good crêpes (€2 to €4).

A handful of more clublike bars stay open longer. There are further bar and club possibilities on Playa de los Lances and outside town.

Bar Misiana BAR
(Hotel Misiana, Calle Sancho IV El Bravo 18) This fashionable bar in the hotel of the same name is one of *the* places to be seen. DJs spin till 3am or 4am.

Café del Mar BAR
(Polígono La Vega; ☺from 6pm Mon-Sat) Top of the late and cool list, though oddly located, this Ibiza-inspired place includes a couple of bars and a nikkei (Japanese-Peruvian) restaurant, and a nightclub with resident house DJs.

Bar Almedina BAR
(Calle Almedina) Built into the old city walls, this place has a cavernous feel and squeezes a flamenco ensemble into its clamorous confines every Thursday at 10.30pm.

INTO AFRICA

You can travel to Morocco in Africa from one of two Spanish ports – Tarifa and Algeciras – arriving in either Tangier or the Spanish enclave of Ceuta. The company **FRS** (☑956 68 18 30; www.frs.es; Avenida Andalucía, Tarifa) runs the fastest and most comprehensive service. Buy your ticket in the port or at the agencies on Avenida de la Marina: prices are the same everywhere.

Tarifa–Tangier	passenger/car/motorcycle one-way €37/93/31	35 minutes	eight times daily
Algeciras–Tangier	passenger/car/motorcycle one-way €37/93/31	70 minutes	eight times daily
Algeciras–Cueta	EU citizen passenger/car/motorcycle one-way €33.50/84/31; non-EU citizen passenger/car/motorcycle one-way €14/60/22	35 minutes	four daily

FRS also offers tours to Tangier including ferry ride, guide and lunch, for one/two days €65/96. Three-day trips to the nearby Moroccan coastal town of Asilah cost €98. For non-EU passengers on organised excursions a passport is required. For EU citizens a national ID card is sufficient.

Information

Centro de Salud (Health Centre; ☎956 02 70 00; Calle Amador de los Ríos) Has emergency service.

Pandora (Calle Sancho IV El Bravo 13A; internet per hr €2; ⏰10am-2.30pm & 5-9.30pm)

Policía Local (☎956 61 21 74; Ayuntamiento, Plaza de Santa María)

Tourist office (☎956 68 09 93; www.aytotarifa.com, in Spanish; Paseo de la Alameda; ⏰10am-2pm daily, 6-8pm Mon-Fri Jun-Sep)

Getting There & Around

Comes (☎902 19 92 08, 956 68 40 38; Calle Batalla del Salado 13) runs six or more daily buses to Cádiz (€8.45, 1¾ hours), Algeciras (€2, 30 minutes) and La Línea de la Concepción (€3.83, 45 minutes), four to Seville (€17.05, three hours), two each to Jerez de la Frontera (€8.95, 2½ hours) and Málaga (€12.75, two hours) and one to Zahara de los Atunes (€3.37, 40 minutes).

In July and August local buses run about every 1½ hours northwest along the coast as far as Camping Jardín de las Dunas on Ensenada de Valdevaqueros. There's a bus stop at the bottom of the Paseo de Alameda; another stop is at the Comes bus station, where a timetable and prices should be posted.

Algeciras

POP 111,300

The major port linking Spain with Africa is an ugly industrial town and fishing port notable for producing the greatest flamenco guitarist of the modern era, Paco de Lucía, who was born here in 1947. New arrivals usually make a quick departure by catching a ferry to Morocco. If you're going to arrive in Morocco after dark, take some dirham. Exchange rates for buying dirham in Algeciras are best at banks. There are banks and ATMs on Avenida Virgen del Carmen and around Plaza Alta, plus a couple of ATMs inside the port.

It should be said that in the tradition of seedy ports the world over, Algeciras isn't entirely safe; keep your wits about you in the port, bus station and market. Bags can be secured at **Left Luggage** (Estación Maritima; per item €2-3; ⏰7am-9-30pm) or there are lockers (€3) nearby. There is also luggage storage at the bus station. The English-speaking **tourist office** (Calle Juan de la Cierva; ⏰9am-7.30pm Mon-Fri, 9.30am-3pm Sat & Sun) also has a message board.

During summer the port is hectic, as hundreds of thousands of Moroccans working in Europe return home for summer holidays.

The bus station is on Calle San Bernardo. **Comes** (☎956 65 34 56) has buses for La Línea (€2, 30 minutes) every half-hour, Tarifa (€2, 30 minutes, 13 daily), Cádiz (€11, 2½ hours, 13 daily) and Seville (€17, 2½ hours, six daily).

The adjacent **train station** (☎956 63 10 05) runs services to/from Madrid (€68.70, six or 11 hours, two daily) and Granada (€20.20, four hours, three daily).

MOVING ON?

For tips, recommendations and reviews, head to shop.lonelyplanet.com to purchase a downloadable PDF of the Morocco chapter from Lonely Planet's *Mediterranean Europe* guide.

La Línea de la Concepción

POP 63,000

La Línea, 20km east of Algeciras, is the stepping stone to Gibraltar. A left turn as you exit the bus station brings you onto Avenida 20 de Abril, which runs the 300m or so from the main square, Plaza de la Constitución, to the Gibraltar border. The **municipal tourist office** (Avenida Príncipe Felipe; ⏰8am-8pm Mon-Fri, 9am-2pm Sat) faces the border.

Buses run about every 30 minutes to/from Algeciras (€1.86, 30 minutes).

To save queuing at the border, many visitors to Gibraltar park in La Línea, then walk across. The underground **Parking Fo Cona**, just off Avenida 20 de Abril, is the safest place to leave your wheels.

Gibraltar

POP 30,000

Red pillar boxes, fish-and-chip shops, bobbies on the beat, and creaky seaside hotels with 1970s furnishings; Gibraltar – as British writer Laurie Lee once opined – is a piece of Portsmouth sliced off and towed 500 miles south. As with many colonial outposts, 'The Rock', as it's invariably known, tends to overstate its underlying Britishness, a bonus for lovers of pub grub and afternoon tea, but a confusing double-take for modern Brits who thought that their country had moved on since the days of stuffy naval prints and Lord Nelson memorabilia. Stuck strategically at the jaws of Europe and Africa, Gibraltar's Palladian architecture and camera-hogging Barbary apes make an interesting break from the tapas bars and white towns of Cádiz province. Playing an admirable supporting role is its swashbuckling local history; lest we forget, the Rock has been British longer than the United States has been American.

History

In 711 Tariq ibn Ziyad, the Muslim governor of Tangier, landed at Gibraltar to launch the Islamic invasion of the Iberian Peninsula. The name Gibraltar is derived from Jebel Tariq (Tariq's Mountain).

Castilla wrested the Rock from the Muslims in 1462. Then in 1704 an Anglo-Dutch fleet captured Gibraltar during the War of the Spanish Succession. Spain ceded the Rock to Britain in 1713, but didn't abandon military attempts to regain it until the failure of the Great Siege of 1779–83. Britain developed it into an important naval base (bringing in a community of Genoese ship repairers). During the Franco period, Gibraltar was an extremely sore point between Britain and Spain: the border was closed from 1967 to 1985. In 1969 Gibraltarians voted – 12,138 to 44 – in favour of British rather than Spanish sovereignty, and a new constitution gave Gibraltar domestic self-government. In 2002 the UK and Spain held talks about a possible future sharing of sovereignty over Gibraltar, but Gibraltarians expressed *their* feelings in a referendum (not recognised by Britain or Spain), which voted resoundingly against any such idea.

In December 2005 the governments of the UK, Spain and Gibraltar set up a new, trilateral process of dialogue. The three parties reached agreement on some issues but tricky topics remain, not least Britain's military installations and 'ownership' of Gibraltar airport. Gibraltarians want self-determination and to retain British citizenship, making joint sovereignty improbable. Few foresee a change in the status quo but at least relations are less strained these days. On 18 September 2006 a three-way deal was signed by Spain, Gibraltar and Britain relating to telecommunications on the Rock, Gibraltar airport and other issues, but not sovereignty. Gibraltar airport is currently being expanded, and flights from Spanish cities and other European destinations direct to Gibraltar airport were re-introduced in 2006 (though they had been suspended at the time of writing due to lack of demand). In December 2009 a ferry link to mainland Algeciras was reactivated after lying dormant for 40 years.

The mainstays of Gibraltar's economy are tourism, the port and financial services. Investment on the Rock continues apace with a huge luxury waterfront development on its western side. Much of the demand for space is being met through extensive land reclamation (reclaimed land currently comprises approximately 10% of the territory's total area).

◎ Sights & Activities

THE TOWN

Pedestrianised Main St has a typically British appearance (including pubs, imperial statues and familiar British shops), though you'll catch Spanish inflections in the shuttered windows, narrow winding side streets and bilingual locals who have a tendency to start their sentences in English and finish them in Spanish. Most Spanish and Islamic buildings on Gibraltar were destroyed in 18th-century sieges, but the Rock bristles with British fortifications, gates and gun emplacements.

Gibraltar Museum   MUSEUM
(Bomb House Lane; adult/under 12yr £2/1; ◎10am-6pm Mon-Fri, to 2pm Sat) In this fine museum – comprising a labyrinth of rooms large and small – the story of Gibraltar unfolds from Neanderthal to medieval artefacts, with plenty more of its later military and naval history. Don't miss the well-preserved Muslim bathhouse and an intricately painted 7th-century-BC Egyptian mummy washed up here in the late 1800s.

Trafalgar Cemetery   CEMETERY
(Prince Edward's Rd; ◎9am-7pm) Gibraltar's cemetery gives a more poignant history lesson, with its graves of British sailors who died at Gibraltar after the Battle of Trafalgar in 1805.

FREE **Alameda Botanic Gardens** GARDENS
(Europa Rd; ◎8am-sunset) These lush gardens make a refreshing break from Gibraltar's inexplicably manic traffic.

Gibraltar

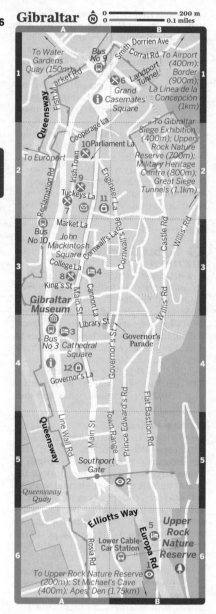

Gibraltar

thing about Gibraltar is the Rock itself. The bulk of the upper Rock, starting just above the town, is a nature reserve, with spectacular views and several interesting spots to visit. A great way to get up here is by the cable car (p719). During a westerly wind the Rock is often a fine spot for observing migrations of birds, especially raptors and storks, between Africa and Europe. January to early June is the time for northbound migrations, and late July to early November for southbound migrations. White storks sometimes congregate in flocks of 3000 to cross the strait.

The Rock's most famous inhabitants are its colony of Barbary macaques, the only wild primates in Europe (probably introduced from North Africa in the 18th century). Some of these hang around the Apes' Den, near the middle cable-car station; others lurk at the top cable-car station or the Great Siege Tunnels. Touchingly human in their ways, they groom their young with frowns of absorption, snack on blackened banana skins, or pose for your camera, looking wistfully out to sea. However, do note that the apes are wild animals and potentially dangerous if approached. Under no circumstances should they be offered food.

About 20 minutes' walk south down St Michael's Rd from the top cable-car station

THE ROCK

🌿 **Upper Rock Nature Reserve**

NATURE RESERVE

(adult/child incl attractions £10/5, vehicle £2, pedestrian excl attractions £0.50; ⏰9.30am-7.15pm, last entry 6.45pm) The most exciting (or 20 minutes up from the Apes' Den), **St Michael's Cave** is a big natural grotto that was once home to Neolithic inhabitants of the Rock. Giant fingers of stone plunge deep and soar high, with atmospheric lighting to add drama as you pace the walkway on a 15-minute tour. Princess Caroline's Battery, a half-hour walk north (downhill) from the top cable-car station, houses a **Military Heritage Centre**. From here a road leads up to the impressive **Great Siege Tunnels**, hand-hewn by the British for gun emplacements during the siege of 1779–83. They constitute a tiny proportion of the more than 70km of tunnels in the Rock, most of which are off limits.

On Willis's Rd, which leads down to the town from Princess Caroline's Battery, are the **Gibraltar, A City under Siege** exhibition (visit at twilight for maximum waxwork spookiness) and the **Tower of Homage**, the last vestige of Gibraltar's Islamic castle, built in 1333.

Tours

The Bahía de Algeciras has a sizeable population of **dolphins** and, from about April to September, several boats make two or more daily trips out to see them; at other times of the year there's usually at least one in daily operation. You'll be unlucky not to get plenty of close-up dolphin contact. Most boats go from Watergardens Quay or adjacent Marina Bay. The trips last about 1½ hours and cost around £20 per adult. Tourist offices have full details.

Sleeping

Bristol Hotel HOTEL €€
(200 76800; www.bristolhotel.gi; 10 Cathedral Sq; s/d/tr £63/81/93; P✹☏☒) Veterans of bucket-and-spade British seaside holidays can wax nostalgic at the stuck-in-the-70s Bristol with its creaking floorboards, red patterned carpets and Hi-de-Hi reception staff. Arrivals from other climes will enjoy the attractive walled garden, small swimming pool and prime just-off-Main St location.

Rock Hotel HOTEL €€€
(20 07 30 00; www.rockhotelgibraltar.com; 3 Europa Rd; d/ste £160/195; P✹@☏☒) Gibraltar's grand dame is looking a little worn these days, though the rooms still have sea views and the general facilities offer much, including gym, pool, welcome drink, bathrobes and that all-important trouser press you'll never use. Mingle among the conference delegates and retired naval captains and rekindle the empire spirit.

Cannon Hotel HOTEL €€
(200 51711; www.cannonhotel.gi; 9 Cannon Lane; s/d without bathroom £26.50/38.50, d with bathroom £47, all incl breakfast) This small, budget-priced hotel right in the main shopping area recalls a kind of Britain of yesteryear with its flowery decor.

Eating

Maybe it's the British influence, but Gibraltar isn't legendary for its food. Though there are a few Spanish-influenced places, the emphasis is on pub grub from the drinking establishments on or just off Main St. Grand Casemates Sq has a profusion of cooler, more modern cafes.

Gibraltar has a whole host of British-style pubs serving food. The usual rule of thumb in these places is: stick to the pub grub (roast beef, fish and chips, etc) and avoid anything that sounds exotic. Places to try include the **Gibraltar Arms** (184 Main St), which does all-day English breakfasts, and the **Star Bar** (12 Parliament Lane; mains £5-11; ☉24hr), the oldest pub on the Rock. **Café Solo** (200 44449; Grand Casemates Sq 3; pastas £8-12; ☏) is a little more refined and has a variety of interesting pastas and salads, including vegetarian fare.

Clipper BRITISH €€
(78B Irish Town; mains £3.50-9; ☏) Full of that ubiquitous naval decor, the Clipper offers real pub grub, genuine atmosphere and Premier League football on big-screen TV. Picture a little piece of Portsmouth floated round the Bay of Biscay to keep the Brits happy. Full English breakfast is served from 9.30am to 11am.

House of Sacarello INTERNATIONAL €€
(57 Irish Town; daily specials £7-11.50; ☉9am-7.30pm Mon-Fri, 9am-3pm Sat, closed Sun) In a converted coffee warehouse, this restaurant with many hats (and nooks) serves light lunches, pastas, salads, quiche and soup. Or you can linger over afternoon tea between 3pm and 7.30pm.

Shopping

Gibraltar has lots of British high-street stores, such as Next, Marks & Spencer, Monsoon and Mothercare (all on or just off Main St) and a huge Morrisons store (in Europort at the northern end of the main harbour). Shops are normally open 9am to

7.30pm weekdays, and until 1pm Saturday. There are a couple of good bookshops, including **Bell Books** (☑200 76707; 11 Bell Lane) and **Gibraltar Bookshop** (☑200 71894; 300 Main St).

ℹ Information

Electricity

Electric current is the same as in Britain: 220V or 240V, with plugs of three flat pins. You'll thus need an adaptor to use your Spanish plug lead, available for £3 to £4 from numerous electronics shops in Main St.

Emergency

Emergency (☑199) For police or ambulance.
Police station (120 Irish Town)

Internet Access

Cyberworld (International Commercial Centre, Queensway; per 30min £2.50; ◷noon-midnight)

Medical Services

St Bernard's Hospital (☑200 79700; Europort) 24-hour emergency facilities.

Money

The currencies are the Gibraltar pound (£) and pound sterling, which are interchangeable. You can spend euros (except in payphones and post offices), but conversion rates are poor. Change unspent Gibraltar currency before leaving. Banks are generally open from 9am to 3.30pm weekdays; there are several on Main St.

Post

Post office (104 Main St; ◷9am-4.30pm Mon-Fri & 10am-1pm Sat, closes at 2.15pm Mon-Fri mid-Jun–mid-Sep)

Telephone

To dial Gibraltar from Spain, you now precede the five-digit local number with the code ☑00350; from other countries, dial the international access code, then the Gibraltar country code (☑350) and local number. To phone Spain from Gibraltar, just dial the nine-digit Spanish number.

Tourist Information

Gibraltar has several helpful tourist offices.

Gibraltar Tourist Board (www.gibraltar.gov.uk; Duke of Kent House, Cathedral Sq; ◷9am-5.30pm Mon-Thu, to 5.15pm Fri)

Information booths Airport (airport; ◷Mon-Fri, mornings only); Customs House (Customs House, Frontier; ◷9am-4.30pm Mon-Fri, 10am-1pm Sat)

Tourist office (Grand Casemates Sq; ◷9am-5.30pm Mon-Fri, 10am-3pm Sat, to 1pm Sun & holidays) Several information desks provide all

the information you need about Gibraltar, with plenty of pleasant cafes in the same square where you can read through it all at leisure.

Visas

To enter Gibraltar, you need a passport or EU national identity card. EU, USA, Canadian, Australian, New Zealand and South African passport-holders are among those who do not need visas for Gibraltar. For further information contact Gibraltar's **Immigration Department** (☑51725).

ℹ Getting There & Away

Air

Three operators currently fly in and out of Gibraltar. As of October 2010 there was no direct air connection to Spain. **Easyjet** (www.easyjet.com) flies approximately 15 times weekly from London, Gatwick, **British Airways** (www.iberia.com) operates seven weekly flights from London Heathrow and **Monarch Airlines** (www.flymonarch.com) flies daily to/from London Luton and three times a week to/from Manchester, UK. At the time of writing, Gibraltar's airport terminal was undergoing a major revamp with a road tunnel being built under the runway.

Bus

There are no regular buses to Gibraltar, but La Línea de la Concepción bus station (p714) is only a five-minute walk from the border.

Car & Motorcycle

Snaking vehicle queues at the 24-hour border and congested traffic in Gibraltar often make it easier to park in La Línea and walk across the border. To take a car into Gibraltar (free) you need an insurance certificate, registration document, nationality plate and driving licence.

Ferry

A new ferry run by **Transcoma** (☑200 61720; www.transcomalines.com; Suite 22, 6 Watergardens Suite) between Algeciras and Gibraltar began operation in December 2009. Tickets cost one-way/return €8/14. The ferry runs five times daily between 9.30am and 6.30pm.

ℹ Getting Around

The 1.5km walk from the border to the town centre crosses the airport runway. A left turn off Corral Rd takes you through the pedestrian Landport Tunnel into Grand Casemates Sq. Alternatively, several local bus lines (adult/child/senior 70p/50p/40p) run from the border into town about every 15 minutes (every 30 minutes on Saturday and Sunday), until 9pm. Bus 9 goes to Market Pl; number 3 goes to Cathedral Sq and the lower cable-car station; and number 10, a red double-decker, runs to Europort (stopping

There's no easy way to find good authentic flamenco. Committed aficionados rely on luck, patience and a little bit of street-savvy. Here are a few tips.

» Search on posters, ask around in bars, read the local papers and listen to the word on the street to find out where the best performances are taking place.

» Flamenco thrives on spontaneity – excellent performances often break out unannounced at ferias, *romerías* and other public gatherings.

» Flamenco feeds off its audience: the presence of more aficionados at a venue enhances the mood and improves your chances of inspiring *duende* (see the boxed text, p760).

» Flamenco *peñas* are private clubs, but they put on some of the best shows in town – try to worm yourself an invite.

» The best flamenco shows rarely charge an entry fee. Good music is played for passion not profit.

» Flamenco was originally the music of Roma people. Gravitate towards the old Roma quarters of Triana (Seville), San Miguel (Jerez), Santa María (Cádiz) and Sacromonte (Granada) to seek out better venues and performances.

» Understand that traditional flamenco performances aren't like normal concerts. Players warm up slowly, tuning their guitars and clearing their throats while the gathered throng talk among themselves. It is up to the dancers/musicians to grab the audience's attention and gradually suck them in. *Duende* is the ultimate goal.

» Regional styles are important and often reflect the personality of the city from which they originate. Listen out for upbeat *alegrías* in Cádiz, cheeky *bulerías* in Jerez, tragic *soleares* in Seville, classic fandangos in Huelva, sparse *tarantos* in Almería and ornamental *granainas* in Granada.

at Morrisons), then Reclamation Rd near the city centre.

All of Gibraltar can be covered on foot, if you're energetic. You can also ascend to the upper Rock, weather permitting, by the **cable car** (Red Sands Rd; adult/child return £8/4.50, incl entry to Nature Reserve £16/12.50; ☉every few min 9.30am-8pm Mon-Sat; last cable up, 7.15pm, last cable down 7.45pm, to 5pm Oct-Apr). For the Apes' Den, disembark at the middle station.

MÁLAGA PROVINCE

Misty-eyed old men on park benches reminisce about whitewashed fishing villages as blue-eyed invaders from the north pick up the keys to their new Costa del Sol condominiums. Málaga province is where Spain's great tourist experiment went viral, leaving a once-tranquil coastline covered in concrete and a local populace fighting to maintain a semblance of its traditional culture. Odd snippets of the old way of life still exist. The provincial capital, Málaga, is an oasis of old-fashioned Spanishness while, further inland, outside encroachments have been kept to a minimum in eye-catch-

ing towns like Antequera and Ronda, and equally spectacular natural features such as the Garganta del Chorro (Chorro Gorge).

Málaga
POP 558,000

The Costa del Sol can seem wholly soulless until you decamp to Málaga, an unmistakably Spanish metropolis curiously ignored by the lion's share of the 11 million tourists who land annually at Pablo Ruíz Picasso International Airport before getting carted off to the golf courses and beaches of 'Torrie' and Fuengirola. Their loss could be your gain. Stubborn and stalwart, Málaga's history is as rich as its parks are green, while its feisty populace challenges *sevillanos* as 24-hour party people. Not known for their timidity in battle, the *malagueños* (residents of Málaga) held out until 1487 against the invading Christian armies and employed equal tenacity when Franco's fascists came knocking in the Spanish Civil War. More recently, Málaga has fought off the less attractive effects of mass tourism and placed a strong bid to become Europe's 2016 Capital of Culture. Work has already started to re-develop its weathered port area.

Málaga endowed the world with another priceless gift – Pablo Picasso, the 20th century's most ground-breaking artist, who was born in a small house in Plaza de Merced in 1881. A couple of excellent museums guard his gigantic legacy.

History

Probably founded by Phoenicians, Málaga has long had a commercial vocation. It flourished in the Islamic era, especially as the chief port of the Emirate of Granada, later reasserting itself as an entrepreneurial centre in the 19th century when a dynamic middle class founded textile factories, sugar and steel mills and shipyards. Málaga dessert wine ('mountain sack') was popular in Victorian England. During the civil war Málaga was initially a Republican stronghold. Hundreds of Nationalist sympathisers were killed before the city fell in February 1937 after being bombed by Italian planes. Vicious reprisals followed.

Málaga has enjoyed a steadily increasing economic spin-off from the mass tourism launched on the nearby Costa del Sol in the 1950s. In recent years, the city has become an important destination in itself.

◉ Sights

TOP CHOICE **Museo Picasso Málaga** ART GALLERY
(☏902 44 33 77; www.museopicassomalaga.org; Palacio de Buenavista, Calle San Agustín 8; permanent collection €6, temporary exhibition €4.50, combined ticket €8; ☺10am-8pm Tue-Thu & Sun, to 9pm Fri & Sat) The hottest attraction on Málaga's tourist scene is tucked away on a pedestrian street in what was medieval Málaga's *judería*. The Museo Picasso Málaga has 204 Picasso works, donated and lent by his daughter-in-law Christine Ruiz-Picasso and grandson Bernard Ruiz-Picasso, and also stages high-quality temporary exhibitions on Picasso themes. The Picasso paint-

Málaga Province

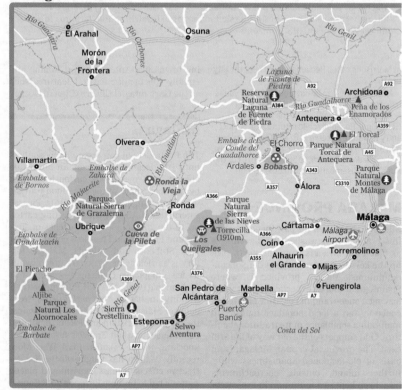

ings, drawings, engravings, sculptures and ceramics on show (many never previously on public display) span almost every phase and influence of the artist's colourful career – blue period, cubism, surrealism and more, with a fascinating emphasis on early, formative works. Gaze at *Niña con su muñeca* (Girl with her doll) and marvel. The museum is housed in the 16th-century Palacio de Buenavista, sensationally restored at a cost of €66 million. Picasso was born in Málaga in 1881 but moved to northern Spain with his family when he was nine.

Catedral
CATHEDRAL

(www.3planalfa.es/catedralmalaga; Calle Molina Lario, entrance Calle Císter; admission €3.50; ⏲10am-5.30pm Mon-Fri, to 5pm Fri, closed Sun & holidays) Preserved rather magnificently, like an unfinished Beethoven symphony, Málaga's cathedral was begun in the 16th century on the former site of the main mosque and never properly completed. Consequently the

building exhibits a mishmash of architectural styles absorbed during more than two centuries of construction. For example, the northern door, **Portada de la Iglesia del Sagrario**, is Gothic; the interior, with a soaring 40m dome, is Gothic/Renaissance; while the facade is 18th-century baroque. The cathedral is known as La Manquita (the One-Armed), since its southern tower was never completed. Inside, note the 17th-century wooden choir stalls, as dark and smooth as chocolate, finely carved by the popular Andalucian sculptor Pedro de Mena. The chapels vie with each other in splendour. Pause at the Chapel of the Virgin of the Kings (numbered 18 in the cathedral guide) to look at a large painting depicting the beheading of St Paul – violent, graphic and strangely beautiful.

Alcazaba
CASTLE

(Calle Alcazabilla; admission €2.10, incl Castillo de Gibralfaro €3.40; ⏲9.30am-8pm Tue-Sun Apr-Oct, closed Mon & major holidays) At the lower, western end of the Gibralfaro hill, the wheelchair-accessible Alcazaba was the palace-fortress of Málaga's Muslim governors, dating from 1057. The brick path winds uphill, interspersed with arches and stone walls and is refreshingly cool in summer. Roman artefacts and fleeting views of the harbour and city enliven the walk, while honeysuckle, roses and jasmine perfume the air. Go before noon during the hot months, to avoid the crowds as well as the worst of the heat, and watch out for low, unprotected parapets, especially if you are taking kids. A lift (elevator) from Calle Guillén Sotelo brings you out in the heart of the Alcazaba.

Below the Alcazaba is a Roman theatre discovered and excavated in 1951.

Castillo de Gibralfaro
CASTLE

(admission €2.10; ⏲9am-9pm Apr-Sep) Above the Alcazaba rises the older Castillo de Gibralfaro, built by Abd ar-Rahman I, the 8th-century Cordoban emir, and rebuilt in the 14th and 15th centuries. Nothing much remains of the interior of the castle, but the walkway around the ramparts affords exhilarating views and there's a tiny museum with a military focus.

To walk up to the Castillo, take the road immediately right of the Alcazaba entrance, and where it bends left into a tunnel, take the steps on the right; or take bus 35 from Avenida de Cervantes (roughly every 45 minutes). The walk is long and steeply uphill. There is a small cafe with outdoor seating and toilets at the Castillo.

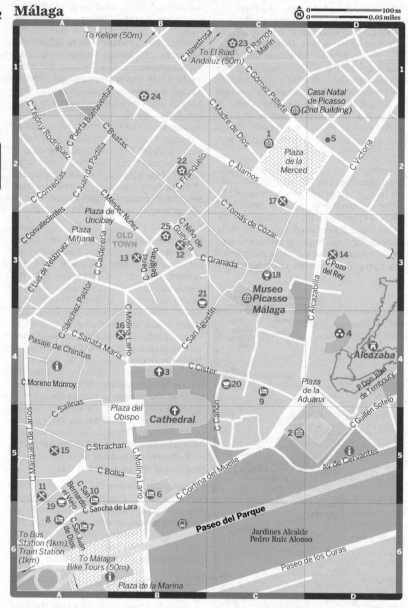

Other Museums MUSEUMS

Casa Natal de Picasso (Plaza de la Merced 15; €1; 9.30am-8pm, closed major holidays), Picasso's birthplace, is a centre for exhibitions and academic research on contemporary art, with a few compelling items of personal memorabilia and a well-stocked shop. A couple of doors away at Plaza de la Merced 13 you can view temporary art exhibitions (a large collection of Dalí magazine covers was showing at the time of writing). Entrance is free with the Picasso museum combined ticket.

The **Centro de Arte Contemporáneo** (Calle Alemania; admission free; ⊘10am-2pm & 5-9pm Tue-Sun) is a coolly minimal museum of international 20th- and 21st-century art housed in a skilfully converted 1930s market. To get here head west on the Alameda Principal from the city centre and turn left when you get to the Río Guadalmedina. The large and diverse museum shop and suitably stark cafe are good stops to complete your visit.

Located in a 17th-century inn, the speciality of **Museo de Artes y Costumbres Populares** (Museum of Popular Arts & Customs; www.museoartespopulares.com; Pasillo de Santa Isabel 10; adult/under 14yr €2/free; ⊘10am-1.30pm & 4-7pm Mon-Fri Jun-Sep, to 8pm Oct-May, 10am-1.30pm Sat year-round) is everyday rural and urban life of the past; note the painted clay figures *(barros)* of characters from Málaga folklore. To get here head west on the Alameda Principal from the city centre and turn right when you get to the Río Guadalmedina.

The **Palacio de la Aduana** (Paseo del Parque) is set to become the permanent home of the city's museum, but not until 2012. Art exhibitions have been suspended, but meanwhile you can marvel at one of Andalucía's largest and most magnificent patios, and take shelter from the sun under glossy, broad-leafed plants.

Beaches
BEACHES
Sandy city beaches stretch several kilometres in each direction from the port. **Playa de la Malagueta**, handy to the city centre, has some excellent bars and restaurants close by. **Playa de Pedregalejo** and **Playa del Palo**, about 4km east of the centre, are popular and reachable by bus 11 from Paseo del Parque.

Jardín Botánico La Concepción
BOTANICAL GARDEN
(adult/under 16 yr/senior €4/2/2; ⊘9.30am-8.30pm (last entry 7pm) Apr-Sep, closed Mon) The largely tropical Jardín Botánico, 4km north of the city centre, features towering trees (including hundreds of palms), 5000 tropical plants, waterfalls, lakes and spectacular seasonal blooms – especially the purple wisteria in spring. You can visit solo or by 1½-hour guided tour in English, costing an extra €2.50.

By car, take the N331 Antequera road north from the Málaga ring road (A7) to Km166 and follow the signs. Alternatively, the Málaga Tour bus runs from the bus station to the gardens.

📷 Courses

There are many private language schools in Málaga; try the **Instituto Picasso** (⊡952 21 39 32; www.instituto-picasso.com; Plaza de la Merced 20), which runs two-/three-/four-week courses for €285/400/515 starting every fortnight on a Monday. There are four 50-minute lessons a day and the price includes access to cultural activities such as flamenco and cookery courses. Accommodation is also available.

👉 Tours

To pick up the child-friendly, open-topped **Malaga Tour bus** (✆902 10 10 81; www.malaga-tour.com; adult/child €16/8; ⊙every 30min 9.30am-8pm), head for Avenida Manuel Agustín Heredia or the eastern end of the Paseo del Parque. This hop-on-hop-off tour does a circuit of the city, stopping at all the sights. Tickets are valid for 24 hours. If you're happier on two wheels, you can try **Malaga Bike Tours** (✆606 978513; www.malagabiketours.eu; Calle Trinidad Grund 1; tours €23). Open tours leave from outside the municipal tourist office in Plaza de la Marina at 9.50am daily. You can book 24 hours ahead. Alternatively, you can travel in old-fashioned style, with a **horse-and-carriage tour** of the city that lasts 45 minutes and costs €30. Carriages line up at the Plaza de la Marina end of the Jardines Alcalde Pedro Ruiz Alonzo, along the Paseo del Parque.

🎊 Festivals & Events

Semana Santa   HOLY WEEK
Solemn and spectacular: the platforms bearing the holy images *(tronos)* are large and heavy, each needing up to 150 bearers. Every night from Palm Sunday to Good Friday, six or seven *tronos* are carried through the city, watched by big crowds. Witness this event on the Alameda Principal, between 7pm and midnight.

Feria de Málaga   SUMMER FAIR
Lasting nine days (mid- to late August), this is the biggest and most ebullient of Andalucía's summer fairs. During daytime, especially on the two Saturdays, celebrations take over the city centre, with music, dancing and horses. At night the fun switches to large feria grounds at Cortijo de Torres, 4km southwest of the city centre, with fairground rides, music and dancing.

🛏 Sleeping

El Riad Andaluz   HOTEL €€
(✆952 21 36 40; www.elriadandaluz.com; Calle Hinestrosa 24; s/d €70/86; ✳@?) Colourful and exotic, this gorgeous restored monastery offers eight Moroccan-style rooms set around an atmospheric patio, with tea and coffee on tap all day. Situated in the rapidly gentrify-

ing Centro Histórico, it's an easy stroll to all the funkiest bars and restaurants in surrounding plazas. The French owner and his family infuse the Riad with a special magic.

AC Málaga Palacio   HOTEL €€€
(✆952 21 51 85; www.achotels.com; Calle Cortina del Muelle 1; d €137; P✳?≋) This sleek, 15-storey hotel has sensational views over the busy seafront. Design in the public areas tends towards bling, but the rooms are quietly elegant, there is a top-floor terrace for drinks and dining, a fitness centre and an outdoor pool on the roof.

Parador Málaga Gibralfaro   HOTEL €€€
(✆952 22 19 02; www.parador.es; Castillo de Gibralfaro; r €160-171; P✳?≋) With an unbeatable location up on the pine-forested Gibralfaro hill, Málaga's modern but rustic *parador* provides spectacular views of the city and harbour from its upper floors, an excellent terrace restaurant and a rooftop pool.

Hotel Sur   HOTEL €€
(✆952 22 48 03; www.hotel-sur.com; Calle Trinidad Grund 13; s/d/tr with bathroom €52/76/100; s/d without bathroom €39/49; P✳?) A good location a goal kick away from the Plaza de la Marina adds kudos to the plain but pristine Hotel Sur's portfolio. More are added with friendly, polite staff and the availability of wi-fi in all rooms.

Hotel Carlos V   HOTEL €
(✆952 21 51 20; www.hotel-carlosvmalaga.com; Calle Císter 10; s/d €36/59; P✳@) Close to the cathedral and Picasso museum, the Carlos V is enduringly popular. Renovated in 2008, bathrooms sparkle in their new uniform of cream-and-white tiles. Excellent standard for the price plus helpful staff make this hotel a winner.

Hotel Don Curro   HOTEL €€
(✆952 22 72 00; www.hoteldoncurro.com; Calle Sancha de Lara 7; s/d €63/74; P✳@?) Big, busy Don Curro is efficient, comfortable and central, with well-appointed, spacious rooms, and substantial breakfasts just a few steps away at its own Café Moka.

Hostal Derby   HOTEL €
(✆952 22 13 01; www.hostalderbymalaga.com, in Spanish; Calle San Juan de Dios 1, 4th fl; s/d €36/48; @) A friendly, well-run, and good-value *hostal* with spacious rooms and big windows, some overlooking the harbour.

Hostal Victoria   HOTEL €
(✆952 22 42 24; www.hostalvictoriamalaga.com; Calle Sancha de Lara 3; s/d €43/55; ✳)

Centrally located, the Victoria provides basic, comfortable rooms with bathtubs.

Eating

Málaga's restaurants are well priced and of a good standard due to the largely local clientele. A speciality here is fish fried quickly in olive oil. *Fritura malagueña* consists of fried fish, anchovies and squid. Most of the best eating places are sandwiched in the narrow streets between Calle Marqués de Larios and the cathedral.

La Rebaná
TAPAS €

(Calle Molina Lario 5; tapas €4.20-8.50, raciones €7-11.50) A great, noisy tapas bar near the Picasso museum and the cathedral. Dark wood, tall windows and exposed-brick walls create a modern, minimal, laid-back space. Try the unique foie gras with salted nougat tapa.

Gorki
TAPAS €€

(Calle Strachan 6; platos combinados €7.50-16) A popular upmarket tapas bar with pavement tables and a modern interior full of wine-barrel tables and stools. Creative tapas have a more *sevillano* twist and the clientele is young and trendy.

Café Lepanto
COFFEE, SNACKS €

(Calle Marqués de Larios 7) An old-world Italianite coffee/ice-cream bar that serves as Málaga's top *confitería* (sweets and pastries shop), Lepanto is insanely popular probably because most of its sweets and pastries are highly addictive. Enjoy them in the art nouveau embellished interior, being served by athletic waiters in waistcoats.

Comoloco
MODERN SPANISH €

(Calle Denis Belgrano 17; salads €8-10, pittas €5-6; ⊘1pm-1am, ⊘) This place with huge windows onto the little street is packed out at lunchtime. The menu also features a vegetarian's delight of salads and generously filled pitta wraps at a good price amid industrial decor.

Clandestino
INTERNATIONAL €

(Calle Niño de Guevara 3; mains €9-17; ⊘1pm-1am; ⊘) A trendy warehouse-style restaurant with an exciting menu that fuses northern European and Latin cuisines. A good selection of vegetarian dishes is headed by silky felafel patties on a salad dressed with alfalfa sprouts and a dill yoghurt vinaigrette.

Café de París
INTERNATIONAL €€€

(⊘952 22 50 43; www.rcafedeparis.com; Calle Velez-Málaga 8; mains €12-36; ⊘1.30-5pm & 8.30pm-12.30am Tue-Sat) There are reasons why La Malagueta neighbourhood is considered 'posh', and here's one of them. Just as it name implies, Café de París is politely refined, upmarket, and very, well, Parisian. But, none of it's an act. With a Michelin-starred Spanish chef, this is where you come with your rich friends to enjoy fried lobster and hope they pick up the bill.

Restaurante Antonio Martín
SEAFOOD €€€

(⊘952 22 73 98; Playa de la Malagueta; mains €22-29; ⊘closed Sun Nov-Apr) On the beach and with a large terrace, Antonio Martín is a somewhat stuffy dress-up-and-be-seen restaurant serving a range of fried fish and meat in a starched-tablecloth zone. If you want something cheaper and more down-to-earth, walk a few hundred metres along the promenade to one of the tented beach dives.

Lechuga
TAPAS, VEGETARIAN €

(Plaza de la Merced 1; tapas €2.50-3.50, raciones €8-10; ⊘) In this calm retreat, vegetables reign supreme and the chef does wonderful things with them, such as hummus, Indian-style *bhajis* and various inventive salads.

El Vegetariano de la Alcazabilla
VEGETARIAN €€

(Calle Pozo del Rey 5; mains €9.50-12.50; ⊘closed Sun; ⊘) Laid-back veggie/vegan restaurant combining friendly service with good food in a shabby-chic setting just a cannonball shot from the Alcazaba walls. Do try the 'meatballs of Seitan'.

☿ Drinking

On weekend nights, the web of narrow old streets north of Plaza de la Constitución comes alive. Look for bars around Plaza de la Merced, Plaza Mitjana and Plaza de Uncibay.

TOP CHOICE Bodegas El Pimpi
BAR

(Calle Granada 62; ⊘11am-2am) A Málaga institution with a warren of charming rooms and mini-patios, El Pimpi attracts a boiterous crowd of all nationalities and generations with its sweet wine and traditional music. Look out for the flamenco (last Monday of the month) and the signed photo of a young-looking Tony Blair.

La Tetería
TEAROOM

(Calle San Agustín 9; teas from €2.50; ⊘9am-midnight) Emulating many of Granada's *teterías*, this inviting establishment near the Picasso museum complements a full menu of exotic teas with some heavenly homemade cakes and one of the best bowls of breakfast granola you're ever likely to taste.

Café Moka
CAFE

(Calle San Bernardo El Viejo 2) Just off Calle Larios, this busy little retro cafe caters to a mainly Spanish crowd. In the mornings, it does brisk breakfast business with savoury-filled soft rolls *(molletes)*, croissants and strong, creamy coffee, starting at around €3.50.

El Jardín
CAFE, BAR

(Calle Cañón 1; mains €12.50; ⊗9am-midnight Mon-Thu, 9am-2pm & 5pm-midnight Fri & Sat, 5pm-midnight Sun) A beautiful Viennese-style cafe next to palm-filled gardens behind the cathedral, full of ancient *malagueños* plus the odd inebriated Picasso lookalike. Art-nouveau flourishes and old photographs evoke a pleasant ambience, but not great food. Instead, come for wine or coffee and listen to some young-at-heart septuagenarian pound away on the upright piano.

☆ Entertainment

Málaga's substantial flamenco heritage has its nexus to the northwest of Plaza de la Merced. Venues here include Kelipe (☑692 82 98 85; www.kelipe.net; Calle Peña 11), a flamenco centre which puts on *muy puro* performances Thursday to Saturday at 9.30pm; entry of €15 includes one drink and tapa – reserve ahead. Kelipe also runs intensive weekend courses in guitar and dance. Amargo (Calle Franquelo 3) offers Friday and Saturday night gigs, while Vino Mio (Calle Álamos) is a small restaurant with an international menu where musicians and dancers fill the wait for the food.

Teatro Cervantes
THEATRE

(☑952 36 02 95; www.teatrocervantes.com; Calle Ramos Marín; ⊗closed mid-Jul–Aug) The palatial Cervantes has a fine program of music, theatre and dance.

Warhol
NIGHTCLUB

(Calle Niño de Guevara; ⊗11pm-late Thu-Sat) A stylish haunt for gay clubbers who want an upmarket atmosphere in which to enjoy the funky house beats mixed by dreadlocked DJs.

❶ Information

There are plenty of banks with ATMs on Calle Puerta del Mar and Calle Marqués de Larios, and ATMs in the airport arrivals hall.

5 á Sec (Calle Granada 15) Laundry loads with drying and folding included from approximately €10 a bag.

Ciberbocutorio (Calle Frailes 38; internet per 30min €0.50; ⊗9am-midnight) Numerous internet terminals.

Hospital Carlos Haya (☑951 03 01 00; Avenida de Carlos Haya) The main hospital, 2km west of the centre.

Municipal tourist office (www.malagaturismo.com, in Spanish; ⊗9am-8pm Mar-Sep, 9am-6pm Oct-Feb) Plaza de la Marina (Plaza de la Marina) Also information booths at the bus station and around town.

Policía Local (☑952 12 65 00; Avenida de la Rosaleda 19)

Post office (Avenida de Andalucía 1; ⊗8.30am-8.30pm Mon-Fri, 9.30am-2pm Sat)

Regional tourist office (Pasaje de Chinitas 4; www.andalucia.org; ⊗9am-7.30pm Mon-Fri, 10am-7pm Sat, to 2pm Sun) There is another branch at the airport; these cover the whole of Málaga and all of Andalucía.

❶ Getting There & Away
Air

Málaga's busy **airport** (☑952 04 88 38), the main international gateway to Andalucía, receives flights by dozens of airlines (budget and otherwise) from around Europe.

Boat

Trasmediterránea (☑952 22 74 77, 902 45 46 45; www.trasmediterranea.com; Estación Marítima, Local E1) operates a fast ferry (four hours) and a slower ferry (7½ hours) daily year-round to/from Melilla (passenger, fast ferry/ferry €55/33.50; car, fast ferry/ferry €174/156).

Bus

Málaga's **bus station** (Paseo de los Tilos) is just 1km southwest of the city centre. Frequent buses travel along the coasts, and others go to Seville (€16, 2½ hours, nine or more daily), Granada (€9.75, 1½ to two hours, 17 daily), Córdoba (€12.50, 2½ hours, five daily), Antequera (€5, one hour, 13 daily) and Ronda (€9.50, 2½ hours, nine or more daily). Nine buses also run daily to Madrid (€21.50, six hours), and a few go up Spain's Mediterranean coast. There are services to France, Germany, Holland, Portugal and Morocco too.

Car

Numerous international and local agencies have desks at the airport, many with small cars for around €170 per week.

Train

The main station, **Málaga-Renfe** (Explanada de la Estación), renamed the María Zambrano in 2007, is round the corner from the bus station. The superfast AVE service runs to Madrid (€76.40 to €85, 2½ hours, six daily).

Trains also go to Córdoba (€21 to €44, one hour, 10 daily), Seville (€19.10 to €36.40, two to 2½ hours, five daily) and Barcelona (€62.70 to €138, two daily; the cheaper train takes 13 hours, while the more expensive takes only half that). For Granada (€15, 2½ hours) and Ronda (€9.75, 1½ hours minimum) you need to change at Bobadilla.

ⓘ Getting Around

To/From the Airport

The Aeropuerto train station on the Málaga–Fuengirola line is a five-minute walk from the airport (follow signs from the departures hall). Trains run about every half-hour, from 6.49am to 11.49pm, to Málaga-Renfe station (€2, 11 minutes) and Málaga-Centro station. Trains depart for the airport between 5.45am and 10.30pm.

Bus 19 to the city centre (€1.10, 20 minutes) leaves from the 'City Bus' stop outside the arrivals hall, every 20 or 30 minutes, 6.35am to 11.45pm, stopping at Málaga-Renfe train station and the bus station en route. Going out to the airport, you can catch the bus at the western end of Paseo del Parque and from outside the stations, about every half-hour from 6.30am to 11.30pm.

A taxi from the airport to the city centre costs €20 to €24 depending on traffic and pick-up location.

Málaga is responding to green issues and citizen pressure by building its own metro system, **Metro Málaga** (www.metrodemalaga.info), with the first section of track, from the port towards the city centre and including the train station, set to launch in 2011.

Tricosol (☑657 440605; www.bike2malaga. com; Calle Victoria 15, ☺11am-8pm) Trixi hire offers another fun way to get around Málaga. These curvaceous electric-powered cars can be hired for short journeys in the city centre (€2.50), or to the beach (€5), or train station (€7). They offer a green and pleasant way of touring Málaga, and can normally be hailed from in front of the cathedral.

Costa del Sol

Splaying from Nerja in the east to Gibraltar in the west, the Costa del Sol juxtaposes cheesy (Torremolinos) with swanky (Marbella) on a coastline that is not renowned for its subtlety. Though the sprawling suburbs and overdeveloped beaches provoke extreme responses from different types of travellers, the Costa – to coin one of its favourite tourist-brochure clichés – really does have 'something for everyone'. If your idea of a good holiday is sandy beaches, pulsating nightclubs, and large, kid-friendly amusement parks, then this famously mild coastline has them all in abundance. If, on the other hand, the very mention of the word 'Torremolinos' sends you into fits of depression, thank your lucky stars that, by sucking up approximately 70% of the region's annual tourists, the Costa del Sol unwittingly keeps the likes of Tarifa, Vejer de la Frontera and Grazalema deliciously tranquil.

A convenient train service links Málaga's Renfe and Aeropuerto stations with Torremolinos (€1.35), Arroyo de la Miel (€1.55) and Fuengirola (€2.15). Buses from Málaga link all the resorts, and services to places such as Ronda, Cádiz, Seville and Granada go from the main resorts.

TORREMOLINOS

POP 48,000

Like an overexposed film star with a fame addiction, Torremolinos' reputation precedes it. Think T-shirt suntans and Union Jack swimming trunks, beer over fish and chips and permanently inebriated 18–30 year olds on elongated stag weekends. Yet, despite being the butt of everything from Monty Python jokes to hysterical tabloid holiday exposés, 'Terrible Torrie' refuses to die. Reinvention is its perennial hallmark. Dogged by a lager-loutish reputation in the 1990s, the resort has successfully embraced its kitsch side and started attracting an older demographic backed up by a strong gay following. Make no mistake; the town of towers (*torres*) and windmills (*molinos*) has life in it yet.

◉ Sights & Activities

Torrie's beaches are wider and longer than some on the *costa,* but way inferior (and more crowded) than those on the Costa de la Luz. Away from the beach/bar scene, the local attractions are mostly child-oriented.

Sea Life AQUARIUM
(www.sealifeeurope.com; adult/child €13.75/ 10.50; ☺10am-10pm Jun, to midnight Jul-Sep) In the more upmarket Puerto Deportivo (marina) at Benalmádena Costa, just southwest of Torremolinos, this is a good modern aquarium of mainly Mediterranean marine creatures, with organised games and shark feeding.

Tivoli World　　　　　AMUSEMENT PARK
(www.tivoli.es; Avenida de Tivoli; admission €7; ☺6pm-1am) Just five minutes' walk from Benalmádena-Arroyo de la Miel train station, this is the biggest amusement park on the *costa*. The Supertivolino ticket (€12) gives unlimited access to more than 35 rides.

🛏 Sleeping & Eating

Torremolinos lists 55 hotels in its tourist-office brochures, and as well as British breakfasts and beer, Torremolinos has no shortage of good seafood places, many of them lining the Paseo Marítimo in La Carihuela.

Hotel El Pozo　　　　　HOTEL
(☎952 37 54 45; www.hotelelpozo.com; Avenida Los Manantiales 4; s €35-50, d €46-60; ❉🤖🖼) This two-star place is handily located close to the train station and the beach. The no-frills rooms are clean, and the clientele young, European and budget-oriented.

☆ Entertainment

Torrie's nightlife is famous. Hit **Palladium** (Avenida Palma de Mallorca 36) for hard partying and international DJs. The gay 'in crowd' gravitates towards the trendy **El Gato Lounge** (La Nogalera; ☺from 4pm till late).

❶ Information

Tourist office (www.ayto-torremolinos.org; Plaza Pablo Picasso; ☺10am-2pm & 6-8pm Jun-Sep) In the town hall. There are also offices on Playa Bajondillo (☺10am-2pm) and Playa Carihuela (☺10am-2pm).

FUENGIROLA
POP 65,000

Fuengirola, 18km down the coast from Torremolinos, is sold as a more family-friendly alternative to its upstart sibling, but it's splitting hairs really – the towns are two wings of the same bird. Attractions are generally either beach- or child-oriented.

The **Hipódromo Costa del Sol** (www.hipodromocostadelsol.es; Urbanización El Chaparral; admission €5; ☺10pm-2am Sat Jul-Sep, 11.30am-4pm Sun Oct-Jun), Andalucía's leading horse-racing track with regular racing, is off the N340 at the southwestern end of Fuengirola.

If you're staying the night, **Hostal Marbella** (☎952 66 45 03; www.hostalmarbella.info; Calle Marbella 34; s/d €45/62; ❉@🤖), run by a dedicated Swedish couple, has blue and yellow rooms plus wi-fi and a coffee machine in reception. It's in the centre of town, just minutes from the beach.

The **tourist office** (Avenida Jesús Santos Rein 6; ☺9.30am-2pm & 5-7pm Mon-Fri, 10am-1pm Sat) is about a block from the **train station** (Avenida Jesús Santos Rein), which runs half-hourly trains to Torremolinos, Málaga airport and Málaga city.

MARBELLA
POP 132,000

Long a favourite bolthole for criminals on the so-called 'Costa del Crime', Marbella is an unholy melange of wealth-flaunting 'celebrities' and water-guzzling golf courses that has traditionally provided an antidote to the cheap package-tour heaven (or hell?) of Torremolinos. A little more authentic than the resorts further east, Marbella has retained something of its Spanish identity in a pretty town centre, though corruption through the issuing of illegal building permits has marred local politics in recent years.

◉ Sights & Activities

Pretty **Plaza de los Naranjos**, with its 16th-century town hall, is at the heart of the largely pedestrianised, postcard-perfect old town. **Puerto Banús**, the Costa del Sol's flashiest marina, is 6km west of Marbella and has a slew of glamorous boutiques and busy restaurants strung along the waterfront.

There are good **walks** in the Sierra Blanca, starting from the Refugio de Juanar, a 17km drive north of Marbella.

Museo del Grabado Español Contemporáneo　　　　　MUSEUM
(Museum of Contemporary Spanish Prints; Calle Hospital Bazán; admission €3, Sat free; ☺9am-2pm & 6-9pm Tue-Fri, 9am-2pm Mon & Sat). Near Plaza de los Naranjos, this museum has beautifully uncluttered vaulted rooms, where you can see work by Picasso, Joan Miró and Salvador Dalí, among others.

🛏 Sleeping & Eating

Hostal/Restaurant El Gallo　　　　　HOTEL €
(☎952 82 79 98; Calle Lobatas 46; s/d €35/55; ❉@) A slice of the pre-celebrity Marbella hides a few blocks from the Plaza de los Naranjos. The restaurant offers fine home-cooking made with *amor* (nothing over €10) and is a local favourite. The economical rooms have all the necessary comforts, including wi-fi, TVs and friendly owners.

Hotel La Morada Mas Hermosa
　　　　　HOTEL €€
(☎952 92 44 67; www.lamoradamashermosa.com; Calle Montenebros 16A; r €97; ❉@🤖)

MIJAS

Welcome to a bit of light relief. Of all the clamorous urban developments on the Costa del Sol, sparkling Mijas remains the most traditional and pretty – although with a municipal population pushing 70,000, the label 'white town' is pushing it. Surrounded by *urbanizaciones* (housing estates), amusement parks and enough golf courses (seven, and four more in the works) to start a Tiger Woods academy, Mijas' days as an antidote to the raucous 'fun in the sun' package holidays could well be numbered. For the time being, come here to escape the beach mania, inhale the scent of blossoming jasmine and wander winding streets of Muslim origin. The Casa Museo de Mijas (Calle Málaga; admission free; ☺10am-2pm & 4-7pm Sep-Mar, afternoons 5-8pm Apr-Jun, 6-9pm Jul-Aug) gives a poignant glimpse into life in the area before the 1960s tourist deluge. There are good hotels and lots of restaurants, cafes and craft shops. Frequent buses run from Fuengirola, 8km away.

A small, personable hotel on a tranquil, flowery, old-town street. Just six rooms, some with spiral stairs up to the bathrooms, and it's genuinely nonsmoking.

El Balcón de la Virgen ANDALUCIAN €€
(☑952 77 60 52; Calle Virgen de los Dolores; mains €9-18; ☺closed Sun) One of the best restaurants near Plaza de los Naranjos, this has a lovely summer *terraza* overlooked by a 300-year-old grieving Virgin and a large bougainvillea, vibrant pink against the bright-blue paintwork. The fare is typical Andalucian.

La Comedia INTERNATIONAL €€€
(www.lacomedia.net; Plaza de la Victoria; mains €10.50-20) Along with popular 1st-floor tables looking down on the little plaza, a charming candlelit room, and a mix of interesting art and photography on the walls, you get a very warm welcome from the Irish hosts, and a good selection of classic, Spanish and international dishes for carnivores and vegetarians alike.

🍷 Drinking & Entertainment

The busiest nightlife zone in the Marbella area is at Puerto Banús, where dozens of pubs and varied dance clubs cluster along a couple of narrow lanes behind the marina.

ⓘ Information

Municipal tourist office (www.marbella.es, in Spanish; ☺9am-9pm Mon-Fri, 9.30am-2.30pm Sat, closed Sun); Fontanilla (Glorieta de la Fontanilla); Naranjos (Plaza de los Naranjos 1)

ⓘ Getting There & Around

Half-hourly buses to Fuengirola (€2.65, 1¼ hours), Puerto Banús (€1.10, 20 minutes) and Estepona (€2.51, 1¼ hours) have stops on Avenida Ricardo Soriano. Other services use the **bus station** (Avenida Trapiche), 1.2km north of Plaza de los Naranjos. Bus 7 (€1.10) runs between the bus station and the central **Fuengirola/Estepona bus stop** (Avenida Ricardo Soriano); returning to the bus station, take bus 2 from Avenida Ramón y Cajal.

Marbella's streets are notoriously trafficclogged. Fortunately there are a number of pay car parks where you can take refuge on arrival.

El Chorro & Bobastro

POP (EL CHORRO) 100

Fifty kilometres northwest of Málaga, Río Guadalhorce and the main railway in and out of Málaga both pass through the awesome Garganta del Chorro, which is 4km long, up to 400m deep and as little as 10m wide. The gorge is a magnet for rock climbers, with hundreds of varied routes of almost every grade of difficulty. Anyone can view the gorge by walking along the railway from the tiny El Chorro village (ask locally for directions). The view provides an adrenalin rush all by itself.

The gorge is particularly famous for the Camino del Rey, a 1m-wide white-knuckle path similar to an Italian *via ferrata* that contours across the sheer rockface on a ledge 100m above the ground. Initially built in 1905 (and traversed by King Alfonso XIII in 1921 – hence the name, Path of the King), the path had fallen into severe disrepair by the late 1990s and was closed in 2000 after a couple of tourist deaths. In 2006 €7 million was earmarked by the Andalucian government to restore it. The work is still pending.

Swiss-owned Finca La Campana, popular with adventure lovers, offers half-day climbing courses (€45), caving (€180 for a group of up to four people), kayaking (€20 per person) and mountain-bike rentals (€12 to €18 per day).

Near El Chorro is Bobastro, the hilltop redoubt of the 9th-century rebel Omar ibn Hafsun, a sort of Islamic Robin Hood, who led a prolonged revolt against Cordoban rule. Ibn Hafsun at one stage controlled territory from Cartagena to the Strait of Gibraltar. From El Chorro village, follow the road up the far (western) side of the valley and after 3km take the signed Bobastro turn-off. Nearly 3km up here, an 'Iglesia Mozárabe' sign indicates a 500m path to the remains of a remarkable little Mozarabic church cut from the rock, the shape so blurred by time that it appears to have been shaped by the wind alone. It's thought that Ibn Hafsun converted from Islam to Christianity (thus becoming a Mozarab) before his death in 917 and was buried here. When Córdoba finally conquered Bobastro in 927, the poor chap's remains were taken for grisly posthumous crucifixion outside Córdoba's Mezquita. At the top of the hill, 2.5km further up the road and with unbelievable views, are faint traces of Ibn Hafsun's rectangular *alcázar* (Muslim-era fortress).

Rockfax publishes a comprehensive guidebook, *El Chorro* by Mark Glaister, featuring El Chorro and the surrounding crags – listing routes, grades and access information.

Sleeping & Eating

Complejo Turistico Rural La Garganta
TOP CHOICE
APARTMENTS €

(📞952 49 50 00; www.lagarganta.com; 2-/4-person apt €75/115; mains €12; P❄❅) The best option in El Chorro, this converted flour mill has beautifully decorated apartments and excellent food. Extra bonuses include a view-embellished outdoor pool with a mini-waterfall shower, and the raft of activities that can be organised in the vicinity.

Finca La Campana
HOSTEL, COTTAGES €

(📞952 11 20 19; www.el-chorro.com; dm €12, d €29, 2–8-person apt €42-96; ❄❅) More than just a great place to stay, with cottage-style accommodation in one of Andalucía's most stunning landscapes, this is also a club of like-minded adrenalin junkies, with a cult following to prove it. During the climbing season (October to March) the Finca is very busy, so book ahead. To get there follow signs from behind Apartamentos La Garganta.

🛈 Getting There & Away

Trains run to El Chorro from Málaga (€4.05, 45 minutes, two daily except Sunday and holidays), Ronda (€6.40, 70 minutes, one daily except Sunday and holidays) and Seville (€15.90, two hours, one daily). No buses run to El Chorro. Drivers can get there via Álora (south of El Chorro) or Ardales (west of El Chorro).

Ronda

POP 37,000 / ELEV 744M

Stamped in infamy in chapter 10 of the novel *For Whom the Bell Tolls*, Ronda attracts a predictable contingent of Ernest Hemingway buffs on the lookout for Papa-once-got-sloshed-in-here bars. But it's a sideshow to the real deal: a yawning chasm of a gorge, premier white-town status, and a bullfighting legacy enshrined in the tale of two pugnacious families – the Romeros and the Ordóñezes. Surrounded by glowering mountains, the settlement was once a favoured escape route for bandits, smugglers and – later on – rugged macho writers. These days, Costa del Sol day trippers make up the bulk of the body count, but stick around after the last bus has departed and you'll get a sense of the old mountain-inspired magic.

For most of the Islamic period, Ronda was the capital of an independent statelet, and its near-impregnable position kept it out of Christian hands until 1485.

🎯 Sights

Plaza de España & Puente Nuevo
SQUARE & BRIDGE

The majestic Puente Nuevo (New Bridge), spanning El Tajo from Plaza de España, the main square on the north side of the gorge, was completed in 1793. Folklore claims that its architect, Martín de Aldehuela, fell to his death while trying to engrave the date on the bridge's side. Chapter 10 of Hemingway's *For Whom the Bell Tolls* tells how, early in the Spanish Civil War, the 'fascists' of a small town were herded into the town hall before being clubbed and flailed by townspeople 'in the plaza on the top of the cliff above the river', then thrown over the cliff. The episode was based on real events in Ronda, though the perpetrators were from Málaga. The town hall is now a *parador*.

La Ciudad
OLD TOWN

The old Muslim town retains a typical medieval Islamic character of twisting narrow streets.

The first street to the left, after you cross the Puente Nuevo, leads down to the Casa del Rey Moro (Calle Santo Domingo 17). This romantically crumbling 18th-century house, supposedly built over the remains of an Islamic palace, is itself closed, but you can visit its clifftop gardens and descend the 200 dimly lit steps of La Mina (gardens & La Mina adult/child €4/2; ☉10am-7pm), an Islamic-era stairway cut inside the rock right down to the bottom of the gorge (take care!).

Back uphill, enjoy the views from Plaza María Auxiliadora. Nearby is Palacio de Mondragón (admission €3; ☉10am-7pm Mon-Fri, to 3pm Sat & Sun), now an engaging museum, built for Abomelic, the ruler of Ronda in 1314. Of its three courtyards, the Patio Mudéjar still preserves an Islamic character. A horseshoe arch leads into a small clifftop garden. Various displays draw you into prehistoric caves, with hilarious wax figures depicting early lifestyles.

A minute's walk southeast is Plaza Duquesa de Parcent, where the Iglesia de Santa María La Mayor (adult/senior/student €4/3/2; ☉10am-8pm Apr-Oct), as grand as a cathedral, stands on the site of Islamic Ronda's main mosque. The church's tower and the handsome galleries beside it date from Islamic times, and just inside the entrance is an arch, covered with Arabic inscriptions, which was the mosque's mihrab.

Nearby, the amusing Museo del Bandolero (Calle de Armiñán 65; admission €3; ☉10.30am-8pm Apr-Sep) is dedicated to the banditry for which central Andalucía was renowned during the 19th century. One dashing mannequin vaguely resembles Bryan Ferry, and there are plenty of striped blankets flung over shoulders, together with the tools of the bandit trade, and some of their spoils. The museum is wheelchair accessible.

Beside the museum, a long flight of cobbled steps leads down to an impressive stretch of La Ciudad's old walls. Follow the path down to the beautiful horseshoe arches of the 13th- and 14th-century Baños Árabes (Arab Baths; Hoyo San Miguel; admission €3, Sun free; ☉10am-7pm Mon-Fri, to 3pm Sat & Sun), the best-preserved baths on the whole Iberian Peninsula. From the northern side of the nearby Puente Viejo (1616) you can make your way back up to Plaza de España via a small park along the gorge's edge.

Plaza de Toros & Around   BULLRING
(☎952 87 41 32; Calle Virgen de la Paz; admission €6; ☉10am-8pm Apr-Sep) Ronda's elegant bullring is one of the oldest in Spain – it opened in 1785 – and has seen some of the most important events in bullfighting history. It was here, in the 18th and 19th centuries, that three generations of the Romero family – Francisco, Juan and Pedro – established the basics of modern bullfighting on foot. The bullring's museum is crammed with memorabilia, spectacular costumes and photos of famous fans including Hemingway and Orson Welles.

Vertiginous clifftop views open out from Paseo de Blas Infante, behind the Plaza de Toros, and the leafy Alameda del Tajo nearby.

Walks   WALKS
The tourist office publishes a series of brochures (€5) highlighting eight easy hikes around Ronda, all of which start in the town itself. Distances range from 2.5km to 9.1km and visit viewpoints, old hermitages and parks. One of the best is the 4.6km SL-A38, which starts at Plaza Campillos near the Palacio de Mondragón before tracking down below the gorge (for the classic bridge photo). After winding past some old mills, it loops back uphill into the New Town.

✶✶ Festivals & Events
During the first two weeks of September Ronda's Feria de Pedro Romero (an orgy of partying, including the important flamenco Festival de Cante Grande) takes place. It culminates in the Corridas Goyesca (bullfights in honour of legendary bullfighter Pedro Romero).

🛏 Sleeping
Hotel San Francisco   HOTEL €
(☎952 87 32 99; www.hotelsanfranciscoronda.com; Calle María Cabrera 18; s/d incl breakfast €38/60; ✳) This is possibly the best budget option in Ronda, offering a warm welcome. Once a hostal, it has been refurbished and upgraded to hotel, with facilities to match – including wheelchair access.

Hotel Alavera de los Baños   HOTEL €€
(☎952 87 91 43; www.alaveradelosbanos.com; Hoyo San Miguel; s/d incl breakfast €70/95; ✳☒) A magical hotel echoing the style of the Arab baths next door, this one-time tannery looks like it was decorated by a departing Moor, with a flower-filled patio and pool. The sultan-sized baths are carved from a

type of stucco, and their pink tinge is due to natural pigments. Get comfortable and don't move until your credit runs dry.

Jardín de la Muralla
HOTEL €€

(☎952 87 27 64; www.jardindelamuralla.com; Calle Espíritu Santo 13; s/d incl breakfast €85/95; P❄@☎) Relatively new on the hotel scene but actually dating from the Moorish era, this unique private house has a huge terraced garden overlooking the *serranía* (mountain region or highlands). Six rooms are bedizened with antiques but it's neither staid nor cluttered; rather the opposite. It's central and popular – book ahead.

Parador de Ronda
HOTEL €€€

(☎952 87 75 00; www.parador.es; Plaza de España; r €160-171; P❄@☎☎) Acres of shining marble and deep-cushioned furniture give this modern *parador* a certain appeal. The terrace is a wonderful place to drink in views of the gorge with your coffee or wine, especially at night.

Enfrente Arte
HOTEL €€

(☎952 87 90 88; www.enfrentearte.com; Calle Real 40; r incl breakfast & all drinks from €75-110; ❄@☎) Everything about this bohemianstyle hotel is vivid and fun, from the modernoriental decor clash to the rainbow colours and variety of the (superb) breakfast, to the quirky rooms. There's even a bright-green parakeet terrorising the white bunnies in the patio pet corner. Definitely different.

Hotel San Gabriel
HOTEL €€

(☎952 19 03 92; www.hotelsangabriel.com; Calle José M Holgado 19; r €82; ❄@☎) This charming, historic hotel with a country-house ambience is filled with antiques and photographs chronicling Ronda's history. There is a poetry collection and deep armchairs to read in, you can watch old movies in the miniature cinema, and your breakfast croissant comes from an artisan baker. This attention to detail extends to the elegant rooms.

Hotel Morales
HOTEL €

(☎952 87 15 38; www.hotelmorales.es; Calle de Sevilla 51; s/d €30/45; ❄) A small hotel with 18 pleasant rooms and thorough information on the town and nearby parks.

✖ Eating

Traditional Ronda food is hearty mountain fare that's big on stews, trout, game such as rabbit, partridge and quail, and, of course, oxtail. The largest concentration of restaurants are situated in the grid east of Plaza de España, though there are some less-heralded gems just south of the old town in the Barrio San Francisco.

⌐TOP⌐ Bodega San Francisco
CHOICE
TAPAS €€

(Calle Ruedo Alameda; raciones €6-10) Taking price, food quality, ambience and local-to-tourist ratio into account, this is the best eating joint in town – hands down. It's situated in the Barrio San Francisco just outside the old Carlos V gate and gets regular rave reviews from travellers who have sought it out.

Bar Restaurant Almocábar
ANDALUCIAN €€€

(☎952 87 59 77; Calle Ruedo Alameda 5; tapas €2, mains €12-20; ⊙1.30-5pm & 8pm-1am Wed-Mon, closed Aug; ✎) In the Barrio San Francisco a little off the tourist path, tiny Almocábar features inspired and exceptional cooking with a surprising range of vegetarian salads as well as classic fish and meat dishes. The salad with goat's cheese, walnuts, apples and mango purée is outstanding. Finish your meal with a tangerine sorbet that tastes like all the tangerines in the world concentrated into one shimmering scoop. Booking is advisable.

Nonno Peppe
ITALIAN €

(Calle Nueva 18; pasta dishes from €6) If you're on a long haul and need a break from tapas, you can't go wrong with the genuine Italian fare served up in this economical place run by a couple from Salerno near Naples. There's great *spaghetti alla vongole* (with clams), pesto and pizzas, along with homey Italian-style service.

Restaurante Tragabuches
MODERN SPANISH €€€

(☎952 19 02 91; Calle José Aparicio 1; mains €27-32; ⊙closed Mon) Sleek, modern Tragabuches is Ronda's poshest restaurant. Points for creativity are won for the venison and sweet potatoes and the pork trotters with squid and sunflower seeds.

Restaurante Pedro Romero
ANDALUCIAN €€€

(☎952 87 11 10; Calle Virgen de la Paz 18; mains €17.50-22; ⊙closed Sun & Mon dinner Jul & Aug) This celebrated eatery, dedicated to bullfighting, turns out classic Ronda dishes – a good place to try the famous oxtail dish, *rabo de toro*.

Chocolat
BREAKFAST, SNACKS €

(Carrera de Espinel 9; breakfasts from €2.20) A funky modern cafe where you can choose from a long list of teas, coffees, breakfasts and a boggling array of cakes and pastries. Prices are refreshingly reasonable.

☕ Drinking

In Calle Los Remedios you can stop for a cold *cerveza* (beer) at ever-popular **Taberna del Antonio** (Calle Los Remedios 22). Several ebullient cafes and restaurants spill out on pedestrianised Calle Nueva in the newer northern side of town.

Tetería Al Zahra   TEAROOM
(Calle Las Tiendas 17; teas from €3) This atmospheric, dark, typically Granadian tea house has sweet desserts, *shisha* pipes and silver teapots full of exotic brews.

☆ Entertainment

Círculo de Artistas   FLAMENCO TABLAO
(Plaza de Socorro; admission €25; ☉10pm Mon & Wed) Ronda's flamenco space is rather steep in price and low in authenticity. Shows run twice weekly.

ℹ Information

Banks and ATMs are mainly on Calle Virgen de la Paz and Plaza Carmen Abela.

Municipal tourist office (www.turismo deronda.es; Paseo de Blas Infante; ☉10am-7.30pm Mon-Fri May-Sep, 10.15am-2pm & 3.30-6.30pm Sat, Sun & holidays) Helpful and friendly staff with a wealth of information on the town and region.

Regional tourist office (www.andalucia.org; Plaza de España 1; ☉9am-7.30pm Mon-Fri May-Sep, 10am-2pm Sat)

Tintorería (Calle María Cabrera 14; ☉10am-1.30pm & 5-8pm Mon-Fri, 10am-1.30pm Sat) Laundry washed, dried and folded for €12 per bag.

Virtual System Informática (Calle Sevilla 46; ☉10am-2pm & 5-8.30pm Mon-Fri, 10.30am-1pm Sat) Internet terminals available here.

ℹ Getting There & Away

Bus

From the **bus station** (Plaza Concepción García Redondo 2), **Los Amarillos** (☎952 18 70 61) buses go to Málaga (€9.20, two hours, at least four daily), Grazalema (€2.47, 35 minutes, two daily) and Seville (€10.85, 2½ hours, three to six daily); **Comes** (☎952 87 19 92) has three or four buses daily to Arcos de la Frontera (€8.14, two hours), Jerez (€10.75, 2½ hours) and Cádiz (€13.85, 2½ hours); and **Portillo** (☎952 87 22 62) runs to Málaga (€10.21, 1½ hours, at least three daily) via Marbella.

Train

The **train station** (Avenida de Andalucía) is on the highly scenic Granada–Algeciras line. Trains run to/from Algeciras (€7.40 to €18.70, 1¾ hours, six daily), Granada (€13.50, 2½ hours, three daily) via Antequera, Córdoba (€31.50, 2½ hours, two daily) and Málaga (€9.75, two hours, one daily except Sunday). For Seville, change at Bobadilla or Antequera.

ℹ Getting Around

Minibuses operate every 30 minutes to Plaza de España from Avenida Martínez Astein, across the road from the train station.

Around Ronda

Ronda is more than just a destination in itself. Surrounded by beautiful mountains, it acts as an ideal launching pad for trips into the parks and white towns of Málaga and Cádiz provinces. Hire a car or, even better, a bike, and strike out in earnest. **Cycle Ronda** (☎952 87 78 14; www.cycleronda.com; Calle Serrato 3, Ronda) can loan you a good pair of wheels for €20 per day.

This area has many traditional houses converted into gorgeous rural accommodation. For information try Ronda's municipal tourist office or www.serraniaronda.org.

CUEVA DE LA PILETA

Palaeolithic paintings of horses, goats, fish and even a seal, dating from 20,000 to 25,000 years ago, are preserved in this large **cave** (☎952 16 73 43; www.cuevadela pilata.org; adult/student/child €8/5/5; ☉hourly tours 10am-1pm & 4-6pm), 20km southwest of Ronda. You'll be guided by kerosene lamp and one of the knowledgeable Bullón family from the farm in the valley below. A family member found the paintings in 1905. The Cueva de la Pileta is 250m (signposted) off the Benaoján–Cortes de la Frontera road, 4km from Benaoján. Guides speak a little English. If it's busy, you may have to wait, but you can phone ahead to book a particular time.

PARQUE NATURAL SIERRA DE LAS NIEVES

This precious area of rare natural diversity, a Unesco Biosphere Reserve, also has an unusual history of human endeavour. For hundreds of years before refrigeration, the snow sellers of the region would gather at the end of the winter to shovel tonnes of snow into containers and transport it to huge pits, where it was pressed and compacted to form ice, and tightly covered until summer. Mule teams would then transport huge blocks of ice into neighbouring towns, to sell at astronomical prices. Today, this 180-sq-km protected area, southeast of Ronda, offers some excellent walks. Torrecilla (1910m), the highest peak in the western half of Andalucía, is a five- to six-hour (return) walk from Área Recreativa Los Quejigales, which is 10km east by unpaved road from the A376 Ronda–San Pedro de Alcántara road.

Cerro de Hijar ([🖉]952 11 21 11; www.cerro dehijar.com/eng; Carretera del Balneario, Sierra de las Nieves; d €80; [P][❄][@][🌐][🏊]), just above the dazzling white village of Tolox and just within the park, sits at 650m above sea level. This tastefully decorated hotel is generous with its room sizes, decoration, sweeping views and the range of activities it cheerfully organises for guests, including mountain biking, guided walks and 4WD excursions.

Antequera

POP 43,000 / ELEV 575M

'*Y que salga el sol en Antequera*' ('And let the sun rise in Antequera') announced King Ferdinand I of Aragon when he stole the town back from the Moors in 1410. Rise it did, and rise it still does over a settlement embellished with 32 churches, two Bronze Age burial mounds, some of the region's best Mudéjar architecture, and a countryside covered in weird karstic land formations.

◎ Sights

Alcazaba & Around FORTRESS
The main approach to the **Alcazaba** (admission free; ◎10.30am-2pm & 4-6pm Tue-Fri, 10.30am-2pm Sat, 11.30am-2pm Sun) passes through the **Arco de los Gigantes**, built in 1585 and incorporating stones with Roman inscriptions. What remains of the Alcazaba affords great views. Just below it is the **Colegiata de Santa María la Mayor** (Plaza Santa María; ◎10am-2pm & 4.30-6.30pm Tue-Fri, 10.30am-2pm Sat, 11.30am-2pm Sun), a 16th-century church with a beautiful Renaissance facade.

Museo Municipal MUSEUM
(Plaza del Coso Viejo; tours €3; ◎10am-1.30pm & 4.30-6.30pm Tue-Fri, 10am-1.30pm Sat, 11am-1.30pm Sun) The pride of this museum is

Efebo, a beautiful 1.4m bronze Roman statue of a patrician's 'toy boy', unearthed near Antequera in the 1950s – one of the finest pieces of Roman sculpture found in Spain.

Iglesia del Carmen CHURCH
(Plaza del Carmen; admission €2; ◎10.30am-1.30pm & 4.30-6pm Tue-Fri, 11am-1.30pm Sat & Sun) Only the most jaded would fail to be impressed by this church and its marvellous 18th-century Churrigueresque *retablo*. Carved in red pine and in beautiful detail by Antequera's Antonio Primo, it is encrusted with angels, saints, popes and bishops who seem to fly through the air, so finely rendered are their garments.

Dolmen de Menga & Dolmen de Viera
FREE MEGALITHIC TOMBS
(◎9am-5.45pm Tue-Sat, 9.30am-2.15pm Sun) Some of Europe's largest megalithic tombs stand on the fringes of Antequera. These two are 1km from the city centre, on the road leading northeast to the A45. In about 2500 or 2000 BC the local folk managed to transport dozens of huge rocks from nearby hills to construct these earth-covered tombs for their chieftains. Menga is 25m long, 4m high and composed of 32 slabs, the largest weighing 180 tonnes. You can walk across the utterly modern marble courtyard to enter this simple yet powerful relic of an unimaginably distant past. It could have been built yesterday to house one of Andalucía's proliferating dance venues.

🛏 Sleeping & Eating

Hotel San Sebastián HOTEL
([🖉]952 84 42 39; Plaza de San Sebastián 5; s/d €25/40; [❄][@]) You can't get much more central than this smartly refurbished hotel. Its terrace is the best perch on the plaza to watch the evening *paseo*.

Hotel Coso Viejo HOTEL
([🖉]952 Calle Encarnación 9; www.hotelcoso viejo.es; s/d incl breakfast €50/65; [P][❄][@][🌐]) Rooms at this converted 17th-century neoclassical palace are set around a handsome patio with a fountain. There's also a pleasant cafeteria and restaurant.

Parador de Antequera HOTEL
([🖉]952 84 02 61; www.parador.es; Paseo García del Olmo; s/d €95/118; [P][❄][🌐][🏊]) In a quiet area north of the bullring, this ultramodern hotel is set amid pleasant gardens with wonderful views.

TOP CHOICE **Restaurant La Espuela**

MODERN SPANISH

(📞952 70 30 31; Calle San Agustín 1; mains €12-21; ⊙closed Mon) In a quiet cul-de-sac off Calle Infante Don Fernando, this place plays background jazz and offers a fine selection of Anterqueran specialities, some of which are prepared by smartly attired waiters-cum-cooks in front of your eyes.

Restaurante Plaza de Toros

TRADITIONAL ANDALUCIAN

(Paseo María Cristina; mains €12-22; ⊙closed Sun pm) Traditional food in a unique setting right inside the bullring.

🛈 Information

Tourist office (www.antequera.es; Plaza de San Sebastián 7; ⊙11am-2pm & 5-8pm Mon-Sat, to 2pm Sun)

🛈 Getting There & Away

The **bus station** (Paseo Garcí de Olmo) is 1km north of the city centre. At least 12 daily buses run to/from Málaga (€5, one hour), and three to five each to/from Osuna (€6.50, one hour), Seville (Prado de San Sebastián; €12, two hours), Granada (€7.55, 1¼ hours) and Córdoba (€8.25, 1½ hours). The ticket offices shut down completely between 2pm and 5pm.

The **train station** (Avenida de la Estación) is 1.5km north of the city centre. Two to four trains a day travel to/from Granada (€19.90, 1½ hours), Seville (€29.40, 1¾ hours) and Ronda (€16.10, 1¼ hours). For Málaga or Córdoba, change at Bobadilla.

El Torcal

Sixteen kilometres south of Antequera, nature has sculpted this 1336m mountain into some of the weirdest, most wonderful rock formations you'll see anywhere. Its 12 sq km of gnarled, pillared and deeply fissured limestone began life as seabed about 150 million years ago.

Two marked walking trails, the 1.5km 'Ruta Verde' (Green Route) and the 3km 'Ruta Amarilla' (Yellow Route), start and end near the information centre.

East of Málaga

The coast east of Málaga, sometimes called the Costa del Sol Oriental, is less developed than the coast to the west, although there's an unnerving feeling that the bulldozers are never too far away.

Behind the coast, **La Axarquía**, a region dotted with white villages (of Islamic origin) linked by snaking mountain roads, climbs to the sierras along the border of Granada province. There's good walking here (best in April and May, and from mid-September to late October). Once impoverished and forgotten, La Axarquía has experienced a surge of tourism and an influx of expat residents in recent years.

NERJA
POP 16,500

Nerja, 56km east of Málaga, is where the Costa del Sol becomes a little easier on the eye, with more precipitous topography and prettier vistas allowing a peek into the Spain that once was. Though locals like to distance themselves from the gaudy resorts further west, Nerja has been similarly inundated by (mainly British) tourists in recent years. Those seeking solitude might want to look elsewhere.

The town's pièce de résistance, right in the centre, is the spectacular **Balcón de Europa**, a palm-shaded walkway that protrudes out into the ocean.

🛏 Sleeping & Eating

Rooms in the better hotels get booked up well in advance for the summer period.

Hotel Carabeo HOTEL €€

(📞952 52 54 44; www.hotelcarabeo.com; Calle Carabeo 34; d/ste incl breakfast €75/110; P ❋ @ ☲) This small hotel is the result of a sympathetic restoration of an old schoolhouse. The seven chic rooms are named after local coves and the well-tended gardens sit right on the cliff edge. Its **Restaurante 34** (mains €17.50-25.50; ⊙closed Nov-Apr) offers delicious and exotic food combinations in lovely seating alcoves in a stunning setting overlooking the sea.

Hotel Balcón de Europa HOTEL €€

(📞952 52 08 00; www.hotelbalconeuropa. com; Paseo Balcón de Europa 1; s/d €82/115; P ❋ @ ☲) Stealing the position of best digs in town, this terraced hotel with private room balconies overlooks a snug section of beach lapped by the translucent Mediterranean. A pool, sauna, piano bar and restaurant with a view all add value.

Hostal Marissal HOTEL €

(📞952 52 01 99; www.hostalmarissal.com; Balcón de Europa; s/d €45/60; ❋ @) Right by the Balcón de Europa, the Marissal delights with its soothingly clean, quiet and comfortable rooms decked with tasteful art, and a good restaurant. This is hotel accommodation at hostel prices.

Merendero Ayo　　　　SEAFOOD €€
(Playa Burriana; mains €9-13) One of the best feeds in town can be had at this always-busy open-air restaurant on Nerja's best beach. You can down a plate of paella, cooked on the spot in great sizzling pans, then go back for a refill.

Casa Luque　　　　MEDITERRANEAN €€€
(☎952 52 10 04; www.casaluque.com; Plaza Cavana 2; mains €15-21; ⊙closed Sun lunch & Wed) Casa Luque has a wonderfully panoramic terrace and, with an elegant haute-Med menu, more character than most Nerja eateries. The interior, with its high ceilings, is a cool and classy refuge from the ever-bustling streets.

❶ Information

Tourist office (www.nerja.org; Puerta del Mar; ⊙10am-2pm & 6-10pm Mon-Sat, 10am-2pm Sun May-Oct) Just off the Balcón de Europa promenade and lookout point, which has gorgeous coastal vistas.

❶ Getting There & Away

From the N340 near the top of Calle Pintada, **Alsina Graells** (☎952 52 15 04) runs to Málaga (€3.86, one hour, 14 daily), Almuñécar (€2.50, 25 minutes, up to 13 daily), Almería (€12.15, 2½ hours, nine daily) and Granada (€9.20, 1½ hours, two to three daily).

AROUND NERJA

The big tourist attraction is the Cueva de Nerja (☎952 52 95 20; www.cuevaden erja.es; adult/child €8.50/4.50; ⊙10am-2pm & 4-6.30pm, to 7.30pm Jul & Aug), just off the N340, 3km east of town on the slopes of the Sierra Almijara. This enormous cavern remains impressive, like some vast underground cathedral, 225 million years in the making. Large-scale performances including ballet and flamenco are staged there throughout the summer. About 14 buses run daily from Málaga and Nerja, except Sunday. The whole site is very well organised for large-scale tourism and has a huge restaurant and car park. A full tour of the caves takes about 45 minutes.

Further east the coast becomes more rugged, and with your own wheels you can head out to Playa El Cañuelo and other scenic, if stony, beaches down tracks from the N340, about 8km to 10km from Nerja.

CÓMPETA & AROUND
POP 3500 / ELEV 640M

The hill village of Cómpeta, 17km inland, is a popular base for exploring La Axarquía and the mountains, although it's in danger of being overwhelmed by heavy construction traffic and estate agents as the *costa* building boom spreads uncontrollably up the inland valleys. It is very popular with summer home owners from northern Europe, with a sizeable Danish community.

◉ Sights & Activities

A few kilometres down the valley from Cómpeta, Árchez has a beautiful Almohad minaret next to its church. From Árchez a road winds 8km southwest to Arenas, where a steep but driveable track climbs to the ruined Islamic Castillo de Bentomiz, which crowns a hilltop. Los Caballos del Mosquín (☎608 658108; www.horseriding-andalucia.com), just outside Canillas de Albaida, 2km northwest of Cómpeta, offers horse rides in the mountains lasting from one hour (€30) to three days (€565). An exhilarating long walk is up the dramatically peaked El Lucero (1779m), from whose summit, on a clear day, you can see both Granada and Morocco. This is a demanding full-day return walk from Cómpeta, but it's possible to drive as far up as Puerto Blanquillo pass (1200m) via a slightly hairy mountain track from Canillas de Albaida. From Puerto Blanquillo a path climbs 200m to another pass, the Puerto de Cómpeta. One kilometre down from there, past a quarry, the summit path (1½ hours), marked by a signboard, diverges to the right across a stream bed.

🛏 Sleeping & Eating

You can book houses, apartments and rooms through Cómpeta Direct (www.com petadirect.com).

The two best restaurants, both serving excellent and varied Spanish/international food, are El Pilón (www.elpiloncompeta.com; Calle Laberinto; mains €11-18.50; ⊙8pm-midnight) and Cortijo Paco (Avenida Canillas 6; mains €10-15; ⊙8pm-midnight, closed Mon). In summer ask for an upstairs terrace table at either place.

Hotel Balcón de Cómpeta　　　HOTEL €€
(☎952 55 35 35; www.hotel-competa.com; Calle San Antonio 75; s/d €51/73; P❄≋) Cómpeta's only hotel has comfortable rooms with balconies, a good restaurant, a bar, a big pool and a tennis court. Staff are friendly and helpful and speak good English. It's also wheelchair accessible.

Information

Tourist office (Avenida de la Constitución; ⏱10am-2pm & 3-6pm Wed-Sun, Tue-Sat Jul-Sep) By the bus stop at the foot of the village.

Getting There & Away

Three or four buses run daily from Málaga (€3.50, two hours) via Torre del Mar.

CÓRDOBA PROVINCE

Ascending over the Sierra Morena from La Mancha, the window into northern Andalucía is Córdoba province, a largely rural area renowned for its olive oil, wine and historic Roman-founded city that at its zenith was the capital of Al-Andalus and home to the glittering court of Abd ar-Rahman III.

Córdoba

POP 306,000 / ELEV 110M

Picture a city 500,000 strong embellished with fine architecture and fuelled by a prosperous and diverse economy. Picture universities and libraries filled with erudite artists and wise philosophers. Picture an Islamic caliphate more advanced and civilised than anything else the world had ever known. Picture Córdoba c AD 975.

OK, so this slightly grainy image may be over 1000 years old now, but enough of ancient Córdoba remains to place it in the contemporary top three drawcards of Andalucia. The centrepiece is the gigantic Mezquita, an architectural anomaly and one of the only places in the world where you can worship Mass in a mosque. Surrounding it is an intricate web of winding streets, geranium-sprouting flower boxes and cool intimate patios that are at their most beguiling in late spring.

History

The Roman colony of Corduba, founded in 152 BC, became capital of Baetica province, covering most of today's Andalucía. In 711 Córdoba fell to Muslim invaders and became the Islamic capital on the Iberian Peninsula. It was here in 756 that Abd ar-Rahman I set himself up as emir of Al-Andalus.

Córdoba's heyday came under Abd ar-Rahman III (912–61). The biggest city in Western Europe had dazzling mosques, libraries, observatories and aqueducts, a university and highly skilled artisans in leather, metal, textiles and glazed tiles. And the multicultural court was frequented by Jewish, Arab and Christian scholars.

Towards the end of the 10th century, Al-Mansour (Almanzor), a fearsome general, took the reins of power and struck terror into Christian Spain with over 50 *razzias* (forays) in 20 years. But after his death bands of Berber troops terrorised Córdoba and the caliphate descended into anarchy.

Córdoba's intellectual traditions, however, lived on. Twelfth-century Córdoba produced two of the most celebrated of all Al-Andalus scholars: the Muslim Averroës (Ibn Rushd) and the Jewish Maimonides. These polymaths are best remembered for their philosophical efforts to harmonise religious faith with reason.

In 1236 Córdoba was captured by Fernando III of Castilla and became a provincial town of shrinking importance. The decline began to be reversed only with the arrival of industry in the late 19th century. In common with other Andalucian cities in recent years, the culture, artefacts and traditions of Al-Andalus have enjoyed a growing revival of scholarly and popular interest.

Córdoba, along with 14 other Spanish cities (including Málaga), is aspiring to be the 2016 European Capital of Culture. You can check the campaign's status at www.cordoba2016.es.

Sights & Activities

Opening hours for Córdoba's sights change frequently, so check with the tourist offices for updated times. Most places (except the Mezquita) close on Monday. Closing times are generally an hour or two earlier than summer.

TOP CHOICE **Mezquita** CHURCH, MOSQUE (adult/child €8/4, 8.30-10am Mon-Sat free; ⏱10am-7pm Mon-Sat Apr-Oct, 9-10.45am & 1.30-6.30pm Sun year-round) Founded in 785, Córdoba's gigantic mosque is an architectural hybrid that has experienced two big 'modern' changes: a 16th-century cathedral plonked right in the middle; and the closing of 19 once-important doorways, which would have filled the original Mezquita with light.

The main entrance is the **Puerta del Perdón**, a 14th-century Mudéjar gateway on Calle Cardenal Herrero, with the ticket office immediately inside. Beside the Puerta del Perdón is a 16th- and 17th- century tower built around the remains of the Mezquita's minaret. Inside the gateway is the aptly named **Patio de los Naranjos** (Courtyard

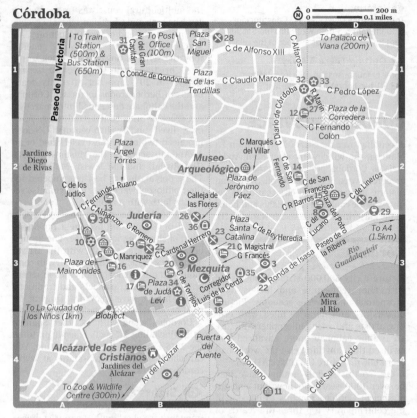

of the Orange Trees), originally the mosque's ablutions courtyard, from which a door leads inside the prayer hall itself.

From this door you can see straight ahead to the mihrab, the prayer niche in a mosque's kiblah (the wall indicating the direction of Mecca) that is the focus of prayer. The first 12 transverse aisles inside the entrance, a forest of pillars and arches, comprise the original **8th-century mosque**. The columns support two tiers of arches, necessary to give the building sufficient height and maintain its sense of openness.

In the centre of the building is the Christian cathedral. Just past the cathedral's western end, the approach to the mihrab begins, marked by heavier, more-elaborate arches. Immediately in front of the mihrab is the **maksura**, the royal prayer enclosure (today enclosed by railings) with its intricately interwoven arches and lavishly decorated domes created by Caliph Al-Hakam II in the 960s. The decoration of the **mihrab portal** incorporates 1600kg of gold mosaic cubes, a gift from the Christian emperor of Byzantium, Nicephoras II Phocas. The mosaics give this part of the Mezquita the aura of a Byzantine church.

After the Christians captured Córdoba, the Mezquita was used as a church. In the 16th century the centre of the building was torn out to allow construction of a cathedral comprising the **Capilla Mayor**, now adorned with a rich 17th-century jasper and marble *retablo,* and the **coro** (choir), with fine 18th-century carved mahogany stalls.

Judería NEIGHBOURHOOD

Jews were among the most dynamic and prominent citizens of Islamic Córdoba. The medieval *judería,* extending northwest from the Mezquita almost to Avenida del Gran Capitán, is today a maze of narrow streets and whitewashed buildings with flowery window boxes.

◎ Top Sights
Alcázar de los Reyes Cristianos................... B4
Judería B3
Mezquita B3
Museo Arqueológico C2

◎ Sights
1 Casa Andalusí A3
2 Casa de Sefarad A3
3 Hammam Baños Árabes........................ C3
4 Islamic Water Wheel.............................. B4
   Museo de Bellas Artes.................. (see 5)
5 Museo Julio Romero de
   Torres D2
6 Museo Taurino A3
7 Patio de los Naranjos B3
8 Posada del Potro D2
9 Puerta del Perdón................................... B3
10 Sinagoga A3
11 Torre de la Calahorra C4

◎ Sleeping
12 Casa de Los Azulejos C1
13 Hostal el Reposo de Bagdad................ A2
14 Hostal La Fuente.................................... C2
15 Hotel Maestre D2
16 Hotel Amistad Córdoba B3
17 Hotel González.. B3

18 Hotel Hacienda Posada de
   Vallina... C3
19 Hotel Lola... B3
20 Hotel Maimonides B3
21 Hotel Mezquita... C3

◎ Eating
22 Amaltea... C3
23 Bar Santos.. C3
24 Bodega Campos.. D2
25 Casa Pepe de la Judería B3
26 Mesón de las Flores................................ B3
27 Taberna Salinas.. D1
28 Taberna San Miguel El Pisto................. C1

◎ Drinking
29 Amapola... D2
30 Bodega Guzmán.. A3

◎ Entertainment
31 Gran Teatro de Córdoba....................... B1
32 Jazz Café.. C1
33 Mesón La Bulería..................................... D1
34 Tablao Cardenal...................................... B3

◎ Shopping
35 Ghadamés... C3
36 Meryan.. B3

The beautiful little 14th-century **Sinagoga** (Calle de los Judíos 20; adult/EU citizen €0.30/free; ☺9.30am-2pm & 3.30-5.30pm Tue-Sat, to 1.30pm Sun & holidays) is one of only three surviving medieval synagogues in Spain and the only one in Andalucía. In the late 1400s it became a hospital for hydrophobics. Translated Hebrew inscriptions eroded in mid-sentence seem like poignant echoes of a silenced society. The **Casa Andalusí** (Calle de los Judíos 12; admission €2.50; ☺10.30am-8.30pm, to 6.30pm Nov-Mar) is a 12th-century house furnished with objects from Córdoba's medieval Islamic culture and a Roman mosaic.

In the heart of the *judería,* and once connected by an underground tunnel to the Sinagoga, is the 14th-century **Casa de Sefarad** (www.casadesefarad.es; admission €4; ☺10am-6pm Mon-Sat, 11am-2pm Sun). Opened in 2008 on the corner of Calles de los Judíos and Averroes, this small, beautiful museum is devoted to reviving interest in the Sephardic-Judaic-Spanish tradition. There is a refreshing focus on music, do-

mestic traditions and on the women intellectuals (poets, singers and thinkers) of Al-Andalus. A specialist library of Sephardic history is housed here, and there's also a well-stocked shop. A program of live music recitals and storytelling events runs most of the year.

Nearby, the **Museo Taurino** (Bullfighting Museum; ☎957 20 10 56; Plaza de Maimónides) was being renovated at the time of writing.

Alcázar de los Reyes Cristianos CASTLE (Campo Santo de Los Mártires; adult/child €4/2, Fri free; ☺10am-2pm & 5.30-7.30pm Tue-Sat May-Jun & Sep–mid-Oct, 8.30am-2.30pm Tue-Sat Jul-Aug, 9.30am-2.30pm Sun & holidays year-round) Just southwest of the Mezquita, the Alcázar, or Castle of the Christian Monarchs, began as a palace and fort for Alfonso X in the 13th century. From 1490 to 1821 the Inquisition operated from here. Today the castle's gardens are among the most beautiful in Andalucía. The building houses an old royal bathhouse, the Baños Califales. Take time to gaze at the 3rd-century Roman sarcophagus, with its reflections on life and death.

Mezquita

A TIMELINE

AD 600 Foundation of the Christian Visigothic church of St Vincent on the site of the present Mezquita.

AD 785 Salvaging Visigoth and Roman ruins, Emir Abd ar-Rahman I converts the Mezquita into a mosque.

AD 822-5 Mosque enlarged in reign of Abd-ar-Rahman II.

AD 912-961 A new minaret is ordered by Abd ar-Rahman III.

AD 961-6 Mosque enlarged by Al-Hakam II who also enriches the mihrab **1**.

AD 987 Mosque enlarged for the last time by Al-Mansur Ibn Abi Aamir. With the addition of the Patio de los Naranjos **2**, the building reaches its current dimensions.

1236 Mosque reconverted into a Christian church after Córdoba is recaptured by Ferdinand III of Castile.

1271 Instead of destroying the mosque, the overawed Christians elect to modify it. Alfonso X orders the construction of the Capilla de Villaviciosa **3** and Capilla Real **4**.

1300s Original minaret is replaced by the baroque Torre del Alminar **5**.

1520s A Renaissance-style cathedral nave **6** is added by Charles V. 'I have destroyed something unique to the world' he laments on seeing the finished work.

2004 Spanish Muslims petition to be able to worship in the Mezquita again. The Vatican doesn't consent.

TIPS BOX

» **Among the oranges** The Patio de los Naranjos can be enjoyed free of charge at any time.

» **Early birds** Entry to the rest of the Mezquita is offered free every morning except Sunday between 8.30am and 10am.

» **Quiet time** Group visits are prohibited before 10am meaning the building is quieter and more atmospheric in the early morning.

Capilla de Villaviciosa
Sift through the building's numerous chapels till you find this gem, an early Christian modification added in 1277 which fused existing Moorish features with Gothic arches and pillars. It served as the Capilla Mayor until the 1520s.

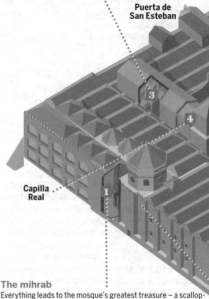

Puerta de San Esteban

Capilla Real

The mihrab
Everything leads to the mosque's greatest treasure – a scallop-shell-shaped prayer niche facing Mecca that was added in the 10th century. Cast your eyes over the gold mosaic cubes crafted by imported Byzantium sculptors.

The cathedral choir

Few ignore the impressive *coro* (choir): a late-Christian addition dating from the 1750s. Once you've admired the skilfully carved mahogany choir stalls depicting scenes from the bible, look up at the impressive baroque ceiling.

Torre del Alminar

This is the Mezquita's cheapest sight because you don't have to pay to see it. Rising 93m and viewable from much of the city, the baroque-style bell tower was built over the mosque's original minaret.

The Mezquita arches

No, you're not hallucinating. The Mezquita's most defining characteristic is its unique terracotta-and-white striped arches that support 856 pillars salvaged from Roman and Visigoth ruins. Glimpsed through the dull light they're at once spooky and striking.

Puerta del Perdón

Patio de los Naranjos

Abandon architectural preconceptions all ye who enter here. The ablutions area of the former mosque is a shady courtyard embellished with orange trees that acts as the Mezquita's main entry point.

Capilla Mayor

A Christian monument inside an Islamic mosque sounds beautifully ironic, yet here it is: a Gothic church commissioned by Charles V in the 16th century and planted in the middle of the world's third largest mosque.

The maksura

Guiding you towards the mihrab, the maksura is a former royal enclosure where the caliphs and their retinues prayed. Its lavish, elaborate arches were designed to draw the eye of worshippers towards the mihrab and Mecca.

CÓRDOBA FOR CHILDREN

When you and the kids just don't want to look at old stones a moment longer, it's time to head a little way out of town and leave the past behind. Just southwest of Córdoba's city centre and adjoining the Zoo and Wildlife Centre (Avenida de Linneo; adult/child €4/2; ⊙10am-7pm Tue-Sun Apr & May, to 8pm Jun-Aug, to 7pm Sep), historic buildings morph into brightly coloured climbing equipment. Welcome to La Ciudad de los Niños (☑663 035709; Avenida Menéndez Pidal; admission free; ⊙10am-2pm & 7-11pm Jun–mid-Sep), Córdoba's City for Kids. A calendar of special events aimed at four- to 12-year-olds runs throughout the summer – check the website for details, or ask at the regional tourist office. Buses 2 and 5 (heading to Hospital Reina Sofía) from the city centre stop here.

Puente Romano & Around   ROMAN BRIDGE

The much-restored Puente Romano (Roman Bridge) crosses the Guadalquivir just south of the Mezquita. Not far downstream, near the northern bank, is a restored Islamic water wheel.

At the southern end of the bridge is the Torre de la Calahorra (☑957 29 39 29; Puente Romano; adult/child €4.50/3; ⊙10am-6pm), a 14th-century tower with the curious Roger Garaudy Museum of the Three Cultures highlighting the intellectual achievements of Islamic Córdoba.

Plaza del Potro   SQUARE

This pedestrianised plaza, 400m northeast of the Mezquita, was a celebrated hang-out for traders and adventurers in the 16th and 17th centuries. Miguel de Cervantes lived for a while in the Posada del Potro (Plaza del Potro 10; admission free; ⊙5-9pm Tue-Fri, 10am-2pm Sat), then an inn (which he described in *Don Quijote* as a 'den of thieves') and today a more respectable exhibition hall.

A former hospital houses what is, surprisingly enough, Córdoba's most visited museum, the Museo Julio Romero de Torres (Plaza del Potro 1; admission €4, Fri free; ⊙2.30-8.30pm Tue, 9am-8.30pm Wed-Sat, to 2.30pm Sun & holidays), devoted to revered local painter Julio Romero de Torres

(1873–1930). Romero de Torres specialised in sensual yet sympathetic portraits of Cordoban women. In the same building is the Museo de Bellas Artes (Fine Arts Museum; adult/EU citizen €1.50/free; ⊙2.30-8.30pm Tue, 9am-8.30pm Wed-Sat, to 2.30pm Sun & holidays), which exhibits Cordoban artists' work from the 14th to the 20th century.

Hammam Baños Árabes   HAMMAM

(☑957 48 47 46; www.hammamspain.com/cordoba; Calle Corregidor Luis de la Cerda 51; bath €26, bath & massage €33; ⊙2hr sessions at 10am, noon, 2pm, 4pm, 6pm, 8pm & 10pm) Follow the lead of the medieval Cordobans and dip your toe in these beautifully renovated Arab baths, where you can enjoy an aromatherapy massage, with tea, hookah and Arabic sweets in the cafe afterwards.

Palacio de Viana   MUSEUM

(☑957 49 67 41; Plaza de Don Gome 2; admission whole house/patios only €6/3; ⊙10am-1pm & 4-6pm Mon Fri, 10am-1pm Sat) Córdoba is famous for its patios and nowhere are they better exhibited than in this Renaissance palace with a dozen tranquil courtyards, a formal garden and a gilded house (with guided tours). It's 500m north of the Plaza de la Corredera. Opening times are extended in July and August.

Museo Arqueológico   MUSEUM

(Plaza de Jerónimo Páez 7; adult/EU citizen €1.50/free; ⊙3-8pm Tue, 9am-8pm Wed-Sat, to 3pm Sun & holidays) Córdoba's excellent archaeological museum provides a real insight into pre-Islamic Córdoba in the suitably historic setting of a Renaissance palace. The upstairs is devoted to medieval Córdoba.

Festivals & Events

Spring and early summer are the chief festival times for Córdoba.

Concurso & Festival de Patios Cordobeses   PATIOS

(Early May) A 'best patio' competition with many private patios open for public viewing; there's also a concurrent cultural program.

Feria de Mayo   SPRING FAIR

(Last week of May/first days of June) Ten days of party time for Córdoba, with a giant fair, concerts and bullfights.

Festival Internacional de Guitarra   MUSIC

(Late June/early July) Two-week celebration of the guitar, with live classical, flamenco, rock, blues and more; top names play in the Alcázar gardens at night.

Semana Santa   HOLY WEEK
Every evening during Holy Week, between around 8pm and midnight, up to 12 processions accompany their *pasos* on an official route through the city. Processions peak between 4am and 6am on Good Friday.

🛏 Sleeping
There is plenty of budget accommodation in Córdoba (though finding single rooms for a decent price is not easy). Booking ahead is wise from March to October and essential during the main festivals.

🔝 Hotel Hacienda Posada de Vallina   HOTEL €€
(📞957 49 87 50; www.hhposadadevallinacordoba.com; Corregidor Luís de la Cerda 83; s/d €50/70; P 🌼 @ 🛜) In an enviable nook on the quiet side of the Mezquita (the building actually pre-dates it), this cleverly renovated hotel uses portraits and period furniture to enhance a plush and modern interior. There are two levels overlooking a salubrious patio and the rooms make you feel comfortable but in-period (ie medieval Córdoba). Columbus allegedly once stayed here.

Hotel Amistad Córdoba   HOTEL €€€
(📞957 42 03 35; www.nh-hoteles.com; Plaza de Maimónides 3; s/d €125; P 🌼 @ 🛜) Occupying two 18th-century mansions with original Mudéjar patios, the Amistad is part of the modern NH chain, with elegant rooms and all the requisite luxury hotel facilities including babysitting. Although it was closed at the time of research, renovations will have been completed by the time you read this.

Hostal La Fuente   HOTEL €
(📞957 48 78 27; www.hostallafuente.com; Calle de San Fernando 51; s/d €35/50; 🌼@🛜) A journeyman hotel, though in Córdoba this means you get an airy patio, azulejos tiles, exposed brick and interesting architectural details. The rooms are clean and comfortable and the staff quietly helpful. There's some street noise, but it all adds to the brew.

Hotel Maimonides   HOTEL €€
(📞957 47 15 00; Calle de Torrijos 4; r from €65; P 🌼 @) As close as you can get to the Mezquita without actually sleeping in it, the Maimonides has a businesslike sheen inside, meaning it's not quite as deep and meaningful as its philosopher-inspired name suggests. Nonetheless, it has clean, competent facilities,

a coffee and gift shop, minibars, newspapers and that all-important hairdryer.

Hotel Mezquita   HOTEL €€
(📞957 47 55 85; hotelmezquita.com; Plaza Santa Catalina 1; s/d €42/74; 🌼) One of the best-value places in town, this hotel is right opposite the Mezquita itself. The 16th-century mansion has sparkling bathrooms and elegant rooms, some with views of the great mosque across the street.

Casa de los Azulejos   HOTEL €€
(📞957 47 00 00; www.casadelosazulejos.com; Calle Fernando Colón 5; s/d €90/110; 🌼@) Andalucía meets Mexico in this stylish hotel, where the patio is all banana trees, fluffy ferns and tall palms. The rooms are in a colonial style, and there's a good Mexican restaurant downstairs.

Hotel Lola   HOTEL €€
(📞957 20 03 05; www.hotelconencantolola.com; Calle Romero 3; d incl breakfast €119; P 🌼🛜) A quirky hotel with large antique beds and full of smaller items that you just wish you could take home. You can eat your breakfast on the roof terrace overlooking the Mezquita bell tower.

Hotel Maestre   HOTEL €
(📞957 47 24 10; www.hotelmaestre.com; Calle Romero Barros 4; s/d €38/52, apt €58; P 🌼@) This place has comfortably furnished rooms with all the mod cons, although bathrooms are grudging of both space and supplies. The reception staff speak some English.

Hotel González   HOTEL €€
(📞957 47 98 19; www.hotel-gonzalez.com; Calle Manríquez 3; s/d €40/70; 🌼@🛜) Rich baroque decor lends a graciousness to this well-priced hotel. The restaurant is set in the pretty flower-filled patio and the friendly proprietors speak fluent English.

Hostal El Reposo de Bagdad   HOTEL €
(📞957 20 28 54; Calle Fernández Ruano 11; s/d €30/45) Hidden in a tiny street in the *judería,* this 200-year-old house feels thrillingly Moorish. The rooms are simple but clean.

🍴 Eating
Córdoba has its share of signature food including *salmorejo,* a very thick tomato-based gazpacho (cold vegetable soup), and *rabo de toro* (oxtail). Some restaurants feature recipes from Al-Andalus, such as garlic soup with raisins, honeyed lamb, or meat stuffed

with dates and nuts. The local tipple is wine from the nearby regions of Montilla and Moriles, similar to sherry but unfortified.

There are lots of places to eat right by the Mezquita, but beware inflated prices and uninspired food.

TOP CHOICE Taberna San Miguel El Pisto

TAPAS €€

(Plaza San Miguel 1; tapas €3, media-raciones €5-10; ⊘closed Sun & Aug) Stand aside Seville. Fine wine, great atmosphere, professional old-school waiters, zero pretension, and a clamorous yet handsome decor, make El Pisto (the Barrel) a Cordoban and Andalucian tapas classic. You can squeeze in at the bar or grab a jug of wine and grab a table out back.

Bodega Campos

ANDALUCIAN €€€

(✆957 49 75 00; Calle de Lineros 32; tapas/raciones €6.50-16, mains €17.50-29; ⊘closed Sun dinner) This many-roomed, atmospheric winery-cum-restaurant offers one of the peak dining experiences in Córdoba. Corridors and rooms are lined with oak barrels, signed by the Spanish royal family and Tony Blair (gets around, does Tone), among other celebs, and the establishment offers its own house Montilla.

Mesón de las Flores

TAPAS €

(Calleja de las Flores; tapas €2-5, media raciones €5-10) Tucked up a *judería* side street and seemingly oblivious to the Mezquita hordes, Las Flores carries on as if Franco's tourism project never happened. Push in next to the festival crowd and enjoy some of the simplest but best tapas in town (the prawns are tremendous).

Taberna Salinas

TAPAS €

(Calle Tundidores 3; tapas/raciones €2.50/8; ⊘closed Sun & Aug) Dating back to 1879, this large patio restaurant fills up fast. Try the delicious aubergines with honey or potatoes with garlic. The tavern side is quieter in the early evening, and the friendly bar staff will fill your glass with local Montilla whenever you look thirsty.

Casa Pepe de la Judería

ANDALUCIAN €€€

(✆957 20 07 44; Calle Romero 1; tapas/media raciones €2.50-9.50, mains €11-18, menús €27) A great roof-terrace with views of the Mezquita and a labyrinth of busy dining rooms. Down a complimentary glass of Montilla before launching into the house specials, including Cordoban oxtails or venison fillets.

Bar Santos

TORTILLAS €

(Calle Magistral González Francés 3; tortillas €2.50) The legendary Santos serves the biggest *tortilla de patata* (potato and onion omelette) in town – eaten with plastic forks on paper plates, while gazing at the Mezquita. Don't miss it.

Amaltea

INTERNATIONAL, VEGETARIAN €€

(Ronda de Isasa 10; mains €8-16; ⊘closed Mon & Sun pm; ✐) Possibly Córdoba's best vegetarian-friendly place (although the meat's also good), with a strong emphasis on organic produce (try the Lebanese-style tabouli). It's down by the river.

Drinking & Entertainment

Córdoba's liveliest bars are mostly scattered around the newer parts of town and ignite around 11pm to midnight at weekends. Most bars in the medieval centre close around midnight.

Amapola

BAR

(Paseo de la Ribera 9; ⊘9am-3pm Mon-Fri, 5pm-4am Sat & Sun) This is where the young and beautiful lounge on green leather sofas and consume elaborate cocktails. DJs spin until the small hours.

Bodega Guzmán

BAR, PUB

(Calle de los Judíos 7) Don't miss this atmospheric old-city favourite, with Montilla from the barrel.

FREE Jazz Café

BAR

(Calle Espartería; ⊘8am-late) This fabulous, cavernous bar full of black-and-white jazz photos puts on regular live jazz and jam sessions. It's also a good place for an early-morning (8am) hangover cure.

Gran Teatro de Córdoba

THEATRE

(✆957 48 02 37; www.teatrocordoba.com, in Spanish; Avenida del Gran Capitán 3) This theatre hosts a busy program of concerts, theatre, dance and film, mostly geared to popular Spanish tastes.

FLAMENCO

Córdoba has two regular flamenco spots.

Tablao Cardenal

FLAMENCO VENUE

(Calle de Torrijos 10; admission incl drink €20; ⊘10.30pm-late Mon-Sat) In an old building opposite the Mezquita, this place offers a variable mix of music and dance in a firm tourist setting.

Mesón La Bulería

FLAMENCO VENUE

(Calle Pedro López 3; admission incl drink €12) Slightly less known and more edgy (and

MEDINA AZAHARA

Even in the cicada-shrill heat and stillness of a summer afternoon, the Medina Aza-hara (Madinat al-Zahra; ☑957 32 91 30; adult/EU citizen €1.50/free; ☉10am-6.30pm Tue-Sat, to 8.30pm May–mid-Sep, to 2pm Sun) whispers of the power and vision of its founder, Abd ar-Rahman III. The self-proclaimed caliph began the construction of a magnificent new capital 8km west of Córdoba around 936, and took up full residence around 945. Medina Azahara was a resounding declaration of his status, a magnificent trapping of power.

The new capital was amazingly short-lived. Between 1010 and 1013, during the caliphate's collapse, Medina Azahara was wrecked by Berber soldiers. Today, less than a tenth of it has been excavated, and only about a quarter of that is open to visitors.

The visitor route leads down to the Dar al-Wuzara (House of the Viziers), a substantial building with several horseshoe arches, fronted by a square garden, and on to the most impressive building, the painstakingly restored Salón de Abd ar-Rahman III, the caliph's throne hall, with delicate horseshoe arching framing elaborate gardens, and exquisitely carved stuccowork, of a lavishness hitherto unprecedented in the Islamic world.

Medina Azahara is signposted on Avenida de Medina Azahara, which leads west out of Córdoba onto the A431.

A taxi costs €37 for the return trip, with one hour to view the site, or you can book a three-hour coach tour for €6.50 to €10 through many Córdoba hotels.

cheaper) than Tablao Cardenal; 10.30pm performances kick off nightly.

🛍 Shopping

Córdoba is known for its *cuero repujado* (embossed leather) goods, silver jewellery (particularly filigree) and attractive pottery. Craft shops congregate around the Mezquita. Meryan (Calleja de las Flores) is good for quality embossed leather, although it's factory-produced (on a relatively small scale).

Ghadamés   LEATHER GOODS
(www.cuerrosghadames.com; Corregidor Luis de la Cerda 52; ☉10am-1pm & 5.30-8pm, to 1pm Apr-Sep) This is the workshop of Rafael Varo, one of a handful of dedicated craftsmen reviving the lost art of *guadamecíes*, a technique invented in Córdoba during the 13th century for curing leather so that intricate designs can be painted, engraved or inlaid on it. Pieces start at around €200.

ℹ Information

Most banks and ATMs are around Plaza de las Tendillas and Avenida del Gran Capitán. The bus and train stations have ATMs.

Ch@t (Calle Claudio Marcelo 15; per hr €1.80; ☉9.30am-1.30pm & 5.30-8.30pm Apr-Oct, 10am-1.30pm Sat) Many terminals and efficient internet access (although no internet access for Macs).

Hospital Reina Sofia (☑957 21 70 00; Avenida de Menéndez Pidal) Located 1.5km southwest of the Mezquita.

Municipal tourist office (Plaza de Judá Levi; ☉8.30am-2.30pm Mon-Fri)

Policía Nacional (☑95 747 75 00; Avenida Doctor Fleming 2)

Post office (Calle José Cruz Conde 15)

Regional tourist office (☑957 35 51 79; Calle de Torrijos 10; ☉9am-7.30pm Mon-Fri, 9.30am-3pm Sat, Sun & holidays) Facing the western side of the Mezquita, this helpful office offers information on the city and surrounding countryside.

ℹ Getting There & Away

Bus

The **bus station** (Glorieta de las Tres Culturas) is 1km northwest of Plaza de las Tendillas, behind the train station. Destinations include Seville (€10.36, 1¾ hours, six daily), Granada (€12.52, 2½ hours, seven daily), Málaga (€12.75, 2¾ hours, five daily) and Baeza (€10, three hours, one daily).

Train

Córdoba's **train station** (Avenida de América) is on the high-speed AVE line between Madrid and Seville. Rail destinations include Seville (€10.60 to €32.10, 40 to 90 minutes, 23 or more daily), Madrid (€52 to €66.30, 1¾ to 6¼ hours, 23 or more daily), Málaga (€21 to €39.60, one hour to 2½ hours, nine daily), Barcelona (€59.40 to €133, 10½ hours, four daily) and Jaén (€11.45, 1½ hours, one daily). For Granada (€34.30, four hours), change at Bobadilla.

ℹ️ Getting Around

Bus 3 (€1.20), from the street between the train and bus stations, runs to Plaza de las Tendillas and down Calle de San Fernando, east of the Mezquita. For the return trip, you can pick it up on Ronda de Isasa, just south of the Mezquita.

Taxis from the bus or train station to the Mezquita cost around €6.

For drivers, Córdoba's one-way system is nightmarish, but routes to many hotels and *hostales* are fairly well signposted with a 'P' if they have parking. Hotels charge about €12 to €18 per day for parking.

Blobject (☑957 76 00 33; www.blobject.es; Avenida Dr Fleming; from €30 for 1st 2hr) is an American-made Gem electric car (top speed around 32km/h). Equipped with GPS technology and a USB port for plugging in flash-drive information in your chosen European language, the jaunty, rounded Blobject is a safe, environmentally friendly and fun way to see, hear and smell this city of flowers. Blobjects for one, two or four passengers can be collected and returned to several major tourist sites around the city. Ask at a tourist information office for details of routes. The same company is experimenting with the strange-but-cute Segway, an electrical scooter controlled by leaning movements of the driver, with full training and safety helmets provided before setting off.

GRANADA PROVINCE

Who goes to Granada province without first visiting the eponymous city? But once you've paid your respects to Lorca, the Albayzín, and the foppish ghosts of the Alhambra, there's a whole different world waiting on the sidelines. Much of it is rugged and mountainous. Granada is home to the mainland's highest mountain peaks (the Sierra Nevada) and its only ski station, while on the range's southern flanks lies the sleeping beauty of the valleys of Las Alpujarras, sprinkled with snaking footpaths and time-stood-still white villages. Granada's coastline, the Costa Tropical, is centred on salt-of-the-earth Almuñécar, an evocative but little-visited Spanish seaside town.

Granada

POP 300,000 / ELEV 685M

Boabdil the Moor wasn't the last departing traveller to shed a farewell tear for Granada, a city of sun-bleached streets and parched earth interspersed with soothing splashes of green, including the woods and gardens that embellish the sultry Alhambra. For those who dig deeper, Granada hides a more elusive allure. This is a place to put down your guidebook and let your intuition lead the way – through mysterious labyrinthine streets and shady Moroccan *teterías,* under-the-radar flamenco experiences and the *duende*-stoked cocoon of the Albayzín.

What keeps Granada interesting is its lack of any straightforwardness. Here stands a traditionally conservative city sprinkled with counterculture bohemians, a place where modern graffiti has been sprayed provocatively onto 500-year-old walls. Make no mistake, you'll fall in love here, but you won't always be able to work out why; best idea – don't bother. Instead, immerse yourself in the splendour, and leave the poetic stanzas to the aesthetes. 'Your elegy, Granada, is spoken by the stars which from the heavens perforate your black heart', wrote Federico García Lorca, Granada's most famous man of letters. It's the perfect coda.

History

Granada's history reads like a thriller. Granada began life as an Iberian settlement in the Albayzín district. Muslim forces took over from the Visigoths in 711, with the aid of the Jewish community around the foot of the Alhambra hill in what was called Garnata al Jahud, from which the name Granada derives; *granada* also happens to be Spanish for pomegranate, the fruit on the city's coat of arms.

After the fall of Córdoba (1236) and Seville (1248), Muslims sought refuge in Granada, where Mohammed ibn Yusuf ibn Nasr had set up an independent emirate. Stretching from the Strait of Gibraltar to east of Almería, this 'Nasrid' emirate became the final remnant of Al-Andalus, ruled from the increasingly lavish Alhambra palace for 250 years. Granada became one of the richest cities in medieval Europe.

However, in the 15th century the economy stagnated and violent rivalry developed over the succession. One faction supported the emir, Abu al-Hasan, and his harem favourite Zoraya. The other faction backed Boabdil, Abu al-Hasan's son by his wife Aixa. In 1482 Boabdil rebelled, setting off a confused civil war. The Christian armies invading the emirate took advantage, besieging towns and devastating the countryside, and in 1491 they finally laid siege to Granada. After eight months, Boabdil agreed to surrender the city in return for the Alpujarras and 30,000 gold coins, plus political and religious freedom for his subjects. On 2 January 1492 the conquering Catholic Monarchs, Ferdinand and Isabella, entered Granada ceremonially in Muslim dress. They set up court in the Alhambra for several years.

Jews and Muslims were steadily persecuted, and both groups had been expelled by the 17th century. Granada sank into a deep decline until the Romantics revived interest in its Islamic heritage during the 1830s, when tourism took hold.

When the Nationalists took over Granada at the start of the civil war, an estimated 4000 *granadinos* (residents of Granada) with left or liberal connections were killed, among them Federico García Lorca. Granada has a reputation for political conservatism.

◉ Sights & Activities

Most major sights are within walking distance of the city centre, though there are buses to save you walking uphill.

TOP CHOICE **Alhambra** PALACE COMPLEX
(Map p754; ☏902 441221; advance ticket purchase: www.alhambra-tickets.es & www.servicaixa.com; adult/EU senior & EU student €12/9, Generalife only €6; ⊗8.30am-8pm 16 Mar–31 Oct, closed 25 Dec & 1 Jan) Stretched along the top of the hill known as La Sabika, the Alhambra is the stuff of fairy tales. From outside, its red fortress towers and walls appear plain, if imposing, rising from woods of cypress and elm, with the Sierra Nevada forming a magnificent backdrop.

Try to visit first thing in the morning (8.30am) or late in the afternoon to avoid the crowds, or treat yourself to a magical night by visiting the Palacio Nazaríes.

The Alhambra contains two outstanding sets of buildings: the Palacio Nazaríes and the Alcazaba (Citadel). Also within its walls you'll find the Palacio de Carlos V, the Iglesia de Santa María de la Alhambra, two hotels, several bookshops and souvenir shops – as well as lovely gardens, including the supreme Generalife.

There are a couple of cafes by the ticket office, but only the two hotels offer full-scale meals.

The Alhambra, from the Arabic *al-qala'at al-hamra* (red castle), was a fortress from the 9th century. The 13th- and 14th-century Nasrid emirs converted it into a

fortress-palace complex adjoined by a small town (medina), of which only ruins remain. Yusuf I (1333–54) and Muhammad V (1354–59 and 1362–91) built the magnificent Palacio Nazaríes.

After the Christian conquest the Alhambra's mosque was replaced with a church and the Convento de San Francisco (now the Parador de Granada) was built. Carlos I, grandson of Ferdinand and Isabella, had a wing of the Palacio Nazaríes destroyed to make space for a huge Renaissance palace, the Palacio de Carlos V (using his title as Holy Roman Emperor).

In the 18th century the Alhambra was abandoned to thieves and beggars. During the Napoleonic occupation it was used as a barracks and narrowly escaped being blown up. In 1870 it was declared a national monument as a result of the huge interest stirred by Romantic writers such as Washington Irving, who wrote the entrancing *Tales of the Alhambra* in the Palacio Nazaríes during his brief stay in the 1820s. Since then the Alhambra has been salvaged and very heavily restored. Together with the Generalife gardens and the Albayzín, it now enjoys Unesco World Heritage status.

Alcazaba

The cross and banners of the Reconquista were raised here in January 1492. In the past the bell chimes of the main tower, the **Torre de la Vela**, controlled the irrigation system of Granada's fertile plain, the Vega.

Palacio Nazaríes

Full of mesmerising, symbolic, geometrical patterns, this is the Alhambra's true gem. Arabic inscriptions proliferate in the stuccowork.

The **Mexuar**, through which you normally enter the palace, dates from the 14th century and was used as a council chamber and antechamber for audiences with the emir. The public would have gone no further.

From the Mexuar you pass into the **Patio del Cuarto Dorado**, a courtyard where the emirs gave audiences, with the **Cuarto Dorado** (Golden Room) on the left. Opposite the Cuarto Dorado is the entrance to the Palacio de Comares through a beautiful facade of glazed tiles, stucco and carved wood.

Built for Emir Yusuf I, the **Palacio de Comares** served as a private residence for the ruler. It's built around the lovely **Patio de los Arrayanes** (Patio of the Myrtles)

Alhambra

A TIMELINE

900 The first reference to *al-qala'at al-hamra* (red castle) atop Granada's Sabika Hill.

1237 Founder of the Nasrid dynasty, Muhammad I, moves his court to Granada. Threatened by belligerent Christian armies he builds a new defensive fort, the Alcazaba **1**.

1302-09 Designed as a summer palace-cum-country estate for Granada's foppish rulers, the bucolic Generalife **2** is begun by Muhammad III.

1333-54 Yusuf I initiates the construction of the Palacio Nazaríes **3**, still considered the highpoint of Islamic culture in Europe.

1350-60 Up goes the Palacio de Comares **4** taking Nasrid lavishness to a whole new level.

1362-91 The second coming of Muhammad V ushers in even greater architectural brilliance exemplified by the construction of the Patio de los Leones **5**.

1527 The Christians add the Palacio de Carlos V **6**. Inspired Renaissance palace or incongruous crime against the Moorish art? You decide.

1829 The languishing, half-forgotten Alhambra is 'rediscovered' by American writer Washington Irving during a protracted sleep-over.

1954 The Generalife gardens are extended southwards to accommodate an outdoor theatre.

TIPS BOX

» **Queue-dodger** Reserve tickets in advance online at www.alhambra -tickets.es.

» **Money-saver** You can visit the general areas of the palace free of charge any time by entering through the Puerta de Justica.

» **Stay over** Two fine hotels are encased in the grounds: Parador de Granada (expensive) and Hotel América (more economical).

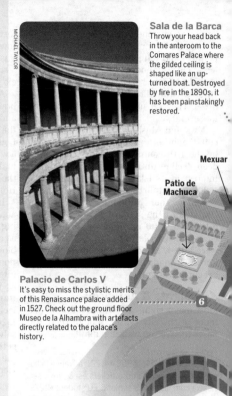

MICHAEL TAYLOR

Sala de la Barca
Throw your head back in the anteroom to the Comares Palace where the gilded ceiling is shaped like an up-turned boat. Destroyed by fire in the 1890s, it has been painstakingly restored.

Mexuar

Patio de Machuca

Palacio de Carlos V
It's easy to miss the stylistic merits of this Renaissance palace added in 1527. Check out the ground floor Museo de la Alhambra with artefacts directly related to the palace's history.

6

Palacio Nazaríes

3

Detail

Puerta de Justica

1

2

Alcazaba
Find time to explore the towers of the original citadel, the most important of which – the Torre de la Vela – takes you, via a winding staircase, to the Alhambra's best viewpoint.

DAVID TOMLINSON

Patio de Arrayanes
If only you could linger longer beside the rows of myrtle bushes (arrayanes) that border this calming rectangular pool. Shaded porticos with seven harmonious arches invite further contemplation.

Torre de Comares

4

Patio de Arrayanes

Palacio de Comares
The neck-ache continues in the largest room in the Comares Palace renowned for its rich geometric ceiling. A negotiating room for the emirs, the Salón de los Embajadores is a masterpiece of Moorish design.

Sala de Dos Hermanas
Focus on the dos hermanas: two marble slabs either side of the fountain, before enjoying the intricate cupola embellished with 5000 tiny moulded stalactites. Poetic calligraphy decorates the walls.

Baños Reales

Washington Irving Apartments

5

Jardín de Lindaraja

Sala de los Abencerrajes

Palacio del Partal

Jardines del Partal

Patio de los Leones
Count the 12 lions sculpted from marble holding up a gurgling fountain. Then pan back and take in the delicate columns and arches built to signify an Islamic vision of paradise.

Generalife
A coda to most people's visits, the 'architect's garden' is no afterthought. While Nasrid in origin, the horticulture is relatively new: the pools and arcades were added in the early 20th century.

ANDALUCÍA GRANADA PROVINCE

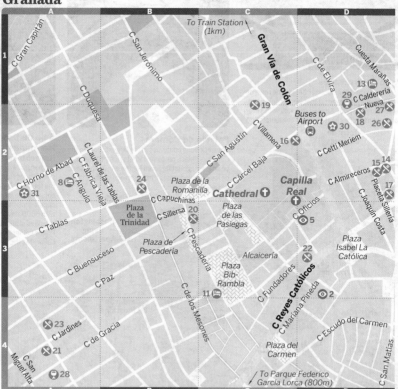

with its rectangular pool. The southern end of the patio is overshadowed by the walls of the Palacio de Carlos V. Inside the northern **Torre de Comares** (Comares Tower), the **Sala de la Barca** (Hall of the Blessing), with a beautiful wooden ceiling, leads into the **Salón de los Embajadores** (Ambassador's Hall), where the emirs would have conducted negotiations with Christian emissaries. This room's marvellous domed marquetry ceiling contains more than 8000 cedar pieces in a pattern of stars representing the seven heavens of Islam.

The Patio de los Arrayanes leads into the **Palacio de los Leones** (Palace of the Lions), built under Muhammad V – by some accounts as the royal harem. The palace rooms surround the famous **Patio de los Leones** (Lion Courtyard), with its marble fountain channelling water through the mouths of 12 marble lions. The palace symbolises the Islamic paradise, which is divided into four parts by rivers (represented by water channels meeting at the fountain). Of the four halls around the patio, the southern **Sala de los Abencerrajes** is the legendary site of the murders of the noble Abencerraj family, whose leader, the story goes, dared to dally with Zoraya, Abu al-Hasan's favourite. At the eastern end of the patio is the **Sala de los Reyes** (Hall of the Kings), with leather-lined ceilings painted by 14th-century Christian artists. The name comes from the painting on the central alcove, thought to depict 10 Nasrid emirs. On the northern side of the patio is the richly decorated **Sala de Dos Hermanas** (Hall of Two Sisters), probably named after the slabs of white marble at either side of its fountain. It features a fantastic *muqarnas* dome with a central star and 5000 tiny cells, reminiscent of the constellations. This may have been the room of the emir's favourite paramour. At its far end is the **Sala**

of Islamic artefacts from the Alhambra, Granada province and Córdoba, with explanatory texts in English and Spanish.

Upstairs, the **Museo de Bellas Artes** (958 22 48 43; adult/EU citizen €1.50/free; 2.30-8pm Tue, 9am-8pm Wed-Sat, 9am-2.30pm Sun & holidays Mar-Oct) is worth a visit for its impressive collection of Granada-related paintings and sculptures.

Other Christian Buildings

The **Iglesia de Santa María** was built between 1581 and 1617 on the site of the former palace mosque. The **Convento de San Francisco**, now the Parador de Granada hotel (p756), was erected over an Islamic palace. Isabella and Ferdinand were buried in the patio before being transferred to the Capilla Real.

Generalife

Within the palace of the 'Architect's Garden', the **Patio de la Acequia** (Court of the Water Channel) has a long pool framed by flower beds and 19th-century fountains, whose shapes sensuously echo the arched porticos at each end. Off this patio is the **Jardín de la Sultana** (Sultana's Garden), with the trunk of a 700-year-old cypress tree, where Abu al-Hasan supposedly caught his lover, Zoraya, with the head of the Abencerraj clan, leading to the murders in the Sala de los Abencerrajes.

Realejo   NEIGHBOURHOOD
The Realejo lies below the Alhambra hill to the south. Its beautiful homes are enhanced by the **Carmen de los Martires** (Paseo de los Martires; admission free; 10am-2pm & 4-8pm Jun-Sep Mon-Fri) Romantically dishevelled 19th-century gardens and a restored mansion much in use for posh weddings reside on the site of the splendidly named Convent of the Discalced (barefoot) Carmelites.

Capilla Real   CHAPEL, MAUSOLEUM
(Map p750; www.capillareal.granada.com; Calle Oficios; admission €3.50; 10.30am-1.30pm & 4-7.30pm Mon-Sat, 11am-1.30pm & 4-7pm Sun Apr-Oct) The **Royal Chapel**, adjoining the cathedral, is Granada's outstanding Christian building. Catholic Monarchs Isabella and Ferdinand commissioned this elaborate Isabelline-Gothic-style mausoleum. It was not completed until 1521, hence their temporary interment in the Convento de San Francisco.

The monarchs lie in simple lead coffins in the crypt beneath their marble monuments in the chancel, which is enclosed

de los Ajimeces, with low-slung windows through which the favoured lady could look over the Albayzín and countryside while reclining on ottomans and cushions.

From the Sala de Dos Hermanas a passage leads through the **Estancias del Emperador** (Emperor's Chambers), built for Carlos I in the 1520s, some of them later used by Washington Irving. From here, descend to the **Patio de la Reja** (Patio of the Grille) and **Patio de Lindaraja** and emerge into the **Palacio del Partal**, an area of terraced gardens. Leave the Partal gardens by a gate facing the Palacio de Carlos V, or continue along a path to the Generalife.

Palacio de Carlos V

This imposing building is square but contains a surprising circular, two-tiered courtyard with 32 columns.

On the ground floor, the **Museo de la Alhambra** (958 22 75 27; admission free; 9am-2.30pm Tue-Sat) has an absorbing collection by a stunning gilded wrought-iron screen created in 1520 by Bartolomé de Jaén. The sacristy contains a small but impressive museum with Ferdinand's sword and Isabella's sceptre, silver crown and personal art collection, which is mainly Flemish but also includes Botticelli's *Prayer in the Garden of Olives*. Felipe de Vigarni's two fine early-16th-century statues of the Catholic Monarchs at prayer are also here.

Just opposite is La Madraza (Map p750; admission free; ☉8am-10pm), founded in 1349 by Sultan Yusuf I as a school and university. You can gaze into the splendid prayer hall with its elaborate mihrab where the light here has a special mellow quality. The building was closed for renovations at the time of writing.

Catedral   CATHEDRAL
(Map p750; admission €3.50; ☉10.45am-1.30pm & 4-8pm Mon-Sat, 4-8pm Sun, to 7pm Nov-Mar) Adjoining the Capilla Real but entered separately from Gran Vía de Colón, the cavernous Gothic-Renaissance cathedral was begun in 1521 and directed by Diego de Siloé from 1528 to 1563. Work was not completed until the 18th century. The main facade on Plaza de las Pasiegas, with four heavy buttresses forming three great arched bays, was designed in the 17th century by Alonso Cano.

Alcaicería & Plaza Bib-Rambla   SQUARE
Just south of the Capilla Real, the Alcaicería was the Muslim silk exchange, but what you see now is a restoration after a 19th-century fire, filled with tourist shops. Just southwest of the Alcaicería is the large and picturesque Plaza Bib-Rambla. Nearby, the handsome, horseshoe-arched 14th-century Corral del Carbon (Map p750; Calle Mariana Pineda) was once an inn for coal dealers (hence its modern name, meaning Coal Yard). It houses a government-run crafts shop, Artespaña (p759).

Albayzín   NEIGHBOURHOOD
On the hill facing the Alhambra across the Darro valley, Granada's old Muslim quarter, the Albayzín, is an open-air museum in which you can lose yourself for a whole morning. The cobblestone streets are lined with gorgeous *cármenes* (large mansions

with walled gardens, from the Arabic *karm* for garden). It survived as the Muslim quarter for several decades after the Christian conquest in 1492.

Plaza del Salvador, near the top of the Albayzín, is dominated by the Colegiata del Salvador (admission €0.75; ⊕10.30am-1pm & 4.30pm-7.30pm Mon-Sat), a 16th-century church on the site of the Albayzín's main mosque; the mosque's horseshoe-arched patio, cool and peaceful, survives at its western end.

The Arco de las Pesas, off Plaza Larga, is an impressive gateway in the Albayzín's 11th-century defensive wall. If you follow Callejón de San Cecilio from here you'll end up at the Mirador San Nicolás, the Albayzín's premier (and perennially crowded) lookout, with unbeatable views of the Alhambra and Sierra Nevada. Come back here with the world and his wife for sunset, but beware of skilful, well-organised wallet-lifters and bag-snatchers.

Just east of Mirador San Nicolás, off Cuesta de las Cabras, the Albayzín's first new mosque in 500 years, the Mezquita Mayor de Granada (⊕gardens 11am-2pm & 6-9.30pm), has been built to serve modern Granada's growing Muslim population.

Another well-placed lookout is the Placeta de San Miguel Bajo, with its lively cafe-restaurants. Close to this square off Callejón del Gallo and down a short lane is the 15th-century Palacio de Dar-al-Horra (Callejón de las Monjas; admission free; ⊕10am-2pm Mon-Fri), a romantically dishevelled mini-Alhambra that was home to the mother of Boabdil, Granada's last Muslim ruler.

Downhill from Placeta de San Miguel Bajo you'll find the lovely Alminar de San José (Map p750) in Calle San José, a minaret that survives from an 11th-century mosque. Calle San José meets the top of Calle Calderería Nueva, a narrow street famous for its *teterías*, but also a good place to shop for slippers, hookahs, jewellery and North African pottery from an eclectic cache of shops redolent of a Moroccan souk.

Buses 31 and 32 both run circular routes from Plaza Nueva around the Albayzín about every seven to nine minutes from 7.30am to 11pm.

Plaza de Santa Ana   SQUARE

Plaza Nueva extends northeast into Plaza de Santa Ana, where the Iglesia de Santa Ana (Map p750) incorporates a mosque's minaret in its bell tower. Along narrow Carrera del Darro is the 11th-century Muslim bathhouse, the Baños Árabes El Bañuelo (Carrera del Darro 31; admission free; ⊕10am-2pm Tue-Sat). Further along is the Museo Arqueológico (Carrera del Darro 43; adult/EU citizen €1.50/free; ⊕2.30-8.30pm Tue, 9.30am-8.30pm Wed-Sat, to 2.30pm Sun), displaying finds from Granada province.

ALHAMBRA ADMISSION

Some areas of the Alhambra can be visited at any time without a ticket, but the highlight areas can be entered only with a ticket. Up to 6600 tickets are available for each day. About one third of these are sold at the ticket office on the day, but they sell out early and you need to start queuing by 7am to be reasonably sure of getting one.

It's highly advisable to book in advance (€1 extra per ticket). You can book up to three months ahead in two ways:

Alhambra Advance Booking (☎902 88 80 01 for national calls, 0034 934 92 37 50 for international calls; www.alhambra-tickets.es; ⊕8am-9pm)

Servicaixa (www.servicaixa.com) Online booking in Spanish and English. You can also buy tickets in advance from Servicaixa cash machines, but only in the Alhambra grounds (⊕8am-7pm Mar-Oct, 8am-5pm Nov-Feb).

For internet or phone bookings you need a Visa card, MasterCard or Eurocard. You receive a reference number, which you must show, along with your passport, national identity card or credit card, at the Alhambra ticket office when you pick up the ticket on the day of your visit.

The Palacio Nazaríes is also open for night visits (⊕10-11.30pm Tue-Sat Mar-Oct). Tickets cost the same as daytime tickets: the ticket office opens 30 minutes before the palace's opening time, closing 30 minutes after it. You can book ahead for night visits in the same ways as for day visits.

Alhambra & Generalife

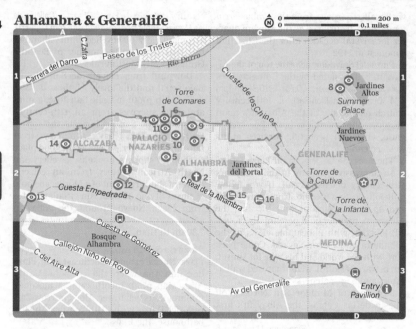

Alhambra & Generalife

TOP CHOICE **Hammams de Al-Andalus** HAMMAM
(☎902 33 33 34; www.granada.ham
mamspain.com; Calle Santa Ana 16; bath/bath &
massage €21/30) A long way from the back-
slapping, skin-stretching hammams of Fez
and Marrakech, Granada's best bathhouse
nonetheless feels a shade more exotic than
your stress-absorbing shopping-mall spa
back home. Relent to Alhambra-like luxury
in dimly lit underground pools as you sip
mint tea and imagine you're Alec Guinness
in *Lawrence of Arabia*. Advance reservations and bathing costumes are mandatory.

Monasterio de San Jerónimo MONASTERY
(Calle Rector López Argueta 9; admission €3.50;
⊙10am-2pm & 4-7.30pm Apr-Oct) This 16th-
century monastery, 500m west of the cathedral, is the burial place of El Gran Capitán
(the Great Captain), Gonzalo Fernández de
Córdoba, the military right-hand man of
the Catholic Monarchs. It's a treat for fans
of Gothic and Renaissance architecture and
stone carving. The formal gardens are as
beautiful in winter as in summer.

Monasterio de La Cartuja MONASTERY
(Paseo de la Cartuja; admission €3.50; ⊙10am-
1pm & 4-8pm Apr-Oct) Another architectural
gem stands 2km northwest of the city
centre, reached by bus 8 from Gran Vía de

Colón. La Cartuja Monastery was built between the 16th and 18th centuries and features a church bursting with gold, marble and sculptures and an exuberantly baroque sacristy.

TOP CHOICE **Huerta de San Vicente** MUSEUM
(958 25 84 66; Calle Virgen Blanca; admission €3; ⊙guided tours 10.15am, 11am, 11.45am, 12.30pm, 5.15pm, 6pm, 6.45pm, 7.30pm) This house where Federico García Lorca spent summers and wrote some of his best-known works is only 1.5km south of the city centre, but still retains the evocative aura of an early-20th-century country villa. Today the modern but handsome Parque Federico García Lorca separates it from whizzing traffic.

To get there, head 700m down Calle de las Recogidas from Puerta Real, turn right along Calle del Arabial, then take the first left into Calle Virgen Blanca.

🐎 Courses

Granada is a great place to study Spanish. It also has several Spanish dance schools. The provincial tourist office has lists of schools, or check out www.granadaspanish.org and www.spanishcourses.info.

Escuela Carmen de las Cuevas
SPANISH LANGUAGE
(958 22 10 62; www.carmencuevas.com; Cuesta de los Chinos 15, Albayzín) This private school attracts students from as far away as the USA, and no wonder. The passion and enthusiasm of staff and students is extraordinary. The school teaches Spanish language and culture, and flamenco dance and guitar from beginners to advanced. A two-week intensive language course (40 hours) costs €330.

Centro de Lenguas Modernas
SPANISH LANGUAGE
(Modern Languages Centre; 958 21 56 60; www.clm-granada.com; Placeta del Hospicio Viejo) Granada University's modern-language department offers a variety of popular Spanish-language courses, at all levels, starting from 10 days (40 hours of classes) for €381.

👉 Tours

Granada Tapas Tours FOOD TOURS
(619 444984; www.granadatapastours.com) Friendly and fluent in both Scots and Spanish, your guide will steer you to independently chosen favourite bars for drinks, tapas and information about the city, starting at around €65 for two, including drinks and tapas.

City Sightseeing Granada BUS TOURS
(902 10 10 81) Operates Granada's double-decker city tour bus, with 20 stops at the main sights. Hop on and off where you like; the ticket (€16) is valid for 24 hours.

🎊 Festivals & Events

Semana Santa HOLY WEEK
This and the Feria de Corpus Christi are the big two. Benches are set up in Plaza del Carmen to view the Semana Santa processions.

Día de la Cruz RELIGIOUS
(Day of the Cross) Squares, patios and balconies are adorned with floral crosses (the Cruces de Mayo) and become the setting for typical *andaluz* revelry on 3 May.

Feria de Corpus Christi SPRING FAIR
(Corpus Christi Fair) Fairgrounds, bullfights, more drinking and *sevillanas*. Next celebrated 23 June 2011, 7 June 2012, 30 May 2013.

Festival Internacional de Música y Danza MUSIC, DANCE
(www.granadafestival.org) Running for 2½ weeks from late June to early July, this festival features mainly classical performances, some free, many in historic locations. Explore the website early as popular performances are sold out very quickly.

🛏 Sleeping

Granada's strong Moorish bent is reflected in its hotels, many of which have taken old medieval mansions and converted them into Moroccan-style riads. Most of these establishments reside in the Albayzín quarter. Equally beguiling are Granada's handful of restored *cármenes*.

As in all Andalucian cities, it's worthwhile booking ahead during Semana Santa and Christmas.

TOP CHOICE **Casa Morisca Hotel**
HISTORIC HOTEL €€€
(958 22 11 00; www.hotelcasamorisca.com; Cuesta de la Victoria 9; d interior/exterior €118/148; ❄@🖿) With its 14 Alhambra-esque rooms occupying a gorgeous late-15th-century Albayzín mansion, the Morisca could easily compete with the finest of Marrakech's riads. Everything is arranged around an atmospheric patio with an ornamental pool and overlooking wooden

GRANADA FOR CHILDREN

With four buildings and eight interactive exhibition areas, Granada's popular **Parque de las Ciencias** (☑958 13 19 00; www.parqueciencias.com; Avenida del Mediterráneo; adult/under 18yr €6/5; ⏱10am-7pm Tue-Sat, 10am-3pm Sun & holidays) should keep the kids happily absorbed for hours. Playing giant chess or threading the Plant Labyrinth are just two activities they can do here. It's about 900m south of the centre, near the Palacio de Congresos conference centre.

If even less intellectual exertion is called for, then **Parque Federico García Lorca** (p761) offers refreshing, flat open space for both children and parents. The park abounds in broad paved paths and is also a great place to study *granadinos* at leisure.

---

galleries. The pinnacle: an exquisite Mirador suite, affording views of the great palace itself.

Carmen de la Alcubilla   HISTORIC HOTEL €€
(☑958 21 55 51; www.alcubilladelcaracol.com; Aire Alta 12; s/d €100/120; ✳@✈) Tranquil Granadian beauty, this time perched on the Realejo hill in a restored *cármene* with a terraced garden overflowing with jasmine and lemon trees. The house is (almost refreshingly) light on antiques, but the views of the Sierra Nevada are stunning and the service flawless.

Parador de Granada   HISTORIC HOTEL €€€
(Map p754; ☑958 22 14 40; www.parador.es; Calle Real de la Alhambra; r €315; P✳@✈) The most expensive *parador* in Spain can't be beaten for its location within the walls of the Alhambra and its historical connections (it was a former convent). Live like a Nasrid king, for one night at least. Book ahead.

Palacio de Los Patos   BOUTIQUE HOTEL €€€
(☑902 29 22 93; www.ac-hotels.com; Solarillo de Gracia 1; r from €200; P✳@✈✈) As if all the rest wasn't enough, Granada hits five stars with this inspired fusion of neoclassical traditionalism and modern-industrial. The hotel's princely price tag brings you a spa, a snazzy restaurant, lush gardens, a pool, numerous fancy soaps and a red carnation

on your bed when you return for an afternoon siesta.

Hotel Guadalupe   HOTEL €€
(☑958 22 34 23; www.hotelguadalupe.es; Avenida Los Alixares; s/d €75/92; P✳✈✈) Almost on the Alhambra's doorstep, Guadalupe has a bright atmosphere. Rooms are subdued and elegant in shades of pumpkin and cream, with Alhambra or olive-grove views. Prices dive out of season.

Hotel Zaguán del Darro   HISTORIC HOTEL €€
(Map p750; ☑958 21 57 30; www.hotelzaguan. com; Carrera del Darro; s €55; r €95; ✳@✈). Here you get the classic location (right at the foot of the Alhambra hill) and a creeping history (a restored 16th-century house) without the usual Granada boutique prices. Snap it up!

Hostal Molinos   HOTEL €
(☑958 22 73 67; www.hotelmolinos.es; Calle Molinos 12; s/d/tr €29/32/45; ✈) Don't let the 'narrowest hotel in the world' moniker put you off (and yes, it actually is – and has a certificate from the *Guinness Book of Records* to prove it), there's plenty of breathing space in Molino's nine rooms, and warm hospitality in its information-stacked lobby. Situated at the foot of the Realejo, it makes an economical central option.

Oasis Backpackers' Hostel   HOSTEL €
(Map p750; ☑958 21 58 48; www.oasisgranada. com; Placeta Correo Viejo 3; dm/d €18/40; ✳@✈) Bohemian digs in a bohemian quarter, Oasis is seconds away from the *teterías* and bars on Calle Elvira. There's free internet access, a rooftop terrace and personal safes. As backpacker hostels go, it's a gem.

Camping Sierra Nevada   CAMPING GROUND €
(☑958 15 00 62; www.campingsierranevada.com; Avenida de Madrid 107; sites per adult/child/tent €5.95/5.05/5.95; ✳) Close to the bus station, 2.5km northwest of the centre, this camping ground is big, jolly and well run. Bathrooms are plain and clean, and there is a laundrette, supermarket and kids play area. Gates close at midnight and reopen at 7am. Bus 3 runs between here and the centre.

Hotel Carmen de Santa Inés
    HISTORIC HOTEL €€
(Map p750; ☑958 22 63 80; www.carmensan taines.com; Placeta de Porras 7; s/d €85/95, r with sitting room €140; ✳) This Moorish-era house, extended in the 16th and 17th centuries, offers a lovely breakfast patio

in a garden of full of myrtles, fruit trees and fountains.

Hotel Casa del Capitel Nazarí
HISTORIC HOTEL **€€**
(Map p750; ☑958 21 52 60; www.hotelcasacapi tel.com; Cuesta Aceituneros 6; s/d €88/110; ❄@☎) More Albayzín magic in a 1503 Renaissance palace that's as much architectural history lesson as plush hotel. Rooms have Moroccan inflections and the courtyard hosts art exhibits.

Hotel América
HOTEL **€€**
(Map p754; ☑958 22 74 71; www.hotelameri cagranada.com; Calle Real de la Alhambra 53; d €81-116; ☺Mar-Nov; ❄@☎) Within the Alhambra grounds, the early-19th-century building creates a restful ambience in contrast to the busy Alhambra foot traffic. Reserve well in advance, as rooms are limited.

Hotel Los Tilos
HOTEL **€€**
(Map p750; ☑958 26 67 12; www.hotellostilos. com; Plaza Bib-Rambla 4; s/d/tr €50/80/90; ❄@☎) Recently restored and right in the heart of the city, Los Tilos is a reasonable if uninspiring central option with a roof terrace.

Puerta de las Granadas
HOTEL **€€**
(Map p754; ☑958 21 62 30; www.hotelpuert adelasgranadas.com; Calle Cuesta de Gomérez 14; d €104-170; ❄@☎) This 19th-century building, renovated in modern-minimalist style, has wooden shutters and elegant furnishings.

Hostal Landázuri
HOTEL **€**
(Map p750; ☑958 22 14 06; www.hostallanda zuri.com; Cuesta de Gomérez 24; s/d €36/45, s/d without bathroom €24/34, t €60, q €70; P€10) This homely place boasts a terrace with Alhambra views, a cafe and a helpful mother–daughter team.

Hostal Meridiano
HOTEL **€**
(Map p750; ☑958 25 05 44; www.hostalpen sionmeridiano.com; Calle Angulo 9; r €38, s/d without bathroom €17/27, d/tr with bathroom €40/60; P❄@) The energetic couple who run this hotel seem to genuinely like helping their guests.

Hostal La Ninfa
HOTEL **€€**
(☑958 22 79 85; www.hostallaninfa.net; Calle Campo del Príncipe; s/d €46/70; ❄☎) A rustic place covered inside and out with brightly painted ceramic stars and plates. It has clean, cosy rooms, friendly owners and an attractive breakfast room.

✖ Eating

Granada is one of the last bastions of that fantastic practice of free tapas with every drink, and some have an international flavour. There are also some good Moroccan and Middle Eastern restaurants, particularly in the Albayzín. There's a revived *granadino* trend for *teterías,* most of which serve light desserts – others offer fuller menus.

NEAR PLAZA NUEVA
Plaza Nueva is rimmed with restaurants most with alfresco seating. The more obvious places can be a little touristy. For the better nooks hunt around the backstreets or head up Carrera del Darro.

For fresh fruit and veg, head for the large covered **Mercado Central San Agustín** (Map p750; Calle San Agustín; ☺8am-2pm Mon-Sat), a block north of the cathedral.

Parador de Granada
INTERNATIONAL **€€€**
(Map p754; ☑958 22 14 40; Calle Real de la Alham bra; mains €19-22; ☺8am-11pm) Even a jaded, jilted, world-weary cynic would come over all romantic in this dreamy setting. The Spanish food has Moroccan and French inflections and it tastes all the better for being taken inside the Alhambra.

Bodegas Castañeda
TAPAS **€€**
(Map p750; Calle Almireceros; raciones from €6) An institution and reputedly the oldest bar in Granada, this kitchen whips up traditional food in a typical bodega setting. The free tapa of paella is almost enough for a light lunch. Get a table before 2pm as it gets very busy then. Sharing the same block but a little less authentic is **Antigua Castañeda** (Map p750; Calle de Elvira; raciones €8-16).

Café Lisboa
PASTRIES **€**
(Map p750; cnr Calle Reyes Catolicos & Plaza Nueva) The pastries here are huge.

ALBAYZÍN
The labyrinthine Albayzín holds a wealth of eateries all tucked away in the narrow streets. Calle Calderería Nueva is a fascinating muddle of *teterías,* leather shops and Arabic-influenced takeaways.

⌐TOP⌐ Restaurante Arrayanes
 CHOICE
MOROCCAN **€€**
(Map p750; ☑958 22 84 01; Cuesta Marañas 4; mains €8.50-19; ☺from 8pm) The best Moroccan food in a city that is well known for its Moorish throwbacks? Recline on lavish patterned seating, try the rich, fruity tagine

casseroles and make your decision. Note that Restaurante Arrayanes does not serve alcohol.

Samarkanda
LEBANESE €€
(Map p750; Calle Calderería Vieja 3; mains €12-16) While everyone else is satisfying their Arabic aspirations in the Moorish *teterías*, only a savvy few seek out this fine family-run Lebanese restaurant with indoor and outdoor seating. The aubergine dips, avocado salad, felalefs and cinnamon-dusted chicken pie could well have you planning your next holiday around a trip to Beruit.

El Ají
MODERN €€
(San Miguel Bajo 9; mains €12-20;) A cool, modern (tiny) interior, soft jazz and a menu of nontraditional meat and vegetarian choices make Ají different in the way that only Granada can be.

Kasbah
PASTRIES €
(Map p750; Calle Calderería Nueva 4; mains €8-12) This *tetería* is unusual in that it serves light snacks. It also stands out for its intricate stucco arches and well-camouflaged seating nooks.

Tetería Nazarí
PASTRIES €
(Map p750; Calle Calderería Nueva 13) Compliments its aromatic brews with some delicate Arabic pastries.

PLAZA BIB-RAMBLA & AROUND
In the heart of modern Granada, the plaza and its surrounding network of streets cater to a range of tastes and pockets from student to executive. Don't miss the excellent ice cream and *churros*.

Pastelería López-Mezquita
PASTRIES €
(Map p750; Calle Reyes Católicos 39; pastries €2-6; ⊗9am-6.30pm Mon-Fri) The on-the-go-snacks served at this pastry shop with cafe seating out back will allow you to enjoy Plaza Bib-Rambla and a flaky bacon-and-date *empanadilla* at the same time – ingenious.

Poë
ANGOLAN, BRAZILIAN €
(Map p750; Calle Paz; media raciones €3-5) British-Angolan Poë offers Brazilian favourites such as *feijoada* or chicken stew with polenta, and a trendy multicultural vibe.

Om-Kalsum
ARABIC €
(Map p750; Calle Jardines 17; media raciones €3-6) A few doors away from Poë, Om-Kalsum sticks to Arabic-influenced favourites such as lamb mini-tagines and chicken kebabs.

Reca
TAPAS €€
(Map p750; Plaza de la Trinidad; raciones €8; ⊗closed Tue) A tapas classic rightly famous for its *salmorejo* and its all-through-the-afternoon food service.

Oliver
SEAFOOD €€
(Map p750; Calle Pescadería 12; mains €12-18; ⊗closed Sun) Sandwiched between Plazas Bib-Rambla and Trinidad, this is a favourite lunchtime office-worker-stop revered for its fried fish.

Café Gran Vía de Colón
BREAKFAST €
(Map p750; Gran Via 13) Breakfasts here are substantial.

Café Fútbol
PASTRIES €
(Plaza Mariana Pineda 6, opposite tourist office) No Raúl or Fábregas, but plenty of art nouveau decor and fresh *churros*.

Drinking
The best street for drinking is the rather scruffy Calle de Elvira (try above-average Taberna El Espejo at No 40), but other chilled bars line Río Darro at the base of the Albayzín, and Campo del Príncipe attracts a sophisticated bunch.

Bodegas Castañeda (Map p750; Calle Almireceros) and Antigua Castañeda (Map p750; Calle de Elvira) are the most inviting and atmospheric, with out-of-the-barrel wine and generous tapas to keep things going.

Bar Pacurri
BAR
(Map p750; Calle de Gracia 21; tapas €2.50-5; ⊗1pm-1am) Perch at this small, arty bar, and munch on above-average tapas with well-chosen wines.

☆ Entertainment
The excellent monthly *Guía de Granada* (€1), available from kiosks, lists entertainment venues and places to eat, including tapas bars.

Clubs
Look out for posters and leaflets around town advertising live music and non-touristy flamenco.

Planta Baja
NIGHTCLUB
(Map p750; Calle Horno de Abad 11; www.plantabaja.net; admission €5; ⊗12.30am-6am Tue-Sat) Planta Baja's popularity never seems to wane, and it's no wonder since it caters to a diverse crowd *and* has top DJs like Vadim. There's old school, hip hop, funk and electroglam downstairs, and lazy lounge sessions on the top floor.

Granada 10 NIGHTCLUB

(Map p750; Calle Cárcel Baja; admission €6; ☺from midnight, closed mid-Jul & Aug) A glittery converted cinema is now Granada's top club for the glam crowd, who recline on the gold sofas and go crazy to cheesy Spanish pop tunes.

Afrodisia BAR, NIGHTCLUB

(www.afrodisiaclub.com; Edificio Corona, Calle Almona del Boquerón; admission free; ☺11pm-late) If you dig Granada's ganja-driven scene, this is where you'll find a like-minded lot. DJs spin hip hop, ska, reggae, funk and even jazz on Sunday.

Flamenco

Situated above and to the northwest of the city centre, and offering panoramic views over the Alhambra, the Sacromonte is Granada's centuries-old *gitano* quarter. The Sacromonte caves harbour touristy flamenco haunts for which you can prebook through hotels and travel agencies, some of whom offer free transport. Try the Friday or Saturday midnight shows at Los Tarantos (☎958 22 45 25 day, 958 22 24 92 night; Camino del Sacromonte 9; admission €24) for a lively experience.

Peña de la Platería FLAMENCO CLUB

(Placeta de Toqueros 7) Buried deep in the Albayzín warren, this is a genuine aficionados' club, with a large outdoor patio. Dramatic 9.30pm performances take place on Thursday or Saturday in an adjacent room and cost €12.

El Eshavira MUSIC VENUE

(Postigo de la Cuna 2; ☺from 10pm) Duck down a spooky alley to this shadowy haunt of flamenco and jazz. It is jam-packed on Thursday and Sunday, the performance nights.

Other Entertainment

Teatro del Generalife THEATRE

(Map p754; Generalife Gardens, Alhambra) Created in 1954 by extending the Generalife gardens southward, this outdoor theatre is a Granada rite of passage for summer performances of Lorca plays or live shows by great such as Paco de Lucía.

Teatro Alhambra THEATRE

(☎958 22 04 47; Calle de Molinos 56) Both Teatro Alhambra and the more central Teatro Isabel La Católica (☎958 22 15 14; Acera del Casino) have ongoing programs of theatre and concerts (sometimes flamenco); you may pick up a Lorca play here.

Centro Cultural Manuel de Falla MUSIC VENUE

(☎958 22 00 22; Paseo de los Mártires) A haven for classical-music lovers, this venue near the Alhambra presents weekly orchestral concerts in a leafy and tranquil setting.

 ## Shopping

Granadino crafts include embossed leather, *taracea* (marquetry), blue-and-white glazed pots, handmade guitars, wrought iron, brass and copper ware, basket weaving and textiles. Look out for these in the Alcaicería and Albayzín, on Cuesta de Gomérez and in the government-run Artespaña (Map p750) in Corral del Carbón.

The Plaza Nueva area is awash with jewellery vendors, selling from rugs laid out on the pavement, and ethnic-clothing shops.

For general shopping try pedestrianised Calle de los Mesones or expensive department store El Corte Inglés.

Metro BOOKSHOP

(☎958 26 15 65; Calle de Gracia 31) Stocks an excellent range of English-language novels, guidebooks and books on Spain, plus plenty of books in French.

❶ Information

Dangers & Annoyances

Despite all this charm and beauty, the Albayzín is still a work in progress and, unfortunately, its narrow streets are often havens for thieves and muggers. Muggings, some violent, sometimes happen in the Albayzín, so be discreet about valuables and proceed with care especially during siesta time (3pm to 5pm).

Emergency

Policía Nacional (☎958 80 80 00; Plaza de los Campos) The most central police station.

Internet Access

Thanks to Granada's 60,000 students, internet cafes are cheap and stay open for long hours.

Cyberlocutorio (Puerta Elvira, Plaza del Triunfo 5; per hr €1; ☺9am-midnight Mon-Thu, 9am-2am & 4pm-midnight Fri, 11am-midnight Sat, Sun & holidays)

Cyberlocutorio Alhambra (Calle Joaquín Costa 40; per hr €1.50; ☺10.30am-midnight)

Media

Where2 Magazine Excellent free English-language pocket guide to Granada, published bimonthly. *Where2* is stuffed with information on 'where to' indulge your eyes, ears and taste buds in Granada. It's available at tourist offices and at major sights.

Medical Services
Hospital Ruiz de Alda (☑958 02 00 09, 958 24 11 00; Avenida de la Constitución 100) Central, with good emergency facilities.

Money
There are plenty of banks and ATMs on Gran Vía de Colón, Plaza Isabel La Católica and Calle Reyes Católicos.

Post
Post office (Puerta Real; ⏰8.30am-8.30pm Mon-Fri, 9.30am-2pm Sat) Often has long queues.

Tourist Information
Municipal tourist office (www.granadatur. com; Calle Almona del Campillo, 2; ⏰9am-7pm Mon-Fri, to 6pm Sat, 10am-2pm Sun, holidays) Sleek, efficient centre opposite the city's Parque Federico García Lorca.

Provincial tourist office (www.turismode granada.org; Plaza de Mariana Pineda 10; ⏰9am-8pm Mon-Fri, 10am-2pm & 4-7pm Sat, 10am-3pm Sun May-Sep) Helpful staff with information on the whole Granada region; a short walk east of Puerta Real.

Regional tourist office Plaza Nueva (Map p750; Calle Santa Ana 1; ⏰9am-7.30pm Mon-Sat, 9.30am-3pm Sun & holidays); Alhambra (Map p754; ticket-office bldg, Avenida del Generalife; ⏰8am-7.30pm Mon-Fri, 8am-2pm & 4-7.30pm Sat & Sun, 9am-1pm holidays) Information on all of Andalucía.

Websites
Where2 (www.where2.es) Excellent, comprehensive English-language website with information on 'where to' eat, sleep, find entertainment or even buy property in Granada.

Turismo de Granada (www.turismodegranada. org) Good website of the provincial tourist office, although deeper layers of information are sketchy.

Getting There & Away
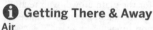

Air
Iberia (☑902 40 05 00; www.iberia.com) flies daily to/from Madrid and Barcelona. **Ryanair** (www.rynanair.com) flies daily to Milan and Bologna.

Bus
Granada's **bus station** (Carretera de Jaén) is nearly 3km northwest of the city centre. All services operate from here, except those going to a few nearby destinations, such as Fuente Vaqueros. **Alsina Graells** (☑902 42 22 42; www.alsa. es) runs to Córdoba (€12.52, 2¾ hours direct, nine daily), Seville (€19.32, three hours direct, eight daily), Málaga (€9.75, 1½ hours direct, 16 daily) and Las Alpujarras. Alsina also handles buses to destinations in Jaén province, Granada, Málaga, Almería, on to Madrid (€16.30, five to six hours, 10 to 13 daily) and up the Mediterranean coast to Barcelona (€68.65, seven to 10 hours, four daily) and many international destinations.

Car
Car rental is expensive. **ATA** (☑958 22 40 04; Plaza Cuchilleros 1) has small cars (eg Renault Clio) for approximately €75/48/36 per day for one/two/seven days. You would be better advised to take a taxi to the airport (€18 to €22), where four or five good car-hire operators have offices.

Train
The **train station** (Avenida de Andaluces) is 1.5km west of the centre, off Avenida de la Constitución. Four trains run daily to/from Seville

---

DUENDE

'There are neither maps nor exercises to help us find the *duende*', wrote Spanish poet Federico García Lorca in the 1920s in an early snub to cartographers, rationalists and future guidebook authors. An ambiguous term that lacks a direct English translation, the concept of *duende* has enthralled and perplexed visitors to Andalucía for aeons. Flamenco purists refer to it as the musical spirit that reaches out and touches your soul during an ecstatic live performance; Goethe – hinting at extra-musical links – described it as 'a physical power that all may feel but no philosophy can explain'.

The beauty of *duende* is that no book or person can predict exactly when or where it might occur. Its elusiveness is part of its mystical attraction. Some might find it in the sound of a full choir raising the roof in a Renaissance cathedral; others, in the play of light and water at dusk in an Alhambra-esque patio; more still, in the hypnotic fusion of guitar and dance at an obscure village *romería*. There is but one ineffable fact: *duende* – whether it transpires in Cádiz, Córdoba, Almería or Arcos de la Frontera – is a hugely powerful and uniquely Andalucian form of magic. Once you've felt its force, there's no going back. Andalucía (and all its cultural exoticisms) has trapped you in its spell.

GETTING TO THE ALHAMBRA

Buses 30 and 32 (€1.10) both run between Plaza Nueva and the Alhambra ticket office every five to nine minutes from 7.15am to 11pm.

If you opt to walk up Cuesta de Gomérez from Plaza Nueva you soon reach the **Puerta de las Granadas** (Gate of the Pomegranates), built by Carlos I. Above this are the Bosque Alhambra woods. If you already have your Alhambra ticket, you can climb the Cuesta Empedrada path up to the left and pass through the austere **Puerta de la Justicia** (Gate of Justice), constructed in 1348 as the Alhambra's main entrance.

If you need to go to the ticket office, in the **Pabellón de Acceso** (Access Pavilion), continue on for about 900m from the Puerta de las Granadas. From the Pabellón de Acceso you can enter the Generalife, and move on from there to other parts of the complex.

For drivers coming from out of town, 'Alhambra' signs on the approach roads to Granada direct you circuitously to the Alhambra car parks (per hr/day €1.40/14) on Avenida de los Alixares, above the ticket office.

(€23.85, three hours) and Almería (€15.90, 2¼ hours) via Guadix, and six daily to/from Antequera (€19.90, 1½ hours). Three go to Ronda (€13.50, three hours) and Algeciras (€20.10, 4½ hours). For Málaga (€15, 2½ hours) or Córdoba (€34.30, 2½ hours) take an Algeciras train and change at Bobadilla (€9, 1½ hours). One or two trains go to each of Madrid (€66.80, four to five hours), Valencia (€50.60, 7½ to eight hours) and Barcelona (€62.10, 12 hours).

Getting Around

To/From the Airport

The **airport** (958 24 52 23) is 17km west of the city on the A92. **Autocares J González** (958 49 01 64) runs buses between the airport and a stop near the Palacio de Congresos (€3, five daily), with a stop in the city centre on Gran Vía de Colón, where a schedule is posted opposite the cathedral, and at the entrance to the bus station. A taxi costs €18 to €22 depending on traffic conditions and pick-up point.

Bus

City buses cost €1.20. Tourist offices have leaflets showing routes. Bus 3 runs between the bus station and the Palacio de Congresos conference centre, via Gran Vía de Colón in the city centre. To reach the city centre from the train station, walk to Avenida de la Constitución and pick up bus 4, 6, 7, 9 or 11 going to the right (east). From the centre (Gran Vía de Colón) to the train station, take number 3, 4, 6, 9 or 11. Routes 30, 31, 32 and 34 are special tourist minibuses plying in and around the Alhambra and the Albayzín. Route 33 takes you to/from the bus station, through the centre of the city, and northeast towards the Sierra Nevada.

Car & Motorcycle

Vehicle access to the Plaza Nueva area is restricted by red lights and little black posts

known as *pilonas,* which block certain streets during certain times of the day. If you are going to stay at a hotel near Plaza Nueva, press the button next to your hotel's name beside the *pilonas* to contact reception, which will be able to lower the *pilonas* for you.

Many hotels, especially in the midrange and above, have their own parking facilities. Central underground public car parks include **Parking San Agustín** (Calle San Agustín; per hr/day €1/16), **Parking Neptuno** (Calle Neptuno; A44-E902, exit 129) and **Parking Plaza Puerta Real** (Acera del Darro; per hr/day €1/12). Free parking is available at the Alhambra car parks.

Taxi

If you're after a taxi, head for Plaza Nueva, where they line up. Most fares within the city cost between €4.50 and €8.50.

Around Granada

Granada is surrounded by a fertile plain called La Vega, planted with poplar groves and crops ranging from melons to tobacco. The Vega was an inspiration to Federico García Lorca, who was born and died here. The Parque Federico García Lorca, between the villages of Víznar and Alfacar (about 2.5km from each), marks the site where Lorca and hundreds, possibly thousands, of others are believed to have been shot and buried by the Nationalists, at the start of the civil war.

FUENTE VAQUEROS

The touchingly modest house where Lorca was born in 1898, in this otherwise unremarkable suburb 17km west of Granada, is now the Casa Museo Federico García

Teterías & Hammams

It's 500 years since the Moor uttered his last sigh, but the civilised habits of Al-Andalus' erstwhile rulers live on in many Andalucian cities, in dark, atmospheric *teterías* (tearooms) and elaborate *hammams* (bathhouses). While away lazy evenings in shadowy Moorish leisure facilities embellished with puffed cushions, stuccoed arches and winking lanterns.

Tetería Almedina

1 Liquid refreshment in this Almería establishment (p778) could include anything from an aromatic tea-tray of global brews. Try the Moroccan mint or Indian chai accompanied by a plate of delicate Arabic sweets.

Tetería Nazarí

2 A Granada tearoom (p758) popular among students and bohemians, who huddle in the dark corners sharing furtive puffs on the ubiquitous *shishas* (water-pipes).

La Tetería

3 Unbeknownst to many, Málaga remained Moorish almost as long as Granada did, meaning that its revitalised *teterías* can claim equal authenticity. You'll find stand-out brews and cakes at the rather unadventurously named La Tetería (p725), near the Museu Picasso Málaga.

Hammams de Al-Andalus

4 Moroccan *hammams* often resemble one-sided wrestling tournaments, but in Andalucía they're a shade more relaxing. Sample the hot baths at Hammams de Al-Andalus (p754) before cooling down with a glass of mint tea.

Hammam Andalusi

5 Underrated in almost every department, Jerez harbours plenty of Moorish exoticism, including the Hammam Andalusi (p699) with its unusual 'chocolate bath'.

Right
1. Tea in a *tetería* 2. Hammam Andalusi (p699)

JERÓNIMO ALBA/ALAMY

ANDREAS VON EINSIEDEL/HAMMAMANDALUSI.COM

National & Natural Parks

Andalucía's national and natural parks provide visitors with much-needed 'breathing space' between heavy doses of art, culture and history. They also act as important bulwarks against the encroaching development that plagues much of Spain's Mediterranean coast.

Parque Nacional Sierra Nevada

1 Peak-baggers can make for the easily accessible summits of Veleta and Mulhacén (p764), the Spanish mainland's highest peak. The less height-obsessed can ski, cycle, horse-ride, canyon or trek from park access points in Pradollano (p764) and Capileira (p767).

Parque Nacional de Doñana

2 A World Heritage–listed rare European wetland, the 542-sq-km Doñana National Park (p684) features copious bird species, large coastal sand dunes and vital water-based ecosystems.

Parque Natural Sierra de Grazalema

3 You can debate all day about Andalucía's finest park, or you can vote with your feet and get up onto the dreamy hiking trails and craggy mountains of this one (p703).

Parque Natural Sierra de Aracena y Picos de Aroche

4 Northern Huelva's *dehesa* ecosystems are the bastion of its finest cured hams, produced in the bucolic oak pastures of one of Andalucía's least-known parks (p687).

Parque Natural de Cabo de Gata-Níjar

5 Remember Spain before mass tourism? No? Then come to Almería's undeveloped littoral (p780) and reacquaint yourself with deserted coastlines and sleepy fishing villages.

Left
1. Sierra Nevada (p764) 2. Cabo de Gata-Níjar (p780)

Lorca (958 51 64 53; www.museogarcialorca. org, in Spanish; Calle Poeta Federico García Lorca 4; admission €1.80; guided visits hourly 10am-2pm & 5-7pm Tue-Sat). The place brings his spirit to life, with numerous charming photos, posters and costumes from his plays, and paintings illustrating his poems. A short video captures him in action with the touring Teatro Barraca.

Ureña (958 45 41 54) buses to Fuente Vaqueros (€1.55, 20 minutes) leave from Avenida de Andaluces in front of Granada train station, roughly once an hour from 9am during the week, and at 9am, 11am, 1pm and 5pm at weekends and holidays.

Sierra Nevada

True to their name, Spain's highest mountains rise like icy sentinels behind the city of Granada culminating in the rugged summit of Mulhacén (3479m), mainland Spain's highest peak. But the snowcapped mountains you see shimmering in the background of all those scenic Alhambra postcards are just the tip of the iceberg. The Sierra Nevada proper stretches 75km west to east from Granada into Almería province. The upper reaches of the range form the 862-sq-km Parque Nacional Sierra Nevada, Spain's biggest national park, with a rare high-altitude environment that is home to about 2100 of Spain's 7000 plant species. Andalucía's largest ibex population (about 5000) is here too. Surrounding the national park at lower altitudes is the 848-sq-km Parque Natural Sierra Nevada. The mountains and Las Alpujarras valleys comprise one of the most spectacular areas in Spain, and the area offers wonderful opportunities for walking, horse riding, climbing, mountain biking and, in winter, good skiing and snowboarding.

ESTACIÓN DE ESQUÍ SIERRA NEVADA

The Sierra Nevada Ski Station (www.sierra nevadaski.com; 10am-2pm & 4-6pm), at Pradollano, 33km southeast of Granada, is one of Spain's biggest and liveliest ski resorts. It can get overcrowded at weekends and holiday times. The ski season normally lasts from December to April.

The resort has 70 marked downhill runs (mainly red and blue with a few black and green) totalling over 80km, a dedicated snowboarding area and some cross-country routes. Some runs start almost at the top of Veleta, the Sierra Nevada's second-highest peak. A one-day lift ticket costs €37 to €41 depending when you go. Rental of skis, boots and stocks or snowboard is extra. The resort has several ski and snowboard schools: five days of skiing instruction in group classes costs approximately €130.

Nonskiers can ride cable cars up from Pradollano (2100m) to Borreguiles (2645m) for €10 return, and then ice-skate, dogsled or snowshoe. One cable car has wheelchair access. Outside the ski season Sierra Nevada Activa (www.sierranevadaactiva.com, in Spanish) operates a host of warmer-weather activities, such as mountain biking, trekking, horse riding and canyoning.

The ski station has around 20 hotels, *hostales* and apartment-hotels. None of these options is cheap (double rooms mostly start at €80) and reservations are always advisable. For cheaper digs look in Granada. Ski packages, which can be booked through the station's website or phone number, start at around €150 per person for two days and two nights, with half-board and lift passes. Book two weeks ahead, if you can.

Dorm rooms at youth hostel Instalación Juvenil Sierra Nevada (958 57 51 16; Calle Peñones 22; dm incl breakfast under/over 26yr €25/30; P) sleep from two to four, including six doubles with wheelchair access. The stark modern exterior encloses a stark, modern interior, and many school groups use this *hostal*. Albergue Universitario (958 48 01 22; Peñones de San Francisco, Monachil; dm €40, d €45 half-board; year-round; P), a big chalet-style *hostal*, offers plain, comfortable accommodation in a remote setting. Adventure days out can be booked here. At Hotel Apartamentos Trevenque (958 48 08 62; www.cetursa.es; Plaza de Andalucía 6; studios from €80; P), studios for two come complete with kitchenette, TV and DVD player, plus good food and views.

ℹ Information

The Centro de Visitantes El Dornajo (958 34 06 25; 9.30am-2.30pm & 4.30-7.30pm), about 23km from Granada, on the A395 towards the ski station, has plenty of information on the Sierra Nevada. Knowledgeable, English-speaking staff are happy to help.

ℹ Getting There & Away

In the ski season Autocares Bonal (958 46 50 22) operates three daily buses (four at weekends) from Granada bus station to the ski station (one-way/return €4.50/8, one hour). Outside the ski season there's just one bus daily (9am

Western Sierra Nevada & Las Alpujarras

Road Closed (special permit required)

5 km
3 miles

To Centro de Visitantes
El Dornajo (8km);
Granada (30km)

Borreguiles
(2645m)

Pradollano (Estación de
Esquí Sierra Nevada;
2100m)

Río Dílar

To Dílar

Tosal del Cartujo
(3152m)

Caballo
(3010m)

Parque Natural
Sierra Nevada

To Granada
(45km)

Lanjarón

Path No E4

Río Lanjarón

Caratáunas

Bayacas

Cáñar Soportújar

Órgiva

Río Guadalfeo

Ermita del
Padre Eterno

Parque Nacional
Sierra Nevada La Cebadilla

Central de
Poqueira

Pampaneira

Bubión

Capileira

Path No 4

Río Mulhacén

Refugio Vivac
La Caríguela

Veleta
(3395m)

Las Posiciones
del Veleta (3020m)

Hoya de la
Mora

Sierra   Nevada

Mulhacén
(3479m)

Refugio Vivac
La Caldera

Refugio
Poqueira

Cortijo Las
Caldera

El Chorrillo

Puerto Molina

Puntal de
Vacares
(3129m)

El Cuervo
(3152m)

Cañada de Siete
Lagunas

Alcazaba
(3366m)

Río Culo de Perro

Mirador de
Trevélez (2680m)

Puerto
(2727m)

Hoya del
Portillo

To Jerez
del Marquesado (10km)

Puerto de Trevélez
(2800m)

Sierra

Río Chico

Río Grande

Peñón del
Puerto
(2750m)

San Juan
(2786m)

Nevada

Parque Nacional
Sierra Nevada

Trevélez

Río Trevélez

Capilerilla

Pórtugos

La Tahá

Pitres

Mecina

Atalbéitar

Ferreirola

Fondales

Busquístar

Portichuelo
de Cástaras

Cástaras

Nótaez

Almegíjar

A348

Río Guadalfeo

A7210

L A S   A L P U J A R R A S

Notáez

Bérchules

Alcútar

Juviles

Tímar

Lobras

Narila

Cádiar

A345

Mecina
Bombarón

Golco

Río de Mecina

Parque Natural
Sierra Nevada

Yegen

Yátor

Río Yátor

Joiairátar

To Albuñol
(22km)

GRANADA

ALMERÍA

Nechite

Válor

Ugíjar

Cherín

Laujar de Andarax (9km);
Almería (86km)

Lucainena

Darrical

Mairena

Bayárcal

Laroles

Río de Laroles

Río Bayárcal

Chullo
(2612m)

from Granada, 5pm from Pradollano). A taxi from Granada to the ski station costs around €65.

A road climbs right over the Sierra Nevada from the ski station to Capileira village in Las Alpujarras, on the southern side of the range, but it's snowbound much of the year and in any case always closed to private motor vehicles between Hoya de la Mora (2550m), 3km up from Pradollano, and Hoya del Portillo (2150m), 12.5km above Capileira. From about late June to the end of October the national park shuttle-bus services, called the Servicio de Interpretación Ambiental Altas Cumbres (High Peaks Environmental Interpretation Service), run about 6km up the road from Hoya de la Mora (to the Posiciones del Veleta, at 3020m) and some 21km up from Capileira (to the Mirador de Trevélez, at 2680m). Tickets (one-way/return €4.80/8 on either route) and further information are available from the national park information posts at **Hoya de la Mora** (☺during bus-service season approx 8.30am-2.30pm & 3.30-7.30pm) and at Hoya del Portillo, **Capileira** (☺year-round approx 9am-2pm & 4.30-7.30pm).

Las Alpujarras

Below the southern flank of the Sierra Nevada lies the 70km-long jumble of valleys known as Las Alpujarras. Arid hillsides split by deep ravines alternate with oasis-like white villages set beside rapid streams and surrounded by gardens, orchards and woodlands. An infinity of good walking routes links valley villages and heads up into the Sierra Nevada: the best times to visit are between April and mid-June, and mid-September and early November.

A recent upsurge in tourism, New Age and foreign (mainly British) settlers has given the area a new dimension.

History

In the 10th and 11th centuries Las Alpujarras, settled by Berbers, was a great silkworm farm for the workshops of Almería. But after Granada fell to Ferdinand and Isabella in 1492, the industry languished and many villages were abandoned. *South from Granada* by Gerald Brenan, an Englishman who lived in Las Alpujarras village of Yegen in the 1920s and '30s, gives a fascinating picture of what was then a very isolated, superstitious corner of Spain. Another Englishman, Chris Stewart, settled here more recently, as a sheep farmer near Órgiva. His entertaining best-selling *Driving over Lemons* tells of life as a foreigner in Las Alpujarras in the '90s.

LANJARÓN

Known as 'the gateway to the Alpujarras', Lanjarón's heyday was during the late 19th and early 20th centuries, when it was a fashionable *balneario* or spa. Today, although Lanjarón water is sold all over Spain, the Balneario (☎958 77 00 137; www.balneariodelanjaron.com; Avenida de la Constitución; 1 hr bath €25) is visited largely by elderly Spanish cure-seekers. Yet the town has authentic charms. Traditional family life is lived along its main streets, Avenida de la Alpujarra and Avenida Andalucía. The recently inaugurated Museo de Agua (Water Museum; ☺10am-2pm & 6-9pm Tue-Sun) explores water's link to agriculture, industry and health, along with medicinal qualities of Lanjarón's water. There's an exhibition hall and an audiovisual show.

There are plenty of hotels. Hotel Andalucía (☎958 77 01 36; www.hotelandalucia.com; Avenida de la Alpujarra 15-17; r from 54 🅿✳@✳) close to the *balneario* is a good budget option, with clean if bland rooms and an outdoor pool. Eat at seafood restaurant Los Mariscos (Avenida de la Alpujarra), where everything is cooked with fresh ingredients.

The tourist office (Avenida de la Alpujarra), opposite the *balneario,* provides comprehensive information on outdoor activities and accommodation for the entire Alpujarras region.

ÓRGIVA

POP 6500 / ELEV 725M

The western Alpujarras' main town, Órgiva, is a scruffy but bustling place with a big hippie/New Age element. Good places to eat include El Limonero, where the chef's passion for local ingredients is put to good use in a handsome room; La Almazara (Avenida González Robles; menús €12), with inventive dishes and excellent pizza served in an orange grove all summer; and vegetarian brunch/lunch options at welcoming Café Libertad (Calle Libertad).

Stay at Hotel Taray Botánico (☎958 78 45 25; www.hoteltaray.com; A348 Km18.5; s/d €60/79; 🅿✳@✳✳), where the owners love their hotel and it shows. It's set in lush gardens just south of the centre, with rustic-style rooms and a good restaurant, plus two lovely big pools; book well ahead in summer. A cheaper option is Camping Puerta de las Alpujarras (☎958 78 44 50; www.campingpuertadelaalpujarra.com; A348 Carretera Lanjarón-Orgiva; sites per adult/under 11yr/tent & car €5/3.50/9.50), handily located for the High Alpujarras with a big pool, pleasant restaurant.

PAMPANEIRA, BUBIÓN & CAPILEIRA
POP 1270 / ELEV 1200-1440M

These small villages clinging to the side of the deep Barranco de Poqueira valley, 14km to 20km northeast of Órgiva, are three of the prettiest, most dramatically sited (and most touristy) in Las Alpujarras. Capileira is the best base for walks.

⊙ Sights & Activities

All three villages have solid 16th-century Mudéjar churches (⊙Mass times). They also have small weaving workshops, descendants of a textile tradition that goes back to Islamic times, and plentiful craft shops. In Bubión, get a marvellous glimpse of bygone Alpujarras life at the excellent little folk museum, Casa Alpujarreña (Calle Real; admission €2; ⊙11am-2pm Sun-Thu, to 2pm & 5-7pm Fri, Sat & holidays), beside the church.

Eight walking trails, ranging from 4km to 23km (two to eight hours), are marked out in the beautiful Barranco de Poqueira with little colour-coded posts. Their starting points can be hard to find, but they are marked and described on Editorial Alpina's *Sierra Nevada, La Alpujarra* map. Nevadensis (☑958 76 31 27; www.nevadensis. com), at the information office in Pampaneira, offers hikes and treks, 4WD trips, horse riding, mountain biking, climbing and canyoning, all with knowledgeable guides.

🛏 Sleeping & Eating

Book ahead for rooms around Easter and from July to September. Many villages have apartments and houses for rent; ask in tourist offices or check websites such as Turgranada (www.turgranada.es) or Rustic Blue (www.rusticblue.com).

PAMPANEIRA
A good-value *hostal* at the entrance to the village, Hostal Pampaneira (☑958 76 30 02; www.hostalpampaneira.com; Avenida Alpujarra 1; s/d/tr incl breakfast €31/42/49) has a friendly local owner. Restaurante Casa Diego (Plaza de la Libertad 3; mains €6.50-13.50), along the street, has a pleasant upstairs terrace and serves local trout and ham.

BUBIÓN
Hostal Las Terrazas (☑958 76 30 34; www. terrazasalpujarra.com; Plaza del Sol 7; s/d €22/31, 2-/4-/6-person apt €45/55/72; 🛜) is located below the main road and near the car park. Traditional Teide Restaurant (Carretera de

Sierra Nevada 2; menús €10) has a good *menú del día*, while Estación 4 (Calle Estación 4; mains €7-12) inhabits an old village house.

CAPILEIRA
Hostal Atalaya (☑958 76 30 25; www.hostala talaya.com; Calle Perchel 3; s/d with view €30/38, without view €18/30) is a good budget option, while Finca Los Llanos (☑958 76 30 71; www. hotelfincalosllanos.com; Carretera de Sierra Nevada; s/d €53/75; P @ 🛋) has tasteful rooms, a pool and a good restaurant. It's also an official Sierra Nevada information point. Renovated farmhouse Cortijo Catifalarga (☑958 34 33 57; www.catifalarga.com; d €76-104, apt for 2/4/6 people €99/118/141; P 🅿) is stunning and serves meals (mains €9 to €17). The driveway begins 750m up the Sierra Nevada road from the top of Capileira, and both the views and its eclectic food are way up there. At Restaurante Ibero-Fusión (Calle Parra 1; salads €7-10, mains €10-12.50 ⊙dinner, closed Tue; 🅿), just below the church, enjoy a rare *andaluz*, Arabic and Indian fusion restaurant with plenty of vegetarian specialities and great views from the pleasant upstairs dining room.

ⓘ Information

You'll find ATMs outside the car-park entrance in Pampaneira, and in Capileira at **La General** (Calle Doctor Castilla).

Punto de Información Parque Nacional de Sierra Nevada (www.nevadensis.com; Plaza de la Libertad, Pampaneira; ⊙10am-2pm & 4-6pm Tue-Sat, to 3pm Sun & Mon, Oct-March) Plenty of information about Las Alpujarras and Sierra Nevada; outdoor gear, maps and books for sale.

Servicio de Interpretación de Altos Cumbres (⊙approx 9am-2pm & 4.30-7.30pm) By the main road in Capileira; information mainly about the national park, but also on Las Alpujarras.

PITRES & LA TAHA
POP 800

Pitres (elevation 1245m) is a break from the tourism and souvenirs in the Poqueira Gorge villages, although not quite as pretty. The beautiful valley below it, with five tranquil hamlets (Mecina, Mecinilla, Fondales, Ferreirola and Atalbéitar), all grouped with Pitres in the *municipio* called La Taha, is particularly fascinating to explore. Its ancient pathways are a walker's delight.

Above Pitres in the tiny hamlet of Capilerilla (and on the E4 footpath) lies Hotel Maravedi (☑958 76 62 92; www.hotelmaravedi. com; s/d/tr €60/80/102; P ✳🛜), rustic but with all home comforts including satellite

THE GR7 THROUGH LAS ALPUJARRAS

Unbeknownst to many, one of Europe's most scenic highways cuts straight across Las Alpujarras. But this is no normal traffic-clogged motorway. This, rather, is the E4 (or the GR7, as it's known in Spain), a cross-continental long-distance footpath that runs from Tarifa in Spain to Athens in Greece, passing through eight countries en route.

Picking up the small segment of the GR7 between Lanjarón and Pitres is one of the best ways to arrive in Las Alpujarras on a simple day trip from Granada. Moving at a slower pace, you get the opportunity to experience the mountains viscerally as vertiginous valleys reveal hidden waterfalls, small hillside farms and little-visited villages.

After a carb-loading breakfast in Lanjarón, proceed to the far eastern end of town, where a bridge crosses a river just past the Museo de Agua (p766). Follow the road for approximately 300m before turning left at an E4/GR7 signpost. The trail heads steeply uphill initially but soon flattens out and starts to contour the scrubby hillside as spectacular views unfold. Regular red-and-white signposts indicate the route. Cáñar is the first village you come to – a mesh of twisted lanes and distinctive arcades where animal stabling has been built into the houses – followed 5km later by Soportújar. After crossing the Dique 24 dam and waterfall built in 1942 to control flash flooding, you enter the magical Barranco de Poqueira where the three villages of Pampaneira, Bubión and Capileira sit stacked up on top of one another in the shadow of Spain's highest mountains. Food and accommodation can be procured in any of the villages, where there are also several late-afternoon/early-evening buses back to Granada. To elongate the trip you can continue over a craggy ridge and descend into the more pastoral La Taha valley, finishing in the somnolent village of Pitres the following day.

TV and private bar–restaurant for clients. In nearby Mecina, welcoming French-run guesthouse L'Atelier (958 85 75 01; www.ivu.org/atelier; Calle Alberca 21, Mecina; s/d incl breakfast €35/50; dinner Wed-Mon;) in an ancient village house also serves gourmet vegetarian/vegan meals and has an art gallery. It also runs vegetarian cooking courses (€50 per day). In peaceful Ferreirola, Sierra y Mar (958 76 61 71; www.sierraymar.com; Calle Albaicín, Ferreirola; s/d/tr incl breakfast €42/62/84) has just nine rooms, set around patios and gardens.

TREVÉLEZ
POP 1150 / ELEV 1476M

Trevélez, in a valley almost as impressive as the Poqueira Gorge, claims to be the highest village in Spain (although Valdelinares, Aragón, reaches above 1700m) and produces famous *jamón serrano*.

On a leafy, terraced hillside 1km west of Trevélez, Camping Trevélez (/fax 958 85 87 35; www.campingtrevelez.net; Carretera Trevélez-Órgiva Km1; sites per adult/tent/car/cabin €4.50/5/3.80/19; closed Jan–mid Feb;) has ecologically minded owners and a good-value restaurant. Walkers' favourite Hotel La Fragua I (958 85 86 26; Calle San Antonio 4; s/d €33.50/45;) provides

pine-furnished rooms, with a more upmarket annex at La Fragua II (doubles/triples €55/72). Its restaurant, Mesón La Fragua (mains €7.50-12.50), a few doors away, is one of the best in town and worth searching out. More-central Hotel Pepe Álvarez (958 85 85 03; www.hotelpepealvarez.es; Plaza Francisco Abellán; s/d €25/45;) has some terraces overlooking the busy plaza, and serves meals (mains €6 to €11).

EAST OF TREVÉLEZ
East of Trevélez the landscape becomes barer and more arid, yet there are still oases of greenery around the villages. The central and eastern Alpujarras have their own magic but see far fewer tourists than the western villages.

❶ Getting There & Away

Alsina Graells (958 18 54 80) runs three daily buses from Granada to Órgiva (€4.38, 1½ hours), Pampaneira (€5.17, two hours), Bubión (€5.25, 2¼ hours), Capileira (€5.25, 2½ hours) and Pitres (€5.80, 2¾ hours). Two of these continue to Trevélez (€6.85, 3¼ hours) and Bérchules (€8.10, 3¾ hours). The return buses start from Bérchules at 5am and 5pm, and from Pitres at 3.30pm. Alsina also runs twice-daily buses from Granada to Cádiar (€7.50, three hours) and Yegen (€8.50, 3½ hours).

The Coast

Granada's cliff-lined, 80km-long coast has a hint of Italy's Amalfi about it and is definitively Spanish in flavour. A sprinkling of attractive beach towns are linked by several daily buses to Granada, Málaga and Almería.

ALMUÑÉCAR
POP 23,000

More interesting and certainly more Spanish than anything on the Costa del Sol, Almuñécar is well worth a day's diversion. There's easy access from either Granada or Málaga. The attractive old town, which hugs the coast amid small coves and precipitous cliffs, huddles around the 16th-century Castillo de San Miguel (Santa Adela Explanada; adult/child €2.35/1.60; ⊙10.30am-1.30pm & 4-6.30pm Tue-Sat, 10.30am-2pm Sun) and ajoining Museo Arqueológico (Calle San Joaquín) situated in the basement of an old Roman construction (same schedule and prices as Castillo). The breezy seafront is an excellent place to *dar un paseo* (go for a slow evening stroll). Make for the steep pointed headland that divides the two beaches known as the Peñon del Santo.

Just behind Playa de San Cristóbal is a tropical-bird aviary, Parque Ornitológico Loro-Sexi (adult/child €4/2; ⊙11am-2pm year-round, plus 6-9pm Jul–mid-Sep, 5-7pm mid-Sep–Oct & Apr-Jun).

You can paraglide, windsurf, dive, sail, ride a horse or descend canyons in and around Almuñécar and nearby La Herradura. The tourist office and its website have plenty of information.

Just off the winding N340 coast road, Hostal California (☎958 88 10 38; www.hotel californiaspain.com; Carretera N340 Km313; s/d €43/58; P☒) is refreshingly different, with colourful touches of Moroccan style and tasty food, including vegetarian options. The hotel offers special packages for paragliders as the owner is an expert and enthusiast. In town, streamlined Hotel Casablanca (☎958 63 55 75; www.hotelcasa blancaalmunecar.com; Plaza de San Cristóbal 4; s/d €50/64; P☀☎) is furnished in distinctive Al-Andalus style, with sea views from some rooms.

The best food is on the eastern beach. Try La Última Ola (Paseo Puerta del Mar 4-6; mains €15-24) for its grilled monkfish with mushrooms and almonds.

The main tourist office (www.almunecar. info; Avenida Europa; ⊙10am-2pm year-round, plus 6-9pm Jul–mid Sep, 5-8pm mid-Sep–end Oct) is 1km southwest, just back from Playa de San Cristóbal, in a rose-pink neo-Moorish Palacete La Najarra with lovely gardens that is a tourist sight in its own right. The bus station (Avenida Juan Carlos I 1) is just south of the N340.

❶ Getting There & Away

ALSA (☎902 42 22 42; www.alsa.es) runs 12 daily buses to Granada (€7.20, 1½ hours). There are also regular connections west along the coast to Málaga (€6.35, two hours, nine daily) via Nerja.

JAÉN PROVINCE

Jaén province is rarely included in standard Andalucía itineraries, a crying shame for lovers of olive oil, Renaissance architecture, and rugged mountain scenery strafed with rare flora and fauna. The architecture is courtesy of the historic towns of Baeza and Úbeda, the nature is encased in the expansive Parque Natural de Cazorla (Spain's largest single protected area), while the olive oil is everywhere you look; indeed, it is doubtful if there's a vista in Jaén that doesn't include at least one neat patchwork of olive plantations (the province *alone* accounts for about 10% of the world's olive oil production).

Jaén

POP 120,000 / ELEV 575M

You don't need to be a genius to deduce what is the pillar of Jaén's economy. With olive plantations pushing right up against the city limits, the health-enhancing 'liquid gold' has long filled the coffers of the local economy and provided rich topping for one of the most dynamic (and least heralded) tapas strips in Andalucía. Surrounding a sentinel-like castle in Jaén's centre is a magnificent Renaissance cathedral worthy of a city twice the size, from which emanate narrow alleys, smoky bars, cavernous tabernas and *mucho alegría* (joy). Welcome to Andalucía at its grittiest and understated best.

◎ Sights

Catedral   CATHEDRAL
(adult/child €5/1.50; ⊙10am-6pm Mon-Sat 10am-noon Sun) Jaén's huge cathedral was

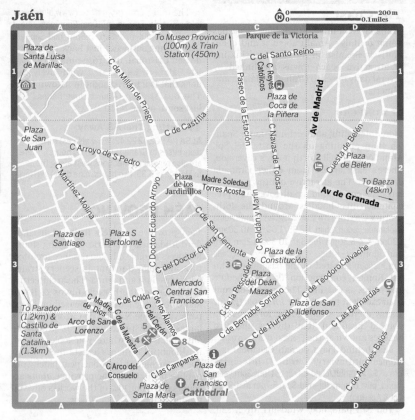

built mainly in the 16th and 17th centuries, and mainly to the Renaissance designs of Andrés de Vandelvira – though the south-western facade on Plaza de Santa María sports a dramatic array of 17th-century baroque statuary.

FREE Palacio de Villardompardo   PALACE
(Plaza de Santa Luisa de Marillac; admission free with passport; ⊙9am-8pm Tue-Fri, 9.30am-2.30pm Sat & Sun, closed holidays) The Renaissance palace houses three excellent attractions and is worth tracking down: the beautiful 11th-century **Baños Árabes** (Arab Baths), with a transparent walkway for viewing the excavated baths; the **Museo de Artes y Costumbres Populares**, devoted to the artefacts of the harsh rural lifestyle of pre-industrial Jaén province; and the **Museo Internacional de Arte Naïf**, with a large international collection of colourful and witty Naive art. You can spend hours

lost in the everyday detail so playfully depicted in these works.

Museo Provincial   MUSEUM
(Paseo de la Estación 27; adult/EU citizen €1.50/ free; ⊙2.30-8.30pm Tue, 9am-8.30pm Wed-Sat, to 2.30pm Sun) This museum has the finest collection of 5th-century-BC Iberian sculptures in Spain. Found in Porcuna, they show a clear Greek influence in their fluid form and graceful design.

Castillo de Santa Catalina   CASTLE
(admission €3; ⊙10am-2pm & 5-9pm Tue-Sun Apr-Sep, 3.30-7pm Tue-Sun Oct-Mar) Jaén's most exhilarating spot is the top of the Cerro de Santa Catalina, where the castle was surrendered to Fernando III in 1246 by Granada after a six-month siege. Audiovisual gimmicks add fun to the visit to the castle's keep, chapel and dungeon. The castle is a circuitous 4km drive from the city centre (€6.50 by taxi), but you

Jaén

◉ Top Sights
Cathedral...B4

◉ Sights

🛏 Sleeping

⊗ Eating

◉⊜ Drinking

can walk up in 45 minutes using a steep path almost opposite the top of Calle de Buenavista.

🛏 Sleeping

Parador Castillo de Santa Catalina

HOTEL €€€

(☑953 23 00 00; www.parador.es; r €160; P ✳ @ 🛜 ⌖) Next to the castle at the top of the Cerro de Santa Catalina, this hotel has an incomparable setting and theatrically vaulted halls. Rooms are luxuriously dignified, featuring four-poster beds. There is also an excellent restaurant (mains €17 to €32).

Hostal Carlos V

HOTEL €

(☑953 22 20 91; Avenida de Madrid 4, 2nd fl; s/d without bathroom €24/38; ✳ @) The best budget option in town, the well-located family-run Carlos V provides pleasant rooms with wrought-iron beds and TV, near the bus station. Ring the buzzer at the communal street entrance.

Hotel Xauen

HOTEL €€

(☑953 24 07 89; www.hotelxauenjaen.com; Plaza del Deán Mazas 3; s/d €66/89; P ✳ @ 🛜) The 35 rooms at the central, business-oriented Xauen have adequate facilities for a stopover, but it's a little overpriced.

✕ Eating

The Jaén tapas trail is full of pleasant surprises, especially along tiny Calle del Cerón and Arco del Consuelo

Taberna Casa Gorrión

TAPAS €€

(www.tabernagorrion.es, in Spanish; Calle Arco del Consuelo 7; ⊙1.30-5pm Tue, Wed, Thu, 8am-12.30pm Sun & Mon) A Jaén institution since 1888, with its original tiled floor, copper sink and long bar. Aficionados come here for the topaz-yellow *queso manchego* (Manchego cheese) and sweet wine aged in the taverna's own barrels.

Taberna La Manchega

TAPAS €€

(Calle Bernardo López 12; platos combinados €7.50; ⊙lunch & dinner Wed-Mon) If you can squeeze behind the bar at this insanely smokey and crowded old-town tavern you can descend a flight of stairs to an equally cramped but earthy dining room.

🍷 Drinking

Cool drinking spots include stylish El Azulejo (Calle de Hurtado 8), playing everything from pop to electronic to jazz, and Iroquai (Calle de Adarves Bajos 53), which usually has live rock, blues, flamenco or fusion on Thursday. At the Italianesque La Columbiana (Calle La Parra) you can pick up your espresso, moka or frappuccino.

ℹ Information

There's no shortage of banks or ATMs around Plaza de la Constitución.

Cyber Cu@k (Calle de Adarves Bajos 24; per 30min €1.20; ⊙10.30am-3pm & 5pm-1am Mon-Fri, 11am-3pm & 4.30pm-12am Sat, Sun)

Tourist office (Calle Ramón y Cajal 1; ⊙10am-8pm Mon-Fri, to 7pm Oct-Mar, to 1pm Sat, Sun & holidays) Helpful, multilingual staff with plenty of free information about the city and province.

ℹ Getting There & Away

The **bus station** (Plaza de Coca de la Piñera) is 250m north of Plaza de la Constitución. Destinations include Granada (€7.60, 1½ hours, 14 daily), Baeza (€5, 45 minutes, up to 11 daily), Úbeda (€5.50, 1¼ hours, up to 12 daily), Córdoba (€8.22, 1½ hours, seven daily) and Cazorla (€7.85, two hours, two daily).

Most days there are only five departures from the **train station** (☑902 24 02 02); one, at 8am, goes to Córdoba (€11.45, 1½ hours) and Seville (€22.25, three hours), and up to four go to Madrid (€30.20, four hours).

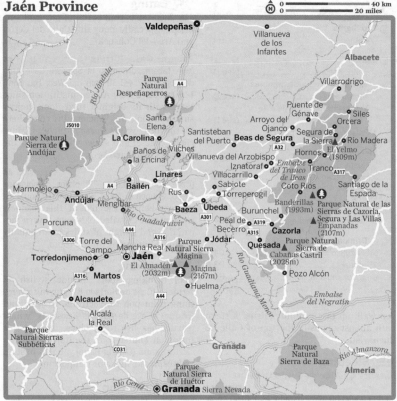

N 0 ————— 40 km
0 ————— 20 miles

Map labels:
Valdepeñas
Villanueva de los Infantes
Albacete
Parque Natural Despeñaperros A4
Villarrodrigo
Río Jándula J5010
Santa Elena
Santisteban del Puerto
Arroyo del Ojanco
Puente de Génave
Siles
Orcera
Segura de la Sierra
Río Madera
Parque Natural Sierra de Andújar
La Carolina
Beas de Segura A32
El Yelmo (1809m)
Baños de la Encina
Vilches
Villanueva del Arzobispo
Hornos
Iznatoraf
Embalse del Tranco de Beas
Tranco A317
Marmolejo
Linares
Villacarrillo
Coto Ríos
Santiago de la Espada
Andújar A4 Bailén
Rus
Sabiote
Banderillas (1993m)
Parque Natural de las Sierras de Cazorla, Segura y Las Villas
Menjíbar
Río Guadalquivir
Baeza Úbeda A301
Torreperogil
Burunchel
Porcuna A306
A44 A316
Peal de Becerro A319
A315
Cazorla
Empanadas (2107m)
Torre del Campo
Mancha Real
Parque Natural Sierra Mágina
Jódar
Quesada
Parque Natural Sierra de Cabañas Castril (2028m)
Torredonjimeno
Jaén
Magina
Río Guadiana Menor
A316 Martos
El Almadén (2032m)
Magina (2167m)
Pozo Alcón
Embalse del Negratín
Alcaudete
A44
Huelma
Alcalá la Real
Parque Natural Sierras Subbéticas
CO31
Granáda
Parque Natural Sierra de Baza
Río Almanzora
Almería
Río Genil
Parque Natural Sierra de Huétor
Granada Sierra Nevada

Baeza

POP 17,000 / ELEV 790M

Baeza is where the Moors beat an earlier retreat than elsewhere in the region. Consequently, it often looks more Italian than Andalucian – a small town with big ambitions that exhibits one of the most complete ensembles of Renaissance buildings in Andalucía, if not Spain. Perched on a well-protected escarpment, Baeza also affords stunning views over endless olive groves towards the aptly named Sierra del Mágica.

Sights

Opening times of some buildings vary unpredictably.

In the centre of beautiful Plaza del Pópulo is the Fuente de los Leones (Fountain of the Lions), topped by an ancient statue believed to represent Imilce, a local Iberian princess who was married to Hannibal. On the southern side of the plaza is the Plat-eresque Casa del Pópulo from about 1540 (housing Baeza's helpful tourist office).

Catedral   CATHEDRAL
(Plaza de Santa María; donations welcome; ⊙10.30am-1pm & 5-7pm Apr-Sep) Baeza's eclectic cathedral is chiefly in 16th-century Renaissance style, with an interior designed by Andrés de Vandelvira and Jerónimo del Prado. One chapel displays a life-sized Last Supper, with finely detailed wax figures and Mary in Victorian flounces of cream lace and pearls.

FREE **Antigua Universidad**   OLD UNIVERSITY
(Calle Beato Juan de Ávila; ⊙10am-1pm & 4-6pm Thu-Tue) Now a high school, Baeza's former university was founded in 1538. The main patio has two levels of elegant Renaissance arches.

FREE **Palacio de Jabalquinto**   PALACE
(Plaza Santa Cruz; ⊙9am-2pm Mon-Fri) Round the corner from the old university,

this early-16th-century mansion has a flamboyant Isabelline-Gothic facade and lovely Renaissance patio with a fantastically carved baroque stairway.

Iglesia de la Santa Cruz   CHURCH
(⊙11am-1pm & 4.30-6pm Mon-Sat, 11am-1pm Sun) This 13th-century church was one of the first to be built in Andalucía after the Reconquista. It may be the only Romanesque church in Andalucía.

Ayuntamiento   TOWN HALL
(Paseo del Cardenal Benavides 9) A block north of Paseo de la Constitución, the town hall has a marvellous Plateresque facade.

🛏 Sleeping & Eating
With such a wealth of building heritage, there are several beautifully restored hotel conversions to choose from in Baeza. Eating-wise, Paseo de la Constitucíon is a good place to start, though there are a few gems hidden in the old town.

Hotel Palacete Santa Ana
HISTORIC HOTEL €€
(☑953 74 16 57; www.palacetesantana.com; Calle Santa Ana Vieja 9; s/d €45/70; ❀⊛) Undergoing a renovation at the time of writing (though still open), this place occupies what was a 16th-century nunnery. When finished, it will sport its own museum and restaurant. Rooms are a little austere, but it's clean and the owner's an enthusiastic history buff.

Hotel Puerta de la Luna   HOTEL €€
(☑953 74 70 19; www.hotelpuertadelaluna.com, in Spanish; Calle Canónigo Melgares Raya; s/d Mon-Thu €75/95, Fri-Sun €105/129; ❘P❙⊛@⊛⊛) With its lantern-lit courtyards and luminous pool, the Luna is proof that the Christians of the Reconquista could replicate heaven almost as well as the Nasrid kings of the Alhambra.

Hospedería Fuentenueva   HOTEL €€
(953 74 31 00; www.fuentenueva.com; Calle del Carmen 15; s/d incl breakfast €55/78; ⊛@⊛⊛) Occupying a former women's prison, Fuentenueva now has big, beautiful rooms with matte-black slate shower rooms.

La Góndola   ANDALUCIAN €€
(☑953 74 29 84; Portales Carbonería 13, Paseo de la Constitución; mains €12-20) Hearty meals can be found at this local staple, where a fine Baezan atmosphere is helped along by the glowing wood-burning grill, cheerful

service and good, healthy food. Enjoy the smooth, nutty olive oil, rich red wine and plates piled up with vegetables.

Torre Al Bayyassa   ANDALUCIAN €
(Comendadores 6; menús €9; ⊙closed Mon dinner & Tue) The best old-town option is situated near the glorious cathedral but is not as Moorish as the name implies. Traditional Andalucian food comes with a Baeza twist, read: cod in a *baezana* sauce and *rabo de toro* croquettes.

ℹ Information
Tourist office (Plaza del Pópulo; ⊙9am-7.30pm Mon-Fri, 9.30am-3pm, Sat, Sun & holidays Apr-Sep) Situated just southwest of Paseo de la Constitución in the 16th-century Plateresque Casa del Pópulo, a former courthouse.

ℹ Getting There & Away
The **bus station** (Paseo Arco del Agua) has recently moved further east along Avenida Puche Pardo to a location next to the hospital. There are plans to redevelop it permanently. Buses go to Jaén (€5, 45 minutes, 11 daily), Úbeda (€1.20, 30 minutes, 15 daily), Cazorla (€4.80, 2¼ hours, two daily) and Granada (€11.34, 2¼ hours, five daily)

    Linares-Baeza train station (☑953 65 02 02) is 13km northwest. Buses connect with most trains Monday to Saturday; a taxi is €15.

Úbeda
POP 35.000 / ELEV 760M

Just 9km east of Baeza, Úbeda's architecture rivals its neighbour's. Sixteenth-century grandee Francisco de los Cobos y Molina became first secretary to Carlos I; his nephew, Juan Vázquez de Molina, succeeded him in the job and kept it under Felipe II. They lavished their wealth on a profusion of Renaissance mansions and churches – many of them designed by Jaén's Renaissance master, Andrés de Vandelvira (b 1509).

◉ Sights
Plaza Vázquez de Molina   SQUARE
This plaza, Úbeda's crown jewel, is surrounded by beautiful 15th- and 16th-century buildings.

    The **Capilla del Salvador** (admission €3; ⊙10am-2pm & 4-6.30pm Mon-Sat, 11.15am-2pm & 4-7pm Sun) faces the eastern end of the plaza. Founded in the 1540s by Francisco de los Cobos y Molina as his family funerary chapel, it was Vandelvira's first commission in Úbeda. The basic concept is by Diego de Siloé, architect of Granada cathedral, but Vandelvira added plenty of his own touches, including the elaborate main facade, an outstanding piece of Plateresque design. Lit up at night, the whole facade seems to come to life. The sacristy, by Vandelvira, has a portrait of Francisco de los Cobos y Molina. The Cobos family crypt lies beneath the nave.

Next to the Capilla de El Salvador stands what was the abode of its chaplains – in fact one of Vandelvira's best palaces, the Palacio del Deán Ortega. It's now Úbeda's *parador*.

The harmonious proportions of the Italianate Palacio de Vázquez de Molina (☼8am-8pm Mon-Fri, 10am-2pm Sat), at the western end of the plaza, make it one of the finest buildings in the town. Now Úbeda's town hall, it was built around 1562 by Vandelvira for Juan Vázquez de Molina, whose coat of arms surmounts the doorway.

Plaza 1 de Mayo & Around   SQUARE

Plaza 1 de Mayo used to be Úbeda's market square and bullring, and the Inquisition burnt heretics where its kiosk now stands. Worthies would watch from the gallery of the elegant 16th-century Antiguo Ayuntamiento (Old Town Hall) in the southwestern corner. Along the top (northern) side of the square is the Iglesia de San Pablo (☼11am-1.30pm & 7-8pm Mon-Sat), with a fine late-Gothic portal from 1511.

The Museo de San Juan de la Cruz (Calle del Carmen 13; admission free; ☼11am-1pm & 5-7pm Tue-Sun) is devoted to the mystic and religious reformer St John of the Cross, who died here in 1591. Even if you can't understand the Spanish-speaking monks who guide all visits, you'll still get to marvel at some of the saint's mystical memorabilia.

FREE Hospital de Santiago
CULTURAL CENTRE

(Calle Obispo Cobos; ☼8am-2.30pm & 3.30-10pm Mon-Fri, 10am-2.30pm & 4-9.30pm Sat & Sun) Completed in 1575, Andrés de Vandelvira's last building is on the western side of town. This impressive late-Renaissance masterpiece has been dubbed the 'Escorial of Andalucía'. Off the classic Vandelvira two-level patio are a chapel, now restored as an auditorium (the hospital is now a busy cultural centre), and a staircase with colourful frescoes.

🛏 Sleeping & Eating

TOP CHOICE Palacio de la Rambla
HISTORIC HOTEL €€

(☎953 75 01 96; www.palaciodelarambla.com; Plaza de Marqués 1; s/d incl breakfast €96/120; ✴ @) Another converted palace, but you're really *doing* Úbeda by staying in this elaborate Renaisaance-era building with just eight guestrooms, a huge ivy-clad courtyard, suits of armour and precious antiques. The included breakfast is substantial and the silence and privacy precious.

Parador Condestable Dávalos
HISTORIC HOTEL €€€

(☎953 75 03 45; www.parador.es; Plaza Vázquez de Molina; r €171; ✴@☎) This hotel overlooks the magnificent Plaza Vázquez de Molina and its restaurant serves up elegant dishes (around €14 to €22). Try local specialities such as *carruécano* (green peppers stuffed with partridge) or *cabrito guisado con piñones* (stewed kid with pine nuts).

Museo Agrícola Restaurant/La Posada de Úbeda
HOTEL, ANDALUCIAN €€

(☎953 79 04 73; Calle San Cristóbal 18; r from €80; ✴@) Bedecked inside and out with agricultural paraphernalia, this hotel/restaurant combo brings the rustic into the urban. Seven rooms upstairs have all mod cons, while the downstairs restaurant spills out into a courtyard that doubles as an agricultural museum.

Hotel El Postigo
BOUTIQUE HOTEL €€

(☎953 79 55 50; www.hotelelpostigo.com; Calle Postigo 5; s/d €60/90; ✴@☎✳) There's always something vaguely exciting about finding a sleek modern hotel in an old historic town. El Postigo is cool, sharp, well designed and very user friendly, with added bonuses such as a small pool, garden and private salon with a fireplace.

Taberna Zayta
TAPAS €

(Calle Cronista Pascual 6; tapas €2-3, raciones €6-9) Part of a cluster of good tapas bars near the bullring, Zatya is a no-nonsense, real, spit-and-sawdust place with strung hams decorating the ceiling, and a signature dish: *andrajos* (cod, squid, pasta and broth).

Mesón Restaurante Navarro
TAPAS €€

(Plaza del Ayuntamiento 2; raciones €6-14) This no-frills local favourite is great fun. Best *ración* is *tortitas de camarones* (crisply fried prawn mini-omelettes).

La Imprenta
MODERN €€€

(☑953 75 55 00; Plaza del Doctor Quesada 1; mains €16-25; ⊘closed Tue) A renovated number, formerly Úbeda's print works, La Imprenta serves an inspired fusion menu of local ingredients.

🛍 Shopping
The typical green glaze on Úbeda's attractive pottery dates back to Islamic times. Several workshops on Cuesta de la Merced and Calle Valencia in the Barrio San Millán, the potters' quarter northeast of the old town, sell their wares on the spot, and the potters are often willing to explain some of the ancient techniques they still use. Alfarería Tito (Plaza del Ayuntamiento 12) has a large selection too. Tito's intricately made blue-and-cream ware is particularly covetable.

ℹ Information
Tourist office (Calle Baja del Marqués 4; ⊘9am-2.450pm & 4-7pm Mon-Fri, 10am-2pm Sat) In the 18th-century Palacio Marqués de Contadero in the old town.

ℹ Getting There & Away
The **bus station** (Calle San José 6) is in the new part of town. Destinations include Baeza (€1.20, 30 minutes, 15 daily), Jaén (€5.50, 1¼ hours, up to 12 daily), Cazorla (€3.60, 45 minutes, up to 10 daily) and Granada (€11.34, 2¾ hours, seven daily).

Cazorla

POP 8173 / ELEV 885M

Cazorla, 45km east of Úbeda, is a gorgeous foot-of-the-mountains village with a hunting obsession that acts as a gateway to Spain's largest protected park.

👁 Sights
At one end of lovely Plaza de Santa María is the large shell of the Iglesia de Santa María. It was built by Andrés de Vandelvira in the 16th century but wrecked by Napoleonic troops. A 3.5km round-trip hike starts here to the Ermita San Sebastián via a mirador. Look out for the many species of birds along the route. Alternatively you can take the shorter walk up to the ancient Castillo de la Yedra, which houses the Museo del Alto Guadalquivir (adult/EU citizen €1.50/free; ⊘2.30-8pm Tue, 9am-8pm Wed-Sat, to 2pm Sun & holidays), with art and relics of past local life.

🛏 Sleeping & Eating

Check out some new and wonderful tapas including *rin-ran* (mixed salted cod, potatoes and red peppers), *talarines* (pasta), *gachamiga* (a kind of Spanish polenta), *carne de monte* (meat – usually venison); and Sierra de Cazorla's memorable olive oil – fresh, fruity and slightly bitter.

Hotel Guadalquivir
HOTEL €

(☑953 72 02 68; www.hguadalquivir.com, in Spanish; Calle Nueva 6; s/d €35/48; ❄🛜) A family-run, 17-room affair just off the main drag, the Guadalquivir has comfortable, pine-furnished rooms and big bathrooms. New floor tiles and flat-screen TVs add a modern touch to the good old-fashioned hospitality.

Hotel Ciudad de Cazorla
HOTEL €€

(☑953 72 17 00; Plaza de la Corredera 9; s/d incl breakfast €61/70; P❄@🛜🏊) This modern structure on mansion-ruled Plaza de Corredera has faced some resistance from tradition-minded locals, but it sort of blends in. Modern facilities include spacious rooms, a restaurant and outdoor pool.

Bar Las Vegas
TAPAS €

(Plaza de la Corredera 17; raciones €8) Several bars on Cazorla's three main squares serve good tapas and *raciones*. Las Vegas is the most popular, with the litter of countless satisfied lunchers covering the floor after a busy session.

Mesón Don Chema
MEAT DISHES €€

(Calle Escaleras del Mercado 2; mains €10-18) Down a lane off Calle Doctor Muñoz, this hunting-themed restaurant in a hunting-mad town serves up classic local game. All OK, if you don't mind being watched by their unnerving likenesses mounted on the wall.

ℹ Information
Oficina de Turismo Municipal (Paseo del Santo Cristo 19; ⊘10am-1pm & 5-7.30pm) The tourist office is located 200m north of Plaza de la Constitución.

ℹ Getting There & Away
Alsina Graells runs buses to/from Úbeda (€3.60, 45 minutes, up to 10 daily), Jaén (€7.88, two hours, two daily) and Granada (€15, 3½ hours, two daily). The main stop in Cazorla is Plaza de la Constitución; the tourist office has timetables.

Parque Natural de Cazorla

Filling almost all the eastern side of Jaén province, the Parque Natural de las Sierras de Cazorla, Segura y Las Villas is a stunning region of rugged mountain ranges divided by high plains and deep, forested valleys, and it's one of the best places in Spain for spotting wildlife. At 2143 sq km, it's also the biggest protected area in the country. Walkers stand a good chance of seeing wild boar, red and fallow deer, ibex and mouflon (a large wild sheep). The park also supports 2300 plant species.

The Guadalquivir, Andalucía's longest river, rises in the south of the park and flows north into the Embalse del Tranco de Beas reservoir, then west towards the Atlantic.

Admittedly, you do need wheels to reach some of the most spectacular areas and walks. The best times to visit are between late April and June, and September and October, when the vegetation flourishes and the weather is at its best. In spring, the flowers are magnificent. Peak visitor periods are Semana Santa, July and August.

◉ Sights & Activities

The tourist office in the village of Cazorla has maps and descriptions of six park hikes (from 8km to 23km) and seven drives.

RÍO BOROSA WALK

Though it gets busy at weekends and holidays, this walk of about seven hours return (plus stops) is the park's most popular for good reason. It follows the course of Río Borosa upstream to two beautiful mountain lakes: an ascent of 500m in the course of 12km from Torre del Vinagre. Using the bus to Torre del Vinagre, you can do it as a day trip from Cazorla (but confirm bus schedules before setting off). You can top up your water bottle at good, drinkable springs along the walk; the last is at the Central Eléctrica hydroelectric station.

A road signed 'Central Eléctrica', opposite Torre del Vinagre, soon crosses the Guadalquivir and, within 1km, reaches the marked start of the walk, on your right beside Río Borosa. The first section is an unpaved road, crisscrossing the tumbling river on bridges. After 4km, where the road starts climbing to the left, take a path forking right. This takes you through a beautiful 1.5km section, where the valley narrows to a gorge, Cerrada de Elías, and the path takes you to a wooden walkway to save you from swimming. Rejoining the main track, continue for 3km to the Central Eléctrica hydroelectric station. Just past this, a sign points you on up towards the Laguna de Valdeazores. This path will lead you, via some dramatic mountain scenery and two tunnels supplying water to the power station (there's room to stay dry as you go through), to reservoir Laguna de Aguas Negras, then the natural Laguna de Valdeazores.

HORNOS & EL YELMO

The small village of Hornos sits atop a high rocky outcrop with a romantic ruined castle and panoramic views over the northern end of the Embalse del Tranco. The southern approach is awe-inspiring. About 10km northeast of Hornos is the Puerto de Horno de Peguera pass and junction. One kilometre north from here, a dirt road turns left to the top of El Yelmo (1809m), one of the most distinctive mountains in the north of the park. It's 5km to the top, an ascent of 360m – driveable, but better as a walk, with superb views and griffon vultures wheeling around the skies (plus paragliders and hang-gliders at weekends). At a fork after 1.75km, go right.

SEGURA DE LA SIERRA

The most spectacular village inside the park, Segura sits 20km north of Hornos, perched on an 1100m hill crowned by a castle. When taken in 1214 by the Knights of Santiago, Segura was one of the very first Christian conquests in Andalucía.

As you reach the upper part of the village, there's a tourist office (◷10.30am-2pm & 6.30-8.30pm) beside the Puerta Nueva arch. Segura's two main monuments are normally left open all day every day, but you should check this before proceeding.

The Baño Moro (Muslim Bathhouse; Calle Caballeros Santiaguistas), built about 1150, has three elegant rooms (for cold, tepid and hot baths) with horseshoe arches and barrel vaults studded with skylights. The castle, at the top of the village, has Islamic (or maybe even earlier) origins. From its three-storey keep there are great views across to El Yelmo and far to the west.

☞ Tours

A number of operators offer trips to some of the park's less accessible areas, plus other activities. Hotels and camping grounds in the park can often arrange for them to pick you up.

Excursiones Bujarkay   ADVENTURE GUIDES
(☑953 72 11 11; www.guiasnativos.com; Calle Martinez Falero, 28, Cazorla) Walking, 4WD, biking and horse-riding trips with 'native' guides.

Tierraventura   ADVENTURE GUIDES
(☑953 72 20 11/953 71 00 73; www.aventuraca zorla.com, in Spanish; Calle Ximénez de Rada 17, Cazorla) Multiadventure activities including canoeing, hiking, canyon descents and rock climbing.

🛏 Sleeping & Eating

There's plenty of accommodation in the park, much of it dotted along the A319 north of Empalme del Valle. At peak times it's worth booking ahead. Most restaurants in the park are part of hotels or *hostales*.

Camping is not allowed outside the organised camping grounds.

Parador de Cazorla   HOTEL €€€
(☑953 72 70 75; www.parador.es; s/d €109/128; P❄🐾🛜) This hunting-lodge-style *parador* has a lovely pine-forest setting, grassy garden and good pool, but only nine of the 33 rooms have views. It's at the end of the JF7094, near Vadillo Castril.

Complejo Puente de las Herrerías
    CAMPING GROUND €
(☑953 72 70 90; www.puentedelasherrerias. com; near Vadillo Castril; sites per adult/tent/car €5.15/4.70/4.70, caravan €5.56-6.64, 2-person cabin €51.36, rooms s/d €36.40/53.30; P❄🐾) This is the largest camping ground in the park, with room for about 1000 people, plus a restaurant and a pool. You can arrange horse riding, canoeing, canyoning and climbing here. It's open from Easter to 1 November.

Los Huertos de Segura   APARTMENTS €
(☑953 48 04 02; www.loshuertosdesegura.com; Calle Castillo 11, Segura de la Sierra; 2-/4-person apt €58/78; P❄🛜) Excellent apartments whose genuinely friendly and helpful owners are full of information about tours and walking in the area. Excellent English spoken.

ℹ Information

The main information centre is the **Centro de Interpretación Torre del Vinagre** (☑953 71 30 40; ⏱10am-2pm & 4-7pm Apr-Jun, 10am-2pm & 5-8pm Jul-Aug), 16km north of Empalme del Valle on the A319. Kids will enjoy the interactive AV exhibits about the park's flora and fauna. The **Museo de Caza** (Hunting Museum) with stuffed

park wildlife, is in an adjoining building; a more-cheerful **botanic garden** is just along the road.

Editorial Alpina's 1:40,000 *Sierra de Cazorla*, which covers the south of the park and is available in English, and *Sierra de Segura*, which covers the north, are the best maps, showing selected walks that are described in accompanying booklets. You may be able to get the maps locally, but don't count on it.

ℹ Getting There & Away

Carcesa (☑953 72 11 42) runs two daily buses (except Sunday) from Cazorla's Plaza de la Constitución to Empalme del Valle (€2, 30 minutes), Arroyo Frío (€2.40, 45 minutes), Torre del Vinagre (€3.60, one hour) and Coto Ríos (€3.60, 70 minutes). Pick up the latest timetable from the Cazorla tourist office.

ALMERÍA PROVINCE

Way out east, the gritty working port of Almería and its arid hinterland lie half-forgotten on Andalucía's most unblemished stretch of coastline. Defiantly Spanish with a strong Moorish history, the Costa del Sol–style tourist juggernaut has yet to arrive in this neck of the woods, although Clint Eastwood dropped by in the 1960s to make his trilogy of Spaghetti Westerns amid scenery more reminiscent of the Wild West than southern Spain. Lying in the rain shadow of the Sierra Nevada, Almería is the Iberian Peninsula's sunniest and driest region, and the site of Europe's only desert. Modern greenhouse farming techniques have recently turned its parched landscapes into a horticultural powerhouse and a huge centre for immigrant labour.

Almería

POP 188,000

Don't underestimate sun-baked Almería, a tough waterside city with an illustrious history and a handful of important historical monuments to prove it. While the queues form outside Granada's Alhambra, mere trickles of savvy travellers claim their free tickets for Almería's equally hefty Alcazaba fortress, which lords it over a city that once served as chief sea outlet for the 10th-century Córdoba caliphate. Today Almería is an increasingly prosperous port with a thriving agribusiness sector and a strong flamenco tradition enshrined in its distinctive *tarantos*.

◉ Sights & Activities

Alcazaba CASTLE

(Calle Almanzor; adult/EU citizen €1.50/free; ◷9am-8.30pm Tue-Sun Apr-Oct, 9am-6.30pm Tue-Sun Nov-Mar) The founding of the Alcazaba by the Córdoba caliph Abd ar-Rahman III in 955 was what turned Almería into the major port of Al-Andalus. It still rises triumphantly from impregnable cliffs and commands exhilarating views, though earthquakes and time have spared little of its internal splendour.

The lowest of the Alcazaba's three compounds, the Primer Recinto, originally served as a military camp in times of siege. The Segundo Recinto was the heart of the Alcazaba. At its eastern end is the **Ermita de San Juan** chapel, which was converted from a mosque by the Catholic Monarchs, who took Almería in 1489. On its northern side are the remains of the Muslim rulers' palace, the **Palacio de Almotacín**. The Tercer Recinto, at the top end of the Alcazaba, is a fortress added by the Catholic Monarchs.

Catedral CATHEDRAL

(Plaza de la Catedral; admission €3; ◷10am-2pm & 4pm-5.30pm Mon-Fri, 10am-2pm Sat) Almería's weighty cathedral is at the heart of the old part of the city below the Alcazaba. Begun in 1524, its fortresslike appearance, with six towers, reflects the prevalence of pirate raids from North Africa during this era.

The interior has a Gothic ribbed ceiling and is trimmed with jasper and local marble. The chapel behind the main altar contains the tomb of Bishop Diego Villalán, the cathedral's founder, whose broken-nosed image is the work of Juan de Orea, who also created the Sacristía Mayor with its fine carved stonework.

FREE Centro Andaluz de Fotografía GALLERY

(Andalucian Photographic Centre; Calle Pintor Díaz Molina, 9; ◷11am-2pm & 5.30pm-9.30pm) Whether you are a keen photographer or an overheated sightseer, you will enjoy the edgy and memorable images here.

Museo Arqueológico MUSEUM

(Carretera de Ronda 91; non-EU/EU citizen €1.50/free; ◷2.30-8.30pm Tue, 9am-8.30pm Wed-Sat, 9am-2.30pm Sun) Presents artefacts from Moorish, Roman and ancient Copper Age civilisations using interesting multimedia technology.

Walks WALKS

The regional tourist office gives out a map with four monumental walks around the city, including Muslim, Christian and cinematic routes (parts of *Lawrence of Arabia* and *Patton* were filmed here).

Beaches BEACHES

A long, grey-sand beach fronts the palm-lined Paseo Marítimo, east of the city's centre.

⊨ Sleeping

TOP CHOICE Hotel Costasol HOTEL €

(☎950 23 40 11; www.hotelcostasol.com; Paseo de Almería 58; r €54; P❄@🖀) It's amazing what some red colour accents and a clean, simple but funky refurb can do. Factor in the sleek reception, enormous (for Spain) bathrooms, spacious communal areas, and stylish basement restaurant and you won't find a better hotel for this price in Andalucía.

Hotel Catedral BOUTIQUE HOTEL €€€

(☎950 27 81 78; www.hotelcatedral.net; Plaza de la Catedral 8; s/d €110/140; ❄@🖀🏊) Superbly located, this elegant if slightly pretentious restored former 19th-century house offers spacious rooms all with broadband and satellite TV. A smart bar and restaurant with funky touches serves light modern Mediterranean dishes.

Hotel Torreluz HOTEL €€

(☎950 23 43 99; www.torreluz.com; Plaza de las Flores 2 & 3; s/d 2-star €39/64, 3-star €56/74; P❄🖀) Burnt-plum-coloured walls, comfortable beds and good prices make this one of Almería's best-value places to stay.

Hotel Sevilla HOTEL €

(☎950 23 00 09; www.hotelsevillaalmeria.es; Calle de Granada 23; s/d €32/40; ❄🖀) This best budget bet is a cheerful and efficient place that offers clean rooms and a good central location. Bathrooms are minuscule but modern.

✕ Eating

Most of the best tapas bars lie in the triangle between Plaza Pablo Cazard, Puerta de Putchería and the cathedral.

TOP CHOICE Tetería Almedina MOROCCAN €

(☎629 277827; Calle Paz 2; teas €2-3, mains €7-10; ◷11am-11pm) A much-heralded nook in the old city that could give any *tetería* in Granada a run for its money. And it serves food too (try the couscous). Decor is cool and Moorish with a heavy Islamic feel.

Casa Puga
TAPAS €€

(Calle Jovellanos 7; tapas from €2, raciones from €8) In the heart of the old town, this is one of Almería's best eating establishments, with tapas served in a crowded bar out front and more-substantial fare (try the smoked fish roe) in an equally crowded restaurant behind.

Plaza de Cañas
TAPAS €€

(Calle Martín 20; tapas €2.20, raciones €6-12; ⊘closed Mon & Sep) When you've had one smoky, cavernous tapas bar too many, head to Cañas, a modern, stylish version of those ham-filled havens of yore. The food, service and ambience here are definitely 21st century. Sit out in the square and let it come to you.

Casa Joaquín
SEAFOOD €€

(☑950 26 43 59; Calle Real 111; mains €14-21; ⊘closed Sat pm, Sun & Sep) Down towards the water, this place specialises in all kinds of usual fish cooked in all kinds of unusual ways. Grab a seat and take your chances, or squeeze in at the bar and wait for a free sample to come your way.

La Charka
TAPAS €€

(Calle Trajano 8; tapas from €2) This very popular tapas haunt in Almería's busiest bar area is loud, busy with the rattle of plates and the chatter of its youngish clientele.

Drinking & Entertainment

El Quinto Toro
BAR

(Calle Juan Leal 6; ⊘noon-4pm & 8pm-midnight, closed Sat pm & Sun) Authentic, bullfight-flavoured tapas bar that has been a local institution since 1947. Good selection of tapas, and friendly third-generation owner.

Peña El Taranto
FLAMENCO CLUB

(☑950 23 50 57; Calle Tenor Iribarne 20) Hidden in the renovated Aljibes Árabes (Arab Water Cisterns), this is Almería's top flamenco club. Live performances (€20), open to the public, often happen at weekends. Local hero Tomatito still sometimes plays here.

Peña Flamenco 'El Morato'
FLAMENCO CLUB

(☑950 25 09 14; www.elmorato.com; Calle Manuel Vicente; ⊘10pm-late) Scooped out of a cave on the edge of town, this bar–club is about as local as it gets flamenco-wise in Andalucía. Slip in for weekend performances over tapas and wine and you'll soon feel like one of the family.

ⓘ Information

There are numerous banks on Paseo de Almería.

Main post office (behind Plaza Ecuador)

Policía Local (☑950 21 00 19; Calle Santos Zárate)

Regional tourist office (☑950 27 43 55; Parque de Nicolás Salmerón; ⊘9am-7pm Mon-Fri, 10am-2pm Sat & Sun)

ⓘ Getting There & Away

Air
Almería **airport** (☑950 21 37 00), 10km east of the city centre, receives flights from several European countries. **Easyjet** (www.easyjet.com) flies from London Gatwick and Stansted, **Ryanair** (www.ryanair.com) from Stansted and Madrid, **Thomas Cook Airlines** (www.thomascook airlines.co.uk) from Manchester, Birmingham and London Gatwick, and **Monarch Airlines** (www.flymonarch.com) from Birmingham and Manchester. **Air-Berlin** (www.airberlin.com) flies from Berlin and **Transavia** (www.transavia.com) from Amsterdam. **Iberia** (www.iberia.com) flies direct to/from Barcelona, Madrid and Melilla.

Boat
Trasmediterránea (☑950 23 61 55; www. trasmediterranea.es; Estación Marítima) sails daily to/from Melilla and twice daily most days from June to September. The trip takes up to eight hours on the slow ferry and three hours on the fast ferry. A *butaca* (seat) costs €33.20 one-way; car fares start at €189.20 for a small vehicle and driver. Three Moroccan lines sail to/from Nador, the Moroccan town neighbouring Melilla, with similar frequency and prices. Trasmediterránea also has summer sailings to Ghazaouet, Algeria.

Bus
Destinations served from the clean, efficient **bus station** (☑950 26 20 98) include Granada (€13.45, 2¼ hours, 10 daily), Málaga (€16, 3¼ hours, 10 daily), Murcia (€17.25, 2½ hours, 10 daily), Madrid (€25, seven hours, five daily) and Valencia (€35.65, 8½ hours, five daily).

Train
Four daily trains run to Granada (€15.90, 2¼ hours) and Seville (€38.15, 5½ hours); two run to Madrid (€44.10, 6¾ hours).

ⓘ Getting Around
The airport is 8km east of the city; the number 20 'Alquián' bus (€0.90) runs from Calle Doctor Gregorio Marañón to the airport every 40 to 50 minutes from 6.35am to 10.40pm (but less frequently on Saturday and Sunday). The last bus from the airport to the city leaves at 10.33pm (10.22pm Saturday and Sunday).

Around Almería

Beyond Benahadux, north of Almería, the landscape becomes a series of canyons and rocky wastes that look straight out of the Arizona badlands, and in the 1960s and '70s movie-makers shot around 150 Westerns here.

The movie industry has left behind three Wild West town sets that are open as tourist attractions. Mini Hollywood (950 36 52 36; adult/child €19/9; 10am-9pm Apr-Oct), the best known and best preserved of these, is 25km from Almería on the N340 Tabernas road. Parts of more than 100 movies, including *A Fistful of Dollars* and *The Good, the Bad and the Ugly,* were filmed here. At 5pm (and 8pm from mid-June to mid-September) a hammed-up bank hold-up and shootout is staged (dialogue in Spanish of course). Rather bizarrely, the ticket also includes entry to the adjoining Reserva Zoológica. You will need your own vehicle to visit from Almería.

Cabo de Gata

If you can find anyone old enough to remember the Costa del Sol before the bulldozers arrived they'd probably say it looked a bit like Cabo de Gata. Some of Spain's most beautiful and least crowded beaches are strung between the grand cliffs and capes east of Almería city, where dark volcanic hills tumble into a sparkling turquoise sea. Though Cabo de Gata is not undiscovered, it still has a wild, elemental feel and its scattered fishing villages (remember them?) remain low-key. You can walk along, or not far from, the coast right round from Retamar in the northwest to Agua Amarga in the northeast (61km); but beware – the sun can be intense and there's often little shade.

It's worth calling ahead for accommodation over Easter and in July and August.

Parque Natural de Cabo de Gata-Níjar covers Cabo de Gata's 60km coast plus a slice of hinterland. The park's main information centre is the Centro de Interpretación Las Amoladeras (950 16 04 35; 10am-2pm & 5.30-9pm mid-Jul–mid-Sep, to 3pm Tue-Sun mid-Sep–mid-Jul), about 2.5km west of Ruescas.

SAN MIGUEL DE CABO DE GATA

Fronted by a long straight beach, this scruffy village isn't the best introduction to the park. It's composed largely of holiday houses and apartments (deserted out of season), and resembles a detached suburb of Almería. Press on to the Faro, or start hiking in San José and use this as your finishing point.

South of the village stretch the Salinas de Cabo de Gata, which are salt-extraction lagoons. In spring many migrating greater flamingos and other birds call in here: by late August there can be 1000 flamingos here. An 11km trail circumnavigates the *salinas* equipped with strategically placed viewing hides. You should see a good variety of birds from here any time except in winter, when the *salinas* are drained, but you really need binoculars to appreciate the scene.

There are a couple of decent options for accommodation: Hostal Las Dunas (950 37 00 72; www.lasdunas.net; Calle Barrio Nuevo 58; s/d €40/55; P), a friendly, family-run hotel with spotless modern rooms, huge bathrooms and crazy balustraded balconies carved in marble and wreathed with flowers. For camping, try the extremely well-run Camping Cabo de Gata (950 16 04 43; sites per adult, caravan, car & power supply €17.28, bungalow €71-112; P), 1km from the beach; it has all the necessary amenities, including a restaurant. It's 2.5km north of the village by dirt roads.

Located right at the entrance to the village, El Naranjero (Calle Iglesia 1; mains €12-27; closed Sun) specialises in fish and seafood dishes.

FARO DE CABO DE GATA & AROUND

Beyond the Salinas de Cabo de Gata, a narrow road winds 4km round the cliffs to the Faro de Cabo de Gata, the lighthouse at the promontory's tip. A turn-off by Café Bar El Faro, just before the lighthouse, leads to the Torre Vigía Vela Blanca, an 18th-century watchtower atop 200m cliffs, with awesome views. Here the road ends but a walking and cycling track continues down to Playa de Mónsul (one hour on foot).

SAN JOSÉ
POP 550

San José, spreading round a bay on the eastern side of Cabo de Gata, is a mildly chic resort in summer, but it remains a small, pleasant, low-rise place and is a base for both watery and land-bound activities. Out of season you may have the place almost to yourself.

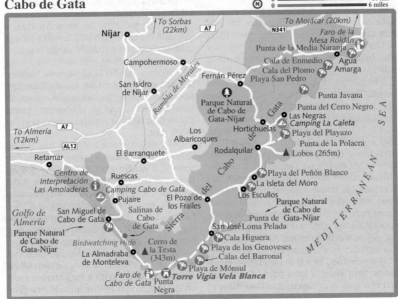

The road from the north becomes San José's main street, Avenida de San José, with the beach and harbour a couple of blocks down to the left.

Some of the best beaches on Cabo de Gata lie along a dirt road southwest from San José. Playa de los Genoveses, a broad strip of sand about 1km long with shallow waters, is 4.5km away. Playa de Mónsul, 2.5km further from town, is a shorter length of grey sand, backed by huge lumps of volcanic rock. Away from the road, the coast between these two beaches is strung with a series of isolated, sandy, cove beaches, the Calas del Barronal, which can be reached only on foot.

On Avenida de San José you'll find a Natural Park information office (Avenida de San José 27; ⊙10am-2pm & 5-8pm), a bank and an ATM. The information office can tell you about bicycle rental, horse riding, boat trips and diving.

🛏 Sleeping & Eating

Santuario San José   HOTEL €€
(📞902 87 73 88; www.elsantuariosanjose.es; Camino de Calahiguera 9; s/d €64/79; P ❋) This refurbished 28-room brilliant-white hotel offers minimal yet friendly design with attractive lounging and dining

terraces. Its Restaurante Aniceto (mains €15-24) has a strong reputation locally.

Hostal Sol Bahía   HOTEL €€
(📞950 38 03 07; Avenida de San José; d €40-70; ❋) The Sol Bahía and its sister establishment, Hostal Bahía Plaza, across the street, are in the centre of San José and have functional, clean rooms in bright, modern buildings.

Hotel Cortijo el Sotillo   HOTEL €€
(📞950 61 11 00; www.cortijoelsotillo.com; Carretera Entrada a San José; r €75; P ❋ 🛜 ☜) This smart but fun ranch-style complex, popular with families, has a host of great facilities, on-site riding and an excellent restaurant (mains €15-25).

Camping Tau   CAMPING GROUND €
(📞950 38 01 66; www.campingtau.com; sites per adult/tent/car €6.50/9.50/6; ⊙Apr-Sep) Set 250m from the beach, the small but shady Tau is very popular with families.

Restaurante Mediterraneo   SEAFOOD €€
(📞950 38 00 93; Puerto Deportivo de San José; mains €10-22) Last stop in a run of similarly good seafood restaurants near the marina, this one has particularly friendly staff and a less frantic atmosphere than some of its neighbours.

The rugged coast northeast of San José allows only two small settlements, the odd fort and a few beaches before the village of Las Negras, 17km away as the crow flies. The road spends most of its time ducking inland.

The hamlet of Los Escullos has a short beach. You can walk here from San José, along a track starting at Cala Higuera bay. One kilometre beyond Los Escullos, La Isleta del Moro is a tiny village with a beach and a couple of fishing boats. Casa Café de la Loma (☑950 38 98 31; www.degata.com/laloma; s/d €40/60), on a small hill above the village and five minutes from the beach, is a 200-year-old house restored in Al-Andalus style with airy rooms and terrific views. From here the road heads inland past the spooky former gold-mining village of Rodalquilar, worth a detour. About 1km past Rodalquilar is the turn-off to Playa del Playazo, a good beach between two headlands, 2km along a level track. From here you can walk near the coast to the village of Las Negras, which is set on a pebbly beach and largely given over to seasonal tourism.

On Las Negras' main street, Hostal Arrecife (☑950 38 81 40; Calle Bahía 6, Las Negras; s/d €28/40) has cool, quiet, well-maintained rooms, some with sea views from their balconies. Camping La Caleta (☑950 52 52 37; www.vayacamping.net/la caleta; sites per adult/tent/car €5.60/6.70/5.60; ☉year-round; P☀) lies in a separate cove 1km south of Las Negras. It can be fiercely hot in summer, but there is a good pool. Other accommodation in Las Negras is mostly holiday apartments and houses to let. Restaurante La Palma (mains €12-24), overlooking the beach, plays good music and serves a huge array of fish dishes.

LAS NEGRAS TO AGUA AMARGA

There's no road along this secluded, cliff-lined stretch of coast, but walkers can take an up-and-down path of about 11km, giving access to several beaches. Playa San Pedro, one hour from Las Negras, is the site of a ruined hamlet (with castle), inhabited erratically by hippies and naturists. It's 1½ hours on from there to Cala del Plomo beach, with another tiny village, then 1½ hours further to Agua Amarga.

Drivers must head inland from Las Negras through Hortichuelas. A mostly unsealed road heads northeast, cross-country from the bus shelter in Fernán Pérez. Keep to the main track at all turnings, and after 10km you'll reach a sealed road running down from the N341 to Agua Amarga, a chic and expensive but still low-key former fishing village on a straight sandy beach.

Breezy, beachfront Hostal Restaurante La Palmera (☑950 13 82 08; www.hostalrestaurantelapalmera.com; Calle Aguada; d low/high season €60/90; ☀) has 10 bright rooms all with sea views, and its restaurant (mains €11 to €19) is Agua Amarga's most popular lunch spot.

Chic, slick MiKasa Suites & Spa (☑950 13 80 73; www.mikasasuites.com; Carretera Carboneras; d incl breakfast €125-240; P☀☎☂☀) is an elegant, comfortable, romantic hideaway for the long-weekend crowd. There's a poolside restaurant, Restaurante La Villa (☑950 13 80 73), and more-expensive food (by the sound of it) in the on-site spa – ever heard of caviar facials or algae wraps?

Top spot for food is the minimal but courteous Restaurante Playa (mains €8-23; ☉closed Jan & Feb), with a long terrace right on the beach. Specialities include rice dishes and – not surprisingly – 'catch of the day'.

❶ Getting There & Away

From Almería bus station buses run to El Cabo de Gata (€2, 30 minutes, 10 daily), San José (€3.16, 1¼ hours, four daily Monday to Saturday), Las Negras (€4.25, 1¼ hours, one daily Monday to Saturday) and Agua Amarga (€4.95, 1¼ hours, one daily Monday to Friday).

Mojácar

Tucked away in an isolated corner of one of Spain's most traditional regions lies Mojácar, a town that was almost abandoned in the mid-20th century until a foresightful local mayor started luring artists and others with giveaway property offers. Although the tourists have arrived, Mojácar has retained its essence.

There are actually two towns here; old Mojácar Pueblo, a jumble of white, cube-shaped houses on a hilltop 2km inland, and Mojácar Playa, a modern beach resort.

◉ Sights & Activities

Exploring Mojácar Pueblo is mainly a matter of wandering the mazelike streets, with their bougainvillea-swathed balconies, stopping off at craft shops, galleries and boutiques. The Mirador El Castillo, at the topmost point, provides magnificent views.

The fortress-style Iglesia de Santa María (Calle Iglesia) dates from 1560 and may have once been a mosque.

The most touching spot is the Fuente Mora (Moorish Fountain; Calle La Fuente) in the lower part of the old town. Though remodelled in modern times, it maintains the medieval Islamic tradition of making art out of flowing water. For good windsurfing equipment (per hour €12), canoeing, sailing and water-skiing (per session €20), check out Samoa Surf (☑666 442263; Playa de las Ventánicas) in Mojácar Playa.

🛏 Sleeping & Eating

El Mirador del Castillo   HOTEL
(☑950 47 30 22; www.elcastillomojacar.com; Mirador El Castillo; d €60-68; @🛜🌊) A laid-back *hostal* with a no-fuss bohemian atmosphere and fantastic views.

La Taberna   TRADITIONAL ANDALUCIAN
(Plaza del Cano 1; tapas & platos combinados from €4; ☑) This thriving little eatery, inside a warren of cavelike rooms, serves extremely well-prepared meals, with plenty of tasty vegetarian options.

ℹ Information

Tourist office (☑950 61 50 25; www.mojacar. es; Calle Glorieta 1; ⊙10am-2pm & 5-7.30pm Mon-Fri, 10.30am-1.30pm Sat) Very helpful tourist office; just off Mojácar Pueblo's Plaza Nueva.

ℹ Getting There & Around

Local buses link Mojácar Pueblo with Mojácar Playa every 30 minutes. Long-distance buses run to Murcia (€10.17, 2½ hours, five daily), Almería (€6.67, 1¾ hours, two daily), Granada (€15, four hours, two daily) and Madrid (€34.13, eight hours, two daily).

Extremadura

Best Places to Eat

» Restaurante La Troya (p801)

» Mesón El Asador (p796)

» Restaurante Torre de Sande (p796)

» Tabula Calda (p806)

Best Places to Stay

» Parador Jarandilla (p787)

» Hospedería del Real Monasterio (p803)

» Hotel Casa Don Fernando (p796)

» La Flor de al-Andalus (p805)

» Hotel Adealba (p806)

» Posada Dos Orillas (p800)

Why Go?

Visiting Extremadura is like traversing old Spain, from the country's finest Roman ruins to medieval cities and villages that have yet to fully enter the 21st century. Mérida, Cáceres and Trujillo rank among the country's best-preserved historical settlements, while *extremeño* villages have a timeless charm, from the remote valleys of the north to beguiling Zafra on the cusp of Andalucía in the south.

This is a region of big skies and vast swathes of sparsely populated land with isolated farmhouses. Wooded sierras rise along the region's northern, eastern and southern fringes while the raptor-rich Parque Nacional de Monfragüe is arguably Extremadura's most dramatic corner.

Best of all, relatively few foreign travellers make it this far. Spaniards, however, know it as a place to sample some of inland Spain's finest food, especially roasted meats and the pungent and creamy Torta de Casar cheese.

When to Go
Caceres

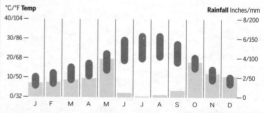

April The Feria del Queso (Cheese Fair) arrives in Trujillo on the last weekend in April.

May The Valle del Jerte blossoms with the spring cherry harvest.

July–August Mérida's 2000-year-old Roman theatre hosts the Festival de Teatro Clásico.

NORTHERN EXTREMADURA

The western reaches of the Cordillera Central mountain range arch right around Plasencia from the Sierra de Gredos in the east to the Sierra de Gata in the west. In the region's northeast you'll find three lovely valleys: La Vera, Valle del Jerte and Valle del Ambroz. Watered by mountain streams and dotted with ancient villages, the valleys offer fine walking routes and accommodation.

The once-remote Las Hurdes region in the northernmost tip of Extremadura has a harsh beauty, while the Sierra de Gata in the northwest is pretty, wooded and more fertile.

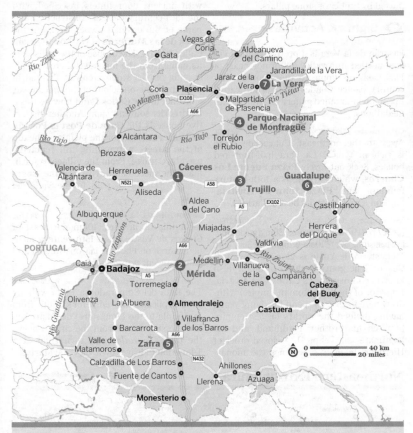

Extremadura Highlights

❶ Stroll the Ciudad Monumental's evocative cobbled streets in **Cáceres** (p793)

❷ Clamber over Spain's finest Roman ruins in **Mérida** (p804)

❸ Travel to **Trujillo** (p798), medieval home town of some of Latin America's most (in)famous conquistadors

❹ Spot majestic birds of prey as they wheel over the **Parque Nacional de Monfragüe** (p792)

❺ Wander among the gleaming white buildings in the southern town of **Zafra** (p810)

❻ Join the pilgrims on the road to **Guadalupe** (p802), with its extraordinary monastery complex nestled in a valley

❼ Explore the half-timbered villages of **La Vera** (p786), one of Spain's least-visited areas

La Vera

Surrounded by mountains often still capped with snow as late as May, the fertile La Vera, on the northern side of Río Tiétar valley, produces raspberries, asparagus and, above all, paprika *(pimentón)*, sold in charming old-fashioned tins. Typical, too, of La Vera are half-timbered houses leaning at odd angles, their overhanging upper storeys supported by timber or stone pillars.

◉ Sights & Activities

Pasarón de la Vera   VILLAGE
Pasarón de la Vera is a pretty, tranquil village nestled in a valley 32km northeast of Plasencia. It's home to the emotive 16th-century palace Condes de Osorno, featuring an open-arcaded gallery decorated with medallions.

Cuacos de Yuste   VILLAGE
Away to the northeast, Cuacos de Yuste is rich in typical La Vera half-timbered houses. Seek out lovely **Plaza Fuente Los Chorros**, which surrounds a 16th-century fountain, and **Plaza Juan de Austria**, built on a rock, with its bust of Carlos I.

Monasterio de Yuste   MONASTERY
(☑927 17 21 97; admission free, 30min guided tour in Spanish €2.50; ◷10am-6.15pm Tue-Sun) The Monasterio de Yuste is 2km northwest of Cuacos. The gouty Carlos I of Spain (also known, confusingly, as Carlos V of Austria, Emperor of the Holy Roman Empire) withdrew here in 1557 to spend his dying years, having divided the world's biggest empire between his brother, Ferdinand, and his legitimate son, Felipe II. A closed order of Hieronymite monks occupies the monastery itself, but you can visit the outlying **church**, with its Gothic and Plateresque cloisters, and the modest **royal chambers**, where the ailing monarch's bed was placed to give him a direct view of the altar.

Garganta la Olla   VILLAGE
A narrow road with fine views continues 7km beyond the monastery to Garganta la Olla, a picturesque, steeply pitched village with ancient door lintels inscribed with the 16th-century date of construction and name of the original owner. Seek out the **Casa de las Muñecas** at No 3 on the main Calle Chorillo. The 'House of the Dolls' gets its name from the much-weathered female carving on the stone archway. Painted in blue, the come-on colour of the time, it was a brothel under Carlos I and now houses a far drearier souvenir shop. Another distinctive house is the **Casa de Postas Posada de Viajeros** (look for the plaque at the top of the street), a travelling inn reputedly used by Carlos I. From the village, you can make the spectacular drive over the 1269m **Puerto de Piornal** pass to the Valle del Jerte.

Jarandilla de la Vera   VILLAGE
Jarandilla de la Vera, 10km northeast of Cuacos de Yuste, has a 15th-century fortified church on Plaza de la Constitución and a magnificent *parador* (p787).

Ruta del Emperador   WALKING TRAIL
The Ruta del Emperador, a 10km walking trail, replicates the emperor's route from Jarandilla to the Monasterio de Yuste. Follow the sign south from the church below the town's *parador* and turn right at a T-junction to leave town via Calle Marina.

Northeastern Extremadura

EASTER SUFFERING

On the day before Good Friday, Villanueva de la Vera is the scene of one of the more bizarre of Spain's religious festivities, **Los Empalaos** (literally 'the Impaled'). Several penitent locals strap their arms to a beam (from a plough) while their near-naked bodies are wrapped tight with cords from waist to armpits, and all along the arms to the fingertips. Barefoot, veiled, with two swords strapped to their backs and – to top it all – wearing a crown of thorns, these 'walking crucifixes' follow a painful Way of the Cross. Hanging from the timber are chains of iron that clank in a sinister fashion as the penitents make their painful progress, watched by the crowds. Guided by *cirineos* (guides who light the way and help them if they fall), the *empalaos* occasionally cross paths. When this happens, they kneel and rise again to continue their laborious journey. Doctors stay on hand, as being so tightly strapped does nothing for blood circulation.

Valverde de la Vera & Villanueva de la Vera
VILLAGES

Other La Vera villages with fine traditional architecture are Valverde de la Vera and Villanueva de la Vera. The former is particularly engaging; lovely Plaza de España is lined with timber balconies, and water gushes down ruts etched into the cobbled lanes.

Sleeping & Eating

Most of the villages have well-signposted camping grounds and *casas rurales* (country home, village or farmstead accommodation) with rooms to let.

Parador Jarandilla
HOTEL €€

(927 56 01 17; www.parador.es; Avenida de García Prieto 1, Jarandilla de la Vera; d €70-137; P🅿❄🏊) Be king of the castle for the night at this 15th-century castle-turned-hotel. Apparently Carlos I hung out here for a few months while waiting for his monastery digs to be completed. Within the stout walls and turrets are period-furnished rooms, plus a classic courtyard where you can dine on royal fantasies from the gourmet restaurant menu.

La Vera de Yuste
CASA RURAL €€

(927 17 22 89; www.laveradeyuste.com, in Spanish; Calle Teodoro Perianes 17, Cuacos de Yuste; s/d €40/60; ❄) This real gem is set in two typical 18th-century village houses near Plaza Major. The beamed rooms have chunky rustic furniture and the garden is a delight, surrounded by rose bushes with a small courtyard and vegetable patch. Dinner is available.

La Casa de Pasarón
HOTEL €€

(927 46 94 07; www.pasaron.com; Calle de La Magdalena 18, Pasarón de la Vera; d €80-95;

P❄) Follow the signs through the village to this handsome family house, where the ground floor dates from 1890. Rooms are bathed in light with terracotta tiles and lashings of white linen and paintwork. The restaurant is excellent, but only opens if there are enough people; there are small bars serving food in the village.

Casa Rural Parada Real
CASA RURAL €

(927 17 96 05; www.paradareal.com; Calle Chorrillo 28, Garganta La Olla; s/d €40/50; ❄) Painted a fetching dark pink, this attractive *casa rural* at the top of the main street has wrought-iron balconies and bright no-fuss rooms. There's a fine downstairs restaurant (meals €15 to €20).

Hotel Don Juan de Austria
HOTEL €€

(927 56 02 06; www.donjuandeaustria.com; Avenida Soledad Vega Ortiz 101, Jarandilla de la Vera; d from €60; ❄@🏊) This long-standing hotel has a modest spa complex, with hot tub, saunas (including Finnish and Turkish) and massages. Rooms (renovated in 2007) are warmly bathed in ochre, with old-fashioned detail and hardwood floors.

Camping Jaranda
CAMPING €

(927 56 04 54; www.campingjaranda.es; Jarandilla de la Vera; sites per adult/tent/car €4.70/4.80/4.80; ☉mid-Mar–mid-Sep; 🏊) Located beside a gurgling brook, 1.25km west of Jarandilla, Camping Jaranda provides sketch maps for local walks. There's a terraced restaurant, plenty of shade and bungalows and cabins (€64 to €104).

Information

Asociación de Turismo de la Vera (www. aturive.com, in Spanish) Useful website for activities.

Comarca de la Vera (www.comarcadelavera. com) Another recommended website.

Tourist office (☑927 56 04 60; www.jaran dilla.com, in Spanish; Plaza de la Constitución 1, Jarandilla de la Vera; ☉10am-2pm & 4-6pm Tue-Sun)

ⓘ Getting There & Away

Up to three buses daily run between lower La Vera villages and Plasencia. There is one daily bus from Plasencia to Madrigal de la Vera (€7.85, 1¾ hours), the most distant village.

Valle del Jerte

This valley, separated by the Sierra de Tormantos from La Vera, grows half of Spain's cherries and is a sea of white blossom in early spring. Visit in May and every second house is busy boxing the ripe fruit.

◉ Sights & Activities

Piornal   VILLAGE
Piornal (1200m), on the southeast flank of the valley and famous for its Serrano ham, is well placed for walks along the Sierra de Tormantos.

Cabezuela del Valle   VILLAGE
In Cabezuela del Valle, the Plaza de Extremadura area has some fine houses with overhanging wooden balconies. A spectacular, winding 35km road leads from just north of Cabezuela over the 1430m Puerto de Honduras to Hervás in the Valle del Ambroz.

Jerte   VILLAGE
Jerte has another excellent base for walks within the nature reserve: Reserva Natural de la Garganta de los Infiernos ('Hell's Gorge'). The Centro de Interpretación de la Naturaleza (☑927 01 49 36; ☉9am-2pm & 5-8pm), beside Camping Valle del Jerte, has an illustrated display and can provide a map highlighting 12 walks. An easy 1½-hour 7km return walk from the office takes you to **Los Pilones**, with its strange, smooth rock formations and winding emerald-and-sapphire-coloured stream.

Tornavacas   VILLAGE
Tornavacas, yet another Extremaduran village with a huddled old quarter, is the starting point of the Ruta de Carlos V (www.ruta delemperador.com, in Spanish). Twenty-eight kilometres long, the trail (PR1) follows the route by which Carlos I was borne over the mountains to Cuacos de Yuste via Jaran-

dilla de la Vera. You can walk it in one day – just as Carlos' bearers did in the 1550s. The route crosses the Sierra de Tormantos by the 1479m Collado (or Puerto) de las Yeguas.

🛏 Sleeping & Eating

Camping Río Jerte   CAMPING €
(☑927 17 30 06; www.campingriojerte.com; sites per adult/tent/car €4.60/4.60/4.60, 4-6 person bungalows €64-105; ⊛) Located 1.5km southwest of Navaconcejo, facilities include a volleyball court. To cool off, choose from the adjacent natural riverside pool or a standard artificial one.

El Cerezal de los Sotos   CASA RURAL €€
(☑927 47 04 29; www.elcerezaldelossotos.net, in Spanish; Calle de las Vegas, Jerte; d incl breakfast €76; P ❄ ⊛) The valley is known for *casas rurales* like this one. It is a homey stone house dating from 1890, with beams, open fireplace and spacious attractive rooms set amid cherry orchards and sweeping lawns above the river. Follow the signs over the bridge from Jerte and the N110. Dinner is available (€19).

Valle del Jerte   TRADITIONAL €€
(☑927 47 04 48; Gargantilla 16, Jerte; meals €25-30) This family-run traditional restaurant is *the* place to taste local specialties like trout and *cabrito* (kid). The superb desserts include a classic cherry-and-goat's-cheese tart topped with cherry-flavoured honey.

ⓘ Information

Tourist office (☑927 47 25 58; www.turismo valledeljerte.com, in Spanish; ☉10am-5.30pm Mon-Fri, to 2pm Sat & Sun) Located 600m north of Cabezuela del Valle on the N110; covers the whole valley.

Valle del Jerte tourism (www.elvalledeljerte. com) Another useful website.

ⓘ Getting There & Away

On weekdays, there's one bus daily from Plasencia to Piornal (€2.80, one hour) and up to five daily along the valley as far as Tornavacas (€3.25, one hour and 20 minutes).

Valle del Ambroz

This broader valley west of the Valle del Jerte was once split by the Roman Vía de la Plata, whose name lives on in the A66 motorway that runs through the valley. The area's tourist office (☑927 47 36 18; www.valle ambroz.com, in Spanish; Calle Braulio Navas 6;

⊙10am-2pm & 4.30-7.30pm Tue-Fri, 10am-2pm Sat & Sun) is in Hervás.

HERVÁS
POP 4130

⊙ Sights & Activities
Hervás has Extremadura's best surviving **barrio judío** (Jewish quarter); it thrived until the tragic 1492 expulsion of the Jews, when most families fled to Portugal. Seek out Calles Rabilero and Cuestecilla, then, for a fine view, climb up to the **Iglesia de Santa María**, on the site of a ruined Knights Templars castle.

Museo Pérez Comendador-Leroux
ART MUSEUM
(☑927 48 16 55; Calle Asensio Neila; admission €1.20; ⊙4-8pm Tue, 11am-2pm & 4-8pm Wed-Fri, 10.30am-2pm Sat & Sun) Within an impressive 18th-century mansion, the Museo Pérez Comendador-Leroux houses works of Hervás-born 20th-century sculptor Enrique Pérez Comendador and his wife, the French painter Magdalena Leroux.

Museo de la Moto Clásica
VEHICLE MUSEUM
(☑927 48 12 06; www.museomotoclasica.com; Carretera de la Garganta; adult/12-25yr/under 12yr €10/5/free; ⊙10.30am-1.30pm & 5-9pm Mon-Fri, 10.30am-9pm Sat & Sun) Set in distinctive conical-roofed buildings 200m north of the river, this museum has classic motorcycles, cars and horse-drawn carriages.

⌂ Sleeping & Eating

Albergue de la Via de la Plata
HOSTEL €
(☑927 47 34 70; www.alberguesviaplata.es; Paseo de la Estación; per person €18-20; P @) Owner Carlos runs this delightful hostel with warmth and enthusiasm. The setting is an evocative converted train station overlooking the overgrown tracks, not in use since 1984. Rooms and the communal areas are brightly furnished and there's a bar, as well as self-catering facilities.

El Jardín del Convento
HOTEL €€
(☑927 48 11 61; www.eljardindelconvento.com, in Spanish; Plaza del Convento 22; r €60-90, cottage €110; P ❄ 🅿) Dating from 1860, this stunningly restored former convent has just six rooms, plus a small cottage. The former are large with wooden floors, exposed stone walls, period furniture and a well-concealed TV. Several rooms overlook the exquisite gardens, with beds of roses, a vegetable patch and plenty of tranquil seating space. Dinner is available in summer.

❶ Getting There & Away
Up to five buses daily run between Cáceres, Plasencia and Salamanca via the Valle del Ambroz, calling by Hervás (€3.15).

GRANADILLA
About 25km west of Hervás, the ghost village of **Granadilla** (admission free; ⊙10am-1pm & 4-8pm), overlooking the Embalse de Gabriel y Galán, is a beguiling reminder of how Extremadura's villages must have looked before the rush to modernisation. Founded in 1170 but abandoned in the 1960s, the village is slowly coming back to life through a student project designed to restore Granadilla's architecture; many of the students now live in the village.

After entering through the **Puerta de Villa**, climb up the cobblestone **Calle Mayor** into the delightfully rustic **Plaza Mayor**, then wind your way back to the 15th-century **Torre de Defensa**; from the summit, there are evocative views of the village, its 12th-century **Almoravid walls** and the surrounding pinewoods.

Las Hurdes
One of inland Spain's least-traversed corners, Las Hurdes has taken nearly a century to shake off its image of poverty, disease and chilling tales of witchcraft, and even cannibalism. In 1922 the miserable existence of the *hurdanos* prompted Alfonso XIII to declare during a horseback tour, 'I can bear to see no more'.

The austere, rocky terrain yields only small terraces of cultivable land along the riverbanks. The few remaining original, squat stone houses resemble slate-roofed sheep pens as much as human dwellings. In the hilly terrain, donkeys and mules remain more practical than tractors while clusters of beehives produce high-quality honey.

The valley of **Río Hurdano**, slicing northwest from Vegas de Coria and cut by the EX204, is at the heart of Las Hurdes. From **Nuñomoral**, 7.5km up the valley, a road heads west up a side valley to **El Gasco**, from where there's a particularly good one-hour return walk to **El Chorro de la Meancera**, a 70m waterfall. This side valley, the most picturesque of the area, has farming terraces carved out of the ravine's steep banks and clusters of traditional stone and slate-roofed houses huddled together in hamlets such as **Cottolengo** and **La Huetre**.

SIERRA DE GATA

The Sierra de Gata is a remote land of wooded hills and valleys, punctuated by spectacular outcrops of granite, the building material of choice in the vernacular architecture.

Hoyos, formerly the summer residence of the bishops of Coria, has some impressive *casas señoriales* (mansions). The solid sandstone mass of its 16th-century Iglesia de Nuestra Señora del Buen Varón is surrounded on three sides by wide plazas and balconies bright with cascading flowers.

Santibáñez el Alto, high on a lonely windswept ridge to the east, has some lovely cobblestone streets beneath the partially ruined walls of the mostly 13th-century castle.

Of all the hamlets in the sierra, the most delightful is San Martín de Trebejo. Beside cobblestone lanes with water coursing down central grooves, traditional houses jut out upon timber-and-stone supports. The pick of the village's *casas rurales* is Casa Antolina ([ ]927 51 05 29; www.casa-antolina.com, in Spanish; Calle La Fuente 1, San Martín de Trebejo; s/d/ste €60/65/95), with its tastefully restored rustic rooms. On the northern edge of the village, you can stroll out along an original Roman road. Here and in the two next villages looking west, Elvas and Valverde del Fresno, the folk speak their own isolated dialect, a strange mix of Spanish and Portuguese.

Other pretty villages in the area include Trebejo and Torre de San Miguel.

Buses run daily between Coria and Hoyos, and from Plasencia to Valverde del Fresno, San Martín de Trevejo, Hoyos and Santibáñez El Alto.

To get a feel for Las Hurdes at the pace it demands, set aside a day to walk the PR40, a near-circular 28km route that follows ancient shepherd trails from Casares de las Hurdes to Las Heras.

Other fascinating (and isolated) villages include Riomalo de Arriba, Ladrillar, Cabezo and Las Mestas, at the junction of the forest-lined road that leads up into the Peña de Francia towards La Alberca (p142). Tiny Las Mestas proudly advertises its honey as being the best in the world; several stores sell it by the jar.

For hotels and *casas rurales,* check out the website of the tourist office ([ ]927 43 53 29; www.todohurdes.com; Avenida de Las Hurdes, Caminomorisco; ⊗10am-2pm & 4.30-7pm Tue-Sat, 11am-1.30pm Sun) or visit them in person in Caminomorisco.

Public transport is infrequent in these parts. On weekdays, one bus runs daily between Plasencia and Vegas de Coria (€5.95, 1½ hours) and Casares de las Hurdes (€7.25, 2¼ hours). Another runs between Riomalo de Arriba and Vegas de Coria (€3.20, 30 minutes), connecting with the Plasencia service. Two Coria–Salamanca buses call by Caminomorisco Monday to Saturday and one bus connects the town with Plasencia on weekdays.

Coria

POP 12,900

This pretty, small market town lies south of the Sierra de Gata. Massive and largely intact protective walls, marked by four gates, enclose the historic quarter of town. The Romans called the place Caurium; after a period of decay, its splendour was revived under the Moors, when it was briefly the capital of a small Muslim state. Today it seems an altogether more modest place.

◉ Sights & Activities

FREE Catedral   CATHEDRAL
(Plaza de la Catedral; ⊗10.30am-2pm & 4.30-7pm) The primarily Gothic catedral has intricate plateresque decoration around its north portal. Attached is a small ecclesiastical museum (admission €2). On the plain below is a fine stone bridge, abandoned in the 17th century by Río Alagón, which now takes a more southerly course.

Museo de la Carcel Real   MUSEUM
(Calle de las Monjas 2; admission €1.50; ⊗10.30am-2pm & 5.30-8.30pm Wed-Sun) The Museo de la Carcel Real, once the town prison, houses Coria's tiny two-storey archaeological museum. Step inside the dark, poky *celda del castigo* (punishment cell),

then see how the cushy 1st-floor cells differed from the plebs' prison below.

Convento de la Madre de Dios CONVENT
(Calle de las Monjas; admission €1.50; ☺10am-12.45pm & 4.15-6.45pm Sun-Fri, 4.15-6.45pm Sat) The Convento de la Madre de Dios is a thriving 16th-century convent with an elegant cloister. The sisters sell a variety of delicious homemade sweets and pastries.

🛏 Sleeping & Eating

Palacio Coria HOTEL €€
(☎927 50 64 49; www.hotelpalaciocoria.es; Plaza de la Catedral; s/d from €70/85; 🅿 ❀ 🛜) Opened in early 2008 in a 17th-century former bishop's palace next to the cathedral, this sumptuous accommodation successfully couples modern comfort and convenience with heady palatial surrounds. There are excellent weekend deals.

El Bobo de Coria TRADITIONAL EXTREMEÑO €€
(Calle de las Monjas 6; meals €25-30; ☺Tue-Sun) Particularly strong on local mushroom dishes in season, 'the Idiot of Coria' (named after a Velázquez painting), with its eclectically rustic decor, is also rich in traditional Extremadura dishes.

ℹ Information
Tourist office (☎927 50 13 51; http://turismo.coria.org, in Spanish; Avenida de Extremadura 39; ☺9.30am-2pm & 5-7pm Mon-Fri, 10am-2pm Sat & Sun)

ℹ Getting There & Away
The **bus station** (☎927 50 01 10; Calle de Chile) is in the new part of town. Buses run to/from Plasencia (€5.35, 50 minutes, three daily) and Cáceres (€7.15, 3½ hours, five daily).

Plasencia
POP 41,150

This pleasant, bustling town is the natural hub of northern Extremadura. Rising above a bend of Río Jerte, it retains long sections of its defensive walls. Founded in 1186 by Alfonso VIII of Castilla, Plasencia lost out to Cáceres as Extremadura's premier town only in the 19th century. It has an earthy and attractive old quarter of narrow streets and stately stone buildings, many emblazoned with noble coats of arms. Plasencia seems to be competing with Madrid with its number of bars, particularly around the historic centre.

◉ Sights

Plaza Mayor SQUARE
In Plasencia life flows through the lively, arcaded Plaza Mayor, meeting place of 10 streets and scene of a Tuesday farmers market since the 12th century. The jaunty fellow who strikes the hour on top of the much-restored Gothic transitional town hall is El Abuelo Mayorga (Grandpa Mayorga), an unofficial symbol of the town.

Catedral CATHEDRAL
(Plaza de la Catedral; ☺9am-1pm & 5-7pm Mon-Sat, 9am-1pm Sun) Plasencia's cathedral is actually two in one. The 16th-century Catedral Nueva (under restoration until 2011) is mainly Gothic, with a handsome plateresque facade. Within the Romanesque Catedral Vieja (admission €1.50; ☺9am-1pm & 5-7pm) are the classic 13th-century cloisters surrounding a trickling fountain and lemon trees. Also on view is the soaring octagonal Capilla de San Pablo with the dramatic 1569 Caravaggio painting of John the Baptist.

FREE Centro de Interpretación Torre Lucia MULTIMEDIA DISPLAY
(Calle Torre Lucia; ☺10am-2pm & 5-7pm Tue-Sat) The Centro de Interpretación Torre Lucia, located just off Avenida del Ejército, tells the history of medieval Plasencia through a video, models and artefacts and provides access to a hunk of the city wall, which you can walk along.

🛏 Sleeping

Parador HOTEL €€
(☎927 42 58 70; www.parador.es; Plaza San Vicente Ferrer; d €70-137; 🅿 ❀ ❀) This *parador* is a classic – still oozing the atmosphere and austerity of its 15th-century convent roots, with massive stone columns, soaring ceilings and a traditional Renaissance cloister. The rooms are far from monastic, being luxuriously furnished with rugs and rich fabrics.

Hotel Rincón Extremeño HOTEL €
(☎927 41 11 50; www.hotelrincon.com, in Spanish; Calle Vidrieras 6; s/d €35/45; ❀ 🛜) This unpretentious hotel just off Plaza Mayor has clean, if unmemorable, rooms, although its popular restaurant is more daring, with frogs legs and white truffles with garlic on the menu (meals €25).

🍴 Eating
At lunchtime and sunset, the bars and terraces surrounding Plaza Mayor fill up with eager punters, downing *cañas* (a small

draught beer) or the local *pitarra* red while munching complimentary *pintxos* (tapas) and watching life pass by.

Corral

TRADITIONAL EXTREMEÑO €

(☑927 41 52 69; Calle Vidrieras 11; meals €10) This no-frills restaurant has paper table-cloths and bright lights, but the food is good and astonishingly cheap. Try the *sopa extremeño,* with garlic, bread, ham, aspara-gus and egg (€4).

Casa Juan

EXTREMEÑO, FRENCH €€

(☑927 42 40 42; Calle Arenillas 5; meals €25-30; ☺Fri-Wed) Tucked down a quiet cobbled lane, French-owned Casa Juan does well-prepared *extremeño* meat dishes, such as shoulder of lamb and suckling pig. Try the homemade melt-in-the-mouth *foie gras* or Parisian authentic *escargots au gratin.* Eat in the vast dining room or on the smaller rear terrace surrounded by pot plants.

ⓘ Information

Municipal tourist office (☑927 42 38 43; www.aytoplasencia.es/turismo, in Spanish; Calle Santa Clara 2; ☺9am-2pm & 4-9pm Mon-Fri, 10am-2pm & 4-8pm Sat & Sun)

Regional tourist office (☑927 01 78 40; www.turismoextremadura.com; Calle Torre Lucia; ☺9am-2pm & 4-6pm Mon-Fri, 9.45am-2pm Sat & Sun)

ⓘ Getting There & Away

The **bus station** (☑927 41 45 50; Calle de Tornavacas 2) is about 750m east of Plaza Mayor. The train station is off the Cáceres road, about 1km southwest of town.

Up to five buses daily run to/from Cáceres (€4.05, 50 minutes), Madrid (€28.08, 5½ hours) and Salamanca (€8.43, 2½ hours). Local services, weekdays only, include La Vera, Hervás, Coria, Hoyos, Caminomorisco and Valverde del Fresno.

Trains depart from Plasencia to Madrid (€20.15, three to 3½ hours, two to six daily), Cáceres (€5.55, 1½ hours, up to five daily) and Mérida (€8.75, 2½ hours, two to three daily).

Parque Nacional de Monfragüe

Spain's 14th and newest national park, created in 2007, is a hilly paradise for birdwatchers. Straddling the Tajo valley, it's home to some of Spain's most spectacular colonies of raptors and more than 75% of Spain's protected species. Among some 175 feathered varieties are around 300 pairs of black vultures (the largest concentration of Europe's biggest bird of prey) and populations of two other rare large birds: the Spanish imperial eagle and the black stork. The best time to visit is between March and October, since storks and several raptors winter in Africa.

Signed walking trails of between 2½ and 3½ hours criss-cross the park, with shorter loops also possible; maps are available from the park's information centre in the pretty hamlet of Villareal de San Carlos. The EX208 Plasencia–Trujillo road also traverses the park and you can drive to several of the hides and lookout points. The hilltop Castillo de Monfragüe, a ruined 9th-century Muslim fort, has sweeping views; the castle can also be reached via an attractive 1½-hour walk from Villareal. Arguably the best spot is the Mirador del Salto del Gitano, a lookout point along the main road. From here, there are stunning views across the river gorge to the Peña Falcón crag, where you may spot griffon vultures, black storks, black vultures, Egyptian vultures, peregrine falcons, golden eagles and eagle owls.

Research is still being carried out as to whether the highly endangered Iberian lynx (which was previously thought to be present in only two small populations in Andalucía) is present in the park.

ⓒ Tours

The Centro de Información in Villareal de San Carlos runs free guided walks of two to three hours on Friday, Saturday and Sunday; prior reservations by telephone are required.

Many of the hotels and *casas rurales* that surround the park also offer guided tours, either on foot or by 4WD. Other private organisations offering a range of tours include the following:

Birding in Extremadura BIRDWATCHING
(☑609 684719; www.birdingextremadura.com) Run by British ornithologist Martin Kelsey

Iberian Nature BIRDWATCHING
(☑676 784221; www.extremadurabirds.net)

Monfragüe Natural BIRDWATCHING, WILDLIFE
(☑638 520891; www.monfraguenatural.com, in Spanish)

Monfragüe Vivo BIRDWATCHING
(☑620 941778; www.monfraguevivo.com, in Spanish)

Rutas Dehesas de Monfragüe

HIKING, BIRDWATCHING

(☑605 732252; www.rutasdehesasde
monfrague.com, in Spanish)

🛏 Sleeping

Casa Rural Monfragüe   CASA RURAL €

(☑927 19 90 02; www.monfraguerural.com, in
Spanish; Calle de Villareal 15, Villareal de San Carlos; d incl breakfast from €55; ✱🕸) Opened in
2008, this light-filled *casa rural* has large,
brightly painted rooms in a lovely blue
building directly opposite the park's information centre. There's a bar-restaurant
downstairs, and the owners have another
casa rural a few doors down.

Hospedería Parque de Monfragüe

HOTEL €€

(☑927 45 52 78; www.hospederiasdeextre
madura.es; Km37, Torrejón el Rubio; d incl breakfast €63-132; ✱🕸🏊) This tranquil four-star
hotel on the northern edge of Torrejón el
Rubio looks out across the plains to the national park. The rooms (most with views)
have slate walls and modern furnishings,
and there's a decent on-site restaurant.

Camping Monfragüe   CAMPING €

(☑927 45 92 33; www.campingmonfrague.com, in
Spanish; Malpartida de Plasencia; sites per adult/
tent/car €4.20/4.20/3.80, 4-person bungalows
€90; ☺year-round; 🐾) Precisely 14km north
of Villareal on the EX208 is this shady
camping ground, with restaurant, shop and
pool, plus homey bungalows complete with
front porches. It rents out bikes and does
inexpensive four-hour 4WD guided tours of
the park (€25), including a picnic.

❶ Information

**Centro de Información del Parque Nacional
de Monfragüe** (☑927 19 91 34; www.mon
frague.com, in Spanish; Villareal de San Carlos;
☺9.30am-7.30pm) Staff also run interpretation
centres at various points around the park.

❶ Getting There & Away

Public transport through the park is restricted
to one **bus** each on Monday and Friday between
Plasencia and Torrejón el Rubio; it stops in Villareal de San Carlos. The nearest **train** station
is at Monfragüe, 18km north of Villareal de San
Carlos. On Friday, Saturday, Sunday and public
holidays, there's a free **minibus** service between
Villareal de San Carlos and Castillo de Monfragüe at 10am, noon, 3pm and 5pm, returning
30 minutes later.

If you have time to visit just one region,
make it this one; the heart of Extremadura
is home to some of inland Spain's prettiest
towns: Cáceres, Trujillo and Guadalupe.

Cáceres

POP 93.130

The Ciudad Monumental (old town) of Cáceres is truly extraordinary. The narrow
cobbled streets twist and climb among
ancient stone walls lined with palaces and
mansions, while the skyline is decorated
with turrets, spires, gargoyles and enormous storks' nests. Protected by defensive
walls, it has survived almost intact from its
16th-century heyday. Established by the Romans, adapted by the Moors and enriched
by migrating nobles from León in the wake
of the Reconquista, the old town retains
tangible evidence of all three cultures. At
dusk or after dark when the crowds have
gone, you'll feel like you've stepped back
into the Middle Ages. Stretching at its feet,
the lively and arcaded Plaza Mayor is one of
Spain's finest public squares.

◉ Sights

Ciudad Monumental's name captures it all.
The churches, palaces and towers of the
'Monumental City' are indeed huge and
hugely impressive although, ironically, few
people actually live here and there are just
a handful of bars and restaurants.

Plaza de Santa María   PUBLIC SQUARE
Enter the Ciudad Monumental from Plaza
Mayor through the 18th-century Arco de
la Estrella, built this wide for the passage
of carriages. The Concatedral de Santa
María (Plaza de Santa María; admission €1;
☺9.30am-2pm & 5.30-8.30pm Mon-Sat, 9.30-
11.50am & 5.30-7.15pm Sun), a 15th-century
Gothic cathedral, creates an impressive
opening scene. On its southwestern corner
is a modern statue of San Pedro de Alcántara, a 16th-century *extremeño* ascetic (his
toes worn shiny by the hands and lips of
the faithful). Inside, there's a magnificent
carved 16th-century cedar altarpiece, several fine noble tombs and chapels, and a
small ecclesiastical museum. Climb the bell
tower (€1) for stunning views.

Also on the plaza are the Palacio Episcopal (Bishop's Palace), the Palacio de May-
oralgo and the Palacio de Ovando, all in

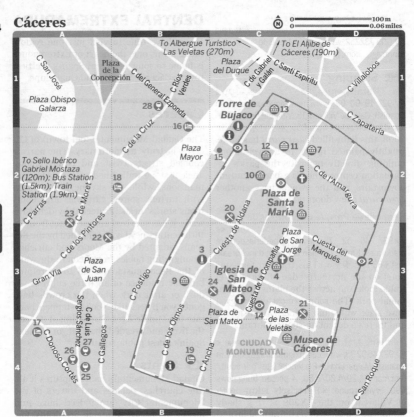

16th-century Renaissance style. Just off the plaza's northeastern corner is the Palacio Carvajal (Calle de l'Amargura 1; admission free; ⏱9am-9pm Mon-Fri, 10am-2pm & 5-8pm Sat, 10am-2pm Sun). Within this late-15th-century mansion, rooms have been restored with period furnishings and artwork.

Just to the west of the plaza lies the domed Palacio Toledo-Moctezuma (Calle Canilleros), once the home of a daughter of the Aztec emperor Moctezuma, who was brought to Cáceres as a conquistador's bride; the palace now houses the municipal archives. Heading back through Arco de la Estrella, you can climb the 12th-century Torre de Bujaco (Plaza Mayor; adult/under 12yr €2/ free; ⏱10am-2pm & 5.30-8.30pm Mon-Sat, 10am-2pm Sun). From the top of this tower, there's a good stork's-eye view of the Plaza Mayor.

Plaza de San Jorge SQUARE
Southeast of Plaza de Santa María, past the Renaissance-style Palacio de la Diputación, is Plaza de San Jorge, above which rises the Iglesia de San Francisco Javier (Iglesia de la Preciosa Sangre; Plaza de San Jorge; adult/under 12yr €1/free; ⏱10am-2pm & 5.30-8.30pm Mon-Sat), an 18th-century Jesuit church; the views from the towers would be wonderful, were it not for the chicken wire. Around the corner, the Centro Divulgación Semana Santa (Cuesta de la Compañía; admission free; ⏱10am-2pm & 5.30-8.30pm) has exhibits on Easter celebrations in Cáceres atop 18th-century cisterns. Due east of the plaza on Cuesta del Marqués is the Arco del Cristo, a Roman gate.

Plaza de San Mateo & Plaza de las Veletas SQUARE
From Plaza de San Jorge, Cuesta de la Compañía climbs to Plaza de San Mateo and the Iglesia de San Mateo, traditionally the church of the land-owning nobility and built on the site of the town's Islamic mosque.

EXTREMADURA CÁCERES

Just to the east is the Torre de las Cigüeñas (Tower of the Storks). This was the only Cáceres tower to retain its battlements when the rest were lopped off in the late 15th century.

Below the square is the excellent Museo de Cáceres (Plaza de las Veletas 1; non-EU/EU citizens €1.20/free; ⊙9am-2.30pm & 5-8.15pm Tue-Sat, 10.15am-2.30pm Sun) in a 16th-century mansion built over an evocative 12th-century *aljibe* (cistern), the only surviving element of Cáceres' Muslim castle. It has an impressive archaeological section and an excellent fine-arts display (open only in the mornings), with works by Picasso, Miró, Tàpies and other renowned Spanish painters and sculptors.

Other nearby buildings along the western side of the Ciudad Monumental include the Palacio de los Golfines de Arriba (Calle de los Olmos 2), where Franco was declared head of state in 1936, and the Casa Mudéjar (Cuesta de Aldana 14), which still reflects its Islamic influence in its brickwork and 1st-floor window arches.

Activities

El Aljibe de Cáceres　　　HAMMAM
(☎927 22 32 56; www.hammamcaceres.com; Calle de Peña 5; ⊙10am-2pm & 6-10pm Sun-Thu, 10am-2pm & 6pm-midnight Fri & Sat) This beautifully indulgent recreation of an Arab-style bath experience combines soothing architecture and range of treatments. The basic thermal bath with aromatherapy starts from €15; throw in a massage and you'll pay €22.

Tours

Asociación de Guías Turísticas
　　　　　　　　　　　　　WALKING TOURS
(Tourist Guides Association; ☎927 21 72 37; Plaza Mayor 2) The Asociación de Guías Turísticas leads regular 1½- to two-hour tours (€5) in Spanish of the Ciudad Monumental at least twice daily from Tuesday to Saturday, with only morning tours on Sunday. Tours start from its office on Plaza Mayor, and tours in English can be arranged with advance notice.

Cáceres de Leyenda　　　NIGHT TOURS
(www.caceresdeleyenda.com) In May and June 2010, Cáceres de Leyenda offered up to five terrific nightly tours (€20) of the Ciudad Monumental which begin at the Arco de la Estrella, included street theatre by actors in period dress and ended with a tasting session of local foods. It's a wonderful way to experience the old town; check the website to see if/when the tours are still operating.

✿ Festivals & Events

Womad   WORLD MUSIC
(World of Music, Arts and Dance; www.womad
caceres.com, in Spanish) For three fiesta-
fuelled days in early May, Cáceres stages
the Spanish edition of Womad, with
international bands playing in the old
city's squares.

Fiesta de San Jorge   PATRON SAINT FESTIVAL
From 21 to 23 April the town celebrates
the Fiesta de San Jorge in honour of its
patron saint.

🛏 Sleeping

Hotel Casa Don Fernando   HOTEL **€€**
(☎927 21 42 79; www.casadonfernando.com;
Plaza Mayor 30; d €60-140; P❋🤖) Arguably
the classiest midrange choice in Cáceres,
this boutique hotel sits on Plaza Mayor
directly opposite the Arco de la Estrella.
Spread over four floors, the designer rooms
and bathrooms are tastefully chic; there are
rooms on each floor with plaza views. Parking costs €9.

Hotel Don Carlos   HOTEL **€€**
(☎927 22 55 27; www.hoteldoncarloscaceres.
net, in Spanish; Calle Donoso Cortés 15; s €39-
48, d €56-74; P❋🤖) Rooms are tastefully
decorated with bare brick and stone at this
welcoming small hotel, sensitively created
from a long-abandoned early-19th-century
house. There are two artists among the
owner's family, hence plenty of original art
work. Parking costs €9.

Hotel Iberia   HOTEL **€€**
(☎927 24 76 34; www.iberiahotel.com, in Spanish;
Calle de los Pintores 2; s/d €46/60; ❋) Located
in an 18th-century former palace just off
Plaza Mayor, this friendly and family-run
36-room hotel has public areas that look
like an old-world museum piece, decorated
with antique furnishings. The rooms are
more subdued, with parquet floors, cream
walls and pale-grey tiled bathrooms. It's
a good, more traditional choice in a good
location.

Alameda Palacete   HOTEL **€€**
(☎927 21 16 74; www.alamedapalacete.com; Calle
General Margallo 45; s/d/ste €50/65/85; ❋)
This tastefully restored early-20th-century
town house has traditionally styled rooms
that are comfortable, have original richly
patterned floor tiles and high ceilings, and
are bathed in light. You're a short walk
north from the Ciudad Monumental.

Albergue Turístico Las Veletas   HOSTEL **€**
(☎927 21 12 10; lasveletas@hotmail.com; Calle del
General Maragallo 36; dm €18; ⊖@) This modern hostel, with its homey rear garden with
flowers, offers agreeable accommodation in
rooms with between three and six beds. Reserve in advance, especially out of season,
since it works primarily with groups.

Parador de Cáceres   HOTEL **€€€**
(☎927 21 17 59; www.parador.es; Calle Ancha 6;
P⊖❋) A grand 14th-century Gothic stone
building houses this elegant accommodation located deep in the walled town across
from the tourist office. It was closed for major renovation works when we visited and is
due to reopen in spring 2011.

✗ Eating

From the restaurants and cafes flanking
Plaza Mayor, you can watch the swallows
and storks swoop and glide among the
turrets of the old city. Stick to a drink and
simple tapa, however, as the food here tends
to be overpriced and indifferent.

Mesón El Asador   TRADITIONAL EXTREMEÑO **€€**
(☎927 22 38 37; Calle de Moret 34; raciones €6-8,
meals €20-30, menús €15-26; ⊙closed Sun) Enter the dining room and you get the picture
right away: one wall is covered with hung
hams. It's often packed to the rafters with
locals, not least because you won't taste
better roast pork (or lamb) in town. Its bar
also serves *bocadillos* (bread rolls with filling) and a wide range of *raciones,* while the
menú especial (€26) is terrific value.

Restaurante Torre de Sande
                            EXTREMEÑO FUSION **€€**
(☎927 21 11 47; www.torredesande.com, in Spanish; Calle Condes 3; meals €35-45; ⊙lunch &
dinner Tue-Sat, lunch Sun) Dine in the pretty
courtyard on dishes like *salmorejo de ce-
rezas del jerte con queso de cabra* (cherry-
based cold soup with goat's cheese) at this
elegant gourmet restaurant. More modestly, stop for a drink and a tapa (€4) at the
interconnecting *tapería* (tapas bar). It's
the pick of the places within the Ciudad
Monumental.

El Corral de las Cigüeñas   CAFE **€**
(www.elcorralcc.com, in Spanish; Cuesta de Aldana 6; ⊙8am-1pm Mon & Tue, 8am-1pm & 7pm-
3am Wed-Fri, 10am-3pm & 6pm-3am Sat, 5-11pm
Sun) The secluded courtyard with its lofty
palm trees and ivy-covered walls just inside
the Ciudad Monumental is the perfect spot
for one of the best-value breakfasts around:

there are six versions to choose from, including the basic *madrileño* (fresh orange juice, coffee and *porras* – doughnut type pastries) for just €2.20. It also has snacks at other times and sometimes live music in the evenings.

El Racó de Sanguino   EXTREMEÑO FUSION €€
(📞927 22 76 82; www.racodesanguino.es, in Spanish; Plaza de las Veletas 4; meals €35-40; ⊙lunch & dinner Tue-Sat, lunch Sun) Tables and wicker chairs spread beneath the sloping, timber ceiling within, while romantics can head for the candlelit tables outside. Carlos Sanguino has created a traditional *extremeño* menu with innovative twists like wild boar with mashed potato and thyme-scented olive oil.

Figón de Eustaquio   TRADITIONAL EXTREMEÑO €€
(📞927 24 43 62; Plaza de San Juan 14; menús €17-19, meals €30-40) The walls are papered with photos of famous diners, including Spanish royalty, at this venerable, multi-roomed option. You'll be treated to such dishes as *solomillo de cerdo a la Torta de Casar* (pork sirloin with the creamy local cheese). There are a range of set menus, including the *menú regional* (€22), which takes you on a short journey through some of Extremadura's signature dishes.

 Drinking

The streets at the northern end of Plaza Mayor are lined with lively late-night bars. Just beyond the walls on the southern side of the Ciudad Monumental are more popular hang-outs, all of which open at around 4pm and stay open until around 3am. If you are after atmosphere, El Corral de las Cigüeñas occasionally stages live music. The new part of the city also offers plenty of action, including several clubs, in an area known as La Madrila on and around Calle Doctor Fleming.

La Traviata   BAR
(Calle de Luis Sergios Sánchez) Has floral wallpaper, original tiles, arches and a terrace.

María Mandiles   BAR
(Calle de Luis Sergios Sánchez) This place packs them in, with its dark red interior and funky artwork.

Babel Café-Bar   CAFE, BAR
(Calle de Luis Sergios Sánchez 7) Does coffees, cocktails, art exhibitions and film screenings depending on the day and the hour.

Room   CAFE, BAR
(Calle de la Cruz) A block back from the Plaza Mayor, Room is a similar deal to Babel Café-Bar.

 Shopping

Plenty of places around town sell *extremeño* cheeses (especially the strong, creamy Torta de Casar), cured meats and other foods.

Sello Ibérico Gabriel Mostaza
                DELICATESSEN
(📞927 24 28 81; www.gabrielmostazo.com; Calle de San Antón 6; ⊙9am-2pm & 5-8.30pm Mon-Sat, 10am-2pm Sun) Our pick of the delis.

 Information

Junta de Extremadura tourist office (📞927 01 08 34; www.turismoextremadura.com; Plaza Mayor 3; ⊙8.30am-2.30pm & 4-6pm Mon-Fri, 10am-2pm Sat & Sun)

RUTA DE LA PLATA

The name of this ancient highway, also called the Vía de la Plata, derives from the Arabic *bilath*, meaning tiled or paved. But it was the Romans in the 1st century who originally laid this 1000km-long artery, linking Seville in the south with the coast of Cantabria and Bay of Biscay. Along its length moved goods, troops, travellers and traders. Later, it also served as an alternative pilgrim route for the faithful walking from Andalucía to Santiago de Compostela.

Nowadays it's closely paralleled by the A66 highway, although much of the original remains and alternative walking tracks have been introduced. Entering Extremadura south of Zafra, it passes through Mérida, Cáceres and Plasencia, then heads for Salamanca in Castilla y León.

Neglected and virtually abandoned when cars arrived on the scene, it's now justifiably promoted. Take a look at www.rutadelaplata.com or pick up the guide (€3) from tourist offices on the route. And should you be tempted to trek a stretch or two, pack *Walking the Vía de la Plata* by Ben Cole and Bethan Davies.

Municipal tourist office (☑927 25 58 00; Calle de los Olmos 3; ☻10am-2pm & 4.30-7.30pm)

❶ Getting There & Away

The **bus station** (☑927 23 25 50; Carretera de Sevilla) has services to Trujillo (€4.19, 40 minutes, eight daily), Plasencia (€4.05, 50 minutes, up to five daily), Guadalupe (€10.55, 2½ hours, one daily) and Mérida (€5.35, 50 minutes, two to four daily).

Up to five trains per day run to/from Madrid (€25.80 to €38.50, four hours), Plasencia (€5.55, 1½ hours) and Mérida (from €4.30, one hour).

❶ Getting Around

Bus L-1 from the stop outside the train station – close to the bus station – will take you to the central Plaza Obispo Galarza.

Valencia de Alcántara

POP 6180

This pretty town is 7km short of the Portuguese frontier and its well-preserved old centre is a curious labyrinth of whitewashed houses and mansions. One side of the old town is watched over by the ruins of a medieval castle and the 17th-century Iglesia de Rocamador.

The surrounding countryside is known for its cork industry and some 50 ancient dolmens (stone circles of prehistoric monoliths).

Up to three buses run daily from Cáceres (€5, 1½ hours).

Alcántara

POP 1650

Alcántara is Arabic for 'the Bridge'. West of town, a six-arched Roman bridge – 204m long, 61m high and much reinforced over the centuries – spans Río Tajo below a huge dam retaining the Embalse de Alcántara. An inscription above a small Roman temple on the river's left bank honours the bridge's original architect, Caius Julius Lacer.

The town retains some of its old walls, the remains of a castle and several imposing mansions. From 1218 it was the headquarters of the Orden de Alcántara, an order of Reconquista knights that ruled much of western Extremadura as a kind of private fiefdom.

Up to four buses run daily to/from Cáceres (€5.10, 1½ hours).

Trujillo

POP 9820

Wander into Plaza Major here and you could be forgiven for thinking that you had stumbled onto the filmset of a medieval blockbuster. The square is surrounded by baroque and Renaissance stone buildings topped with a skyline of towers, turrets, cupolas, crenulations and nesting storks. Stretching beyond the square, the illusion continues with a labyrinth of mansions, leafy courtyards, fruit gardens, churches and convents; Trujillo truly is one of the most captivating small towns in Spain.

The town came into its own only with the conquest of the Americas. Then, Francisco Pizarro and his co-conquistadors enriched the city with a grand new square and imposing Renaissance mansions that look down confidently upon the town today.

❂ Sights

Plaza Mayor

Pizarro   STATUE

A large equestrian Pizarro statue by American Charles Rumsey looks down over Plaza Mayor. Apparently Rumsey originally sculpted it as a statue of Hernán Cortés to present to Mexico, but Mexico, which takes a dim view of Cortés, declined it, so it was given to Trujillo as Pizarro instead.

Palacio de la Conquista   MANSION

On the plaza's south side, carved images of Pizarro and his lover Inés Yupanqui (sister of the Inca emperor Atahualpa) decorate the corner of the 16th-century Palacio de la Conquista. To the right is their daughter Francisca Pizarro Yupanqui with her husband (and uncle), Hernando Pizarro. The mansion was built in the 1560s for Hernando and Francisca after Hernando – the only Pizarro brother not to die a bloody death in Peru – emerged from 20 years in jail for murder. Higher up, a bas relief carving shows the Pizarro family shield (two bears and a pine tree), the walls of Cuzco (in present-day Peru), Pizarro's ships and a group of Indian chiefs.

FREE Palacio Juan Pizarro de Orellana
                                                   MANSION

(☻10am-1pm & 4.30-6.30pm Mon-Sat, 10am-12.30pm Sun) Through a twisting alley above the Palacio de la Conquista is the Palacio Juan Pizarro de Orellana, converted from miniature fortress to Renaissance mansion by one of the Pizarro cousin conquistadors.

Its patio is decorated with the coats of arms of the two most famous local families: the Pizarros and the Orellanas (Francisco Orellana was the first European to explore reaches of the Amazon).

Iglesia de San Martín
CHURCH

(adult/under 12yr €1.40/free; ⊘10am-2pm & 4-7pm) Overlooking the Plaza Mayor from the northeast corner is the 16th-century Iglesia de San Martín, with delicate Gothic ceiling tracing, stunning stained-glass windows and a grand organ (climb up to the choir loft for the best view). It's one of the few churches in Trujillo still functioning as a place of worship.

Palacio de los Duques de San Carlos
MANSION, CONVENT

(admission €1.40; ⊘9.30am-1pm & 4.30-6.30pm Mon-Sat, 10am-12.30pm Sun) Across the street rears the solid presence of the 16th-century Palacio de los Duques de San Carlos, nowadays a convent for the Jerónimo order, but open for visits and for selling its homemade biscuits. Its treasures are the sober classical patio and a grand granite staircase crowned with a painting of the family crest: a two-headed eagle. The distinctive brick chimneys were built in late Mudéjar and Gothic style.

Other Sights

City Walls
CITY WALLS

The 900m of walls circling the upper town date from Muslim times and it was here the newly settled noble families built their mansions and churches after the Reconquista. The western end is marked by the Puerta del Triunfo (Gate of Triumph), through which it is said conquering Christian troops marched in 1232, when they wrested the city from the Muslims.

Iglesia de Santiago
CHURCH

(adult/under 12yr €1.40/free; ⊘10am-2pm & 4-7pm) Coming up from Plaza Mayor, you pass through the Puerta de Santiago. To its right is the deconsecrated Iglesia de Santiago, founded in the 13th century by the Knights of Santiago (look for their scallop-shell emblem). The ground level has displays of mainly Bronze Age and Roman artefacts found locally and you can climb the bell tower.

Iglesia de Santa María la Mayor
CHURCH

(adult/under 12yr €1.40/free; ⊘10am-2pm & 4-7pm) The 13th-century Iglesia de Santa

The Trujillo tourist office sells **combined tickets** (€4.70 or €5.30), which include a comprehensive guidebook (mostly in Spanish, with some English text at the back), and covers entry to most sights, including the castle, Museo de Queso y el Vino and Iglesia de Santiago. It's €7.95 if you want to join one of the **guided tours** (in Spanish); they leave from the tourist office daily at 11am and 4.30pm.

In summer, most of the sights in Trujillo listed open later and stay open longer in the afternoons (ie from 5pm to 8.30pm).

María la Mayor has a mainly Gothic nave and a Romanesque tower that you can ascend (all 106 steps) for fabulous views. It also has tombs of leading Trujillo families of the Middle Ages, including that of Diego García de Paredes (1466–1530), a Trujillo warrior of legendary strength who, according to Cervantes, could stop a mill wheel with one finger. The church's magnificent altarpiece includes 25 brilliantly coloured 15th-century paintings in the Flemish style.

Castle
CASTLE

(adult/under 12yr €1.40/free; ⊘10am-2pm & 4-7pm) At the top of the hill, Trujillo's castle of 10th-century Muslim origin (evident by the horseshoe-arch gateway just inside the main entrance) and later strengthened by the Christians, is impressive, although bare but for a lone fig tree. Patrol the battlements for magnificent 360-degree sweeping views. One of the towers contains the hermitage of Our Lady of the Victory, the patron saint of Trujillo.

Museo de Queso y el Vino
CHEESE & WINE MUSEUM

(www.quesovino.com, in Spanish; Calle de la Encarnación; admission €2.30; ⊘11am-3pm & 6-8pm) Cheese-and-wine aficionados may enjoy this museum where you can have a taster of both and take a look at the informative display (in Spanish) of wine and cheese in Spain. Set in this fine former convent, the 4m 3-D picture of a jolly Don Quijote is the stunning work of local artist Francisco Blanco. It's just a short walk down the hill south of Plaza Mayor.

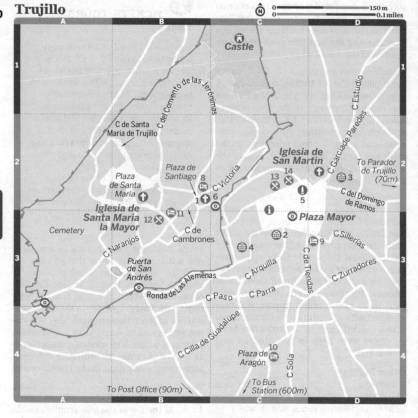

✹ Festivals & Events

Feria del Queso   CHEESE FAIR

The last weekend in April is a pungent period as cheesemakers from all over Spain converge on Trujillo for the Feria del Queso (Cheese Fair).

Fiestas de Trujillo   TOWN FESTIVAL

The town's annual Fiestas de Trujillo, with music, theatre and plenty of partying, are spread over a few days around the first Saturday in September.

🛏 Sleeping

Posada dos Orillas   POSADA €€

(☏927 65 90 79; www.dosorillas.com; Calle de Cambrones 6; d €69.55-107; ✿🗗) This tastefully renovated 16th-century mansion in the walled town once served as a silk-weaving centre. The rooms replicate Spanish colonial taste; those in the older wing bear the names of the 'six Trujillos'

of Extremadura and the Americas. Unsurprisingly, 'Extremadura' is the largest and most luxurious. There's a pleasant courtyard restaurant.

Parador de Trujillo   HOTEL €€

(☏927 32 13 50; www.parador.es; Calle Santa Beatriz de Silva 1; d from €90; 🅿➠✿🗗✉) No surprise that this *parador* is also a former 16th-century convent; there's an agreeable overdose in this town. Rooms are large with terracotta-tiled floors and understated historical touches. It's in the winding back streets of the old town east of the Plaza Mayor.

El Mirador de las Monjas   HOSTERÍA €€

(☏927 65 92 23; www.elmiradordelasmonjas. com, in Spanish; Plaza de Santiago 2; s/d incl breakfast from €50/60; ✿) High in the old town, this contemporary six-room *hostería* has large, minimalist rooms with clean lines and stylish bathrooms.

Trujillo

Isla del Gallo HOTEL €€
(☏927 32 02 43; www.isladelgallo.com; Plaza de Aragón 2; d €65-75; ✳✳) Yet another 17th-century former convent tastefully restored as a boutique-style hotel. Rooms are large with parquet floors, wrought-iron beds and dark-wood furniture. The colour scheme throughout is warm earth colours, and the tranquil patio is shaded by lemon and olive trees.

Hostal Nuria HOSTAL €
(☏927 32 09 07; www.hostal-nuria.com; Plaza Mayor; s/d €30/45, apt €60-90; ✳) Rooms here are no frills, but the location on Plaza Mayor is hard to beat. Although rooms are simple, you'll spend most of the time looking out the window onto the plaza if you're in rooms 204 or 205. There's a busy downstairs bar-restaurant.

 Eating

Restaurante La Troya TRADITIONAL €
(Plaza Mayor 10; menú €15) Mention Trujillo to anyone in Spain and chances are that they'll have heard of La Troya – the restaurant and its founder, the late Concha

Álvarez, are *extremeño* institutions. You will be directed to one of several dining areas and there, without warning, you will be presented with plates of tortilla, chorizo, cheese and salad, followed by a three-course *menú* (with truly gargantuan portions) and including wine and water. Food is simple home cooking, but it's all about quantity and queues stretch out the door on weekends. If it all sounds a bit too girth expanding, opt for one of the tapas at the bar (€2) instead.

Restaurante Pizarro TRADITIONAL €€
(☏927 32 02 55; Plaza Mayor 13; meals €30-40; ✹Wed-Mon) Next door to La Troya, Restaurante Pizarro is much quieter and has arguably better food (they've been winning gastronomic awards since 1985). The dining room is pleasantly unpretentious, while the menu includes dishes like chicken stuffed with truffles, and *frito de cordero* (lamb stew).

Posada Restaurante Dos Orillas
MODERN €€
(www.dosorillas.com; Calle de Cambrones 6; meals €25-30; ✹lunch & dinner Tue-Sat, lunch Sun) Just as the hotel is a gem, so the restaurant is a place of quiet, refined eating, whether alfresco on the patio or in the dining room, with its soft-hued fabrics. Fresh tastes are what it's all about here, with dishes like courgettes stuffed with mushrooms and prawns.

Mesón Alberca TRADITIONAL €€
(Calle de Cambrones 8; meals €30-40, menús €15-24.50; ✹Thu-Sun) A pretty ivy-clad terrace or dark-timber tables laid with gingham tablecloths create a choice of warm atmospheres for sampling classic *extremeño* cooking. The specialities here are oven roasts and *solomillo ibérico con Torta del Casar* (pork sirloin with creamy sheep's-milk cheese).

ⓘ Information
Tourist office (☏927 32 26 77; www.trujillo.es, in Spanish; Plaza Mayor; ✹10am-2pm & 5-8pm)

ⓘ Getting There & Away
The **bus station** (☏927 32 12 02; Avenida de Miajadas) is 750m south of Plaza Mayor. There are services to/from Madrid (€19.34 to €31.40, three to 4¼ hours, five daily), Guadalupe (€6.25, 1½ hours, two daily), Cáceres (€4.19, 40 minutes, eight daily) and Mérida (€8.15, 1½ hours, three daily).

Guadalupe

POP 2100

This sparkling white village is like a bright jewel set in the green crown of the surrounding ranges and ridges of the Sierra de Villuercas. There are thick woods of chestnut, oak and cork meshed with olive groves and vineyards. Guadalupe (from the Arabic meaning 'hidden river') appears as though from nowhere, huddled around the massive stone hulk of the Real Monasterio de Santa María de Guadalupe. It's a small place, and you can easily visit the sights and stroll its cobbled streets in a day.

◉ Sights

Real Monasterio de Santa María de Guadalupe MONASTERY & CHURCH, MUSEUM

(☏927 36 70 00; www.monasterioguadalupe.com, in Spanish; Plaza Santa María de Guadalupe; ⊘8.30am-9pm) The Real Monasterio de Santa María de Guadalupe, a Unesco World Heritage site, was founded in 1340 by Alfonso XI on the spot where, according to legend, a shepherd found an effigy of the Virgin, hidden years earlier by Christians fleeing the Muslims. It remains one of Spain's most important pilgrimage sites.

In the 16th century, the Virgin of Guadalupe was so revered that she was made patron of all Spain's New World territories. On 29 July 1496, Columbus' Indian servants were baptised in the fountain in front of the monastery, an event registered in the monastery's first book of baptisms. The Virgin of Guadalupe, patron of Extremadura, remains a key figure for many South American Catholics.

Inside the church (admission free), the Virgin's image occupies the place of honour lit up within the soaring *retablo* (altarpiece). There's a five-minute audio explanation available in several languages for €1 (to the right of the entrance), plus a 45-minute guided tour (adult/under 12yr €3/free; ⊘tours in Spanish 9.30am-1pm & 3.30-6.30pm). To get the most out of the latter, buy the English version of the visitors guide (€2) in advance, which, in stilted English, describes the route followed.

At the centre of the monastery is a 15th-century Mudéjar cloister with three museums. The Museo de Bordados displays wonderfully embroidered altar cloths and vestments from the 14th to 18th centuries. The Museo de Libros Miniados has a fine collection of illuminated choral songbooks

EXTREMADURA & AMERICA

Extremeños jumped at the opportunities opened up by Columbus' discovery of the Americas in 1492.

In 1501 Fray Nicolás de Ovando from Cáceres was named governor of all the Indies. He set up his capital, Santo Domingo, on the Caribbean island of Hispaniola. With him went 2500 followers, many of them from Extremadura, including Francisco Pizarro, the illegitimate son of a minor noble family from Trujillo. In 1504 Hernán Cortés, from a similar family in Medellín, arrived in Santo Domingo.

Both young men prospered. Cortés took part in the conquest of Cuba in 1511 and settled there. Pizarro, in 1513, accompanied Vasco Núñez de Balboa (from Jerez de los Caballeros) to Darién (Panama), where they 'discovered' the Pacific Ocean. In 1519 Cortés led a small expedition to what's now Mexico, rumoured to be full of gold and silver. By 1524, with combined fortitude, cunning, luck and ruthlessness, Cortés and his band had subdued the Aztec empire.

Pizarro returned to Spain and, before returning to Panama, visited Trujillo, where he received a hero's welcome and collected his four half-brothers, as well as other relatives and friends. Their expedition set off from Panama in 1531, with just 180 men and 37 horses, and managed to capture the Inca emperor Atahualpa, despite the emperor having a 30,000-strong army. The Inca empire, with its capital in Cuzco and extending from Colombia to Chile, resisted until 1545, by which time Francisco had died (he is buried in the cathedral of Lima, Peru).

About 600 people of Trujillo made their way to the Americas in the 16th century, so it's no surprise that there are at least five further Trujillo towns in Central and South America. There are even more Guadalupes, for conquistadors and colonists from all over Spain took with them the cult of the Virgen de Guadalupe in eastern Extremadura, one that remains widespread throughout Latin America.

from the 15th century onwards, and the Museo de Pintura y Escultura includes three paintings by El Greco, a Goya and a beautiful little ivory crucifixion attributed to Michelangelo.

In the elaborately decorated baroque sacristía (sacristy) hang eight portraits (1638–47) by Francisco de Zurbarán of leading monks of the Hieronymite order. The Relicario-Tesoro houses a variety of treasures, including a 200,000-pearl cape for the Virgin. The camarín, a chamber behind the altarpiece, has an image of the Virgin that is revolved for the faithful to kiss a fragment of her mantle.

Activities

The tourist office has maps describing other shorter and easier circular routes of three to five hours.

Ruta de Isabel la Católica   HIKE

One splendid walking option is to take the Madrid–Miajadas bus to the village of Cañamero, southwest of Guadalupe, and hike back along a well-signed 17km trail. The Ruta de Isabel la Católica retraces the steps of pilgrims coming to Guadalupe from the south (including Isabel and Fernando after the fall of Moorish Granada).

Festivals & Events

Colourful processions wind through the heart of the town during Easter Week, between 6 and 8 September in honour of the Virgin of Guadalupe, and on 12 October, the Día de la Hispanidad, celebrated throughout the Spanish-speaking world. Wednesday is the local market day.

Sleeping

TOP CHOICE Hospedería del Real Monasterio
HOSPEDERÍA €€

(☎927 36 70 00; www.monasterioguadalupe. com; Plaza Juan Carlos I; s/d/tr €45.50/65/87; P ✱) Centred on the monastery's beautiful 16th-century Gothic cloister with high-ceilinged rooms (all different), this is *the* sleeping option in Guadalupe. The prices are astonishingly reasonable and the public areas are stunning; don't miss the flower-filled patio just off the lobby.

Posada del Rincón   POSADA €€

(☎927 36 71 14; www.posadadelrincon.com, in Spanish; Plaza Mayor 11; s €45-49, d €68-75; ✱) Behind its tiny facade, Posada del Rincón, first mentioned in writing in the late 15th

century, has 20 warm-coloured rooms with exposed brick and stonework, dark-timber furniture and oak ceilings. Rooms 3, 4 and 5 overlook the bijou internal patio.

Parador de Guadalupe   PARADOR €€

(☎927 36 70 75; www.parador.es; Calle Marqués de la Romana 12; d €90-137; P ✱ ≋) Also known as Parador Zurbarán, this place occupies a converted 15th-century hospital and 16th-century religious school opposite the monastery. Spacious rooms are tastefully decorated and the cobbled courtyard is delightful, with its lemon and orange trees surrounded by a cloisterlike colonnade with arches.

Camping Las Villuercas   CAMPING GROUND €

(☎927 36 71 39; sites per adult/tent/car €3.50/3.50/3; ◷Apr-Dec; ≋) This is the nearest camping option to Guadalupe, with a tennis court, swimming pool, bar-restaurant and sites shaded by lofty mature trees. It's 3km south of the village off the EX102.

Cerezo II   HOSTAL €

(☎927 15 41 77; www.hostalcerezo2meson.com; Plaza Mayor 23; s/d €35/48; ✱) On the main square, Cerezo II has attractive modern rooms, decorated in earthy colours with classy thick quilts.

Eating

In addition to the following, the restaurants in the Parador de Guadalupe and Posada del Rincón are quality eateries. There are several tempting-looking bakeries around Plaza Mayor in town, selling freshly made *tortas de anís* (aniseed biscuits).

Panadería Nuestra Señora de Guadalupe   BAKERY €

(Calle Alfonso el Onceno 11) Join the queue at this tiny place, dating from 1933 and serving delicious traditional cakes and pastries (as well as fresh bread).

La Marina   CENTRAL SPANISH €

(☎927 36 71 30; Gregorio López 21; meals €15-20, mains €4.80-9) An earthy, dress-down restaurant, where toothy wild boars and antlers decorate the dining room. Hearty starters, like the tasty *lentejas estofadas* (lentil stew) and *garbanzos guisados con chorizo* (chickpeas with chorizo), will set you up for the day for the price of a couple of *vinos*.

Hospedería del Real Monasterio
TRADITIONAL EXTREMEÑO €€

(☎927 36 70 00; www.monasterioguadalupe.com; Plaza Juan Carlos I; meals €25-35) Dine grandly under the arches of the magnificent Gothic cloister or in the dining halls, rich with 17th-century timber furnishings and antique ceramics. There's a competent range of both meat and fish dishes, and most of the desserts are rustled up in the kitchen.

ℹ Information

Tourist office (☑927 15 41 28; www.puebla deguadalupe.net; Plaza Mayor; ⊙10am-2pm & 4-6pm Mon-Fri)

ℹ Getting There & Away

Buses stop on Avenida Conde de Barcelona near the town hall, a two-minute walk from Plaza Mayor. **Mirat** (☑927 23 48 63) runs two daily services to/from Cáceres (€10.55, 2½ hours) via Trujillo (€6.25). **La Sepulvedana** (☑902 222282) has two daily buses to/from Madrid (€16, 3¾ hours). Timetables are displayed in the tourist-office window.

SOUTHERN EXTREMADURA

The landscape in this region is a beguiling combination of flat plains, which, further south, subtly change to a gentle, more pastoral, landscape. The main attraction is the Roman city of Mérida, but don't miss the lovely towns of Olivenza and Zafra.

Mérida

POP 56,400

Mérida is remarkable for having the most impressive and extensive Roman ruins in all of Spain. The ruins lie sprinkled around the town, often appearing in the most unlikely corners, and one can only wonder what still lies buried beneath the modern anonymous city that is Mérida today. Apart from the ruins, there are some attractive streets around the pretty Plaza de España.

◉ Sights
Roman Remains

Teatro Romano   THEATRE, AMPHITHEATRE
(Calle Álvarez Sáenz de Buruaga; adult/under 12yr €8/free; ⊙9.30am-7.30pm) The Teatro Romano, built around 15 BC to seat 6000 spectators and set in lovely gardens, has a dramatic and well-preserved two-tier backdrop of Corinthian stone columns; the stage's facade (scaenae frons) was inaugurated in AD 105. The only Roman building

in Mérida to be used for its original purpose, the theatre hosts performances during the Festival del Teatro Clásico in summer. The adjoining **Anfiteatro**, opened in 8 BC for gladiatorial contests, had a capacity of 14,000. Outside the main gate, the **Casa del Anfiteatro**, the remains of a 3rd-century mansion, has some reasonable floor mosaics.

Los Columbarios   TOMBS
(Calle del Ensanche; adult/under 12yr €4/free; ⊙9.30am-1.45pm & 5-7.15pm) Los Columbarios is a Roman funeral site, well documented in Spanish and illustrated. A footpath connects it with the **Casa del Mitreo** (Calle Oviedo; adult/under 12yr €4/free; ⊙9.30am-1.45pm & 5-7.15pm), a 2nd-century Roman house with several intricate mosaics (especially the partial but beautiful remains of the *mosaico cosmológico,* with its allegories and bright colours) and a well-preserved fresco.

Puente Romano   BRIDGE
Don't miss the extraordinarily powerful spectacle over the Río Guadiana of the Puente Romano, which, at 792m in length with 60 granite arches, is one of the longest bridges built by the Romans. There are good views from the altogether more modern Puente Lusitania, a sleek suspension bridge designed by the famed Spanish architect Santiago Calatrava away to the northwest.

Arco de Trajano   MONUMENTAL ARCH
The 15m-high Arco de Trajano over Calle de Trajano may have served as the entrance to the provincial forum, from where Lusitania province was governed.

Templo de Diana   TEMPLE
(Calle de Sagasta) The Templo de Diana stood in the municipal forum, where the city government was based. Parts were incorporated into a 16th-century mansion, built within it, and it now stands surrounded by modern Mérida along a quiet street. The restored **Pórtico del Foro**, the municipal forum's portico, is just along the road.

FREE **Centro de Interpretación Las VII Sillas**   INTERPRETATION CENTRE
(Calle de José Ramón Mélida 20; ⊙9.30am-2pm & 5pm-7.30pm) The Centro de Interpretación Las VII Sillas has the remains of a noble mansion and a sizeable hunk of Roman, Visigothic and Arab wall. A 13-minute DVD in Spanish takes you on a virtual tour of the Roman city.

Circo Romano
HIPPODROME

(Avenida Juan Carlos; adult/child €4/free; ⊘9.30am-1.45pm & 5-7.15pm) Northeast of the amphitheatre are the remains of the 1st-century Circo Romano, the only surviving hippodrome of its kind in Spain, which could accommodate 30,000 spectators. Inside you can see brief footage in Spanish about Diocles, a champion *auriga* (chariot racer) who served his apprenticeship in Mérida before going on to the big league in Rome.

Acueducto de Los Milagros
AQUEDUCT

(Calle Marquesa de Pinares) Further west, the Acueducto de Los Milagros, highly favoured by nesting storks, once supplied the Roman city with water from the dam at Lago Proserpina, about 5km out of town.

Other Sights

Museo Nacional de Arte Romano
ARCHAEOLOGICAL MUSEUM

(http://museoarteromano.mcu.es; Calle de José Ramón Mélida; adult/child, EU senior & student €3/free; ⊘9.30am-3.30pm & 5.30-8.30pm Tue-Sun) On no account miss this fabulous museum, which has a superb collection of statues, mosaics, frescoes, coins and other Roman artefacts. Designed by the architect Rafael Moneo, the soaring brick structure makes a remarkable home for the collection.

Alcazaba
FORTRESS

(Calle Graciano; adult/child €4/free; ⊘9.30am-1.45pm & 5-7.15pm) This large Muslim fort was built in AD 835 on a site already occupied by the Romans and Visigoths. Down below, its *aljibe* (cistern) incorporates marble and stone slabs with Visigothic decoration that were recycled by the Muslims, while the ramparts look out over the Guadiana and down into the Alcazaba's gardens. The 15th-century monastery in its northeast corner now serves as the Junta de Extremadura's presidential offices.

Basílica de Santa Eulalia
RUINS, CHURCH

(Avenida de Extremadura; adult/child €4/free; ⊘9.30am-1.45pm & 5-7.15pm Mon-Sat) Built in the 5th century in honour of Mérida's patron saint, the basilica was reconstructed in the 13th century. Beside it, a museum and excavated areas enable you to identify Roman houses, a 4th-century Christian cemetery and the original 5th-century church.

FREE Museo de Arte Visigodo
ARCHAEOLOGICAL MUSEUM

(Calle de Santa Julia; ⊘10am-2pm & 5-7pm Mon-Sat, 10am-2pm Sun) Many of the Visigothic

COMBINED TICKET

805

The cheapest way to gain entry to Mérida's Roman sites is to purchase the 'Entrada Conjunta' ticket (€12) that includes entry to the Teatro Romano and Anfiteatro (which otherwise costs €8 for an individual ticket), Casa del Anfiteatro, Los Columbarios, Casa del Mitreo, Alcazaba, Circo Romano, Basílica de Santa Eulalia and the Zona Arqueológica de Morería (otherwise, entry to each of these costs €4). The combined ticket also includes a comprehensive guide (available in English) to the monuments. Please note that the combined ticket does not include entry to the Museo Nacional de Arte Romano or the Museo de Arte Visigodo. The ticket is available from the ticket office of the Teatro Romano.

objects unearthed in Mérida are exhibited in this museum, just off Plaza de España. It's a fascinating insight into a little-known period of Spanish history.

Zona Arqueológica de Morería
RUINS

(Avenida de Roma; adult/child €4/free; ⊘9.30am-1.45pm & 5-7.15pm) This excavated Moorish quarter contains the remains of a cemetery, walls and houses dating from Roman to post-Islamic times.

✦ Festivals & Events

Festival de Teatro Clásico
CLASSICAL THEATRE

(www.festivaldemerida.es, in Spanish; admission €12-39; ⊘around 11pm most nights Jul & Aug) This prestigious summer festival, at the Roman theatre and amphitheatre, features Greek and more recent drama classics, plus music and dance.

Feria de Septiembre
TOWN FAIR

Mérida lets its hair down a little later than most of Extremadura at its Feria de Septiembre (September Fair; 1 to 15 September).

🛏 Sleeping

La Flor de al-Andalus
HOSTAL €

(📞924 31 33 56; www.laflordeal-andalus.es, in Spanish; Avenida de Extremadura 6; s/d €33/45; 🌐🈵) If only all *hostales* were this good. Opened in May 2010 and describing itself as a 'boutique

EXTREMADURA SOUTHERN EXTREMADURA

hostal', La Flor de al-Andalus has beautifully decorated rooms in an Andalucian style, friendly service and a good location within walking distance of all of the main sites. The buffet breakfast costs just €3.

Hotel Adealba
BOUTIQUE HOTEL €€
(☏924 38 83 08; www.hoteladealba.com; Calle Romero Leal 18; d incl breakfast from €96.30; P⊖❋⊛) Mérida has been crying out for a boutique midrange hotel in the centre and at last it has arrived. Opened in 2009, this stunning hotel occupies a 19th-century town house close to the Templo de Diana and does so with a classy, contemporary look. The designer rooms have strong, contrasting colours and there's a pillow menu to choose from. Parking costs €12.

Parador Vía de la Plata
HOTEL €€
(☏924 31 38 00; www.parador.es; Plaza de la Constitución 3; d €90-137; P⊖❋⊛⊛) You're sleeping on the site of a Roman temple in a building that started life as a convent; the lounge was a former chapel, then served as both hospital and prison. In the gardens, the assembled hunks of Roman, Visigothic and Mudéjar artefacts give a brief canter through Mérida's architectural history. Rear-room balconies look onto a quiet garden with fountains.

Hotel Nova Roma
HOTEL €€
(☏924 31 12 61; www.novaroma.com, in Spanish; Calle Suárez Somonte 42; s/d €72/89; ❋) A rather uninspiring facade, a marble lobby with pseudo-Roman decor (including headless statues) and reasonable rooms are how we'd sum up this place. The rooms range from modern and spacious to older ones, which are fine without being exciting; the bathrooms are excellent. We resent paying for wi-fi (€2 for three hours), which cheapens an otherwise reasonable package.

Hotel Cervantes
HOTEL €€
(☏924 31 49 61; www.hotelcervantes.com; Calle Camilo José Cela 8; s €45-55, d €65-75; P❋) The rooms are starting to show their age, but it's still a good deal in this price bracket and the service is friendly. The bar-restaurant serves a bacon-and-egg breakfast.

✕ Eating

Tabula Calda
TRADITIONAL €€
(www.tabulacalda.com; Calle Romero Leal 11; meals €20-25; ⊙lunch & dinner Mon-Sat, lunch Sun) This inviting space, with tile work and abundant greenery, serves up well-priced meals (including set menus from €12 to €24.50) that cover most Spanish staples. It effortlessly combines traditional home cooking, thoughtful presentation and subtle innovations.

Mérida

◎ Top Sights

◎ Sights

🛏 Sleeping

✖ Eating

◎ Drinking

Convivium TAPAS, TRADITIONAL SPANISH €
(Calle de Sagasta 21; tortillinas €1, meals €15-20; 🛜) Head straight for the pretty patio with tables set under a large lemon tree at this informal place where the speciality is *tortillinas* (mini-omelettes with fillings including cod, salami, spinach, aubergine and prawns). The *tortillina,* gazpacho and drink for €2.50 has to be Mérida's best deal. The *raciones* (€9 to €14) are more traditional.

Casa Nano TRADITIONAL EXTREMEÑO €€
(Calle San Salvador Castelar 3; meals €25-35; ⊙Mon-Sat) Tucked behind Plaza de España, the *simpático* staff here serve dishes like *cordero a la ciruela* (lamb with plums; €18) and *patatas al rebujón* (wedges of thick potato omelette). We also recommend the

three-course *menú extremeño* (€23). Don your shades and brave the bright lights of the dining room or head outside for a table on the quiet pedestrian street.

Casa Benito TRADITIONAL €€
(Calle San Francisco 3; tapas €2.60) Squeeze onto a tiny stool in the wood-panelled dining room, prop up the bar or relax on the sunny terrace for tapas at this bullfighting enthusiasts' hang-out, its walls plastered with photos, posters and memorabilia from the ring. The adjacent *asador* specialises in roasts including *rabo de toro* (bull's tail; €13.75) – no surprises there.

🍷 Drinking

The best place to enjoy an early evening drink is at one of the four kiosk-bars on Plaza de España. You'll find a more diverse selection of bars in and around Plaza de la Constitución.

La Moett KIOSK-BAR
(Plaza de España 2; ⊙4pm-late) Under the arches of the Ayuntamiento on the Plaza de España's northeastern side, La Moett is a classier option, with tables on the square.

La Tahona Nueva BAR, LIVE MUSIC
(Calle Alvarado 5; ⊙5pm-late) There's a classy courtyard draped with bougainvillea at La Tahona, plus a cavernous bar area with a stage for regular live gigs ranging from flamenco to blues and jazz.

Raw Café-Club LIVE MUSIC
(Plaza de la Constitución 2A; ⊙7pm-3.30am Tue-Sat) A spirited and edgily grungy bar in an incongruous lavishly tiled and historic town house. It attracts the teens and early 20s gang with live gigs nightly.

Jazz Bar BAR, LIVE MUSIC
(Calle Alvarado 10; ⊙4pm-2am Tue-Sat) This jazz stalwart has a more sophisticated scene with regular exhibitions, and live jazz once or twice a week at 10pm.

ℹ Information

Municipal tourist office (☏924 33 07 22; www.merida.es, in Spanish; Calle Álvarez Sáenz de Buruaga; ⊙9.30am-2pm & 5-7.30pm) Next to the Teatro Romano.

ℹ Getting There & Around

From the **bus station** (☏924 37 14 04; Avenida de la Libertad), across the river via the Puente Lusitania, destinations include Badajoz (€4.46, one hour, five to nine daily), Seville (€13.10,

The Roman city of Emerita Augusta, centred on the site of modern Mérida, was founded by Emperor Augustus in 25 BC as a colony for veterans of Rome's campaigns in Cantabria; the Roman name translates roughly as 'bachelors' or 'discharged soldiers' from the army of Augustus. The city's location also served the strategic purpose of protecting a nearby pass and the bridge over the Río Guadiana. The city prospered and became the capital of the Roman province of Lusitania and one of the empire's most important cultural and political centres, with a population of 40,000 in its heyday. After the fall of the Western Roman Empire, the city became the Visigothic capital of Hispania in the 6th century and its monuments remained largely intact. The city later passed into Muslim hands in the 8th century and has been Christian since 1230. During Napoleon's 19th-century invasion of Spain, many of Mérida's monuments were destroyed.

2½ hours, five daily), Cáceres (€5.35, 50 minutes, two to four daily), Trujillo (€8.15, 1¼ hours, three daily) and Madrid (€22.15 to €27, four to five hours, eight daily).

There are trains to Madrid (€31.80 to €36.30, 4½ to 6½ hours, five daily), Cáceres (from €4.30, one hour, six daily) and Seville (€14.10, four hours, one daily) via Zafra (€4.60).

Badajoz

POP 148,330

Just 4km from Portugal, the sprawling industrial city of Badajoz is not Extremadura's prettiest. At its heart, however, it does have a historic town topped by the Alcazaba fortress and a sprinkling of interesting museums and monuments. As such, while you wouldn't cross Spain to visit Badajoz, it may be worth an overnight stay if you're en route to Portugal.

Founded by the Muslims in the 9th century, Badajoz has been battled over by invading armies for centuries – the Portuguese, French, Spanish and British all wreaked their fury upon the city. During the Spanish Civil War, the Nationalists carried out atrocious massacres when they took Badajoz in 1936.

⊙ Sights

Alcazaba   FORTRESS

The magnificent walled Alcazaba lords it on the hilltop, north of the centre. You can climb the ramparts that enclose the eight-hectare site that was once a thriving community, with *medinas,* baths, mosques and houses. Guarding all is the **Torre Espantaperros** (Scare-Dogs Tower), symbol of Badajoz, constructed by the Arabs and topped by a 16th-century Mudéjar bell tower. At its feet is the unusual **Plaza**

Alta, dating back to 1681, with its highly decorative burgundy, grey and white dizzily painted facades. Within the fort area, a restored Renaissance palace houses the Museo Arqueológico Provincial (admission free; ⊙10am-3pm Tue-Sun), with artefacts from prehistoric times through to Roman, Islamic and medieval Christian periods.

Catedral de San Juan   CATHEDRAL
(Plaza de España; ⊙Mass 10-10.30am) The Catedral de San Juan was built in the 13th century on the site of a mosque and subsequently much altered. Its Museo Catedralicio (Calle de San Blas; adult/student €3/1; ⊙11am-1pm & 5-7pm Tue-Sat) contains a treasure chest of religious objects and artworks.

FREE **Museo Extremeño e Iberoamericano de Arte Contemporáneo**   CONTEMPORARY ART MUSEUM
(MEIAC; www.meiac.es; Calle Virgen de Guadalupe 7; ⊙10am-1.30pm & 5-8pm Tue-Sat, 10am-1.30pm Sun) Badajoz' pride and joy, this commanding modern building, dedicated to Spanish, Portuguese and Latin American contemporary art, houses a wide-ranging collection of avant-garde painting and sculpture.

FREE **Museo de Bellas Artes**
                                      FINE ART MUSEUM
(Calle del Duque de San Germán 3; ⊙10am-2pm & 4-6pm Tue-Fri, 10am-2pm Sat & Sun) This excellent gallery has works by Zurbarán, Morales, Picasso and Dalí, plus striking works by the 19th-century Badajoz-born artist Felipe Checa.

Lusiberia   THEME PARK
(www.lusiberia.com; Avenida de Elvas, Antigua Frontera de Caya; adult/child €15/11; ⊙11.30am-8.30pm) Lusiberia is a gigantic family theme park and (summer only) water park, next to the Portuguese frontier.

Activities

Baraka Al Hammam   HAMMAM
(924 25 08 26; www.baraka-al-hammam.com, in Spanish; Plaza de la Soledad 14; 10am-2pm & 5-10pm) This beautiful recreation of the Arab-style bath experience has beguiling architecture and a range of treatments – the 30-minute bath, aromatherapy treatment and massage together costs €30.

Festivals & Events

Feria de San Juan   TOWN FAIR
Badajoz' big bash is the Feria de San Juan, celebrated for a full week around 24 June.

Carnaval   CARNAVAL
Running a close second are the town's Carnaval celebrations in the build-up to Lent, among the most elaborate in Spain.

Sleeping

Hotel Husa Zurbarán   HOTEL €€
(924 00 14 00; www.husa.es; Paseo Castelar; d €55-100; P) Something of a concrete monster from street level, the four-star Zurbarán is considerably warmer and more attractive within. The majority of the rooms have been tastefully reformed, with lots of dazzling white and soft earth colours. The hotel's Restaurante Los Monjes is excellent.

Hostal Niza II   HOSTAL €
(924 22 31 73; www.hostal-niza.com; Calle del Arco Agüero 45; s/d €27/43;) Look beyond the bland chip marble floors and anaemic colour scheme, as the rooms here are clean and comfortable. Hostal Niza I across the road at No 34 is basically an overspill in a more recent building, with virtually identical decor.

Eating

Gran Café Victoria   CAFE €
(Calle Obispo San Juan de Ribera 3; breakfasts €2-3) With its huge central lamp arrangement, tall dark pillars and wine-red couches, this cafe has a dignified ambience for your morning coffee and croissant, but it's good for a quiet drink at any time of the day.

El Claustro   TAPAS €€
(924 20 17 21; Plaza de Cervantes 13A; tapas from €2.50; meals €25-30; noon-midnight Mon-Sat) The fashionable stone-clad interior, hung with edgy artwork, is fronted by a buzzy tapas bar serving generous, innovative snacks. The chandelier-lit dining room dishes up larger portions in more formal surrounds.

Taberna La Casona Alta   TAPAS, IBERIAN €€
(Plaza Alta; raciones from €6.50; meals €25-30; lunch & dinner Mon-Sat, lunch Sun) With chairs on the square and a bustling bar area with barrel tables, you can choose from a healthy menu of *raciones* or more substantial dishes in the downstairs Moorish-influenced restaurant, like Portuguese-style *bacalao* (cod), prepared a variety of ways.

Drinking

Late-night bars are scattered around the streets near the cathedral.

Espantaperros Café   JAZZ CAFE
(Calle Hernán Cortés 14; 7pm-3am Mon-Thu & 4pm-4am Fri-Sun) Among the liveliest near the cathedral, it has live jazz nightly.

El Arrabal   BAR
(Calle de San Blas 14; 10pm-2.30am Mon-Fri, 6pm-2.30am Sat) Sophisticated El Arrabal has a garden bar.

Samarkanda   BAR
(www.cafesamarkanda.com, in Spanish; Calle Virgen de la Soledad 9; 4.30pm-2.30am) Moody dark-red paintwork and cushions overlooked by a serene Buddha statue.

Blues Center   BAR, LIVE MUSIC
(www.bluescenter.es; Calle de San Juan Bautista 8; 4pm-4.30am) Another good choice for nightly live music.

Information

Municipal tourist office (924 22 49 81; www.turismobadajoz.es; Pasaje de San Juan; 10am-2pm & 4-6pm Mon-Fri, 10am-2pm Sat)

La Guía de Badajoz (www.laguiadebadajoz.com) Useful online guide to the city.

Getting There & Around

Buses run to/from Mérida (€4.46, one hour, five to nine daily), Madrid (from €27, 4½ to 5½ hours, nine daily), Lisbon (€31, three hours, three daily) and Seville (€14.50, three hours, six daily) via Zafra (€6, 1¼ hours).

MOVING ON?

For tips, recommendations and reviews, head to shop.lonelyplanet.com to purchase a downloadable PDF of the Alentejo chapter from Lonely Planet's *Portugal* guide.

Around Badajoz

ALBUQUERQUE
POP 5700

Looming large above the small town, 38km north of Badajoz, is the intact Castillo de la Luna (admission free; ⊘guided visits in Spanish 11am-1pm & 4-6pm Tue-Sun). The centrepiece of a complex frontier defence system of forts, the castle was built on the site of its Muslim predecessor in the 13th century and subsequently expanded. From the top, views take in the Portuguese frontier (the Portuguese actually took the town for a few years in the early 18th century). Among many curiosities is a hole set in the wall of one of the towers. It was used by the castle's masters as a toilet – sending an unpleasant message to hostile forces below when under siege.

Up to four buses a day (€4.15, 45 minutes) between Badajoz and San Vicente de Alcántara stop by.

OLIVENZA
POP 11,850

Pretty Olivenza, 24km south of Badajoz, clings to its Portuguese heritage – it has only been Spanish since 1801. The cobbled centre is distinctive for its whitewashed houses, typical turreted defensive walls and penchant for blue-and-white ceramic tile work.

Smack-bang in its centre is the 14th-century castle, dominated by the **Torre del Homenaje**, 37m high, from which there are fine views. The castle houses an ethnographic museum (admission €1; ⊘11am-2pm & 4-7pm Tue-Fri, 10am-2pm Sun), with a collection of toy cars on the 1st floor. The most impressive section of the original defensive walls is around the 18th-century **Puerta del Calvario**, on the western side of town.

Restaurante Hostal Dosca (✆924 49 10 65; www.hoteldosca.com; Plaza de la Constitución 15; s/d €40/50; ❈ @), on the corner of one of the town's most evocative squares, complete with fountain, makes an excellent lunch stop (menús del día €13 to €26) or an overnight stay. The rooms here are prettily furnished and most have lovely views.

Buses to Badajoz (€1.40, 30 minutes) run almost hourly during the week.

Zafra

POP 16,420

Gleaming white Zafra resembles an Andalucian *pueblo blanco* and it's a serene, attractive stop between Seville and Mérida. Originally a Muslim settlement, Zafra's narrow streets are lined with baroque churches, old-fashioned shops and traditional houses decorated by brilliant red splashes of geraniums. The modern town sprawls somewhat, but leave it behind for the old town at its core and step into an altogether different world.

⊙ Sights

Zafra's 15th-century castle, now the town's *parador,* was built over the former Muslim *alcázar* and dominates the town. Plaza Grande and the adjoining Plaza Chica, arcaded and bordered by bars, are the places to see Zafra life, from old men in flat caps playing dominoes to children playing football and decorating the ground with *pipas* (sunflower) shells. Peek into the courtyard of the ayuntamiento (town hall; Plaza Pilar Redondo), its brick arches supported by slender pillars and the 16th-century Iglesia de la Candelaria (Calle Tetuán; ⊘10.30am-1pm & 5.30-7.30pm Mon, Tue & Thu-Sat, 11am-1pm Sun), with its fine altarpieces. The Museo Santa Clara (admission free; 10.30am-1.30pm & 4.30-6.15pm Tue-Sun) has a gilded chapel and there's an interesting video on convent life; the resident nuns also sell their pastries.

⌸ Sleeping

Hotel Plaza Grande　　　　HOTEL €€
(✆924 56 31 63; www.hotelplazagrande.com; Calle Pasteleros 2; s incl breakfast €35-55, d incl breakfast €55-75; ❈⌾) The owner has created a gem of a hotel here. Go for room 108, with its corner balconies overlooking the plaza (room 208 is the same but with windows instead of balconies). Decor is terracotta accentuated by cream paintwork and muted earth colours. The downstairs restaurant and bar are reliably good.

Parador Hernán Cortés　　　HOTEL €€
(✆924 55 45 40; www.parador.es; Plaza Corazón de María 7; d €90-155; ⊖❈⌾⌇) They say a man's home is his castle: here it's the reverse. The large rooms are richly decorated with burgundy-coloured fabrics and antiques. The marble-pillared courtyard is truly magnificent, while the secluded pool is surrounded by ivy and turrets. The restaurant is excellent.

Hotel Huerta Honda　　　　HOTEL €€
(✆924 55 41 00; www.hotelhuertahonda.com; Calle López Asme 1; s €59, d €74-96, ste €120-150; Ⓟ⊖❈⌾⌇) There are two grades of rooms here: standards are contemporary, stylish and supremely comfortable, with lots

of browns and beiges; while 'Gran Clase' are sumptuous, with four-poster beds, timber ceilings and antiques. Whichever you choose, this place is outstanding. The bougainvillea-draped courtyard has views of the castle. Parking costs €5.

Albergue Convento San Francisco
HOSTEL €

(☎924 02 98 17; Calle Ancha 1; dm €18-32; @) Open to all, this former monastery is the choice of walkers along the Ruta de la Plata (see the boxed text, p797). It has a choice of doubles with private bathrooms or dorms in pleasant, brightly furnished surroundings.

Eating

Gastro-Bar Baraka
TAPAS €

(Plaza Grande 20; meals €15-20; ⊙7pm-midnight Mon-Wed, 7pm-3am Thu, 1pm-3am Fri-Sun) Opened in 2009, Gastro-Bar Baraka adds a touch of sophistication to Plaza Grande's charm. The food here ranges from creative *tostas* (€2.85 to €3.75) to more substantial *raciones,* such as the pork sirloin in a sauce of creamy Torta de Casar cheese on a bed of thinly sliced potatoes (€8.75). Enjoying these dishes on a balmy summer's evening with a glass of red in the lamp-lit square – bliss. Downstairs, there's a groovy bar (open Thursday to Sunday) inhabiting the 15th-century cisterns.

La Rebotica
TRADITIONAL SPANISH €€

(☎924 55 42 89; Calle Boticas 12; meals €35; ⊙lunch & dinner Tue-Sat, lunch Sun) This restaurant offers a traditional meaty menu, including *rabo de toro* (ox tail) and five different pork fillet dishes, subtly prepared by Dutch chef Rudy Koster. It's just off delightful Plaza Chica.

ⓘ Information

Municipal Tourist Office (☎924 55 10 36; www.turismodezafra.blogspot.com, in Spanish; Plaza de España 8A; ⊙9.30am-2pm & 4-7pm Mon-Fri, 10am-1.30pm & 5-7pm Sat & Sun)

ⓘ Getting There & Away

Zafra is on the main bus routes linking Seville to the south with Mérida (€5.35, 65 minutes) and Badajoz (€6, 1¼ hours). Trains also pass through.

Around Zafra

Roads through the rolling Sierra Morena into Andalucía head southwest through Fregenal de la Sierra into northern Huelva province, and southeast into the Parque Natural Sierra Norte in Seville province.

In Fregenal de la Sierra, highlights include the 13th-century castle with seven turrets and adjacent Santa María church. On Tuesday and Friday mornings there is a lively market in the main square.

Walled and hilly Jerez de los Caballeros, 42km west of Zafra, was a cradle of conquistadors. It has a Knights Templars castle and several handsome churches, three with towers emulating the Giralda in Seville.

Quiet Burguillos del Cerro, southwest of Zafra, is overlooked by a 15th-century castle atop a grassy hill. Just outside Casas de Reina on the Guadalcanal road are impressive remains of a Roman theatre and a hilltop Muslim castle.

One weekday bus runs between Zafra and Fregenal de la Sierra (€3.25, one hour), Jerez de los Caballeros (€3.45, one hour) and Burguillos del Cerro (€1.85, 30 minutes).

Teatro Romano (p804), Mérida
The Teatro Romano was built around 15 BC and is the only Roman building in Mérida used for its original purpose

Understand Spain

population per sq km

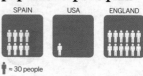

SPAIN   USA   ENGLAND

👤 ≈ 30 people

Spain Today

Boom & Bust

Spain was, not so long ago, the poster-child for a prosperous Europe. Its booming economy was a source of great pride to Spaniards who for decades had been playing catch-up with the rest of Europe. And then came the fall. The economy suddenly shrank alarmingly in 2008 and unemployment has soared from around 6% to close to 20%. It is, even the government admitted, 'the deepest recession in half a century'. The country's reliance on two industries vulnerable to economic downturns – construction (16% of GDP) and tourism (5%) – suggests that the country's economy will continue to be the singlemost important challenge facing Spain for some years to come.

Remaking Spain

Spain's Socialist government, which came to power in 2004 and was re-elected in 2008, has been responsible for nothing less than a social revolution. Its raft of reforming legislation has, in this once-staunchly Catholic country, made Spain one of Europe's most liberal. Gay marriage was legalised, divorce and abortion laws were liberalised and the powerful Catholic Church was stripped of its power over school curricula. Despite fierce opposition from the church and conservative political parties, the reforms proved overwhelming popular among the wider Spanish populace. More controversially, the decision to reopen investigations into crimes committed during the Spanish Civil War and the subsequent Franco years, coupled with a drive towards greater autonomy for Spain's restive regions, has left many Spaniards uneasy. Such has been the ferocity of the opposition that many Spaniards fear that the country is more divided than it has been in decades.

» Population: 46 million (2010)

» GDP: 1.466 trillion

» GDP per capita (2009): US$33,700

» Annual inflation (2009): -0.8%

» Unemployment (2009): 18%

» Internet domain: es

» Area: 505,370 sq km

Top Books

Ghosts of Spain (Giles Tremlett) An account of modern Spain and the hangover from its past.
Roads to Santiago (Cees Nooteboom) A fascinating journey along the Camino de Santiago.
A Handbook for Travellers (Richard Ford) This 1845 classic is witty, informative and downright rude.
Between Hopes and Memories: A Spanish Journey (Michael Jacobs) Amusing reflection on modern Spain.
Spanish Steps (Tim Moore) The Camino with plenty of laughs.

Top Films

¡Bienvenido, Mr Marshall! (1952)
Jamón, Jamón (1992)
Flamenco (1995)
Todo Sobre Mi Madre (1999)
Mar Adentro (2004)
Volver (2006)
Alatriste (2006)

belief systems
(% of population)

94 — Roman Catholic

6 — Other (mostly Islam)

if Spain were 100 people

74 would speak Castilian Spanish
17 would speak Catalan
7 would speak Galician
2 would speak Basque

Terrorism

On 11 March 2004, just three days before Spain was due to vote in national elections, Madrid was thrown into chaos by 10 bombs planted on four rush-hour commuter trains by supporters of al-Qaeda; 191 people were killed and almost 1800 wounded. Spanish prosecutors in the trial that followed alleged the attack was in retribution for Spain's deeply unpopular support for the war in Iraq. It was the biggest terror attack in the nation's history and shocked even this country which has become accustomed to the violence carried out by Euskadi Ta Askatasuna (ETA; Basque Homeland and Freedom, labelled terrorists by the EU and US).

Although ETA has been weakened over the last few years, it remains a sinister presence. Two people were killed in a bombing at Madrid's Barajas airport on 30 December 2006 (the bombing broke a promising ETA ceasefire) and a former Basque councillor was killed by ETA during the 2008 election campaign. It's highly unusual to meet a Spaniard who lives in fear of ETA or any other form of terrorism – the risks of being caught up in an attack are no higher than in any other Western country. Nonetheless, the majority of Spaniards, including peaceful Basque nationalists, look forward to the day ETA is no longer a threat.

» Highest point on mainland: Mulhacen (3479m)

» Number of national parks: 14

» Length of coastline: 4964km

» Longest border: 1214km (Portugal)

» Shortest border: 1.2km (Gibraltar)

Sporting Success

It has been a torrid few years for Spain, but thankfully its sportspeople have given Spaniards some much-needed good news to cheer about. In particular, Rafael Nadal's 2008 victory at Wimbledon (and again in 2010), and the Spanish football team's victories at the 2008 European Championship and 2010 World Cup, have united the country, albeit briefly, like never before. And boy did they party...

Top Flamenco

Una Leyenda Flamenca (El Camarón de la Isla) Great music by the all-time flamenco master.
Canciones Hondas (Ketama) Rocky flamenco fusion.
Lágrimas Negras (Diego El Cigala) Flamenco with Cuban rhythms.

Flamenco (Enrique Morente) Modern flamenco's creative talent joined by guitar greats.
Paco de Lucía Antología (Paco de Lucía) The life's work of the great flamenco guitarist.
Flamenco Chill (Chambao) Flamenco chill.

Top Conversations

Too many immigrants? From 2% to 12% of the population in the last 15 years.
The economy How did it all go so wrong so quickly?
The 2010 World Cup Spaniards will be talking about this for generations.

History

Early Spaniards painted some of the world's great prehistoric art at the Cueva de Altamira and other sites between 15,000 and 10,000 BC. After 1000 BC, Phoenician and Greek traders from the eastern Mediterranean established settlements on Spain's southern and eastern coasts. They were supplanted by the Carthaginians, who in turn were replaced by the Romans. Rome ruled the Iberian Peninsula (Spain and Portugal) from about 200 BC to AD 400, bringing stability and prosperity. After the Roman Empire disintegrated, the Visigoths, a Germanic tribe, took control of the peninsula until Muslim forces invaded from North Africa in AD 711 and rapidly overran the peninsula. The Muslims (often referred to as Moors) were to be the dominant power for four centuries, and a potent one for four centuries after that. Islamic political power and cultural developments centred first on Córdoba (756–1031), then Seville (c 1040–1248) and lastly Granada (1248–1492). Between wars and rebellions, Islamic Spain developed the most cultured society of medieval Europe.

From small beginnings in Asturias, on Spain's northern coastal strip, Christian kingdoms such as León, Castilla (Castile), Aragón and Portugal gradually regained territory in the eight-centuries-long Reconquista. The last Muslim kingdom, Granada, fell in 1492 to the Reyes Católicos (Catholic Monarchs), Isabel (Isabella) of Castilla and Fernando (Ferdinand) of Aragón, whose marriage had united the two most powerful Christian states. The same year, Genoese sailor Christopher Columbus (Cristóbal Colón to Spaniards) found several Caribbean islands on a voyage financed by the Spanish crown, leading to the Spanish conquest of large parts of the Americas and a flood of silver from the new empire. The 16th century saw Spain at the peak of its power under kings Carlos I and Felipe II, who also ruled large parts of Europe.

Silver shipments shrank drastically in the 17th century, initiating three centuries of decline in which Spain lost all of its foreign possessions and sank into stagnation and widespread poverty. Internal wars

For a colourful survey of the whole saga of Spanish history, read *The Story of Spain* by Mark Williams.

TIMELINE	c 1.2 million BC	c 22,000 BC	c 15,000–10,000 BC
	Europe's earliest-known humans leave their fossilised remains in the Sima del Elefante at Atapuerca, near the northern city of Burgos.	Neanderthal humans die out on the Iberian Peninsula – possibly due to climatic changes during the last Ice Age, possibly because they were displaced by *Homo sapiens* arriving from Africa.	Palaeolithic (Old Stone Age) hunters of the Magdalenian culture paint beautiful, sophisticated animal images in caves at Altamira and other sites along Spain's northern coastal strip.

and a widening wealth gap between rich and poor fomented social unrest and political radicalisation in the late 19th and early 20th centuries. Spain became irretrievably polarised between left and right during the Second Republic (1931–36). This led to the Spanish Civil War (1936–39), in which the right-wing Nationalists, led by General Francisco Franco, defeated the left-wing Republicans. Franco then ruled as a dictator until his death in 1975, after which King Juan Carlos I engineered a return to democracy. Three decades of steady economic progress followed.

The Original Spaniards

In 2007 archaeologists unearthed an assortment of bones and stone tools in the Sima del Elefante (Elephant Chasm) at Atapuerca, near the northern Spanish city of Burgos. Dating revealed that a fossilised human jawbone, arm bone and teeth were approximately 1.2 million years old – the oldest human remains ever found in Europe. Scientists reckon these bones come from the species *Homo antecessor,* which may have been a common ancestor of both the Neanderthals and *Homo sapiens sapiens* (modern humanity). Debate continues about how these early humans reached Spain – whether direct from Africa or via Asia – but until an older find is made, Spain can certainly claim to be the cradle of European humanity. See p189 for more on Atapuerca.

Caves and archaeological sites all round the country – many of them open for visits today (as is Atapuerca) – reveal plenty more about Spain's prehistoric inhabitants. The much-visited Cueva de Nerja in Andalucía was one of many haunts of the earliest *Homo sapiens sapiens* on the Iberian Peninsula, the Cro-Magnons, who probably arrived from Africa around 35,000 years ago. Wonderful cave paintings from the Palaeolithic (Old Stone Age) in northern Spain are the country's most superb legacy of prehistoric humanity. The finest art was produced by the Solutrean and Magdalenian cultures of about 20,000 to 15,000 and 15,000 to 10,000 BC respectively. Altamira's beautiful, sophisticated images of bison, stags, boars and horses make it the finest of 18 separate Palaeolithic cave-art sites along northern Spain's coastal strip that are now on the Unesco World Heritage list (see p467).

After the end of the last Ice Age in about 8000 BC, further new peoples arrived, again probably from North Africa, and the rock-shelter paintings of hunting, gathering, combat, daily life and mythology that survive all down the eastern side of Spain from the following 5000 years provide a unique record of Stone Age life. Over 700 separate rock-painting sites from Aragón to Andalucía are included in another World Heritage listing.

The Neolithic (New Stone Age) reached Spain from Mesopotamia and Egypt around 6000 BC, bringing revolutionary innovations such

Top Prehistoric Sites

» Cueva de Altamira, near Santillana del Mar

» Atapuerca, near Burgos

» Cueva de Tito Bustillo, Ribadesella

» Dolmens, Antequera

» Cueva de la Pileta, near Ronda

The Iberian Peninsula's best-known Neanderthal relic is 'Gibraltar woman', a skull found in 1848.

MICHAL BOUDIN/ALAMY

» Cueva de Altamira (p467)

3000–1900 BC	c 800–600 BC
Spaniards begin to work metal: people at Los Millares near Almería smelt and shape copper. Then people at El Argar learn to alloy copper with tin, initiating the Bronze Age.	The fabled Tartessos culture, influenced by Phoenician and Greek traders, flourishes in western Andalucía. The Phoenicians in the south and the Celts in the north usher in the Iron Age.

as the plough, crops, livestock, pottery, textiles and permanent villages, especially in the east. Contacts with northern Europe are evident with the appearance of megalithic tombs (dolmens), constructed of large rocks, in several places around the perimeter of the Iberian Peninsula between 3000 and 2000 BC – the same era as the megalithic age in France, Britain and Ireland. The best dolmens in Spain are at Antequera in Andalucía. At the same time, the southeastern province of Almería saw the beginnings of metal technology in Spain, ushering in first the Copper then the Bronze Age.

Early Traders & Invaders

Spain's rich natural resources and settled societies eventually attracted the interest of more sophisticated societies around the Mediterranean. A series of newcomers arriving between 1000 BC and AD 600 brought huge technological, social and political changes, and left some of Spain's most impressive monuments and indelible, lasting imprints on the Spanish way of life. The first arrivals came chiefly to trade; later, emerging Mediterranean imperialist states sought not just to tap Spain's wealth but also to exert military control.

Phoenicians, Greeks, Celts

By about 1000 BC a flourishing culture rich in animals, agriculture and metals had arisen in western Andalucía. Phoenicians, a Semitic people from present-day Lebanon, came to exchange perfumes, ivory, jewellery, oil, wine and textiles for Spanish silver and bronze, and established coastal trading colonies at places like Almuñécar (which they called Ex or Sex), Cádiz (Gadir) and Huelva (Onuba). Museums in those cities preserve many Phoenician artefacts today. In the 7th century BC, Greek traders reached Spain too, trading much the same goods as the Phoenicians and establishing settlements mainly along the Mediterranean coast – the biggest was Emporion (Empúries) at L'Escala in Catalonia.

The Phoenician- and Greek-influenced culture that developed in western Andalucía in the 8th and 7th centuries, with Phoenician-type gods, is known as the Tartessos culture. The Tartessians developed advanced methods of working gold, but it was iron that replaced bronze as the most important metal. Tartessos was described centuries later by Greek, Roman and biblical writers as the source of fabulous riches. Whether it was a city, a state or just a region no one knows. Some argue that it was a trading settlement near modern Huelva; others believe it may lie beneath the marshes near the mouth of the Río Guadalquivir.

As well as iron, the Phoenicians and Greeks brought with them several things now considered quintessentially Spanish – the olive tree,

Spanish History Index (vlib.iue.it/hist-spain) provides countless internet leads for those who want to dig deeper.

6th century BC	218 BC	1st to 3rd centuries AD	AD 53
Carthage, a former Phoenician colony in North Africa, supplants the Phoenicians and Greeks as the major trading power in the western Mediterranean.	Roman legions arrive in Spain during the Second Punic War against Carthage, initiating the 600-year Roman occupation of the Iberian Peninsula; it takes two centuries to subdue all local resistance.	Pax Romana (Roman Peace), a period of stability and prosperity. The Iberian Peninsula is divided into three provinces: Baetica (capital: Córdoba); Lusitania (Mérida) and Tarraconensis (Tarragona).	Future Roman Emperor Trajan is born in Itálica to a wealthy senator. His imperial rule will begin in 98 and see the Roman Empire reach its greatest extent.

the grapevine and the donkey – along with other useful items such as writing, coins, the potter's wheel and poultry.

Around the same time as the Phoenicians brought iron technology to the south, the Celts (originally from Central Europe) brought it – and beer-making – to the north. In contrast to the dark-featured Iberians (the general name given to most inhabitants of the peninsula at this time), the Celts were fair. Celts and Iberians who merged on the *meseta* (the high tableland of central Spain) are known as Celtiberians. Celts in northwestern Spain typically lived in sizeable hill-fort towns called *castros,* some of which can still be seen.

The Carthaginians

From about the 6th century BC the Phoenicians and Greeks were pushed out of the western Mediterranean by Carthage, a former Phoenician colony in modern Tunisia that established a flourishing settlement on Ibiza.

Unhappily for the Carthaginians, the next new power to rise in the Mediterranean was Rome. After losing out to Rome in the First Punic War (264–241 BC), which was fought for control of Sicily, Carthage conquered southern Spain. The Second Punic War (218–201 BC) saw Carthaginian general Hannibal march his elephants on from here and over the Alps to threaten Rome, but also saw Rome bring legions to fight Carthage in Spain. Rome's victory at Ilipa, near Seville, in 206 BC, gave it control of the Iberian Peninsula. The first Roman town in Spain, Itálica, was founded near the battlefield soon afterwards.

The Romans

The Romans held sway on the Iberian Peninsula for 600 years. It took them 200 years to subdue the fiercest local tribes, but by AD 50 most of Hispania (as the Romans called the peninsula) had adopted the Roman way of life. The major exception was the Basques, who, though defeated, were never Romanised like the rest.

Rome's legacy was huge, giving Hispania a road system, aqueducts, temples, theatres, amphitheatres and bathhouses, along with the religion that still predominates today – Christianity – and a Jewish population who were to play a big part in Spanish life for over 1000 years. The main languages still spoken on the Iberian Peninsula – Castilian Spanish, Catalan, Galician and Portuguese – are all versions of the colloquial Latin spoken by Roman legionaries and colonists, filtered through 2000 years of linguistic mutation. It was also the Romans who first began to cut (for timber, fuel and weapons) the extensive forests that in their time covered half the *meseta.* In return, Hispania gave Rome gold, silver, grain, wine, fish, soldiers, emperors (Trajan, Hadrian,

Dating back to at least the 9th century BC, Cádiz is the oldest continually inhabited city in the whole of the Iberian Peninsula.

CÁDIZ

4th to 7th centuries AD	711	718	756
Germanic tribes enter the Iberian Peninsula, ending the Pax Romana. The Visigoths establish control and bring 200 years of relative stability in which Hispano-Roman culture survives.	Muslims invade Iberia from North Africa, overrunning it within a few years, becoming the dominant force on the peninsula for nearly four centuries, then a potent one for four centuries more.	Christian nobleman Pelayo establishes the Kingdom of Asturias in northern Spain. With his victory over a Muslim force at the Battle of Covadonga around 722, the Reconquista begins.	Abd ar-Rahman I establishes himself in Córdoba as the emir of Al-Andalus (the Islamic areas of the peninsula) and launches nearly three centuries of Cordoban supremacy.

Theodosius) and the literature of Seneca, Martial, Quintilian and Lucan. Another valuable export was *garum*, a spicy sauce derived from fish and used as a seasoning.

The Pax Romana (Roman Peace; the long, prosperous period of stability under the Romans) in Spain started to crack when two Germanic tribes, the Franks and the Alemanni, swept across the Pyrenees in the late 3rd century AD, causing devastation. When the Huns hit Eastern Europe from Asia a century later, further Germanic peoples moved westward. Among these were the Suevi and Vandals, who overran the Iberian Peninsula around 410.

The Visigoths

The Visigoths, another Germanic people, sacked Rome itself in 410. Within a few years, however, they had become Roman allies, being granted lands in southern Gaul (France) and fighting on the emperor's behalf against the barbarian invaders in Hispania. When the Franks pushed the Visigoths out of Gaul in the 6th century, they settled in the Iberian Peninsula, making Toledo their capital.

The roughly 200,000 Visigoths, who let their hair grow long and had a penchant for gaudy jewellery, had a precarious hold over the millions of more-sophisticated Hispano-Romans, and their position was undermined by strife among their own nobility. The Hispano-Roman nobles still ran the fiscal system and their bishops were the senior figures in urban centres. Ties between the Visigoth monarchy and the Hispano-Romans were strengthened in 587 when King Reccared converted to Roman Christianity from the Visigoths' Arian version (which denied that Christ was identical to God). Culturally, the Visigoths tended to ape Roman ways and they left little mark on the Spanish landscape, although the Visigothic church at Baños de Cerrato, near Palencia, which dates from 661, is reckoned to be the oldest surviving church in the country. The Visigoths' principal lasting impact on Spanish history lies in the fact that Visigothic nobility headed the small Christian kingdoms that survived the Muslim conquest of 711 and began the eight-century Reconquista, which eventually reasserted Christianity in the Iberian Peninsula. Common names of Visigothic origin, such as Fernando, Roderigo, Fernández and Rodríguez, are still reminders of the Visigoths' role in the Spanish story.

Moorish Spain

Following the death of the prophet Mohammed in 632, Arabs had carried Islam through the Middle East and North Africa. With the disintegration of the Visigothic kingdom through famine, disease and strife among the aristocracy, the Iberian Peninsula was ripe for invasion. If

---

Top Roman Remains

» Mérida
» Segovia
» Itálica
» Tarragona
» Baelo Claudia, Bolonia
» Lugo

Richard Fletcher's *Moorish Spain* is an excellent short history of Al-Andalus (the Muslim-ruled areas of the peninsula).

801	929	1031
Barcelona is taken by Frankish troops and becomes a buffer between the Christians to the north and the Muslims to the south.	Abd ar-Rahman III inaugurates the Córdoba Caliphate, under which Al-Andalus reaches its zenith and Córdoba, with up to half a million people, becomes Europe's biggest and most cultured city.	The Córdoba Caliphate disintegrates into dozens of *taifas* (small kingdoms) after a devastating civil war. The most powerful *taifas* include Seville, Granada, Toledo and Zaragoza.

OLIVER STREWE

» *Alcázar (p668), Seville*

you believe the myth, the Muslims were ushered into Spain by the sexual adventures of the last Visigoth king, Roderic, who reputedly seduced Florinda, the daughter of the governor of Ceuta on the Moroccan coast. The governor, Julian, sought revenge by approaching the Muslims with a plan to invade Spain, and in 711 Tariq ibn Ziyad, the Muslim governor of Tangier, landed at Gibraltar with around 10,000 men, mostly Berbers (indigenous North Africans). Roderic's army was decimated, probably near Río Guadalete or Río Barbate in western Andalucía, and he is thought to have drowned while fleeing the scene. Visigothic survivors fled north and within a few years the Muslims had conquered the whole Iberian Peninsula, except for small areas behind the mountains of the Cordillera Cantábrica in the north. Their advance into Europe was only checked by the Franks at the Battle of Poitiers in 732.

The name given to Muslim-controlled territory on the peninsula was Al-Andalus. Its frontiers shifted constantly as the Christians strove to regain territory in the stuttering 800-year Reconquista. Up to the mid-11th century the frontier between Muslim and Christian territory lay across the north of the peninsula, roughly from southern Catalonia to northern Portugal, with a protrusion up to the central Pyrenees.

Islamic cities such as Córdoba, Seville and Granada boasted beautiful palaces, mosques and gardens, universities, public baths and bustling *zocos* (markets). Al-Andalus' rulers allowed freedom of worship to Jews and Christians (known as *mozárabes,* Mozarabs) under their rule. Jews mostly flourished, but Christians had to pay a special tax, so most either converted to Islam (to be known as *muladíes* or *muwallad*) or left for the Christian north. The Muslim settlers themselves were not a homogeneous group. Beneath the Arab ruling class was a larger group of Berbers, and tension between these two groups broke out in numerous Berber rebellions.

The Cordoban Emirate & Caliphate

Initially Al-Andalus was part of the Caliphate of Damascus, which ruled the Islamic world. In 750 the caliphal dynasty in Damascus, the Omayyad, was overthrown by a rival clan, the Abbasids, who shifted the caliphate to Baghdad. However, one aristocratic Omayyad survivor managed to make his way to Spain and establish himself in Córdoba in 756 as the independent emir of Al-Andalus, Abd ar-Rahman I. It was he who began construction of Córdoba's Mezquita, one of the world's greatest Islamic buildings. Most of Al-Andalus was more or less unified under Cordoban rule for long periods. In 929 the ruler Abd ar-Rahman III gave himself the title caliph, launching the Caliphate of Córdoba (929–1031), during which Al-Andalus reached its peak of power and lustre. Córdoba in this period was the biggest and most dazzling city in

Best Moorish Monuments

» Alhambra, Granada

» Mezquita, Córdoba

» Albayzín, Granada

» Alcázar, Seville

» Giralda, Seville

» Aljafería, Zaragoza

» Alcazaba, Málaga

1035	1085	1091	1137
Castilla, a county of the northern Christian Kingdom of León (successor to the Kingdom of Asturias), becomes an independent kingdom and goes on to become the leading force of the Reconquista.	Castilla captures the major Muslim city of Toledo in central Spain after infighting among the *taifas* leaves them vulnerable to attack.	North African Muslim Almoravids invade the Peninsula, unifying Al-Andalus, ruling it from Marrakesh and halting Christian expansion. Almoravid rule crumbles in the 1140s: Al-Andalus splits into *taifas*.	Ramón Berenguer IV of Catalonia marries Petronilla, heiress of Aragón, creating a formidable new Christian power bloc in the northeast, the Crown of Aragón, with Barcelona as its power centre.

Western Europe. Astronomy, medicine, mathematics and botany flourished and one of the great Muslim libraries was established in the city.

Later in the 10th century the fearsome Cordoban general Al-Mansour (or Almanzor) terrorised the Christian north with 50-odd forays in 20 years. He destroyed the cathedral at Santiago de Compostela in northwestern Spain in 997 and forced Christian slaves to carry its doors and bells to Córdoba, where they were incorporated into the great mosque. But after Al-Mansour's death the caliphate collapsed in a devastating civil war, ending Omayyad rule, and in 1031 it finally broke up into dozens of *taifas* (small kingdoms).

The Almoravids & Almohads

Political unity was restored to Al-Andalus by the invasion of a strict Muslim sect of Saharan nomads, the Almoravids, in 1091. The Almoravids had conquered North Africa and were initially invited to the Iberian Peninsula to support Seville, one of the strongest *taifas,* against the growing Christian threat from the north. Sixty years later a second Berber sect, the Almohads, invaded the peninsula after overthrowing the Almoravids in Morocco. Both sects roundly defeated the Christian armies they encountered in Spain.

THE MOORISH LEGACY

Muslim rule not only set Spain's destiny quite apart from that of the rest of Europe, but left an indelible imprint on the country, despite the fact that Islam itself was effectively eradicated from the 16th century until the late 20th century, when it returned with new immigrants from North Africa. Great architectural monuments such as the Alhambra in Granada and the Mezquita in Córdoba are the stars of the Moorish legacy, but thousands of other buildings large and small are Moorish in origin (including the many churches that began life as mosques). The tangled, narrow street plans of many a Spanish town and village, especially in the south, date back to Moorish times, and the Muslims also developed the Hispano-Roman agricultural base by improving irrigation and introducing new fruits and crops, many of which are still widely grown today. The Spanish language contains many common words of Arabic origin, including the names of some of those new crops – *naranja* (orange), *azúcar* (sugar), *arroz* (rice). Flamenco song, though brought to its modern form by Roma people in post-Moorish times, has clear Moorish roots. Muslim and local blood quickly merged after the conquest, adding a new ingredient to the Spanish genetic mix: many Spaniards today are partly descended from medieval Muslims. It was also through Al-Andalus that much of the learning of ancient Greece and Rome – picked up by the Arabs in the eastern Mediterranean – was transmitted to Christian Europe, where it would exert a profound influence on the Renaissance.

1160–73	1195	1212	1218
The Almohads, another strict Muslim sect from North Africa, conquer Al-Andalus. They make Seville their capital and revive arts and learning.	The Almohads inflict a devastating defeat on Alfonso VIII of Castilla at the Battle Of Alarcos, near Ciudad Real – the last major Christian reverse of the Reconquista.	Combined armies of the northern Christian kingdoms defeat the Almohads at Las Navas de Tolosa in Andalucía, and the momentum of the Christian–Muslim struggle swings decisively in favour of the Christians.	The University of Salamanca is founded by Alfonso IX, King of León, making it the oldest – and still the most prestigious – university in the country.

Almohad rule saw a cultural revival in Seville, and the great Cordoban philosopher Averroës (1126–98) exerted a major influence on medieval Christian thought with his commentaries on Aristotle, trying to reconcile science with religion.

The Last Redoubt: Granada

Almohad power eventually disintegrated because of internal disputes and Christian military advances. Seville fell to the Christians in 1248, reducing Muslim territory on the Iberian Peninsula to the Emirate of Granada, which occupied about half of modern Andalucía. Ruled from the lavish Alhambra palace by the Nasrid dynasty, Granada saw Muslim Spain's final cultural flowering, especially in the 14th century under Yusuf I and Mohammed V, both of whom contributed to the splendours of the Alhambra.

The Reconquista

The Christian Reconquest of the Iberian Peninsula began in about 722 at Covadonga, Asturias, and ended with the fall of Granada in 1492. It was a stuttering affair, conducted by Christian kingdoms that were as often at war with each other as with the Muslims. But the Muslims were gradually pushed back as the Christian kingdoms of Asturias, León, Navarra, Castilla and Aragón in the north, and Portugal in the southwest, developed. The Christians eventually succeeded in turning the whole Iberian Peninsula into a redoubt of Roman Catholicism, which it has remained ever since. Spain today is littered with reminders of the Reconquista era, especially in the shape of thousands of picturesque castles and churches.

An essential ingredient in the Reconquista was the cult of Santiago (St James), one of the 12 apostles. In 813 the saint's supposed tomb was discovered in Galicia. The city of Santiago de Compostela grew around the site, to become the third-most popular medieval Christian pilgrimage goal after Rome and Jerusalem. Christian generals experienced visions of Santiago before forays against the Muslims, and Santiago became the inspiration and special protector of soldiers in the Reconquista, earning the sobriquet Matamoros (Moor-slayer). Today he is the patron saint of Spain.

Castilla Rises

Covadonga lies in the Picos de Europa mountains, where some Visigothic nobles took refuge after the Muslim conquest. Christian versions of the battle there tell of a small band of fighters under their leader, Pelayo, defeating an enormous force of Muslims; Muslim accounts make it a rather less important skirmish. Whatever the facts of Covadonga, by 757 Christians controlled nearly a quarter of the Iberian Peninsula.

Spanish Castles on the Web

» Castles of Spain (www.castillosnet.org)

» Castles of Spain (www.castlesofspain.co.uk)

» Castles in Spain (http://spainforvisitors.com/archive/features/castlesinspain.htm)

1229–38	1248	1366–69	1469
Catalonia enjoys its golden age under King Jaume I of Aragón, who takes the Balearic Islands and Valencia from the Muslims and makes Catalonia the major power in the western Mediterranean.	Having captured Córdoba 12 years earlier, Castilla's Fernando III takes Seville after a two-year siege, making the Nasrid Emirate of Granada the last surviving Muslim state on the peninsula.	Civil war erupts in Castilla as Pedro (nicknamed 'the Just' by supporters but 'the Cruel' by enemies) fights his half-brother Enrique for the throne. Enrique eventually kills Pedro and becomes king.	Isabel, the 18-year-old heir to Castilla, marries Fernando, heir to Aragón and one year her junior, uniting Spain's two most powerful Christian states.

The Asturian kingdom eventually moved its capital south to León and became the Kingdom of León, which spearheaded the Reconquista until the Christians were set on the defensive by Al-Mansour in the 10th century. Castilla, initially a small principality within León, developed into the dominant Reconquista force as hardy adventurers set up towns in the no-man's-land of the Duero basin, spurred on by land grants and other *fueros* (rights and privileges). The capture of Toledo in 1085, by Alfonso VI of Castilla, led the Seville Muslims to call in the Almoravids from North Africa.

The counter-attack against the Almoravids was led by Alfonso I of Aragón, on the southern flank of the Pyrenees. Alfonso took Zaragoza in 1118. After Alfonso's death Aragón was united through royal marriage with Catalonia, creating a formidable new Christian power block known as the Crown of Aragón.

In 1212 the combined armies of the Christian kingdoms routed a large Almohad force at Las Navas de Tolosa in Andalucía. This was the beginning of the end for Al-Andalus: León took the key towns of Extremadura in 1229 and 1230; Aragón took Valencia in the 1230s; Castilla's Fernando III El Santo (Ferdinand the Saint) took Córdoba in 1236 and Seville in 1248; and Portugal expelled the Muslims in 1249. The sole surviving Muslim state on the peninsula was now the Emirate of Granada.

The Lull

Fernando III's son, Alfonso X El Sabio (the Learned; r 1252–84), proclaimed Castilian the official language of his realm and gathered around him scholars of all religions, particularly Jews who knew Arabic and Latin. Alfonso was, however, plagued by uprisings and plots, even from within his own family. Indeed, the Castilian nobility repeatedly challenged the crown until the 15th century. In a climate of xenophobia spawned by the struggle against the Muslims, intolerance also developed towards the Jews and Genoese, who came to dominate Castilian commerce and finance while the Castilian nobility were preoccupied with low-effort, high-profit wool production. In the 1390s anti-Jewish feeling culminated in pogroms around the peninsula.

Castilla and Aragón laboured under ineffectual monarchs from the late 14th century until the advent of Isabel and Fernando, the Catholic Monarchs, a century later.

Granada Falls

In 1476 Emir Abu al-Hasan of Granada refused to pay any more tribute to Castilla, spurring Isabel and Fernando to launch the Reconquista's final crusade, against Granada, with an army largely funded by Jewish

1478	1492 (January)	1492 (April)	1492 (October)
Isabel and Fernando, the Reyes Católicos (Catholic Monarchs), stir up religious bigotry and establish the Spanish Inquisition that will see thousands killed between now and 1834 when it's finally abolished.	Isabel and Fernando capture Granada, completing the Reconquista. Boabdil, the last Muslim ruler, is scorned by his mother for weeping 'like a woman for what you could not defend like a man'.	Isabel and Fernando expel Jews who refuse Christian baptism. Some 200,000 leave, establishing Jewish communities around the Mediterranean; Spain's economy suffers from the loss of their knowledge.	Christopher Columbus, funded by Isabel and Fernando, lands in the Bahamas, opening up the Americas to Spanish colonisation. The bulk of Spanish maritime trade shifts from Mediterranean to Atlantic ports.

loans and the Catholic Church. The Christians took full advantage of a civil war within the Granada emirate, and on 2 January 1492 Isabel and Fernando entered the city of Granada at the beginning of what turned out to be the most momentous year in Spanish history.

The surrender terms were fairly generous to Boabdil, the last emir, who got the Alpujarras valleys south of Granada and 30,000 gold coins. The remaining Muslims were promised respect for their religion, culture and property, but this didn't last long.

THE CATHOLIC MONARCHS

Few individuals in any time or place have had quite such an impact on their country's history as Spain's Reyes Católicos (Catholic Monarchs), Isabel (Isabella) of Castilla and Fernando (Ferdinand) of Aragón. Indeed, Spain owes its very existence to their marriage in 1469 (which effectively united the Iberian Peninsula's two biggest Christian kingdoms) and to their conquest of Granada (1492) and annexation of Navarra (1512).

Isabel, by all accounts, was pious, honest, virtuous and very determined, while Fernando was an astute political operator – a formidable team. Though not celebrated for their religious or racial tolerance (this was Spain's eighth successive century of intercommunal war), they did provide an early example of gender equality within marriage, in keeping with their motto *Tanto monta, monta tanto, Isabel como Fernando* (roughly translated: 'Isabel and Fernando are equal'). Isabel resisted her family's efforts to marry her off to half a dozen other European royals before her semi-clandestine wedding to Fernando at Valladolid – the first time the pair had set eyes on each other. They were second cousins; she was 18 and he 17. Isabel succeeded to the Castilian throne in 1474, and Fernando to Aragón's in 1479. By the time Isabel died in 1504, the pair had:

» set up the Spanish Inquisition (1478)

» completed the Reconquista by conquering Granada (1492)

» expelled all Jews (1492) and Muslims (1500) who refused to convert to Christianity

» helped to fund Columbus' voyage to the Americas (1492), opening the door to a vast overseas empire for Spain

» crushed the power of Castilla's rebellious nobility.

The Castilian throne passed from Isabel to their daughter Juana, dubbed Juana la Loca (the Mad), who proved unfit to rule. Her husband, Felipe El Hermoso (Philip the Handsome), heir to the Low Countries and the lands of the powerful Habsburg family in Central Europe, took over as regent, but died in 1506, leaving Fernando as regent until his death in 1516.

Today Isabel and Fernando still lie beside Juana and Felipe in the beautiful Gothic church they commissioned as their own mausoleum, Granada's Capilla Real.

1494	1500	1512	1517–56
The Treaty of Tordesillas (near Valladolid) divides recently discovered lands west of Europe between Spain and Portugal, giving the Spanish the right to claim vast territories in the Americas.	Persecution of Muslims in the former Granada emirate sparks rebellion. Afterwards, Muslims are forced to adopt Christianity or leave. An estimated 300,000 undergo baptism.	Fernando, ruling as regent after Isabel's death in 1504, annexes Navarra, bringing all of Spain under one rule for the first time since Roman days.	Reign of Carlos I, Spain's first Habsburg monarch, who comes to rule more of Europe than anyone since the 9th century, plus rapidly expanding areas of South and Central America.

Jews & Muslims Expelled

The Catholic Monarchs' Christian zeal led to the founding of the Spanish Inquisition to root out those believed to be threatening the Catholic Church. The Inquisition focused first on *conversos* (Jews converted to Christianity), accusing many of continuing to practise Judaism in secret. Then, in April 1492, under the influence of Grand Inquisitor Tomás de Torquemada (p158), Isabel and Fernando ordered the expulsion of all Jews who refused Christian baptism. Up to 100,000 converted, but some 200,000 – the first Sephardic Jews – left Spain for other Mediterranean destinations. The bankrupt monarchy seized all unsold Jewish property. A talented middle class was gone.

Cardinal Cisneros, Isabel's confessor and overseer of the Inquisition, tried to eradicate Muslim culture too. In the former Granada emirate he carried out forced mass baptisms, burnt Islamic books and banned the Arabic language. After a revolt in Andalucía in 1500, Muslims were ordered to convert to Christianity or leave. Most (around 300,000) underwent baptism and stayed, becoming known as *moriscos* (converted Muslims), but their conversion was barely skin-deep and they never assimilated. The *moriscos* were finally expelled between 1609 and 1614.

Medieval Jewish Sites

» *Judería* (Jewish quarter), Toledo

» The Call, Girona

» Ribadavia, Galicia

» *Judería*, Córdoba

» Hervás, Extremadura

Spain & the Americas

The conquest of Granada coincided neatly with the opening up of a whole new world of opportunity for a confident Christian Spain. Columbus' voyage to the Americas, in the very same year as Granada fell, presented an entire new continent in which the militaristic and crusading elements of Spanish society could continue their efforts. It also opened up vast new sources of wealth for the Spanish crown, nobility and individual adventurers. But in the end the bulk of the population reaped little benefit, and society became completely polarised between the haves and have-nots.

The Catholic Monarchs' hopes for a liaison between Spain and England went wrong when their youngest child, Catalina, or Catherine of Aragón, was divorced by England's Henry VIII.

Conquering a New World

In April 1492 the Catholic Monarchs granted the Genoese sailor Christopher Columbus funds for his long-desired voyage across the Atlantic in search of a new trade route to the Orient.

Columbus sailed from the Andalucian port of Palos de la Frontera on 3 August 1492, with three small ships and 120 men. After a near mutiny as the crew despaired of sighting land, they finally arrived on the island of Guanahaní, in the Bahamas, and went on to find Cuba and Hispaniola. Columbus returned to a hero's reception from the Catholic Monarchs in Barcelona, eight months after his departure. Columbus made three more voyages, founding the city of Santo Domingo on Hispaniola, finding Jamaica, Trinidad and other Caribbean islands, and reaching

1520–21	1521	1533	1556–98
Carlos I crushes rebellious Castilian cities in the Guerra de las Comunidades (War of the Communities), definitively establishing Habsburg rule in Spain.	Hernán Cortés, from Medellín, Extremadura, conquers the Aztec empire in present-day Mexico and Guatemala with a small band of conquistadors, in the name of the Spanish crown.	Francisco Pizarro, from Trujillo, Extremadura, conquers the Inca empire in South America with a small band of conquistadors, in the name of the Spanish crown.	Reign of Felipe II, the zenith of Spanish power. The American territories expand into the modern United States and enormous wealth arriving from the colonies is used for grandiose architectural projects.

the mouth of the Orinoco and the coast of Central America. But he died impoverished in Valladolid in 1506 – still believing he had reached Asia.

Brilliant but ruthless conquistadors such as Hernán Cortés and Francisco Pizarro followed Columbus' trail, seizing vast tracts of the American mainland for Spain. With their odd mix of brutality, bravery, gold lust and piety, these men were the natural successors to the crusading knights of the Reconquista. By 1600 Spain controlled Florida, all the biggest Caribbean islands, nearly all of present-day Mexico and Central America, and a large strip of South America. The new colonies sent huge cargoes of silver, gold and other riches back to Spain, where the crown was entitled to one-fifth of the bullion (the *quinto real,* or royal fifth). Seville enjoyed a monopoly on this trade and grew into one of Europe's richest cities.

Entangled in the Old World

Isabel and Fernando embroiled Spain in European affairs by marrying their five children into the royal families of Portugal, the Holy Roman Empire and England. After Isabel's death in 1504 and Fernando's in 1516, their thrones passed to their grandson Carlos I (Charles I), who arrived in Spain from Flanders in 1517, aged 17. In 1519 Carlos also succeeded to the Habsburg lands in Austria and was elected Holy Roman Emperor (as Charles V) – meaning he now ruled all of Spain, the Low Countries, Austria, several Italian states, parts of France and Germany, and the expanding Spanish colonies in the Americas.

Carlos spent only 16 years of his 40-year reign in Spain and at first the Spanish did not care for a king who spoke no Castilian, nor for his appropriations of their wealth. Castilian cities revolted in 1520–21 (the Guerra de las Comunidades, or War of the Communities), but were crushed. Eventually the Spanish came round to him, at least for his strong stance against the new threat of Protestantism, and his learning of Castilian.

European conflicts soaked up the bulk of the monarchy's new American wealth and a war-weary Carlos abdicated shortly before his death in 1556, retiring to the Monasterio de Yuste in Extremadura and dividing his many territories between his son Felipe II (Philip II; r 1556–98) and his brother Fernando. Felipe got the lion's share, including Spain, the Low Countries and the American possessions, and presided over the zenith of Spanish power, though his reign is a study in contradictions. He enlarged the American empire and claimed Portugal on its king's death in 1580, but lost Holland after a long drawn-out rebellion. His navy defeated the Ottoman Turks at Lepanto in 1571, but the Spanish Armada of 1588 was routed by England. He was a fanatical Catholic, who spurred the Inquisition to new persecutions, yet readily allied

HISTORY SPAIN & THE AMERICAS

Echoes of America

» Trujillo, Extremadura

» Lugares Colombinos, near Huelva

» Casa-Museo de Colón, Valladolid

» Columbus' Tomb, Seville Cathedral

» Tordesillas, near Valladolid

» Palacio de Sobrellano, Comillas

OLIVER STREWE

» Columbus' Tomb, Seville Cathedral (p665)

1561	1571
The king makes the minor country town of Madrid capital of his empire. Despite many new noble residences, the overwhelming impression of the new capital is one of squalor.	The Holy League fleet, led by Spain and Venice and commanded by Felipe II's half-brother Don Juan de Austria, defeats the Ottoman fleet at Lepanto, ending Ottoman expansion into Europe.

Spain with Protestant England against Catholic France. He received greater flows of silver than ever from the Americas, but went bankrupt. Felipe too died in a monastery – the immense one at San Lorenzo de El Escorial, which he himself had had built and which stands as a sombre monument to his reign.

Riches to Rags

Spain's impotent response to its American windfall came home to roost over the 17th, 18th and 19th centuries. Under a series of comically inept rulers, it lost nearly all its foreign possessions, sank into deep economic malaise and internal wars, and wound up as a stagnant backwater untouched by the currents of industry, democracy, national unification and colonial expansion that swept Western Europe. All this eventually led to the social unrest and political polarisation that culminated in the Spanish Civil War of the 1930s.

Hapless Habsburgs

Seventeenth-century Spain was like a gigantic artisans workshop, in which architecture, sculpture, painting and metalwork consumed around 5% of the nation's income. The age was immortalised on canvas by great artists such as Velázquez, El Greco, Zurbarán and Murillo, and in words by the likes of Miguel de Cervantes (author of *El ingenioso hidalgo Don Quijote de la Mancha*) and the prolific playwright Lope de Vega. But while the arts enjoyed a golden age, a trio of weak, backward-looking Habsburg monarchs, a highly conservative Church and an idle nobility allowed the economy to stagnate, leading to food shortages. Felipe III (Philip III; r 1598–1621) left government to the self-seeking Duke of Lerma. Felipe IV (Philip IV; r 1621–65) – whose royal circle is inimitably recorded in paint by Velázquez – concentrated on his mistresses and handed over affairs of state to Count-Duke Olivares, who tried bravely but retired a broken man in 1643. Spain lost Portugal and faced revolts in Catalonia, Sicily and Naples. Silver shipments from the Americas shrank disastrously. And the sickly Carlos II (Charles II; r 1665–1700), known as El Hechizado (The Bewitched), failed to produce children, a situation that led to the War of the Spanish Succession.

Enlightened Bourbons

Carlos II bequeathed his throne to his young relative Felipe V (Philip V; r 1700–46), who also happened to be second in line to the French throne. Meanwhile the Austrian emperor Leopold wanted to see his own son Charles (a nephew of Carlos II) on the Spanish throne. The resulting War of the Spanish Succession (1702–13) was a contest for the balance of power in Europe. Spain lost its last possessions in the Low

Bourbon Baubles

» Palacio Real, Madrid

» Palacio Real, Aranjuez

» La Granja de San Ildefonso, near Segovia

1580	1588	c 1600–1660	1609–14
Spain exploits succession disputes in Portugal to bring its neighbour under its rule. John, Duke of Braganza, will eventually restore Portuguese independence as John IV in 1640.	Felipe II's 'invincible Armada' sails to England as part of a Spanish invasion force. English attacks and bad weather destroy up to half the fleet; the rest limps home.	Spain enjoys a cultural golden age with the literature of Cervantes and the paintings of Velázquez, Zurbarán and El Greco scaling new heights of artistic excellence as the empire declines.	The *moriscos* (converted Muslims) are expelled from Spain in a final purge of non-Christians that undermines an already faltering economy.

Countries to Austria, and Gibraltar and Menorca to Britain. Felipe V renounced his right to the French throne but held on to Spain. He was the first of the Bourbon dynasty, still in place today.

This was Europe's Age of Enlightenment, but Spain's powerful Church and Inquisition were at odds with the rationalism that trickled in from France. Two-thirds of the land was in the hands of the nobility and Church, and underutilised; and large numbers of males, from nobles to vagrants, were unwilling to work.

Under Fernando VI (Ferdinand VI; r 1746–59) the economy took an upturn thanks to a revitalised Catalonia and the Basque shipbuilding industry. But agricultural Castilla and Andalucía were left behind. Carlos III (Charles III; r 1759–88) expelled the backward-looking Jesuits, transformed the capital Madrid, built new roads to the provinces and tried to improve agriculture, but food shortages still fuelled unrests.

BUILD, BUILD, BUILD

History throws up some strange parallels. When Spain received its great windfall of silver and gold from the Americas back in the 16th and 17th centuries, it notoriously failed to use this wealth as a foundation for lasting prosperity. Instead of investing in early industries and developing commerce, Spain spent the windfall on costly and unsuccessful European wars and on building hundreds of elaborate palaces, mansions, cathedrals and monasteries (many of which figure among its most splendid monuments today). It has been joked that Spain had actually discovered the magical 'reverse alchemy' formula for turning silver into stone. Its nobility was famously unwilling to soil its hands with anything so lowly as industry, trade or even agriculture. The country duly sank into three centuries of economic decline.

Spain's next windfall didn't come for a long time – not until the late 20th century, when the country was showered with money from the European Union (EU) after joining it in 1986, and then enjoyed two long economic booms. The second boom lasted a full decade, until the international financial meltdown of 2008. Which sector of the economy boomed most spectacularly during this period? Construction. Along the coasts and around the cities and towns, cranes speckled every skyline as developers and investors poured endless billions of euros into erecting new homes and office blocks, on the apparent principle that any piece of land is worth more with a building on it than without, never mind whether anyone wanted to use it. Between 1997 and 2008, four million new homes came on to the market, and despite the glut, Spanish house prices doubled. Around one-fifth of all new jobs created during the boom were in construction, so the country's economic downturn was all the more severe when the housing bubble burst in 2008. By 2010 an estimated 1.5 million recently built homes were still standing empty. Another case of silver into stone – or rather, this time, concrete?

1676	1701	1702–13	1761
The devastation caused by the third great plague to hit Spain in a century is compounded by poor harvests. In all, more than 1.25 million Spaniards die through plague and starvation during the 17th century.	Felipe V, first of the Bourbon dynasty, takes the throne after the Habsburg line dies out with Carlos II. Felipe being second in line to the French throne causes concern across Europe.	Rival European powers support Charles of Austria against Felipe V in the War of the Spanish Succession: Felipe survives as king but Spain loses Gibraltar and the Low Countries.	Spain becomes involved in the Seven Years' War (1756–63), fighting alongside France against Britain and her allies. The latter's eventual victory sees Spain hand over Florida to the British.

Echoes of the Napoleonic Wars

» Cabo de Trafalgar, Los Caños de Meca

» Trafalgar Cemetery, Gibraltar

» Museo de las Cortes de Cádiz, Cádiz

» Xardín de San Carlos, A Coruña

The Peninsular War

Carlos IV (Charles IV; r 1788–1808) was dominated by his Italian wife, Maria Luisa of Parma, who saw to it that her favourite, the handsome royal guard Manuel Godoy, became chief minister. This unholy trinity was less than suited to coping with the crisis presented by the French Revolution of 1789. When France's Louis XVI, cousin to Carlos IV, was guillotined in 1793, Spain declared war on France – only for Godoy to make peace with the French Republic two years later, promising military support against Britain. In 1805 a combined Spanish–French navy was beaten by the British fleet, under Admiral Nelson, off the Cabo de Trafalgar, putting an end to Spanish sea power.

In 1807 Napoleon Bonaparte and Godoy agreed to divide Britain's ally Portugal between them. French forces poured into Spain, supposedly on the way to Portugal, but by 1808 this had become a French occupation of Spain, and Carlos IV was forced to abdicate in favour of Napoleon's brother Joseph Bonaparte (José I). In Madrid crowds revolted and across the country Spaniards took up arms guerrilla-style, reinforced by British and Portuguese forces led by the Duke of Wellington. A national Cortes (Parliament) meeting at Cádiz in 1812 drew up a new liberal constitution, incorporating many of the principles of the American and French prototypes. The French were finally driven out after their defeat at Vitoria in 1813.

My Throne – No, Mine

An increasingly backward and insular Spain in the 19th century frittered its energies on internal conflicts between liberals (who wanted vaguely democratic reforms) and conservatives (the Church, the nobility and others who preferred the earlier status quo), and sank to depths of poverty and exploitation that spawned growing social unrest.

Fernando VII (Ferdinand VII; r 1814–33) revoked the Cádiz constitution, persecuted liberals and cheerily re-established the Inquisition. Meanwhile Spain's American colonies took advantage of its problems and seized their independence. Fernando's dithering over his successor resulted in the First Carlist War (1833–39), between supporters of his brother Carlos and those loyal to his infant daughter Isabel. Carlos was supported by conservatives and regional rebels, together known as the Carlists, while the Isabel faction had the support of liberals and the army. During the war violent anticlericalism emerged, religious orders were closed and, in the Disentailment of 1836, church property and lands were seized and auctioned off by the government. It was the army that emerged victorious from the fighting.

In 1843 Isabel, now all of 13, declared herself Queen Isabel II (Isabella II; r 1843–68). Business, banking, mining and railways brought some

1793	1805	1808–13
Spain declares war on France after Louis XVI is beheaded, but within a couple of years the country is supporting the French in their struggles against the British.	A combined Spanish–French fleet is defeated by British ships under Nelson at the Battle of Trafalgar. Spanish sea power is effectively destroyed and discontent against the king's pro-French policies grows.	French forces occupy Spain; Carlos IV abdicates in favour of Napoleon's brother, José I. The ensuing Peninsular War sees British forces helping the Spanish defeat the French.

DENNIS JOHNSON

» *Trafalgar Cemetery (p715)*

economic progress, but this didn't stop radical liberals and discontented soldiers from overthrowing Isabel in the Septembrina Revolution of 1868.

Spain still wanted a monarch, however, and in 1870 a liberal-minded Italian prince, Amadeo of Savoy, accepted the job. But the Spanish aristocracy opposed him, which led to another Carlist War (1872–76), fought between not just two but three factions each supporting different claimants to the throne. Amadeo abandoned Spain in 1873 and the liberal-dominated Cortes proclaimed the country a federal republic. But this First Republic had lost control of the regions and the army put Isabel II's son Alfonso on the throne as Alfonso XII (r 1874–85), in a coalition with the Church and landowners.

The Great Divide
By the late 19th century industry had finally arrived in Barcelona, Madrid and some Basque cities, attracting migrants from the countryside and bringing both prosperity and squalid slums to the cities. In rural areas the old problems of underproduction, oligarchic land ownership and mass poverty persisted. Many Spaniards emigrated to Latin America; those who stayed seized eagerly on revolutionary ideas arriving from elsewhere in Europe, and society and politics became increasingly polarised between left and right.

Revolutionaries & Separatists
The anarchist ideas of the Russian Mikhail Bakunin reached Spain in the 1860s and rapidly gained support in cities as well as in the countryside. Bakunin looked forward to a free society of voluntary cooperation – a state of affairs to be achieved through strikes, sabotage and revolts. In the 1890s and the 1900s anarchists bombed Barcelona's Liceu opera house, assassinated two prime ministers and killed 24 people with a bomb at King Alfonso XIII's wedding to Victoria Eugenie of Battenberg in May 1906. In 1910 the anarchist unions were organised into the powerful Confederación Nacional del Trabajo (CNT; National Labour Confederation).

Socialism grew more slowly than anarchism because of its less dramatic strategy of steady change through parliamentary processes. The Unión General de Trabajadores (UGT; General Union of Workers), established in 1888, was moderate and disciplined.

Parallel with the rise of the left was the growth of Basque and Catalan separatism. In Catalonia this was led by big business interests. In the Basque country, nationalism emerged in the 1890s in response to a flood of Castilian workers into Basque industries: some Basques considered these migrants a threat to their identity.

During the First Republic some Spanish cities declared themselves independent states, and some, such as Seville and nearby Utrera, even declared war on each other.

FIRST REPUBLIC

1809–24	1814	1833–39	1860s
Most of Spain's American colonies win independence as Spain is beset by problems at home. By 1824 only Cuba, Puerto Rico, Guam and the Philippines are under Spanish rule.	Fernando VII becomes king and revokes the 1812 Cádiz Constitution (an attempt by Spanish liberals to introduce constitutional reforms) just weeks after agreeing to uphold its principles.	The First Carlist War, triggered by disputes over the succession between backers of Fernando VII's infant daughter, Isabel, and his brother, Carlos. Isabel will eventually become queen.	Anarchist ideas reach Spain and soon gain a wide following. In 1868 the inept Isabel II is overthrown by liberals and goes into exile in Paris.

In 1909 a contingent of Spanish troops was wiped out by Berbers in Spanish Morocco, leading the government to call up Catalan reservists to go and fight. This sparked off the so-called Semana Trágica (Tragic Week) in Barcelona, which began with a general strike and turned into a frenzy of violence. The government responded by executing many workers.

Spain stayed neutral during WWI and enjoyed an economic boom, but anarchist and socialist numbers grew, inspired by the Russian Revolution, and political violence and mayhem continued, especially in lawless Barcelona.

First Dictatorship

Alfonso XIII (r 1902–30) had a habit of meddling in politics (his reign saw 33 different governments), and when 10,000 Spanish soldiers were killed by Berbers at Anual in Morocco in 1921, the finger of blame pointed directly at the king. However, just as a report on the event was to be submitted to parliament in 1923, General Miguel Primo de Rivera, an eccentric Andalucian aristocrat, led an army rising in support of Alfonso and established his own mild dictatorship.

Primo was a centralist who censored the press and upset intellectuals but gained the cooperation of the socialist UGT. Anarchists went underground. Primo founded industries, improved roads, made the trains run on time and built dams and power plants. But in 1930, facing increasing opposition and an economic downturn following the Wall Street Crash of October 1929, he resigned.

Second Republic

When a new republican movement scored sweeping victories in local elections in 1931, the king left for exile in Italy. The tumultuous Second Republic that followed – called La Niña Bonita (Pretty Child) by its supporters – split Spanish society down the middle and ended in civil war.

National elections in 1931 brought in a government composed of socialists, republicans and centrists. A new constitution gave women the vote, granted autonomy-minded Catalonia its own parliament, legalised divorce, stripped Catholicism of its status as official religion, and banned priests from teaching. But anarchist disruption, an economic slump, the votes of women and disunity on the left all contributed to right-wing parties winning the next election, in 1933. One new force on the right was the fascist Falange, led by José Antonio Primo de Rivera, son of the 1920s dictator.

By 1934 violence was spiralling out of control. Catalonia declared itself independent (within a putative federal Spanish republic), and workers' committees took over the northern mining region of Asturias after

The Oscar-winning film *Belle Epoque*, telling the story of a Spanish army deserter finding love in 1930s rural Spain, was actually filmed in Portugal.

1872–76	1888	1898	1909
The Second Carlist War, between three different monarchist factions, brings Isabel II's son, Alfonso XII, to the throne after the brief, chaotic First Republic of 1873.	As a new industrial working class emerges in cities such as Madrid, Bilbao and Barcelona, the socialist Unin General de Trabajadores (UGT; General Union of Workers) is formed.	Spain loses Cuba, Puerto Rico, Guam and the Philippines, its last remaining colonies, after being defeated in the Spanish-American War by the US, which declared war in support of Cuban independence.	The Semana Trágica (Tragic Week) in Barcelona begins after Catalan reservists are called up to fight in Morocco; a general strike becomes a violent riot, dozens of civilians are killed.

attacking police and army posts. A violent campaign against the Asturian workers by the Spanish Legion (set up to fight Moroccan tribes in the 1920s), led by generals Francisco Franco and José Millán Astray, split the country firmly into left and right.

In the February 1936 elections the right-wing National Front was narrowly defeated by the left-wing Popular Front, with communists at the fore. Violence continued from both sides. Extremist groups grew and peasants were on the verge of revolution. But when the revolt actually came, on 17 July 1936, it was from the other end of the political spectrum. On that day the Spanish army garrison in Melilla, North Africa, rose up against the Popular Front government, followed the next day by garrisons on the mainland. The leaders of the plot were five generals, among them Francisco Franco. The civil war had begun.

The Civil War

Some pundits postulate that the Spanish Civil War might not have happened without the Great Slump: Miguel Primo de Rivera might have somehow succeeded in holding Spain together. Others see the civil war as a long-term consequence of Spain's failure over several centuries to modernise and distribute any wealth beyond the ruling class. Most agree that given the extreme polarisation of society and politics by the early 20th century, Spain could not work out its contradictions without a conflagration of some kind.

The civil war split communities, families and friends, killed an estimated 350,000 Spaniards (some writers say 500,000), and caused untold damage and misery. Both sides committed atrocious massacres and reprisals, and employed death squads to eliminate opponents. The rebels, who called themselves Nationalists because they believed they were fighting for Spain, shot or hanged tens of thousands of supporters of the republic. Republicans did likewise to Nationalist sympathisers, including some 7000 priests, monks and nuns. Political affiliation often provided a convenient cover for settling old scores.

At the start of the war many of the military and of the Guardia Civil police force went over to the Nationalists, whose campaign quickly took on overtones of a crusade against the enemies of God. In Republican areas, anarchists, communists or socialists ended up running many towns and cities, and social revolution followed.

Nationalist Advance

The basic battle lines were drawn within a week of the rebellion in Morocco. Most cities with military garrisons fell immediately into Nationalist hands – this meant almost everywhere north of Madrid except Catalonia and the north coast, as well as parts of Andalucía. Franco's

---

Civil War Reads

» *For Whom the Bell Tolls* – Ernest Hemingway

» *Homage to Catalonia* – George Orwell

» *Blood of Spain* – Ronald Fraser

» *The Spanish Civil War* – Hugh Thomas

1910	1914–18	1923–30	1931
Anarchist trade unions set up the powerful Confederación Nacional del Trabajo (CNT; National Labour Confederation). Anarchism appeals to rural and urban workers and remains a force until the civil war.	Spain remains neutral during WWI and experiences a financial boom as the shift from an agricultural to an industrial economy accelerates to meet wartime needs.	General Miguel Primo de Rivera launches an army rising in support of King Alfonso XIII and then establishes himself as dictator. He retires and dies in 1930.	Alfonso XIII goes into exile after Republicans score sweeping gains in local elections. Spain's Second Republic is launched, left-wing parties win a national election, and a new constitution enfranchises women.

force of legionnaires and Moroccan mercenaries was airlifted to Seville by German warplanes in August. Essential to the success of the revolt, they moved northward through Extremadura towards Madrid, wiping out fierce resistance in some cities. At Salamanca in October, Franco pulled all the Nationalists into line behind him.

Madrid, reinforced by the first battalions of the International Brigades (armed foreign idealists and adventurers organised by the communists), repulsed Franco's first assault in November and then endured, under communist inspiration, over two years' siege.

Foreign Intervention

The International Brigades never numbered more than 20,000 and couldn't turn the tide against the better-armed and -organised Nationalist forces.

Nazi Germany and Fascist Italy supported the Nationalists with planes, weapons and men (75,000 from Italy, 17,000 from Germany), turning the war into a testing ground for WWII. The Republicans had some Soviet planes, tanks, artillery and advisers, but other countries refused to become involved (although some 25,000 French fought on the Republican side).

Republican Quarrels

With Madrid besieged, the Republican government moved to Valencia in late 1936 to continue trying to preside over the quarrelsome factions on its side, which encompassed anarchists, communists, moderate democrats and regional separatists.

In April 1937 German planes bombed the Basque town of Guernica (Gernika), causing terrible casualties; this became the subject of Picasso's famous pacifist painting. All the north coast fell to the Nationalists that year, while Republican counter-attacks near Madrid and in Aragón failed. Meanwhile divisions among the Republicans erupted into fierce street fighting in Barcelona, with the Soviet-influenced communists completely crushing the anarchists and Trotskyites who had run the city for almost a year. The Republican government then moved to Barcelona in autumn 1937.

Nationalist Victory

In early 1938 Franco repulsed a Republican offensive at Teruel in Aragón, then swept eastward with 100,000 troops, 1000 planes and 150 tanks, isolating Barcelona from Valencia. In July the Republicans launched a last offensive in the Ebro valley. This bloody encounter, won by the Nationalists, cost 20,000 lives. The USSR withdrew from the war in September 1938, and in January 1939 the Nationalists took Barcelo

Films Set in Franco's Spain

» *Pan's Labyrinth* (2006)

» *The Spirit of the Beehive* (1973)

» *¡Bienvenido, Mr Marshall!* (Welcome, Mr Marshall!; 1952)

» *Las 13 Rosas* (The 13 Roses; 2007)

1933–35	1936	1936–39	1937
Right-wing parties win a new election; political violence spirals and a ruthless army operation against workers in Asturias irrevocably polarises Spain into left- and right-wing camps.	The left-wing National Front wins a national election. Right-wing 'Nationalist' rebels led by General Francisco Franco rise up against it, starting the Spanish Civil War.	The Spanish Civil War: the Nationalist rebels, under Franco, supported by Nazi Germany and Fascist Italy, defeat the USSR-supported Republicans. About 350,000 people die in fighting and atrocities.	Nazi German planes saturation-bomb the Basque town of Guernica, killing 1645 civilians. Guernica later becomes the subject of Pablo Picasso's most famous painting.

na unopposed. The Republican government and hundreds of thousands of supporters fled to France. The Republicans still held Valencia and Madrid, and had 500,000 people under arms, but in the end their army simply evaporated. The Nationalists entered Madrid on 28 March 1939 and Franco declared the war over on 1 April.

Franco's Dictatorship

Instead of postwar reconciliation, more blood-letting ensued. An estimated 100,000 people were killed or died in prison after the war. The hundreds of thousands imprisoned included many intellectuals and teachers; others fled abroad, depriving Spain of a generation of scientists, artists, writers, educators and more. For 36 years Franco maintained absolute power by never allowing any single powerful group – the Church, the Movimiento Nacional (the only legal political party), the army, monarchists or bankers – to dominate. Regional autonomy aspirations were simply not tolerated.

The army provided many government ministers and enjoyed a most generous budget. Catholic supremacy was fully restored, with secondary schools entrusted to the Jesuits, divorce made illegal and church weddings compulsory. Franco won some working-class support offering job security and paid holidays, though workers had no right to strike.

WWII & the Years of Hunger

Franco promised Hitler an alliance but never committed himself to a date and Spain took no active part in WWII. In 1944 Spanish leftists launched a failed attack on Franco's Spain from France; small leftist guerrilla units continued a hopeless struggle in parts of the north, Extremadura and Andalucía until the 1950s.

After WWII Franco's Spain was excluded from the UN and NATO, and suffered a UN-sponsored trade boycott that helped turn the late 1940s into Spain's *años de hambre* (years of hunger). With the onset of the Cold War, however, the US wanted bases in Spain, and Franco agreed to the establishment of four, in return for large sums of aid. In 1955 Spain was admitted to the UN.

Economic Miracle

In 1959 a new breed of technocrats in government, linked to the Catholic group Opus Dei, engineered a Stabilisation Plan, which brought an economic upswing. Spanish industry boomed and thousands of young Spaniards went abroad to study. Modern machinery, technology and marketing were introduced; transport was modernised; new dams provided irrigation and hydropower.

GENERALÍSIMO

Franco styled himself Generalisimo (Supreme General) and, later, *caudillo*, which is roughly equivalent to the German Führer.

BRUCE BI

» *Centro de Arte Reina Sofía (p68), Madrid*

1938	1939
The Nationalists defeat the Republicans' last major offensive, in the Ebro Valley, with 20,000 killed. The Soviet Union ends its support for the Republican side.	The Nationalists take Barcelona in January. The Republican government flees to France, Republican forces evaporate and the Nationalists enter Madrid on 28 March. Franco declares the war over on 1 April.

FRANCO

Paul Preston's *Franco* is the big biography of one of history's little dictators – and it has very little to say in the man's favour.

The recovery was funded in part by US aid, and remittances from more than a million Spaniards who had gone to work abroad, but above all by tourism, which was developed initially along Andalucía's Costa del Sol and Catalonia's Costa Brava. By 1965 the number of tourists arriving in Spain was 14 million a year.

A huge population shift from rural regions to the cities and tourist resorts took place. Many Andalucians went to Barcelona. In the cities, elegant suburbs developed as well as the drab apartment blocks for the workers that are still a none-too-inspiring feature of most Spanish cities.

The Final Decade

The year 1964 saw Franco celebrating 25 years of peace, order and material progress. However, the jails were still full of political prisoners and large garrisons were still maintained outside every major city. Over the next decade, labour unrest grew and discontent began to rumble in the universities and even the army and Church. Regional problems resurfaced too. The Basque-nationalist terrorist group Euskadi Ta Askatasuna (ETA; Basque Homeland and Freedom) gave cause for the declaration of six states of emergency between 1962 and 1975.

Franco chose as his successor Prince Juan Carlos, the Spanish-educated grandson of Alfonso XIII. In 1969 Juan Carlos swore loyalty to Franco and the Movimiento Nacional. Cautious reforms by Franco's last prime minister, Carlos Arias Navarro, provoked violent opposition from right-wing extremists. Spain seemed to be sinking into chaos when Franco died on 20 November 1975.

New Democracy

Juan Carlos I, aged 37, took the throne two days after Franco died. The new king's links with the dictator inspired little confidence in a Spain now clamouring for democracy, but Juan Carlos had kept his cards close to his chest and takes much of the credit for the successful transition to democracy that followed. In July 1976 he appointed Adolfo Suárez, a 43-year-old former Franco apparatchik with film-star looks, as prime minister. To general surprise, Suárez got the Cortes to approve a new, two-chamber parliamentary system, and in 1977 political parties, trade unions and strikes were all legalised. The Movimiento Nacional was abolished.

Suárez's centrist party, the *Unión de Centro Democrático* (UCD; Central Democratic Union), won nearly half the seats in the new Cortes in 1977. A new constitution in 1978 made Spain a parliamentary monarchy with no official religion. In response to the fever for local autonomy after the stiflingly centralist Franco era, by 1983 the country was divided into 17 'autonomous communities' with their own regional governments controlling a range of policy areas. Personal and social life

1939–50	1955–65	1959	1975
Franco establishes a right-wing dictatorship, imprisoning hundreds of thousands. Spain stays out of WWII but is later excluded from NATO and the UN and suffers a damaging international trade boycott.	Spain is admitted to the UN after agreeing to host US bases. The economy is boosted by US aid and mass tourism on the Costa Brava and Costa del Sol.	The ETA is founded with the aim of gaining Basque independence. The terrorist group will go on to murder more than 800 people, including Franco's prime minister in 1973.	Franco dies and is succeeded by King Juan Carlos I. The monarch had been schooled by Franco to continue his policies but soon demonstrates his desire for change.

enjoyed a rapid liberation after Franco. Contraceptives, homosexuality and divorce were legalised, and the Madrid party and arts scene known as the *movida* formed the epicentre of a newly unleashed hedonism that still looms large in Spanish life.

The Suárez government granted a general amnesty for deeds committed in the civil war and under the Franco dictatorship. There were no truth commissions or trials for the perpetrators of atrocities. For the next three decades Spain cast barely a backward glance. Spaniards seemed to agree on an instinctive pact to bury old differences and get on with building a better future. Only in very recent years have some of them started to raise civil-war grievances again.

Through the 1980s and '90s, under their new constitution and multiparty political spectrum, Spaniards became steadily richer, better educated and more liberated than ever before. But not everything in the orchard was orange blossom: ETA terrorism cost many hundreds of lives (see p400 for more on ETA), economic progress was sometimes stained by corruption, and the tussles over regional autonomy between Madrid and the Basque Country and Catalonia seemed to have no end. But Spain's changes of government were orderly, electoral affairs, the economic graphs moved in a general upward direction and the improvement in ordinary people's lives was steady.

SPAIN REINVENTED

The Spain that entered the 21st century would have been unrecognisable to most of its citizens at the end of the dictatorship just a quarter of a century earlier. Spain had joined the modern world of shiny shopping malls, high-speed trains, fast highways, internet, mobile phones, ATMs, reality TV, globalised business, eye-catching contemporary architecture, figure-hugging fashions and dance-till-dawn nightclubs with thumping electronic music. Spaniards could now get divorced and use contraception and be gay without breaking the law. They had better schools and better medical services. Many more people went to university, fewer went to church. Women had fewer children and more jobs. Huge areas of countryside had been placed under environmental protection. Spaniards went abroad not as economic migrants but as tourists, and ever more foreigners came to Spain, as tourists *and* economic migrants: hundreds of thousands of Africans, Latin Americans and other Europeans came seeking work – including plenty of Muslims, who had had no significant presence in Spain for the previous 500 years. The arts flourished under the new freedoms and government funding. If one single creative figure could be said to represent the age, it has to be the Oscar-winning film director Pedro Almodóvar, whose quirky, colourful, provocative movies on themes of passion, sexuality and personal identity would have been utterly inconceivable in the old Spain.

1976	1978	1981	1982–96
The king appoints Adolfo Suárez as prime minister. Suárez engineers a return to democracy. Left-wing parties are legalised, despite military opposition, and the country holds free elections in 1977.	A new constitution, overwhelmingly approved by referendum, establishes Spain as a parliamentary democracy with no official religion and the monarch as official head of state.	On 23 February a group of armed Guardia Civil led by Antonio Tejero attempt a coup by occupying the parliament building. The king denounces them on national TV; the coup collapses.	Spain is governed by the centre-left PSOE led by Felipe González. The country experiences an economic boom but the government becomes increasingly associated with scandals and corruption.

The PSOE & the PP

A new left-of-centre party, the Partido Socialista Obrero Español (PSOE; Spanish Socialist Workers' Party), led by a charismatic young lawyer from Seville, Felipe González, came second in the 1977 election and then won power with a big majority in 1982. González was to be prime minister for 14 years. The PSOE's young and educated leadership came from the generation that had opened the cracks in the Franco regime in the late 1960s and early 1970s. It persuaded the unions to accept wage restraint and job losses in order to streamline industry. Unemployment rose from 16% to 22% by 1986. But that same year Spain joined the European Community (now the EU), bringing on a five-year economic boom. The middle class grew ever bigger, the PSOE established a national health system and improved public education, and Spain's women streamed into higher education and jobs.

Around halfway through the boom, the good life began to turn a little sour. People observed that many of the glamorous new rich were making their money by property or share speculation, or plain corruption. In 1992 – the 500th anniversary of the fall of Granada and Columbus' first voyage to the Americas – Spain celebrated its arrival in the modern world by staging the Barcelona Olympics and the Expo 92 world fair in Seville. But the economy was in a slump and the PSOE was mired in scandals. By 1996 unemployment was running at 23%, the highest in Western Europe. Most damaging was the affair of the Grupos Antiterroristas de Liberación (GAL), death squads that had murdered 28 suspected ETA terrorists (several of whom were innocent) in France in the mid-'80s. A stream of GAL allegations contributed to the PSOE losing the 1996 general election, and in 1998 a dozen senior police and PSOE men were jailed in the affair.

The party that won the 1996 election was the centre-right Partido Popular (PP; People's Party), led by José María Aznar, a former tax inspector from Castilla y León. The PP had been founded by a former Franco minister, Manuel Fraga, something its opponents never let it forget. Aznar promised to make politics dull, and he did, but he presided over eight years of solid economic progress, winning the 2000 election as well. The PP cut public investment, sold off state enterprises and liberalised sectors such as telecommunications, and during the Aznar years Spain's economy grew a lot faster than the EU average, while unemployment fell dramatically.

Modern Spain Reading

» *Ghosts of Spain* – Giles Tremlett

» *The New Spaniards* – John Hooper

» *Juan Carlos: Steering Spain from Dictatorship to Democracy* – Paul Preston

The Spanish government can be found on the web at www.lamoncloa.es, while Juan Carlos I has his site at www.casareal.es.

1986	1992	1996	2000
Spain joins the European Community (now the EU). Along with its membership of NATO since 1982, this is a turning point in the country's post-Franco international reacceptance.	Barcelona holds the Olympic Games, putting Spain in the international spotlight and highlighting the country's progress since 1975; Madrid is European Capital of Culture; and Seville hosts a world Expo.	Disaffection with PSOE sleaze gives the centre-right Partido Popular (PP), led by José María Aznar, a general election victory, at the start of a decade of sustained economic growth.	The PP under Aznar wins a second election victory; the PSOE chooses a young lawyer from Valladolid, José Luis Rodríguez Zapatero, as its new leader.

Architecture

As you look up at the arches of the great Roman aqueduct in Segovia, you can almost see centurions marching beneath it. With the gentle bubbling of its cool fountains, the Alhambra conjures up Spain's Islamic era as if from a dream. On a grey winter's day, along the echoing corridors of the Monasterio de Santo Domingo de Silos' Romanesque cloisters, the Middle Ages seem to return with their mystical fervour. Towering, at times half-ruined, castles dot the countryside from Catalonia to Castilla. To gaze up, eyes turned to God, at the great Gothic cathedrals of Burgos, Palma de Mallorca and Toledo, you can feel the awe they must have inspired when first raised. And who isn't carried away by the whimsy of Gaudí's Modernista fantasies dotting the streets of Barcelona?

Spain's architecture presents one of the broadest and richest testimonies in Europe to thousands of years of building ingenuity, starting with the simple stone housing of the Celtiberian tribes. Unique within western Europe is Spain's long Islamic history. The fusion of Middle Eastern and European aesthetics that occurred on the peninsula gave rise to distinct styles, both during the Moorish heyday and after the Reconquista, when architects reacted strongly against Islamic styles with austere Romanesque structures. Meanwhile, others slyly integrated them, as in the case of Mozarabic and Mudéjar designs. The love of ornament established in the Islamic era carried on well into the Renaissance, when Spanish designers developed the ornate plateresque style, which in turn paved the way for the staggering confections of the baroque period. In the late 19th century, Modernista geniuses in Barcelona pushed walls and ceilings into all-new shapes – effectively paving the way for the country's contemporary architecture scene, where both Spanish and foreign architects have been given free rein to make their oddest visions a reality.

Ancient Spain

The tribes that first inhabited the Iberian Peninsula, collectively known as Celtiberians, made a lasting mark on the land once they moved out of cave dwellings. In the northwest part of the country (and in Portugal), the so-called Castro culture of the Bronze Age (9th century BC) is named for its most common living

210 BC–AD 409 Roman

Bridges, waterworks, walls, whole cities – the Romans build to last, and to inspire later traditions.

409–711 Visigothic

Invaders from the north build sturdy stone churches with simple decoration and horseshoe arches.

711–1492 Moorish

Horseshoe arches, square minarets, intricate geometric design – this synthesis of styles from across the Islamic empire includes Mozarabic (Islamic-look buildings in Christian territory).

1100–1700 Mudéjar

Post-Reconquista work by Muslims, carrying on the Moorish tradition of decoration and adapting it to more common materials.

1100–1300 Romanesque

Essentially the anti-Moorish, with spare decoration and proportions based on Byzantine churches. Look for heavy, perfectly semicircular arches.

1200–1600 Gothic

Churches nearly take flight: flying buttresses enable ceilings to soar, and arches become pointy to match.

arrangement: the *castro,* or walled hamlet made up of circular stone houses, clustered together like cupcakes in a bakery box. Among the better preserved *castro* ruins are those at A Guarda, on Galicia's southern coast, and near Coaña in Asturias.

When the Greeks and Carthaginians arrived (around 500 BC and 200 BC, respectively), they remained primarily on the coast and left little behind. The Romans, however, made more of an impact – architectural and otherwise – across the peninsula after the 2nd century BC. The 1st-century emperor Trajan, who expanded the empire to its furthest limits and left many landmarks in Rome, was born at Itálica, near modern-day Seville, and in Extremadura, Augusta Emerita (now Mérida), was one of the most influential cities in the western Roman Empire, and continued to hold sway until it was conquered by the Arabs in 713 AD. It has the longest Roman bridge still standing, working reservoirs and a vast amphitheatre.

The Visigothic Period

The Visigoth reign lasted fewer than three centuries between the last vestiges of the Roman Empire and the rise of the Islamic one, beginning in 711 AD. Similarly, the architectural legacy is small, as very little survived. During the Islamic era, many of these churches were neglected, and during the Catholic Reconquista, many more were destroyed to make way for grander structures.

But what remains shows a remarkably attractive style – humbler than the Romans', but solidly built with smooth dressed stones and decorated with reliefs of abstract plant forms and crosses that are reminiscent of Byzantine styles. Another characteristic of the period is the arch with slightly indented sides, creating a faint horseshoe shape. It would later become associated purely with Moorish architecture, as Syrian architects had also developed the arch.

Reputedly the oldest Visigothic church in Spain, the Basílica de San Juan in Baños de Cerrato, in the province of Palencia, was constructed in 661 and consecrated by King Recceswinth. It has a horseshoe-shaped entrance door and friezes of intertwined circles. Ermita de Santa María de Lara, at Quintanilla de las Viñas in Burgos province, is probably the last church built under the Visigoths, as archaeologists have dated it to around 700. Only about a third of it survives, but in the outline of the building one can see numerous smaller rooms, another characteristic of Visigoth structures.

The Introduction of Islam

About 70 years after the first Islamic incursion into Spain, Córdoba was well established as the new capital of the western end of the empire. In 784 Syrian architects set to work on the grand Mezquita, conjuring their homeland with details that echo the Umayyad Mosque in Damascus, such as delicate horseshoe arches and exquisite decorative tiles with floral motifs. But even from the beginning, this Islamic architecture in Spain was a synthesis: the building's most distinctive feature – more than 500 columns that crowd the interior of the mosque – were repurposed from Roman and Visigothic ruins.

In the centuries that followed, Moorish architecture incorporated trends from all over the Islamic empire. The technique of intricately carved stucco detailing was developed in 9th-century Iraq, while *muqarnas* vaulting arrived via Egypt in the 10th century. Square minarets, such as the Giralda in Seville (now a church tower), came with the Almohad invasion from Morocco in the 12th century.

The better remnants of the Islamic era are in Andalucía, although the Aljafería in Zaragoza is a beautiful exception. Perhaps the most

Roman relics

» Aqueduct, Segovia

» Bridge, Alcántara

» City walls, Lugo, Galicia

» Tarraco (Tarragona), Catalonia

» Itálica, Seville

» Sagunto, Valencia

Ildefonso Falcones' bestselling historical novel *La Catedral del Mar* (The Cathedral of the Sea) tells the juicy tale of the construction of the Santa María del Mar cathedral in Barcelona in the 13th century.

magnificent creation is the core of Granada's Alhambra, the Palacios Nazaríes (Nasrid Palaces). From the 13th to the 15th century, architects reached new heights of elegance, creating a study in balance between inside and outside, light and shade, spareness and intricate decoration. But the construction is also effectively a stylistic dead end. Eschewing innovation, the Alhambra refined well-tried forms, as if in an attempt to freeze time and halt the collapse of Moorish power, which, at the time, was steadily eroding across the peninsula.

Hybrid Styles: Mozarabic & Mudéjar

The real creativity in architecture came as a byproduct of the *convivencia,* when Muslim, Christian and Jewish cultures cross-pollinated. By the 10th century, Moorish rule had produced a class of people called Mozarabs – practicing Christians who lived in Islamic territory and spoke Arabic. When Mozarab artisans moved or travelled north into Christian Spain, they took elements of classic Islamic construction with them. As a result, the 1913 Iglesia de San Miguel de Escalada, east of León, imitates the Mezquita, with horseshoe arches atop leafy Corinthian capitals reused from Roman buildings. Many arches are boxed in by an *alfiz,* a rectangular decorative frame typically filled with geometric or abstract vegetal decoration, around the upper portion of the arch. This became a signature detail in Mozarabic architecture.

The 11th-century Ermita de San Baudelio, beyond Berlanga de Duero in Soria province, resembles Visigoth churches in its constricted layout – no grand cathedral hall here. But it was covered in lavish frescoes of Middle Eastern camels and elephants, as well as hunting scenes that resemble those in old Syrian Umayyad palaces. (Most of the frescoes have since been removed to museums.) Because these Mozarabic buildings crossed religious boundaries, they could be called the first truly Spanish architectural style to emerge after the rise of Islam.

Later, as the Reconquista started to gain ground, another border-crossing class emerged: Mudéjars, the Muslims who stayed on in now-Catholic Spain. Mudéjar artisans, largely disenfranchised, offered cheap labour and great talent. The fundamentalist nature of the Catholic campaign gave the impression that Spain was being 'reverted' to an essential Christian nature, but Mudéjar architecture from this period tells a different story: the *convivencia* would never be fully reversed.

The Mudéjar style, in evidence from the 12th century on, is notable first for the use of relatively inexpensive materials – gone were the days of lavish government commissions, and the Roman stones had all been used up. Instead, brick, tile and plaster were worked with incredible skill to conjure opulence, with some of the best extant examples in Aragon and Castile. The city of Teruel in particular is dotted with intricate brick towers, trimmed with glazed tiles.

Another telltale Mudéjar feature is extravagantly decorated timber ceilings done in a style called *artesonado.* They can be barrel vaults, but the most typical style is a flat wood ceiling made of interlocking beams that are inset with multicoloured wood panels in geometric patterns. In the Alhambra, the ceilings installed by later Catholic occupants may

ARCHITECTURE

1400–1600 Plateresque

The pinnacle of Spain's Renaissance, a dazzling ornate style of relief carving on facades.

1650–1750 Churrigueresque

Spain's special twist on baroque – literally, as spiral columns were all the rage, along with gold-leaf everything.

1888–1911 Modernisme

The Spanish version of art nouveau took a brilliant turn in Barcelona, and the city hasn't been the same since.

Only one unruly part of northern Spain, in what is now Asturias, was never conquered by the Muslims. During the 9th century a unique building style emerged, exaggerating Visigothic styles. The Palacio de Santa María del Naranco, for instance, has dramatically elongated proportions, delicate relief carvings and tall, thin arches.

not be quite as intricate as earlier Islamic work in the same complex, but the style is remarkably consistent, even as it incorporates the new rulers' coats of arms.

From Romanesque to Gothic

While the tide was turning against the Muslims, the Romanesque style was sweeping medieval Europe. It probably took root in Spain in part because it was the aesthetic opposite of Islamic fashions – architect and art historian Josep Puig i Cadafalch posited that each Romanesque detail was a systematic riposte to an Islamic one. These buildings were spare, angular and heavy, inspired by the proportions of classical structures. From about the 12th century, the Romanesque churches, monasteries, bridges and pilgrims' hospices that were erected served their intended functions, but they were also not-so-subtle statements about the success of the Reconquista.

In particular, Romanesque structures had perfectly semicircular arches – none of the stylised horseshoe look that had come before. In churches, this was expressed in a semicylindrical apse (or, in many cases, triple apse), a shape previously found in Byzantine churches. The round arch also graced doorways, windows, cloisters and naves. Entrances supported stacks of concentric arches – all the more eye-catching because they were often the only really decorative detail. Later, during the 12th century, the Spanish began to modify these semi-circles, edging toward the Gothic style, as they added pointed arches and ribbed vaults. The Monasterio de la Oliva in Navarra was among the first to show such features, and cathedrals in Ávila, Sigüenza, Tarragona and Tudela all display at least some transitional elements.

Meanwhile, in northern Europe, everyone was marvelling at the towering cathedrals made possible by the newfangled flying buttresses. The idea caught on in Spain by the 13th century, when the cathedrals at Burgos, León and Toledo were built. Their models were basically French, but the Spaniards soon introduced other elements. Some changes were subtle, such as placing choir stalls in the centre of the nave, but one was unmissable: the towering, decorative *retablo* (altarpiece) that graced the new churches. Spanish Gothic architects also devised the star vault, a method of distributing weight with ribbed vaults projecting out from a central point.

Many great buildings were begun at the height of Romanesque fashion but not completed until long after the Gothic style had gained the upper hand. The cathedral in Burgos, for instance, was begun in 1221 as a relatively sober construction, but its 15th-century spires are a product of German-inspired late-Gothic imagination. Mudéjar influences also still made themselves felt, particularly in the use of brick rather than stone. Toledo boasts many gloriously original buildings with a Gothic–Mudéjar flair, as does part of Aragón, where the fanciful brick structures have been declared a Unesco World Heritage Site.

Gothicism displayed odd local variants. The Catalan approach was more sober, bereft of pinnacles. Architects developed incredibly broad, unsupported vaults without the use of flying buttresses. In contrast, the Isabelline Gothic look, inspired by the Catholic queen, is a decorative mash-up, reflecting her fondness of Islamic exotica and heraldic imagery. It's on display in Toledo's San Juan de los Reyes, where Gothic arches meet intricately carved and painted wood ceilings, and the Capilla Real in Granada, where she and King Ferdinand are buried, and their initials form a decorative band around the outside, perhaps inspired by the calligraphy in the Alhambra.

It wasn't only religious buildings that flourished during this period. Most of the innumerable castles scattered across the country went up

The Camino de Santiago is also an architecture pilgrimage route, for such Romanesque beauties as the Monasterio de Santo Domingo de Silos, the smaller cloister in the Monasterio de las Huelgas in Burgos, the restored Iglesia de San Martín in Frómista and the cathedral itself in Santiago de Compostela.

CAMINO

in Gothic times. Many never saw action and were not intended to – an extraordinary example is the sumptuous castle at Coca, in Segovia. In Barcelona, some marvellous civil Gothic architecture can be admired, including the Saló del Tinell in the one-time royal palace in the Barri Gòtic and the Reials Drassanes, the once-mighty shipyards now home to the Museu Marítim.

The Gothic fascination lasted into the 16th century, when there was a revival of pure Gothic, perhaps best exemplified in the new cathedral in Salamanca, although the Segovia cathedral was about the last, and possibly most pure, Gothic structure raised in Spain.

The Renaissance & Plateresque

The effects of the pan-European Renaissance began to show in Spain at the end of the 15th century. The intellectual boom did not yield a single unified style, but inspired the uniquely Spanish vision of plateresque, which drew on Italian styles in part but was also an outgrowth of the Isabelline Gothic look. It is so named because facade decoration was so ornate that it looked as though it had been wrought by *plateros* (silversmiths). To visit Salamanca, where the Spanish Renaissance first took root, is to receive a concentrated dose of the most splendid work in the genre. The university facade is a virtuoso piece, featuring busts, medallions and a complex floral design that covers the wall like an unfurled carpet. Not far behind in intensity comes the facade of the Convento de San Esteban, where the main facade arch is studded with a thousand flowerlike forms, glowing in the warm local sandstone. Little of the work can be convincingly traced to any one hand, and it appears that the principal exponent of plateresque, Alonso de Covarrubias, was at the time busier in his home city of Toledo with the Alcázar and the Capilla de Reyes Nuevos in the cathedral.

A more purist Renaissance style, reflecting classical proportions and styles already established in Italy and France, prevailed in Andalucía. Symbolically and physically, the aesthetic finds its maximum expression in the Palacio de Carlos V that the emperor erected smack in the middle of the Moorish pleasure palaces in the Alhambra of Granada. It's the only example of the Renaissance circle-in-a-square ground plan in Spain.

The Renaissance wild card was Juan de Herrera, whose work bears almost no resemblance to anything else of the period because it is so austere. His masterpiece is the palace-monastery complex of San Lorenzo de El Escorial, a study in cubes (he had written a book on this very subject). He discarded typical classical decorative orders, leaving vast granite surfaces bare. The look was imitated in numerous monasteries for more than a century.

Baroque & Churrigueresque

Beginning in the late 17th century, Spanish architects took to the heady frills and spills of baroque in a big way. Aside from the late-18th-century Cádiz cathedral, there are very few from-scratch baroque buildings in Spain. But no matter: the exuberant decoration is so eye-catching that it easily overtakes the more sober earlier buildings to which it's attached. The leading exponents of this often overblown style were the Churriguera brothers, three sons of a respected sculptor who specialised in *retablos*, the enormous carved-wood altar backdrops. José Benito, Joaquín and Alberto picked up their father's work and elaborated on it exponentially. José Benito was court architect for Carlos II from 1690 to 1702; in his obituary he was dubbed 'the Michelangelo of Spain'.

In the 1920s, a replica of Seville's Giralda jutted above the old Moorish-looking Madison Square Garden in New York City; it was later torn down. Another replica fares better, standing tall above Kansas City, Missouri – a sister city to Seville.

(Continued on page 848)

Decorative Details

The history of architecture in Spain seems to be an ongoing struggle between austere simplicity and mind-boggling decoration. Perhaps it's too soon to declare a winner, but all things baroque, intricate and elaborate appear to have the edge.

Alhambra, Granada

1 The pinnacle of Islamic architecture in Spain, the Alhambra piles on the ornament in the form of plaster so finely carved it resembles lace and repetitive calligraphy that makes wallpaper-like patterns. Richly coloured ceramic tiles are quintessential Andalucía.

Aljafería, Zaragoza

2 Wood ceilings with a complex inlay in geometric patterns were perfected under Islamic rule and carried into the Reconquista by Mudéjar artisans. Lie down in the middle of the room to gawk properly – it's worth it.

Park Güell, Barcelona

3 Catalonia's capital bursts with Antoni Gaudí's vision's, especially the eye-popping tiles in Park Güell. Structure and surface merge perfectly: the mosaics seem to grow organically from the odd bulging forms to which they're applied.

Monasterio de La Cartuja, Granada

4 The Carthusian monks went for baroque in a big way – the whole monastery is extreme. The sacristy, where the priests would dress, is trimmed in mirrors, marquetry cabinets and dizzying black-and-white tiles.

Universidad Civil, Salamanca

5 Plateresque craftsmen carved Salamanca's rich sandstone within an inch of its life; the facade crawls with crests, lions, griffins, skulls, the pope and a tiny frog, said to bring luck to whoever can spot it.

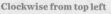

Clockwise from top left

1. Alhambra, Granada (p744) 2. Aljafería, Zaragoza (p365) 3. Park Güell, Barcelona (p257)

Awesome Arches

Horseshoes, scallops, parabolas, Gothic peaks, Romanesque semicircles – Spanish builders put the 'arch' in 'architecture'. It's perhaps the single most creative element in the tradition.

Roman aqueduct, Segovia

1 Later arches may be more decorative, but the simplest Roman approach has staying power; the immense waterworks in Segovia date from the 1st century AD. Just within the city, the aqueduct incorporates 167 arches.

Monasterio de Sigena, east of Zaragoza

2 The entrance to the Sigena monastery may be the most extreme and wonderful example of Romanesque arches in Spain – the doorway is framed by 14 concentric semicircles, creating an odd sense of receding perspective.

La Mezquita, Córdoba

3 The interior of the Umayyads' first mosque in Spain is a forest of arches. It set the standard for the use of the horseshoe arch in later Islamic architecture, and the triple-lobed arches and alternating coloured stones just add to the fun.

Sinagoga de Santa María La Blanca, Toledo

4 Like La Mezquita, this 13th-century synagogue is a study in horseshoe arches, showing the skill of Mudéjar architects in adapting Islamic forms to other contexts. The round windows align perfectly with the centre of each arch.

Mercat de Santa Caterina, Barcelona

5 The arch obsession continues in the modern age, as architects build on previous innovations. Enric Miralles refurbished the city's first public market with a playful, swooping roofline that Gaudí would have admired.

Right
1. La Mezquita (p737) 2. Roman aqueduct (p145), Segovia

Modern Marvels

Contemporary Spanish architecture (which includes many foreign designers) may not have a single identifiable look, but it embraces beauty. New buildings shimmer, swoop and glow from within.

Torre Agbar, Barcelona

1 French architect Jean Nouvel envisioned his tower as a Gaudí-like parabola in the round. The bullet-shaped tower rises 34 storeys over the city and is trimmed in iridescent glass. After dark, it puts on a bold light show.

Ciudad de las Artes y las Ciencias, Valencia

2 Spanish starchitect Santiago Calatrava never met a curve he didn't like, and his vast arts and science complex, unveiled in 1998, inspires wonder. The opera house resembles a giant eye, staring out over a reflecting pool.

Palacio de Congresos, Zaragoza

3 A citywide expo in 2008 brought together brilliant architects from around the world. Nieto Sobejano Arquitectos designed the main building, remarkable for its angular silhouette, which conjures warehouses, escalators and city towers.

Kursaal Palace, San Sebastián

4 Spain's Pritzker Prize–winner Rafael Moneo imbues his buildings with subtle natural logic. This angular glass auditorium on the waterfront reflects the ocean and the mountains and creates a visual link between the two.

Camp Nou, Barcelona

5 In keeping with the forward-thinking Spanish vision, one of the more exciting architectural visions is one that has yet to be built: Norman Foster's revamp of the venerable home of the Barça team. Look for the rainbow-glow wrapping in late 2011.

Left
1. Torre Agbar (p256), Barcelona 2. Hemisfèric (p546), Valencia

(Continued from page 843)

The hallmark of Churrigueresque is the so-called Solomonic column, a delightful twisting pillar that, especially when covered in gold leaf or vines, seems to wiggle its way to the heavens. Near the end of his life, José Benito's designs became more sober, as when he pioneered the more severe estipite column, shaped like an inverted cone.

Later practitioners took the Churrigueras' innovations and ran with them. The Carthusian monks of Granada, for instance, built the Monasterio de Nuestra Señora de la Asunción (more commonly called La Cartuja) by hand. The *sancta sanctorum* around the tabernacle is mind-boggling, crammed with saints, gilt skulls and intricate marble inlay. Likewise, Narciso Tomés' gold-leaf-trimmed altarpiece in the Catedral de Toledo is a later baroque masterwork. It glimmers under a skylight, giving it the nickname El Transparente.

Modernisme & Art Deco

At the end of the 19th century, Catalonia was the powerhouse of Spain, and Barcelona's prosperity unleashed one of the most imaginative periods in Spanish architecture. The architects at work here, who drew on current art nouveau trends as well as earlier Spanish styles, came to be called the Modernistas. Chief among them, Antoni Gaudí sprinkled Barcelona with jewels of his singular imagination. They range from his immense, unfinished Sagrada Família to the simply weird Casa Batlló and the only slightly more sober La Pedrera. Though Gaudí is most associated with a certain, well, gaudiness, his structural approach owed more to the austere era of Catalan Gothic, which inspired his own inventive work with parabolic arches.

Two other Catalan architects, Lluís Domènech i Montaner and Josep Puig i Cadafalch, don't have the immediate name recognition, but their works are Barcelona landmarks. Domènech i Montaner's Palau de la Música Catalana, for instance, matches Gaudí in exuberance and use of decorative tile. Puig i Cadafalch, who studied under Domènech i Montaner, built town houses such as Casa Amatller, as well as the cafe Els Quatre Gats, where Modernistas brainstormed until it shut in 1903 (it eventually reopened in 1989).

While Barcelona went all wavy, Madrid embraced the rigid glamour of art deco. This global style arrived in Spain just as Madrid's Gran Vía was laid out in the 1920s – the boulevard was the perfect blank slate for architectural creation. One of the more overwhelming caprices from that era is the Palacio de Comunicaciones on Plaza de la Cibeles.

The playful nature of Modernisme and art deco came to a quick end shortly after Franco took over in 1936, stifling architectural creativity for decades.

Contemporary Innovation

Post-Franco, Spain has made up for lost time. Ambitious urban redevelopment programs revamped cityscapes such as Barcelona, where the 1992 Olympics inspired a harbour makeover. More recently in Madrid, the Cuatro Torres business area (CTBA) sprouted skyscrapers by international star architects, such as César Pelli (best known for the Petronas Towers in Kuala Lumpur), as well as Spaniards Carlos Rubio Carvajal and Enrique Álvarez-Sala Walter.

Local heroes include Santiago Calatrava, who built his reputation with swooping, bone-white bridges. In 1996 he designed the whole futuristic Ciudad de las Artes y las Ciencias (City of Arts and Sciences) complex in Valencia. In 2000 he also built the Sondika Airport, in Bil-

---

Baroque Baubles

» Monasterio de Nuestra Señora de la Asunción, Granada

» Plaza Mayor, Salamanca

» Cathedral facade, Santiago de Compostela

» Cathedral, Murcia

» Real Academia de Bellas Artes de San Fernando, Madrid

Robert Hughes' *Barcelona* is a thorough, erudite history of the city, with an emphasis on architecture. The Gaudí chapters provide special insight into the designer's surprisingly conservative outlook.

bao, which has been nicknamed La Paloma (the Dove), for the winglike arc of its aluminium skin.

Catalan Enric Miralles had a short career, dying of a brain tumour in 2000 at the age of 45, but his Mercat de Santa Caterina in Barcelona shows brilliant colour and inventive use of arches. His Gas Natural building, also in Barcelona, is a poetic skyscraper that juts both vertically and horizontally. Both were completed after his death by his widow, Italian architect Benedetta Tagliabue.

One great showcase for Spanish architects was the 2008 Expo in Zaragoza. Many somewhat loopy buildings were created for the event, including the soaring, glittering Torre del Agua, by Enrique de Teresa and Julio Martínez Calzón; its floor plan resembles a drop of water. Madrileño duo Fuensanta Nieto and Enrique Sobejano built the Palacio de Congresos for the Expo, with its jaunty, angular elevation, like a quirky city skyline in miniature.

In 1996 Rafael Moneo won the Pritzker Prize, the greatest international honour for living architects, largely for his long-term contributions to Madrid's cityscape, such as the revamping of the Atocha railway station. His renovation of the Palacio Villahermosa into the Thyssen-Bornemisza Museum in Madrid blends in subtly with the urban fabric. The Kursaal Palace in San Sebastían, finished in 1999, is eye-catching – still staunchly functional, but shining, like two giant stones swept up from the sea.

Moneo may so far be the only Pritzker winner from Spain, but the country has become something of a Pritzker playground. It's perhaps this openness – even hunger – for outside creativity that marks the country's built environment today. Norman Foster designed the metro system in Bilbao, completed in 1995; the transparent, wormlike staircase shelters have come to be called *fosteritos*. But it was Frank Gehry's 1998 Museo Guggenheim in the same city that really sparked the quirky-building fever. Now the list of contemporary landmarks includes Herzog & de Meuron's deep-blue Edifici Fòrum on Barcelona's waterfront; Jean Nouvel's spangly, gherkin-shaped Torre Agbar, also in Barcelona; Richard Rogers' dreamy, wavy Terminal 4 at Madrid's Barajas airport; Oscar Niemeyer's flying-saucerish Centro Cultural Internacional in Asturias; and Zaha Hadid's whalelike bridge-cum-pavilion for the Zaragoza Expo.

Before the economic crash of 2008, the number of buildings under construction in Spain was second only to China. Since then, many ambitious projects have been cancelled or delayed. But look to Barcelona to pull the country out of a slump. On the drawing board or under construction are, among other things, Norman Foster's facelift of the Camp Nou Stadium in Barcelona, where coloured glass will create a modern cathedral, and Zaha Hadid's Spiral Tower, which resembles a precarious stack of rectangular dinner plates.

Outside Spain, Rafael Moneo is best known for the 2002 Cathedral of Our Lady of Angels, in downtown Los Angeles, California.

MONEO

Spain's Food & Wine

Spanish cuisine is, quite simply, wonderful. Paella, the wines of La Rioja and tapas are all the rage in restaurants around the world, and Spain's celebrity chefs are undisputed global superstars. These icons of the Spanish kitchen are merely the tip of an extremely large iceberg; few countries can match Spain's gastronomic variety, innovation and sheer culinary excellence.

Spaniards love to travel in their own country and, given the riches on offer, they especially love to do so in pursuit of the perfect meal. Tell a Spaniard that you're on your way to a particular place and they're sure to start salivating at the mere thought of the local speciality and a favourite restaurant at which to enjoy it. That's because eating is more than a functional pastime to be squeezed between other more important tasks; it's one of life's great pleasures, a social event to be enjoyed with friends and one always taken seriously enough to have adequate hours allocated for the purpose and savoured like all good things in life.

Having joined Spaniards around the table for years, we've come to understand what eating Spanish-style is all about. If we could distil the essence of how to make food a highlight of your trip into a few simple rules, it would be this: *always* ask for the local speciality; *never* be shy about looking around to see what others have ordered before choosing; *always* ask the waiter for his or her recommendations; and, wherever possible, make your meal a centrepiece of your day.

¡Buen provecho! (Enjoy your meal!)

Rich in anecdotes and insight, *A Late Dinner – Discovering the Food of Spain*, by Paul Richardson, is arguably the best and most readable book in English about Spanish food.

The Laws of Spanish Cooking

The laws of traditional Spanish cooking are deceptively simple: take the freshest ingredients and interfere with them as little as possible. While the rest of the world was developing sophisticated sauces, Spanish chefs were experimenting with subtlety, creating a combination of

---

PRACTICAL INFORMATION

Throughout this guidebook, the order of restaurant listings follows the author's preference, and each place to eat is accompanied by one of the following pricing symbols.

» €   <€20 per meal per person

» €€   €20 to €50 per meal per person

» €€€   >€50 per meal per person

We define a meal as three courses (including dessert) and house wine. Restaurant hours in Spain are lunch from 1pm to 4pm, dinner from 8.30pm to midnight or later.

Plenty of places that serve food and drink go by the name of *bar* or *restaurante,* but there are variations on the theme.

» *asador* – a restaurant specialising in roasted meats.

» *bar de copas* – gets going around midnight and primarily hard drinks are served.

» *cervecería* – the focus is on *cerveza* (beer) and there's plenty of the foamy stuff on tap.

» *horno de asador* – a restaurant with a wood-burning roasting oven.

» *marisquería* – a bar or restaurant specialising in seafood.

» *tasca* – a tapas bar.

» *terraza* – an open-air bar, for warm-weather tippling only.

» *taberna* – usually a rustic place serving tapas and *raciones* (large tapas servings): expect to see barrels used as tables and tile decor.

» *vinoteca* – slightly more upmarket wine bars where you can order by the glass.

tastes in which the flavour of the food itself was paramount. Nowhere is this more evident than in the humble art of tapas – bite-sized morsels whose premise is so simple as to have the hallmarks of genius – where carefully selected meats, seafood or vegetables are given centre stage and allowed to speak for themselves. Such are the foundations on which Spanish cooking is built.

If simplicity is the cornerstone of Spanish cooking, it's the innovation and nouvelle cuisine emerging from Spanish kitchens that has truly taken the world by storm. Celebrity chefs have developed their own culinary laboratories, experimenting with all that's new while never straying far from the principles that underpin traditional Spanish cuisine.

Staples & Specialties

Desayuno (breakfast) is generally a no-nonsense affair taken at a bar on the way to work. A *café con leche* (half coffee and half warm milk) with a *bollo* (pastry) is the typical breakfast. Croissants or a cream-filled pastry are also common. Some people prefer a savoury start – try a *sandwich mixto,* a toasted ham and cheese sandwich; a Spanish *tostada* is simply buttered toast. Others, especially those heading home at dawn after a night out, go for an all-Spanish favourite, *churros y chocolate,* a deep-fried stick of plain pastry immersed in thick hot chocolate.

The typical *carta* (menu) begins with starters such as *ensaladas* (salads), *sopas* (soups) and *entremeses* (hors d'oeuvres). The latter can range from a mound of potato salad with olives, asparagus, anchovies and a selection of cold meats – a meal in itself – to simpler cold meats, slices of cheese and olives.

The basic ingredients of later courses can be summarised under the general headings of *pollo* (chicken), *carne* (meat), *mariscos* (seafood), *pescado* (fish) and *arroz* (rice). Meat may be subdivided into *cerdo* (pork), *ternera* (beef) and *cordero* (lamb). If you want a *guarnición* (side order), such as *verduras* (vegetables), you may have to order separately.

When it comes to fish, the Spanish mainstays are *bonito* (tuna), *sardinas* (sardines), *anchoas* (anchovies), *merluza* (hake), *dorada* (bream) and *lenguado* (sole). Shellfish is another favourite. But the fish with which Spaniards have the closest relationship historically is *bacalao* (dried and salted cod). For many centuries roving Spanish fishermen have harvested the codfish from Newfoundland and Norway, salting it and bringing it home looking more like a rock than food. After soaking

The Food of Spain & Portugal – A Regional Celebration, by Elisabeth Luard (2005), demystifies the food and wine of the various Spanish regions with recipes and the context from which they arise.

it several times in water it's rehydrated and relieved of its salt content, which enriches the flavour and improves the texture. Originally it was considered food for the poor and some called it 'vigil day beef' for its use during fasts. The best place to enjoy it is in the Basque Country, where it's revered. Try sweet red peppers stuffed with *bacalao* and we're sure you'll be inclined to agree.

Inland, you're far more likely to encounter *legumbres* (legumes) such as *garbanzos* (chickpeas), *judías* (beans) and *lentejas* (lentils). Of the hearty stews, the king is *fabada* (pork and bean stew) from Asturias, although *cocido,* a hotpot or stew with a noodle broth, carrots, cabbage, chickpeas, chicken, *morcilla* (blood sausage) beef and lard is a special favourite in Madrid and León. Other popular staples in Spain's interior include *cordero asado* (roast lamb), *cochinillo asado* (roast suckling pig) and *patatas con huevos fritos* (baked potatoes with eggs).

Tapas

Many would argue that tapas are Spain's greatest culinary gift to the world. While devotees of *paella* and *jamón* can make a strong counter-claim, what clinches it for us is the fact that the potential variety for tapas is endless.

Anything can be a tapa: a handful of olives, a slice of ham and cheese on bread, a piece of *tortilla de patatas* (potato and onion omelette). Other common orders include: *boquerones en vinagre* (fresh anchovies marinated in white vinegar, which are delicious and tangy); *boquerones fritos* (fried fresh anchovies); *albóndigas* (good old meat balls); *pimientos de Padrón* (little green peppers from Galicia – some are hot and some not); *gambas* (prawns, either done *al ajillo,* with garlic, or *a la plancha,* grilled); *chipirones* (baby squid, served in various ways); *calamares a la Romana* (deep-fried calamari rings)...the list goes on.

The undoubted king of tapas destinations is the Basque Country in general (where they call tapas *'pintxos'*), and San Sebastián in particular. Although good tapas can be found anywhere, other places with especially fine tapas include Madrid (see the boxed text) and Zaragoza and most cities in Andalucía.

Ordering Tapas

Too many travellers miss out on the joys of tapas because, unless you speak Spanish, the art of ordering can seem one of the dark arts of Spanish etiquette. Fear not – it's not as difficult as it first appears.

In the Basque Country, Zaragoza and many bars in Madrid, Barcelona and elsewhere, it couldn't be easier. With so many tapas varieties lined up along the bar, you either take a small plate and help yourself or point to the morsel you want. If you do this, it's customary to keep track of what you eat (by holding on to the toothpicks for example) and then tell the bar staff how many you've had when it's time to pay. Otherwise, many places have a list of tapas, either on a menu or posted up behind the bar. If you can't choose, ask for *'la especialidad de la casa'* (the house speciality) and it's hard to go wrong. Another way of eating tapas is to order *raciones* (rations; large tapas servings) or *media raciones* (half-rations; smaller tapas serving). These plates and half-plates of a particular dish are a good way to go if you particularly like something and want more than a mere tapa. Remember, however, that after a couple of *raciones* you'll almost certainly be full; the *media ración* is a good choice if you want to experience a broader range of tastes. Tapas are always taken with a drink, and almost always while standing at the bar. In some bars you'll also get a small (free) tapa when you buy a drink.

OLIVE OIL

Spain is the world's largest producer of olive oil and much of the Italian olive oil sold around the world is made from Spanish olives.

There are many stories concerning the origins of tapas.

One of the most common explanations derives from the fact that medieval Spain was a land of isolated settlements and people on the move – traders, pilgrims, emigrants and journeymen – who had to cross the lonely high plateau of Spain en route elsewhere. All along the route, travellers holed up in inns where the keepers, concerned about drunken men on horseback setting out from their village, developed a tradition of putting a 'lid' *(tapa)* of food atop a glass of wine or beer. The purpose was partly to keep the bugs out, but primarily to encourage people not to drink on an empty stomach.

Another story holds that in the 13th century, doctors to King Alfonso X advised him to accompany his small sips of wine between meals with small morsels of food. So enamoured was the monarch with the idea that he passed a law requiring all bars in Castile to follow suit.

In Andalucía in particular, it is also claimed that the name 'tapa' attained widespread usage in the early 20th century when King Alfonso XIII stopped at a beachside bar in Cádiz Province. When a strong gust of wind blew sand in the king's direction, a quick-witted waiter rushed to place a slice of *jamón* atop the king's glass of sherry. The king so much enjoyed the idea (and the *jamón*) that, wind or no wind, he ordered another and the name stuck.

Jamón

Another essential presence on the Spanish table is cured ham from the high plateau, known as *jamón*. Every *tasca* (tapas bar) has it. The *jamón* from Extremadura or Salamanca is considered to be the finest, although the Teruel region of Aragón makes a convincing claim for membership to such an elite group. *Chorizo, salchichón* and *lomo* (different types of pork sausages) are also made from acorn-fed pigs.

Jamón – a Primer

Spanish *jamón* is, unlike Italian prosciutto, a bold, deep red and well marbled with buttery fat. At its best, it smells like meat, the forest and the field. Like wines and olive oil, Spanish *jamón* is subject to a strict series of classifications. *Jamón serrano* refers to *jamón* made from white-coated pigs introduced to Spain in the 1950s. Once salted and semidried by the cold, dry winds of the Spanish sierra, most now go through a similar process of curing and drying in a climate-controlled shed for around a year. *Jamón serrano* accounts for approximately 90% of cured ham in Spain.

Jamón ibérico – more expensive and generally regarded as the elite of Spanish hams – comes from a black-coated pig indigenous to the Iberian Peninsula and a descendant of the wild boar. Gastronomically, its star appeal is its ability to infiltrate fat into the muscle tissue, thus producing an especially well-marbled meat. If the pig gains at least 50% of its body weight during the acorn-eating season, it can be classified as *jamón ibérico de bellota,* the most sought-after designation for *jamón*.

Paella

We'll let you into a secret: a *really* good paella can be surprisingly hard to come by in Spanish restaurants. Why? For a start, saffron is extremely expensive, prompting many restaurants to cut corners by using yellow dye number 2. Secondly, many restaurant owners play on the fact that every second foreign visitor to Spain will order a paella while in the country, but few will have any idea about what a good paella should

The recipe for cured meats such as *jamón* (ham) is attributed to a noble Roman, Cato the Elder, who changed the course of Spanish culinary history with his tome *De Re Rustica*.

taste like. Spaniards are much more discerning when it comes to their national dish, so check out the clientele before sitting down and ordering – if there are plenty of locals in residence, you can order with more confidence. The places where we recommend the paella throughout this book are also among the better places to try.

The base of a good paella always includes short-grain rice, garlic, parsley, olive oil and saffron. The best rice is the *bomba* variety, which opens out accordion fashion when cooked, allowing for maximum absorption while remaining firm. Paella should be cooked in a large shallow pan to enable maximum contact with the bottom of the pan where most of the flavour resides. And for the final touch of authenticity, the grains on the bottom (and only on the bottom) of the paella should have a crunchy, savoury crust known as the *socarrat*. Beyond that, the main paella staples are *paella valenciana* (from Valencia, where paella has its roots and remains true to its origins), which is cooked with chicken, beans and sometimes rabbit, and the more widespread *paella de mariscos* (seafood paella), which should be bursting with shellfish.

Regional Specialties
Basque Country & Catalonia

The Basque Country and Catalonia are Spain's undoubted culinary superstars. Partly this is because of the area's gastronomic innovation; its avant-garde chefs – Ferran Adrià, Sergi Arola, Mari Arzak, Oriol Balaguer and Pedro Subijana, to name just a few – are famous throughout the world for their food laboratories, their commitment to food as art and their crazy riffs on the themes of traditional local cooking. But the Basque Country and Catalonia are also a gastronome's paradise because food here runs deep into every aspect of culture. If Spaniards elsewhere in the country love their food, the Basques and Catalans are obsessed with it. They talk about it endlessly. They plan their day around it. And then they spend the rest of their time dreaming about it.

The confluence of sea and mountain has bequeathed to the Basque Country an extraordinary culinary richness, a cuisine as much defined by the fruits of the Bay of Biscay as by the fruits of the land. You're as likely to find great *anchoas*, *gambas* and *bacalao* as you are heaving steaks and *jamón*, and often in surprising combinations. The food is exceptional wherever you go in the region. But it's in San Sebastián that you understand how deeply ingrained food is in Basque culture, home as the city is to everything from secret gastronomic societies and exclusive sit-down restaurants with the full complement of Michelin stars to the more accessible *pintxos* bars of the Parte Vieja. If we could choose one place to sample the creativity, variety and sheer excitement of Basque cuisine, it would be here. It's from the kitchens of San Sebastián that *nueva cocina vasca* (Basque nouvelle cuisine) has emerged, announcing Spain's arrival as a culinary superpower. The results are, quite simply, extraordinary.

Food & Wine Festivals

» Feria del Queso, Trujillo (April)

» Fiesta de la Sidra Natural, Gijón (August)

» Fiesta de San Mateo, Logroño (September) Celebrates La Rioja's grape harvest

Considered by many to be the Basque Country's equal when it comes to food excellence, Catalonia blends traditional Catalan flavours and extraordinary geographical diversity with an openness to influences from the rest of Europe, a trait that Barcelona has turned into a way of life. All manner of seafood, paella, rice and pasta dishes are regulars on Catalonian menus and, this being Catalonia, always with a creative local twist. Sauces are more prevalent here than elsewhere in Spain, and the further you head inland, the more likely you are to see the mainstays of Pyrenean cooking with *jabalí* (wild boar), *conejo* (rabbit), *caracoles* (snails, especially in Lleida) and delicious hotpots such as *suquet* (fish and potato stew). If you prefer to self-cater, with the finest produce

TOP FIVE BASQUE EATING EXPERIENCES

» **Pintxos** (Basque tapas; p423) in the bars of San Sebastián's Parte Vieja, washed down with *txacoli* (a sharp, local white wine).

» **Bacalao al pil-pil** – salt cod and garlic in an olive-oil emulsion.

» **Chipirones en su tinta** – baby squid served in its own ink.

» **Chuleton de buey** – enormous steaks at various *sidrerías* (cider bars) in the mountains around San Sebastián.

» **Nueva cocina vasca** (Basque nouvelle cuisine) at Arzak, one of Spain's best restaurants.

in the land, look no further than Barcelona's Mercat de la Boqueria, arguably Spain's finest food market. Here you'll find *botifarra* (the local version of cured pork sausage) and *garrotxa,* a formidable Catalan cheese that almost lives up to its name. Desserts are also a feature, notably *crema catalana* (the Catalan version of *crème brûlée*). For more on Catalan cuisine, turn to the boxed text, p305.

Inland Spain

Central Spain's high *meseta* (plateau) has a food culture all its own. The best *jamón ibérico* comes from Extremadura and Salamanca, while *cordero asado lechal* (roast spring lamb) and *cochinillo asado* (roast suckling pig) are winter mainstays right through the heart of Spain to such an extent that Spaniards will travel for hours on a winter weekend in search of the perfect *cochinillo* or *cordero*.

Beyond these iconic dishes, each region has its own speciality.

In Aragón it's all about meat, where a love for *ternasco* (suckling lamb, usually served as a steak or ribs with potatoes) is elevated almost to the status of a local religion. Another signature dish, especially in Teruel, is *jarretes* (stewed Mozarabic hock of lamb). Teruel's *jamón* is also considered to be among Spain's finest, and the Pyrenean fare in the north closely resembles that of neighbouring Catalonia. For more on Aragonese cuisine, see the boxed text, p367.

In Extremadura you should always order *solomillo ibérico con Torta del Casar* (pork sirloin with creamy Torta del Casar cheese made from sheep's milk) if it's on the menu, while *frito de cordero* (lamb stew), *migas* (breadcrumbs, often cooked with cured meats and served with grapes) and even frog legs are other delicacies to watch for.

Castilla-La Mancha is famous for its *queso manchego* (a hard cheese made from sheep's milk; see the boxed text, p205), as well as snails and quirky dishes such as bread embedded with sardines that you'll find in Alcalá de Júcar. Castilla y León is even more devoted to the cult of meat with *carnes asadas* (roasted meats) and *embutidos* (cured meats) weighing down every bar and restaurant across the region. For more on eating in Castilla y León, see the boxed text, p130.

In Madrid the local *cocido a la madrileña* (meat and chickpea stew) inspires considerable passion among its devotees; it's echoed in Astorga in northern Castilla y León, where the elements (soup, meats etc) are eaten in reverse order and known as *cocido maragato*. *Madrilieños* are also passionate about fish and seafood; it's often said Madrid is the best 'port' in Spain because the seafood arrives fresh daily from both the Atlantic and the Mediterranean. In fact, inland Madrid has the world's second-largest fish market (after Tokyo)...

In January the country's most prestigious chefs showcase the latest innovations in Spain's world-famous cuisine at the Madrid Fusion (www.madridfusion.net) gastronomy summit.

More than half of Spain's wine production comes from Castilla-La Mancha, with Catalonia, Extremadura and Valencia making up the top four. Better-known wine-producing regions such as La Rioja and Castilla y León trail in fifth and sixth place respectively.

(Continued on page 860)

GUY MOBERLY

GREG ELMS

1. Paella (p853)
The base of a good paella always includes short-grain rice, garlic, parsley, olive oil and saffron.

2. Jamón (p853)
The high-plateau cured ham from Extremadura and Salamanca is considered to be the finest in Spain.

OLIVER STREWE

3. Chocolate con churros

No Madrid night is complete without deep-fried doughnut strips dipped in hot chocolate.

4. Basque Country tapas (p852)

The undoubted king of tapas destinations is the Basque Country, where they call tapas 'pintxos'.

5. Ordering tapas (p852)

Take a small plate and help yourself or point to the morsel you want.

GUY MOBERLY

1. Tapas (p852)
Tapas are always taken with a drink, and almost always while standing at the bar.

2. Wine (p863)
Spanish wine is subject to a complicated system of wine classification, marked on the bottle.

3. Tetilla cheese (p504)
Galicia's iconic tetilla cheese ('titty cheese') was supposedly inspired by Queen Esther's breasts.

4. Alambique cooking school (p83)
Offers cooking classes in Madrid covering Spanish and international themes.

JONAS KALTENBACH

(Continued from page 855)

Galicia & the Northwest

Perhaps more than any other Spaniards, *gallegos* (Galicians) are defined by their relationship with the sea. A large proportion of them make their livelihoods from fishing, and their cuisine, their fiestas and, some would say, their whole reason for living revolves around fish and seafood. Yes, they're proud of their *empanadas* (savoury pies) and *pimientos de padron* (grilled and often spicy green capsicum). But these are merely diversions from the main event, which is *pulpo gallego* (spicy boiled octopus), a dish whose constituent elements (octopus, oil, paprika and garlic) are so simple yet whose execution is devilishly difficult. The trick is in the boiling; dipping the octopus into the water, then drawing it out and dipping again cooks it at just the right rate. Other Galician mainstays include a litany of bewildering sea creatures such as *navajas* (razor clams), *coquinas* (large clams), *percebes* (goose barnacles), *mejillones* (mussels), *berberechos* (cockles), *almejas* (baby clams) and *vieiras* (a form of scallop).

Not to be outdone, neighbouring Asturias and Cantabria also give to Spain a handful of seafood delicacies, the best known of which are *anchoas*. If you're anywhere in Spain and you spy *anchoas de santoña* on the menu, don't hesitate for a second. Better still, go straight to the source and visit Santoña where the little fellas come ashore.

In the high mountains of the Cordillera Cantábrica in the coastal hinterland, the cuisine is as driven by mountain pasture as it is by the daily comings and goings of fishing fleets. Cheeses are particularly sought-after, with special fame reserved for the untreated cows-milk cheese, *queso de Cabrales*. River fish (trout, eels and salmon in particular) are also popular. But if *asturianos* (Asturians) get excited about one food above all others, then it would have to be *fabada asturiana* (a stew made with pork, blood sausage and white beans). This is winter food, the sort of meal that will have you rising from the table on suddenly heavy legs and longing for a siesta. The saving grace is that the fresh taste of *sidra* (cider) straight from the barrel will not, unless you overindulge, cast such a long shadow over the rest of your afternoon. Asturian cuisine is covered in the boxed text on p483, while for Cantabria see the boxed text, p461.

Valencia, Murcia & the Balearic Islands

There's so much more to the cuisine of this region than oranges and paella, but these signature products capture the essence of the Mediterranean table. There's no dish better suited to a summer's afternoon spent with friends overlooking the sea than paella, a dish filled with flavour and, very often, full of seafood. You can get a paella just about anywhere in Spain, but to get one cooked as it should be cooked, look no further than the restaurants in Valencia's waterfront Las Arenas district or La Albufera. For the noodle variety of *fideuá* (noodles with fish and shellfish), the alternative that many travellers prefer with a dollop of *alioli* (garlic mayonnaise), your first stop should be Restaurante Emilio in Gandia. For more on Valencian cooking, see the boxed text, p561.

The cooking style of the Balearic Islands owes much to its watery locale and to its cultural similarities with Catalonia and Valencia. As such, paella, rice dishes and lashings of seafood are recurring themes, with a few local variations, notably the preponderance of eel, sometimes in the most unlikely places (the Mallorcan *espinagada,* eel and spinach pie, for instance). One particularly tasty local dish in Ibiza is *arròs caldós* (saffron rice cooked in the broth of local fish, herbs and potatoes). We cover the cooking of the Balearics in more detail in the boxed text, p625.

For an authoritative and comprehensive periodical on Spanish gastronomy, check www.spaingourmetour.com, which overflows with recipes and ideas for culinary explorations of Spain.

Dishes often served during Semana Santa include *monas de pascua* (chocolate figurines), *torta pascualina* (spinach and egg pie) and *torrija* (French toast). A popular Easter dish in Mallorca is *flan de pascuas* (Easter cheese flan), and *cordero pascual* (spring lamb) is common fare everywhere.

The moist, cool climate of northwestern Spain produces rich grasses that make for fat, contented cows and flavour-filled milk. Some of the more widely available varieties of cheese include:

» **San Simón** – a slightly smoked Galician mountain cheese that's dense, yellow and has a creamy texture.

» **Cabrales** – a creamy, powerful blue cheese from Asturias cured in the cool, deep caves of the Picos de Europa.

» **Afuega'l Pitu** – an Asturian valley cheese that's drier and nuttier than most Atlantic cheeses and sometimes made with paprika.

» **Tetilla** – literally 'nipple', this Galician cheese is so-named for its remarkable resemblance to a perfectly shaped breast; it's mild, sweet and creamy.

» **Ahumado de Aliva** – a Cantabrian cheese smoked over juniper wood and with a mild, smoky taste.

Murcia's culinary fame brings us back to the oranges. The coastal littoral is known simply as 'La Huerta' ('the garden'). Since Moorish times, this has been one of Spain's most prolific areas for growing fruit and vegetables, but you'll also come across rice, tomatoes, peppers and olives. Great plates of grilled vegetables are, not surprisingly, a common order, but *arroz caldoso* (rice cooked in fish stock), *arroz con conejo* (rice with rabbit) and *zarangollo* (omelette of courgettes, onion and potatoes cooked in olive oil) are tasty variations on the theme.

Andalucía

It's difficult to reduce a region as large and diverse as Andalucía to a few words, but there are a few overarching culinary themes. Seafood is an obvious and consistent presence the length and breadth of the coast. While many of the national and well-known Mediterranean varieties of seafood are found here, the long reach of local fishing fleets into deep Atlantic waters adds depth to your eating experience. The result is all the usual suspects, alongside *pez espada* (swordfish), *cazón* (dogfish or shark that feeds on shellfish to produce a strong, almost sweet flavour), *salmonetes* (red mullet) and *tortilla de camarones* (shrimp fritters).

Another governing principle is that the temperature rarely drops below the tolerable and in summer the region bakes with a ferocity unmatched elsewhere on the peninsula. As such, a primary preoccupation of its inhabitants is keeping cool, and there's no better way to do so than with a *gazpacho andaluz* (Andalucian gazpacho), a cold soup with many manifestations. The base is almost always tomato, vinegar and olive oil, but also often incorporates green peppers and soaked bread, and you'll find cooks who won't use anything but sherry vinegar. Our opinion? They're all good. Other similar cold soups typical of the region include *ajo blanco* (white gazpacho, cooked using almonds and no tomato), and *salmorejo cordobés* (a cold tomato-based soup from Córdoba where soaked bread is essential). And one final thing: yes, it's supposed to be cold. *Please* don't make the mistake of one traveller in Seville who returned his gazpacho and asked for it to be heated.

Andalucía is also Spain's spiritual home of bullfighting. In season (roughly May to September), bars and restaurants will proudly announce '*hay rabo de toro*', which roughly translates as, 'yes, we have bull's tail for those of you who not only like to see the bull chased around the ring but also like to pursue it to its ultimate conclusion'. If you don't think about where it came from, it's really rather tasty.

At Christmas, *turrón* is a countrywide favourite. It's a uniquely Spanish kind of nougat, whose recipe goes back to the 14th century and incorporates honey, almonds and sugar.

Vegetarians & Vegans

Such is their love for meat, fish and seafood, many Spaniards, especially the older generation, don't really understand vegetarianism. As a result, dedicated vegetarian restaurants are still pretty thin on the ground outside the major cities.

That said, while vegetarians – especially vegans – can have a hard time, and while some cooked vegetable dishes can contain ham, the eating habits of Spaniards are changing; an ever-growing selection of vegetarian restaurants is springing up around the country. Barcelona and Madrid in particular have plenty of vegetarian restaurants to choose from. Restaurants offering a good vege selection are easy to find throughout this book – they're marked with a 🖉 symbol.

Otherwise, salads are a Spanish staple and often are a meal in themselves. You'll also come across the odd vegetarian paella, as well as dishes such as *verduras a la plancha* (grilled vegetables); *garbanzos con espinacas* (chickpeas and spinach); and potato dishes, such as *patatas bravas* (potato chunks bathed in a slightly spicy tomato sauce) and *tortilla de patatas*. The prevalence of legumes ensures that *lentejas* and *judías* are also easy to track down, while *pan* (bread), *quesos* (cheeses), *alcachofas* (artichokes) and *aceitunas* (olives) are always easy to find. *Tascas* usually offer more vegetarian choices than do sit-down restaurants.

If vegetarians feel like a rarity among Spaniards, vegans will feel as if they've come from another planet. To make sure that you're not misunderstood, ask if dishes contain *huevos* (eggs) or *productos lácteos* (dairy).

The New Spain – Vegetarian & Vegan Restaurants, by Jean Claude Juston, should be a bible for vegetarian and vegan visitors. It's available from L'Atelier (www.ivu.org/atelier).

Habits & Customs

Love them or hate them, Spanish waiters are unlikely to leave you indifferent. In smarter establishments waiters are often young, attentive and switched on to your needs. In more traditional places, waiting is a career, often a poorly paid one, which is the preserve of old men (sometimes one old man, sometimes one grumpy old man) in white jackets and bow ties, for whom service with a smile is not part of the job description. In such places they shuffle amid the tables, the weight of the world upon their shoulders, struggling with what seems a Sisyphean task. Getting their attention can be a challenge. On the other hand, they know their food and, if you speak Spanish, can help tailor your order in the best possible way.

Somewhere in between are Spanish bartenders, who can be as informal as they are informed and who love to shout their orders to the kitchen and generally create a breezy atmosphere.

In simpler restaurants you may keep the same knife and fork throughout the meal. As each course is finished you set the cutlery aside and your plates will be whisked away.

TRAVELLERS' FRIEND – MENÚ DEL DÍA

One great way to cap prices at lunchtime Monday to Friday is to order the *menú del día,* a full three-course set menu (usually with several options), water, bread and wine. These meals are priced from around €10, although €12 and up is increasingly the norm. You'll be given a menu with five or six starters, the same number of mains and a handful of desserts – you choose one from each category; it is possible to order two starters, but not two mains. Filling as it may be, it's worth remembering that the *menú del día* usually doesn't include the most exciting dishes on the menu; for those you'll need to order à la carte.

The philosophy behind the *menú del día* is that during the working week few Spaniards have time to go home for lunch. Taking a packed lunch is just not the done thing, so most people end up eating in restaurants, and all-inclusive three-course meals are as close as they can come to eating home-style food without breaking the bank.

There are numerous terrific cooking courses throughout Spain:

Alambique (p83) Cooking classes in Madrid covering Spanish and international themes.

Apunto – Centro Cultural del Gusto (p85) Fun and varied classes in Madrid, although you'll probably need decent Spanish.

Catacurian (USA ☑1-866 538 3519, Spain ☑93 802 2660; www.catacurian.com; Carrer del Progres 2, El Masroig, Tarragona, Catalonia) Head down to the rural wine region of Priorat for one- to six-day wine and cooking classes. Catalan chef Alicia Juanpere and her American partner Jonathan Perret lead tours and teach the classes (in English).

Cook and Taste (p271) One of Barcelona's best cooking schools with half-day courses and more.

Cooking Club (☑91 323 29 58; www.club-cooking.com, in Spanish; Calle de Veza 33, Madrid) The regular, respected program of classes here encompasses a range of cooking styles.

Dom's Gastronom Cookery School (☑93 674 51 60; www.domsgastronom.com; Passeig del Roser 43, Valldoreix, Barcelona) Cordon-bleu chef Dominique Heathcoate runs the full gamut of Catalan, Spanish and French cuisine.

L'Atelier (p768) Award-winning vegetarian chef Jean-Claude Juston (formerly of Neal's Yard Bakery and other celebrated veggie eateries in London) runs vegetarian cookery courses at his welcoming little guesthouse in the magical Alpujarras valleys of Andalucía.

Most visitors complain not about the quality of Spanish food but its timing. *Comida/Almuerzo* (lunch) is the main, leisurely meal of the day and rarely begins before 2pm (kitchens usually stay open until 4pm). For *cena* (dinner), few Spaniards would dream of turning up before 9.30pm. Many bars serve tapas and *raciones* throughout the day. *Bocadillos* (filled rolls) are another option. If you can't face a full menu, a simpler option is the *plato combinado,* basically a meat-and-three-veg dish.

When it comes to tipping, most Spaniards leave small change or around €1 per person.

Wine

Spaniards invariably accompany their meal with a Spanish wine. Extremely loyal to the local drop, they often wonder, with considerable justification, what need they have for foreign wines when their own vineyards produce prodigiously and to such high quality.

Probably the most common premium red table wine you'll encounter will be from La Rioja, in the north. The principal grape of Rioja is the tempranillo, widely believed to be a mutant form of the pinot noir. Its wine is smooth and fruity, seldom as dry as its supposed French counterpart. Look for the 'DOC Rioja' classification on the label and you'll find a good wine. Not far behind are the wine-producing regions of Ribera del Duero (Castilla y León), Navarra, the Somontano wines of Aragón (see the boxed text, p388), and the Valdepeñas region (see the boxed text, p211) of southern Castilla-La Mancha, which is famous for its quantities rather than quality, but is generally well priced and remains popular.

For white wines, the Ribeiro wines of Galicia (p538) are well regarded. Also from the area is one of Spain's most charming whites – Albariño (see p526). This crisp, dry and refreshing drop is a rare wine as it's designated by grape rather than region. The Penedès region in Catalonia produces whites and sparkling wine such as *cava,* the traditional champagnelike toasting drink of choice for Spaniards at Christmas.

Sherry, the unique wine of Andalucía, is Spain's national dram and is found in almost every bar, *tasca* and restaurant in the land. Dry Sherry, called *fino,* begins as a fairly ordinary white wine of the Palomino grape, but it's 'fortified' with grape brandy. This stops fermentation and gives the wine taste and smell constituents that enable it to age into

Wines from Spain (www.winesfromspain.com) is the best website covering Spanish wine, with detailed but accessible sections on history, grape varieties and all the Spanish wine-producing regions.

SPAIN'S BEST WINE MUSEUMS

Although tourist offices in Spain's major wine regions can help point you in the direction of local bodegas (wineries) and many also organise winery tours, the following museums are where you really should start your journey in getting to know the local drop. Most are interactive, allowing you to familiarise yourself with the various grape aromas, many host tastings, and all put the wineries you're about to visit into their proper historical context.

» Museo del Vino, Haro (p451) – La Rioja
» Dinastía Vivanco, Briones (Museo de la Cultura del Vino; p452) – La Rioja
» Quaderna Via, Estella (see the boxed text, p452) – Navarra
» Museo de la Viña y el Vino de Navarra, Olite (p443) – Navarra
» Museo Provincial del Vino, Peñafiel (p187) – Ribera del Duero
» Espacio de Vino, Barbastro (p388) – Somontano, Aragón
» Museo del Vino, Cariñena (p369) – Cariñena, Aragón's largest wine-growing area

something sublime. It's taken as an *aperitivo* (apéritif) or as a table wine with seafood. Amontillado and Oloroso are sweeter Sherries, good for after dinner. Manzanilla is grown only in Sanlúcar de Barrameda near the coast in southwestern Andalucía and develops a slightly salty taste that's very appetising. When ordering it be sure to say *'vino de Manzanilla'*, since *manzanilla* alone means chamomile tea. It's possible to visit a number of bodegas (wineries) in Sanlúcar, as well as in Jerez de la Frontera and El Puerto de Santa María.

Then there is that famous Spanish wine drink, sangria. Don't expect too much from it and remember that it was developed as a way to make use of bad wine. It's usually a red wine mixed with citrus juice and zest, a bit of cinnamon, sometimes some rum and always diabetes-inducing amounts of sugar.

Spanish Wine Classification

All of Spain's autonomous communities, with the small exceptions of Asturias and Cantabria, are home to recognised wine-growing areas. With so many areas to choose from, and with most Spanish wines labelled primarily according to region or classificatory status rather than grape variety, a little background knowledge can go a long way.

Spanish wine is subject to a complicated system of wine classification with a range of designations marked on the bottle. These range from the straightforward *vino de mesa* (table wine) to *vino de la tierra,* which is a wine from an officially recognised wine-making area. If an area meets certain strict standards for a given period and covering all aspects of planting, cultivating and ageing, it receives Denominación de Origen (DO; Denomination of Origin) status. There are currently over 60 DO-recognised wine-producing areas in Spain.

An outstanding wine region gets the much-coveted Denominación de Origen Calificada (DOC), a controversial classification that some in the industry argue should apply only to specific wines, rather than every wine from within a particular region. At present, the only DOC wines come from La Rioja in northern Spain and the small Priorat area (see the boxed text, p349) in Catalonia.

Other important indications of quality depend on the length of time a wine has been aged, especially if in oak barrels. The best wines are often, therefore, marked with the designation *'crianza'* (aged for one year in oak barrels), *'reserva'* (two years ageing, at least one of which is in oak barrels) and *'gran reserva'* (two years in oak and three in the bottle).

Wine production in Spain has a long history, having first been introduced into Andalucía by the Phoenicians, possibly as early as 1100 BC.

WINE

Spain's Passions

The clichés of Spain present the country as a land of flamenco dancers, bullfighters and zany artists, but in reality this image is pretty far off the mark. Flamenco music, it is true to say, is a growing power in Spanish and world music, but you're just as likely to hear American or English music playing on the radio. Bullfighting doesn't even register with many Spaniards and the real sport of choice is football. And as for the art, well the arty days of the *movida* (late-night bar and club scene) of the late '70s are long gone and a crashing economy has meant a probable end to the construction of daring, but expensive, art galleries such as Bilbao's Guggenheim.

Here we examine a few of Spain's passions and clichés.

Football

Fútbol seems to be many a Spaniard's prime preoccupation. Hundreds of thousands of fans attend the games in the *primera división* (first division) of the *liga* (league) every weekend from September to May, with millions more following the games on TV.

Spanish football fans thought the world couldn't get any better when they won the European Cup against Germany in 2008, the first time Spain had managed this since beating Russia in the 1964 tournament. However, the world did get better and all Spaniards went into a state of delirium when for the first time the national team won the World Cup against the Netherlands in 2010. So big an event was this that many commentators speculated on how it would help lift the country out of its recent depression or even that the rush of pride in being Spanish would do away with old regional differences. But, on the same weekend of the finals, a million people gathered in Barcelona calling for greater autonomy for Catalonia. It's going to take more than football to cure Spain.

Almost any *primera división* match is worth attending, if only to experience the Spanish crowd. Those matches involving eternal rivals Real Madrid and FC Barcelona stir even greater passions. These two clubs have something approaching a monopoly on the silverware: between them they have carried off the league title 51 times (Real Madrid has won 31 times), but in the past couple of years FC Barcelona have had the upper hand winning La Liga in both 2009 and 2010. In 2009 FC Barcelona became the first team ever to win all six major football titles open to them (La Liga, Copa del Rey, Supercopa de España, Champions League, UEFA Super Cup and the FIFA Club World Cup).

Other leading football clubs include Valencia, Athletic Bilbao, Deportivo La Coruña, Real Betis (of Seville), Málaga and Real Sociedad of San Sebastián.

Bullfighting

An epic drama of blood and sand or a cruel blood 'sport' that has no place in modern Spain? This most enduring and controversial of Spanish traditions is all this and more, at once compelling theatre and an an-

REAL MADRID

Real Madrid was voted the most successful football club of the 20th century by FIFA. It is also the second-richest club in the world (after Manchester United) and has an estimated worldwide fan base of 283 million.

cient ritual that sees 40,000 bulls killed in around 1000 fights every year in Spain. Perhaps it was best summed up by Ernest Hemingway – a bullfighting aficionado – who described it as a 'wonderful nightmare'.

La lidia, as bullfighting is known, took off in the mid-18th century. King Carlos III stopped it temporarily late in the century, but his successors dropped the ban. By the mid-19th century, breeders were creating the first reliable breeds of *toro bravo* (fighting bull), and a bullfighting school had been launched in Seville.

The bullfighting season begins in the first week of February with the fiestas of Valdemorillo and Ajalvir, near Madrid, to mark the feast day of San Blas. All over the country, but especially in the two Castillas and Andalucía, *corridas* (bullfights) and *encierros* (running of the bulls through town), as in Pamplona, are part of town festivals.

The matador is the star of the team. Above all it is his fancy footwork, skill and bravery before the bull that has the crowd in raptures, or in rage, depending on his (or very occasionally her) performance.

A complex series of events takes place in each clash, which can last from about 20 to 30 minutes. *Peones* (the matadors' 'footmen' whose job it is to test the strength of the bull) dart about with grand capes in front of the bull; horseback *picadores* (horsemen) drive lances into the bull's withers and *banderilleros* (flagmen) charge headlong at the bull in an attempt to stab its neck. Finally, the matador kills the bull, unless the bull has managed to put him out of action, as sometimes happens.

The most extraordinary matador of the moment is Madrid's José Tomás who, at the fiestas of San Isidro in Madrid on 5 June 2008 (after five years in retirement), cut four bulls' ears (the cutting off of an ear, or in rare cases both ears, of the dead bull is a mark of admiration) for his performance – something that hadn't been seen for decades. Says the austere Tomás: 'Living without bullfighting isn't living.' Two weeks later, in another epic afternoon, bulls gored him severely in the thighs three times. After recovering from his injuries he once again returned to the ring and continued to dazzle audiences, but in April 2010, during a fight in Mexico, he was severely injured after being gored in the groin. At the time of writing he is still recovering.

Other great fighters include El Cordobés, El Juli, Manuel Jesú (El Cid) and Miguel Ángel Perera.

La lidia is about many things – death, bravery, performance. No doubt the fight is bloody and cruel, but aficionados say the bull is better off dying at the hands of a matador than in the *matadero* (abattoir). To witness it is not necessarily to approve of it, but might give an insight into the tradition and thinking behind *la lidia*.

The popular image of Spain would have us all believe that every Spaniard is a die-hard *la lidia* fan, but this couldn't be any further from

The Asociación para la Defensa de los Derechos del Animal (ADDA; www.addaong.org) is a Spanish animal-rights and antibullfighting organisation. Other antibullfighting organisations are the World Society for the Protection of Animals (WSPA; www.wspa.org.uk) and People for the Ethical Treatment of Animals (PETA; www.peta.org).

GREAT ANGLO-AMERICAN BULLFIGHTERS

Ernest Hemingway loved watching the bullfight, but some of his countrymen preferred action to observation. Sidney Franklin was the first English-speaking *torero* (bullfighter) to take the alternative, in 1945 in Madrid's Las Ventas, one of the largest rings in the bullfighting world. He was followed by Californian John Fulton (a painter and poet) in 1967. Best of all was Arizona-born Robert Ryan. Now retired, he is a man of many facets – writer, poet, painter, sculptor and photographer. Englishman Henry Higgins, known in Spain as Enrique Cañadas, something of an adventurer and pilot, was also keen to take to the ring, while his countryman, Mancunian Frank Evans (known as 'El Inglés'), only retired in 2005.

Another great love of the Spanish is the cinema. Though state aid is limited and Spanish films only attract around 15% of Spanish audiences, the industry has evolved in leaps and bounds recently with Spanish cinema becoming a staple of art-house cinemas the world over. Much of this success can be put down to one man: Pedro Almodóvar (b 1949). The Castilian director with the wild shock of hair, whose personal, camp cinema was born in the heady days of the Madrid *movida* (the late-night bar and club scene) in the years after Franco's death, is inimitable.

Almodóvar's first films were all silent short films made on a hand-held Super 8 and containing overtly sexual narratives. In 1978 he made his first full-length (though still silent) Super-8 film, *Folle, Folle, Fólleme, Tim* (Fuck me, Fuck me, Fuck me, Tim), a magazine style melodrama. His first feature film, made in 1980, was *Pepi, Luci, Bom y Otras Chicas del Montón,* which had such a low budget he relied on a team of volunteers at weekends.

In 2000 Almodóvar became one of the few Spaniards to take an Oscar, in this case for possibly his best movie, *Todo Sobre Mi Madre* (All About My Mother; 1999). Other Almodóvar classics include *Hable Con Ella* (Talk to Her), which revolves around two men who become friends whilst caring for a comatose woman they both love, *Volver* (Return; 2006), which is a typically unhinged tale partly set (as usual) in Madrid, in which Almodóvar lines up a series of his favourite actresses (including Carmen Maura and Penélope Cruz) to rattle the skeletons in a village family's closet. His latest release, *Los Abrazos Rotos* (Broken Embraces) is the tragic story of a former film director. At the time of writing filming was underway on his next production, *La Piel que Habito* (The Skin I Live In), due for release in spring 2011.

the truth. While bullfighting remains strong in some parts of the country, notably Andalucía, in other areas such as Galicia, Cantabria and other northern regions it's never really been a part of local culture. Few opinion polls have been conducted to measure the strength of support for bullfighting in Spain, but in 2006 a Gallup poll revealed that 72% expressed 'no interest' in bullfighting and just over 7% 'a lot of interest'. The poll also showed that support levels were much higher amongst older generations of Spanish than younger.

Today there is a large and growing antibullfighting movement in Spain. The current government has banned children under the age of 14 from attending bullfights and state-run TV has stopped broadcasting live coverage of bullfights (although the TVE state-run channel does still broadcast Tendido Cero, a weekly magazine-style bullfighting program, and various private broadcasters continue to screen live fights). The bullfighting world was given a further blow when in 2010 the Catalan government banned bullfighting in Catalonia altogether. On the flip side, though, bullfighting does still have some fans in high places. In 2008 around €600 million of public money, including some from European funds, was given to the bullfight breeding industry and King Juan Carlos is on record as saying that 'The day the EU bans bullfighting is the day Spain leaves the EU'.

Painting

Humans have been creating images in Spain for at least as long as 14,500 years, as the cave paintings in Altamira attest, and Spain now has an artistic legacy almost unmatched anywhere else.

With such a distinguished artistic tradition there are many candidates for the title of 'master', but there are six whose talents shine just a little brighter than the others and it is they that we profile here.

Manolete (The Passion Within; completed in 2007, general release 2010), starring Adrien Brody and Penélope Cruz, is a beautifully filmed portrayal of the tragic last days of legendary matador Manuel Laureano Rodríguez Sánchez (Manolete). Anti-bullfight groups have called for a boycott of the film.

VELÁZQUEZ

The Golden Century – Velázquez & Friends

The star of the 17th-century art scene, which became known as an artistic Golden Age, was the genius court painter from Seville, Diego Rodríguez de Silva Velázquez (1599–1660). With him any trace of the idealised stiffness that characterised the previous century's spiritless mannerism fell by the wayside. Realism became the key, and the majesty of his royal subjects springs from his capacity to capture the essence of the person, king or *infanta* (princess), and the detail of their finery. His masterpieces include *Las Meninas* (Maids of Honour) and *La Rendición de Breda* (Surrender of Breda), both in the Museo del Prado.

Another shining light of the period was Francisco de Zurbarán (1598–1664), who is best remembered for the startling clarity and light in his portraits of monks. Despite his talent Zurbarán fell on hard times in the 1640s and was compelled by the plague to flee Seville. He died in poverty in Madrid.

Goya & the 19th Century

Francisco José de Goya y Lucientes (1746–1828), a provincial hick from Fuendetodos in Aragón, went to Madrid to work as a cartoonist in the Real Fábrica de Tapices. In 1792 an illness left him deaf and it was this condition, many critics speculate, that was responsible for his wild and merciless style that would become increasingly unshackled from convention. Despite this, by 1799 he was Carlos IV's court painter.

Several distinct series and individual paintings mark the progress of his life and work. At the end of the 18th century he painted such enigmatic masterpieces as *La Maja Vestida* and *La Maja Desnuda,* identical portraits of an unknown woman but for the lack of clothes in the latter. At about the same time he did *Los Caprichos,* a series of 80 etchings lambasting the follies of court life and ignorant clergy.

The arrival of the French and the war in 1808 profoundly affected his work. He makes unforgiving portrayals of the brutality of war in *El Dos de Mayo* (Second of May) and, more dramatically, *El Tres de Mayo* (Third of May). The latter depicts the execution of Madrid rebels by French troops and both hang in the Museo del Prado.

Picasso, Dalí & the Others – the Shock of the New

Like a thunderclap came the genius of the mischievous *malagueño* (person from Málaga), Pablo Ruiz Picasso (1881–1973). A child when he moved with his family to Barcelona, Picasso was formed in an atmosphere laden with the avant-garde freedom of Modernisme.

Picasso must have been one of the most restless artists of all time. His work underwent repeated revolutions as he passed from one creative phase to another. From his gloomy Blue Period, through the brighter Pink Period and on to cubism – in which he was accompanied

Velázquez so much wanted to be made a Knight of Santiago that in *Las Meninas* he cheekily portrayed himself with the cross of Santiago on his vest, long before his wish was finally fulfilled.

GOYA'S BLACK PAINTINGS

Goya saved his most confronting paintings to the end. After he retired to the Quinta del Sordo (Deaf Man's House) in Madrid, he created his nightmarish *Pinturas Negras* (Black Paintings), which now hang in the Museo del Prado in Madrid. The *Saturno Devorando a Su Hijo* (Saturn Devouring His Son) captures the essence of Goya's genius and *La Romería de San Isidro* and *El Akelarre (El Gran Cabrón)* are profoundly unsettling. The former evokes a writhing mass of tortured humanity, while the latter are dominated by the compelling individual faces of the condemned souls of Goya's creation.

It was market day in the small Basque town of Guernica on the morning of 26 April 1937. At the same time that market-goers poured into the town from outlying villages a squadron of aeroplanes was also making its way to Guernica. Over the next few hours Hitler's Condor Legion, in agreement with Franco, dropped hundreds of bombs on the town and killed some 1645 civilians.

Shortly afterwards, Picasso, who was based in Paris at the time, was commissioned by the Republican government of Madrid to produce the paintings for the Spanish contribution to the Paris Exposition Universelle. As news of the bombings filtered out of Spain, Picasso committed his anger to canvas: it was a poignant memorial to the first use of airborne military hardware to devastating effect. You can see *Guernica* in Madrid's Centro de Arte Reina Sofía.

by Madrid's Juan Gris (1887–1927) – Picasso was nothing if not a surprise package.

By the mid-1920s he was dabbling with surrealism. His best-known work is *Guernica,* a complex canvas portraying the horror of war. Picasso consistently cranked out paintings, sculptures, ceramics and etchings until the day he died. A good selection of his early work can be viewed in Barcelona's Museu Picasso. Other of his works are scattered about different galleries, notably Madrid's Centro de Arte Reina Sofía.

Separated from Picasso by barely a generation, two other artists reinforced the Catalan contingent in the vanguard of 20th-century art: Dalí and Miró. Although he started off dabbling in cubism, Salvador Dalí (1904–89) became more readily identified with the surrealists. This complex character's 'hand-painted dream photographs', as he called them, are virtuoso executions brimming with fine detail and nightmare images dragged up from a feverish and Freud-fed imagination. Preoccupied with Picasso's fame, Dalí built himself a reputation as an outrageous showman and shameless self-promoter. The single best display of his work can be seen at the Teatre-Museu Dalí in Figueres.

Slower to find his feet, Barcelona-born Joan Miró (1893–1983) developed a joyous and almost childlike style that earned him the epithet 'the most surrealist of us all' from the French writer André Breton. His later period is his best known, characterised by the simple use of bright colours and forms in combinations of symbols that represented women, birds (the link between earth and the heavens), stars (the unattainable heavenly world, source of imagination) and a sort of net, which entraps all these levels of the cosmos. Galleries of his work adorn Barcelona and Palma de Mallorca.

Reach into the tortured mind of one of Spain's greatest artists with the help of Robert Hughes' riveting work *Goya.*

GOYA

Spain's Best Contemporary Artists

The death of Franco acted as a catalyst for the Spanish art movement. New talent sprang up, and galleries enthusiastically took on anything revolutionary, contrary or cheeky. The 1970s and 1980s were a time of almost childish self-indulgence. Things have since calmed down but there is still much activity.

The Basques Eduardo Chillida (1924–2002) and Jorge Oteiza (1908–2003) were two of Spain's leading modern sculptors, active throughout their lives almost to the end of their days.

Joan Hernández Pijuan (1931–2005) was one of the most important abstract painters to come out of Barcelona in the latter decades of the 20th century.

Seville's Luis Gordillo (b 1934) started his artistic career with surrealism, from where he branched out into pop art and photography. His later work in particular features the serialisation of different versions of the same image.

Antonio López (b 1936) is considered the father of the so-called Madrid hyperrealism. One of his grandest works is the incredibly detailed *Madrid desde Torres Blancas* (Madrid from Torres Blancas).

Mallorcan Miquel Barceló (b 1957) is one of the country's big success stories. His work is heavily expressionist, although it touches on classic themes, from self-portraiture to architectural images.

Barcelona's Susana Solano (b 1946) is a painter and above all sculptor, considered to be one of the most important at work in Spain today.

Jaume Plensa (b 1955) is possibly Spain's best contemporary sculptor and has displayed his work around the world.

Seville's Curro González (b 1960) creates big canvases full of hallucinatory figures, allegory and allusions to contemporary society. Distortion, surrealism and a good dose of irony are among his arms.

The figure of the woman lies at the heart of much of the recent work by Madrid's José Manuel Merello (b 1960), paintings full of broad sweeps of primal colour and blurred detail.

www.arteespana.com is an interesting website (in Spanish) that covers broad swathes of Spanish art history (and where you can buy art books or even models of monuments).

Flamenco

Flamenco, Spain's soul-stirring gift to the world of music, provides the ever-present soundtrack to Spanish life. The passion of flamenco is clear to anyone who has heard its melancholy strains in the background of a crowded Spanish bar or during an uplifting live performance. At the same time, flamenco can seem like an impenetrable world of knowledgeable but taciturn initiates. But love it or hate it, a flamenco performer who successfully communicates their passion will have you on the edge of your seat. The gift of sparking this kind of response is known as *duende* (spirit).

The Birth of Flamenco

Flamenco's origins have been lost to time. Some have suggested that flamenco derives from Byzantine chants used in Visigothic churches. But most musical historians speculate that it probably dates back to a fusion of songs brought to Spain by the *gitanos* (Roma people formerly known as Gypsies) with music and verses from North Africa crossing into medieval Muslim Andalucía. Flamenco as we now know it first took recognisable form in the 18th and early 19th centuries among *gitanos* in the lower Guadalquivir valley in western Andalucía. Suitably, for a place considered the cradle of the genre, the Seville, Jerez de la Frontera and Cádiz axis is still considered the flamenco heartland and it's here, purists believe, that you must go for the most authentic flamenco experience.

Flamenco – the Essential Elements

A flamenco singer is known as a *cantaor* (male) or *cantaora* (female); a dancer is a *bailaor* or *bailaora*. Most of the songs and dances are performed to a blood-rush of guitar from the *tocaor* or *tocaora* (male or female flamenco guitarist). Percussion is provided by tapping feet, clapping hands and sometimes castanets. Flamenco *coplas* (songs) come in many different types, from the anguished *soleá* or the intensely despairing *siguiriya* to the livelier *alegría* or the upbeat *bulería*. The first flamenco was *cante jondo* (deep song), an anguished instrument of expression for a group on the margins of society. *Jondura* (depth) is still the essence of pure flamenco.

The traditional flamenco costume – shawl, fan and long, frilly *bata de cola* (tail gown) for women, flat Cordoban hats and tight black trousers for men – dates from Andalucian fashions in the late 19th century.

Possibly the most important flamenco singer of all time, José Monge Cruz aka Camarón de la Isla (Shrimp of the Island) did more to popularise flamenco over the last 30 years than anyone else. Born to *gitano* (Roma people, formerly known as Gypsies) parents, Camarón started his career at a young age by singing in local bars. Eventually he met that other great of flamenco, the guitarist Paco de Lucía, with whom he recorded nine much-praised albums between 1969 and 1977. Later in his career Camarón worked with one of Paco's students, Tomatito.

Camarón was an intense introvert and hated publicity, but so extraordinary was his talent that publicity was to hound him everywhere he went and, so many say, it was eventually to lead him to an early grave in the best live fast, die young rock-star fashion. Idolised for his voice by flamenco fans across the world it was his fellow *gitanos* who really elevated him almost to the status of a god. It's said that *gitano* women would bring their children to meet him just in the hope that he would touch them and pass on some of his magic.

Eventually Camarón's life descended into a spiral of drugs and self-abuse and he died of lung cancer in 1992 at the age of just 42. It's estimated that over 100,000 people attended his funeral.

The Shrimp's best recordings include *La Leyenda del Tiempo, Soy Gitano* and *Una Leyenda Flamenca*.

The *sevillana,* a popular dance with high, twirling arm movements, is not, for purists at least, flamenco at all. Consisting of four parts, each coming to an abrupt halt, the *sevillana* is probably an Andalucian version of a Castilian dance, the *seguidilla*.

Flamenco Legends

The great singers of the 19th and early 20th centuries were Silverio Franconetti and La Niña de los Peines, from Seville, and Antonio Chacón and Manuel Torre, from Jerez de la Frontera. Torre's singing, legend has it, could drive people to rip their shirts open and upturn tables.

The dynamic dancing and wild lifestyle of Carmen Amaya (1913–63), from Barcelona, made her the *gitana* dance legend of all time. Her long-time partner Sabicas was the father of the modern solo flamenco guitar, inventing a host of now-indispensable techniques.

After a trough in the mid-20th century, when it seemed that the *tablaos* (touristy flamenco shows emphasising the sexy and the jolly) were in danger of taking over, *flamenco puro* got a new lease of life in the 1970s through singers such as Terremoto, La Paquera, Enrique Morente, Chano Lobato and, above all, El Camarón de la Isla (whose real name was José Monge Cruz) from San Fernando near Cádiz. El Camarón's incredible vocal and emotional range and his wayward lifestyle made him a legend well before his tragically early death in 1992.

Some say that Madrid-born Diego El Cigala (b 1968) is El Camarón's successor. This powerful singer's biggest hitting albums are *Lágrimas Negras* (Black Tears; 2003) and *Dos Lágrimas* (Two Tears; 2008), which mixes flamenco with Cuban influences.

Paco de Lucía, born in Algeciras in 1947, is the doyen of flamenco guitarists. So gifted is he that by the time he was 14 his teachers admitted that they had nothing left to teach him. De Lucía has transformed the flamenco guitar into an instrument of solo expression with new techniques, scales, melodies and harmonies that have gone far beyond traditional limits.

Many of the most talented flamenco stars have spent time in prison and each year Spain's penitentiary system holds the *El Concurso de Cante Flamenco del Sistema Penitenciario* (Prison Flamenco Competition).

SPAIN'S PASSIONS FLAMENCO

FLAMENCO

Flamenco Today

Rarely can flamenco have been as popular as it is today, and never so innovative. While long-established singers such as Enrique Morente (who is also an inspirational force behind flamenco's fusion with other musical styles), Carmen Linares and José Menese remain at the top of the profession, new generations continue to broaden flamenco's audience.

Universally acclaimed is José Mercé, from Jerez. Estrella Morente from Granada (Enrique's daughter) and internationally best known for being the 'voice' behind the 2006 film *Volver,* Miguel Poveda (from Barcelona) and La Tana from Seville are young singers steadily carving out niches in the first rank of performers.

Dance, always the readiest of flamenco arts to cross boundaries, has reached its most adventurous horizons in the person of Joaquin Cortés, born in Córdoba in 1969. Cortés fuses flamenco with contemporary dance, ballet and jazz in spectacular shows with music at rock-concert amplification. The most exciting younger dance talent is Farruquito (Juan Manuel Fernández Montoya), born into a legendary flamenco family in Seville in 1983.

Among guitarists, listen out for Manolo Sanlúcar from Cádiz; Tomatito from Almería; and Vicente Amigo from Córdoba and Moraíto Chico from Jerez, who both accompany today's top singers.

Seville's new Museo del Baile Flamenco trawls through flamencos past and present and, with its frequent flamenco classes, gives you the chance to perfect your *sevillana.*

Flamenco Fusion

What started with the experimentation of Paco de Lucía, has seen musicians mixing flamenco with jazz, rock, blues, rap and other genres. This 'flamenco fusion' has taken Spain by storm and presents perhaps the easiest way into flamenco for newcomers, but it sends die-hard purists into shivers of disapproval.

The seminal recording was a 1977 flamenco-folk-rock album *Veneno* (Poison) by the group of the same name, centred on Kiko Veneno and Raimundo Amador, both from Seville. Kiko remains an icon of flamenco fusion, mixing rock, blues, African and flamenco rhythms with witty lyrics focusing on snatches of everyday life. Amador later formed the group Pata Negra, which produced four fine flamenco-jazz-blues albums, before going solo.

The group Ketama, originally from Granada, has successfully mixed flamenco with African, Cuban, Brazilian and other rhythms for two decades. Cádiz's Niña Pastori arrived in the late 1990s with an edgy, urgent voice singing jazz- and Latin-influenced flamenco.

Eleven-strong Barcelona-based band Ojos de Brujo mixes flamenco with reggae, Asian and even club dance rhythms.

FLAMENCO RESOURCES

» Flama (www.guiaflama.com, in Spanish) Good for upcoming live concerts and background information.

» *Duende* (Jason Webster) The author's gripping journey through the underbelly of flamenco.

» *Camarón* (Director Jaime Chávarri; 2005) A terrific biopic of El Camarón de la Isla.

» *Bodas de Sangre* (1981) and *Flamenco* (1995) These two Carlos Saura films are flamenco classics; the former is a film version of Federico García Lorcas's dramatic play of the same name.

» Centro Andaluz de Flamenco (www.centroandaluzdeflamenco.es, in Spanish) The website of the Andalucian Centre for Flamenco.

» *Paco de Lucía Antología* – Paco de Lucía (1995)
» *Una Leyenda Flamenca* – El Camarón de la Isla (1993)
» *Cañailla* – Niña Pastori (2000)
» *Del Amanecer* – José Mercé (1999)
» *Niña de Fuego* – Concha Buika (2008)
» *Noche de Flamenco y Blues* – Raimundo Amador, BB King et al (1998)
» *Blues de la Frontera* – Pata Negra (1986)
» *Cositas Buenas* – Paco de Lucía (2004)
» *Lágrimas Negras* – Bebo Valdés and Diego El Cigala (2003)
» *Sueña La Alhambra* – Enrique Morente (2005)
» *Flamenco Chill* – Chambao (2002)
» *Malamarismo* – Mala Rodríguez (2007)

Málaga's Chambao successfully combines flamenco with electronic beats on its albums such as *Flamenco Chill* (2002) and *Pokito a Poko* (Little by Little; 2005). Their latest is 2009's *En el Fin del Mundo*.

Concha Buika, a Mallorcan of Equatorial Guinean origin, possesses a beautiful, sensual voice. Her albums *Buika* (2005) and *Mi Niña Lola* (2006) are a captivating melange of African rhythms, soul, jazz, hip hop, flamenco and more.

Probably nobody upsets the purists quite as much as Mala Rodríguez does with her socially aware combination of flamenco and rap. *Malamarismo* (2007) is a classic of her unique genre and her latest *Dirty Bailarina* (2010) looks set to repeat on her earlier successes.

Flamenco World (www.flamenco-world.com) is an online shop that stocks absolutely everything and anything flamenco based. Its website also contains numerous interviews and news features.

Seeing Flamenco

Flamenco is easiest to catch in Seville, Jerez de la Frontera, Granada and Madrid. Aside from widely advertised concerts held in large arenas, the best places for live performances are *peñas,* clubs where flamenco fans band together. The atmosphere in such places is authentic and at times very intimate and proof that flamenco feeds off an audience that knows its flamenco. Most Andalucian towns have dozens of *peñas,* and most tourist offices have lists of those open to visitors. The other, easier, option is to attend a performance at a *tablao,* which hosts regular shows put on for largely undiscriminating tourist audiences. However, don't knock these places as the quality of the flamenco in a *tablao* can be top-notch, even if the gritty atmosphere of the *peñas* is lacking.

In many towns in the south, summer *ferias* (fairs) and fiestas include flamenco performances, and some places stage special night-long flamenco festivals. The following are some of the best flamenco festivals:
» Festival Flamenco, Madrid (February)
» Festival de Jerez, Jerez de la Frontera (February to March)
» Suma Flamenca, Madrid (May)
» Festival Internacional de la Guitarra, Córdoba (June to July)
» Festival Internacional del Cante de las Minas, La Unión, Murcia (August)
» Bienal de Flamenco, Seville (September)

Cáceres (p793), Extremadura
Protected by defensive walls, the Ciudad Monumental (old town) of Cáceres has survived almost intact from its 16th-century heyda

Survival Guide

Directory A-Z

Accommodation

Spain's accommodation is generally outstanding, from small, family-run *hostales* to the old-world opulence of *paradores*.

Officially, places to stay are classified into *hoteles* (hotels; one to five stars), *hostales* (one to three stars) and *pensiones* (basically small private hotels, often family businesses in rambling apartments; one or two stars). These are the categories used by the annual *Guía Oficial de Hoteles*, sold in bookshops, which lists almost every such establishment in Spain, except for one-star *pensiones*, with approximate prices.

Checkout time is generally noon.

Reservations

Although there's generally no need to book ahead for a room in the low or shoulder seasons, booking ahead is always a good idea, if for no other reason than to avoid a wearisome search for a room. Most places will ask for a credit-card number or will hold the room for you until 6pm unless you let

them know that you'll be arriving later.

Seasons

Prices throughout this guidebook are high-season maximums. You may be pleasantly surprised if you travel at other times. What constitutes low or high season depends on where and when. Most of the year is high season in Barcelona or Madrid, especially during trade fairs that you're unlikely to be aware of. August can be dead in the cities. Winter is high season in the Pyrenees and low season in the Balearic Islands (indeed, the islands seem to shut down between November and Easter). July and August in the Balearics offer sun and fun, but finding a place to stay without booking ahead can be a pain. Weekends are high season for boutique hotels and *casas rurales*

(rural homes), but low season for business hotels (which often offer generous specials then) in Madrid and Barcelona.

Prices

Throughout this guidebook, the order of accommodation listings is by author preference, and each place to stay is accompanied by one of the following symbols (the price relates to a double room with private bathroom):

€ <€60 per double room (<€70 for Madrid and Barcelona)

€€ €60 to €120 per double room (€70 to €200 for Madrid and Barcelona)

€€€ >€120 per double room (>€200 for Madrid & Barcelona)

At the lower end of the budget category, expect dorm beds (from €17 per person) in youth hostels or private rooms with shared bathrooms in the corridor. If you're willing to pay a few euros more, there are many budget places with good, comfortable rooms and private bathrooms. In relatively untouristed or rural areas, the prices of some boutique or other hotels can sometimes drop into the budget category, especially during low season.

Spain's midrange hotels are generally excellent and you should always have your own private bathroom, and breakfast is sometimes included in the room price. Boutique hotels, including many that occupy artfully converted historical buildings, largely fall into this

---

BOOK YOUR STAY ONLINE

For more accommodation reviews by Lonely Planet authors, check out hotels.lonelyplanet.com/spain. You'll find independent reviews, as well as recommendations on the best places to stay. Best of all, you can book online.

category and are almost always excellent choices.

And a final word about terminology. A *habitación doble* (double room) is frequently just that: a room with two beds (which you can often shove together). If you want to be sure of a double bed (*cama matrimonial*), ask for it!

ACCOMMODATION TYPES

Apartments, Villas & Casas Rurales

Throughout Spain you can rent self-catering apartments and houses from one night upwards. Villas and houses are widely available on the main holiday coasts and in popular country areas.

A simple one-bedroom apartment in a coastal resort for two or three people might cost as little as €30 per night, although more often you'll be looking at nearly twice that much, and prices can jump even further in high season. More luxurious options with a swimming pool might come in at anything between €200 and €400 for four people.

Rural tourism has become immensely popular, with accommodation available in many new and often charming *casas rurales*. These are usually comfortably renovated village houses or farmhouses with a handful of rooms. They often go by other names, such as *cases de pagès* in Catalonia, *casas de aldea* in Asturias, *posadas* and *casonas* in Cantabria and so on. Some just provide rooms, while others offer meals or self-catering accommodation. Lower-end prices typically hover around €30/50 (single/double) per night, but classy boutique establishments can easily charge €100 or more for a double. Many are rented out by the week.

Agencies include the following:

Apartments-Spain (www.apartments-spain.com)

PRACTICALITIES

» **Currency**: euro

» **Weights & Measures**: metric

» **Electric Current**: 220V, 50Hz

» **Plugs**: European-style, two-pin (see p881)

» **Major newspapers**: centre-left *El País* (www.elpais.com, in Spanish); centre-right *El Mundo* (www.elmundo.es, in Spanish); right-wing *ABC* (www.abc.es, in Spanish). The widely available *International Herald Tribune* includes an eight-page supplement of articles from *El País* translated into English (www.elpais.com/misc/herald/herald.pdf).

» **Radio**: Radio Nacional de España (RNE)'s Radio 1, with general interest and current affairs programs; Radio 5, with sport and entertainment; and Radio 3 ('Radio d'Espop'). Stations covering current affairs include the left-leaning Cadena Ser, or the right-wing COPE. The most popular commercial pop and rock stations are 40 Principales, Kiss FM, Cadena 100 and Onda Cero.

» **TV**: Spain's state-run Televisión Española (TVE1 and La 2) or the independent commercial stations (Antena 3, Tele 5, Cuatro and La Sexta). Regional governments run local stations, such as Madrid's Telemadrid, Catalonia's TV-3 and Canal 33 (both in Catalan), Galicia's TVG, the Basque Country's ETB-1 and ETB-2, Valencia's Canal 9 and Andalucía's Canal Sur. Cable and satellite TV is becoming widespread.

Associació Agroturisme Balear (www.agroturismo-balear.com)

Atlas Rural (www.atlasrural.com, in Spanish)

Casas Cantabricas (www.casas.co.uk)

Cases Rurals de Catalunya (www.casesrurals.com)

Fincas 4 You (www.fincas4you.com)

Guías Casas Rurales (www.guiascasasrurales.com, in Spanish)

Holiday Serviced Apartments (www.holidayapartments.co.uk)

Owners Direct (www.ownersdirect.co.uk)

Ruralka (www.ruralka.com)

Rustic Rent (www.rusticrent.com)

Rusticae (www.rusticae.es)

Secret Destinations (www.secretdestinations.com)

Secret Places (www.secretplaces.com)

Top Rural (www.toprural.com, in Spanish)

Traum Ferienwohnungen (www.traum-ferienwohnungen.de, in German)

Villas 4 You (www.villas4you.co.uk)

Vintage (vintagetravel.co.uk)

CAMPING & CARAVAN PARKS

Spain has around 1000 officially graded *campings* (camping grounds). Some of these are well located in woodland or near beaches or rivers, but others are on the outskirts of towns or along highways. Few of them are near city centres, and camping isn't particularly convenient if you're relying on public transport. Tourist offices can always direct you to the nearest camping ground.

Camping grounds are officially rated as first class (1ªC), second class (2ªC) or third class (3ªC). There are also a few that are not officially graded, usually equivalent to third class. Facilities generally range from reasonable to very good, although any camping ground can be crowded and noisy at busy times (especially July and August). Even a third-class camping ground is likely to have hot showers, electrical hook-ups and a cafe. The best ones have heated swimming pools, supermarkets, restaurants, laundry service, children's playgrounds and tennis courts.

Camping grounds usually charge per person, per tent and per vehicle – typically €5 to €9 for each. Children usually pay a bit less than adults. Many camping grounds close from around October to Easter.

You sometimes come across a *zona de acampada* or *área de acampada*, a country camping ground with minimal facilities (maybe just tap water or a couple of barbecues), little or no supervision and little or no charge. If it's in an environmentally protected area, you may need to obtain permission from the local environmental authority to camp there.

With certain exceptions – such as many beaches and environmentally protected areas and a few municipalities that ban it – it is legal to camp outside camping grounds (but not within 1km of official ones!). Signs usually indicate where wild camping is not allowed. If in doubt you can always check with tourist offices. You'll need permission to camp on private land.

Useful websites:

Guía Camping (www. guiacampingfecc.com) Online version of the annual *Guía Camping* (€13.60), which is available in bookshops around the country.

Campinguía (www.campin guia.com) Contains comments (mostly in Spanish) and links.

Campings Online (www. campingsonline.com/espana) Booking service.

CAMAS, FONDAS & HOSPEDAJES

At the budget end of the market, places listing accommodation use all sorts of overlapping names to describe themselves. In broad terms, the cheapest are usually places just advertising *camas* (beds), *fondas* (traditionally a basic eatery and inn combined, though one of these functions is now often missing) and *casas de huéspedes* or *hospedajes* (guest houses). Most such places will be bare and basic. Bathrooms are likely to be shared, although if you're lucky you may get an in-room *lavabo* (washbasin). In winter don't hesitate to ask for extra blankets.

PENSIÓNES

A *pensión* is usually a small step up from the above types in standard and price. Some cheap establishments forget to provide soap, toilet paper or towels. Don't hesitate to ask for these necessities.

HOSTALES

Hostales are in much the same category, although a small step up again from *pensiónes*. In both cases the better ones can be bright and spotless, with rooms boasting full en suite bathroom (*baño complete*, most often with a shower (*ducha*) rather than bathtub), usually a TV and air-conditioning and/or heating.

HOTELS

The remainder of establishments call themselves *hoteles* and run the gamut of quality, from straightforward roadside places, bland but clean, through charming boutique gems and on to superluxury hotels. Even in

the cheapest hotels, rooms are likely to have an attached bathroom and there'll probably be a restaurant.

Among the more tempting hotels for those with a little fiscal room to manoeuvre are the 90 or so **Paradores** (🖉in Spain 902 547 979; 🖥 www.parador.es) a state-funded chain of hotels in often stunning locations, among them towering castles and former medieval convents. Similarly, you can find beautiful hotels in restored country homes and old city mansions, and these are not always particularly expensive. A raft of cutting-edge, hip design hotels with cool staff and a feel à la New York can be found in the big cities and major resort areas. At the top end you may pay more for a room with a view (especially sea views or with a *balcón* (balcony) and will often have the option of a suite.

Many places have rooms for three, four or more people where the per-person cost is lower than in a single or double, which is good news for families. And many hotels can also be booked online at some of the sites listed under Apartments, Villas & Casas Rurales.

MONASTERIES

An offbeat possibility is staying in a monastery. In spite of the expropriations of the 19th century and a sometimes rough run in the 20th, plenty of monastic orders have survived (albeit in diminishing numbers) across the country. Some offer rooms to outsiders – often fairly austere monks' or nuns' cells.

Monastery accommodation is generally a single-sex arrangement, and the idea in quite a few is to seek refuge from the outside world and indulge in quiet contemplation and meditation. On occasion, where the religious order continues ancient tradition by working on farmland, orchards and/or vineyards, you may have the opportunity to work too.

Useful resources:

Guía de Monasterios (www.guiasmonasterios.com, in Spanish)

Alojamientos Monásticos de España A guidebook by Javier de Sagastizabal and José Antonio Egaña to Spain's monasteries, although it's in need of an update.

REFUGIOS

Mountain shelters (refugios) for walkers and climbers are liberally scattered around most of the popular mountain areas (mainly the Pyrenees), except in Andalucía, which has only a handful. They're mostly run by mountaineering and walking organisations. Accommodation, usually bunks squeezed into a dorm, is often on a first-come, first-served basis, although for some refugios you can book ahead. In busy seasons (July and August in most areas) they can fill up quickly, and you should try to book in advance or arrive by mid-afternoon to be sure of a place. Prices per person range from nothing to €15 or more a night. Many refugios have a bar and offer meals (dinner typically costs around €8 to €12), as well as a cooking area (but not cooking equipment). Blankets are usually provided, but you'll have to bring any other bedding yourself. Bring a torch too.

The Aragonese Pyrenees are particularly well served with refugios; check out the following:

Albergues & Refugios de Aragón (www.alberguesyrefu giosdearagon.com, in Spanish) To make reservations in refugios and albergues.

Federación Aragonesa de Montañismo (FAM; ☑976 22 79 71; www.fam.es, in Spanish; 4th fl, Calle Albareda 7, Zaragoza) Provides information and a FAM card that

entitles you to substantial discounts on refugio stays.

YOUTH HOSTELS

Spain's 250 or so youth hostels – albergues juveniles, not be confused with hostales (budget hotels) – are often the cheapest places for lone travellers, but two people can usually get a double room elsewhere for a similar price.

The hostel experience in Spain varies widely. Some hostels are only moderate value, lacking in privacy, often heavily booked by school groups, and with night-time curfews and no cooking facilities (although if there is nowhere to cook there is usually a cafeteria). Others, however, are conveniently located, open 24 hours and composed mainly of double rooms or small dorms, often with a private bathroom. An increasing number have rooms adapted for people with disabilities. Some even occupy fine historic buildings.

Most Spanish youth hostels are members of the **Red Española de Albergues Juveniles** (REAJ, Spanish Youth Hostel Network; www.reaj.com), the Spanish representative of **Hostelling International** (HI; www.hihostels.com).

Most of the REAJ member hostels are also members of the youth hostel association of their region (Andalucía, Catalonia, Valencia etc). Each region usually sets its own price structure and has a central booking service where you can make reservations for most of its hostels. You can also book directly with hostels themselves. Central booking services include:

Andalucía (☑902 510 000; www.inturjoven.com, in Spanish)
Catalonia (☑93 483 83 41; www.xanascat.cat)
Valencia (☑902 225 552; www.ivaj.es in, Spanish)

Prices at youth hostels often depend on the season, and vary from about €15 to

€21 for under-26s (the lower rate is usually applied to people with ISIC cards too – see p881) and between €18 and €28 for those 26 and over. In some hostels the price includes breakfast. A few hostels require you to rent sheets (around €2 to €5 for your stay) if you don't have your own or a sleeping bag.

Most hostels require you to have a HI card or a membership card from your home country's youth hostel association. You can obtain a HI card in Spain at most hostels.

A growing number of hostel-style places not connected with HI or REAJ often have individual rooms as well the more typical dormitory options. Prices can vary greatly as, not being affiliated to any organisation, they are not subject to any pricing system. A good resource for seeking out hostels, affiliated or otherwise, is **Hostel World** (www.hostelworld.com).

Finally, you will sometimes find independent albergues offering basic dormitory accommodation for around €10 to €18, usually in villages in areas that attract plenty of Spanish walkers and climbers. These are not specifically youth hostels – although the clientele tends to be under 35. They're a kind of halfway house between a youth hostel and a refugio. Some will rent you sheets for a couple of euros if you need them.

Business Hours

Reviews in this guidebook won't list business hours unless they differ from the following standards. These standard opening hours are for high season only and tend to decrease outside that time. See regional chapters for their respective high-season periods.

Banks: 8.30am-2pm Mon-Fri; some also open 4-7pm Thu and 9am-1pm Sat

Central Post Offices: 8.30am-9.30pm Mon-Fri, 8.30am-2pm Sat

Nightclubs: midnight or 1am to 5am or 6am

Restaurants: lunch: 1-4pm, dinner: 8.30pm-midnight or later

Shops: 10am-2pm & 4.30-7.30pm or 5-8pm; big supermarkets and department stores generally open 10am-10pm Mon-Sat

Children

Spain is a child- or family-friendly destination and there are loads of attractions designed specifically with children in mind, such as zoos and theme parks, as well as beaches. They're all over the country, but in this guidebook we've highlighted these especially in Madrid (see the boxed text, p86), Barcelona (see the boxed text, p272), Valencia (see the boxed text, p547), Seville (see the boxed text, p671), Córdoba (see the boxed text, p742) and Granada (see the boxed text, p756). We also cover attractions for children in the Basque Country, Navarra and La Rioja in the boxed text, p420.

Other places the kids will love include Catalonia's Port Aventura (p356), Terra Mítica in Benidorm (p580), and Mini Hollywood (p780) and other Western movie sets in the Almería desert.

But there are also plenty of 'adult' sights that seem designed to capture a child's imagination, among them castles, horse shows, fiestas and *ferias* (fairs), interactive museums, flamenco shows and even the Semana Santa (Holy Week) processions to name just a few. Numerous major sights (such as the Alhambra and most art galleries) also have guidebooks aimed specifically at children.

Practicalities

Most hotels (but rarely *hostales* and other budget places) have cots for small children, although most only have a handful, so reserve one when reserving your room. In top-end hotels you can sometimes arrange for childcare and in some places child-minding agencies cater to temporary visitors.

You cannot rely on restaurants having high chairs, although many do. Very few have nappy-changing facilities. That said, few Spanish restaurants will turn up their noses to families and children.

You can hire car seats for infants and children from most car-rental firms, but you should always book them in advance.

Discounts are available for children (usually under 12) on public transport and for admission to sights. Those under four generally go free.

You can buy baby formula in powder or liquid form, as well as sterilising solutions such as Milton, at *farmacias* (pharmacies). Disposable nappies (diapers) are widely available at supermarkets and *farmacias*. Fresh cow's milk is sold in cartons and plastic bottles in supermarkets in big cities, but can be hard to find in small towns, where UHT is often the only option.

Throughout the book, we have added a child-friendly icon (👶) to sights and sleeping options that seem to be particularly appropriate for children or go out of their way to welcome kids. This does not imply that other places in the book are not child-friendly. As most restaurants are child-friendly but few make any special effort to, say, cater for infants, we have not used such icons there.

For further information, see Lonely Planet's *Travel with Children* or visit the websites www.travelwith yourkids.com and www.familytravelnetwork.com.

TIPS FOR TRAVELLING WITH CHILDREN

Some of our authors have travelled throughout Spain with their children. Here are a few of their tips:

» Expect your children to be kissed, offered sweets, have their cheeks pinched and their hair ruffled (especially if it's anything lighter than black) at least once a day.

» Always ask for extra tapas in bars, such as olives or raw-cut carrots.

» Adjust your children to Spanish time (ie late nights) as quickly as you can – otherwise they'll miss half of what's worth seeing.

» Pray for the day when all bars and restaurants are made nonsmoking – it's on its way and may even have begun by the time you read this.

» Unlike in the US, crayons and paper are rarely given out in restaurants – bring your own.

» If you're willing to let your child share your bed you won't incur a supplement. Extra beds usually (though not always) incur a €20 to €30 charge.

» Always ask the local tourist office for the nearest children's playgrounds.

Customs Regulations

Duty-free allowances for travellers entering Spain from outside the EU include 2L of wine (or 1L of wine and 1L of spirits), and 200 cigarettes or 50 cigars or 250g of tobacco.

There are no duty-free allowances for travel between EU countries but equally no restrictions on the import of duty-paid items into Spain from other EU countries for personal use. You *can* buy VAT-free articles at airport shops when travelling between EU countries.

Discount Cards

At museums, never hesitate to ask if there are discounts for students, young people, children, families or seniors.

Senior Cards Reduced prices for people over 60, 63 or 65 (depending on the place) at various museums and attractions (sometimes restricted to EU citizens only) and occasionally on transport.

Student Cards Discounts (usually half the normal fee) for students. You will need some kind of identification (eg an International Student Identity Card; www.isic.org) to prove student status. Not accepted everywhere.

Youth Card Travel, sights and youth hostel discounts with the Euro<26 (www.euro26.org) card (known as Carnet Joven in Spain). The International Youth Travel Card (IYTC; www.istc.org) offers similar benefits.

Electricity

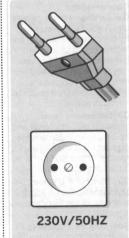

230V/50HZ

240V/50HZ

Electrical plugs in Spain can also be round, but will always have two round pins. The bottom graph is for Gibraltar (p718).

Embassies & Consulates

The embassies are located in Madrid. Some countries

also maintain consulates in major cities, particularly in Barcelona. Embassies and consulates include:

Australia Madrid (📞91 353 66 00; www.spain.embassy. gov.au; 24th fl, Paseo de la Castellana 259D); Barcelona (📞93 490 90 13; 1st fl, Plaça de Galla Placidia 1)

Canada Madrid (📞91 382 84 00; www.espana.gc.ca; Torre Espacio, Paseo de la Castellana 259D); Barcelona (📞93 204 27 00; Carrer d'Elisenda de Pinós 10); Málaga (📞95 222 33 46; Plaza de la Malagueta 2)

France Madrid (📞91 423 89 00; www.ambafrance-es.org; Calle de Salustiano Olózaga 9); Barcelona (📞93 270 30 00; www.consulfrance-barcelone. org; Ronda de l'Universitat 22B) Further consulates in Bilbao and Seville.

Germany Madrid (📞91 557 90 00; www.madrid.diplo.de; Calle de Fortuny 8); Barcelona (📞93 292 10 00; www. barcelona.diplo.de; Passeig de Gràcia 111)

Ireland Madrid (📞91 436 40 93; www.embassyofireland. es; Paseo de la Castellana 46); Barcelona (📞93 491 50 21; Gran Via de Carles III 94)

Japan (📞91 590 76 00; www. es.emb-japan.go.jp; Calle de Serrano 109, Madrid)

Morocco Madrid (📞91 563 10 90; www.embajada-marrue cos.es; Calle de Serrano 179); Barcelona (📞93 289 25 30; Calle Bejar 91) Further consulates-general in Algeciras, Almería, Bilbao, Seville, Tarragona and Valencia.

Netherlands Madrid (📞91 353 75 00; www.embajada paisesbajos.es; Torre Espacio, Paseo de la Castellana 259D; Avenida del Comandante Franco 32); Barcelona (📞93 363 54 20; Avinguda Diagonal 601) Further consulates in Palma de Mallorca, Seville and Torremolinos.

New Zealand (📞91 523 02 26; www.nzembassy.com; Calle del Pinar 7, Madrid)

UK Madrid (📞91 714 63 00; www.ukinspain.com; Torre

Espacio, Paseo de la Castellana 259D); Barcelona (☎93 366 62 00; Avinguda Diagonal 477); Palma de Mallorca (☎971 71 24 45; Carrer del Convent dels Caputxins 4, Edifici B) Further consulates in Alicante, Bilbao, Ibiza and Málaga.

USA Madrid (☎91 587 22 00; www.embusa.es; Calle de Serrano 75); Barcelona (☎93 280 22 27; Passeig de la Reina Elisenda de Montcada 23-25; FGC Reina Elisenda) Consular agencies in A Coruña, Fuengirola, Palma de Mallorca, Sevilla and Valencia.

Gay & Lesbian Travellers

Homosexuality is legal in Spain and the age of consent is 13, as for heterosexuals. In 2005 the Socialist president, José Luis Rodríguez Zapatero, gave the country's conservative Catholic foundations a shake with the legalisation of same-sex marriages in Spain.

Lesbians and gay men generally keep a fairly low profile, but are quite open in the cities. Madrid (see the boxed text, p89), Barcelona (see the boxed text, p282), Sitges, Torremolinos and Ibiza have particularly lively scenes. Sitges is a major destination on the international gay party circuit; gays take a leading role in the wild Carnaval there in February/ March. As well, there are gay parades, marches and events in several cities on and around the last Saturday in June, when Madrid's gay and lesbian pride march takes place (p86).

Useful Resources

In addition to the following resources, Barcelona's tourist board publishes *Barcelona – The Official Gay and Lesbian Tourist Guide* biannually, while Madrid's tourist office has a useful 'Gay & Lesbian Madrid' section on the front page of its website (www.esmadrid.com).

Chueca (www.chueca.com in Spanish) Forums, news and reviews

Coordinadora Gai-Lesbiana (www.cogailes. org) A good site presented by Barcelona's main gay and lesbian organisation, with nationwide links. Here you can zero in on information ranging from bar, sauna and hotel listings through to contacts pages.

GayBarcelona (www. gaybarcelona.com) News and views and an extensive listings section covering bars, saunas, shops and more in Barcelona and Sitges.

Gay Madrid 4 U (www. gaymadrid4u.com) A good overview of gay bars and nightclubs.

Guía Gay de España (guia. universogay.com in Spanish) Countrywide listings.

LesboNet (www.lesbonet. org, in Spanish) A lesbian site with contacts, forums and listings.

Night Tours.com (www. nighttours.com/madrid/) A reasonably good guide to gay nightlife and other attractions in Madrid.

Orgullo Gay (www.orgullogay .org, in Spanish) Website for the gay and lesbian pride march and links to gay organisations across the country.

Shangay (www.shangay.com, in Spanish) For news, upcoming events, reviews and contacts. It also publishes *Shanguide*, a Madrid-centric biweekly magazine jammed with listings (including saunas and hardcore clubs) and contact ads. Its companion publication *Shangay Express* is better for articles with a handful of listings and ads. They're available in gay bookshops and gay and gay-friendly bars.

Organisations

Casal Lambda (☎93 319 55 50; www.lambdaweb.org; Carrer de Verdaguer i Callis 10). A gay and lesbian social,

cultural and information centre in Barcelona.

Colectivo de Gais y Lesbianas de Madrid (☎91 522 45 17, 91 523 00 70; www. cogam.es; Calle de la Puebla 9, Madrid) Has an information office, social centre, and runs an information line (☎91 523 00 70; ☺5-9pm Mon-Fri).

Coordinadora Gai-Lesbiana (☎93 298 00 29; www.cogailes.org; Carrer de Violant d'Hongria 156, Madrid). Barcelona's main coordinating body for gay and lesbian groups. It also runs an information line, the Línia Rosa (☎900 60 16 01).

Federación Estatal de Lesbianas, Gays, Transexuales & Bisexuales (Felgt; ☎91 360 46 05; www.felgt.org; 1st fl, Calle de las Infantas 40, Madrid) A national advocacy group that played a leading role in lobbying for the legalisation of gay marriages.

Fundación Triángulo (☎91 593 05 40; www.fundacion triangulo.es; 1st fl, Calle de Melendez Valdés 52, Madrid) Another source of information on gay issues in Madrid; it has a separate information line, Información LesGai (☎91 44 66 394).

Health

Spain has an excellent health-care system.

Availability & Cost of Health Care

If you need an ambulance, call ☎061. For emergency treatment, go straight to the *urgencias* (casualty) section of the nearest hospital.

Farmacias offer valuable advice and sell over-the-counter medication. In Spain, a system of *farmacias de guardia* (duty pharmacies) operates so that each district has one open all the time. When a pharmacy is closed, it posts the name of the nearest open one on the door.

Medical costs are lower in Spain than many other European countries, but can still mount quickly if you are uninsured. Costs if you attend casualty range from nothing in some regions to around €80.

Altitude Sickness

If you're hiking at altitude, altitude sickness may be a risk. Lack of oxygen at high altitudes (over 2500m) affects most people to some extent. Symptoms of Acute Mountain Sickness (AMS) usually develop during the first 24 hours at altitude but may be delayed up to three weeks. Mild symptoms include headache, lethargy, dizziness, difficulty sleeping and loss of appetite. AMS may become more severe without warning and can be fatal. Severe symptoms include breathlessness, a dry, irritative cough (which may progress to the production of pink, frothy sputum), severe headache, lack of coordination and balance, confusion, irrational behaviour, vomiting, drowsiness and unconsciousness. There is no hard-and-fast rule as to what is too high: AMS has been fatal at 3000m, although 3500m to 4500m is the usual range.

Treat mild symptoms by resting at the same altitude until recovery, usually for a day or two. Paracetamol or aspirin can be taken for headaches. If symptoms persist or become worse immediate descent is necessary; even 500m can help. Drug treatments should never be used to avoid descent or to enable further ascent.

Hypothermia

The weather in Spain's mountains can be extremely changeable at any time of year. Proper preparation will reduce the risks of getting hypothermia: always carry waterproof garments and warm layers, and inform others of your route.

Hypothermia starts with shivering, loss of judgment and clumsiness. Unless rewarming occurs, the sufferer deteriorates into apathy, confusion and coma. Prevent further heat loss by seeking shelter, warm dry clothing, hot sweet drinks and shared body warmth.

Bites & Stings

Bees and wasps only cause real problems to those with a severe allergy (anaphylaxis). If you have a severe allergy to bee or wasp stings, carry an 'epipen' or similar adrenaline injection.

Other nasty insects to be wary of are the hairy reddish-brown caterpillars of the pine processionary moth (touching the caterpillars' hairs sets off a severely irritating allergic skin reaction) and some Spanish centipedes have a very nasty but nonfatal sting. Scorpions are found in Spain and their sting can be distressingly painful, but are not considered fatal.

Jellyfish, which have stinging tentacles, are an increasing problem at beaches along the Mediterranean coastline.

The only venomous snake that is even relatively common in Spain is Lataste's viper. It has a triangular-shaped head, grows up to 75cm long, and is grey with a zigzag pattern. It lives in dry, rocky areas, away from humans. Its bite can be fatal and needs to be treated with a serum, which state clinics in major towns keep in stock.

Water

Tap water is generally safe to drink in Spain. If you are in any doubt, ask ¿Es potable el agua (de grifo)? (Is the (tap) water drinkable?). Do not drink water from rivers or lakes as it may contain bacteria or viruses that can cause diarrhoea or vomiting.

Insurance

A travel-insurance policy to cover theft, loss, medical problems and cancellation or delays to your travel arrangements is a good idea. Paying for your ticket with a credit card can often provide limited travel-accident insurance and you may be able to reclaim the payment if the operator doesn't deliver. Worldwide travel insurance is available at lonelyplanet. com/travel_services. You can buy, extend and claim online anytime – even if you're on the road.

For details of car insurance, see p897.

Internet Access

Wi-fi Increasingly available at most hotels and in some cafes, restaurants and airports; generally (but not always) free. Connection speed often varies from room to room in hotels, so always ask when you check in. Hotels offering wi-fi are indicated throughout this book with an icon (🛜). If they instead have a public-access computer terminal, the icon is @.

Internet Cafes Good cyber-cafes that last the distance are increasingly hard to find; ask at the local tourist office. Prices per hour range from €1.50 to €3.

Language Courses

Among the more popular places to learn Spanish are Barcelona (p269), Granada (p755), Madrid (p83), Salamanca (p136) and Seville (p670). In these places and elsewhere, a number of Spanish universities offer good-value language courses.

The **Escuela Oficial de Idiomas** (EOI; www.eeooiinet. com in Spanish) is a nationwide language institution where you can learn Spanish and other local languages. Classes can be large and busy but are generally fairly cheap. There are branches in many major cities. On the website's opening page, hit 'Centros' under 'Comunidad' and then 'Centros en la Red' to get to a list of schools.

Private language schools as well as universities cater for a wide range of levels, course lengths, times of year, intensity and special requirements. Many courses have a cultural component as well as language. University courses often last a semester, although some are as short as two weeks or as long as a year. Private colleges can be more flexible. One with a good reputation is **Don Quijote** (www.donquijote .com), with branches in Barcelona, Granada, Madrid, Salamanca and Valencia.

It's also worth finding out whether your course will lead to any formal certificate of competence. The Diploma de Español como Lengua Extranjera (DELE) is recognised by Spain's Ministry of Education and Science.

Legal Matters

If you're arrested you will be allotted the free services of an *abogado de oficio* (duty solicitor), who may speak only Spanish. You're also entitled to make a phone call. If you use this to contact your embassy or consulate, the staff will probably be able to do no more than refer you to a lawyer who speaks your language. If you end up in court, the authorities are obliged to provide a translator.

In theory, you are supposed to have your national ID card or passport with you at all times. If asked for it by the police, you are supposed to be able to produce it on the spot. In practice it is rarely an issue and many people choose to leave passports in hotel safes.

The Policía Local or Policía Municipal operates at a local level and deals with such issues as traffic infringements and minor crime. The **Policía Nacional** (☑091) is the state police force, dealing with major crime and operating primarily in the cities. The military-linked Guardia Civil (created in the 19th century to deal with banditry) is largely responsible for highway patrols, borders, security, major crime and terrorism. Several regions have their own police forces, such as the Mossos d'Esquadra in Catalonia and the Ertaintxa in the Basque Country.

Other legal issues include the following:

Age of Consent 13 years for both heterosexual and homosexual relations. Note that there are limitations on sexual relations between adults and minors, and the age of consent for young teenagers is understood as consent between two minors. Travellers should note that they can be prosecuted under the laws of their home country regarding age of consent, even when abroad.

Drugs Cannabis is legal but only for personal use and in very small quantities. Public consumption of any drug is illegal. Travellers entering Spain from Morocco should be prepared for drug searches, especially if you have a vehicle.

Legal Voting Age: 18
Legal Driving Age: 18
Legal Drinking Age: 18

Maps
Small-Scale Maps

Some of the best maps for travellers are by Michelin, which produces the 1:1,000,000 *Spain Portugal* map and six 1:400,000 regional maps covering the whole country. These are all pretty accurate and are updated regularly, even down to the state of minor country roads. Also good are the GeoCenter maps published by Germany's RV Verlag.

Probably the best physical map of Spain is *Península Ibérica, Baleares y Canarias* published by the **Centro Nacional de Información Geográfica** (CNIG, www.cnig. es), the publishing arm of the **Instituto Geográfico Nacional** (IGN, www.ign.es). Ask for it in good bookshops.

Walking Maps

Useful for hiking and exploring some areas (particularly in the Pyrenees) are Editorial Alpina's *Guía Cartográfica* and *Guía Excursionista y Turística* series. The series combines information booklets in Spanish (and sometimes Catalan) with detailed maps at scales ranging from 1:25,000 to 1:50,000. They are an indispensable hikers' tool but have their inaccuracies. The Institut Cartogràfic de Catalunya puts out some decent maps for hiking in the Catalan Pyrenees that are often better than their Editorial Alpina counterparts. Remember that for hiking only maps scaled at 1:25,000 are seriously useful. The CNIG also covers most of the country in 1:25,000 sheets.

You can often pick up Editorial Alpina publications and CNIG maps at bookshops near trekking areas, and at specialist bookshops such as these:

Altaïr (☑93 342 71 71; www. altair.es; Gran Via de les Corts Catalanes 616, Barcelona)

La Tienda Verde (☑91 535 38 10; tiendaverde.es; Calle Maudes 23, Madrid)

Librería Desnivel (☑902 248 848; www.libreriadesnivel. com, in Spanish; Plaza de Matute 6, Madrid)

Quera (☑93 318 07 43; www. llibreriaquera.com; Carrer de Petritxol 2, Barcelona)

Some map specialists in other countries, such as **Stanfords** (☑020-7836 1321; www.stanfords.co.uk; 12-14

Long Acre, London WC2E 9LP) in the UK, also have a good range of Spain maps.

Money

The most convenient way to bring your money is in the form of a debit or credit card, with some extra cash for use in case of an emergency. You'll find information on exchange rates and costs on p18.

ATMs Many credit and debit cards can be used for withdrawing money from *cajeros automáticos* (automatic teller machines) which display the relevant symbols such as Visa, MasterCard, Cirrus etc. Remember that there is usually a charge (around 1.5% to 2%) on ATM cash withdrawals abroad.

Cash Most banks and building societies will exchange major foreign currencies and offer the best rates. Ask about commissions and take your passport.

Credit & Debit Cards Can be used to pay for most purchases. You'll often be asked to show your passport or some other form of identification. Among the most widely accepted are Visa, MasterCard, American Express (Amex), Cirrus, Maestro, Plus, Diners Club and JCB. If your card is lost, stolen or swallowed by an ATM, you can call the following telephone numbers toll free to have an immediate stop put on its use: **Amex** (☑902 375 637 or 900 994 426); **Diners Club** (☑901 101 011); **MasterCard** (☑900 971 231); and **Visa** (☑900 991 216, 900 991 124).

Moneychangers You can exchange both cash and travellers cheques at exchange offices – which are usually indicated by the word *cambio* (exchange). Generally they offer longer opening hours and quicker service than banks, but

worse exchange rates and higher commissions.

Taxes & Refunds In Spain, value-added tax (VAT) is known as IVA (ee-ba; *impuesto sobre el valor añadido*). Visitors are entitled to a refund of the 16% IVA on purchases costing more than €90.16 from any shop if they are taking them out of the EU within three months. Ask the shop for a cash back (or similar) refund form showing the price and IVA paid for each item, and identifying the vendor and purchaser. Then present the refund form to the customs booth for IVA refunds at the airport, port or border from which you leave the EU.

Tipping Menu prices include a service charge. Most people leave some small change if they're satisfied: 5% is normally fine and 10% extremely generous. Porters will generally be happy with €1. Taxi drivers don't have to be tipped but a little rounding up won't go amiss.

Travellers Cheques Can be changed (you'll often be charged a commission) at most banks and building societies. Visa, Amex and Travelex are widely accepted brands with (usually) efficient replacement policies. Get most of your cheques in fairly large denominations (the equivalent of €100 or more) to save on any per-cheque commission charges. It's vital to keep your initial receipt, and a record of your cheque numbers and the ones you have used, separate from the cheques themselves.

Post

The Spanish postal system, **Correos** (☑902 197 197; www.correos.es), is generally reliable, if a little slow at times.

Sellos (stamps) are sold at most *estancos* (tobacconists' shops with 'Tabacos' in yellow letters on a maroon background), as well as post offices.

A postcard or letter weighing up to 20g costs €1.07 from Spain to other European countries, and €1.38 to the rest of the world. For a full list of prices for certified (*certificado*) and express post (*urgente*), go to www.correos.es (in Spanish) and click on 'Calculador de Tarifas'.

Receiving Mail

Lista de correos (poste restante) mail can be addressed to you anywhere that has a post office. It will be delivered to the main post office unless another is specified in the address. Take your passport when you pick up mail. A typical *lista de correos* address looks like this:

    Your name
    Lista de Correos
    28014 Madrid
    Spain

Delivery times are similar to those for outbound mail. All Spanish addresses have five-digit postcodes; using postcodes will help your mail arrive more quickly.

Sending Mail

Delivery times are erratic but ordinary mail to other Western European countries can take up to a week (although often as little as three days); to North America up to 10 days; and to Australia or New Zealand (NZ) between 10 days and three weeks.

Public Holidays

The two main periods when Spaniards go on holiday are Semana Santa (the week leading up to Easter Sunday) and August. At these times accommodation in resorts can be scarce and transport heavily booked, but other places are often half-empty.

There are at least 14 official holidays a year – some observed nationwide, some locally. When a holiday falls close to a weekend, Spaniards like to make a *puente* (bridge), meaning they take the intervening day off too. Occasionally when some holidays fall close, they make an *acueducto* (aqueduct)! National holidays:

Año Nuevo (New Year's Day) 1 January

Viernes Santo (Good Friday) March/April

Fiesta del Trabajo (Labour Day) 1 May

La Asunción (Feast of the Assumption) 15 August

Fiesta Nacional de España (National Day) 12 October

La Inmaculada Concepción (Feast of the Immaculate Conception) 8 December

Navidad (Christmas) 25 December

Regional governments set five holidays and local councils two more. Common dates include:

Epifanía (Epiphany) or **Día de los Reyes Magos** (Three Kings' Day) 6 January

Día de San José (St Joseph's Day) 19 March

Jueves Santo (Good Thursday) March/April. Not observed in Catalonia and Valencia.

Corpus Christi June. This is the Thursday after the eighth Sunday after Easter Sunday.

Día de San Juan Bautista (Feast of St John the Baptist) 24 June

Día de Santiago Apóstol (Feast of St James the Apostle) 25 July

Día de Todos los Santos (All Saints Day) 1 November

Día de la Constitución (Constitution Day) 6 December

Safe Travel

Most visitors to Spain never feel remotely threatened, but a sufficient number have unpleasant experiences to warrant an alert. The main thing to be wary of is petty theft (which may of course not seem so petty if your passport, cash, travellers cheques, credit card and camera go missing). What follows is intended as a strong warning rather than alarmism. In other words, be careful but don't be paranoid.

Scams

There must be 50 ways to lose your wallet. As a rule, talented petty thieves work in groups and capitalise on distraction. More imaginative strikes include someone dropping a milk mixture on to the victim from a balcony. Immediately a concerned citizen comes up to help you brush off what you assume to be pigeon poo, and thus suitably occupied you don't notice the contents of your pockets slipping away.

Beware: not all thieves look like thieves. Watch out for an old classic: the ladies offering flowers for good luck. We don't know how they do it, but if you get too involved in a friendly chat with these people, your pockets always wind up empty.

On some highways, especially the AP7 from the French border to Barcelona, bands of delinquents occasionally operate. Beware of men trying to distract you in rest areas, and don't stop along the highway if people driving alongside indicate you have a problem with the car. While one inspects the rear of the car with you, his pals will empty your vehicle. Another gag has them puncturing tyres of cars stopped in rest areas, then following and 'helping' the victim when they stop to change the wheel. Hire cars and those with foreign plates are especially targeted. When you do call in at highway rest stops, try to park close to the buildings and leave nothing of value in view. If you do stop to change a tyre and find yourself getting unsolicited aid, make sure doors are all locked and don't allow yourself to be distracted.

Even parking your car can be fraught. In some towns fairly dodgy self-appointed parking attendants operate in central areas where you may want to park. They will direct you frantically to a spot. If possible, ignore them and find your own. If

---

GOVERNMENT TRAVEL ADVICE

The following government websites offer travel advisories and information for travellers:

» **Australian Department of Foreign Affairs & Trade** (www.smartraveller.gov.au)

» **Canadian Department of Foreign Affairs & International Trade** (www.voyage.gc.ca)

» **French Ministere des Affaires Etrangeres Europeennes** (www.diplomatie.gouv.fr/fr/conseils-aux -voyageurs_909/index.html)

» **New Zealand Ministry of Foreign Affairs & Trade** (www.mft.govt.nz/travel)

» **UK Foreign & Commonwealth Office** (www.fco. gov.uk)

» **US Department of State** (www.travel.state.gov)

unavoidable, you may well want to pay them some token not to scratch or otherwise damage your vehicle after you've walked away. You definitely don't want to leave anything visible in the car (or open the boot (trunk) if you intend to leave luggage or anything else in it) under these circumstances.

Terrorism

Despite the terrorist attack on Madrid which left 191 people dead in March 2004, the chances of being in the wrong place at the wrong time are not much greater nowadays than in any other Western country.

The Basque terrorist organisation ETA frequently issues warnings to tourists to stay away from Spain, although bombings by ETA are now extremely rare.

Theft

Theft is mostly a risk in tourist resorts, big cities and when you first arrive in a new city and may be off your guard. You are at your most vulnerable when dragging around luggage to or from your hotel. Barcelona, Madrid and Seville have the worst reputations for theft and, on very rare occasions, muggings.

Anything left lying on the beach can disappear in a flash when your back is turned. Avoid dingy, empty city alleys and backstreets, or anywhere that just doesn't feel 100% safe, at night.

Report thefts to the national police. You are unlikely to recover your goods but you need to make this formal *denuncia* for insurance purposes. To avoid endless queues at the *comisaría* (police station), you can make the report by phone (☑902 102 112) in various languages or on the web at www.policia. es (click on Denuncias). The following day you go to the station of your choice to pick up and sign the report, without queuing.

Telephone

The ubiquitous blue payphones are easy to use for international and domestic calls. They accept coins, phonecards *(tarjetas telefónicas)* issued by the national phone company Telefónica and, in some cases, various credit cards. Calling from your computer using an internet-based service such as Skype is generally the cheapest option of all.

Collect Calls

International collect calls *(una llamada a cobro revertido)* are simple. Dial ☑99 00 followed by the code for the country you're calling:

Australia ☑900 99 00 61
Canada ☑900 99 00 15
France ☑900 99 00 33
Germany ☑900 99 00 49
Ireland ☑900 99 03 53
Israel ☑900 99 09 72
New Zealand ☑900 99 00 64
UK for BT ☑900 99 00 44
USA for AT&T ☑900 99 00 11, for Sprint and various others ☑900 99 00 13

Mobile Phones

You can buy SIM cards and prepaid time in Spain for your mobile (cell) phone (provided you own a GSM, dual- or tri-band cellular phone). This only works if your national phone hasn't been code-blocked; check before leaving home. Only consider a full contract if you plan to live in Spain for a while.

All the Spanish mobile phone companies (Telefónica's MoviStar, Orange and Vodafone) offer *prepagado* (prepaid) accounts for mobiles. The SIM card costs from €50, which includes some prepaid phone time. Phone outlets are scattered across the country. You can then top up in their shops or by buying cards in outlets, such as tobacconists *(estancos)* and newsstands.

Spain uses GSM 900/1800, which is compatible with the rest of Europe and Australia but not with the North American GSM 1900 or the system used in Japan. From those countries, you will need to travel with a tri-band or quadric-band phone.

On 1 July 2010 the EU's new Roaming Regulation came into force. It reduced roaming charges and set in place measures designed to prevent travellers from running up massive bills. Check with your mobile provider for more information.

Phone Codes

Mobile (cell) phone numbers start with 6. Numbers starting with 900 are national toll-free numbers, while those starting 901 to 905 come with varying costs. A common one is 902, which is a national standard rate number, but which can only be dialled from within Spain. In a similar category are numbers starting with 800, 803, 806 and 807.

International access code ☑00
Spain country code ☑34
Local area codes None (these are incorporated into listed numbers)

Phonecards

Cut-rate prepaid phonecards can be good value for international calls. They can be bought from *estancos*, small grocery stores, *locutorios* (private call centres) and newsstands in the main cities and tourist resorts. If possible, try to compare rates because some are better than others. Many of the private operators offer better deals than those offered by Telefónica. *Locutorios* that specialise in cut-rate overseas calls have popped up all over the place in bigger cities. Again, compare rates – as a rule the phonecards are better value and generally more convenient.

Useful Phone Numbers

Emergencies ☏112

English-speaking Spanish international operator ☏1008 (for calls within Europe) or ☏1005 (rest of the world).

International directory inquiries ☏11825 (A call to this number costs €2!).

National directory inquiries ☏11818

Operator for calls within Spain ☏1009 (including for domestic reverse-charge (collect) calls).

Time

Time zone Same as most of Western Europe (GMT/UTC plus one hour during winter and GMT/UTC plus two hours during the daylight-saving period)

Daylight-saving From last Sunday in March to last Sunday in October

UK, Ireland, Portugal & Canary Islands One hour behind mainland Spain

Morocco Morocco is on GMT/UTC year-round. From the last Sunday in March to the last Sunday in October, subtract two hours from Spanish time to get Moroccan time; the rest of the year, subtract one hour.

USA Spanish time is USA Eastern Time plus six hours and USA Pacific Time plus nine hours.

Australia During the Australian winter (Spanish summer), subtract eight hours from Australian Eastern Standard Time to get Spanish time; during the Australian summer, subtract 10 hours.

12-24-hour clock Although the 24-hour clock is used in most official situations, you'll find people generally use the 12-hour clock in everyday conversation.

Tourist Information

Local Tourist Offices

All cities and many smaller towns have an *oficina de turismo* or *oficina de información turística*. In the country's provincial capitals you will sometimes find more than one tourist office – one specialising in information on the city alone, the other carrying mostly provincial or regional information. National and natural parks also often have their own visitor centres offering useful information.

Turespaña (www.spain.info) is the country's national tourism body.

Tourist Offices Abroad

Information on Spain is available from the following branches of Turespaña abroad:

Canada (☏416-961 3131; www.spain.info/ca/tourspain; 2 Bloor St W, Ste 3042, Toronto M4W 3E2)

France (☏01 45 03 82 50; www.spain.info/fr/tourspain; 43 rue Decamps, 75784 Paris)

Germany (☏030-882 6543; www.spain.info/de/TourSpain; Kurfürstendamm 63, 10707 Berlin) Branches in Düsseldorf, Frankfurt am Main and Munich.

Netherlands (☏070-346 59 00; www.spain.info/nl/tourspain; Laan van Meerdervoort 8a, 2517 The Hague)

Portugal (☏21-315 3092; www.spain.info/pt/tourspain; Avenida Sidónio Pais 28 3° Dto, 1050-215 Lisbon)

UK (☏020-7317 2010; www.spain.info/uk/tourspain) You may visit the office by appointment only.

USA (☏212-265 8822; www.spain.info/us/tourspain; 666 Fifth Ave, 35th fl, New York, NY 10103) Branches in Chicago, Los Angeles and Miami.

Travellers with Disabilities

Spain is not overly accommodating for travellers with disabilities but some things are slowly changing. For example, disabled access to some museums, official buildings and hotels represents something of a sea change in local thinking. In major cities more is slowly being done to facilitate disabled access to public transport and taxis; in some cities, wheelchair-adapted taxis are called 'Eurotaxis'. Newly constructed hotels in most areas of Spain are required to have wheelchair-adapted rooms. With older places, you need to be a little wary of hotels who advertise themselves as being disabled-friendly, as this can mean as little as wide doors to rooms and bathrooms, or other token efforts.

Organisations

Accessible Barcelona (☏93 428 52 27; www.accessiblebarcelona.com) Craig Grimes, a T6 paraplegic and inveterate traveller, created this Barcelona-specific accessible travel site, easily the most useful doorway into the city for the disabled. It can also help with the surrounding region of Catalonia.

Accessible Travel & Leisure (☏01452-729739; www.accessibletravel.co.uk; Avionics House, Naas Lane, Quedgeley, Gloucester GL2 2SN) Claims to be the biggest UK travel agent dealing with travel for the disabled and encourages the disabled to travel independently.

Madrid Accessible (www.esmadrid.com) Not a patch on the Barcelona service, but Madrid's tourist office website allows you to download a list of wheelchair-accessible hotels, and a pdf called 'Lugares Accesibles', a list of wheelchair-friendly restaurants, shopping centres and museums.

ONCE (☎91 577 37 56; www.once.es; Calle de Prim 3, Madrid) The Spanish association for the blind. You may be able to get hold of guides in Braille to a handful of cities, including Madrid and Barcelona, although they are not published every year.

Society for Accessible Travel & Hospitality (☎212 447 7284; www.sath.org; 347 Fifth Ave, Ste 605, New York, NY 10016) Although largely concentrated on the USA, this organisation can provide general information.

Visas

Spain is one of 25 member countries of the Schengen Convention, under which 22 EU countries (all but Bulgaria, Cyprus, Ireland, Romania and the UK) plus Iceland, Norway and Switzerland have abolished checks at common borders. Cyprus has signed the Schengen agreement, but full membership has been postponed until at least late 2010.

The visa situation for entering Spain is as follows:

Citizens or residents of EU & Schengen countries No visa required.

Citizens or residents of Australia, Canada, Israel, Japan, NZ and the USA No visa required for tourist visits of up to 90 days.

Other countries Check with a Spanish embassy or consulate.

To work or study in Spain A special visa may be required – contact a Spanish embassy or consulate before travel.

Extensions & Residence

Schengen visas cannot be extended. You can apply for no more than two visas in any 12-month period and they are not renewable once in Spain. Nationals of EU countries, Iceland, Norway and Switzerland can enter and leave Spain at will and don't need to apply for a *tarjeta de residencia* (residence card), although they are supposed to apply for residence papers.

People of other nationalities who want to stay in Spain longer than 90 days have to get a residence card, and for them it can be a drawn-out process, starting with an appropriate visa issued by a Spanish consulate in their country of residence. Start the process well in advance.

Volunteering

Possibilities for volunteering to participate in projects in Spain include:

Earthwatch Institute (www.earthwatch.org) Check to see if there are any Spanish conservation projects on its program.

Global Vision International (www.gvi.co.uk) Monitor the presence of the bearded vulture in Andalucía or participate in whale or dolphin research.

Go Abroad (www.goabroad.com) At last count it had links to 52 different volunteering opportunities in Spain.

Pueblo Inglés (www.puebloingles.com) Volunteers spend their days conversing with Spaniards in English at various locations in Spain.

Sunseed Desert Technology (www.sunseed.org.uk) A UK-run project, developing sustainable ways to live in semi-arid environments, and is based in the hamlet of Los Molinos del Río Agua in Almería.

Transitions Abroad (www.transitionsabroad.com) A good website to start your research.

Women Travellers

Travelling in Spain as a woman is as easy as travelling anywhere in the Western world. That said, you should be choosy about your accommodation. Bottom-end fleapits with all-male staff can be insalubrious locations to bed down for the night. Lone women should also take care in city streets at night – stick with the crowds. Hitching for solo women travellers, while feasible, is risky.

Spanish men under about 40, who've grown up in the liberated post-Franco era, conform far less to old-fashioned sexual stereotypes, although you might notice that sexual stereotyping becomes a little more pronounced as you move from north to south in Spain, and from city to country.

The Socialist Zapatero government has introduced measures to promote equality in employment for women and took a lead in 2008 when it appointed a cabinet in which women ministers outnumbered their male counterparts eight to seven. Zapatero also named the country's first ever woman defence minister. Still, few women reach top positions in private enterprise and women's wages remain lower than those of men for the same kind of work.

Work

Nationals of EU countries, Switzerland, Norway and Iceland may work freely in Spain. If you are offered a contract, your employer will normally steer you through any bureaucracy.

Virtually everyone else is supposed to obtain, from a Spanish consulate in their country of residence, a work permit and, if they plan to stay more than 90 days, a residence visa. These procedures are well-nigh impossible unless you have a job contract lined up before you begin them.

You could look for casual work in fruit picking, harvests

or construction, but this is generally done with imported labour from Morocco and Eastern Europe, with pay and conditions that can often best be described as dire.

Translating and interpreting could be an option if you are fluent in Spanish and a language in demand.

You can start a job search on the Web, for instance at **Think Spain** (www.thinkspain. com).

Language Teaching

This type of work is an obvious option for which language-teaching qualifications are a big help. Language schools abound and are listed under 'Academias de Idiomas' in the Yellow Pages. Getting a job is harder if you're not an EU citizen

and the more reputable places will require prospective teachers to have TEFL qualifications. Giving private lessons is another avenue, but is unlikely to bring you a living wage straight away.

Sources of information on possible teaching work – in a school or as a private tutor – include foreign cultural centres such as the British Council and Alliance Française, foreign-language bookshops, universities and language schools. Many have noticeboards where you may find work opportunities or can advertise your own services.

Tourist Resorts

Summer work on the Mediterranean coasts is a possibility, especially if you

arrive early in the season and are prepared to stay a while. Check any local press in foreign languages, such as the Costa del Sol's *Sur In English*, which lists ads for waiters, nannies, chefs, babysitters, cleaners and the like.

Yacht Crewing

It is possible to stumble upon work as crew on yachts and cruisers. The best ports to look include (in descending order) Palma de Mallorca, Gibraltar and Puerto Banús.

In summer the voyages tend to be restricted to the Mediterranean but, from about November to January, many boats head for the Caribbean. Such work is usually unpaid and about the only way to find it is to ask around on the docks.

Transport

GETTING THERE & AWAY

Spain is one of Europe's top holiday destinations and is well linked to other European countries by air, rail and road. Regular car ferries and hydrofoils run to and from Morocco, and there are ferry links to the UK, Italy, the Canary Islands and Algeria.

Flights, tours and rail tickets can be booked online at lonelyplanet.com/bookings.

Entering Spain

Immigration and customs checks usually involve a minimum of fuss, although there are exceptions.

Your vehicle could be searched on arrival from An-

dorra. Spanish customs look out for contraband duty-free products destined for illegal resale in Spain. The same generally goes on arrival from Morocco or the Spanish North African enclaves of Ceuta and Melilla. In this case the search is for controlled substances. Expect long delays at these borders, especially in summer.

The tiny principality of Andorra is not in the European Union (EU), so border controls (and customs checks for contraband) remain in place.

Passport

Citizens of the 27 EU member states and Switzerland can travel to Spain with their national identity card alone. If such countries do

not issue ID cards – as in the UK – travellers must carry a full valid passport. All other nationalities must have a full valid passport.

For more information on visa requirements for Spain, turn to p889.

By law you are supposed to carry your passport or ID card with you at all times.

Air

There are direct flights to Spain from most European countries, as well as North America, South America, Africa, the Middle East and Asia. Those coming from Australasia will usually have to make at least one change of flight.

High season in Spain generally means Christmas, New Year, Easter and roughly June to September. This varies depending on the specific destination. You may find reasonably priced flights to Madrid available in August because it is stinking hot and everyone else has fled to the mountains or the sea. As a general rule, November to March is when airfares to Spain are likely to be at their lowest, and the intervening months can be considered shoulder periods.

Airports & Airlines

All of Spain's airports share the user-friendly website and flight information telephone number of **Aena** (☎902 40 47 04; www.aena.es), the national

---

CLIMATE CHANGE & TRAVEL

Every form of transport that relies on carbon-based fuel generates CO_2, the main cause of human-induced climate change. Modern travel is dependent on aeroplanes, which might use less fuel per person than most cars but travel much greater distances. The altitude at which aircraft emit gases (including CO_2) and particles also contributes to their climate change impact. Many websites offer 'carbon calculators' that allow people to estimate the carbon emissions generated by their journey and, for those who wish to do so, to offset the impact of the greenhouse gases emitted with contributions to portfolios of climate-friendly initiatives throughout the world. Lonely Planet offsets the carbon footprint of all staff and author travel.

airports authority. To find more information on each airport, choose English and click on the drop-down menu of airports. Each airport's page has details on practical information (such as parking and public transport) and a full list of (and links to) airlines using that airport.

Madrid's Aeropuerto de Barajas is Spain's busiest (and Europe's fourth-busiest) airport. Other major airports include Barcelona's Aeroport del Prat and the airports of Palma de Mallorca, Málaga, Alicante, Girona, Valencia, Ibiza, Seville and Bilbao. There are also airports at A Coruña, Almería, Asturias, Jerez de la Frontera, Murcia, Reus and Seville.

Land

Spain shares land borders with France, Portugal and Andorra.

Apart from shorter cross-border services, **Eurolines** (www.eurolines.com) are the main operators of international bus services to Spain

from most of Western Europe and Morocco.

In addition to the rail services connecting Spain with France and Portugal, there are direct trains between Zurich and Barcelona (via Bern, Geneva, Perpignan and Girona), and between Milan and Barcelona (via Turin, Perpignan and Girona). For these and other services, visit the website of **Renfe** (☑ for international trips 902 24 34 02; www.renfe.com), the Spanish national railway company.

Andorra

Regular buses connect Andorra with Barcelona (including winter ski buses and direct services to the airport) and other destinations in Spain (including Madrid) and France. Regular buses run between Andorra and Estació d'Autobusos de Sants bus station (€21, 3¼ to four hours).

France
BUS
Eurolines (www.eurolines.fr) heads to Spain from Paris and more than 20 other French cities and towns. It

connects with Madrid (17¾ hours), Barcelona (14¾ hours) and many other destinations. There is at least one departure per day for main destinations.

CAR & MOTORCYCLE
The main road crossing into Spain from France is the highway that links up with Spain's AP7 tollway, which runs down to Barcelona and follows the Spanish coast south (with a branch, the AP2, going to Madrid via Zaragoza). A series of links cut across the Pyrenees from France and Andorra into Spain, as does a coastal route that runs from Biarritz in France into the Spanish Basque Country.

TRAIN
The principal rail crossings into Spain pierce the Franco-Spanish frontier along the Mediterranean coast and via the Basque Country. Another minor rail route runs inland across the Pyrenees from Latour-de-Carol to Barcelona.

In addition to the options listed below, two or three TGV (high-speed) trains leave from Paris-Montparnasse for Irún, where you change to a normal train for the Basque Country Zand on towards Madrid. Up to three TGVs also put you on track to Barcelona (leaving from Paris Gare de Lyon), with a change of train at Montpellier or Narbonne. For more information on French rail services check out the **SNCF** (www.voyages-sncf.com) website.

There are plans for a high-speed rail link between Madrid and Paris by 2012. In the meantime, these are the major cross-border services:

Paris-Austerlitz to Madrid-Chamartín (chair/sleeper class €166.50/194.20, 13½ hours, one daily) *Trenhotel Francisco de Goya* runs via Orléns, Blois, Poitiers, Vitoria, Burgos and Valladolid.

Paris-Austerlitz to Barcelona–Estacio de Franca (sleeper class €188, 12

BUS PASSES

Travellers planning broader European tours that include Spain could find one of the following passes useful.

Busabout (☑ in the UK 084 5026 7514; www.busabout. com; 7-11 Bressenden Place, London) is a UK-based hop-on, hop-off bus service aimed at younger travellers. It has passes of varying duration allowing you to use a network of 33 cities in nine countries. The main passes are of interest only to those travelling a lot beyond Spain (where there are four stops). A West Loop pass (adult/student €399/385) takes in Spain and France, while other passes take in many of the countries in continental Western Europe.

Eurolines (www.eurolines.com) offers a low-season pass valid for 15/30 days that costs UK£205/310 (UK£175/240 for under-26s and seniors over 60). This pass allows unlimited travel between 43 European cities. The only Spanish cities included are Barcelona and Madrid. Fares increase to UK£345/455 (UK£290/375) between June and mid-September.

Seniors travelling from the UK should ask at the **Rail Europe Travel Centre** (☑0844 848 4064; www.raileurope.co.uk) about possible discounts on rail travel in continental Europe. Another source of rail information for all of Europe is **Rail Choice** (www. railchoice.com).

InterRail Passes

InterRail (www.interrail.net) passes are available to people who have lived in Europe for six months or more. They can be bought at most major stations and student travel outlets, as well as online.

InterRail has a **Global Pass** encompassing 30 countries that comes in four versions, ranging from five days' travel in 10 days to a full month's travel. These in turn come with three prices: adult 1st class, adult 2nd class and youth 2nd class. The one-month pass costs, respectively, €792/528/352; children travel for half the cost of the adult fare.

The InterRail **one-country pass** for Spain can be used for three, four, six or eight days in one month. For the eight-day pass you pay €384/256/167 for adult 1st class/ adult 2nd class/youth 2nd class. Children's passes (half the cost of the adult fare) are for children aged four to 11, youth passes for people aged 12 to 25 and adult passes for those 26 and over. Children aged three and under travel for free.

Eurail Passes

Eurail (www.eurail.com) passes are for those who've lived in Europe for less than six months and are supposed to be bought outside Europe. They're available from leading travel agencies and online.

Eurail Global Passes are good for travel in 21 European countries (not including the UK); forget it if you intend to travel mainly in Spain. Passes are valid for 15 or 21 days, or for one, two or three months. These cost €511/662/822/1161/1432, respectively, for the 1st-class adult pass. The 2nd-class youth version comes in at €332/429/535/755/933. Children aged between four and 11 pay half-price for the 1st-class passes. The 1st-class saver is for groups of two or more and brings a 15% reduction in the standard Global Pass adult prices. Another option is a Global Pass for 10/15 days' travel within two months, which costs €603/792 for adults, or €313/515 if you're 25 or under.

The **Eurail Select Pass** provides between five and 15 days of unlimited travel within a two-month period in three to five bordering countries (from a total of 23 possible countries). As with Global Passes, those aged 26 and over pay for a 1st-class pass, while those aged under 26 can get a cheaper 2nd-class pass. The basic five-day pass for three countries costs €324/275/211 for the 1st-class adult/saver/2nd-class youth version.

Eurail also offers a **Spain national pass** and several **two-country regional passes** (Spain-France, Spain-Italy and Spain-Portugal). You can choose from three to 10 days' train travel in a two-month period for any of these passes. The 10-day national pass costs €401/321 for 1st/2nd class. Regional passes come in five versions: 1st- and 2nd-class adult, 1st- and 2nd-class adult saver and 2nd-class youth.

As with all Eurail passes, you want to be sure you will be covering a lot of ground to make these worthwhile. Check some sample prices in euros for the places you intend to travel on the **Renfe** (www.renfe.com) website to compare.

---

hours, one daily) *Trenhotel Joan Miró* runs via Orléns, Limoges, Figueres and Girona.

Montpellier to Valencia (from €82, 7¾ to 9¾ hours, twice daily) Talgo service

along the Mediterranean Coast via Girona, Barcelona, Tarragona and Valencia.

Portugal
BUS
Avanza (☑in Spain & Portugal 902 02 09 99; www.avanzabus.

com) runs two daily buses between Lisbon and Madrid (€55.25, 7½ to nine hours, two daily).

Other bus services run north via Porto to Tui, Santiago de Compostela and A Coruña in Galicia, while local buses cross the border from towns such as Huelva in Andalucía, Badajoz in Extremadura and Ourense in Galicia.

CAR & MOTORCYCLE

The A5 freeway linking Madrid with Badajoz crosses the Portuguese frontier and continues on to Lisbon, and there are many other road connections up and down the length of the Hispano-Portuguese frontier.

TRAIN

From Portugal, the main line runs from Lisbon across Extremadura to Madrid.

Lisbon to Madrid (chair/sleeper class €58.60/83.20, 10½ hours, one daily)

Lisbon to Irún (chair/sleeper class €68.80/96.60, 14½ hours, one daily)

Sea

Ferries run to mainland Spain regularly from the Canary Islands, Italy, North Africa (Algeria, Morocco and the Spanish enclaves of Ceuta and Melilla) and the UK. Most services are run by the Spanish national ferry company, **Acciona Trasmediterránea** (☎902 45 46 45; www.trasmediterranea.es). You can take vehicles on the following routes.

Algeria

Acciona Trasmediterránea runs Almería to Ghazaouet (eight hours, four weekly) from late June to mid-September. See p779 for details.

Italy

For each of the following services, see p292.

Genoa to Barcelona (18 hours, three weekly)

Civitavecchia (near Rome) to Barcelona (20½ hours, six to seven weekly)

Livorno (Tuscany) to Barcelona (19½ hours, three weekly)

Porto Torres (Sardinia) to Barcelona (12 hours, one daily)

Morocco

In addition to the following services, there are also ferries to the Spanish enclaves of Melilla (from Almería and Málaga) and Ceuta (from Algeciras). For details, see the relevant sections of the Andalucía chapter, p779, p726 and p713).

Tangier to Algeciras (70 minutes, up to eight daily) See the boxed text, p713. Buses from several Moroccan cities converge on Tangier to make the ferry crossing to Algeciras, and then fan out to the main Spanish centres.

Tangier to Barcelona (24 hours, weekly) See p292.

Tangier to Tarifa (35 minutes, up to eight daily) See the boxed text, p713.

Nador to Almería (five to eight hours, up to three daily) See p779.

UK

From mid-March to mid-November, **Brittany Ferries** (☎0871 244 0744; www.brittany-ferries.co.uk) runs the following services. See p462 for more information.

Plymouth to Santander (24 to 35 hours, weekly)

Portsmouth to Santander (24 to 35 hours, three weekly)

GETTING AROUND

Spain's network of train and bus services is one of the best in Europe and there aren't many places that can't be reached using one or the other. The tentacles of Spain's high-speed train network are expanding rapidly with every passing year, while domestic air services are plentiful over longer distances and on routes that are more complicated by land.

Air

Spain has an extensive network of internal flights. These are operated by both Spanish airlines and a handful of low-cost international airlines which include:

Air Berlin (☎902 320 737; www.airberlin.com) German budget airline with flights from Madrid to Valencia, Palma de Mallorca, Seville, Jerez de la Frontera and Asturias

Air Europa (☎902 401 501; www.aireuropa.com) Dozens of domestic Spanish routes

EasyJet (☎807 260 026; www.easyjet.com) To Ibiza from Madrid and Bilbao

Iberia (☎902 400 500; www.iberia.es) Spain's national airline and its subsidiary, Iberia Regional-Air Nostrum, have an extensive network covering all of Spain

Ryanair (☎807 220 032; www.ryanair.com) More than a dozen domestic Spanish routes

Spanair (☎902 131 415; www.spanair.com) Numerous domestic Spanish services

Vueling (☎807 200 200; www.vueling.com) Spanish low-cost company with loads of domestic flights within Spain

Bicycle

Years of highway improvement programs across the country have made cycling a much easier prospect than it once was, although there are few designated bike lanes. There are plenty of options, from mountain biking in the Pyrenees to distance riding along the coast. Cycling on *autopistas* (tollways) is forbidden. Driver attitudes are not always so enlightened, so beware.

Few of the big cities offer much in the way of encouragement to cycle. Barcelona is an exception, where cycling lanes (albeit insufficient) have been laid out along main roads and various hire outlets make it possible for visitors to enjoy them.

If you get tired of pedalling it is often possible to take your bike on the train. All regional trains have space for bikes (usually marked by a bicycle logo on the carriage), where you can simply load the bike. Bikes are also permitted on most *cercanías* (local-area trains around big cities such as Madrid and Barcelona). On long-distance trains there are more restrictions. As a rule you have to be travelling overnight in a sleeper or couchette to have the (dismantled) bike accepted as normal luggage. Otherwise, it can only be sent separately as a parcel. It's often possible to take your bike on a bus – usually you'll just be asked to remove the front wheel.

In the UK, the **Cyclists' Touring Club** (CTC; ☏0844 736 8451; www.ctc.org.uk; Parklands, Railton Rd, Guildford, Surrey GU2 9JX) can help you plan your own bike tour or organise guided tours. Membership costs UK£36 per annum (UK£12 for those under 18).

Hire & Purchase

Bicycle rental is not as common as you might expect in Spain, although it is becoming more so, especially in the case of mountain bikes *(bici todo terreno)* and in the more popular regions, such as Andalucía and coastal spots like Barcelona. Costs vary considerably, but you can be looking at around €10 per hour, €15 to €20 per day, or €50 to €60 per week.

Zaragoza and Seville are among those cities to have introduced public bicycle systems with dozens of automated pick-up/drop-off points around the city. These schemes involve paying a small subscription fee which then allows you to pick up a bicycle at one location and drop it off at another.

You can purchase any kind of bicycle you want in the bigger centres, and prices are average by European standards.

Boat

Ferries and hydrofoils link the mainland (La Península) with the Balearic Islands (see p620) and Spain's North African enclaves of Ceuta and Melilla. For details of the latter, see the relevant sections in the Andalucía chapter (p779, p726 and p713).

The main national ferry company is **Acciona Trasmediterránea** (☏902 45 46 45; www.trasmediterranea. es). It runs a combination of slower car ferries and modern, high-speed, passenger-only fast ferries and hydrofoils. On overnight services between the mainland and the Balearic Islands you can opt for seating or sleeping accommodation in a cabin.

Bus

There are few places in Spain where buses don't go. Numerous companies provide bus links, from local routes between villages to fast intercity connections. It is often cheaper to travel by bus than by train, particularly on long-haul runs, but also less comfortable.

Local services can get you just about anywhere, but most buses connecting villages and provincial towns are not geared to tourist needs. Frequent weekday services drop off to a trickle, if they operate at all, on Saturday and Sunday. Often just one bus runs daily between smaller places during the week, and none operate on Sundays. It's usually unnecessary to make reservations; just arrive early enough to get a seat.

On many regular runs (say, from Madrid to Toledo) the ticket you buy is for the next

bus due to leave and *cannot* be used on a later bus. Advance purchase in such cases is generally not possible. For longer trips (such as Madrid to Seville or to the coast), and certainly in peak holiday season, you can (and should) buy your ticket in advance. On some routes you have the choice between express and all-stops services.

In most larger towns and cities, buses leave from a single bus station *(estación de autobuses)*. In smaller places, buses tend to operate from a set street or plaza, often unmarked. Locals will know where to go. Usually a specific bar sells tickets, although in some cases you may have to purchase tickets on the bus.

Bus travel within Spain is not overly costly. The trip from Madrid to Barcelona starts from around €29 one way. From Barcelona to Seville, one of the longest trips you could do (15 to 16 hours), you pay up to €89 one way.

People under 26 should inquire about discounts on long-distance trips. Occasionally a return ticket is cheaper than two singles.

Among the hundreds of bus companies operating in Spain, the following have the largest range of services:

ALSA (☏902 42 22 42; www. alsa.es) By far the biggest player, this company has routes all over the country, which it operates in association with various other companies.

Avanza (☏902 02 09 99; www.avanzabus.com) Operates buses from Madrid to Extremadura, western Castilla y León and Valencia via eastern Castilla-La Mancha (eg Cuenca), often in association with other companies.

Socibus & Secorbus (☏902 22 92 92; www.socibus. es) These two companies jointly operate services between Madrid and western

Andalucía, including Cádiz, Córdoba, Huelva and Seville.

Car & Motorcycle

Every vehicle should display a nationality plate of its country of registration and you must always carry proof of ownership of a private vehicle. Third-party motor insurance is required throughout Europe. A warning triangle and a reflective jacket (to be used in case of breakdown) are compulsory.

Automobile Associations

The **Real Automóvil Club de España** (RACE; ✆902 40 45 45; www.race.es; Calle de Eloy Gonzalo 32, Madrid) is the national automobile club. They may well come to assist you in case of breakdown, but in any event you should obtain an emergency telephone number for Spain from your own insurer.

Driving Licence

All EU member states' driving licences are fully recognised throughout Europe. Those with a non-EU licence are supposed to obtain a 12-month International Driving Permit (IDP) to accompany their national licence, which your national automobile association can issue. People who have held residency in Spain for one year or more must apply for a Spanish driving licence.

Fuel & Spare Parts

Petrol (*gasolina*) in Spain is pricey, but generally cheaper than in its major EU neighbours (including France, Germany, Italy and the UK). About 30 companies, including several foreign operators, run petrol stations in Spain, but the two biggest are the home-grown Repsol and Cepsa.

Petrol is about 10% cheaper in Gibraltar than in Spain and 15% cheaper in Andorra. It's about 35% cheaper in Spain's tax-free enclaves of Ceuta and Melilla in North Africa.

You can pay with major credit cards at most service stations.

Hire

To rent a car in Spain you have to have a licence, be aged 21 or over and, for the major companies at least, have a credit or debit card. Smaller firms in areas where car hire is particularly common (such as the Balearic Islands) can sometimes live without this last requirement. Although those with a non-EU licence should also have an IDP, you will find that national licences from countries like Australia, Canada,

ROAD DISTANCES (KM)

	Alicante	Badajoz	Barcelona	Bilbao	Córdoba	Granada	A Coruña	León	Madrid	Málaga	Oviedo	Pamplona	San Sebastián	Seville	Toledo	Valencia	Valladolid
Badajoz	696																
Barcelona	515	1022															
Bilbao	817	649	620														
Córdoba	525	272	908	795													
Granada	353	438	868	829	166												
A Coruña	1031	772	1118	644	995	1043											
León	755	496	784	359	733	761	334										
Madrid	422	401	621	395	400	434	609	333									
Málaga	482	436	997	939	187	129	1153	877	544								
Oviedo	873	614	902	304	851	885	340	118	451	995							
Pamplona	673	755	437	159	807	841	738	404	407	951	463						
San Sebastián	766	768	529	119	869	903	763	433	469	13	423	92					
Seville	609	217	1046	933	138	256	947	671	538	219	789	945	1007				
Toledo	411	368	692	466	320	397	675	392	71	507	510	478	540	458			
Valencia	166	716	349	633	545	519	961	685	352	648	803	501	594	697	372		
Valladolid	615	414	663	280	578	627	455	134	193	737	252	325	354	589	258	545	
Zaragoza	498	726	296	324	725	759	833	488	325	869	604	175	268	863	396	326	367

New Zealand and the USA are usually accepted.

The following companies are useful if you're considering hiring a car:

Auto Europe (www.auto-europe.com) US-based operator that acts as a clearing house for deals with major car rental agencies

Autos Abroad (www.autosabroad.com) The same deal but from a UK base

Ideamerge (www.ideamerge.com) Information on the Renault company's car-leasing plan, motor-home rental and much more.

The following multinational car rental agencies operate in Spain:

Avis (✆902 18 08 54; www.avis.es)

Europcar (✆902 10 50 30; www.europcar.es)

Hertz (✆91 749 77 78; www.hertz.es)

National/Atesa (✆902 10 01 01; www.atesa.es)

Pepecar (✆807 41 42 43; www.pepecar.com in Spanish) A local low-cost company.

Insurance

Third-party motor insurance is a minimum requirement in Spain and throughout Europe. Ask your insurer for a European Accident Statement form, which can simplify matters in the event of an accident. A European breakdown-assistance policy such as the AA Five Star Service or RAC Eurocover Motoring Assistance is a good investment.

Car-hire companies also provide this minimum insurance, but be careful to understand what your liabilities and excess are, and what waivers you are entitled to in case of accident or damage to the hire vehicle.

Road Rules

Blood-alcohol limit: 0.05%. Breath tests are common, and if found to be over the limit you can be

judged, condemned, fined and deprived of your licence within 24 hours. Fines range up to around €600 for serious offences. Nonresident foreigners will be required to pay up on the spot (at 30% off the full fine). Pleading linguistic ignorance will not help – your traffic cop will produce a list of infringements and fines in as many languages as you like. If you don't pay, or don't have a Spanish resident to act as guarantor for you, your vehicle could be impounded.

Legal driving age for cars: 18

Legal driving age for motorcycles & scooters: 16 (80cc and over) or 14 (50cc and under). A licence is required.

Motorcyclists: must use headlights at all times and wear a helmet if riding a bike of 125cc or more.

Overtaking: Spanish truck drivers often have the courtesy to turn on their right indicator to show that the way ahead of them is clear for overtaking (and the left one if it is not and you are attempting this manoeuvre).

Roundabouts (traffic circles): vehicles already in the circle have the right of way

Side of the road: drive on the right

Speed limits: in built-up areas, 50km/h (and in some cases, such as inner-city Barcelona, 30km/h), which increases to 100km/h on major roads and up to 120km/h on *autovías* and *autopistas* (toll-free and tolled dual-lane highways, respectively). Cars towing caravans are restricted to a maximum speed of 80km/h.

Hitching

Hitching is never entirely safe in any country in the world, and we don't recommend it. Travellers who decide to hitch should understand that they are taking

a small but potentially dangerous risk. People who do choose to hitch will be safer if they travel in pairs and let someone know where they are planning to go.

Hitching is illegal on *autopistas* and *autovías*, and difficult on other major highways. Choose a spot where cars can safely stop before highway slipways or on minor roads. The going can be slow on the latter, as the traffic is often light.

Local Transport

Most of the major cities have excellent local transport. Madrid and Barcelona have extensive bus and metro systems, and other major cities also benefit from generally efficient public transport. By European standards, prices are relatively cheap.

Bus

Cities and provincial capitals all have reasonable bus networks. You can buy single tickets (usually €1) on the buses or at tobacconists, but in cities such as Madrid and Barcelona you are better off buying combined 10-trip tickets (see Metro, p897) that allow the use of a combination of bus and metro, and which work out cheaper per ride. These can be purchased in any metro station.

Regular buses run from about 6am to shortly before midnight and even as late as 2am. In the big cities a night bus service generally kicks in on a limited number of lines in the wee hours. In Madrid they are known as *búhos* (owls) and in Barcelona more prosaically as *nitbuses* (night buses).

Metro

Madrid has the country's most extensive metro network. Barcelona follows in second place with a reasonable system. Valencia,

Schematic map of the subway network

Metro Lines

1. PINAR DE CHAMARTÍN / VALDECARROS
2. LA ELIPA / CUATRO CAMINOS
3. VILLAVERDE ALTO / MONCLOA
4. ARGÜELLES / PINAR DE CHAMARTÍN
5. ALAMEDA DE OSUNA / CASA DE CAMPO
6. CIRCULAR
7. HOSPITAL DEL HENARES / PITIS
8. NUEVOS MINISTERIOS / AEROPUERTO
9. HERRERA ORIA / ARGANDA DEL REY
10. HOSPITAL INFANTA SOFÍA / PUERTA DEL SUR
11. PLAZA ELÍPTICA / LA PESETA
M. METROSUR
R. PRÍNCIPE PÍO

Keys

- Metro Interchange station
- Interchange station with long walking distance
- Station with restricted opening times
- Change of trains
- Madrid-Barajas Airport
- Airport extra charge
- Renfe suburban railway station
- Travel information centre
- Parking
- Suburban bus station
- Interregional bus station
- Railway station
- Transfer Terminal
- Light Rail
- B1. Change of fare
- B2.
- B3.

Light Rail

1. PINAR DE CHAMARTÍN / LAS TABLAS
2. COLONIA JARDÍN / ESTACIÓN DE ARAVACA
3. COLONIA JARDÍN / PUERTA DE BOADILLA

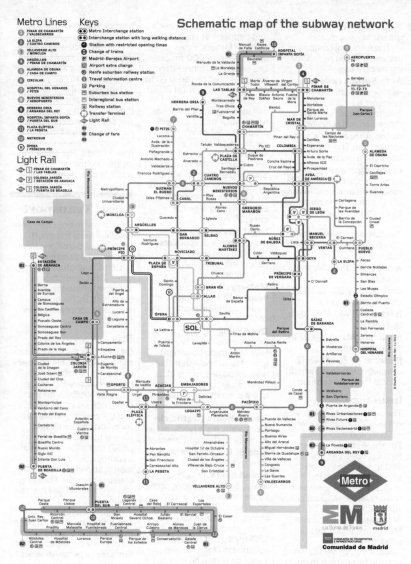

© Diseño Rofis S.L. 2008. Ref. 11/2010

Metro

EM La Suma de Todos · madrid

CONSEJERÍA DE TRANSPORTES E INFRAESTRUCTURAS
Comunidad de Madrid

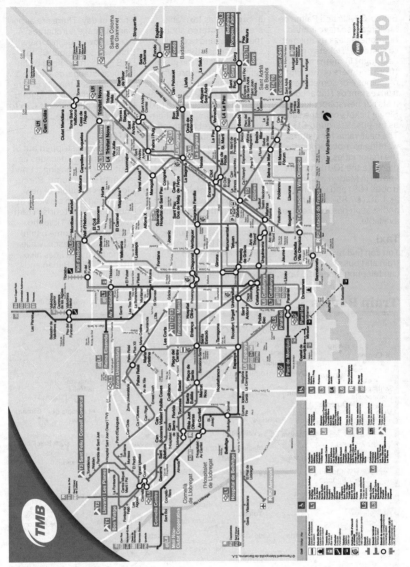

Bilbao, Seville and Palma de Mallorca also have limited but nonetheless useful metro systems. Tickets must be bought in metro stations (from counters or vending machines), or sometimes from *estancos* (tobacconists) or newspaper kiosks. Single tickets cost the same as for buses (around €1). The best value for visitors wanting to move around the major cities over a few days are the 10-trip tickets, known in Madrid as Metrobús (€9) and in Barcelona as T-10 (€7.85). Monthly and season passes are also available.

Taxi

You can find taxi ranks at train and bus stations, or you can telephone for radio taxis.

In larger cities taxi ranks are also scattered about the centre, and taxis will stop if you hail them in the street – look for the green light and/or the *libre* sign on the passenger side of the windscreen. The bigger cities are well populated with taxis, although finding one when you need to get home late on a Friday or Saturday night in places such as Madrid and Barcelona can be tricky. No more than four people are allowed in a taxi.

Daytime flagfall (generally to 10pm) is around €1.40 to €2.05. After 10pm and on weekends and holidays (in some cities, including Madrid and Barcelona), the price can rise to €3.10. You then pay up to €1 per kilometre depending on the time of day. There are airport and luggage surcharges. A cross-town ride in a major city will cost about €5 to €8 – absurdly cheap by European standards – while a taxi between the city centre and airport in either Madrid or Barcelona will cost €25 to €30 with luggage.

Tram

Trams were stripped out of Spanish cities decades ago, but they are making a timid comeback in some. Barcelona has a couple of new suburban tram services in addition to its tourist Tramvia Blau run to Tibidabo. Valencia has some useful trams to the beach, while various limited lines also run in Seville, Bilbao and Murcia.

Train Routes

Train

Renfe (☎902 24 02 02; www.renfe.com) is the excellent national train system that runs most of the services in Spain. A handful of small private railway lines are noted throughout this book.

You'll find consignas (left-luggage facilities) at all main train stations. They are usually open from about 6am to midnight and charge from €3 to €4.50 per day per piece of luggage.

Spain has several types of trains and long-distance trains (largo recorrido or Grandes Líneas) in particular have a variety of names.

Alaris, Altaria, Alvia, Arco and Avant Long-distance intermediate-speed services.

Cercanías For short hops and services to outlying suburbs and satellite towns in Madrid, Barcelona and 11 other cities.

Euromed Similar to the AVE trains, they connect Barcelona with Valencia and Alicante.

Regionales Trains operating within one region, usually stopping all stations.

Talgo and Intercity Slower long-distance trains.

Tren de Alta Velocidad Española (AVE) High-speed trains that link Madrid with Barcelona, Burgos, Córdoba, Cuenca, Huesca, Lerida, Málaga, Seville, Valencia, Valladolid and Zaragoza. There is also a Barcelona–Seville service. In coming years Madrid–Cádiz and Madrid–Bilbao should also come on line.

Trenhotel Overnight trains with sleeper berths.

Classes & Costs

All long-distance trains have 2nd and 1st classes, known as turista and preferente, respectively. The latter is 20% to 40% more expensive. Some services have a third, superior category, called club.

Fares vary enormously depending on the service (faster trains cost considerably more) and, in the case of some high-speed services such as the AVE, on the time and day of travel. Tickets for AVE trains are by far the most expensive. A one-way trip in 2nd class from Madrid to Barcelona (on which route only AVE trains run) could cost as must as €115 (it works out slightly cheaper if you book online).

Children aged between four and 12 years are entitled to a 40% discount; those aged under four travel for free (except on high-speed trains, for which they pay the same as those aged four to 12). Buying a return ticket often gives you a 10% to 20% discount on the return trip. Students and people up to 25 years of age with a Euro<26 Card (Carnet Joven in Spain) are entitled to 20% to 25% off most ticket prices.

On overnight trips within Spain on trenhoteles it's worth paying extra for a litera (couchette; a sleeping berth in a six- or four-bed compartment) or, if available, single or double cabins in preferente or gran clase class. The cost depends on the class of accommodation, type of train and length of journey. The lines covered are Madrid–La Coruña, Barcelona–Córdoba–Seville, Barcelona–Madrid (and on to Lisbon) and Barcelona–Málaga, as well as international services to France.

Reservations

Reservations are recommended for long-distance trips, and you can make them in train stations, Renfe offices and travel agencies, as well as online. In a growing number of stations you can pick up prebooked tickets from machines scattered about the station concourse.

A MEMORABLE NORTHERN TRAIN JOURNEY

The romantically inclined could opt for an opulent and slow-moving, old-time rail adventure in the colourful north of Spain.

Catch the **Transcantábrico** (www.transcantabrico.feve.es) for a journey on a picturesque narrow-gauge rail route, from Santiago de Compostela (by bus as far as O Ferrol) via Oviedo, Santander and Bilbao along the coast, and then a long inland stretch to finish in León. The eight-day trip costs €3500/5200 per single/double, and can also be done in reverse. There are departures around twice a month from April to October. The package includes various visits along the way, including the Museo Guggenheim in Bilbao, the Cuevas de Altamira, Santillana del Mar, and the Covadonga lakes in the Picos de Europa. The food is as pleasurable for the palate as the sights are for the eyes, with some meals being eaten on board but most in various locations.

The trains don't travel at night, making sleeping aboard easy and providing the opportunity to stay out at night.

Language

WANT MORE?

For in-depth language information and handy phrases, check out Lonely Planet's *Spanish Phrasebook*. You'll find it at **shop. lonelyplanet.com**, or you can buy Lonely Planet's iPhone phrasebooks at the Apple App Store.

Spanish (*español*), or Castilian (*castellano*) as it is also called, is spoken throughout Spain, but there are three regional languages as well: Catalan (*català*), spoken in Catalonia, the Balearic Islands and Valencia; Galician (*galego*), spoken in Galicia; and Basque (*euskara*), which is spoken in the Basque Country and Navarra.

Most Spanish sounds are pronounced the same as their English counterparts. Note that the kh in our pronunciation guides is a gut-tural sound (like the 'ch' in Scottish *loch*), ly is pronounced as the 'lli' in 'million', ny is pro-nounced as the 'ni' in 'onion', th is pronounced with a lisp, and r is strongly rolled. Some Span-ish words are written with an acute accent (eg *días*) – this indicates a stressed syllable. In our pronunciation guides, the stressed syllables are in italics. If you follow our pronunciation guides given with each phrase in this chapter, you will be understood.

Spanish nouns are marked for gender (masculine or feminine). Feminine nouns generally end with -a and masculine ones with -o. Endings for adjectives also change to agree with the gender of the noun they mod-ify. Where necessary, both forms are given for the words and phrases in this chapter, separated by a slash and with the masculine form first, eg *perdido/a* (m/f).

If a noun or adjective ends in a vowel, the plural is formed by adding -s to the end. If it ends in a consonant, add *-es* instead.

When talking to people familiar to you or younger than you, use the informal form of 'you', *tú*, rather than the polite form *Usted*. The polite form is used in the phrases pro-vided in this chapter; where both options are given, they are indicated by the abbreviations 'pol' and 'inf'.

BASICS

Hello.	*Hola.*	o·la
Goodbye.	*Adiós.*	a·dyos
How are you?	*¿Qué tal?*	ke tal
Fine, thanks.	*Bien, gracias.*	byen gra·thyas
Excuse me.	*Perdón.*	per·don
Sorry.	*Lo siento.*	lo see·en·to
Yes./No.	*Sí./No.*	see/no
Please.	*Por favor.*	por fa·vor
Thank you.	*Gracias.*	gra·thyas
You're welcome.	*De nada.*	de na·da

My name is ...
Me llamo ...   me *lya*·mo ...

What's your name?
¿Cómo se llama Usted? ko·mo se *lya*·ma oo·ste (pol)
¿Cómo te llamas? ko·mo te *lya*·mas (inf)

Do you speak (English)?
¿Habla (inglés)?   a·bla (een·gles) (pol)
¿Hablas (inglés)?   a·blas (een·gles) (inf)

I (don't) understand.
Yo (no) entiendo.   yo (no) en·tyen·do

ACCOMMODATION

I'd like to book a room.
Quisiera reservar una habitación.   kee·sye·ra re·ser·var oo·na a·bee·ta·thyon

How much is it per night/person?
¿Cuánto cuesta por noche/persona?   kwan·to kwes·ta por no·che/per·so·na

Does it include breakfast?
¿Incluye el desayuno?   een·kloo·ye el de·sa·yoo·no

campsite	terreno de cámping	te·re·no de kam·peeng
hotel	hotel	o·tel
guesthouse	pensión	pen·syon
youth hostel	albergue juvenil	al·ber·ge khoo·ve·neel
I'd like a ... room.	Quisiera una habitación ...	kee·sye·ra oo·na a·bee·ta·thyon ...
single	individual	een·dee·vee·dwal
double	doble	do·ble
air-con	aire acondicionado	ai·re a·kon·dee·thyo·na·do
bathroom	baño	ba·nyo
bed	cama	ka·ma
window	ventana	ven·ta·na

DIRECTIONS

Where's ...?
¿Dónde está ...? · don·de es·ta ...

What's the address?
¿Cuál es la dirección? · kwal es la dee·rek·thyon

Could you please write it down?
¿Puede escribirlo, por favor? · pwe·de es·kree·beer·lo por fa·vor

Can you show me (on the map)?
¿Me lo puede indicar (en el mapa)? · me lo pwe·de een·dee·kar (en el ma·pa)

at the corner	en la esquina	en la es·kee·na
at the traffic lights	en el semáforo	en el se·ma·fo·ro
behind ...	detrás de ...	de·tras de ...
far away	lejos	le·khos
in front of ...	enfrente de ...	en·fren·te de ...
left	izquierda	eeth·kyer·da
near	cerca	ther·ka
next to ...	al lado de ...	al la·do de ...
opposite ...	frente a ...	fren·te a ...
right	derecha	de·re·cha
straight ahead	todo recto	to·do rek·to

EATING & DRINKING

What would you recommend?
¿Qué recomienda? · ke re·ko·myen·da

What's in that dish?
¿Que lleva ese plato? · ke lye·va e·se pla·to

I don't eat ...
No como ... · no ko·mo ...

That was delicious!
¡Estaba buenísimo! · es·ta·ba bwe·nee·see·mo

KEY PATTERNS

To get by in Spanish, mix and match these simple patterns with words of your choice:

When's (the next flight)?
¿Cuándo sale (el próximo vuelo)? · kwan·do sa·le (el prok·see·mo vwe·lo)

Where's (the station)?
¿Dónde está (la estación)? · don·de es·ta (la es·ta·thyon)

Where can I (buy a ticket)?
¿Dónde puedo (comprar un billete)? · don·de pwe·do (kom·prar oon bee·lye·te)

Do you have (a map)?
¿Tiene (un mapa)? · tye·ne (oon ma·pa)

Is there (a toilet)?
¿Hay (servicios)? · ai (ser·vee·thyos)

I'd like (a coffee).
Quisiera (un café). · kee·sye·ra (oon ka·fe)

I'd like (to hire a car).
Quisiera (alquilar un coche). · kee·sye·ra (al·kee·lar oon ko·che)

Can I (enter)?
¿Se puede (entrar)? · se pwe·de (en·trar)

Could you please (help me)?
¿Puede (ayudarme), por favor? · pwe·de (a·yoo·dar·me) por fa·vor

Do I have to (get a visa)?
¿Necesito (obtener un visado)? · ne·the·see·to (ob·te·ner oon vee·sa·do)

Please bring the bill.
Por favor nos trae la cuenta. · por fa·vor nos tra·e la kwen·ta

Cheers!
¡Salud! · sa·loo

I'd like to book a table for ...	Quisiera reservar una mesa para ...	kee·sye·ra re·ser·var oo·na me·sa pa·ra ...
(eight) o'clock	las (ocho)	las (o·cho)
(two) people	(dos) personas	(dos) per·so·nas

Key Words

appetisers	aperitivos	a·pe·ree·tee·vos
bar	bar	bar
bottle	botella	bo·te·lya
bowl	bol	bol
breakfast	desayuno	de·sa·yoo·no
cafe	café	ka·fe

Signs

Abierto	Open
Cerrado	Closed
Entrada	Entrance
Hombres	Men
Mujeres	Women
Prohibido	Prohibited
Salida	Exit
Servicios/Aseos	Toilets

children's menu	menú infantil	me·*noo* een·fan·*teel*
(too) cold	(muy) frío	(mooy) *free*·o
dinner	cena	*the*·na
food	comida	ko·*mee*·da
fork	tenedor	te·ne·*dor*
glass	vaso	*va*·so
highchair	trona	*tro*·na
hot (warm)	caliente	ka·*lyen*·te
knife	cuchillo	koo·*chee*·lyo
lunch	comida	ko·*mee*·da
main course	segundo plato	se·*goon*·do *pla*·to
market	mercado	mer·*ka*·do
menu (in English)	menú (en inglés)	oon me·*noo* (en een·*gles*)
plate	plato	*pla*·to
restaurant	restaurante	res·tow·*ran*·te
spoon	cuchara	koo·*cha*·ra
supermarket	supermercado	soo·per·mer·*ka*·do
with/without	con/sin	kon/seen
vegetarian food	comida vegetariana	ko·*mee*·da ve·khe·ta·*rya*·na

Meat & Fish

beef	carne de vaca	*kar*·ne de *va*·ka
chicken	pollo	*po*·lyo
duck	pato	*pa*·to
fish	pescado	pes·*ka*·do
lamb	cordero	kor·*de*·ro
pork	cerdo	*ther*·do
turkey	pavo	*pa*·vo
veal	ternera	ter·*ne*·ra

Fruit & Vegetables

apple	manzana	man·*tha*·na
apricot	albaricoque	al·ba·ree·*ko*·ke
artichoke	alcachofa	al·ka·*cho*·fa
asparagus	espárragos	es·*pa*·ra·gos
banana	plátano	*pla*·ta·no
beans	judías	khoo·*dee*·as
beetroot	remolacha	re·mo·*la*·cha
cabbage	col	kol
carrot	zanahoria	tha·na·o·*rya*
celery	apio	*a*·pyo
cherry	cereza	the·*re*·tha
corn	maíz	ma·*eeth*
cucumber	pepino	pe·*pee*·no
fruit	fruta	*froo*·ta
grape	uvas	*oo*·vas
lemon	limón	lee·*mon*
lentils	lentejas	len·*te*·khas
lettuce	lechuga	le·*choo*·ga
mushroom	champiñón	cham·pee·*nyon*
nuts	nueces	*nwe*·thes
onion	cebolla	the·*bo*·lya
orange	naranja	na·*ran*·kha
peach	melocotón	me·lo·ko·*ton*
peas	guisantes	gee·*san*·tes
(red/green) pepper	pimiento (rojo/verde)	pee·*myen*·to (*ro*·kho/*ver*·de)
pineapple	piña	*pee*·nya
plum	ciruela	theer·*we*·la
potato	patata	pa·*ta*·ta
pumpkin	calabaza	ka·la·*ba*·tha
spinach	espinacas	es·pee·*na*·kas
strawberry	fresa	*fre*·sa
tomato	tomate	to·*ma*·te
vegetable	verdura	ver·*doo*·ra
watermelon	sandía	san·*dee*·a

Other

bread	pan	pan
butter	mantequilla	man·te·*kee*·lya
cheese	queso	*ke*·so
egg	huevo	*we*·vo
honey	miel	myel
jam	mermelada	mer·me·*la*·da
oil	aceite	a·*they*·te
pasta	pasta	*pas*·ta
pepper	pimienta	pee·*myen*·ta
rice	arroz	a·*roth*
salt	sal	sal
sugar	azúcar	a·*thoo*·kar
vinegar	vinagre	vee·*na*·gre

Drinks

beer	cerveza	ther·ve·tha
coffee	café	ka·fe
(orange) juice	zumo (de naranja)	thoo·mo (de na·ran·kha)
milk	leche	le·che
tea	té	te
(mineral) water	agua (mineral)	a·gwa (mee·ne·ral)
(red) wine	vino (tinto)	vee·no (teen·to)
(white) wine	vino (blanco)	vee·no (blan·ko)

EMERGENCIES

Help!	¡Socorro!	so·ko·ro
Go away!	¡Vete!	ve·te

Call ...!	¡Llame a ...!	lya·me a ...
a doctor	un médico	oon me·dee·ko
the police	la policía	la po·lee·thee·a

I'm lost.
Estoy perdido/a.   es·toy per·dee·do/a (m/f)

I had an accident.
He tenido un   e te·nee·do oon
accidente.   ak·thee·den·te

I'm ill.
Estoy enfermo/a.   es·toy en·fer·mo/a (m/f)

It hurts here.
Me duele aquí.   me dwe·le a·kee

I'm allergic to (antibiotics).
Soy alérgico/a a   soy a·ler·khee·ko/a a
(los antibióticos).   (los an·tee·byo·tee·kos) (m/f)

SHOPPING & SERVICES

I'd like to buy ...
Quisiera comprar ...   kee·sye·ra kom·prar ...

I'm just looking.
Sólo estoy mirando.   so·lo es·toy mee·ran·do

May I look at it?
¿Puedo verlo?   pwe·do ver·lo

I don't like it.
No me gusta.   no me goos·ta

Question Words		
How?	¿Cómo?	ko·mo
What?	¿Qué?	ke
When?	¿Cuándo?	kwan·do
Where?	¿Dónde?	don·de
Who?	¿Quién?	kyen
Why?	¿Por qué?	por ke

How much is it?
¿Cuánto cuesta?   kwan·to kwes·ta

That's too expensive.
Es muy caro.   es mooy ka·ro

Can you lower the price?
¿Podría bajar un   po·dree·a ba·khar oon
poco el precio?   po·ko el pre·thyo

There's a mistake in the bill.
Hay un error en la cuenta.   ai oon e·ror en la kwen·ta

ATM	cajero automático	ka·khe·ro ow·to·ma·tee·ko
credit card	tarjeta de crédito	tar·khe·ta de kre·dee·to
internet cafe	cibercafé	thee·ber·ka·fe
post office	correos	ko·re·os
tourist office	oficina de turismo	o·fee·thee·na de too·rees·mo

TIME & DATES

What time is it?	¿Qué hora es?	ke o·ra es
It's (10) o'clock.	Son (las diez).	son (las dyeth)
Half past (one).	Es (la una) y media.	es (la oo·na) ee me·dya

morning	mañana	ma·nya·na
afternoon	tarde	tar·de
evening	noche	no·che
yesterday	ayer	a·yer
today	hoy	oy
tomorrow	mañana	ma·nya·na

Monday	lunes	loo·nes
Tuesday	martes	mar·tes
Wednesday	miércoles	myer·ko·les
Thursday	jueves	khwe·bes
Friday	viernes	vyer·nes
Saturday	sábado	sa·ba·do
Sunday	domingo	do·meen·go

January	enero	e·ne·ro
February	febrero	fe·bre·ro
March	marzo	mar·tho
April	abril	a·breel
May	mayo	ma·yo
June	junio	khoo·nyo
July	julio	khoo·lyo
August	agosto	a·gos·to
September	septiembre	sep·tyem·bre
October	octubre	ok·too·bre
November	noviembre	no·vyem·bre
December	diciembre	dee·thyem·bre

Numbers

1	uno	oo·no
2	dos	dos
3	tres	tres
4	cuatro	kwa·tro
5	cinco	theen·ko
6	seis	seys
7	siete	sye·te
8	ocho	o·cho
9	nueve	nwe·ve
10	diez	dyeth
20	veinte	veyn·te
30	treinta	treyn·ta
40	cuarenta	kwa·ren·ta
50	cincuenta	theen·kwen·ta
60	sesenta	se·sen·ta
70	setenta	se·ten·ta
80	ochenta	o·chen·ta
90	noventa	no·ven·ta
100	cien	thyen
1000	mil	meel

TRANSPORT

Public Transport

boat	barco	bar·ko
bus	autobús	ow·to·boos
plane	avión	a·vyon
train	tren	tren
tram	tranvía	tran·vee·a
first	primer	pree·mer
last	último	ool·tee·mo
next	próximo	prok·see·mo

I want to go to ...
Quisiera ir a ... kee·sye·ra eer a ...

Does it stop at (Madrid)?
¿Para en (Madrid)? pa·ra en (ma·dree)

What stop is this?
¿Cuál es esta parada? kwal es es·ta pa·ra·da

What time does it arrive/leave?
¿A qué hora llega/sale? a ke o·ra lye·ga/sa·le

Please tell me when we get to (Sevilla).
¿Puede avisarme pwe·de a·vee·sar·me
cuando lleguemos kwan·do lye·ge·mos
a (Sevilla)? a (se·vee·lya)

I want to get off here.
Quiero bajarme aquí. kye·ro ba·khar·me a·kee

a ... ticket	un billete de ...	oon bee·lye·te de ...
1st-class	primera clase	pree·me·ra kla·se
2nd-class	segunda clase	se·goon·da kla·se
one-way	ida	ee·da
return	ida y vuelta	ee·da ee vwel·ta
aisle seat	asiento de pasillo	a·syen·to de pa·see·lyo
cancelled	cancelado	kan·the·la·do
delayed	retrasado	re·tra·sa·do
platform	plataforma	pla·ta·for·ma
ticket office	taquilla	ta·kee·lya
timetable	horario	o·ra·ryo
train station	estación de trenes	es·ta·thyon de tre·nes
window seat	asiento junto a la ventana	a·syen·to khoon·to a la ven·ta·na

Driving & Cycling

I'd like to hire a ...	Quisiera alquilar ...	kee·sye·ra al·kee·lar ...
4WD	un todo-terreno	oon to·do-te·re·no
bicycle	una bicicleta	oo·na bee·thee·kle·ta
car	un coche	oon ko·che
motorcycle	una moto	oo·na mo·to
child seat	asiento de seguridad para niños	a·syen·to de se·goo·ree·da pa·ra nee·nyos
diesel	gasóleo	ga·so·lyo
helmet	casco	kas·ko
mechanic	mecánico	me·ka·nee·ko
petrol/gas	gasolina	ga·so·lee·na
service station	gasolinera	ga·so·lee·ne·ra

Is this the road to ...?
¿Se va a (Barcelona) se va a (bar·the·lo·na)
por esta carretera? por es·ta ka·re·te·ra

(How long) Can I park here?
¿(Por cuánto tiempo) (por kwan·to tyem·po)
Puedo aparcar aquí? pwe·do a·par·kar a·kee

The car has broken down (at Valencia).
El coche se ha averiado el ko·che se a a·ve·rya·do
(en Valencia). (en va·len·thya)

I have a flat tyre.
Tengo un pinchazo. ten·go oon peen·cha·tho

I've run out of petrol.
Me he quedado sin me e ke·da·do seen
gasolina. ga·so·lee·na

Unless otherwise indicated, these terms are in Castilian Spanish.

agroturismo – rural tourism; see also *turismo rural*

ajuntament – Catalan for *ayuntamiento*

alameda – tree-lined avenue

albergue – refuge

albergue juvenil – youth hostel

alcázar – Muslim-era fortress

aljibe – cistern

artesonado – wooden Mudéjar ceiling with interlaced beams leaving a pattern of spaces for decoration

autonomía – autonomous community or region: Spain's 50 *provincias* are grouped into 17 of these

autopista – tollway

autovía – toll-free highway

AVE – Tren de Alta Velocidad Española; high-speed train

ayuntamiento – city or town hall

bailaor – male flamenco dancer

bailaora – female flamenco dancer

baile – dance in a flamenco context

balneario – spa

barrio – district/quarter (of a town or city)

biblioteca – library

bici todo terreno (BTT) – mountain bike

bodega – cellar (especially wine cellar); also a winery or a traditional wine bar likely to serve wine from the barrel

búhos – night-bus routes

cabrito – kid

cala – cove

calle – street

callejón – lane

cama – bed

cambio – change; also currency exchange

caña – small glass of beer

capilla – chapel

capilla mayor – chapel containing the high altar of a church

carmen – walled villa with gardens, in Granada

Carnaval – traditional festive period that precedes the start of Lent; carnival

carretera – highway

carta – menu

casa de huéspedes – guesthouse; see also *hospedaje*

casa de pagès – *casa rural* in Catalonia

casa rural – village, country house or farmstead with rooms to let

casco – literally 'helmet'; often used to refer to the old part of a city; more correctly, *casco antiguo/histórico/viejo*

castellano – Castilian; used in preference to *español* to describe the national language

castellers – Catalan human-castle builders

Castile – Castilla (the province)

castillo – castle

castro – Celtic fortified village

català – Catalan language; a native of Catalonia

catedral – cathedral

cercanías – local train network

cervecería – beer bar

churrigueresco – ornate style of baroque architecture named after the brothers Alberto and José Churriguera

ciudad – city

claustro – cloister

CNIG – Centro Nacional de Información Geográfica; producers of good-quality maps

cofradía – see *hermandad*

colegiata – collegiate church

coll – Catalan for *collado*

collado – mountain pass

comarca – district; grouping of *municipios*

comedor – dining room

completo – full

comunidad – fixed charge for maintenance of rental accommodation (sometimes included in rent); community

comunidad autónoma – see *autonomía*

conquistador – conqueror

copa – drink; literally 'glass'

cordillera – mountain range

coro – choir: part of a church, usually the middle

correos – post office

Cortes – national parliament

costa – coast

cruceiro – standing crucifix found at many crossroads in Galicia

cuesta – lane, usually on a hill

custodia – monstrance

día del espectador – cut-price ticket day at cinemas; literally 'viewer's day'

dolmen – prehistoric megalithic tomb

embalse – reservoir

encierro – running of the bulls Pamplona-style; also happens in many other places around Spain

entrada – entrance

ermita – hermitage or chapel

església – Catalan for *iglesia*

estació – Catalan for *estación*

estación – station

estación de autobuses – bus station

estación de esquí – ski station or resort

estación marítima – ferry terminal

estany – lake

Euskadi Ta Askatasuna (ETA) – the name stands for Basque Homeland & Freedom

extremeño – Extremaduran; a native of Extremadura

fallas – huge sculptures of papier-mâché (or nowadays more often polystyrene) on wood used in Las Fallas festival of Valencia
farmacia – pharmacy
faro – lighthouse
feria – fair; can refer to trade fairs as well as to city, town or village fairs that are basically several days of merrymaking; can also mean a bullfight or festival stretching over days or weeks
ferrocarril – railway
festa – Catalan for *fiesta*
FEVE – Ferrocarriles de Vía Estrecha; a private train company in northern Spain
fiesta – festival, public holiday or party
fútbol – football (soccer)

gaditano – person from Cádiz
gaita – Galician version of the bagpipes
gallego – Galician; a native of Galicia
gitanos – the Roma people
glorieta – big roundabout/ traffic circle
Gran Vía – main thoroughfare
GRs – (senderos de) Gran Recorrido; long-distance hiking paths
guardia civil – military police

hermandad – brotherhood (including men and women), in particular one that takes part in religious processions
hórreo – Galician or Asturian grain store
hospedaje – guesthouse
hostal – cheap hotel
hostal-residencia – *hostal* without any kind of restaurant
huerta – market garden; orchard

iglesia – church
infanta/infante – princess/ prince

IVA – *impuesto sobre el valor añadido*, or value-added tax

jai-alai – Basque name for *pelota vasca*
jardín – garden
judería – Jewish *barrio* in medieval Spain

levante – easterly
librería – bookshop
lidia – the art of bullfighting
locutorio – private telephone centre

madrileño/a – a person from Madrid
manchego – La Manchan; a person from La Mancha
marcha – action, life, 'the scene'
marismas – wetlands
marisquería – seafood eatery
medina – Arabic word for town or city
mercado – market
mercat – Catalan for *mercado*
meseta – plateau; the high tableland of central Spain
mihrab – prayer niche in a mosque indicating the direction of Mecca
mirador – lookout point
Modernisme – literally 'modernism'; the architectural and artistic style, influenced by art nouveau and sometimes known as Catalan Modernism, whose leading practitioner was Antoni Gaudí
Modernista – an exponent of *modernisme*
monasterio – monastery
morería – former Islamic quarter in a town
movida – similar to *marcha*; a *zona de movida* is an area of a town where lively bars and discos are clustered
Mozarab – Christian living under Muslim rule in early medieval Spain
Mozarabic – style of architecture developed by Mozarabs, adopting elements of classic Islamic construction to Christian architecture

Mudéjar – Muslims who remained behind in territory reconquered by Christians; also refers to a decorative style of architecture using elements of Islamic building style applied to buildings constructed in Christian Spain
muelle – wharf or pier
municipio – municipality, Spain's basic local administrative unit
muralla – city wall
murgas – costumed groups
museo – museum
museu – Catalan for *museo*

nitbus – Catalan for night bus

oficina de turismo – tourist office; also *oficina de información turística*

Pantocrator – Christ the All-Ruler or Christ in Majesty, a central emblem of Romanesque art
parador – luxurious state-owned hotels, many of them in historic buildings
parque nacional – national park; strictly controlled protected area
parque natural – natural park; a protected environmental area
paseo – promenade or boulevard; to stroll
paso – mountain pass
pasos – figures carried in Semana Santa parades
pelota vasca – Basque form of handball, also known simply as *pelota*, or *jai-alai* in Basque
peña – a club, usually of flamenco aficionados or Real Madrid or Barcelona football fans; sometimes a dining club
pensión – small private hotel
pincho – snack
pintxos – Basque tapas
piscina – swimming pool
plaça – Catalan for *plaza*
plateresque – early phase of Renaissance architecture

noted for its intricately decorated facades

platja – Catalan for *playa*

playa – beach

plaza – square

plaza de toros – bullring

poniente – westerly

port – Catalan for *puerto*

PP – Partido Popular (People's Party)

PRs – *(senderos de) Pequeño Recorrido;* short distance hiking paths

PSOE – Partido Socialista Obrero Español (Spanish Socialist Workers Party)

pueblo – village

puente – bridge; also means the extra day or two off that many people take when a holiday falls close to a weekend

puerta – gate or door

puerto – port or mountain pass

punta – point or promontory

rambla – avenue or riverbed

rastro – flea market; car-boot sale

REAJ – Red Española de Albergues Juveniles, which is the Spanish HI youth hostel network

real – royal

Reconquista – the Christian reconquest of the Iberian Peninsula from the Muslims (8th to 15th centuries)

refugi – Catalan for *refugio*

refugio – mountain shelter, hut or refuge

Renfe – Red Nacional de los Ferrocarriles Españoles; the national rail network

retablo – altarpiece

Reyes Católicos – Catholic monarchs; Isabel and Fernando

ría – estuary

río – river

riu – Catalan for *río*

rodalies – Catalan for *cercanías*

romería – festive pilgrimage or procession

ronda – ring road

sacristía – sacristy; the part of a church in which vestments, sacred objects and other valuables are kept

sagrario – sanctuary

sala capitular – chapter house

salinas – salt-extraction lagoons

santuario – shrine or sanctuary

Semana Santa – Holy Week, the week leading up to Easter Sunday

Sephardic Jews – Jews of Spanish origin

serranía – mountain region or highlands)

seu – cathedral (Catalan)

sidra – cider

sidrería – cider house

sierra – mountain range

s/n – sin número (without number), sometimes seen in addresses

tablao – tourist-oriented flamenco performances

taifa – small Muslim kingdom in medieval Spain

tasca – tapas bar

techumbre – roof; specifically a common type of *armadura*

teleférico – cable car; also called *funicular aereo*

terraza – terrace; pavement cafe

terrazas de verano – open-air late-night bars

tetería – teahouse, usually in Middle Eastern style, with low seats around low tables

toreros – bullfighters

torre – tower

trascoro – screen behind the *coro*

turismo – means both tourism and saloon car; *el turismo* can also mean 'tourist office'

turismo rural – rural tourism; usually refers to accommodation in a *casa rural* and associated activities, such as walking and horse riding

urbanización – suburban housing development

urgencia – emergency

vall – Catalan for *valle*

valle – valley

villa – small town

VO – abbreviation of versión original; a foreign-language film subtitled in Spanish

zarzuela – Spanish mix of theatre, music and dance

behind the scenes

SEND US YOUR FEEDBACK

We love to hear from travellers – your comments keep us on our toes and help make our books better. Our well-travelled team reads every word on what you loved or loathed about this book. Although we cannot reply individually to postal submissions, we always guarantee that your feedback goes straight to the appropriate authors, in time for the next edition. Each person who sends us information is thanked in the next edition – and the most useful submissions are rewarded with a free book.

Visit **lonelyplanet.com/contact** to submit your updates and suggestions or to ask for help. Our award-winning website also features inspirational travel stories, news and discussions.

Note: We may edit, reproduce and incorporate your comments in Lonely Planet products such as guidebooks, websites and digital products, so let us know if you don't want your comments reproduced or your name acknowledged. For a copy of our privacy policy visit lonelyplanet.com/privacy.

OUR READERS

Many thanks to the travellers who used the last edition and wrote to us with helpful hints, useful advice and interesting anecdotes:

Leon Alsemgeest, Javier Anton, Mona Arain Crites, Chiara Architta, Manuela Arigoni, Karine Baillet, Reinier Bakels, Lina Bangash, Terri Baumgart, Irene Billeter Sauter, Natalie Bladon, Scott Blake, Lena Bledau, Robert Blom, Miquel Bosch, Marinus Bosters, Mark Brayne, Paul Bristow, Joshua Brower, Birgit Cachet, Paolo Campegiani, Tristan Cano, Nerea Casas, Deep Charan, Alba Codes, Aisling Collins, Stephen Daly, Peter Damm, Juan de Antonio Rubio, Bie De Keulenaer, Desiree de los Reyes, Max De Stefani, Jose Antonio Díaz, Marie Dumonceau, Lisa Duncan, Frank Eisenhuth, Ana Eraso de Castro, Carmen Espinosa Vilar, Kate Evans, Jim Eychaner, Mario Falzon, Lorenzo Fragola, Mandy Gaggero, Caroline Garrido, Antoine Gautier, David Glass, Alison Godlewski, Mercedes Gomez, Isabel Gomis Tatay, Miren Gonzalez, Jim Green, Tom Haesebrouck, Doug Hall, Emma Haller, Jane Hawkins, Keith Hughes, Laura Jörger, Kr Kaffenberger, Alex Klaushofer, Stephan Koetting, Gayle Lanthier, Joe Ledesma, Alan Leigh, Rodrigo Lema, Wade Letts, David Lewis, Eduardo Licciardi, Liliam, Jill Linderwell, James Luce, Vincent Mahon, Laura Manganotti, Zaida Mantis, Maricruz, David Martin, Paqui Martín, Sergi Maya Agusti, Claire McGinley, Martin McNally, Mary Metzger, Zoe Meyer, Adrián Milá, Nicholas Milner, Alba Monedero, Frances Morris, Maureen Moss, Beba Naveira, John Oliden, Carlos Ortiz, Martin Page, Despoina Papadopoulou, Nadia Parbo, Trent Paton, Clive Paul, Nieves Pérez, Susan Permut, Kerstin Pohle, Jamie Poole, David Radin, Jorge Ramos, Paul Rankin, Laura Raurell, Javier Re, Joy Rennie, Amanda Rice, Emilio Robres, Jos Rooijackers, Malcolm Rushan, Mazinka Rutherford, Emma Rutledge, Paul Sampson, Sandra Schmidt, Johannes Schuler, Don Shirley, Mara Smaldone, Art Smith, Michael Sonsini, Mary Stewart, Kerry Strom, Joao Teixeira, Dan Tomas, Tracy Tomlin, Iñigo Ullmann, Elske van Dijk, Dirk van Norren, Rob van Oijen, Cecce & Enrico Ullmann, Amalia Vidal Vázquez, Vincenzo Vigilante, Paul Wagner, Yvonne Welzen, Thomas Wetzer, Marc Wisselo, Robert Wouterlood, Sana Younis

AUTHOR THANKS

Anthony Ham

In eight years of living in Madrid, I have been welcomed and assisted by too many people to name. A huge thank you to my wonderful coauthors, and to Lucy Monie and Joe Bindloss at Lonely Planet. It was my great fortune a week after arriving in Madrid to meet my wife and soulmate, Marina, who has made this city a true place of the heart. And to my daughters, Carlota and Valentina: truly you are Madrid's greatest gifts of all.

Stuart Butler

First and foremost I must once again thank my wife, Heather, for everything she does and for giving us the gift of our son, Jake. I would also like to thank all my friends in the Basque regions for their help and advice, in particular to Olatz. In Catalonia thanks to Imma Masià Idiarte in the Ebro delta and finally I must single out Cristina Joher-Fita in Girona for help above and beyond the call of duty.

John Noble

Thank you to the people of the northwest for their heart-warming good humour, courtesy and warm welcome, even during Asturias' heaviest rains ever recorded! Cyclist JP Chamness, good to run into you (five times!). Thanks to all the LP team, a pleasure to work with, and to all my LP predecessors in the northwest for their accumulated wit and wisdom. And thank you Jack for putting up with my absence, and to Jack, Izzy and Sarah for your support and encouragement throughout!

Zora O'Neill

Thanks to Lucy Monie for offering me the chance to look at pictures of Spain's most beautiful buildings, as well as to Heidi Liebes for geeking out over fosteritos and Jean Nouvel. And of course thanks to the Lonely Planet editing staff, especially Barbara Delissen, for pulling the whole thing together.

Josephine Quintero

Special thanks to the especially helpful tourist offices in Cuenca, Burgos and Salamanca, as well as the local experts in León who introduced me to some great places and provided invaluable advice. Thanks too to Isabel and Luís for a bed and inside info on Segovia, and to Robin for his superb proofing, map reading and for sharing a bottle of wine at the end of days on the road. A mega gracias to Anthony Ham for being such a terrific coordinating author.

Miles Roddis

To Ingrid, for her chauffeuring and proofing and to Marcos Puig and Julia for sharing their Menorca secrets. And to informed tourist office staff: Teresa Dolz (Vinaros), Ester and Marisa (Peñiscola), Guillem Monferrer (Vilafranca), Pilar and Vanessa (Morella), Iván (Sant Mateu), Raquel Moreno (Benicàssim), Sylvia (Oropesa), Marta (Castellón),

THIS BOOK

This 8th edition of Spain was researched and written by a dedicated team of authors. Anthony Ham coordinated the group, which comprised Damien Simonis, Miles Roddis, Stuart Butler, John Noble, Josephine Quintero, Brendan Sainsbury and Zora O'Neill, who wrote the architecture chapter. Anthony, Damien, Miles, Stuart, John and Josephine all contributed to previous editions, as did Sarah Andrews, Arpi Armenakian Shively, Susan Forsyth, Fiona Adams, Mark Armstrong, Fionn Davenport, Tim Nollen, Andrea Schulte-Peevers, Corinne Simcock, Daniel C Schecter, Des Hannigan, Richard Sterling, Elizabeth Swan and Dr Caroline Evans. This guidebook was commissioned in Lonely Planet's London office, and produced by the following:

Commissioning Editors Joe Bindloss, Lucy Monie, Dora Whitaker

Coordinating Editor Barbara Delissen

Coordinating Cartographer Andras Bogdanovits

Coordinating Layout Designer Paul Iacono

Managing Editors Imogen Bannister, Sasha Baskett

Managing Cartographers David Connolly, Amanda Sierp, Herman So

Managing Layout Designer Indra Kilfoyle

Assisting Editors Holly Alexander, Andrew Bain, Andrea Dobbin, Elizabeth Harvey, Kim Hutchins, Robyn Loughnane, Katie O'Connell, Susan Paterson, Simon Sellars, Elizabeth Swan, Angela Tinson

Assisting Cartographers Sonya Brooke, Hunor Csutoros, Corey Hutchison, Jennifer Johnston, Jolyon Philcox, Peter Shields

Assisting Layout Designer Kerrianne Southway

Cover Research Naomi Parker

Internal Image Research Sabrina Dalbesio

Illustrator Javier Zarracina

Language Content Branislava Vladisavljevic

Thanks to Mark Adams, Jane Atkin, Stefanie Di Trocchio, Janine Eberle, Brigitte Ellemor, Joshua Geoghegan, Mark Germanchis, Michelle Glynn, Liz Heynes, Lauren Hunt, Laura Jane, David Kemp, Lisa Knights, Nic Lehman, Alison Lyall, John Mazzocchi, Annelies Mertens, Wayne Murphy, Trent Paton, Adrian Persoglia, Piers Pickard, Lachlan Ross, Michael Ruff, Julie Sheridan, Laura Stansfeld, John Taufa, Sam Trafford, Juan Winata, Emily K Wolman, Celia Wood, Nick Wood

María (Segorbe), Carolina (Elche), Begoña (Novelda), Luis-Ángel Ruiz (Alicante), Carmen (Orihuela), José-Manuel Gomez (Torrevieja), Virginia (Benidorm), Mari-Carmen (Denia), Miguel (Xàbia), Amparo (Alcoy), Manuca (Xàtiva), Laura and Carlos (Ciutadella), Marián (Maó), Rafa (Palma de Mallorca) and Lorena (Ibiza).

Brendan Sainsbury

Many thanks to all the untold bus drivers, tourist info volunteers, restaurateurs, flamenco aficionados and innocent bystanders who helped me during my research, particularly to Lucy Monie for offering me the gig in the first place, Joe Bindloss for smoothing it along, and Anthony Ham for being a supportive coordinating author. Special thanks to Toni Vilchez in Seville, and to my wife, Liz, and four-year-old son, Kieran, for their company in countless bars, buses, music clubs and hotel rooms.

Damien Simonis

Thanks to friends for their good company and frequent tips. They include: Alexa Botines, Sandra Canudas, Josep Cerdà & Maite Zaldivia, Dominique Cerri, Rebecca & Elsa Daraspe, Oscar Elias, Ferran Esteves, Ralf Himburg & Lilian Müller, Edith López García, Teresa Moreno Quintana & Carlos Sanagustín, Steven Muller, Sonja Müller, Nicole Neuefeind, Brian O'Hare, Cristina Pedraza, Susana Pellicer, Gemma Sesplugues, Peter Sotirakis, Armin Teichmann, José María Toro, Joan Trujillo, Michael van Laake, Nuria Vilches, Simona Volonterio and Sarah Whitehouse.

ACKNOWLEDGMENTS

Climate map data adapted from Peel MC, Finlayson BL & McMahon TA (2007) 'Updated World Map of the Köppen-Geiger Climate Classification', *Hydrology and Earth System Sciences*, 11, 163344.

Barcelona Metro Map © TMB Metro 2010

Madrid Metro Map © Diseño Raro S.L. 2010

Illustrations pp70-1, pp248-9, pp264-5, pp666-7, pp740-1 and pp748-9 by Javier Zarracina.

Cover photograph: Advertising sign, Toledo, Spain, Felix Stenson/Photolibrary. Many of the images in this guide are available for licensing from Lonely Planet Images: www.lonelyplanetimages.com.

NOTES

index

Map Pages **p000**
Image Pages **p000**

how to use this book

These symbols will help you find the listings you want:

👁 Sights   🎎 Festivals & Events   ☆ Entertainment

🏃 Activities   🛏 Sleeping   🛍 Shopping

🛋 Courses   🍴 Eating   ℹ Information/Transport

👉 Tours   🍷 Drinking

These symbols give you the vital information for each listing:

📞	Telephone Numbers	📶	Wi-Fi Access	🚌	Bus
🕐	Opening Hours	🏊	Swimming Pool	⛴	Ferry
🅿	Parking	🥗	Vegetarian Selection	Ⓜ	Metro
⊝	Nonsmoking	📖	English-Language Menu	Ⓢ	Subway
❄	Air-Conditioning	👪	Family-Friendly	⊖	London Tube
@	Internet Access	🐾	Pet-Friendly	🚋	Tram
				🚆	Train

Reviews are organised by author preference.

Look out for these icons:

TOP CHOICE   Our author's recommendation

FREE   No payment required

🌿   A green or sustainable option

Our authors have nominated these places as demonstrating a strong commitment to sustainability – for example by supporting local communities and producers, operating in an environmentally friendly way, or supporting conservation projects.

Map Legend

Sights

- 🏖 Beach
- ☸ Buddhist
- 🏰 Castle
- ✝ Christian
- 🕉 Hindu
- ☪ Islamic
- ✡ Jewish
- 🏛 Monument
- 🖼 Museum/Gallery
- ⊙ Ruin
- 🍷 Winery/Vineyard
- 🦁 Zoo
- ⊙ Other Sight

Activities, Courses & Tours

- 🤿 Diving/Snorkelling
- 🛶 Canoeing/Kayaking
- ⛷ Skiing
- 🏄 Surfing
- 🏊 Swimming/Pool
- 🚶 Walking
- 🏄 Windsurfing
- • Other Activity/Course/Tour

Sleeping

- 🛏 Sleeping
- ⛺ Camping

Eating

- 🍴 Eating

Drinking

- ☕ Drinking
- ☕ Cafe

Entertainment

- 🎭 Entertainment

Shopping

- 🛍 Shopping

Information

- 📮 Post Office
- ℹ Tourist Information

Transport

- ✈ Airport
- ⊗ Border Crossing
- 🚌 Bus
- ++⊕++ Cable Car/Funicular
- –◉– Cycling
- –⊝– Ferry
- Ⓜ Metro
- ═×◉═ Monorail
- 🅿 Parking
- Ⓢ S-Bahn
- 🚕 Taxi
- +–◉–+ Train/Railway
- ═◉═ Tram
- ⊝ Tube Station
- Ⓤ U-Bahn
- • Other Transport

Routes

- Tollway
- Freeway
- Primary
- Secondary
- Tertiary
- Lane
- Unsealed Road
- Plaza/Mall
- Steps
- ⊃ ⊏ Tunnel
- Pedestrian Overpass
- Walking Tour
- Walking Tour Detour
- Path

Boundaries

- – – – International
- ––––– State/Province
- – – Disputed
- Regional/Suburb
- Marine Park
- Cliff
- Wall

Population

- ● Capital (National)
- ◉ Capital (State/Province)
- ● City/Large Town
- ○ Town/Village

Geographic

- 🏠 Hut/Shelter
- 🔦 Lighthouse
- ● Lookout
- ▲ Mountain/Volcano
- ⊙ Oasis
- ❶ Park
-)(Pass
- ⊕ Picnic Area
- 💧 Waterfall

Hydrography

- River/Creek
- Intermittent River
- Swamp/Mangrove
- Reef
- Canal
- Water
- Dry/Salt/Intermittent Lake
- Glacier

Areas

- Beach/Desert
- +⊹+ Cemetery (Christian)
- ×××× Cemetery (Other)
- Park/Forest
- Sportsground
- Sight (Building)
- Top Sight (Building)

Josephine Quintero

Castilla y Léon, Castilla-La Mancha, Murcia Josephine Quintero moved to Spain after a seven-year stint in Kuwait where she was editor of the *Kuwaiti Digest* until the Iraq invasion. Some 20 years on, the relaxed way of life in Andalucía continues to appeal. Josephine loves exploring Spain, seeking out hidden corners, appreciating the unsung glories and meeting some extraordinary people along the way. During researching this book one of the highlights was discovering a little-known Roman archaeological site in the middle of a field near Cuenca which was fabulously evocative and memorable.

Read more about Josephine at:
lonelyplanet.com/members/josephinequintero

Miles Roddis

Valencia & the Costa Blanca, Mallorca, Menorca & Ibiza Miles and his wife, Ingrid, have lived for nearly 20 years in a shoebox-sized apartment in the Barrio del Carmen, Valencia's oldest and most vital quarter. These days, he writes about Mediterranean lands – Spain, France and Italy – and is author or coauthor of more than 50 Lonely Planet guidebooks, including *Valencia & the Costa Blanca, Valencia Encounter, Walking in Spain, Canary Islands* and six editions of the book you're holding.

Brendan Sainsbury

Andalucía Brendan has logged many achievements while in Spain, including meeting his future wife, learning to play flamenco guitar, holding down a job as a travel guide and realising that Granada is his favourite city on the planet. He first visited the country by train in the late 1980s, returned on a bike in the '90s, and came back to lead hiking trips around Andalucía in the early 2000s. He researched this book accompanied by his wife and four-year-old son.

Read more about Brendan at:
lonelyplanet.com/members/brendansainsbury

Damien Simonis

Barcelona In 1990, Damien found himself in pre-Olympics Barcelona. The place left a mark and, eight years later, Damien turned up in a Rambla-side *pensión* on assignment for Lonely Planet. He has called the city home since 2000 and wrote Lonely Planet's *Barcelona,* which he has continued to update. Long the coordinating author of *Spain,* he is amazed at the discoveries one can make in deepest Barcelona, like the excellent Cerveseria Gallega restaurant, a stalwart he had never stumbled across before.

Read more about Damien at:
lonelyplanet.com/members/damiensimonis

OUR STORY

A beat-up old car, a few dollars in the pocket and a sense of adventure. In 1972 that's all Tony and Maureen Wheeler needed for the trip of a lifetime – across Europe and Asia overland to Australia. It took several months, and at the end – broke but inspired – they sat at their kitchen table writing and stapling together their first travel guide, *Across Asia on the Cheap*. Within a week they'd sold 1500 copies. Lonely Planet was born.

Today, Lonely Planet has offices in Melbourne, London and Oakland, with more than 600 staff and writers. We share Tony's belief that 'a great guidebook should do three things: inform, educate and amuse'.

OUR WRITERS

Anthony Ham

Coordinating Author, Madrid, Aragón, Extremadura In 2002, Anthony arrived in Madrid on a one-way ticket, has called the city home ever since and now lives with his *madrileña* wife and two daughters overlooking their favourite plaza in the city. He has written more than 50 guidebooks for Lonely Planet, including *Spain* and *Madrid,* and writes and photographs for newspapers and magazines around the world. Apart from rediscovering his home city afresh while research-ing this guide (Malasaña is his new favourite *barrio*), his happiest moments were losing himself again in the quiet streets of Albarracín after the tour buses had gone home.

Stuart Butler

Catalonia, Basque Country, Navarra & La Rioja, Spain's Outdoors, Spain's Pas-sions Stuart's first childhood encounters with Spain, in Parque Nacional de Doñana and on family holidays along the north coast, left lasting impressions. When he was older he spent every summer on the Basque beaches until one day he found himself unable to tear himself away – he has been there ever since. When not writing for Lonely Planet he hunts for uncharted surf on remote coast-lines. The results of these trips appear frequently in the world's surf media. His website is www.oceansurfpublications.co.uk.

John Noble

History, Cantabria & Asturias, Santiago de Compostela & Galicia John, originally from England, has lived in an Andalucian mountain village since 1995. In that time he has travelled all over Spain and helped write every edition of Lonely Planet's *Spain* and *Andalucía* guides. He loves getting to faraway parts of the country like Galicia and the north coast and being reminded just how diverse, in culture, landscape and climate, Spain is. He doesn't think he could stay away from Andalucía's sunny skies for ever, though.

Read more about John at:
lonelyplanet.com/members/ewoodrover

Zora O'Neill

Architecture Zora studied 11th-century Andalucian Arabic literature in graduate school, so when she visited Córdoba, it was like walking into a poem. She finds the cultural mix of modern-day Spain just as intriguing – because it involves walking, eating and ogling architectural confections. Zora has been a guidebook author since 2003; in 2009, she contributed to *Andalucía* and, in a new adven-ture for this city mouse, *Hiking in Spain*. She lives in New York City and blogs at www.rovinggastronome.com.

Read more about Zora at:
lonelyplanet.com/members/zoraoneill

OVER MORE
PAGE WRITERS

Published by Lonely Planet Publications Pty Ltd
ABN 36 005 607 983
8th edition – March 2011
ISBN 978 1 74179 599 8
© Lonely Planet 2011   Photographs © as indicated 2011
10 9 8 7 6 5 4 3 2
Printed in China

Although the authors and Lonely Planet have taken all reason-able care in preparing this book, we make no warranty about the accuracy or completeness of its content and, to the maxi-mum extent permitted, disclaim all liability arising from its use.

All rights reserved. No part of this publication may be copied, stored in a retrieval system, or transmitted in any form by any means, electronic, mechanical, recording or otherwise, except brief extracts for the purpose of review, and no part of this publication may be sold or hired, without the written permission of the publisher. Lonely Planet and the Lonely Planet logo are trademarks of Lonely Planet and are registered in the US Patent and Trademark Office and in other countries. Lonely Planet does not allow its name or logo to be appropriated by commercial establishments, such as retailers, restaurants or hotels. Please let us know of any misuses: lonelyplanet.com/ip.